STUDIES IN ARCHITECTURE

Edited by Anthony Blunt, John Harris, and Howard Hibbard

Volume XVIII

Carlo Fontana: The Drawings at Windsor Castle

Allan Braham and Hellmut Hager

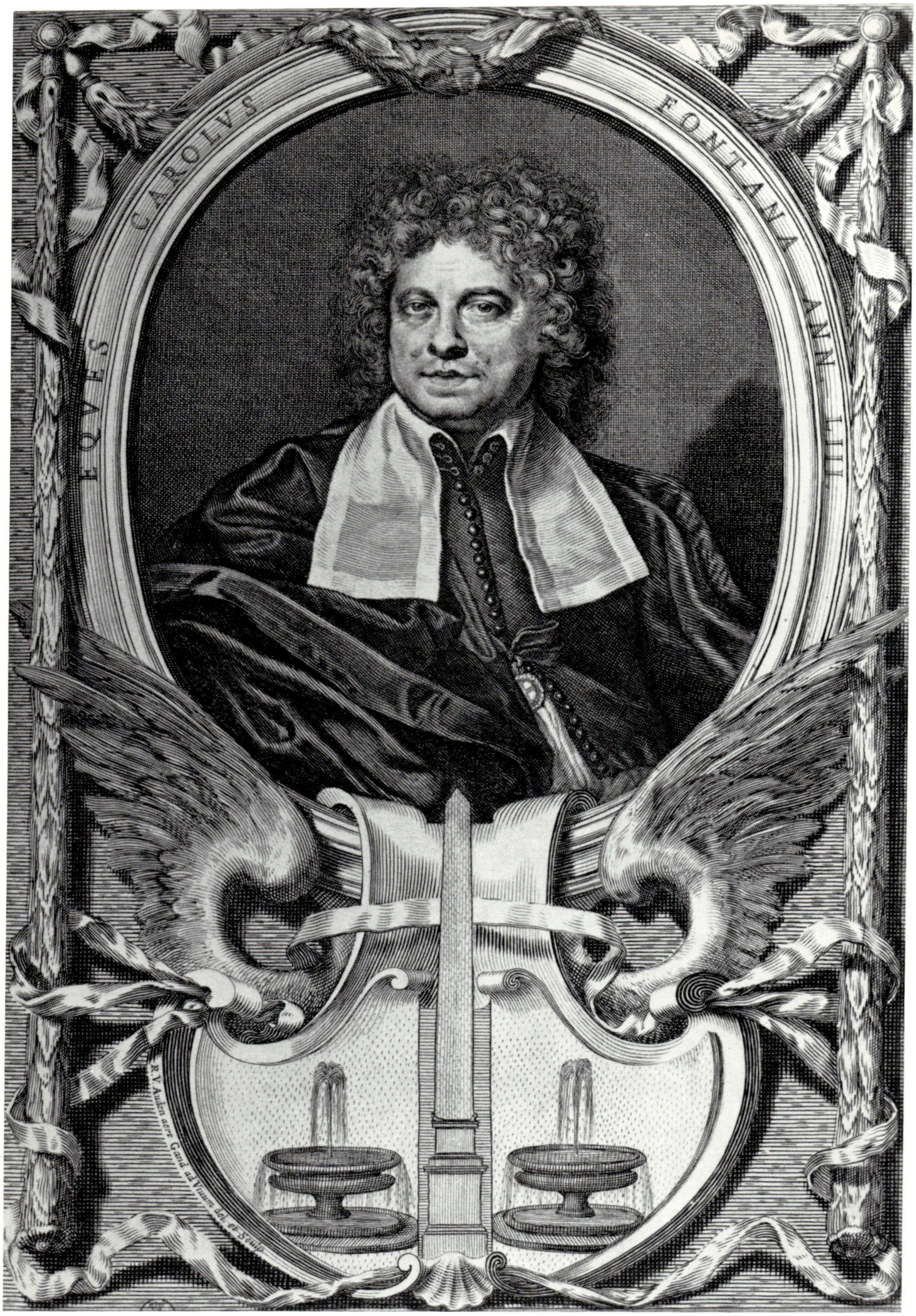

Portrait of Carlo Fontana, aged 53 (1691), engraving by Robert van Audenaerd (Florence, Uffizi)

CARLO FONTANA
The Drawings at Windsor Castle

by Allan Braham and Hellmut Hager

A. Zwemmer Ltd

Published by A. Zwemmer Ltd, 76–80 Charing Cross Road, London, WC2

ISBN 0 302 02780 7

Designed by Graham Johnson/Lund Humphries

Printed in Great Britain by Lund Humphries, London and Bradford

Table of Contents

Preface and Acknowledgements

The present catalogue of 783 drawings in the Royal Library covers the contents of thirteen bound volumes of drawings by Carlo Fontana and two volumes of drawings referring to building activities in the Papal States during the reign of Pope Clement XI (1700–1721). Work on the catalogue was begun many years ago by Professor Arnold Noach, whose notes were kindly put at our disposal. In certain cases his material has been absorbed in the catalogue entries, but we have noted those occasions where we are especially indebted to him for giving us valuable leads. The catalogue has also benefited from work on the drawings subsequently undertaken by Mr Brian Sewell. The completion of the catalogue in its present form has been carried out in collaboration with Dr Hellmut Hager, now Professor of the History of Art at The Pennsylvania State University, to whom are due the entries on the church projects, as well as the sections on the Baptistry of S. Peter's, Urbino – Pesaro – Colbordolo, the introduction to the entries for the Ospizio di San Michele, and the biographical section of the introduction. The majority of the other entries have also greatly benefited from research carried out by Dr Hager, with the active assistance of Mrs Hager (Dr Maria Antonietta Hager).

The encouragement and help of Sir Anthony Blunt has been unstinted throughout the course of the preparation of the catalogue, and an especial debt to him is most gratefully acknowledged. Work at Windsor has been facilitated by the kind help of Miss Scott-Elliot, Sir Robin Mackworth-Young, Miss Janet Holt and Miss Jennifer Sherwood. The task of translating Dr Hager's entries from the German was accomplished with the greatest efficiency by Miss Elsa Scheerer. The photography of the vast majority of the drawings was organized by Miss Amanda Tomlinson and the staff of the Conway Library and the photographic department of the Courtauld Institute. To those who have kindly communicated information on specific occasions acknowledgement is made in the text. On matters relating to the sculpture of the period Dr Jennifer Montagu and Mr Frederick den Broeder have been especially generous in sharing their knowledge with us. Mr Peter Ward-Jackson kindly facilitated work on an album of drawings in the Victoria and Albert Museum related to Fontana's decoration for the funeral service to Leopold I, and provided photographs of many of the sheets. Mr Adrian Ward-Jackson kindly made available photographs of three recently discovered drawings by Fontana, formerly with Messrs Colnaghi. Dr Olga Pujmánova and Dr Emmanuel Poche have taken a great interest in Fontana's two projects for Prague and provided invaluable assistance in matters appertaining to these works.

The publication of this volume would have been impossible without generous financial assistance provided by the Armand Hammer Foundation, the Trustees of the M.A. Cotton Trust and the British Academy. In its preparation we have greatly appreciated the interest and care of our publisher and editor, Mr Desmond Zwemmer, and his assistant, Mr Kevin Stower, and the typographical skills of Mr Graham Johnson. At Windsor the Hon. Mrs Roberts kindly supplied last-minute help. The task of typing the text was carried out by Mrs Kay Butterworth and that of checking and creating the index by Mrs Braham.

Dr Hager, endorsing these acknowledgements, also wishes to extend his thanks to the Deutsche Forschungsgemeinschaft, Bonn-Bad Godesberg, and the Kultusministerium of Nordrhein-Westphalen, Düsseldorf, for the financing of his research, to Professor Dr Franz Graf Wolff Metternich, Professor Dr Wolfgang Lotz, and Professor Dr Herbert von Einem, Bonn, for continuous help during the period of his research. Professor Jack Wasserman, Milwaukee, mentioned the Fontana volume in Modena, Biblioteca Estense, whilst Dr Hans Ost, Bonn, supplied the reference to Fontana's report on the history of the "Templum Vaticanum et ipsius Origo" in the Biblioteca Comunale at Como, and Professor Henry Millon, Director of The American Academy in Rome, drew our attention to some drawings by Carlo Fontana which have survived in a Juvarra Album in a private collection in Turin.

Dr Hager is also grateful to Mons. Lionello Razza and Dr Nello Nobilone, who facilitated his work in the archives at Frascati, to Can. D. Bramante Ligi for advice at Urbino, and he remembers with appreciation conversations with Professors Eugenio Battisti, The Pennsylvania State University, Robert Enggass, University of Kansas, Christoph Luitpold Frommel, University of Bonn, Gerhard Eimer, University of Frankfurt, David Bershed, Calgary University, Dr Sabine Jakob, Herzog Anton Ulrich Museum, Brunswick, Dr Werner Oechslin, University of Zürich. And a special word of thanks from both authors must finally be reserved for Dr Don Cipriano Cipriani, O. S. B. Olivet, archivist of the Archivio della R. Fabbrica di S. Pietro and Dr Marcello del Piazzo, director of the Archivio di Stato di Roma, as well as to Dr Paulo Tournon, and Dr Anna Maria Corbo, of the same institution, for valuable advice in the use of the archive.

Since the preparation of the text of the volume a resurgence of interest in the work of Fontana and his contemporaries has witnessed the appearance of a number of new publications. We have tried where possible to include references to such recent studies, without attempting to discuss them in detail.

List of Illustrations

I S. Peter's

III Secular Buildings

IV The 'Albani' Volumes and additional illustrations

Introduction

1 The drawings in the present catalogue and their history

The drawings discussed in the present catalogue comprise for the most part the contents of fifteen volumes in the Royal Library. The volumes belonged to Pope Clement XI, who probably acquired them in 1716; they were bought by George III from the Pope's nephew, Cardinal Alessandro Albani, in 1762 with the Albani collection. Of the fifteen volumes thirteen contain drawings by Carlo Fontana (1638–1714), and two consist mainly of drawings made in the early years of the 18th century on behalf of Clement XI and members of the Albani family. Many of Fontana's latest works were carried out for Clement XI, who reigned from 1700 to 1721, and the two 'Albani' volumes are to a great extent complementary to the thirteen Fontana volumes. They contain a number of sheets by Fontana and his workshop, as well as a large proportion of drawings by his pupils.

The volumes of drawings by Fontana at Windsor cover in full the last two decades of his activity, from about 1690 to 1710. This was the period of Fontana's greatest success, when he acted, during the reigns of Popes Innocent XII (Pignatelli, 1691–1700) and Clement XI, as chief papal architect, and when his reputation attracted both pupils and commissions from many parts of Italy and from abroad. The volumes comprise in addition to drawings a large number of manuscripts, and it is evident that, so far from containing merely a random assemblage of material, the volumes were each put in order and bound at the instigation of Fontana himself. There were originally 26 of these volumes, according to an inventory of 1716 which accompanies one of the Windsor volumes, and in addition to the thirteen albums at Windsor seven other volumes of the series can be traced. These, it is hoped, will be discussed in greater detail in a supplementary volume to the present catalogue.

Fontana was unusual as an architect in the number of books that he published. Those who knew him spoke of him as being an excessively voluble man, and his books are not treatises on the orders, but tracts dealing with his own works and the difficulties he encountered in carrying them out, as well as books calculated to show off his knowledge of historical and antiquarian matters. In some cases the volumes of drawings were clearly intended to join the body of Fontana's published work; they deal with single projects and are equipped with title pages (cf. Fig.343) and carefully written introductions. Most of the volumes contain drawings and papers relating to many different projects, but even here the material is usually set out in an orderly manner, the drawings for each project being grouped together and enclosed within interleaving sheets which are in many cases inscribed by Fontana with a note of the commission and the date. Beyond this point, however, no particular system seems to have been followed in organizing the drawings; they would appear simply to have been grouped according to size and sent off to the binders. The volumes are still in their original bindings of red morocco with gilt tooling of several different patterns (Figs 559–562).

The Fontana volumes thus represent an almost unique episode in the history of art. As a result of Fontana's passion for self-promotion, almost the entire output of a famous architect over a period of some twenty years is preserved. Many of the drawings are for commissions that would otherwise be totally unknown; they range in subject matter from the building of palaces and churches, to the construction of water conduits; many are designs for sculpture and others show in some detail how schemes of temporary decoration for funerals and festivals were organized. The detailed catalogue of such a body of material must inevitably take on the character of a monograph, and must include some discussion of the considerable contribution which the drawings make to what is known of the patronage of the period. They reflect especially the interests of the Popes for whom Fontana worked and the needs of his foreign clients. Some attempt has been made in the present catalogue to discuss in the text as fully as possible all the commissions covered in Fontana's drawings and manuscripts, and to give in the illustrations some impression of the range of Fontana's work.

The interest of the two 'Albani' volumes extends beyond the area of papal patronage to that of politics. All the architectural drawings which can be identified in these volumes (and a large proportion are identifiable) record the state of buildings, or refer to building projects, in the papal states during the reign of Clement XI. Many are connected with commissions in Urbino and the neighbourhood undertaken by members of the Pope's family. Datable drawings or manuscripts in the volumes range between the years 1702 and 1713. In addition there are many maps, some of them illustrating battles and sieges in the War of the Spanish Succession. One group records the siege of Comacchio (1708), where Alessandro Albani fought against the Imperial army; others show plans of a number of towns in Italy and Europe, giving details of their defences.

The inventory of 1716 in which all 26 volumes are listed, was made by the architect Giovanni Battista Contini. The volumes were shown to him at the request of the Pope by Battelli – this must be Archbishop G. C. Battelli who was librarian to Pope Clement XI (see Clough p.15, Posterla, 1707, p.329) – and he was asked to give a valuation. The value of the books, judged by Contini at 160 *scudi*, was presumably established to enable the Pope to buy the volumes from Fontana's heirs. The numbers given to the volumes in Contini's list coincide with figures, still clearly visible, on the covers of the existing volumes, and in the following transcription of the list the Windsor volumes are included in their appropriate places:

> 'Hauendo uisto, e riconosciuto uentisei libri di disegni di / diuerse sorti fatti dalla bona memoria del Caualier / Carlo fontana esibitimi da Mons Ill Battelli di / ordine di Nos^{t} Sig^{re} e ben considerati chiascheduno di essi / e riconosciuti li disegni, e piante in essi espressi dico / seconda mia peritia esser il suo prezzo – Cento ses: / santa sc(udi). dico–160:sc(udi). questo di 24 7br^{e} 1716
>
> Gio Batta Contini

– 1: Libro che contiene diuersi pensieri del porto / d'Anzio, la ueduta di Ciuitauecchia, Pon/te rotto da restaursi, diuersi pensieri di / barche dà farsi in mare in occasione di / feste

– 2: Diuersi disegni di S Michele

– 3: Disegno del Catafalcho del Rè di Portogallo (WINDSOR VOLUME 171)

– 4: Disegno, e Scritture dell' acqua felice

– 5: Disegni delle Carcerette di S. Michele à Ripa (WINDSOR VOLUME 181)

– 6: Diuersi disegni d Altare, Machine, macine / d oglio trombe, et altri ordegni mattema(ti)ci

– 7: Disegni della facciata di S.ª M.ª in Trasteuere / anticha, e moderna, Ponte dell Abbadia / e granari di Termini (WINDSOR VOLUME 172)

– 8: Disegni del palazzo di Egemberch, la fac / ciata di S.ª M.ª in Trasteuere, Chiesa de / Gesuiti di Frascati, S: Domenico Maggiore / di Napoli, Ciuita uecchia con l'Arsenale (WINDSOR VOLUME 170)

– 9: Stallone di Caprarola, Casino di Venetia / Fonte Batismale di S. Pietro, Forma di / Ciuita Vecchia, S. Michele a Ripa, disegno / della Cuppola di S. Pietro con sua descrittione / Terracina con la ueduta di Euolo Varij / disegni, S. Teodoro, Galera di Ciuita Vecchia, / Carcerette di S. Michele (WINDSOR VOLUME 176)

– 10: Diuersi disegni di Tempij (WINDSOR VOLUME 180)

– 11: Teatro di Tordinona, et altri

– 12: Antemurale, e Lanterna di Ciuita Vecchia (WINDSOR VOLUME 178)

– 13: Disegni del Deposito della Regina di Suetia, / con altri di Papa Innocenzo XII, Altri / di Chiese, Tabernacolo delli Apostoli in S. / Gio: Laterano, Chiesa, et Altare di Parma, / Altare p(er) Venetia (WINDSOR VOLUME 179)

– 14: Disegni diuersi

– 15: Diuersi disegni d Altari, e Stampe d'Ornati

– 16: Disegni d'una Inscrittione da farsi p Nostro / Sig^{re} Papa Clemente XI

– 17: Disegni dell'Ornamenti della Fontana di / Treui (WINDSOR VOLUME 169)

– 18: Cappella di S. Bastiarno

– 19: Acqua Paola

– 20: Conclaue Circondario Vaticano Seminario di / Siena Ruscellai

– 21: Originale del libro delle Acque Correnti

– 22: Depositi, Altari, et Altro (WINDSOR VOLUME 173)

Questo Tomo Manca – 23: Cuppola di Monte Fiascone, Cuppola della / Chiesa nuoua, Conuento di S. Sabina, Fiume / frà Ponte quattro Capi e Ponte Sisto, ed Altro

– 24: Alcuni disegni de Siti, et altro di S Michele à / ripa

– 25: Disegni p il Prencipe di Leictrestein in Germa/nia, disegni p il Pn'pe Martinitz in Praga / et Altri disegni comme nella sua tauola (WINDSOR VOLUME 174)

– 26: Catafalco dell' Imperatore (WINDSOR VOLUME 177)

–[27] [Di più] Originale del Tempio Vaticano

The final number on the list is crossed out, and it is apparently not included by Contini at the start of his manuscript, where the total number of volumes is given as twenty-six.

The next record of the volumes is of a quite different kind. Two books of drawings by the Piedmontese architect Bernardo Vittone (1704/5–1770) in the Musée des Arts Décoratifs in Paris contain, amongst drawings related to Vittone's own projects, an extraordinary number of copies after the Fontana drawings at Windsor. The copies are in some cases more neatly drawn than the originals, and they are closely related in technique to Vittone's independent projects. They were probably made by Vittone when he was in Rome in 1732, Fontana's drawings providing for the young architect a course in architectural design and draughtsmanship, as well as a repertoire of motifs. The Fontana volumes were probably at this time in the collection of Cardinal Alessandro Albani, who had inherited them on the death of his uncle, Pope Clement XI, in 1721.

The thirteen volumes at Windsor were acquired as part of the collection of Cardinal Alessandro Albani for King George III in 1762 through the agency of James Adam (see especially Fleming, pp.164ff.). With the Fontana volumes came the two 'Albani' volumes, and these were certainly bound before 1762, probably in the last years of Clement XI's reign or shortly after his death. The binding of these volumes, in white vellum, and the lettering on their spines corresponds with that of the single volume of Fontana's own drawings which is not included in Contini's list of 1716. This is Volume 168, which contains drawings connected with Fontana's work on the Curia Innocenziana (1694/5). Fontana published two books on this work and for this reason he may not have troubled to have the remaining drawings for the Curia sent to the binders, leaving them as an unbound sheaf, in which condition they passed to the collection of Pope Clement XI, and thus escaped mention in Contini's inventory.

Of the Fontana drawings that are not at Windsor a relatively small number, now in many different collections, consist of unbound sheets. These are mainly early drawings and later designs that Fontana sent out from Rome to meet commissions coming to him from other towns in Italy and abroad. The majority of drawings in other collections are contained in bound volumes most of which originally formed part of the set that is now mainly at Windsor. No clear distinction can be drawn between the Windsor and non-Windsor material, and in certain cases drawings for a single project are to be found in volumes in different collections. A short guide to the history of the other volumes known at present is therefore outlined here.

The first volume to leave the set owned by Fontana was probably the one which is now at Leipzig. The drawings it contains were discussed and in part illustrated in Coudenhove-Erthal's monograph of 1930 on Fontana, it being the only volume known to the author at that time. In binding the Leipzig volume is uniform with those at Windsor, but none of the entries in Contini's list gives an adequate description of the contents of the book and no number is to be seen on the cover. It probably left the collection before 1716 and there are no copies in the Vittone volumes of the drawings it contains. The second volume to have left the set was probably the one recently discovered by Professor Jack Wasserman in the Biblioteca Estense at Modena. This is volume 23 of Contini's list and the words '*Questo / Tomo manca*' are written in a later hand in the margin of his manuscript against this item. Copies of several of the drawings in the volume were made by Vittone in 1732, and it presumably left the collection at some time between then and 1762. It can be assumed from the note in the margin that Contini's list must have been checked during this period and that only one volume was found to be missing. Volume 14 of Contini's list is in the Biblioteca dell' Istituto Nazionale di Archeologia e Storia dell' Arte in Rome, acquired with the Lanciani collection (MSS, Lanciani 101), and many of its drawings were published by Donati (1942). Although there are no copies by Vittone of the drawings in this volume, it seems likely that it was removed after the one now at Modena, and before the series was acquired for George III.

The number of volumes of Fontana drawings acquired by Adam from the Albani collection may therefore have totalled twenty-four, and it is certain that there were more than the thirteen at present in the Royal collection. Adam himself appears by some means to have acquired two of the volumes – items 11 and 21 in Contini's list, which certainly belonged to his brother, Robert – and he may have owned others (see Fleming, pp.186f., on Adam's acquisition of some of the volumes). These two volumes are now in the Soane Museum, and as inscriptions in the volumes show, they were bought at Robert Adam's book sale in May 1818 by Sir John Soane. (There are in addition at the Soane Museum the original manuscript and drawings of Fontana's book on the Colosseum, the *Anfiteatro Flavio* which was published in The Hague in 1725. This volume is not mentioned in Contini's list and it was probably not in the Albani collection.)

The final loss to the Windsor set of Fontana's drawings consisted of three volumes which are now in the British Museum – Contini nos 1, 19 and 20. Like the volumes at Windsor, they have the insignia of George III embossed in the centre of the covers, and they were probably sent to the British Museum when the King's library of printed books and the King's topographical collection were established at the Museum in the early nineteenth century. Contini volume 1 contains for the most part drawings made by Fontana for Civitavecchia and Porto d'Anzio, drawings which have a direct bearing on a number of sheets remaining in the Windsor volumes. For this reason it must be regarded, together with the volume at Leipzig, as the most serious loss to the set of Fontana volumes, as it existed in the lifetime of the architect. The volumes remaining at Windsor are entered in Inventory A on fo.138 (Vol.169) and fo.140 *recto* and *verso* (the remaining twelve volumes).

Of the twenty-six volumes listed by Contini in 1716, seven are at present missing; it is to be hoped that some of these, existing perhaps in English or American collections, may yet come to light. They comprise Contini no.2 – drawings for S. Michele a Ripa; no.4 – drawings of altars, machines, and mathematical material; no.6 – drawings of the Acqua Felice; no.15 – projects for altars and ornaments; no.16 – projects for an inscription for Pope Clement XI; no.18 – projects presumably connected with the building of the Cappella Albani in S. Sebastiano; and finally no.24 – drawings of sites, including that of S. Michele a Ripa. In some cases sheets in the Vittone volumes in Paris can be related without difficulty to these missing drawings by Fontana; as a result of Vittone's seemingly tireless interest in the work of his predecessor the contents of Contini volume 16, for example, are probably recorded in full on three of the sheets of the Paris albums (Figs 565/6; vol. I, fos 90 to 92).

2 The literature on Fontana and an outline biography

The first *vita* of Carlo Fontana was published in the *Notizie degli Arcadi morti* in 1720, a few years after his death (1714). It was written by Giovanni Maria Crescimbeni, *Arciprete* of S. Maria in Cosmedin, historian and custodian of the Arcadian Academy originally founded by Queen Christina of Sweden in 1656 and re-established in 1690, of which Fontana had been a member since 1694 under the name of Olmano Falesio. It is, however, in the form of an obituary rather than a biography. Except for giving the correct year of birth (1638) – confirmed by Donati – Crescimbeni limits himself mainly to recording Fontana's work, which, in view of its immense quantity, had to be done concisely, and was restricted to the most important phases of his career. The works are divided into categories and listed in accordance with the author's ideas of their importance. Buildings outside Rome, and those in which Fontana played only a secondary part, are listed separately.

The first biography proper was published in 1736 by Lione Pascoli in the second volume of his *Vite*. Curiously enough he gives the year of Fontana's birth as 1634. He tells us about Fontana's apprenticeship with Bernini and to a certain extent describes his works chronologically, but without giving their dates. The value of his biography lies in the fact that it contains a far more comprehensive list of Fontana's buildings than Crescimbeni's, and in the information he gives about Fontana's numerous pupils.

In Francesco Milizia's biography of Fontana, first published in 1768, the author applied to his works the same criticisms that he had made against other Roman Baroque architects, and adds little to our knowledge of the architect's career.

The first modern attempt at a monograph was made by Conrad Escher in 1916, in his article in Thieme Becker, which was necessarily condensed, and is inaccurate in some details. He took note of the recent work of Gurlitt (1887) and Schubert (1908) and the article by Misciatelli in *Vita d'Arte* (1909), which included drawings by Fontana. A brief study by M. Guidi followed in 1925.

The only monograph on Fontana is that of Eduard von Coudenhove-Erthal, published in 1930. The author drew on much wider sources, and particularly on the reports sent to Paris by La Teulière, the Director of the French Academy in Rome and the *Avvisi* in the Vatican Library. He refers to three groups of drawings: a series in the Chigi archives in the Vatican (Chigiana P. VII, 9–13), the volume in Leipzig, and some separate drawings in the Albertina, but he remained in ignorance of the drawings at Windsor (cf. review by R. Wittkower, *Kritische Berichte*, III, 1930–31, pp.142–145).

Wittkower's essay of 1937 on Carlo Rainaldi and the Roman full Baroque threw new light on Fontana's relations with the architect Carlo Rainaldi, and two years later Vincenzo Golzio published the *Documenti Artistici* in the Chigi Archives, thus providing important documents about Fontana's part in the building activities of the Chigi family, in particular those of Cardinal Flavio. Ugo Donati in his *Artisti Ticinesi* of 1942 published in part the album of Fontana drawings in the Biblioteca Nazionale di Archeologia e Storia dell' Arte in Rome. Lina Montalto (1955) provided important information about Fontana's work for Cardinal Benedetto Pamphili, and the architect's relationship to Carlo Rainaldi was further explored by Furio Fasolo in his book on Hieronimo and Carlo Rainaldi (1961). In the chapter 'Late Baroque Classicism' in his *Art and Architecture in Italy 1600–1750* (1958; 1965 and 1973, 3rd ed.) Rudolf Wittkower once again returned to the theme of Fontana, and discussed his position in Roman Baroque architecture and the sources of his style. Paolo Portoghesi, in his book on the Roman Baroque (1966; English ed., 1970), adds little to our knowledge of Fontana, whom he regards as 'diluting' the style of the true Baroque. Thus it appears that a complete monograph on Carlo Fontana is still lacking and the authors hope that the present catalogue will prove the first step towards filling this gap.

The date of Carlo Fontana's birth was established by Ugo Donati on the basis of a manuscript of 1698 by Padre Sisto Sassi in the Biblioteca Cantonale at Lugano, which includes a copy of the certificate of baptism. This states that Carlo Fontana, the son of Francesco Amedeo Fontana and Cecilia Pizzalmore, was born on 22 April 1638 at Rancate near Como.

According to Pascoli, Carlo Fontana first came to Rome as an adult, but Sassi's statement that he moved there when he was twelve years old, in 1650, is more reliable, since it is obviously based on first-hand sources. It follows that Fontana must have received his training as an architect in Rome. The statement in the guides to Rome, that he was involved in the restoration of S. Marco in 1653, is still not proved by documentary evidence, but it is possible that his training began at this time or a little later, since by 1658 Carlo Fontana had become an extremely capable draughtsman in Pietro da Cortona's studio, and assisted the master with drawings at the time of his remodelling of S. Maria della Pace (H. Ost, *Römisches Jahrbuch für Kunstgeschichte*, 13, 1971, pp.248–257). Already then, Fontana was evidently so proud of his accomplishments that he began to sign his drawings, in itself a rather unusual practice at that time, and one which he continued throughout his life (sometimes his signature has not been preserved because the sheets were cut for binding – see Catalogue).

There is no doubt that Pietro da Cortona was his first teacher. Pollak's statement (s.v. Thieme Becker, Pietro da Cortona, VII, 1912, p.495) that Fontana in 1660, at the age of twenty-two, was entrusted with the direction of the work for S. Carlo al Corso, which he continued till 1665, remains unconfirmed despite recent research in the archives of the Lombard brotherhood (cf. G. Drago and L. Salerno, *SS. Ambrogio e Carlo al Corso e l'arciconfraternita dei Lombardi in Roma* (CRI 96), Rome, 1967, pp.60, 71 note 17).

Fontana's long association with Bernini began soon after the completion of the façade of S. Maria della Pace, probably with the erection of the colonnades of S. Peter's on which, according to Brauer/Wittkower, Fontana was engaged in 1659. In 1663 he assisted Bernini in the building of the Scala Regia and took over from him work on the Arsenal of Civitavecchia. Fontana also drew up the plans for the palace of Cardinal Flavio Chigi on the Piazza SS. Apostoli (1664–67), for the extension of the Chigi palace, and the church of S. Maria dell' Assunta in Ariccia (1662–64). When Bernini was directing the creation of the monument with the elephant in front of S. Maria sopra Minerva (1665–66), Carlo Fontana provided the plans for its position in front of the church, where it was erected in 1667.

With Carlo Rainaldi his relations were completely different. In the case of Pietro da Cortona and Bernini, he was the pupil and assistant; to Carlo Rainaldi he became a competitor, who, in connection with the façade of S. Andrea della Valle and the twin churches on the Piazza del Popolo, S. Maria di Monte Santo and S. Maria dei Miracoli, attempted to have the plans of his master modified, actually undermining Rainaldi's scheme by producing counter-projects. In spite of this, their collaboration continued over a number of years and only completely collapsed in 1677, though there had been a lapse for some time after 1667.

Carlo Fontana's first completely independent work is probably the façade of SS. Faustino e Giovita (*c.*1664),* which was demolished when the embankment of the Tiber was built. The plan of this building in the Ashmolean Museum, Oxford, shows that it was a fairly conventional work, with few original traits. The façade of S. Biagio in Campitelli (S. Rita da Cascia), formerly in the Via Giulio Romano and after its demolition in 1928 re-erected on the Piazza Campizucchi (1940), was finished about 1665, and in its arrangement recalls Bernini's façade of S. Bibiana. In order to compensate for the oblique view which the site afforded, Fontana placed the concave side bays of the upper storey on a diagonal, a device which must have caught the attention of those interested in architecture and aroused their interest in the young architect, then only twenty-seven. To the end of Fontana's early period belongs the restoration of S. Spirito dei Napolitani, commissioned in 1666, which was replaced in 1702–1708 by a more complete reconstruction by the same architect.

In 1664 Carlo Fontana was appointed coadjutor and successor-designate to Bernini in the post of *misuratore e stimatore della Camera Apostolica*, and two years later, in 1666, he became *misuratore della Rev. Fabbrica di S. Pietro*. This post brought in only a small revenue, but was of great importance for Fontana's future, since it was his first contact with the building authorities of S. Peter's.

Carlo Fontana's early phase, which coincides almost exactly with the period of Alexander VII's pontificate (1655–67), ends with his unanimous election as *architetto di merito* of the Accademia di San Luca on 15 May 1667, constituting his official approbation by the Academy and entitling him to teach architecture (see Archivio dell'Accademia di S. Luca, vol.44, fo.40).

With this nomination his really independent activities began, but, as so often in his future career, external events were to hinder him. With the death of Alexander VII there followed a lull in building activities which lasted, almost uninterrupted, till the end of the century. Two of the great masters of the High Baroque died, Borromini in 1667 and Pietro da Cortona two years later, and Bernini, with the rejection of his Louvre project in 1666, had passed his zenith. In these circumstances it is not, therefore, surprising that although Fontana was able to undertake so many varied commissions with remarkable results, up to the end of the seventies he was restricted to more or less minor works.

On the occasion of a reception on 15 August 1668 in the gardens of the Casino Chigi, near the Via delle Quattro Fontane, he was responsible for the decoration, which is recorded in engravings (Bjurström, pp.68, 144f.). He was in charge of work at the Villa of Cardinal Flavio Chigi, near Formello, which, in spite of its grandiose name, Versaglia (Versailles), was a fairly simple country seat (Felice della Greca's chapel there had already been finished).

*Many of the works mentioned in this outline biography are discussed below in the main part of the catalogue, where full bibliographical references are to be found. On SS. Faustino e Giovita and S. Biagio in Campitelli (S. Rita da Cascia), see Hager in *Commentari,* 1972, pp.261ff.; M. Myers, pp.24f.; Tafuri in *Via Giulia* pp.233f, 530f.

As regards Fontana's share in the work, the documents published by Golzio refer to a granary, a shed for sheep, and waterworks, but the plan of the house, with open arcades towards the court – now only a ruin – also goes back to a design by Fontana, of which his assistant, Simone Felice del Lino, made a model in 1681. He was also commissioned with the restoration of the nearby church of the Madonna del Sorbo (1682). Fontana erected another palace for Cardinal Flavio Chigi in S. Quirico d'Orcia in 1678–79, and at the same time he carried out the alterations to the Villa Cetinale, near Siena, for Don Mario Chigi.

Fontana's most illustrious patron at this time was Queen Christina of Sweden. She entrusted him with the building of the Teatro Tor di Nona, of which she was patron (1669–71). The site belonged to the Arciconfraternità della Carità di S. Girolamo, for which Fontana worked as architect during the same period. The design for the church of the Brigittine Convent on the Piazza Farnese, which the Queen commissioned from Fontana in 1676, was not carried out for reasons of economy (Hager, *Zwillingskirchen*, p.246, n.110). The monument to Queen Christina in S. Peter's, commissioned by Innocent XII and finished under Clement XI, for which the drawings are at Windsor, was Fontana's last work connected with the Queen (on the theatre see Cametti; p.183 below).

It was probably owing to the patronage of the Altieri family, who had become very influential after the elevation of Cardinal Emilio Altieri to the papacy as Clement X in 1670, that Fontana received the commission for completing the dome of the cathedral at Montefiascone, damaged by fire in 1670, of which Cardinal Paluzzo Altieri had been bishop. In the last years of the reign of Alexander VII, about 1666–67, Fontana had already submitted plans for the reconstruction of the castle (Vatican Library, Chigi P. VII 12, fos. 40–44). Coudenhove-Erthal was misled by the fact that the related perspective drawings show the cathedral in its earlier form and connected them with the erection of the cupola. According to Crescimbeni, Fontana also worked on a palace for the Altieri "nella Terra dell' Oriuolo", and this presumably refers to the addition of a gallery at the castle of Oriolo, to house Clement X's important collection of papal portraits (A. Schiavo, *Palazzo Altieri*, 1964, pp.187f.). The commission for extending the Roman palace of the family on the Piazza del Gesù, for which Fontana had submitted designs, was given to Giovanni Antonio de'Rossi, who was almost twenty years his senior (for Montefiascone, see A. Serra; Hager, 1975).

Fontana also designed a palace for Count Bigazzini, but, according to Pascoli, his first projects did not meet with approval; finally he presented two alternative proposals which pleased the patron so much that he found it difficult to choose between them. The project, carried out between 1676 and 1680, involved an extension of the palace, which was destroyed when the Piazza Venezia was cleared. The Palazzo Grimani in the Via Rasella, to which Pascoli also refers, likewise fell a victim to nineteenth-century rebuilding.

Fontana's most important commission in the field of church architecture in the early seventies was the continuation of the church of S. Maria di Monte Santo on the Piazza del Popolo, on which work had stopped in 1667, when the drum was at window level. Taken up again in 1671, it was given new impetus by a donation from Cardinal Gastaldi. Fontana's scheme, although it had already been accepted for execution, was soon discarded in favour of one by Bernini, Fontana being again reduced to the capacity of assistant. In the case of the sister church, Santa Maria dei Miracoli, however, he was able to get his modifications to the Rainaldi project accepted and on his own carried out the interior of the choir of the church. Towards the end of the decade, in 1678–80, Fontana erected the small church of S. Margherita in Trastevere at the order of Cardinal Gastaldi, whose sister lived in the Franciscan convent attached to the church (Hager, *Zwillingskirchen*, and in *Commentari*, 1974, pp.225ff.).

The commission for S. Maria Maddalena was an unhappy one for Fontana. The apse was begun after his plans in 1668, but work was discontinued in 1674, when it had reached the crossing. After six years building activities were resumed, starting with the erection of the convent, and Fontana had to make way for his pupil Carlo Francesco Bizzaccheri, who was in his turn replaced by other architects when the church was completed (L. Mortari, *S. Maria Maddalena,* CRI 104, Rome, 1969).

During the years 1670–74 Fontana redecorated S. Marta, a small church of 1570 on the Piazza del Collegio Romano, and he enlarged it by the addition of chapels to the nave. In 1675, on the orders of Ascanio Sforza, he restored the mediaeval collegiate church of Lanuvio, near Genzano, the façade of which is almost a replica of Bernini's at S. Maria di Galloro, near Ariccia. The Fontana degli Scogli, on the 'Piazza Carlo Fontana', also recalls Bernini in its imitation of natural rock (see M. Guidi; A. Galieti. On S. Marta see Hager in *Commentari,* 1974, pp.225ff.).

A great part of Fontana's activities in the decade after the death of Alexander VII was directed towards the solution of problems of engineering, which also played a considerable role in his later life, as the drawings at Windsor attest.

About 1669, when the Via Flaminia was threatened by flooding near S. Andrea, where the waters of the Tiber endangered the dam built under Julius III, Fontana provided plans and expert evidence, which, in spite of his youth, prevailed against those of the engineer Negrisoli, a specialist who had been called in from Ferrara. The commission was, however, finally given in 1671 to the Dutch hydraulic expert, Cornelius Meyer, who provided a much lower estimate (see d'Onofrio, *Tevere*, pp.83ff.).

Under Clement X Fontana was entrusted with the repair of the water-supply system which fed the Fontana Paola on the Janiculum, a commision which stimulated him to discuss the problems involved in an exhaustive treatise (cf. below).

Fontana was, however, most successful in the treatment of interiors during this period. The ciborium for the high altar of S. Maria in Traspontina, commissioned by Matteo Orlandi, General of the Carmelite Order, was executed in 1674 in the shape of a columnar tempietto on a circular ground plan, with the cupola representing a crown, an allusion to the Roman tradition of having especially venerated icons crowned by the Chapter of S. Peter's. In 1671 he began work on the Cappella Ginetti in S. Andrea della Valle, but, owing to delays in the sculptors' and masons' work, it was completed only in 1684. This chapel was the first of several in which Fontana used coloured marble.

The first period of his career, ending in the 1670's, can be seen as the phase of his development and establishment as an architect, during which he was also already training pupils. He is recorded as a teacher in architecture at the Academy of S. Luke in 1675, but as early as 1673 the Swede, Nicodemus Tessin, was training with him, the first of his numerous pupils coming from northern Europe who, after their return home, made their special mark. Two Italian pupils, Simone Felice del Lino and Carlo Francesco Bizzaccheri, have already been mentioned. The latter seems to have started to work independently about 1676–77, when he was given the commission for the Vivaldi Chapel in S. Maria di Monte Santo (for Fontana's beginnings as a teacher, see Archivio dell' Accademia di S. Luca, vol.45, fo.17).

By the end of the 1670's Fontana's position was not yet spectacular, but he managed to assert himself at a time which was very difficult for all Roman architects, because of the financial stringency which ensued after the lavish pontificate of Alexander VII, and he had two notable achievements – the last-named commissions – to his credit. After Alexander VII's death even Bernini had to be content with the decoration of chapels (Cappella Altieri in S. Francesco a Ripa, Cappella Fonseca in S. Lorenzo in Lucina), since his large projects were abandoned for reasons of economy.

At Bernini's death in 1680, it was Mattia de' Rossi, not Fontana, who was accepted as his successor. De' Rossi was appointed Architect of S. Peter's, while Fontana was put in charge of the secular papal buildings. Mattia de' Rossi was elected Principe of the Accademia di S. Luca in 1681, and received what important commissions arose, including the Ospizio di S. Galla with the attached church (1684–86), and the original building of the Ospizio di S. Michele (1686–89). Other works that he carried out were the remodelling of San Francesco a Ripa (1682–89) and S. Maria delle Vergini (façade completed in 1697), and the new Collegiata at Valmontone (1686–89).

On Mattia de' Rossi's resignation as Principe of the Accademia di S. Luca in 1682, Carlo Fontana was one of the candidates for the post, but the painter Luigi Garzi was elected. It was only in 1686 that Fontana became Principe, after Filippo Lauri had declined the post. One of Carlo's pupils, Domenico Martinelli of Lucca, had already begun to play a prominent part in the Academy, where he taught regularly from 1683 till 1689, when he left Rome for some time (see Archivio dell' Acc. di S. Luca, vol.45 and Missirini). Giovanni Battista Contini, a fellow pupil of Fontana's in Bernini's studio, had already been elected Principe in 1683, but had not been very successful in that capacity. His architectural work during this period was mainly concerned with interiors of chapels, except for the commission for the Abbey of Montecasino, where he began to enlarge the 'Loggia del Paradiso' with subsidiary cloisters (Hager in *Commentari*, 1970, pp.92ff.).

Owing to the continuing unfavourable economic and political conditions during Innocent XI's pontificate (1676–89), which prevented extensive building activities, Fontana and his followers worked mainly for private patrons and on commissions outside Rome.

The construction of the chapel for the tombs of Cardinals Lorenzo and Alderano Cybo in S. Maria del Popolo, which had originally been given to Bernini, was executed by Carlo Fontana after his master's death. The first design was circular with concentric chapels. A similar form was used by Fontana about the same date for the church of the Jesuit College at Loyola, and for the church commissioned for the Colosseum by Innocent XI, but never executed owing to the war with the Turks of 1683 (plan in the Soane Museum, London). Important commissions like the last two projects are proof of the reputation which Fontana had already gained for himself. Oliva, the General of the Jesuit Order, was the originator of the Loyola project, which, owing to its association with St Ignatius' birth-place, was one of the most important commissions to be given by the

Order. Oliva died in 1681 without seeing the plans, which were presented to his successor, Charles de Noyelles (General from 1681 to 1686). When the building was actually carried out, after 1689, many deviations in detail were made from Fontana's plan (On the Cybo chapel, see Hager in *Commentari*, 1974, pp.47ff., and on the work at Loyola and the project for the Colosseum, see di Macco; Hager, *Colosseum,* and *Loyola,* 1973 and 1974).

The Cappella Cybo, actually built on a cruciform ground-plan, was Fontana's first work of importance. In spite of the fact that all the subsidiary annexes, except for the entrance vestibule, are cut off short, the chapel has the appearance of a small domed church, in which the polychrome and sculptural decoration is in every detail part of a comprehensive scheme in emulation of Raphael's Chigi Chapel opposite. Fontana's work is one of the most mature achievements in Roman chapel architecture, as his contemporaries were quick to acknowledge: 'dicendosi . . . hauer luogo tra le principali di Roma' (Cartari-Febei, vol.90, 1684, fo.287). It was soon followed by the somewhat less spectacular Cappella dell' Assunta which Fontana added to the Collegio Clementino (1685–87; see below, and L. Montalto, 1938, p.164; Zambarelli, pp.28f).

At the same time Fontana was able to create a work of equal importance in the field of façade architecture, the front of S. Marcello al Corso, commissioned by Mons. Marc' Antonio Buoncompagni, and essentially completed in 1682–84 on a concave ground plan (Figs 563/4). It established a type for the late Roman Baroque façade.

The Cappella Cybo and the façade of S. Marcello represented the real break-through in Fontana's career and put him at the head of contemporary Roman architects, with the exception perhaps of Mattia de' Rossi, who was still more revered especially in the circle of the Accademia di S. Luca.

Fontana's rise to fame can be clearly followed in the titles and privileges accorded him. By 1670 the title *Cavaliere* had been conferred upon him (Arch. dell' Acc. di S. Luca, vol. 45, fo.56). In 1681 he was already in the position of having a medal struck with his portrait on the obverse and on the reverse the allegorical figure of architecture with the inscription: SUPEREMINET OMNES (Figs 567/8). On the completion of the Ginetti Chapel in 1684 Fontana was referred to as 'architetto rinomato' (Cartari-Febei, vol.90, fo.220*v*).

Other chapels that can be attributed to Fontana during these years are those for Michelangelo Ricci (d. 1682) in S. Francesco a Ripa, and the Cappella Montioni in S. Maria di Monte Santo, the latter executed by his pupil Tomaso Mattei and completed in 1687. Both these works contain certain Borrominesque elements.

Lina Montalto has established that in 1683 Fontana became architect to Cardinal Benedetto Pamphili, one of the most influential patrons of the time, whom he served till the end of his life, but the commissions he obtained from him were of limited importance. He carried out the alterations to the family palace on the Corso, which included the decoration of the 'teatro stabile', opened in 1684, the technical direction of which was Fontana's responsibility; the remodelling of the library (*c.*1686), and the construction of two chapels. In 1685 he built a pulpit in S. Francesco a Ripa (now destroyed), and during the second half of the eighties Fontana produced plans for the cupola of the cathedral at Como (1688) and for completing the cathedral at Bergamo (1688–92), erected the Cappella del SS. Sacramento in the cathedral at Albano (1688–89; A. Galieti), and enlarged in

1690 the cathedral at Porto near Fiumicino (Golzio, *Documenti*). The patron for the two last-named buildings was again Cardinal Flavio Chigi.

It was only at the end of the decade, which nearly coincided with the end of the pontificate of Innocent XI (1689), that Fontana once more received an important commission, the project for the Casino 'per Ventia', with its highly original ground plan, for which the drawings are preserved at Windsor.

In 1690, during the short reign of Alexander VIII (1689–91), Fontana began the reconstruction of the Fontana Paola on the Janiculum which he extended by the still extant 'fontanone', in imitation of Bernini's basin for the Trevi Fountain. In spite of the fact that an engraving of the fountain by Alessandro Specchi was published in 1694, the work seems to have continued during most of the pontificate of Innocent XII, who inspected the completed fountain on 17 July 1700, a few months before his death. Fontana also made plans for the extension of the Piazza in front of S. Peter's and for the replanning of the Borgo; this was carried out to a different plan in modern times (Hager, 1968; T. K. Kitao, *Circle and Oval in the Square of S. Peter's*, New York, 1974, pp.61–66).

Innocent XII, though in general anxious to prolong the economies of Innocent XI, was, like Alexander VIII, interested in artistic matters, and the competence of his judgement is shown by his comments on a model for the Baptismal Chapel in S. Peter's and by those on the campanile for the Palazzo di Montecitorio (see Catalogue).

Although Fontana's model for the Baptistry had been rejected by the Pope in 1693, it was he who eventually won the commission in competition with Mattia de' Rossi, first architect of S. Peter's, and Maratta, who then stood in high favour. On 23 March 1697, two years after Mattia de' Rossi's death, Fontana was appointed architect of S. Peter's. The Baptistry was then nearing completion, the tomb of Queen Christina of Sweden had been begun in 1696, and the very humble monument to the Pope himself had been designed in 1692.

Fontana's reputation did not, however, rest solely on these works. His long service as *misuratore* in connection with S. Peter's and especially, at the request of Innocent XII, as expert in connection with the threatened collapse of the dome, a problem which had overshadowed Bernini's last years, brought him renown. This long association with S. Peter's led to his most important literary work, *Il Tempio Vaticano e sua origine*, of which the manuscript was essentially completed by 1687, but which was only published in 1694, with engravings by Specchi after Fontana's drawings (on the consequences of the publication, leading to Fontana's promotion to the rank of Polish Count, see Catalogue).

In 1692 the *Discorso del Mons. Carlo Vespignano sopra la facile riuscita di restaurare il Ponte Senatorio* had appeared with illustrations from his own hand. These were followed in 1696 by his *Discorso sopra le cause delle innondationi del Tevere,* which deals with the floods near S. Andrea in the Via Flaminia and in which Fontana refers to his recommendations of 1669 mentioned above. His proposals were, however, attacked by Francesco Maria Onorati in a treatise, published in 1698, who convincingly defends the work of the Dutch engineer: 'Apologia per la passonata fatta sopra il Tevere fuori di Porta del Popolo in difesa della Strada della Flaminia con la direttione del signor Cornelio Meyer famoso ingegniere olandese'. Fontana's *Utilissimo trattato delle Acque Correnti,* of which the manuscript is preserved in the Soane Museum, London, also appeared in 1696. The *Anfiteatro*

Flavio (manuscript and drawings in the same museum) must also have been completed in 1696, since it is referred to in the *Utilissimo trattato* (Coudenhove-Erthal, p.85). The series of theoretical treatises of these years ends with the *Descrizione della nob. Cappella della Fonte Battesimale in S. Pietro*, published in 1697. These works provide evidence of Fontana's historical and technical knowledge, gained as a result of his practical activities. His concern is not primarily to establish academic principles but to record the wisdom acquired in four decades of experience as an architect.

Under Innocent XII, who caused the harbours of Civitavecchia and Anzio to be repaired, Fontana had ample opportunity to gain experience in the field of hydraulic works.

The plans in the *Tempio Vaticano* for the Piazza of S. Peter's had little chance of being carried out under Innocent XII, but those in the *Discorso sopra l'antico Monte Citatorio* were executed as far as the completion of the palace itself was concerned, although those for the semi-circular open space in front of it were not realized.

In 1693 Fontana was elected Principe of the Accademia di S. Luca, because Mattia de' Rossi refused re-election, and he was reappointed every year till 1699. The pontificate of Innocent XII must be regarded as the zenith of Fontana's career, but even then there were disappointments. In the second version of his report about the events connected with the reconstruction of the Baptistry in 1704 (published below), and in his expanded *Discorso sopra . . . Monte Citatorio* of 1708, he tells us of the constant difficulties that he had to face.

In 1693 it was decided not to execute his plans for the new sacristy of S. Peter's, and in 1696 his project for the Jesuit church at Frascati, presented and approved in 1694, was discarded. A further scheme for a church, projected in 1694 for Cardinal Giovanni Francesco Negroni, seems also not to have been realized. The limitations imposed on his plans for the Curia Innocenziana have already been mentioned. A tragedy from the architectural point of view was the demolition for moral reasons in 1697 of the Teatro Tor di Nona, which had had to close its doors in the Holy Year of 1675, and had just been re-erected on a larger scale in 1695–97 (Cametti).

A further work of Fontana's to be dated to these years was a private commission for the 'abellimento e rimodernamento' of the Palazzo Massimo at the foot of the Capitol.

Cardinal Benedetto Pamphili continued to be Fontana's patron. As protector of the Collegio Clementino he commissioned alterations to the College, which included the fitting-up of the 'Teatrino dei Convittori'. In 1681, as Grand Prior of the Order of Malta, Pamphili had already instructed Fontana to complete the Loggia of S. Maria del Priorato, which had been left unfinished by Mattia de' Rossi, and in 1696 he ordered him to restore the Casino Cecchignola belonging to the Order (Montalto, 1953). From 1697 onwards he was also Fontana's superior for the work mentioned in Civitavecchia and Anzio.

During this phase commissions outside Rome increased in number. The designs for the apse of the cathedral of Naples (1691–96?) were followed by plans for the high altar of the Steccata at Parma (1697). The Martinitz Palace in Prague appears to have been built from Fontana's plans (1700), though probably modified by a local architect. His scheme for the Liechtenstein Palace at Landskron (1696), a monumental project with several court-yards, was rejected, probably because, like Bernini's Louvre, it was regarded as being alien to local traditions.

The building activities during the pontificate of Innocent XII end with a competition for the façade of S. Giovanni in Laterano, in which Fontana seems to have been involved. A studio drawing or copy of a project for it is preserved at Oxford (see Hager in *The Burlington Magazine*, 1975, pp.105f.).

At the beginning of the eighteenth century Fontana's position was indisputably that of the leading architect in Rome. In a certificate of authorship of 1703 for the Casa Correzionale (see below) he is referred to as 'maggior Virtuoso nella sua Professione de' nostri tempi'. Of his contemporaries in Bernini's studio only Giovanni Battista Contini was still alive, working mainly outside Rome (Vetralla, Ravenna, etc.) and obtaining only small commissions in the Holy City. Antonio Valeri, younger by a generation, became Fontana's pupil after he had worked with Bernini for a time, and eventually succeeded him as first architect of S. Peter's. Andrea Pozzo, who was occasionally Fontana's competitor, moved to Vienna in 1702.

The election of Clement XI (1700–21), a pope deeply interested in artistic affairs which he pursued with initiative and eagerness, brought important changes for Carlo Fontana. The Pope preferred Carlo Maratta to him as Principe of the Accademia di S. Luca, and in 1702 founded the so-called 'Concorsi Clementini', which regularized the competitions of the Academy under the supervision of the Pope, who sometimes even suggested the themes for them. In this way he officially gave the Accademia di S. Luca the importance that had already in fact been conceded to it, and which was publicly acknowledged when in 1676 the French Academy was associated with it.

In the practical sphere, however, the patronage of this enthusiastic Pope was limited by external circumstances: the Spanish War of Succession threatened the Holy City with occupation in 1708, and when the Turkish War started again in 1716, the Pope was faced with the payment of high subventions.

Carlo Fontana was 63 years old when Clement XI became Pope and already suffered from gout; he said in a letter of 1703 (fo.1 in Vat. Lat. 8635, fos 47ff., see Coudenhove-Erthal, p.95, n.165) that gout made it very difficult for him to write). His replacement by Maratta at the Academy had been a hard blow for him, and relations between the two artists remained strained in spite of the Pope's attempts at a reconciliation. Fontana was now given the post of Primo Consigliere, which he occupied till the end of his life, and was therefore still able to exert considerable influence in the field of architecture. His son Francesco, born in 1668 and a member of the Academy since 1694, was made Vice-President in 1703 and invested with full authority to represent the ageing Maratta.

Although the building activities of the Pope were restricted by economic and political difficulties, he was active in the restoration of ancient monuments and buildings of a practical character and in the embellishment of his home town, Urbino. He sent Fontana to Urbino in 1703 to prepare plans for the high altar of the cathedral, for the restoration of the Palazzo Albani, and for a family chapel in S. Francesco. As, however, in the scheme for the Ripetta harbour in Rome (carried out by Alessandro Specchi), the final planning and execution were handed over to other artists – in the case of the cathedral altar again to Specchi – or were postponed to a later date. The portico of S. Maria in Trastevere was the first restoration scheme carried out by Fontana for Clement XI (1702), while those for S. Teodoro al Palatino were to a large extent executed by his assistants. The most important project in the field of church architecture in Rome under Clement XI, the rebuilding of

SS. Apostoli, was undertaken in 1702 by Francesco Fontana, the son, who had already been engaged in reconstructing the Temple of Neptune as the Dogana di Terra in 1694 (finished 1705). After his early death in 1708 the work was completed by his father and his pupil, Nicola Michetti. Francesco Fontana was also responsible for the restoration of S. Pietro in Vincoli and for strengthening the upper church of S. Clemente, the modernisation of which was carried out by Carlo Stefano Fontana, a nephew of Carlo Fontana. This latter work was undertaken after Carlo's death, as were the alterations to S. Maria in Monticelli by his pupils Matteo Sassi and Giuseppe Sardi, and the redecoration of S. Maria in Cosmedin by the latter in 1718, which was removed at the end of the 19th century.

Soon after the turn of the century, therefore, the generation of Fontana's pupils was preparing to succeed him, though he himself remained remarkably active, in spite of his partial disablement. For this and other reasons he had recourse to assistants, and young pupils are mentioned on various occasions assisting Fontana and making drawings especially of sites etc. The erection of the Casa Correzionale of the Ospizio di S. Michele (1701–04), an innovation in the field of prison architecture, attracted a 'grand. mo concorso di forastieri, a vedere d.a Casa di Corrett.ne' even as early as 1725 (see A.S.R. Osp. di S. Michele, vol.338, fo.496). The alterations and extension of the hospice itself after 1708 were carried out after his plans and under his supervision almost until his death. The same was true of the granary on the site of the Baths of Diocletian, which had been erected between 1703 and 1705. One of the most remarkable works of the late phase of his career are the designs for the Fontana di Trevi (1706). The plans for the Casino Vaini on the Janiculum, which, on the orders of the Presidenza delle Strade, was demolished in 1703 because it blocked the view of the Fontana Paola, were executed by his pupil, Romano Carapecchia, for a private patron (Tonna and de Lucca, p.7). A donation of Cardinal Girolamo Casanata, who died on 2 March 1700, provided for the erection of the Biblioteca Casanatense in the Convent of S. Maria sopra Minerva, in which Fontana continued the tradition of the two great libraries of the High Baroque, the Alessandrina and Vallicelliana. The building was planned during the life-times of the Cardinal and of Innocent XII, as was that for the church of S. Spirito dei Napolitani, belonging to a Neapolitan fraternity, the renovation of which (1702–08) was made possible by the generous support of Innocent XII. At the same time Fontana worked on the designs for the façade of S. Maria dell' Umilità at the foot of the Quirinal (erected in 1703) and for the Albani Chapel in S. Sebastiano fuori le mura (begun in 1706).

Another field in which Carlo Fontana's artistic inventiveness played a great part was that of decorations for festivities. For Innocent XII (1692) and Clement XI (1701) he had erected the triumphal arches on the occasion of their taking possession of the Lateran. More important were the decorations which he provided for the memorial services to the Emperor Leopold I in S. Maria dell' Anima (1705) and King Pedro II of Portugal in S. Antonio de' Portoghesi (1707; Braham, *Funeral Decorations*).

Even in his last years Fontana was still working for patrons outside Rome. The Palazzo Capponi in Florence was built after his plans in 1705, and the Conte Durazzo commissioned him to carry out the alterations to his palace in Genoa, which included the insertion of a new staircase and a loggia on the court façade (1705; G. de Angelis d'Ossat in Rivista Municipale 'Genova', 8, August 1935).

Under Leopold I Fontana had presented plans for the royal stables in Vienna, which do not seem to have been executed, and his project for the cathedral at Fulda seems to have suffered the same fate. The present whereabouts of the drawings for the latter are not known, and the model for the cathedral, which was sent from Rome to Fulda in 1706 (Dettweiler, p.1, n.1) – probably that mentioned by Pascoli – is also lost.

Another very carefully worked out Roman project, which would have been Carlo Fontana's masterpiece in church architecture, never got beyond the planning stage. This is the church which was to be erected in the Colosseum in honour of the early Christian martyrs, with the arena transformed into an open approach, for which Fontana submitted plans to Clement XI. The earlier version, produced under Innocent XI (cf. above), had been revised considerably at the turn of the century. Although a project like this must have been of the greatest interest to a Pope like Clement XI, economic conditions prevented its realisation, as they had done under Innocent XI. Only a fence to safeguard the consecrated ground, was erected. When in 1725 the project was published in the form of engravings as a complement to his historical treatise on the amphitheatre, Fontana was already dead.

According to Pascoli, Carlo Fontana never recovered from the death of his son Francesco. On 16 February 1714 Fontana met his own death before being able to receive the sacraments of the Holy Eucharist and Extreme Unction (Arch. del Vicar., S. Lorenzo ai Monti, 21, Liber Mortuorum, VIII, fo.47). Fontana died in his house, opposite the monastery of S. Spirito alla Colonna Traiana (cf. no.114 on the Map of Nolli). At that time the members of his household comprised his son Gaspare (a priest), his grand-children Mauro and Anna Teresa, and the servants Giovanna Ruggieri, Antonio and Michelangelo (Arch. del Vicar., S. Lorenzo ai Monti, 35, Status Animarum, 1711–1719, fo. 238 *vo.*). Pascoli reports that 'decorose esequie' took place in Fontana's honour in S. Lorenzo ai Monti, his parish church which was destroyed in modern times when the whole area was cleared. In fact, however, the ceremony was simple, considering the important position Fontana had held and his long and successful career as an architect. The reason for this may have been that he had made few friends, and a report preserved in the Accademia di S. Luca indicates the cool reaction of his colleagues to his death which differed so much from the compassionate attitude which prevailed when Mattia de' Rossi died. Carlo Fontana '. . . fù sepelito nella sua Parrocchia di S. Lorenzolo con mediocre pompa, postigli in giro 24 facoletti da tre libre per ciascuno, fu vestito col sacco della Compagnia del S. mo Nome di Maria; gli fu cantata Messa semplice senza Musica parato con le sue Insegne il sito solo dell' Altar maggiore, e ui interuennero il Principe con diecenoue Accademici, à quali fù data una Candela di mezza libra per ciascheduno, Requiescat in pace, amen' (Arch. Acc. S. Luca, vol.46a, fo.166).

Success and recognition do not seem to have come easily to Fontana; he had to strive for them. This is reflected in his literary works, which often contain extensive *apologie*, in particular in his highly polemical report of 1704 about Mattia and Domenico de' Rossi and Maratta in connection with the alterations to the Baptistry (published below).

Fontana's fundamental attitude in his professional life seems to have been a determination to succeed. With frankness and lively eloquence he drew attention to his achievements, thus giving rise to Pascoli's well-known remark: 'Parlava bene e meglio parlato avrebbe, se men parlato avesse di se, e dell' opere sue'. It was in keeping with his striving for recognition that he presented to the Academy Congregation on 28 December 1708 a volume containing copies of certificates and letters of appreciation which he had received from the Emperor Leopold I, the Empress and King Augustus II of Poland, on the pretext that any honour accorded to a member of the Academy would reflect on the Academy itself. Although these documents, still in the archives of the Academy (vol.35), do not mention definite building projects, they testify to Fontana's extensive connections and his influence north of the Alps. They did not, however, smooth the way for him again to the summit of the Academy of S. Luke.

The evaluation of his achievements outside his professional circle was much more positive, as is shown by the passage from the certificate of 1703 quoted above in connection with the affair of the Casa Correzionale. Crescimbeni in his obituary considers Fontana worthy of being listed among the 'principali professori' and ends his list of architectural works with the remark: 'Opere tutte, dalle quali si conosce la vastità del suo talento, il suo molto sapere e quanto se fosse contradistinto dagli altri professori del suo tempo'. This opinion was unaffected by the ill-feeling caused between them by Fontana when he refused to sign a resolution, for which the Academy of the Arcadia as a penalty withdrew the name of 'Falesio', which had been assigned to him.

Carlo Fontana had a greater number of pupils than any other architect of the Roman Baroque before or after him. The complex problem of his influence on the activities of the Accademia di S. Luca can here only be touched upon and deserves a special investigation (see the recent publication of the drawings by Marconi, etc., 1974, and Carlo Pietrangeli, *et al., L'Accademia Nazionale di San Luca,* Rome, 1974).

Pascoli has already provided a list of pupils, which included, besides Carlo's son, Francesco, and his nephews, Carlo Stefano and Girolamo Fontana, the following names: Simone Felice del Lino, Romano Carapecchia, Carlo Francesco Bizzaccheri, Carlo Buratti, Tomaso Mattei, and Alessandro Specchi. Pascoli, being aware that the number was far greater, adds Matteo Sassi and Antonio Canevari and indicated that these are only the names of those he remembered. In fact he had forgotten Fontana's most famous Italian pupil, Filippo Juvarra. An anonymous life of Juvarra (ed. Rovere-Viale-Brinckmann, p.23) mentions the studio, Fontana's advice and the 'Giovani' (sic), whose circle Juvarra joined. Owing to his talent and the support which he received from Carlo and Francesco Fontana, Juvarra won the Academy competition in architecture in 1705. He paid tribute to Fontana in the design of a funeral monument (Fig.569).

To Pascoli's list of pupils or direct successors can be added the names of the following architects: Domenico Martinelli, Sebastiano Cipriani, Nicola Michetti, Filippo Barigioni, Domenico Antonio de Sanctis, Nicola Rossini, Ludovico Rusconi Sassi and Antonio Valeri, and probably many more, like Giacomo Amato, who was active in Sicily (see Anthony Blunt, *Sicilian Baroque,* 1968, p.32). During his last years Fontana worked on particularly close terms with Nicola Michetti, originally a *giovane* of his son, Francesco Fontana, and he held Michetti in high esteem (A.S.R., Ospizio di S. Michele, vol.237, fo.257). Pascoli omits from the list Fontana's foreign pupils, as, for instance, Nicodemus Tessin the Younger, who worked with him in 1673 (O. Siren, *Nicodemus Tessin D.Y.S.*, 1914, pp.42, 44, 164). Fischer von Erlach, who, although not documented as a pupil (H.

Sedlmayr, *Johann Bernhard Fischer von Erlach*, 1956, pp.13, 18f., 306), almost certainly worked in Fontana's studio about 1680; Lukas von Hildebrandt joined it in 1690 (B. Grimschitz, *Lukas von Hildebrandt*, 2nd ed., 1959, pp.8, 188, 201), and the Scotsman James Gibbs was there about 1705–08 (B. Little, *Life and Work of James Gibbs,* 1955, pp.19ff.).

In Rome Fontana's direct influence made itself felt till about the middle of the 18th century. His grandson Mauro was also an architect and Principe of the Accademia di S. Luca between 1761 and 1763. Bernardo Antonio Vittone, winner of the Concorso Clementino of 1732, can be regarded as one of Carlo's pupils in a wider sense, because of his many copies of Fontana's drawings.

3 The style of Fontana and his pupils as architects and draughtsmen

Fontana is probably the least appreciated of the major Roman architects of the Baroque period. His work has that confidence and lack of intensity characteristic of the late 17th century, but it can too easily be dismissed as architecture which is superficial, or merely 'scenographic' and theatrical. Fontana is characteristic too of the late 17th century in the extent of his patronage and power, having his counterparts outside Italy in Jules Hardouin Mansart, architect to Louis XIV, and in Sir Christopher Wren. The success of Fontana in his career cannot be dissociated from the nature of his temperament. The facility of the courtier, his wish to please and his willingness to compromise are especially apparent in Fontana's drawings; they show how he was capable of producing, with little apparent effort, any number of different designs in the hope of satisfying his patrons. Many of the characteristics of the 18th-century artist are present in Fontana, and a close study of his work makes intelligible the extent of his influence on the generation of architects that followed after him.

The qualities of Fontana's style, as well as its weaknesses, are well illustrated in what is probably his most famous and certainly his most discussed work, the façade of S. Marcello al Corso (Figs 563/4; see Muñoz Gasparini, pp.24f; Hager in *Commentari*, 1973, pp.58ff.). It has been shown how Fontana, in contrast to the architects of the High Baroque, here makes the façade easily readable – how all the elements of the top storey have their exact counterpart in the lower storey, giving the façade a static quality. The aedicule framing the door, flanked by free-standing columns joined to the main part of the façade, appears to be easily detachable and it thus has a scenic quality, a quality of unrelatedness characteristic of theatrical scene painting.

This, the conventional view of Fontana's style, is in many ways apt, but too little stress is thereby laid on the historical importance of Fontana as a pioneer of the style, on his personal contribution to its development, and on the variety and visual sophistication of his work. As the Windsor drawings make abundantly clear, Fontana's style must really be understood in relation to that of his principal master, Bernini, and not least because of the important role which sculpture played in his work. Many of his surviving drawings are designs not for buildings but for sculptural monuments, and to most of Fontana's architectural works sculpture and decoration are of vital importance.

As a consequence of this breadth of approach Fontana assumed at the end of his life a part approaching that of director of arts which Bernini had played at an earlier date, although Fontana in this position remained primarily an architect whereas Bernini's main concern had been sculpture. Because of his relationship to Bernini Fontana must be distinguished from his less gifted contemporaries, and even from Maratta, who was in many ways Fontana's counterpart in painting. Maratta remained almost exclusively a painter, and as a pupil of Sacchi he developed the classical tradition within the Baroque; his work is to this extent less varied than Fontana's and it may be said to have been well suited almost from the start to the standards prevailing in the later part of the 17th century.

In relation to the work of Bernini the façade of S. Marcello presents a number of important innovations. The façade is in the first place well set back from the street and it can be taken in at a glance. The plan is based on a broken concave curve like that used by Bernini, for example, in his second project for the east façade of the Louvre. Fontana, however, leaves out the contrast which Bernini had obtained between the concave curves in the centre of his façade and the straight walls compressing the centre, and in this way the intensity of the High Baroque, based on the juxtaposition of contrasting shapes and masses, is largely dispersed. The double concave form, uninterrupted by straight or convex projections, is to be encountered in many of Fontana's works – at Windsor, for example, in the designs for a casino for the Veneto and in those for the Fontana di Trevi. The psychological effect at S. Marcello is that of the façade appearing to yield – courtier-like – before the spectator, offering no resistance as he walks up to the church. The clarity and neatness of the elevation matches the lack of tension in the plan, but the impression it gives is not well conveyed by the word 'static'. Fontana's design must be distinguished from the many truly static façades of the late 16th century not merely because it is diverse or 'scenographic', but because it embodies an extension of the principles of design developed during the Baroque period. The façade has pronounced sculptural density, which increases towards the centre where the projecting columns of the doorway stand. In these respects Fontana's façade is a late descendant of Maderno's façade of S. Susanna, and however distinguished intellectually Maderno's façade may be Fontana's is visually much the livelier. Both architects may be said to have established coherent styles relative to their historical positions, Maderno tightening, as it were, and Fontana loosening the rules of composition.

The focal point of the façade of S. Marcello lies in the empty frame over the main entrance, a frame which was originally to be attached to the wall (Fig.563) and intended to enclose a relief panel. The emphasis which should have been given, had the relief been executed, to a work of sculpture in Fontana's design betrays the disciple of Bernini, and the disposition of the columns in relation to the frame which they enclose within a broken pediment recalls the central motif within Bernini's church of S. Andrea al Quirinale. It is characteristic of Fontana's architectural approach to sculpture that Bernini's dynamic tableau, with the figure of S. Andrea caught in flight within the pediment, should be replaced by a relief, enclosed within a frame, the frame repeating in miniature the neat disposition of the architectural members of the façade. The effect of the relief frame inserted within a broken pediment seems clumsy, an error of judgement of the kind that Fontana as an architect who had inherited the mantle of Bernini could sometimes make, but one of the happiest features of the façade is also sculptural. This is the use of the martyr's palms at the sides of the upper storey, where consoles or regular swags would be attached in a less imaginative work. They are juxtaposed in Fontana's façade with the statues of martyrs at the corners of the upper storey. The irregular curve of their leaves coincides with the shape of a conventional console, and the uneven pattern so produced, silhouetted against the sky, is already rococo in its effect.

Fontana's professionalism is well shown in his drawings, and here too he developed a technique which was in use in Bernini's workshop. Fontana's drawings differ from the architectural drawings of the earlier 17th century in their extreme neatness, in their use of colour and in the relative isolation of the design in the centre of the page – characteristics which can be paralleled in Fontana's architecture. The drawings were in most cases laid out with guide lines in black chalk (cf. Fig.236), the organization of the design based on loose geometrical relationships of lines and circles. Brown ink was then applied over the chalk to show the main outlines of the building, and this was followed by an application of coloured wash, grey being the colour most often present. The chalk lines then appear to have been rubbed out, although in some cases the geometrical structure of a design is outlined in ink (cf. Fig.236) and in other cases lines are overdrawn in wash to indicate the sight lines on the main axes of the plans (cf. Fig.200). It is perhaps in their use of colour that Fontana's drawings are of the greatest significance. Colour makes a timid appearance in the architectural drawings of Bernini's studio, in the plan drawings for the Louvre, for example, where the existing parts of the palace are outlined in yellow and Bernini's proposed additions in brown wash. This system of colour notation is fully developed by Fontana so that his drawings, like his buildings, are easily legible as well as being pleasing to the eye. In Fontana's system the colour grey usually denotes the fabric due to be built, and yellow or brown show existing walls. Many other colours are introduced in the drawings in a rational way to denote other architectural features, blue for water, red for brickwork in an elevation, or for the site of a stove in a plan, and so on. It is perhaps not surprising that Fontana was able when necessary to produce competent landscapes in watercolour (cf. Fig.418). Fontana's contribution to the practice of architecture in the 18th century is well shown in the technique of his drawings no less than in the style of his architecture.

Though Fontana had many pupils, and though he must have employed assistants in his studio, the drawings at Windsor are remarkably homogeneous in style. It is likely that many of the drawings are the work of assistants, but they cannot be distinguished from Fontana's autograph drawings. Often a single design is recorded in several versions, and it seems improbable that Fontana would have put his own hand to the making of copies and variants, but even here it is usually impossible to decide which version is the original, and therefore presumably by Fontana, and which the copy. Amongst the drawings, however, are a small number that differ in style from the large majority. They are slightly freer in technique, more delicate in appearance and in them all traces of chalk have usually been carefully erased (cf. Fig.107). These drawings are not so unlike Fontana's that it is always possible to distinguish between the two hands, but the draughtsman may be said to play the part of Guardi in relation to Fontana's Canaletto.

It has been proposed by Noach that this secondary hand be identified with that of Alessandro Specchi, but the evidence for such an attribution is slight. The association between Fontana and Specchi was a close one, for Specchi engraved the illustrations to many of Fontana's treatises. The engravings in the *Tempio Vaticano* of 1694 are by him, and many of the drawings at Windsor for this book (see below; Fig.1), though they are in pen and ink, have certain of the characteristics of the secondary hand amongst the main group of Fontana drawings. However, the drawings amongst the main group are later in date than the *Tempio Vaticano* drawings and the majority appear to have been made in connection with building projects on which Fontana was employed in the first years of the 18th century. At least by 1703, with the design of the Porto di Ripetta, Specchi had begun an independent career as an architect, and in his architectural style he proved himself one of the least dependent of Fontana's pupils. The only drawings at Windsor which have a definite connection with one of Specchi's works are two sheets in the second of the two 'Albani' volumes showing a project for the stables of the Palazzo del Quirinale (Figs 411/2). The near-rococo style of the project architecturally, with the spacious and delicate treatment of the elevation and the shallow curves of the plan, recalls the style of the Porto di Ripetta, and this would seem to support the attribution of the drawings to Specchi. They are in a style which is vaguely similar, but not precisely like the secondary drawings of the Fontana volumes. It may be that in his independent works Specchi took leave of Fontana in the technique of his drawings, as in his architectural style. The problem of identifying this particular assistant of Fontana seems difficult to solve, and it is not beyond the bounds of possibility that the drawings are by Fontana himself.

Two of Fontana's pupils are represented in the 'Albani' volumes by signed drawings – Nicola Michetti and Romano Carapecchia. Michetti assisted Fontana in the early 1700's, especially in the work on the Ospizio di S. Michele (Fig.336). One drawing by him at Windsor records the state of SS. Apostoli in 1708 when Fontana took over the building at the death of his son (Fig.472), and there are three drawings by him of 1703(?) for a project for the Fontana di Trevi (Figs 481–483). The drawings are close to Fontana in style, but extensively heightened with wash, and clumsier in execution. Architecturally too Michetti is clumsier than Fontana and eccentric in the squat proportions in his elevations. Carapecchia was praised by Pascoli for his draughtsmanship, but the group of Windsor drawings show him in only a modest capacity. They are projects for booths to be erected on the Piazza del Pantheon (Figs 468–470), and consequently limited in the scope of the architecture. As drawings they are much influenced by Fontana's style of draughtsmanship. Surviving drawings by Fontana's son, Francesco, of two of the altars in SS. Apostoli (Fig.570), cannot be easily related in style to any of the drawings at Windsor.

Many of the drawings in the 'Albani' volumes are by architects who have so far unfortunately escaped identification. It is to be hoped that the publication of these may lead to the discovery of the names of the artists. Some of the more competent of the drawings appear to be by architects who were not directly influenced by Fontana. The drawings of the arsenal at the Forte Urbano, near Bologna (Figs 533–537) and the two studies for an Albani villa (Figs 553/4) are amongst these. In both cases the drawings are executed in grey monochrome, and the architectural details, such as they are, seem north Italian in style. However, the best of the unattributed drawings appear to be by pupils or close associates of Fontana. The name of the architect who designed the executed version of the church at Morciola, near Colbordolo (Figs 519–523), would be worth discovering, and even more so the name of the architect responsible for the unexecuted project for this church (Figs 524–532). A number of drawings for other projects appear to be by this second artist, and he is clearly to be ranked amongst the more accomplished pupils of Fontana. By his hand appear to be drawings for the high altar of the Cathedral of Urbino (Figs 499–501), and probably also drawings for the chapel in the Palazzo Albani at Urbino (Fig.504), as well as the elevation of the altar of the Blessed Michelina Metelli in S. Francesco at Pesaro (Fig.513). He thus seems to have worked for some length of time on commissions for the Albani family in and around Urbino. His drawings are close to Fontana's in their precision, and in a certain largeness of scale which departs from the 18th-century lightness of Specchi(?) and Michetti. The drawings go beyond Fontana in their use of colour, containing in some cases representations in facsimile of polychrome marble, and in the plainer drawings yellow wash is much in evidence, in place of the more sober grey which Fontana would have used. It is tentatively suggested below that these drawings may be the work of Filippo Barigioni.

A number of lesser architects and craftsmen are represented by signed drawings in the 'Albani' volumes. A plan project for S. Maria in Monticelli is by Domenico Antonio de Sanctis (Fig.480). There are maps by a certain Charles Smith of Carington (Fig.546), by the Polish architect Benedykt Renard (Fig.547) and by Antonio Ludovisi, and a drawing of an engineering project is signed by a certain 'Michel Angeli Scappi da Mondolfo' of Urbino (Fig.486). Mention must finally be made of a group of drawings in the Fontana volume relating to the Curia Innocenziana, signed by Mattia de' Rossi, who was Fontana's main rival in Rome after the death of Bernini. The drawings must have been made shortly before de' Rossi's death in 1695. They are unfortunately not projects for architecture, but plans – all but one of them – recording the offices of lawyers due to be moved to the Curia (Figs 259–60). The drawings are in coloured wash and not unlike Fontana in technique, but they can be seen to lack the clarity and elegance of comparable drawings by Fontana himself.

General Bibliography and List of Abbreviations

Books, articles and unpublished sources containing useful information about single buildings or groups of projects are listed or mentioned in the main part of the catalogue in conjunction with the entry for the building to which they refer.

J. S. Ackerman, *Il cortile del Belvedere*, 1954

G. R. Ansaldi, see E. Lavagnino

T. Ashby, 'Alessandro Specchi', *The Town Planning Review*, 1927, 4, pp.237ff.
See also Platner and Ashby

ASR., Archivio di Stato, Rome

G. Baglione, *Le vite de' pittori, scultori e architetti*, 1649

R. Battaglia, *La Cattedra berniniana di S. Pietro*, 1943

L. Bianchi, 'Disegni di Ferdinando Fuga e di altri architetti del settecento', *Catalogo della XLIII esposizione del Gabinetto Nazionale delle Stampe*, Rome, 1955

P. Bjurström, *Feast and theatre in Queen Christina's Rome*, 1966

A. Blunt, 'The drawings of Carlo Fontana in the Royal Library at Windsor Castle', *Barocco europeo, barocco italiano, barocco salentino*, Atti del Congresso internazionale sul Barocco, Lecce, 1969, pp.89ff.

A. Blunt and H. L. Cooke, *The Roman Drawings of the XVII and XVIII centuries in the Collection of Her Majesty the Queen at Windsor Castle*, 1960

F. Bonanni, *Numismata summorum Pontificum Templi Vaticani fabricam . . .*, 1696 and 1700; *Numismata Pontificum Romanorum quae a tempore Martini V. usque ad annum M.DC.XCIX . . .*, 2 vols, 1699

A. Braham, *Funeral Decorations in Early Eighteenth Century Rome*, Victoria and Albert Museum Brochure, no.7, 1975

A. Braham and H. Hager 'The Tomb of Christina', *Queen Christina of Sweden: Documents and Studies*, 1966, pp.48ff.

H. Brauer and R. Wittkower, *Die Zeichnungen des Gianlorenzo Bernini*, 1931

G. Briganti, *Il Palazzo del Quirinale*, 1962

A. E. Brinckmann, see L. Rovere

C. Calisse, *Storia di Civitavecchia*, 1898

L. Callari, *I palazzi di Roma*, 1944, 3rd ed.

A. Cametti, *Il teatro di Tordinona*, 2 vols., 1938

P. Campello della Spina, *Diario . . .*, 1887

G. Carandente, *Il Palazzo Pamphilj*, 1975, pp.148ff.

Cartari-Febei, *Diario di Giulio Cartari*, Rome, Archivio di Stato, Fondo Archivi Gentilizi, Archivio Cartari-Febei

C. Cecchelli, *S. Clemente* (CRI. 24/5), 1930

G. P. Chattard, *Nuova descrizione del Vaticano o sia Palazzo Apostolico di S. Pietro*, 3 vols, 1767

L. Chracas, *Racconto istorico de terremoti sentiti in Roma e in parte dello Stato ecclesiastico, e in altri luoghi la sera de' 14. Gennajo, e la mattina de' 2. Febbrajo dell'anno 1703*, 1703

A. Ciacconius, *Vitae, et res gestae Pontificum Romanorum et S·R·E·Cardinalium Ab initio nascentis Ecclesiae usque ad Clementem IX P.O.M.*, 4 vols, 1677. For the continuation, see Guarnacci

A. Cipriani, see P. Marconi

O. Piselli Ciuccioli, *Notizie istoriche della Chiesa Parrochiale di S. Maria in Monticelli di Roma, Col Ristretto della Vita del Regnante Pontifice Clemente XI, Restauratore della medesima*, 1719

C. H. Clough, 'The Albani Library and Pope Clement XI', *Librarium*, XII (1969), pp.13ff.

H. L. Cooke, see A. Blunt

Correspondance des Directeurs de l'Académie de France à Rome . . ., ed. A. de Montaiglon, vols. I–IV, 1887/9.

E. Coudenhove-Erthal, *Carlo Fontana und die Architektur des Römischen Spätbaroks*, 1930
'Zum Problem Carlo Fontana', *Wiener Jahrbuch für Kunstgeschichte*, IX, 1934, pp.157/8
'Römisches Stadtbaudenken zu Ende des Seicento', *Festschrift für Hermann Egger*, 1933, pp.95–103

M. Crescimbeni, *Notizie degli Arcadi morti*, vol. II, 1720 (no. CXXVI)

CRI., 'Le Chiese di Roma illustrate' series

F. Dettweiler, *Die Stuckarbeiten im Dom zu Fulda und ihre Meister*, Frankfurt am Main thesis, 1928

U. Donati, *Artisti ticinesi a Roma*, 1942

G. Eimer, *La Fabbrica di S. Agnese in Navona*, vol. 1, p.210

R. Enggass, 'Laurentius Ottoni Rom. Vat. Basilicae Sculptor', *Storia dell' Arte*, 15/16, 1972, pp.236f., 335f.
'Un problème du baroque romain tardif. Projets de sculptures par des artistes non sculpteurs', *Revue de l'Art*, No.31, 1976, pp.21ff.
Early Eighteenth Century Sculpture in Rome, 1976

G. Falda, *Il nouvo teatro delle fabriche . . . di Roma moderna*, 1665–99

F. Fasolo, *Le chiese di Roma nel' 700*, vol. I (Trastevere), 1949
L'opera di Hieronimo e Carlo Rainaldi, 1961

J. Fleming, 'Cardinal Albani's Drawings at Windsor: Their purchase by James Adam for George III', *The Connoisseur*, 1958, pp.164ff.

V. Forcella, *Iscrizioni delle chiese ed altri edifici di Roma*, 13 vols, 1869–78

A. Frangipani, *Istoria dell'antichitissima città di Civitavecchia*, 1759

S. Fraschetti, *Il Bernini*, 1900

C. Galassi Paluzzi, *San Pietro in Vaticano*, 3 vols, 1963 (CRI. no.66)

A. Galieti, *Contributi alla storia della diocesi suburbicaria di Albano Laziale*, 1948, pp.197ff.

GBA. *Gazette des Beaux-arts*

V. Golzio, *Documenti artistici sul seicento nell' Archivio Chigi*, 1939

M. Guarnacci, *Vitae, et res gestae Pontificum Romanorum et S.R.E. Cardinalium a Clemente X. usque ad Clementem XII.*, 2 vols, 1751 (continuation of Ciacconius)

M. Guidi, 'Notizie intorno all' architetto Carlo Fontana', *Roma*, III, 1925, pp.453–464

H. Hager, 'Zur Plannungs und Baugeschichte der Zwillingskirchen auf der Piazza del Popolo: S. Maria di Monte Santo und S. Maria dei Miracoli in Rom', *Römischen Jahrbuch für Kunstgeschichte*, 1967/8, pp.191ff.
'Projetti del tardo barocco romano per il terzo braccio del colonnato della piazza S. Pietro', *Commentari*, 1968, pp.299ff.
Filippo Juvarra e il concorso di modelli del 1715 bandito da Clemente XI per la nuova sacrestia di S. Pietro, 1970
'Carlo Fontana's project for a Church in Honour of the 'Ecclesia Triumphans' in the Colosseum Rome', JWCI, XXXVI, 1973, pp.319ff.
'Carlo Fontana and the Jesuit Sanctuary at Loyola', JWCI, XXXVII, 1974, pp.280–289
'Die Kuppel des Domes in Montefiascone', *Römisches Jahrbuch für Kunstgeschichte*, 15, 1975, pp.144ff.
'Carlo Fontana e l'ingrandimento dell'Ospizio di S. Michele. Contributo allo sviluppo architettonico di un' istituzione caritativa del Tardo Barocco Romano', *Commentari*, XXVI, 1975, pp.344–359
'G .B. Contini o Carlo Fontana? Osservazioni sui disegni e l'altare Berninesco della "Madonna delle Grazie" nel Palazzo Venezia di Roma', *Commentari*, XXVII, 1976, pp.89–92
Un riesame di tre cappelle di Carlo Fontana', *Commentari*, XXVII, 1976 (in course of publication)
See also Braham and Hager, and Introduction, pt.2, *passim*

C. Hülsen, *Le chiese di Roma nel Medio Evo*, 1927

S. Jakob, *Katalog der italienischen Handzeichnungen in der Kunstbibliothek Staatliche Museen*, Berlin, 1976

JWCI, Journal of the Warburg and Courtauld Institutes

R. Krautheimer, S. Corbett and W. Frankl, *Corpus Basilicarum Christianarum*, II, 1962, V, 1970

A. Kubíček, *The Palaces of Prague*, 1946

E. Lavagnino, G. R. Ansaldi and L. Salerno, *Altari Barocchi in Roma*, 1959

M. Loret, 'I lavori artistici nel Vaticano durante il Pontificato di Clemente XI (1700–1721)' *Archivi*, 1936

D. de Lucca, see J. Tonna

M. di Macco, *Il Colosseo. Funzione simbolica, storica, urbana*, 1971, pp.82/9, 385–431

N. A. Mallory, *Roman Rococo Architecture from Clement XI to Benedict XIV (1700–1758)*, New York, Garland Publishing, Inc., 1977

P. Marconi, A. Cipriani, and E. Valeriani, *I disegni di architettura dell' archivio storico dell' Accademia di San Luca*, 2 vols., Rome, 1974

G. Matthiae, *Ferdinando Fuga e la sua opera romana*, 1953

P. Misciatelli, 'Un documento inedito dell'architetto Carlo Fontana', *Repertorium für Kunstwissenschaft*, XXXII, 1909, pp. 453-464

F. Milizia, *Le vite de' più celebri architetti*, 1768

H. Millon, *Corpus Juvarrianum*, vol.1 (in preparation)

M. Missirini, *Memorie per servire alla storia della Romana Accademia di S. Luca fino all morte di A. Canova*, 1823

L. Montalto, *Il Clementino 1585–1875*, 1938
Un mecenate in Roma barocca: Il Cardinale Benedetto Pamphilj (1653–1730), 1955

G. Moroni, *Dizionario di erudizione storico-ecclesiastica* . . ., 103 vols, 1840–1861

L. Muñoz Gasparini, *S. Marcello* (CRI. no.16)

M. L. Myers, *Architectural and Ornament Drawings: Juvarra, Vanvitelli, the Bibiena Family and Other Italian Draughtsmen.* Exhibition Catalogue, The Metropolitan Museum of Art, New York, 1975, pp.24f.

K. Noehles, *La chiesa dei SS. Luca e Martina nell'opera di Pietro da Cortona*, 1969

W. Oechslin, *Bildungsgut und Antikenrezeption in frühen Settecento in Rom, Studien zum römischen Aufenthalt Bernardo Antonio Vittones*, 1972

C. d'Onofrio, *Le fontane di Roma*, 1957
Gli obelischi di Roma, 1965
Il Tevere e Roma, 1968
Castel S. Angelo, 1971
Roma val bene un' abjuria. Storie romane tra Cristina di Svezia, Piazza del Popolo e l' Accademia d' Arcadia, 1976, pp.262–290

R. Pane, *Ferdinando Fuga*, 1956

L. Pascoli, *Vite de' pittori, scultori, ed architetti moderni*, 2 vols, 1730, 1736

L. von Pastor, *Geschichte der Päpste seit dem Ausgang des Mittelalters*, 16 vols, 1885 –1933; Eng. ed., *The History of the Popes*, 40 vols, 1891–1953

P. Pecchiai, *Il Gesù di Roma*, 1957

C. B. Piazza, *La Gerarchia Cardinalizia*, 1703

J. Pinto, *Nicola Michetti*, Harvard thesis, 1975

S. B. Platner and T. Ashby, *A topographical dictionary of ancient Rome*, 1929

F. Posterla, *Roma sacra e moderna*, 1707

D. Redig de Campos, *I Palazzi Vaticani*, 1967

D. de Rossi, *Studio d'architettura civile*, 3 vols, 1701, 1711 and 1721

P. Rossini, *Il mercurio errante* . . ., 1760

L. Rovere, V. Viale and A. E. Brinckmann, *Filippo Juvarra*, 1937

L. Salerno, *Piazza di Spagna*, 1957

L. Salerno, L. Spezzaforo, M. Tafuri, *Via Giulia, una utopia urbanistica del '500*, 1973 2 ed., 1975, p.130 n.113; pp.392–404

See also E. Lavagnino

A. Schiavo, *La Fontana di Trevi e le altre opere di Nicola Salvi*, 1956
'Notizie biografiche sui Fontana', *Studi Romani*, 19, 1971, pp.56–61

C. Serafini, *Le monete . . . del medagliere Vaticano*, III, 1913

A. Serra, 'L'attività giovanile di Michele Sammicheli e di Carlo Fontana a Montefiascone', *Annuario, Università degli Studi*, Istituto di Storia dell'Arte, 1973/4, pp.211–235

L. Spezzaforo, see L. Salerno

M. Tafuri, see L. Salerno

U. Thieme and B. Becker *Allgemeines Lexikon der bildenden Künstler* . . ., 37 vols, 1907–1950

F. Titi, *Studio di Pittura, Scoltura, et Architettura, Nelle Chiese di Roma*, 1674 and later editions

J. Tonna and D. de Lucca, *Romano Carapecchia*, Studies in Maltese Architecture, 1, 1975

E. Valeriani, see P. Marconi

Valesio, Diary in the Archivio Capitolino, Rome (published only in extracts)

G. Vasi, *Delle magnificenze di Roma*, 5, 1747

A. Venturi, *Storia dell'arte italiana*, 25 vols, 1901–1939

P. Verzone, 'L' opera di Carlo Fontana e Filippo Juvarra', *Arte in Europa. Scritti di storia dell'arte in onore di Edoardo Arslan*, vol.1, 1966, pp.783/5

Via del Corso (L. Salerno and others), 1961

V. Viale, see L. Rovere

B. Vittone, *Istruzioni diverse concernanti l'officio dell'architetto civile*, 1766(?)

L. Vogel, *The Column of Antoninus Pius*, 1973

R. Wittkower, review of Coudenhove in *Kritische Berichte, III*, 1930/1, pp. 142–5
'Carlo Rainaldi and the Roman Architecture of the full Baroque', *The Art Bulletin*, 1937, pp. 242ff.
Art and architecture in Italy, 1600–1750, 2nd ed., 1965
'Vittone's Drawings in the Musée des Arts Décoratifs', *Studies in Renaissance and Baroque Art presented to Anthony Blunt*, 1967, pp.165ff.
See also Brauer and Wittkower

C. von Wurzbach, *Biographisches Lexicon des Kaiserthums Oesterreich*, 60 vols, 1856–1891

L. Zambarelli, *Il Collegio Clementino di Roma*, Rome, 1936

The Catalogue: Table of Contents

I S. Peter's

II Other Ecclesiastical Works

III Secular Buildings

IV The 'Albani' Volumes

Rome: Ecclesiastical works

Rome: Secular works

Urbino, Pesaro and Colbordolo

Other parts of Italy

Maps connected with fortification and warfare

Unidentified drawings

Notes and list of Watermarks

For reasons of economy it has not been possible to give printed transcriptions of all the manuscripts by Fontana that accompany the drawings, though a few of the more interesting texts are included below, those dealing mainly with the ecclesiastical projects.

The measurements of the drawings are given in millimetres, height preceding width.

The majority of the drawings have been cut at the edges when the volumes were bound. This is not mentioned in the catalogue unless part of a drawing or an inscription is evidently missing. Where inscriptions have been cut a line followed by dots (/ . . .) appears in the transcription.

If it is not clear in which of the volumes a particular drawing is to be found the concordance of the old and new numbers at the end of the catalogue can be consulted, where the drawings are listed in the order in which they appear in the various volumes.

Mention of copies by Vittone which appear frequently in the text refer to two volumes of Vittone drawings in the Musée des Arts Décoratifs, Paris.

The word 'pen' in the descriptions of the drawings denotes pen and brown ink.

Numbers are given for the watermarks that appear most frequently, mainly watermarks of Roman paper manufacturers, according to the following table:

1 Dove and letters A and N in circle
2 Anchor in oval with six-pointed star and letter F
3 Lily in oval with crown
4 Kneeling S. John in a shield
5 Dove on *monti* in oval with letter F
6 Dove on *monti* in oval with letter N
7 Lily in double oval with letter V
8 Lily in double oval
9 Lily in oval with letter V
10 Dove on *monti* and letters A and P in circle
11 Dove on *monti* in circle with letters F and I
12 Star in oval with cross
13 Dove on *monti* in oval with letters A and N
14 Anchor in oval with letters A and N
15 Dove on *monti* in oval with letter S
16 Agnus Dei in double oval with letter V
17 Dove on *monti* in oval with letter R
18 Agnus Dei in double oval with letters A and N
19 Anchor in oval with star and letter N
20 Deer in circle with letter P
21 Six-pointed star in circle with cross and letter N
22 Dove on *monti* in oval with letter G
23 Lily in double oval with cross
24 Star in oval with letter F
25 Dove on *monti* in oval with letter V
26 Agnus Dei in double oval with letter A
27 Lily on *monti* in oval with letter B
28 Lily in oval with letter A
29 Lily in oval with letter P
30 Lily in double oval with letter F
31 Animal in circle

I

S. Peter's

The *Tempio Vaticano* (1680–1694)

Volume 180 at Windsor contains material collected by Fontana in preparation for the publication of his book on S. Peter's and the Vatican, *Il Tempio Vaticano e sua origine*, printed in 1694 with illustrations engraved by Specchi after Fontana and parallel texts in Italian and Latin. The volume contains in Fontana's handwriting a list of contents and several headed pages (not transcribed below), and it is roughly divided into three sections: 1) drawings and written texts dealing with buildings which Fontana wished to compare with S. Peter's, 2) drawings of S. Peter's itself, and 3) drawings supposedly of the Piazza of S. Peter's. Fontana clearly put the book together without much care and the last two groups of drawings are not as strictly divided as he apparently supposed when preparing this material for the binders and when writing the title pages. The interest of the drawings themselves is indeed strictly limited, the more so since the majority were merely to form the basis for engravings, and little more than an inventory of the volume is given in the catalogue below.

An account of the origin of the *Tempio Vaticano* is touched upon by Fontana in two interesting manuscripts, one in Volume 176 at Windsor (see below: Surveys of the Cupola of S. Peter's 1695), and one in the Biblioteca Communale at Como (Baserga and Cassiani Ingoni). The Como manuscript is divided into two parts, the first giving details of the origin of the book and the second describing how the book played a part, or so Fontana believed, in the conversion to Catholicism of Augustus II of Saxony, King of Poland. In 1680 a rumour was spread by a certain Fra Giuseppe Paglia (or Palia) that the cupola of S. Peter's was cracking. Pope Innocent XI ordered an enquiry and Paglia's theories were declared to be unfounded. Mattia de' Rossi, the capomaestro of S. Peter's, composed a report which Fontana dismisses as a '. . . lieue relazione, che non compiua pienamente al bisogno, . . .', and Fontana himself was asked for an account of the affair. From this arose the conception of writing a book on S. Peter's. On the advice of Cardinal Vespignani Fontana decided, unwisely as it proved, to mention in the text the cost of the building, in comparison with that of the Temple of Solomon. Fontana says little more about the preparation of the book, though a certain amount of evidence is provided by the drawings below.

The book was ready for the printers in February 1693 and in February of the following year the Pope (Innocent XII) received the first published copy. It was then represented to the Pope that the publication of the cost of the building would provide a weapon in the hands of enemies of Catholicism, and after an interview with the Pope Fontana contemplated fleeing from Rome. The Pope's fears were finally calmed by Cardinal Albani (the future Clement XI) who pointed out that what Luther had said about S. Peter's was that donations for the building of the church had been misappropriated. This theme is touched upon in the second part of the manuscript, where Fontana is at pains to justify his book, trying to show how, so far from being a weapon for anti-Catholics, the book had actually brought about the conversion of Augustus II.

The manuscript in Volume 176 describes at greater length the inspection of the cupola of S. Peter's in 1680 (see below, and in Pascoli's life of Mattia de' Rossi).

Such is the background to the drawings in volume 180 at Windsor. The first group contains the only dated sheet in the volume – a plan of Milan Cathedral of 1686 by the Milanese architect Giovanni Battista Quadrio. The long description of Milan Cathedral which accompanies this drawing was apparently written in 1691, the date given in the last page of the text (it is published by Braham and Gatti Perrer). Other drawings, engravings and sheets of notes in this first section of the volume refer to the Cathedral of Florence, S. Giustina of Padua, and old S. Paul's in London. The drawings of the first two churches, like that of Milan cathedral, were clearly made by local architects and sent to Fontana in Rome. In most cases the drawings and engravings of this section are inscribed with figures in Fontana's hand, and it appears from these that he was mainly interested in establishing the heights of the churches. When it came to writing his book, he chose to discuss and illustrate only the cathedral of Florence (pp.479ff.).

The last two groups of drawings – directly related to the illustrations of the *Tempio Vaticano* – are in two styles, the first comprising small sheets bearing very rough measured sketches of details of the basilica and the Piazza, and the second consisting of folded sheets representing larger areas of the church (Fig.1), profiles of mouldings and similar details. Drawings in the second style are annotated by Fontana, but they appear to be by an assistant (possibly Specchi) who prepared the engravings.

There are at Windsor other drawings which may have been originally produced in preparation for the book (see below, Surveys of the lantern and cupola of S. Peter's, The Piazza of S. Peter's, diagram). Fontana's interest in the publication of the book was in part to make known his own ideas for the improvement of the basilica and the Piazza, though nothing came of these projects (on the Piazza, see Hager, 1968). There are no drawings at Windsor connected with Fontana's scheme for the *terzo braccio* of the colonnade, but the volume contains (Fig.3) sheets referring to his project for adding oval *cupolini* over the aisle bays of the church, as illustrated in a simplified way on pp.423, 425 and 427 of the *Tempio Vaticano*.

The publication of the book was a major factor in establishing an international reputation for Fontana, and hence in extending the range of his patrons. According to the Como manuscript Fontana was asked to send copies to many heads of state and Cardinals and this is also referred to in several passages of the *Correspondance des Directeurs* (8 and 22 December 1693, 27 April 1694, etc.). The effect of the book on Augustus II of Saxony is described in the second part of Fontana's treatise at Como. Augustus was travelling incognito in Rome in 1694 and he visited S. Peter's in Fontana's company, his interest in the church stimulated by a copy of Fontana's book. After his return to Saxony, Fontana received the news that the Academy of Leipzig had published a Latin version of his text. Augustus became Elector of Saxony and then King of Poland, after being converted to Catholicism. Fontana then learnt through the King's emissary in Rome that his book on the Vatican had played a large part in the conversion of the King, and he seems on the evidence of the Como manuscript to have believed this very improbable story. Later he had the further satisfaction of being created a Count by the newly-appointed King (August 1699).

ADDITIONAL BIBLIOGRAPHY:

G. Baserga, in *Periodico della Società Storica . . . di Como*, 26, 1926, pp.113ff.

A. Braham and M. L. Gatti Perrer, in *Il Duomo di Milano*, I, 1969, pp.265ff.

A. Cassiani Ingoni in R. Liceo–Ginnasio "A. Volta", Como, *Annuario*, 1928/9, VII, pp.105ff.

1 Florentine School, late 17th Century
LONGITUDINAL SECTION OF FLORENCE CATHEDRAL [9920]
425×*c*.455 mm. Watermark, letters D M P in a triangle. Chalk, coloured washes. Inscribed in chalk with measurements in 'B(raccia ?)', referring to the height and width of the crossing and dome, and inscribed in Fontana's writing with a sum and *dal Pauimento sino alla / Cima della Crocie p(almi). 539.*

This rather crude drawing was presumably executed in Florence by a local architect and sent to Fontana in Rome. The note in Fontana's hand must refer to the height of the dome in terms of *palmi romani*. On the *verso* are five unidentified sketches, which may be by Fontana.

2 Giovanni Battista Quadrio
PLAN OF MILAN CATHEDRAL [9921]
288×190 mm. (irregular). Laid down. Pen, grey wash, traces of chalk. With scale labelled: *Scala de b*(racci)*a* (?) *cento Milanesi* and index letters referring to the sheet of measurements. Signed: *Gio: Batta quadrio Architetto d'/ esso Tempio Della Citta di Mil^o^.*, and dated: *Mil^o^. il 21 Decemb^e^. 1686.* With sums, upper left, in Fontana's hand.
Braham and Gatti Perrer, Pl.2. Quadrio is recorded as an architect who worked on Milan cathedral from 1686 to 1728 (Thieme Becker).

3 D. Modesto Albanesi
PLAN OF S. GIUSTINA OF PADUA [9922]
415×*c*.275mm. Watermark, no.14 and six-pointed star. Pen. With scales in Roman *palmi* and Paduan feet, and index. Inscribed: *Pianta della Chiesa di S. Giustina di Padoua formata da D. Modesto Albanese Monacho del medemo monasterio.*

4 PLAN OF THE *SCALA REGIA*, WITH PLANS OF DETAILS [9923]
280×*c*.595 mm. Two sheets joined horizontally. Watermark no.1. Pen. Some of the measurements in chalk.

Compare *Tempio Vaticano*, p.239. On the *verso* is a rough ink plan of two columns.

5 SHEET OF MEASUREMENTS, WITH DIAGRAMS OF THE DOME OF S. PETER'S [9924]
276×*c*.195 mm. Pen, chalk.

The notes and measurements refer to the height of the dome and they are continued on the *verso*.

6 TRANSVERSE SECTION THROUGH THE PORTICO OF S. PETER'S, WITH PLAN OF THE BENEDICTION LOGGIA (*VERSO*) AND OTHER STUDIES [9925]
C.275 × 423 mm. Pen, chalk.

7 ELEVATION OF TWO BAYS OF A SIDE FAÇADE, WITH OTHER STUDIES (*VERSO*) (*Figure* 1) [9926]
279 × *c*.195 mm. Watermark no.2. Pen, chalk. Measured in full and annotated.

The drawing on the *recto* (Fig.1) is of two of the bays of the side elevations of S. Peter's (compare p.391 of the *Tempio Vaticano*, Fig.2). The *verso* contains a part elevation of the entrance wall of the left aisle (compare p.299 of the *Tempio Vaticano*).

8 STUDIES OF S. PETER'S, MAINLY OF THE *CUPOLINI* (*Figure* 3) [9927]
424 × *c*.265 mm. Watermark no.3. Pen, chalk.

The main studies on the *recto* are of the oval *cupolini* that Fontana planned for the oval bays of nave aisles of the basilica (*Tempio Vaticano*, p.423). The studies on the *verso* are for the most part related to Vignola's *cupolini* (*Tempio Vaticano*, p.359).

9 STUDIES OF S. PETER'S, MAINLY OF THE *CUPOLINI* AND LANTERN [9928]
C.270 × 422 mm. Pen, chalk, with inscriptions and measurements.

The *recto* contains studies of one of Vignola's *cupolini* (*Tempio Vaticano*, p.359), and the *verso* has studies related to the lantern of the main dome, and a section of the area adjacent to one of Fontana's proposed oval cupolas.

10 PLAN OF THE NORTHERN HALF OF S. PETER'S [9929]
424 × *c*.730 mm. Two sheets joined vertically. Watermark no.4. Pen, chalk.

Compare p.383 of the *Tempio Vaticano*.

11 PART PLAN OF THE FAÇADE, WITH PLAN OF FOUNTAIN [9930]
C.265 × 420 mm. Pen, chalk. With measurements.

Compare *Tempio Vaticano*, p.191.

12 ENGRAVING OF S. PETER'S, OVERDRAWN WITH A PLAN OF THE WATER SYSTEM [9931A]
Pen, yellow wash, chalk.

The sheet is made up of two engravings, the lower one with the inscription, *Franc. Bufalinus delin. Nicolaus Belin Sculp*. The water conduits of the whole area are drawn on the engravings in brown ink and several of the houses around the Piazza have been added in the same technique. Inscriptions on the sheet appear to be in Fontana's hand.

13 SKETCH OF THE BALDACCHINO [9931]
C.320 × *c*.215 mm. (irregular). Laid down. Pen. With measurements.

14 STUDIES OF SCAFFOLDING [9932]
380 × *c*.480 mm. Watermark no.4. Pen, some chalk. With scale.

15 STUDIES OF SCAFFOLDING [9933]
380 × *c*.480 mm. Watermark no.4. Pen, chalk. With scale.

The drawings may illustrate the scaffolding of the Scala Regia, to which Fontana refers on pp.233f. of the *Tempio Vaticano*, where he claims that he drew the scaffolding in order to explain its structure to Pope Alexander VII. The drawings may be copies of studies made by Fontana at that time.

16 SHEET OF STUDIES, MAINLY OF ONE OF THE FOUNTAINS OF THE PIAZZA [9934]
303 × *c*.214 mm. (irregular). Laid down. Chalk, pen.

17 STUDIES OF THE ALTAR UNDER THE BALDACCHINO [9935]
320 × *c*.224 mm. (irregular). Laid down. Chalk. With measurements.

For the measured elevation at the bottom of the sheet showing the entrance arch compare *Tempio Vaticano*, p.409, and for the rough sketch on the upper part of the sheet of a section of the altar compare no.31 below.

18 DIAGRAMMATIC HALF PLAN OF THE PIAZZA [9936]
C.325 × *c*.220 mm. (irregular). Laid down. Chalk, pen.

With measurements.

19 STUDIES OF ONE OF THE FOUNTAINS OF THE PIAZZA [9937]
C.297 × *c*.217 mm. (irregular). Laid down. Chalk, pen.

Compare *Tempio Vaticano*, p.205.

20 PROFILE OF THE PODIUM OF THE SIDE ELEVATIONS OF S. PETER'S [9938]
C.271 × *c*.198 mm. (irregular). Laid down. Pen, chalk.

Compare p.391 of the *Tempio Vaticano*. The same profile occurs in drawing no.22 below.

21 STUDIES OF DETAILS OF THE SIDE ELEVATIONS [9939]
C.199 × *c*.272 mm. (irregular). Laid down. Pen, chalk. For the main drawing on the sheet compare

Tempio Vaticano, p.391. The two smaller studies on the sheet are perhaps connected with the framing of the first-floor windows.

22 SHEET OF STUDIES, INCLUDING DETAILS OF THE SIDE ELEVATIONS [9940]
278 × 204 mm. Laid down. Chalk.

Some of the studies are connected with the engraving on p.391 of the *Tempio Vaticano*.

23 SHEET OF STUDIES OF DETAILS OF THE SIDE ELEVATIONS [9941]
207 × 280 mm. Laid down. Chalk.

Most of the studies appear to be of details of the frames of the windows and niches.

24 STUDIES OF THE COLONNADE [9942]
260 × *c*.192 mm. (irregular). Laid down. Chalk. Some inscriptions in pen.

On the left a sketch of one of the columns and on the right a section of a colonnade.

25 DIAGRAMMATIC PLAN OF THE FORECOURT [9943]
273 × 196 mm. Laid down. Pen, chalk.

26 STUDY OF ONE OF THE DOORWAYS LEADING INTO THE CHURCH [9944]
275 × 198 mm. Laid down. Pen. Some chalk. With measurements and sums.

Compare p.281 of the *Tempio Vaticano*.

27 STUDIES OF THE ENTRANCE WALL OF THE CHURCH [9945]
270 × 198 mm. Laid down. Pen and chalk.

Compare *Tempio Vaticano*, p.299.

28 PLAN OF ONE OF THE FOUNTAINS OF THE PIAZZA [9946]
272 × 192 mm. Laid down. Pen, grey washes, traces of chalk. With two scales (one in chalk, unfinished).

Possibly a copy of a drawing made by Fontana when he built the southern fountain of the Piazza in the 1670's.

29 SHEETS OF STUDIES, INCLUDING ONE OF A SPIRAL STAIRCASE [9947]
280 × *c*.195 mm. (irregular). Laid down. Pen, chalk. With inscriptions by Fontana.

The sheet contains three rough studies in ink. The figure walking up a ramp was perhaps included to demonstrate the angle of incline of the staircase drawn on the left. For the doorway in the centre compare *Tempio Vaticano*, p.298.

30 DIAGRAM IN SECTION OF THE STEPS IN FRONT OF THE CHURCH [9948]
C.184 × 272 mm. (irregular). Laid down. Chalk. Measured, mainly in pen.

To the left is a sketch of the obelisk of the Piazza (compare no.32 below). On the *verso* is a caricature in ink of the head of a Pope, bearing some resemblance to Innocent XI. Fontana himself was a practitioner of caricature as is shown by a drawing of Borromini by him (P. Portoghesi, in *The Burlington Magazine*, 1967, p.709).

31 STUDY OF THE ALTAR UNDER THE BALDACCHINO [9949]
185 × *c*.272 mm. (irregular). Laid down. Chalk. Compare no. 17 above.

32 STUDY OF THE PIAZZA [9950]
C.192 × 273 mm. (irregular). Pen. With a signed inscription which is legible only in part: *Sge Gioseppe luchese fami fauore di liuellare quella ..... di / questo mio ..... della* R*a* *fab*[*ric*]*a / Carlo fontana*.

The inscription appears to refer to a possible levelling of the slope up to the church. A sketch plan in ink appears to be present on the *verso*.

33 DIAGRAM OF A COLUMN [9951]
272 × *c*.187 mm. (irregular). Laid down. Pen.

The order is probably that of the Piazza (compare no.24 above).

The Piazza, a diagram and a letter

Drawing no.34, which is bound amongst a group of studies of the Baptistry of S. Peter's in Volume 176, is a geometrical diagram which demonstrates a method of placing rows of columns on curving lines. In a short text explaining the working of the diagram, Fontana says that this method was used by him in planning 'the portico of the part opposite the Palazzo de Cesis', presumably the palace facing the southern frontispiece of the southern wing of the colonnade of S. Peter's. Fontana's drawing confirms that he had been one of the architects assisting Bernini in the building of the colonnade (see Brauer and Wittkower, 1931, p.82, n.5), and suggests that Fontana worked out methods whereby Bernini's project could be carried into execution. Brauer and Wittkower illustrate (pl.162b) a drawing for the colonnade with axial lines included.

The letter connected with the Piazza is a short undated text, also in Volume 176, in which Fontana reports to Cardinal Spinola that permission is sought by the Marchese Francesco Riccardi to lay a pipe to conduct water from one of the fountains of the Piazza.

34 DIAGRAM OF THE SCALE [9715]

*C.*210×300 mm. Watermark no.5. Inscribed at bottom: *Il Semidiametro del Circolo minore che dal Centro del Circolo giunge sino al uiuo delle Colonne / del primo giro sono pmi. 29 6⁷/12 ridotti a minuti sono no. 17795.*

On the next sheet, which originally formed the lower half of the sheet bearing the diagram, the following text is written:

'Nel modo sopra delineato fù operato dà mè in piantare il portico della parte uerso il Palazzo de Cesis e formai la Centina del' Primo giro delle Colonne poì feci la medema operatione nelle Colonne del quarto giro con la meda: spartitione seruendomi del' semidiametro del' medo: che sono pmi: 373, e formai la Centina di do: quarto giro alla sua giusta distanza determinata dal' primo al quarto giro, poi tirai paralello il mezzo delle Colonne di do: quarto giro, et il mezzo delle Colonne del' primo giro è sopra di quello feci la partitione delle Colonne dà un mezzo all' altro tanto nel' po.giro come nel quarto giro, è poi tirai li mezzi dà una all' altra li quali tutti (?) poi uennero à ferire (?) al suo punto p quanto portauano le Colonne che sono poste al punto del Circolo minore.

Il medo.tenni nel Circolo mage.p la mage. distanza del' punto con la meda. partitione è poi le Colonne et Entrate a suo luogo sempre con la misura sopra la Centina del' mezzo delle Colonne del' po. è quarto giro e li mezzi delle mede. uennero a Corispondere al suo punto. Tutta questa operatione fù fatta nelle parte oposte de Circoli come destintamente disopra si dimostra.'

The Baptistry (1690–1699)

Very few of the many designs by Fontana and his assistants for the Cappella Battesimale of S. Peter's are preserved, and only one of those of his competitors (Windsor, 5597; reproduced by Dowley, p.69, no.2). The vast gaps in the existing series of drawings are only in part filled by Bonanni's engravings (Bonanni, pls 41, 42), and by the Fontana drawings in Volumes 176 and 179 at Windsor.

Planning and building history

The remodelling of the Baptistry of S. Peter's under Innocent XII was a costly architectural enterprise, in the planning of which every important Roman architect was involved. F. H. Dowley has done much to clarify its complicated history. But Fontana's own report of 23 pages and related documents in the archives of the Fabbrica have not as yet been studied in extenso (cf. d' Onofrio, 1971). The report (published in full below), dated 1704, is much more comprehensive than the published version of 1697. The early Christian sarcophagus of the Prefect Anicius Probus had previously served as the font in the Baptismal Chapel (see nos 79/80 below); the appearance of the chapel before Fontana's alterations is recorded in a drawing by Domenico Castelli (Battaglia, pl. VII, fig.1, and Dowley, pp.68f.). Pope Alexander VIII (1689–91) had already commissioned Fontana to design "una Sontuosa opera", and "con ogni attentione per un nobil Fonte". In May 1690 it seemed that a start was about to be made after a design with two gilded metal statues, for 3,000 *scudi* had been made available (Cartari-Febei, vol. 101, fo.134, 1 May 1690). It is not known why this project was not carried out.

Innocent XII made another beginning with a competition, the result of which was 'trenta, e più pensieri', a far larger number than was indicated by La Teulière, who on 25 March 1692 reported that twelve architects had been involved. The projects of Fontana and Maratta were closely considered by the Congregation of Cardinals of the Fabbrica, as well as one by 'fù Cau. Langardi' (Algardi), who on 23 February 1646 had been commissioned to make a design for the font: 'Fiat ex metallo nouus fons Baptismalis in pulchriorem formam ab Alessandro Algardi excitandam' (Arch. Fabbr. Decr. et Resolut. Sac. Cog.nis R.F.S. Petri Ab Anno, ser. III, vol.162, fo.74 *verso*; cf. vol.163, fo.72 *verso*). La Teulière does not name Maratta as a competitor but only Mattia de' Rossi, of whom Fontana says later in his own report – almost in passing – that his 'Modelli, e Disegni' were rejected.

According to Fontana his project was the one selected: 'e benche tutti degni d'estimatione, piaque però alla Congregat.ne d'elegere il mio, di che scriue il P. Bonanni erudito scrittore Giesuita nel suo libro delle Medaglie Vaticane'. The quotation from Bonanni gives an indication of the scheme which was probably evolved at this first stage (op. cit., p.100): a design with the personifications of the four rivers of Paradise, of which Dowley has made an iconographical examination. The design is unknown, but seems to be a variant of that with the angels surrounding the font, into which one of them pours the holy water (cf. Bonanni, pl.42). According to Bonanni it found general approval but was rejected – contrary to Fontana's statement – as being more suited to a garden than to a church. This remark and Fontana's engraved project suggest that it might have had some resemblance to Tribolo's fountain in a grotto of the Villa Medici at Castello near Florence, and also because the form of the grotto shows some affinity with the Baptismal Chapel, especially before Carlo Fontana intervened (cf. Luigi Dami, *The Italian Garden*, Milan/Rome, 1925, Pls XLIIf; Liliane Chatelet-Lange, 'The Grotto of the Unicorn and the Garden of the Villa di Castello', *The Art Bulletin*, L. 1968, pp.51–58).

Fontana tells us that Maratta 'pieno d'ambitione Architettonica' was not defeated and tried to get a second design accepted. This was criticized by Fontana as 'piu tosto Chimerico, et Ideale, che Geometrico nelle misure' and he says that it was weaker than the first and was absolutely rejected.

As a result of this competition, Fontana was commissioned to produce further ideas: 'Onde io m'auanzai p. picca à farne altri numero 13. tutti uariati, e Nobili, i quali diedero affatto sepoltura à quelli del Maratta con gl'altri concorrenti'. Of these, Fontana states, Bonanni used some as illustrations for his work, evidently referring to the two engravings with four stags which serve as a pedestal for the font (Bonanni, pls 41, 42), although the engravings include the porphyry *tazza* from the undercroft of S. Peter's, which, according to Fontana, was not ordered to be raised until 20 May, 1693, and led to a complete replanning of the scheme (see below). Complaining of the severe conflict which followed the rejection of Maratta's projects, Fontana states that the last of his own designs succeeded and that a model was made after it: 'con tutto ciò preualse l'ultimo disegno fatto da me, sopra il quale si fece dentro la med.a Cappella in S. Pietro il Modello in grande, doue apunto e hora l'opera, e questo Modello, e Disegno in grande, era ornato di statue all'uscita al sacro fonte fatte con somm' intelligenza, et Arte dalli scultori Lorenzo Ottone, Gio: Teodoro, Michele Maglia'. Fontana insists the model after his design was accepted while that of Domenico Guidi was rejected: 'Fu anche fatto un Modello di Creta in grande nella facciata propria della Cappella dal Sig.e Dom.o Guidi, ma per non essere piaciuto fù leuato d'opera, et hora si conserua nella Fonderia di S. Marta'.

The scornful way in which Fontana mentions Domenico Guidi's model suggests that it was designed in competition with his own, but La Teulière in his letter of 25 March 1692 only refers to one model and states that the main group was allotted to Guidi and the remaining figures to Théodon and others. On 11 November 1692 La Teulière further says that Guidi's model represented the Baptism and gives the names of the other sculptors involved and the meaning of the allegorical figures: Religion by Ottone and Faith by Théodon, Innocence by Maglia and Chastity by Lucenti (cf. Coudenhove-Erthal, pp.66f.). Girolamo Lucenti had to withdraw and is not mentioned by Fontana. His figure was executed by the other sculptors after a new design (Reg. Liste, cf. below). According to La Teulière these figures were over life-size and seated on a three-stepped pedestal, but Innocent XII had neither seen the model nor given a decision.

It is evident from La Teulière's letter that Mattia de' Rossi's project had also advanced to the model stage, since he says that Lorenzo Ottone worked on two wax models, after Fontana and Mattia de' Rossi. This information is confirmed by Fontana's own statement that Mattia de' Rossi's 'Modelli e Disegni' were rejected. These two small models and the large models in clay, were presented for selection and it was then that the decision went against de' Rossi, and Fontana's project was accepted. Six further designs for the font are mentioned in the Avviso of 31 May 1692: 'Tiene ordine il Cav.re Fontana, Architetto di Palazzo, di fare disegni e particolarmente per un fonte Battesimale in S. Pietro, del quale vi sono 6 modelli fatti finhora' (cf. Rossi, *Roma*, XX, p.374).

Work on Fontana's large model with the figures of Virtues seems to have begun only in the summer of 1692. A payment of 23 July was made to '3 manuali che hanno lauorato a raccomodare li tetti sop. a la fabrica, e principiare a fare il nuouo modello p. il Battesimo' (Reg. Liste, fo.34 *verso*) and on the same date a payment is recorded to a carpenter. Notes about delivery of materials to the sculptors of the single figures appear from 16 September 1692 (Usc. Monit. no.765), and on 13 October 1692 for deliveries to Domenico Guidi, the sculptor of the Baptism group (op. cit., no.784). Théodon, Ottone and Maglia received their first payments on 26 September 1692, followed by a second on 4 March 1693. The models were probably more or less finished at this time, but the final payment was only made on 10 March 1700 (Reg. Liste, fos 202 *verso*, 203 *verso*; cf. Decr. et Resol., vol.167, fos 123f., 126; 198ff., 206).

The Pope inspected the large model on 14 June 1693, and it seems that Domenico Guidi's group received most of the criticism, apparently owing to its size: '. . . vedutane la figura del Christo disse essere si grande che se si levava in piedi toccava il cuppolino . . .' (Rossi, *Roma*, XX, p.375), and the Pope ordered it to be destroyed. Dowley (p.69) doubts whether this and the subsequent Avvisi refer to the same model that La Teulière describes in 1692, since the side figures are not mentioned. The documents of the Fabbrica referred to above prove, however, that work on the model mentioned by La Teulière continued until 1693. And a later model, which could not have been ready by the date of the Pope's examination (14 June 1693), is not mentioned in the accounts.

Fontana's share in the model was judged more favourably than Guidi's figure group, and artistically there were only small details that the Pope did not approve. His main objection concerned the cost and he asked for alterations to be made: 'Hauendo Sua Stà osseruata la fabrica del nuouo Fonte Battesimale, e disapprouato in qualche parte il disegno, ordinò la reforma, e la prosecutione con premura a proportione della Spesa . . .' (Avv. Marescotti, Bibl. Naz., Rome, Fondo: Vitt. Em., Ms.788, fo.430 *verso*, 20 June 1693; Pastor, German ed., XIV, 2, p.1091, note 8, mistakenly states that it was a "first design" by Fontana which the Pope found too expensive).

The Avviso of 27 June 1693 is especially important because it states that Innocent XII commissioned a design from yet another 'virtuoso' – 'di spesa asai minore dell' altro principiato' (Rossi, *Roma*, XX, p.375; Dowley, loc. cit.). At the end of the year (8 December 1693) La Teulière also reports about the failure of the model and its figures, which for a time remained in the Cappella del Battesimo, and in later letters (18 January 1695, 10 January 1696) he returns to these events.

The Pope's order, made in anger, to destroy the models, was not carried out. When Clement XI had founded his museum of material produced by the Fabbrica (cf. H. Hager, *Juvarra*) near the Belvedere, the model for the Baptismal chapel decorated the short side of the long rectangular hall (to the left from the Nicchione) called "Stanzone detto del Battesimo" facing the entrance – a drawing (Fig.7) in the British Museum (75K, I, fo.5) published by Ackerman and dated 1720–1727 (*Cortile del Belvedere*, p.25, note, fig.39) shows the ground plan of a convex pedestal and the projections of the pilasters which embraced the group of the Baptism. This composition, probably still the original, was described in detail by Chattard before it disappeared: '. . . un piedestallo grande centinato, con due risalti quadri, uno per parte, zoccolo e cimasa, che ricorre attorno; nel mezzo del quale vi è un riquadro scorniciato, con un ovato, in cui vedesi espresso *l'Agnello Pasquale* con bandiera dorata, e due rami di gigli per di fuori, uno per parte, di stucco; esistendo sopra il riferito piedestallo *tre grandi Statue* rappresentanti il Battesimo di *Nostro Signore*, il tutto di stucco, opera di *Domenico Guidi*.' Théodon's statue of Purity was placed 'nella metà della facciata dell' ingresso' in the same hall, the three others were preserved in one of the neighbouring rooms (Chattard, III, pp.157f., 167f.).

All the sources seem to indicate that the commission was mainly concerned with a new font rather than a new chapel but even in Fontana's first design with the personifications of the four rivers of Paradise the figure sculpture is already prominent, and in the large model it plays a predominant part. The sources describing this model, it is worth noting, only speak of the statues and do not mention the appearance of the font itself.

Dowley (p.59) has suggested that the Berninesque drawing (Windsor no.5597) is connected with the model rejected by Innocent XI, but in view of the above mentioned sources this is no longer tenable, and the drawing is in no way connected with Fontana. As the form of the altar recalls that of the Cappella Cornaro in S. Maria della Vittoria, Bernini's former assistant Mattia de' Rossi might be considered as a possible author. In this case – and it seems that the attribution to de'Rossi can be endorsed by a comparison with his analogously conceived altar in S. Maria di Monte Santo of *c.*1678 (Hager, *Zwillingskirchen,* p.233, fig.171) – at least one of the projects which competed with Fontana's designs, has become identifiable.

When Fontana produced his design in 1693 Innocent XII was not prepared to burden the Fabbrica of S. Peter's with the expenses of such a huge project, and he therefore rejected a plan in which the furnishings of the chapel had won precedence over the original commission for a font. The Pope could not foresee that he would ultimately undertake far greater financial commitments. Innocent evidently tried to reduce the costs by cancelling the project for the statues, and to concentrate on the design of the font.

Even before the submission of the model to the Pope an event had occurred that influenced him in this direction, the discovery of the porphyry basin, which Hadrian had brought to Rome and which was later taken to the undercroft of S. Peter's, where it covered the sarcophagus of the Emperor Otto II (Fig.6). Fontana mentions that on a walk through the lower church he saw a 'pietra incauata . . . di Marmo numidico, cioè Porfido' and was then commissioned 'd'applicare si rara Pietra per Seruitio del Sacro Fonte'. Bonanni, who does not mention the phase which featured Guidi's rejected model, reports the discovery of the porphyry basin in direct connection with Carlo Fontana's four-river project.

The inclusion of the porphyry basin into the scheme was, according to Fontana, the reason for a completely new start: 'non ostante con l'incaminato del già fatto Modello à propalare la nouità in applicarla al nuouo Fonte, per il quale cominciassimo da Capo à formare nuoui, e numerosi Disegni, e l'adattai cosi bene in un Disegno in modo, che la Sacra Cong.ne l'approuò e si ordinò, che si leuasse d'opera quello di già principiato, non ostante gia fatto, benche fossero di tutta bellezza, et intelligenza, che hora si conseruano in Fabrica, e l'ordinò, che si distruggesse quello gia fatto'. Fontana was apparently not the only architect who thought of using the basin as the font, since in the original version of his text he says that the Sacra Congregazione preferred his design to the others. Thus he confirms, omitting any reference to the Pope's criticism of his model, the content of the Avviso of 27 June 1693, namely that Innocent XII had also commissioned other 'virtuosi' to make designs.

Fontana tells us that on 20 May 1693 orders were given for the removal of the *tazza*, confirming the date given by Bonanni after the Economo of S. Peters, Vespignani, had agreed that the basin was suitable as a font.

This decision was reached a few weeks before the Pope saw the model, and it is therefore not certain whether designs for the font that included the porphyry basin were already presented for his opinion on 14 June 1693. The silence of the sources about the designs for the font seems to indicate that this question was still open at the time of the Pope's inspection of the model.

Fontana's 'nuoui e numerosi disegni' made after this decision must have included the two variants known through Bonanni's engravings, in which four stags support the font. The first of these shows the structure attached to the rear wall, with two angels kneeling on a pedestal holding a bowl and towel; the second shows a free-standing font, with the two angels standing beside it and a third pouring water into the basin.

An Avviso of 6 March 1694 records the discontent of Roman artists, who resented that the 'quattro gran statue di metallo che vanno poste con una bellissima conca' were given to four northern artists (Rossi, *Roma*, XXI, p.60; Dowley, pp. 66f.), but the accounts show that the only northerners were Théodon and Maille, called 'Maglia'. It is possible, therefore, that, although four large statues are mentioned, the Avviso really refers to the four angels in the final design (Fig.4), which Bonanni published in a third plate. In this the font rests on a curved pedestal and has a monumental cover of gilt bronze. The 'intreccio de' cherubini' which surrounds the lower part of the basin has a technical as well as an aesthetic function, which will be discussed below.

Fontana also mentions 20 May 1693 for the transport of the basin to the Fonderia near S. Marta, but according to a note on a loose sheet in the archives of the Fabbrica the actual move was only begun on 8 February 1694 (l. P°. Ser. III. pacco 4a). During this operation the porphyry basin was accidentally broken into five pieces, an accident for which Fontana blamed Mattia de' Rossi, who as architect of S. Peter's was responsible for the transport. Some of the workmen concerned were imprisoned, but de' Rossi got away with the excuse that he was 'p. la Città' at the time and had left precise instructions for the operation. The repair of the basin was difficult and, according to Fontana, took twelve men about 120 days (Bonanni gives the names of two workmen). Payments are recorded from 16 June 1694, those for the stone-mason's work being made to 'Marcello Bigeri' (Reg. Liste, fos 63 *verso*, 86, 88). On 3 March 1695 the Pope went to the above-mentioned workshop to inspect the basin (Campello, p.80).

Fontana's difficulties in obtaining suitable material for the execution of the base of the font and the 'labro o uero Cornicione' to enlarge the rim of the basin (see Fig.6) were solved by the discovery of a piece of marble of the right colour during excavations for the Dogana di Terra (cf. d'Onofrio, 1971). The 'mezza Colonna di Porfido' was passed to the above-named mason and the work paid for on 2 March 1695 (Reg. Liste, fo.78). On 16 June 1695 Théodon received the material 'per fare le teste delli Cherubini sotto la tazza di Porfido p.il Battisterio' (Uscit. Monit., no.1085). The accounts of the founder begin on 1 September 1695 (Giardini, *Esposti*). Fontana's statement that 'Diposto attorno d.o piedestallo l'intreccio de Cherubini, e Festoni di Metallo dorato p. maggior pompa e decoro, e Compito, fù posto in opera alli 10. di Nou.e 1694 nel luogo, doue ora dimora' must therefore be wrong. The Pope visited the restored basin in its chapel on 1 January 1696 (Campello, pp.91f.) but the actual positioning took place only on 16 February 1696 (Reg. Liste degli honerarij 1695–1725, Arch. Fabbr., 1 P°., Ser. Arm., vol. 396). About a month later, on 14 March 1696, the founder, Giardini, received a part-payment for the 'Cherubini, e festoni', etc. and at the same time Théodon, Maglia and Ottone received 30 *scudi* each, 'p. li lauori fatti all' piede e Coperchio di porfido' (Reg. Liste, fo.98 *recto* and *verso*). The remaining metal pieces were attached much later (payment to the workmen was made on 23 July 1698 (cf. Reg. Liste, fo.157 *verso*).

The work on the superstructure of the font covered about the same period of time. Many designs were inspected before a decision was made about the shape of the final design and its execution in bronze: 'Non ui essendo materiale più nobile, ne più proprio della gran Basilica Vaticana, quanto è il metallo dorato, fu stabilito dopo molti disegni . . .' (Carlo Fontana, ed. 1697). On 14 March 1696 the accounts mention a 'Modello in grande del Coperchio della tazza di Porfido' (Reg. Liste, fo.98), and those for the cast and the gilding respectively cover the years 1697 and 1698 (the inscription on the rear side of the medallion has the latter year: Forcella, *Iscriz.*, VI, p.163, no.605; Coudenhove-Erthal, p.65). The putti and the tondo are the joint work of Lorenzo Ottone, Michele Maglia and Jean Théodon, who were each paid 180 *scudi* on 6 June 1696 (Reg. Liste, fo.106). As early as 2 March 1696 the keenly interested Innocent XII returned 'per vedere lavorare il coperchio del fonte battesimale, che ha fatto in S. Pietro' (Campello, p.93). The Agnus Dei, which was originally planned in alabaster, was the sole responsibility of Lorenzo Ottone, and payments for the material ('Alabastro bianco orientale') were made to Marcello Bigeri on 8 April 1697, and for the execution to Lorenzo Ottone on 24 September 1698 (Reg. Liste, fos 127 *verso*, 165). It did not, however, meet with the approval of the Cardinals of the building commision, and a clay model was made which eventually was cast in bronze (final payment on 29 July 1699; ibid., fo.188). The cover, which had obviously been inspired by the lid added in 1622 to the 'Terrina' fountain by Giacomo della Porta (d'Onofrio, *Fontane,* pl.44), had already been put in place in March of the same year. For an earlier project, existing among the Juvarra drawings in a private collection in Turin, Fontana had envisaged in lieu of the lid a superstructure similar in shape to that of the font in the Lateran Baptistry. The front of it was to be decorated with a relief showing the Baptism of Christ (H. Millon).

Even after the death of Mattia de' Rossi (2 August 1695) Fontana's difficulties with the Fabbrica continued. Domenico de' Rossi had stepped into his brother's position and had raised apparently valid objections with the "Cardinali Deputati" about the weight (*c.* 'ottomila libre') of the additions to the basin and its cover. The figure quoted by Fontana in the 1697 edition of his report, 12,000 *libre*, represented the total weight of the metal parts (according to Giov. Giardini, *Esposti*: *c.*13,000 *libre*). Fontana demonstrated to the Cardinals a 'Modello dell'Armatura di ferro' which suspends the superstructure at a distance of about two fingers above the font (no.44, Fig.5). The 'Intreccio de Cherubini' has therefore the function of a circular clamp.

Fontana caused the cover to be cast by Giovanni Giardini in one piece and fire-gilded ('oro Macinato di Zecchino con Mercurio a fuoco') instead of using the 'ad uso di spadaro' gilding which had been employed for the Cathedra, the ciborium and the tabernacle of the Cappella del SS. Sacramento and had blackened owing to the damp.

Among the other fittings of the chapel designed by Fontana and cast in bronze, were the cartouches with the coat-of-arms of Innocent XII (cf. nos 39–41) above the side-tables, and the heads of putti on their bases: 'Questi tavolini servono per le funzioni solenni di Batesimi di Persone Nobilissime, per li quali si fà apparecchio di Vasi d'argento e si posano sopra li detti tavolini' (Fontana, ed. 1697). On 23 July 1698 five workmen were paid for the mounting of the coat-of-arms, and on 19 November 1698 Théodon was paid 25 *scudi* 'per hauer fatto più uolte il modello d'una testa di Cherubino con sue ali e festoni dalle parti che orna li riquadri delli due piedestalli delli tauolini . . .' (Reg. Liste, fos 157 *verso*, 169).

The work on the chapel and its ornamentation was carried out at the same time as that on the font. According to Fontana, the repaired basin was so much admired by the Pope, the Congregation of the Fabbrica and the people that Innocent XII ordered the further decoration of the chapel.

Such a scheme had already been possible in 1692, when the old altar was demolished (22 March payment to the 'manuali', Reg. Liste, fo.29 *verso*), but the crisis over the model in 1693 had caused a delay. Directions for the construction of a lantern over the cupola, which Fontana had suggested in order to improve the lighting, were according to him already given on 10 July 1694. Since, however, at that time the restoration of the basin had hardly begun, the date must either be incorrect, or the statement that the Pope commissioned the redecoration of the chapel following the favourable impact made by the restored basin must be doubted.

To compensate for the walled-up window above the former altar, Fontana opened the vault with a big transverse elliptical oculus, which was already carried out when the well-known perspective view of the chapel was published in 1697 (Fig.9). This engraving shows no trace of any scheme for the room above, with the window giving light to the Baptistry. To avoid creating an unfavourable impression, at least for the view from the northern aisle, Fontana had recourse to a stage-set device, augmenting the rear wall with the window on its inside and shaping it in the manner of a drum (cf. no.36, Fig.12) articulated by Paolo Albertoni's grisaille decoration, feigned windows and statues in niches (see Hager, *Un riesame . . .*, figs 17f.). For the view through the window above the entrance of the chapel Fontana provided a stucco decoration with the half-length figure of God the Father blessing.

Fontana's opponents had tried to hinder the execution of his plans, for structural reasons, referring to 'defetti, e rouine causata dall'incarco pesante del Campanile demolito', and warning him not to make any alterations. Fontana argued that it was exactly for this reason that it was advisable to reduce the weight considerably by the opening of the vault and the removal of the heavy staircase above it, which led to the Benediction Loggia: 'e feci costare euidentem.te, ch'era necessaria la demolitione di d. uolta p. sleggerire il gran peso, che sosteneua una gran Scala, che conduceua alla Loggia della Benedittione' (cf. no.36). As regards the other parts of the chapel, Fontana was forced by the existing structure to limit his alterations to decorative features. The blocking of the lunette window gave Fontana the whole surface to the top of the arcade for a monumental painting, which was commissioned from his rival, Carlo Maratta, as were the pictures on the side walls (see below).

The principal payments to the *Scarpellino* Bigeri, which included work on the decoration of the chapel as well as that on the font, were made between 5 November 1695 and 30 June 1699 (final settlement 29 July 1699; Reg. Liste, fos 117 *verso*, 118, 188 *verso*, 194). At about the same time payments were made to the *Capo Muratore* Giacomo Patriarca, i.e. between 5 November 1695 and 13 December 1697 (settlement 21 May 1698; Reg. Liste, fo.196). On 6 June 1696 four 'manuali' received payment for the transport of blocks of marble to the chapel ('marmi mischi ed altro lauorato da Scarpellini'). This was followed by further deliveries, until payment was made on 13 November 1697 for the marble for the 'finimento all'occhio' (Reg. Liste, fos 102, 137 *verso*).

As regards colour, Fontana was largely committed by the existing decoration of S. Peter's, but in the frames to the paintings and in the oculus he was able to follow his preference for yellow and green marbles.

Maratta's projects for the decoration of the Baptistry have been discussed by Dowley, Schaar and recently by Difederico (publishing the relevant documents in the Fabbrica Archives). In the spring of 1696 Maratta began work on the main composition, the *Baptism of Christ* (payment for the canvas on 14 April; Reg. Liste, fo.98 *verso*), which some months before had been transposed from small to large-scale by his pupil Paolo Albertoni (payment 23 November 1695; Reg. Liste, fo.92). Maratta was paid for the canvas for the side paintings on 13 November 1697 (Reg. Liste, fo. 139), and received the final payment for the *Baptism of Christ* on 14 September 1698. The fact that the artist was paid 100 *scudi* above the agreed amount (900 *scudi*), '. . . p. particolare consideratione hauuta alla qualità dell'opera e del soggetto . . .', is surprising, in view of the criticism which the painting received, according to Fontana, after it had been put in place in June 1699 (compare the document of 1699 published by Rossi, *Roma*, XXI, 1943, p.360). The *Baptism* had from the beginning been commissioned as a model for the mosaic now in its place. The remaining scenes were completed in 1711 after Maratta's designs by Andrea Procaccini ('St Peter baptizing Cornelius') and Giuseppe Passeri ('Baptism of SS. Processus and Martinianus'; cf. di Federico, pp. 195f.).

Paolo Albertoni was responsible for the chiaroscuro decoration of the drum, including the two angels with candle-sticks in the feigned niches beside the window (main payments between 22 January 1698 and 29 July 1699; Reg. Liste, fos 145 *verso*, 154, 160 *verso*, 165, 188). The stucco relief of God the Father in Glory was carried out by Carlo Giorgio Roncati (payments 22 January 1698 and 23 July 1698; Reg. Liste, fos 145 *verso*, 160 *verso*).

Fontana quotes the sum of about 43,480 *scudi* for work on the chapel, excluding the payments due to him. This still left the container for the holy oil, which, according to a decision of 19 February 1705, was to go beneath the mosaic of the *Baptism* (for Fontana's designs in the Leipzig volume, cf. Coudenhove-Erthal, p.68, pl.46) and the balustrade, for which a model was made in 1710 (Arch. Fabbr. 1 P°., Ser. III, pacco 4a; cf. no. 45 below). The oil-container, as illustrated in Fontana's drawings, was later replaced by a tablet with an inscription, which refers to the lowering of the font in 1725 (Forcella, *Iscriz.*, VI, p.172, no.632). As stated in the inscription, the alteration was due to Benedict XIII, who felt that, in accordance with tradition and the nature of baptism, it was more appropriate to step down to the font than up to it. All attempts to persuade him that this alteration would mean sacrificing the aesthetic effect and endangering the basin were of no avail (Scatassa quoting Valesio, 18 August 1725). The alterations were completed on 8 June 1726.

Maratta's mosaic was the only feature to benefit from Benedict XIII's alteration, since it is no longer obscured by the upper part of the cover, but the modification destroyed the aesthetic effect of a complete work of art from the end of the Seicento on which so many artists worked under Fontana's direction, as they were later to work on his design for the tomb of Queen Christina (begun 1696/97, see below). It was to the architect Carlo Fontana, and not to a sculptor, that Innocent XII entrusted the overall design.

On 23 March 1697, in appreciation of his work on the baptismal chapel, etc., Fontana was made 'architetto di S. Pietro', which, however, did not change his financial position. He continued to receive the 10 *scudi* a month for his activities as 'revisore delle misure'. His son Francesco was given Carlo's previous post and, as a token of respect for his father's achievements requested the Fabbrica on 26 March 1697 to reduce his own payments to 5 *scudi* (Reg. Mandati, 1674–1712, 1° Piano, Serie Armadi, vol.373, fo.166). Fontana ends his 'Veridico racconto' with the regretful statement: '. . . sin'al pnte anno 1704 non ho ancora potuto hauere la douerosa mercede, se no che trauagli, e rammarichi, e qui taccio'. His efforts to extract payment for the work on the tomb of Queen Christina in S. Peter's were also unsuccessful (cf. Misciatelli, p.256).

ADDITIONAL BIBLIOGRAPHY:

Sources:

ROME, ARCHIVIO DELLA REV. FABBRICA DI S. PIETRO.

Decreta et Resolutiones, Sac. Cong.nis. R.F.S. Petri Ab anno 1642 ad Annum 1653 (1.P°., Ser. III, vol.162; also 163 (1653–1660), 167 (1680–1700), and 168 (1700–1702).

Registro de Mandati della RR. Fabrica di S. Pietro, 1674–1712 (1.P°., Ser. Armadi, vol.373).

Registro delle Liste, 15 November 1690–28 November 1703 (1.P°., Ser. Armadi, vol.391).

Registro delle Liste degl' honerarij e Speditioni de' Conti à medemi, 1695–1725 (1.P°., Ser. Armadi, vol.396).

Uscita di Monitione, Principiata li 13.Mag.o 1685 (1.P°., Ser. Armadi, vol.390).
Basilica restauri ecc. (1.P°., Ser. III, pacco 4a, Fasc. 12):
Carlo Fontana, Veridico racconto di ciò ch'è accaduto in far l'opera del Fonte Baptismale dentro il Tempio Vaticano (Ms. reproduced below).
Esposti, che fà Gio: Giardini all'Emi. e Remi. Sig.i Cardinali della R.da fabrica di S. Pietro sopra il Particolare del lauoro di Metallo del Fonte Battismale di già nel tempio Vaticano.
Conto Della Reud. fabrica di S. Pietro In Vaticano Delli Lauori di metallo Dorato à macinato fatti da Gio: Giardini, Argente.e e fonditore p.Seruitio del Battesimo, che ua posta in detta Basilica.
Nota Adi 19.2.1705: Vacuo da farsi p.riporre l'oglio Santo per il Fonte Battismale.
Pro Fonte (8 February 1694): Li Muratori della Fabrica di S. Pietro cominciarono a leuare dal Sepolcro di Ottone II Imperatore il coperchio di porfido . . . (on a loose sheet).

LITERATURE:

Francis H. Dowley, *The Art Bulletin*, 1965, pp.57–81.
R. Enggass, *Ottoni*, pp.325–327, 335.
d'Onofrio, 1971, pp.162–165, 262–269.
F. R. Difederico, *The Art Bulletin*, 1968, pp.194–197.
Carlo Fontana, *Descrizione della Nobilissima Cappella del Fonte Batismale nella Basilica Vaticana*, Rome, 1697.
Ermete Rossi in *Roma*, XX, 1942, XXI, 1943.
Ercole Scatassa in *Rassegna bibliografica dell' Arte Italiana*, XVI, 1913, p.114 (Valesio).
Eckart Schaar in *The Art Bulletin*, 1966, pp.414–415.

35 ELEVATION OF THE ENTRANCE (*Figure* 10) [9716]
300×*c*.210 mm. Watermark no.5. Pen, some chalk. With scale, measurements and sums in margin.

A chalk sketch inside the central opening shows an altar on the rear wall of the chapel, above which are two columns which support sections of the broken pediment and enclose a figure with a halo. Behind is a large oval, perhaps representing a window (cf. no.37). To the left, in front of one of the columns, stands a figure, probably connected with the projected font. The drawing occupies half of a double sheet folded in the binding of Volume 176; on the *verso* of the other half of the sheet is a rapid sketch of the front view of the chapel.

The project probably influenced Juvarra's conception of a statue set against a luminous foil above the altar in the Cappella Antamoro in S. Girolamo dell Carità in Rome (see R. Preimesberger, *Römische Historische Mitteilungen,* 10, 1966/7, pp.205f.; Myers, p.33).

36 SKETCH PLAN AND SECTION OF THE SPACE ABOVE THE CHAPEL (*Figure* 12) [9721]
300×*c*.210 mm. Pen, traces of chalk. With scale and measurements. Inscribed with notes on features of the site.

The space serves as passage between a spiral staircase and a corridor which leads to the Benediction Loggia. The plan contains a sketch for the lighting arrangement of the Baptistry mentioned above and a plan for the feigned drum (indicated in chalk).

37 ELEVATION OF THE ENTRANCE, SHOWING FONT (*Figure* 11) [9916]
396×245 mm. Laid down. Pen, grey wash.

The oval on the back wall sketched on no. 35 is here formed by extending the lunette window. The drawing is probably one of the first efforts by Fontana to tackle the commission given him by Alexander VIII. The domed top of the font is reminiscent of the tabernacle in the Sacrament Chapel. The relief on the front, particularly the figure of Christ, is nearer to the Cafà model in the Vatican Library than to Windsor drawing 5597 (see p.41). The paper on which the drawing is executed is considerably discoloured.

38 PROJECT FOR THE FACING OF AN ARCADE [9714/9722]
C.420×300 mm. Watermark no.5. Pen, traces of chalk. With scale on no.9722.

The two parts of this drawing form halves of a single sheet fixed in the binding of Volume 176. The upper part of the sheet (9714) bears inscriptions referring to two levels of the chapel: *Cima della Cornice sopra le Colonne*, and *Piano del disotto dell' Architraue*.

39 PROJECT FOR THE FACING OF A SIDE WALL (*Figure* 14) [9719]
300×*c*.210 mm. Pen, grey wash, traces of chalk. With measurements (in chalk).

The papal coat-of-arms appears over the dado, as executed, but the tables underneath it are not indicated.

40 PROJECT FOR A WALL FACING (*Figure* 15) [9717]
300×*c*.210 mm. Pen, grey wash, traces of chalk.

The design corresponds in the main to the executed version, but the arms are not on the walls.

This and the following drawing are related to a cross-section of the chapel in the Biblioteca Nacional, Madrid (Dib.8159; Fig.8), discovered by Dr Jennifer Montagu, which shows in the oculus above the chapel the coat-of-arms of Innocent XII supported by two angels (laid down on the

basic sheet). The font already has the cover, but the figures of the angels and the medallion vary slightly. The drawing must therefore have been executed before the date of casting, probably at the beginning of 1696, when work was still in progress on the cover of the font.
Copy by Vittone, vol. I, fo.30.

41 VERSION OF THE PRECEDING [9718]
300×*c*.210 mm. Pen, grey wash, traces of chalk.

In this drawing the putti are omitted.

42 PROJECT FOR A WALL FACING (*Figure* 16) [9749]
300×*c*.210 mm. Watermark no.6. Pen, grey wash, traces of chalk. With scale.

An alternative design, which also differs in its proportions from the previous drawings.

43 HALF-PLAN WITH PROJECT FOR FLOOR DECORATION (*Figure* 13) [9720]
300×*c*.210 mm. Pen, traces of chalk, With scale inscribed on right (in ink): *Mezzo Principale dell' Opera*, and in chalk, upper right, with an index of materials to be used.

This ground-plan agrees only in part with the original state as known from the engraving of 1697 (Fig.9). On the *verso* of the half-sheet following the present drawing are a pencil sketch for a console and calculations in pen.

44 SECTION OF THE FONT (*Figure* 5) [9915A]
415×265 mm. Watermark no.7. Pen, coloured washes, traces of chalk. With index letters.

The drawing is to the same scale as an engraved elevation of the font (Fig.4) which acts as a flap to the section. The drawing was submitted by Carlo Fontana to the Commission of the Fabbrica; he described it in his report of 1704 to explain the arrangement by which the heavy lid to the basin is supported. On the same sheet is an inscription of 14 November 1696 explaining by means of the index letters on the drawing the method whereby the lid was supported over the basin.

45 Unidentified draughtsman
PROJECT FOR THE ENTRANCE SCREEN (*Figure* 17) [10583]
280×349 mm. Watermark no.8. Pen, coloured washes, traces of chalk.

The design, probably by a pupil of Fontana, incorporates the emblems of the Albani coat-of-arms and it is probably of about 1710 when a model (see introduction) was made. The present scheme was not executed.

A document of 5 February 1710 left the decision 'tanto circa l'elezione del disegno, quanto circa l'elezione de' ministri, che haueranno da operare' to the discretion of the Cardinal Acquaviva (Decr. et Resol., vol.168, fos.74 *verso*, 75).

Fontana's Report of 1704: (Archivio della Rev. Fabbrica di S.Pietro, l. Piano, Serie III, Pacco4 .A, fasc.12; published in part by d'Onofrio, 1971):

Veridico Racconto, di ciò ch'è accaduto in far l'opera del Fonte Baptismale dentro il Tempio Vaticano.
[Cap: 117]

A Cagione che dentro il Tempio Vaticano si faceuano li Battesimi in un Vaso di Marmo antico molto abietto, et ordinario, che si dice fosse Vn Sepolcro di Probo Anicio Prefetto di Roma diede motiuo à Mon. Vespignani Economo, e Seg.io della R.da Fabrica di d.o Tempio, di rappresentare a i Pontefici, che il m.o Sacramento della S.Sede esercitato nel Tempio il più rinomato del Mondo hauesse il sacro Fonte di si bassa conditione, quando in ogni ordinaria Chiesa ui sono Vasi più ornati, e decorosi, e furono tali li stimoli, che indussero la Sa.me .di Aless.o. 8.o ad ordinare una sontuosa opera à corrispondenza secondo la conuenienza del Tempio, e di quelle Cerimonie Sacramentali.

Sepolcro di Probo Aniccio Prefetto di Roma

Papa Aless. 8.o ordina sontuosa opera p.il Fonte

Indotto dunque S.Sta. all'effettuat.ne dell' opera fece chiamare a se io Cau.e Carlo Fontana, acciò delineassimo con ogni attentione per un nobil Fonte, com' anche ordinò à Mons.e Vespignani, che sentisse, e facesse disegnare per tal opera à più celebri, ed esperti Periti della Città di Roma, onde tutti feruorosam.te mostrorono il loro talento, e se n'ottenne da quel stuolo di Virtuosi circa numero trenta, e più pensieri, li quali tutti poi furono portati in una piena Congreg.ne di Card.li della Reu. Fabrica à tal' effetto deputata, acciò con ogni maturità ne facessero la scelta, ed un estratto d' essi, e fra i quali ui fù un Disegno che fece il Sig.e Carlo Maratta Pittore, et altro del gia fù Cau.e Langardi, e benche tutti degni d'estimatione, piacque però alla Congregat.ne d'elegere il mio, di che scriue il P. Bonanni erudito scrittore Giesuita nel suo libro delle Medaglie Vaticane.

Il Cau.Carlo Fontana riceuè ordini di far il disegno.

Disegno del Maratta improprio

Si come il d.o Maratta era pieno d'ambitione Architettonica, li parue li fosse fatto torto, e non uoleua soffrire tall' elettione, et arriuò ad impegnarsi uoler sostenere il suo Disegno, il quale era più tosto Chimerico, et Ideale, che Geometrico nelle misure, e non Contento riprouò con altro disegno, che p.esser più debole del p.mo anche il secondo ebbe la totale esclusione. Onde io m' auanzaj p.picca à farne altri numero 13; tutti uariati, e nobili, i quali diedero affatto sepoltura à quelli del Maratta con gl' altri concorrenti, de quali pensieri se ne ualse il Pre.Bonanni Giesuita d'alcuni p. arricchire la sua opera stampata, che tratta delle Medaglie Vaticane; si che dall' esclusione data al Maratta, ne naquero molti dissapori con publici

Pre filippo Bonanni

uarij pensieri e disegni fatti da me

Dissapori tra me e Maratta

contrasti, in modo tale, che trascese l Maratta ali segno della conuenienza in qual tempo che stauano le cose molto contrastate, con tutto ciò preualse l'ultimo disegno fatto da me, sopra il quale si fece dentro la med.a Cappella in S.Pietro il Modello in grande, doue apunto e hora l'opera, e questo Modello, e Disegno in grande, era ornato di statue allusiue al sacro fonte fatte con somm' intelligenza, et Arte dalli scultori Lorenzo Ottone, Gio:Teodoro, Michel Maglia, e dto.Modello riusciua con sommo piacere; Fù anche fatto un Modello di Creta in grande nella facciata propria della Cappella dal Sig.re Dom.Guidi, ma per non essere piaciuto fù leuato d'opera, et hora si conserua nella Fonderia di S.Marta; Era di gia Modellata l'opera, che si poteua dire finita, restaua solo di porui mano à i lauori di Marmo, e Metalli con li scorniciam.i delle Pietre.

Modello in grande non eseguito

Succede il caso, che a me conuenne uisitare per alcuni bisogni le sacre Grotte Vaticane, et in tal congiuntura trouassimo Vna Pietra incauata di buona larghezza, et altezza di Marmo numidico, cioè Porfido, che seruì ne tempi antichi per Coperchio dell' Vrna sepolcrale d' Adriano Imperatore nel suo gran Mausoleo, che hoggi uien denominato Castel Sant.' Angelo, che fù gettato assieme con statue marmoree, e Colonne in tempo delle Guerre Gotiche che l'ornauano; Indi poi fù trasportata da sommi Pontefici alle predette sacre Grotte, e giaceua molto uilm.te, e considerata inutile; Da si fatto ritrouamento, diede motiuo a me d'applicare si rara Pietra per seruitio del sacro Fonte, e uedendo che la grandezza della Pietra, qualità nobile della Materia sarebbe riuscita l'opera decorosa, e m'inoltrai non ostante conl' incaminato del gia fatto Modello à propalare la nuouità in applicarla al nuouo Fonte, per il quale cominciassimo da capo à formarne nuoui, e numerosi Disegni, e l'adattai così bene in un Disegno in modo, che la Sacra Cong.ne lo [preelesse à tutti gl' altri con la totale approuatione] approuò, e si ordinò, che si leuasse d'opera quello di già principiato, non ostante gia fatte, benche fossero di tutta bellezza et intelligenza, che hora si conseruano in Fabrica, e s'ordinò, che si distruggesse quello gia fatto.

Ritrouam. della Pietra di Porfido Numidico da me

noui dissegni fatti da me data alla Pietra numidica

Estratione della d. Pietra dalle Sacre grotte

Della Figura e luogo doue risiedeua la detta Pietra Numidica.
[Cap: 118.]

Staua come s'è detto ne i sotterranei del Tempio appoggiata ad un Anello di Marmo quadro, ch'ora serue per ricetto del Cadauere d' Ottone Secondo Imperatore, e si trouauano le sue latitudini nelle misure seguenti con il palmo Moderno di Architetto, fù lunga palmi 16, e mezzo e larga palmi 8.½. e grossa nel Maggior piano pm.2 con un Incauo, che esteriorm. ueniua ad esser conuessa, et in Vna Testa era di figura quadrata, e nell'altra tonda à similitudine d'una Porta in piedi, che habbia il suo Arco tondo; et haueua esteriorm.e attorno alla medesima Vna piccola Cornice, che gli faceua Orlo=Prima di muouerla si fece una diligentissima ricognit.ne p.uedere la sua saldezza, e si trouò, che haueua due peli transuersali, quasi inuisibili all'occhio, e fù uista ch'era del più bel Porfido che habbia prodotto quelle Fodine Numidiche.

[Lu]oco e modo [c]ome giaceua d.Pietra nelli sotteranej

Che però sotto li 20.Maggio 1693 fù ordinato di leuare la d.a Pietra da i sotterranei con portarla nel luogo destinato p.poterla lauorare secondo il nostro bisogno.

Si come à Mattia de Rossi, soprastante della Fabrica anche à lui furono esclusi li suoi Modelli, e Disegni che fece p.il primiero modo e considerando egli che questa nuouità di pensiero faceuano crescer sempre piu fama [maggiore a me] p.il ritrouam.to di si nobil [Disegno] composto; mosso egli non so da qual proprio genio s'unì con altri à suscitare uarie contrarietà insossistenti all'Emo Sig.e Card.Carlo Barberini Arciprete della Basilica Vaticana p.impedire si bell' Opera, però con un special Chirografo di Papa Inn:XII pieno di facoltà fu p. messo di prendere instantem.te la detta Pietra in seruitio del sacro fonte Battismale p.disporla secondo il bisogno nostro, escludendo tutti li Disegni fatti da altri Professori, e come il de Rossi era soprastante, fe ne chieder la cura al medemo p.il trasporto, onde gl'operarij posero li Canapi, e Corde p.il d.trasporto dei più Vecchi, e fracidi che hauesse la Reu.Fabrica, e nell' atto del p.mo moto si strapparono, e fù causa che crollò la Pietra, e si spezzò in cinque parti. A tal disordine il Papa, e la Sac.Cong.e ordinorono la Carceratione d'alcuni Manuali della med.a Reu. fabrica impiegati dal sud. de Rossi à tal effetto, che si scusò di non esser sciente di tal fatto, asserendo, che in quel tempo era p.la Città, e che haueua dato gl'ordini opportuni agl'operarij, nulla di meno prouò molti disgusti; onde non p.questo accidente restò indietro l'esecutione di si bell' opera.

Maratta, è Rossi s' uniscono contro li miei disegni

A Causa di si fatto disordine S.Sant.tà deputò tre Card.li Anziani della Fabrica p.meglio gouerno, et assistenza dell'opera, e furono l'Em.mi seguenti, cioè Galeazzo Marescotti, Girolamo Casanatta, Gio.Batta Costaguti con piena facoltà Pontificia.

Del Trasporto della d.a Pietra e sua ridutione, e ritaccatura.
[Cap. 119.]

Fù alli 20 di Maggio 1693 tirato sù dalle Sacre Grotte la detta Pietra diuisa in cinque parti a causa dell' accennato disordine, e portata nella Fonderia contigua alla Chiesa di S.Marta, e si riunì con molta diligenza a suo luogo, riempitosi l'incauo di legante Bitume, in modo che diuenne un Corpo bene consolidato, e fù capouoltata con la faccia piana uerso Terra, et il conuesso uerso il Cielo, e si contrasegnorno i luoghi doue si doueuano fare i forami p.li Perni di Bronzo p.il suo ritaccam.to fù doppo quel corpo ammassato messo in un recinto di fuoco, il quale liquefece quei Bitumi, e se n'hebbe la libertà di slogare quelli prefati pezzi di Porfido, disposi l'ordegni come sta appresso, indi poi furono posti in cortello sopra alcuni posam.ti di saldi Trauertini, e ben fermati d'un ottima legatura di gesso, e sopra de quali à corrispondenza del contrasegnato luogo furono poste le sue Canne di Rame di Diametro circa tre dita à foggia di Cilindri imbellicate con ruote che p.Via di braccio dauano il moto continuo, sopra le quali u'era un colcante peso di Piombo, che premeua p.pendicolarmente, onde p.il moto, e peso l'acqua, e smeriglio se n'ottenne il sforachiam.to di quei buchi destinati a riceuere i Perni, le di cui Canne con quel moto consumauano a guisa de Cerchi il Porfido, restaua nel Vacuo della Canna un Anima tonda à similitudine di pezzi di Bastoni, che poi con ferri fatti à posta larghi, ueniua slogata, et estratta dal suo luogo, e molti pezzi de quali se ne conseruano in Fabrica, e s'impiegarono à tal operationi giorni Cento Venti in circa con dodici huomini di continuo, e li buchi furono internati ne detti Porfidi circa palmi due, certo è che rendeua molta Curiosità a i riguardanti in uedere si belle, et ingegnose machine così ben regolate di moto, et altro.

Arrivati i fori al fondo destinato furono con somma diligenza posti i Perni di Bronzo dentro essi constringenti di Piombo, che riunirono tutti quei pezzi con tal diligenza, che quasi la Vista non riconosceua i loro distacchi, e si uedeua come intiera a guisa del suo primiero Stato, e sta di nuouo riempito il Vacuo di materie tenaci con staffe di ferro, che compaginorono il tutto con ottima sicurezza p.resistere al trauaglio del lauoro p.ridurre la ristata quadra simile all' altra tonda: e p.togliere affatto il timore di qualche slogatura à causa de i colpi di scarpello presi ripiego di smembrare quelle soprabondanti Parti non con scarpelli, ne à colpi di Mazzuola, ma con Martelline pontate con moderati moti, che scagliauano minuti pezzi, et à poco a poco p. le quali scagliature furono necessitati li Mastri scarpellini di prouedersi d' Vna maschera di Corame con suoi Occhiali nel mezzo p.non essere offesi nel Viso, e negl' Occhi, e con tali diligenze fù lauorata la Tazza da tutti i lati uniformi.

Dei Membri accresciuti per rendere il detto Coperchio in propria figura di Tazza.
[Cap. 120]

Doppo hauer ridotto circolare nelle Testate, e riattacato il d.Coperchio conoscessimo noi stante la tenuità dell'Altezza non hauerebbe fatto in quel ambito la Comparsa, che meritaua, onde pigliassimo ripiego d'accrescerla con un riportato labbro à foggia di Cordone p.dargli maggior eleuatione.

Si come anche ad essa Tazza mancaua il suo piede p.far questo, furono diuerse le propositioni, Bronzo, o di Variate Pietre, ma riconobbi con giuste cause, e motiui che doueuasi fare di Porfido p.l'unione di quel composto, doue la Sac.Cong.ne de Card.li Deputati acconsentirono alle propositioni dell' Architetto, che si facesse tutto di Porfido secondo il mio Disegno.

Si che ci conuenne affaticare di molto p.trouare pezzi di Porfido di simil Pasta, e colore, e doppo infinite diligenze si trouò à caso ne i fondam.ti della nuoua Dogana di Terra un pezzo di Porfido simile, et Vniforme di colore, e passa à quello della Tazza; Il tutto s'eseguì di modo tale, pare, che la d.opera sià uscita tutta da un luogo dalle fodine Numidiche.

Contribuì anche alla natura l'Arte, mentre delineassimo il piede, e Labro in Vbbidienza di quel gusto antico della propria Tazza, acciò fosse il tutto uniforme come di presente s'ammira, ma p.chè doueua detta Tazza reggere un pezzo di ottomila libbre in circa del Coperchio di Bronzo p.suo finim.to, giudicai di prolongare il piede di figura ovale formato da quattro semicircoli, acciò potessero riceuere sopra il loro Dorso la pesante Machina, e furono quelli Vniti pezzi concatenati con spranghe di Bronzo, con il suo spianato letto di Piombo, che rende in stato di sicurezza si della Tazza, come anche del suo finimento, s'è Disposto attorno d. piedestallo l'intreccio de Cherubini, e Festoni di Metallo dorati p.maggior pompa, e decoro, e compito, fù posto in opera alli 10.di Nou.e 1694 nel luogo, doue ora dimora, e ui s'impiegò circa mesi quindici p.fare d.Lauoro con molti operarij.

Fù pochi giorni doppo à vederla la San.tà Sua Papa Innocenzo XII con numeroso corteggio de Porporati, et altri, e suggerì S.Stà à me Cau. Fontana p.qual cagione non si riconosceua in uerun modo quell' attaccature, Disposi che egli procedeua dalla qualità d'un Bitume messo in quelle commissure molto disseccante composto da tali colori, che non si riconosceua il Porfido finto dal Vero, ed hora con tutta Vmidità di quel Tempio opera ancora il suo effetto.

Innouatione degl' Ornati e suo Lume procacciato dalla Cappella oue ora risiede il Sacro Santo Fonte.
[Cap. 121]

Fù cosi grande la sodisfatt.ne, che hebbe S.Stà, Sac.Collegio, et il Popolo della Comparsa di questa riunita gran Tazza, che diede motiuo all' ordinatione degl' ornamenti, e suoi Lumi, che uestono ora la Cappella, doue risiede l'amministratione del Sacro Santo Battesimo, in modo, che io pensai alla contributione decorosa d'un commodo reggio di due Tauolini nobilissimi di Porfido per simili funtioni di stima maggiore parim.te guarniti di riportati Bronzi intagliati et indorati p.esporre le regie, e sacri suppellettili, sopra delle quali collocassione anche le due Arme di Bronzo dorate di quel Regnante Pontefice Inn.XII delineate, e modellate da me medemo.

Disposi nelle tre Parieti spatiosi uani con nobili ornam.ti di Cornici p.sontuose pitture, com'al pnte la Vista gode, ma p.che quest'ambito ueniua alimentato pouerам.te da quel Fosco, e debole lume compartito dal Tempio non sufficiente p. così graue opera, risoluei di demolire la uolta ceca primiera, e feci riedificare quella di pnte costrutta con un gran Vano nel mezzo di figura ouale, quale da passaggio di Lume uiuo riceuuto dal Finestrone del Tempio uerso il S.Offitio, che tramanda abondantem.te uiuezza di Luce p.discernere quei Lauori si nobili.

Doppo demolito la primiera uolta trouai un disordine ineuitabile, et è ch'il mezzo della Cappella d'esso Sacro Fonte è distante uerso la Piazza circa palmi 4. dal mezzo del Finestrone esteriore, che tramanda d.Lume mediante l'industriose operationi seguite nel luogo di quella Variatione de mezzi, hanno tolto affatto il discuoprim.to del diffetto, mentre ne di dentro, ne di fuori nulla si scorge, se non venisse indicata da Professori, e qsto fù fra l'altre Vna briga fastidiosa che hauessimo à coprire il difetto.

Saputosi dall' Emoli nostri la risolutione dell' innouatione in proseguim.to dell'opera, s'unirono à suscitare, e Portare querele all' Emi Card.li della Fabrica contro l'Efettuatione, adducendo questi che in esso Angolo, e residenza di d.Cappella regnauano diffetti, e rouine causate dall' incarco pesante del Campanile demolito, che p.ciò non si doueua innouare cosa alcuna in d.luogo. Parue in p.mo faccia da non rigettarsi tal obiettione, ma si come io p.ma di uenire all'atto della demolitione ero preparato nelle risposte, e feci costare euidentem.te, ch' era necessaria la demolitione di d. uolta p. sleggerire il gran peso, che sosteneua una gran scala, che conduceua alla Loggia della Benedittione; e fù dalli sopradetti tre Card.li ciò uisto, e riconobbero benissimo essere, le querele molto Vane, e senza Verun fondam.to; diedero ordine sotto li 10.Luglio 1694, che immediatè si demolissero in essecutione delle direttioni mie, in modo tale, che ne uscirono precetti contro di loro d'un fermo silentio. Tuttauia non già s'acquietorono nel machinare contro d.opera et à me p.altre strade indirette come in appresso.

Del Coperchio di Metallo, et altri Lauori nella Cappella del detto Sacro Fonte.
[Cap. 122.]

Di già restaua stabilita la parte principale della Tazza p. uso del Sac.Fonte si Venne all' esecut.ne della fonditura del Coperchio di Bronzo secondo il Modello di Creta gia fatto, et approuato da Sua San.tà, e Sacra Cong.ne, quale si lauorò nello stanzione del Palazzo dell' Ecc.mi Cesarini, che auanti seruiua p. commodo de Cursori p.tale esecutione s'elesse Gio:Giardino Fonditore, et Argentiere di grido ordinandogli, che gettasse, e fondesse di Metallo la d.a opera con ogni prestezza, e celerità, il qual Mastro non si sgomentò all' Instanza fattagli da me, cioè che si gettasse tutta d'un pezzo, acciò l'opera fosse più resistente all' ingiurie, et accidenti del tempo, benche sia di Vasta misura, e di straordinario intaglio, e fattura con li proprij lauori, che la uestiuano molto sontuosam.te d'ornati tutto eseguì, e cominciando dal labro della sua residenza sin' al piedestallo che sostiene l'Agnello Pasquale. Furono tali le diligenze usate nell'operationi benche broccardiche, ouero zardose, che se ne ottenne il bramato intento dell' intiero gettito di tutta la Machina, nulla di meno p. far comparire all' occhio sempre più la bellezza de lauori, uolsi che tutte quelle porosità fossero ripiene in gettito à croccioli p.empire quelle tozze, e picciole concauità, solite crearsi dalla natura di quei Metalli di p.mo gettito p.la pulitia dell' Indoratura, e se n'ottenne generalm.te in quelle superficie un perfettissimo lauoro, come nell'opera s'ammira.

Furono anche pratticate, et usate simili diligenze nelle dette due bellissime Armi di Bronzo, che risiedono sopra l'accennati Tauolini, et altri lauori di Metallo attorno.

Era di già passato à miglior Vita Mattia de Rossi, e subentrò in luogo d'esso nella carica di soprastante Domenico de Rossi fratello d'esso, il quale come nuouo in queste Materie di difficile intendim.to e prattica scrupolizzandoui sopra l'ideata mia opera, indusse questo à produrre una relatione all' Emi Card.li Deputati, la quale conteneua quel Coperchio di Bronzo pesante d'ottomila libre in circa posto che fosse nella sua residenza hauerebbe quel grauante peso premuto li sporti, e Proietti della Tazza, e consequentem.te si sarebbero discompagnati, e slogati quelli riuniti pezzi di Porfido. Alla comparsa di questa fece qualche senso alli Sig.i Cardinali Deputati, quali concorrono una Cong.ne particolare sopra tal affare. Auuisato io di ciò che di gia tutto haueuamo prouisto formai subito da i Disegni formar un Modello dell' Armatura di ferro, che doueua reggere la d.a Machina, e portato in Cong.ne feci uedere demostratiue, che quella Pesante Machina ueniua sostenuta non dalla Tazza, ma da due Bachi di Marmo, che posauano a corrispondenza perpendicolarm.te nel uiuo del Piedestallo di Porfido, e che il detto Coperchio sarebbe restato dal Piano della Tazza circa due dita d'Aria d'Altezza per far restare illesa, e libera, le proietture, et orli di d.a Tazza.

Riconosciutosi da questi Emi il ripiego ordinorono, che si proseguisse l'opera secondo i Modelli, et ordinationi mie, con reiterato ordine, ch'ogn' altro oppositore si quietasse, e che non s'ingerisse più in simil' affare.

Fù posto il Coperchio in opera, ma solleuato in Aria secondo il modo che dimostrai in Cong.ne, e quell' Aria, che corre tra la Tazza, e Coperchio uiene nobilm.te chiusa con cerchi mouibili circolari, quali fingono come Vna Base di quel ornato, doue che alla giornata uengano quei cerchi leuati, e rimessi p. far uedere alli Forastieri con somma ammiratione, che quella grauità resti per aria, e non sopra la d.Tazza, uiene però sostenuta dall' Armatura di Ferro posata sopra li due Bachi, li quali non appariscono all' occhio mediante l'ornato Piramidale, che le cuopre.

Dell' Indoratura, et altre Querele fatte suscitare contro me Cau.Fontana.
[Cap. 123.]

Conoscei che le tre opere di Metallo dentro il Tempio Vaticano, cioè Catedra, Ciborio, e la Confessione, e Tabernacolo del' SS.mo Sacramento, sono offese, et annegrite nella propria Indoratura p.essere indorate ad uso di spadaro non resistente à quell' ambiente così Vmido, che p.euitare tal causa insinuai alli SS.i Card.li Deputati, ch'era bene d'indorare quella Machina d'oro Macinato di Zecchini con Mercurio a fuoco, che s'hauerebbe ottenuto quel Indoratura più perfetta, e perpetua, tanto più che simil modo ammetteua in ogni tempo il ripulim.to, e la separat.ne de i Metalli iui posti, cioè l'Oro, e Bronzo, al contrario l'Indoratura à spadaro non ammette queste particolarità.

Riconobbero detti Emi Deputati esser la proposit.ne nostra ottima, e giusta, ordinorono, che s'indorasse d'oro macinato, comandando anche a Gio:Giardini, atteso la sollecitudine di S.Stà. indorasse di subito; Per tal causa li ueniuano somministrati mandati per buona somma di Zecchini p.ottenere con prestezza i lauoro; E ciò diede motiuo alli contrarij di dare altra querela, che la fecero passare p.Persona Terza a due Card.li della Cong.ne piena di bugie contro il Giardini, e de i med. tre Card.li Deputati sparlando che alla cieca si gettaua l'oro della Fabrica, che doueuasi indorare dallo spadaro l'altr' opere, che sarebbe stato di minor spesa in modo tale, che li due Card.li che haueuano riceuto tal' auuiso, fecero ordinare una Cong.ne nel mese di sett.e, nella quale fù risoluto la sospensione dell' Indoratura, e anche la facoltà, che haueuano li tre Card.li Deputati dal Papa. Furono poi fieram.te dibattute, e contrastate le cose, e si supplì, mediante le raggioni addotte da tutti li Periti della Città con esempio d' altre simili opere, Vna Verità così patente, si scoperse poi che furono Trame p.abbattere, et oscurare la candidezza di quei tre Card.li; e doppo lunghe dispute, e litigij apparue il sole della Verità, e Giustitia, e dileguò quelle Caligini, che offendeuano d.i Porporati, che p.esser indecenza si tace l'Istoria, basta il dire, che i litigij seguiti canonizzorono d'una somma gloria li d.ti tre Card.li con l'Architetto, et il Giardini, onde poi ordinorono, che si proseguisse l'Indoratura nel modo stabilito dalli sud.i tre Card.li Deputati, li quali acciò restasse al publico Vna dimostrat.ne delli loro buoni ordini, fecero dar fine all' opera, finita che fù de fatto s'alienorono dalla Cong.ne di d.a Fabrica, p.toglier di mezzo qualche accidente che potesse partorire li dissapori contro i querelanti.

Vedendo il Maratta abbattute, et annientate anche quelle Machine s'indusse liuorosam.te à sparlare male di quest'opera, ciò peruenuto alle mie orecchie feci intendere molto sensitiuam.te, che io haueua di gia la fortuna in quella sua opera dell'applauso generale, e Lodi infinite da tutto il Popolo Romano, e Forastieri di qualunque genere, e che p.ciò douesse quietarsi, e che auuertisse bene, poichè anche lui dipengeua la sua tauola del Battesimo che uà collocata sopra, che operasse con studio p.riceuere il med.o onore, e che non era da uirtuoso le Maledicenze, e che però à suo tempo si sarebbero contracambiate le Palle; e finalm.te qsta Tauola fù posto in opera nel mese di Giugno 1699, doue fù il Papa con li Porporati a uederla, e non hebbe quell' applauso che si supponeua, e le censure andauano al Quadro, e non all'opera del Sac.Fonte; Onde dalla Critica popolare contro qsto Quadro con uerità se ne riporta qui presente la copia, in modo che scemò affatto la stimatione, che con troppa baldanza pretendeua il Maratta di qsta sua opera, che però p.ma di censurare il prossimo, bisogna misurare se stesso.

Descrittione del Nobilissimo Coperchio di Metallo dorato posto per finimento a detto Sacro Fonte.
[Cap. 124.]

Non essendo materiale più nobile, ne più proprio della gran Basilica Vaticana, quant'è il Metallo dorato fù stabilito, come s'è detto doppo molti Disegni di fare un coperchio nobilissimo alla pretiosa Tazza di Porfido gettato di Metallo senza risparmio alcuna di spesa. Quasi che sia l'Anello d'oro, che terrà p.petuam.te legata la gioia di d. Porfido, ed il Vero finim.to dell'opera.

S'inalza dunque sopra il piano della Tazza un maestoso ornam.to di Cornici, Festoni, e Fogliami di Metallo, li quali con uago intreccio di risalti Vanno a diminuirsi in un piedestallo quadrilongo dorato doue riposa un Agnellino con fascia scritta

Ecce Agnus Dei Ecce qui tollit peccata Mundi.

Ma in mezzo al prospetto di faccia u'è un medaglione parim.te di Metallo dorato, che rappresenta la SS.ma Triade per le parole necessarie al Sacramento del Battesimo

Baptizo te in nomine Patris, et filij, et Spiritus Sancti.

Questa gran Medaglia uien sostenuta da due

Angeli con tanta attitudine, e tenerezza, che rendono sodisfatte le persone nell' Arte, e deuotione alla sagra operatione che rappresentano; Ammirando all'ingegnoso Anello dorato, doue si ritiene l'Acqua Benedetta, aggiustato in forma commodissima p.il sacerdote da poterlo sempre tirar in fuori, e riporlo al suo luogo senza che si ueda tra gl'ornam.ti delli sud.Metalli.

E p.ornam.to ancora del med.coperchio dalla parete della muraglia sotto il Quadro magg.e di d.a Cappella ui sono due altri Putti di Metallo dorato, li quali sostengono un tondo parim.te dorato, nel quale sono scolpite le seguenti parole

Innocentius XII
Pont:Max.
Regenerandis
filijs Hominum
Et in Dei Filios
Adoptandis
MDCXCVII.

Spese dell' Opera sudetta.
[Cap. 125.]

Tutto il lauoro di Metallo sono libre 12438 ualutato raguagliatam.te, secondo la qualità delle fatture a sc.1.25 la libra, che montano sc.15547. Zecchini andatiui nell' Indoratura n.o 2503 che con costo, e fattura sc.7509, e con lauori di Modelli, cere caui, et altro ascende a sc.24456 in circa. Aggiuntoui poi li lauori di scarpello, e ualore delle Pietre, opere di Muro, Pitture, ferram.ti, Vetri con il Quadro del Maratta con altre spese, che rendono finita la d.opera ascende a sc.43480 m.ta in circa.

Non si sono potute qui registrare nel n. delle spese le recognit.ni, che si deuono con tanta rag.e a me Cau.Fontana, com' Architetto p.le nostre laboriose fatiche, assistenze, Modelli, e Disegni à causa, che sin'al pnte anno 1704 non ho ancora potuto hauere la douerosa mercede, se non che trauagli, e rammarichi, e qui taccio.

The tomb of Innocent XII (1692 and (?) after 1700)

Innocent XII had a simple tomb built for himself during the course of his papacy – a plain sarcophagus in deep relief, inscribed with his name and placed over the doorway leading into the Cappella di S. Nicola, a small enclosed chapel between the first and second open chapels of the right aisle of the basilica. It was here that his body was placed on 1 October 1700 (Pastor, Eng. ed., XXXII, p.689 and Arch. Vat. Cod. Urb. 1654, fo.362 *v*/363 – this reference kindly provided by Mr Frederick den Broeder). There was at this time some difficulty in lowering the coffin into a sarcophagus of such small dimensions (ibid.) The monument, which no longer exists, was illustrated (pl.32; Fig.19) in the second (1700) edition of Bonanni. It was replaced in the 18th century by a grander monument in an adjacent bay opposite Bernini's monument to Contessa Matilda, carried out by Filippo della Valle to the designs of Ferdinando Fuga.

In a short account of the history of Fontana's monument, published in connection with his drawings for the tomb of Queen Christina, it was suggested that the work should be dated in the years 1696–1700 (Braham and Hager), but the documents show that the work was carried out from 31 October to 14 November 1692 (S. Peter's, Arch. Fabr., Uscita di Monitione, principiata li 13. Mag°. 1685, 1. piano, Ser. Arm., vol.390, fos 794–802). The monument is recorded as completed when the Pope visited the site on 22 November 1692 (document quoted in Galassi Paluzzi, vol.2, p.79: '. . . Viene questo [sepolcro] collocato dirimpetto à quello della Contessa Matilda, e consiste in una bella urna di pietra mischia, con una cartella nel mezo dove à lettere d'oro vi è il semplice suo nome . . .' (It is here strangely implied that the monument was placed directly opposite Bernini's Contessa Matilda, and the same is stated in Gizzi in his *Breve Descrizzione della Basilica Vaticano*, 1721 (p.12), but this cannot have been literally true.)

There are at Windsor six projects for the tomb of Innocent, distributed in three volumes. Five are connected with the final design and they contain projects for placing a full-length standing figure in a niche above the sarcophagus (Figs 20 and 21). This was an extravagance of which the Pope would presumably have disapproved – the final tomb is said to have cost a mere 300 *scudi* (Pastor) and the drawings may date from after the Pope's death in 1700, being projects for embellishing the tomb of 1692. Three of the drawings (9533/5, nos 47 to 49) are enclosed within Fontana's group of projects for the decoration of the piers of S. Peter's (nos 83–96, see below) which appears to date from after 1700. All five drawings are close in style to the projects for the piers, and they may have formed part of the same campaign of embellishment in the basilica. They differ in style from the remaining project (the sixth, no.46, Fig.18) which is almost certainly a preliminary project for the tomb of 1692. This is a study for an elaborate monument in a bay of the aisle which contained no doorway. It is laid down on a sheet amongst the drawings for the tomb of Queen Christina in Volume 179. Drawing 121 below is of another monument probably in honour of Innocent XII.

46 PROJECT WITH A KNEELING FIGURE, PERSPECTIVE VIEW (*Figure* 18) [9904]
319×209 mm. Laid down. Pen, grey wash, traces of chalk. With scale.

Alterations to the sarcophagus are shown on small tabs. Since the figure of the pope faces to the right – presumably towards the 'east' end of the basilica – the project may have been intended for the bay of the aisle adjacent to the Contessa Matilda monument.

47 ELEVATION OF THE (?) EXISTING TOMB [9534]
414×272 mm. Pen, traces of chalk. With scale.

The drawing corresponds closely with the finished tomb, as recorded in Bonanni (Fig.19)

48 ELEVATION OF THE (?) EXISTING TOMB, WITH NICHE ABOVE [9535]
414×272 mm. Pen, some chalk. With unfinished scale.

The doorway and the *urna sepolcrale* above are drawn in ink. The sarcophagus corresponds with the one constructed in 1692, but the door-frame has no ears. In the area above the door there is an extremely rough chalk sketch of a niche containing a standing figure with an escutcheon at the top of the composition. A copy in the first of the Vittone albums in Paris (fo.13) shows the upper part of the composition worked out in ink, with an allegorical female figure standing in the niche. This suggests that other versions of the present design may have existed in the early 18th century.

49 PROJECT WITH A NICHE (1), ELEVATION (*Figure* 20) [9533]
414×273 mm. Pen, grey wash, traces of chalk.

50 PROJECT WITH A NICHE (2), ELEVATION (*Figure* 21) [9485]
420×273 mm. Pen, traces of chalk.

A version of the foregoing drawing in which the lid of the sarcophagus is omitted. It may here have been Fontana's intention to change the programme of the sculpture.

51 PROJECT SHOWING SARCOPHAGUS, ELEVATION [9486]
420×273 mm. Watermark no.7. Pen, chalk.

The drawing appears to be a version of the foregoing, or a preliminary drawing in which only the sarcophagus is included.

Projects for the Sacristy (1693 and 1706)

After the rebuilding of S. Peter's the only remaining part of Old S. Peter's, the circular early Christian church of the Madonna della Febbre (Fig.25), became the Sacristy on the orders of Gregory XIII in about 1575 (Cancellieri, p.7). This was to be a provisional arrangement, and Maderno, and later Bernini and Borromini, all made designs for a new structure. In 1693 Carlo Fontana produced a further project, of which nothing is known except that it would have involved the demolition of the early Christian church. This idea did not meet with Innocent XII's approval and, further, he was not prepared to face the expenses involved. Fontana's models for the Sacristy and Baptistry were viewed by the Pope on 14 June 1693 and turned down (cf. above, p.40): 'Dopo volse vedere il modello della sacrestia e vedutolo disse, che non gli pareva bene demolire si bella antichità' (cf. Rossi, p.375; Galassi Paluzzi, pp.169, 173).

The drawing at Windsor (Vol.176, no.52) is however not connected with the model of 1693, for it refers not to a new building, but to restoration of the existing structure, the level of which was to conform with that of the basilica. This second project is recorded in a document of 4 March 1693 which seems to exclude a dating for the drawing after 1700 (*pace* Hager, *Juvarra*, p.11). The document (Arch. Fabbr. Decreta et Resolutiones, vol.167, fo.123) refers to a relatively inexpensive proposal for the adaptation of the *tempietto* of the Madonna della Febbre, but the proposal seems not to have been carried out. An entry of 28 June 1708 mentions measurements taken by Fontana's assistants in connection with the new Sacristy, the realization of which was, however, prevented by difficulties caused by the Spanish War of Succession (Hager, loc.cit.).

At the request of Pope Clement XI the Academy of S. Luke held a competition for a Sacristy in 1711, in which the first prize was awarded to a remarkable project by Nicolas Besnier, which resembles in some respects Fontana's project for a church for Cardinal Negroni (Vol.179; nos 111/2 below), and perhaps even reflects some of his lost or unknown plans for the new Sacristy (Hager, p.12). With the competition of 1715, in which Domenico Paradisi, Antonio Valeri, Filippo Juvarra, Nicola Michetti and Antonio Canevari were involved, the period of planning reached its climax with Juvarra's scheme (Rovere-Viale-Brinckmann, pp.127ff.; Hager, op.cit.). Other plans that did not come to realization were those by Filippo Raguzzini for Benedict XIII (Windsor drawings nos 9238–40) and those produced for another competition in 1732 under the auspices of

Clement XII, in which Juvarra again was involved.

The existing building was designed and executed by Marchionni for Pius VI between 1776 and 1784 (Gaus).

ADDITIONAL BIBLIOGRAPHY:

Francesco Cancellieri, *La Sagrestia Vaticana eretta dal Regnante Pontefice Pio Sesto*, Rome, 1784.
Joachim Gaus, *Carlo Marchionni*, Studi Italiani, vol.9, Cologne, 1967, chapters III and IV.
Ermete Rossi, in *Roma*, XX, 1942, p.375.

52 SECTION OF THE 'MADONNA DELLA FEBBRE' (*Figure* 22) [9784]
275×*c*.410 mm. Watermark no.6. Pen, chalk. With scale, measurements and inscriptions, referring to features of the site.

In this section, drawn by an assistant, Fontana himself seems to have indicated in pencil his ideas for the restoration. In order to eliminate the difference in level between the church and the basilica, a floor was to be inserted 18 *palmi* above the original floor, supported on low vaults, and the chapels in the niches were to be raised to the same extent. As in S. Teodoro (see below), the walls were to be articulated by single pilasters, which were here to be continued by ribs above the entablature and round windows were to be opened in the vault.

On the *verso* of this drawing is a rapid pencil sketch (Fig. 23) which probably represents the first draft of a design for a big rectangular building containing in the centre the Sacristy with its upper parts projecting above the roof level of the first tier.

53 PROJECT FOR AN INSCRIBED TABLET (*Figure* 24) [9482]
422×*c*.275 mm. Pen, grey wash, traces of chalk. With scale. Inscribed, upper right: *Em*[o]. *e Reve:*[mo] *Sig*[re]*/Card: Nerli*, and, lower right: *Adi 19 febro 1706 per/ liscrittione della Sagrestia/ Vaticano C:F.*

The inscription refers to Cardinal Francesco Nerli, secretary to Clement XI and Prefetto della Fabbrica. The drawings are probably connected with the tablet placed in the chapel of SS. Lamberto and Servazio which the Cardinal had chosen for his burial place (cf. Forcella, *Iscriz.*, vol. VI, p.167, no.645).

54 VERSION OF THE PRECEDING [9481]
422×*c*.275 mm. Pen, grey wash, traces of chalk. scale.

Surveys of the lantern, damaged by lightning (1694, 1699 and 1709)

The fourteenth subject in Volume 176 concerns damage, caused by lightning, to the lantern of S. Peter's in 1694, 1699 and 1709. A text and a single drawing for each of the first two years are bound in the volume, while a loose text, not illustrated by a drawing, deals with the damage of 1709. The title on the preceding blank sheet reads: *Relatione delli Danni Causati da fulmini / Dati nella Lanterna della Cuppola / Vaticana Anno 1694 e 1699*'. Since the damage of 1709 is not referred to in this title, it seems likely that the volume itself was made up and bound sometime before 1709, when the last of the texts was inserted in the book.

The first text, of 5 May 1694, is a copy of a document composed by officers of S. Peter's, which describes the damage done on 4 May to the area around one of the pairs of columns of the lantern. The text of 1699 is a simple description of the ravages made by lightning on 12 July 1699. The third text refers to a *saetta* which struck the lantern on 8 December 1709. It is the latest autograph text by Fontana in the Windsor volumes and betrays great infirmity of hand.

The present section of Volume 176 also includes an engraving of the dome of S. Peter's, like that illustrated as p.311 of the *Tempio Vaticano*. This has been numbered as a drawing (no.9765) and was presumably placed with the two drawings of the lantern by Fontana himself. This engraving is omitted from the catalogue below.

55 ELEVATION AND SECTION OF THE LANTERN (1694) (*Figure* 26) [9763]
275×*c*.195 mm. Chalk, grey wash, some pen. With index.

The lantern is shown half in elevation and half in section (compare p.337 of the *Tempio Vaticano*). The damaged bay of the lantern is indexed with letters from A to G in the elevation, referring to Fontana's text of 1694.

56 ELEVATION AND SECTION OF THE LANTERN (1699) [9764]
275×*c*.205 mm. Watermark no.5. Chalk, grey wash.

The drawing is closely similar to the preceding. The index comprises the numbers 2, 3, 4, and 7, referring to Fontana's text of 1699.

Survey of the cupola (1695)

The seventh subject in Volume 176 consists of four texts and two drawings bearing on the stability of the cupola. The whole section in

Volume 176 is entitled, rather misleadingly, on the preceding blank sheet: *Relatione della Cuppola Vaticana con / Quella di S Ma. del fiore di / firenze.*

The first text, made at the request of the *Illmo: Sigr. Paolo Falconieri* and dated 6 August 1695, is a long and interesting *discorso* which concerns the quarrel about the condition of the dome dating from 1680. The first part of the text gives a more detailed account of this quarrel than that in the Como manuscript (see first section of Catalogue). It describes how a rumour had gained currency to the effect that Bernini had placed a great circle of iron around the cupola (i.e. around the outside of the inner shell of the dome) to counteract a crack which was visible from the interior of the church. This and other 'lies' are attributed by Fontana to a certain Fra Giuseppe Palia 'Siciliano Laico dell'Ordine di S. Domco:' who had apparently published an account of his views. At the request of Pope Innocent XI, Cardinal Vespignani, accompanied by Palia, the architects (Mattia de') Rossi and Fontana himself, and others, made a tour of inspection on 12 September 1680. Asked to point out Bernini's iron brace, Palia pointed to one of the three braces which had been placed in position by Domenico Fontana in the time of Sixtus V (cf. the *Tempio Vaticano*, p.331). Palia, as Fontana says, made an ass of himself, and after the visit the nature of the crack in the dome was explained to him. It is, Fontana claims, a perfectly natural manifestation, held in check by the three iron braces mentioned above, and for various reasons not to be considered a danger. Monsignore Vespignani was able to reassure the Pope about the stability of the cupola.

Fontana then goes on to mention his own book on S. Peter's, 'il libro Famoso intitolato il Tempio Vaticano', saying that he was encouraged by Monsignore Vespignani to undertake this task. He describes the section in his book dealing with the dome of Florence Cathedral – a cupola which, being pointed, is more stable than a lower dome. To show what can be done in cases of real danger, Fontana then cites examples of two domes that he himself had repaired. The dome of the Chiesa Nuova had been weakened by the piercing of windows to shed light on Pietro da Cortona's fresco in the cupola, and a fairly wide crack had appeared in the fabric. In this case a *Cerchio di Ferro* was placed around the cupola in order not to damage the fresco. At Montefiascone the cracking of the dome of the Cathedral was checked by reinforcing the fabric with chains (see Hager, *Montefiascone*, and in *Commentari*, 1973, pp.300ff.).

Fontana's second text is a short and hastily written description of the crack in the cupola of S. Peter's and the iron braces.

There follow – texts three and four – the list of 30 questions about the condition of the cupola and Fontana's replies to these questions, which are illustrated by the two drawings. Fontana's text is addressed to Dottor Basetti, secretary to the Grand Duke of Tuscany, and the questions were therefore presumably sent to Fontana on the Grand Duke's behalf. Fontana's letter and the two drawings are presumably copies of the original papers which are still in existence in Florence (Bibl. Nazionale, Fondo Nazionale, II–21). One of the Windsor drawings bears the date 1695 on the *verso* and the letter in Florence is dated 22 September 1695, the month following the *discorso* made for Paolo Falconieri.

Fontana begins his letter by explaining that the reason for writing the *Tempio Vaticano* was to make known to the public the composition of the cupola and to allay any fears about its condition. He then refers to the pages and illustrations of the book dealing with the cupola, and goes on to answer one by one the thirty questions, describing again the crack and the iron braces, and referring to the indexes on the two drawings. In these drawings only two of the three braces are described, one fully visible and one embedded in the fabric just above the level of the drum. Disputes about the stability of the dome continued into the eighteenth century, when a campaign of reinforcement was undertaken by Vanvitelli (1743–8; see Galassi Paluzzi, II, pp.54f.).

Together with the original of Fontana's letter in Florence is a report of 13 June 1696 by the architect's son, Francesco, on the dome of Florence cathedral. This report presumably arose from the correspondence of 1695 between Fontana and the Grand Duke of Tuscany, Francesco being sent to Florence to report on the stability of Brunelleschi's dome. The report has no direct bearing on Fontana's work.

57 PLANS OF THE CUPOLA WITH DIAGRAMS OF AN IRON BRACE (*Figure* 27) [9737]

387×255 mm. (unfolded). Two sheets joined horizontally. Watermark no.9. Pen, grey and yellow wash, traces of chalk. With scale and index of letters.

The lower sheet shows a half plan of the dome at the level of the drum, and the upper sheet a half plan of the cupola (compare *Tempio Vaticano*, pp.309 and 321). The first is indexed with the letter R, and the second with letters between A and L. The position of the crack in the dome is marked with a short zigzag line, numbered 1/2. At the top of the sheet on the left is a drawing, indexed M, N and O, of one link of the *cingola* of iron around the cupola, as described in Fontana's letter. The rectangle of grey in the upper right-hand corner (index S) is a full-scale section through one of the links of the *cingola*.

58 SECTION THROUGH THE CROSSING AND CUPOLA (*Figure* 28) [9738]

386×225 mm. (unfolded). Two sheets joined horizontally. Watermark no.9. Pen, grey, brown and yellow wash, some chalk. Dated on the *verso*: 1695.

Possibly made originally for an engraving (compare *Tempio Vaticano*, p.331), and with a border (cut at top and bottom). The sheet is indexed with various letters from A to F and from T to X. The crack in the dome is indexed 1–2–3, and coloured yellow. The two iron braces around the cupola are indexed T (the visible one) and V (the one embedded in the fabric).

Surveys of the tomb of Alexander VIII (1696 and 1699)

Two texts and three drawings in Volume 176 are connected with the construction of the tomb of Pope Alexander VIII (Ottoboni). This monument, of which the design is attributed to Count A. di San Martino, was carved by Angelo de Rossi and occupies the bay adjacent to the choir of S. Peter's on the left, matching the tomb of Clement X to the right (Galassi Paluzzi, II, pp.115f.). Fontana was apparently called upon as architect of S. Peter's on two occasions to report on technical difficulties arising from the construction of the tomb. Drawings 59 and 61 and the two texts which accompany them are bound together as the fifteenth subject in Volume 176. They are entitled, on the preceding blank sheet: 'Relatione e Peritia per la Collocatione del / Sepolcro di Papa Aless: VIII in / S. Pietro' (and a similar title also occurs on the sheet following the drawings).

The first text, of 6 June 1696, is a document drawn up by Fontana, as representative of S. Peter's, with Domenico de Rossi and Antonio Valeri. They had been asked to decide whether the construction of the large niche, which was to form the background of the tomb, replacing an existing doorway, would be harmful to the fabric of the basilica. They report that the niche is to be only 9½ *palmi* deep, in contrast to the niche behind the tomb of Clement X with its 12 *palmi*, and that it will not be prejudicial to the church. Their findings are illustrated by drawing no.59 (Fig.29), which originally formed the upper half of the sheet bearing the text.

The second text, signed by Fontana and dated 20 September 1699, is a report of a meeting held on 19 August 1699 to consider the problem of making a new doorway and passage at the side of the tomb leading to the space behind the niche. The site was examined by Cardinal Negroni, representing the Confraternity of S. Peter's, and the Conte di San Martino, who is described as the director of work on the tomb, acting on behalf of Cardinal Ottoboni, the heir of Alexander VIII. Their findings are illustrated by drawing 61, which is not by Fontana, but, as explained in an inscription on the sheet in his hand, a drawing provided by the Conte di San Martino. It was apparently decided that a doorway already existing in the pedestal of the tomb, which must have been a temporary door (index B on the plan), should be left open so that a permanent opening at the side of the tomb (index A on the plan) could be pierced from the inside. By this means the necessary work would cause the minimum disturbance within the church. The door of the new opening, as proposed by San Martino, was to be made to correspond with the adjacent walls and thus made as unobtrusive as possible. Fontana reports, finally, that work carried out on these lines would not be prejudicial to the church. The construction of the tomb must have been quite far advanced by this date, but it was apparently still not completed in 1701, when a speedy end to the work was requested by Pope Clement XI in his first *chirografo* dealing with the tomb of Queen Christina (see below).

The third drawing connected with the tomb of Alexander VIII, no.60, is separated from the others in Volume 176. It corresponds closely in style and technique with drawing 59 and shows a method of giving access to the space behind the site chosen for the tomb by means of two symmetrical passages. The drawing may represent an attempt by Fontana to provide access to the room behind the site of the tomb, when he knew that the central door was to be replaced, but before he was aware of the design on which the tomb was to be constructed.

59 PLAN OF THE TOMB (1696) (*Figure* 29) [9765A]

*C.*210×300 mm. Pen, coloured washes, some chalk. With scale and index letters.

The doorway to be replaced by the tomb is indexed A and the walls to each side of the door are labelled C and shown in pale grey wash. The back wall of the tomb is labelled E and shown in pink wash. It is directly compared with the shape of the deeper niche of the tomb of Clement X, labelled B and shown in yellow wash.

60 PLAN OF THE SITE OCCUPIED BY THE TOMB (*Figure* 30) [9747]

*C.*210×302 mm. Watermark no.5. Pen, coloured washes, traces of chalk.

The drawing closely resembles no.59 in technique and is probably by Fontana himself. It shows the doorway later replaced by the tomb and a method of piercing two 'L'-shaped passageways (shown in cream wash) to the space behind the site.

61 Unidentified draughtsman
PLAN OF THE TOMB (1699) (*Figure* 31) [9766]
278×*c*.335 mm. (unfolded). Pen, grey and pink wash, traces of chalk. With scale and index letters A and B. Inscribed, upper left, in Fontana's hand: *Pianta originale consegniata / dal S. Conte S. Martino li / 19 Agosto prima della Cong*ne*. / e si mostrò in piena congreg.*ne */ è se nè diede copia all' Em*mo*. / è Reu*mo*. Negroni alli 2 7bre / – 1699.*
The drawing is not in Fontana's style, and, as explained in his inscription, it was provided by the Conte di San Martino for the meeting of 19 August 1699, which is described in Fontana's text of 2 September. The plan shows the tomb itself and the whole of the empty area behind. The new passage to be cut to the left of the tomb is coloured pink and indexed A. The tomb itself is coloured pink and inscribed with the letter B and parallel lines in dotted ink. These must refer to the opening in the base of the monument described in the text of 1699.

The tomb of Queen Christina of Sweden (1696–1702)

A group of 17 drawings in Volume 179 at Windsor are projects by Fontana for the tomb of Queen Christina of Sweden. The majority have been illustrated and discussed in a recent publication (Braham and Hager) and the present introduction is confined to a summary of that paper, with some additions and corrections outlined in greater detail.

The tomb of Queen Christina lies at the back of the first pier on the right in the nave of S. Peter's (Fig. 32). Its long inscription (Forcella, VI, p.609) records that the work was begun for Innocent XII and finished for his successor, Clement XI, in 1702. The Queen died in Rome in 1689 and her body was placed in the crypt of the basilica in a tomb which is still in existence (Bonanni, plan of crypt, pl.47, no.56; Galassi Paluzzi, I, pp.144f.). (The Queen had asked in her will to be buried simply in the Pantheon – Cartari Febei, vol.99, fos 87f.)

The Pope intended to have a 'bello e ricco deposito' constructed in her honour (Cartari Febei, loc.cit.; Bibl. Vat., *Lat. Urb.* 1665, fos 177f.), but both he and Cardinal Decio Azzolino, the Queen's heir, died shortly after, and nothing further, as far as is known, was done at the time (see Stockholm Catalogue, p.342).

During the pontificate of Innocent XII, a certain Conte di Vasno, one of the Queen's courtiers, obtained the Pope's approval for a design for a monument costing 1,000 *scudi* (Bibl. Vat., loc.cit.; Braham and Hager, p.56). But on 17 November 1696 the Pope gave notice that a monument costing 6,000 *scudi* was to be constructed 'a somiglianza di quello della Contessa Matilde' to the designs of Carlo Fontana (Pastor, Eng. ed., XXXII, pp.587f.; the *avviso* quoted by Rossi). It was probably agreed that the tomb should incorporate a full-length standing figure like that of the Contessa Matilda.

The tomb was finally built in the bay adjacent to Bernini's monument, and bearing relatively little resemblance to his work. The progress of the construction is recorded in a series of documents ranging in date from 1697 to 1702 (Braham and Hager, pp.56f.). In July of the former year the sculptors Jean Théodon and Lorenzo Ottone received material to enable them to start work on the sculpture of the tomb, and in the following month Giovanni Giardini, who cast the metal accoutrements of the monument, received the first of several disbursements of metal. But this campaign of work had almost come to a halt by the time of Innocent's death (27 September 1700) – perhaps as a consequence of the mounting costs – and it was left to Clement XI to complete the monument.

While still a Cardinal Clement had been closely associated with the circle of Queen Christina (Pastor, Eng. ed., XXXIII, pp.7f.) and he had the work quickly restarted (Valesio, 28 November 1700 – passage quoted by Scatassa). On 12 March 1701 Clement issued his first *chirografo* on the subject of the monument, and the second followed on 31 May 1702, by which time the work was almost finished. The unveiling took place on 8 June, as reported by Valesio (quoted by Scatassa), and the final payments to the sculptors were made in July and September.

The final cost of the construction exceeded the original estimate of 6,000 *scudi* for the first design by several thousand, and a figure of 12,000 *scudi* was given in 1760 (Rossini, p.148). Valesio (journal entries for 28 November 1700 and 27 November 1701, quoted by Scatassa) apparently believed that the original estimate was of 2/3,000 *scudi*, and this may indeed have been true of the final design, since a number of Fontana's projects appear to be inscribed with estimates of cost in the region of 3,000 *scudi*. Fontana later complained that he himself had received no payment for all the work he had undertaken on the tomb: '. . . ha fatti infiniti modelli e disegni per il fonte battesimale e Deposito della regina di Svezia senza verun pagamento . . .' (Misciatelli, p.256).

The sculptors appear to have fared better than Fontana. To the documents already mentioned (Braham and Hager, p.56) must be added the following references (of which the first was kindly pointed out by Dr Jennifer Montagu): from 9 August 1697 to 3 January 1698 large quantities of metal were made available to Giardini for his work (Arch. della Rev. Fabbr. di S. Pietro, Entrata di monitione, 1° piano, Serie Armadi, vol.339 (1659–1698) fos 54ff.); on 20 January 1698, when Théodon was paid for the 'modelli della medaglia' and the 'modello della morte', Ottone at the same time received payment for 'li modella di Creta di tre Putti da scolpirsi' – the reference to three *putti* must be an error, and a later reference, of 18 March, mentions only two (loc.cit., Registro delle liste, 1° piano, Serie Armadi, vol.391); on 24 September 1698, finally, a payment is recorded for marble supplied for the two bas-reliefs 'nelle testate del Vrna del deposito della già Regina di Suetia', and these are presumably the reliefs at the two ends of the sarcophagus (ibid. fo.163).

Théodon seems therefore to have started work on the main relief, representing Queen Christina's adjuration of Protestantism in the Cathedral of Innsbruck (1655), after July 1697, and two *modelli* for this have been discovered by Dr Hager (Figs 50 and 51). By 20 January 1698 he had made the models for the portrait medallion and the death's head, and material was ready in September of this year, probably, for the side reliefs of the sarcophagus to be started. These represent 'Disprezzo delle grandezze' (on the left) and 'La fede che scaccia via l'eresia' (on the right), and their appearance is recorded in Fontana's drawing no.76 below. By 20 January 1698 Ottone too had made models, in clay, of his two *putti*. The medallion portrait was almost finished by November 1700 (Valesio, quoted by Scatassa; see also de Bildt, pp.125/7). It was estimated by February 1701 that 2274.38 *scudi* had so far been spent on the monument (Braham and Hager, p.56). Further money was then made available to the sculptors, and the work rapidly finished off, final payments being settled in 1702, when Giardini's bill was cut to 6,300 *scudi*, Ottone's to 300 *scudi* (5 July 1702), and Théodon's to 750 *scudi* (15 September 1702) (ibid. p.57).

The monument was first illustrated as the frontispiece to the second edition of Bonanni's *Numismata Pontificum* (1700), in a form close to the final design. It is one of the few works by Fontana to be illustrated in Domenico de Rossi's *Studio d'architettura civile*, II (1711), pl.36, and Vittone produced no less than four engravings of it in his *Istruzzione diverse*.

The drawings surviving at Windsor must represent only a part of the 'infiniti modelli e disegni' mentioned by Fontana. They can be divided into four groups: a single drawing of a project with a full-length standing figure of the Queen (Fig.33); two projects comprising a medallion fixed over a doorway (Figs 35 and 36), the doorway being later covered over and a sarcophagus superimposed; a large group of preliminary studies for the final design; and lastly drawings showing the final design itself.

The first drawing appears to fulfil the terms of the *avviso* of November 1696 for a monument resembling that of Contessa Matilda, and it is probably one of a number of such projects made by Fontana for a monument of this character. A second such project must be that recorded in a pen tracing in the Busiri Vici collection (Fig.34), actually published as a project by Bernini for the Contessa Matilda monument (Schiavo, p.154, fig.1). The drawing is a copy, made on *carta trasparente*, and it came to the Busiri Vici collection from that of the architect Vanvitelli in the 18th century. This project shows a sarcophagus relief corresponding closely, though in reverse, with that of drawing 71 below (Fig.43) and it may correspond with a model by Fontana to which a document refers (Braham and Hager, p.57). In both the above-mentioned drawings the figure of the Queen faces to the left, and it may be supposed that the monument was intended at this stage to occupy the then vacant bay opposite Contessa Matilda's monument.

The site chosen for the tomb represented in the second group of drawings – the two projects incorporating a doorway in the basic designs – is more problematic. It has been assumed (Braham and Hager) that the bay diagonally opposite the Contessa Matilda monument, which contained a real doorway, and which Fontana used as the site of his *urna sepolcrale* of Innocent XII, was allocated to Queen Christina in these two drawings, but this theory was based on a mistaken dating for the construction of Innocent's sarcophagus – 1696, instead of 1692 (see entry for the tomb of Innocent above). It may be that the two drawings refer to the bay opposite Innocent's tomb, the one finally chosen for Queen Christina's monument, and that Fontana here intended to introduce a fake doorway matching the real door beneath the *urna sepolcrale* of Innocent. Such a scheme, consisting of little more than a medallion, would clearly have been much cheaper to erect than any of Fontana's other projects; lacking a sarcophagus, it may have been intended to place the Queen's remains behind the doorway, or at least to give the impression that the doorway, as in Bernini's tomb of Alexander VII, led to a sepulchral room.

One of the two drawings bears an inscription referring to a certain *Conte di Suasio*, who may be identifiable with the Conte di Vasno, the Swedish courtier who obtained the Pope's approval for a monument to be erected costing only 1,000 *scudi* at some time before 1696, and it seems possible that the project is the one worked out on his behalf. The basic projects of the two drawings may therefore date from before November 1696, when the full-length composition costing 6,000 *scudi* was decided upon by the Pope, and in this case Fontana apparently returned to these drawings later on, using them as the basis on which the final design was worked out. The rectangles of paper pasted over the doorways probably lead up to the projects of group 3 below, and these are entered in a purely hypothetical sequence leading up to the final design, represented in the sheets of group 4.

Since Dr Hager's discovery of two *modelli* by Théodon for the main relief of Queen Christina's sarcophagus (Figs 50 and 51), the relationship between Fontana, as architect, and the sculptors who worked with him on this, as on other works, can be determined more exactly than has been possible hitherto. One of Théodon's models corresponds closely with the relief designed by Fontana and recorded in the drawings of group 4 below, while the other incorporates slight changes – an alteration in the shape of the bishop's hat is the most important difference visible in photographs – which make their appearance in the finished work. Théodon, one may assume, while keeping to the design worked out by Fontana, was at liberty to suggest slight improvements of his own. It is therefore probable that many other small discrepancies between Fontana's latest drawings and the final work, can be attributed to Ottone and Théodon. One of the most moving motifs in the final design, the winged death's-head which appears to fly away carrying the medallion and portrait upon its back with the scroll apparently rippling over his wings, may derive from an idea of Théodon, since in Fontana's final drawings (Figs 46 and 48) the head of death seems to be appended to an entirely static scroll (cf. Enggass, 1976, pp.26–28, and 1972, pp.236f. 236f., 335f.).

Volume 179, containing Fontana's projects for the tomb of Queen Christina, was exhibited at Stockholm in 1966 (Stockholm catalogue, no.811, p.342 in the first edition).

ADDITIONAL BIBLIOGRAPHY:

Stockholm Catalogue, *Christina Queen of Sweden*, Stockholm, 1966, 1st edition.

F. Bianchini, *Opuscula Varia*, 1754, vol. II.

C. N. D. de Bildt, *Les médailles romains de Christine de Suède*, 1908.

F. Cancellieri, *Il mercato al lago dell'Acqua Vergine* . . ., 1811, p.225 (quotation from Valesio).

R. Enggass, 1972, and 1976.

E. Rossi in *Roma*, XXI, 1943, p.118 (the *avviso* of 17 November 1696).

E. Scatassa in *Rassegna bibliographica dell' arte italiana*, 1914, pp.179/80 (quotations from Valesio's diary).

A. Schiavo in *Palladio*, 1953, pp.153ff.

Group 1

62 PROJECT WITH A FULL-LENGTH STATUE (*Figure* 33) [9903]

415×*c*.272 mm. Watermark no.7. Pen, grey and brown wash, traces of chalk. With scale. Inscribed, lower left, in chalk: *s* (scudi?) *4600* –, and in ink: *s* (scudi?) *3250* –

Two versions of the roundel are present in the drawing: the final design, with its rays emanating from a central circle, stuck down over the basic version, which seems to show a smaller variant of the same device. The sums inscribed on the present sheet appear to refer to the estimated cost of Fontana's design, and both are considerably lower than the 6,000 *scudi* officially mentioned in November 1696. The drawing (Fig.34) published by Schiavo appears to record a more advanced stage in the development of the same project, and this was perhaps incorporated in the model. In the latter drawing the sarcophagus is equipped with a relief resembling that of drawing 71 below (Fig. 43), but in the reverse sense, the action moving towards the left, in the same direction as the glance of the full-length figure.

Group 2

63 FIRST PROJECT ORIGINALLY OVER A DOORWAY (*Figure* 35) [9893]

415×*c*.270 mm. Watermark, probably no.6. Pen, grey wash, some chalk. With scale. Inscribed, lower left: *Ill.mo Sigr Conte di / Suasio li manda / il Disegno Consaputo* (?) / . . . . . (?) *C. fontana. / plm 15 di largezza* (the last line added in a different ink).

The basic drawing is covered by three flaps showing, in descending order, an enlarged design of the medallion bearing the Queen's portrait in profile facing right, an enlarged version of the scroll beneath the medallion, and finally a design for a plain trapezoidal sarcophagus topped by a crown and a cushion, replacing a doorway in the basic drawing. The basic design for the medallion and its scroll probably corresponded with those in the following drawing, no.64, where only the doorway is covered over. The *Conte di Suasio* (see above) may be the Conte di Vasno, and the basic version of this project may antedate the full-length project of November 1696.

64 SECOND PROJECT ORIGINALLY OVER A DOORWAY (*Figure* 36) [9901]

370×*c*.235 mm. Pen, grey wash, traces of chalk. With scale. Inscribed in chalk, lower right: *s* (scudi?) *3500*.

The basic design of the present drawing appears to be a version of the design of the preceding sheet, showing a doorway surmounted by an inscribed scroll and a medallion. In the present case only the doorway is covered over. The inscription probably refers to the estimated cost of this second design.

Copy by Vittone, vol. I, fo.9.

Group 3

65 PROJECT WITH A CONCAVE TABLET (*Figure* 37) [9895]
415 × *c*.270 mm. Pen, grey wash, traces of chalk.

The design is close to two of the preceding three projects in having an undecorated trapezoidal sarcophagus. The tablet above has a concave upper edge and it gives the impression (perhaps falsely) of being slightly concave throughout its height.

66 PROJECT WITH AN URN (*Figure* 38) [9894]
414 × *c*.270 mm. Pen, grey wash, traces of chalk. With scale. Inscribed in chalk, lower right: *s* (scudi?) *3500*.

The sarcophagus is again a plain trapezoidal vessel, here surmounted by an urn, decorated with a wheatsheaf. The tablet behind has a concave upper edge, as in the preceding design. This part of the drawing is executed on a flap pasted down on to the basic sheet. The figure given in the inscription is the same as that in drawing 64 above.

67 PROJECT WITH A RECTANGULAR PLINTH (*Figure* 39) [9897]
414 × *c*.270 mm. Pen, grey wash, traces of chalk. With scale. Inscribed in chalk, lower right: *s* (scudi?) *3000*.

As in the flap of the project over a doorway (no.64 above) the crown and cushion are placed over a rectangular sarcophagus or plinth. This is here decorated with a wheatsheaf in relief. The estimated cost appears to be 500 *scudi* lower than that of the project set down in drawing 64. There is a rough chalk sketch of a pyramid on the *verso*.

68 PROJECT WITH TWO MOURNERS (*Figure* 40) [9900]
415 × *c*.270 mm. Pen, grey wash, traces of chalk.

The medallion is placed above a trapezoidal sarcophagus, and to each side of a console beneath there sits uncomfortably the figure of a female mourner. The console is drawn on a flap of paper pasted to the basic sheet, as is also the lid of the sarcophagus.
Copy by Vittone, vol. I, fo.9.

69 PROJECT WITH *PUTTI* SUPPORTING THE MEDALLION (*Figure* 41) [9898]
415 × *c*.270 mm. Pen, grey wash, traces of chalk. With scale.

A high rectangular plinth, decorated with a wheatsheaf in relief, supports a trapezoidal sarcophagus. To each side of the crown over the sarcophagus *putti* are now present, in this case supporting the medallion.
Copy by Vittone of the left half of the drawing, vol. I. fos 84/5.

70 PROJECT WITH A RECTANGULAR SARCOPHAGUS (*Figure* 42) [9902]
414 × *c*.270 mm. Pen, grey wash, traces of chalk.

A low rectangular sarcophagus decorated with a relief supports a tapering pedestal with a *putto* to each side. The design is close to one for the tomb of Innocent XII (no.46).

71 PROJECT WITH THREE CROWNS (LOWER HALF) (*Figure* 43) [9905]
412 × *c*.270 mm. Pen, grey wash, traces of chalk. With scale. Inscribed in chalk on right with a sum, probably referring to the dimensions of the tomb.

The drawing may have been cut considerably and it shows only a detail of the lower part of the tomb. The relief on the sarcophagus corresponds in reverse with that designed earlier in conjunction with a full-length statue (Fig.34).

72 PROJECT WITH RECLINING *PUTTI* (*Figure* 44) [9896]
415 × *c*.270 mm. Pen, grey wash, traces of chalk.

The present design is close to the final one, but the *putti* are in reclining attitudes, and a wheatsheaf has been added at the top of the composition. Swags, later covered over, were beneath the medallion on the basic sheet.

73 PROJECT WITH A FRONTAL DEATH'S-HEAD (*Figure* 45) [9899]
415 × *c*.270 mm. Two sheets joined horizontally. Watermark no.7. Pen and grey wash, some chalk. With scale.

The composition, although not shown in full, is close to the final design. The panel behind the crown is decorated at the top with a frontal death's-head in relief. At frieze level a *putto* is drawn roughly in chalk. Several measurements occur in chalk.
Copy by Vittone, vol. I, fos 84/5.

Group 4

74 PERSPECTIVE VIEW OF THE FINAL DESIGN (*Figure* 46) [9889]
413 × *c*.265 mm. Pen, grey and brown wash, traces of chalk.

Within a heavy ruled outline, and possibly drawn for an engraving. The sculptural decoration is close to, but not exactly the same as, that of the final design. The winged death's-head, for example, here looks towards the scroll, as though reading the text.

75 ELEVATION OF THE LOWER HALF OF THE FINAL DESIGN (*Figure* 47) [9891]
414×*c*.270 mm. Watermark no.7. Pen, grey and brown wash, traces of chalk. With scale.

The drawing corresponds with the lower half of the preceding and likewise had a ruled outline.

76 STUDIES OF THE SARCOPHAGUS RELIEFS (*Figure* 49) [9890]
C.270×414 mm. Watermark no.7. Pen, grey and brown wash, traces of chalk. With scale.

The composition of the main relief corresponds with that of Théodon's first *modello* (Fig.50; see Introduction).

77 STUDY OF THE PORTRAIT MEDALLION, SCROLL AND DEATH'S-HEAD (*Figure* 48) [9892]
410×*c*.270 mm. Two sheets joined horizontally. Watermark no.7. Pen, grey and brown wash, some chalk. With scale.

The treatment of the death's-head differs in many small particulars from Théodon's bronze figure (see Introduction). A larger, measured drawing of the scroll is indicated faintly in chalk beneath the main drawing.
Copy with variations by Vittone, vol. I, fo.107.

78 STUDY OF THE INSCRIPTION OF THE MEDALLION [9906]
413×*c*.270 mm. Watermark no.7. Pen, grey wash, traces of chalk.

The medallion is shown with a shortened (and smudged) variant of the final inscription. (A large letter 'B' is drawn in the ink below, as a suggestion presumably for the type and scale of script to be used.)

Drawings of the sarcophagus of Anicius Probus (1704)

The sarcophagus of Anicius Probus is the subject of a manuscript in Volume 172 at Windsor, illustrated by two drawings (Figs 52/3). This section of the volume is entitled on the preceding blank page 'Memorie e Sepolcro di Probo Annicio'. Fontana explains at the start of his manuscript that the text was given on 20 May 1704, together with drawings, to Cardinal Nerli, who transmitted it to the Pope. This led to the production of the treatise on the sarcophagus by Archbishop Battelli, published in August 1705 (J. C. Battellus, *De Sarcophago marmoreo Probi Anicii, et Probae Faltoniae in Templo Vaticano*, 1705). Here as elsewhere in his writings Fontana appears anxious to reflect credit upon himself as the moving spirit behind the work, in this case the work of Battelli. He goes on in his manuscript to outline the facts known about the life of Anicius Probus (died 393), and the tomb built for him on the site of what was to become the Vatican. The tomb was demolished during the reign of Nicholas V to make way for the building of S. Peter's, and the sarcophagus was transported to the church and used as a font, until the completion of Fontana's Baptistry (see above). The manuscript ends with a description of the sarcophagus, giving in full the inscriptions which it bears.

The drawings record the front side with its relief of Christ as the Redeemer with Apostles, and the left side. Three engravings at the end of Battelli's treatise show the reliefs of all four sides. The sarcophagus is still in existence in S. Peter's (Galassi Paluzzi, III, pp.213f.).

79 ELEVATION OF THE FRONT (*Figure* 52) [9414]
267×408 mm. Watermark no.8. Pen, grey wash, traces of chalk. With scale.

The drawing forms half of a double sheet folded in the binding of the volume with part of the manuscript occupying the other half.

80 ELEVATION OF THE LEFT SIDE (*Figure* 53) [9415]
267×408 mm. Watermark no.8. Pen, grey wash, traces of chalk.

Drawings of the 'Throne of S. Peter' (1705)

Two drawings and a written text in Volume 172 at Windsor comprise a survey made by Fontana of the famous relic of S. Peter's – the chair that was considered to have been the throne used by St Peter. This section of the volume bears a title on the preceding blank sheet and on the sheet following the section: Relazione, e disegno del Cauallier Carlo Fontana a N'ro Sig^{re}. / Papa Clemente XI. Fontana's survey seems therefore to have been made at the request of the Pope, and his text is dated 1705. Clement XI is recorded as having ordered a model of the chair, which was kept in the Casino del Belvedere '. . . e pur ha fatto per conseruarsi et à deuotione delli fedeli in custodie dorate, il modello della uera Sedia dell' Apostolo S. Pietro . . .' (Loret, *Lavori artistici*, pp.54ff.; Battaglia, p.241) – and Fontana's drawings are probably connected with this work. His text consists for the most part of a detailed description of the chair and its damages, with an index of numbers and letters referring to drawing no.82 (Fig.54). He explains at the start that the relic is kept within Bernini's bronze monument in the choir of S. Peter's and that it had been moved from the Baptistry of S. Peter's to the apse in 1656 at the time when Bernini's monument was projected. Fontana himself appears to have made several drawings of the chair not long afterwards, being paid for his work in 1665 (Battaglia, pls XXV–XXVIII, pp.222 and 237ff. – the inscriptions on the drawings (Cod. Chigi, D VII 110) seem clearly to be in Fontana's hand).

Fontana's later survey of the chair was made known to the British public in 1861 in a paper read before the Society of Antiquaries by Arthur Ashpitel, and drawing no.82 was apparently lent to the Society on this occasion (11 April 1861 – see *Vetusta Monumenta*, vol.6, 1885). Ashpitel's researches were followed up by those of A. Nesbitt, who found that the chair had been further examined in 1784 (ibid.; Battaglia, pl. XLI). A further investigation of the chair has been carried out in the recent past (see *Atti della Pontificia Accademia Romana di Archeologia, Memorie,* vol.X, 1971).

Fontana's second drawing, probably based on the first, was reproduced in 'chromolitho' in Ashpitel (op. cit., 1885, pl. XL; Battaglia, pl. XL) and Fontana's text is also transcribed by this author (pp.2f.).

81 FRONT ELEVATION AND FOUR DETAILS (*Figure* 55) [9411]
314×445 mm. Watermark no.5. Chalk. With scale, measurements and annotations.

The present drawing occupies both halves of a double sheet folded in the binding of Volume 172. The left side shows a measured sketch of the front elevation of the chair, but including in part the lower tier of arcading at the back. The missing piers of the upper tier of the arcade are labelled 'm', presumably an abbreviation for *manca.* The right side of the page shows four sketches of which three are connected with the chair.

82 PERSPECTIVE VIEW (*Figure* 54) [9412]
376×482 mm. (unfolded). Pen, coloured washes, some chalk. With scale and index letters.

A large sheet folded at both sides. The index letters and numbers are explained in Fontana's text of 1705.

Projects for the decoration of the piers

Volume 174 at Windsor contains fourteen studies connected with the decoration of the piers of S. Peter's. The drawings are not dated, or accompanied by any texts, but the scheme of decoration includes in three cases the *monti* and star of the Albani arms, which suggests that the drawings were made on behalf of Pope Clement XI and therefore in the first decade of the 18th century.

The piers of S. Peter's are articulated with two pilasters framing two niches, one near floor level and the other beneath the level of the capitals. There were in all twenty such surfaces in need of decoration and the niches near the crossing contained panels surmounted by a shell in the hoods. The appearance of the piers and niches in this undecorated state is recorded in three of Fontana's drawings (nos 83, 84 and 85), and no alteration appears to have been made to their basic structure when the niches were finally equipped with statues in the later 18th century (Galassi Paluzzi, II, pp.42f.).

Fontana proposed no less than ten different ways in which these piers could be decorated, each illustrated in a single drawing, but it is not clear whether each design was intended to be a model for the decoration of all the piers of the basilica, or whether Fontana's drawings referred in the first instance only to the piers adjacent to the crossing. The decoration of the crossing appears to play an increasingly important part in the development of the projects.

The earliest drawings must be those which record the appearance of the piers in their undecorated state, and in what is evidently his first project (no.86, Fig.57) Fontana makes no alteration to the basic structure, merely equipping the niches with statues. The second group of drawings comprises three projects, in which the appearance of the niches is altered and a pedestal, rising from the floor of the church, is introduced beneath the lower niche. At this point Fontana seems to have decided that the pedestal he wished to have below the lower niche must be made to correspond with the pedestals of the statues of the crossing of the church, and representations of these statues are included on the left in the drawings of the third group of projects, their pedestals matching those in Fontana's projects. Drawing no.90, which appears to act as an introduction to the group of projects is a measured plan and profile of the pedestal of the St Andrew.

In some of the drawings of the third group Fontana allowed the statues of the lower tier to equal in height those of the crossing, but having only a narrow niche at his disposal his figures became unnaturally elongated. In what appear to be the last two drawings of the group Fontana first omits the lower niche altogether (no.95), and then reverts (no.96) to the size of niche he had used in the second group of drawings, combining this with a pedestal resembling those of the crossing statues, but with a long neck added at the top of the pedestal so as to absorb part of the height of the niche. The repetition of decorative motifs in the drawings would seem to give a fairly precise idea of the sequence in which they were executed within these three groups, confirming at the same time the sequence from group to group.

Group 1

83 ELEVATION OF A PIER (1) [9531]
413×273 mm. Watermark no.7. Pen, grey wash, traces of chalk. With scale.

The pier is shown in its undecorated state. On the *verso* is a small rough sketch in chalk.

84 ELEVATION OF A PIER (2) (*Figure* 56) [9536]
413×271 mm. Watermark no.7. Pen, some chalk. With scale.

The drawing corresponds closely with the preceding, but grey wash is not present. A series of additions to the basic drawing in chalk and ink appear to have been made in preparation for the drawings of groups 2 and 3 below. The mouldings enclosing the two niches are struck through with chalk lines, anticipating the second group of drawings, and statues are faintly indicated in chalk in the two niches. To the left of the sheet at the bottom is a rough measured sketch in ink of the pedestal of the statue of St Longinus in the crossing of the church, anticipating the third group.

85 PLAN AND ELEVATION OF A NICHE OF THE LOWER TIER [9520]
413×272 mm. Watermark no.7. Pen, chalk. With scale.

The niche is decorated internally and corresponds with the niches near the crossing of the church. A plan, at the bottom of the sheet, has the inscription: *Pilastro.*

86 PROJECT INCORPORATING THE EXTANT NICHES (ELEVATION) (*Figure* 57) [9527]
413×272 mm. Watermark no.7. Pen, grey wash, traces of chalk. With scale.

The drawing corresponds in its architecture with nos 83 and 84 above.

Group 2

87 PROJECT WITH TWO PLAIN ROUND-HEADED NICHES (1 – ELEVATION) (*Figure* 58) [9522]
413×272 mm. Pen, grey wash, traces of chalk. With scale.

The shape of the niches remains the same as in the preceding design, but they are here framed in a different way, and differ slightly in size.

88 PROJECT WITH TWO PLAIN ROUND-HEADED NICHES (2 – ELEVATION) (*Figure* 59) [9526]
413×272 mm. Watermark no.7. Pen, grey wash, traces of chalk. With scale.

The present drawing differs from the preceding mainly in the character of its sculptural decoration (in the lower niche St Francis appears).

89 PROJECT WITH A RECTANGULAR UPPER NICHE (1 – ELEVATION) (*Figure* 60) [9524]
413×272 mm. Watermark no.7. Pen, grey wash, traces of chalk. With scale.

The upper niche as in the preceding drawing again contains a bust-length figure of a saint on a pedestal, but the niche itself is rectangular in shape.

Group 3

90 PROFILE AND HALF PLAN OF THE PEDESTAL BENEATH THE CROSSING STATUE OF ST ANDREW [9521]
263×206 mm. Laid down. Pen. Measured in full. Inscribed on plan: *Pianta del Piedestallo / sotto la statua del / S. Andrea.*

The sheet is stuck down on the *verso* of drawing no.85 and another sheet – now missing – was apparently fixed in the space below.

91 PROJECT WITH A RECTANGULAR UPPER NICHE (2 – ELEVATION) (*Figure* 61) [9532]
413×272 mm. Watermark no.7. Pen, grey wash, traces of chalk. With scale.

The design of the upper niche and its sculpture is close to that of drawing 89 above. A study of the St Longinus is included to the left of the drawing, the profile of its pedestal exactly matching the pedestal beneath the lower niche, as is shown by dotted ink lines. It is possible that the present drawing is a study for the pier immediately to the left of the St Longinus, but the statue is shown from the front and closer to the pier than is the case in reality.

92 PROJECT WITH A PEDIMENTED LOWER NICHE (1 – ELEVATION) (*Figure* 62) [9528]
413×272 mm. Watermark no.7. Pen, grey wash, traces of chalk. With scale.

The upper niche is close in treatment to that of the foregoing drawing, but part of the decoration includes the three *monti* and the star of the Albani arms. A statue within the lower niche is supported by a convex pedestal rising from the floor of the nave, as in the preceding drawing, and a representation of the crossing statue of St Helena is included on the left. Dotted lines show that this figure is equal in height to the figure in Fontana's lower niche, which is in consequence very attenuated.

93 PROJECT WITH A PEDIMENTED LOWER NICHE (2 – ELEVATION) (*Figure* 63) [9529]
413×272 mm. Pen, grey wash, traces of chalk. With scale.

The lower niche in the present project corresponds closely with that of the preceding drawing. The crossing statue of St Andrew is included on the left and dotted lines again show that Fontana's statue is equal in height to those of the crossing. Fontana's statue now stands upon a rectilinear pedestal, exactly resembling those beneath the statues of the crossing. The field above the lower niche contains a representation of the *monti* and star of the Albani arms. The upper niche is replaced by a flat rectangular frame.

94 PROJECT WITH TWO OVAL NICHES (ELEVATION) (*Figure* 64) [9530]
413×272 mm. Pen, grey wash, traces of chalk. With scale.

The pedestal beneath the lower niche closely matches that of the statue of St Veronica, included in the drawing on the left. In the field above the lower niche is a rectangular frame enclosing the *monti* and star of the Albani arms, and including here a coronet supported on the lower two *monti*.

95 PROJECT OMITTING THE LOWER NICHE (ELEVATION) (*Figure* 65) [9525]
413×272 mm. Watermark no.7. Pen, grey wash, traces of chalk. With scale.

In place of the lower niche Fontana here presents a sculptural group of Christ and St Peter on a pedestal which corresponds, though it is fractionally wider, with that of the St Longinus (included on the left – see no.91 above). A roundel occupies the field above the lower niche, while the upper niche is rectangular.

96 PROJECT WITH A HIGH PEDESTAL (ELEVATION) (*Figure* 66) [9523]
413×272 mm. Pen, grey wash, chalk. With scale.

In the present project Fontana appears to have incorporated some of his earliest ideas for the decoration without relinquishing the improvements introduced in the third group of designs. The lower niche is round-headed, but the pedestal below corresponds exactly in profile with the pedestals beneath the statues of the crossing, as in the designs of group 3. As in the preceding drawing a roundel replaces the upper niche.

Projects for decorating the vault roundels

Two drawings in Volume 173 are of a half-dome, pierced with three windows, which corresponds with the vault over the apses of the choir and the transepts at S. Peter's. The present drawings appear to refer to only one of the three vaults (presumably that of the choir). The second of the two drawings (Fig.67) contains, as well as the elevation of the vault, two circular compositions of scenes from the life of St Peter, and these were presumably proposed by Fontana as reliefs or paintings to be inserted in the central roundel. As with Fontana's more ambitious – and perhaps contemporary – designs for the decoration of the nave piers of S. Peter's, nothing appears to have come of his projects for the vault; like the piers, the apse vaults were not decorated until the later 18th century. The roundels were executed by G. B. Maini, under the direction of Vanvitelli, about 1750 (Galassi Paluzzi, II, pp.64, 99).

97 ELEVATION OF THE CHOIR (?) VAULT [9484]
281×209 mm. Laid down. Pen, traces of chalk. Measured in full.
The vault is given in elevation from the crossing.

98 ELEVATION OF THE CHOIR (?) VAULT, AND TWO STUDIES FOR A ROUNDEL (*Figure* 67) [9483]
275×420 mm. Pen, grey wash, traces of chalk. With scale.

A more finished variant of the preceding drawing. The upper corners of the sheet are occupied by studies for medallions: on the right, the Liberation of St Peter, and on the left, a less familiar scene from his life – St Peter causing water to rise from the floor of his prison in order to perform baptism. These two compositions are probably alternative designs for the central roundel.

Drawing of the tomb of Paul III

99 Unidentified draughtsman
PERSPECTIVE VIEW OF THE TOMB [9917]
416×*c*.265 mm. Two sheets joined horizontally. Pen, grey wash, traces of chalk.

This rather fussy and hesitant drawing style is not characteristic of Fontana himself; the drawing was perhaps made on his behalf, for reasons unknown, by a student or another architect.

II

Other Ecclesiastical Works

A project for S. Maria dei Miracoli, Rome (1673–4)

Drawing no.100, a design for the façade of S. Maria dei Miracoli, occurs in Volume 189 at Windsor; this is not one of the Fontana volumes, and the drawing itself is probably not, as assumed earlier (Hager, *Zwillingskirchen*, pp.270ff.), an autograph drawing by Carlo Fontana. Perhaps made by an assistant or other contemporary architect for the purpose of an engraving, it reproduces a scheme of Fontana's which can be attributed to a precise point within the intricate history of the planning of the twin churches on the Piazza del Popolo (Hager, *Zwillingskirchen*, loc. cit.).

On 16 November 1661 Alexander VII gave instructions for the building of both churches after the design of Carlo Rainaldi. The scheme having been changed substantially several times with the intervention of Carlo Fontana, work came to a halt when the Pope died in 1667. S. Maria di Monte Santo had then reached the level of the windows in the drum while the work on S. Maria dei Miracoli had been interrupted on the façade. Taken up again about 1671, work began in earnest only after a donation on 27 October 1673 from Cardinal Girolamo Gastaldi, whose intention it was that the church of S. Maria di Monte Santo should be finished first (cf. Golzio, doc. 3), and obviously in conformity with a design produced by Carlo Fontana for Matteo Orlandi, General of the Carmelites between 1666–1672, which has come down to us in an engraving dedicated by Fontana to Orlandi (Wittkower, 1937, p.248, fig.10; Hager, *Zwillingskirchen*, p.209, fig.154). Fontana's project provided for the extension of the transverse axis of the oval drum so that the whole dome became nearly circular to match that of the sister church which was planned to be raised on a circular ground plan.

Owing to the proximity of the churches, however, two round cupolas of the diameter proposed by Fontana would have seemed very heavy, and it is probably for this reason that Bernini, who was put in charge of the second building phase, rejected this scheme and returned to a dodecagon, which was related to an earlier project by Rainaldi, in the Archivio Segreto Vaticano (Golzio, 1941, pl. II; Hager, op. cit., p.209, fig.154). He replaced the attic with a low balustrade, thus increasing the importance of the pediment and so distracting attention from the drum.

The presence on the Windsor drawing (Fig.68) of the coat-of-arms of Girolamo Gastaldi, who became Cardinal on 12 June 1673 and made his donation in October of the same year, is evidence that the project belongs to the second building phase and was probably made in the period of transition between Fontana's 'Orlandi' project and Bernini's final design. The first indication of changes in the plans was already given in the *misure* dating between 24 January and 24 March 1674 (cf. Golzio, doc. 8). Details, such as the concave moulding at the base of the cupola, or the fact that the windows still have a projecting entablature, are still reminiscent of the Orlandi engraving, which enable us to attribute the scheme of the Windsor drawing to Fontana. Since the churches were to be identical in elevation, the drawing must antedate the final modifications to S. Maria di Monte Santo, the cupola of which was erected between 20 November 1674 and the end of February 1675 (cf. Golzio, doc. 12).

The drawing was apparently executed according to Bernini's directions, since, as architect in charge, he was the only person in a position to reject the Orlandi project – a fact which Fontana laments in the text on his engraving of the elevation (Hager, *Zwillingskirchen*, p.240, n.98). It is easy to deduce the instructions given to Fontana: replacing the dodecagon by an octagon, to see how the projected adjustments for S. Maria di Monte Santo would affect the sister church before arriving at a final plan for the Carmelite church.

On 6 October 1675 a second foundation stone was laid for S. Maria dei Miracoli (cf. Golzio, doc. 24). About the middle of 1675 Rainaldi was again in charge of the building activities, having taken over from Bernini (cf. Golzio, 1941, p.127), and his ground plan for S. Maria dei Miracoli in the Archivio Segreto Vaticano of the time of Alexander VII, with modifications, formed the basis for the execution (Hager, op. cit., p.265, fig.

189). When in mid-1677 the work had progressed to the tambour Rainaldi again departed (cf. Golzio, loc. cit.) and the work was completed under Fontana, according to his own ideas (consecration 1681). Carlo Fontana was also partly responsible for the interior of the church, the high altar, and the tombs of Cardinals Girolamo Gastaldi and his brother Benedetto, who was buried in 1681. The sculptural decoration (Donati, figs 394, 415, 388–391; cf. M. L. Casanova) was carried out by Antonio Raggi.

ADDITIONAL BIBLIOGRAPHY:
Sources:
Notitiae Historicae Conuentus M. S. de Urbe, Archivio della Biblioteca Carmelitana, Rome, via Sforza Pallavicini, 10. II. Mons. Sanctus, 1. Begun in 1709.
Maria Letizia Casanova, *S. Maria di Monte Santo e S. Maria dei Miracoli*, Rome, 1960 (CRI, vol.58).
Vincenzo Golzio in *Archivi d'Italia*, ser. II, vol. VIII, 1941, pp.122–148; and ser.II, vol. X, 1943, p.58.

100 ELEVATION (*Figure* 68) [10740]
309 × 201 mm. Pen, brown wash.

The drawing is similar in technique to Fontana's designs in the Archivio Segreto Vaticano (Golzio, 1941, pp.124f.; Hager, *Zwillingskirchen*, pp.209, 211, 222). A later phase of the project is reproduced by a drawing in the Staatliche Kunstbibliothek in Berlin (Fig.69) which has been attributed to Gabriele Valvassori (cf. Hermann Schmitz, *Baumeisterzeichnungen des 17. und 18. Jahrhunderts in der Staatlichen Kunstbibliothek in Berlin*, Berlin–Leipzig, 1937, p.12, pl.3; S. Jacob, pp.153f., no.781).

Naples Cathedral, projects for the decoration of the apse (between 1691 and 1696)

Five drawings connected with this project are bound in Volume 170 at Windsor – two plans of the apse with scales in Neapolitan *palmi*, and three elevations of the interior walls. The volume was listed as no.8 in Contini's inventory and the drawings are wrongly connected by him with the church of S. Domenico Maggiore at Naples (see p.3). The sheets have no dates or inscriptions, but they can presumably be connected with the pontificate of the Neapolitan Innocent XII (Pignatelli).

The first of the two plans (Fig.70) shows the seven-sided apse in its existing condition, superimposed on a plan of the crypt of the Cappella Carafa. It is unlike Fontana's drawings in technique, has a scale in Neapolitan *palmi* only, an exceptional watermark, and was once apparently folded to letter size – all of which suggests that it was drawn by a local architect and sent to Fontana in Rome. The second plan (Fig.72), with scales in both Neapolitan and Roman *palmi*, shows the existing apse outlined beneath a new project for the treatment of the interior walls. The three elevations are of projects for a scheme of decoration consisting of four projecting bays articulated with pediments, alternating with three recessed bays. They are drawn in pure elevation with no suggestion of the shape of the plan, but they all clearly correspond in a general way with Fontana's actual plan project.

The design was unfortunately not carried out. The apse of the cathedral was restored and redecorated in the 1740's following a project by Paolo Posi (Strazullo, pp.254ff. and fig.105). Previously it contained a number of monuments, of which the most important were an altarpiece of the *Assumption* attributed to Perugino (ibid., fig.53), and the tombs of Cardinals Alfonso Gesualdo and Alfonso Carafa. These monuments were all removed from the apse at the time of its restoration, together with Domenico Guidi's monument of 1696 to Innocent XII (ibid., fig.101).

In one (probably the first) of Fontana's three elevations (no.103, Fig.71) the Gesualdo and Carafa monuments are incorporated into the design in the recessed bays at the sides of the apse (a photograph of the former is illustrated in Venturi, X, vol.2, fig.493). This project shows no trace of the memorial to Innocent XII and Fontana's drawings may therefore date from before its unveiling in December 1696 (Strazullo, p.250). The memorial may even have been planned as a cheaper alternative to Fontana's scheme of redecoration (a preliminary drawing attributed to Maratta is in the British Museum), and it may have been ordered for the same patron, Cardinal Cantelino, the archbishop of Naples.

The elevation drawing showing the two existing tombs corresponds with the plan drawing in its size and unfinished technique, and this provides a further reason for supposing it was probably the first of the architect's three elevation projects. The order of the other two is more difficult to determine, but in one (no.104, Fig.73) there is a sarcophagus on each side of the nave, replacing the two existing monuments, and this perhaps represents the second stage in the development of Fontana's ideas.

ADDITIONAL BIBLIOGRAPHY:
F. Strazullo, *Saggi storici sul Duomo di Napoli*, 1956.

101 Unidentified draughtsman
PLAN OF THE APSE AND CAPPELLA CARAFA, WITH A SECTION (*Figure* 70) [9357]
448×322 mm. Watermark, leaping deer, in oval, letter P. Pen, pink and grey wash, traces of chalk. With scale in Neapolitan *palmi*, index and measurements.

The drawing was probably made on Fontana's behalf in Naples. The measurements and index letters appear to be in Fontana's hand. The plan of the apse is superimposed on that of the crypt, while the section at the bottom is taken through the left-hand staircase and shows the first bay of the lower chapel in elevation.

102 PLAN PROJECT (*Figure* 72) [9358]
479×368 mm. Two sheets joined horizontally. Watermark no.7. Pen, chalk. With scales in Roman and Neapolitan *palmi*.

The existing plan is indicated with dotted lines and numerous *pentimenti* in the new design are concealed beneath flaps of paper. Fontana adds a series of engaged columns to break up the wall surfaces into seven roughly equal sections, and introduces a semi-circle at the east. Other features of the site are indicated in chalk.

103 PROJECT WITH TWO EXISTING TOMBS, ELEVATION (*Figure* 71) [9361]
370×479 mm. Pen, chalk.

The order may be of columns, as in the plan, or pilasters. The recessed bays to each side contain the Gesualdo (left) and Carafa monuments (right). The bust over the altarpiece probably represents St Gennaro and the sarcophagus above the altar is to contain his relics.
Copy by Vittone of the left half of the drawing, vol. I, fo.19.

104 PROJECT WITH TWO SARCOPHAGI, ELEVATION (*Figure* 73) [9359]
334×478 mm. Two sheets joined vertically. Watermark no.7. Pen, grey wash, traces of chalk. With scale in Roman *palmi*.

The design is close to the foregoing in its basic structure, but the order is now clearly one of pilasters and the decoration is richer – approaching Neapolitan standards in its elaboration (some alterations to the decoration are concealed beneath flaps of paper). The sarcophagus above the altar appears – in this finished drawing – to be equipped with a glass front; further sarcophagi occupy the recessed bays at the sides.
Copy by Vittone of the right half of the drawing, vol. I, fo.37.

105 PROJECT WITHOUT TOMBS, ELEVATION (*Figure* 74) [9360]
332×480 mm. Two sheets joined vertically. Watermark no.7. Pen, grey wash, traces of chalk. With scales (unlabelled) in Roman and Neapolitan *palmi*.

In this design the lower cornice of each pediment breaks backwards in the centre. The decoration above is a transcription of the sketch in the first drawing, and the six medallions at the sides contain pairs of portrait busts drawn in chalk.
Copy by Vittone of the left half of the drawing, vol. I, fo.37.

Project for the Jesuit Church at Frascati (1694)

The Jesuit church at Frascati is built on a site acquired by the Order in 1559 (Sacchini, pp.88ff.). They proceeded to erect a new building which was expected to be ready before winter 1562 (Pirri, pp.215ff.) and in 1608 a new church was begun (Santovetti, p.182). It was finished by 1610 (Farnetti Salvatori, pp.53, 56) and dedicated to Sta Maria Assunta. In addition to the high altar it contained two side altars, one dedicated to Mary Magdalen, the other to St Ignatius and St Francis Xavier (Sacr. Visit., 1636, fos 160f.; 1660, fos 198ff.). Greutter's plan of 1620 (Fig.76) shows the buildings of the college, which abutted on the town walls, and near them the church, with a small bellcot and on the façade a feature which might be a small round window or a coat of arms. Plans of the church and college are recorded in drawings in the Bibliothèque Nationale in Paris (Fig.75; Vallery-Radot, p.16, nos 55/6). The dimensions are as follows: overall length 85 *palmi*; nave 53 *palmi* long, and 40 *palmi* wide (53 *palmi* including the chapels).

Three drawings by Carlo Fontana at Windsor (106–108) bear the approval of the General of the Order, Thyrsus Gonzales, and are dated 30 December 1694. The connection of these drawings with the Frascati College is established by the fact that the drawings are identified in Contini's inventory, and further that the earlier buildings shown in Fontana's drawing no.106 correspond with the Paris plan of the college. The design of the new church is based in its general form on the old one, though the dimensions are considerably greater.

The church as actually carried out (Fig.82) differs from Fontana's project and therefore the question remains: who was responsible for the alterations and when was the building actually begun? This cannot have happened before November 1696, because at that date the Jesuits acquired a strip of the present Via Cairoli which runs along the left side of the church. The grant of this strip was later annulled as the result of a complaint lodged on 17 July 1697 (cf. Atti Cons., vol.8, fos 94ff.). Santovetti maintains that the building of the new church was already well advanced by 1697, but the document just referred to proves that this cannot have been the case: "... hanno incominciato à fabricare, et alzare li muri ...".

It is not clear why Fontana's plans had to be abandoned, but the withdrawal of the grant meant that the site available for the new church was reduced to the 40 *palmi* of the original church. The width of 52 *palmi* mentioned in the Sacra Visita document of 1703 (fo.444) corresponds neither with the width of the nave of the actual church (40 *palmi*), nor with the entire width of 73 *palmi* inclusive of the side chapels. How far parts of the preceding church have been incorporated into the new building remains to be established. The building of the new church was carried out rapidly, and ran almost parallel with the completion of the cathedral, the façade of which was erected between 1697 and 1700 by Girolamo Fontana, Carlo's nephew. The structure of the Jesuit church must have been ready by the end of the 17th century. On 26 December 1699 the fathers asked the town council for a loan to enable them to build a dormitory "sopra la chiesa" (Atti Cons., vol.8, fo.124 *vo.*). This was in fact over the transept. But it can be assumed that the nave was also already vaulted by the same time (see below).

In the second volume of his *Prospettiva* (no.64), published in 1700, Andrea Pozzo speaks of the fresco of the Jesuit church as already finished (J. Braun in Thieme Becker, XXVII, p.335, refers to an edition of 1698, but this seems to be a mistake). At the date of the Sacra Visita of 28 April 1703 Cardinal d'Aste indicates the building as "reedificata, et ampliata aere" (fo.444; cf. Farnetti-Salvatori, pp.56f.) and mentions the frescoes in the transept and the side chapels (rep. Kambo, pp.41f., and de Angelis, pl. III). According to the report of 1703 the decoration of the Magdalen Chapel and the vaulting of the nave had taken place three years previously.

The church as actually built is basically like Fontana's project, but differs from it in several ways: it is on a narrower site; it includes a transept; the low dome is replaced by a barrel-vault and the wall pilasters are coupled.

In the absence of documentary evidence only a stylistic analysis can provide a clue to the identity of the artist responsible for the modifications. Farnetti-Salvatori (p.58) suggested the name of Pozzo, on the grounds that the architecture of the frescoes is consonant with that of the church, but she finally concluded that Pozzo was only responsible for the paintings.

Fontana's relations with Pozzo were not unclouded. In 1696, as architect to the Farnese, he had raised objections to Pozzo's design for the altar of St Ignatius in the Gesù (cf. Pecchiai, p.172), and one can easily imagine that as a member of the Order Pozzo was well placed to dislodge Fontana from the Frascati commission. We know of still another project of Fontana for a Jesuit church; of this there have survived a copy of the elevation of the apse in the Nationalmuseum at Stockholm (C.C. 878 *recto*) and a longitudinal section of the nave (with a preparatory drawing) in the Cooper-Hewitt Museum of Design (Smithsonian Institution), New York (1901–39–2207), but it seems rather improbable that a connection with the Gesù at Frascati can be established.

The scheme of the ground plan of the present nave of the church is essentially a repetition of that of S. Margherita in Trastevere built by Fontana in 1678–1680 (see H. Hager in *Commentari*, 1974, p.239, figs 13ff.) and it may, for this reason, be credited to him as a new proposal when the execution of his project in Windsor Castle had been suspended about 1697. The introduction of the transept and the decorative details in the interior of the church, however, point to Andrea Pozzo. The first plate in volume one of Pozzo's *Prospettiva* (Fig.80) shows a church which is in many ways strikingly similar to the existing church at Frascati and it is perhaps not by chance that in the text to this plate Pozzo discusses the problem of how to enlarge the apparent space of the choir by a painted perspective, as happens at Frascati. The architectural decoration of the church also corresponds with details represented in some of Pozzo's other plates, and it seems therefore likely that the architect chiefly responsible for the church was Andrea Pozzo. There is, furthermore, evidence that Pozzo was concerned with architectural activity in Frascati; Monsignor Leonello Razza, who is preparing a monograph on the cathedral, has kindly communicated his discovery in the town archives of a letter dated 4 August 1696 from the governor of Frascati, Carlo Colonna, to the town council, which shows that Pozzo had submitted designs for the façade of the cathedral, as well as Girolamo Fontana.

The existing church contains a small chapel to the left of the choir, designed to house the "Madonna Refugium Peccatorum", the site of which corresponds, though on a slightly smaller scale, to the oratory shown in no.106 below.

ADDITIONAL BIBLIOGRAPHY:

Sources:

FRASCATI, ARCHIVIO VESCOVILE:

Acta Apostolicae, ac Generalis Visitationis Tusculanen. Episcopatus ac Diocesis, factae per Reuerendiss.m in Christo Patrem Dominum D. Joannem Baptistam de Alterijs Romanum olim Episcopum Camerini, ac Sacrae Penitent. Sigil-

latorem Delegatum Apostolicum Anno Domini 1636, fo.160–162.
Acta Apostolicae, ac Gn'alis Visitationis Tusculanen. Episcopatus ac Diocesis factae per R.mum in X'sto Patrem D.Antonio Seuerolum Fauentinum Archiepiscopum Nazarenum Delegatum Apostolicum Anno Dne 1660, fos 198–205.
Atti della Sacra Visita compiuta dal Ecc.mo Monsig. Franciscus Maria De Aste nel 1703, fos 432–461.
FRASCATI, ARCHIVIO COMUNALE:
Atti consigliari, vol.7 (1657–1689), vol.8 (1690–1721).

LITERATURE:

Monumenta Historica Societatis Jesus, Litterae Quadrimestres, 6 (1559–1560), Madrid, 1925, pp.252 ff., no.280.
Alberto de Angelis in *Studi Romani*, 6, 1958, pp.163f., pls IIf.
Angela Farnetti-Salvatori, *L'Opera del Pozzo a Frascati in relazione alla sua attività romana.* Tesi di laurea, Università degli Studi di Roma, Facoltà di Magistero, Anno Accademico 1944–1945 (unpublished manuscript kindly mentioned by Dr Nello Noblioni, Frascati).
Saverio Kambo, *Il Tuscolo e Frascati*, Bergamo, 1929.
Bernhard Kerber, *Andrea Pozzo*, 1971, pp.47–51.
H. Millon, *Corpus Juvarrianum.*
Pietro Pirri, *Giov. Tristano e i primordi dell' architettura gesuitica*, Rome 1955.
Francesco Sacchini, *Historiae Societatis Jesus, Pars Secunda*, Antwerp, 1620.
Pietro Santovetti, *Tuscolo moderno*, vol.II, fo.180–240 (unpublished manuscript, written about 1865, in the library of the Abbey of Grottaferrata – Codex Cryptensis, 126; information supplied by Mons. Leonello Razza, Frascati).
Dom. Seghetti, *Memorie di Tuscolo antico e nuovo*, Rome, 1891, pp.323 f; id. *Frascati nella natura – nella storia – nell'arte*, Frascati, 1906, pp.198–206.
Giuseppe Toffanello, *Frascati Civitas Tusculana*, Frascati, 1958.
Jean Vallery-Radot, in *Bibliotheca Instituti Historici S.J.*, vol.XV, Rome, 1960, p.16, nos 55/6.

106 PLAN (*Figure* 77) [9354]
483×371 mm. Pen, coloured washes, traces of chalk. With scale. The cut inscription, lower right, corresponds with that of nos 107/8, and the seal of the order is affixed below.

The existing buildings on the site are indicated in yellow wash, the projected church in grey. Of the existing fabric the rear façade was to remain intact, as well as the line of the flank (on the left) facing the Via Cairoli. An earlier project with the main front enclosed by paired columns is preserved in an album of drawings by Juvarra in a private collection (Millon).

Copy by Vittone of the right half of the drawing, vol.II, fo.212.

107 LONGITUDINAL SECTION (*Figure* 78) [9355]
483×421 mm. Two sheets joined horizontally. Watermark no.7. With scale. Inscribed on right: *Ideam hanc approbamus, die 30:/Decembris 1694./ Thyrsus Gonzalez*, and with the seal of the order affixed below.

The church as actually built was considerably lower, having a height to the vault of 65 *palmi* as opposed to that of 100 shown in the present section (cf. *Atti della Sacra Visita*, 1703, fo.444).
Copy by Vittone of the left half of the drawing, vol.II, fo.210.

108 TRANSVERSE SECTION (*Figure* 79) [9356]
482×420 mm. Two sheets joined horizontally. Watermark no.7. Pen, grey wash, traces of chalk. With scale. With inscription and seal as before.
Copy by Vittone of the right half of the drawing, vol.II, fo.210.

Parma, S. Maria della Steccata, project for the high altar (1696)

Two drawings in Volume 179 at Windsor (nos 109, 110; Figs 83, 84) are connected with Fontana's projects for the high altar of S. Maria della Steccata at Parma. Another project for this work, a drawing in the Leipzig volume (fo.20), was published by Coudenhove-Erthal (pp.80f., pl.29). The Windsor drawings comprise a section and an elevation of a more carefully elaborated project, which differs in many ways from the Leipzig design. That it too is connected with the Steccata project is shown by the inscription on the section drawing (no.110 below).

It was decided by the congregation of the church in the last decade of the 17th century to lengthen the choir, replacing the original altar with a larger structure to be erected on the site of the existing east wall of the church (Testi, pp.90ff.). The congregation asked for projects from several architects at this time, but in 1698 the work was apparently entrusted to Mauro Oddi, a local architect who died in 1702 (ibid.). His successor, Edelberto della Nave, had constructed the extension to the choir by 1729 (ibid., pp.95f.), while the new high altar was not begun until 1753, to the design of the architect Maurizio Lotici (ibid., p.223).

Fontana was apparently one of several outsiders who were asked at an early stage to provide designs for this work, the others recorded being (Simone?) Felice Delini of Rome, and Ferdinando Galli Bibiena who was paid for a design in 1704 (ibid., p.100, n.350). Fontana is apparently first mentioned in connection with the work in a letter of 9 December 1695 from the President of the congregation of the church to Duke Francesco Farnese: 'Secondando noi i piissimi cenni di V.A.S di consultare valenti uomini per accertare disegno proprio nel collocare maestosamente l'Imagine di N.a Sig.ra nello Orat.io con nuova fabbrica, habbiamo fatto mettere in carta le Piante de'siti, et una di questa copie desideraressimo inviare a Roma per riceverne il parere dall'Architetto Fontana sovra tutti accreditato nella professione.' (ibid., p.99). Drawings were sent to Fontana in Rome, and he was paid for his work in connection with the altar on 4 January 1697: 'Al Sig.r Cavag.re Fontana per haver operato intorno al disegno nel nuovo Altare. Doppie 12. L. 648' (ibid., pp.99f, n.350). There is finally a reference of 1724 to a project by Fontana connected with the extension of the choir of the church: 'Disegno della Chiesa della Steccata per la giunta dalla parte del coro', though this may be no more than an oblique description of his altar project (ibid., pp.95f., n.329).

These documents quoted by Testi suggest that Fontana's project, or projects, for the altar were made in 1696 (after December 1695 and before January 1697), that he was given precise instructions about the site, that he may perhaps have provided a separate project for extending the choir, and finally that the altar itself was to be a showplace for a picture of the Virgin (*l'Imagine di N.a Sig.ra*). This is presumably the rectangular picture incorporated in the final altar as built in 1753.

The Windsor drawings for the altar bear no relation to the choir of the Steccata plan, and they have a tabernacle instead of a painting as the central feature of the composition. This is corrected in the Leipzig drawing where an oval painting is incorporated in a structure like that of the Windsor drawings. It seems likely that the Windsor drawings were originally made not with the Steccata in mind, but some other church, and then adapted for the commission for Parma. When the Leipzig drawing was made Fontana was apparently unaware that the image of the Virgin in the Steccata was rectangular in shape, but the Leipzig drawing probably formed the basis for Fontana's final project which was sent off in due course to Parma.

(A drawing attributed to Fontana, showing a half elevation and half section of S. Maria della Steccata, in a recent sale – Sotheby's, Palazzo Capponi, Florence, 18 October 1969 (lot D99) – seems unconnected with the architect).

ADDITIONAL BIBLIOGRAPHY:

L. Testi, *Santa Maria della Steccata*, 1922.

109 ELEVATION OF THE ALTAR (*Figure* 83) [9914]

412 × *c*.270 mm. Two sheets joined horizontally. Pen, grey wash, traces of chalk.

The altar occupies a rectangular space unlike any part of the church of the Steccata. The main features of the altar are the large tabernacle, the baldacchino and, above the altar, an undecorated sphere.

110 SECTION OF THE ALTAR (*Figure* 84) [9913]

412 × *c*.270 mm. Pen, grey wash, traces of chalk. With index letters. Inscribed at top: *Profilo dell'Opera della Santissima/Vergine della Steccata di/Parma.*

The drawing gives the tabernacle of the altar in elevation from the side, with the deeply projecting baldacchino above it in section. Both are supported on beams fixed in the wall and shown with dotted lines. The altar itself was to enclose a shrine visible through a window.

A church design for Cardinal Negroni (1697)

Volume 179 contains two drawings (nos 111, 112; Figs 85, 86), which, according to the inscription on no.111, were commissioned by Cardinal Giovanni Francesco Negroni (1629–1713) and are to be dated 21 March 1697.

The arrangement of the ground plan (Fig.85) suggests North Italian influence, which may be due to Fontana's renewed contact with the north when he was working on the plans for the cathedral at Bergamo in 1688. Some of the unpublished drawings submitted for the cathedral by other architects, now in the State Archives in Milan (cf. Elia Fornoni, *Le Cattedrali di Bergamo*, Bergamo, 1907, p.62), are similar to Fontana's church, notably two, of which one is signed by Giovanni Cristoforo Battera.

The section at Windsor (Fig.86) is even more unusual than the plan. The main space is flanked by two arcaded storeys, suggesting a banqueting hall rather than a church, and the altarpieces of the upper storey have pedimented frames. This central space is covered by a low cupola, with space for a ceiling painting. The façade has two storeys, and the portico is arcaded.

The numerous altars suggest that the plans were intended for a convent or monastery. Giovanni Francesco Negroni was born in Genoa in 1629, became Chierico di Camera under Clement IX, and was made Tresoriere by Innocent XI and a Cardinal on 2 September 1686 (cf. Moroni, *Diz. Eccl.*, 47, pp.261f.). It is possible that he met Fontana in connection with the Altar of St. Ignatius which Negroni commissioned for the

Gesù in Rome (cf. Pecchiai, p.132). On his elevation to the purple Negroni first went to Bologna as papal legate and in 1687 became Bishop of Faenza, where he extended the Seminary, altered the bishop's palace (both dated 1689; cf. Strocchi, pp. 222 ff.), and built the prison for convicted priests (cf. Vaglimiglio, p.19).

Given the date of the Windsor drawings, it could be surmised that they were probably made for Faenza, but research in the Archivio Comunale has yielded no information confirming this, and no further help is provided by the *Vite succinte* in the Biblioteca Corsiniana, Rome, the *Vita critica* at Vaduz, Liechtenstein, or the *Memoriale* (1696) and the slightly earlier diary of Negroni (both Biblioteca Nazionale, Rome, 34–5, L. 11–36, quoted by Micci, p.93 note 25 and p.146 note 84). Similarly no information was forthcoming in the Cardinal's will (1713) and related documents in the Roman State Archives. Of the churches of which Negroni was made titular abbot in 1687 (Vaglimiglio, fo.11), the medieval building of S. Croce at Sassoferrato has to be excluded as lacking a suitable site (cf. Serra, p.296), and there is no reason to think that he rebuilt the church of Ponte Santo near Imola (1580–1585) (see Gaddoni, pp. 22f.), or S. Lorenzo in Campo at Fabriano (see Micci, pp. 147ff., on Negroni's appointment – Vaglimiglio appears to confuse S. Lorenzo with S. Maria in Campo at Fabriano), where the church was later restored by Cardinal Alessandro Albani.

ADDITIONAL BIBLIOGRAPHY:
Sources:
Vite Succinte di diversi Cardinali, Ms. Biblioteca Corsiniana, Rome (Cod. 39.D.18, fos.43ff., dated 1699 – see fo.45).
Vita critica de' Cardinali che vivevano circa l'anno 1696, Liechtenstein, Schloss Vaduz (formerly at Vienna – cited by Pastor, German ed. XIV, 2).
Rome, Archivio di Stato, Fondo Notari del Trib. A.C., Pelusius Marcus Joseph, vols 5619, 5621, 5622.

LITERATURE:
Serafino Gaddoni, *La Madonna di Ponte Santo presso Imola*, Quaracchi, 1922.
Brocardi Galeati, *Memoria istorica della divozione alla miracolosa Immagine della Beatissima Vergine Maria di Ponte Santo,* Imola, 1817 (copy in Archivio Tozzoni, via Garibaldi 18, Imola: Tit.42, Cart.I, fasc.1).
P. F. Kehr, *Italia Pontificia*, Berlin, 1909 (Reprint Berlin, 1961), IV, pp. 123f.
Costanzo Micci and Francesco Medici, *S. Lorenzo in Campo nella sua storia antica e nella vita di oggi,* Ancona, 1965, pp.146f.
Filippo Montano, *Lettere su le origini di Fabriano*, Fabriano, 1922, p.152.
Luigi Serra, 'Riflessi bizantini nell' Architettura delle Marche', *Architettura e Arti Decorative*, V, 1925/1926, p.296.
Andrea Strocchi, *Serie cronologica storico-critica de' Vescovi Faentini*, 1841.
Gian Marcello Vaglimiglio, *Memorie storiche di Faenza*, (Ms. Bibl. Com. di Faenza; Invent. Gen. Ms.62. – 1/16).

111 PLAN (*Figure* 85) [9909]
413 × 270 mm. Pen, grey and buff wash, traces of chalk.

112 LONGITUDINAL SECTION (*Figure* 86) [9908]
274 × 413 mm. Watermark no.7. Pen, grey wash, traces of chalk. With scale. Inscribed, lower left; *Adi 21 Marzo 1697/Emmo. C: Negroni.*

The bay on the extreme right, showing the side elevation of the choir, is executed on a rectangle of paper stuck down over the basic drawing. In the design on the basic drawing the roof sloped downwards over the choir towards the rear of the building.
Copy in reverse of the left half of the drawing by Vittone, vol.II, fo.217.

Venice, SS. Giovanni e Paolo, a project for the Valier Monument (*c.*1700?)

Volume 176 contains a short manuscript referring to a project for the tomb of a doge. It forms a section of the book which is entitled on the preceding sheet '*Per Venetia*', and beneath this title is a faint sketch in chalk (no.113) which appears to correspond with the tomb described in the manuscript. The text must presumably be a copy of a letter which Fontana sent off to Venice together with his final drawing of the project. In it he explains that the drawings sent to him from Venice gave him too little information about the site but that he had assumed that two round-headed doorways (*Porte tonde*) at ground level were unalterable and that three effigies had to be incorporated with other decoration in the design.

His description of the main features in his own project is difficult to follow in the absence of a clear drawing, and it is possible that his final project differed from the chalk sketch which now accompanies the text. The doorways were surmounted by a pedestal, with space on it for an inscription and this acted as a base for the three effigies. This lower part of the composition also had figures of Justice and Strength, circular ornaments carried by figures representing Fame, and the arms of the family. The upper part of the design was occupied by what Fontana calls a 'meta Istoriata . . . à guisa delle Colonne Romane mete'. This may mean that he finally incorporated an obelisk with spiralling reliefs, like those *mete* which occur in the funeral decorations for the Emperor Leopold I (see below) or it may refer to the elongated pyramid visible in the drawing. Above this was a crown (as in the drawing) and to its sides Turkish standards. The monument was apparently flanked by columns supporting further representations of Fame, and Fontana recommends finally that the monument should be crowned by a semicircular arch in place of the existing pointed arch 'per caminare con il moderno, e sfuggire l'antico modo, che discorda molto.' He ends his letter with a promise to make further designs if more details about the patron's wishes are sent to him.

Fontana's project has been convincingly identified by Noach as a design for the Valier monument in SS. Giovanni e Paolo in Venice. This occupies a site with two round-headed doorways at ground level, it is of roughly the same scale in relation to the doors as Fontana's design, and it too has three effigies: Doge Bertucci Valier (d.1660), Doge Silvestro Valier (d.1700), and his wife, Elizabetta Querini Valier (d.1708) (see G. Fogolari, *I Frari e i SS. Giovanni e Paolo*, 1931, pl.35, and A. Ravà, 'Un architetto sfortunato. Marco Torresini (1668–17..)' in *L'Arte*, 1910, pp.48ff.). This monument was designed by Andrea Tirali; it is believed to have been commissioned on the death of Doge Silvestro in 1700 by his widow, and completed in 1708. Tirali had certainly prepared a model by 1702, when his design was attacked by Torresini, who hoped to secure the commission for himself (Ravà, pp.49ff.). Fontana was presumably approached when the decision was first made to erect the monument, which is to say about 1700. There would seem to be only the most general connection between his design and Tirali's monument.

113 ELEVATION OF THE MONUMENT [9766A]
304×*c*.215 mm. Watermark no.5. Chalk. Inscribed at top: *Per Venetia.*

The drawing is too faint to be clearly legible, but the main feature is a large pyramid supported on a wide pedestal. Nine figures are visible, including two angels (?) supporting a coat-of-arms and at the top a pair of winged figures supporting a large coronet. The architectural background appears to consist of a pointed vault above the structure, columns to each side and the round-headed doors at the base of the composition.

The restoration of S. Spirito dei Napolitani, Rome (*c*.1700/2–1708)

History of the building

The year 1572 saw the foundation of the Arciconfraternità di S. Spirito dei Napolitani, which did not have its own church till 1574, when Gregory XIII assigned to them S. Aurea in the Via Giulia, which is first mentioned in 1367 but about which nothing is known. The rebuilding 'quasi da fondamenti' was begun about 1581–82 (Fanucci, p.365) and was not completed till 1589 (Pecchiai, pp.64ff.). One of the architects concerned with the planning was Ottaviano Mascherino (Golzio, pp.177ff.; Lotz, p.69; Wasserman, pp. 71ff.). The building as erected at the time is shown on the maps of Tempesta (1593) and Maggi (1625); it was given a new façade by Cosimo Fanzago in 1649 recorded in an engraving (Fig.90 here; published by Giov. Batt. Cipriani in 1835, pl.92), which was demolished in 1835–1854 when the present façade was built to a design by Antonio Cipolla (Lancellotti, pp. 40ff.). It is doubtful whether any extensive renovation of the interior was undertaken in Fanzago's time, since very soon afterwards it became necessary to carry out such work.

Giovanni Antonio Bruzio, who saw the church 'prima, che ponessero l'anno presente (1666) la mano a restaurarla e dargli altra forma' (Bruzio, fos 277ff.; see Hülsen, p.XLVIII), describes it as a building with one nave, protected by a roof resting on six 'traui marcati' and fitted with seven altars, including the *altare maggiore*. The latter was located in a special recess (*tribuna*), which was flanked by two side chapels (*choretti*), and above the *mensa* there was a painting of the Spirito Santo contained in a wooden structure illuminated by a big semi-circular window. The side altars at that time were dedicated to Christ Crucified, St Francis, St Thomas Aquinas (left), and Sta Maria della Concezione, Sta Maria delle Grazie, St Michael (right). The most precious of the altar paintings was probably the 'St Francis' by the Cavaliere d' Arpino, decorating the altar of the saint, and still mentioned as being in the church (on the second altar to the right) by Titi in the editions of 1675 (p.66), 1686 (p.90) and 1721 (p.107). The oratory then adjacent to the church on the left opened into an apse for the altar, which was decorated with a painting of the Annunciation.

On 23 May 1666 three members of the fraternity were instructed by the General Congregation to collect donations 'p la fabrica della nra chiesa', among them the future Cardinal Giovanni Battista de Luca, at the time still 'Auocato' (Archives of the Arciconfraternita S. Spirito dei Napolitani, Congregationi, Decreti 1628–1676, fo.217). The work must have been nearly completed by 1668, since on 13 July 1668 a resolution was passed to get further financial help 'p. poter finire la nra fabrica' (loc. cit., fo.200 *verso*). The work was executed according to designs by Carlo Fontana (*Roma Antica e Moderna*, 1697, II, p.246).

Pecchiai assumed that at this time the building was given the form which it had till the 19th century restoration and believed that two plans in the archives of the fraternity, not executed, were preliminary studies for the work (Pecchiai, pl.II). A second restoration, also ascribed to Carlo Fontana (Titi, ed. 1721, pp.106f.), is referred to in an inscription of 1708, now destroyed (cf. Forcella, *Iscriz.*, VII, p.333, no.681; cf. also Coudenhove-Erthal, p.115), which stated that an undertaking begun by Innocent XII had been completed. Pecchiai (pp.86f.) believed that this refers only to 'nuovi restauri ed abbellimenti'.

The Guide of 1697, quoted above, gives a fairly definite account of the extent of the restoration carried out between 1666 and 1668: 'Nell' anno 1667 ingrandirono la medesima di nuovo adornandola con bel Soffitto e con altre Cappelle', that is to say, the alterations seem to have involved heightening the existing building (cf. Falda's plan of 1676) – possibly by the inclusion of the 'bel Soffitto' – and adding further chapels, or substituting or enlarging earlier ones. The plans, which Pecchiai tentatively ascribed to Carlo Fontana, have nothing to do with his work and belong, like Mascherino's projects, to the time of the first rebuilding of the church.

The present state of the interior is due to fundamental alterations carried out at the beginning of the eighteenth century (which included a completely new choir) and not to that of the years 1666–68, as can be proved by documents preserved in the archives of the fraternity (Giustificazioni e Mandati, 1701–1708). The accounts covering the work of the craftsmen, checked and signed by Carlo Fontana, mainly cover the years 1702–1708. Payments for the foundation of the chapel for the high altar had already been made on 13 August 1702 (Giustif. e Mand., fos 3678ff.).

In 1697 Innocent XII attached three abbeys to the fraternity, in order to increase the revenues of the Arciconfraternità and so enable them to finance projected work. This intention is not clearly expressed in the fraternity memorandum (Regolamenti, e Statuti della Ven. Arciconfraternità dello Spirito Santo della Nazione del Regno di Napoli, I, ch.V, p.10, note 13) quoted by Pecchiai (p.86), but appears 'precisam. expressa' on fo.2172 of the document already mentioned, which states that the donation was made 'p. ingrandire, et abelire la loro Chiesa dllo Spirito Santo posta in Roma nella Strada Giulia' (Giustif. e Mand., 1701–1708).

Innocent XII (Pignatelli), of a noble Neapolitan family and previously Archbishop of Naples, had held the position of Primicerio of the Arciconfraternity between 1643 and 1646 and, in appreciation of his services, the Congregation decided on 18 October 1698 to erect a memorial tablet to him after his death (Reg. e Stat., loc. cit.).

The dates of the building of the choir, together with the alterations to the nave, the side-chapels, etc., are given by the dated records of accounts for the masons' work, which run from 14 August 1702 to 31 March 1705 (Giustif. e Mand., fos 1893–2003). The second main settlement with the masons (between 1 April 1704 and 15 September 1708) covered in great part decorative and stucco work, etc. (ibid., fos 1821–1879), which was not finished till 1709 (ibid., fos 2011ff.). The final account of the stone masons, who executed the bases of the pilasters, capitals, altars, etc., is dated 15 September 1708 (ibid., fos 2035–2077).

The earlier chancel with the main altar and its flanking chapels was replaced by the new domed structure designed by Carlo Fontana. A section of this chapel with Carlo Fontana's handwriting and the date 28 October 1706 has been preserved in a volume of drawings by Filippo Juvarra in a private collection in Turin (cf. Rovere-Viale-Brinckmann, p.48; Millon); the walls of the church were heightened and the whole decoration of the interior removed '... spicconato via tutti gli stucchi uecchij e colle uecchie di detta chiesa, compresoui anche li due uani, doue sono li coretti' (Giustif. e Mand. fo.1971). The walls of the nave were articulated by coupled pilasters, continued by the ribs of the barrel vault, into three arched bays of equal height, two of them separated by the closed central interval (see drawing 128, Fig.104), opening into chapels unified in size and decoration.

The 19th-century restoration by Antonio Cipolla removed Fontana's stucco-work (cf. Lancellotti, pp.47ff.; Pecchiai, pp.96ff.), and included the restoration of the chapel of the high altar, but the accounts and a perspective view (Fig.88) in the Nationalmuseum of Stockholm (THC 2000) enable us to imagine what it must have looked like originally.

The corner pilasters flanking the choir arch, which are now single, were originally clustered (cf. Lancelotti's plan (Fig.87) which shows the old plan but also indicates the 19th-century alterations as projected). The oval medallion of the Holy Ghost in Glory was accompanied by full-size stucco figures of angels covered with *scagliola* in high relief (cf. designs for altars, nos 130, 124), with a curved tablet ending in volutes underneath them. Over the arch was a fringed stucco curtain. The choir was nearly square and its arch was supported by double pilasters (cf. no.118; Fig.95), still visible in Lancelotti's ground plan (Fig.87).

The insertion of large semicircular windows in the lunettes on the side-walls underneath the 'arconi maestri' is reminiscent of the Ginetti and Cybo chapels. The four Evangelists in the pendentives, which had been repainted soon after the erection of the building, were again restored by Gagliardi in the 19th century. The insertion by Fontana of the low cylindrical drum, octagonal on the outside, and the almost square windows (cf. S. Maria dei Miracoli), foreshadow to some extent his Albani Chapel, begun in 1706. The eight *candelieri* which decorated the interior of the drum between the real and blind windows, executed by Domenico Belletti (Giustif. e Mand., fo.2139), are still preserved. The fresco of the Trinity in Glory in the cupola survives, though in a very damaged state. The traditional attribution to Maratta's pupil, Giuseppe Passeri, is confirmed by the accounts (Giustif. e Mand., fo.2135).

The high altar itself – with an inlay of green and white marble – corresponds to that recorded in the documents and must therefore date from the period of Carlo Fontana's activity, and the date inscribed on it, 18 September 1725 (Forcella, *Iscriz.*, VII, p.333, no.684), must consequently refer to the consecration of the altar and not to its erection.

The superstructure of the altar, now lost, showed the same contrasts of colour as the *mensa*. The round-headed altarpiece was flanked on each side by a column and a pilaster of 'Diaspro di Sicilia', 20 *palmi* high and $2\frac{1}{3}$ *palmi* in diameter, supporting fragments of an entablature, crowned by a large arch, probably like that in no.124, Fig.100.

'Sopra il finimento di d. Altar maggiore' were six stucco angels, two 'di tutto relieuo isolati' by Vincenzo Felice, the successor of Domenico Guidi, who had made the tomb of Cardinal de Luca (cf. below). The remaining angels, who held gilt festoons, were the work of Giuseppe Napolini.

Giuseppe Ghezzi's altarpiece of the 'Descent of the Holy Ghost' (indicated on the drawing in Stockholm, Fig.88) was removed when the altar was destroyed during the 19th-century alterations, and was given to the Italian church of S. Peter, Clerkenwell Road, London, on 20 August 1856 (size 27×14 *palmi*; cf. Lancellotti, p.61). It was probably sold some years ago with other pictures (I am indebted for this information to Don Mario Moriconi of S. Peter's Church).

The tomb of Cardinal Giovanni Battista de Luca, which in the middle of the 19th century was placed in the second chapel on the right, dates from before the renovations of 1702–1708. His will stipulated that he should be buried in the church of S. Girolamo degli Schiavoni, of which he was titular cardinal. His heir and executor was Cardinal Benedetto Pamphili, who arranged for the construction of the tomb in 1690 (Rapolla). By the end of January 1690 the sculptor was already at work on the monument (Cartari-Febei, vol.101, fo.23).

The Cardinal's last wish, to be buried in his own church, was not, however, fulfilled, as the site for the erection of the tomb was refused. The General Congregation of S. Spirito dei Napolitani thereupon decided on 23 November 1692 to offer space in their church for the tomb (Regol. e Statuti, I, ch.XXI, fo.34, note 17) in appreciation of de Luca's loyal membership (from 1645–48 Guardiano, later Sindaco and Consigliere). On 17 April 1693 permission was sought for the transfer of the Cardinal's body from S. Girolamo degli Schiavoni, which means that the tomb must have been finished about that time (Arch. del Vicariato, Segreteria del Tribunale, vol.4, fo.134).

The Guide of 1697 refers to the monument as 'a mano destra entrando', and the Giustif. e Mand. fo.1939, gives further indications of its position, 'uicino la porta', that is to say, on the right side of the entrance wall (see also Giustif. e Mand., fo. 1971). When work began on the alterations, the tomb was transferred to the right wall of the choir, where it remained till the 19th-century restorations.

The two removals caused a certain amount of damage to the tomb. The side figures of Justice and Prudence formerly stood on grey projecting pedestals, flanking a green and yellow marble structure, while today they share a pedestal with the statue of the Cardinal (cf. Forcella, *Iscriz.*, VII, p.332, no.677). The architectural frame of the superstructure is, however, original.

The position of the tomb after its transfer to the choir can be seen on the Stockholm drawing (Fig.88), where it is shown on the right wall. The change of location raised the difficulty of the direction of the head of the statue, which had been brought into proximity with the high altar. In the presence of the sculptor the statue was 'alzata in aria prouate più uolte per metterla come uolse il scultore' and elevated by the insertion of a marble block underneath it (Giustif. e Mand., fos 2012 f., *misura* of 20 February 1709). Domenico Guidi had died in 1701, and this note must therefore refer to his successor, Vincenzo Felice.

When the choir was altered in the nineteenth century, the tomb was moved to its present position in the walled-up middle right-hand bay of the nave. The accompanying figures, as the pedestals indicate, were originally turned more towards the centre than is the case today.

Postscript

Tafuri (*Via Giulia*) independently discovered the documents discussed above in the archives of the fraternity, and refers to accounts of 1668 and 1669 which he found in the Roman State Archives for masonry and stucco work of fairly extensive, yet limited, volume concerning mainly the decoration of chapels, especially the one of the main altar. But he does not offer a comprehensive picture of the nature of Fontana's two clearly distinguishable restorations, the second one of which superseded the modifications of about thirty-five years earlier (for the decorations see Salerno, *Via Giulia*).

The dating of the drawings

The earliest possible date is the beginning of the pontificate of Innocent XII (1690), who had taken the initiative in the extensive remodelling of S. Spirito dei Napolitani. More likely, however, is a date around 1697, when the Pope took decisive administrative steps to support the realization of his intentions financially. The planning must have been essentially completed by 1702 when work on the construction began.

Grouping of the drawings

The drawings can be divided into two main sections, with a transitional group connecting the two principal stages. The connection with the church of S. Spirito dei Napolitani is established by the text on no.114.

Evidence for the connection between the longitudinal section no.114 (Fig.91) and the detail section no.115 (Fig.93) is supplied by the position of the choir and the tomb for the Cardinal on its left wall. The scale of the latter drawing corresponds with those of three ground plans, nos 117, 116 (Fig.94), 118 (Fig.95), almost square in shape. Of these no.117 is connected directly with section no.115 (Fig.93) and no.116 is a variant. No.118 differs from these in the reduction of the number of columns, but a design for the high altar (no.119, Fig.96) and the drawing for the chapel entrance (no.120, Fig.97) are connected with it.

The drawings grouped round no.114 (Stage 1) represent the first stage in the designing. Subordinated to these is a small group of drawings for the choir with the monument of the Pope, planned on a square ground plan (nos 121 (Fig.98), 122 and 123, of which the last differs slightly from the others in scale). With these goes the altar design no.124 (Fig.100), identifiable by the medallion with the Holy Ghost, and the sketch for the chapel entrance, no.125 (Fig.101). In spite of the completely new conception for the choir, these drawings are directly connected with the previous series of designs, as the measurements of the bases clearly indicate. The longitudinal section no.126 (Fig.102), however, in which the space above the main entablature has gained *c.*10 *palmi* in height (cf. below), represents a fundamental modification of the plan of the nave, no.114. No.127 (Fig.103) is a variant of no.126, which in Vittone's copy (vol.I, fo.30) is shown alongside a detail section after the final project no.128. These two drawings represent a transition to the second planning stage, which includes the plan of the nave, no.128 (Fig.104), the section of the choir chapel belonging to it, no.130 (Fig.106) and designs for the bay with the confessional under the centre nave arcade (nos 131, 132, 133). These plans were, with modifications, the basis for the alterations actually carried out.

ADDITIONAL BIBLIOGRAPHY:

Sources:

ROME, ARCHIVIO DELL' ARCICONFRATERNITA DI S. SPIRITO DEI NAPOLITANI: congregationi, decreti, 1628–1676.

Regolamenti, e Statuti della Ven.Arciconfr. dello Spirito Santo della Nazione del Regno di Napoli (cited by Pecchiai, p.86).

Giustificazioni e Mandati, 1701–1708 (AL 37, 28).

ROME, ARCHIVIO DI STATO:

Camerale III, Chiese e Monasteri, Busta 1982, fasc.2 (for the palace near the church, *c.*1660)

ARCHIVIO DEL VICARIATO.

Segreteria del Tribunale, vol. 4, fo.134.

ARCHIVIO VATICANO:

Giov. Antonio Bruzio, *Opera*, Vat.Lat. 11889, fos 269/79.

LITERATURE:

Giov. Batt. Cipriani, *Itinerario figurato negli Edifizi più remarchevoli di Roma*, Rome, 1835, pl.92.

Camillo Fanucci, *Trattato di tutte l'opere pie dell' alma città di Roma*, Rome, 1602, p.365.

Vincenzo Golzio in *Dedalo*, X, 1929/1930, pp.177ff.

Luigi Lancellotti, *La Regia Chiesa dello Spirito Santo dei Napolitani in Roma ampliata e rifatta*, Naples, 1868.

Wolfgang Lotz in *Röm. Jahrbuch für Kunstgesch.*, 7, 1955, p.69.

H. Millon, *Corpus Juvarrianum.*

Pio Pecchiai, *La Chiesa di S.Spirito dei Napolitani e l'antica Chiesa di S.Aurea in Via Giulia*, Rome, 1958, pp.64ff.

Diego Rapolla, *Del Card. Giov. Batt. di Luca, Giureconsulto Venosino, del suo tempo e della sua Patria, Monografia storica*, Portici, 1899.

Jack Wassermann, *Ottaviano Mascherino and his Drawings in the Accademia Nazionale di S.Luca*, Rome, 1966, pp.71–75.

Stage 1.

114 LONGITUDINAL SECTION OF NAVE AND CHOIR (*Figure* 91) [9918]

410×790 mm. Two sheets joined vertically. Watermark no.7. Pen, grey wash, chalk. With scale. Inscribed on *verso*: *Spirito Sant| Strada Giulia.*

The wall arrangement of the nave is centred on a

large chapel (for a sketch of a similar project, cf. fo.43 *verso* of the Fontana volume of the Biblioteca dell' Istituto Nazionale di Archeologia e Storia dell'Arte, Collezione Lanciani, Ms.110). The sketch shows a regular division into bays by single supports, while in no.114 these have been changed to double pilasters, with reversed segmental fragments to serve as pedestals for seated angels. The choir (cf. ground plan no.118) is treated in a similar manner to the larger side-chapels of the nave, though it is larger and has a higher arch (for the monument of the Cardinal, cf. no.115).
Copy by Vittone of the elevation of the choir wall, with wash added, vol.I, fos 101/2.
For the smaller side-chapels, with oval altarpieces carried by putti, cf. the copy by Vittone, vol.I, fo.97.

115 SECTION OF THE CHOIR (*Figure* 93) [9502]
410×271 mm. Watermark no.7. Pen, grey wash, traces of chalk. With scale.
This drawing differs from no.114 only in that it shows columns instead of coupled pilasters at the chapel entrance, and a somewhat simpler version of the tomb.
Copy by Vittone, vol.I, fos 101/2.

The tomb is almost certainly not the de Luca Monument, begun about 1690 for S. Girolamo degli Schiavoni, which antedates the transformation of S. Spirito dei Napolitani under Innocent XII, and shows the figure of the Cardinal in a completely different attitude. The design must, therefore, be connected with another cardinal, who has still to be identified.

116 PLAN OF THE CHOIR (*Figure* 94) [9505]
410×271 mm. Watermark no.7. Pen, grey wash, some chalk. With scale, and measurements (in chalk). The plan corresponds with the foregoing section.

117 PLAN OF THE CHOIR [9507]
410×271 mm. Pen, grey and yellow wash, traces of chalk. With scale.

The plan corresponds closely with the foregoing, though it differs slightly in shape, and provides for engaged columns on the side walls. Both plans are variants of the type used by Fontana for the Ginetti and Cybo chapels.
Copy by Vittone of the left half of the plan, vol.I, fo.67.

118 PLAN OF THE CHOIR (*Figure* 95) [9503]
410×271 mm. Watermark no.7. Pen, grey wash, some chalk. With scale and measurements. Inscribed at top: *Il Vano dell' Arcone sopra laltare è pm. 30 | il Vano delli Arconi laterali sono pm. 28⅔ | li si darà pm. 1⅓ di dritto p Caminare al | piano della Crociera e piano della Cima | delli Arconi accio uolendo fare scudella | piana sopra tonda uolendo disparegiarla | come mostra la Circonferenza.*

The text explains the project – to balance the larger width of the arch over the high altar by stilting the other arches by 1⅓ *palmi*. The proportions are the same as in no.117, but the chapel is conceived with pilasters rather than columns. The simplification of the earlier ground-plans marks a transition to stage 1a.
Copy by Vittone, vol.II, fo.172.

119 ELEVATION OF THE ALTAR WALL (*Figure* 96) [9498]
410×271 mm. Pen, grey wash, some chalk. With scale, cut on left.

This design agrees exactly with the foregoing plan. A cross and figures of angels are indicated in pencil (cf. no.124). A similar, slightly later stage of the project is recorded in a drawing hitherto unpublished in the Cooper Hewitt Museum of Design (Smithsonian Institution) in New York (no.1938–88–5157) in which the window surrounding the arch of the altarpiece has been replaced by a pedimental structure and where the two sketchily indicated angels with a cross reappear (Fig.92).

120 ELEVATION OF THE ENTRANCE WALL OF THE CHOIR (*Figure* 97) [9497]
410×268 mm. Watermark no.7. Pen, grey wash, chalk.
Corresponding with plan 118 above.

Stage 1a

121 SECTION OF THE CHOIR SHOWING MONUMENT TO INNOCENT XII (*Figure* 98) [9501]
410×270 mm. Watermark no.7. Pen, grey wash. traces of chalk.

The present sheet forms a group with the four following drawings. See under 125 below.
Copy by Vittone, vol.I, fo.9.

122 PLAN OF THE CHOIR (*Figure* 99) [9504]
410×270 mm. Pen, grey, yellow and brown wash, some chalk. With scale, and measurements (in chalk).

Dotted lines on the plan appear to show the fabric existing on the site. The choir is increased in width on strips of paper pasted to the sheet. A large flap (133×167 mm.) attached near the base of the sheet contains a measured sketch of the site of the choir.

123 VERSION OF THE PRECEDING [9506]
410×271 mm. Pen, grey and yellow wash, traces of chalk. With scale, and measurements (in chalk).

A fair copy of the preceding plan in its final condition.
Copy by Vittone of the left half of this, or of the preceding sheet, vol.II, fo.141.

124 ELEVATION OF THE ALTAR WALL (*Figure* 100) [9495]
410×268 mm. Watermark no.7. Pen, grey wash. With measurements (in chalk).

Copy by Vittone, together with improvised plan, vol.I, fos 21/2.

125 ELEVATION OF THE ENTRANCE WALL OF THE CHOIR (*Figure* 101) [9496]
410×268 mm. Pen, grey wash, traces of chalk.

Copy by Vittone, omitting balustrade, vol.I, fos 58/9.
In the scheme represented in the present group of drawings the chapel was to be slightly broader than it was long and had a simple barrel-vault and lunettes.

The monument is probably intended to be a memorial to Innocent XII rather than his actual tomb.

Transitional Stage

126 PLAN, SECTION AND ELEVATION OF A SIDE CHAPEL (*Figure* 102) [9500]
410×270 mm. Watermark no.7. Pen, grey and buff wash, traces of chalk. With scale and measurements. A measured ink sketch, upper left, is inscribed: '*quadro d. Spir^{to}*.

This design represents a step towards the unification of the nave walls by continuing the entablature over the side-chapels. The height of the arcade (41⅔ *palmi*) is between those of the smaller and larger chapels (30½ and 49 *palmi*) in no.114. Compare the side altars in the Ospizio di S. Michele, Rome, built by Carlo Fontana between 1710 and 1714 (see below).
Copy by Vittone of the elevation but with the small order supplied on both sides of the chapel, vol.I, fo.30.

127 PART ELEVATION OF THE NAVE, SHOWING A SIDE CHAPEL IN PLAN AND ELEVATION (*Figure* 103) [9499]
410×270 mm. Chalk, grey wash. With scale sketched in ink.

A variant of the previous project, but the arch is here 39 *palmi* high, instead of 41⅔. Above the chapel, very faintly sketched in, is a large triangular pediment carried by a tapering pilaster.
Copy by Vittone, vol.II, fo.211 (omitting the plan and changing the order of the pilasters).

Stage 2

128 SECTION OF THE NAVE (*Figure* 104) [9493]
410×274 mm. Pen, grey wash, traces of chalk. With scale, partly covered by the binding. A correction to the drawing, to the left of the central window, is drawn on a small rectangle of paper pasted to the sheet.

Copy by Vittone of the left half of the drawing, vol.II, fo.211.

In the final stage the length of the nave is 109 *palmi*, slightly less than in no.114 (120 *palmi*). The total height corresponds roughly (64 to 66 *palmi*), but the archivolt is given greater importance and now breaks the entablature. The three chapels are now of equal height and are separated by pairs of pilasters enclosing statues standing on consoles.

The elevation, in part inspired by Maderno's nave of S. Peter's, has a humble predecessor in Fontana's remodelling of the mediaeval collegiate church of S. Maria Maggiore at Lanuvio near Genzano, of which he was in charge (dated by an inscription on the façade 1675; cf. Galieti, pp.197ff.).

In the actual execution of S. Spirito, however, the elevation was modified and a continuous entablature was introduced (cf. Giustif. e Mand., fos1969ff.; renewed in the 19th century). The pilasters are broader than in the drawings and this involved the omission of the projected statues. In the execution the last two bays were combined into a single unit. The barrel-vault was changed in the 19th-century restorations, but the medallion-windows are Fontana's, though the decoration of those in the middle has been changed. Fontana has blocked the central chapel-bay up to the top of the pilasters, sustaining the arch, and in front of it a relief and a confessional have been placed, above which is a *coretto*.

This curious project is probably only a makeshift arrangement, since the site required for the second side-chapel on the right was claimed by the Collegio Ghislieri (see Lancelotti, p.48). During the execution an alteration became necessary. The supports ('due modelli e due sottomodelli') for the *coretto* balcony on the right, which had already been carried out, had to be replaced (cf. Giustif. e Mand., fo.1973).

At the time of Lancellotti S. Spirito had only four side altars, and the two centre chapels were occupied by 'due palchi in legno ai quali ascendevasi dalla Chiesa stessa, e non da parte interna, mercè scale pur di legno, i quali palchi nelle solennità di Corte erano destinati ad accogliere gl'invitati' (Lancellotti, p.48). The *palchi* removed at that time were probably those designed by Carlo Fontana.

Two of the altarpieces mentioned by Titi (1763, p.464), the 'Martyrdom of St Gennaro' by Luca Giordano, and the 'Miracle of St Thomas Aquinas' by Domenico Maria Muratori, are still in their original positions, in the first and third chapels to the left, but the 'Madonna del Fulmine' by Antoniazzo Romano and a 'Miracolo di S. Francesco' by Paolo del Lamberti are in different positions.

129 SKETCH OF ONE BAY OF THE NAVE, ELEVATION (*Figure* 105) [9492]
410×268 mm. Watermark no.7. Chalk, pen. With measurements and sums (some in ink).

130 ELEVATION OF THE ENTRANCE WALL OF THE CHOIR (*Figure* 106) [9494]
410×268 mm. Pen, grey wash, traces of chalk. With scale.

The height of the choir is here increased to equal that of the nave and has a barrel-vault, as in stage 1a. The altar-niche, 5 *palmi* deep (cf. ground plan of Vittone copy, vol.I, fo.22), has a semicircular arch. The high altar and the tall painting correspond to the side-chapels in no.128. The columns with two seated angels, which again rise from the floor, refer back to no.119. The windows in the nave on no.128 and the decorative motives are variants of those in earlier designs (particularly of no.124). After the replanning of the choir as a low rectangular space with dome, the decoration of the semicircular space above the high altar was transferred to the wall of the triumphal arch, where it adjoins the medallion with the dove in the design just mentioned, no.124. The only element of this design to survive is the curious repetition of the arches.
Copy by Vittone, with improvised plan, vol.I, fos 21/2.

131 PLAN AND ELEVATION OF THE CENTRAL NAVE BAY (*Figure* 107) [9508]
323×225 mm. Pen, coloured washes, some chalk.

The drawing occupies half of a folded page. It shows a variant of the central bay of no.128.
Copy by Vittone, vol.I, fos 32–35 (top right), omitting the pilaster capitals.

132 VERSION OF THE PRECEDING [9509]
370×237 mm. Pen, grey and buff wash, chalk. With measurement on pilaster.

On the same scale as the foregoing and probably a preliminary sketch. On the *verso* is a sketch for the balustrade.

133 PLAN AND ELEVATION OF THE CENTRAL NAVE BAY (*Figure* 108) [9748]
302×215 mm. Pen, grey, yellow and brown wash, some chalk.
With scale. Sums and notes inscribed in chalk to left and right.

This drawing is connected with nos 131/2, but is a studio work and on a different scale. It shows further simplification.

The portico of S. Maria in Trastevere, Rome (1701)

The drawings at Windsor for the façade of S. Maria in Trastevere belong to a project for which most of the studies are preserved in the Fontana volume at Leipzig. Volume 172 at Windsor contains a short description of the scheme by Fontana, and the drawings are distributed between this volume and Volume 174. Of the drawings at Leipzig Coudenhove-Erthal published the elevations (pls 38–42), but none of the ground plans.

History of the building

The original portico of S. Maria in Trastevere dated from the time of Innocent II (1130–42), who replaced the early church by a new building. The present portico was the first building commissioned by Clement XI as Pope. He had a special connection with the church, since members of his family were buried there. In view of the bad condition of the old portico and 'p.euitare quelle disonestà che ui si commetteuano', Fontana was asked to produce designs for a new portico, on condition that the mediavel façade mosaics were preserved and the sum of 4,600 *scudi* not exceeded. Thus doubly restricted in his planning Fontana complained bitterly that he was prevented 'di poter inestare e disporre l'opera con quelle belle parti secondo nostro Intelletto'.

In June 1701 the new foundations for the columns were begun; as Fontana planned to attach them to pillars, the foundations had to be extended slightly forward. During excavations for the first column on the right on June 21, a marble vase with bones was found at a depth of 20 *palmi* (cf. Valesio, quoted by Cecchelli, p.67), together with other marble fragments, which were used in a strip decorating the pavement underneath the architrave (no longer extant). A second entry in Valesio's Diary (cf. Fasolo, 1949, pp.88, 92 n. 6) states that the work began with the demolition of the old portico, and that the Pope, after considering several *disegni*, decided in favour of Fontana's project because it was the cheapest. But Valesio was no friend of Fontana and if the architect in fact produced the least expensive design, he was only following the instructions of the Pope.

Unfortunately the names of other architects involved in the project are unknown, and Fontana gives no indications of a competition having taken place. Two earlier drawings for the façade, dating from the reign of Alexander VII (1655–67), exist in the British Museum (King's Topography, LXXV, 68, fos 37, 38).

The building operations were started on 1 July 1701, and two of the drawings at Windsor are dated slightly later in the same year. According to Fontana's statement the building costs amounted to 6,800 *scudi*, but Fil. Mallerini (*Storia della Basil. di S. Maria in Trastevere*, 1870, Ms in the Archivo Capitolare of the Basilica, Arm. I, sc. I, fo.52) asserts that an amount of 8,000 *scudi* was spent on work for the church. On the Feast of Assumption 1701 the Pope visited the site for the first time while work on the plans was still in progress. Drawing no.138 below bears the date 12 August 1701, and in the same month the last of the Leipzig plans for the façade was produced (cf. Coudenhove-Erthal, p.108, note 183); drawing no.136, on the other hand, seems to have been completed in November of the same year (cf. below). By November the portico was nearly completed '... ridotto hoggi quasi a compim.o con poca sodisfazzione Vniuersale come troppo basso è poco magnifico ...' (cf. Valesio, 27 November 1701). All that remained was to find a solution for the upper part of the façade, which is shown in nos 136 and 137. On 14 October 1701 Clement XI had made available for the new vestibule 21 blocks of Travertine, originally destined for the Campanile of S. Peter's (cf. Fraschetti, p.169). The vestibule was unveiled in 1702 in the presence of the Pope: 'Contemplò S.S.tà il portico fatto fabbricare ... hoggi scoperto e terminato con hauer'fatto accomodare il mosaico ...'.

The figures on the balustrade were carried out by the sculptors who had worked for Fontana on the Baptistry of St Peter's and the tomb for Queen Christina: Jean Théodon (St Callisto), Michele Maglia (St. Cornelio), and Lorenzo Ottone (St Giulio; cf. *Roma Ant. e Mod.*, ed. 1708, p.136, and Cecchelli, p.66). They were assisted by a pupil of Domenico Guidi, Vincenzo Felice, who was responsible for St Calepodius and who later worked for Fontana elsewhere (see pp.73 and 86). Fontana's decoration of the upper part of the façade was removed under Pius IX, when three arched windows were inserted and the mediaeval frieze was completed with new paintings (cf. Cecchelli, pp. 44, 46).

The vestibule was influenced by Soria's portico to S. Crisogono, commissioned by Cardinal Scipione Borghese in 1626. The architect had to re-use the four columns of the old vestibule shown in no.135. The five Leipzig drawings (Coudenhove-Erthal, pp.109ff.) represent the first stages of the design, and the two Windsor drawings (nos 136, 137) follow closely on the last of them (Coudenhove-Erthal, fig.42); they differ only in that they show sculpture on the attic. In the executed building, as shown in the Roman guide of 1708 (Fig.111), Fontana followed no.137 in all essentials, except that he inserted two extra windows in the façade.

ADDITIONAL BIBLIOGRAPHY:

Sources:

ARCHIVIO DELLA REV. FABBRICA DI S. PIETRO

Registro de Mandati della RR. Fabrica di S. Pietro, 1674–1712, 1º. Piano, Armadio VII, vol.373 (*chirografo* of Clement XI of 14 October 1701, cited by Fraschetti, *Bernini*, p.169, n.1).

LITERATURE:

Carlo Cecchelli, *S. Maria in Trastevere*, Rome, 1933 (CRI, nos 31/32).

Drawings of the old church

134 PLAN (*Figure* 110) [9417]

298 × 393 mm. Watermark no.7. Pen, yellow wash, traces of chalk. With scale. Measured in full. Inscribed: *Portico antico distrutto di S.M.ª in trastevere*, and *La Colonna presi con Base e capitello alta p. 28½ / Dalla corda dell encaual cione dal di sotto p. 35½.*

Comparative sections of the old and new portico are sketched in ink on the right.

135 ELEVATION (*Figure* 109) [9418]

292 × 388 mm. Pen, coloured washes. With scale and notes in chalk on right.

No.135 corresponds in all important details to a drawing at Leipzig, which is a rough sketch for it. The old façade is also shown in Falda (I, pl.33).

Drawings for the new portico

136 PROJECT WITH ALBANI *MONTI*, ELEVATION (*Figure* 112) [9416]

481 × 371 mm. Pen, grey wash, traces of chalk. With scale. Inscribed, lower right: *Adi 7 9bre/ ... C:F.*

The drawing corresponds with the final project, but shows the Albani *monti* as the main feature of the decoration of the balustrade; in this it agrees with one of the Leipzig drawings (fo.78; Coudenhove-Erthal, pl.42).

137 PROJECT WITH STATUES, ELEVATION [9353]

481 × 371 mm. Pen, grey and brown wash, traces of chalk.

The design corresponds closely with the executed one (Fig.111). Panels are sketched lightly in chalk

to each side of the window in the first storey of the façade.
Copy by Vittone of the right half of the drawing, vol.II, fo.212.

138 SECTION (*Figure* 113) [9537]
410×271 mm. Pen, grey wash, traces of chalk. With scale and measurements. Inscribed, lower right: *Adi 12 Agosto 1701 / Profilo del Portico di S.M.a in Trasteuere.*

A flap covering part of the drawing (117×233 mm.; not shown in Fig.113) gives a variant – rather flattened – design for the vault of the portico.

139 VIEW OF THE FAÇADE, DESIGN FOR A MEDAL [10597]
131×129 mm. Watermark no.5. Pen, grey wash, traces of chalk.

One of a group of four medal designs in Volume 188.

Fontana's description

(Windsor Vol. 172; preceding drawing 136 above): [9416]
[Parte decima quinta]
Rinouazione del Portico, e facciata auanti la Basilica di S. Maria in T:re Disegno del Cau. Carlo Fontana.
Cap: 137.
Risiedeua il Portico antico auanti la Basilica di SM.a in Trasteuere molto diforme, et abietto con quattro Colonne di granito con base in Terra, e Capitelli di Varie sorti di goffa maniera, e pezzi di pilastro rozzamente costrutti senza uerun ordine e si nella situazione, come nella Corrispondenza con le porte della Basilica sorrette. n'erano le predette Colonne alcuni pezzi di marmo auanzo di frammenti dell' antichi edificij di pessimo disegno, e di Varie forme, quali facceuano l'offitio d'Architraue, e sop.a ui staua un tetto molto uile, il quale rendeua poca soddisfatione all'occhio in guardarlo, e sicome questo portico era esposto al publico, et haueua alcuni Angoli, quali renderiano oscurità, e stante l'apertura libera ammetteua un ridotto di gente pessima, unito poi l'Asilo di quei ritirati fugitiui della Corte né succedeua, che nei Tempi notturni si commetteuano in quell'ambiti delle disonestà indecenti. Si spiccaua sopra d.o Portico la fronte eleuata della chiaue molto imperfetta, e di pessima cattiua figura, e contorno senza uerun ornamento con un Sporto Trasuersale di muro fuori del uiuo senza disegno, nel quale ui sono alcuni mosaichi, che rappresentano le uergini in atto d'offerire al Saluatore uasi pieni di liquore.

In occasione, che fù assunto al Gloriosissimo Pontificato l'Emo Sig. Card. Gio: Francesco Albani, hoggi il Regnante Clemente XI. mosso di uero Zelo, e dall' affetto, che portaua à quella Chiesa à causa di essere in essa sepelliti alcuni antichi nobili della sua Casa prouidde à quei disordini, che iui si cometteuano, e fece chiamare a se noi Cauallier Carlo Fontana, ordinandoci, che di Subito si facesse distruggere quel Diforme Portico, e che si disegnasse p.la rinouazione d'un altro abile à liberare quel luogo da tali disordini, e p. euitare quelle disonestà, che iui si commetteuano, e che anche restassero illesi quei musaichi, che ui sono di pnte nella fronte di essa Chiesa, che la spesa non eccedesse Sc.4600: in Circa.

Dal Precetto della Spesa, et improprietà de siti, uariazioni di misure, e distanze disuguali alli mezzi delle porte non corrispondenti, ma la Chiesa, et il Portico con il pessimo Contorno della facciata con infinite irregolarità, e nelle misure, e con lasciare illesi quei musaichi con precetto della poca Spesa p.tali Cause ci rendessimo pieno di confusione à causa di non poter inestare, e disporre l'opera con quelle belle parti secondo il nostro Intelletto, con tutto ciò con numerosi, e faticosi disegni ci Schermissimo nel disporre il Portico, che di presente s'ammira con suo Cancellato di ferro, che lo chiude p.euitarne nelli notturni Tempi quelle indecenze, usassimo molti ripieghi nella disposizione p. occultare all' occhio quell' errori primieri, e con riportati ornati alla deforme fronte, et attorno à quei mosaichi nel modo in cui si amira, onde quanto meritano esser compatiti gl'Artefici delli riguardanti in uedere tal uolta l'Edificij priui di quelle belle parti, tanto più nel Composto del d.o Portico, e fronte, che fà facciata, ci seruissimo delle medeme quattro Colonne antiche solleuate con il suo Zoccolo con cinque aperture, e sopra la sua balaustrata, e quattro statue, che rappresentano quattro Papi Santi che li loro Corpi, e reliquie iui dimorano, si diede principio all' opera al p.o Luglio 1701, e fù terminato nell' ano 1702. con Spesa di Sc. 6800 in circa, doue S.S.tà ha spurgato quel luogo da quelle frequenze uitiose, e restituito il commodo del nobil Portico con magnifiche Cancellate, che lo chiudono, et ha ornato la detta fronte attorno alli mosaichi con appagamento del publico più che si è potuto, e p. Benemerenza l'Illmo, e Rmo Capitolo di d.a basilica ha posto una bella Iscrizione in rendimento di grazie à Sua Santità, la quale Iscrizione uiene seguentemente registrata.

The restoration of S. Teodoro al Palatino, Rome (1702–1704)

According to tradition the little church of S. Teodoro was established in a late antique temple built on the spot where Romulus and Remus were exposed to the waters of the Tiber, which at that time reached this area (cf. Piazza, pp. 733 ff.). The date of the origin and consecration is unknown (cf. Cecchelli), but the apse mosaic, with St Theodore being presented to Christ enthroned (Matthiae, pp. 86 ff.), dates from the middle of the 6th century, and gives a date *ante quem* for the original church (cf. Torrigio, pp.155f., 160ff.) which is situated in a courtyard in the Horrea Agrippiniana. The present circular structure, according to Krautheimer and Corbett (1970, pp.279–288) was rebuilt in its entirety under Nicholas V (1453/4). At the same time the oculus over the choir was inserted. Cardinal Francesco Barberini's restoration of 1674 (*Roma moderna*, ed. 1697, pp.201f.) had little effect (Relat. della Chiesa di S. Toto, Archiv. del Vicar. di Roma) and did not stop the dampness with which the Tempietto was constantly threatened owing to its low position.

Carlo Fontana's description of the state of the interior before he took over as architect is attached to the drawings in Volume 176 at Windsor (transcribed below), and the *Relatione* by Torrigio in the Archivio del Vicariato di Roma provides further information. There was only one small altar, with a painting of St Theodore. The visits of sick children who received blessing from a priest on Sundays and Thursdays probably gave Clement XI the idea of commissioning Fontana to provide an elaborate drainage system and a dignified and comfortable flight of steps leading down to the church. But he had also selected S. Teodoro to become the national church of his home town Urbino in Rome, and he intended to establish a Confraternity there, but was prevented from doing so by his death (cf. Calvani, fo.8, no.22).

On 7 July 1702 work began on clearing the ground around the church (cf. Valesio). On 20 September of the same year Clement XI gave 2,000 *scudi* 'per erogarli nella restaurat.e dell' antico tempio di S. Teodoro in Campo Vaccino, ed altre spese necessarie p. ridurlo in stato decente . . .' (Rom. Archiv. di Stato). Pastor's statement (German ed., XI, p.375, note 1) that the Pope saw the finished work on 23 September 1702 cannot be correct, since a note in Valesio's Diary on 23 November 1702 proves that work was still in progress. The external restoration of the church was finished on 11 May 1703 and included a curved retaining wall, a forecourt, and a monumental staircase leading down to it.

The designs at Windsor for the restoration of S. Teodoro can be divided into two groups. The first, which is concerned with the clearing of the area round the church, is contained in Volume 188, one of the two Albani volumes. The remaining drawings, which concern the interior of the church are distributed among the Fontana Volumes 173, 174 and 176. In the first series the church, surrounded by a wall, is given a courtyard (stage 1), which is changed into an elongated approach on no.144 (stage 2) and assumes a trefoil-shape on no.145 (stage 3). The final phase is not represented at Windsor, but the design for the gate, no.147, is related to it. The interior (ground plans 148, 149) is represented by only two design stages, the sections nos 150, 155 and 156 respectively, for which the sketches (nos 151 to 154) are intermediary. There are further designs for the high altar and the framing of the entrance. In the execution of these designs Fontana employed an assistant, but the inscriptions on the drawings are all in Fontana's hand.

The drawing for the medal struck for the laying of the foundation stone (no.146) proves that the scheme shown in stage 3 was to be the basis for the execution, but a second medal design in the Leipzig album records further alterations and bears the date *Adi 5 Giung:o*, from which the year, 1702, has probably been cut (Leipzig, fo.103; Coudenhove-Erthal, p.115). It is not known who initiated these modifications, including the omission of the *exedrae*, but probably the Pope disliked the emphasis on the transverse axis and personally ordered the change. Clement seems also to have disliked the atrium and the staircase, since Valesio writes on the occasion of the Pope's inspection on 23 November 1702: '. . . uidde la fabrica delle Scale e Cortile che ui fà formare mostrò di non piacerli molto il disegno posto in opera dal Cau.re fontana Architetto . . .'. In the arrangement of the interior, too, Carlo Fontana had to yield to the obstinate demands of his patron.

A view of the early eighteenth century (*Descrizione di Roma moderna*, ed. 1708, II, p. 209; Fig.115), which corresponds almost exactly with the second medal design, shows the wall surrounding the forecourt as a relatively low enclosure, but the heightening of this wall, which in no.141 reaches the height of the gate on the street, probably goes back to Fontana's designs. The new edition of the *Descrizione*, published in 1725 with the title *Roma sacra e moderna*, has an engraving (p.476) which shows a higher wall broken by windows (Fig.120). Behind it was the 'vaga Sagrestia' and a house for one of the two canons of the church. These alterations, made at the order of Clement XI, must have taken place before 1716, since they are mentioned by Cecconi. On 11 February 1729 these buildings became the property of the Arciconfraternità del SS. Cuore di Gesù (cf. Lumbroso-Martini, p.113), which immediately began to alter the buildings to serve its particular purpose (cf. Calvini, fo.9, nos 23f.). A little later, on 22 November 1738, Clement XII transferred the church to the confraternity (Archiv. Arciconfr., I, V. 9), and in 1739 a new chapel and vestry, as well as a vault underneath the sacristy were added (cf. Calvini, fo.217, no.389).

The appearance of the court after the first phase of execution seems after all to have satisfied

Clement XI, since he was now prepared to consider the alterations to the interior of the church (cf. Valesio, 11 May 1703). This is confirmed by another diarist, Chracas (cf. *Terremoto*, p.228), who reports that on the occasion of an inspection on 20 July 1703 Clement expressed satisfaction with the results of Fontana's efforts.

The date of 20 September 1703 given by Fontana for the order to commence building refers to the renovation of the interior. At the end of the year, on 15 December 1703, the Pope gave a further sum of 700 *scudi*, so that the workmen could be paid and the restorations completed (A.S.R., Camerale I, Chirografi, vol.XVIII, Reg.171, fo.67). Fontana was in favour of drastic alterations to the church and would have preferred to replace the vault of Nicholas V with a new one and to remove the windows and the niches. These intentions were, however, quite contrary to the wishes of the Pope.

The respect shown by the Pope for ancient works of art was remarkable and was later praised at the time of the classical revival. It would be a mistake, however, to regard his attitude as solely antiquarian. Fontana emphasizes in his text that Clement XI 'con tanta pietà paterna' appreciated old and abandoned sacred buildings and that the restoration of S. Teodoro was part of a campaign for the preservation of such monuments. His attitude at S. Teodoro was paralleled at S. Maria in Trastevere (see above), at S. Maria Antiqua (cf. Eva Tea, *La Basilica di S. Maria Antiqua*, Milan, 1937, pp.4f, and Valesio, 2 August, 1702), at S. Maria in Cosmedin (Valesio, 25 September 1706, including plan and section), and at S. Clemente, where Fontana worked (see below). Unexecuted designs for the crypt of S. Maria in Cosmedin (Figs.118/9) are in the Archivio Segreto Vaticano (Fondo Albani, vol.12, fos 191 ff.). After the completion of the drainage system for S. Teodoro, work of the same kind was carried out at SS. Marcellino e Pietro (see below).

The drawings preserved at Windsor demonstrate the degree to which Fontana was able to adjust his own ideas to the demands of Clement XI. In no.150 the masonry is only visible in a few places, over the choir-arch and below the ogival windows. In the drawings of details, nos 151, 152, the pilasters and capitals are eliminated and the ribs are supported on consoles. Fontana paid particular attention to this part of the building and tells us that he solved the problem presented by the irregularities of the vault by a skilful distribution of the consoles. The sections, nos 155 and 156, incorporate the results of these experiments. The masonry is now visible across the whole wall, as the Pope had desired, and in the oculus he placed the Albani arms.

Perhaps following the example of Pietro da Cortona's first project for the façade of S. Maria della Pace (H. Ost, *Römisches Jahrbuch für Kunstgeschichte,* 13, 1971, p.235, fig.4), the motive is also anticipated in the papal coats-of-arms fitted into the medallions which surmount the windows of the uppermost storey of the Sapienza building facing the courtyard (P. Portoghesi, *The Rome of Borromini,* 1968, pl.78).

This design was made the basis for the execution, as is confirmed by a description of the church dating from 1739 (Archiv. Arciconfr., I, V.4) and by the accounts for the restoration of 1851/52 (cf. below), although the ribs ended in stucco decoration instead of volutes: 'Stabbiliti con cartelle a piedi' (cf. no.154). According to the description of 1739, there were medallions with coats-of-arms in the intervals between the ribs (loc.cit., no.19). In the intervals between the pilasters there were 'no.8 Finestre, quattro delle quali sono finte' (loc.cit., no.21). It appears that blind windows alternated with real openings.

Clement inspected the completed interior of S. Teodoro on 9 November 1704. The three marbled altars, of which the *mensae* were replaced in the later Settecento, were already completed (Valesio). The tablet with the inscription dedicated to the Pope (cf. Forcella, *Iscriz.*, X, p.286, no.451), shown in drawings nos 170 to 172, dates from the same year. The painting 'col Santo in mezzo alle fiamme', attributed to one of the Zuccari, which was then over the high altar, was replaced by another in the 18th century. The paintings for the two side-altars, representing the patron saints of Urbino – St Giuliano by Baciccio (now lost) and St Crescentino by P. L. Ghezzi (still in the church) – were missing but are reported as in place on 9 March 1706 by Valesio.

In spite of the strict limitations imposed by the Pope, the arrangement of the interior won general acclaim, especially in the guides of 1708 and 1725 (see above). But most of what Fontana's 'difficultosa, e rarissima Invenzione' had created, time and later restorations have destroyed. The insertion in 1763 of the wooden gallery over the door (Archiv. Arciconfr., I, V.7) made it necessary to close the lower half of the windows and to transfer the tablet with the Pope's coat-of-arms (shown on no.172) to its present position underneath the entablature. A thorough restoration of the interior was carried out in 1777–79, and the altars were rebuilt in the mid-1780's (cf. Calvani, fos 180 f., nos 323 ff.; Archiv. Arciconfr., I, VI.6). In 1769 the campanile with two bells was added (Archiv. Arciconfr., I, V.8), and in 1823–24 the sacristy was rebuilt and a wall added between the forecourt and the neighbouring gardens (Archiv. Arciconfr., I, V.16; I, VIII.11, no.6). The interior of the church, the forecourt, and the cemetery were again restored about 1825 (report of 21 September – Rome, Archivio di Stato), when Valadier opposed the modernization of the entrance front. The greatest harm to Fontana's work was done during the restoration of 1851/52 which is responsible for its present state (Fasolo, p.119). It destroyed 'con molto scommodo' the 'aggetti delle costole della Cuppola', and the consoles belonging to it (Archiv. Arciconfr., I, V.12, no.8). The surface of the vault and the 'modinature del Cornicione reale alto pmi 5' were scraped down (loc.cit., no.10). At the same time the oculus over the choir-arch was replaced by a rectangular opening and the windows received their present round-headed shape. The only remains of Carlo Fontana's work are the angel-tabernacle of the high altar, the frames of the altarpieces on the side-altars, and the inscribed tablet.

ADDITIONAL BIBLIOGRAPHY:
Sources:
ARCHIVIO DELL' ARCICONFRATERNITA DEL SS. CUORE DI GESÙ (ROME, VIA S. TEODORO).
Gian Francesco Cecconi, *Memorie istoriche dell' insigne, e antichissima Diaconia di S. Teodoro Martire situata alle radici di Monte Palatino*, Roma nella Stamperia Camerale, 1716 (I. V.3).
Ab. Calvini, *Storia dell' Arciconfraternita del SS. Cuore di Gesù compilata da Fr. Francesco di S. Reginaldo dalla sua fondazione a tutto Maggio 1784, e non proseguita attesa la di lui morte* (Manuscript; I. I.22).
Inventario della chiesa, e delle suppellettili donate dalla S.M. di Clemente XII. L' inventario è compilato in seguito di risoluzione del Consiglio segreto del 23 Gennaio 1739 (I. V.4).
Carlo Cecchelli, *Notizie storiche-archeologiche-artistiche* (Manuscript dated 10 October 1925; I.I. 22 bis).
ARCHIVIO DEL VICARIATO DI ROMA.
Eccl.arum Partium Regularium Alma Urbis Nec non Eccl.ae et Capellae Rurales, vol. 45, fo.540 (Relatione della Chiesa di S. Toto).
ARCHIVIO DI STATO DI ROMA.
Cam.I., Chirografi Ser. A., Tomo XVIII, Reg.171, fo.67 (Chirografo of Clement XI of 20 September 1702), fo.112 (Chirografo of Clement XI of 15 December 1703).
Camerlengato, Parte 2., Titolo IV, Antichità e Belle Arti, fasc.306.

LITERATURE:
'La prima Confraternità del Sacro Cuore di Gesù in Roma, 1729', in *La Civiltà Cattolica*, Quad.1637, September 1918.
Robert Enggass, *The Painting of Baciccio, Giovanni Battista Gaulli, 1639–1709*, 1964, pp.148f.
Furio and Orseolo Fasolo in *Palladio*, V, 1941, pp. 112–119.
Matizia Maroni Lumbroso – Antonio Maritini, *Le Confraternite Romane nelle loro Chiese*, Rome, 1963, pp. 112 ff.
Francesco Maria Torrigio, *Historia del Martirio di S. Teodoro soldato seguito nella Città d' Amazia*, Rome, 1643.
Günter Urban, in *Röm. Jahrb. für Kunstgesch.*, 9/10, 1961/62, pp. 205–208.

I. The drainage and arrangement of the forecourt

Stage 1:

140 PROJECT WITH SHORT FORECOURT, PLAN (*Figure* 121) [10603]
300 × 227 mm. Watermark no.6. Pen, coloured washes, some chalk. With scale.

141 PROJECT WITH SHORT FORECOURT, SECTION (*Figure* 122) [10602]
182 × 312 mm. Chalk, coloured washes, pen.

142 FRONT ELEVATION, SHOWING EXISTING STATE (*Figure* 123) [10604]
186 × 224 mm. Watermark, no.6. Chalk, coloured washes.

The drawing records the difference in level of 14 *palmi* between the church and its surroundings, which Fontana mentions in his text. The existing octagonal superstructure (cf. a drawing in the Staatl. Kunstbibliothek in Berlin, no.3675) is shown with oblong oval windows. The drawing appears to be a pair to the following.

143 FRONT ELEVATION, WITH PROJECTED SCREEN (*Figure* 125) [10605]
187 × 269 mm. Chalk, brown and grey wash, pen. The system of the curved stairways set in a semicircular retaining wall recalls the arrangement of the steps in front of a *confessio* in front of a high altar (S. Peter's, S. Susanna, etc.).

Stage 2:

144 PROJECT WITH LONG FORECOURT, PLAN (*Figure* 124) [10601]
300 × 224 mm. Watermark no.1. Pen, chalk, coloured washes. Inscribed, lower right, in Fontana's hand: *Dato il scandaglio*/ *s*(cudi) *1850*–.

In the middle of the side walls of the forecourt are shallow rectangular recesses, which Fontana intended to develop into *exedrae*, as indicated in additions in black chalk. These lead up to the next phase represented by no.145.

Stage 3:

145 PROJECT WITH *EXEDRAE* FOR FORECOURT (*Figure* 126) [10606]
412×278 mm. Pen, chalk, coloured washes. With scale and measurements.

The narrow forecourt is here developed by means of *exedrae* which offered accommodation for the mothers arriving with their sick children and, though on a very modest scale, they look back to the two *exedrae* of the Forum of Augustus.

146 PROJECT WITH *EXEDRAE* FOR FORECOURT, DESIGN FOR A MEDAL (*Figure* 128) [10600]
129×128 mm. Pen, grey wash, traces of chalk.

Stage 4: Final project

147 PLAN AND ELEVATION OF THE SCREENING WALL (*Figure* 129) [9512]
235×315 mm. Pen, grey wash, traces of chalk. With scale and measurements.

This drawing was followed in all essentials in the execution of the wall (Fig.115), which bears the arms of Clement XI. It corresponds to the description of 1739 (Archiv. Arciconfr. I, V.4, fo.1, no.1).

II. Interior

148 SKETCH PLAN OF THE CHURCH [9517]
210×269 mm. Watermark, no.7. Chalk. With scale.

The drawing occupies the right half of a large sheet, folded in the binding, of which the following drawing takes up the left half. Drawings 9511 to 9516 are enclosed inside the double sheet.

149 PLAN OF THE CHURCH (*Figure* 127) [9510]
210×*c*.540 mm. Pen, grey wash, chalk. With scale and measurements.

Three trial positions for the altar are indicated in chalk. This ground plan shows the problems arising from the uneven distribution of the openings. As a result the pilasters must either be unevenly spaced, or not placed at the centre of each section of the wall. Fontana's various ideas are indicated in pencil. In the execution (cf. no.155) he solves the problem by placing pilasters next to the openings, which at the same time minimizes the conflict with the existing ribs. The words *Palme* and *Monti* inscribed beside the pilasters refer to the decoration of the springs of the ribs (cf. nos 153, 154).
Copy by Vittone of the left half of the drawing, vol.II, fo.167.

150 TRANSVERSE SECTION (*Figure* 130) [9511]
410×268 mm. Watermark no.7. Chalk, brown and grey wash, pen.

The octagonal superstructure has oval windows and a tiled roof, which still exist (for the previous state cf. G. Urban, pp.205 ff.). The high altar has as yet no frame for the altarpiece (cf. no.158).

151 SKETCH OF PART OF THE CORNICE, SHOWING A CONSOLE [9513]
410×270 mm. Watermark no.7. Chalk, pen. With scale.

152 ELEVATION AND SECTION OF PART OF THE CORNICE, SHOWING A CONSOLE (*Figure* 131) [9516]
407×265 mm. Pen, grey wash, chalk. With scale and measurements.

The decoration above the cornice is shown in the two following drawings. The present drawing appears to have formed the basis for two drawings by Vittone, vol.I, fo.7 and vol.II, fo.153 (cf. 153 below).

153 PROJECT FOR THE DECORATION OF A RIB (1) [9514]
132×*c*.190 mm. Pen, grey wash.

The present drawing appears to have formed the basis for two drawings by Vittone, vol.I, fo.7 and vol.II, fo.153.

154 PROJECT FOR THE DECORATION OF A RIB (2) [9515]
135×271 mm. Pen, grey wash, chalk.

Nos 153 and 154 were originally attached as flaps to the preceding drawing (no.152).

155 TRANSVERSE SECTION (*Figure* 132) [9756]
302×215 mm. Pen, brown and grey wash, traces of chalk. With scale.

Fontana's text, dealing with S. Teodoro, in Vol.176 at Windsor (see below) was originally attached to the sheet bearing this drawing.

156 VERSION OF THE PRECEDING [9760]
302×215 mm. Pen, grey and brown washes, traces of chalk. With scale.

In the present section the old walls of the church are left uncovered, except for bands which stand on a continuous base and support the consoles. The oculus contains the *monti* of the Albani arms, while the star replaces the shell on no.150.
Copy by Vittone of the right half of this or the preceding drawing, vol.II, fo.217.

157 PLAN OF THE CHOIR, WITH PROJECT FOR THE HIGH ALTAR (*Figure* 133) [9761]
302×215 mm. Pen, grey and yellow washes, traces of chalk. With scale, and measurements (in chalk).

The altar is placed almost exactly under the middle of the choir vault, as in one scheme shown on no.149. It is shown at the bottom of the sheet in elevation, and consists of little more than a plain *mensa*.

158 PROJECT FOR THE HIGH ALTAR, ELEVATION (*Figure* 134) [9469]
417×275 mm. Pen, grey wash, some chalk. With scale, and measurements (in chalk). On the *verso* is a sketch in ink and chalk connected with the Fontana di Trevi (see below).

The *mensa* is the same as in no.157, surmounted by a pedimented tabernacle, which is reminiscent of Fontana's S. Marcello al Corso façade. In a separate chalk sketch at the top left Fontana shows a less symmetrical design, with one angel higher than the other. The altar, as executed, was 'tutto di Pietre mischie tanto nella facciata uerso la porta, quanto nelle due fianchate', and had on its front a medallion with the Cross in a radiance (Archiv. Arciconfr., I, V.4, fo.4, nos 33, 38). In 1786/87 the altar had been completely reconstructed by Camillo Buti, since it had no proper foundations (cf. Calvini, fo.217, no.389, and Fasolo, pl.119). The existing altar decoration corresponds to no.158, except for the slightly larger scale of the figures ('Dalle bande di detto Quadro ui sono due Angioli grandi di stucco, e p.di sotto u'è un Ornato simile di stucco, con Palme, Conchiglia, e Fettuccia svolazzata'; Archiv. Arciconfr., I, V.4, fo.3 *verso*, no.31; cf. also *Roma sacr. e mod.*, 1725, loc.cit.). The altarpiece, attributed in the Guides to 'Zuccari', was replaced in the 18th century (Calvini, fo.179 *verso*, no.119). It is described in the 1739 inventory (Archiv. Arciconfr., I, V.4, fo.3, no.40). During the restoration of the church of 1779 a painting of the Immaculata by Pietro Angeletti was placed above that of St. Theodore (cf. Calvini, loc.cit., and Archiv. Arciconfr., I. VII.9).

159 PROJECT FOR A SIDE ALTAR, ELEVATION (1) (*Figure* 135) [9480]
420×270 mm. Chalk, grey wash, pen. With measurements (in chalk). Scribbles in brown ink are present on the *verso*.

The frame over the altar is executed on a flap (217 (including top)×120 mm.; watermark no.7); on the basic sheet below it the articulation of the back wall of the chapel is sketched in chalk (not shown in Fig.135). The system of proportions based on a circle is clearly visible. On the *verso* of the sheet is a sketch in ink related to Fontana's project for the Fontana di Trevi of 1706 (see below).

160 PROJECT FOR A SIDE ALTAR, ELEVATION (2) [9477]
422×270 mm. Watermark no.7. Pen, grey wash, some chalk. With scale.

The basic scheme of this and the following eight drawings is taken over from no.159, though slightly simplified. The crowning feature varies from drawing to drawing.

161 PROJECT FOR A SIDE ALTAR, ELEVATION (3) [9478]
422×270 mm. Pen, grey wash, some chalk. With scale.

162 PROJECT FOR A SIDE ALTAR, ELEVATION (4) [9471]
422×270 mm. Watermark no.7. Pen, grey wash, some chalk. With scale.

163 PROJECT FOR A SIDE ALTAR, ELEVATION (5) [9476]
422×270 mm. Watermark no.7. Pen, grey wash, some chalk.

164 PROJECT FOR A SIDE ALTAR, ELEVATION (6) [9470]
422×270 mm. Watermark no.7. Pen, grey wash, traces of chalk.

165 PROJECT FOR A SIDE ALTAR, ELEVATION (7) [9479]
422×270 mm. Watermark no.7. Pen, grey wash, traces of chalk.

166 PROJECT FOR A SIDE ALTAR, ELEVATION (8) [9475]
422×270 mm. Pen, grey wash, chalk. With scale.

167 PROJECT FOR A SIDE ALTAR, ELEVATION (9) [9472]
422×270 mm. Pen, grey wash, some chalk. With scale.

168 PROJECT FOR A SIDE ALTAR, ELEVATION (10) [9474]
422×270 mm. Pen, grey wash, some chalk.

169 PROJECT FOR A SIDE ALTAR, ELEVATION (EXECUTED DESIGN) (*Figure* 136) [9473]
422×270 mm. Watermark no.7. Pen, grey wash, traces of chalk.

This design corresponds to the executed altar, except that the bow-motive has been replaced by a star on the medallion. The stucco decorations were partly gilt (Archiv. Arciconfr., I, V.4, fo.3, no.22). In 1784 (not 1786, as wrongly stated by Fasolo, p.119) both altars were completely rebuilt (Archiv. Arciconfr., I, V. 10; Calvini, fo. 217, no.389).

170 SKETCH FOR THE FRAMING OF THE ENTRANCE DOOR [9759]
263×*c*.185 mm. Chalk. With scale and measurements.

171 PROJECT FOR THE FRAMING OF THE ENTRANCE DOOR (1) (*Figure* 137) [9757]
302×215 mm. Watermark no.10. Pen, grey wash, traces of chalk. Inscribed lower left: *L'arme alta dalli p^mi^ 7½ a p^m^ 9 – se si trouasse uecchia / si potrebbe aiutarla con qualche cosa quando non / fosse tanto piccola.*

A finished drawing based on the foregoing sketch.

172 PROJECT FOR THE FRAMING OF THE ENTRANCE DOOR (2) [9758]
302×215 mm. Pen, grey wash, traces of chalk. With scale, and measurement, lower left. Inscribed lower right, *Alta da terra /p^m^ 20.*

The project corresponds closely with the preceding one, but the tablet above the door has an eared frame. On the right are letters referring to the type of lettering for the inscription.
Copy by Vittone of the right half of the doorway design, vol.II, fo.217.

Fontana's description

(Windsor Vol.176; preceding drawing 9756–no.155):

Restauratione del Tempietto di S:
Teodoro, situato in Campo
Vaccino con Disegno di noi
Cav.^r^ Carlo Fontana
Cap:

Il Tempietto circolare di S: Teodoro situato nel Campo Bovario, hà il suo piano molti p.^m^ sotto la superficie della Terra, e strada, si era reso quàsi impraticabile à causa delle grandi trapellationi dell' acque in esso provenienti dalle pioggie, e terreno, che immediatàm.^e^ accostava alli suoi muri antichi, il qual Terreno si è inalzato dal continuo riporto di stabbii p coltura dell' orti, et altre cause, che sollevano li piani della Città, essendo arrivato in altezza già dal piano della soglia della sua Porta postali da Niccola Papa V. circa p.^m^ 14, e si discendeva à foggia di caverna con una scala di 15: scalini attaccata alla propria Porta, si che dal fondo, e scarsezza dè lumi la rendeva non solo tenebroso, mà ànche umido molto dannevole alla frequenza di quei ammalati fanciulli portati dalli devoti di quel Santo nell' ora de Santi Sacrificii per ricevere la salute.

Si còme la Stà di N.S. Papa Clemente XI. tutto propensa, et attento con tanta pietà paterna à restaurare, e restituire al publico le Fabriche Ecclesiastiche antiche abbandonate, non mancò in qsto, còme nè gl' altri di beneficare qsto Tempio dòve fece chiamare noi Cav.^r^ Carlo Fontana ordinandoci che pensassimo alli rimedii p liberarlo da quei danni, e renderlo al publico più salutifero, che si puole, ondè seguissimo gl' ordini di S. Stà, e con un' esatto esame delle cause de i danni riferissimo, che era necessario p togliere quell' Umidi di circonvallarlo con una trascenda, ò vero forma circolare ben larga p ricevere in essa le trapellationi dell' acque, e liberare il Tempio con scavare il Terreno avànti la Porta p stendervi un gran cortile p introdurre l' aria, e ventillatione purificata dèntro il Tempio e allontanare le scale, e con accrescere alcuni sfori in augumento del lume p migliorare quell' ambito.

Piaceva a S. Stà la nostra propositione, dòve alli 20: di Sett.^re^ dell' anno 1703: ordinò l' esecutione dè i lavori, e viene hora dunque d. Tempio riparato dalla forma fabricata di nuovo, la quale tiene lontano dal Tempio quell' Acque et umidi, che li erano vicini, e si è benificato nell' aria dall' amplo Cortile al piano del Tempio con muri attorno, che sostentano il terreno, che li stà alli lati con una nobil scala orbicolata molto lontana dal Tempio.

Restava con un brutto vedere l' interno di qsto Tempietto à causa della rozzezza dè muri spogliati dall' ornamenti, sòpra il quale risiede hòra la volta fatta fare da Niccola Papa V.^o^ positàm.^e^ senzà la giusta spartitura della costole d' essa, non corrispondente alle nicchie, e Tribuna, màggiorm.^e^ disuguali nelle distanze delle finestre, ònde S. Stà ci ordonò, che pensassimo à qualche ornato semplice p dargli qualche vaghezza., si che p disporre il pred. ornati con le vere uniformationi delle misure, necessitava rimover la volta con li Sfori delle Nicchie, e finestre antiche, il tutto còntro la mente di S. Stà, il quale desidera, e vole la conservatione di qlle antichità, e che non si levasse affatto quell' apparenza, e veneratione di quei muri antichi, ònde pigliassimo espediente p non impedire, et occupare il sito frequentato del Tempio di riportare in parte sòpra d. muri semplici fascie con un cornicione [nel] sotto imposta della volta, risolato con protiridi, òvero mensole, che sostengano a corrispondenza delle costole disposte con tall' arte, che l' occhio non scuopre le disugualianze, e ciò non si è potuto praticarsi cosi nelli vani delle finestre p esser troppo esorbitante le misure delle loro varie distanze, còme il fatto lo dimostra, e quei campi trà gl' ornati si sono lasciati con la propria antichità, solo che una semplice picchiatura acciò si vedessero con pulizia il loro antico essere.

Ònde la dispositione dè i pred. ornati hà levato la total diturpatione con sommo piacere di chi l' ammira, volendo S. Stà, che qsta rinovatione à riuscita molto approvatamènte da tutti, ordinò di far di nuovo l' Ara principale, et accrescer li due altri nelle Nicchie di mischii con l' Effigie di due Santi miracolosi con suoi Quadri, che si pensa farli di Mosaico, e S. Stà vi hà fatto porre sòpra la Porta una bellissima Iscrittione uscita dalla sua gran penna qui registrata.

The façade of S. Maria dell'Umilità, Rome (1703)

Two drawings for a church façade (nos 173 and 174, Figs 138/9), 49 *palmi* in width, correspond in size and character with the façade of S. Maria dell' Umilità, a work which is known from the sources to have been built by Fontana (Titi, ed. 1763, p.327; Crescimbeni, p.345, reprint in Donati, p.284). A photograph of the façade in its present condition is given by Donati (p.323, fig.279 and Cicinelli, fig.10). The drawings at Windsor show also that the street slopes upwards and this corresponds with the site of the church of S. Maria dell'Umilità.

The original monastery and church was founded in 1601 by Francesca Baglioni Orsini and seems to have been completed by 1609 when Paul V confirmed the Dominican rule. The monastery was subsequently enlarged and the church rebuilt by Paolo Maruscelli, 1641–1646 (Cicinelli, pp.27, 34ff.), slightly nearer to the Quirinal (*Roma Antica e Moderna*, ed. 1653, p.120). About two decades later the interior was adorned with statues by Antonio Raggi, according to Cicinelli (p.39), who also established that Carlo Fontana was already architect of the monastery in 1681, and was then apparently involved with its enlargement and later with the decoration of the interior of the church. This circumstance led Cicinelli (pp 42, 48–55) to the erroneous assumption that the church front was already built about 1681.

The dates for the construction of Fontana's façade, which took only three months (7 May 1703 – 12 August 1703), are given by Valesio. He was as usual hostile to the achievements of Fontana, and he comments critically on the completion of the work: 'Dom.a 12 E stata scoperta la nuova facciata della chiesa delle monache dell'Umilità che non è stata punto applaudita fatta con disegno del Cau.re Fontana.' Vincenzo Felice is mentioned in the Guide book of 1708 as the author of the relief on the façade.

ADDITIONAL BIBLIOGRAPHY:

Aldo Cicinelli, *S. Maria dell' Umilità e la Cappella del Collegio Americano del Nord* (CRI 111), Rome, 1970.

173 ELEVATION OF THE FAÇADE (*Figure* 138) [9518]

272 × 410 mm. Watermark no.7. Pen, grey wash, traces of chalk. With scale (covered by binding strip) and measurements. Inscribed, lower right: *scandagliata la spesa/ . . . ? Scudi quattro Cento senz*(a)/ *il fusto della Porta Cfontan*, and on left: *Dal piano della/Cimasa al piano / del Collare p*^{m} *35⅜*.

The façade is designed in a similar way to the openings of the side chapels of S. Spirito in drawing 128 above. Apart from the present drawing other projects for the façade by Fontana must have existed. One appears to be recorded in a copy at Stockholm (Nationalmuseum, THC 8027, Fig.141), which shows alternative designs, that on the left resembling the present drawing, and that on the right recalling an altar project for S. Spirito (no.124). Coudenhove-Erthal (p.115) dismisses the present façade with its triangular pediment as *akademisch*, without taking into consideration what may have been its original appearance, which is recorded by Vasi (*Magnificenze*, VIII, fig.144; Fig.140 here; cf. Cicinelli, pp.48–52–reconstruction after Vasi, fig.12); it was changed in the 19th century when the façade was raised by a storey (the buildings are now incorporated into a single big edifice – the Collegio Americano degli Stati Uniti). The lower part of the façade was also changed at this time, and the original height of the entrance can still be deduced from scars on the frames of the opening and on the doors. A variant of the finished design is in the Albertina (no.1317; Fig.142). A further project by Fontana for the central part of the façade may be recorded in a copy by Vittone, vol.I, fos 82/3, which occurs next to a copy of the present drawing.

174 DIAGRAM OF THE LOWER PART OF THE FAÇADE, PLAN AND ELEVATION (*Figure* 139) [9519]

273 × 410 mm. Pen, chalk. With scale and measurements (cut on left). Inscribed on right with notes on measurements.

Rome, S. Giovanni in Laterano, drawings of the nave niches (1703) and of an altar project after Borromini

Volume 179 at Windsor contains a manuscript of 20 October 1703, addressed to Cardinal (Benedetto) Pamphili, in which Fontana outlines his ideas on the type of statue he considers suitable for filling the niches, designed by Borromini, in the nave of the Lateran. His theories are illustrated in an accompanying drawing, no.175 (Fig.143). A copy of the same manuscript is to be found in Volume 172 at Windsor, with a copy (no.176; Fig.144) of part of drawing no.175. The text and drawing in Volume 172 are entitled on the preceding blank page: *Per le Statue di S. Gio Laterano / Dentro li Tambernacoli / o nicchie.* Both of the Windsor texts are based on an earlier treatise by Fontana, which is dated 16 March 1703 and addressed to Cardinal Corsini, later Pope Clement XII, who was then Treasurer to Clement XI (Arch. Vat., Fondo Albani, published by M. Loret in *Archivi*, 1935, pp. 75ff.). The Windsor texts follow this treatise almost word for word, but they contain two sections, one short and one longer, which do not occur in the earlier text in the Vatican.

The work of filling the niches of the Lateran with statues of the Apostles was instigated by Cardinal Benedetto Pamphili, the recipient of Fontana's Windsor treatises, who was made Archpriest of the Lateran in 1699, and by Pope Clement XI after his election in 1700 (on the history of the work see Montalto, pp. 433ff. and den Broeder). The work was supervised by a committee consisting of Cardinal Pamphili, Monsignore Curzio Origo, Don Orazio Albani, the brother of the Pope, Count Giulio Bussi, and it had as architectural consultant Fontana's nephew, Carlo Stefano, *l'abbate* (Balestra, pp.9 f.). Money to pay for the statues was raised by subscription, and drawings for the statues were provided by Carlo Maratta (M. Loret in *Archivi*, 1935, pp.104ff.; a drawing for one of the statues is at Windsor, no.737, attributed to Rusconi). The project was not finally completed until 1718. The first of the statues appear to have been commissioned in 1703, or slightly before, and in 1703 full-scale models for two of the statues (St John and St Peter) were put up. A model for the niche for the St John was apparently constructed with the help of Carlo Stefano Fontana in February 1703 (Montalto, p.279) and the model of the St Peter is mentioned by Valesio on 17 May 1703 (E. Scatazza, in *Arte e storia*, 1916, p.335). This statue, commissioned by the Pope from Monnot, was in 1705 the first of the twelve to be completed; Rusconi's St John, commissioned by Cardinal Pamphili, was not completed until 1713.

Fontana's treatise of March 1703 was therefore written at the time when experiments were being carried out with models in the church, and it was presumably made at the request of Cardinal Corsini, and then copied out in October for Cardinal Pamphili. Cardinal Corsini commissioned the statue of St Bartholomew from Pierre Legros, which is said to date from between 1703 and 1713 (P. d'Espezel in *GB–A*, XII, 1934, p.154; den Broeder, pl.5). The Fontana drawings in the Windsor volumes refer to a figure of St Bartholomew, though to one which differs considerably from the statue finally executed by Legros.

In his treatise Fontana begins by insisting that the niches of the Lateran are strictly tabernacles. He stresses that the statues must be kept in proportion to the scale of the architecture, and to that of the bas-reliefs over the tabernacles. He recommends at this stage a height of 18 *palmi* for the statues, excluding a low and preferably elliptical base, and this height he arrives at by comparison with that of the columns flanking the tabernacles. There follows a list of fifteen tabernacles or altars related to those of the Lateran, where in each case the height of the statue is either equal to or less than that of the framing columns. Most of these examples are drawn from the work of Bernini, and Fontana also names two of his own earlier works: the Cappella Ginetti in S. Andrea della Valle, and the tabernacle or *ciborio* – presumably the high altar – in S. Maria in Traspontina (*opera molto imitata dà professori in altre simili*). 18½ *palmi* is then given as the maximum height for the Lateran statues. There follows a short list of statues in S. Peter's, statues which Fontana gives as being in 'ambiti grandi'. Finally, he sets out rules for the creation of the Lateran sculptures. He calculates the size in relation to the height of the columns, and then gives his reflections on what constitutes a good sculpture: a lightness achieved by the best ancient and modern artists in which the structure of the body is revealed beneath the drapery. The recommended height is then given as about 18½ *palmi* and the question of perspective is touched upon. As finally completed the height of the Lateran statues appears to be slightly greater than that recommended by Fontana.

The third drawing below is a copy after a project by Borromini for the high altar of S. Giovanni in Laterano; the same design was engraved by Domenico de Rossi in the *Studio d'architettura civile*, III (1721), pl.49 left. The engraving and a related drawing by Borromini are illustrated in E. Hempel, *Francesco Borromini*, 1924, pl.67. The purpose for which Fontana had this copy made is not known, nor the date when it was copied.

ADDITIONAL BIBLIOGRAPHY:

A. Balestra, *Stato della Chiesa Papale Lateranense nell'Anno MDCCXXIII.*

F. den Broeder in *Apollo*, 1967, pp. 360ff.

R. Enggass, *Revue de l'Art*, 1976, pp.21–25.

175 PLAN AND ELEVATION OF A TABERNACLE (*Figure* 143) [9919]
711 × 263 mm. Three sheets joined horizontally. Watermark no.7. Pen, grey wash, some chalk. With scale.

The lowest of the three sheets contains a plan of the tabernacle, with chalk lines to indicate its relation to an oval pedestal in the centre. Two sizes are given for this pedestal in the elevation. In the basic drawing (shown in Fig.143) it is unusually high, so that the head of the statue overlaps the upper frame of the niche. On a flap covering this version of the elevation there is a similar statue on a lower plinth. In this case the figure bears a knife and must therefore be a representation of St Bartholomew. The relief in the rectangular field above the tabernacle is that of the Baptism of Christ.

176 ELEVATION OF A TABERNACLE (*Figure* 144) [9413]
407 × 277 mm. (the left edge folded in the binding). Watermark no.7. Pen, grey wash, traces of chalk. Inscribed within a frame of leaves, upper right: *Emo e Rmo Sig.^{re} / Il Cau.^{r} Carlo Fontana / soggiunge oltrè la / scrittura a v. Em.^{za} come / il Telaro À destina il / suo uano, la misura / della statua à guisa / delle communi Pittu: / :re, che sono negl' / Altari, il presente / Disegno nè fà la dimos:/:tratione.*

The statue and its pedestal correspond with those shown on the flap of the preceding drawing. The frame of the tabernacle behind the statue is indexed '*A*'.

177 PROJECT FOR THE HIGH ALTAR, ELEVATION (AFTER BORROMINI) [9910]
414 × 270 mm. Pen, grey wash, traces of chalk. Inscribed on the frieze: 'ALEXANDER · VII · PONT · MAXI · FE'

Projects for SS. Marcellino e Pietro, Rome (1703?)

The success of the measures taken to preserve S. Teodoro seems to have encouraged Clement XI to turn his attention to another church of early Christian origin, SS. Marcellino e Pietro (for a reconstruction etc., see Krautheimer, *Corpus Basilicarum*, II, pp. 201ff.). Its position in the valley between the Caelian and the Esquiline made it, like S. Teodoro, liable to dampness and restorations were frequently necessary. Fundamental restorations had been undertaken in the Middle Ages (Cecchelli/Persico, pp.11ff.); later efforts at preservation were made by Cardinal Mariano Pierbenedetti (after 1589) and, in the Holy Year of 1700, by Cardinal Giacomo Buoncompagni. The last restoration cannot have been radical, since it was immediately followed by that undertaken by Clement XI.

Coming from S. Teodoro, the Pope visited SS. Marcellino e Pietro on 20 July 1703 'anch'essa dall'antichità oltre misura oltragiata' and immediately gave instructions for its restoration (Chracas, *Terremoto*, p.228). When he again visited the church on 8 November 1703, the feast of S. Teodoro, the site in front of the building had already been cleared (Valesio).

Fontana's name is not mentioned in the sources, but he was the obvious choice as an architect for the commission, and the first of the two Windsor drawings catalogued below (no.178; Fig.145) confirms the connection. It shows the area in front of the building after the levelling of the site, with pencil indications of proposed decorations for the façade with coats-of-arms over rectangular niches for statues, probably of the two patron saints.

Clement XI is said to have given the church a new façade ('l'ornò di facciata'; *Roma ant. e mod.*, ed. 1750, II, p.490), and it may be this façade which is recorded on one of a group of recently discovered drawings by Filippo Juvarra for the Palazzo del Conclave (1725; Vat. Lat. 137. 50, III; Fig.147, detail) where there is a resemblance to S. Maria dell'Umilità (cf. V. Viale, in *Atti delle Scienze di Torino*, 103, 1968/1969, fig.4). A survey drawing, however, in the Albertina (no.817; Fig.148) shows a flat surface broken only by the door and the window.

According to O. P. Ciuccioli (p.141), SS. Marcellino e Pietro was 'ristorata a fundamentis' by Clement XI, but this statement is no doubt exaggerated. The 1725 Guide (p.76) gives a more convincing account of the situation: 'Ma la Santa Memoria di Clemente XI senza rimovere cosa alcuna dell' antichità, la fece abbellire, ponendola in Isola, e liberandola dagl' orti vicini . . .', which brings out the desire of the Pope to preserve as much of the old building as possible. In connection with the restoration of the church, the Guides also mention Cardinal Francesco Pignatelli, who was made a Cardinal by Clement XI on 17 December 1703 and was resident in Rome till 1707 (Guarnacci, *Hist. Pont. Rom.*, II, pp. 42ff.).

Unfortunately no drawings are known for the renovation of the interior of the church, but a plan for the façade (no.179 in Vol.188 at Windsor; Fig.146) may represent Cardinal Pignatelli's project. The façade shows a polychrome scheme, with columns enclosing niches for statues. The connection of this unsigned and undated drawing with SS. Marcellino e Pietro seems to be indicated by the arms of Sixtus V flanked by griffons in the tympanum (cf. no.178), which refer to the restoration by Mariano Pierbenedetti, who has griffons in his coat-of-arms (cf. top right of no.178; Ciacconius, *Hist. Pont. Rom.*, IV, p.194).

The new design for the façade, which has the arms of Clement XI over the portal, is clearly derived from no.178, but the niches and panels have been transposed.

Clement XI transferred the church in 1703 to the Monaci Maroniti Libanesi di S. Antonio Abbate and added monastic buildings. He contributed to the income of the monks by appointing the rector to the Chair of Syrian Language at the Sapienza (cf. Valesio, 13 December 1707). A note in the Cod. Terribilini, quoted by Cecchelli/Persico, shows, however, that the erection of a new building soon became necessary: 'la fabrica del Monistero fu principata nell' 1729 dall' Architetto Nicola Michetti' (Bibl. Casanatense, Ms. 2185, fo.121).

By the middle of the 18th century the basilica was 'ridotta inistato da poter, da un giorno all' altro rovinare' (*Rom. ant. e mod.*, ed. 1750, II, p.490). It was demolished under Benedict XIV, who made the sum of 4,000 *scudi* available to the architect Girolamo Theodoli for the erection of a new church. The existing centralized church with a stepped cupola has the date 1752 on the entablature. Vasi (*Magnificenze*, 1753, III, pl.50; detail Fig.149) reproduces a view of the building immediately after its completion.

In 1753 Benedict XIV ordered the transfer to SS. Marcellino e Pietro of the Carmelite Scalze of S. Lucia alle Botteghe Oscure, who altered and extended the convent building (Rome, Archivio di Stato, Cam. I, Corp. Ord. Rel. Femm., vols 4314, 4361, 4364).

ADDITIONAL BIBLIOGRAPHY:

C. Cecchelli and E. Persico, *SS. Marcellino e Pietro, La Chiesa e la Catacomba*, Rome, 1938 (CRI, vol.36, with further bibliography).

178 VIEW OF THE FAÇADE AND FORECOURT (*Figure* 145) [9750]

302×*c.*215 mm. Chalk, coloured washes, pen. Inscribed lower right: *S. Pietro è Mar*(cellino).

The drawing was presumably made between the Pope's first visit to the site on 20 July 1703 and the second on 8 November 1703, by which time the approach shown in the drawing was cleared. Pen appears to have been used in the drawing to indicate existing features of the façade.

179 Unidentified draughtsman.
PROJECT FOR THE FAÇADE, PERSPECTIVE VIEW (*Figure* 146) [10582]

332×268 mm. Watermark no.7. Pen, coloured washes, traces of chalk.

A design for a similar façade with the inscription *Divo Silvestro* in the architrave over the door, is in the Royal Institute of British Architects, London (box A/2, no.6).

Rome, S. Maria dell'Anima, the decoration for the memorial service to the Emperor Leopold I (1705)

Volume 177 at Windsor consists of 53 drawings made in preparation for the decoration of S. Maria dell' Anima for the funeral service of the Emperor Leopold I. The drawings must have been executed in the latter half of 1705, between 5 May, when the Emperor died, and 19 December, the day of the service itself. The sheets fall into two groups, nos 180 to 201 (Figs 150–171) which are finished drawings of 22 roundels for reliefs containing allegorical scenes, and nos 202 to 231 which are rough studies directly related to the final scheme of decoration for the church and the construction of an elaborate catafalque in the centre of the nave. The book has a title-page, dated 1705, and an introduction by Fontana which was clearly intended for publication, together with engravings of the roundels, although neither was apparently committed to print.

The text consists largely of a long description of the 22 roundels with a shorter passage bearing on the funeral decoration at the end: *Motiui, e Riflessione, che mi hanno indotto al sopra d.º Componiment: figurato.* This passage makes it clear that the roundels were to have formed the most important part of an early project for the decoration of the church. Fontana explains that he attempted to show in the roundels the *uirtù intrinseche* of Leopold rather than to describe the events of his life, which had been the subject of medals designed for the funeral service at Vienna. Leopold had been especially important to the papacy as an opponent of the Turks, and amongst conventional allusions in Fontana's allegories, there occur a number of anti-Ottoman references.

Fontana's first idea appears to have been more interesting than the final scheme of decoration. He wished to turn the whole church into a catafalque ('di fare che l'istessa Chiesa rapresentasse totalmente il Catafalco') and arrange the roundels along the walls. The church of S. Maria dell'Anima has no crossing, and Fontana appears to refer to this fact when he explains that the building seemed to him to impede the construction of a proper catafalque. The details of this early project are difficult to visualize without the help of drawings, but Fontana's description contains some hints. The coffin, in the centre of the nave, was to be draped, and encircled by bronze torches borrowed from S. Peter's. The Imperial regalia were to be placed with a crucifix on a cushion over the coffin, surmounted by an Imperial eagle with a representation of the Madonna in its breast. The draperies of the Madonna were to fall around the cushion. This whole composition was to be raised on three steps, with four pedestals decorated with emblems and surmounted by an eagle. Incense was to burn in crystal vases, following the method recorded on antique medals, and in four large *conconi* placed above the steps of the bier.

At this point Fontana cuts short his description of the interior of the church and goes on to describe the exterior. This was to be decorated with reference to the *parti estrinseche* of the Emperor – his victories thus making an epilogue (or rather he should say a prologue) to the *uirtù intrinseche* in the interior. The façade was to bear simulated inscriptions based on antique monuments; the house of Hapsburg, or so Fontana explains in his concluding paragraph, is related to the Roman family of Anicius. This connection apparently led Fontana to take as the subject of the first two roundels events from the life of the Emperor Rudolf I, the founder of the Hapsburg dynasty.

The final scheme for the decoration of the church was more conventional than that described in Fontana's text, and it was not apparently considered a success (see below). This is perhaps the reason why he wished to publish an account of his earlier scheme, but he refrains, unfortunately, from explaining why the change took place. The final design was centred upon the type of catafalque (Fig.176) that Fontana had hoped to avoid; it was unsuitable for the church and many of the roundels had to be altered in shape and fitted round the base of the new construction. The most striking feature of the final scheme were the four *mete* – small columns in imitation of those used by the Romans as winning posts in circuses, and decorated by Fontana with spiralling reliefs – which stood one at each corner of the catafalque. The catafalque as finally built, including the *mete*, Fontana seems to have derived from the scheme of decoration supplied by his pupil Sebastiano Cipriani for James II of England whose funeral service took place in S. Lorenzo in Lucina in 1702. These decorations are recorded in engravings by Specchi in C. de Aquino *Sacra Exequialia in funere Jacobi II. Magnae Britanniae Regis*, 1702. The design of Cipriani's catafalque may have been based in turn on earlier structures of this kind, but it is difficult to reconstruct in any detail the history of the temporary structures of the period in the absence of adequate visual records (see Braham). What appears to be a small sketch of Fontana's catafalque occurs in one of the sketch books of Juvarra (Biblioteca Nazionale, Turin, 59/4, fo.117, labelled wrongly as 'Funerale di Leopoldo–II–'), and it may have been the existence of this drawing which has led some authors to attribute the decorations for Leopold's funeral to Juvarra.

The second group of drawings in Volume 177 at Windsor, with one exception, appear to refer to Fontana's final design, but there are unfortunately no detailed drawings amongst them. A description of the funeral service was, however, published in 1705, and by the greatest good fortune there have recently come to light, through the efforts of Mr Brian Sewell, several drawings which record in some detail the final scheme of decoration for the church and catafalque. The drawings form part of an album recently acquired by the Victoria and Albert Museum which contains for the most part studies for the decoration of S. Maria dell' Anima for the memorial service to the Emperor Joseph I in 1712 (see Braham). This scheme of decoration, by Ferdinando Poletti, was based on that devised by Fontana for Leopold, and it is probably for this reason that drawings for the two schemes are to be found in the same volume. Fontana's design is recorded in drawings on seven of the pages of the volume: no.4, plan of the catafalque (Fig.175); no.5, perspective view of the nave (Fig.176); nos 6/7, elevation and section of the base of the catafalque and the bier (Fig.174); nos 8/9, drawings of the battle scenes decorating the sides of the bier; and nos 101, 104 and 106, drawings which record three of the roundels designed by Fontana in his early project.

The published text of Leopold's funeral service is by Francesco Posterla; *ISTORICA, E VERIDICA RELAZIONE | Della Mole funebre fatta inalzare in occasione delle solenne Essequie | fatte all'Augustissimo Imperadore LEOPOLD I. . . . Con Disegno, Disposizione, & Invenzione dell'Illustrissimo Sig. Cavalier Carlo Fontana | Architetto, & Ingegnero Pontificio, e di Sua Maestà Cesarea, . . .* Fontana had worked for the Emperor on the design of the imperial coach houses at Vienna (Pascoli, II, p.548 and Donati, p.282 and fig.295), and he had also received commissions from Austrian nobles (see below). Leopold had conferred upon Fontana the title of count (see below, Fontana's coat-of-arms) and the text of Fontana's treatise, the *Utilissimo trattato dell'acque correnti* (1696), is dedicated to the future Emperor Joseph. Posterla, the author of the description of the funeral, apparently collaborated with Fontana on the work for he says at one point that he had devised the various quotations that were applied to the catafalque. These quotations are listed in the Windsor volumes on two sheets bound with the second group of drawings.

The catafalque as described by Posterla can be visualized from the drawings in the Victoria and Albert Museum album (Fig.176) and from those of the second group at Windsor. The colours used were black, gold and yellow and the structure stood 76 *palmi* high, measuring 50×42 *palmi* across the first, *obliquo*, base. There was a second, circular, base over the first, 4 *palmi* high, with arcs cut towards the centre on the four main axes. Four square pedestals stood out from the projections between these four arcs, each decorated on three sides with one of Fontana's allegorical compositions, changed from a round to a rectangular format ('Pitture di chiaro oscuro lumeggiate d'oro'). The four *mete* stood on the pedestals, each 25 *palmi* high, and at the base of each there was a pair of bronze-coloured cannon emitting smoke and incense. Beneath each cannon a quotation was affixed (index letters F to FFFF and H to HHHH in the Windsor text, excepting HH for which a different quotation was apparently supplied). An eagle, 5 *palmi* high, stood at the summit of each of the *mete*, their heads turned to face the centre of the catafalque. At the junction of the *mete* and their pedestals were placed four of Fontana's roundels.

The cavities in the circular base facing the door and the altar each supported a pedestal, placed diagonally, and apparently decorated with paintings on the front representing the standards and arms of Austria. Each urn was supplied with two quotations ('Alla Prima Urna uerso la Porta 1' and '2' in the Windsor text). At this point in his narrative Posterla mentions that all the quotations, chosen by himself, came from the Psalms and the writings of the Holy Fathers. On each of these bases (behind the urns, see Fig.174) there was a *putto* made of stucco, dressed in black and carrying a cross and standards decorated with roundels painted with crosses and chalices. The pedestals in front of the *putti* supported large candles and, according to the text, a hollow crown decorated with leaves and emitting smoke and incense. The side cavities of the catafalque also contained figures of *putti*, seated and holding *fasces*, and at their feet lay drums, Ottoman standards and two (inscribed) silver moons; the drums bore inscriptions (I and III in the Windsor text). The printed text goes on to speak of the other decorations of the '4 lati interni' and the '4 lati esteriori', but it is difficult at this point to follow the sequence of the description in full. The 'lati interni' were decorated with representations of crosses and chalices, and the 'lati esteriori' (i.e. at the base of the *mete*, cf. Fig.174) with quivers and turbans. The four turbans were inscribed with quotations (index E to EEEE in the Windsor text).

In the centre of the circular base there rose a rectangular pedestal supported on six balls and decorated at the sides with representations of the four most important victories of Leopold over the Turks (nos 8/9 of the Victoria and Albert Museum drawings). At the corners were four stucco cornucopias with further candles. Over this was the bier festooned with silver laurel and inscribed: *LEOPOLDUS I. semper Augustus Austriacae Domus Imperator XV*. Above the coffin a cushion was placed, with long tassels at the corners, and this supported the regalia, the whole being covered like a tent with a black drapery, 'con somma gloria del Sig. Cavalier Carlo Fontana, una grandezza, & una Maestà non mai ne' tempi passati in consimili occasione veduta' (Posterla).

A large medallion hung over the coffin, 7 *palmi* in diameter, and supported by four 'Fame scherzanti in atto di volò'. There was a portrait of Leopold in relief on one side, and on the other a painted portrait of the Emperor with an inscription (that headed 'Sopra alla Medaglia dell' Imp^{re}.' in the Windsor text). Over the medal was the baldacchino with four long black draperies held in position by four silvered skeletons which stood behind the *mete*. Between the draperies crystal chandeliers were placed so as to give the impression of tears falling from heaven. Near each of the skeletons further inscriptions were written ('Alle 4. Morti' in the Windsor text). The cornice of the baldacchino was decorated with clocks and death's heads, and at this level were further medallions, 6 *palmi* in diameter (inscriptions in the Windsor text labelled: 'Alle 4. Medaglie pendenti dal Baldacchino'). The composition ended finally with an array of flags, a panel of arms and a crown.

The decoration of the four *mete* was intended to illustrate the following general themes: *divozione* – left from door, *carità* – right from door, *giustizia* – right facing altar, and *ingrandimento del Imperio* – left facing altar. They bore inscriptions related to these themes (index letters B to BBBB in the Windsor text), as did the roundel attached to each *meta* (index A to AAAA). The three rectangular reliefs on the pedestal of the *mete* also bore inscriptions (see below).

The interior of the church was festooned with mourning draperies and one of Fontana's roundels was placed over the chancel arch, to be removed later to the wall above the entrance. The chancel itself had richer decoration than the nave, since here the *porporati* were to sit during the services. Four of the pilasters of the nave had decorations of standards, and over the main entrance a long inscription was written on two canvases. The façade was likewise draped and carried an inscription on a large canvas, with a further canvas (24 *palmi* high) containing a representation of the Imperial eagle holding at its breast a skull with the Austrian arms. Posterla ends his description with a short account of the ceremony and a word of praise for the 'non mai abbastanza lodato Sig. Cavalier Carlo Fontana'.

According to Valesio the decoration of the church was not considered successful: 'Vi fù gran concorso p uedere quella machina funebre architettura del Cau.^{re} Carlo Fontana, ma non piacque ad alcuno mancando d'Idea et ripiena di superfluità e di motti di scrittura così generici che rassebraua più tosto un'Catafalco p anniuersario de morti che particolare p un'Imp.^{re} le 4 mete poste negl' angoli oltre non confarsi punto a materia funebre danaro campo a belli ingegni di dargli simiglianze oscene e ridicole . . .' (19 December 1705, fo.172). The cost of the decoration is recorded as not less than 3,792 *scudi* (Schmidlin, p.275, referring to *Avvisi Marescotti* 506 and 508).

The drawings are catalogued below in two groups, the first consisting of the roundels, and the second of the remaining drawings, related for the most part to the catafalque of the final scheme. The roundels are of great interest as the largest surviving group of figurative drawings by Fontana. The compositions are described thus by Posterla: 'Sappiasi per tanto che l'Invenzione di questo Figurativo, e Rappresentativo, con tutto l'Inalzamento della Machina fù del celebre Sig. Cavalier Fontana che in quest'Opera insigne non solo si fè vedere da quel grande Architetto che Egli è, ma anche da Pittore, e da Erudito rappresentando, & inventando can la sublimità del suo Ingegno tutto quello che in detta Mole funebre si rimirava, seguendo sempre la scorta degl'Antichi Romani, sù la di cui Imitazione egli corre à gran passi . . .' The compositions amount, in fact, to a dictionary of 17th-century allegory – undiluted adulation, of the kind that the Emperor is shown in the drawings to have trampled underfoot (no.196).

For the second group of drawings no attempt has been made to work out an exact order for the sheets, except in the case of a section of the nave of S. Maria dell'Anima (no.202) which appears to refer to Fontana's first projects, and is placed first in the catalogue of the second group. The majority of the other drawings correspond in a general way with the final design of the catafalque. Fontana appears to have established the plan and the general character of the catafalque and then to have worked out the details of the decoration. The drawings closest to the final design are those connected with the placing of the inscriptions and they are grouped together at the end.

Copies of the majority of the drawings are to be found in the Vittone volumes in Paris – evidence of the great interest of Vittone in the temporary architecture of Fontana.

ADDITIONAL BIBLIOGRAPHY:

A. Braham, *Funeral decorations*, with further bibliography.

J. Schmidlin, *Geschichte der Deutschen Nationalkirche in Rom, S. Maria dell'Anima*, 1906.

The Roundels

The 22 drawings of the roundels are arranged in Volume 181 in the order in which Fontana describes them in his text, and the entries below follow this sequence. In the final design for the funeral decoration the compositions were arranged in the following way: for the *meta di divozione*, left from entrance to church, 183 (*tondo* affixed to *meta* – on right in Fig.176), 184, 188 and 185 (rectangles at sides and front of pedestal); for the *meta della carità*, right from entrance to church, 197 (*tondo* – on left in Fig.176), 194, 192 and 186 (rectangles on pedestal); for the *meta della giustizia* on the right facing altar, 201 (*tondo*), 195, 193 and 189 (rectangles on pedestal); for the *meta dell'ingrandimento dell'Imperio*, 187 (tondo), 199, 191 and 200 (rectangles on pedestal). Composition no.190 was used for the roundel over the doorway from the street. The remainder were apparently not used (nos 180, 181, 182, 196 and 198), and these are the only drawings where no biblical text is written on the sheet.

The drawings all measure *c*.415×*c*.270 mm., and all are executed in pen, grey wash and chalk. Each bears an explanatory title in the upper right-hand corner and these have been taken as the titles under which the drawings are listed below. The subject matter of each composition is described in detail in Fontana's text. The 17 drawings used in the final scheme of decoration are inscribed on the right with the shape finally assumed by each composition, and the motto attached to each is inscribed on the sheet in the upper left-hand corners. These *motti*, drawn mainly from the Psalms, correspond with those listed in the second Windsor text.

180 1: *Azzione religiosa, e caritatiua / del Co: d'Ausperg, al Sacerdote, / che portaua il Venerabile.* (*Figure* 150) [9807]

The word '*Habsburg*' is written beside the title, as a correction to '*Ausperg*'. A second inscription, upper left, partly hidden by the binding strip, reads: . . . (cont) *e d'Ausper* / . . . (sac) *erdote*.

181 2: *Assunzione all'Imperio del Co: d' / Auspurg detto Ridolfo Primo / Austriaco.* (*Figure* 151) [9808]
Watermark no.7. A second inscription, upper left, is partly hidden by the binding strip.

Copy, with frame added, in the Victoria and Albert Museum album, no.101.

182 3: *Leopoldo Primo uisitato nell'In:/fantia dall' Imbasciatore Ottomano, / e uaticinij di detto Ministro Turco.* (*Figure* 152) [9809]
Watermark no.7.

Copy, with frame added, in the Victoria and Albert Museum album, no.104.

183 4: *Leopoldo, da Fanciullo sempre / deddito alle cose de' Sagri Tempj.* (*Figure* 153) [9810]
Also inscribed: *Gressus meos dirige- S:., Tondo* and *A I.*

The *motto* is indexed 'A' in the second Windsor text.

184 5: *Leopoldo sempre più applicato al sos:|tengo dell' Autorità Pontificia, et ab:|battere la Setta Ottomana.* (*Figure* 154) [9811]
Watermark, no.7. Also inscribed: *Irritauerunt Te Domine :S:5, Figura quadra* and *Laterali del Piedestallo.*

The *motto* is indexed 'G' in the second Windsor text.

185 6: *Leopoldo indefesso Sostenitore | della Fede, e Chjesa* Romana. (*Figure* 155) [9812]
Also inscribed: *Fortitudo mea es Tu. S:30, figura rettiangolo, A 3* and *laterali.*

The *motto* is indexed 'C' in the second Windsor text.

186 7: *Leopoldo tutto Clemente, e pio à be:|neficare il suo Prossimo.* (*Figure* 156)[9813]
Watermark no.7. Also inscribed: *Extendit manum in* Retribuendo. *Ps: 54* and F. Rettiangolo.

The *motto* is indexed 'GGGG' in the second Windsor text.

187 8: *Leopoldo angelicamente guidato | nell'intraprendere le Guerre non injuste.* (*Figure* 157) [9814]
Also inscribed: *Justitia plena est dextera tua S:47* and *Tondo.*

The *motto* is indexed 'AAA' in the second Windsor text.

188 9: *Leopoldo sempre attento alla deuotione | uerso Dio, la SS'ma Vergine, e Suoi Santi | Auuocati.* (*Figure* 158) [9815]
Watermark no.7. Also inscribed: *Semper laus eius in Ore meo. S: 39, F rettiangolo, Fronte del Piedestallo* and *A 2.*

The *motto* is indexed 'D' in the second Windsor text.

189 10: *Vita pudica, & onesta di* Leopoldo. (*Figure* 159) [9816]
Also inscribed: *Ambulans in Via inmaculata | P.s:100* and *F rettiangolo.*

The *motto* is indexed 'GG' in the second Windsor text.

190 11: *La Virtù Eroica hà costituito Leopol:|do nel Tempio dell'Immortalità| con il corteggio dell' Arti Liberali* (*Figure* 160) [9817]
Also inscribed: *Date Nomini eius Magnificentia–| Eccles.39–* and *F rettiangolo.*

191 12: *Vittorie riportate da Leopoldo con:|tro l'Ottomana Potenza.* (*Figure* 161) [9818]
Also inscribed: *In Umbra Alarum Tuaru': Ps:56* and *F rettiangolo.*

The *motto* is indexed 'DDD' in the second Windsor text.

192 13: *Leopoldo che perdona l'offese | à suoi Traditori.* (*Figure* 162) [9819]
Also inscribed: *Ostende Misericordiam Tuam. Ps:84* and *F rettiangolo.*

The *motto* is indexed 'DDDD' in the second Windsor text.

193 14: *Leopoldo sempre penitente, e paziente | in soffrire tante Traversità tramategli.* (*Figure* 163) [9820]
Watermark no.7. Also inscribed: *Eripe me de Inimicis | P:s: 58, F rettiangolo* and *A 4.*

The *motto* is indexed 'DD' in the second Windsor text.

194 15: *La Magnanimità e Gratitudine | praticata sempre da Leopoldo.* (*Figure* 164) [9821]
Also inscribed: *Intelligit super Egen'um et Pauperum | Ps:40* and *F rettiangolo.*

The *motto* is indexed 'CCCC' in the second Windsor text.

195 16: *Leopoldo sempre mansueto, e | benigno* (*Figure* 165) [9822]
Also inscribed: *Mansuetis dabit Gratiam. Prou: 3º* and *F rettiangolo.*

The *motto* is indexed 'CC' in the second Windsor text.

196 17: *Leopoldo sempre Inimico dell'abo:|mineuole Adulatione & Inganno.* (*Figure* 166) [9823]
Also inscribed: *F rettiangolo.*

197 18: *Leopoldo pieno di Carità, e Mi:|sericordia.* (*Figure* 167) [9824]
Watermark no.7. Also inscribed: *Aures eius in Preces Eorum P:s:33* and *Tondo.*

The *motto* is indexed 'AAAA' in the second Windsor text.

198 19: *Leopoldo tutto attento alli* Re:|*scritti de' Memoriali, acciò | non sia fraudata la Gjustizia | à Suditti.* (*Figure* 168) [9825]
Watermark no.7. Also inscribed: *F rettiangolo.*

Copy, with slight variations and with frame added, in the Victoria and Albert Museum album, no.106.

199 20: *Leopoldo, che hà ingrandito l'/Impero con guista ragione.* (*Figure* 169) [9826]
Also inscribed: *Justitia de Caelo prospexit. P:s:84* and *F rettiangolo.*

The *motto* is indexed 'CCC' in the second Windsor text.

200 21: *Fortezza di Leopoldo in soffrire / le Tribolazioni.* (*Figure* 170) [9827]
Also inscribed: *In Deo speraui, Non timebo P:s:55* and *rettiangolo.*

The *motto* is indexed 'GGG' in the second Windsor text.

201 22: *Realità e Sincerità di Leopoldo* (*Figure* 171) [9828]
Watermark no.7. Also inscribed: *Misericors, Patiens, et Verax / Ps: 85* and *Tondo.*

The *motto* is indexed 'AA' in the second Windsor text.

The remaining drawings

1. Drawings of the Church, plans and sections of the catafalque

202 ELEVATION OF THE NAVE ARCADE (*Figure* 172) [9829]
271×*c*.415 mm. Watermark no.7. Pen, chalk. Inscribed, in ink over chalk: *Profilo della / Chiesa dell'/Anima,* and with sum on right.

The four arches of the nave are drawn in outline in ink, and over this a scheme of decoration is superimposed very roughly in chalk. It consists of roundels hanging in the arches and, in two cases, affixed to the piers. The present drawing is probably connected with Fontana's first design (see introduction).

203 ELEVATION OF TWO PIERS OF THE NAVE, DETAIL [9839]
270×*c*.415 mm. Watermark no.11. Pen, some chalk. With scale.

The drawing shows the lower part of the two piers. The distance between them is given as 37½ *palmi*. Rough chalk sketches occur in the vicinity of the pier on the left, and further, unidentifiable sketches on the *verso*.

204 PLAN OF THE CHURCH (*Figure* 173) [9830]
270×*c*.415 mm. (including a strip added on the right). Pen, grey wash, traces of chalk. With scale. Inscribed, ink over chalk: *Pianta della Chiesa dell'Anima / però è fuori di squadro.*

205 PLAN OF THE CENTRAL NAVE BAYS WITH ROUGH PLAN OF THE CATAFALQUE [9831]
265×*c*.415 mm. Watermark no.11. Pen, chalk. With scale.

The drawing shows a rough plan of the curvilinear upper base of the catafalque, with the positions of the *mete* established, and two measurements given.

206 ROUGH PLAN OF THE CATAFALQUE [9835]
270×*c*.415 mm. Chalk, pen. With two measurements.

207 PLAN OF THE CENTRAL NAVE BAYS AND OF THE CATAFALQUE (*Figure* 177) [9833]
271×*c*.415 mm. Watermark no.7. Pen, grey washes, chalk. With scale. Inscribed, ink over chalk: *Prima pianta del detto / funerale.*

A finished plan of the upper base of the catafalque; one of the incense cannon (lower right) is indicated in chalk.

208 PLAN OF THE CATAFALQUE AT BASE AND BALDACCHINO LEVEL, SHOWING STRUCTURAL SUPPORTS (*Figure* 178) [9834]
270×*c*.415 mm. Pen, brown wash, some chalk. With scale and measurements. Inscribed, in ink over chalk: *Pianta ingrandita,* and on the left, above the scale: *Dal centro A al B dlle* (?) *mete* p^{mi} *18½ / Dal centro A al Viuo dell'Armatura C* p^{mi} *14 / Dal Viuo dell'Armatura maestra al Viuo / dell'Armatura delle mete* p^{mi} *3⅛.*

The main features of the plan are drawn in outline in ink at base level on the left, and at baldacchino level on the right. The beams supporting the structure both vertically and horizontally are indicated in brown wash.

209 DIAGONAL HALF SECTION OF THE CATAFALQUE, SHOWING STRUCTURAL SUPPORTS (*Figure* 179) [9840]
C.415×271 mm. Watermark, no.7. Pen, brown, yellow and grey wash, some chalk. With scale, measurements and annotations. Inscribed, in ink over chalk: *Armatura della Machina.*

Rough copy by Vittone, vol.I, fo.89.

210 DIAGONAL HALF SECTION OF THE CATAFALQUE, SHOWING STRUCTURAL SUPPORTS [9847]
C.415 × 270 mm. Watermark no.7. Pen, brown wash, chalk. With measurements. Inscribed on left: *Si deue auertire quella che / ua sotto terra* and on right *Dal piano della Chiesa sino sop la uolta* p^{mi} *76½*.

The present drawing appears to be a study for the foregoing. On the *verso* in ink and chalk is a schematic plan of the catafalque, showing its supporting beams.

2. Studies of the Mete

211 ELEVATION OF THE CATAFALQUE (*Figure* 180) [9832]
C.415 × 270 mm. Watermark, no.7. Pen, chalk.

The eagles over the *mete* face outwards, as in 209 above, and not inwards as in the final design. The baldacchino is simpler than that finally constructed, and the incense cannon were apparently to be placed at the junction of the *mete* and their pedestals (cf. no.213 below).

212 ELEVATION OF A *META* ,WITH PLAN (*Figure* 181) [9838]
C.415 × 270 mm. Watermark no.7. Pen, grey wash, some chalk. With scale and measurements.

On the right is an elevation of the lower half of a *meta*, including the pedestal, and on the left one of a *meta* in its entirety, but without the pedestal. The drawing in the bottom left-hand corner of the sheet is probably a plan of the *meta* at the level of its base.

213 ELEVATION OF A *META*, WITH BIER AND MEDALLION [9837]
C.415 × 270 mm. Pen, chalk. Inscribed, in ink over chalk: *Mete*.

In character the present drawing is like no.211 above, and it appears to occupy a position between 211 and no.214 (below) in the development of the decoration of the catafalque.

214 ELEVATION OF A *META* (*Figure* 182) [9836]
C.415 × 270 mm. Watermark no.7. Pen, grey wash, some chalk. Inscribed in ink over chalk: *Meta*, and with a sum on left, and an illegible mark in chalk, upper left.

The drawing includes on the left a measured sketch of a flag. The roundel on the *meta* is here placed at the junction of the column and its base, as in the final group of drawings below, and the incense cannon are at the base of the pedestal.

215 STUDIES FOR THE DECORATION OF A PEDESTAL (*Figure* 183) [9850]
C.415 × 270 mm. Watermark no.7. Pen, grey wash, some chalk. With scale.

The drawing is possibly an early study for one of the pedestals under the *mete*; dotted lines cutting through the centre perhaps indicate the position of the support within the structure. The scale probably refers to the measured sketch plan at the top of the sheet corresponding in shape with one of the shields on the pedestal. The shield measures 6½ by 3½ *palmi*, and the pedestal would thus measure approximately 6 *palmi* in width. On the left of the sheet are sketches of two turbans.
Copy of the pedestal by Vittone, vol.I, fo.89.

3. Studies for the decoration of the concave bays of the catafalque, and of the bier

216 ELEVATIONS OF THE BIER AND AN INCENSE URN (*Figure* 184) [9842/3]
C.415 × 270 mm. Two sheets joined horizontally. Watermark no.7. Pen, grey wash, traces of chalk. 9842 with scale.

Putti carrying standards, and closely resembling the figure in drawing 217 below, sit one in each cavity at the sides of the bier, on the transverse axis of the catafalque. The positions of the incense cannon and the *mete* are not shown in the drawing and it is possible that the present study dates from before the stage at which they were introduced. The lower half of the sheet appears to mark a stage in the development of the pedestal and crown motif between the drawing on the upper half of the present sheet and drawing no.218 below.
Copies of both drawings by Vittone, vol.I, fo.8.

217 STUDY OF A *PUTTO* BEARING STANDARDS [9845]
C.415 × 271 mm. Watermark no.7. Pen, grey wash, traces of chalk.

The design closely resembles that of the *putti* in drawing 216 above.
Copy by Vittone, vol.I, fo.89.

218 ELEVATION OF A CROWN ON A PEDESTAL [9841]
C.415 × 271 mm. Watermark no.7. Pen, grey wash, some chalk. With scale.

The structure resembles in shape the pedestal in drawing 216 above. The crown itself is executed on a sheet of paper pasted over the basic sheet.

219 ELEVATION OF A PEDESTAL WITH INCENSE CROWN (*Figure* 185) [9846]
C.415 × 270 mm. Pen, grey and pink wash, some chalk. With scale. Inscribed, upper right: *Urna porfido / l'arme di Argento / Corona Doro / Niello doro.*

The present drawing is enclosed by faint sketches in chalk, and on the *verso* are further rough sketches including one apparently of a wreath of oak leaves with acorns.
Copy by Vittone, vol.I, fo.8.

220 PLAN AND PERSPECTIVE VIEW OF A CONCAVE BAY OF THE CATAFALQUE (*Figure* 186) [9854]
C.415 × 271 mm. Pen, grey wash, some chalk. With scale.

The bay is flanked by incense cannon and in the perspective view, at the top of the sheet, a *putto* sits between the cannon. Beneath his feet is a crescent moon, two quivers, and an object resembling a kettle-drum.

221 SECTION OF AN INCENSE CANNON (*Figure* 187) [9855]
271 × *c*.415 mm. Watermark no.7. Pen, grey wash, some chalk. With scale and index. Inscribed: *Profilo delle nº 8 machine p fare gettare fumi oder/* (osi)...*nel funerale*... (?) *alli otto Cannoni*, followed by explanations of the index letters.

222 STUDIES OF A DRUM (?), CRESCENT AND QUIVER [9852]
C.415 × 271 mm. Pen, grey wash, some chalk. With scale, index and measurements.

The sheet shows objects connected with those disposed at the feet of the *putto* in drawing 220 above (on the left is probably a rough plan and elevation of a kettle-drum).

223 STUDY OF A CRESCENT [9853]
C.415 × 271 mm. Watermark no.7. Pen, chalk. With measurements.

Probably made in preparation for the preceding drawing.

224 PLAN AND HALF ELEVATION OF THE BIER [9844]
C.415 × 271 mm. Pen, some chalk. With scale, index and measurements.

The design is close to that shown in no.216 above.

225 STUDIES FOR THE INSCRIPTIONS ON THE BIER [9851]
C.417 × 271 mm. Watermark no.7. Pen, some chalk. With index. Inscribed, with notes on the colours to be used.

The lower drawing shows the lid of the bier, which is inscribed: *LEPOLDVS* [*sic*] *PRIMVS*, and indexed with the letters A and B. At the top is a study probably for the opposite end of the lid of the bier, inscribed: *SEMPER AVGVST.*
Copy by Vittone of the right half of the main study, vol.I, fo.89.

4. Studies of the baldacchino

226 ELEVATION OF THE BALDACCHINO, DECORATED WITH AN IMPERIAL CROWN (*Figure* 188) [9849]
C.415 × 270 mm. Watermark no.7. Pen, grey wash, traces of chalk.

The cornice of the baldacchino lacks the clocks, the medallions and the other decorative elements added in the final design.
Copy of the left half of the drawing by Vittone, vol.I, fo.89.

227 ELEVATION AND HALF PLAN OF THE BALDACCHINO, DECORATED WITH A DEATH'S HEAD (*Figure* 189) [9848]
C.415 × 270 mm. Watermark no.7. Pen, grey wash, chalk.

The supports of the hour-glass are clearly intended to resemble bones. Two variants are given for the draperies suspended from the cornice (the basic design is shown in Fig.189 and this is replaced, in a flap, by an inscribed medallion).
Copy of the right half of the basic design by Vittone, vol.I, fo.89.

228 STUDIES OF MEDALLIONS AND TABLETS FOR INSCRIPTIONS [9859]
271 × *c*.416 mm. Watermark no.7. Pen, grey wash, traces of chalk. With scale.

The sheet bears three studies. The medallion of the left is probably one of the four which hung from the baldacchino. The inscription reads: *nº 4 Cartelle Doro / lettere Bianche / Ramo Bianco.* The studies for two tablets for inscriptions are inscribed: *Cartelle Doro nº 8 / lettere Bianche / Rami Bianchi*, and *Cartelle Doro nº. 4 / lettere Bianche / Rami Bianchi.* It is probable that these tablets were to be used with the reliefs at the bases of the *mete*. The present sheet is inscribed on the extreme left: *Tutti salmi / e Salamon*, and this presumably implies that the texts for the tablets and the medallions were to be drawn from the Psalms and the Song of Solomon.

5. Sketches connected with the placing of the inscriptions, etc.

229 SKETCH PLAN OF THE CATAFALQUE [9856]
205 × 290 mm. Chalk, pen.

The drawing occupies the *verso* of the second page containing the list of inscriptions to be used for the decoration of the catafalque. It is indexed in ink with the letters A to D, referring to this list of inscriptions. The letters in chalk on the sheet are for the most part counterproofs of the *recto* side of the following drawing. In this plan, as in the final design, the urns in the concave bays facing the altar and the door were set diagonally. The plan is inscribed at the top '*Corno Euangelio*', and at the bottom '*Corno Epistola*'.

230 STUDIES OF A *META* PEDESTAL AND OF THE BIER [9857]
270 × 197 mm. Chalk, pen. With indexes.

The *recto* of the present sheet contains a sketch of the surfaces which make up the area around the base of one of the *mete*. They are indexed from AAA to HHH referring to the index of the list of inscriptions. A rough sketch near to the top of the sheet appears to represent a tablet, or scroll, like those shown in drawing 228 above. The *verso* contains rough measured sketches in chalk of various parts of the catafalque and studies in ink of the bier.

231 STUDIES OF A *META* PEDESTAL AND OF STANDARDS AND MEDALLIONS [9858]
265 × *c*.415 mm. Watermark no.12. Pen, chalk. With index and measurements.

The right half of the sheet is occupied by a chalk sketch of the area around the base of one of the *mete* – a rather clearer version of that in the foregoing drawing. An index of letters in ink, from A to I, refers to the text giving the list of the inscriptions. On the left of the sheet are four measured studies, two of standards like those carried by a *putto* in drawing 217 above, and two of medallions. The latter are inscribed: *medaglia pendente . ./al baldachino*, and: *medaglia sopra li piedestalli*. On the *verso* is a rough sketch in chalk of the catafalque.

Rome, S. Egidio in Trastevere, the Origo Monument (1706)

A group of nine drawings in Volume 173 at Windsor are projects for the monument to Marchesa Veronica Rondanini Origo (Fig.198) in the church of S. Egidio in Trastevere (on the entrance wall of the church to the right of the doorway) (see the catalogue for the 'Exhibition of Architectural and Decorative Drawings', The Courtauld Institute, 1941, pp.13f.; exhibit no.24 is a related drawing in the collection of Sir Anthony Blunt. The identification of the tomb has recently been confirmed by Mr Frederick den Broeder). The monument is dated 1706 and attributed to Lorenzo Ottone. It is to be discussed by Mr den Broeder in a forthcoming publication, and only a short analysis of the drawings is attempted in the following paragraphs.

The monument is simple in design and remarkable mainly for the principal moulding that frames the portrait bust, which is movingly conceived in the shape of a rosary. Of Fontana's nine drawings four correspond closely with the executed monument, and of these no.240 (Fig.197) is closest of all, although the features of the portrait bust are more generalized, the appearance and age of the 'sitter' differing greatly from drawing to drawing. Other differences within this group of four drawings are confined largely to the area at the base of the monument, where the design of the urn appears to have caused Fontana difficulty. The architect appears in the present series of drawings to have made six experimental studies on small sheets and three larger drawings of the final design.

Preliminary studies

232 PROJECT WITH A SQUARE FRAME (*Figure* 190) [9460]
283 × 217 mm. Laid down. Pen, grey wash, traces of chalk.

The present design resembles the tomb of Marchesa Origo in showing a female portrait bust in a circular frame, which penetrates into the zone of the inscription, and in the type of coronet present. It foreshadows the following two designs in showing the portrait bust as a relief on a medallion.

233 PROJECT WITH AN EXTENDED SCROLL (*Figure* 191) [9459]
304 × 219 mm. Laid down. Pen, grey wash, traces of chalk. With figures and letters roughly inscribed in chalk (bottom right).

The three main elements of the final design of the Origo monument – the portrait, the scroll and the urn – are present in this drawing in the sequence in which they appear in the executed work.

234 PROJECT WITH A SARCOPHAGUS (*Figure* 192) [9457]
290 × 219 mm. Laid down. Pen, grey wash, traces of chalk.

The portrait medallion and its inscription are set out, together with an escutcheon, on a tablet which resembles that of the final design except in the presence of large ears at the sides.

235 PROJECT WITH A FREE-STANDING PORTRAIT BUST (1) (*Figure* 193) [9453]
318×221 mm. Laid down. Pen, grey wash, traces of chalk.

The outer frame of the monument is here close in shape to that of the final design, and the portrait bust is free-standing.

236 PROJECT WITH A FREE-STANDING PORTRAIT BUST (2) (*Figure* 194) [9458]
303×214 mm. Laid down. Pen, grey wash, traces of chalk.

Late projects

237 PROJECT WITH AN URN FLANKED BY LAUREL BRANCHES (*Figure* 195) [9455]
315×225 mm. Laid down. Pen, grey wash, traces of chalk. With three scales, of which two appear to be crossed out, and the last marked with a chalk star.

The word *BONVS* written at the base of the sheet, with the letter *L* above, appears to be an experiment for the type and scale of the lettering to be used on the scroll. An inscription referring to the lettering occurs along the bottom margin of the sheet: *Righe nº 12 stendono p.mi 55 lettere nº 6 il p.mo sono 330 Parole circa 35* —'. The bust portrait with its circular frame and encircling rosary is present in this design.

238 PROJECT WITH AN URN FLANKED BY EAGLES (1) (*Figure* 196) [9454]
420×*c*.275 mm. Pen, grey wash, traces of chalk. With scale.

At the bottom of the sheet appear the letters *A* and *B*, referring to the size of script to be used.

239 PROJECT WITH AN URN FLANKED BY EAGLES (2) [9452]
422×*c*.275 mm. Watermark no.7. Pen, grey wash, traces of chalk. With scale.

The present drawing closely resembles the preceding, the portrait bust being again that of a very young girl. The inscription, however, is now backed by a scroll, rolled over at the top as in the executed design. Two versions of the urn below the inscription are present, the first covered by the second.

240 FINAL PROJECT (*Figure* 197) [9456]
421×*c*.275 mm. Pen, grey wash, traces of chalk. With scale.

The present drawing differs from the finished monument mainly in the treatment of the portrait bust.

Rome, S. Antonio de'Portoghesi, the decoration for the memorial service to King Pedro II of Portugal (1707)

Volume 171 is devoted to 44 drawings connected with the decoration of S. Antonio de' Portoghesi in Rome for the memorial service to King Pedro II of Portugal. The King died in December 1706 and the service took place on 13 September 1707 (Valesio, see below). The volume contains no introduction or explanatory notes, but a description of the decoration, with twelve illustrations, was published in Rome in 1707, *Funerale celebrato nella chiesa di Santo Antonio Della Nazione Portoghese in Roma per la morte del Re di Portogallo Don Pietro Secondo* . . . According to this book the decoration was ordered by King John V, who succeeded to the throne on the death of Pedro; Fontana is said to have been chosen as architect because he had acted for the Portuguese Royal family for some time, and he had been awarded the Portuguese order of Giesù Cristo. The nature of work he had undertaken for Portugal is unknown.

Fontana organised the decoration in the following way. The façade of the church (Fig.199) was draped in black and at first-floor level a portrait medallion of the dead king appeared in the centre with statues of Magnanimity and Valour to the sides. The doors of the church were surmounted by death's heads with the arms of Portugal over the side doors, and medallions above them, one with an eagle looking at the sun, and one with a rainbow. Over the pediment were skeletons holding an hour glass and two figures representing Fame, blowing trumpets. In the nave (Fig.222) the lunette over the entrance had a representation of the globe with figures of the four continents and an inscription held by figures representing Authority and Dominion. Below the cornice the royal arms appeared again, supported by angels, and to each side of the door was an inscribed scroll surmounted by death's heads. The three clerestory windows on each side of the nave (Fig.221) were flanked by figures (twelve in all) symbolizing the countries subject to Portugal, and six square plaques along the cornice of the nave (over the arcades of the side chapels) bore symbols of the benefits of Pedro's reign – a palm tree for Felicity, scales for Justice, a laurel tree for Victory, smoke for Good Fortune, a river for Glory and stars for Watchfulness. Boat-shaped lamps hung from the arcades of the side chapels and medallions attached to the pilasters of the nave were inscribed in allusion to Pedro's victories over the Infidel. Silvered brackets for candles were attached to the nave pilasters, beneath the medallions, and to the pilasters of the crossing. The arch dividing the nave from the crossing (Fig.212) supported a curved tablet, inscribed and draped.

Pedro's personal virtues were the subject of the decoration of the crossing, beginning with the medallions hanging from the arches dividing the crossing from the transepts and choir. These showed the King refusing the Crown, distributing the gold of Brazil, and the Arts and Sciences in procession with his portrait. The catafalque (Fig.211) was circular and placed in the centre of the crossing. The regalia, draped in black, were placed on a low base which was encircled by four pedestals. The pedestals supported figures representing Faith (holding a flame), and Human Charity (accompanied (?) by a pelican). Each pedestal was decorated with reliefs representing ideas associated with these four main virtues and with candles in sockets shaped like cornucopias. Consoles projected to the rear of each pedestal and a large draped skeleton stood upon each, supporting a cylindrical sarcophagus (the *urna*). This was surmounted by a portrait bust of the King in a free-standing frame composed of a snake, enmeshed in olive branches, devouring its tail, in allusion to Eternity and Peace. The bottom part of the sarcophagus was encircled by four reliefs alluding to the piety of the King, who was shown on his knees before an altar of the Virgin (opposite the altar), accompanying the Host carried by a priest to the dying (opposite the nave), sleeping in penitance upon a wooden board, and rewarding converted slaves. Over the sarcophagus was a huge baldacchino in the shape of a royal crown, supported invisibly; it was in fact held up by beams rising from the piers of the crossing and masked by draperies, which were to all appearances held away from the catafalque by *putti*.

The printed text of the funeral contains illustrations of the decoration, engraved by Domenico Franceschini, Giovanni Girolamo Frezza, and Nicola Oddi. All but two are inscribed with Fontana's name as draughtsman; a certain Pietro Razina is given as draughtsman for the two plates (IX and X) which show the four reliefs of the sarcophagus; the drawings connected with these in the Windsor volume (group 5 below) seem clearly to be by Fontana.

The date of the service is given in Valesio's diary as 13 September 1707 (fos 454 and 460). A *relazione* of the funeral but without illustrations is bound with his text (fos 456–9). Valesio mentions in connection with the funeral an ode by Posterla, and gives the estimated cost of the decorations as 7,000 *scudi*, while acknowledging that Fontana's design was considered a success: 'L'inuenzione della machina et apparato è stata opera del Cau.re fontana uniuersalm.te lodata, e la spesa in tutto uedesi ascenderà à $\frac{m}{7}$ scudi.' He reports the dismantling of the 'bel catafalco' on 12 October 1707 (fo.472).

Indeed the funeral decoration of S. Antonio appears to be one of the more successful of such works by Fontana (on its likely importance, see Braham). In its general scheme and in some of the decoration the design is related to that carried out for the memorial service to Leopold I (see above), but the church of S. Antonio with its short nave and spacious crossing was better suited to showing off Fontana's catafalque. The huge crown-shaped baldacchino (Fig.212) appeared to be suspended miraculously in the crossing, with winged *putti* holding back its draperies to reveal the catafalque. The circular sarcophagus also appeared to be suspended beneath the baldacchino, supported only by the arms of the four skeletons. Beneath it was an aperture through which the high altar of the church was visible from the nave.

The Windsor drawings suggest that Fontana had considerably less trouble in designing this scheme of decoration than was the case with the funeral decorations for Leopold I. The main structure of the catafalque appears to have been established from the beginning and the decoration shown in the drawings varies only to a limited extent from that finally carried out. The drawings are arranged below in the seven groups. Many of the sheets are related to the engravings of the printed book, but none can be described with certainty as the originals from which the engravings were made. In cases where the correspondence between the drawing and engraving appears to be extremely close, it is probable that the drawing in question is a copy of one sent by Fontana to the engraver.

The majority of the drawings are laid down on the pages of Volume 171 and many bear numbers in ink which must have been added before the volume was made up. The sequence now runs from no.6 (9370–no.280) to no.36 (9410–no.255), with many interruptions between the two. It was presumably Fontana himself who numbered and arranged the sheets in preparation for the binding of the book; his order is vaguely logical, but it is not apparently worked out with great care.

A sketch of the catafalque occurs in one of Juvarra's albums of drawings (Biblioteca Nazionale, Turin, 59/4, fo.104, inscribed 'Per il funerale del Ré di Portogallo Piero I [*sic*]–'). The existence of this drawing is probably the cause of some scholars mistakenly attributing Fontana's scheme of decoration to Juvarra.

ADDITIONAL BIBLIOGRAPHY:
A. Braham, *Funeral decorations*, with further references.

1 Drawings of the church, showing the catafalque in plan

241 PLAN OF THE INTERIOR (*Figure* 200) [9367]
752×524 mm. Watermark no.9. Pen, coloured washes, some chalk. With scale and a few measurements. Inscribed in chalk: *medaglie n 3* – . . . (?), in reference probably to the medallions hanging in the final decoration from the transept and the choir arches (see Group 6 below).

Guide lines for the shaping of the catafalque and lines of vision from various parts of the church are indicated in chalk, and in yellow and pink wash. Rough sketches in chalk are present on the *verso*, one showing a crown on a globe.

242 LONGITUDINAL SECTION OF THE CHURCH [9368]
526×744 mm. Watermark no.9. Chalk. With scale (numbered in ink).

243 PLAN OF THE CHURCH [9374]
423×280 mm. Laid down. Pen, coloured washes, traces of chalk. With scale. Inscribed in Fontana's hand, top left: *Auanzare il sito p la facciata*, and signed, bottom right: *Carlo C: fontana / D. franceschini.*

The drawing must presumably be related to the engraving on pl.II of the printed book of the funeral, which is signed, like the drawing, by Fontana as draughtsman and Franceschini as engraver. The inscription, upper left, must refer to the need to finish off the façade of the church, which is completed only on one side.

244 PLAN OF THE CHURCH [9402]
424×277 mm. Laid down. Pen, coloured washes, traces of chalk. With scale.

A version of the preceding, with the façade completed.

245 PLAN OF THE CROSSING [9378]
423×281 mm. Laid down. Pen, coloured washes, some chalk. With scale.

A similar plan is given as pl.XI of the printed book of the funeral, engraved by Franceschini.
Copy of the left half of the drawing by Vittone, vol.I, fos 111/2.

2 Plans and sections of the catafalque, showing the scaffolding

246 SECTION OF THE CATAFALQUE AND BALDACCHINO (*Figure* 201) [9391]
426×280 mm. Laid down. Pen, coloured washes, traces of chalk. With scale.

The catafalque and its baldacchino are indicated in blue wash and the wooden scaffolding which supports them in brown wash. The cylindrical sarcophagus is supported by beams rising diagonally from the four pedestals around the catafalque and by an iron framework (shown in dark grey wash) across its base.
Copy by Vittone, vol.II, fo.181.

247 VERSION OF THE PRECEDING [9405]
421×281 mm. Laid down. Pen, coloured washes, traces of chalk. With scale.

248 HALF PLAN AND SECTION OF THE BALDACCHINO (*Figure* 202) [9392]
420×280 mm. Laid down. Pen, coloured washes, traces of chalk. With scale.

A representation on a larger scale of the baldacchino as shown in the two foregoing sections. Beneath it is a half plan of the baldacchino seen from above.

249 VERSION OF THE PRECEDING (1) [9406]
426×278 mm. Laid down. Pen, coloured washes, traces of chalk. With scale.

250 VERSION OF THE PRECEDING (2) [9407]
422×282 mm. Laid down. Pen, coloured washes, traces of chalk. With scale.

251 PLAN OF THE SCAFFOLDING OF THE CATAFALQUE (*Figure* 203) [9389]
342×281 mm. Laid down. Pen, coloured washes, traces of chalk. With scale.

The iron parts of the scaffolding are omitted in the present plan.

252 VERSION OF THE PRECEDING [9403]
422×280 mm. Laid down. Pen, coloured washes, traces of chalk. With scale.

253 SECTION OF THE CATAFALQUE [9404]
427×280 mm. Laid down. Pen, coloured washes, some chalk. With scale.

A representation on a larger scale of the catafalque as it is shown in sections 246 and 247 above.

254 SECTION OF THE CATAFALQUE, SHOWING SCULPTURAL DECORATION (*Figure* 204) [9390]
420×279 mm. Laid down. Pen, coloured washes, traces of chalk. With scale and index of letters.

The drawing corresponds with the preceding but it shows parts of the sculptural decorations which were to be supported on the scaffolding. The key to the index is given on a sheet laid down on the reverse side of the drawing: *Indice dell'Armatura qui seguente de legni che sosteneua:/no la Machina ò Vrna sotto la Corona,* followed by explanations of the letters.

3 Three early sketches connected with the preceding group

255 ELEVATION OF A PEDESTAL, SHOWING SCAFFOLDING AND SOME DECORATION (*Figure* 205) [9410]
C.427×*c*.285 mm. Laid down. Pen, yellow and brown wash, some chalk. With measurements and sums. A three line inscription is present on the *verso*.

A beam partly of wood and partly of iron (indicated in dark brown wash) runs horizontally beneath the sarcophagus in the present drawing. In the absence of the diagonal beams which Fontana later adopted (see preceding group) the skeleton has been left undraped.

256 PLAN OF THE SCAFFOLDING OF THE CATAFALQUE (*Figure* 206) [9409]
312×*c*.245 mm. Laid down. Pen, grey and yellow wash, some chalk. With scale and measurement. Several lines of inscription appear to be present on the *verso*.

Just over half of the plan is shown. The drawing corresponds in its general character with the preceding. The structure of the scaffold is slightly less complex than in plans 251 and 252 above.

257 HALF PLAN AND HALF SECTION OF THE BALDACCHINO (*Figure* 207) [9408]
502×*c*.375 mm. Laid down. Pen, brown wash, traces of chalk. With scale, index, measurements and notes referring to measurements.

4 Elevations and perspective views of the catafalque

258 ELEVATION OF THE CATAFALQUE (*Figure* 208) [9379]
420×278 mm. Laid down. Pen, grey wash, traces of chalk. With scale.

The catafalque is close in its general character to that finally constructed, but there are many discrepancies in detail.

259 PLAN AND ELEVATION OF A PEDESTAL (*Figure* 209) [9393]
421×278 mm. Laid down. Pen, grey wash, traces of chalk. With scale.

The pedestal is of the same plain type as those of the preceding drawing. The part of the pedestal beneath the skeleton shows a *pentimento* whereby a base in the shape of a console is substituted for a rectangular base.

260 STUDIES OF CANDLE HOLDERS (*Figure* 210) [9394]
422×280 mm. Laid down. Pen, grey wash, traces of chalk.

The type of candle shown on the right, on a base resembling a cornucopia, was used for the catafalque in the final design. Consoles like those supporting the candles in the main study on the present sheet were used finally for the candle decoration on the walls of the church.

261 PERSPECTIVE VIEW OF THE CATAFALQUE AND BALDACCHINO IN THE CROSSING (*Figure* 212) [9380]
477 (irregular)×277 mm. Two sheets joined horizontally. Laid down. Pen, grey wash, traces of chalk.

The drawing corresponds with plate XII in the printed book of the funeral service, engraved by Oddi and Franceschini. Corrections to the drawing of the sarcophagus and of the decoration of the chancel are executed on pieces of paper pasted on to the basic sheet.

262 VERSION OF THE PRECEDING [9381]
479×284 mm. Laid down. Two sheets joined horizontally. Pen, grey wash, traces of chalk.

263 PERSPECTIVE VIEW OF THE CATAFALQUE (*Figure* 211) [9382]
525×383 mm. Four sheets joined. Watermark no.13. Pen and brown ink, grey wash, traces of chalk.

5 Drawings of the reliefs on the sarcophagus

Each of the four compositions is shown once in a simple ruled frame and two are also shown in more elaborate frames (nos 267, 269). Each drawing is trapezoidal in shape and executed in pen and grey wash. The four reliefs are illustrated on pls IX and X of the book of the funeral, drawn by Pietro Razina and engraved by Frezza. The compositions in all the present drawings are shown in the reverse sense to the engravings. They are all close in style to Fontana (cf. the following group), and they could not be safely attributed to Razina.

264 KING PEDRO ACCOMPANIES THE HOST (*Figure* 213) [9383]
154×218 (top edge) mm.

The composition was that seen from the nave of the church.

265 KING PEDRO KNEELS IN WORSHIP BEFORE A STATUE OF THE VIRGIN AND CHILD (*Figure* 214) [9384]
153×212 (top edge) mm.

The composition was that seen from the choir of the church.

266 KING PEDRO ASLEEP ON A WOODEN BOARD (*Figure* 215) [9387]
153×212 (top edge) mm.

The composition was that seen from one of the transepts of the church.

267 VERSION OF THE PRECEDING [9385]
173×235 (top edge) mm.

The drawing is inscribed within a ruled frame of many lines, as is the corresponding engraving on pl.X of the printed text. A winged hour-glass is roughly drawn in chalk at the base.

268 KING PEDRO DISTRIBUTES REWARDS TO CONVERTED SLAVES (*Figure* 216) [9388]
154×215 (top edge) mm.

The composition was that seen from one of the transepts of the church.

269 VERSION OF THE PRECEDING [9386]
173×242 (top edge) mm.

Like no.267 above the present composition has a ruled frame of many lines, like the corresponding engraving on pl.X of the printed text.

6 Drawings of the roundels suspended in the crossing

The three roundels are illustrated on pls VI to VIII of the printed text, with Fontana named as draughtsman and Frezza as engraver. In the engravings and the drawings the arch above the medallion is included and the draperies behind the medallions. The drawings are all laid down, and executed in pen and grey wash with traces of chalk.

270 THE ARTS AND SCIENCES WITH A PORTRAIT OF KING PEDRO (*Figure* 217) [9395]
227×332 mm.

The composition was that used for the medallion to the left side of the catafalque (pl.VIII of the printed text). It is here represented in the same sense as the engraving, but the drapery is in the reverse sense.

271 VERSION OF THE PRECEDING [9396]
232×325 mm.

In this composition the drapery also corresponds with that of the engraving.
Copy by Vittone, vol.I, fo.108.

272 HERCULES (?) WITH A PORTRAIT OF KING PEDRO, ACCOMPANIED BY THE ARTS AND SCIENCES (*Figure* 218) [9399]
225×325 mm.

The composition is probably Fontana's first idea for the medallion represented in the preceding two drawings. It corresponds with one he used for the funeral decorations for the Emperor Leopold (see above, no.190). The movement in the composition takes place in the opposite sense to that in the two preceding drawings.

273 KING PEDRO REFUSES THE CROWN (*Figure* 219) [9397]
230×348 mm.

The composition (pl.VI of the printed text) was that used either for the medallion suspended from the arch of the choir (according to the text) or for that to the right of the catafalque (according to the caption of the engraving). It is in the same sense as the engraving.

274 VERSION OF THE PRECEDING (IN REVERSE) [9398]
225×338 mm.

275 PEDRO DISTRIBUTING THE GOLD OF BRAZIL (*Figure* 220) [9400]
275×329 mm.

This composition (pl.VII of the printed text) was that used either for the medallion to the right of the catafalque (according to the text), or for that of the choir arch (according to the caption on the engraving). It is in the same sense as the engraving. A suggestion for enlarging the scroll beneath the medallion is roughly indicated in chalk and ink.

276 VERSION OF THE PRECEDING (IN REVERSE) [9401]
230×331 mm.

7 Drawings for the decoration of the nave and the façade

277 ELEVATION OF A WALL OF THE NAVE [9375]
426×318 mm. (including strips added at each side). Laid down. Pen, grey wash, traces of chalk.

This appears to be the earliest of the drawings of the nave decoration. It differs from the final decoration (pl.V of the printed text) mainly in the absence of the square panels affixed to the cornice. The presence of medallions at both sides of the present sheet would appear to suggest that the drawing refers to both sides of the nave.

278 ELEVATION OF THE LEFT WALL OF THE NAVE (*Figure* 221) [9376]
328×415 mm. Two sheets joined horizontally. Laid down. Pen, grey wash, traces of chalk. With scale.

The project differs from the final scheme of decoration mainly in the absence of the medallion on the pier of the crossing, and in the treatment of the figures standing over the cornice at clerestory level.
Copy of part of the drawing by Vittone, vol.I, fos 111/2.

279 VERSION OF THE PRECEDING [9377]
327×440 mm. Laid down. Pen, grey wash, traces of chalk.

The figures standing on the cornice correspond more closely with the engraved illustration than those of the preceding drawing.

280 ELEVATION OF THE ENTRANCE WALL OF THE NAVE (detail, *Figure* 222) [9370]
422×276 mm. Laid down. Pen, grey wash, traces of chalk. Signed, lower right: *Carlo fontana.*

The drawing corresponds, despite slight differences, with the engraving on pl.III of the printed text, executed by Oddi.
Copy by Vittone, vol.I, fos 111/2.

281 VERSION OF THE PRECEDING [9371]
425×283 mm. (torn, bottom left). Laid down. Pen, grey wash, traces of chalk. With scale.

A radiant sun is lightly sketched in the doorway of the church.

282 STUDY OF THE LUNETTE OVER THE DOORWAY: THE GLOBE WITH THE FOUR CONTINENTS, DOMINION AND AUTHORITY (*Figure* 223) [9373]
202×308 (bottom edge) mm. Laid down. Pen, grey wash, traces of chalk.

It differs from the engraving on pl.IV of the printed text, executed by Franceschini, mainly in the treatment of the signs of the Zodiac on the rainbow at the top of the composition.

283 VERSION OF THE PRECEDING (IN REVERSE) [9372]
202×311 (bottom edge) mm. Laid down. Pen, grey wash, traces of chalk.

The present drawing corresponds more closely with Franceschini's engraving than the foregoing; it is in the reverse sense to both.

284 ELEVATION OF THE MAIN FAÇADE (*Figure* 199) [9369]
526×383 mm. Watermark no.4(?). Pen, grey wash, traces of chalk. With scale.

The decoration of the façade corresponds closely with that shown on pl.I of the printed text, engraved by Frezza and Franceschini.
Copy of the left half by Vittone, vol.I, fo.109.

A manuscript on the Colosseum church project (between 1700 and 1707)

A volume in the Sir John Soane Museum (AL/7A) contains Carlo Fontana's drawings pertaining to the Colosseum, most of which served for the engravings of his "L'Anfiteatro Flavio" published posthumously in 1725 (The Hague), but ready in manuscript before 1696 (cf. E. Coudenhove-Erthal, pp.84f.). The volume also includes the drawings for the church to be erected in honour of the martyrs in the Arena of the amphitheatre. A short text in Volume 176 at Windsor is an early draft for the introduction to this book (see Hager, *Colosseum*, 1973).

Undated projects for altars: Venice, S. Maria dei Frari (?), an altar project

Drawing 285, in Volume 179, is a project for an altar containing a sculptural representation of the Crucifixion. The project has two scales, one labelled *Piedi Veneti*, and the project is therefore likely to be one designed by Fontana for a Venetian patron. The patron and the site for which the design was made are uncertain (for Fontana's other Venetian patrons see below, projects for a Casino for the Veneto). The drawing looks different from Fontana's other drawings at Windsor because the paper on which it is executed is brown and faded. In this it resembles one other sheet, one of Fontana's early projects for the Baptistry of S. Peter's (no.37), which is also laid down in Volume 179. It is possible that the two drawings are approximately contemporary, in which case the altar project would date from the early 1690's.

Postscript: The altar bears a close resemblance to the first altar on the left in the nave of the Frari.

285 ELEVATION OF THE ALTAR (*Figure* 224) [9915]
394 × *c*.242 (irregular) mm. Laid down. Pen, grey wash. With two scales, the lower one in ink and inscribed: *Piedi: Veneti nº: 20,* the upper one in chalk and probably of *palmi romani*.

The altar is in the shape of a sarcophagus and it has a decoration of martyrs' palms.
Copy of the right half of the drawing by Vittone, vol.I, fo.48.

Manduria (?), plan of an altar for Cardinal Ferrari

A single drawing in Volume 176 at Windsor is a plan of an altar, which is accompanied by a short manuscript, and entitled on the preceding page: 'Per il Card. Ferrari / p. la sua patria'. The patron referred to in this title was presumably Cardinal Tommaso Maria Ferrari (1649–1716), a native of Manduria, a small town in Apulia (Guarnacci, col.435ff.), and the altar was possibly commissioned for the cathedral in this town. Ferrari was created a Cardinal in 1695 and the present project may have been intended to commemorate this event.

The text and the accompanying plan (Fig.225) must be copies of those sent to the Cardinal, and in the text Fontana speaks of an elevation (*alzata*), of which he apparently had no copy to include with the plan. At the start Fontana explains that the narrowness of the 'Navata laterale', where the altar was to stand, prevented him from giving the altar any great projection. In elevation the structure was twice as high as it was wide, with a space left in the centre for a painting. Statues were to be included and a column at each side supporting an inverted broken pediment (?) ('frontispizii piegati') enclosing a circular window. Fontana suggests that if permission for the piercing of such a window was withheld, then a medallion could be substituted. Alternative positions are suggested for the coat of arms.

286 PLAN OF THE ALTAR (*Figure* 225) [9739]
C.215 × 303 mm. Watermark no.6. Pen, yellow and grey wash, traces of chalk. With scale and index letters *A* and *B*.

The drawing forms the first half of a double sheet wrapped around the text and folded in the binding of the volume. The altar table is inscribed with the letters 'A' and 'B', referring to Fontana's text. Copy by Vittone, vol.I, fo.41.

Design for an altar with two martyrs

Volume 179, which contains the drawings for the Baptistry of S. Peter's, the rebuilding of S. Spirito dei Napolitani, the church project of Cardinal Negroni of 1697, etc., also includes two designs for an altar with a reliquary sarcophagus over the *mensa* (nos 287, 288). Like Bernini's tabernacle in the Cappella del S. Sacramento in S. Peter's, it has two kneeling angels, a motive which Fontana had already taken up in his plans for the Baptistry of S. Peter's (cf. especially Bonanni, pl.41). In spite of the differences in proportions, these two drawings must be alternatives for the same altarpiece. The flanking figures – a young saint wearing a tunic and a bearded soldier martyr, both without attributes and so unidentifiable – are the same, and the medallions on no.287, with the bust of a female saint holding a branch, are repeated in the second design. The rounded top of the whole arrangement suggests that it was to be placed at the end of a barrel-vaulted choir or transept.

The usual position of a reliquary sarcophagus is below the *mensa*, and the present arrangement is therefore exceptional. It goes back to a mediaeval tradition, but a more recent example is Pietro da Cortona's high altar in SS. Luca e Martina, where the figure of S. Martina is placed above the *mensa*, though in a kind of open reliquary niche. Fontana's solution is closer to Andrea Pozzo's design for the altar of the Blessed Lodovico Gonzaga in S. Ignazio (completed in the Holy Year 1700; cf. *Prospectiva Pictorum*, Rome, 1700, II, fig.65), which it may actually have inspired. It is not possible at present to identify the church for which this altar was designed.

The two drawings, of which no.287 is probably the earlier, contain elements from both Bernini and Pietro da Cortona. There is some resemblance to the altar in the right transept of SS. Luca e Martina, which had been converted into a family chapel by Lazzaro Baldi in 1680, and in this connection it is worth noting that Carlo Fontana intended to erect an altar in SS. Luca e Martina, and that permission was given on 24 November 1697 'da fabricarui una Cappella da erigersi da Sua Sig.ia à proprie spese incontro à quella di S. Lazaro, il qual sito è in stato rustico e uacante nel modo e forma, che parerà, e piacerà alla no'ra Accad.a . . .'. The material was to be 'pietre dure e mischi', but Fontana was permitted to choose his patron saint (cf. Noehles, *SS. Luca e Martina*, pp.114, 360, doc.146). For reasons unknown to us this project was never carried out. The altar shown in the drawing would not actually fit the position in SS. Luca e Martina, but it may have been influenced by designs for the latter. A dating about 1700 would be confirmed by the connection between the drawings and other works by Fontana.

287 ELEVATION (1) (*Figure* 226) [9912]
413×271 mm. Watermark no.7. Pen, grey wash, traces of chalk.

The design of the window above the altar and the area around it is executed on a sheet pasted on the basic drawing.
Copy by Vittone, vol.I, fo.19.

288 ELEVATION (2) (*Figure* 227) [9911]
413×271 mm. Watermark no.7. Pen, grey wash, traces of chalk. With scale.

France, project for a cloistered building for Cardinal de Forbin Janson

Five drawings in Volume 170 at Windsor (three plans and two sections) form part of a project that was apparently commissioned for a site in France, as is revealed by the inscription on the *verso* of plan no.290: *Em.mo di Gianson / p(er) / francia*. The 'Em.mo di Gianson' referred to in this inscription must be Cardinal Toussaint de Forbin Janson (1634–1713), the French *chargé d'affaires* at the papal court in the mid–1690's and early 1700's. Fontana's drawings may be copies of sheets sent to France, or they could represent a preliminary project that formed the basis for a final design of which Fontana kept no record.

Fontana provides in his project for a large block with a square court in the centre surrounded by a cloister or covered gallery at ground-floor level, which is surmounted by two tiers of *loggie* along the sides of the court. The block is of three main stories, but includes a mezzanine over the first floor and an attic storey over the second floor. Most of the space is made over to rows of small cells. The block itself is roughly square, but with projections, or pavilions, of varying size at three of the corners. It was apparently intended to form an extension to an existing building, of which the side walls are indicated in the plans (Figs 228, 229) in buff wash to the right of Fontana's building. The walls of the older building appear to have abutted on the new block at ground and first-floor level. The existing building may have been a relatively low medieval structure, with corner towers of different sizes that are matched by the projections at the corners of Fontana's block. They constitute an irregularity that Fontana must in normal circumstances have hoped to avoid. The deepest of Fontana's corner projections lies to the left of the main entrance and here are disposed the largest rooms of his block, those presumably destined for communal use and as the private appartments of the head of the community.

The inscription on drawing 290 gives precise information neither about the site, nor about the date of Fontana's project. Forbin Janson came from near Marseilles and he had been made Bishop of Beauvais in 1679 (C. Doyen, *Histoire de la ville de Beauvais*, 1842, II, pp.156ff.; Guarnacci, 1751, I, col.339ff.); it is possible that Fontana's building was destined to form an extension to a monastery or convent in these neighbourhoods. It seems doubtful that his designs were carried out. Created a Cardinal in 1690 (Pastor, Eng. ed., XXXII, p.543), Forbin Janson succeeded Cardinal d'Estrées as French *chargé d'affaires* at the papal court in October 1693 (ibid., p.601). He was replaced four years later by Cardinal de Bouillon and left Rome in July 1697 (ibid.). He was in personal contact with Fontana in 1694, when the architect gave him a presentation copy of the *Tempio Vaticano* destined for Louis XIV (*Correspondance des Directeurs*, II, pp.10, 21f., 36f.). Forbin returned to Rome for the conclave of 1700 (Pastor, op.cit., XXXIII, p.3) and he seems to have remained there until 1706 (*Corr. des Directeurs*, I, p.xiv). Fontana's drawings are perhaps more likely to date from the mid-1690's; they are alike in style and character to the projects for the Sternberg palace in Prague, datable to 1696/1700, which immediately precede them in Volume 170 (see below).

289 GROUND-FLOOR PLAN (*Figure* 228) [9348]
480×371 mm. Watermark no.7. Pen, grey and buff wash, traces of chalk.

The main vestibule, articulated with columns, leads to a cloister of five by five bays, with concave corner piers. Sight lines across the court are drawn in buff wash. Walls, also in buff wash, are indicated to the right of the main axis of the cloister and they presumably indicate the positions of buildings already existing on the site. A large block projects on the corner of Fontana's building to the left of the main entrance, and contains the largest rooms in Fontana's plan – each was to be vaulted as is shown by the section no.293 below. On the diagonally opposite corner the main staircase forms a small projection and on the intervening corner a smaller projection occurs, containing a wash room or lavatory. A curious *pentimento* is present in all the outer walls of the plan, except those adjacent to the existing building, whereby the wall appears to be halved in thickness; the narrower wall may refer (see the sections below) to the tapering of the wall from first-floor level upwards.

290 FIRST-FLOOR PLAN (*Figure* 229) [9349]
481×371 mm. Watermark no.7. Pen, grey and yellow wash, traces of chalk. Inscribed on the *verso*: *Em.mo di | Gianson | p | francia.*

At first-floor level the plan is made over for the most part to small cells. The large projecting corner block to the left of the main entrance contains relatively large rooms. The three projecting corners of the cloister block are linked by dotted ink lines emphasized with grey wash, and these perhaps represent projected terraces. The wall adjacent to the existing buildings has window openings for part of its length.

291 SECOND-FLOOR PLAN [9350]
482×370 mm. Pen, grey and yellow wash, traces of chalk.

According to the two sections below, Fontana's block was to have a mezzanine over the first floor, extending over the whole plan with the exception of the two open sides of the court *loggie*. It corresponded in plan with that of the first floor and was almost equally high. According to the section no.293, the second floor presented some slight differences in plan, mainly in the organization of the block projecting to the left of the main entrance, and these reveal that the present plan is that for the second floor. At this level windows are pierced in the wall adjacent to the existing buildings throughout its length.

292 LONGITUDINAL SECTION (1) (*Figure* 230) [9351]
371×480 mm. Pen, grey wash, traces of chalk.

The section is drawn on an axis parallel to the main entrance axis, not through the entrance itself. It shows in elevation the three tiers of arcades on the left side of the court and the side elevation of the large projection on the left of the main entrance. The masonry of the ground-floor walls is considerably thicker than that of the floors above. The ground floor has two tiers of windows, although there is no evidence on any of the other drawings of a mezzanine floor at this level. Decoration throughout the building is reduced for the most part to pilaster strips, plain mouldings and panelling.
Copy of the left half of the drawing by Vittone, vol.II, fo.147.

293 LONGITUDINAL SECTION (2) (*Figure* 231) [9352]
371×481 mm. Watermark no.7. Pen and brown ink, traces of chalk.

The section is taken on the centre line of the passages running behind the court arcade to the left of the entrance axis. The section continues to the left to include the block projecting on the left of the main entrance. A series of doors at attic level suggests that further cells were to be inserted beneath the roof.

III

Secular Buildings

Projects for a Casino in the Veneto (1689)

Volume 176 at Windsor contains seven drawings for a Casino, together with a copy of a letter of 5 March 1689, in which the design is explained to a certain Abbate Ugolini. On a blank page preceding the drawings is the slightly puzzling inscription: 'Casino per Ventia' [*sic*], which presumably denotes that the project was intended for a site in the neighbourhood of Venice. This seems to have been Contini's reading of the title which is given in his hand list under Volume no.9, *Casino di Venetia*.

The project, one of Fontana's most attractive and influential designs, is shown in two stages of development. A sheaf of folded pages bound into the volume contains five drawings for a building consisting of a hexagonal central hall, with entrances on three sides and projecting T-shaped blocks on the other three (Figs 232 to 234). According to the section and elevation drawings, the projecting blocks were of three floors over a basement, while the central hexagon rose above them and a row of attic windows was visible below a roof. The *piano nobile* of the hexagon was level with the top storey of the wings and balconies joining the wings at this height were inserted over the entrances. Below the balconies there was a hexagonal corridor linking the three wings at mezzanine level.

The second design is shown in only two plans (Figs 236, 237), both apparently of the ground floor and differing only slightly from each other. In these the central part of the villa is circular, the projecting blocks are wider, and the inset bays between them curve inwards. This design apparently corresponds closely with the project described in Fontana's letter and it may be assumed that the two plans formed the basis for the final drawings, sent off with the original of the letter.

Fontana explains at the start of his letter that the project is based on multiples of three – three projecting blocks ('tomi'), each with three floors divided into three rooms. The central entrance was circular (not hexagonal as in the early project) and the six niches lining its walls were to be used for parking carriages (stables and horses are not mentioned). The basement area was reserved for kitchens, etc. The *scala maestra* (a curved double staircase, according to the plans, which was placed behind one of the inward curving façades) led to a circular corridor at mezzanine level, and to the main *salone* of the first floor. This was decorated with columns and six niches 'p(er) uso di Cappella, Libreria, . . .' etc. There were also three doors which led to *loggie* 'p ottener l'amenità della uista'. The *loggie* were presumably balconies between the three T-shaped blocks and they would probably have been supported from below by the ceiling of the circular corridor of the mezzanine. The rooms in the principal floor of the three wings consisted of a *sala*, a bedroom and a gallery for pictures, and each had also a *gabinetto* and a private staircase leading out of the villa. The *salone*, finally, was vaulted and lit from windows 'nel sesto della uolta'.

In the final paragraphs of his letter Fontana mentions a possible enlargement of the scale of the villa (which is measured, he says, in *palmi romani*) but he gives warning that all parts must be enlarged to the same scale: the creation of the 'armonia delle parte' is the most difficult of the architect's tasks. In conclusion he recommends the design to the Abbate and an unnamed Cavaliere, saying that he believes it to be unique ('unica, e non più uista') and not expensive because it is so compact in character ('tutti li muri operano a più cose').

The letter is reticent about the Cavaliere for whom the villa was designed, and his connection with the Abbate Ugolini (his agent ?) is not made clear. However, Fontana is known to have worked for at least one Venetian ambassador to Rome, namely Niccolò Erizzo, for whom he designed a monument in S. Marco, Rome, for a dead son, Francesco (Coudenhove-Erthal, pl.33). The ambassador to Rome in 1689 was a certain Cavaliere Girolamo Lando, whose office lasted from 1684 to 1691, and it is possible that it was for him that the villa was designed (Barozzi and Berchet, pp 405/7). Other known Venetian patrons of Fontana, apart from Erizzo, included members of the Valier family (see above, the tomb of Doge

Valier). A connection between the present design and the family of the Venetian pope, Alexander VIII (Ottoboni), seems doubtful, since his election took place in October of 1689 and Fontana's letter is dated March.

Fontana was probably justified in claiming that his design was 'unica, e non più uista'. The plan has more resemblance to the kind of elaborate pedestal found in his work than to any existing villa plan (there are analogies, for example, with the base of the Fontana di Trevi in Fontana's design of 1706, see below). Fontana may have regarded the commission as an opportunity to experiment in an unfamiliar context, and thus to produce a modern Roman equivalent of the Venetian villa design. The project appears to have remained unexecuted, although the drawings themselves must have been known. Several copies (of the first design) occur in the Vittone volumes in Paris (Fig.235), and these were later engraved by Vittone for his *Istruzioni diverse*... (vol.II, pl.XXXII). This is a case where the interest of Vittone in Fontana's projects is fully understandable, and the design has recently been taken in error as an independent work of the Piedmontese architect (Portoghesi, p.171). Fontana's drawings also appear to have suggested the subject of the Concorso Clementino (first class) of 1705: a 'palazzo in villa per tre personaggi', which was won by Juvarra and Fontana's nephew Carlo Stefano. Triangular plans became of increasing importance during the course of the 18th century (see Arndt), and what is of special interest in the case of Fontana's project is the adaptation made by Carlo Stefano Fontana in a church project of 1721/2 (Accad. di S. Luca, Cartella Y., nos 275/6; Figs 238/9). The church is based on the second stage of Fontana's design (mezzanine level), and it refers at the same time to the triangular *impresa* of the Academy. In two later projects for the Curia Innocenziana (nos 345/6) Fontana employs, as in the present drawings, angles of 120 degrees in the organization of the plan, and in this respect the design can be related to later 18th-century buildings like Juvarra's palace of Stupinigi.

ADDITIONAL BIBLIOGRAPHY:

H. and K. Arndt in *Beiträge zur Kunstgeschichte, Eine Festgabe für Heinz Rudolf Rosemann*, 1960.

N. Barozzi and G. Berchet, *Le relazione degli stati europei lette al Senato dagli ambasciatori veneziani nel secolo XVII*, ser.III, vol.II (Rome), 1878.

H. Hager, *Juvarra*, p.56, n.135.

W. Oechslin, in *Barocco europeo, barocco italiano, barocco salentino* (*Atti del Congresso internazionale sul Barocco*), Lecce, 1969, pp.141ff.

R. Pommer, *Eighteenth Century Architecture in Piedmont*, 1967, pp.69, 75f., n.27.

P. Portoghesi, *Bernardo Vittone*, 1966.

The first project

The drawings of the early stage measure approximately 270×200 mm. Nearby the drawings is a rough sketch plan, which is included in the catalogue below, although it is probably not related to the drawings for the villa. The copy of Fontana's letter was originally attached to drawing no.298 (9708) and it is written on half sheets of approximately the same size as those containing the early drawings for the villa. It clearly refers, however, not to the first, but to the later project.

294 GROUND-FLOOR PLAN [9711]
Chalk. With annotations in ink.

The central hexagon is labelled *Entron.e o Portico*. Two of the wings have three rooms labelled *Stanza*, and the third contains the main staircase together with three rooms labelled *Cucina Dispensa* and *Pasticiaria*. In the later project these services were relegated to the basement.

295 GROUND-FLOOR PLAN (*Figure* 232) [9712]
Pen, grey wash, some chalk. With two scales, one partly erased.

A finished version of the foregoing, without inscriptions. A chapel has been added in one of the projecting wings. One of the inset entrance bays is overdrawn roughly with curved chalk lines, incorporating on one side a double flighted staircase – a precise anticipation of the changes made in the later project. The drawing is exceptional in the present group in its finished appearance and in having a scale.
Two copies of the ground-floor plan by Vittone, vol.I, fo.68/9 and vol.II, fo.174 (Fig.235).

296 PLAN AT MEZZANINE LEVEL [9710]
Watermark no.14. Chalk and grey wash.

The plan shows a corridor passing around the villa on the exterior of the central hexagon, linking the projecting wings by sections passing over the entrances, and accessible from the main staircase. An altar is introduced here in the same position as that in the preceding ground-floor plan.
Copy by Vittone, vol.II, fo.174 (Fig.235).

297 SECTION (*Figure* 233) [9709]
Watermark no.14. Chalk and grey wash.

The area of the section over the entrance bay (right) appears to have been reworked by Fontana to clarify the construction of the mezzanine corridor and the covered *loggia* (?) at first-floor level. The section reveals that both floors of the central hexagon were to be surmounted by six-part vaults.

298 ELEVATION (*Figure* 234) [9708]
Chalk and grey wash.

The elevation appears to correspond with the plans except in the area above the entrance (centre) where the mezzanine corridor seems to be missing (it is clear from the plan no.296 that the design of this corridor, which was essential to the plan and certainly a feature of the final project, caused Fontana a good deal of trouble). The present drawing is difficult to read in the centre at first-floor level, but there appears to be a balcony opening from the *salone*, supported on a low vault. The main entrance below is placed at the summit of a ramp which slopes away to each side revealing the windows of the basement. The ground-floor walls slope inwards as they rise.
Copy by Vittone, vol.II, fo.174 (Fig.235).

299 SKETCH PLAN [9713]
Chalk.

A rough drawing on the *verso* of the sheet following the plan 295. It shows a figure based on a square with a semi-circular projection on each side. A group of fountains is perhaps indicated, but Fontana's letter makes no reference to the grounds of the villa and it is perhaps unlikely that the sketch has any connection with the adjacent drawings.

The later project

The later project, based on the chalk sketch in plan 295 above and corresponding with the building described in Fontana's letter, is illustrated in two closely-related plans. Both contain features mentioned in the letter as being at first-floor level, but the plans are both apparently at ground level. This is shown by the extreme width of the openings from the central circular room to the exterior and the absence of any indication, except single dotted lines, of the mezzanine corridor and the first-floor balconies.

300 GROUND-FLOOR PLAN (*Figure* 236) [9706]
298 × 210 mm. Watermark no.15. Pen, grey wash, some chalk. Inscribed: *Non entra con li altri/3 seguenti* (perhaps referring to the drawings to be sent off).

The curved façade of the main entrance conceals the double *scala maestra*. The central room is circular with six niches and six doors lining the circumference. Three of the niches contain spiral staircases (roughly drawn) and one contains an altar. In the letter the *cappella* of the Casino is described as occupying one of the niches of the first-floor *salone*, and the spiral stairs (as in the following drawing) were incorporated in the projecting blocks. The axes of the plan and the curves on which it is based are indicated with dotted lines; the concave façades are formed by circles equal in diameter to the central room of the Casino.

301 GROUND-FLOOR PLAN (*Figure* 237) [9707]
298 × 210 mm. Pen and brown ink, grey wash, traces of chalk. With scale.

The circular entrance in the basic design was ringed with free-standing columns. On a circular flap pasted down in the centre of the plan heavy piers projecting from the walls are substituted for the columns. The letter mentions columns as being a feature of the first-floor *salone*, not of the entrance below, and the present drawing suggests that this idea had also been considered (and rejected) for the ground floor. In its final state the present plan probably corresponded very closely (if not exactly) with the final design.

Civitavecchia, the aqueduct (1692–1702)

The start of Fontana's work on the restoration of the Roman aqueduct of Civitavecchia, the *acqua trajana*, is recorded in a single drawing at Windsor (Fig.242), which is bound together with two short texts in Volume 176 (Contini, vol.9. 'Forma di Ciuita Vecchia'). This section of the volume is entitled on the preceding blank sheet: 'Struczione del Cond di Ciuita Vecchia / li 10 luglio 1692'. Many further drawings connected with Fontana's work on the aqueduct are preserved in one of the Fontana volumes at the British Museum (Contini, volume 1) and these were probably intended as illustrations in a book which Fontana hoped to publish, 'Il Libro della Toscana antica, con la narrativa della Condottura dell'Acqua Trajana a Civita Vecchia'. This book was apparently never printed but it is mentioned as forthcoming in Fontana's *Utilissimo trattato dell'acque correnti* (1696). In 1699 Fontana published an engraving showing a number of views of the aqueduct and bearing the title *Veduta de nuovi aquedotti di Civitavecchia delineata dal Cavalier Carlo Fontana, ingegniere* . . . (figs 276/7 in Donati, who mentions the existence of further drawings).

Fontana was working at Civitavecchia under the direction of Bernini during the papacy of Pope Alexander VII (cf. the drawing for the arsenal in Coudenhove-Erthal, fig.6), and he apparently undertook some work on the aqueduct at this time (reference in his book *Antio e sua antichità* (1711) noted by Donati). The complete restoration of the aqueduct was begun in 1692 (*chirografo* of Innocent XII, 24 May 1692; see Calisse, pp.482ff.). The moving spirit behind the idea of restoring, and where necessary rebuilding, the Roman aqueduct was apparently Giuseppe Rocchi, a prominent citizen of Civitavecchia, who supervised the work. The engineer chosen to carry out the work was Ferdinando Padrone, and the papers at Windsor provide information about Fontana's relationship at this time with both Padrone and Rocchi. In 1694 the Pope sent Cardinal Negroni (for Fontana's other connections with this Cardinal see above, pp.69f.) to inspect the work (Calisse, p.484, n.2), and he himself paid a visit to Civitavecchia, the first papal visit for many years, in 1696 (Pastor, Eng. ed., XXXII, p.580; Calisse, pp.485ff.). This visit is described in the journal of P. Campello della Spina, and an illustration of Fontana presenting his project for the aqueduct to the Pope on this occasion is included in his engraving of 1699. The Pope's inspection of the aqueduct is recorded by Campello and he describes (p.100) how on 1 June 1696 Fontana interrupted the Pope at table with the news that all the bridges of the aqueduct had been completed. In the year when Fontana's engraving was printed there was published a written account of the work: *Perizia fatta d'ordine della S. Congregatione . . . sopra l'acquedotto che fa fare il Sig. Ferdinando Padrone per condurre l'acqua dentro la città di Civitavecchia*.

On the succession of Pope Clement XI, Cardinal Pamphili, who had been in charge of work being carried out at Porto d'Anzio, was appointed to supervise the completion of the aqueduct (Calisse, p.489; Montalto, pp.409ff.). At this time the architect Antonio Bufalini appears to have taken over from Fontana (Montalto, pp.412f.) and this may be the reason why Pascoli (II, p.545) gives the aqueduct as a work by Fontana carried out by another architect. The engineer appointed at this time was Filippo Leti (see the Granary, below). The aqueduct was completed in 1702, water running to the port on 22 November (inscription in Frangipani, p.257 (3); Montalto, p.542, n.28) and a commemorative medal was issued in 1703 (Guarnacci, col.373/4, no.XVI).

The aqueduct of Civitavecchia must have occupied a good deal of Fontana's time in the 1690's. He mentions it as one of the four most important tasks undertaken for the Holy See for which he had received no payment (Misciatelli, p.253). As well as the drawings and papers at Windsor and in the British Museum and those noted by Donati, others are recorded in the Inventory of Cardinal Pamphili of 1725 (Montalto, p.412). The first of the Windsor papers is a list of instructions worked out by Fontana and Patrone [*sic*] which were sent to Giuseppe Rocchi to be passed to Patrone for the guidance of the workmen. This is dated 10 July 1692, two months after the *chirografo* of Innocent XII. The second text is a copy of a letter of 16 July 1692 sent to Fontana by Rocchi to thank him for his instructions.

Fontana lists seventeen rules to be observed in the reconstruction of the aqueduct, both when its course lay at ground level and when it crossed valleys. He mentions several general points – that the remains of the *condotto antico* should be used where possible etc. – but the instructions deal mainly with engineering problems. These are illustrated in the accompanying drawing (no.302) which represents a section through the aqueduct as it passes through a cutting.

Three further drawings at Windsor that are apparently connected with various stages of the building of the aqueduct are included in the present section of the catalogue. The first is a project by Fontana for a fountain in the harbour wall of Civitavecchia (Fig.240). This is probably a version of the fountain project which he included in his engraving of views of the aqueduct of 1699. The second two come from the first of the 'Albani' volumes; both appear to record the completion of the aqueduct, but have no other connection with Fontana.

302 SECTION THROUGH THE AQUEDUCT (*Figure* 242) [9723]

300×*c*.210 mm. Pen, coloured washes, some chalk. With scale, index and measurement. Dated: *Adi 10 luglio 1692* and inscribed with notes.

303 PROJECT FOR A FOUNTAIN, PERSPECTIVE VIEW (*Figure* 240) [9450]

230×370 mm. Watermark no.7. Pen, coloured washes, traces of chalk. With scale.

The drawing is bound in Vol.172 with a plan of the south-east end of the breakwater (entered below with the other drawings for the breakwater). The fountain lies in a rectangular recess in the harbour wall. The design is probably a variant, simpler in its general character, of the *Fontana da situarsi nel Porto* which is illustrated in Fontana's engraving of 1699 (lower right). Nothing appears to have come of Fontana's designs for this fountain; the fountain which exists now is probably the work of Nicola Salvi (see Schiavo, *Salvi*, pp.18f.). It is possible that a triple arcade existed on the site chosen for the fountain by Fontana (see drawing 306 in the following section of the catalogue).

304 Unidentified draughtsman

VIEW OF THE AQUEDUCT (*Figure* 243) [10628]

253×386 mm. Watermark no.7. Pen, coloured washes. With index.

The drawing shows a small site plan of Civitavecchia and a view of the route of the aqueduct. An angel blowing a trumpet, upper right, carries a shield bearing the arms of Pope

Clement XI. The key to the index, bottom right is entitled: 'Descritione dell'Acquedotto che porta l'Acqua in Civitavecchia in / distanza di Miglia uenti due'. The drawing may have been intended to form the basis of an engraving to commemorate the completion of the aqueduct in 1702. It differs in style from the workshop technique of Fontana.

305 CIVITAVECCHIA: DESIGN FOR A MEDAL (*Figure* 241) [10599]
133 × 132 mm. Pen, grey wash, traces of chalk.

One of four small designs for medals in Volume 188. The aqueduct is visible beyond the port at the top of the roundel, and the medal may have been intended to commemorate the completion of the aqueduct (cf. Guarnacci, II, 1751, col.374, no.XVII, 1703).

Civitavecchia, project for the arsenal and the Piazza

Five drawings in Volume 170 are related to projects for alterations to the arsenal at Civitavecchia (Contini, vol.8, 'Civita Vecchia con l'Arsenale'). Two of the sheets (Figs 244, 245) are studies in perspective of the port and the arsenal showing the existing condition of the site. The remaining three drawings show a project for radical alterations in the neighbourhood of the Arsenal. In this the back wall of the hollow containing the three halls of the arsenal is made straight, the two side halls are extended into the space thus made available at the corners, a new tower is added in the centre of the back wall, and the *piazza* above the arsenal is considerably improved. A similar project for the *piazza* probably made by Fontana for Bernini in the 1660's as part of his work on the construction of the arsenal is illustrated by Coudenhove-Erthal (fig.6), and other drawings of this date for the Arsenal are discussed by M. Fagiolo dell'Arco (*Arte Illustrata*, 1971, IV, pp.26ff.). There is no evidence to suggest that any of these alterations was carried out.

The drawings, to judge from their style, would appear to be relatively early, and they probably date from the 1690's, like the other dated drawings in the same volume. It is known from Campello's diary that some improvements to the town of Civitavecchia were carried out in time for the visit of Innocent XII in 1696; he mentions specifically a new *palazzo publico*, and a wall initiated by Cardinal Negroni (p.98).

306 PERSPECTIVE VIEW OF CIVITAVECCHIA (*Figure* 244) [9362]
369 × 481 mm. Pen, grey wash.

The scale is too small to permit close comparisons with the drawings below. The site of the fountain in the harbour wall is occupied by an arcade of three arches. The aqueduct, visible in the perspective view 305 above, is not present, but dotted lines on the drawing apparently indicate the existing or projected routes of the aqueduct. A more detailed view, without the triple arcade in the harbour wall, is illustrated by Bonnani, II, p.585 (engraving of 1699 by Girolamo Frezza).
Copy by Vittone, vol.I, fo.14.

307 PERSPECTIVE VIEW OF THE ARSENAL (*Figure* 245) [9366]
368 × 481 mm. Watermark no.7. Chalk, grey wash.

Possibly made for an engraving – a large blank scroll on the left is cut slightly at the edge. The view is taken from the *piazza* facing out to sea and shows the roofs of the arsenal in the centre and the towers of the *rocca* on the left.
Copy by Vittone, vol.I, fo.14.

308 PLAN OF THE ARSENAL AND THE *PIAZZA* (*Figure* 246) [9365]
481 × 368 mm. Pen, coloured washes, traces of chalk. With scale, inscribed in scroll.

The arsenal itself is drawn in grey wash and the area behind indicated with brown wash enclosed in dotted lines. Over this in yellow is superimposed a project for a straight back wall surmounted by a rampart with a relatively large octagonal tower in the centre. The inner naves of the side halls of the arsenal are extended in yellow to fill the space made available at the corners. Fontana's intentions for the *piazza* above the arsenal are less clear. There is a fountain in the centre and the buildings at the sides may incorporate additions and improvements proposed by Fontana.
Copy by Vittone, vol.II, fo.183.

309 SECTION THROUGH THE ARSENAL (*Figures* 247, 249) [9364]
368 × 481 mm. Pen, coloured washes, traces of chalk. With scale, inscribed on the *verso: Arsenale di Civita Vecchia*.

The section corresponds in scale with the plan. It is taken on the central axis of the arsenal, though not through the piers. The roof of the proposed new tower behind the arsenal corresponds with the level of the upper string courses of the palaces on the *piazza*, which are here given exactly matching façades.
Copy by Vittone, vol.I, fo.14.

310 STUDIES OF THE TOWER AND RAMPART (*Figure* 248) [9363]
368×482 mm. Watermark, no.7. Pen, grey and pink wash, traces of chalk. With two scales.

The design of the tower is worked out in greater detail than in the two foregoing drawings and differs slightly in composition.
Copy by Vittone, vol.II, fo.175.

The Curia Innocenziana, Palazzo di Montecitorio, Rome (1694–98)

One of the most important domestic reforms brought about by Pope Innocent XII was the centralization of the papal tribunals in the Palazzo Ludovisi (Curia Innocenziana); the replanning of the site and the completion of the palace formed the most ambitious task undertaken by Fontana in Rome in the 1690's. It furnished the subject of two of his treatises, published in 1694 and 1708, and two surviving books of drawings contain further material which remained for the most part unpublished. The first is a volume formerly (?) in the Pignatelli collection, which Fontana presumably presented to Pope Innocent (Pignatelli) – published by Misciatelli in 1909, and the second is Volume 168 at Windsor which contains 41 further studies of various kinds connected with the project.

The Palazzo Ludovisi had been designed by Bernini in 1653 for Niccolò Ludovisi, nephew of Pope Innocent X. Left uncompleted at the time of the Pope's death in 1655, it had remained uninhabited for almost forty years. It occupied the north side of a triangular site divided by narrow streets from the Palazzo Chigi on the north side of the Piazza Colonna, while across the road to the left lay the monastery of the Missione. This part of the site has in fact been little altered. The ground sloped upwards to the north of the triangular site behind the Palazzo Ludovisi, and in the centre lay an area of open land, bordered on the left and at the top by buildings attached to the Somaschian church of S. Biagio, and on the right by a group of private houses. Behind the monastery of the Missione were lands belonging to the Palombara family. The road leading across the front of the palace was bordered on the south by the following sites: a monastery of Filippini fathers, facing the Missione monastery; a large garden behind the Palazzo Capranica, opposite the left half of the façade of the Palazzo Ludovisi; a street leading up to the Palazzo on its central axis; some small properties, and finally, bordering the Piazza Colonna, a small palace belonging to the Baldinotti family (Fontana's site plan illustrated by Misciatelli and Coudenhove-Erthal, fig.26; site plans in outline in the plates of Fontana's treatises of 1694 and 1708; Windsor drawings, below – especially groups 4, 5 and 6; the Nolli plan – for the Palombara site).

The half-completed state of the Palazzo Ludovisi itself in 1694 is recorded in elevation in two of Fontana's drawings (Misciatelli, illustrated in Coudenhove-Erthal, fig.25; Windsor, no.317, Fig.263), and the height at which the building was left by Bernini is clearly visible on the pilasters of the present façade. Bernini's intentions for completing the palace are known only from a painting (illustrated by Fraschetti) which plausibly suggests that the whole building was to be of three storeys and an attic beneath an uninterrupted cornice, with a simple balustrade surmounting the central projecting block, and a single round-headed doorway in the centre with a caryatid to each side. According to Fontana's plans work had already started on a rectangular stair-chamber which projected at the rear of the building on the left of the central axis. In his treatise of 1708 (p.24) Fontana claims that Bernini intended to provide a small courtyard at the back of the palace (cf. no.316; Fig.261), and this would presumably have been hemmed in on the left by the inner wall of the stairchamber. The far wall of the cage was interrupted by the apse of the church of S. Biagio. Fontana was later, and with good reason, to alter Bernini's design in several important respects, but he would presumably have been familiar with Bernini's intentions for the palace, if only through the agency of Bernini's pupil Mattia de' Rossi (1637–1695), who worked on the early stages of the Curia project (see below).

The complicated story of the creation of the Curia Innocenziana can be divided into three sections: the events of 1694, leading up to the publication of Fontana's first treatise with its ambitious projects for the development of the whole site on 16 October 1694; the first campaign of work and the modification of Fontana's projects, late 1694 and 1695; and the final building activity, when the court behind the Curia was laid out, 1695 onwards.

The history of the work can be reconstructed in outline from documents, some of them published by E. Rossi, from the diary of Campello, and from the summary given by Pastor (Eng. ed., XXXII, pp.584ff.). In addition to these sources many documents have recently come to light in the preparation of the exhibition, organized by Dr Marcello del Piazzo in 1970, on the Palazzo di Montecitorio. All this evidence shows that Fontana's own account of the work, published in his book in 1708, is not a reliable one (the book is reprinted in Borsi (1967)).

1) As early as 14 February 1694 materials were apparently being collected for work on the completion of the palace (Rossi, pt.1). In the first days of June the palace was acquired for the sum

of 30,000 *scudi* and the Pope's wish at this time was to convert the ground floor for use as the Dogana di Terra and to use the upper floors for the Curia (Rossi, pt.1; exhibition documents, 71, 84f.; Bonanni, p.826; Campello, p.67, where mention is made of the precedent of the Vicaria of Naples). The Pope's idea was that the profits from the *dogana* should help to support the poor houses of Rome, under the jurisdiction of the Ospizio di San Michele (exhibition document 82). In writing of the acquisition of the palace Campello suggests that there was an open competition for the completion of the building. It seems, however, that the architect responsible for the work at this time was Mattia de' Rossi, who is reported to have given the Pope on 28 August 1694 an estimate for 200,000 *scudi* for completing the palace (Rossi, pt.1). By October the work was sufficiently far advanced for an inscription to have been placed on the palace wall, explaining its connection with the Lateran Poor House (cf. Forcella, XIII, p.184, no.371), and at this time a part of the cornice apparently fell to the ground (Rossi, pt.1). According to Pascoli (I, p.327), Mattia de' Rossi built the staircase, the portico and the topmost storey of the palace. Group 1 of the Windsor drawings below shows that he was certainly involved in the early stages of the planning of the Curia. It is possible that de'Rossi finished off the staircase and the top storey of the palace, but the portico in its present state is by Fontana; Pascoli may have been referring to a portico replaced by Fontana's structure (see further below). Mattia de' Rossi is mentioned in the documents on 8 December 1694 in connection with a bas-relief which was to be made for the palace, and on 5 March 1695 in connection with a model of a cross designed in conjunction with Fontana (exhibition documents 105f.).

In his treatise of 1708 (pp.15ff.) Fontana gives a rather different account of the events of 1694, one in which the architect himself plays so important a part that doubts about his accuracy must immediately be aroused. Fontana claims for himself the honour of reviving in the 1690's the idea of a central Curia in Rome, following popes Julius II, Sixtus V and Alexander VIII, and he gives the impression that the commissioning of the Curia came about as the result of a conspiracy organized by himself and Cardinal Nuzzi, who suggested to Innocent XII the acquisition of the Palazzo Ludovisi as a suitable building for a poor house. Fontana was asked to complete the building for this purpose, spending as little as possible, and it was also apparently part of the plan to use the building for storehouses. From this arose the idea of converting it to a Dogana, and thus seeing some return for the money spent, Fontana having realized that the design of a customs house was akin to that of a Curia and having made plans of the palace and the surrounding area. At this stage he says that work had begun on the *pilastri* [*sic*] of the portico (this is presumably not the final design – see below). The Pope, when the idea of a Curia was finally suggested to him, drew back because of the cost. At this stage, we are told, Fontana prepared a treatise on his Curia projects, showing how in Roman times the site had been used for buildings of similar functions (Fig.257). So impressed was the Pope that he ordered the publication of Fontana's treatise, which took place on 16 October, and decided, with the approval of members of the Curia, to use the palace for their benefit. On a later page (20) Fontana mentions that on 5 October, some days before the publication of his treatise, two models of his project had been shown to the Pope.

It may be true that the publication of Fontana's book stimulated enthusiasm for a splendid Curia building with the Palazzo Ludovisi as its nucleus, but that the idea of using the palace as a Curia was new at the time cannot be true, since this had been acknowledged as a possible use for the site since June at least. Fontana makes no mention of the part played by Mattia de' Rossi in the work carried out at the palace, and the role ascribed by Fontana to himself can be sensed to be greatly exaggerated. It is however possible that the Pope originally wished to use the palace as a poor house, since it seems always to have been an important part of his intention that the Curia should contribute to the poor, and the rents of the final building were destined for this purpose. What may have happened in 1694 is that Mattia de' Rossi, as Bernini's principal disciple, and Fontana, as architect of the secular papal buildings, consulted together about the completion of the palace, Fontana hoping to see an ambitious scheme of his own devising substituted for the simple project for completing the palace as a Dogana/Curia. Mattia de' Rossi would presumably have been concerned to see that Bernini's intentions were respected as far as possible, and at one stage a single doorway was apparently built or projected for the building, as Bernini had intended (Windsor drawing no.318, Fig.262). The state of the work in October 1694 is not known, but the palace itself may have been nearly completed with a single doorway and without the *campanile* added later by Fontana.

Fontana's treatise of October 1694 is clearly the result of months of preparation, and two elaborate projects for the development of the whole site are given in the engraved illustrations (Figs 254, 256). In both projects Fontana proposed to develop the whole of the triangular site behind the Palazzo Ludovisi. The *piazza* of the second project (Fig.254) is a huge semi-circular space, occupying all the land between the monastery of the Filippini and the Palazzo Baldinotti. Around its edge were to be rooms for the notaries of the Curia and in the centre Fontana hoped to erect the column of Antoninus Pius, which lay largely embedded in the ground in 1694 on land owned by the fathers of the Missione (Platner and Ashby, p.131). According to Fontana's elevation (Fig.255) the Curia was to have a triple entrance bay surmounted by four statues, and a large belfry framing a clock surmounting the cornice. These two alterations to Bernini's design were essential if the Curia was to function smoothly – the bell of the tower to give warning of the opening of the tribunals, and the doorway to allow easy ingress and egress to the officials of the Curia and the general public. Certain of the features of Fontana's project in elevation and plan are paralleled in his attempted reconstruction of the site as it appeared in Roman times (Fig.257), and the appeal of his design may have resided in part in these connections (Fontana's text of 1694, reprinted as the first part of his treatise of 1708, and ibid., p.17).

2) The story of the Curia in the months following October 1694 is outlined by Pastor. Fontana's project was estimated at a cost of 250,000 *scudi*, and on 20 November a model of the Piazza was ordered, presumably a large scale version of one of the models presented in 5 October. Campello gives the date 8 December for the unveiling of the model (p.75), and work on the demolition of the houses on the site of the Piazza began on the following day. At about this time an even more elaborate project (presumably not designed by Fontana) was apparently contemplated, which involved the moving of Trajan's column, to be set up with the Colonna Antonina and an obelisk, this last to be incorporated in a fountain to which the Acqua Felice was to be re-directed from the Piazza di Trevi. Scarcely had work begun on the demolition of the houses on the site of the Piazza, when a change of plan was decided whereby a rectangular Piazza was to be constructed (14 December, Campello, p.76). This was presumably an alternative to Fontana's project and in the following weeks buildings bordering the site were taken over to house lawyers who would in Fontana's project have been provided with houses around the Piazza. On 24 December the church of S. Biagio was taken over, the fathers receiving in exchange S. Niccolò ai Cesarini (exhibition document 47), and on 1 January 1695 the takeover of the Filippini monastery is mentioned (Rossi, pt.2); a *motu proprio* about this change is dated 6 April (exhibition document 63) and a drawing at Windsor for the allocation of rooms in the monastery to lawyers, no.328, is dated 18 April 1695.

From December 1694 work continued on the Piazza, though its final shape apparently remained undetermined, while work on the palace itself progressed slowly (Fontana's *campanile* was probably the main feature carried out at this time). On 26 December Fontana was reprimanded by the Pope because of the slowness of the work (Campello, p.77). By 21 February 1695 a site for the Dogana di Terra had apparently been chosen in the nearby Piazza di Pietra, incorporating the remains of the temple of 'Neptune', and this building was erected by Francesco Fontana before October of the same year (Campello, pp.78 and 86). By April 1695 Fontana's *campanile* for the Curia had been completed and the bell it was to contain was blessed on 17 (?) April (Campello, p.80; Rossi pt.3, 23 April). The Pope visited the site at this time and expressed anger at the smallness of the bell; he criticized Fontana's *campanile* because it was too large (*smisurato* – according to Ms. Ottoboni 3359, fo.51r., section not quoted by Rossi), and poorly conceived (*meschino* – according to Campello, p.80). A larger bell was made for the *campanile* in 1696/8 (Campello, pp.91 and 122). Fontana appears gradually to have enlarged his *campanile* in his projects, beginning with the engraved design (Fig.255) and Windsor drawing no.324 (Fig.264), which is dated 10 March 1695. The finished building differs from this drawing in the greater height of the parapet enclosing the clock.

By 1 June 1695 the department of the Auditore della Camera had apparently moved into the palace and the papal tribunals began to function on the following day (Campello, p.82; the date 7 April 1697 [*sic*] is given by Paston op. cit., p.585 n.). The distribution of the floors of the palace between the various sections of the Curia is shown in a series of drawings by Michetti of 1715 (exhibition doc. no.100; Fig.253; see also Pastor, Eng. ed., p.586). Though the tribunals of the Curia may have been functioning by June 1695, it appears that parts of the palace remained to be completed, and the main doorway was not inspected by the Pope until 23 October 1695 (Campello, p.86). Groups 3 and 6 of the Windsor drawings suggest that before the doorway was carried out the openings had been pierced and that the vestibule was constructed and part of the court arcade.

Fontana in his treatise of 1708 writes at length of some of the difficulties encountered at this time and of the hostility directed at him as the architect of the scheme. Objections to the project (Ch. II) came from the landlords of the lawyers who were to be moved from 'i loro antichi Nidi', and from the Somaschian fathers of S. Biagio (Ch.III), but these were overcome by the efforts of Cardinals Nuzzi and Spada, and Leonardo Libri. More serious was the criticism voiced by two *Professori* that Fontana's project, which he had apparently estimated at 350,000 *scudi* (not 250,000) would cost half a million (pp.20f.), and this, according to Fontana, was the *colpo mortale*. The Pope ordered a cheaper project, and it was later decided to put the notaries in the monastery of the Filippini (Ch.V). This new development was opposed by the Filippini fathers, but their premises were taken over, and Fontana claims bitterly that this raised the cost of the project to a sum equal to that estimated for his original scheme.

3) Fontana next speaks of the completion of the Curia and its court (Ch.VI) – the final phase of the building. As finally built the Curia had only one main staircase, that started by Bernini, and this was balanced by a screen wall on the opposite side of the court, with an arcade of three tiers joining screen and staircase at the rear of the palace. A semicircular space was excavated at the back of the court, articulated by two curved screens of six bays each with a fountain in the centre (see Fig.253 – one of the series of plans of 1715, by Michetti, kindly communicated by Dr del Piazzo). The Piazza in front of the palace was roughly rectangular; it extended from the site of the Palazzo Baldinotti to the monastery of the Filippini, but occupied only about half of the depth which would have been taken up by the semicircular court of Fontana's original project (see the plans in Borsi, fig.119, p.76 and fig.2, p.259 (plan of 1855), also the engravings of the court by Specchi (Figs 251, 252), and the Nolli plan which shows how Specchi improved Fontana's design; the plan illustrated by Coudenhove-Erthal, fig.30, taken from Bonanni, appears to derive from Fontana's project of 1694, and it bears only the most general resemblance to the finished building).

Opposition was voiced against this project of Fontana's, but it was eventually silenced by Cardinal d'Adda, who had taken charge of the operation. It was claimed that the courtyard would cost too much to carry out, so much earth having to be excavated. As for the palace itself, the side doors of the main entrance would weaken the fabric supporting the weight of the *campanile*. Fontana points out that the Curia needed a large entrance, being no longer a private palace, and that Bernini himself would in these circumstances have done the same. This passage in Fontana's treatise would seem to imply that the main entrance was not built until the final design for the courtyard was carried out, but the doorway was probably finished in October 1695, and the Windsor drawings (Groups 3 and 6) show that the side openings had already been pierced; Fontana's critics presumably hoped to force the architect to have the side entrances filled up before the external decoration of the doorway was carried out.

Fontana goes on (Ch.VIII) to speak of the large fountain of 350 *oncie* of water from the Acqua Felice which was projected for the palace by himself and his son, Francesco. A model of the fountain was apparently made, but no drawings of the project appear to be known. One project of this period may be recorded in a drawing at Stockholm (Fig.258), inscribed *Fontaine au Monte Citorio Architecture du Cau Ch Fontana*. Finally, a small fountain of 25 *oncie* was built, using a granite basin which Fontana says he found at Ostia. This was brought to Rome in June 1696 and on 15 August the fountain was inaugurated (an old photograph of the fountain is illustrated in Borsi, figs 114/7, p.74). Fontana gives the total cost of the project as 300,000 *scudi* (see below for further discussion). Ultimately Fontana refused payment for his work (Chs IX, X), giving the money to the poor (declaration of 20 December 1698).

Fontana then describes his project of 1694, which is illustrated in both treatises, and he mentions that by the addition of *mezzanini* the number of floors in the main building would have been increased to six (Ch.XI). In the last of his chapters (XII) he mentions that the amount of earth excavated in the construction of the court and Piazza of the Curia was so great that it would have exceeded the capacity of the Pantheon. He goes on finally to describe the raising of the Colonna Antonina, a task begun on the orders of Clement XI in 1704. The work was undertaken by Carlo and Francesco Fontana, and the base of the column apparently came to light during the excavations (Platner and Ashby, p.131; Huelsen, p.44). Fontana says that at 66 he himself was too old for the work and suffering from gout. After several unsuccessful attempts, causing damage to the column, it was finally raised by Francesco Fontana in September 1705 (engraving illustrated in *Via del Corso*, 1961, fig.29), but the site on which the column was to be set up was left undecided (see entry below for the Fontana di Trevi). The final two chapters in Fontana's book are accounts by Francesco Posterla of the raising of the column (for another account of this see the extracts of Valesio's diary published by Cancellieri; cf. also d'Onofrio, *Obelischi*, pp.238ff.).

The course of the building after the middle of 1695 can be followed in part in the documentary sources. Pastor mentions a new project for the Piazza made in July 1695, but abandoned in October. On 29 October the Pope inspected the doorway of the palace (see above) and a stable and *rimesse* (Ms. Ottoboni 3359, fo.63 – passage not quoted by Rossi). The stable referred to may be the one which Fontana added behind the Filippine monastery (see group 4 of the Windsor drawings). In this same month the cost of the building was apparently estimated as 500,000 *scudi* (Campello, p.86; the same figure is given by Pastor for October 1697 and by Fontana in the declaration of December 1697 – Ospizio di S. Michele Decrete, vol.234). This sum presumably refers to the whole work, including the building of 1694; it is 150,000 *scudi* in excess of the sum given by Fontana in his book of 1708, which may possibly refer to the money spent on the palace itself. On 5 November 1695 the street between the Curia and the Missione monastery was being levelled (Rossi, pt.4, and see the Windsor documents discussed below). According to Pastor an extra 100 workmen were employed on the site on 26 November; they were possibly recruited to work on the excavation of the courtyard, the largest part of the work which remained to be done. Much of the work on the courtyard must have been completed before the summer of 1696, when the fountain at the back was built. Payments for setting up the fountain and connecting it with the Acqua Felice are dated 4 June and 6 and 29 September (Rome, Archivio di Stato, Cam. I°, Registri Mandati, vol. 1046, fos 317, 328 (naming Francesco Fontana) and 329).

For some time after August 1696, when the fountain was unveiled, work continued on the Piazza, the forecourt and some of the less important parts on the palace were still being finished off as late as 1698 (Rossi, pts 4 and 5). Work on the 'semicircolo' of the courtyard is mentioned in the Decrete of the Ospizio di San Michele on 17 April and 11 November 1698 (vol.234), and as late as 2 August 1699 (vol.235). On 2 December 1696 the Pope inspected the Piazza and the *gradinata* leading up to the entrance (Campello, p.104), and shortly after the new bell, replacing the one blessed in October 1695, was installed (ibid., p.122). On 10 May 1698 the Pope issued a *chirografo* for the opening of a road opposite the palace (ibid., p.126) but this remained unbuilt (see the plans in Borsi, pp.76/7). In 1701, finally, Fontana planned the installation of a statue of Innocent XII which was placed in the principal room of the first floor (dated drawing in the Leipzig volume, fo.96); the statue was unveiled on 7 April (Decrete of the Ospizio di S. Michele, 29 September 1701, vol.235; Valesio, fos 82v and 83r).

Only the façade of the main Curia building survives now in an unaltered condition, as part of the Camera dei Deputati of the Italian Parliament. The Piazza in front of the palace was improved for Clement XII by Ferdinando Fuga beginning in 1734 (see Borsi, figs 122/3ff.); the same architect set up the base of the Colonna Antonina in the Piazza for Benedict XIV (1740–58). Both base and column had apparently lain in or near the Piazza since 1705 and in 1764 the column itself was damaged by fire and later destroyed (Platner and Ashby, p.131, and *Roma antica e moderna*, 1767, 1, pp.172ff.). It may have been part of Fontana's intention for the final design of the Piazza to have the column set up in the centre as in his earlier project, but no drawings of such a scheme are known (the *Descrizione di Roma* of 1708, p.458, would appear to show a project for erecting the column with a statue of a saint at the summit, like that of S. Paul on the column of Marcus Aurelius in the Piazza Colonna). The base of the Colonna Antonina was finally removed to the Vatican, and in 1789 the obelisk of Augustus was set up in its stead (Platner and Ashby, pp.131, 366; on the column and its history see also Vogel, pp.5ff.).

By the mid-18th century the allocation of rooms in the Curia may also have been altered. As described in various guide books of the period, the main Curia building appears to have absorbed notaries and other officers destined, according to the Windsor drawings, for buildings on the Piazza (for a fuller discussion see below, groups 4, 5 and 6). At this time the rent paid by the Curia was still allocated to the poor. Since 1870 the palace has been used for the Camera dei Deputati, the civil tribunals of the papacy having been transferred elsewhere, and in 1918 the architect Basile converted Fontana's courtyard into a covered hall, and altered the rear part of the site, extending it further backwards to the present northern elevation on the Piazza del Parlamento (on the later history of the building see Borsi, pt.2).

Volume 168 at Windsor, containing 41 drawings and a number of written texts concerning the Curia, is exceptional amongst the Fontana volumes in several respects: it is not mentioned in Contini's hand list of 1716, and the binding – of undecorated white vellum – corresponds with that of the two Albani volumes (the volume is labelled on the spine '. . . e Piant / Del Fabric / Della Nuou / Curia'). It is therefore likely that the volume was not bound during Fontana's lifetime, but at some time after the drawings had been acquired by the Albani and probably before 1732, when Vittone copied one of the sheets. The book contains for the most part drawings connected with the less important stages of Fontana's project. Having already written two treatises on the Curia and assembled for Pope Innocent a book of those drawings related to the engraved projects (Misciatelli, op.cit.), the task of making up a book of the remaining drawings was one which Fontana presumably considered scarcely worthwhile.

The drawings were probably assembled into their present order by the anonymous writer who placed bold inscriptions on the *verso* of many of the sheets. They refer sometimes to the drawing on the *recto*, and sometimes to groups of as many as five drawings preceding the inscription (e.g. nos 9307 (315) to 9311 (332)). These inscriptions must have been added before the volume was bound because in two cases (nos 346 (9287) and 335 (9301)) sheets folded horizontally were opened out for binding and the inscriptions, written originally on the *verso* of the second half page, now occur upside down at the bottom of the bound sheet. It is clear from the inscription on no.332 that the writer was not completely familiar with the significance of the drawings, since he uses the phrase 'si puo credere'.

The texts occurring in the volume are written on nine small sheets bound at the start of the book (fos 1 to 9, of which the first and the last three are blank, except for the *verso* inscription on fo.9). They represent what is clearly a very small part of the documentation that must have been prepared for the whole project. The longest text (fos 3/4) is a *scandaglio* of 26 November 1695 of the cost 'che potra andare in leuare la Terra nel Vicolo della Missione'. The document apparently refers to the levelling of the street dividing the Curia from the monastery of the Missione, including the lowering of the doorway which leads from this street to the cloister of the monastery and the provision of a staircase. It is possible that the excavation of this area of the site was connected with the excavation of the courtyard behind the main Curia building, and that the latter work was being carried out at about this time (cf. the reference in Pastor to the extra workmen engaged on 26 November 1695, the exact date of the present *scandaglio*). The last text (fo.6) is apparently connected with the first and it consists largely of an estimate of work necessary on the interior of the Missione monastery, connected presumably with the lowering of the side door. The short and partly illegible text on fo.5 must refer to drawing no.333, a project for extending the monastery of the Filippini by several feet on to the Piazza in front of the Curia.

There is little logic in the present ordering of the drawings in Volume 168, but bearing in mind the complicated history of the Curia in 1695/6, they can be considered most conveniently in seven groups.

ADDITIONAL BIBLIOGRAPHY:

Sources:

Documents assembled for the exhibition *Il Palazzo di Montecitorio*, Rome, 1970, including extracts from A.S.R., Ospizio di S. Michele, Decreti, 1692–1703 (vols 233–5).

LITERATURE:

F. Borsi etc., *Il Palazzo di Montecitorio*, Rome I, 1967.

F. Cancellieri, *Effem. Lett.*, Feb. 1821.

C. Fontana, *Alla Santita di nostro signore Innocenzo XII. Discorso del Cavalier Carlo Fontana Sopra il Monte Citatorio . . .*, 1694.

Discorso sopra l'antico Monte Citatorio . . ., 1708.

S. Fraschetti in *L'Arte*, 1899, II, pp.277ff.

C. Huelsen in *Mittheilungen des Kaiserlich Deutschen Archeologischen Instituts*, 1884, 4.

P. Misciatelli in *Vita d'arte*, Siena, 1909, 2.

E. Rossi, *Roma, Revista di studi e di vita romana*, XXI, 1943, pt.1, pp.59ff.; pt.2, pp.116ff.; pt.3, pp.174ff.; pt.4, pp.207ff.; pt.5, pp.262ff.

The present text and photographs of the drawings catalogued below were sent to Rome with the drawings themselves in 1970 on the occasion of the exhibition *Il Palazzo di Montecitorio*. The authors of the present catalogue were concerned to see what advantage had been taken of their co-operation, on finding the drawings published inadequately, but illustrated in their entirety, on the basis of the analysis below in a second attempt at the history of the Curia by Franco Borsi in *Montecitorio, Richerche di storia urbana*, 1972.

1. Drawings by Mattia de' Rossi

The presence of five drawings by Mattia de' Rossi in Volume 168 might suggest that they were made on Fontana's orders, or rather that they were inherited when he took charge of the building in October 1694, but the circumstances of the collaboration between the two architects are obscure. Four of the drawings record the plans of the offices in the Strada di Banchi of five of the papal notaries – the notaries of the *Aud*(ito)*re della Camera*, according to the inscription on the *verso* of a later drawing (no.338). A proposed identification of the notaries offices is suggested by Dr del Piazzo with houses demolished to make way for the Corso Vittorio Emanuele. Inscriptions on the Windsor sheets record the capacity of the offices, and two are signed by de' Rossi. The final drawing, in the same style as the preceding four, and inscribed in the same handwriting, shows a project apparently designed for housing the notaries in buildings belonging to the Somaschians at the top of the triangular site of the Curia. The drawings must date from before August 1695, when de' Rossi died, and if they were made independently of Fontana, they must presumably date from before October 1694. In this case the scheme for new quarters for the lawyers might seem to be a rival project to Fontana's extravagant idea for housing the lawyers around his semi-circular Piazza.

311 THE OFFICES OF BELLI, PLAN [9290]

310×430 mm. Pen, grey wash, traces of chalk. With scale and annotations.

Inscribed: 'Disegno è pianta della Casa che tiene Lorenzo Belli Notaro A: C: in Banchi', followed by an account of the space he used and signed: 'Il tutto reconosciuto deligentemente dà me Matthia de Rossi'.

The rooms, shown at first-floor level, have a frontage of nine bays on to the Strada di Banchi, including those occupied by a barber to the left of Belli's offices.

312 THE OFFICES OF OLIVIERI, PLAN [9291]
424×277 mm. Pen, grey and blue wash, some chalk. With scale and annotations.

Inscribed: 'Casa che tiene l'Oliuieri Capo Notaro A: C. in Banchi', followed by an account of the space he used. The offices are shown at first-floor level and they have a frontage of four bays on to the Strada di Banchi.

313 THE OFFICES OF FATII AND FRANCESCHINI, PLAN (*Figure* 259) [9292]
433×314 mm. Watermark no.16. Pen, yellow and pink wash, traces of chalk. With scale and annotations.

Inscribed: 'Il colorito di Giallo dimostra Il disegno è Pianta della Casa che tiene Il Fatij/ Il colorito di Rosso dimostra Il disegno è Pianta della Casa che tiene Il Franceschinj', followed by an account of the space each lawyer used, and signed: 'Il tutto reconosciuto con ogni deligenza da / me Matthia de Rossi'.
The plans are taken at first-floor level and each office has a frontage of four bays on to the Strada di Banchi.

314 THE OFFICES OF PELOSI, WITH THE *SCRITTURE* OF FATII, PLAN [9293]
447×330 mm. Watermark no.16. Pen, grey and yellow wash, traces of chalk. With scale and annotations. Inscribed on *verso*: *Piante 4 dell' Abitatione che godevano li notari in Banchi cioe, Olivieri Fatij / Pelosi, e Belli.*'

Inscribed on *recto*: 'Dimostra il Disegno è pianta della Casa che tiene Il Pelosi Notaro A. C. In Banchi ch'è tutto Il Colorito di negro, è Il Colorito di Giallo dimostra le Stanze terrene che tiene Il Fatij anesse con la Casa già descritta del. med.º', followed by an account of the space used by Pelosi. Pelosi's offices have a frontage of five bays on the Strada di Banchi, and a part of the ground floor of his house is occupied by the *Scritture* of Fatii, as explained in the inscription.

315 GROUND-FLOOR PLAN OF THE BUILDINGS AT THE NORTHERN BORDER OF THE CURIA SITE (*Figure* 260) [9307]
270×428 mm. Watermark no.17. Pen, yellow and pink wash, traces of chalk. With scale, index and inscriptions. Inscribed *Prima* (the first of a group of five drawings to which the inscription on the *verso* of no.332 refers).

The plan shows the houses along the northern edge of the Curia site, stretching from the wall beside the church of S. Biagio (*Muro della Chiesa*) to include the houses occupying the point of the triangular site. The existing walls are indicated in yellow wash, as can be seen in comparison with Fontana's drawings (no.336 below, for example) and proposed additions are in pink wash. The site is divided into five sections, each with a small *cortile* and the rooms of the first are all inscribed with the number 1, and so on up to the number 5. It is probable that the houses are to be allocated to the five lawyers of the Auditore della Camera.

2. Early plans and elevations

316 GROUND-FLOOR PLAN WITH SQUARE COURT, AFTER BERNINI(?) (*Figure* 261) [9304]
477×750 mm. Two sheets joined vertically. Watermark no.7. Pen, coloured washes, traces of chalk. With scale.

A simplified version of the drawing in the Albertina reproduced by Coudenhove-Erthal (fig.24), probably drawn by Fontana – and on paper of the kind he generally used – possibly after Bernini's project or after that of Mattia de' Rossi. The present sheet is puzzling in that it shows part of the plan of the palace in yellow wash, though there seems to be no very clear reason for distinguishing this area from the others which are indicated in grey. The plan differs in several small ways from that established by Bernini, and recorded in Fontana's plan in the Pignatelli volume (Misciatelli, illustrated by Coudenhove-Erthal, fig.26). The project may have influenced Fontana in choosing a square shape with five bay arcades on each side in the second of the two projects for the Curia published in October 1694 (Fig.254).

317 ELEVATION IN UNFINISHED STATE (*Figure* 263) [9272]
459×326 mm. Watermark no.9. Pen, grey wash, traces of chalk. With scale.

The drawing occupies the upper half of the sheet and is inscribed within a ruled outline, as though intended for engraving. It shows the state of the façade before Fontana's work, and corresponds with the central part of a drawing, signed by Fontana and dated 1694, in the Pignatelli volume (Misciatelli, reproduced by Coudenhove-Erthal, fig.25).

318 ELEVATION WITH SINGLE DOORWAY (*Figure* 262) [9271]
278×425 mm. Pen, grey wash, chalk.

The drawing shows a hitherto unrecorded stage in the development of the work, probably a design by Fontana, but from before his projects published in October 1694 and probably before the function of the building had been decided. Eight doors are pierced into the main building along the terraces, suggesting that the ground floor was to be split up into many separate sections. It is possible that the main door shows what had actually been built by the time that the drawing was made. According to Fontana's text of 1708 (p.16) the door had been given *pilastri* at some time before October 1694. In his project for the façade published in the latter month the central entrance is roundheaded, but in two more detailed projects (drawings 325 and 326 below) and in the building as executed the central door is rectangular.

3. Later plans and elevation of the Curia (1695)

Group 3 of Fontana's drawings comprises a series of five plans of the different floors of the Curia executed in yellow wash, an elevation dated 10 March 1695, and two drawings of the doorway. The plans probably date from before Fontana started working on his projects for completing the court behind the Curia (group 6 below), and on comparison with the latter plans the present drawings appear to show the state of the building in the early part of 1695. The drawings are not executed with great precision, but the main outlines of the work carried out from October 1694 can be appreciated. According to the ground-floor plan (Fig.265) the side entrances flanking the central doorway had been pierced and the four piers of the vestibule constructed. The half-columns of Fontana's project for the decoration of the main doorway are not shown, but the central entrance would appear to be flanked by pilasters – those (?) mentioned by Fontana as having been executed before October 1694 (see introduction above). Three openings led from the vestibule to the court and a five-bay arcade screening the rear of the Curia building had been constructed at ground and first-floor level, and the passage behind the arcade gave access to Bernini's staircase, now rising the full height of the building. The court arcading had not been extended around the sides of the court, though the corner piers had apparently been shaped with this in mind. The plans therefore help to explain the origin of Fontana's final design for the rear façade of the Curia block. According to Specchi's engraving (Fig.251) an extra projecting bay was added to the arcade on each side, one of which took up the space beside the staircase, and a third tier of arcades was added at second-floor level. Only the five floors of the executed design are recorded in the present drawings, not the extra floor(s) which Fontana, according to the treatise of 1708, intended in October 1694 to add to the palace. The plans are all numbered and labelled in chalk overdrawn in ink.

319 BASEMENT PLAN [9281]
317×450 mm. Watermark no.17. Chalk, yellow wash. With annotations in chalk. Inscribed upper right: *sotterranio* (chalk) and *Pianta del piano Terreno al piano / della strada uerso Chigi e Piazza colonna.* Numbered *5.*

The plan shows the basement windows, present beneath all but the central seven bays of the façade, and it includes the basement level of the staircase.

320 GROUND-FLOOR PLAN (*Figure* 265) [9280]
317×450 mm. Watermark no.5. Chalk, yellow wash. Inscribed, upper right in ink over chalk: *Pianta del piano tereno*, and numbered *4.* Inscribed on *verso: Pianta delli 4 Piani et una del sotteraneo del Palazzo di M'te Citorio* (referring to the whole group of drawings, nos 9277–9281 (323–319).

321 FIRST-FLOOR PLAN (*Figure* 266) [9279]
317×450 mm. Watermark no.17. Chalk, yellow wash. With scale and measurements in chalk. Inscribed in ink: *Pianta del primo piano nobile*, over chalk: *Piano Nobile*, and numbered *3.*

The central part of the Curia block is occupied by a room over the ground-floor vestibule five bays wide. The remainder of the plan is divided into relatively large rooms.

322 SECOND-FLOOR PLAN [9278]
317×450 mm. Watermark no.5. Chalk, yellow wash. With scale and measurements in chalk. Inscribed in ink over chalk, upper right: *Pianta del 2º piano nobile*, and numbered *2.*

The planning of the second floor corresponds closely with that of the first, but the piers of the arcade across the court, later built at second-floor level, are not present on the plan.

323 PLAN OF THE ATTIC [9277]
317×452 mm. Watermark no.17. Chalk, yellow wash. With scale and measurements in chalk. Inscribed, upper right: *Mezzanili* (chalk), *Pianta de mezzanili di Cima* (ink), and numbered *1.*

The attic is divided into many small rooms, and a number of corrections to the plan are indicated in chalk.

324 ELEVATION (*Figure* 264) [9273]

276×423 mm. Watermark no.7. Pen, grey wash, traces of chalk. With scale. Inscribed, upper left: *p l'Em.mo Dada / Adi 10 Mar.o 1695*, and lower right: *Carlo fontana Archo / manda*. Inscribed on *verso: Tre Piante diuerse della facciata del Palazzo p la nuoua Curia* (referring to drawings 9271–9273; nos. 317, 318 and 324). The *verso* also bears rough sketches in chalk.

Cardinal 'Dada' is presumably the d'Adda referred to in Fontana's treatise of 1708, who supervised the completion of the building of the Curia. March 1695 was the month before the bell of the *campanile* of the Curia was blessed (see above). The design of the *campanile* in the present drawing is close to the final design; several slight differences (size of clock etc.) may be due to the relatively small scale of the drawing. This design for the *campanile* must have been worked out some time after October 1694, when a less extensive structure made its appearance in the engraving of the Curia in perspective. The main doorway in the present drawing is like that of the engraved design, but the roundels over the side entrances are omitted. In the present sheet the hill on which the Curia stood has been made to slope on both sides of the main entrance of the building, whereas in the engraved perspective it sloped only on the right. The lowering of the ground to the left of the Curia was carried out about the month of November 1695, as the *scandaglio* for lowering the Via della Missione, bound at the start of the volume and dated 25 November, reveals. The drawing was possibly to be engraved as a pair showing with no.317 the state of the main building before and after Fontana's work.

325 PROJECT FOR THE MAIN DOORWAY (1), ELEVATION (*Figure* 267) [9284]

280×422 mm. Pen, grey wash, traces of chalk. With scale.

None of the decoration of the doorway (probably not completed until October 1695) is included.

326 PROJECT FOR THE MAIN DOORWAY (2), ELEVATION (*Figure* 268) [9285]

324×453 mm. Two sheets joined vertically. Watermark no.9. Pen, grey wash, traces of chalk. With scale. Inscribed on *verso*: (D)*ue Piante del Portone, e ringhiera di Monte Citorio* (referring to this and the preceding drawing).

Slight differences in structure from the foregoing drawing are present. The upper part of the decoration shown in the drawing was entirely omitted in the finished building, but the reliefs over the side doors, of Justice and Mercy, were carried out by Lorenzo Ottone. A version or copy of this drawing, bearing apparently the strange attribution to Ciro Ferri, is in the Uffizi (repr. in Borsi, fig.110, p.71).

4. Drawings of the monastery of the Filippini

Seven drawings in Volume 168 are connected with the project to house papal notaries in the monastery of the Filippini on Monte Citorio. In style they differ from Fontana's own drawings, and resemble a little Mattia de' Rossi's. The monastery lay to the left of the Piazza in front of the Curia, its main façade facing north on the street running across the front of the Curia and into the Piazza Colonna. The first floor appears to have been intended by Fontana to contain the rooms of the five notaries of the Auditore della Camera, those whose houses in the Strada di Banchi were measured by Mattia de' Rossi (see Group 1 above), and part of the ground floor is made over in his drawings to four notaries who are described as those *del Vicaro*. Fontana also wished to provide a new stable block in the garden behind the monastery, and to enlarge the plan slightly, extending the eastern wall of the monastery by several feet into the Piazza in front of the Curia (drawing 333). One of the drawings bears the date 18 April 1695 (no.328) and this provides a definite *terminus ante quem* for the abandonment of Fontana's project for a semicircular Piazza in front of the Curia, where he had at first intended to house the notaries. How far Fontana's proposals for the alteration of the monastery were carried out seems difficult to determine. The building itself was certainly made into an annexe for the Curia, as Fontana's treatise of 1708 reveals (Ch.V), but in his later projects for completing the main Curia building (Group 7 below), the names of the five notaries of the Auditore della Camera are inscribed in the rooms of the ground-floor plan. This would suggest that their quarters had not yet been fixed at the monastery, and in the 18th century these lawyers in fact occupied the ground-floor rooms of the main Curia building (*Roma antica e moderna*, 1767, I, p.175). According to Nolli's plan of Rome, the courtyard behind the monastery was made tidy but not in the way suggested by Fontana in the drawings below. A stable like that suggested in Fontana's drawings was, however, built and it is still in existence, accessible from the Vicolo della Guardiola; it is now used as a printing works. This building may have been completed or in construction in October 1695 (see main introduction).

327 GROUND-FLOOR PLAN OF THE MONASTERY (*Figure* 269) [9282]
278 × 423 mm. Chalk, yellow and other coloured washes. With scale, index and annotations.

Inscribed, upper right: 'Habitatione delle filippine spartite in una / portione del Pian terreno per li n.° 4 notari / del Vicario', and with an account (upper left), indexed E to H, of the space available.

The monastery is indicated in yellow wash, and the indexed rooms, the walls of which are each coloured differently, occupy the central part of the ground floor. A small church lies between the rooms labelled 'G' and those labelled 'H'. The land to the left of the monastery, actually to its east, is marked *Capranica*, denoting the garden of the Palazzo Capranica, which formed part of the Piazza in front of the Curia. Behind the buildings of the monastery to the right a plot of land is labelled *Giardino*. It is probable that the present sheet was intended by Fontana to be read in conjunction with the plans for the Palazzo Baldinotti (Group 5 below); they are drawn in the same style with inscriptions arranged in the same manner, and one of the plans (no.334, Fig.274) bears the index letters 'A' to 'D' – those missing in the present sheet.

328 FIRST-FLOOR PLAN [9276]
275 × 426 mm. Chalk, yellow and some grey wash. With scale index and annotations.

Inscribed in chalk, upper right: 'Filippine Per n.° 4 notari li 18 Aprile 1695' and upper left with two indices describing the rooms and staircases. Inscribed on the *verso*: 'Pianta delle filippine quando fu repartita alli notari'. The plan corresponds closely with the preceding, but the absence of doorways appears to show that this is of the first floor, and all the rooms of the building are apparently to be made over to the lawyers in the present plan. The rooms were originally lettered neatly in chalk from A to D, corresponding with the text of the index inscribed above the plan, but over this a second series of index letters was added ranging from A to E. This latter method of dividing the rooms into five sections forms the basis for the layout of the following plan, also of the first floor. Finally on the present sheet an index of three letters clumsily formed in ink, C, D, and E, appears in some of the rooms and in the same hand the names of three of the lawyers of the Auditore della Camera – *Pelosi*, *Fatij* and *Belli* – are inscribed.

Walls indicated in grey wash and a number of chalk lines on the plan would appear to indicate projected additions and alterations to the existing building.

329 FIRST-FLOOR PLAN (*Figure* 270) [9283]
280 × 422 mm. Watermark no.5. Pen, coloured washes, some chalk. With scale, indexes, inscriptions and measurements. Inscribed on *verso*: *Pianta del M'ro delle filippine, et altra Pianta de terreni* [*de terreni*] *delle med.*[me] (referring to this and the preceding, ground-floor, plan, no.327).

The building is divided into five parts, each indexed and coloured separately, and each part is presumably intended for one of the notaries of the Auditore della Camera, three of whose names are inscribed on the foregoing drawing. A projected stable occupies the far side of the garden behind the monastery on the right. It is indicated in grey wash at ground level, and divided into two sections, following the uneven edge of the site. New walls to be built inside the monastery are apparently those coloured grey in the plan. Inscribed, upper right: 'Monastero delle filippine', and lower right and upper left with a description of the rooms.

330 SITE PLAN, SHOWING NEW STABLES (*Figure* 272) [9310]
452 × *c*.680 mm. Watermark no.9. Pen, coloured washes, traces of chalk. With scale. Inscribed *quarto* (ink) and *curia* (?) (chalk). The first inscription is one of the series of cardinal numbers written on drawings 9307 (no.315) – 9311 (no.332).

The monastery is shown in plan in what is evidently its existing condition and the adjacent sites are indicated in washes of differing colours, including the large garden of the Palazzo Capranica. A new stable at the rear of the garden of the monastery is drawn in strong grey wash. It occupies the same position as the stable projected in the foregoing drawing, but now consists of a single rectangular block which encroaches on land forming part of the property behind the monastery.

331 PLAN OF THE STABLES [9308]
465 × 330 mm. Watermark no.9. Pen, coloured washes, some chalk. With scale, annotations and index numbers, and letters (in chalk). Inscribed *seconda*.

A version of the right-hand part of the preceding drawing.

332 PLAN, TWO SECTIONS AND TWO ELEVATIONS OF STABLES (*Figure* 271) [9311]
729 × *c*.470 mm. Four sheets joined. Watermark no.9. Pen, grey and yellow wash, traces of chalk. With scale. Inscribed on *verso*, referring to the present sheet and the four preceding drawings in the volume: *Piante cinque diuerse nelle quali non stà notato che siano ma si puo credere la p*[ma] *Abitatione, e Chiesa de / P'ri somaschi, seconda Pia'ta delle Case doue*

stà la nuoua Piazza, Terzo disegno della scaletta che ua alle Cucine, quarto / Pianta di tutte le Case che stauano, e stanno in prospetto al Palazzo della Curia, quinto Prospetti delle rimesse / e Stalle dietro alle filippine.

The stable is close in plan to that shown in the preceding drawings, though a staircase has been added in the upper left-hand corner of the block. Dotted lines on the transverse section show alternative designs for the roof. The block (7 by 3 bays) is decorated externally with pilaster strips and plain heavy window surrounds.

333 HALF PLAN OF THE PIAZZA IN FRONT OF THE CURIA (*Figure* 273) [9302]

436×285 mm. Watermark no.18. Pen, coloured washes, traces of chalk. With index, annotations and measurements. Drawn on the *recto* of the first half of a large sheet folded in the binding; the *verso* of the second half of the sheet is inscribed with various calculations in ink and chalk, and inscribed: *Pianta della nuoua Piazza e come si debba fabbricare.*

The drawing shows a project for altering the left half of the Piazza in front of the Curia. The projecting corner block of the Curia is shown in outline on the right in the drawing. As explained in the index it is proposed to allow the end wall of the monastery to encroach on the Piazza up to the line marked 'D'. A wall dividing the line 'D' from the *Piazza nuoua* is not explained in the index. The line marked 'C' refers to what was then the present edge of the Piazza. This drawing presumably dates from a later period than the other drawings of the present group where the site is shown before the *Piazza nuoua* was built, when it was occupied by the garden of the Palazzo Capranica. This change to the *piazza* may be the one referred to in the *decreti* of the Ospizio di San Michele of 7 June 1696 (vol.233). A short text bound at the start of the Windsor volume (fo.4) apparently refers to the same project.

5. Drawings of the Palazzo Baldinotti

Drawings 334 and 335 *recto* and *verso* contain three plans of part of the Palazzo Baldinotti which was intended to be used for housing officers of the papal Treasury. According to the site plan given in outline with Fontana's project for a semicircular Piazza in his treatises of 1694 and 1708 this palace consisted of two rectangular blocks occupying the entire west side of the Piazza Colonna. The present drawings refer to the upper block, whose garden wall faced across the Piazza in front of the Curia towards the west wall of the Filippini monastery. The drawings are not dated but they probably formed part of the same scheme as the Filippini drawings (the revised Piazza scheme of April 1695), and the present mezzanine (?) floor plan (334) was probably devised in conjunction with the ground-floor plan of the Filippini monastery. It was probably this part of the Palazzo Baldinotti which in the 18th century housed the rooms of *Monsignor Vicegerente* on the first floor and on the ground floor four secretaries, or *Notari di Camera*, and the *Archivio Urbano* (*Roma antica e moderna*, 1767, I, pp.199f.). The offices of the Treasury were at this time housed on the second floor of the Curia building. Nothing now remains of the building; the site is occupied by the 19th-century Palazzo Wedekind.

334 PLAN AT (?) MEZZANINE LEVEL (*Figure* 274) [9300]

473×325 mm. Watermark no.9. Chalk, red and yellow wash. With scale, index and annotations.

Inscribed, upper left: 'Palazzo di Baldinotti spartito nel pian terreno è mezzanili superiori / per li n.º 4 offitij del Tesoriero /', followed by an account, indexed A to D, of possible uses and alterations for the rooms. The plan occupies the upper half of a once folded sheet. The palace fronts on to the Piazza Colonna, and the absence of doorways suggests that the plan is at mezzanine level. In the centre at the back of the block is a small garden or courtyard divided by a wall from the Piazza in front of the Curia. The front part of the block is occupied by eight rooms (those indexed from A to D). Each index letter corresponds with a name inscribed clumsily on the plan: *Antamoro* – A, *Liberati* – B, *Belucci* – C, and *Galloppi* – D.

335 PLANS OF THE FIRST AND SECOND FLOORS [9301]

530×415 mm. Watermark no.7. Pen, coloured washes, some chalk. With scales, indexes and annotations.

The first-floor plan occupies the upper part of the *recto*, and the second-floor plan occupies the lower part of the *verso*. The sheet was once folded in half horizontally and bears a general inscription which occurs upside down at the bottom of the *recto*: 'Piante tre del Palazzo dell' Ma(r)ch Baldinotti cioè Terreni p li Notari, Primo, e secondo Appartam^{to} Nobile' (referring to drawings 334 and 335). Inscribed on *recto*, at top: 'Pianta del P.^{mo} App:^{to} Nobile del'Palazzo in Piazza Colonna, doue sono gl' Offiti del'Thesoriero' and on left with a description, indexed A to D, of the rooms. At first-floor level almost the whole of the plan is made over to rooms for the use of the Treasury (those indexed from A to D). Rough chalk lines on the plan probably indicate small improvements which were contemplated at this time. Inscribed on the *verso* at the top: 'Pianta del 2.º App.^{to} Nobile del Medemo Palazzo', followed by an account (on left), indexed A to E, of the rooms.

6. Projects for the final design of the courtyard

The exact date of Fontana's design for the semicircular court behind the Curia is not known, but work probably started on the court during the second half of 1695; it continued after August 1696, when the fountain was installed (see above). The present group of drawings includes four plan projects which appear to run in the following order: the first showing a design for a rectangular court resembling those of Fontana's engraved projects; the second incorporating curved screens in a rather primitive composition; the third – most ambitious – design incorporating behind the screens a building which is curved on both its inner and outer faces (two variants); and the fourth apparently corresponding fairly closely with the project as built except in the absence of the fountain (cf. Figs 252, 253). In the plan of the second design, and an allied plan (no.339), which is catalogued with it below, the rooms of the ground floor of the Curia are divided between the five notaries of the Auditore della Camera, who, in an earlier project, had been placed on the first floor of the Filippini monastery.

336 COURT PROJECT 1, GROUND-FLOOR PLAN (*Figure* 275) [9305]
477×751 mm. Two sheets joined vertically. Watermark no.7. Pen, coloured washes, chalk. With scale, and annotation: *Piazza*.

Inscribed, upper right: 'Pianta del Palazzo della Curia, e Case contigue, che gli fan Isola / Tutto il Colorito di giallo, e nero denota la Stato della Curia / Tutto il colorito di Persichino denota l'habitatione de PP. di S. Biagio / Tutto il colorito turchino denota le casette contigue de Particolari'.

The plan is of the whole triangular site, showing the existing buildings in washes of different colours. The plan of the Curia itself, in yellow and black, corresponds with that shown on the ground-floor plan of Group 3 above (320). The black wash is reserved for the vestibule and the arcade in order, presumably, to show Fontana's additions to the building, carried out from late 1694 to early 1695. The main doorway has three openings, but no indication is given of its external decoration having yet been carried out. Fontana proposes in chalk to add a rectangular court of five by seven bays behind the Curia, resembling that of the first engraved project of 1694 (three by seven bays), but here apparently enclosed by a simple wall. A curved line in chalk to the rear of the court hints at the final, semicircular, plan.

337 VERSION OF THE PRECEDING [9306]
475×743 mm. Two sheets joined vertically. Watermark no.7. Pen, coloured washes. With scale. Inscribed on *verso*: *Due Piante del Palazzo di Monte Citorio con le Case, e Conuento de P'ri di S. Biagio che le fanno / Isola* (referring to this and the preceding plan).

The drawing reproduces only those parts of the previous plan which are indicated in wash; the actual colours used here are different.

338 COURT PROJECT 2, GROUND-FLOOR PLAN (*Figure* 276) [9303]
442×624 mm. Two sheets joined vertically. Watermark no.16. Chalk, yellow and grey wash. With scale, index of letters and inscriptions. Inscribed on the *verso*: *Pianta del Palazzo di Monte Citorio con la repartitione delli Notari dell' Aud.e della Camera*.

The Curia block with its staircase and the adjacent arcade is drawn in yellow wash, and the project for completing the court in grey wash. Fontana proposes to add a new staircase to the right of the court, balancing the existing one, and a semicircular wall across the rear part of the site. In chalk is a project for extending the arcade behind the Curia by adding three bays along each side of the court. The majority of the ground-floor rooms of the Curia are numbered from 1 to 5 and inscribed with the names of the five lawyers of the Auditore della Camera. Figures in chalk in the rooms reserved for the lawyers to the right of the vestibule probably refer to the cubic capacity of the respective rooms.

339 GROUND-FLOOR PLAN, RELATED TO THE PRECEDING [9294]
315×453 mm. Watermark no.17. Chalk, grey and other coloured washes.

The plan shows only the main Curia block, and it is related to the preceding in showing the rooms of the Curia divided into five sections (coloured differently and indexed from 1 to 5).

340 COURT PROJECT 3, FIRST VERSION, GROUND-FLOOR PLAN (*Figure* 277) [9296]
387×482 mm. Pen, some chalk. Inscribed on *verso*: *Piante due di Monte Citorio, e un sbozo tutte di diferenti disegni* (referring to this drawing and no.343).

The rear of the site is occupied in the present drawing by a semicircular block curved on its inner and outer sides. The rooms and staircase in the new block are trapezoidal, like those around the semicircular Piazza of Fontana's original project, and it is probable that the present rooms too are intended for the use of the notaries. In giving the present plan a curved outer wall

Fontana incorporates a feature of his two engraved projects, where a semicircular block was placed to the rear of the court behind the Curia.

341 COURT PROJECT 3, SECOND VERSION, GROUND-FLOOR PLAN (*Figure* 278, detail) [9289]
383×466 mm. Watermark no.9. Pen, traces of chalk. Inscribed on *verso*: *Due Piante del Cortile à semicircolo del Palazzo della Curia* (referring to this and no.342, catalogued below).

The drawing corresponds in technique with the preceding, and shows a slightly different project for the semicircular block to the rear of the courtyard in which stables are incorporated. The main Curia building is omitted in the present drawing, suggesting that the present project follows the former in point of time.

342 COURT PROJECT 4, GROUND-FLOOR PLAN (*Figure* 279) [9288]
350×457 mm. Watermark no.7. Chalk, pink and grey wash, with scale.

The drawing shows only the rear part of the site, and appears to be at ground level, though doorways are hard to find in the plan. The two curved screens stand before two curved walls. At the top of the site Fontana incorporates a block of houses, indicated in grey wash, which existed on the site, having been taken over from the fathers of S. Biagio (cf. drawing 336 above), and the screens, also in grey, may already have been built although no fountain is indicated on the drawing.

343 PLAN OF THE AREA BESIDE THE MAIN STAIRCASE (*Figure* 280, detail) [9295]
466×390 mm. Chalk, some pen and brown ink.

The present drawing is a study for the treatment of the area to the left of the main staircase, incorporating a part of the site behind the curved walls at the rear of the court. The border of the site and the main axial lines are indicated with dotted ink lines. A drawing of this detailed character might be expected to record adjustments to be made to a project which had already been established, and perhaps carried out in part. It is possible that the rooms above the transverse axis of the site correspond with those actually built, but below this line Fontana proposes to incorporate a small rectangular staircase running at right angles to the main staircase. According to the engraving by Specchi (Fig.251), which is corroborated by the following drawing (no.344), a staircase was built on this site, but on an axis parallel with that of the main staircase.

344 SECTION THROUGH AN AREA BESIDE THE MAIN STAIRCASE (*Figure* 281) [9309]
468×327 mm. Watermark no.9. Pen and brown ink, grey wash, traces of chalk. With scale and measurements. Inscribed: *Terzo* (i.e. the third of the last five drawings in the volume).

The present section covers the same part of the site as the preceding plan. On the right is a part of the main Curia building, shown in section, and next to it in elevation the side wall of the main staircase. This is interrupted to the left by the section of Fontana's new staircase, of which the flights run parallel with those of the main staircase. To the left again is the passageway on the transverse axis of the court and finally the first of the houses occupying the area between the street and the curved walls at the rear of the Curia courtyard. The design of the upper part of the new staircase is left undecided.

The new staircase appears to correspond with the final design as shown in Specchi's engraving (Fig.251), but Specchi appears to be inaccurate in showing the same structure repeated on the left in his plate; according to the Nolli plan Fontana had to make do with a screening wall here.
Copy by Vittone – the only drawing in Vol.168 copied by him – vol.II, fo.176.

345 PERSPECTIVE VIEW OF THE REAR PART OF THE COURT (1) (*Figure* 282) [9286]
448×314 mm. Watermark no.17. Pen, grey and blue wash, traces of chalk.

The drawing occupies the upper half of a once-folded sheet. The screens at the back of the court are close in design to those built, but elsewhere (especially in the absurdly large clock) the drawing appears to be less a project than a picturesque invention.

346 PERSPECTIVE VIEW OF THE REAR PART OF THE COURT (2) (*Figure* 283) [9287]
445×314 mm. Watermark no.17. Pen, grey wash, chalk. Inscribed upside down at base: *Due Prospetti del Cortile à Semicircolo nel Palazzo della Curia Romana* (referring to this and the preceding drawing, no.345).

A variant of the preceding drawing.

7. Drawings of the internal furnishings for the Curia

The following five drawings are bound amongst the other sheets in Vol.168, and it can be assumed that they are all connected with the Curia. The drawings appear to be by several different hands, those presumably of the craftsmen Fontana employed for the furnishing of the building. The inscriptions on drawing 347 are clearly in Fontana's hand and the drawing itself may be by him, but the second drawing for a similar structure (348) appears to be in a different style. The Fontana volume at Leipzig contains (fo.96) a drawing by Fontana of 1701 of the statue of Innocent XII placed in the Curia.

347 PERSPECTIVE VIEW OF A SEAT FOR A JUDGE AND TWO NOTARIES (*Figure* 284) [9274]
396×268 mm. Watermark no.19. Pen, grey wash, traces of chalk. Inscribed with notes.

The drawing occupies the upper half of a once-folded sheet.

348 PERSPECTIVE VIEWS OF A DAIS (*Figure* 285, detail) [9275]
264×410 mm. Watermark no.20. Pen, brown wash, traces of chalk. Inscribed on *verso*: *Risega di diuerse sedie p l'udienza di Monte Citorio.*

Perhaps by the same hand as no.351 below.

349 DESIGNS FOR AN ORNAMENTAL PEDESTAL (*Figure* 286) [9297]
269×405 mm. Watermark no.21. Pen.

A once-folded sheet which bears four designs for extremely elaborate pedestals. Two are given in alternative halves, one on the upper half of the *recto* and the other on the bottom half of the *verso*.

350 DESIGNS FOR SIMPLE PEDESTALS (*Figure* 287) [9298]
411×271 mm. Watermark no.2. Pen, brown wash, chalk. With scale.

A once-folded sheet turned upside down in the process of binding, and containing three studies for simple pedestals on the bottom half of the *recto*.

351 DESIGNS FOR LAMPS (*Figure* 288) [9299]
280×422 mm. Pen, coloured washes. Half of a double sheet, watermark no.7, folded in the binding and inscribed on the *verso* of the second half-sheet: *Diuersi modelli.*

With nine studies for lamps attached to gilt (?) back-plates of differing patterns, and matching studies in the bottom corners of a lamp in the form of a cornucopia.

Projects for the Liechtenstein palace, Landskron, Bohemia (1696)

Two drawings by Fontana for this palace, in the Liechtenstein archives, were made known by Tietze, together with documents connected with their commissioning. It was assumed by Tietze that the drawings were for the Liechtenstein Garden Palace in Vienna, the palace which was built to the designs of Domenico Martinelli. It is, however, convincingly shown by Passavant (1967, p.110) that Fontana's drawings were for the Liechtenstein country palace at Landskron in Bohemia. This is suggested in the first place by the documents quoted by Tietze (see below), and it is made clearer still by the character of Fontana's drawings, especially those at Windsor, which seem unacceptable as designs for a town palace. Fontana sent to Vienna a plan and an elevation for a large square building with a central courtyard containing an octagonal tower and divided by arcades into three sections (Tietze, fig.5 – plan, and fig.7 – elevation). To the plan was attached a flap whereby the basic drawing could be nearly halved, and transformed into a rectangular palace, the tower making a projection in the centre of the rear elevation (ibid., fig.6). Fontana's project apparently failed to win approval and Martinelli was given the commission for Landskron, as for Vienna; his palace there is dateable 1698 (Passavant, p.110).

The patron was Johann Adam Andreas (1656–1712), the reigning prince of Liechtenstein. He approached Fontana through Count George Adam Martinitz, who had arrived in Rome in January 1696 as Imperial ambassador to the court of Innocent XII in succession to Count Anton Liechtenstein, a cousin of the reigning prince (Pastor, Eng. ed., XXXII, p.668; on Martinitz, see below, The Martinitz Palace in Prague). Johann Adam Andreas sent to Martinitz a letter containing detailed instructions for Fontana to follow (Tietze, pp.16f., no.37, and below), and on 4 December 1696 Fontana apparently sent his drawings to Martinitz with the following letter (Tietze, p.17):

"Illmo et ecc^{mo} Sig^{re} e Padrone Col^{mo} Il Signore Conte di Martinitz Ambasciadore Cesareo in Roma.

Invio all Ecc^{za} V^{ra} li Disegni del Palazzo richiesto da quel gran Prenzipe, che è in Germania di Leictrestein, li quali ho procurato farli secondo il medesimo Signore accenna il suo desiderio bensì doppo procurato di sodisfare alle richieste, hò disposto l'edificio regolato alla Romana, per accrescergli magnificenza, come anche l'ho delineato di figura quadrata, volendo l'edificio di maggior ampiezza e ridotto a figura Paralellograma per la minore estensione, e spesa in modo, che quando anche fosse fabricato il primo tomo del ridotto paralellograma, si puole aggiungere il restante del quadrato corrispondente di proportioni correlative all'uno et all'altro. E se la debolezza delle mie Linee non fosse per sodisfare al un Signore di quella gran sorte et all' imposizione che mi ha fatta V^{ra} Ecc^{za} con tanta premura, ne sara cagione il mio poco talento. Mi perdonerà V^{ra}

Ecc^{za} della tardanza non già per difetto di volontà, ma delle grandi occupazioni ben note all' Ecc^{za} V^{ra}. Ritengo appresso di me le copie precise degl'acclusi Disegni in caso, che il Sig^{r} Prencipe di Leichtrestein volesse muovere, ò variare, accrescere ò diminuire qualche cosa, si possa qui sodisfare alla volantà di questo Sig^{re} con il carteggiare, benchè la struttura dell'opera mi pare, che habbia un composto di perfetto complesso, e capacità per un Palazzo di Villa nel modo, che chiede. E faccio all'Ecc^{za} V^{ra} hum^{ma} e profond^{ma} riverenza.

Di Casa li 4 X^{mbre} 1696
Dell'Ecc^{za} V^{ra} Umill^{mo} Divot^{mo} et Oblig^{mo} Ser^{re}
Carlo Cavaliere Fontana".

Volume 174 at Windsor (Contini, vol.25) contains copies of the two drawings sent to Vienna (presumably the copies mentioned in Fontana's letter) and twelve further studies for the Liechtenstein palace: in all seven plans, four elevations, a section and two studies of the staircase. The fourteen drawings are bound as a consecutive series at the end of the volume and two are inscribed with the patron's name – as interpreted by Fontana. The drawings can be divided into two groups; firstly those connected with the project sent to Vienna and secondly a group of four closely inter-related plans where the tower in the centre is larger than before and linked by four broad passages to the outer wings of the palace. Though it was the first project which Fontana chose to send to Vienna, the second group of drawings are clearly the more advanced, more polished and academic in character and even less suited to the needs of a dwelling place.

The drawings for Liechtenstein are problematical in that the architect appears to have disregarded most of the instructions contained in his patron's letter to Martinitz, and hence the ideas set out in the drawings are of uncertain parentage. It is further obscure why Fontana should have gone on to produce a second group of drawings, about which the patron apparently knew nothing.

Liechtenstein's letter to Martinitz contains the most detailed instructions about the type of building required. It reads, in Tietze's transcription:

"Havendomi Vra Ecc^{za} promesso di scriverle piu diffusamente interno al Disegno, che io desidero dal sig. cavalier Fontana, ingiongo quà il sito, pregandola di fargli raccomandare quest' affare da qualche duno di sua Casa: Acciò però egli mi possa intender meglio, hò voluto ricordar, al detto Sig.^{r} Fontana, che nel fare il Disegno, deve regolarsi secondo la nostra misura di un Klaffter di Vienna, e poiche il sito, in cui io penso di far fabricare è assai grande, cioè longo cento, e largo cinquanta in sessanta Klaffter, così sarei di parere di farvi fare due Cortili, nel primo de'quali vi doverebbero essere Rimesso di Carrozze, Cantine, Stalle, con sopra le habitazioni per la gente bassa, e sarebbe sufficiente, se queste fossero alti due Piani, cioè l'altezza delle stalle con sopra Mezzanini. Nell' altro Cortile gli vi potrebe fare tre Appartamenti, cioè l'Appartamento terreno, e poi due Appartamenti nobili, e poichè in Italia e particolarmente in Roma si sogliono fabricare le stanze assai alte, il che non sarebbe a proposito per questo Paese, a causa de gran freddi così basterebbe se egli alzasse le stanze sino all'altezza di ventine piedi. Fa bisogna ancora una Cappella nella quale si possa vedere dalle superiori, l'entrata però potrebbe essere al disotto. Si deve ancora osservare, che li volti della scala venghino alti, e che detta scala venga commoda, larga e lucida. Nel mezzo piano potrebbe fare una sala e dargli l'altezza di due Appartamenti. Dal ingionta pianta si può vedere, dove sia il miglior prospetto, ed ivi si dovrebbero fare le stanze principali: e poichè le stanze doppie sono molto commode, per causa della communicazione e stanno meglio che li corridori, che hauno del convento, perciò anche questo gli si dovrebbe avvisare, ma quelle, che guarderanno nel cortile non sarebbe necessario che fossero tanto grandi come le altre, poichè servono piutosto di passaggio che di habitazione. Di più non sarà forse noto al Signor Fontana, che noi qui si serviamo di forni di stufe, chè però prego fargli spiegare, che Bestia sia un forno di stufa, e che cerchi il modo di poter scaldare le stufe senza pregiudizio delle stanze. Per collocare l'orlogio sarà anche necessaria una torre. Il Vestibolo in questo secondo cortile potrebbe essere un poco ornato. Il Portone, e le finestre di buon gusto e che la fabrica havesse un bel cornicione: Nel resto io non desidero ornamenti superflui, mentre io voglio far fabricare più per necessità che per adornamento. Ma già che si fabrica aggradirei ancora che la cosa fosse commoda e di buon gusto. Finalmente stante che il sito è alguanto discosto dalla città e vicino ai monti, è necessaria una Fossa per sicurezza, che lo cinga, la quale non fa bisogno, che rassomigli quelle delle fortezze. Prego Vra Ecc^{za} di far l'accordo con detto signor Fontana prima di metterlo in opera, mentre talvolta non restono sodisfatti con la discrezione che se li da."

On only one of Fontana's drawings is the scale supplied in *Klaffter* (Fig.298); his plans are for a building just under fifty *Klaffter* square, which would have occupied under half of the available site; in the basic plans there is no stable court; no *piano nobile* is provided at second-floor level (the section (Fig.296) shows that the highest rooms are those of the ground and first floors); there is apparently no chapel, and no room two storeys in height, except for that in the tower itself; no stoves are marked on the plans and no provision is made for stoves passages; corridors, however, which the prince disliked, are present in the majority of the plans, but not a moat. The only requirements which Fontana consistently meets are those for a clock-tower and for restraint in the decoration.

The project introduced, however, on the flaps of the design sent to Vienna (Fig.291) and in the corresponding first-floor plan (Fig.293) fulfils the Prince's demand for a separate stable court with a single storey of rooms above the stables, and in these flaps Fontana introduces a moat (present also in the elevations) which extends on to the paper of the basic sheet. In the elevation connected with this stage of the planning (361; Fig.300), the clock-tower, projecting in the centre of the rear elevation, is transformed into a *campanile*, containing three bells and decorated with the figures of two angels – the only direct reference to a chapel in Fontana's projects.

It seems likely that Fontana received full instructions from the patron only after he had started work on the plans. Several references in the Prince's letter to Martinitz seem rather obscure but the phrase '*più diffusamente*' in the first sentence carries the implication that less detailed instructions had already been sent to Martinitz, and it was perhaps on the basis of these that Fontana began work on his drawings. If this is so, it can be imagined that he may already have begun work on his second group of drawings when the second letter arrived, and that he decided at this juncture to adapt the drawings of the first project to meet the Prince's new demands, adding flaps to the two plans of the palace and drawing the first-floor plan of the stable blocks. In the corresponding elevation drawing the tower became the *campanile* of the chapel, and the alternative project for the staircase was probably also drawn up at this time to satisfy the Prince's demand for a staircase *commoda, larga e lucida.* When deciding finally which drawing to send to Vienna, Fontana apparently chose only the ground-floor plan and the last of the three front elevations.

The exact nature of the instructions with which Fontana, on this analysis, began work can only be guessed at, but the need for a clock-tower, the strangest element in his projects, must have been known to him. In placing this in the centre of the court and adding at the top a *belvedere* Fontana may have had in mind his drawings of 1689 for a casino for the Veneto (see above), but the general character of his project – four wings around a large court with a domed tower – seems French or German; Fontana's assurance that his project was *regolato alla Romana* seems true only of the elevations. For a reason so far unknown, they are drawn in such a way as to suggest that the tower was placed in the centre of the roof over the entrance wing of the palace, in the orthodox northern manner. In spite of this, the project has a strangely hybrid character, and this can be attributed mainly to the Roman treatment of the wall surface up to cornice level.

It is perhaps not surprising that the Prince chose not to carry out Fontana's project but it would be wrong to suppose that the drawings themselves were of no further importance. The type of plan evolved by Fontana in a polished and academic form in the second group of studies is one which was further developed by architects of the following century. Vanvitelli's palace at Caserta, to take the most obvious example, is remarkably close to Fontana's second project both in its general character and in such a detail as the placing of the main staircase (see de Seta). Vittone too was interested in Fontana's drawings for the Liechtenstein palace and amongst copies in the two Vittone albums in Paris a whole sheet is devoted to each of the second series of plans.

ADDITIONAL BIBLIOGRAPHY:

G. Passavant, *Studien über Domenico Egidio Rossi . . .*, 1967.

M. Petzet in *Alte und moderne Kunst*, II, 1957, no.5, pp.16f.

C. de Seta in *Storia dell'Arte*, 1974, pp.267ff. (where Michetti's drawing, no.620 below, is also published, as a Fontana drawing (fig.19), and no.243 above is given as a church project (fig.24)).

H. Tietze in *Jahrbuch des Kunsthistorischen Instituts,* Vienna, 1919, pp.1ff.

First group of drawings

352 GROUND-FLOOR PLAN (*Figure* 289) [9558]
413×*c*.410 mm. Two sheets joined vertically. Pen, grey wash, some chalk.

The plan, including its large flap, is identical with that sent by Fontana to Vienna (Tietze, figs 5 and 6). All four façades have a central doorway and a vestibule leading to the court, but the one to the right in the drawing is apparently intended to be the principal one, since its vestibule leads to the staircase chamber.

On the flap (Fig.291; 413×321 mm., two sheets joined vertically) the rear wing of the palace is omitted, together with six bays of each side wing. A moat is introduced on the flap and extended round the palace on the paper of the basic sheet. In the space gained by the halving of the plan two 'L'-shaped blocks are introduced, each with stables and a small chapel.
Copy by Vittone, showing half of the basic plan and half of the flap, omitting the stable block, vol.II, fo.169.

353 FIRST-FLOOR PLAN OF THE STABLES (*Figure* 292) [9564]
418 × *c*.217 mm. Pen, grey wash, some black and yellow (?) chalk.

The plan is of the two stable blocks shown at ground level in the flap of the foregoing drawing. They contain the 'sopra habitazioni per la gente bassa' mentioned in Prince Liechtenstein's letter.
Copy by Vittone, vol.II, fo.139.

354 FIRST-FLOOR PLAN (*Figure* 290) [9559]
413 × 421 mm. (including folded edge on right). Two sheets joined horizontally. Watermark no.7. Pen, grey wash, some black and yellow(?) chalk.

The basic drawing corresponds with that of 352 and a project on a flap (Fig.293; 369 × 205 mm.) corresponds with the flap project of 352, though the stable blocks, being of only two, relatively low storeys, are omitted.
Copy by Vittone of the basic plan, vol.II, fo.154.

355 PLAN OF A STAIRCASE (*Figure* 294) [9565]
C.267 × 415 mm. Watermark no.7. Pen, grey wash, traces of chalk. With scale.

The project differs from that shown in the previous plans in that the open wells of the two staircases are omitted and the junction of the stairchamber with the central, in this case circular, *salone* is worked out with greater care.
Copy by Vittone of half the plan, vol.II fo.168.

356 SECTION OF THE STAIRCASE (*Figure* 295) [9557]
415 × 273 mm. Pen, grey and brown wash, chalk.

The section is taken across the passage dividing the flights of the two staircases at ground and first-floor level.

357 TRANSVERSE SECTION (*Figure* 296) [9556]
415 × 273 mm. Watermark no.7. Pen, grey and brown wash, traces of chalk.

The section is taken through the centre of the octagonal tower and the arcades and corridors to each side of it; it corresponds with the basic plans 352 and 354. Though Prince Liechtenstein asked Fontana to provide over the ground floor two *piani nobili*, it is the ground and first floor which are the highest storeys in the palace, the second floor being relatively low. The central cupola is an undecorated hemisphere, unlike the domes of the elevations, and in dotted ink lines a low pitched roof is suggested as an alternative to the cupola.
Copy by Vittone of just over half the drawing, vol.II, fo.176.

358 FRONT ELEVATION (1) (*Figure* 297) [9555]
274 × 415 mm. Pen, grey and brown wash, traces of chalk.

The fifteen bays of the façade, enclosed by a moat (shown in section), are divided, as in the plans, into five sections of three bays, pilaster-strips framing the central three bays and double pilaster-strips the corner blocks. The roof over these three blocks is designed so as to give the appearance of a series of pediments supported on the pilaster-strips. The elevation is exceptionable only for the strange super-structure surmounting the octagonal tower in the court and its two flanking arcades. This is drawn in pure elevation and in such a way as to suggest that it was to break through the roof of the front wing, though, as the plans show, it lay in reality some way back in the court.
Copy by Vittone, vol.II, fos213/4, published by Petzet as an original project by Fontana.

359 FRONT ELEVATION (2) (*Figure* 298) [9552]
272 × 415 mm. Two sheets joined horizontally. Watermark no.7. Pen, grey and brown wash, some chalk. With two scales, one labelled *Palmi* R. and one (in capitals) *Klaffter*.

The lower half-sheet is a version of the preceding elevation cut off at a level just above the cornice. Attached to the upper half-sheet in the centre is the elevation of a dome, equally deriving from the preceding elevation, and probably cut from the upper part of the same sheet which forms the lower half of the present drawing. The result of this work with scissors and paste is a version of the foregoing elevation with a simple dome surmounting the façade, and on this basic design a number of embellishments are suggested roughly in ink and chalk. The presence of a scale in *Klaffter* suggests that this and the following elevation were made after Fontana had received Liechtenstein's letter, and that they are therefore connected with the halved project of the flaps of plans 352 and 354 (see Introduction).

360 FRONT ELEVATION (3 – FINAL DESIGN) (*Figure* 299) [9553]
272 × 415 mm. Watermark no.7. Pen, grey and brown wash, traces of chalk. Inscribed, upper left, with the patron's name, now covered by the binding strip.

The present elevation corresponds with that sent to Vienna and illustrated by Tietze (fig.7). It is based on the left half of the foregoing drawing.

361 REAR ELEVATION (*Figure* 300) [9554]
272 × 415 mm. Pen, grey and brown wash, traces of chalk.

This elevation corresponds with the design shown on the flaps of plans 352 and 354. The drum of the

central tower functions as a *campanile* (three bells being visible beyond the central window) and it is decorated with a clock supported by angels.
Copy by Vittone, vol.II, fo.150.

Second group of drawings

362 GROUND-FLOOR PLAN (*Figure* 301) [9562]
414×544 mm. (including folded strip on right). Two sheets joined vertically. Watermark no.7. Pen, grey wash, some black and yellow(?) chalk. With scale (left) and measurements (right). Many small alterations drawn on flaps and pasted on the basic sheet.

In its general character the plan corresponds with those of the preceding group, but, as far as the elevations are affected, the central projecting blocks on each façade are no longer present. Each entrance leads to a vestibule, divided into 'nave' and 'aisles', and on all four sides the vestibules are extended towards the centre of the plan, giving access to a circular *salone* in the centre, larger than that of the preceding group of plans and sited within a block which is nearer to a square than to an octagon. The main staircase remains in the same position as before, but the open rectangular wells on each side of the central passageway are shorter, and the stair-chamber smaller, and approached from a short flight of steps projecting into the vestibule. Columns were at first used for the arcades of the four courts, but these were replaced by piers, drawn in some cases on flaps pasted on to the basic sheet. Similarly the central *salone* had an articulation of columns lining its walls, which are covered by flaps.
Copy by Vittone, vol.II, fo.139.

363 FIRST-FLOOR PLAN (1) (*Figure* 302) [9563]
414×536 mm. Two sheets joined vertically. Watermark no.7. Pen, grey and brown wash, some black and yellow(?) chalk. Inscribed on *verso*: *Dissegni p Lechtestein / Germania*.

The present drawing is probably the first of two plans showing the first-floor disposition of the design recorded at ground-floor level in the preceding drawing, although the courts no longer have rounded corners. Fontana may have intended the courts to have rounded corners only at ground-floor level, becoming square from the level of the first floor upwards. This interpretation is borne out by the character of the following plan.
Copy by Vittone, vol.II, fo.156.

364 FIRST-FLOOR PLAN (2) (*Figure* 303) [9560]
413×538 mm. Two sheets joined vertically. Watermark no.7. Pen, grey and brown wash, some chalk.

The present plan corresponds closely with the foregoing, but the windows overlooking the courts have wide openings in the centre flanked by double pilasters and narrower openings in the corners. This articulation corresponds with that suggested in the ground-floor plan (362), and the present drawing is probably an improved design for its first floor. A further improvement in planning lies in the introduction of long corridors in two of the wings of the palace. In the previous plan Fontana had followed Prince Liechtenstein's instructions about corridors, but here he seems to have been unable completely to restrain his liking for open passages.
Copy by Vittone, vol.II, fo.157.

365 GROUND-FLOOR PLAN (SECOND VERSION) (*Figure* 304) [9561]
413×*c*.332 mm. Two sheets joined vertically. Watermark no.7. Pen, grey and blue wash, some black and yellow(?) chalk.

The differences between this and the preceding ground-floor plan are few but important: only one wing has a central entrance and a vestibule (that to the left in the drawing), two staircases are now present, and they are to be approached from the entrance *via* the central *salone*. The courtyards have rounded corners and are articulated with wide central openings divided by columns from the smaller flanking openings. Rough chalk sketches show proposed additions and alterations in front of the entrance wing of the palace, but these stop short where the sheet has evidently been cut. Ruled lines in chalk correspond with the position of the moat.
Copy by Vittone, vol.II, fo.158.

Projects for a Sternberg palace on the Hradčany, Prague (*c.* 1696–1700)

A group of eleven drawings at the beginning of Volume 170 are connected with a site on the Hradčany in Prague. They comprise two drawings, a site plan (no.366) and a plan project (no.367) which were evidently sent to Fontana from Prague and are by an anonymous German draughtsman, and nine drawings containing Fontana's own suggestions for the design of the palace. The site can be identified on the basis of the site plan and its inscriptions as that on the extreme corner of the square, directly opposite the present Nationalgalerie. It lies immediately beside the famous Schwarzenberg palace, built in the 16th century, and is now occupied by the Levy or Salm palace, which was constructed about 1810 by the architect František Pávíček (Merhout and Wirth, fig.28).

When the site plan at Windsor was made the land was occupied by an untidy group of buildings, fronting on to the Hradčany and bounded to the left and at the rear by a road curving down towards the town centre of Prague. There was thus a considerable drop in the level of the land from the front of the site to a series of gardens at the rear. These buildings are shown in perspective from the rear in an 18th-century view of the Hradčany (Merhout and Wirth, fig.29) and the correspondence with the site plan at Windsor is extremely close. The identification of the site can be corroborated on the evidence of the inscriptions on the plan. According to these the neighbouring site belonged to the Eggenberg family, and this family is indeed recorded in the 18th century as the owner of the Schwarzenberg palace (for example in an early 18th-century plan of the Hradčany by Frid(eric) Probst, index no.6, 'Fürste Eggenberg: jetzt Schwartzenburg Haus').

Notes on the history of the site have been most kindly provided by Dr Emmanuel Poche, and from these it transpires that Fontana's patron was in all probability Count Ignaz Karl von Sternberg (d.1700). The collection of buildings shown on the site plan referred apparently to two houses, a 16th-century corner house and, between this and the Schwarzenberg palace, a second house which was built for the Trautson family and was also of the 16th century. In the 17th century the site came into the possession of the Sternbergs and it was owned in the 18th century by the Paars and Brettfeld families. Ignaz Karl von Sternberg was Stadtholder of Prague and the president of the Court of Appeal from 1696 to his death in 1700 (Wurzbach, vol.37, Sternberg – no.21). He was the younger brother of Wenzel Adalbert (d.1708), *Hofmeister* of the Bohemian court (ibid., Sternberg – no.42), and famous as a patron of the arts; it was he who built the palace of Troja near Prague (1679–85), designed by Jean Baptiste Mathey and the palace behind the present Nationalgalerie on a site opposite the one for which Fontana's projects were designed. This building was constructed in 1698 to 1720 by Domenico Martinelli and Giovanni Aliprandi (see Kubíček, pp.100ff.). Thus had Fontana's palace been constructed the entrance to the Royal Castle of Prague would have been flanked, more or less, by a pair of Sternberg palaces, that of the elder brother near the right-hand corner and that of the younger on the left. Jean Baptiste Mathey was apparently the Sternberg's family architect until he left Prague in 1694; he had made plans for the palace constructed by Martinelli and Aliprandi and had he remained in Prague Fontana would perhaps not have been consulted about the palace of Ignaz Karl.

This analysis presupposes that Fontana's projects date from before 1700, the year of Ignaz Karl's death. Their date is not known for certain, but it seems in the circumstances more likely that they were made at the request of this patron, rather than in the years immediately after his death, when the site was presumably in the possession of his heirs. The accident of his death would provide a reason why no building was carried out. Ignaz Karl had no children to succeed him and on the death of his brother Wenzel Adalbert this elder branch of the family apparently died out (Wurzbach, vol.37, family trees under Sternberg).

Neither of the Sternbergs is recorded as having visited Rome and it is likely that Fontana was approached through the agency, and perhaps on the recommendation, of Count Georg Adam Martinitz, who was in Rome as Imperial Ambassador between 1696 and 1700 (see below); he was related to the Sternbergs through his wife, a member of the younger branch of the family.

It is not difficult to understand from the drawings at Windsor why Fontana was consulted about the design of the palace; the plan designed evidently by a local German architect, which was sent to Rome (Fig.306; 367 below), appears to be extremely clumsy – both as a drawing and in the design of the architecture. This project must be by a very little-known architect; it can scarcely be by anyone as competent as Martinelli. In his own projects Fontana paid scant attention to the ideas present in this plan; and instead he designed one of his most ambitious palaces in the Roman idiom, with a large central court, arcaded at ground level, and a façade of three stories and an attic, articulated with pilaster-strips. Two variants of the design are given, one recorded in two plans (Figs 307, 308) and one in a group of plans, sections and an elevation. The two projects are similar, but that recorded in the two plans must be the earlier. It is clumsier than the other project, especially in the planning of the elevations and Fontana apparently forgot at this stage that stoves and stove-passages would be needed for the palace (see the entries for the Liechtenstein and Martinitz palaces). They are omitted in the ground-floor plan and added only as an afterthought to that of the first floor. In the second group of drawings they occur as an integral part of the design. It is not known, finally, whether Fontana sent any of his drawings for this palace to Prague.

ADDITIONAL BIBLIOGRAPHY:
S. Merhout and Z. Wirth, *Zmizelá Praha*, 1946.

366 Unidentified German draughtsman
SITE PLAN (*Figure* 305) [9337]
318×480 mm. Watermark, an elephant. Pen, yellow and pink wash, on brown paper. With scale (unlabelled). Annotated in full in German

with translations into Italian on flaps of white paper pasted to the plan.

The existing buildings are bounded at the front by the Hradčany ('la piazza di Racino'), and by a side street at the left ('la Strada nuoua'), which continues along the rear of the site. On the right is the Eggenberg (now Schwarzenberg) palace. The existing buildings have three courts, the largest to the right ('questo e la Gran Corte'), a small court in the centre ('la Corta piccola'), and a narrow stable court on the left ('un altra Corta Piccola'). This last court is divided from the side road by a stable block ('La Stalla p i Caualli verso la Strada nuoua'). The site sloped at the back and steps lead down to a small garden and a terrace ('Il giardino piccolo / della piazza di sopra sin al giardino piccolo e la profondezza .9. braccio'). From here further steps led down to a long garden occupying the whole width of the site ('Il gran giardino / della piazza di sopra sin al gran giardino e profondo .14. braccio'). From here there was a further drop to the road behind the garden wall ('della piazza di sopra sin alla strada nuoua è profondo 22½ braccio'). The plan also bears instructions that the corner of the block facing the Hradčany is to be filled out ('la piazza il quale deue tenere dl Racino p la Casa e p fare la Stare in una linia dritta'), and that the Eggenberg palace probably had a right of ancient lights which was to be respected ('Questo luogo dipinto Rosso e la Casa di Echenberg e de la piazza di soppra e auuanti la Casa sin à la Casa di Echenberg e a quella di Echenberg una finestra che ua auuanti et è alta di .17. braccie, è più alta credo che si permeterà a fabricare p che la finestra fa fuora dlla pente di vs: Ill:ma'). On the *verso* of the sheet are sums in chalk, apparently in Fontana's hand.

367 Unidentified German draughtsman
PLAN PROJECT (*Figure* 306) [9338]
321×481 mm. Pen, green, grey and brown wash, on brown paper. With two scales, one in Fontana's hand and thus of *palmi romani*.

The project is by the same hand as the last. The new palace is a rectangular block of 18 by 11 bays, with two courtyards and entrances leading to each one from the Hradčany. The main staircase lies between the two courts. It consists of flights rising on three sides of a central core, which is itself occupied by a circular newel staircase. The plan appears to encroach upon part of the land coloured pink in the preceding drawing and thus belonging to the Eggenberg palace.

Fontana's first project

368 GROUND-FLOOR PLAN (*Figure* 307) [9343]
370×481 mm. Pen, grey, green and yellow washes, some chalk. With scale.

The plan is of a large rectangular block with one main court and a narrow side court lying beside the Eggenberg palace. Like the draughtsman of the foregoing project Fontana would appear to have failed to respect the limitations of the site at its rear corners, and this is indicated on his plan by dotted ink lines and washes. The bay on the left of the main façade is excluded from the composition of the façade by a pilaster strip. The rear wing (incorporating a stable) must have lain considerably below the level of the rest of the plan, but there is no indication of this in the drawing (see plan 370 below). A sketch in chalk in the court suggests that Fontana considered decreasing the size of the court, as happens in the second project.
Copy by Vittone, vol.II, fo.166.

369 FIRST-FLOOR PLAN (*Figure* 308) [9339]
281×418 mm. Watermark no.7. Chalk, grey and pink wash, some pen and brown ink.

A rough plan which corresponds for the most part with the preceding drawing. Some features, not present in the ground-floor plan, are taken up in the following project. One of these is the provision of a second staircase in the wing to the right of the court, and another is the inclusion of stoves which are here marked by ink stars.

Fontana's second project

370 GROUND-FLOOR PLAN (*Figure* 309) [9340]
369×479 mm. Two sheets joined vertically. Watermark no.7. Pen, grey and other coloured washes, traces of chalk. With two scales, the upper one of *palmi romani*.

The plan is organized on roughly the same lines as before, but the court is smaller, and provision is made throughout the plan for stoves with passages behind them for refuelling. The rear wing is covered by a blank flap of paper, which presumably indicates that this part of the plan is at a lower level than the rest (see sections nos 374 and 375 below).
Copy by Vittone, vol.II, fo.140.

371 FIRST-FLOOR PLAN (*Figure* 310) [9341]
370×478 mm. Pen, grey and yellow wash, some chalk. With two scales, the upper one of *palmi romani*.

Long passages for fuelling the stoves are included in the plan. Chalk sketches occur in the rooms at the front corners of the plan, apparently showing methods of dividing each room into two sections. Copy by Vittone, vol.II, fo.141.

372 FIRST-FLOOR PLAN (UNFINISHED) [9342]
370×475 mm. Watermark no.9. Chalk.

An unfinished plan corresponding closely with the preceding.

373 TRANSVERSE SECTION (*Figure* 312) [9345]
370×479 mm. Watermark no.9. Pen, grey and brown wash, traces of chalk.

The section runs from side to side of the site, showing in elevation the rear façade of the court.
Copy by Vittone of right half of drawing, vol.II, fo.161.

374 LONGITUDINAL SECTION (*Figure* 313) [9346]
370×481 mm. Watermark no.9. Pen, grey and and other coloured washes, traces of chalk.

The section runs from the back to the front of the palace, showing the side façade of the courtyard in elevation. The stable at the rear of the site is at a level beneath that of the ground floor. It would seem to be cut off completely from the rest of the palace. Stoves in the front and rear wings, drawn in pink wash, are shown in section.
Copy by Vittone of left half of drawing, vol.II, fo.161.

375 LONGITUDINAL SECTION, SHOWING STAIRCASES (*Figure* 314) [9344]
370×479 mm. Pen, grey and brown wash, traces of chalk.

The section is taken through the wing to the right of the court. Flaps of paper pasted down on the basic sheet cover the whole of the circular staircase and a small section of the landing of the rectangular one.

376 ELEVATION OF THE MAIN FAÇADE (*Figure* 311) [9347]
369×480 mm. Pen, grey wash, traces of chalk.

The bay on the extreme right of the façade is omitted in this drawing.
Copy by Vittone of right half of drawing, vol.II, fo.147.

A study of primitive boats (*c.*1698 ?)

A single drawing in Volume 176 (Fig.315) contains studies in pen and chalk of primitive and antique boats. As was discovered by Noach, the same boats reappear in two sheets in the Fontana volume in the British Museum (Fig.316), the volume which contains for the most part the architect's drawings for Porto d'Anzio and the aqueduct of Civitavecchia. The two sheets form part of a series containing numbered studies in ink and wash of various types of early boats and one is inscribed: 'p(er) la nautica Cfontana'. The contents page written by Fontana for the volume of drawings at Leipzig contains a reference to studies of the same kind which are now missing from the volume: '. . . Nautica e Colonna Rostra Naue primitie p la Nautica . . .', which may be those in the British Museum volume, Fontana having transferred the group to his volume of projects for Porto d'Anzio.

The drawings were probably intended for publication as illustrations in a book which Fontana contemplated writing on the subject of primitive boats ('la Nautica'). This book was never printed, but Fontana appended an analysis of such boats to the short unillustrated book he published in 1710 on Porto d'Anzio, *Antio e sue Antichità*. General interest in the subject of antique boats appears to have arisen when projects for the reconstruction of the Roman harbour at Anzio were in hand, and Fontana at the start of the third part of his book explains that he collected material about the boats on behalf of the Pope (Innocent XII) and in preparation for the Pope's visit to Nettuno and Porto d'Anzio in April 1698: 'stimai bene di stendere in pochi giorni le seguenti notizie per informarne il Papa, acciò potesse discorrerne con gli Eminentissimi Porporati, . . .'

He goes on to speak of the various types of boat, some of which are shown on Trajan's column, beginning with the hollowed tree trunk. The boats in the Windsor drawing are confined to the earliest types. The drawing would seem to antedate the second of the two related sheets in the British Museum (Fig.316), where two further vessels have been added to the collection of seven represented on the Windsor sheet. It may perhaps have been made in 1698, at the time when Fontana began his studies on the subject of primitive boats.

The Windsor drawing occupies the *verso* of the second half of a large page folded in the binding of the volume. The first half of the page contains marks in chalk which may represent unfinished sketches of additional boats, and in ink it contains a dotted line perhaps representing a scale.

377 STUDIES OF SEVEN PRIMITIVE BOATS (*Figure* 315) [9762]
*C.*215×303 mm. Watermark, on preceding half page, no.5. Pen, chalk.

The upper part of the drawing contains four studies of boats in ink, and beneath them three further boats are indicated very faintly in chalk. The seven drawings correspond in reverse with seven of the nine drawings of primitive boats on sheet seven of the British Museum volume. The nine boats are there numbered according to their chronological order, or so it seems. The equivalent numbers for the studies on the present sheet are the following: top row, from left to right, nos 4, 2, 7 and 1; bottom row, from left to right, nos 5, 9 and 3.

Prague, the Martinitz palace (1700)

Eleven drawings in Volume 174 (Contini, vol.25) show projects for the Martinitz palace in Prague. Four sheets are inscribed with the name of the patron, and two are dated 20 March 1700 (nos 383/386). There is every chance that this project of Fontana was actually built, though the palace – still existing in Prague (Fig.317) – is generally attributed to a certain Giuseppe Bartolomeo Scotti, a little-known Italian architect. It is dated about 1705 and lies on the castle hill on the west bank of the Moldau, on the north side of the Loretánská *ulice*, a broad street running from the Hradčany to the Loreto church (Kubiček, p.92).

The palace was built for Count Georg Adam Martinitz, who had been sent as Imperial ambassador to the court of Innocent XII in January 1696 in place of Count Anton Liechtenstein (Pastor, Eng. ed., XXXII, pp.668ff.). Martinitz's intolerable arrogance, however, offended the Pope and Count Leopold Joseph von Lamberg was sent to replace him in January 1700 (ibid., p.682). He returned to Austria in April 1700, in the month following that inscribed on Fontana's drawings (ibid., p.682). Martinitz was again in Rome for a few days in June 1707 (ibid., XXXIII, pp.44f.), returning to Austria at the end of the year (Wurzbach, p.47), and he died in Prague in 1714 (ibid.).

Fontana was evidently asked to alter an existing building for his patron, and he must have been sent detailed plans of the site, though these have not survived. A new front wing for the palace was evidently the main need, and in Fontana's plans two wings running back from the front are shown in their original state, no alterations being attempted. The wing on the left may have contained the kitchens, though the interpretation of certain symbols drawn on the plans is problematic. Fontana produced an interesting series of no less than five projects for the alteration of the front wing, gradually replacing more and more of the existing fabric, and on this principle the ordering of the five projects presents no difficulties. The earliest plan (Fig.318) reveals that the front part of the building consisted of an untidy series of rooms masked by a sloping façade, in character not unlike the earlier Martinitz palace, a 16th-century building on the Hradčany square itself (Kubiček, p.38). The main entrance lay off-centre to the left, with a straight passage behind it which led into a corner of the court; to the right of the passage were the stables.

Fontana concentrated in his projects on making the plan regular, in the design of the façade and in the planning of the rooms behind. A main staircase is provided and at the start a *loggia* screening the court elevation of the front wing. In the later projects a broad vestibule becomes a feature of the plan, but in none of the drawings is provision made for a new stable to replace the old one. In the last two projects Fontana was careful to provide passages between the rooms from which the stoves could be re-fuelled from behind – such passages had been omitted in the drawings for the Liechtenstein palace. The mechanism of the German stove is the subject of one of Fontana's drawings in the album at Leipzig (fo.36).

Apart from the slope of the façade, which Fontana corrected only partially in the first three of the projects, his main difficulty lay in the lack of correspondence between the central axes of the street and court façades of the front wing – a vestibule running through the block on the central axis of the court façade met the front façade considerably to the left of centre. After what was evidently a great struggle with this problem, Fontana decided in his final project (Fig.324) to provide a completely new front façade of eleven bays, with the main doorway on the central axis. A vestibule divided into 'nave' and 'aisles' leads through to the court to the right of its central axis, but by allowing the court façade to remain straight, adding no projections of any kind, the presence of the vestibule is not unduly emphasized.

Fontana's final project is recorded in a ground and two first-floor plans. The former (no.386; Fig.324) is inscribed *risoluta*, and the first of the latter *stabilita* (no.387). These are presumably copies of drawings sent to Prague, or the originals of such copies, as suggested by the word *Duplicata* written on the second of the first-floor plans (no.388; Fig.327). This group unfortunately contains no elevation. An elevation for the preceding project, the fourth, exists (no.385; Fig.325), but its façade differed considerably from that of the final project, being shorter by two bays. The drawing itself is inscribed *stabilita*, but this is apparently an error on Fontana's part since the corresponding plans are labelled *n*(on) *abracciati* (no.383) and *n*(on) *risoluti* (no.384). The ground-floor plans of projects four and five are those dated 20 March 1700; both may have been shown on 20 March to Martinitz, who expressed a preference for the second and decided to have it carried out.

The absence of an elevation drawing for the final project leaves a margin of doubt for the attribution to Fontana of the existing palace in

Prague. In plan, however, its façade corresponds closely with that suggested in his final project – 11 bays divided by pilaster-strips into sections of 3/5/3 with the main doorway in the centre. It has kindly been confirmed by Dr Emmanuel Poche that the plan of the rest of the front wing of the palace corresponds with that given in Fontana's drawings. For the façade itself all that is missing in Fontana's plan is the pair of free-standing columns supporting a balcony over the doorway. The façade of the existing palace is strikingly Roman in character, and more austere than in the elevation drawing of Fontana's fourth project. There is, however, one obviously un-Roman feature, a pedimented attic storey over the central five bays, of which there is no trace in the elevation of the fourth project. This must have been added as a *belvedere*, giving a view over the houses on the opposite side of the street towards the country south of Prague; it recalls especially the pedimented central attic of the Clam-Gallas palace in Prague, designed some years later by Fischer von Erlach. Assuming that the palace was indeed built, all or in part, to Fontana's design it is possible that the attic was added to his final elevation at the special request of the patron, or that this and other modifications were made by the architect (Scotti ?) who supervised the construction of the building.

First project

378 GROUND-FLOOR PLAN (*Figure* 318) [9548]
268×410 mm. Watermark no.22. Pen, chalk, brown and grey wash. With scale, probably of *palmi romani*.

In this and all the following plans the front wing of the palace is shown, including part of a courtyard behind and sections of the wings running back to each side of it. The existing plan is indicated with dotted ink lines, and much of it is filled in with brown wash, denoting the parts to be incorporated in Fontana's design. Fontana's actual additions, confined to the front wing of the palace and the area of the courtyard immediately behind, are relatively few and indicated in grey wash and chalk. A *loggia* is added to the court side of the front wing, with projecting blocks at its sides, of which that on the right accommodates a rectangular staircase.

Second project

379 GROUND-FLOOR PLAN (*Figure* 319) [9546]
307×415 mm. Two sheets joined vertically. Watermark no.22. Pen, chalk, grey, buff and brown wash.

This drawing corresponds in technique and in the type of paper used with the foregoing; the existing walls are again indicated with dotted ink lines, coloured brown where they are incorporated in Fontana's project. The proposed additions are shown in grey, and walls to be demolished are coloured buff. The front elevation has a central section of seven bays, slightly straightened, and the main entrance is moved from the left to the centre. It leads to a new passage, which emerges in a *loggia* with an unusual double staircase (sketched in chalk) projecting outwards into the court.

380 PLAN OF THE STAIRCASE (*Figure* 321) [9550]
179×188 mm. Chalk, grey wash.

A flap of the foregoing plan, which became separated when the upper margin of the basic plan (no.379) was folded around drawings 9547/49 (nos 387 and 382) in the process of binding. The method of ascent is not made clear, though it is most probable that the two halves of the design correspond exactly, the ascent probably beginning with either of the straight flights and continuing with the quarter-circle flights. Access to the rooms of the first floor would in this case have been made *via* a gallery leading from the circumference of the half-circle to the *loggia* stretching across the court elevation.
Copy by Vittone, vol.II, fo.171.

Third project

381 GROUND-FLOOR PLAN (*Figure* 320) [9551]
272×415 mm. Pen, grey, yellow and buff wash, some chalk. With two scales, of which one is probably of *palmi romani* and one, that with a larger unit of measurement, of Austrian *Klaffter* (see no.359).

From the third project onwards Fontana's plans become more finished in technique and first-floor plans are included in each case. The same varieties of wash as before are used in the third project to denote the old and the new parts of the palace. Fontana here proposes to demolish most of the right half of the front block, introducing a new – straight – façade, and, incorporating the old fabric only at the corners. The main doorway and the passage behind are aligned in this case with the central axis of the court elevation, so that the doorway is off-centre in the street elevation. To disguise the uneven distribution of the windows Fontana has added pilaster-strips at both sides of the second and tenth bays of the façade (reading from the left), making a symmetrical composition around the door. The court staircase now occupies the wing to the right of the court. The final stages of the planning are anticipated in the present drawing by a large chalk cross which covers an area made over to a single large entrance vestibule in the fifth project.

382 FIRST-FLOOR PLAN (*Figure* 322) [9549]
268×415 mm. Pen, grey and buff wash, some chalk. With two scales.

At this level the whole front part of the site, except the strip where the wing on the left overlaps the front block, is to be newly built. Rectangles of chalk within the rooms probably indicate trial positions for stoves, and the same is probably true of ink stars in the corners of the four central rooms. A large chalk cross covers the same area of the plan as that drawn on the ground-floor project.

Fourth project

383 GROUND-FLOOR PLAN (*Figure* 323) [9543]
271×415 mm. Pen, grey and pink wash, traces of chalk. With two scales. Inscribed: *Adi 20 Marzo 1700 / Dissegni n*(on) *abracciati / dàl Ecc*mo *Martiniz / Pragha.*

The plan of the old palace is omitted in the present drawing, which shows only Fontana's proposed alterations. These are more extensive than in the earlier projects, for only the strip where the left wing of the palace overlaps the front block is incorporated (i.e. it is omitted in the present plan). As in the preceding project the main doorway from the street is aligned with the centre line of the court elevation, but it leads here to a broad entrance vestibule, which in turn leads directly to the court, where it is flanked by projecting blocks, of which that on the right contains the main staircase. The three main rooms of the ground floor contain stoves (rectangles of pink) and passages running parallel with the central vestibule give access to them from the rear. The main façade is designed on the same principles as that of the third project (see no.385), but the slope is corrected.
Copy by Vittone, vol.II, fo.167.

384 FIRST-FLOOR PLAN (*Figure* 326) [9545]
272×415 mm. Pen, grey and pink wash, traces of chalk. With two scales. Inscribed: *Dissegni n*(on) *risoluti.*

The large room at the front is, like the vestibule below, flanked by passages from which the stoves heating the first floor can be fed. A chapel is apparently introduced on the extreme right, as in the ground and first-floor plans of the third project.

385 FRONT ELEVATION (*Figure* 325) [9541]
270×415 mm. Watermark no.7. Pen, grey wash, traces of chalk. With two scales. Inscribed on *recto* (cut on left): (fa)/*ciata* (?) *stabilita* / (P)/ *ragha dll' Ecc.*mo / *Martiniz*, and on *verso*: *Martiniz Pragha.*

The centre section is set back slightly, and the main entrance and the window above are designed in characteristically Roman fashion. The façade is treated more loosely and pictorially than in most of Fontana's other works, and enclosed within a series of frames.
Copy by Vittone, vol.II, fo.150.

Final project

386 GROUND-FLOOR PLAN (*Figure* 324) [9542]
271×415 mm. Pen, grey and yellow wash, traces of chalk. Inscribed: *Adi 20 Marzo 1700 / Pianta risoluta da / farsi dall' Ecc.*mo *Martiniz à Pragha.*

The principles behind the organization of the plan are close to those of the fourth project but the entrance lies on the centre line of the street façade; its entrance from the court is off-centre. The new court façade is straight, like that of the third project, and the staircase occupies the same position as that of the fourth project, though it is re-orientated. The new eleven-bay street façade incorporates none of the existing fabric and it occupies the whole breadth of the site. It is divided by pilaster-strips into sections of 3/5/3 bays, with the main doorway in the centre.
Copy by Vittone, vol.II, fo.167.

387 FIRST-FLOOR PLAN (1) [9547]
269×415 mm. Watermark no.7. Pen, grey and yellow wash, traces of chalk. Inscribed: *Pianta stabilita / p pragha dall' / Ecc.*mo *Martiniz.*

The rooms of the first floor are laid out to either side of a single passage running across the wing, instead of the two passages (project four) running from front to back. As before, the main *salone* occupies the width of the central three bays of the façade.

388 FIRST-FLOOR PLAN (2) (*Figure* 327) [9544]
272×414 mm. Watermark no.7. Pen, grey, yellow and pink wash, traces of chalk. Inscribed: . . . (?) *serui p essere / Duplicata.*

This plan differs from the foregoing in that the corridor in the centre of the block is extended on the right and runs through the whole breadth of the wing. The space to the rear of the staircase is labelled *Cortiletto.*

Survey of the Torre Olevola, near Terracina (1700 and 1703)

The Torre Olevola is a small tower on the Campagna coast, lying to the south of the Pontine Marshes between the headland, Monte Circeo, and the port of Terracina. One of a number of small, free-standing towers in the area, it was rebuilt for Clement XI and re-christened *torre Clementina* (Contatore, p.318). Two of the towers in the vicinity (one perhaps being the Torre Gregoriana) are believed to have been built as a protection against pirates by Giovanni Fontana in the late 16th century (Gurlitt in Thieme-Becker), and the Torre Olevola may also have been built (or rebuilt) about this time.

There are six drawings of the tower at Windsor – two large sheets in Volume 185, which show the building after its reconstruction for Clement XI (Figs 330 and 331), and four small drawings amongst Fontana's papers in Volume 176 recording the appearance of the tower in 1700. This latter group is entitled on the preceding blank page: 'Per la Torre dell' Euolo / Teracina'. Each sheet was originally double its present size and inscribed with an index to the left of the drawing; the sheets were then bound in such a way that the indices now occur on the *verso* of the page following each drawing.

Fontana's drawings of 1700 may have been made, more precisely, in May of that year (before the death of Innocent XII), for a signed drawing by Fontana at Leipzig of a monument at Terracina is dated 20 May 1700 (Leipzig volume, fo.37; repr. Coudenhove-Erthal, fig.47). Fos 55 and possibly 60 of the Leipzig album contain chalk drawings by Fontana of views at Terracina. Innocent XII is known from other sources to have taken an interest in this area of the Campagna (on the draining of the Pontine Marshes see Pastor, Eng. ed., XXXII, pp.579/80) and he was likewise anxious to improve the coastal defences and amenities of the Papal States (Civitavecchia and Porto d'Anzio). The present drawings made by, or for, Fontana in Volume 176 reveal that the Torre Olevola was badly in need of restoration. Index F on drawing 389 (Fig.328) refers to a "Torre noua" at the foot of Monte Circeo (labelled Torre Vittoria in drawing 393), which is perhaps a hint that a tower in the neighbourhood had already been built (or rebuilt) for the Pope.

The two drawings in Volume 185 are elaborate and fully-annotated studies of the tower newly constructed to a larger plan in 1703 – they were perhaps intended to form the basis for engravings. The name of the architect is not, however, mentioned, though Fontana himself is a likely candidate. The legend on the perspective view (393) mentions the purpose of the tower as being for the protection of coastal trade, and such a building close at hand to the Neapolitan frontier could clearly have been put to other uses in 1703, when the Pope was faced with hostility from the territories of Spain and the Empire (see especially Pastor, Eng. ed., XXXIII, Ch.I). The present tower (illustrated in Rossi, p.36) appears to correspond in essentials with the building of 1703.

ADDITIONAL BIBLIOGRAPHY:
D. A. Contatore, *De Historia Terracinense*, 1706.
A. Rossi, *Terracina e la palude pontina*, 1912.

389 VIEW FROM THE EAST OF THE COAST BETWEEN TERRACINA AND MONTE CIRCEO (*Figure* 328) [9741]

300×*c*.210 mm. Chalk, pen, coloured washes. With index of letters referring to a list of features of the site that occurs on the *verso* of the following page.

390 PLAN OF THE TOWER [9743]

300×*c*.210 mm. Watermark no.1. Chalk, pen, coloured washes. With scale and index of letters referring to a dated (1700) list on the *verso* of the following page.

The drawing reveals that the base of the tower ("Platea") remains on three sides only.

391 SECTION OF THE TOWER [9744]

300×*c*.210 mm. Watermark no.1. Chalk, pen, coloured washes. With index of letters and text on the *verso* of the following page.

The tower is shown with the sea (to the south) in the background. Its south wall is riven with three long cracks on the inside. The platform at the top is occupied by a canon.

392 PERSPECTIVE VIEW OF THE TOWER (*Figure* 329) [9742]

300×*c*.210 mm. Watermark no.1. Chalk, pen, coloured washes. With index of letters and text on the *verso* of the following page; dated 1700.

The tower is apparently shown from the east, with the river behind. Its east wall, like that to the south, is seriously cracked.

393 Unidentified draughtsman

PERSPECTIVE VIEW OF THE TOWER AND THE NEIGHBOURING AREA (*Figure* 330) [10327]

481×743 mm. Laid down in part. Watermark no.7. Pen, grey wash. With title and annotations.

The most important features of the landscape are labelled in ink in capitals, with 'MONTE CIRCELLO' on the left behind the 'TORRE VITTORIA' and the town of 'SANTA FELICE'; on the right are the 'PALUDI PONTINE' and, in the far distance, the port of 'NETTUNO'. A cartouche, held aloft by two *putti* (upper right), contains the following inscription: '1703 / TORRE D'OLEVOLA FATTA RIEDIFICARE DI / NVOVO DALLA SANTITA DI N'RO SIG' PAPA / CLEMENTE XI TRA LI TERRITORI DELLA / CITTA DI TERRACINA E DELLA TERRA DI / SANTA FELICE SV LA SPIAGGIA DEL MARE / PER CVSTODIA DELLA MEDEMA SPIAGGIA / E DE TRAGHETTI DE LEGNAMI ET ALTRO / CHE SERVONO DAL FIUME MORTO AL MARE'.

The tower is shown from the east placed diagonally in the landscape. The main door is surmounted by a plaque bearing the Papal/ Albani arms with the name Clement and the date MCII (for MDCIII).

394 Unidentified draughtsman
SECTION AND FOUR PLANS OF THE TOWER (*Figure* 331) [10326]
482×759 mm. Laid down in part. Watermark no.7. Pen, grey wash, some chalk. With scale, annotated in full.

Entitled: 'PIANTA E SPACCATO DELLA TORRE D'OLEVOLA SU LA SPIAGGIA DEL MARE NE CONFINI DE TERRITORIJ TRA LA CITTÁ DI TERRACINA / E LA TERRA DI S. FELICE FATTA RIEDIFICARE NOVAMENTE DALLA SANTITÁ DI N'RO SIG: PAPA CLEMENE XI. L'AN. 1703'. With further titles for the section and the floor plans, and labelled throughout.

A map of Como and its environs (1701)

A single drawing in Volume 176 illustrates an accompanying text – a short history of Como, Fontana's birthplace. The text and drawing are entitled on the preceding blank page 'Como e la sua Relatione / li 15 Agosto 1701'. The history was clearly intended for publication, though it was apparently not printed. The drawing is perhaps more likely to have been made in Rome than in Como itself and based on an earlier view of the town.

395 OUTLINE PLAN OF COMO [9740]
302×*c*.430 mm. Watermark no.6. Pen, coloured washes.

The sheet is folded in the binding of the volume. Fontana's manuscript was originally attached to the bottom right-hand corner of the drawing. The index of letters (A to L) referring to various features of the site, with which the manuscript ends, has not been transferred to the plan.

Rome, the Ospizio di S. Michele: Introduction

The welfare of the poor in Rome in the second half of the 17th century had become such an immense problem that the only hope for improvement seemed to be a centralized organisation for their care. The existing facilities had for some time proved inadequate (see the decree of the Sac. Congregazione della Visita Apostolica of 29 September 1667 – Arch. del Vicariato di Roma, Segret. del Trib., vol.3, fo.137). The problem was again raised under Clement X (1670–76), when the foundation of a 'Casa della Madonna della Clemenza' was suggested (probably stimulated by the large Albergo dei Poveri which had been founded in Genoa between 1655–61). Men, women and boys without support were to find shelter in the house, and for the boys and the 'Zitelle' vocational training was to be supplied. Even prostitutes were to be given shelter without taking a vow but 'con clausura'. Twelve 'Deputati' were to be entrusted with the running of the hospice and were to remain in office for two years at a time (loc.cit., fo.140).

There were other, less compassionate, proposals to solve the problem of vagrancy: a decree according to which beggars able to work had to find occupation within fourteen days or to leave the city, or to be flogged or sent to the galleys. Those remaining helplessly poor were to be divided between various institutions, the sick to go to S. Sisto, those with infectious diseases to S. Giacomo, the 'lebrosi e simili' to S. Lazzaro, the boys to the 'Letterati', an institution then on the Corso, which was founded by Leonardo Ceruso in 1580 and an antecedent of the Ospizio di S. Michele, or to the 'Orfanelli', and the girls to S. Caterina, etc. (loc.cit., fo.141).

An almshouse for beggars, conceived more or less as a prison, at an unspecified place in Trastevere (loc.cit., fo.151), which offered only a minimum of subsistence, did not come to realisation, nor did the compassionately planned 'Casa della Madonna della Clemenza'. By the time Innocent XI became Pope the position of the poor had not changed, and Rome was overrun with beggars. Attempts were made at the beginning of his pontificate to alleviate the problem by restrictive measures, instituted in 1677 and 1678 (cf. Pastor, German ed., XIV, 2, p.686). A few years later, however, the idea of concentrating the poor in a special place was taken up again: 'Si tratta di ridurre i poueri mendicanti in qualche luogo particolare, p.la gran moltitudine, che se ne uede p. Roma' (Cartari-Febei, vol.88, fo.43, 17 June 1681).

With Innocent XI a man had come to power who, apart from the defence against the Turks, regarded the care of the poor as his special duty.

He postponed all other building projects and encouraged his nephew, Tommaso Odescalchi, in building the nucleus of the Ospizio di S. Michele near the Ripa Grande (cf. Pastor, German ed., XIV, 2, pp.690ff.). The Diary of Giulio Cartari reports on 19 October 1686 the start of work on the foundations which had taken place the previous week (op.cit., vol.94, fo.200 *verso* f.). The favourable location of the Ospizio in vineyards made it especially suitable as a home for the 'Putti', who were not only to be given elementary instruction but also to receive vocational training under the Padri delle Scuole Pie. By the end of August 1688, with an expenditure of 60,000 *scudi*, the building was so far advanced that it was decided to open it the following spring. It was estimated that a further 40,000 *scudi* would be necessary for the furnishing, a wall around the site, and the building of a church, which was to stand on the side facing the Dogana di Terra. It is characteristic of Innocent XI that he did not wish to be mentioned in any way as a benefactor of the enterprise: 'per quanto si dice, non si deue metter Memoria alcuna del regnante Pontefice' (op.cit., vol.97, fo.217; vol.98, fo.8 *verso*). On 4 November of the same year the nucleus of the building was more or less finished (op.cit., fo.191 *verso*), and in 1689 eighty boys were transferred to S. Michele from the Ospizio di S. Galla (*Roma Mod.*, ed.1697, II, pp.120f.). The first building, which is plausibly ascribed to Mattia de' Rossi (cf. Coudenhove-Erthal, p.68; Fasolo, p.91, note 2), ran parallel to the Tiber and had three storeys in the main block, each of nine bays, with a *loggia* on the roof (cf. Fig.332, based on the engraving by Specchi in *Quarto libro del nuovo Teatro delli Palazzi . . .*, Rome, 1699, pl.35; cf. also Bonanni, 1706, II, p.823, and Coudenhove-Erthal, pl.18). The central wing of the court had a two-storey arcaded *loggia* (repr. Donati, p.321, fig.276; Tirincanti, fig.68) and was joined to the street by two other wings.

The name of Tommaso Odescalchi is also connected with the Ospizio di S. Galla, which Marcantonio Odescalchi founded in 1650 in his own house as 'pubblico ricetto' for the poor (Moroni, vol.50, pp.16ff.). He acquired the adjoining convent and church of S. Maria in Portico in 1673 (ibid., vol.4, pp.74ff.) and a new church in honour of S. Galla, with two adjoining wings for the hospice, was erected (Moroni, vol.12, p.158; Cartari-Febei, vol. 90, fo.287). The building was completed by the end of 1688 (Cartari-Febei, vol.98, fo.8 *verso*; for the façade cf. Vasi, *Magnificenze*, IX, 1758, pl.177). It is traditionally attributed to Mattia de' Rossi (*Roma Mod.*, ed.1697, II, p.209), who was also responsible for the nucleus of the Ospizio di S. Michele (see above), which was likewise finished by the end of 1688.

Innocent XII also regarded the welfare of the poor as a primary obligation (Pastor, German ed., XIV, 2, pp.1084f.). His aim was to institute an 'Ospizio Generale', that is to say, the coordination of the asylum for boys at the Ripa Grande with the Ospedale dei Poveri founded by Sixtus V near the Ponte Sisto (cf. Tosti, pp.5ff., doc. III) and the Lateran palace, which was to be transformed into an almshouse (Innocent XI had given this commission to Bernini on 21 November 1676; cf. Fraschetti, p.398; Pastor, German ed., XIV, 2, p.692). On orders of the Pope the 'Letterati' were transferred in 1693 to the hospice on the bank of the Tiber. 150 boys were involved, and by the end of the century the number had increased to 260 (*Roma Mod.*, ed.1697, II, p.121; ed.1708, p.121). The Pope hoped to secure the necessary income for the future maintenance by the transfer of the income of the Curia Innocenziana, which Carlo Fontana was to build (see above and Tosti, p.6, and M. del Piazzo in *Montecitorio*, Rome, 1972, pp.73ff). The Hospice was to house 300 children, but only one wing was actually built, that along the present Via di S. Michele, which closed the court of the 'Cortile dei Ragazzi' (Tirincanti, fig.65). The completion of this wing, planned for 1697 (cf. diary note of 19 January 1697, in E. Rossi, *Roma,* XXI, 1943, p.210), dragged on till the following year. On 26 February 1698 Innocent XII made a gift of 832 *scudi* 'ad affetto che Dett.' Ospizio debba erogarli nella fabbrica dà farsi a Ripa del braccio attaccato alla Nuoua Scale' (A.S.R., Cam. I, Tesor. Segr., vol.1334, fo.40).

There is no direct evidence to show who was the author of the plans. It may have been Fontana; Fea (p.3; cf. Fasolo, p.90, n.3) states that Innocent XII had planned a 'grande ed ornata Fabbrica' called 'Ospizio Apostolico de' Poveri Invalidi di S. Michele' and had commissioned Carlo Fontana to produce a model 'ad oggetto, che quello, che non poteva a' suoi giorni veder compito, dalla Liberalità di' Successori Pontefici si vedesse una volta terminato'. There is of course no doubt that Fontana, succeeding Mattia de' Rossi (1695), was then already in charge of the building affairs of the hospice. He is already indirectly indicated in a diary entry of 7 March 1693, which related the following episode. When Fontana, in a conversation about a visit to the Lateran Hospice, referred to the youths housed there as 'birbi', Innocent XII defended his 'nipoti' angrily, and his reply, 'un birbo siete voi', forced Fontana to leave the room immediately (E. Rossi, in *Roma*, XXI, 1943, p.22).

Contini in his hand-list records two volumes of drawings by Fontana for S. Michele (nos 2 and 24) in addition to the volume (see below) at Windsor. Neither of these albums can now be traced but it is possible that they recorded work undertaken during the reign of Pope Innocent XII as well as during that of his successor. The Fontana volume at Leipzig contains (fo.19) an undated section of part of the Hospice buildings; it is inscribed 'Entrone di S. Michele'. A drawing by Fontana (Fig.341; Albertina, Mappe I (Rome), no.10) for a fountain at the Ospizio, probably the large fountain of the Cortile dei Ragazzi, may have been made before 1693, when Campello (p.53; 11 November 1693) records the inspection of an unspecified fountain at the hospice by Innocent XII.

The congregational record of 14 August 1693 furnishes the information that Mattia de' Rossi and Carlo Fontana were both given the order to prepare the 'modello della fontana p. la mostra dell'acqua a S. Michele' (A.S.R., Osp. S. Mich., vol.233, fo.77), which was examined a week later (21 August 1693; cf. op.cit., fo.78). The fountain is fed by water from the 'fontanone' which Carlo Fontana had added to the Fontana Paola on the Janiculum supplying the Ospizio di S. Michele through a special conduct made by order of Innocent XI (cf. Campello, p.42; Osp. S. Mich., vol.233, fo.59; vol.42, fos 145ff.). Innocent XII's deep interest in the Ospizio di S. Michele lasted to the end of his life. He is recorded as paying 64 visits to the building (Vai, p.29). Only a few months before his death (on 27 September 1700), in the summer of the Holy Year, he visited his orphans (F. Posterla, *Memorie storiche del presente Anno di Giubileo MDCC*, Rome 1700, I, p.209).

Innocent XII's idea of the 'Ospizio Generale' was pursued by his successor, Clement XI, who aimed at the physical connection of the Ospizio di S. Giovanni in Laterano and that near the Ponte Sisto with the institution on the Ripa Grande, thus reverting to the project of a 'Casa della Clemenza', which had been shelved under Clement X. In the execution of this plan (compare the related theme of the Concorso of the Accademia di S. Luca of 1702; cf. Fasolo, p.90; note 1) the 'Casa Correzionale' was the first to be built, between 1701 and 1704, as an annexe on the south west side, in the direction of Innocent XIII's wing, towards the Porta Portese (see Fig.342 and the diagrams by Tirincanti, fig.34, 1–6; Tosti, docs.III and IV; for the building and planning history cf. below). Immediately after the completion of the Casa Correzionale the general enlargement of the Ospizio di S. Michele was envisaged. In the congregational report of 20 January 1704 Fontana is said to have submitted a design 'p. Ridurre a comodo dell' ospizio tutta l'Isola di S. Michele', but this did not meet with approval: 'l'E.E. loro stimarono d'accomodarla in altra forma, e dissero li loro sentim.i al med.o Cau.r Fontana che promesse di rifare d. disegno e portarlo secondo il desiderio dell'E.E. loro nella prima congregazione' (A.S.R., Osp. di S. Michele, vol.236, fo.4). On 4 August 1704 there was a new discussion of a project by Fontana. The record unfortunately refers only to a minor detail, 'quel corridore che diuide le stanze perché restauano le med.e troppo anguste', which was criticized because of a lack of space and also for reasons of economy. But Fontana 'non ostante q.ste valide ragioni' did not intend to give in (ibid., fo.44). When he came with a scheme 'a fine di unire tutta l'opra', on 31 January 1706, it did not please the Congregation either – this time because the authorities wanted the church to be able to serve all the four categories of inmate of the Hospice: 'p.ché si vorrebbe una sola chiesa seruisse a tutti quattro gl'Ospitij' (ibid., fo.115). The same demand was, incidentally, made with regard to the kitchen. It is worth noticing that Fontana was requested to make himself familiar with the scheme of the Albergo dei Poveri at Genoa, where the church had been erected on a Greek cross in the centre of a rectangular court (Gino Chierici, 'L'Albergo dei Poveri a Napoli', *Bollettino d'Arte*, XXV, 1932, p.442). Before long the heads of the Hospice grew unsympathetic towards their architect. When Fontana apologized for missing the Congregation of 18 April 1706 because he was suffering from gout, he met with no understanding at all (A.S.R., op.cit., p.121).

The rest of the year passing with no further contribution from Fontana he was reminded again on 31 January 1707 to produce the amended designs for which he had already received payment of 135 *scudi* (ibid., vol.237; fo.5). Two months later, on 15 March 1707, he presented them to the Congregation, but his proposals still failed to win approval because, instead of extending the existing structure, 'tutta faceua figura di una nuoua fabbrica'. Fontana was ordered to readjust his designs, taking into account the existing buildings (ibid., fo.13), although the necessity was understood of extending the edifice to the area opposite the church of S. Cecilia. Even the 'ornato della città' was considered and despite the estimated cost of 300,000 *scudi*, the order was given to prepare the design to that effect 'p. non pregiudicare alla grandiosità dell' opera p.ché si farà adesso quel poco che si poule e se ne lascerà il compiem.to a Posteri'.

Two months later, 16 May 1707, Fontana again appeared with a new design in the Congregation. His former project had obviously not in the meantime undergone substantial modifications because the same objections were voiced again: 'la Facciata ancora di questo era differente totalm.te da quella che ui è di modo che non si puol dire di una continuazione di fabbrica ma di una nuoua Fabbrica' (ibid., fo.17). Although it had been made clear to Fontana that the Congregation were completely unwilling to accept the design in the form presented, he was obviously not ready to change his mind. When he showed his new projects on 10 June and 19 July 1707 the absence of continuity with the Odescalchi building was again criticized on both occasions (ibid., fos 23, 29).

In his Chirograph of 31 January 1708, directed to the Cardinals Spada, Sacripante and Spinola, Protectors of the Hospice, Clement XI gave the official order for the general enlargement of the Ospizio di S. Michele, to unite the boys and girls from the Lateran Hospice and the old men and women from Ponte Sisto under one roof (Tosti, doc.IV). In the Congregation of 7 March 1708 it was announced that the work had been started and no less than a hundred labourers were engaged on it (A.S.R., loc.cit., vol.237, fo.53); the accounts begin on 13 March 1708 (ibid, vol.73, no.576) and run until 1717 (vol.676). Although the Papal document refers explicitly to a design by Fontana in conformity with which the new structure was to be erected the work on the projects had still not come to an end. The report of 1 July 1708 records that the Heads of the Hospice admonished Fontana 'che non uscisse nel Piantare la Fabrica dall'Idea, che gli era stata data'. The proposal was brought forward to prepare a wooden model, but not accepted because of the expense. For the same reason it was decided to use the cheaper *tauolozza* instead of *peperino* for the piers of the cortile (ibid., vol.237, fo.61).

The complaints about Fontana continued. At the end of the month (30 July 1708) the Congregation protested angrily that Fontana had not delivered the ground plan and criticized his method of carrying out the construction. Fontana's defence was that he could not deliver the project for the church as long as the necessary site had not been acquired by the authorities of the Hospice (ibid., fo.67). A new reminder of 14 November 1708 was also in vain (ibid., fo.77).

It was not before 6 August 1709 that his project for the church could be discussed in Congregation (ibid., fo.99). It goes almost without saying that it did not please the members and Fontana was given the usual order to readjust his proposal. The matter continued to drag on for the rest of the year (cf. ibid., fos 109, 114) until Fontana's commissioners, in the Congregation of 17 January 1710, sent him a strict order to have his design ready for the next meeting and let him know that otherwise something 'di suo poco gusto' would happen (ibid, fo.120). Fontana however did not react immediately and continued to try their patience. On 12 June 1710 it was already feared that the summer would pass, as had happened the year before, without the foundation stone having been laid. For this reason the secretary of the Ospizio, Leonardo Libri, ordered a design 'da un giouane di tutte le fabbriche' which found the approval of the Cardinal Spada, who agreed to speak with Fontana and to order him to proceed in the manner which it provided (ibid., fo.139).

Only at this time (10 June 1710) was the contract made with the Fathers of the Dottrina Cristiana of S. Agata in Trastevere who agreed in conformity with the Chirograph of Clement XI, to give up their church (Madonna della Torre) and the adjacent structures opposite the Dogana Vecchia (cf. map of Falda, no.183; Fig.337) because the site was needed for the extension of the Hospice (cf. ibid., vol.237, fo.137). In exchange they were to obtain a new building which was to be erected near the Dogana Nuova (see below).

Surprisingly enough, on 30 July 1710, Carlo Fontana 'finalmente' brought the ground plan for the church of S. Michele and since only a *bagatella* had to be modified (ibid., fo.143) the foundation stone was laid about a month later, on 28 August 1710 (ibid., vol.43, fo.1; cf. Tosti, p.9). During the work on the foundations and the layout of the road remains of an ancient villa had been found, which is described by Valesio (28 April 1710, cf. Fasolo, p.92, note 3).

Having received the ground plan of the church, the authorities of the Ospizio had still to wait for the elevation, which was urgently requested in the meeting of 17 September 1710 (ibid., fo.149). The struggle about the designs to be delivered went on and even as late as 11 April 1711 Fontana is reported to have still not submitted them. Nonetheless work on the construction advanced steadily because 'il Sig.re Card.le Spada ha comandato lui ciò che si deue fare' (ibid., fo.173). Until 1713 Fontana remained responsible for the building. The accounts for the masons between 1 June 1713 and 31 August 1713 are still signed by him (ibid., vol.673, no.582) and refer to 'tutti li muri, che accompagnano la chiesa dal piano del pauimento della med.a sino alli tetti', etc.

Unfortunately no designs by Fontana have been found, either in the enormous Fondo of the Ospizio in the Archivio di Stato di Roma, or in the Archive of its present seat, where the Hospice has been moved in modern times (see below). This is easy to explain because, as the documents quoted above indicate, Fontana constantly refused to submit his plans to the authorities of the Hospice, who wanted to shelve them in their archive. The conclusion to be drawn is that he retained all the drawings for himself and this is confirmed by a later entry of 9 May 1717, when his son, Gaspare, requested a sum of 1200 *scudi* 'p. le fatiche del Padre'; it was then testified by the workmen that they had never received any plan (ibid., vol.238, fos 95 and 117). Hence it must be assumed that Fontana did not make a new overall plan for the extension of the Hospice, but that he only modified his earlier schemes as the construction progressed. The designs which he kept were evidently later united in the two lost volumes.

Fontana's attitude, which seems rather strange

if it is remembered that he usually furnished his commissioners with designs in abundance, cannot sufficiently be explained by his illness at this date, because he was never short of capable assistants. His behaviour seems to have been deliberate and he probably wished to avoid being committed to a fixed scheme in accordance with the ideas of the Congregation in order to keep as free a hand as possible under the close supervision of Cardinal Spada.

Of course Fontana could not entirely circumvent the conditions imposed on him, especially in so far as the continuation of the scheme of the old Hospice was concerned, the adjustment of the storeys etc. But by transforming the roof loggia into an attic storey and by means of the rhythmical articulation of the river façade, the larger units of which are interrupted by narrower and lower intermediate sections, he succeeded in unifying it to such an extent that the front of the earlier building can no longer be distinguished from the new structure (Fig.333; for a similar view by Giuseppe Pannini cf. d'Onofrio, *Tevere*, fig.163). Thus he opposed successfully the demand of the authorities expressed in the Congregation of 15 March 1707 which had requested the architect to avoid such an impression, that 'ne in minima parte' the Glory of the Founder might be minimized (ibid., vol.237, fo.13).

On the basis of the similarity of the ground plan of the Ospizio with that of the Jesuit College at Loyola, we can suppose that Fontana originally intended to extend the Hospice towards the north-east by two symmetrical courts (one for the *Vecchi* and *Vecchie*, the other for the *Zitelle*), of which the second (on another scheme, see below) was only begun under Clement XI (on Fontana's original plans cf. Hager in *Commentari*, 1975). The new mezzanine provided further dormitories (cf. *misure* of 15 October 1714–30 September 1715; A.S.R, loc. cit., vol.675, no.717; Tosti, p.9). The two courtyards are separated by a church planned by Fontana (Figs.339, 340), in accordance with the demands of the Congregation, as a Greek cross, of which, however, the fourth arm was not executed (for further interior views cf. Tirincanti, figs. 77ff.). The accounts of the stone masons between 1 September 1713 and 31 December 1713, signed by Nicola Michetti, refer to the stucco work on the church. At this time the completion of the fourth arm of the cross must have been already in doubt. The arrangement of the ground plan provided for a division of the inmates of the Hospice into categories as in the Albergo dei Poveri in Genoa (and the Salpetrière in Paris). (For the execution of the altars etc. cf. Arch. Segr. Vat., Fondo Albani, vol.13, fos 148ff.) Since the Pope had gone back on his earlier intention to make a donation of paintings, the Congregation of 10 July 1714 accepted an offer of the Flemish painter Vincenzo Mainardi, 'che non lauora male', who promised to deliver the painting for the *altare maggiore* and to give lessons to the boys of the Hospice (A.S.R., Fondo Osp. S. Mich., vol.237, fo.267). When it became clear that he would not be able to fulfil his obligation (17 November 1715) the Congregation intended to place there a copy of Raphael's *Transfiguration* which the Hospice already possessed (ibid., vol.238, fos 53, 87, 92). The church was consecrated on 2 October 1715 by the Canon Mons. Guggio in the presence of Cardinal Spada (*ibid.*, fo.39). Being intended only for the inmates, the church has no separate access for visitors and is hardly visible from outside. A narrow passage-like courtyard (Cortile delle Carrette) was provided towards the via S. Michele for vehicles serving the Hospice (cf. *Architettura Minore in Italia, Roma*, vol.I, Turin, s.d., pl.19).

After the death of Carlo Fontana, which is registered in the minutes of the Congregation of 23 February 1714 (A.S.R, loc.cit., vol.237, fo.257) without comment, the question of his successor had to be considered. The choice was between Matteo Sassi, who had served Fontana as a *misuratore* at the Hospice, Filippo de' Romanis, who had collaborated with him for about twenty years and represented his master during the last three years, when he was sick, and finally Nicola Michetti, called 'suo architetto'. On 14 May 1714, at the proposal of Cardinal Sacripante, Michetti was appointed architect of the Hospice in company with Filippo de' Romanis (ibid., fo.264).

The work of the extension however soon came to a halt. According to Tosti (p.13) it was because the nuns of S. Cecilia refused a plot of land (cf. also A.S.R., loc.cit., vol.237, fo.266). A survey drawing by Michetti illustrates the situation and shows the plan to extend the north-western part of the Hospice beyond the via di S. Michele (cf. Fig.336; ibid., vol.42, fos47f.). From a protest of the three Cardinal Protectors (November 1715) we learn, however, that the work on the extension had not been interrupted because of this problem about the site, but because of lack of money (ibid., fo.20). Nevertheless it was considered necessary to reserve all rights for the future to be able to finish the edifice for the *Zitelle* which was to include accommodation and places to work – mainly weaving – for four hundred women. At the time of this recommendation (about 1715–1716) the building of the *Zitelle* was already large enough to house about two hundred persons, though towards the north-east it did not continue far beyond the via della Madonna dell'Orto. This state of affairs is recorded in Nolli's map of 1748 (Fig.338), which only shows the corridor beyond the truncated fourth arm of the cross of the church and part of the arcades of the adjoining wing parallel to the via di S. Michele and along the bank of the Tiber (cf. Tirincanti, fig.31). This block is represented on Vasi's engraving in the *Magnificenze* (V, 1745, pl.97) as completed, but a ground plan, prepared by the architect Giovanni Battista Spampani for the Concorso Balestra of the Academy of S. Luke in 1768, shows the situation unchanged (Archiv. Acc. S. Luca, Conc. Architett. vol.XIV, no.779) (Marconi, vol.1, fig.1045).

Tosti (p.13) and Fasolo (p.87) blame Niccolò Forti, the architect responsible for the continuation of the building after 1790, for having prevented the completion of the church but the decision to dispense with the fourth arm of the cross must already have been made in Fontana's time. In order to keep the north-east end of the Hospice at a distance from the river he introduced a slight northward bend of the Tiber façade which was increased by Michetti and his successor.

Michetti, who supervised the architectural affairs of the Hospice until his departure for Russia in the summer of 1718, made some alterations in the plan. During his absence he was represented by his assistant Filippo de' Romanis and resumed his task when he came back. According to Ettore Lo Gatto (*Gli artisti italiani in Russia*, Rome, 1935, p.51) Michetti left Russia in 1723. But as early as 1720 there is an account checked by Michetti in the Archive of the Ospizio di S. Michele (vol.677, no.1174, and vol.238, fo.281 – 1721).

It remains to consider the extension of the original Hospice complex to the south-west. Drawings at Windsor, dated 1704 (see below), provide for the building of the present corner block on the river side of the Ospizio (Fig.372), and these are incorporated in his perspective view of 1706 (Fig.342). In 1708 it was decided to build on the river side parallel to the 'Casa Correzionale' a further annexe for 'Magazzini' (A.S.R., loc.cit., vol. 237, fo.72). It was first illustrated in the Guide of Rome of 1708 (facing p.122), interpolated into Specchi's *vedute* of 1699 (Fig.332). On 10 June 1710 a contract was made with the Padri della Dottrina Cristiana to attach a small church to the western side of the 'Magazzini' for the benefit of the sailors using the Porto a Ripa Grande. The ground plan of the new church, entitled 'Madonna del Buon Viaggio', has survived as an enclosure to the document of the contract (Fig.335), and bears Fontana's signature as 'Perito è Archit°. di S: Michele' together with that of Giacomo Onorato Recalcati, architect of S. Agata della Lungaretta (A.S.R., 30 Not. Cap. Ufficio 18, vol. 595, fos 324–329). The church of the Madonna del Buon Viaggio, which is disposed as a single nave with a small section reserved for the main altar (Tirincanti, figs.49ff.) was erected between 1 November 1710 and 30 April 1712 to Fontana's ground plan (A.S.R., loc.cit., vol.673, no.584). A short time later it was incorporated into the Hospice when the store house was heightened (cf. account with the masons of 1 January 1714, ibid., vol.674, no.622) and the block was further extended downstream towards the Dogana Nuova. The new spaces on top of it were to house the first Roman 'Studio degli Arazzi', with class rooms for elementary instruction in the arts and architecture (Tosti, pp. 9ff. Tirincanti, pp. 76ff.). Then work was directed by Nicola Michetti (A.S.R., loc. cit., vols 675ff.) who also conducted the construction of the 'nuoua fabrica del casino della Dogana' (cf. *misure* of 19 November 1715–30 October 1716; ibid., vol.675, no.694).

In 1735 Clement XII added a prison for women facing the Porta Portese, which had not been included in the original scheme and for which the plans were provided by Ferdinando Fuga. Thus the first step was taken towards closing the 'Cortile delle Arti' which was already flanked by the Casa Correzionale and the Studio degli Arazzi etc. The last gap was filled by a long wing with shops (cf. the engraving published by Matthiae (pl.VIII, 1) by De Liegeay in the *Secondo libro del nuouo teatro delle fabriche fatte in Roma dalla S. di N.S.Clemente XII*, Rome, 1739, pl.21). In 1794, under Pius VI, the prison was enlarged by two bays (Matthiae, p.73; Bianchi, pp. 39ff.; Pane, 1956, p.52). During the pontificate of Leo XII the wing with the shops, shown by De Liegeay, was converted into barracks for the 'Finanzieri' (cf. Tosti, pp. 14ff.).

The Ospizio di S. Michele, the creation of which had caused Carlo Fontana so much trouble, is architecturally almost a purely functional building, as opposed to the Albergo dei Poveri at Genoa, with its deliberately articulated façade commanding the hill. The Hospice continued to fulfil its original function until just before the second world war when the main part was transferred to the Piazzale Antonio Tosti, though the Casa di Correzione continues in use to the present time. In its day the Ospizio was one of the most advanced charitable establishments in Europe and was only followed on a comparable level in Italy in the middle of the century by the Albergo dei Poveri of Ferdinando Fuga in Naples.

ADDITIONAL BIBLIOGRAPHY:
Sources:
A.S.R., Fondo Istituzioni Caritative: Ospizio Apostolico di San Michele, Libro Mastro, vol.671–677.
A.S.R., Ospizio di S. Michele, Libro de' Decreti, vols 233–238 (kindly communicated by Dr Marcello del Piazzo, Rome).
Books:
Alberto Balzani, *L'Ospizio Apostolico dei poveri invalidi, detto il 'S. Michele', dal 1693 al 1718*, Rome, 1969.

Giovanni Di Castro in *L'Urbe*, N.S.32, 1969, 5, pp.19–28.
Hellmut Hager, 'Carlo Fontana e l'ingrandimento dell' Ospizio di S. Michele, contributo allo sviluppo architettonico di un' istituzione caritativa del Tardo Barocco Romano', *Commentari*, XXVI, 1975, pp.344–359.
Ingrid Haug, *Peter Speeth, Architekt, 1772–1831*, University of Bonn, unpublished dissertation, 1961.
Stelio Martini in *Capitolium*, XLIV, June–July 1969, pp.105–122.
Vicenzo Monachino, *La Carità Cristiana in Roma*, Bologna, 1968.
Joselita Raspi Serra in *Italia nostra*, 12, 1968, no.58, pp.27–30.
Giulio Tirincanti in *Capitolium*, XLIV, June–July, 1969, pp.16–107.
Antonio Tosti, *Relazione dell' Origine e dei Progressi dell' Ospizio Apostolico di S. Michele*, Rome, 1832.
(Tosti) *Intorno la Origine e i Progressi dell' Ospizio Apostolico di San Michele. Notizie estratte dall' opera scritta da Monsignore Antonio Tosti, Presidente del medesimo*, Rome, 1835.
(Tosti) P.L.B. Drach, *Notice concernant L'Origine et les Progrès de l'Hospice Apostolique de Saint-Michel a Rome. Extraite par les redacteurs du Journal Arcadique de la Relation publiée en 1832, par Mgr. Antoine Tosti. Président de L'Hospice*, Paris–Rome, 1832.
Giuseppe Vai, *Relazione del Pio Istituto di S. Michele a Ripa Grande*, Rome, 1779.

The prison for young criminals at the Ospizio di S. Michele (1701–1704)

Volume 181 in the Windsor series (no.5 in Contini's inventory) is devoted to 24 drawings of the preliminary stages of the design of the 'Casa di Correzione' at S. Michele a Ripa, and Fontana's final project for the prison is recorded in a series of small drawings in Volume 176. His earliest known design is shown in five drawings in the Leipzig album (fos 3 to 7; two of them are illustrated by Coudenhove-Erthal, figs 45/6). The drawings in Volume 181 show four early stages in the planning of the prison, and an index in the volume, dated 25 June 1701, refers to what appears to be the first of the projects. One of the drawings of the last group is dated 14 September 1701, and it can be assumed that the four projects were conceived during a period of four months, following the project recorded in the Leipzig album. The Windsor volume contains in addition to the drawings a long description of the prison, dated 12 November 1703, which was apparently drafted by Fontana for a publication that never appeared. The text refers to the final stage of the planning and there is also a long index concerning the basement of the final design. The presence of these texts in the volumes suggests that a group of drawings showing the final design may have been removed from the book, which has, incidentally, the appearance of once having contained more sheets than at present.

Fontana had already worked during the papacy of Innocent XII on the building of the Ospizio di S. Michele (see introduction to the present entry). The prison designed for Clement XI in 1701 was intended for young criminals and attached to the north-west corner of the site, adjacent to the west wing of the Cortile dei Ragazzi. It is shown from the end in Fontana's perspective view of 1706 (Fig.342). It is now the only part of the Ospizio still in use. Though unpretentious in its outward appearance, the building is of the greatest interest in its general organization, anticipating many of the features of a modern prison. The main feature of the block is a high 'nave' with single cells disposed in three tiers along each side (cf. views of the interior in Tirincanti, figs 42f.). Fontana apparently conceived this idea not only (as in a modern prison) for purposes of security, but to ensure also that each occupant should be able from the window of his cell to participate in the mass, conducted from an altar in the centre of the nave. The floors below the prison (and the terrace above) were arranged as workshops where the young criminals learnt the useful trade of weaving. This was equally an unusual feature of prison life and has already been noted by Pastor amongst others (Eng. ed., XXXIII, pp.499/500) as an important example of the enlightened reforms of Clement XI.

The early history of the project is described in detail in Fontana's own introduction. Cardinal Giovanni Battista Spinola grew concerned at the bad influence to which young criminals were subjected in the Carceri Nuove and informed the Pope, who, with the help of Cardinal Pallavicino and Leonardo Libri, ordered a separate 'Edificio Caritatiuo' to be built at S. Michele a Ripa. A committee, including representatives of the Ospizio, met in May 1701 and decided on a building with 60 single cells and containing also rooms to be used as workshops etc. for weaving. This conference may have taken place while Fontana was working on his early projects, for in that at Leipzig and in the early Windsor design the number of cells provided is less than 60. Fontana was then formally asked for plans and in August 1701 approval was given for the work to be started. Excavation on the site began on 1 September 1701 and the first stone was laid ceremonially on the 28th of that month.

The progress of the work can be followed in detail in documents which range in date from 27 September 1701 to 31 March 1704 (Archivio di Stato, Fondo Ospizio di S. Michele, Giustificazioni vol.425, fos 236ff.; with additional payments in vols 421, fo.382 (20 March 1703, ironwork), 422, 178v.° (19 May 1703, masonry), 423, 1339 (16 May–3 October 1703, plasterwork (?)), 424, 57 and 81 (28 October 1703, painting) and 425, 47ff. (8 July 1704, metalwork)). The building is referred to in the Decreti of the Ospizio on 2 July and 5 October 1702, and 11 April and 15 September 1703, when the matter of an inscription was discussed (vol.233). In 1704 (20 January, 13 May and 4 August) this subject was still under discussion. The completion of the work of the prison was marked by the issue of a medal in 1704 (see drawing 429) and three engravings of the building were published in the third (1721) volume of de' Rossi's *Studio d'Architettura* (nos 55/7 – Fig.359). The total cost of the building was apparently estimated at 17,000 *scudi* (Posterla, 1707, p.104).

The great interest taken by the Pope in the progress of the work is made clear by the number of his visits to the site, as recorded in the *Diario* of Valesio. On a visit of 2 September 1701 he made a public announcement concerning the prison. Further visits occurred on 14 May and 4 October 1702, 21 June 1703 when the work is described by Valesio as '*quasi terminata*', and 4 October 1704. In the entry for 27 October 1703 Valesio reports a rumour which has become public that the prison was not designed by Fontana. Fontana was defended from this rumour by the publication of a sheet, incorporating a letter of 17 October 1703 of Leonardo Libri. The sheet, of which a copy is bound in Valesio's diary (fos 187f.), gives some impression of the official approbation enjoyed by Fontana's building (cf. d'Onofrio, *Tevere*, pp.255f., n.26).

Fontana's manuscript in Volume 181 at Windsor is dated in the month following this attack and it seems possible that it was prepared as a more substantial counter-attack by Fontana himself to the hostile rumours reported by Valesio. After a short dedicatory preface and an introduction outlining the history of the commission, Fontana describes the building floor by floor in the greatest detail. The basement contained the vats for washing and dyeing the wool; it was accessible from two '. . . scale abbundante di lumi, una per passaggio, e traghetto delle robbe con Animali da somma . . .' The ground floor contained the looms themselves, and the first floor the barred cells and an altar in the middle of the nave. Above this was an open *loggia* to be used for drying the wool. The uses of the smaller rooms in the prison block are fully described, the 'loco di Corettione, e Castighi' etc. and the sewage system with its 'lochi Communi'. The basement was connected with the 'loggia' by means of a lift, the 'gran Pozzo quadrato, che da esso si trasportano sù per via di machine tutte le robbe necess^{e}, che si si lavorano nelli doi ridotti Sotterranei . . .'

The prison occupies the same site in all the projects – attached to the south-west corner of the Cortile dei Ragazzi. In the Leipzig project the prison runs parallel with the existing wing of the Ospizio, while in the Windsor projects and in the finished buildings it projects from the latter at right angles. In the early projects at Windsor doors were pierced between the two buildings at the level of the ground floor, where a room in the Ospizio served as a refectory, and at the level of attics. In the final project (Figs 354, 355) a large part of the ground and basement floor of the existing wing of the Ospizio is used for a vestibule to which is attached the wide semicircular ramp ('per traghetto delle robbe con Animali'). In the early projects the open terrace of the final design is a covered room which is described in the indices as a 'spanditore' (a drying room for wool). There is also in the early designs some variation in the size of the prison, in the number of cells it contains, in the treatment of the staircase and in the appearance of the façade. At one stage Fontana apparently intended to add an annexe to the prison block, probably at the end opposite the Ospizio (see final group of drawings below).

The drawings in Volume 181 all measure approximately 408 × 272 mm. and the watermark occurring on many of the sheets is that of a lily in a double oval with the letter "V" (no.7). An old inscription on the *verso* of the final sheet in the book (see drawing 434 below) reads: *Ca:^{te} 24*, and must refer to the number of drawings in the book. The sizes, etc., of the sheets in Volume 176 are given in the introduction to group 5 below.

Group 1

The first group of drawings contains eight sheets – 4 plans, two sections and two elevations. Seven of these drawings are described in an index which is headed: 'Adi 25 Giugno. 1701 – Indice delli Disegni quì acclusi, per l'Opera Pia, da farsi all'Ospizio de S. Michele per uso di Carceri per Giouinetti, & altro come segue – '. At the end of the last entry the following note is appended: 'Deuesi riflettere, che li muri per l'Opra delle Carceri sono disposti, e spartiti à fare officio per altri usi, come addietro viene espresso, tutto armonizato di proporzioni, con Sesti, e grossezze douuti delle Volte necessarie alla permanenza, e concatenazione di tutto il Complesso, sodo e fermo . . .'. The cells in this project are arranged in groups of four, with an additional cell at each corner of the third tier, and a small circular staircase is placed between each pair of cells (Fig.344). There are double openings at each end of the nave and two bays of the façade break forward at each corner. The overall size of the rectangular plan is approximately 191 × 75 *palmi.*

396 GROUND-FLOOR PLAN [9964]
Pen, coloured washes, some chalk. With scale and index of letters in chalk.

The new prison is shown in grey wash; the adjacent wing of the Ospizio di S. Michele contains a refectory and a single door is pierced between the two. Rectangles of cream coloured wash denote the sites of looms etc. A later addition in chalk (not included in the index) shows an extension on the court side of the prison, resembling a wing of an open cloister in its character.

397 FIRST (PRISON) FLOOR PLAN (*Figure* 344) [9963]
Pen, grey and yellow wash, traces of chalk. With scale and index of letters in chalk.

The cells are arranged in groups of four at each corner of the block. The sections below show that there were to be three tiers of cells and the elevations reveal that on the third tier a further cell was introduced in the extreme corners (making 52 cells in all).

398 PLAN OF ATTIC STOREY [9957]
Pen, cream and grey wash, traces of chalk. With scale.

The present drawing is the only sheet in the first group omitted from the index of June 1701. The *verso* shows an unfinished diagrammatic plan in chalk (with scale), which appears to be connected with the planning of the prison cells, but is too unfinished to be identifiable.

399 PLAN OF TOP STOREY [9962]
Pen, grey and yellow wash, traces of chalk. With scale and index of letters in chalk.

The plan is taken at window level, above the attic storey. The storey is described in the index as a 'Spanditore disgregato totalm.te dalle Carceri, e Lavoratorio Terreno.'

400 TRANSVERSE SECTION (*Figure* 347) [9969]
Pen, grey and cream wash, traces of chalk. With scale and index letters in chalk.

A flap on the section (included in Fig.347) shows an alternative project for the attic and the high room above the nave. The principal change introduced on this is the omission of the windows surrounding the attic, a feature which is incorporated into the elevations below.

401 LONGITUDINAL SECTION (*Figure* 345) [9973]
Pen, grey and brown wash, traces of chalk. With scale and index of letters in chalk.

A flap (now detached but included in Fig.345) contains the same alternative project for the attic and 'spanditore' as the flap of the preceding section. The present section continues to the right into the existing wing of the Ospizio. Measurements are inscribed on the drawing in this area and the method of communication between the old and new buildings is clearly demonstrated.

402 STREET ELEVATION (*Figure* 346) [9970]
Pen, grey wash, traces of chalk. With scale and index of letters in chalk.

As on the flaps of the sections (400,401) the 'spanditore' has large round-headed windows, while the attic below has no openings.

403 COURT ELEVATION [9972]
Pen, grey and brown wash, traces of chalk. With scale and index of letters in chalk.

The already existing wing of the Ospizio is shown in section and measured on the right. The court façade of the prison corresponds closely with the street façade, but it has a central doorway in addition to those at the sides.

Group 2

The second group of drawings is the smallest of the five, consisting of three plans only. The cells are arranged as before in groups of four and the nave has double openings at each end (Fig.348). It is quite possible that the present project was in fact the first to have been executed, but since it corresponds with the final design in having no projecting wall surfaces along the sides, it fits slightly more easily into the second place in the order of projects. Certain features appear only in this design: the pair of double-flight staircases at ground-floor level and the four heavy piers supporting the end wall of the block. The overall size, excluding the piers, is approximately 182 × 75 *palmi.*

404 GROUND-FLOOR PLAN [9965]
Pen, grey and yellow wash, traces of chalk. With scale.

The lay-out of the plan is not radically different from that in the ground-floor plan of the previous project which immediately precedes the present drawing in the volume. But the general effect is simpler both in the conception of the general structure (in grey) and in the arrangement of the sites for the looms etc. (in yellow).

405 FIRST (PRISON) FLOOR PLAN (*Figure* 348) [9967]

Pen, grey and yellow wash, traces of chalk. With scale.

An altar is here indicated in the centre of the nave with radiating lines to the windows of the first tier of sixteen cells.

406 PLAN AT ATTIC LEVEL [9958]

Pen, grey and yellow wash, traces of chalk. With scale.

As in the early stage of the previous project the attic has windows. Here, however, the 'spanditore' in the centre extends to the edge of the block of the prison at the end opposite the Ospizio, and is therefore surrounded by the attic on three sides only.

Group 3

In this third project for the prison Fontana introduces groups of five cells in each quarter of the plan (Figs 349, 350), as had occurred in the first project at top-floor level. Now, however, the cells are accessible from only one staircase at each corner of the nave, and the ends of the nave have triple openings. In these respects the present project corresponds with the final one. The planning at this stage appears to have been more experimental than before. The kernel of the group consists of two plans (nos 407 and 409 – Fig. 350; project A) which have flaps covering each end of the nave whereby a second, shorter, project is introduced (project B, Fig. 349).

407 GROUND-FLOOR PLAN [9961]

Pen, coloured washes, some chalk. With scale and flaps.

In the basic version of the plan (labelled A) Fontana introduces a large room between the prison and the existing wing of the Ospizio. The overall length is approximately 202 *palmi*. On flaps covering each end of the block (one labelled B) this room is omitted and at the opposite end a short open extension is added with a fountain in the centre. The length is approximately 191 *palmi*.

408 GROUND-FLOOR PLAN (PROJECT B) [9960]

Pen, grey and yellow wash, chalk. With measurements. Inscribed: / . . *Fabrica alla Casetta p.* $216\frac{1}{2}$ . . / (f)*abrica nova p.* $187\frac{1}{2}$, . . / (au)*anza* p^{mi} *29 p il Cortile* and *Dal fe(?)*.

The present sheet corresponds closely with the project of the flaps of the last plan.

409 FIRST (PRISON) FLOOR PLAN (*Figure* 349, 350) [9959]

Pen, grey and yellow wash, some chalk. With flaps and scale, and measurements in chalk.

The two versions of the design correspond with those of drawing 407 above.

410 PLAN OF TOP STOREY (PROJECT B) [9966]

Pen, grey and yellow wash, some chalk. With measurements.

411 PLAN OF TOP STOREY (PROJECT A) [9968]

Pen, grey and yellow wash, traces of chalk. With scale.

The 'spanditore' is extended in light grey wash for a further bay at the end opposite the Ospizio. This suggests that Fontana had not yet decided whether the penultimate bay of the prison in the alternative project should be roofed over.

412 STREET ELEVATION (PROJECT A) (*Figure* 351) [9954]

Pen, grey wash, traces of chalk. With scale. Inscribed: *Piano terreno alt* p^{mi} *27* / *Piano sopra alt* p^{mi} $25\frac{1}{4}$ / *Piano di Cima alt* p^{mi} $18\frac{3}{4}$.

413 TRANSVERSE SECTION [9955]

Pen, grey and pink wash, traces of chalk.

The section corresponds in a general way with the plans of this group but the doorways leading to the staircase beyond the balconies of the prison cells are not present.

Group 4

The fourth project consists of two plans and four sections. It differs from the final design in the staircase and the top storey of the block for which it shows a drying room and not an open *loggia* (Fig. 353). In the second design the height of the nave is increased with a vault, as in the final project. The first plan bears the name 'Bend. Roscio' and the date 14 September 1701, a fortnight before the foundation stone was laid. The inscription on the second plan reveals that this design was given to the masons, in which case it must have been shortly afterwards superseded by the final design. The size of the block in this project is 193 × 77 *palmi*.

414 BASEMENT PLAN [9952]

Pen, grey and yellow wash, traces of chalk. With scale. Measured in detail in ink. Inscribed: *Adi 14 7bre 1701. . . .* / *a* mo^{r} *Bend. Roscio* and *Riccordo casse ò feritore delle finestre di Cantine* / *come ancora le sboccature delle canne de | lochi Comuni lasciare nelli fondam:[a] | come anche li Condotti di serra p li lochi | Communi delle 4 stanze.*

415 GROUND AND FIRST (PRISON) FLOOR PLAN (*Figure* 352) [9953]

Pen, grey and yellow wash, traces of chalk. With scale and index. Measured in full and annotated in ink. Inscribed: *Pianta stabilita e | data al mu[re] di S. Michele* and *Ricordo dingrandire la scala | lumaca O – a p[mi] 11½.*

The lower half of the plan is of the ground floor of the prison and areas of yellow wash denote the foundations. The upper half shows the first floor. The plan bears a detailed index.

416 TRANSVERSE SECTION [9956]
Pen, grey wash, traces of chalk. With scale and flap. Measured throughout.

Originally the end of the nave at ground-floor level was left as a single wide opening but the flap shows a door flanked by windows (see 418 below). The 'spanditore' no longer breaks upwards over the roof of the attic.

417 TRANSVERSE SECTION (*Figure* 353) [9975]
Pen, grey wash, traces of chalk. Measured in part.

A copy of the preceding section, incorporating the final design for the ground-floor openings of the latter.

418 DETAIL OF TRANSVERSE SECTION [9971]
Pen, grey wash, traces of chalk. With scale.

This drawing corresponds with the flap of 416.

419 TRANSVERSE SECTION [9974]
Pen, grey wash, traces of chalk. With scale.

The present section corresponds with the earlier sections up to the third tier of cells, but the attic is omitted, the nave extends upwards and ends in a vault, as in the final design (group 5 below) and a simple 'spanditore' is placed over the nave.

Group 5

The fifth group of drawings comprises twelve sheets in Volume 176; on the preceding blank page is the title 'S. Michele Carcerette'. The sheets differ in technique from the earlier drawings, being neater in appearance, and in grey wash only, with the chalk underdrawing usually erased. The size of each drawing is approximately 305 × 210 mm. and the watermark on some of the sheets is that of nos 5 or 17.

These eleven drawings show the final stage of the design and therefore illustrate Fontana's text in Volume 181. Two important new features are introduced at this stage. First, there is an extension which overlaps the existing wing of the Ospizio at basement and ground-floor level and contains vestibules and the broad semi-circular staircase described in the written text. This part of the design may well have been a last minute addition, for it was omitted in the first stages of drawings 420 and 422. Secondly, an open terrace, with a covered bay at one end, replaces the 'spanditore'. The overall size of the block, omitting the extension, is 199 × 77 *palmi.*

The final drawing of the twelve in Volume 176 is a study for the street doorway of the prison (no.431). This is bound amongst the drawings of 1704 for the south-west corner block of the Ospizio (see below) and the door (Fig.363) is surmounted by a tablet dated 1704.

420 BASEMENT PLAN (*Figure* 354) [9791]
Two sheets joined horizontally. Pen, grey and blue wash, traces of chalk. With scale, partially obliterated.

The basement is extended with a large room and a smaller block containing a broad, and probably ramp-like, semicircular staircase which penetrates into the existing wing of the Ospizio. This part of the drawing was added after the rectangle of the prison itself had been drawn and it obliterates most of the scale. The index of the basement in Volume 181 appears to correspond closely with the present plan.
Copy by Vittone, vol.II, fo.168.

421 BASEMENT PLAN [9790]
Pen, grey and blue wash, traces of chalk.

A fair copy, without scale, of the preceding drawing.

422 GROUND-FLOOR PLAN (*Figure* 355) [9785]
Three sheets joined horizontally. Pen, grey wash, traces of chalk. With two scales, one partially obliterated.

As with the first drawing (420) the extension on to the site of the existing wing of the Ospizio is a later addition, covering the scale. A second scale has been added on a fresh slip of paper.

423 GROUND-FLOOR PLAN [9788]
Pen and grey wash.

A fair copy of the preceding, without scales.

424 FIRST (PRISON) FLOOR PLAN (*Figure* 356) [9789]
Pen, grey and blue wash, traces of chalk. With scale.

At this level the plan no longer encroaches on to the site of the Ospizio. The nave of the prison has an altar in the centre and a fountain at the far end.

The structures at the near end of the nave are shown (cf. 429 below) to be benches and blocks for spinning wheels.
Copy by Vittone, vol.II, fo.168.

425 PLAN OF THE LOGGIA (*Figure* 357) [9796]
Two sheets joined horizontally. Pen, grey wash, traces of chalk. With scale.

The open loggia is here shown at parapet level. The broad bay of the loggia, nearest to the site of the existing wing of the Ospizio, was apparently covered and it contains the staircase and lift.

426 TRANSVERSE SECTION (*Figure* 358, detail) [9797]
Pen, grey and brown wash, traces of chalk.

This section, which faces in the opposite direction to the existing buildings of the Ospizio, shows the street on the right, with a project for a gateway which leads into the court on the left. The nave is vaulted, and above it is the terrace with its sloping floor. The vault of the nave is supported by buttresses at the sides.

427 STREET ELEVATION (*Figure* 360) [9786]
Two sheets joined vertically. Pen, grey wash, traces of chalk.

In this drawing three round windows flanked by buttresses are shown in the attic; the covered loggia appears on the left.

428 STREET ELEVATION [9787]
Pen, grey wash, traces of chalk.

A copy of the preceding elevation.

429 PERSPECTIVE VIEW INSIDE THE PRISON: DESIGN FOR A MEDAL (*Figure* 362) [9792]
Pen, grey wash, traces of chalk.

The present drawing corresponds with a medal of 1704 of Clement XI, listed in Guarnacci, 1751, p.374, no.XIX.
Copy by Vittone, vol.II, fo.163.

430 VERSION OF PRECEDING [9793]
Pen, grey wash.

431 ELEVATION OF THE STREET DOORWAY (*Figure* 363) [9735]
C.185 × 270 mm. Pen, grey wash, traces of chalk.

The design corresponds closely with the street door as finally built, though the 'ears' of the door frame were omitted (cf. Fig.364). The inscription over the door is dated 1704 (nine trial wordings for this tablet are recorded in Arch. Segr. Vat., Fondo Albani, 14, fos 134 *recto* and *verso*, and 135).
Copy by Vittone, vol.II, fo.141.

Miscellaneous drawings

This section consists of six drawings – two plans, bound amongst the drawings of group 5 in Volume 176, for an annexe to the prison, two rough sketch plans on the end papers of Volume 181, one of a group of four small designs for medals in Volume 188, and a study in chalk of two kneeling youths in Volume 176.

The annexe is shown in drawings 432 and 433 (Figs 365, 366) at ground and first-floor levels. Each sheet was originally double its present size and also contained a short text explaining the functions of the building. The sheets are now folded in two in the binding, and the texts therefore divided from the relevant plans. The inscriptions show that the building was intended as an extension of the prison block at the end opposite the Ospizio. It is divided into two sections. The first, drawn in grey wash, consists of a court with fountains and flights of steps leading to rooms at first-floor level. In the texts it is described as a 'tintorie'. The second section, an 'ostaria', is drawn in yellow wash and forms an extension to an existing building on its east side. This extension apparently remained unbuilt.

432 THE ANNEXE, GROUND-FLOOR PLAN (*Figure* 365) [9795]

304 × *c*.210 mm. Pen, grey, yellow and brown wash, traces of chalk. With scale, inscriptions and measurements.

The accompanying text, explaining the purpose of the annexe, occurs on the *verso* of the following page.
Copy by Vittone, vol.II, fo.168.

433 THE ANNEXE, FIRST-FLOOR PLAN (*Figure* 366) [9794]

304 × *c*.210 mm. Pen, brown ink, grey, yellow and brown wash, traces of chalk. With scale. Measured and inscribed.

The accompanying text, explaining the purpose of the annexe, occurs (upside down) on the *recto* of the next page but two.

434 SKETCH PLANS [9975 A and B]
Two sketch plans in chalk covering the end papers of Volume 181. 9975B is drawn on the last double-page of the volume. It bears the inscription "Ca:te 24", which must refer to the number of sheets of drawings for the prison in the volume. The plan itself is faintly drawn and appears to be unconnected with the prison. 9975A occupies the *recto* of half of 9975B and resembles the plan of the ending of the nave in Fontana's later projects.

435 VIEW OF THE EXTERIOR OF THE PRISON: DESIGN FOR A MEDAL [10598]
122 × 129 mm. Watermark no.5. Pen, grey wash, traces of chalk.

No corresponding medal is known.

436 Unidentified draughtsman
STUDY OF TWO KNEELING YOUTHS [9754]
*C.*210 × 304 mm. Watermark no.23(?). Red chalk.

The two youths wear capes with hoods like the prison inmates shown in drawing 429 above. The drawing is possibly a design for the habits the boys were to wear.

The south-west corner of the Ospizio di San Michele (1704)

The group of 12 drawings in Volume 176 at Windsor (nos 9724–34 and 9736) are studies for the building at the south-west corner of the Ospizio, the building shown on the right in Fontana's perspective view of 1706 (Fig.342). The group is entitled on the preceding blank sheet 'S. Michele', and it is accompanied by a short text: 'Reflessione hauute nella dispositione della nuoua fabrica cantonale da farsi in S. Michele incontro alla dogana', containing suggestions for the use of the rooms (not transcribed below). One of the sheets (no.443) bears the date 12 November (?) 1704, and a study for the doorway of the prison (no.431 above) dated the same year is bound with the drawings.

According to Fontana's text the height of the building was to correspond with that of another block facing the Dogana di mare, and this must be the building to the north of the Casa cantonale, running towards the site of the Casa di Correzzione (see Fig.342 and no.439), occupying land used later for Fuga's prison. The basement plan for the 'casa cantonale' provides for a simple rectangular block, but the plans of the upper storeys and the river elevations appear to incorporate the final bays of the granary building already in existence on the river wing (see introduction and Fig.332).

The twelve drawings at Windsor can be divided into two groups. The second comprises 6 studies, all in grey wash, which show a block 136½ *palmi* long with a completely symmetrical long façade. This project appears to be the one that was carried out (see Figs 334, 342 and 372), and the dated basement plan of November (?) 1704 belongs to the group. The first group has plans in pink wash which provide for a building of only about 123 *palmi*. One of these plans also includes part of an existing building to the north of the 'casa cantonale'. The main façade in this project is asymmetrical in design in order presumably to blend with the existing building. In the elevations and one of the plans (no.439) this connection between the two blocks is emphasized by the addition of pilaster strips to Fontana's façade, which divide the elevation into sections of seven and two bays.

Group 1

437 GROUND-FLOOR PLAN (*Figure* 367) [9734]
*C.*210 × 301 mm. Pen, pink wash, traces of chalk. With scale. Measured in full. Inscribed, upside down, upper right: *Tutte le porte di uano p^mi^ 5¼ /. . . Tutte le finest di uano p^mi^ 5¼ a/(lt)* . .

The block here measures 123 *palmi* along the front façade, and 99¼ *palmi* along the river façade, a measurement which includes three bays of the granary on the front wing of the Ospizio.
Copy by Vittone, vol.II, fo.147.

438 GROUND-FLOOR PLAN [9732]
*C.*210 × 301 mm. Pen, pink wash, traces of chalk. With scale and annotations. Measured in full.

Inscribed, lower right, with notes on materials to be used and the sizes of the windows and doors. The plan corresponds with the preceding except for slight suggested alterations. The façades are labelled 'uerso la Dogana' and 'uerso fiume'.

439 GROUND-FLOOR PLAN [9733]
*C.*210 × 302 mm. Pen, pink wash, some chalk. With scale, index of letters, and annotations. Measured in full.

Four of the rooms are labelled here: 'Cucina', 'Androne', 'Dispensa' and 'Tinello'. The plan also includes part of the building to the north of the 'casa cantonale', with a dotted line beside it labelled 'filo della Dogana', and rooms labelled 'Pizzigaria' and 'Stanza'.
Copy by Vittone, vol.II, fo.147.

On the *verso* is a schematic plan in chalk, which appears to be unconnected with the 'casa cantonale'.

440 ELEVATION FACING THE *DOGANA* (*Figure* 368) [9731]
209 × 301 mm. Watermark no.9. Pen, grey wash, traces of chalk. With scale, measurements and annotations. Marks at the top of the sheet indicate where an inscription has been cut away.

The positions of the pilaster strips are the same as in the immediately preceding plan, but the pattern of the openings of the façade is that of plans 437 and 438. It is possible that the elevation was drawn so as to correspond with these two plans and then altered. Measurements of height occur to the left of the elevation, labelled 'gronda', 'solaro' and 'Piano', and the slope, bottom right is marked 'Declivio'.

Copy by Vittone of the right half of the drawing, vol.II, fo.147.

441 ELEVATION FACING THE *DOGANA* [9730]
*C.*210×301 mm. Watermark no.9(?). Pen, grey wash, traces of chalk. With scale and measurements. Inscription, upper right, partly cut away: *..(pi)/ano di sopra sarà alt* p^{mi} *18 e* p^{mi} *6 di soffito in pend(enz)a.* This appears to refer to the interior heights of the building.

Apparently a fair copy of the final state of the preceding; the main façade measures 121¼ *palmi.*

442 ELEVATION FACING THE *DOGANA* [9736]
*C.*195×268 mm. Pen, grey wash, some chalk. With measurements.

A small scale version of the preceding elevations.

Group 2

443 BASEMENT PLAN [9724]
*C.*220×301 mm. (including a fold). Pen, grey wash, traces of chalk. With scale and figures (in chalk). Measured in full. Inscribed (upper right): *Fondamenti li 12 9bre* (?) *1704 / Tutti li fondamenti sarano larghi il uano* p^{mi} *4 / Profondi come laltri fatti uerso le fabri* (che).

The building measures 136½×70½ *palmi*; the longer side is inscribed 'Verso la Dogana', the shorter side 'Verso fiume'. A central corridor divides the length of the plan, and the basement on the river front is left open.

444 GROUND-FLOOR PLAN (*Figure* 369) [9726]
*C.*210×301 mm. Watermark no.10. Pen, grey wash, traces of chalk. With scale. Measured in full.

Inscribed (upper right): 'Piano terreno', and above this a longer inscription, of which the first line, incorporating the date 1704, is largely cut away. The remainder refers to materials to be used and measurements. A section of the existing granary is included on the river façade.

445 GROUND-FLOOR PLAN [9725]
*C.*210×301 mm. Watermark no.10. Pen, grey wash, traces of chalk. With scale. Measured in full.

A version of the preceding with several of the measurements altered.

446 FIRST-FLOOR PLAN [9727]
*C.*210×301 mm. Watermark no.6. Pen, grey wash, chalk. With scale.

The building includes, as in the ground-floor plans, part of the fabric of the granary. It is perhaps merely an oversight that windows are introduced on three sides of the granary.

447 ELEVATION FACING THE *DOGANA* (*Figure* 370) [9728]
*C.*210×301 mm. Watermark no.10. Pen, grey wash, traces of chalk. With scale and measurements.

The elevation corresponds with Fontana's perspective view of 1706 (Fig.342) and the existing façade of the corner (Fig.372) corresponds, though it has been altered in the rhythm of the nine openings.

448 ELEVATION OVERLOOKING THE RIVER (*Figure* 371) [9729]
*C.*210×301 mm. Pen, grey wash, traces of chalk. With scale.

Three bays of the granary (Fig.332) at the side of the block are indicated in ink, but without wash. They break off at a point marked on the plan by a rough ink line.

Design for an engraving with a representation of Fontana's coat-of-arms (1702 ?)

Drawing 449 (9419 in Volume 172) shows an elaborate setting for a coat-of-arms which can be connected with Fontana himself on the evidence of a short manuscript note accompanying the drawing and in the presence of fountains – in punning allusions to Fontana's name – in the drawing. The text was evidently written in haste, and it is difficult to read accurately, but it appears to contain instructions about improving the design set out in the drawing: 'Fare l'arme / tutte / Le statue . . . (?) / li scalini . . . (?) / con i nomi sotto / Le fame (?) in Giardino / con due Puttini in alto il zena(?)/. . . (?) uenghino zena . . . (?) uolante / col motto omnes in uno e con un / dito (?) dell'altra mano accenni . . . (?) il/detto motto e la facia guardi / i santi – La Corona sopra la / Fonte, e la croce sotto la / corona giacche la fonte –/ deue haver scudo (?).' The *verso* of this inscribed sheet is signed by Fontana, and it bears a reference to a dedication and an illegible name: 'La dedica / Illmo . . . (?) Roberto & c/ Comitis Fontana . . . tic.ensis / Eques Carlo fontana'.

The drawing probably refers to Fontana's promotion in 1702 to the rank of count in the Imperial service of Leopold I (on Fontana's relations with the Emperor see entry on Leopold's funeral service in 1705). This would explain the phrase 'Comitis Fontana' in the inscription, and the presence on the escutcheon in the drawing of the Imperial double-headed eagle and a count's coronet. Fontana became an Imperial count in February 1702; he had been a Polish count since August 1699 (Rome, Accademia di San Luca, *Copie di diplomi onorifici*, vol.35A and see above, the entry for the Tempio Vaticano). The escutcheon in the present drawing differs from that in earlier representations of Fontana's coat-of-arms (for example, that under the portrait by Audenaerd of 1700 – Frontispiece); the present composition is not known to have been engraved.

449 DESIGN FOR THE COAT-OF-ARMS (*Figure* 373) [9419]
405 × 269 mm. Watermark no.7. Pen, grey wash, some chalk.

Section of the Palazzo del Senatore, damaged by an earthquake (1703)

Drawing no.450 (9538 in Volume 174 – Fig.374), as is explained by dated inscriptions of 14 June 1703 on the drawing, records damage inflicted on the 'Sala del Campi (doglio)' by an earthquake. This was presumably one of the tremors that shook Rome in the early months of 1703, damaging several important buildings which Fontana must have surveyed, although the present drawing is the only record at Windsor of such a survey (Pastor, Eng. ed., vol.XXXIII, pp.492ff.). Fontana's drawing shows the main hall of the Palazzo del Senatore. The damage was apparently not serious and affected only the iron braces supporting the vault from below.

450 TRANSVERSE SECTION OF THE PALAZZO DEL SENATORE (*Figure* 374) [9538]
414 × 271 mm. Pen, coloured washes, traces of chalk. With scale and index. Inscribed on *verso*: *Sala del Campi*/(doglio) . . . *Causa dl terem*/(oto) . . . *Giu*° *14 1703*, and on the *recto* (at the top): . . . / *Giu*° *1703 p il Campidoglio* / . . . *Causato dal teremoto*, and on left: *A muraglia antica* / *B Muraglia antica* / *C uolta fatta da Greg*° *XIII* / *D. inCauallature intatte* / *F. Catene strapate dal teremoto* / *G ferrate ou d Catene* / *H fusti di perpendicolo f 7½ I fusti di perpendicolo f 8½*.

Fontana perhaps meant the areas in grey to represent the additions of Gregory XIII (cf. index C). Index F refers to the iron rods which were disturbed by the earthquake. Dotted pen lines on Fontana's drawing enclosing areas of yellow wash reveal that the walls of the building are not precisely perpendicular.

A project for the Porto di Ripetta, Rome (1703)

A single drawing in Volume 174 at Windsor is a project for the parapet of the Porto di Ripetta, inscribed in Fontana's hand and dated August 1703 (Fig.377). The Porto was destroyed about 1890 (see Saranzi), but is recorded in many 18th-century engravings (for instance in one by Piranesi, Fig.375). The work has always been attributed to Fontana's pupil, Alessandro Specchi (cf. Coudenhove-Erthal, pp.113f.). Francesco Posterla, who worked with Fontana on a number of commissions at this time, illustrates the port in his *Roma sacra e moderna* of 1708 (pp.461f.), giving the date 1704 for the work, and Specchi, 'allievo di Carlo Fontana', as architect.

In his *Discorso sopra l'antico Monte Citatorio*, 1708, p.34, Fontana speaks of his own presence near the port together with the supervisor of the work, Cardinal Giudici, in August 1703, the month in which the present drawing at Windsor was executed. The drawing, which differs substantially from the parapet as it was built (Fig.376 is an old photograph of the fountain and parapet of the port taken from *Architettura minore in Italia*, Turin, (1926?), I, pl.5), may represent a part-project, or a fragment of a more extensive design drawn up by Fontana for Giudici in August 1703.

The first papal *avviso* mentioning the work is of 18 August 1703 (Pastor, Eng. ed. XXXIII, pp.528f., n.4). It is recorded, as Fontana himself explains, that Monsignor Giudici, who was Presidente delle Strade, played a large part in the planning of the port, but the extent of his proposals is not known (see Taja, as mentioned in Ashby, *Specchi*, and as quoted in d'Onofrio, *Tevere*, p.103). D'Onofrio suggests (p.104) that Specchi may have been appointed on the recommendation of Fontana, and the existence of the present drawing at Windsor lends some slight confirmation to this theory.

Work on the construction of the port began in October 1703, and the fabric apparently incorporated stones dislodged from the Colosseum by an earthquake in January 1704 (Ashby, op.cit.). The work was almost completed by 2 August 1704; an *avviso* of this date (Pastor, op.cit.) also contains references to a new store house and to the new customs building, and to the placing of an inscription (cf. Forcella, VI, 612). The customs house lay to the left of the steps of the port (for further information on this building see Busiri Vici). On 23 August 1704 the site was visited by the Pope who apparently found fault with the completed work in the scarcity of water provided by the fountains, and with the difficulty of taking in the whole prospect from the parapet. The finished work was commemorated in an engraving by Specchi (Ashby, op.cit., fig.3) and by Taja's publication of 1704; the cost was estimated at 60,000 *scudi* (Pastor, op.cit.).

ADDITIONAL BIBLIOGRAPHY:

A. Busiri Vici in *Capitolium*, 40, 1965, pp. 490/7.
S. Jacob, no.745, on Specchi's fountain of 1710 at Frosinone.
T. Marder, *The Porto di Ripetta*, Columbia University thesis, 1975.
F. Sarazani in *Il Tempo*, 19 February 1969, p.31.
A. Taja, *Lettera, e poetici componimenti in ragguaglio, e in encomio della nuova ripa* . . ., Rome, 1704.

451 ELEVATION OF THE PARAPET (*Figure* 377) [9539]
269×412 mm. Pen, brown and grey wash, traces of chalk. With scale. Inscription, bottom right, partly covered by the binding strip: *Adi 6 Agosto 1703 / Porto di Ripet/* . . .

The parapet is shown from the street above the port. The central frame is flanked by free-standing ornaments composed of the *monti* and star of the Albani arms.
Copy by Vittone, vol.II, fo.140.

The Granary, near the baths of Diocletian (1703–1705)

Volume 172 at Windsor (Contini, vol.7) contains 27 drawings connected with the design of a new granary near the Baths of Diocletian, a work which was completed in 1705 (Fig.378). The shell of the building is still in existence – a large rectangular block with its main façade overlooking the present Via delle Terme (on the right a small portion was demolished to make way for the eastern wing of the Piazza dell' Esedra). A shallow rectangular court lies behind the block and on the left at the rear a large circular tower overlooking the Via Viminale (detail, Fig.391). The tower originally formed part of the Baths of Diocletian; it marked one corner of the outer wall of the Baths and corresponds to another tower which was converted into the church of S. Bernardo alle Terme in 1598/1600 (Ortolani, p.1).

Fontana's drawings are accompanied by three texts. The first is a transcription of a long poem in praise of the Granary by Francesco Posterla, dated 1703 and dedicated to Ferdinando Nuzzi, the Prefetto dell'Annona. Posterla is lavish with praise and refers by name to the architect; 'Gloria al tuo saggio, e spiritoso Ingegno / Carlo, che sublimò l'eccelsa mole,/ Per cui ti fai veder Figlio ben degno / Delle Latine, e delle Greche Scuole.'

The second text, of 29 February 1704, is a copy of a document signed by Fontana as 'Architetto p l'Annona' and two fellow architects Ludovico Gregorini, 'Architetto dell' Annona' and Filippo Leti, 'Architetto p li PP. di San Bernardo'. It is an estimate of the value of the site to be occupied by the new granary and the history of the commission is briefly described at the start. At the wish of the Pope, the Prefetto dell' Annona, Ferdinando Nuzzi, found an appropriate site for a new granary on land belonging to the monastery of S. Bernardo and in the vicinity of the old granaries (see below). The site was enclosed by the Piazza di Termini at the front and the walls of the garden of the Villa Strozzi at the rear. At one side it included the tower of the Baths of Diocletian, which is described vaguely as an 'Edificio antico in parte diruto di un Mausoleo', and on the corner a 'Fabrica di due fenili'. At the other side the boundary of the site was marked at a line where the exedra of the outer wall of the Baths began its curve. This is described simply as a 'Semicircolo antico' (the present Piazza dell' Esedra).

The major part of the document is occupied by an estimate by the three architects of the value of the site – the existing buildings are valued at 1902.55 *scudi*, and the annual rent for the site itself which measured 852 *canne* is fixed at 102.31 *scudi*. Finally the annual rent received by the monastery of S. Bernardo from the *fabrica delli due fienili*, the two small rectangles on the corner of the site in front of the *mausoleo*, is assessed as fair. The third and final text, of 20 October 1705, is an estimate of the value of a further short strip of land to the west of the site, on to which rain dripped from the eaves of the new granary building. Its annual rent is assessed at a mere 1.67 *scudi*.

The second two texts are illustrated by the site plan (no.452; Fig.379). This also is a copy of a document signed by the three architects and has two dated inscriptions corresponding with the agreements of 29 February 1704 and 20 October 1705.

Although assessment of the value of the land is dated 29 February 1704, Fontana had already started work on his projects by this time. An early drawing (no.459) bears the date 12 January 1704 and the land itself appears to have been ceded to the *Camera Apostolica* in two stages, on 27 December 1703 (the year of Posterla's poem) and 5 March 1704 (Ortolani, p.29). The granary was the subject of two medals of Clement XI, which were dated 1704 and 1705, respectively (Guarnacci, II, col.374, no.XX, and col.375, no.XXII). The work was completed in 1705 – the year of the inscriptions over the main entrance and over the door leading into the tower in the Via Viminale (Forcella, XIII, p.186; Figs 388, 391).

There are several references to the work in Valesio's diary. On 11 March 1704 he speaks of the start of the building, suggesting that it was intended to replace the granary at the Palazzo Laterano which had been converted into an Ospizio. On 15 May 1704 the Pope visited the site; more than 400 workmen were engaged and the building had risen to the height of a man. In the entry for 15 March 1705 the building is described as 'ridotta à buon termine'. Finally a visit by the Pope on 6 October coincides with the unveiling of the inscriptions.

Fontana's design has the same strictly functional character as the slightly earlier project for the prison for young criminals. The drawings are, however, less complete than those for the prison and they present a number of difficulties of order and date. Three of Fontana's drawings are in fact dated, those of 12 January, 19 April and 11 July 1704, but the second two are a good deal later in date than the day on which the building was begun (see Valesio above). The drawing of 19 April (Fig.387) is a study for the doorways of the main façade and that of 11 July a project for using the space of the 'mausoleo' for a large staircase. Although the character of the plan itself must have been established by March at the latest, Fontana had apparently left certain crucial details to be worked out at a later date.

The first dated drawing, like the last, refers to a project for the staircase. It is a section of a staircase (Fig.384), attached to the rear façade of the granary, and the same structure appears in a group of plans of the whole granary (nos 452 etc.). In the plans, to which a single elevation is related, the 'mausoleo' is converted for use as a small storage hall and the façade has five openings on to the Piazza di Termini. The present plan, established by March 1704, has three doors in the main façade and one pierced in the 'mausoleo' at the side. Unfortunately the final stage of the general planning is not recorded in full in the drawings; in its place there are only two sheets of indeterminate date. The two final groups of drawings are those for the doorways, (April and after) and the staircase (July). The plan in its final state is recorde in a drawing cited by Pastor (Eng. ed., XXXIII, p.528, n.2).

Included amongst the drawings, and of great topographical interest, is a detailed plan of the *Granari Vecchii à Termini* (Fig.380). Like Fontana's granary, the old granaries also incorporated a part of the Baths of Diocletian. They were begun by Gregory XIII in a wing of the central block of the baths (inscription of 1575) and subsequently extended by Paul V and Urban VIII. The work of these Popes is recorded in the inscription of the main façade of Fontana's granary, and parts of the older building are still in existence (Paribeni, pp.40 and 44/45). The drawing itself appears to be much earlier in date than Fontana's drawings. It reveals how closely Fontana followed established practice in the organisation of the plan and it was presumably acquired by him for such a purpose.

The staircase appears to have caused Fontana considerably more trouble than the storage halls themselves. There are no less than six different projects for the stairs. The sections reveal that they had sloping and extremely shallow steps, which were clearly intended to make life easier for the granary porters. Not only did the stairs therefore occupy a good deal of space, but it was also important to choose a position for them which was directly accessible from the street. In Fontana's first project, which recalls Fuga's design for the Palazzo della Consultà staircase, they were unadvantageously placed in the court at the back. But in the final design (July 1704; Fig.393) the stair is fitted into the spacious well of the 'mausoleo', directly beside the side entrance into the granary. The basic structure of this staircase is still in existence.

The whole group of drawings is preceded in Volume 172 by a blank sheet entitled at the top 'Granari noui a Termine / Anno 1705 –' and a further general title occurs on the *verso* of the last of the sheets, no.453 [9447]. There are no copies of the Granary drawings in the Vittone albums in Paris.

ADDITIONAL BIBLIOGRAPHY:
S. Ortolani, *S. Bernardo alle Terme* (CRI no.8).
R. Paribeni, *Le Terme di Diocleziano*, 1952.

1. Preliminary drawings

452 PLAN OF THE SITE (*Figure* 379) [9421]
Two sheets joined vertically. 406×535 mm. Watermark no.7. Pen, coloured washes. With scale. Annotated and measured in full and inscribed with an account of the site, in size and value, by Fontana, Gregorini and Leti (see above).

This sheet, with its inscriptions of 29 February 1704 and 20 October 1705, is clearly a copy of an original document bearing autograph signatures by the three architects. The site is bordered at the back by the grounds of the Villa Strozzi; it extends from the 'mausoleo' on the left, with the 'fabrica delli due fienili' in front, across the 'Piazza publica di Termine uerso Tramontana' to the grounds retained by the monastery of S. Bernardo – an area which is enclosed at the back by the 'Semicircolo Antico . .' (now half of the Piazza dell' Esedra). A rectangle of green wash in this area, as explained in the inscription, denotes the site of the extra strip leased in October 1705.

453 Unidentified draughtsman
PLAN OF THE OLD GRANARIES
(*Figure* 380) [9447]
528×778 mm. Watermark no.9. Pen, coloured washes. With scale. Inscribed on *verso*: *Granari à Termine* (referring to the whole section of drawings, probably, of which 9447 is the final sheet).

The drawing is enclosed within ruled ink lines and it probably dates from earlier than the 1700's. It shows the three halls of the old granaries drawn in different coloured washes. They were adapted or built for Gregory XIII, Paul V and Urban VIII (see the medal illustrated in Bonanni, II, 1699, on the second pl. of p.563; the inscriptions of the *granari vecchii* are transcribed on pp.589–591).

2. Project with staircase in court (*c.* January 1704)

454 PLAN (*Figure* 381) [9445]
379×925 mm. Two sheets joined vertically. Watermark no.7. Chalk, coloured washes, pen. With scale.

The central five bays on to the court at the rear are masked by a relatively open staircase, apparently added as an afterthought to the plan. The 'mausoleo' is adapted for use as a small store-room. The *verso* of the sheet has a scale in ink and a rough rectangular plan in chalk.

455 PLAN [9423]
289×406 mm. Watermark no.7. Pen, grey and yellow wash, traces of chalk. With scale. Annotated, and inscribed: *Pianta delli nuoui Granari da farsi alla Piazza de Termini.*

A neater and much smaller variant of the last, with slight differences in the disposition of the doors and windows.

456 PLAN [9422]
270×407 mm. Pen, grey and yellow wash, traces of chalk. With scale. Annotated, and inscribed: *Pianta de nuoui Granari da farsi alla Piazza di Termini.*

A sheet which corresponds closely with the last, but with different positions for the doorways.

457 PLAN (*Figure* 382) [9424]
269×406 mm. Pen, grey and yellow wash, traces of chalk. With scale. Annotated, and inscribed: *Pianta delli nuoui Granari da farsi alla Piazza de' Termini.*

A copy, probably, of the last, with the same arrangement of doors more neatly drawn, and further changes indicated in chalk. The drawing is related to the following elevation (Fig.383).

458 ELEVATION OF THE MAIN FAÇADE
(*Figure* 383) [9426]
267×407 mm. Watermark no.7. Pen, grey wash, traces of chalk. With scale. Inscribed: *Prospetto delli nuoui Granari da farsi à Termine.*

The corresponding elevation for no.457. The pilaster strips framing the central, slightly richer, three bays are not marked in the plan.

459 SECTION OF THE STAIRCASE (*Figure* 384) [9446]
264×408 mm. Watermark no.7. Pen, grey wash, traces of chalk. With scale. Inscribed: *Ill:mo e Rev:mo Nuzzi* and *Adi 12 Genuo 1704 / Scala a Cordonata p li Granari / noui à termine un Pensiero assaij comodo p ascenderui.*

The date of the drawing precedes by more than a month the first date on the site plan 452, above. Ramps leading down to a basement and up to a roof level (above the cornice) are drawn in dotted lines, without wash, suggesting that the full extent of the stair was still in doubt. The presence of the name Nuzzi on the drawing suggests that the *Presidente dell' Annona* took a personal interest in the problem of the staircase.

3. Miscellaneous intermediate drawings

460 PLAN WITH SEVERAL TRIAL STAIRCASES (*Figure* 385) [9443]
405×731 mm. Watermark no.7. Pen, coloured washes, some chalk. With scale.

The plan bears six flaps containing different projects for staircases. The block of the granary is close in character to the preceding designs, but the windows at the back on the right are omitted (as in the first plan, 454 above) and the main façade, like the final building, has only three doorways. In the basic plan the principal changes occur at the back of the granary. A single double-flighted staircase is attached to the rear wall of the block, while the circular wall of the 'mausoleo' is retained only for the side street elevation, the court side is transformed into a rectangular extension to the main storage hall.

A small oval stair is superimposed on the plan at the junction of the main storeroom and the new rectangular extension, and in this sketch Fontana disregards the basic plan and incorporates a part of the circular wall which was in fact to be demolished. This area of the plan is redrawn more neatly on a small flap. In a further flap covering the 'mausoleo' (shown in Fig.385) Fontana restores much of the circular wall, introduces a single door on the street side and adds a long double-flighted staircase on the court side. In the remaining flaps a similar stair is introduced on the opposite side of the court (two flaps) and a more carefully-drawn version of the stair in the centre of the rear façade of the granary (two flaps of which the lower one is blank). The upper flaps of these two projects are shown in Fig.385.

461 ELEVATION OF THE MAIN FAÇADE (*Figure* 386) [9427]
271 × 406 mm. Watermark no.7. Pen, grey wash, traces of chalk. With scale.

This drawing corresponds with the final design in the position of its doorways. The central door was apparently intended to occupy two storeys of the central bay of the façade; they are left blank in the drawing. Elsewhere the elevation differs considerably from the present façade – each window has a heavy plain frame and the roof line is extremely low.

4. Later projects for the doorways

The drawings placed in this section number nine, all of them made after work had started on the granary. The first is the dated sheet of 19 April 1704 and the second a related sketch of the same size. The remaining seven drawings are smaller studies for the final design of the doorways and their frames. They are drawn on four folded sheets bound together; the approximate size of each half sheet is 270 × 205 mm. They are followed by three blank sheets of similar size (perhaps originally wrapped around further small drawings which are now missing) of which the first bears the inscription: 'Per li Granari à termini lanno 1704'.

462 STUDY OF THE DOORS OF THE MAIN FAÇADE, ELEVATION (*Figure* 387) [9441]
267 × 405 mm. Watermark no.7. Pen, grey wash, traces of chalk. With scale. Measured and inscribed: *19 Ap'le 1704/. ./anari à termine.*

The drawing shows the three bays of the left corner of the main façade at ground and first-floor level. It is presumably a study of separate parts of the façade drawn for convenience in adjacent bays. The side doors are low and round-headed like the present doors and those in 461 above. The main door corresponds with that in no.458, and is unlike the present door (Fig.388) which Fontana evolved in the smaller drawings below, 465 etc.

463 STUDY OF THE MAIN DOORWAY [9440]
405 × 264 mm. Watermark no.7. Chalk.

Closely resembling the principal door in the last drawing. On the *verso* are two small rough sketches in chalk.

464 STUDY OF THE DOOR IN THE SIDE OF THE 'MAUSOLEO', ELEVATION (*Figure* 392) [9433]
Pen, coloured washes, traces of chalk. With scale. Inscribed: *G. a termine.*

The grey wash must indicate the extent of the area to be demolished in the wall of the 'mausoleo'. The alternative design on the right corresponds with the present character of the side door (Fig. 391), though the door is larger now in proportion to the size of the plaque.

465 STUDY FOR THE MAIN DOORWAY (*Figure* 389) [9434]
Pen, grey wash, traces of chalk. With scale.

The design is close to the present door (Fig.388).

466 STUDIES OF A DOUBLE WHEAT CORNUCOPIA AND TWO PLAQUES (*Figure* 390) [9435]
Watermark, no.24. Pen, grey wash, some chalk.

467 FOUR STUDIES OF SINGLE WHEAT CORNUCOPIAS [9436]
Pen, grey wash, traces of chalk.

Three rectangles of paper are pasted over the principal design.

468 STUDIES OF FOUR SINGLE AND ONE DOUBLE WHEAT CORNUCOPIA [9437]
Pen, grey wash, traces of chalk.

469 THREE STUDIES OF CORNUCOPIAS [9438]
Watermark no.24. Pen, chalk, grey wash.

One is a rough chalk sketch of a double cornucopia.

470 STUDIES OF A DOUBLE WHEAT CORNUCOPIA AND A (?) WHEAT BASKET [9439]
Pen, chalk, grey wash.

5. Final projects for the staircase (*c.* July 1704)

471 PLAN OF THE EASTERN END OF THE GRANARY (*Figure* 395) [9444]
472 × 271 mm. Pen, grey and brown wash, some chalk. With scale and index.

The basic design of the staircase is a simple double-flight structure extending into the 'mausoleo' from the main hall of the granary, and Fontana presumably intended at this stage to build up the level of the floor of the 'mausoleo' to adjust the discrepancy in level with the granary itself (see the sections 477, 478 below). The three flaps show three floors of an alternative rectangular staircase which corresponds closely with the sections below. The index letters of the basic plan are continued from E to T consecutively through the flaps. On the first flaps (shown in Fig.395) a small flight leads downwards to the level of the 'mausoleo'. Five flights lead up to the first floor, and five from first to second-floor level.

472 PLAN OF THE GRANARY (*Figure* 396) [9425]
270×408 mm. Pen, grey and yellow wash, traces of chalk. With scale.

A plan of the whole granary showing a variant of the second stair design of the preceding drawing. A further small stair is introduced between the rear façade and the wall of the 'Casa Strozzi', extreme right.

473 PLAN OF THE EASTERN END OF THE GRANARY [9442]
555×407 mm. Watermark no.7. Pen, grey and yellow wash, traces of chalk. With scale and index.

A repetition of the first plan in the present group, including (on the basic sheet and two flaps) the second stair project of the latter.

474 PLAN OF THE FOUNDATIONS OF THE STAIRCASE [9428]
406×270 mm. Pen, coloured washes, traces of chalk. Measured in full. With scale and index. Inscribed at top: *Adi 11 lug.o 1704 Pianta delli fondamenti della Scale de/ Granari a Termine* –, and at bottom with an account of measurements.

475 PLAN OF THE FIRST (AND SECOND) LEVELS OF THE STAIRCASE (*Figure* 393) [9429]
406×270 mm. Watermark no.20(?). Pen, coloured washes, traces of chalk. Measured in full. With scale and index. Inscribed at top: . . ./*mezzo del Portone nell . ./ezzi* and at bottom with an account of measurements.

Except for slight differences in the arrangement of the piers the stair corresponds with that shown in the flaps of the early plans of the present group and in the sections below.

476 PLAN OF THE SAME [9430]
406×270 mm. Pen, coloured washes. With scale.

A copy of the preceding, without index, inscriptions, or measurements.

477 SECTION OF THE GRANARY (DETAIL), SHOWING STAIRCASE (*Figure* 394) [9431]
508×405 mm. Two sheets joined horizontally. Watermark no.7. Pen, grey and yellow wash, traces of chalk. With scale.

The arrangement of the stairs which give access to the three floors of the granary from the floor of the 'mausoleo' is clearly demonstrated in this section. The stairs themselves, as in the section of group one, are shallow and sloping, and the flights resemble ramps. The diagram at the top reappears in the following drawing with explanatory inscriptions.

478 TRANSVERSE SECTION [9432]
463×374 mm. Pen, grey and brown wash, traces of chalk. With scale.

A version of the last. The three roof levels in the diagram at the top are inscribed respectively 'loggie p^{mi} 2½/ Armaria p^{mi} 2⅙ / Granari p^{mi} 2'. The relevance of the diagram to the drawing itself is not explained.

Rome, the Palazzo del Quirinale, projects for the decoration of the gallery (*c.* 1703)

There are at Windsor ten drawings connected with Fontana's projects for the decoration of the gallery of the Palazzo del Quirinale, four large sheets in Volume 174 and six small sheets in Volume 176. A series of three very clumsy drawings in Volume 188 are probably connected with the same project and they are included at the end of the present section of the catalogue. The group of large sheets by Fontana comprises a project for placing square pedestals, decorated with bust portraits of various popes, at intervals along the walls of the gallery (cf. Fig.397). The smaller sheets in Volume 176 comprise two projects, one where pairs of pedestals carrying busts are substituted for the single square pedestals (cf. Fig.400), and one where the pedestals are absent altogether, the bust portraits occurring on roundels attached to the walls of the gallery (cf. Fig.403). Fontana's intentions at this last stage of the planning are explained in a short manuscript note in Volume 176. This whole section of the volume is entitled on the preceding blank page: 'Per la Galleria di monte Cauallo'.

This project of Fontana's is mentioned in two *avvisi*, quoted by Pastor (Eng. ed., XXXIII, p.514). The first, of 23 February 1703, reveals that there were to be 24 busts: 'Havendo il papa gran genio a risarcir et ornare li palazzi Apostolici, s'intende che voglia adornare la galleria del Quirinale con li busti in marmo di 24 Pontefici, che in varii tempi hanno sostenuto con travagli la Chiesa, con iscrittioni alli piedestalli, che si dicono fatte alla Certosa'. A second *avviso*, of 8 March 1703 (?), speaks of the busts being allocated to the sculptors: 'Si vanno distribuendo alli maestri li busti marmorei delli 24 Pontefici, che si devono collocare nella galleria del Quirinale, tra quali sarà quello di Alessandro VIII. come benefattore del regnante Pontefice, che vi havrà anco il suo'. A contemporary reference to the project occurs in Domenico de Rossi, *Raccolta di statue antiche e moderne*, 1704, and this suggests more specifically that the project was intended as an anti-Ottoman allegory: '... e finalmente quelle numerose immagini di Pontefici, che contro l'Ottomana potenza si segnalarono, le quali si preparano da nobili scultori per adornare la Pontificia galleria del Quirinale'.

The project seems to have been fairly far advanced in 1703/4, and the sculptors preparing to start work, but nothing appears to have come of Fontana's proposals as is revealed in Posterla's *Roma antica e moderna* (1707, pp.328f.): 'occupata però la gran mente della Santità Sua da più gravi negozii ha procrastinato l'esito di un'opera così famosa'. Posterla mentions Fontana as the author of the project and he explains that the busts were to be placed on gilt-wood pedestals which were to be decorated with Latin inscriptions composed by 'Monsig. Battelli, Cameriere d'Onore, e Bibliotecario di Sua Santità'.

The project mentioned in all these references is probably that with busts on single square pedestals which is recorded in Fontana's large drawings in Volume 174. This project might therefore be supposed to be his final design, but it is in point of fact more likely to have been the first of the three. The text in Volume 176 referring to the project where roundels are substituted for busts on pedestals gives some idea of Fontana's preoccupations in making the designs, and it appears that he was concerned that the busts should not project too far into the gallery. This, he explains, would not happen with medallions *di mezzo rilievo*. They would not disturb the chiaroscuro decoration of columns and pictures on the walls, and the inscriptions could be fitted beneath them 'sotto al dado doue sono li Grifoni finti di chiaro oscuro'. The cost would be half that needed for busts and two medallions could be carved from each piece of marble that a single bust would require. There could, finally, be greater variety in the presentation of the figures if roundels were employed. The text reads very much as though Fontana was proposing a cheaper and more convenient alternative to his project with portrait busts, and the project with roundels is probably the last of the three designs. The project with busts on large square pedestals was probably therefore the one on which work was almost started in 1703, to be superseded by Fontana's second proposal, where the pedestals project only to a limited degree and where the 24 popes may have lined only a single wall of the gallery, and finally by the project with roundels.

Within each group of drawings there is some variation in the shape of the pedestals or the tablets bearing the inscriptions, but in each case Fontana appears to have begun with a relatively simple shape, transforming it into a more complex form, mainly by the addition of consoles or 'ears' at the sides.

The Quirinal gallery is now so altered in character (Briganti, pp. 44ff.) that the site for which Fontana's designs were made is impossible to visualize clearly. One of the drawings, however (Fig.397, no.479 below), records in a diagrammatic way the chiaroscuro decoration of a unit of three bays of the room.

1. Projects with square pedestals

479 ELEVATION OF PART OF THE WALL OF THE QUIRINAL GALLERY (*Figure* 397) [9490]
265×412 mm. Chalk, pen, grey wash.

The bays to each side of the central window are occupied by a portrait bust of a pope on a high pedestal decorated with the Albani arms with a 'cone of vision' directed from the left to the inscription on one of the pedestals.
Copy by Vittone of the left half of the drawing, vol.I, fo.67.

480 ELEVATION OF A PEDESTAL WITH A PORTRAIT BUST (*Figure* 398) [9489]
265×412 mm. Pen, grey wash, some chalk. With scale. Inscribed, lower right: *Versi n. 10 inc.ª* / *lettere n 190 incª* / *Parole n. 22 incª* (referring to the possible length of the inscription).

The left part of the drawing amounts to an enlarged detail of the preceding sheet. The large capital letters are included as an indication, presumably, of the size of script to be used for the inscription.

481 A PORTRAIT BUST ON A PEDESTAL DECORATED WITH CONSOLES, ELEVATION [9491]
413×267 mm. Watermark no.7. Pen, grey wash, traces of chalk. With scale and inscription (cut) at bottom: *sito per l'Iscrittione. lon.pal.3½ alto 3:⅔: Righe, ouero uersi circa n:º 11. lettere circa 190: parole n.º 30: in circa* / ...

On the right are trial letters, in part cut away, referring to the script to be used for the inscription on the pedestal.

482 FRONT AND SIDE ELEVATIONS OF A PEDESTAL DECORATED WITH CONSOLES (*Figure* 399) [9488]
265×415 mm. Pen, grey wash, chalk. With two scales, of which the upper one is struck through. Inscription (cut) bottom right: *v* (?) – *83 A*/...

Copy by Vittone, vol.I, fo.7.

2. Projects with pairs of tapering pedestals

483 PROJECT WITH PLAIN PEDESTALS, ELEVATION [9771]
303 × *c*.210 mm. Chalk. With scale.

The pedestals are much smaller than the single pedestal of the foregoing group of projects both in height and in width and each is tapered at the sides (cf. Fig.400).

484 PROJECT WITH PEDESTALS DECORATED WITH ROUNDELS, ELEVATION (*Figure* 400) [9769]
303 × *c*.210 mm. Watermark no.25(?). Pen, grey wash, traces of chalk. With scale.

485 PROJECT WITH PEDESTALS DECORATED WITH ROUNDELS AND CONSOLES, ELEVATION (*Figure* 401) [9767]
303 × *c*.210 mm. Pen, chalk.

The bases of the busts are decorated with the star of the Albani arms, while the *monti* appear beneath each roundel at the base of the pedestals.

486 FRONT AND SIDE ELEVATION OF A PEDESTAL DECORATED WITH A ROUNDEL AND CONSOLES (*Figure* 402) [9770]
303 × *c*.210 mm. Pen, grey wash, chalk. With scale.

The present drawing stands in relation to the second group of projects in exactly the same way as no.482 to the first group. The consoles at the sides, shown for the most part on a rectangle of paper pasted down over the basic sheet, are decorated in the centre with a large leaf. On the *verso* of the sheet is a rough but measured outline plan in chalk which probably refers to the gallery of the Quirinal.

3. Projects with roundels affixed to the wall

487 PROJECT WITH A SIMPLE RECTANGULAR TABLET, ELEVATION (*Figure* 403) [9772]
303 × *c*.210 mm. Watermark no.10. Pen, some chalk.

The same section of the gallery is shown as in the first three drawings of the previous group.

488 PROJECT WITH A TABLET DECORATED WITH CONSOLES, ELEVATION (*Figure* 404) [9768]
303 × *c*.210 mm. Pen, grey wash, some chalk. With scale.

The roundel contains a bust portrait inscribed at the top: *INNOCENTIVS. P . XI.*
Copy by Vittone, vol.I, fo.32.

4. Related drawings in Volume 188

Drawings 489 to 491 (10619 to 10621 in Volume 188) are clumsy drawings of pedestals supporting busts of Popes. It seems likely that they are connected with the project of Pope Clement XI for the Gallery of the Quirinal Palace. It is suggested by Noach that the drawings may have been executed by Pope Clement XI himself, since this Pope is believed to have been an amateur draughtsman.

489 ELEVATION OF A PEDESTAL WITH BUST OF POPE URBAN VIII (*Figure* 405) [10619]
370 × 165 mm. Pen, grey and brown wash, red chalk.

490 PERSPECTIVE VIEW OF A PEDESTAL WITH A BUST OF POPE CLEMENT XI [10620]
375 × 167 mm. Pen, grey and brown wash, chalk.

The presence of the Imperial eagle in the present drawing seems obscure, unless it refers to the Austrians as allies of the Pope against the Turks (see Introduction).

491 ELEVATION OF A PEDESTAL WITH A BUST OF POPE CLEMENT XI [10621]
385 × 165 mm. Watermark no.7. Pen, brown and grey wash, chalk.

Near the top of the pedestal is an object resembling a bee; its relevance in the present context seems obscure.

Project for the *Fontana dell' Organo* in the Quirinal Gardens

A single drawing in Volume 176 (Fig.406) represents the central part of the *Fontana dell'Organo* in the Quirinal Gardens. The fountain was built for Pope Clement VIII (finished in 1596, see L. Salerno, in *Capitolium*, 1961, no.4, pp. 3ff.). It was subsequently altered for Clement XI, and underwent, finally, a radical restoration in 1833 and further restorations in more recent years. According to Vasi (*Magnificenze*, 1761, I, X – quoted by Salerno, p.6) the organ itself, in the centre of the fountain, was added for Pope Clement XI in the place of figures of the muses. An organ is one of the most prominent features of Fontana's drawing and it can perhaps be assumed that he, as an architect with experience of water engineering, was consulted by the Pope on this, as on other projects for the Quirinal.

In the absence of any detailed record of the appearance of the central bay of the fountain before 1833, it is impossible to say how far the present drawing shows alterations which were actually carried out. The fountain as it exists today (Salerno, fig.7) corresponds in its general character with that shown in Fontana's drawing, but there are many discrepancies in detail.

492 ELEVATION OF THE CENTRAL BAY OF THE FOUNTAIN (*Figure* 406) [9753]
303 × *c*.210 mm. Watermark no.25(?). Pen, grey and coloured washes, traces of chalk. With scale.

Copy by Vittone of the right half of the drawing, vol.II, fo.216.

Drawings of the water drainage of the Quirinal Gardens

Drawings 493 to 498 (9800 to 9806 at the back of Volume 176) are studies evidently connected with water drainage. The group is entitled on the preceding blank page *Grotte di monte Cauallo*, and the drawings can thus be connected with the gardens of the Palazzo del Quirinale. There is no trace in the drawings of anything resembling a grotto in the usual sense; the word *grotte* may here refer to underground chambers shown in the drawings, which appear to be used for the storage of water (Fig.408). The precise location of the site is difficult to determine, and the exact purpose of the drawings is not clear. The drawings probably date from the reign of Pope Clement XI, like Fontana's other projects for the Quirinal.

The drawings comprise four double sheets (nos 9801–4) with a drawing on only one half of each double page. These are wrapped within drawings 9805 (no.495) and 9800/6 (no.493). This last is a double page containing only a single drawing which covers both halves of the sheet; it has been given two numbers in error.

493 PLAN (1) [9800/6]
305 × *c*.430 mm. Watermark, no.17. Pen, coloured washes, traces of chalk. With scale, measurements and annotations.

Nos 9800 and 9806 form halves of a single sheet. It shows what appears to be a plan of a small section of the garden, including walls and staircases. A large rectangle in the space between the walls probably shows some feature beneath the ground.

494 PLAN (2) [9803]
304 × 215 mm. Chalk, coloured washes, pen. With scale.

The drawing appears to show the same section of the garden as the preceding drawing.

495 PLAN (3) [9805]
163 × *c*.255 mm. Chalk, coloured washes. With measurements in ink.

This drawing lies on top of no.493 (9800/6) and it is thus folded around drawings 9801 to 9804. It appears to show a part of the garden but one where walls and staircases are absent.

496 PERSPECTIVE VIEW OF AN UNDERGROUND CONDUIT [9801]
305 × *c*.212 mm. Pen, coloured washes, some chalk.

Water appears to be spilling from the conduit in three places. The conduit may be identical with one of the two shown in the following drawing.

497 SECTION OF PART OF THE DRAINAGE SYSTEM, WITH PERSPECTIVE VIEW OF ONE WING OF THE PALACE (*Figure* 407) [9802]
215 × 305 mm. Pen, chalk, coloured washes.

The wing of the palace appears to be too summarily drawn to be certainly identifiable.

498 SECTION OF PART OF THE DRAINAGE SYSTEM (*Figure* 408) [9804]
305 × 215 mm. Pen, coloured washes, traces of chalk. With scale.

The drawing appears to show on a larger scale one of the underground chambers shown in the preceding drawing, together with a nearby conduit. In this case, however, the water in the chamber is replaced by a barrel and the conduit scatters an even spray of water into the earth beneath it.

The coach houses of the Quirinal (1706) and a project for the stables

A single drawing in one of the two 'Albani' volumes – no.499 (10580 in Volume 188 (Fig.410)) – refers to the modest coach house of the Palazzo del Quirinale which is recorded in a perspective view by Fontana of 1706 of the Piazza di Montecavallo (Fig.409) and is still in existence, although much altered. The drawing is accompanied by a long text explaining certain discrepancies between the work as carried out and the model of the project approved in 1706. It is made clear in the text that Fontana was the architect responsible for the design of the coach house. Also in Volume 188 are two drawings for the stables of the Quirinal (Figs 411, 412), a building at right angles to the coach houses which projects towards the Piazza di Montecavallo and the main entrance of the Quirinal palace. The site of the stables is shown in Fontana's drawing of 1706 (Fig.409) as having a ground-floor articulation matching that of the coach houses. Fontana's name has sometimes been associated with this building, and the disposition shown in his 1706 drawing may be due to him, but the stable project at Windsor is not by him.

The text referring to the coach houses consists for the most part of a very detailed account of the mistakes made by the masons in departing from the model of 1706. These are illustrated in the drawing which shows plans, sections and elevations of the model compared with others of the work as carried out. The style of the architecture closely resembles that of a project published by Donati (p.282, fig.295) as Fontana's design for the Imperial coach houses at Vienna. The errors mentioned in the text concern the faultily constructed roof, the dampness of the building, the darkness of the cubicles, the lack of symmetry in the façade, and changes in its proportion. Fontana is said to have explained the mistakes made by the workmen to the Pope's majordomo and to Urbano Roccis, who was in charge of the work. Certain alterations, which are apparently not recorded in the drawing, were then ordered by the papal authorities. There follows an index referring to the letters on the drawing, and a final paragraph where Fontana, the designer of the model, is absolved from blame. Fontana thus appears not to have been directly involved in the writing of this manuscript, which seems to be an independent report, and the drawing must also be the work of an outsider.

The stables of the Quirinal were later constructed on the site adjacent to Fontana's coach houses (see the engraving from Vasi, reproduced by Matthiae, pl.I, 1). They are usually said to have been begun by Alessandro Specchi for Pope Innocent XIII (1721–4) and interrupted at the death of that Pope in 1724. They were finished off by Fuga, who took over the direction of the work in November 1730 (ibid., pp. 7ff. and 69). At this time Fuga also apparently prepared projects for extending Fontana's coach houses (Bianchi, pp.22ff., nos 3/4). A drawing for the stables in a form close to that which they finally assumed, and attributed to Specchi, is illustrated by Matthiae (pl.I, 2). A drawing attributed to Fontana has also been connected with this work (Donati, p.280, fig.286). Although there is a general resemblance between this drawing and the final building, it seems very doubtful whether it is a project for a stable. It has shops at ground level, and long flights of steps leading to the main entrance, instead of ramps suitable for horses, as in the Quirinal stables. The drawing for a staircase published by Donati (fig.283) appears to be part of the same project as his fig.268.

The two drawings in Volume 188 at Windsor are of a project resembling the one finally built, but one which is more elaborate and ambitious. The very presence of the two drawings in one of the Albani volumes strongly suggests that the project was made not at the request of Innocent XIII, but at that of his predecessor Clement XI. The project is unlike Fontana in the style both of its draughtsmanship and of its architecture. It is faintly reminiscent of Specchi's Porto di Ripetta (see above) in the variety of its curved forms, and, if indeed the stables were finally begun according to a project by Specchi, then the present drawings may represent an early project by the same architect.

499 Unidentified draughtsman
STUDIES OF THE COACH HOUSES
(*Figure* 410) [10580]
424 × 280 mm. Laid down. Pen, coloured washes. With scale, index letters and annotations.

The drawing shows in plan, section and elevation the state of the coach houses as built, compared with that proposed in the model, and the six studies are labelled to this effect.

500 Alessandro Specchi (?)
PROJECT FOR THE STABLES, PLAN
(*Figure* 411) [10592]
347 × 415 mm. Laid down. Watermark no.7. Pen, grey and blue wash, traces of chalk. With scale.

A section of Fontana's coach houses is shown roughly in grey wash in the bottom right-hand corner of the plan. The plinths of the statues of the horse-tamers of the Piazza di Montecavallo are included in part in the plan.

501 Alessandro Specchi (?)
PROJECT FOR THE STABLES,
ELEVATION (*Figure* 412) [10596]
345 × 486 mm. Pen, grey wash.

Fontana's coach houses are shown in section on the right. The arcade beneath the stables corresponds in height with the façade of Fontana's block. On the *verso* of the sheet is a rough chalk plan, apparently of a group of four rooms.

Caprarola, survey of the stables (1704/5)

The Windsor volumes contain seven drawings of Vignola's stables at Caprarola – five in Volume 176 (entitled 'Stallone di Caprarola' on the preceding blank sheet), and two larger drawings in Volume 172 (forming part of the last section of the book, which is entitled 'Diuersi'). The former group of drawings were produced as a result of a survey of the stables made to discover the causes of cracking which was observable in 1704 on the interior walls of the first floor. The drawings are accompanied by five texts.

The first, a description of the stables and the damaged fabric, has a short introduction explaining that Fontana visited the building on 19 November 1704, with Giovanni Battista Contini, and the *capomaestri muratori*, Giacomo Pa(tri)arca and Francesco Cantù. The inspection was made with Cardinals Nuzzi and Cavalieri and Giovanni Battista Valenti. Fontana describes the stables which were found to be generally in good condition, the cracks being confined to the transverse walls of the first floor, the only wall 'non di ottima qualità'. The supporting walls beneath the floor, resting on the vault of the stable, were made of 'Tufi molto Fragili, . . .' and the side of the vault was believed to be faulty. Finally, the floor itself had no firm support and showed signs of cracks.

The second text begins with praise of Vignola; the soundness of structure as a whole is again stressed, and its remarkable capacity to withstand earth tremors. Fontana ends with a reassurance about the dangers of the cracking and suggests that the 'muro sotto cattiuo' (the supporting wall beneath the first floor) should be rebuilt. The third text is an estimate for strengthening the walls (129.40 *scudi*) and putting in twenty supporting chains (1062 *scudi*). The number twenty corresponds with the total number of cracking walls, as shown on the plan 502. At the end of this text Fontana proposed that an experiment be carried out on a single wall – rebuilding only a part to show the improvement more clearly.

The fourth text is a long index referring to the section drawing 504 (Fig.415). It contains no reference to the damaged areas. The final, least legible, text refers to the experiment suggested by Fontana at the end of text three. It is a copy of a letter by Fontana, in which the mason Francesco Cantù is instructed on the orders of Cardinal Lorenzo Corsini to carry out the suggestions of the architect. It is illustrated by the section drawing 506. From the date of this letter it would appear that there was a delay of almost a year between the inspection of the stables and the start of work on the repairs.

Fontana's drawings show two methods of strengthening the walls of the first floor. In the two sections to which the texts refer (Fig.415) the interior walls (shown in pale grey wash) continue downwards beneath the floor, filling the triangular spaces behind the main vault. The upper parts of these triangles are shown in brown wash and are probably the areas to be rebuilt and strengthened with *catene*. The remaining section (a detail) appears to show a short brick vault embedded in the upper part of one of the triangles of wall. This more radical method of strengthening the walls is not referred to in the texts and it may represent an ideal solution to the problem worked out by Fontana, and one which was perhaps too expensive to be put into practice.

The two drawings in Volume 172 (Figs 416, 417) are accompanied by no explanatory texts. They show projects for supporting the vault of the ground floor with a system of ribs. The need for these would seem to contradict the statements made by Fontana about the general soundness of Vignola's structure, though at one point (see above) he suggests that the side of the vault was faulty. The relationship, however, between these two sheets and the first group of drawings is not made clear.

Fontana's survey of the stables appears to be one of a number of such surveys undertaken at this time. In the Biblioteca Corsiniana (MS. vol.661) there are preserved two further *relazioni* connected with the stables. The first is by the architect Sebastiano Cipriani and bears the date 26 June 1703, and the second, of 25 February 1704, is by Giovanni Battista Contini, who assisted Fontana in his inspection of the stables in November 1704. An engraving of the stables was included in vol.III (1721) of D. de' Rossi, *Studio d'architettura civile* (pl.73).

502 PLANS OF THE GROUND AND FIRST FLOORS, AND A LONGITUDINAL SECTION (*Figure* 413) [9703]

298×534 mm. Four sheets joined. Watermark no.9. Pen, pink and grey wash, some chalk.

Streaks of grey wash beside the twenty outer doorways on the first-floor plan probably indicate the positions of the cracks in the walls, rather than those across the floor, the 'varie crepature nel medemo astrico' mentioned in text one.
Copy of right half by Vittone, vol.II, fo.164.

503 ELEVATION AND TRANSVERSE SECTION (*Figure* 414) [9704]

300×473 mm. Two sheets joined horizontally. Pen, pink wash, traces of chalk.

On the right the elevation is turned abruptly into a section.

504 TRANSVERSE SECTION (*Figure* 415) [9701]
299×213 mm. Watermark no.6. Pen, coloured washes, some chalk. With scale and index.

The index of letters and numbers on the drawing refers to the text on the facing page which breaks off before the actual cracks are mentioned. These are indicated by streaks of grey wash sloping across the walls of the first floor, and have no index letters or numbers. The areas of brown immediately beneath the floor level probably indicate the sections of wall which were to be strengthened.
Copy by Vittone, vol.II, fo.191.

505 TRANSVERSE SECTION, DETAIL [9702]
300×213 mm. Watermark no.6. Pen, coloured washes, traces of chalk. With scale and index.

The section is centred upon one of the cracked walls of the first floor, and the index letters and numbers of this area of the structure are copied from 504 (Fig.415). The area above the main vault apparently contains a short vaulted section supporting the wall of the first floor.
Copy by Vittone, vol.II, fo.191 (showing the whole of the left half of the stable).

506 TRANSVERSE SECTION [9705]
298×213 mm. Pen, grey wash, traces of chalk. With scale.

Corresponding with 504 (Fig.415). The drawing is indexed with letters (A to F) and illustrates the instructions of 26 August 1705 (text five) to the masons at Caprarola, corresponding with the experiment outlined by Fontana at the end of the third text.

507 TRANSVERSE SECTION OF THE GROUND FLOOR (*Figure* 416) [9449]
264×407 mm. Pen, coloured washes, some chalk.

The drawing illustrates two methods of supporting the main vault of the stable, one by a rib rising from a pier, the other by one supported on a capital sunk into the wall. The *verso* contains three sketches in ink and chalk which are apparently unconnected with the stable.

508 TRANSVERSE SECTION IN PERSPECTIVE (*Figure* 417) [9448]
266×407 mm. Pen, coloured washes, traces of chalk.

The drawing illustrates a method of supporting the vault on ribs, resembling the project on the left in the foregoing section.

A view of the Ponte dell' Abadia, near Castro (1705)

A single water-colour in Volume 172 shows the Ponte dell'Abadia, and the nearby castle, on the river Fiora below Lake Bolsena. It illustrates a long manuscript treatise entitled: 'Discorso fatto dà noi Cauallier Carlo Fontana circa il Ponte / della Badia situato nelle campagne frà la Citta di Castro / demolita, e la Terra di Canino'. This whole section of the volume is entitled on the preceding blank sheet: 'Adi 10 Maggio 1705 relatione e Dissegnio del / Ponte dell' Abadia nel Stato / di Castro'. Fontana's treatise was published without illustrations in Rome in 1711. Both bridge and castle are still in existence. Fontana, as he explains at the start of his treatise, was engaged on 10 May 1705, with Cardinals Corsini and Cavalieri, and Giovanni Battista Valenti, on a tour of inspection in the Papal states of Castro and Ronciglione, and he was asked to survey the site of the Ponte dell'Abadia. In his treatise Fontana describes the site of the bridge and the sulphurous (? – 'tartarose') water of the river Fiora that infects the air of the region. The beauty of the site and its waterfalls are recommended by Fontana as a subject for landscape painters and he compares it advantageously with other waterfalls he had seen in Italy ('quella di Tiuoli, l'altra della Marmore e dell'Isole di Sora, e quella delle case Nuoue di Fuglino'). Fontana also discusses the nearby castle and the origin and history of the Farnese family whom he believed to have built both the bridge and the castle.

509 PERSPECTIVE VIEW OF THE BRIDGE IN A LANDSCAPE (*Figure* 418) [9420]
408×*c*.537 mm. Watermark no.7. Chalk, water-colour.

Projects for the Fontana di Trevi (1706)

Volume 169 at Windsor consists of twenty-five drawings by Fontana relating to projects for the Fontana di Trevi. The interest of Pope Clement XI in the completion of this monument is attested by the survival of a considerable number of projects by different architects for the fountain, but almost nothing was undertaken during his reign. Bernini had transferred the fountain to its present site on the north side of the Piazza di Trevi (see Brauer and Wittkower, I, pp. 147ff.), and it must be the foundations of his project which are recorded in drawings of the late 17th century (d'Onofrio, *Fontane*, p.239; Cooke, fig.5; Fontana drawing no.510, Fig.419, below).

Many of the projects date from the earlier part of Clement's reign, and show methods whereby the column of Antoninus Pius could be incorporated in the fountain. In 1703 the water system of the fountain had been repaired (Cooke, p.153) and in the same year the order was given for the raising of the Antonine column, which lay near the Palazzo di Montecitorio (on the raising of the column see the entry above for the Curia Innocenziana). Carlo Fontana and his son Francesco worked together in the early stages of the work, and the column was finally raised by Francesco in September 1705. It was hoped during the course of 1704 that the column could be taken to the Fontana di Trevi (discussions about the siting are mentioned in documents kindly communicated by Mr Frederick den Broeder, Arch. Vat., Cod. Ottoboni, beginning on 3 July 1704, vol.2732, fo.142 *verso*). On 2 September 1704 the idea was said to have been abandoned for reasons of cost (loc.cit., fo.158 *verso*), but Valesio reports that measurements were taken at the fountain on 13 September 1704 with the idea of incorporating the column in the fountain and enlarging the Piazza (fo.110). On 28 September (fo.118 *verso*) he speaks of an architectural competition being instigated for the design of the fountain.

Many drawings are known referring to this stage in the development of the planning of the fountain. Some are connected with the Concorso Clementino competitions of 1706, more especially with the second class competition of this year, set by Francesco Fontana, and alluding to a public fountain decorated with a column etc. Other surviving drawings are published by Cooke and in addition to these must be mentioned three drawings by Nicola Michetti at Windsor (catalogued with the Albani drawings below), and a series of derivative and eccentric drawings at Vienna (Albertina, Rome, Mappe I, especially nos 7, 11, and 13). Several of these show a column incorporated into the fountain, and one (not showing a column, no.7) is dated as early as 1701. A project at Stockholm which may record ideas of Fontana for the inclusion of the column in the fountain design is discussed below.

The drawings by Fontana at Windsor are for a project of March to June 1706, which may have been devised as a simpler alternative to the use of the Antonine column. His drawings show various ways in which an obelisk from the Villa Ludovisi and a circular basin from the Campo Vaccino could be set up at the Fontana di Trevi. The obelisk, originally from the gardens of Sallust, was known in the 16th century and lay, broken in two, in the gardens of the Villa Ludovisi in the early 18th century (see drawing 513 and d'Onofrio, *Obelischi*, pp. 268ff.; Platner and Ashby, p.368; Lanciani, p.417). The basin had been discovered in the Forum and incorporated into a simple fountain designed by Giacomo della Porta which is known from drawings (d'Onofrio, *Fontane*, fig.85, pp. 108/9).

Fontana's drawings are preceded by a formal letter of 16 June 1706 addressed to the Pope (Fig.424). Although it is fairly short, the text corresponds in character with those other written introductions to volumes of drawings which were clearly intended for publication. Fontana explains that his 15 [*sic*] projects are intended to improve the appearance of the fountain without disturbing its present character, and using the three jets of water already in existence. Both the obelisk and the basin, he goes on, deserve to be better placed. Fontana mentions preparations which had been made at the fountain 'avanzati del Trasporto della Colonna' and this must refer to the earlier project for using the Antonine column which is mentioned again by Fontana at the end of his introduction. The proportions and the history of the obelisk are then briefly described and Fontana, with a reference to Nardini ('libro LI, fo.191'), explains that the obelisk was moved from the gardens of Sallust by Prince Ludovisi in the pontificate of Innocent X to be used to decorate his villa (cf. Famiano Nardini, *Roma Antica*, 1666, pp. 191/2). Fontana then gives a short account of the history of the fountain, speaking of its foundation by Agrippa and Claudius Drusus to illustrate, presumably, one of the most prominent iconographic motifs in his designs. In the final paragraph Fontana compares the obelisk with the Antonine column in weight etc. ('Il d.º obelisco s' accosta alla metà del Peso della Colonna Citatoria . . .'), and this comparison appears to be the subject of the diagram drawn beneath the letter (no.517, Fig.424). The passage presumably refers (though this is not explicit) to the difficulties encountered by Fontana in raising the column and perhaps to other problems which had arisen with the project for incorporating it in the fountain.

Fontana's projects were not carried into execution by Clement XI, although a model was apparently made (inscription of drawing of 30 May 1706, no.521 below). Apart from some small changes carried out in 1708 whereby the *mostra* was raised (Valesio, fo.65; d'Onofrio, *Fontane*, p.242, n.44; Cooke, p.154, n.37), the fountain appears to have remained undisturbed until the present structure was begun in the 1730's (see especially, Schiavo, *Salvi*, pp. 63ff.). It was carried out with no apparent influence of Fontana, although the final design has in common with some of Fontana's drawings an extensive background of naturalistic rocks (in one drawing, no.532, Fig.436, Fontana conceived the lower basin as a pool completely embedded in rock). Of the ingredients of Fontana's projects, the obelisk was taken to the Lateran in the 1730s and erected finally in front of S. Trinità dei Monti (d'Onofrio, *Obelischi*, pp. 268ff.; Platner and Ashby, p.368; Lanciani, p.417); the basin remained in the Campo Vaccino until 1818 when it was transferred to the fountain in the Piazza del Quirinale (Pietrangeli; d'Onofrio, *Fontane*, p.109, fig.80).

Apart from the studies at Windsor, several other drawings have been, or may be, connected with Fontana's projects for the Fontana di Trevi. There is in the first place a project ostensibly dated 1700 which is believed by d'Onofrio (*Fontane*, p.242, fig.211) to be a version of Bernini's fountain perhaps copied by Fontana. This drawing, despite its date, appears to be of the later 18th century and it is attributed by Cooke to Maini (for this and other projects at Berlin for the fountain, see Jacob, nos 799ff.). A drawing at Stockholm (THC. 5158) shows a project with an obelisk which is extremely close in design to the Windsor studies and has every appearance of being a copy of a lost Fontana design. It is accompanied by a second, similar project incorporating the Antonine column into the design and this sheet may record Fontana's ideas for the fountain *c.*1704 (THC. 5157).

In the Windsor volume Fontana appears to have added notes to the drawings when the book was due to be bound. Five of the perspective views are numbered (nos 9322 (522) to 9326 (529)), but the numbers are not consecutive and three of the drawings show the same project. The inscriptions cannot therefore have been made as the drawings were produced but must have been added at a later stage. Many of the sheets bear dates in March and May 1706 and in one puzzling case the same basic plan reappears with a slightly different date. In general terms, however, the lay-out of the volume has been carefully considered – the plans, for example, proceed chronologically and they are followed by the perspective views. The largest group of sheets are views in perspective (one in elevation) of the new fountain. They are connected with the plans only in a general way and provide a difficult problem of ordering in which Fontana's own numbers are of little assistance. They are arranged below in a tentative sequence beginning with no.522 (9322), Fontana's 'Primo p(ensiero)', which is the only drawing where the site itself is at all recognizable.

One of the perspective drawings (no.534) is a study for an entirely free-standing fountain with giants supporting an obelisk in the centre. Related to this is a further project in another volume, no.535 (9907 in Vol.179). In both drawings the obelisk is decorated not with the *monti* and star, the Albani arms of Clement XI, but with bees and a papal tiara, referring to a Barberini pope. This project probably derives from Bernini (as suggested by Brauer and Wittkower, I, p.148), but its immediate source lies in a project designed by Fontana himself for Cardinal Carlo Barberini (d.1704, see d'Onofrio, *Obelischi*, fig.182). A further, sketch related to Fontana's projects for the fountain occurs on the *verso* of one of his drawings for S. Teodoro (no.159 above).

ADDITIONAL BIBLIOGRAPHY:

H. L. Cooke in *The Art Bulletin*, 1956, pp. 149 ff.
F. Lanciani, *The Ruins and Excavations of Ancient Rome*, 1897.
C. Pietrangeli in *Roma*, XXI, 1942.

Plans of the 17th-century structure

510 PLAN OF THE PIAZZA DI TREVI (*Figure* 419) [9316]

485×612 mm. Watermark no.7. Two sheets joined vertically. Pen, coloured washes, some chalk. With scale. Annotated and inscribed: *Pianta di fontana di treui con Case a Canto | come si troua di presente l'ann*(o) *1706*.

The Piazza and the fountain correspond closely, as far as it is possible to judge, with drawings of the late 17th century (for example, that reproduced by Cooke, fig.5), which probably show the foundations of the fountain as they had been left by Bernini. The water flows between the house of Cardinal Carpegna (left) and a building belonging to Prince Pamphili (right), where corrections to the plan are drawn on flaps pasted to the basic drawing. Drawn over the plan is a sketch in chalk for a free-standing pedestal with a semi-circular wall behind the fountain which cuts deeply into the grounds of the two houses.

511 PLAN OF THE FOUNTAIN (*Figure* 420) [9317]

480×378 mm. Two sheets joined horizontally. Pen, coloured washes, some chalk. With scale. Inscribed: *Pianta in grande come si troua fontana|di Treui, l'anno 1706 CF.*

The drawing amounts to a detail of the preceding plan showing only the fountain. The inscription extends over both sheets of paper and the upper line appears to have been added later, after the sheet had been enlarged.

Copy of left half in outline by Vittone, vol.II, fo.228.

Studies of the obelisk and the basin (dates in March, and 16 June, 1706)

512 FOUR STUDIES OF THE OBELISK AND THE BASIN (*Figure* 421) [9313]

481×374 mm. Three sheets joined horizontally. Pen, coloured washes, traces of chalk. With scale. Inscribed: *Adi 2 di marzo 1706 | Carrettiere che Formentaua | la tazza con La Caretta.*

Of the four drawings on this sheet two show the obelisk and two the fountain in the Campo Vaccino.

513 THREE STUDIES OF THE OBELISK
(*Figure* 422) [9314]
482×374 mm. Two sheets joined horizontally. Watermark no.7. Pen, coloured washes, traces of chalk. With scale. Inscribed on the *verso: G / Simonetti / Bianchini.*

The drawing on the right shows the broken obelisk lying in the ground and is inscribed: *Li 21 Marzo 1706 scopri / mento della Guglia*, and *Giardino Ludouisiano*. A copy of this part of the sheet was reproduced in Lanciani, 1899, p.171.
The drawing on the left half of the sheet shows two studies of the obelisk restored.

514 SEVEN STUDIES OF THE OBELISK AND THE BASIN (*Figure* 423) [9315]
484×377 mm. Two sheets joined horizontally. Watermark no.7. Pen, coloured washes, some chalk. With scale and annotations. Inscribed: *Adi 24 Marzo 1706 proportioni / dell' Guglia con La tazza / C. fontana.*

The sketch in the upper right-hand corner, which is drawn on a small flap, shows the two objects incorporated into the centrepiece of a fountain.
Copy of most of the sketches by Vittone, vol.II, fo.228.

515 DEMONSTRATION OF SAFE METHOD OF TRANSPORTING THE BASIN
(*Figure* 428) [9334]
487×374 mm. Two sheets joined horizontally. Watermark no.7. Pen, coloured washes, some chalk. With scale. Inscribed with three faded words in chalk and in ink: *p trasporto della Tazza / con sicurezza / Cf.*

Copy in outline by Vittone, vol.II, fo.226.

516 DEMONSTRATION OF UNSAFE METHOD OF TRANSPORTING THE BASIN
(*Figure* 429) [9335]
485×377 mm. Two sheets joined horizontally. Watermark no.7. Pen, coloured washes, some chalk. Inscribed: *Trasporto della Tazza. n*(on ?) *sicuro.*

Copy in outline by Vittone of right half, vol.II, fo.227, and of left half, vol.II, fo.226.

517 DIAGRAMMATIC PLANS OF THE OBELISK AND A COLUMN (*Figure* 424)
[9312]
484×375 mm. Two sheets joined horizontally. Watermark no.7. Pen, traces of chalk. With scale.

The two sketches are drawn beneath the letter to the Pope of 16 June 1706, which occupies the upper half of the page. The diagrams presumably refer to the comparison drawn by Fontana in the last paragraph of the letter between the obelisk and the Colonna Citatoria (see introduction).

Plans of the new fountain
(dates of 10 to 30 May, 1706)

518 PROJECT WITH A CIRCULAR LOWER BASIN (*Figure* 425) [9318]
473×381 mm. Two sheets joined vertically. Watermark no.7. Pen, coloured washes, traces of chalk. With scale. Inscribed: *Pensiero di ponere la tazza di Campo Vaccino / a fronte della fontana di treui con / Piedestallo, sopra è Guglia l'anno 1706.*

As suggested in chalk on the plan of the existing fountain (510) Fontana incorporates the three jets of water into a free-standing base. He replaces the old circular basin with the one from the Campo Vaccino and hollows out the buildings behind into a large semi-circular space. The water now flows into the centre of the base of the fountain, not from the right, and the trough on the left of the lower basin has been omitted.
Copy of right half in outline by Vittone, vol.II, fo.228.

519 PROJECT WITH A HEART-SHAPED LOWER BASIN (*Figure* 426) [9319]
482×372 mm. Two sheets joined horizontally. Watermark no.7. Pen, coloured washes, traces of chalk. Inscribed: *Secondo pensiero li 10 Maggio 1706.*

Copy of left half in outline by Vittone, vol.II, fo.228.

520 VERSION OF THE PRECEDING PLAN
[9320]
483×375 mm. Two sheets joined horizontally. Watermark no.7. Pen, coloured washes, some chalk. With three scales, of which one is crossed out. Inscribed: *3º pensiero li 12 Mggº 1706.*

Despite its date this plan appears to be the same as the preceding drawing.
Copy of right half in outline by Vittone, vol.II, fo.228.

521 PROJECT USED FOR A MODEL (*Figure* 427)
[9321]
484×471 mm. (irregular). Watermark no.7. Three sheets joined. Pen, chalk, coloured washes. With three scales, of which two are crossed out. Inscribed: *Pensiero p il modello/li 30 Mgg 1706.*

A sketch plan of the centre of the fountain was used, according to the inscription, for a model. It differs from all the other drawings in having a base with rounded corners and it cannot be connected with any of the perspective views.
Copy of part by Vittone, vol.II, fo.224.

Projects in perspective for the new fountain

522 PROJECT WITH STATUES OF ROMAN EMPERORS (*Figure* 430) [9322]
686×369 mm. Two sheets joined horizontally. Pen, grey and blue wash, traces of chalk. Inscribed: *Primo p | C fontana.*

In this drawing the lower basin is semi-circular with pointed extrusions at the sides (a feature unique to this drawing and its versions), and the buildings behind, shown in full only in the present sheet, lie to each side of a rectangular, not a curved recess. The obelisk is decorated at the summit with the Albani *monti* and star.
Copy by Vittone, vol.II, fo.223.

523 VERSION OF THE PRECEDING PROJECT [9324]
718×379 mm. Three sheets joined horizontally. Watermark no.7. Pen, blue and grey wash, some chalk. Inscribed: *5º pensiere | Cf.*

Despite the inscription the fountain shows only slight changes from the preceding project.
Copy of the left half by Vittone, vol.II, fo.224.

524 VERSION OF THE PRECEDING [9325]
479×381 mm. Pen, blue and grey wash, some chalk. Inscribed on a tablet: *2º pensiere C f.*

525 PROJECT WITH PAIRS OF STATUES OF ROMAN EMPERORS (*Figure* 431) [9323]
699×484 mm. Three sheets joined. Watermark no.7. Pen, chalk, blue and grey wash. Inscribed: *4º abozzo e pensiere.*

The obelisk itself is supported by two giants, an idea deriving from a project by Fontana for Cardinal Carlo Barberini (see introduction) and copied below (nos 534 and 535).
Copy of right half by Vittone, vol.II, fo.224.

526 PROJECT WITH STATUES OF ROMAN EMPERORS IN THE BACKGROUND (*Figure* 432) [9327]
484×380 mm. Pen, blue and grey wash, some chalk. Inscribed on a scroll, lower left: *Ornato p Font. di Treui | con tazza & obelisco.| An.º 1706 C.C.Font.*

The corners of the lower section of the base are surmounted by free-standing ornaments composed of the Albani *monti* and star. As in the preceding drawing the obelisk is supported by giants.

527 PROJECT WITH ROUNDELS OF ROMAN EMPERORS IN THE BACKGROUND (*Figure* 433) [9328]
482×379 mm. Watermark no.7. Pen, blue and grey wash, some chalk. Inscribed on a scroll, upper left: *Ornato p Font. di Treui | con tazza & obelisco| An.º 1706. C.C.Font.*

The correspondence with the preceding drawing is extremely close, and both are inscribed formally.
Copy by Vittone, vol.II, fo.222.

528 PROJECT WITH STATUES OF ROMAN EMPERORS ON PEDESTALS IN THE BACKGROUND (*Figure* 434) [9332]
486×378 mm. Pen, blue and grey wash, some chalk.

On a flap Fontana introduces a surface of imitation rock for the lower section of the base of the obelisk (as shown in Fig.434).

529 PROJECT WITH ROUNDELS OF POPES (*Figure* 435) [9326]
483×377 mm. Pen, blue and grey wash, some chalk. Inscribed: *6: pensiere | Cf.*

Originally Fontana placed the roundels behind the fountain closer together but this was later concealed by flaps pasted over the drawing.
Copy by Vittone, vol.II, fo.220.

530 VERSION OF THE PRECEDING PROJECT [9329]
485×376 mm. Watermark no.9. Pen, blue and grey wash, some chalk.

Copy by Vittone, vol.II, fo.219.

531 PROJECT WITH FIVE JETS (*Figure* 437) [9330]
482×378 mm. Watermark no.7. Pen, coloured washes, some chalk.

Copy by Vittone, vol.II, fo.221.

532 PROJECT WITH A POOL SURROUNDED BY ROCK (*Figure* 436) [9331]
486×381 mm. Pen, chalk, blue and grey wash.

533 A PROJECT IN ELEVATION WITH A PEDIMENTED PEDESTAL (DETAIL) (*Figure* 438) [9333]
484×375 mm. Two sheets joined horizontally. Watermark no.7. Chalk, coloured washes. Inscribed in chalk (mainly illegible) and in ink: *pensiere.*

The drawing is exceptional in technique and in showing only a detail of the fountain. The design is close to that on the flap of no.528 (Fig.434).

534 VIEW OF A SMALL FREE-STANDING FOUNTAIN (*Figure* 439) [9336]
486×380 mm. Watermark no.9. Pen, blue and grey wash, traces of chalk.

The design is based on a project by Fontana for Cardinal Carlo Barberini (see above).
Copy by Vittone, vol.II, fo.226.

535 VERSION OF THE PRECEDING [9907]
414×270 mm. Pen, blue and grey wash, some chalk.

The papal tiara, keys and bees at the summit of the obelisk are indicated in chalk, and in chalk again there is a suggestion (absent in 534) for adding consoles to the pedestal.

Civitavecchia, survey of the 'antimurale' (1708 and earlier)

Volume 178 at Windsor consists of 28 drawings recording the decay of the 'antimurale', the embankment guarding the entrance to the principal harbour at Civitavecchia. The volume corresponds with number 12 in Contini's list, *Antimurale, e Lanterna di Civita Vecchia*. The drawings cover the years 1660 to 1708, and a large group date from the months of February and April in the latter year, when the decay had become extreme and Fontana was presumably asked to make a detailed survey.

In the 17th century the 'antimurale' was still a free-standing embankment – a long curved strip founded on rock and stones and surmounted by a broad wall with parapets on each side. At the northwest end stood a curiously-shaped rock, the so-called 'Marzocco', which was thought to be the remains of a Roman lighthouse (inscription on drawing 536 below). The south-east end was occupied by a lighthouse which was built for Paul V in 1608 and is still in existence (inscription, Frangipani, p.260(4)). The embankment as a whole was a source of constant expense to the papacy, and it had been recently restored for Clement X under the direction of Bernini (medal of 1672, inscriptions quoted by Frangipani, p.259 (9) 1674, and p.264 (3) 1673). Fontana himself recorded that the cost of this restoration had grown to 200,000 *scudi* (Misciatelli, p.253). According to the inscriptions on the early drawings below, further repairs had been made *c.*1691/1692, and a *chirografo* of Innocent XII of 25 September 1692 states: 'Essendo che la lanterna è l'assicuramento della presa del porto... è necessaria una continua spesa' (Calisse, p.473, n.). It appears from Fontana's drawings, however, that no radical improvements were made in the 1690s. By 1708, it seems, the decay had become extremely serious and the lighthouse itself was threatened. It was not until 1714 that the 'antimurale' and the lighthouse were fully restored once again (Calisse, p.450; Frangipani, inscription on p.264 (5)).

The majority of the Windsor drawings are indexed and inscribed, and Fontana dwells with monotonous insistence on the causes of the deterioration, describing how the sea was gradually sucking away the embankment of stones beneath the 'antimurale', undermining the superstructure and causing cracks to appear and then actual breakage (these long notations are not transcribed below). The inscriptions on the later drawings are in Fontana's hand and not easy to read.

The drawings themselves vary greatly in character and they are arranged in a roughly chronological sequence after the fourth page. The first three leaves of the volume were used for fairly rough sketches in pen and ink of which one is dated 17 February 1708. Drawings of 1700 further on in the volume were drawn over in chalk on this day and they are succeeded by drawings of 29 February which record the state of decay on 17/19 February. It may be suggested that the volume was built up over a period of years, possibly for a publication that Fontana had in mind, and that it may have been taken to Civitavecchia in the middle of February 1708 and brought hastily up to date. On the basis of the sketches of the lantern produced then the finished drawings of 29 February appear to have been made. These were then added to the volume together with the two drawings of the 'Marzocco' of 1/2 April with which the volume ends.

This hypothetical analysis of the evolution of the book would also account for the different series of numbers occurring on the early drawings, numbers which required alteration whenever any new record was added to the survey. Several of the early drawings are uniform in character; there is, for example, a series of four small sections in perspective showing the state of decay about 1660, and 1693, and in 1705 and 1707. The drawings recording the early appearance of the breakwater were probably made in Fontana's studio and based on early records of the breakwater.

A single independent text of 8 small pages is bound at the end of the volume – a painstaking list made in June 1707 of 147 large stones suitable for reinforcing the embankment.

The following catalogue contains one drawing from another volume – a large plan of the lantern and south east end of the 'antimurale' (544) which is bound with the fountain project for Civitavecchia in Volume 172 (see above).

Perspective views 1660–1698

536 SECTION IN PERSPECTIVE FACING NORTH WEST (*c.*1660) (*Figure* 440) [9864]
205 × 264 mm. Laid down. Pen, coloured washes, traces of chalk. Inscribed: *Dimostratione dell' antimurale rouinato che si trouò circa l'anno 1660*, followed by index.

The 'antimurale' is shown, several years before the restoration of Clement X, in an extremely dilapidated condition.

537 VIEW OF CIVITAVECCHIA (*c.*1690) (*Figure* 441) [9865]
269 × 412 mm. Two sheets joined vertically. Watermark no.9. Chalk, grey and blue wash.

Annotated and inscribed: 'Dimostratione del Porto di Ciuitauecchia con l'antimurale accresciuto con nuoua/costruttione de Muri per la sicurezza contro il moto Marino perfettionato l'Anno/1690. in circa.'
The drawing, showing the repairs to the 'antimurale' of '*c.*1690', is comparable to the perspective view bound with the drawings for the arsenal (306 above, Vol.170).

538 VIEW OF THE 'ANTIMURALE' FROM THE SOUTH WEST (*c.*1691) [9866]
260 × 402 mm. Watermark no.7. Chalk, coloured washes. Inscribed: *Dimostratione dell' Antimurale perfettionato di muri e scogliere circa l'anno 1691*, followed by index.

539 SECTION IN PERSPECTIVE FACING NORTH WEST (*c.*1693) (*Figure* 442) [9867]
204 × 260 mm. Laid down. Pen, coloured washes, some chalk. Inscribed: *Dimostratione dell' antimurale rinouato con scogliera circa l'anno 1693*, followed by index.

540 VIEW FROM THE SOUTH WEST (1698) (*Figure* 443) [9868]
260 × 407 mm. Chalk, blue and brown wash. Inscribed: *Dimostratione dell' Antimurale come si trouò l'Anno 1698*, followed by index.

The drawing shows a newly-built parapet, and records the weakening of the embankment below.

Sections 1693–1700

541 SECTIONS IN PERSPECTIVE (1693 and 1700) [9869]
256 × 405 mm. Pen, coloured washes, some chalk. Labelled: *An 1693* and *An – 1700*.

The two drawings reveal that the weakening of the embankment between 1693 and 1700 has led to cracking in the parapet above. A flap pasted down over the lower part of the diagram of 1700 shows a greater degree of decay than in the basic drawing beneath. The sheet was originally attached at the edge to the following drawing.

542 SECTIONS IN PERSPECTIVE, 1693, 1694 and 1700(?) [9870]
262 × 405 mm. Watermark no.7. Pen, chalk, coloured washes. Inscribed in ink, with dates in chalk, on left: *1700 Dimostratione proflare dell' antimurale trouato l'Anno [1700] 1693 con scogliera sotratta dal mare*, and on right: *Dimostratione profilare del Antimurale con scogliera parte sotratta dal mare l'Anno/1694*.

The lower parapet is shown with two levels of incline in all three sections. They are indexed in chalk in the upper drawing: 'A linea dal . . .(?)/B linea bassa'.

Drawings of the lighthouse, 1699/1701 (and overdrawings of 17 February 1708)

543 PLAN OF THE LIGHTHOUSE AND SOUTH-EAST END OF THE 'ANTIMURALE' (*Figure* 444) [9871]
260 × 406 mm. Pen, coloured washes, chalk. With scale. Inscribed: *Pianta di una parte dell' Antimurale doue risiede la Lanterna trovato l'anno 1700, 1699* (chalk), *1700* (chalk, lower left), followed by index.

Chalk lines on the plan denote further cracks in the parapet visible in 1708. They are indexed and described in an inscription in chalk: 'Adi 17 febr'o 1708/ A peli e Crepature/ Trouate/–B Distacchi.' The companion drawing, 9872 (545) was also overdrawn at this date, and further independent sheets of 17 February are listed below.

544 PLAN OF THE LIGHTHOUSE AND SOUTH-WEST END OF THE 'ANTIMURALE' [9451]
408 × 532 mm. Watermark no.7. Pen, brown and blue wash, chalk. With scale.

A large plan bound in Volume 172 with the project for the fountain. It corresponds with the foregoing plan. At this date a large piece of the embankment had broken away from the outer side of the 'antimurale'. Chalk marks (undated) on the present plan reveal further decay and a ruled and shaded rectangle in chalk may show the site of a projected new wall.

545 PERSPECTIVE VIEW OF THE LIGHTHOUSE AND SOUTH-EAST END OF THE 'ANTIMURALE' (*Figure* 445) [9872]
262×411 mm. Watermark no.7. Pen, coloured washes, chalk. Inscribed: *1700* (chalk), *Dimostratione dell' Antimurale uerso Leuante doue risiede la Lanternatro uato l'anno* [*1699*] (?) *1700*, followed by index.

As in drawing 543 further cracks are recorded in chalk and labelled: 'Adi 17 febro 1708 AB nove Crepature trovate'. They extend to the base of the lighthouse itself.

546 SECTION OF THE LIGHTHOUSE AND SOUTH-EAST END OF THE 'ANTIMURALE' (*Figure* 446) [9873]
262×406 mm. Watermark no.7. Pen, coloured washes, chalk. Inscribed: *Dimostratione profilare della Lanterna Batteria & spalto trouato l'anno 1700 e 1701*, followed by index.

A chalk overdrawing, presumably of 1708, shows further damage in the area G beneath the wall of the lighthouse itself.

Perspective views 1705–1708

547 SECTION IN PERSPECTIVE FACING NORTH WEST (1705) [9874]
200×265 mm. Laid down. Pen, chalk, coloured washes. Inscribed *1705* (chalk), and *Dimostratione dell' antimurale trouato offeso l'Anno 1705*, followed by index but lacking index letters on the drawing.

The crack in the parapet revealed in the section of 1700 above is shown here to have extended throughout the length of the 'antimurale'.

548 SECTION IN PERSPECTIVE FACING NORTH WEST (1707) (*Figure* 447) [9875]
202×265 mm. Laid down. Pen, coloured washes, chalk. Inscribed: *Dimostratione dell' antimurale trouato l'anno 1707*, followed by index.

The front part of the parapet is shown in this drawing to have fallen into the sea.

549 VIEW OF THE 'ANTIMURALE' FROM THE SOUTH WEST (1708) [9876]
259×402 mm. Chalk, blue and brown wash. Inscribed: *Dimostratione dell Antimurale con spalto, e scogliera diminuita l' Anno 1708* (chalk).

550 VIEW OF THE 'ANTIMURALE' FROM THE SOUTH WEST (1708) [9879]
264×412 mm. Watermark no.7. Pen, chalk, coloured washes. Inscribed in chalk: *1708*.

A version, without inscription, of the foregoing.

551 SECTION IN PERSPECTIVE FACING NORTH WEST [9877]
268×412 mm. Pen, chalk, coloured washes. Inscribed: *Dimostratione come ritornera l' antimurale non abile per la mancanza delle fabriche, e scogliere che li faceuano asistenza.*

The present drawing is stuck together with no.549 above, and likewise shows an advanced state of decay. It is probably datable to 1708.

552 SECTION IN PERSPECTIVE 1707/1708 [9878]
270×412 mm. Two sheets joined vertically. Watermark no.7. Pen, chalk, coloured washes. Inscribed: *Dimostratione profilare dell' Antimurale trouato l' anno 1707 & 1708* (chalk), and with index.

Index letter E refers to a pontoon which is shown in the drawing approaching the 'antimurale' with a cargo of large stones. Further stones have been unloaded on to the parapet. The drawing may be directly related to the text of 1707 in the volume (see above).

553 SECTION IN PERSPECTIVE FACING SOUTH EAST (1708) [9885]
225×319 mm. Pen, chalk, coloured washes. Dated in chalk: *1708*.

554 SECTION OF THE 'ANTIMURALE' [9882]
268×408 mm. Chalk.

A measured sketch occurring on an interleaving sheet which shows an advanced state of decay and is probably therefore datable to 1708. It is possible that the drawing was in fact made on 17 February in this year when chalk seems to have been used for rapid notations of the state of the 'antimurale', see following section and drawings 543 and 545 above.

Drawing of 17 February 1708 and related sketches

555 SECTION OF THE LIGHTHOUSE AND SOUTH-EAST END OF THE 'ANTIMURALE' [9863]
269×415 mm. Watermark no.7. Pen, chalk. Inscribed: *Adi 17 Febr'o 1708/ antimurale trouato in Rouina.*

This sketch bears the same date as the chalk overdrawings on 543 and 545 above.

556 SECTION OF THE LIGHTHOUSE [9862]
264×190 mm. Pen, chalk.

A measured drawing of the lighthouse which is attached to the foregoing sheet and is presumably of the same date. It appears to have been used as the basis for the flap attached to 562 (see below).

557 PLAN AND SECTION OF THE 'ANTIMURALE' [9861]
267×415 mm. Watermark no.7. Pen, chalk.

A rough measured sketch on the second leaf of the volume which probably dates from the same time as 555 above.

558 SECTION OF THE 'ANTIMURALE' (?) [9860]
267×415 mm. Pen.
An extremely rough sketch occupying a part of the first leaf of the volume. It appears to form part of the present group but is too rapidly drawn to be identifiable.

Drawings of 29 February 1708 recording the state on February 17/19

559 PLAN OF THE LIGHTHOUSE AND SOUTH-EAST END OF THE 'ANTIMURALE' [9881]
252×392 mm. Pen and brown ink, chalk, coloured washes. Inscribed in Fontana's hand: *li 29 febr'o 1708* and *Pianta della lanterna e sua Rouina sotto trouato | lanno 1708 alli 17–18 febro*, followed by index.

560 PLAN OF THE LANTERN AND SOUTH-EAST END OF THE 'ANTIMURALE' [9880]
215×380 mm. Three sheets joined. Pen, chalk, coloured washes. With scale. Inscribed in Fontana's hand with index.

The present sheet corresponds in character with the foregoing, slightly larger, sheet and appears originally to have been a flap joined to the latter at the top. It seems to show the state of the decay as it was in 1705 (the year mentioned in index H) and it may have been drawn for purposes of comparison with the basic drawing (559).

561 PERSPECTIVE VIEW OF THE LIGHTHOUSE AND SOUTH-EAST END OF THE 'ANTIMURALE' (*Figure* 448) [9883]
257×386 mm. Pen, chalk, coloured washes. Inscribed: *Stato della Rouina dell' Antimurale e | Lanterna trouato li 17 fbro 1708|con molto Danno come mostra li | qui sotto ueduta*

A section which clearly forms part of the present group of finished drawings of the lighthouse of 29 February showing its state on 17/19 of the month. The sheet bears a flap, shown in Fig.448, which reveals that further pieces of the parapet had fallen by 4 April. It is inscribed: 'A Stato del male acresciuto trouato li 4 Ap'le 1708'. This is the latest date in the volume.

562 SECTION OF THE LIGHTHOUSE AND SOUTH-EAST END OF THE 'ANTIMURALE' (*Figure* 449) [9884]
255×400 mm. Pen, chalk, coloured washes. With scale. Inscribed: *Adi 29 febro 1708 – |Profilo che dimostra lo stato Rouinoso dell' Antimurale|sotto la lanterna trouato lanno 1708 mese di|febr'o alli 18–19 di d.mese*, followed by index.

The proportions of the lantern are amended on a flap to correspond with those given in the section 556 above.

563 SECTION IN PERSPECTIVE TOWARDS THE 'MARZOCCO' (*Figure* 450) [9888]
253×400 mm. Watermark no.26. Pen, chalk, coloured washes. Inscribed: *Adi 29 Febro 1708*, followed by index.

Drawings of 1 and 2 April 1708

564 SECTION IN PERSPECTIVE [9886]
261×411 mm. Watermark no.7. Pen, chalk, coloured washes. With scale. Inscribed: *Adi p^o Aple 1708 stato|dell antimurale trouato | ind. giorno acanto à|Marzocco 2° il qui sotto | profilo.*

565 VIEW OF THE NORTH-WEST END OF THE 'ANTIMURALE' AND THE "MARZOCCO" (*Figure* 451) [9887]
242×389 mm. Watermark no.26. Pen, chalk, blue and grey wash. Inscribed: *Veduta dell' Antimurale|uerso il Porto della . . . (?) di Marzocco li 2 Aple 1708 dico*(?) *1708.*

The last dated drawing in the volume, with the exception of the flap of 4 April on 561 above. The *verso* of the present drawing shows two rough sketches in chalk of the 'Marzocco'.

Civitavecchia, design for a papal galley (before 1704)

Drawings 566–574 (9773 to 9783 in Volume 176 at Windsor) form a group connected for the most part with the design of a galley bearing the Albani arms, which is also the subject of a recently discovered drawing by Fontana of 1704 (Fig.452). The set of drawings at Windsor is entitled on the preceding blank sheet: 'Galera noua Ciuita / Vecchia'. This presumably means that the galley was to be made or used at Civitavecchia, and it suggests that the designs were made in expectation of a visit to the town by Pope Clement XI. The Pope is not recorded as having visited Civitavecchia, but had he planned to do so, the most likely date for such a jouney during the early years of his pontificate must have been in 1702, when Fontana's aqueduct was finally inaugurated (see above, and Calisse, pp.489f.).

The drawings are roughly drawn in brown ink, and are unusual for Fontana in the freedom of the drawing style, but this can perhaps be explained as a result of the unusual subject of the designs. The paper used for the drawings has a watermark that occurs on no other drawings by Fontana at Windsor, and it is possible that it came from Civitavecchia, where the drawings themselves may even have been made. They comprise six large sheets folded in halves in the binding of Volume 176. In two cases these large sheets contain a single drawing spread over both halves of the page: nos 566 and 567, which is the central page of the group. The remaining sheets contain different sketches on each half page, and each half is catalogued separately below. The main design (Fig.456), no.574, is of a figure composition in a rectangular frame, which includes representations of Cardinals together with the Pope, to whom a paper is being presented by a kneeling figure. This composition resembles part of the engraving of 1696 by Sante Bartoli which commemorates the visit of Pope Innocent XII to Civitavecchia and shows Fontana presenting his design for the aqueduct to the Pope (reproduced by Donati, figs 276/7). It is probable that the present drawing is a study for another such engraving, projected in connection with Pope Clement XI.

566 STUDY OF THE GALLEY [9774/80]
*C.*410 × 303 mm. Watermark, a series of capital letters and marks with a crown and a bunch of grapes. Pen, chalk.

At the bottom of the sheet is a study for an oar (?), and between the masts a study for an object which could possibly be a pennant.

567 STUDY OF THE STERN OF THE GALLEY (*Figure* 453) [9777]
303 × *c.*410 mm. Watermark as before. Pen, chalk.

Two projecting beams at the back, supported by tritons blowing conches, form a pedestal for an elaborate display of the Albani coat-of-arms. A large lantern, sketched in chalk, is placed over the stern.
Copy by Vittone, vol.I, fo.15.

568 SKETCH OF THE STERN OF THE GALLEY [9773]
*C.*205 × 303 mm. Pen, chalk.

Possibly a preliminary study for the preceding drawing (567). Drawing no.573 below forms part of the same sheet, though it is not directly related in subject matter.

569 SKETCH OF THE STERN OF THE GALLEY [9775]
*C.*205 × 303 mm. Watermark as before. Chalk.

The sketch is apparently continuous with chalk lines on the *verso* of drawing 572 below, which forms part of the same sheet of paper.

570 STUDIES FOR THE DECORATIONS FOR THE STERN OF THE GALLEY (*Figure* 454) [9776]
*C.*205 × 303 mm. Pen, chalk.

This drawing and no.571 below are on a single sheet folded in the binding.

571 STUDY FOR THE PROW OF THE GALLEY (*Figure* 455) [9778]
*C.*205 × 303 mm. Watermark as before. Pen, chalk.

Copy by Vittone, vol.I, fo.15.

572 STUDY FOR THE HELM (?) OF THE GALLEY [9779]
*C.*205 × 303 mm. Pen, chalk.

The *verso* contains very rough sketches in chalk which form part of the sketch on sheet 569 above.

573 STUDY OF A SEA-GOD ON A SEA-HORSE [9781]
*C.*205 × 303 mm. Watermark as before. Pen, chalk.

The present study resembles one of those in drawing 570 (bottom centre), and the motif may have been intended as that decorating the underside of the stern of the galley (cf. drawing 567).
Copy by Vittone, vol.I, fo.15.

574 STUDY FOR A FIGURE COMPOSITION WITHIN A RECTANGULAR FRAME (*Figure* 456) [9782/3]
*C.*410 × 303 mm. Watermark as before. Pen, chalk.

This and no.9783 (not shown in Fig.456) form parts of a single sheet. 9783 shows four very rough sketches in chalk (one with measurements), but none of them appear to have a direct bearing on the other studies of the present group.

Project for a canopy for the Belvedere Torso

Drawing 575 (9540 in Volume 174) is a representation of the Belvedere Torso beneath a small canopy (Fig.457). The drawing is probably connected with the protection of the statue and its removal on the orders of Clement XI to the Cortile delle Statue. This is mentioned in a list of works carried out by Clement XI in the Vatican:

'Cortile delle Statue Le sei famose statue del Vaticano, che si conseruano dentro le nicchie di d.º Cortile, l'ha fatto rifare di nuouo le porte, per esser quelle molto consumate; e ridotto in buona forma il med.º cortile con abellirlo di altre cose antiche; La statua, cioè il Torso detto di Beluedere, l'ha fatto leuare, e trasportare in stanza contigua, e cingerlo con ferrata attorno (Arch. Vat., Fondo Albani, XII, fos 125ff., quoted in M. Loret, *Lavori artistici*, p.58).

575 PERSPECTIVE VIEW OF THE TORSO AND THE CANOPY (*Figure* 457) [9540]
267 × 412 mm. Pen, grey wash, traces of chalk.

Projects for a doorway

A group of eight sheets in Volume 173 (nos 576 to 583) are projects for a doorway that has not so far been identified. Of the eight sheets, one (no.583) shows only some ruled lines in chalk, and one (no.582) is not in fact a drawing, but only a faint counterproof of a project that has been torn from the volume. In the remaining six drawings the doorway is surmounted by a window with an escutcheon decorated with the papal insignia. In four cases statues of Charity and Justice are placed over the sides of the door frame to each side of the window, and in two cases the positions of these statues are occupied by ornaments comprising the three *monti* and the star of the Albani arms. The doorway was to be approximately eleven *palmi* wide, and it was probably designed for a building that was already in existence, since the doorway was clearly designed in isolation. In one drawing (no.580, Fig.459) indications of a string course and a window frame adjacent to the doorway are given in dotted ink lines, a technique Fontana commonly used to indicate existing fabric (cf. the Martinitz palace). The presence of figures of Charity and Justice would suggest that the building was not a private palace of Pope Clement, but a public building, possibly S. Michele a Ripa. The order in which the drawings were executed is not clear, but two projects are more finished than the others (nos 576 and 580), buff wash being used in both to indicate the wooden doors within the door-frame. These two designs appear to be the simplest and most elegant of the projects.

576 PROJECT WITH THE ALBANI ARMS (1) [9462]
422 × *c*.275 mm. Pen, grey and buff wash, chalk. With scale.

577 PROJECT WITH THE ALBANI ARMS (2) (*Figure* 458) [9466]
422 × *c*.275 mm. Watermark no.7. Pen, grey wash, traces of chalk.

578 PROJECT WITH SEATED FIGURES OF CHARITY AND JUSTICE (1) [9464]
422 × *c*.275 mm. Pen, grey wash, traces of chalk. With scale.

579 PROJECT WITH SEATED FIGURES OF CHARITY AND JUSTICE (2) [9465]
422 × *c*.275 mm. Pen, grey wash, traces of chalk.

580 PROJECT WITH SEATED FIGURES OF CHARITY AND JUSTICE (3) (*Figure* 459) [9467]
422 × *c*.275 mm. Watermark no.7. Pen, grey and buff wash, some chalk. With scale.

The project is close to the preceding, but with a nearly square window and a simplified treatment of the door frame.

581 PROJECT WITH STANDING FIGURES OF CHARITY AND JUSTICE (*Figure* 460) [9468]
422 × *c*.275 mm. Pen, grey wash, traces of chalk.

The design is close to that of drawing 578 in the treatment of the doorway.

582 COUNTER-PROOF OF A MISSING PROJECT [9461]
422 × *c*.275 mm.

583 FRAMEWORK FOR A DOORWAY PROJECT [9463]
422 × *c*.275 mm. Chalk.

Lago Maggiore, Isola Bella, projects for the Palazzo Borromeo

Two drawings in Volume 176 are projects for the Palazzo Borromeo on the Isola Bella, as is made clear by inscriptions on both sheets. As proposed by Noach, one drawing can be connected with the Sala del Trono of the palace and the other with a gallery in the gardens. It would appear that Fontana's designs were carried out in both cases, though for the Sala del Trono Fontana seems, on the evidence of the drawing, to have designed only part of the decoration of the room.

Fontana's name is generally associated with the design of the Palazzo Borromeo, but the exact nature of his work there is never clearly specified. It seems unsafe to guess at its possible extent in the absence of a detailed and reliable account of the history of the building. The Windsor drawings provide precise evidence for his share in designing relatively unimportant parts of the palace, and it may be that they represent the full extent of his work on the building. It is not known whether Fontana travelled to the Lago Maggiore in the 1690s or 1700s, but a drawing by him at Windsor of Como is dated 1701 (see above, no.395).

584 PLAN AND SECTION OF A GARDEN GALLERY (*Figure* 461) [9751]
*C.*210×303 mm. Pen, brown wash, some chalk. With scale. Inscribed, upper left: *Prima Galleria di . . .*(?) *statue / dell' Isola Boromea nel /* (la)*gho magre*.

Copy by Vittone, vol.II, fo.216.

585 SECTIONS OF THE 'SALA DEL TRONO' (*Figure* 462) [9752]
*C.*210×302 mm. Watermark no.5. Pen, grey wash, traces of chalk. Inscribed, upper left: *Ornati di metalli Dorati nelle stanze nobbili / nel Palazzo dell' Isola Boromea nel lagho mag.re*.

The inscription suggests that Fontana designed only the metal ornaments of this and other rooms on the first floor of the palace.

Drawings of streams and of prisms

Two pairs of drawings in Volume 176 are connected with Fontana's activity as a water engineer, though in neither case can these pairs of drawings be related directly to any known work or to any of Fontana's publications. Drawings 586 and 587 are watercolours of streams, entitled on the preceding blank page 'Varij Dissegni'. Drawings 588 and 589 are studies of prisms, entitled on the preceding blank page, '[Prismi]'. They are accompanied by a sheet of measurements and a short text which shows that the prisms are for the purpose of diverting currents of water.

586 TWO SPRINGS WITH A TANK(?) [9745]
*C.*210×302 mm. Watercolour, pen.

587 AN AQUEDUCT CROSSING A STREAM [9746]
*C.*210×302 mm. Watermark no.17. Watercolour, traces of chalk.

588 DIAGRAM OF PRISMS IN OUTLINE [9799]
300×*c.*210 mm. Watermark no.10. Pen, chalk. With two scales.

The seven prisms are drawn to scale and placed one beneath the other on the sheet. Each is measured and accompanied by notes of the material it is to be cut from, its size and weight.

589 COLOURED DIAGRAM OF THE PRISMS [9798]
300×*c.*210 mm. Pen, watercolour. With scale.

The present drawing is clearly that made in conjunction with the manuscript and the prisms are indexed from A to G, matching the index at the start of the manuscript. The various shades of brown and grey wash used to colour the prisms presumably refer to the materials ('Selci, Tufo' etc.) they are to be made of, as given in drawing 588.

Unplaced drawings

590 DESIGN FOR A MEDALLION (UNFINISHED) [9487]
422×273 mm. Watermark no.7. Pen, chalk.

A single drawing at the end of Volume 173. Sketched roughly in the centre of the medallion is what appears to be a female portrait bust. The drawing may be connected with the Origo monument (nos 232ff.) or with the projects for the decoration of the Quirinal Gallery (nos 479ff.).

591 ELEVATION OF AN ARCHWAY (DETAIL) DECORATED WITH A ROUNDEL INSCRIBED: 'CHARITAS' [9755]
304×*c.*210 mm. Pen, grey wash, some chalk.

A single drawing in Volume 176.

IV

The 'Albani' Volumes

Rome: Ecclesiastical works

The Palazzo di Propaganda Fide

592 PERSPECTIVE VIEW OF THE SOUTHERN HALF SHOWING THE NEW ATTIC STOREY, 1704 (*Figure* 463) [10328]
484×763 mm. Watermark no.7. Pen, grey wash, traces of chalk. With scale and index letter *A*.

The drawing is entitled at the top in capitals: 'Prospetto del Collegio di Propoganda Fide, con nuovo piano di cima rialzato, di ordine, et / à proprie spese della Santita di N'ro Sig' Papa Clemente. XI. p.' habitatione, e commodo de missio=/narij sacerdoti da istruirsi alle missioni del Indie, e della China l'an.° 1704 / A – Apartamento rialzato'. Index 'A', the new storey of rooms, refers to the attic over the block to the left of the main part of the façade of the palace. On the significance of the present drawing see Wittkower, *Art and Architecture*, p.352, n.47. It is there suggested that use must have been made in constructing the attic of a project by Borromini. The design corresponds with that of the attic over the northern part of the block. The present drawing appears to be no more than a record of the appearance of the completed work. On work carried out at the palace by Fontana, see Salerno, p.85.

Palazzo del Vaticano, drawings of two rooms near the 'Stanza della Bologna'

Four sheets bound in Volume 188 contain drawings referring to two rooms in the Vatican, the 'Gallaria nell'appartamento de Prencipi' and a 'Stanzione contiguo alla stanza della Bologna'. The 'stanza della Bologna' is presumably identical with the Sala Bologna near the Cortile di S. Damaso of the Vatican (Redig de Campos, pp.170ff.). The drawings appear to have been made in connection with the arrangement of pictures on the walls of the two rooms (see Fig.464), and Pope Clement XI is recorded as having decorated two rooms near the 'Stanze d(et)ta la Bolognia' with cartoons by Pietro da Cortona and Ciro Ferri for mosaics executed in S. Peter's (Loret, *Lavori artistici*, and G. Briganti, *Pietro da Cortona*, 1962, pp.252f.). Each picture on the walls of the rooms in the present drawings is inscribed with a brief title; in some cases these titles appear to correspond with the subjects depicted in Cortona's paintings, but in others there is no painting corresponding with the title given in the drawings.

593 PLAN OF THE 'GALLARIA NELL'APPARTAMENTO DE PRENCIPI' AND ELEVATIONS OF THE TWO END WALLS [10610/11/12]
547×*c*.415 mm. Watermark no.7. Pen, grey wash, traces of chalk. Inscribed.

594 ELEVATIONS OF THE LONGER WALLS OF THE SAME [10613/14]
547×*c*.415 mm. Watermark no.7. Pen, grey wash, traces of chalk. Entitled at the top: *Gallaria nell' Apartamento de Prencipi*. Inscribed.

595 PLAN OF A 'STANZIONE CONTIGUO ALLA STANZA DELLA BOLOGNA', AND ELEVATIONS OF THE TWO END WALLS [10615/16/17]
547×*c*.415 mm. Watermark no.7. Pen, grey wash, traces of chalk. Inscribed.

596 ELEVATION OF THE REAR WALL OF THE SAME [10609]
244×329 mm. Pen, grey wash, traces of chalk. Inscribed.

597 ELEVATION OF THE FOURTH WALL OF THE SAME (*Figure* 464) [10608]
190×327 mm. Watermark no.7. Pen, grey wash, traces of chalk. Inscribed.

Palazzo del Vaticano, projects for a pavilion for the Belvedere

Three drawings in Volume 185 refer to two projects for installing a covered fountain in the centre of the octagonal courtyard of the Belvedere (the present 'cortile delle statue'; cf. the early 18th-century plans of the Vatican in Ackerman, pls 38/9). Both have the *monti* and star of the Albani arms, and these projects, neither of which was carried out, must have been commissioned by Pope Clement XI as part of the improvements he carried out in this area of the Vatican palace (see Loret, *Lavori artistici,* pp.125ff.; for a related drawing at Berlin, see Jacob, no.401). The drawings are unlike Fontana in style and more rococo in the treatment of the architecture. The names of two architects, said to have been employed by Clement XI at the Vatican, are known; one is Francesco Fontana and the other Giovanni Battista Contini, who perhaps took over the supervision of the palace on the death of Francesco Fontana in 1708 (for works by these two architects at the Vatican see Taja, pp.341 and 364; for Contini, see also H. Hager in *Commentari,* 1969, pp.109ff. and 1970, pp.92ff., and L. Vicari in *Bolletino della Deputazione abruzzese di storia patria,* 1967/9, pp.3ff., and in the Acts of the Congresso internazionale di Storia dell'Architettura, Abruzzo, 1975 – in preparation).

598 PROJECT WITH CIRCULAR TEMPLE, PLAN (*Figure* 466) [10351]
423×423 mm. Pen and black ink, grey and pink wash, traces of chalk. With scale. Inscribed at top: *Pianta del Cortile delle Statue di Beluedere.*

599 PROJECT WITH CIRCULAR TEMPLE, ELEVATION (*Figure* 467) [10349]
382×1039 mm. Watermark no.9. Two sheets joined vertically. Pen and black ink, grey and pink wash, traces of chalk. With scale. Inscribed at top: *Larghezza del Cortile delle Statue di Beluedere nel Vaticano.*

600 PROJECT WITH AN OCTAGONAL PAVILION, ELEVATION (*Figure* 465) [10350]
382×310 mm. Watermark no.7. Pen and black ink, grey wash, traces of chalk.

Probably a less costly alternative to the preceding project.

The Pantheon, with projects for stalls in the Piazza (1710?)

Six drawings in Volume 188 are connected with the Pantheon. They comprise a plan of the Pantheon itself (601) and drawings connected with two projects for rebuilding the stalls which surrounded the fountain in the centre of the Piazza. The first of these projects (drawings 602–604) is by the architect Romano Carapecchia, and the second (drawings 605–607) by an unidentified architect. The projects for the Piazza are accompanied by a text (partly in Italian and partly in Latin) which consists of a list of the benefits conferred on the chapter of the Pantheon (S. Maria ad Martyres) by various popes from Benedict IV to Alexander VII. The text ends with a short paragraph in which the present unfavourable situation seems to be compared with the benefactions of the past. It refers to a restoration of the portico and the demolition of houses, leading to the loss of over 1500 *scudi* to the chapter, and in recompense the receipt of one silver chalice and four torches per annum. It mentions a restriction of the *Dominio della Piazza*, the rights enjoyed by the canons of the church over the stalls of the Piazza.

The projects for rebuilding the stalls on the Piazza are probably datable to the summer of 1710. A *chirografo* of Clement XI of 21 September 1710 (Rome, Archivio di Stato, Camerale III, busta 1878, cart. S. Maria ad Martyres, fasc.7, 10/10 bis) refers to the permission given in July 1710 to the canons to rebuild the stalls. A group bordering the fountain in the Piazza had been demolished by September 1710, when it was decided by the Pope that the remaining stalls near the fountain were to be demolished and not rebuilt, the canons to receive 300 *scudi* a year in compensation. Permission was not withdrawn for rebuilding the groups of stalls behind the fountain, but the Pope reserved the right to level this part of the Piazza too, in which case the canons would receive an additional 677 *scudi* a year.

The year following the demolition of the stalls, 1711, saw the embellishment of the fountain, under the direction of Filippo Barigioni, by the addition of an obelisk (d'Onofrio, *Obelischi*, pp.250ff.). The medal issued in 1711 to commemorate the placing of the obelisk appears to show stalls in the square behind the fountain and it is thus possible that new stalls were in existence behind the fountain at this time. Other work carried out at the Pantheon during the reign of Clement XI, including the provision of a new high altar by Alessandro Specchi (unveiled in 1724), is listed by Pastor (Eng. ed., XXXIII, pp.521f.; Jacob, no.746, discusses the high altar, and, no. 748, the fountain; see also Marder).

Romano Carapecchia is named by Pascoli (II, p.549) as one of the most able of Fontana's pupils ('Disegnava a maraviglia . . .'). He attributes to him the façade of the church of S. Giovanni Calabita and the nearby hospital. He speaks of his being taken by Prior Vaini to Malta to become architect to the Knights of Malta, and himself a knight. Carapecchia is said by Pascoli to have built the *palazzino* of Vaini at S. Pietro in Montorio. This must be the work for which Fontana produced designs (Coudenhove-Erthal, p.109, figs 43/4) and Carapecchia may at this stage have been working with him, but he seems to have been active as a draughtsman by 1681 (Accademia di S. Luca, U 329; also 3B 354). A volume of his drawings belongs to the Courtauld Institute of Art, containing dated drawings from 1687. The volume is being studied by Denis de Lucca, who has related many of the drawings to buildings carried out in Malta from 1715 to 1736 (see Tonna and de Lucca). The second group of drawings below are in a less Fontanesque technique than Carapecchia's, and they appear to be more rococo in the style of architecture.

ADDITIONAL BIBLIOGRAPHY:

Silvia Bordini, 'Bernini e Il Pantheon. Note sul classicismo Berniniano', *Quaderni dell'Istituto di Storia dell' Architettura,* Serie XIV, fasc.79–84, 1967, pp.53–84.

Tod Marder, 'Piazza della Rotonda e la Fontana del Pantheon: Un rinnovamento urbanistico di Clemente XI', *Arte Illustrata,* 7, 1974, pp.310–320.

601 PLAN OF THE PANTHEON [10636]

464 × 379 mm. Pen, yellow and pink wash, chalk. With scale and index (in chalk).

The key to the index is written in chalk at the bottom of the sheet. It merely lists the most notable features of the interior, naming in some cases papal benefactors who are dealt with at greater length in the text which accompanies the projects for the stalls of the Piazza.

602 Romano Carapecchia

PLAN OF THE EXISTING SITE (*Figure* 468) [10630]

490 × 378 mm. Watermark no.7. Pen, coloured washes. With scale. Annotated in full and signed, bottom right: *Romano carapecchia.*

The stalls existing behind the fountain in the square are coloured yellow in outline. They are to be rebuilt on behalf of the *Canonici* of the Pantheon, as explained in the inscription at the top of the sheet: 'Pianta colorita di gialdo, indicano lo stato uecchio, delli Casini di legno, spettanti / al Reu'mo Cap'lo de Sig:ri Canonici della Rotonda'.

603 Romano Carapecchia

PROJECT FOR NEW STALLS, PLAN (*Figure* 469) [10631]

485 × 380 mm. Pen, coloured washes. With scale. Annotated in full and signed: *Romano carapecchia.*

The new stalls behind the fountain are indicated in grey washes; they follow roughly the disposition of the existing stalls but on a slightly more regular plan. The stalls are referred to in the inscription at the top of the drawing: 'Pianta dello stato nouo da farsi, nel sito indicato di gialdo delli / casini spettanti al R'mo Cap'lo, de S:ri Canonici della Rotonda'.

604 Romano Carapecchia

PROJECT FOR NEW STALLS, SIDE ELEVATION (*Figure* 470) [10633]

185 × 355 mm. Pen, coloured washes. Inscribed: *Prospetto, è eleuatione delli Casini da farsi di nouo inconformita / della Pianta.*

605 PROJECT FOR NEW STALLS, FRONT ELEVATION SHOWING FOUNTAIN (*Figure* 471) [10634]

235 × 358 mm. Pen, coloured washes, traces of chalk. With scale.

In this project the stalls are disposed on a curved plan behind the fountain. They are more complex in elevation than Carapecchia's and decorated with escutcheons of the Papal/Albani arms. The upper part of the fountain appears to be an invention of the draughtsman.

606 VERSION OF THE PRECEDING [10635]

265 × 405 mm. Watermark no.8. Pen, grey and blue wash, traces of chalk. With scale.

The smudging of the ink apparent in the preceding drawing is not present here.

607 FRONT ELEVATION SKETCH, WITH PLAN [10632]

171 × 216 mm. Pen and brown ink.

The present drawing appears to be a sketch for drawings 605/6; they follow an alteration to the plan indicated in the present drawing with dotted lines, which provides for double stalls at the sides of the composition.

Drawing of SS. Apostoli (1708)

On 11 November 1701 it was decided, after careful investigation, that the 6th century basilica of SS. Apostoli which had been frequently restored could not be saved and that a complete rebuilding was inevitable. The commission was given to Francesco Fontana, who after the death of Carlo Rainaldi (1691) had become the architect of the convent of the Minorites (Santilli, p.29; Zocca, pp.59ff.).

On 19 September 1701, two months before the decision to rebuild was taken, work had already begun on the removal of the *soffitto* which had been given by Cardinal Lorenzo Brancati di Lauria (Scatassa). The demolition of the church meant the loss of many valuable works of art, amongst them the chapel of S. Anthony of Padua with a magnificent altar by Carlo Rainaldi which the Duke of Lorraine undertook to redecorate about 1689 for the considerable cost of more than 20,000 *scudi* (E. Rossi, *Roma,* XX, 1942, p.55). The high altar, attributed in the guides to Carlo Rainaldi, however, survived (Zocca, pp.57, 81), and Cardinal Annibale Albani had it re-erected in the Abbey Church of Casamari (d'Onofrio and Pietrangeli). Domenico Guidi's angels were replaced at that time with the Albani *monti* and star.

The transfer of the commission to Francesco Fontana was welcomed by Valesio, who called him 'architetto alquanto migliore del Padre' (29 November 1701, Scatassa). During the destruction of the pillars – also erected for Cardinal Brancati di Lauria – which supported the walls of the nave, the original columns of the church were discovered, while during the laying of the foundation of the new façade the original level of the church was found. It was more than 6 *palmi* lower than the present one (Scatassa, 6 February 1702; Krautheimer). Soon after, on 27 February 1702, the foundation stone was laid by Clement XI in a ceremony which is described in great detail by C. B. Piazza (*Gerarch. Card.*, pp.474f.). Drawings by Francesco Fontana of 1702 of the altars of the old church (Fig.570) survive (A.S.R., Not. Cur. Cap. Uff. 18, vol.565, fos.453ff.; kindly mentioned by Dr. del Piazzo).

In the following years the building progressed sufficiently for the vault to be begun in August of 1705 (Scatassa). But the foundations for the tribune, which was to be enlarged by ten *palmi*, could be laid only in the summer of 1708; these were inspected by the Pope on the 12 June of that year (Scatassa).

It is easy therefore to determine the exact stage which the building had reached at the time when Carlo Fontana took over after the death of his son, Francesco (3 July 1708). Essentially only the apse had to be completed – it had not progressed much further than its foundations. The hand of Carlo Fontana is recognizable in the arrangement of the figures above the free-standing columns of the *coretti* next to the high altar (cf. the lateral walls of the Ginetti chapel); this differs from the section engraving by Dom. de Rossi (*Arch. Civ.*, III, 1721, pl.17); the original drawing is preserved in the Uffizi (Zocca, fig.16) and was evidently based on an earlier scheme.

Sometime after 1712 Nicola Michetti took over from Carlo Fontana (Zocca, p.64) and soon afterwards he was also entrusted with the extension of the Ospizio di S. Michele (see above). According to Santilli (p.55) and Donati (p.374) he made a modification in the vaulting of the tribune, which was apparently too heavy. As can be deduced from the drawing at Windsor which is datable to 1708 (see below), he seems to have been collaborating on the building for some considerable time. Michetti is also the architect of the later pavilions and façade (altered in the 19th century) of the Palazzo Colonna which face the Piazza SS. Apostoli. The church was dedicated on 17 September 1724.

ADDITIONAL BIBLIOGRAPHY:

R. Krautheimer, *Corpus Basilicarum,* pp.78–83.

C. d'Onofrio and C. Pietrangeli, *Abbazie del Lazio,* 1969, p.254, pl.308

Francesco Santilli, *La Basilica dei SS. Apostoli,* C.R.I. vol.15, Rome, 1925.

E. Scatassa in *Rassegna bibliografica dell'Arte italiana,* XVIII, no.1/3, pp.3–15 (extracts from the diary of Valesio).

E. Zocca, *La basilica dei SS. Apostoli in Roma,* Rome, 1959.

608 Nicola Michetti
PERSPECTIVE VIEW OF SS. APOSTOLI
1708 (*Figure* 472) [10325]
498×725 mm. Two sheets joined vertically. Watermark no.7. Pen, grey wash, some chalk. Signed: *Nicola Michetti* on a plaque in the left foreground.

Since the foundations of the apse were laid only in the summer of 1708 (see above), the present drawing cannot antedate this point. The drawing shows approximately the stage which SS. Apostoli had reached at the time of Francesco Fontana's death on 3 July 1708. Perhaps the drawing is connected with the change of architect which had become necessary then. The internal wall of the façade is complete in all its details with all the decorations finished. The large plaque which has an inscription referring to the decision to rebuild the church and the laying of the foundation stone by Clement XI (Forcella, *Iscriz.*, II, p.272, no.834), is already in place. About 25 workmen are shown in the present drawing, a fact which perhaps gives some idea of the numbers required to construct a building the size of SS. Apostoli. On the left in the drawing a gesticulating figure is visible, probably the architect himself, who explains to his companions details of the construction of the building.

S. Clemente, two drawings of frescoes etc.

Two drawings in Volume 185 record the appearance of medieval frescoes in the basilica of S. Clemente (see A. Noach in *The Burlington Magazine*, 1949, pp.309ff., figs 7 and 8). The basilica was restored for Pope Clement XI between the years 1701 and 1719 (Titi, 1763, p.232; Pastor, Eng. ed., XXXIII, pp.517f.) and Fontana's nephew, Carlo Stefano, was associated with the work, building a new side entrance to the church (Cecchelli, *S. Clemente*). The restoration of the interior, consisting mainly of the construction of a new roof, was probably completed by 1715, the date of a long inscription over the main entrance (Cecchelli; L. Nolan, *The Basilica of S. Clemente in Rome*, 1925, pp.75f.). One, or perhaps both, of the present drawings may have been made to illustrate a MS description of the paintings in the church, ordered by Clement XI and dated 13 May 1715 (Cod. Vat. Lat., 9023, f.212/5; Noach, p.311, n.7). The drawings are clearly by different draughtsmen and it would seem unsafe to give either a definite attribution. Their importance as records of the painted decoration is discussed by Noach (op. cit.). The first shows the fresco of Christ and the Virgin and Saints in the apse behind the altar of the church and records damages which had subsequently been repaired. The second is of the wall of the north aisle of the basilica, showing frescoes and monuments which are now destroyed or covered over.

609 STUDY OF THE APSE FRESCO [10345]
243 × *c*.760 mm. Watermark (cut) no.8. Pen, grey and yellow wash, traces of chalk.

The large areas missing in the fresco are shown in yellow wash.

610 STUDY OF THE DECORATION OF THE NORTH WALL [10346]
372 × 946 mm. Two sheets joined vertically. Watermark no.8(?). Pen, coloured washes, chalk.

S. Maria degli Angeli, plan

611 PLAN SHOWING THE *LINEA CLEMENTINA*, 1702(?) [10590]
418 × 563 mm. Watermark no.8. Pen, pink and yellow wash, traces of chalk. With scale.

The church is shown before the alterations by Vanvitelli of 1749. The most prominent feature of the plan is a series of lines in brown ink traversing the crossing; these represent the *linea clementina*, the meridian designed by Francesco Bianchini and Giacomo Maraldi, which was unveiled by Clement XI on 7 October 1702 (Pastor, Eng. ed., XXXIII, p.506; Titi, 1763, pp.292f.).

S. Maria della Concezione, project for the façade (1712?)

The church of S. Maria della Concezione was built to the order of Cardinal Antonio Barberini the Elder to the designs of Antonio Casone (Baglione, *Vite*, p.181) under the supervision of Michele da Bergamo. The foundation stone was laid in 1626 (O. Pollak, *Die Kunsttätigkeit unter Urban VIII*, I, 1928, p.167). A view of the church made soon after the date of building, in a manuscript in the Vatican Library (Cod. Barb. Lat. 4409, fo.76/77, published by da Isnello, p.96), shows a simple façade, with curved steps leading up to it and the lower part of a clock tower (appearing completed on Falda's map of 1676), at the corner of a wing of the convent which ran along the street (cf. Fig.474).

The commission embodied in the present design (Fig.473), a Fontana workshop drawing, was to erect a belfry over the pediment of the church façade, placing a clock between the pediment and the bell, and crowning the top with the *monti* and star of the Albani arms.

An engraving by Vasi in the *Magnificenze* (VII, 1757, pl.132; Fig.474) shows that the project was never carried out. The date of the plan is not recorded, but it may be connected with the consecration of the Blessed Felice da Cantalice by Clement XI in 1712. He had been a member of the Capuchin Order, and in particular of the Monastery of S. Bonaventura, the monks of which had been transferred to S. Maria della Concezione when it was founded.

The wing of the monastery with the old belfry and the steps in front of the church (originally convex) were swept away when the Via Vittorio Veneto was made in 1890 (Bruni, p.18). At the same time the arms of Urban VIII, which appear in the drawing, were replaced by a window.

ADDITIONAL BIBLIOGRAPHY:

Da Villa Ludovisi a Piazza Barberini, exhibition catalogue, Rome, 1957, p.64; no.2, pl.XII.
Le Chiese di Roma, Cenni religiosi, storici, artistici, LXXXIV (Istituto di Studi Romani).
Igino da Alatri, *Guida della Chiesa della SS. Concezione dei M.M. Cappucini di Roma*, Tivoli, 1930.
Bruno Bruni in *Capitolium*, 35, 1960, 5, pp. 16–19.
Domenico da Isnello, *Il Convento della SS. Concezione de' Padri Cappuccini in Piazza Barberini di Roma*, Viterbo, 1923.
C. d'Onofrio, *Scalinate di Roma*, Rome, 1974, pp.254, 256f.

612 ELEVATION OF THE FAÇADE (*Figure* 473) [10591]
349 × 263 mm. Watermark, lily on *monti* and letters A and N in double oval. Pen, grey wash, traces of chalk. With scale.

S. Maria Maggiore, project for the portico gates

Drawing 613 represents the old porch of S. Maria Maggiore which was erected by Martino Longhi the elder in 1575 on the orders of Pope Gregory XIII in place of the medieval vestibule of Eugenius III, dating from 1150 (cf. Matthiae, *Fuga*, pp.75f.). Under Benedict XIV Longhi's work was replaced by the present double-storey façade designed by Ferdinando Fuga (ibid.; Pane, *Fuga*, pp.84ff.), but it is recorded in several views (cf. Fig.477, and Paolo de Angelis, *Basilicae S. Mariae Maioris de Urbe . . . descriptio*, Rome, 1620, pl. facing p.62, ground plan facing p.56; Hermann Egger, *Römische Veduten*, II, Vienna, 1931, pp.26f.).

The relation of no.613 to S. Maria Maggiore is confirmed by the width of the vestibule (108½ *palmi*) which corresponds to that of the present portico (cf. ground plan by Giacomo Fontana, *Raccolta delle migliori chiese di Roma e suburbane*, III, Rome, 1838, pl.XXIII).

The drawings at Windsor are of projects for the gates, for which two variants are offered. The Albani *monti* and star appear as a crowning feature in no.613 (the variant to the left).

On a view formerly in the Pacetti Collection (cf. Egger, op. cit., II, pl.65) the upper limit of a gate seems to be sketchily indicated but the proposal on the left of the present design does not seem to have been carried out, because a painting in the Museo di Roma (Fig.477) representing the portico shortly before it was pulled down, shows a much simpler version.

613 PLAN AND ELEVATION OF THE PORTICO (*Figure* 475) [10623]
362×478 mm. Watermark no.7. Pen, grey, yellow and brown wash. With scale.

614 PROJECT FOR A GATE (*Figure* 476) [10622]
337×310 mm. Pen, grey wash, traces of chalk. With scale.

The drawing is close in style to the foregoing and the gate corresponds in scale (13 *palmi* wide) with those in the foregoing project.

S. Maria in Monticelli, project for restoration (1714)

Following a report about the decay of the medieva church of S. Maria in Monticelli, Clement XI gave orders for an extensive restoration (cf. the 'supplica' in Arch. Segr. Vat., Fondo Albani, vol.12, fos 276f.; Pastor, German ed., XV, p.375, note 3). A ground plan at Windsor (no.615) by Domenico Antonio de Sanctis, an otherwise unknown architect (not to be confused with Francesco de Sanctis) shows a project for restoring the church incorporating part of the old building.

According to the note which accompanies the ground plan and is dated 29 September 1714, the building costs were estimated at 7,300 *scudi*. This amount seems to have been unacceptable, since a draft contract with the 'Capo Mastro muratore' set a limit of 6,000 *scudi*. Another statement attached to the drawing mentions the sum available at the time, 5,800 *scudi*, of which the Pope himself contributed 500 *scudi*. Since it also states that the columns were to be valued at 1,000 *scudi* and either sold or taken into account at this price ('il muratore le piglierà p.il prezzo della chiesa') this document cannot refer to the plan at Windsor but must be connected with a reduced design on the lines of the one eventually executed.

The architect responsible for the reconstruction of the church was Matteo Sassi and not Domenico Antonio de Sanctis, as we know from Ciuccioli (p.72), who was vicar of S. Maria in Monticelli at the time and involved in the contract. Little is known of this architect, who according to Pascoli (II, pp.549f.) was a pupil of Carlo Fontana and died on 4 November 1723 (loc. cit.; Forcella, *Iscriz.*, IX, p.44, no.74; Golzio, p.70). Sassi's assistant at S. Maria in Monticelli was Giuseppe Sardi.

Domenico Antonio de Sanctis was probably also a pupil of Carlo Fontana. It has so far been impossible to discover the reason for his replacement by Sassi; in the documents in the Archivio di Stato in Rome (Fondo Corp. Ord. Rel. Masch, vols.2515f.), the Archivio Segreto Vaticano (Fondo Albani, vol.12, fos 276f.) and the Archivio del Vicariato di Roma (Segr. del trib., vol.46, fos 559ff.) no information is given.

De Sanctis' design was modified in execution, rather than being entirely discarded. But the width of the nave (measuring 42 *palmi* in his plan) was reduced to the original dimension of 37 *palmi*. This narrowing of the main space probably suggested the exclusion of the engaged columns and explains the mention of their possible sale in the contract. In the arrangement of the side-chapels, now connected to each other by high arches and not the narrow passages in the drawing, the shell of the old building was retained, as de Sanctis had already planned. The width of the church in his plan (85 *palmi*) corresponds exactly to the existing building (18.66 m.), and the distance between the pilasters framing the side-chapels (22 *palmi*, or 4.90 m.) is the same as in his ground plan. Even his curiously-designed choir was retained.

A document of 4 January 1716 (quoted by Ciuccioli, p.17) states that the rebuilding was in the main completed at that date, but it was actually finished by 1715, as we learn from an inscription on the inside of the façade (Forcella, *Iscriz.*, V, p.528, no.1387).

The suggestion for the sale of the columns does not seem to have been followed up, since they were encased in the pillars of the new building (Vasi, *Magnificenze*, VI, 1756, p.XXXIV). Two of the columns were removed during the nineteenth-century restorations and the material was used for the incrustation of the pillars, and the framing of the doors, paintings, etc. (Azzuri, p.52).

The excavations for the foundations of the pillars revealed the mosaic floor of the old church at a depth of 2½ *palmi*, and parts of it were used for the paving of the new porch (cf. Ciuccioli, pp.14ff.). The building of Clement XI differs from the drawing in the façade. A drawing in the Albertina (Fig.478), most probably a copy after Matteo Sassi, shows a straight façade which is open in both storeys, like Cortona's front of S. Maria in Via Lata. The façade as actually built was modified by later restoration, but its original form is recorded in an engraving in Vasi's *Magnificenze* (Fig.479; 1756, VI, pl.112).

On 21 November 1716 Clement XI consecrated the church with a dedication to the Presentation of the Virgin (Ciuccioli, p.82; Forcella, *Iscriz.*, V, p.529, no.1390), and in 1719 the altars were finished, with one exception (op. cit., pp.74ff.). In 1727 alterations were made to the high altar A.S.R., Fondo e Corp. e Ord. Rel. Masch. vol. 2517, busta 9, including accounts). The church was reconsecrated on 12 September 1728 by Benedict XIII (cf. inscription on the high altar), who three years earlier, on 26 February 1725, had transferred the church to the French Padri della Dottrina Cristiana (Archivio del Vicariato di Roma, Segr. del Trib., vol.45, fo.222). For an account of the nineteenth-century restorations (completed in 1860; cf. Forcella, V, p.534, no.1404) the reader is referred to the report of Francesco Azzuri (pp.37ff.), who was in charge of the work.

ADDITIONAL BIBLIOGRAPHY:
Sources:
ARCHIVIO SEGRETO VATICANO:
Fondo Albani, vol.12, fos 276f. (*Notizie Istoriche dell'antica chiesa Parrocchiale di S. Maria in Monticelli e supplica presentata a Clemente XI per muoverlo à ristorarla, essendo rouinosa, e cadente*).
ARCHIVIO DEL VICARIATO DI ROMA:
Segreteria del Tribunale: vol.45, fos 222ff. (Brief of Benedict XIII of 26 February 1725; see Valesio, 22 February 1726); vol.46, fos. 559ff. (*Stato della chiesa Parrocchiale di S. Maria in Monticelli dell' anno 1716*).

LITERATURE:
Le Chiese di Roma, Cenni Religiosi, Storici, Artistici, Rome, n.d., nr.XCI.
Mariano Armellini, *Le Chiese di Roma dal sec. IV al XIX*, Rome, 1942.
Francesco Azzuri (etc.), *La Chiesa Parrocchiale di S. Maria in Monticelli e i suoi restauri*, Rome, 1860.
Vincenzo Golzio in *Dedalo*, 12, 1932, p.70.
Christian Hülsen, *Le Chiese di Roma nel Medioevo*, Florence, 1927, p.349, no.65.
Renate Rieger in *Christliche Kunstblätter*, 92, 1954, p.134.

615 Domenico Antonio de Sanctis
PLAN PROJECT (*Figure* 480) [10342]
491 × 382 mm. Watermark no.7. Pen, grey and violet wash, traces of chalk. With scale and index letters. Inscribed at top: *Die 29 Septembris 1714*, and lower left: *Dominicus Ant.ius de Sanctis Arch.us inveniebat*, and labelled in nave: *Iconografia Ecclesiae edificande* (sic) *S. Mariae in Monticellis*'.

Rome: Secular works

The Colonna Citatoria, projects for raising and siting the column (1703/5 ?)

Four drawings in Volumes 185 and 188 are of projects connected with the raising and siting of the Colonna Citatoria. This lay in the ground near the Palazzo di Montecitorio until raised by Francesco Fontana in 1705 (see entries for the Curia Innocenziana and Fontana di Trevi in the main part of the catalogue). The Pope considered raising the column at the Fontana di Trevi, the Piazza di Montecavallo and in front of the Lateran, and many architectural projects are known which refer to these proposals of the Pope. They date in the main from the years 1703/5, before the column was finally raised and transported to the Piazza di Montecitorio.

The present drawings comprise a project for raising the column (616), an anonymous project for placing the column on the Piazza di Montecavallo (617 and 618) and a project by Nicola Michetti for siting the column at the Fontana di Trevi (to be discussed in greater detail by John Pinto in a forthcoming publication). The plan of this project is drawing 619 (10329 in Volume 185) while the elevation and section are separated from it and bound in Volume 189 at Windsor. This volume differs from the two Albani volumes, which are the subject of the present part of the catalogue, in containing material not for the most part directly connected with the commissions of Pope Clement XI.

616 'Michel Angeli Scappi da Mondolfo'
PROJECT FOR RAISING THE COLUMN (*Figure* 486) [10644]
415 × 624 mm. Watermark no.7. Chalk, coloured washes.

The inscription begins: 'Michel Ange'li scappi da Mondolfo dello stato dUrbino . . .', and goes on to describe the project shown in the drawing, where the column is being lowered on to a pedestal by means of a large winch on one side and a weight on the other.

617 PROJECT FOR RAISING THE COLUMN ON THE PIAZZA DI MONTECAVALLO, ELEVATION (*Figure* 484) [10330]
765×503 mm. Pen, grey wash. With scale.

The column is mounted on a high base decorated with three *monti* and the star of the Albani arms.

618 PROJECT FOR RAISING THE COLUMN ON THE PIAZZA DI MONTECAVALLO, PLAN (*Figure* 485) [10593]
512×355 mm. Pen, coloured washes. With scale.

Probably for the same project as the preceding; it differs in showing a large circular basin in front of the column.

619 Nicola Michetti
PROJECT FOR RAISING THE COLUMN AT THE FONTANA DI TREVI, PLAN (*Figure* 481) [10329]
519×739 mm. Two sheets joined vertically. Watermark no.7. Pen, grey and blue washes, traces of chalk. Signed, lower right: *Nicola Michetti.*

The existing features of the fountain, a large semi-circular basin and three jets of water (see the entry for Fontana's projects for the fountain) are here surmounted by a raised terrace behind the fountain on which the column is placed.

620 Nicola Michetti
PROJECT FOR RAISING THE COLUMN AT THE FONTANA DI TREVI, ELEVATION (*Figure* 482) [10765]
Pen, grey and blue wash, traces of chalk. With scale. Inscribed: *fontana di treui*, and signed on right: *Nicola Michetti.*

The central jet of water is surmounted by the arms of Clement XI.

621 Nicola Michetti
PROJECT FOR RAISING THE COLUMN AT THE FONTANA DI TREVI, SECTION (*Figure* 483) [10769]
280×411 mm. Pen, grey washes, some chalk. With scale and index.

Inscribed, lower right, with key to index.

The Palazzo Albani (Palazzo Nerli), three engravings

Between drawings 10689 and 10690 in Volume 188 are three unnumbered engravings by G. B. Falda showing the Palazzo Nerli as built by Domenico Fontana. This palace (the Palazzo del Drago) is in the Via delle Quattro Fontane, opposite the church of S. Carlo (Callari, pp. 388ff.). It was owned in the early 18th century by Cardinal Alessandro Albani, the youngest nephew of Pope Clement XI, and the heir to his collections of drawings (Fleming, pp.164ff.), and alterations were carried out by Alessandro Specchi (Titi, 1763, p.300; Thieme Becker, sv. Specchi). The presence of these engravings in Volume 188 is probably connected with the acquisition of the palace by the Pope or his nephew. No detailed history of the palace appears to have been written, and it is not recorded when it passed to the Albani family, or which member of the family was its first owner.

Palazzo dei Conservatori, drawings connected with the installation of statues (1708 and 1712?)

Two drawings in Volume 188 and two in Volume 185 record the installation of statues in the Palazzo dei Conservatori. The first pair (nos 622/3) refer to a statue of Paul IV which is placed in the main first-floor room of the palace (Figs 487/8). An inscription on the pedestal of the statue gives the date of its installation as 1708. The restoration of the statue took place before 1704, as is shown by the illustration in Domenico de' Rossi, *Raccolta di statue* . . . of that year (pl.CLXII). According to de Rossi the statue, believed to be by Pirro Ligorio, had lain for over a century near the Capitol. The restoration was made by Vincenzo Felice at the direction of Nicolò Giudice, acting on behalf of the Pope. The drawings in Volume 188 may refer to a site which is different from that at present occupied by the statue; they suggest that the statue was to be sited in front of a window with deeply projecting walls to each side. The drawings are close in style to Fontana and may have been made in his studio.

The pair of drawings in Volume 185 record the sites of statues inside the *loggia* of the palace. As inscriptions on the drawings reveal, two Egyptian statues, given by the Pope, were to be sited in the openings of the *loggia* on each side of its central bay, facing across the *loggia* two Roman statues beside the central doorway. The Roman statues can be identified with those of Caesar and a Roman Admiral, which had stood since the 16th century in the *loggia*. The two Egyptian statues, recorded in drawing 624 are of figures of priests in red granite. They formed part of a group of Egyptian statues found, probably in 1712, in the Vigna Verospi, and given by the Pope to the Capitol. They were moved in 1839 to the Vatican, when the Egyptian Museum there was founded (see Pastor, Eng. Ed., XXXIII, p.512; *Descrizzione delle statue . . . che si custodiscono ne Palazzi di Campidoglio*, 1775 (3rd. ed.), pp.9 and 129; *A Catalogue of the ancient sculptures . . . of the Museo*

Capitolino, ed. H. Stuart Jones, 1906, p.8; *A Catalogue . . . of the Palazzo dei Conservatori*, 1926, p.359 and pl.I).

622 PLAN OF THE SITE OF THE STATUE OF PAUL IV (*Figure* 487) [10587]
269 × 284 mm. Watermark no.9. Pen, grey and yellow wash, traces of chalk. With scale and annotations.

623 PERSPECTIVE VIEW OF THE STATUE ON ITS DAIS (*Figure* 488) [10586]
412 × 287 mm. Pen, grey wash, traces of chalk. With scale. Inscribed on a paper laid down beneath the drawing: *disegno della statua di Paolo IV. / ristorata, e collocata in Campidoglio.*

624 ELEVATION OF THE THREE CENTRAL OPENINGS OF THE *LOGGIA*, SHOWING POSITIONS OF EGYPTIAN STATUES [10348]
464 × 742 mm. Watermark no.9. Pen, grey wash, chalk. With measurements. Inscribed at top: *Per la situazione delle due / statue donate dà N: S: / incontro le due che già ui sono.*

625 ELEVATION OF THE THREE CENTRAL WALL BAYS OF THE *LOGGIA*, SHOWING POSITIONS OF ROMAN STATUES [10347]
462 × 742 mm. Watermark no.7. Pen, grey wash, chalk. Inscribed at top: *Situazione delle statue che già sono sotto la loggia.*

The Palazzo del Quirinale(?)

626 PLAN AND ELEVATION OF A WALL OF A SALA DEL MAPPAMONDO (*Figure* 489) [10618]
*C.*415 × 688 mm. Watermark no.9. Pen, coloured washes, chalk. Inscribed on the *verso*: *Varij disegni del Palazzo del M.te Cauallo'.*

The inscription may possibly refer to the drawings of busts of Popes on pedestals which are laid down in Volume 188 on the pages immediately following the present sheet. The decoration of part of the ceiling would appear to show a project including the Albani arms. The drawing appears to be unconnected in its style with Fontana.

The Palazzo Riario, project for establishing an *Accademia Albana*

Two maps of the grounds of the Palazzo Riario (now the Palazzo Corsini) occur in Volume 185, the first showing the site in what was evidently its existing condition (Fig.490), and the second, as is revealed by inscriptions, incorporating alterations to the gardens and the buildings designed to make them suitable for the establishment of an *Accademia Albana* (Fig.491). The main building of the Palazzo Riario had been inhabited by Queen Christina of Sweden and she had founded there the *Accademia Reale* of which Pope Clement XI had been an important member. In 1690, the year following the Queen's death, a group of poets founded the Arcadia, which met for the first year of its existence in the grounds of the palace (Pastor, Eng. ed. XXXIII, p.554; Catalogue of the exhibition Christina, Queen of Sweden, Nationalmuseum Stockholm, 1966, pp.376ff. and 318ff.; R. Stephan, in *Queen Christina of Sweden, Documents and Studies*, 1966, pp.365ff.). The *Accademia Albana* was presumably an academy to be founded under the patronage of Pope Clement XI, at some time after his election to the Papacy in 1700, in succession to these academies of the Palazzo Riario. Nothing seems to have resulted from the project, or from the architectural ideas embodied in the present drawings, and the palace remained unaltered until transformed by Fuga for Cardinal Corsini (Pane, *Fuga*, pp.58ff.). Projects at Stockholm for the transformation of the palace, dating from the lifetime of Queen Christina, are related in a general way to the present project (S. Vänje, in *Queen Christina of Sweden, Documents and Studies*, Stockholm, 1966, pp.376ff.). It seems possible that these early drawings are by Fontana himself, though their attribution is difficult to decide. The present drawings resemble Fontana in the style of their draughtsmanship, but they differ in small ways from his personal technique. They may be copies of Fontana or the work of a pupil working under Fontana's supervision. The elaborate index panel incorporated in the second of the drawings closely resembles tomb designs by Fontana (cf. above, the Origo monument). Fontana himself was a member of the Arcadia (see introduction).

627 PLAN OF THE GROUNDS OF THE PALAZZO RIARIO (*Figure* 490) [10298]
981 × 708 mm. Four sheets joined. Watermark no.9. Pen, coloured washes. With scale and index.

A key to the index of letters is inscribed within a large circular frame on the right; it bears the title: 'INDICE / Della Pianta dello stato p'nte della Vil=/la dell Ill.mo et Ecc:mo Sig:r March. Riari'. Index letter A refers to the building occupied by Queen Christina: 'Palazzo detto della Regina.'

628 PLAN OF THE GROUNDS OF THE PALAZZO RIARIO, SHOWING PROJECTS FOR ALTERATIONS (*Figure* 491) [10299]
993 × 709 mm. Four sheets joined. Watermark no.9. Pen, coloured washes. With scale and index.

Alterations to the plan of the gardens are indicated in pink wash; they include the provision of an oval riding school, leading to an amphitheatre, which is labelled *Academia*. The palace of Queen Christina (index letter A) is to be transformed into a regular block and balanced by a matching palace. The key to the index is inscribed on an elaborate tablet, surmounted by the Papal/Albani arms. The key is headed: 'ACADEMIA ALBANA'. Index A refers to the 'Palazzo detto della Regina per commodo de m'ri di / Pittura, Scultura, Archittura, e belle Littere'. The bottom of the tablet contains an allegorical figure composition showing representations of these four arts. Index B refers to the palace to be built matching that of Queen Christina: 'Palazzo da farsi di nuouo dall'altra banda per il Tea=/tro per Comedie con suoi annessi con il commodo del:/le Stanze per gl'Alunni'.

Views of Rome and estate plans

629 ENGRAVING: BIRD'S EYE VIEW OF PART OF ROME [10593[a]]
500×356 mm. Watermark, Agnus Dei in double oval.

See T. Ashby, 'Frammenti di due piante ignote di Roma del secolo XVII', *Roma*, 1925, pp.1ff.

630 THE VILLA GIULIA, PLAN [10594]
420×322 mm. Pen, grey wash, traces of chalk. With scale.

The drawing appears to be an exact record of the plan of the villa.

631 PLAN OF S. BIBIANA WITH MAP OF THE NEIGHBOURING PROPERTIES [10317]
765×472 mm. Watermark no.7. Pen, grey and yellow wash, traces of chalk. With annotations.

632 MAP OF AN ALBANI ESTATE OUTSIDE THE PORTA MAGGIORE [10737]
1012×724 mm. Watermark no.9. Pen, coloured washes.

A scroll, lower right, bears a scale in *canne*, an index and the title, in capitals: 'Delineatione in pianta delle vigne / dell' Ecc.[ma] casa Albani poste fuori / di Porta Maggiore'. The site is roughly wedge-shaped, bounded on the two longer sides by the 'Strada che Tende a Tor Piggnatara' and the 'Strada che Tende ad. Acqua Bullicante'.

Urbino, Pesaro and Colbordolo: Introduction

A considerable number of the drawings in Volume 188 are connected with projects made for Pope Clement XI and other members of the Albani family for sites in Urbino, Morciola (near Colbordolo) and Pesaro. Urbino was the birthplace of Clement XI, and he felt the deepest interest in the town throughout his career; his "praecordia" are preserved in Urbino in the family chapel in S. Francesco; they were transferred there in 1755 in execution of a clause in the will of his nephew, Cardinal Alessandro Albani (Ligi, *Mem. Eccl.*, p.14). Clement's scheme for making the church of S. Teodoro in Rome, restored on his orders by Fontana, a national church to be based on a confraternity of citizens from Urbino, has already been discussed. But he evolved and carried through many other projects connected with his native city. In 1699, for instance, when he was still a cardinal, he founded a Collegio dei Nobili in Urbino, directed first by the Jesuits (Ligi, *Mem. Eccl.*, pp.11ff.).

In October 1703 the two Monsignori, Curzio Origi, secretary, and Giovanni Maria Lancisi, doctor to the Pope, were sent to Urbino when Annibale Albani, later a cardinal, received his doctoral degree (a drawing showing the arrival of the *cortège* at the Porta Valbona in Urbino is in the Palazzo Chigi (formerly Albani) at Soriano al Cimino). Their diary records important decisions about papal building projects in connection with which Fontana had already visited Urbino. In these projects Fontana was helped by Francesco Bufalini, an architect who was born in that city (Thieme Becker, V, 1911, p.201). Bufalini had received special orders from the Pope to make drawings of the Ducal Palace in Urbino and in particular of the reliefs (*Diario*, fo.5v. see also G. Eimer in *Festschrift für Ulrich Middeldorf*, Berlin, 1968, pp.187/98, and H. Straub, *Ausgewählte Aufsätze*, 1969, pp.102–104). The Pope had long planned a restoration of the deserted Ducal palace and also of the cathedral (Scatassa/Valesio, p.68). He was particularly interested in a scheme for building a new high altar to hold the relics of S. Crescentinus, the patron saint of the town, and many drawings for this project are amongst those at Windsor.

Other important decisions were made in the last days of October and the first of November 1703. Clement planned to restore the archiepiscopal palace and for the façade of this there is a Fontana workshop drawing, now in the Albertina (Italian drawings no.296; not used in the reconstruction of 1708 – *Diario*, fo.140v., 145r.). In 1705 Annibale Albani visited Urbino again, accompanied by Giacomo Patriarca, master-mason of S. Peter's, in connection with further improvements (Valesio, 8 May and 5 July 1705). Clement also planned to restore and embellish the Palazzo Albani (*Diario*, fo.140v.), and drawings for this are preserved at Windsor. In connection with the Albani chapel in S. Francesco a *risarcimento* (renovation) was planned (*Diario*, fo.143v.), but as a result of the complete remodelling of the chapel about 1730 (Ricotti, pp.55f.), there is no means of telling whether Fontana's project, now lost, was ever carried out. Fontana also prepared plans for the better lighting of Barocci's *Madonna with saints*, now in the Urbino Gallery (Olsen, *Barocci*, cat. no.16, pl.22). There are also at Windsor drawings by a local architect, Giuseppe Gianni, for the library of S. Francesco, datable to 1712, drawings of a Casa Corboli and projects for improving the Porta Valbona.

The campaign of 1703 also entailed projects for the renovation of the Villa Albani at Morciola near Colbordolo, which were completed by May 1704 and designs for a later project, which entailed adding another storey to the house and building a free-standing chapel in front of it, are preserved at Windsor.

Many of the drawings connected with Urbino, Pesaro and Colbordolo, though they are of different dates, appear to be by the same artist, an accomplished architectural draughtsman, who indulged at times in elaborately-coloured studies, rendering the effects of polychromed marble and gilt work. This artist's style appears in the drawing of the Blessed Michelina Metelli altar in Pesaro (Fig.513) and the majority of the drawings for the high altar of Urbino Cathedral (Figs 499–501); the unexecuted project for the church at Colbordolo (Figs 524–532) and drawings for the Palazzo Albani, Urbino (e.g. Fig.504), can be related to the Pesaro drawing. These are amongst the most attractive sheets in Volumes 185 and 188 and they may, as suggested below, be by Filippo Barigioni. Other candidates would be Michetti and Specchi, but these pupils of Fontana appear, both as architects and draughtsmen, to be more independent of their master than the architect of the present sheets (for Specchi, see the Quirinal Stables and the Porto di Ripetta, and for Michetti, SS. Apostoli and the Colonna Citatoria – project for moving the column to the Fontana di Trevi; on Barigioni see Thieme Becker; he was born on 11 January 1672; see Hager, *Juvarra*, p.54, n.88).

ADDITIONAL BIBLIOGRAPHY:
Sources:
Diario, Lettere ecc. concernenti il viaggio dei due prelati Mons. Origi e Mons. Lancisi intrapreso da Roma in Urbino per ordine della Santità di Clemente XI . . . (1703), Urbino, Ms., Bibl. Univ.: Fondo del Comune, vol.72 (cited by A. Tani, see below).
Ubaldo Tosi, *Miscellanea di notizie riguardante la storia di Urbino e dei suoi uomini illustri*, Urbino, Ms., Bibl. Univ.: Fondo del Comune, vol.93.
Memoria per la storia di Urbino e degli uomini illustri della medesima, di diversi autori. Raccolto dal Rosa (1818). Urbino, Ms., Bibl. Univ.: Fondo del Comune, vol.55.

LITERATURE:
Bernadino Baldi, *Memorie concernenti la Città di Urbino*, Rome, 1724.
Egidio Calzini, *Urbino e suoi monumenti*, 2nd. ed., Urbino, 1899.
Jörg Garms, *Disegni di Luigi Vanvitelli* . . . , catalogue, Naples, 1973–74, p.64, no.67.
Andrea Lazzari, *Delle Chiese di Urbino, e delle Pitture in esse esistenti*, Urbino, 1801.
Bramante Ligi, *Memorie ecclesiastiche di Urbino*, vol. I, Urbino, 1938.
Le Chiese monumentali in Urbino, Urbino, 1956.
I Santi protettori di Urbino (Urbania), 1968.
H. Olsen, *Federico Barocci*, 1962.
R. Pane in R. de Fusco, etc., *Vanvitelli*, 1973, pp.41f., pls 39–43.
B. M. Peebles, in *Didascalie*, Studies in Honour of Anselm M. Albareda, New York, 1961, pp.327–351.
Egidio Ricotti, *Il Convento e la Chiesa di S. Francesco di Assisi in Urbino*, Padua, 1954.
Ercole Scatassa, *Rass. Bibl. Ital.*, XVI, 1913, p.68.
Luigi Servolini in *Rassegna di Cultura Urbinum*, VI, no.6, 1932.
Antonio Tani, *Urbino e Clemente XI*, Rome, 1957, pp.14f.

Urbino, the high altar of the Cathedral (1703–1708)

On 24 October 1703 Clement XI allocated 6000 *scudi* for the erection of a new high altar in the Cathedral of Urbino (Tani, p.13, n.2). The altar was to contain the relics of S. Crescentinus, a Roman soldier who suffered martyrdom in the third century, the relics having been brought to Urbino in 1068 (Ligi, *Santi protettori*, pp.16ff.). In order to provide more space for the archbishop's throne, which stood on the edge of the steps (see a drawing in the Archivio Segreto Vaticano, Fondo Albani, vol.20, fo.168), it was decided to move the altar 'a similitudine di quello di S. Pietro' further towards the nave, and in this way the new altar was made to correspond in type with the original altar which faced both ways (*Diario*, fo.108v.)

On 31 October 1703 a discussion was held in the presence of the Cardinal Legate, at which a number of proposals were put forward for submission to the Pope (*Diario*, fo.140). In view of the time involved in the actual execution of the scheme there is no means of knowing how far these suggestions were later modified. On 24 April 1705 Orazio Albani, the Pope's brother, set out for Urbino in connection with the construction of the altar, which was to be decorated with marble taken from a block found in the Tiber near the Ripa Grande in the foundation of the 'Torrione antico', just above the Porta Portese. Orazio presented the chapter of the cathedral on this occasion with a set of silver candlesticks (Valesio, 24 April 1705). Some or all of the drawings for candlesticks catalogued in the final section of the present catalogue may be connected with the set presented to the Cathedral.

About a year later, on 10 March 1706, the project is mentioned again. The Pope visited the Fonderia Vecchia to see the model of the altar and the marble to be used in its construction (Valesio). On 6 March 1708 the pieces of the altar were being dispatched by boat from the Ripa Grande (ibid.). The cargo arrived at Pesaro on 22 May 1708 and was transported thence to Urbino, where it was received with great ceremony, the altar being dedicated on 2 July 1708 (Ligi, *Mem. Eccl.*, p.281, n.1, and *Santi protettori*, pp.36ff.).

The altar is traditionally attributed to Alessandro Specchi (Tosi, fo.382v.; Lazzari, p.6). It is in any case a typical product of the school of Fontana who, after the initial planning on the site in 1703, would no doubt have left the further elaboration of the project and the execution to an assistant. Camillo Rusconi was responsible for the bronze decorations (Ligi, pp.13ff., 102ff.). According to Tosi (fo.388) Specchi was also responsible for the altars of the Cappella del SS. Sacramento and the Cappella dell' Immacolata Concezione.

The high altar was seriously damaged in the earthquake of 1789 and its original appearance is best seen in a medal of 1708 (Ligi, *Santi protettori*, pl.VII; Fig.492 here). This shows a very broad *mensa*, similar to Fontana's altar of the Cappella Cybo in Rome; the table is carried by Rusconi's four *putti* and supports six candlesticks (no doubt those presented by Orazio Albani), a crucifix and two statuettes of saints. Of this altar furniture only the crucifix survived the earthquake (Lazzari, pp.5ff.). The altar stands on a platform raised on three steps, preceded by a further flight of three steps, breaking forward in the middle. The sides are decorated with the Pope's coat-of-arms. The total cost is said traditionally to have amounted to 19,000 *scudi* (Lazzari, loc. cit.). An exact account of the marbles used in the altar (front side: *alabastro orientale*, frame-work and table of *mensa*: *verde antico*) is given by Baldi (*Memorie*, fo.184). Of the decorations of the altar Rusconi's *putti*, his relief of S. Crescentinus and the coats-of-arms seem not to have been seriously damaged in the earthquake. At the time of the reconstruction by Valadier in 1796 the altar was transferred back into the choir (Ligi, *Santi protettori*, pls.XIIf. – the measurements are 5.34× 2·50 m.).

The drawings at Windsor were not used for the executed design and they must represent a relatively early phase in the evolution of the project, but those for the sarcophagus, which is enclosed within the altar, cover all stages of the project up to that immediately preceding the execution.

Two ground plans, one (633) inscribed 'Tribuna del Duomo' and the other (634) inscribed 'Chiesa della Grotta', can be identified as being of the cathedral of Urbino on comparison with the plan published by Baldi (pl.2; for an elevation of the cathedral before Valadier see Servolini, pl. opp. p.10). A drawing for a sarcophagus inscribed with the name of S. Crescentinus (640; Fig.497) can be associated with the altar erected to this saint, and this sheet is associated with a further group of drawings (642–646, including 643 which is in Volume 185 at Windsor; Figs 499–501). It is possible to associate with this project further drawings for an altar (635–637, Figs 494–496, 638/9), which in each case bears on its shorter side the arms of Pope Clement XI.

Stylistically these drawings can be divided into three groups: the two plans of the choir and the crypt, the drawings for the altars, and the designs for the sarcophagus. The plans may be by Bufalini, and the last group may possibly be by Filippo Barigioni, a former pupil of Mattia de' Rossi (Pascoli, I, p.330); he worked with Specchi on the execution of Fontana's Albani chapel in S. Sebastiano fuori le mura (Titi, 1721, p.71) and was later active in Urbino in 1727/32 on the church of S. Domenico (Calzini, *Urbino*, pp.91f.) and in 1740 on S. Francesco. These drawings with their use of grey and yellow wash are close stylistically to the unexecuted projects for the church at Colbordolo. The first of the two altar designs (635–637) may also be by the same architect, since it shows the rich plant forms which characterize the work of Barigioni at S. Marco, Rome. These appear too in the drawing for the altar of the Blessed Michelina Metelli at Pesaro (Fig.513), which is stylistically related to the present group of drawings for the sarcophagus of S. Crescentinus. Specchi might be suggested as the author of the second altar design (nos 638/9), in view of its relation to the altar as executed and also to the high altar of the Pantheon, designed by him on the orders of Clement XI, but the drawings themselves appear to be in the same hand (Barigioni's ?) as those for the first altar project.

ADDITIONAL BIBLIOGRAPHY: see references at end of introduction to present section.

633 PLAN OF THE CHOIR (*Figure* 493) [10654]
546×*c*.415 mm. Watermark no.27. Pen. With scale labelled *Scala di Palmi Romani*. Inscribed: *Tribuna del Duomo*.

634 PLAN OF THE CRYPT BENEATH THE CHOIR [10688]
547×*c*.415 mm. Watermark no.27. Pen. With scale labelled *Scala di Palmi Romani*.

The crypt is inscribed 'Chiesa della Grotta', the space before it 'Cantoria' and 'Andito auanti la Chiesa . . . che passa sotto la Cantoria'.

Design for an altar with a broad *mensa*

635 FRONT ELEVATION (*Figure* 496) [10659]
167×360 mm. Pen, coloured washes, traces of chalk.

Washes of different colours denote various types of marble; the design of the central panel is given in alternate halves.

636 SIDE ELEVATION (*Figure* 495) [10658]
189×280 mm. Pen, coloured washes, chalk.

Alternative designs are again given for each half of the central panel.

637 PLAN (*Figure* 494) [10653]
C.415×547 mm. Watermark no.28. Pen, some chalk. With scale.

This drawing appears to show the plan of the present altar project. In style it resembles the sheets showing the plans of the choir and the crypt, 633 and 634 above, in the type of scale used it corresponds with 638 below.

Design for an altar with a narrow *mensa*

638 FRONT ELEVATION [10661]
233×375 mm. Watermark no.7. Pen, traces of chalk. With scale.

The altar is 13 *palmi* wide, corresponding roughly with the size of the altar in plan 633 above. The right-hand pilaster is decorated with a bishop's mitre, probably in reference to Bishop Mainardi, who had transferred the reliquary to Urbino (Ligi, *Chiese mon.*, pp.5f.).

639 SIDE ELEVATION [10660]
175×172 mm. Pen and brown ink, traces of chalk.

Designs for the sarcophagus

640 PROJECT FOR A CURVED SARCOPHAGUS, ELEVATION (*Figure* 497) [10663]
223×351 mm. Pen, grey and buff wash, gold leaf, traces of chalk. With scale.

The sarcophagus is of grey marble, 9½ *palmi* wide at its broadest point. Its decoration is shown partly in gold leaf, including the Albani arms (half visible at the ends), and the inscription across the front: DIVVS. CRESCENTINVS. MARTIR.

641 SECTION AND PLAN OF THE ALTAR WITH PROJECT FOR SARCOPHAGUS DECORATED WITH FLAGS (*Figure* 498) [10662]
183×125 mm. Pen, grey washes, some chalk.

The sarcophagus is shown within an octagonal chamber inside the altar.

642 SECTION OF THE ALTAR WITH PROJECT FOR URN SARCOPHAGUS (1), ELEVATION (*Figure* 499) [10666]
360×476 mm. Pen, grey and yellow wash, traces of chalk. With scale and ruled ink border.

The block of the altar is shown in section (yellow wash), and the sarcophagus in elevation in the chamber within the altar.

643 PROJECT FOR URN SARCOPHAGUS (1), PLAN (*Figure* 500) [10340]
305×446 mm. Pen, yellow wash, some chalk.

This drawing is placed in Volume 185, but it clearly forms part of the same project as the preceding elevation which is in Volume 188.

644 PROJECT FOR URN SARCOPHAGUS (2), FRONT ELEVATION [10665]
355×469 mm. Pen, grey wash, traces of chalk. With ruled ink border.

As is especially clear in this project the present series of designs are related to the sarcophagus of S. Faustina beneath the altar of the Cybo chapel (illustrated in Lavagnino, p.157; see also the sarcophagus on the catafalque of Clement XI, designed by Filippo Barigioni, engraving by Francesco Aquila).

645 PROJECT FOR URN SARCOPHAGUS (2), REAR ELEVATION (?) [10667]
363×479 mm. Watermark no.9. Pen, grey wash, traces of chalk.

The drawing is closely similar to the preceding and probably shows the same design from the rear.

646 PROJECT FOR URN SARCOPHAGUS (3), ELEVATION (*Figure* 501) [10664]
259×349 mm. Pen, grey wash, traces of chalk. With scale.

The design is related to those of the foregoing projects but the sarcophagus is broader in its proportions and plainer in its decoration. The drawing differs slightly in style but is probably by the same hand.

Urbino, projects for the library in the Franciscan monastery (1712)

Four drawings and two short manuscripts in Volume 188 can be connected with Clement XI's foundation of a public library in the monastery of the Franciscans' Conventual at Urbino (Pastor, Eng. ed., XXXIII, p.531; Clough, *Manuscripta*, XIV (1970), p.162). Drawings 648 and 649 appear to show the building as it was constructed and the first of these is accompanied by a text of 26 November 1712 by a certain Giuseppe Gianni, *Capomaestro de muratori* of Urbino, who gives the estimated cost of the construction as 3,000 *scudi*. The second text is a roughly-written estimate of the cost of constructing the eight windows and the door of the library. Drawings 648 and 649 may perhaps have been drawn by Gianni; they seem too clumsy to be the work of a professional architect. The style of the architecture seems equally primitive and this too may have been left to Gianni.

The remaining two drawings consist of a plan (no.647) which appears to record an earlier stage of the design than that shown in 648, and an elevation of a bookcase. This has the same watermark as that of 647 and may refer to the library here or to the one in the Albani Palace at Urbino (see below).

ADDITIONAL BIBLIOGRAPHY: see Urbino, The Palazzo Albani, below.

647 GROUND PLAN [10624]
350×554 mm. Laid down. Watermark no.29. Pen, pink wash, traces of chalk. With scale in *palmi romani*.

648 PLAN WITH SECTION IN PERSPECTIVE [10647]
420×289 mm. Pen, yellow wash. With scale and index and inscriptions in red wash.

The key to the index is inscribed at the top of the sheet. The section shows that the first floor of the library (D) is to be used as a dormitory. On the *verso* is the plan of the first floor, also indexed and inscribed.

649 ELEVATION IN PERSPECTIVE OF THE EAST WALL WITH SECTION OF THE CLOISTER EXTENSION [10684]
*C.*357×676 mm. Watermark no.4. Pen, yellow and brown wash. With scale, and index and annotations in red wash.

The drawing shows that the library was to be built level with the cloister wing, at first-floor level to the street to the west. Over the cloister wing was to be an extension to the dormitory over the library. Inscribed with keys to the index for the section and the elevation in perspective.

650 ELEVATION OF A BOOKCASE [10668]
540×397 mm. Watermark no.29. Pen, chalk. With scale.

The drawing may refer to the library of the Palazzo Albani in Urbino, for there is some resemblance to the bookcases installed in the palace library as recorded in a drawing of the time (reproduced by Clough, *Librarium*, XII (1969), p.15 and fig.3).

Urbino, drawings of a Casa Corboli

Three drawings in Volume 188 refer to a certain Casa Corboli which can be identified as a house still in existence in the Via Raffaello in Urbino, near the bottom of the street and on its west side. The drawings appear to have been made for the purpose of enlarging and improving the appearance of the façade, together with the façade of a seminary and a chapel of S. Sergius beside the house. The patron who commissioned these drawings and the architect who drew them are unknown, but their very presence in Volume 188 suggests that the drawings have some connection with the Albani family.

651 FIRST-FLOOR PLAN [10686]
296×447 mm. Pen. Inscribed at top: *Primo Piano della Casa della Sig:ra Alda Corboli*, and in the centre: *Cortile*, with a meridian nearby. Inscribed on the *verso*: *Pianta, e Prospetto della Casa Corboli d'Urbin.*

652 ELEVATION [10687]
310×632 mm. Watermark no.7. Pen, traces of chalk. With scale, labelled *Scala di Piedi Venticinque d Urbino.* Inscribed at top: *Casa della Sig:ra Corboli.*

Two narrow buildings to the left of the house are included in the elevation – a *Seminario* and the chapel of *S. Sergio.*

653 ELEVATION: PROJECT FOR ALTERATIONS [10685]
311×632 mm. Pen.

The drawing corresponds in character with the preceding, but the articulation of the façade is made more regular.

Urbino, the Palazzo Albani

The history of the Palazzo Albani at Urbino, where Giovanni Francesco Albani, later Pope Clement XI, was born on 23 July 1649, has still to be investigated. This task will be the more difficult because, before the palace was sold, the library and manuscripts of Clement XI were removed and split up; one part (mainly the section of books on theology) was bought in 1928 by the Catholic University of America in Washington – see catalogue by Canuti; Peebles, pp.327ff.; Clough, 1969 and 1970. A description of the furnishing of the palace, which was much altered at the end of the 18th century, is given by Madiai and Calzini.

A detailed account of the palace in the first years of the 18th century is to be found in a letter from Mons. Giovanni Maria Lancisi, dated 9 September 1703 (*Diario*, fo.56v.–64r.). This letter reveals that as far as the principal rooms are concerned the lay-out corresponded with the present state of the building. Unfortunately the writer says nothing about the history of the palace, and is principally concerned with a proposal for altering the staircase. Lancisi criticizes the existing arrangement ('nel luogo apunto contrario . . . incominciando a sinistra') and he recommends that it could be reversed 'come piace oltremodo al Bufalini', in the belief that Orazio Albani would approve what he considered an economical scheme (ibid., fo.54). Signs of alterations can in fact be detected in the staircase and some elements in the style of Fontana may perhaps be recognized in the door-frames etc. The interior of the palace was redecorated, probably by Vanvitelli, about 1728 (J. Garms, *Disegni di Luigi Vanvitelli . . .*, Catalogue, Naples, 1973–74, pp.59f., nos.55f.).

A considerable number of drawings in Volumes 185 and 188 can be connected in varying degrees of certainty with the palace. Like all the other identifiable drawings in the volume they presumably date from the reign of Clement XI. Two drawings are of the court of the palace and several others are related to a chapel on the second floor. There follow in the catalogue below miscellaneous drawings which are probably connected with the building, while still further drawings listed as unidentified may also be projects for the palace.

One chapel in the palace is mentioned by Lancisi (*Diario*, fo.60). This he describes as 'a mano sinistra della Galleria . . . molto devota ed ornata' and it still exists on the first floor of the palace (Valenti, p.165). The Windsor drawings (nos 656–9; Figs 504–6) show a project which was not carried out in the chapel mentioned by Lancisi, but in the one on the second floor of the palace.

The drawing 658 is close in style to the drawing for the Pesaro altar, and this suggests that the same architect (Barigioni?) worked at the Palazzo Albani. The decoration contains no direct allusion to the Pope and this suggests that the commission was probably given by Cardinal Annibale Albani. It can probably be dated about 1712 (see below, the entry for Colbordolo).

ADDITIONAL BIBLIOGRAPHY:

Egidio Calzini, in *Rass. Bibl. Ital.*, XVI, 1913, p.64.
Francesco Canuti, *Catalogo dei Manoscritti che esistevano in Urbino nella Biblioteca del Papa Clemente XI*, Fano, 1939.
C. H. Clough, in *Manuscripta*, XIV (1970), pp.34ff.; see also general bibliography.
Giov. Maria Lancisi, letter of 9 November 1703 to Clement XI, in *Diario*, fo.56vo.–64ro. (See bibliography following introduction to Urbino above.)
Federico Madiai, in *Nuova Rivista Misena*, VIII, 1895, p.122.
R. Pane in R de Fusco, etc., *Vanvitelli*, 1973, pls 31–8.
Giuseppe Valenti, in *Arte e Storia*, VIII, 1889, pp.164–166, 174–176.

654 PERSPECTIVE VIEW OF THE COURTYARD (*Figure* 502) [10690]
226 × 209 mm. Pen, coloured washes. Inscribed at base: *Prospetto del Stato del' Cortile come si troua di presente . . .*

655 PERSPECTIVE VIEW OF THE COURTYARD, SHOWING PROJECTED ALTERATIONS (*Figure* 503) [10691]
233 × 280 mm. Watermark no.9. Pen, coloured washes. With index and key inscribed on a scroll to the left.

The drawing shows the same view as the preceding, and it records with its inscriptions a number of alterations being made or to be made to the palace. As the inscriptions reveal, many of the modifications shown in the drawings were carried out and are still in existence. The two drawings may be by the same artist as the perspective view of the chapel (658 below). The writing and rather eccentric spelling of the inscriptions are not Fontana's. The drawings were possibly sent to Pope Clement XI as a record of the appearance of the court before and after the restoration.

Drawings of the chapel (656–659)

656 PLAN (*Figure* 505) [10339]
305 × 215 mm. Pen, coloured washes, traces of chalk. With scale and index.

The key to the index is written on a sheet laid down beneath the drawing under the title: 'Pianta della Cappella'.

657 PERSPECTIVE VIEW (UNFINISHED) [10649]
274 × 303 mm. Watermark no.7. Chalk.

The chapel is sketched very faintly. The altar resembles in its shape the sarcophagus of the tomb of Maria Clementina Sobieski in S. Peter's designed by Filippo Barigioni and carried out by Pietro Bracci, 1739/42 (K. von Domarus, *P. Bracci, Zur Kunstgesch. d. Ausl.*, 110, Strasbourg, 1915, pp.26f.).

658 PERSPECTIVE VIEW (*Figure* 504) [10706]
474 (arched top) × 319 mm. Pen, coloured washes, gold leaf.

The drawing shows the same view as the preceding and in style it resembles that of nos 635/6 and 674.

659 STUDY OF THE CEILING FRESCO (*Figure* 506) [10707]
515 × 365 mm. Chalk, grey wash.

There is a close correspondence with the ceiling as represented in the preceding drawing. The present sheet is presumably by the artist who painted the ceiling.

Other drawings probably connected with the palace

660 ELEVATION OF A WALL, WITH PORTRAIT MEDALLIONS OF POPE CLEMENT XI (*Figure* 508) [10337]
209 × 258 mm. Watermark no.5. Pen, traces of chalk.

There can be little doubt in the case of the present drawing that it records the wall of a room towards the rear of the palace. Clement XI was born in this room and it still contains a roundel of the Pope (Fig.509) inscribed: '... HOC IN CVBICVLO NATVS EST ...'. The drawing includes two projects for a portrait roundel of the Pope; that to the left is close in character to the existing medallion.

661 STUDY FOR THE DECORATION OF A BEDROOM (*Figure* 510) [10708]
288 × 417 mm. Five sheets joined. Watermark, escutcheon with star surmounted by crown. Pen, coloured washes.

The arch of the bed alcove is decorated with the Albani arms.

662 SKETCH OF TWO BAYS OF THE DECORATION OF THE SAME [10695]
218 × 343 mm. Watermark no.28. Chalk, brown wash.

663 SKETCH OF ONE BAY OF THE DECORATION OF THE SAME [10693]
331 × 240 mm. Watermark no.28. Chalk.

The drawing is inscribed roughly in chalk with notes on colours and (?) types of materials.

664 STUDIES OF AN INSCRIBED PORTRAIT MEDALLION [10710]
202 × 225 mm. Watermark no.9. Chalk.

The drawing may be by the same hand as no.663 above and for the same scheme of decoration.

665 PROJECT FOR A DOORWAY, HALF PLAN AND ELEVATION (*Figure* 507) [10692]
324 × 233 mm. Watermark no.9. Pen, coloured washes, traces of chalk.

Its design is shown in alternative halves, with the (?) Albani star in the eared corner on the left.

666 STUDY OF A CUPBOARD [10696]
301 × 220 mm. Watermark, crown with a lily and a (?) bunch of grapes. Pen. With scale.

Inscribed at top: 'Prospetto dell' Armaria p mettere nel' Palazzo del' Ecc.[ma] Casa .../' followed by an estimate of the weight. The panels of the doors are decorated with the *monti* and star of the Albani arms.

667 ELEVATION OF A CUPBOARD [10648]
199 × 167 mm. Pen, violet wash, traces of chalk. With scale labelled *Palmi ... 10*.

The panels at the base of the cupboard are decorated with the arms of Clement XI.

668 ELEVATION OF A CUPBOARD ON A STAND [10656]
298 × 202 mm. Pen, grey wash.

The cupboard is surmounted by an elaborate decoration topped by an (?) Albani star.

669 STUDIES OF SILVER UTENSILS [10703]
225 × 186 mm. Watermark no.2. Pen, brown wash, traces of chalk.

The drawing shows a basin and two views of an urn with a spout, the second inscribed: 'La med.[a] / Brocca in / Profilo'. The base of the drawing is inscribed with an estimate of the weight.

670 DESIGN FOR A DOOR-KNOCKER (*Figure* 511) [10704]
164 × 233 mm. Watermark no.12. Pen, brown wash.

The design of the knocker is given in alternative halves, as explained in the inscription. Its boss is decorated with the *monti* and star of the Albani arms.

671 STUDY OF A PAIR OF CANDLESTICKS AND A (?) GRILLE [10705]
260 × 330 mm. Pen, brown and yellow wash, traces of chalk.

The candlesticks are decorated at the base with the *monti* and star of the Albani arms. These designs may be connected with the chapel of the palace.

Urbino, projects for the Porta Valbona

This is the subject of two drawings in Volume 188. Both appear to be projects for decorating the gateway and the second project (no.673) seems to have been carried out in part. The drawings suggest that the fabric of the gate was in existence up to the level of the cornice of the attic and that there were brick walls to each side, both articulated, as now, with a niche. The drawings are perhaps by a Roman architect, but they are not precisely like Fontana in style.

672 ELEVATION OF THE GATE (1) [10651]
472 × 363 mm. Watermark no.7. Pen, grey wash.

The drawing appears to have been executed in two stages, the doorway itself neatly drawn in brown ink in outline, and then decoration applied more clumsily in ink and grey wash.

673 ELEVATION OF THE GATE (2) (*Figure* 512) [10652]
489 × 370 mm. Watermark no.7. Pen, coloured washes. With scale.

The decoration of the attic storey over the gate corresponds roughly with that appearing over the door today.

Pesaro, S. Francesco, the altar to the Blessed Michelina Metelli

We know from a contemporary writer that in 1708, at the request of his aunt, Donna Giulia Albani, Clement XI presented to the church of S. Francesco, Pesaro, an altar for the last chapel in the right aisle, dedicated to the Blessed Michelina Metelli, a tertiary Franciscan, who lived from 1300 to 1356 (Bonucci, ed. 1855, p.107). Her body was originally laid in a sarcophagus made in 1372 by Pandolfo Malatesta, which is still preserved in the right-hand wall of the chapel. The body was transferred to the new altar in 1721 (*Cenni della vita*, pp.7ff.).

Over the altar is an upright medallion within a broken pediment, on which kneel angels carrying the altarpiece. This was originally the painting by Barocci representing the Beata contemplating Christ on the Cross (Olsen, *Barocci*, pp.207f., no.63; Schmarsow). The original was removed by the French in 1797 and is now in the Vatican. It was replaced by a copy by Consoli Luffoli (*Cenni della vita,* p.15).

The chapel was restored in 1773 at the expense of Count Raimondo Santinelli, and the figures of the angels, which had not been executed, were made by Sebastiano Pantanelli (ibid., p.14). It was probably at this time that the upper part of the altar was modified and the curvilinear panel with the dove was replaced by the present more rectilinear arrangement. The whole altar is executed in dark green marble, *giallo antico*, and alabaster.

The altar itself, the reliquary and the broken pediment are to be found in almost precisely the same form in the altar of the chapel dedicated to S. Fabiano in S. Sebastiano fuori le mura, Rome, in which Specchi and Barigioni collaborated (Titi, ed.1721, p.71), and which was originally to have had a painted altarpiece (Coudenhove-Erthal, p.116). In the medal of 1710 it is shown with the painting and without the structure behind the *mensa* containing the oval reliquary. Since the donation of the Pesaro altar took place in 1708, it can be assumed that the Windsor drawing preceded the change in the design for the decoration of the Roman altar, and presumably served as a model for it. The Windsor drawing is not by Fontana, but probably by Barigioni (see above).

ADDITIONAL BIBLIOGRAPHY:
Cenni della vita della B. Michelina Metelli da Pesaro, Pesaro, 1919 (Copy in Bibl. Oliveriana in Pesaro: Misc. A.I. e 5 m.29).
Antonio Maria Bonucci, *Vita della Beata Michelina da Pesaro*, Pesaro, 1708 (new edition, Pesaro, 1855).
H. Hager, 'Un riesame di tre cappelle di Carlo Fontana a Roma', *Commentari, XXVII*, 1976 (in course of publication).
August Schmarsow, 'Federigo Barocci, ein Begründer des Barockstils in der Malerei'. *Abhandlungen der Philologisch-Histor. Klasse der Königl. Sächs. Gesellsch. der Wiss.*, vol.XXVI, no.4, Leipzig, 1909, pp.91ff.

674 PROJECT FOR THE ALTAR, ELEVATION (*Figure* 513) [10650]
510 × 320 mm. Pen, grey and coloured washes, traces of chalk. With scale.

A document of 1705 gives a detailed account of the old tomb and may have been prepared with the alterations in view (Bonucci, p.107). The form of the *mensa* is close to that on the sarcophagus of S. Crescentinus at Urbino, see above.

The church and the Villa Albani near Colbordolo

Orazio Albani, in fulfilment of a vow, planned to build a small church on the estate which he owned in the village of Morciola, near Colbordolo, in the diocese of Urbino, about halfway to Pesaro. The church (see no.676 below) was to be a small centralized building dedicated to S. Anthony of Padua. The whole scheme was obviously inspired by Alexander VII's Assunta at Ariccia, but, whereas the latter church is surrounded by a semicircular screen, Albani's church was to follow the model of S. Andrea al Quirinale and Fontana's plans for S. Teodoro with an open space preceding the church of which the curved sides were to link the chapel with the villa itself. When Orazio died on 23 January 1712 this project was still unfulfilled. An inscription in the hall of the villa, dated May 1704, mentions the restoration of the neglected villa, where Carlo Albani (evidently the father of Clement XI) used to withdraw occasionally.

The villa plans at Windsor, nos 677/8 and the elevations, nos 679/80, show a simple country house, which would have been transformed by the alterations suggested in the drawings into something more sophisticated. This scheme, however, is not related to the 1704 project, for the inscriptions on the plans and on the estimate which accompanies them refer to the house as the 'Casino dell' Em:mo Sig.r. Card:le Albani', and this must refer to Clement XI's nephew, Annibale (born 1682), who was made a Cardinal by Clement XI on 23 December 1711, and who inherited the villa on the death of his father in 1712. The project in these drawings cannot, therefore, be dated earlier than 1712.

The fulfilment of the father's vow was, however, undertaken by Carlo, the brother of Annibale (born in 1687). He caused a so far unidentified Roman architect to prepare a new project for the church (Windsor drawings 681/5). These drawings (Figs 519 to 523) are of a church with a centralized plan, an octagon enclosed in a rectangle, and it was to be preceded by a small semi-circular Piazza, enclosed by a small hedge (as shown in the perspective view 681). The existing church at Morciola was carried out according to these plans, and the inscription over the door of the church gives the date of 1713 for the construction of the building.

There are also at Windsor drawings of an alternative project for the church (Figs 524 to 532) which was either an alternative to the one carried out, or was due to Orazio Albani. The drawings of this project are clearly by another hand, apparently that of an architect who was well acquainted with Fontana's work at S. Teodoro. These drawings (686 to 692) show a circular church on a square, stepped platform, which raises it like a monument above its surroundings. The close connection with S. Teodoro is particularly apparent in the wall articulation and in the peculiar way in which the sacristy or choir is connected with the main body of the church by little passages. Connected with this second project for the church is a further group of drawings in Volumes 185/8; they are large-scale studies of details of the door-frames for the building, and their existence suggests that very serious consideration had been given to this second project for the church.

675 SITE PLAN OF MORCIOLA [10726]
262×295 mm. Watermark no.5. Pen. With annotations, including: *Renicci di/ Colbordolo ridotti in cultura.* Further sketches are present on the *verso* and the words: *uarij disegni.*

676 PLAN OF THE PIAZZA WITH VILLA AND CHURCH (*Figure* 514) [10727]
392×546 mm. Pen, pink wash, some chalk. Inscribed: *Pianta del Casino nella Tenuta dell' Ecc:mo Sig. D. Oratio Albani a Colbordolo con piazza e / Chiesa incontro.*

The drawing must date from before 23 January 1712, when the owner, Orazio Albani, died. The church is based on a Greek cross plan, with short arms, and is closely reminiscent of the Albani chapel in S. Sebastiano fuori le mura, where Orazio was buried, and the drawing can therefore be ascribed to the workshop of Fontana. The conception is probably Fontana's own and it may even be regarded as preliminary to the Roman chapel which was begun in 1706 and structurally well advanced in 1708. The evidence for the dating of the present sheet points to October/November 1703, when Carlo Fontana was in Urbino at the request of the Pope. It is possible that, when Clement XI chose the Albani chapel as the burial place for his family, Orazio's interest in the Morciola church abated and caused him to postpone the fulfilment of his vow, especially since he resided permanently in Rome.

Drawings of the villa

677 GROUND PLAN (*Figure* 515) [10728]
241×418 mm. Watermark no.12. Pen, grey and yellow wash, traces of chalk. Inscribed: *Dimostratione dello stato Vechio, e nouo del Casino dell' Em:mo Sig.r Card.le Albani in Colbordolo.*

The areas of yellow wash indicate the existing state of the plan, and those in grey the projected alterations. The two central rooms at present are combined into a single room connecting the two doors. The staircase shown in the present drawing has gone, and is replaced by a vestibule, which adjoins the new staircase, moved to the adjacent room. The back wall of the vestibule contains the inscription of 1704, mentioned above. The present drawing can be dated about 1713, after Orazio Albani's death, when his son, Carlo, was building the church of S. Anthony.

678 FIRST-FLOOR PLAN, INCORPORATING ALTERATIONS (*Figure* 517) [10729]
241×418 mm. Watermark no.9. Pen, grey wash, some chalk. With scale. Inscribed: *Pianta del Casino dell' Em:mo Sig.r Card.le Albani in Colbordolo.*

The distribution of the rooms on the plan of the first floor corresponds with the modifications proposed in the foregoing drawing. Today the two central rooms, echoing the ground-floor distribution, are combined into a long single room.

679 ELEVATION OF THE FRONT (*Figure* 516) [10730]
244×397 mm. Pen and grey ink, grey and pink wash. With scale. Inscribed: *Prospetto presente del Casino à Colbordolo dell' Ecc:ma Casa Albani.*

Attached to the present drawing is an estimate (862.39 *scudi*) for alterations; entitled: 'Scandaglio della fabrica da rialzarsi in Colbordolo p il Casino dell Em:mo Sig:r Card:le Albani'.

680 ELEVATION OF THE FRONT, INCORPORATING ALTERATIONS (*Figure* 518) [10731]
245×399 mm. Pen and grey ink, grey and pink wash. With scale.

In the present project the third floor is extended the whole length of the building, and the central part is covered with a curved pediment enclosing a clock. This relatively inexpensive part of the project was executed and has survived, except that the pediment was replaced by a straight entablature when a terrace was built in 1961. On the street façade new windows have been inserted to the left of the middle pavilion. The existing building shows in the right-hand side of the façade a recess of half the depth of the building, which is not indicated in the plans 677/8 above.

Drawings of the Church: 1– The executed project (1713)

681 PERSPECTIVE VIEW (*Figure* 519) [10736]
347×470 mm. Pen and grey ink, grey wash. Inscribed at the base with the inscription for the panel above the doorway: *In Honorem S. Antonij Patauini / Carolus Albanus Clementis Vndecimi Nepos/ Paterni Voti memor extruxit. Anno Sal. MDCCXIII*

Stylistically the drawing shows some affinity with the drawing of SS. Apostoli (no.608) which is signed by Michetti.

682 GROUND PLAN (*Figure* 520) [10732]
387×251 mm. Pen and grey ink, grey and buff wash. With scale and annotations.

The church consists of an octagon enclosed in a rectangle, with the sacristy placed behind the high altar. The immediate forerunner of the church is that of S. Sebastiano at Urbino, begun in 1710 for Carlo Albani; the ground plan and elevations of the two buildings are almost identical (Urbino, Bibl. Univ., Fondo del Comune, Busta 179, Fasc.8). The architect of the church cannot, unfortunately, be identified, but the mason was Giuseppe Gianni, who also constructed the library of S. Francesco at Urbino (see above).

683 FRONT ELEVATION (*Figure* 521) [10733]
386×253 mm. Pen and grey ink, grey and buff wash. With scale and annotations. Inscribed: *Facciata della Chiesa.*

The coat-of-arms of the Albani family appears in the tympanum. For the inscription over the door see 681.

684 LONGITUDINAL SECTION (*Figure* 523) [10735]
359×468 mm. Pen and grey ink, coloured washes. With scale. Inscribed: *Spaccato della Chiesa per il longo.*

685 TRANSVERSE SECTION (*Figure* 522) [10734]
394×258 mm. Pen and grey ink, coloured washes. With scale. Inscribed: *Spaccato della Chiesa per il trauerso.*

Drawings of the church: 2– The unexecuted project

686 GROUND PLAN (*Figure* 524) [10718]
364×469 mm. Pen, grey wash. With scale. Inscribed: *Pianta.* With ruled ink border.

The plan is an elaboration of the schemes used by Fontana in his Cappella dell'Assuntra in the Collegio Clementino in Rome (destroyed) and at S. Teodoro (the illumination of the altarpiece, see no.690, Fig.531, approaches the former: Coudenhove–Erthal, pl.21). The drawings, and the others of the present group, closely resemble the projects (by Barigioni ?) for the sarcophagus of S. Crescentinus in the altar of the Cathedral of Urbino. There is an affinity between this plan and one by Michetti on the Vassiliewsky Island at Leningrad (see E. Lo Gatto, *Gli artisti italiani in Russia*, vol.II, *Gli architetti del sec. XVIII a Pietroburgo a nelle tenute imperiale, L'opera del genio italiano all'estero*, Serie prima, Rome, 1935, pl.XXVI).

687 FRONT ELEVATION (*Figure* 525) [10719]
365×464 mm. Pen, grey wash. With scale, inscribed: *Prospetto.* With ruled ink border.

The design of the exterior is based on Bernini's Assunta at Ariccia. A dotted ink line is present in the drawing whereby a wide pediment, as in the final design, is substituted for the dome.

688 REAR ELEVATION (*Figure* 527) [10720]
358×460 mm. Pen, grey wash. Inscribed: *Prospetto dalla parte della Sagristia.* With ruled ink border.

The little *campanili* flanking the apse again recall the disposition of the Assunta at Ariccia.

689 TRANSVERSE SECTION (1) (*Figure* 529) [10721]
364×466 mm. Watermark no.7. Pen, grey and yellow wash. Inscribed: *Spaccato.* With ruled ink border.

The conception of the vista towards the painting over the altar in the apse is reminiscent of that in the Chiesa del Miracolo attached to S. Cristina at Bolsena, which was built by Fontana's pupil Tomaso Mattei.

690 TRANSVERSE SECTION (2) (*Figure* 531) [10722]
395×258 mm. Pen, grey and yellow wash, and ruled ink border. With scale.

A variant of the foregoing, with the pilasters replaced by columns, over which the entablature breaks forward. The small bays next to the altar show alternative projects for the placing of busts (compare model G for the new sacristy of S. Peter's in Rome, attributed to Nicola Michetti; Hager, *Juvarra*, pl.35). The lantern is surmounted by an onion-shaped cupola.

691 SECTION OF THE APSE, SHOWING HIGH ALTAR (1) (*Figure* 532) [10724]
378×247 mm. Pen, grey and yellow wash, chalk. With scale. With ruled ink border.

692 SECTION OF THE APSE, SHOWING HIGH ALTAR (2) (*Figure* 530) [10723]
376×246 mm. Pen, grey and yellow wash, some chalk. With ruled ink border.

A variant of the preceding which shows the altar without columns but flanked by angels carrying palms on pedestals which bear the Albani arms.

Studies for the doorways

693 ELEVATION OF THE MAIN DOOR (*Figure* 526) [10712]
409×256 mm. Pen, traces of chalk. With scale and annotations. Inscribed: *P.*(rim)*o*

The design corresponds with that of the central doorway in 687. The door is inscribed: 'Porta Magiore segnata/ nella pianta, e prospet-/to lettera A –,' and the scale is labelled: 'Palmi *20* per la presente Porta A–.' The inscription on this and the following drawings appears to be in the same hand as those on drawings in the preceding group.

694 PROFILE OF THE CASE OF THE MAIN DOOR [10717]
252×571 mm. Two sheets joined vertically. Watermark no.30. Pen, traces of chalk. With scale. Inscribed: *2o.*

Inscribed: 'Modine del Stipite della Porta Maggiore segnata lettera A', and with labelled scale. This and the following two entries appear to be full-scale drawings of the main doorway for the use of masons or carpenters.

695 PROFILE OF THE CORNICE OF THE MAIN DOOR (*Figure* 528) [10716]
381×336 mm. Watermark no.30. Pen, traces of chalk. Inscribed: *3.o* on the *recto*, and on the *verso: Varie piante della Chiesa di Corboldolo che si pen/saua di fare.*

Inscribed in centre of the sheet: 'Modine della Cimasa della Porta Magiore' etc.

696 PROFILE OF THE FRAME OF THE WINDOW OVER THE MAIN DOORWAY [10607]
184×327 mm. Pen, traces of chalk.

Inscribed: 'Modine del Stipite della Fenestra sopra la Porta Magiore A', and 'Viuo del Muro.'

697 ELEVATION OF A SIDE DOOR [10713]
280×255 mm. Watermark no.30. Pen, traces of chalk. With scale and annotations.

The design corresponds with that of the side doors in 687. It is inscribed 'Porta laterale / segnata nella / Pianta, e prospetto / lettera. B.', and the scale is annotated to the same effect.

698 PROFILE OF THE CASE OF A SIDE DOOR [10714]
188×359 mm. Watermark no.30. Pen, chalk.

Inscribed: 'Modine del Stipito della Porta B. quale si poul' far' dritto – ò cetinato nella / conformità fà il tondo della Chiesa'. This and the following drawing appear to be full scale profiles for the side doors.

699 PROFILE OF THE CORNICE OF A SIDE DOOR [10715]
390×286 mm. Pen, chalk.
Inscribed: 'Modine della Cimasa della Porta B'.

Other parts of Italy

Bologna, an arsenal in the Forte Urbano (1712)

Five sheets in Volume 185 contain drawings of a single long room made over to an arsenal. The plan (no.700) has a scale in Bolognese feet. Details about the work are provided in a Latin inscription on drawing 703 (Fig.537), which is a study for the decoration of the end wall of the arsenal with a bust of Pope Clement XI in an elaborate setting. This inscription bears the date 1712 and refers to the Forte Urbano and the Arsenal newly installed and furnished by the Pope. The bust of the Pope was given by Antonio

Domenico Bussio ('Bussius'), the governor of the fort, on behalf of himself and his family, including a brother, Giovanni Battista, who had recently been made a Cardinal.

The architecture of the arsenal is more obviously rococo in style than any work by Fontana or his followers, and it was probably the work of a good local architect. The drawings themselves give the impression of being presentation sheets and they were presumably sent to the Pope from Bologna. The unusual watermark of the paper (no.31) would, in this case, denote a Bolognese origin.

The year 1628 is given for the foundation of the fort, which became a prison in 1859. The present drawings appear to show that the arsenal and its vestibule formed an extension to the existing structure and that they were accessible from an existing staircase.

700 PLAN, WITH ELEVATION OF MUSKET RACKS (*Figure* 533) [10308]

492×735 mm. Watermark no.31. Two sheets joined vertically. Pen, grey wash. With scale in bolognese *Pertiche* and *Piedi*.

701 CROSS SECTION, WITH PERSPECTIVE VIEW OF INTERIOR (*Figure* 534) [10305]

363×520 mm. Watermark no.31. Chalk, grey wash, pen.

The section and perspective view are presented in a fanciful way which would be suited to engraving.

702 ELEVATION OF THE END WALL (*Figure* 535) [10306]

364×521 mm. Watermark no.31. Chalk, grey washes, pen.

703 ELEVATION OF THE CENTRAL FEATURE OF THE END WALL (*Figure* 537) [10304]

524×372 mm. Watermark no.31. Chalk, grey wash, pen.

A bust of Pope Clement XI stands on a pedestal with a tablet beneath inscribed in small and large capitals:

'Armamentarium Arcis Urbanae Noviter Instauratum / Ampliori Aptioreque Supellectile Instructum / Dispositione Ac Nitore Nobilitatum / SS'MO D'NO N'RO CLEMENTE XI / Feliciter Regnante / Tanti Pontificis Marmorea Effigie Donavit / FR' ANT' DOMINICUS BUSSIUS / Eques Et Commendator Hierosolymitanus / Eiusdem Arcis Praefectus / Exigue Quidem Grati Animi Monumento / Quem Vere Clementissimum / IPSE IOANNES BAPTISTA GERMANUS FRATER / Sacra Purpura Nuper Condecoratus / Totaque Familia De Bussis Sentiunt / Ac Venerantur Anno MDCCXII.'

704 PERSPECTIVE VIEW OF THE ENTRANCE VESTIBULE (*Figure* 536) [10307]

244×399 mm. Chalk, grey wash, pen.

The doors are of metal, decorated with the *monti* and star of the Albani arms. A representation of St Barbara occupies the lunette above the door.

Cervia Nuova, view of the town (1714?)

Drawing no.705 (10331 in Volume 185; Fig.538) is a view of the town of Cervia Nuova, built in the years 1698 to 1714 on the coast of Italy between Ravenna and Rimini (see U. Foschi, in *Studi Romagnoli*, XI, 1960, pp.85–113). The town was intended to replace the old city of Cervia, which had become by the late 17th century too unhealthy to be habitable. In 1692 Bishop Riccamonti of Cervia pleaded with Pope Innocent XII for the rebuilding of the town, and permission for this was granted in a *chirografo* of 9 November 1697 (Foschi, p.86). Plans were sent from Rome by the architect Bellardino Perti (or Berti) and the first stone was laid by the Bishop on 24 January 1698 (ibid., p.88). The town was to be a fortified one, centered upon a cathedral and archiepiscopal palace, and outside the walls to the south were matching convents of the Augustinian and Franciscan Orders (drawings for these are in the Bibl. Corsini, Rome, Cod. 34K, 13; Figs 539, 540). Work continued on the building of the town during the reign of Pope Clement XI, after a temporary halt in 1703, and came to an end in 1714, although by 1710 the town was virtually completed (ibid., p.100). The Windsor drawing, possibly by Perti, probably records the completion of the work; it was possibly made in connection with the publication of an engraving, and it may date from about 1714.

705 PERSPECTIVE VIEW OF CERVIA NUOVA (*Figure* 538) [10331]

511×*c*.1440 mm. Two sheets joined vertically. Pen, coloured washes.

A blank scroll in the centre of the drawing at the top is surmounted by a *putto* carrying an escutcheon with the arms of Clement XI. Scrolls to each side of the drawing are likewise blank.

Ferrara

706 PLANS AND SECTIONS OF FERRARA CATHEDRAL SHOWING THE OLD AND THE NEW STATES OF THE NAVE (*Figure* 541) [10324]

678×496 mm. Pen, some chalk. With scale, annotations and index.

This single drawing in Volume 188 records the modernization of the nave of Ferrara cathedral, as it was carried out from 1712–35 to the designs of the Ferrarese architect Francesco Mazzarelli (Thieme Becker, sv. Mazzarelli). The drawing is un-Roman in its character and it may have been made by a Ferrarese architect and possibly in preparation for an engraving. An engraved section of the cathedral showing the nave before the reconstruction is illustrated in *La Cattedrale di Ferrara 1135–1935*, pl.XIII. Clement XI is recorded as having ordered a restoration of the choir of the cathedral in 1703 (Pastor, Eng. ed., XXXIII, p.529).

Pienza, drawings of the cathedral and the Palazzo Piccolomini

A group of five drawings in Volume 188 record the appearance of the Cathedral and the Palazzo Piccolomini at Pienza. They are accompanied by a short manuscript (not transcribed below) describing some of the features of the two buildings. The drawings must be by a local architect, so clumsy are they in technique; their presence in Volume 188 suggests that they were made on behalf of Clement XI and sent to him in Rome (for Pienza, see E. Carli, *Pienza*, Siena, 1966).

707 PLAN OF THE CATHEDRAL [10639]

483×339 mm. Watermark, Agnus Dei with letters V and B. Pen, mauve wash, traces of chalk. With scale in *palmi romani*, index letters and annotations. Inscribed: *Pianta del Duomo.*

The index letters are explained in the accompanying text.

708 ELEVATION OF THE FAÇADE OF THE CATHEDRAL [10641]

432×308 mm. Watermark, small cross (?). Pen, grey wash, traces of chalk. With scale in *palmi romani*. Inscribed: *prospetto del duomo.*

The campanile is included in the elevation.

709 LONGITUDINAL SECTION OF THE CATHEDRAL [10642]

269×448 mm. Watermark, figure in small oval. Pen, grey washes, traces of chalk. Inscribed: *Spachato del duomo.*

710 GROUND-FLOOR PLAN OF THE PALAZZO PICCOLOMINI [10640]

547×*c.*415 mm. Watermark, small cross on three *monti*. Pen, pink wash, some chalk. With scale in *palmi romani*. Inscribed: *Pianta del Palazzo a terreno* and *Giardino.*

711 ELEVATION OF THE FAÇADE OF THE PALAZZO PICCOLOMINI [10643]

286×412 mm. Pen, grey washes, traces of chalk. With scale in *palmi romani*. Inscribed: *Prospetto del Palazo.*

A correction to the roof is given on a strip of paper pasted to the drawing.

Sora (?)

712 SORA (?), SITE PLAN OF PART OF THE TOWN SHOWING LANDS BELONGING TO THE DUKE OF SORA AND THE CAPUCHINS [10645]

615×434 mm. Two sheets joined horizontally. Watermark no.7. Pen, grey and blue wash, chalk. With scale and index.

The key to the index is inscribed at the top of the page. It includes references to sections of land (N and R) which appear to be the subject of negotiations between the Duke of Sora and the Capuchins. The group of drawings for a library for Sicilian Capuchins, catalogued below as unidentified, may be connected with the Capuchins referred to in the present drawing. Clement XI is recorded as having assisted in the restoration of the church of Sora (Pastor, Eng.ed., XXXIII, p.529).

Sulmona, the Bishop's palace

The earthquake of 1706 severely damaged the mediaeval cathedral outside the town of Sulmona and particularly the Bishop's Palace which adjoined it on the left. Bishop Bonaventura Martinelli, who was appointed to the See in the following year (Ignaz. di Pietro, p.358), planned to re-erect the episcopal palace nearer to the town, together with the Seminary. The project, of which important details are known from a manuscript in the cathedral archives, was supported by a donation of Clement XI, made to the town after the earthquake (cf. Piccirilli, pp.73ff.; Sulmona, Arch. Catt., fo.35, no.29, bambagine).

The building was not far advanced when Martinelli took over: 'non oltrepassava le soglie delle finestre', and it was in 'quella porzione del Palazzo, che racchiude oggidì la metà della Sala e le sole sei camere dell'appartamento che si abita da Monsig. Vescovo'. This refers to the left part of the existing building, the four wings of which enclose a rectangular courtyard: 'unicam.te occupaua una porzione di quel sito, che oggi comprende tutto il Vescouile Palazzo'.

The building project was discussed by the Chapter on 30 November 1707 (Arch. Catt., Liber Cap., fo.157), and agreement was reached in the following month (fo.35, no.29, bambagine). The completion of the building, and its extension to four wings, is therefore the result of Martinelli's initiative. The bishop's plans were more ambitious, however, and included a new cathedral within the complex (on the events leading up to this idea, see Piccirilli p.74, notes 1 and 5).

The Bishop's Palace must have been mainly completed in 1709, as is indicated by the inscription above the central window of the main floor: *MVNIFICENTISSIMIS CLEMENTIS P.P.XI Auspicijs Bonauentura Episcopus Sulmonen. Erexit AD. MDCCVIIII.*

Three drawings for this project, of which only parts were executed, are preserved at Windsor (nos 713 to 715). The 'Seminarium Clementinum' on the right and the Bishop's Palace on the left were to have balanced each other round the Greek cross cathedral. The inscription on drawing no.715, boldly anticipating the future, gives the year 1713 as the date for the consecration. This means that the drawing was probably made soon after 1709, when the Bishop's Palace was completed. The author of the Windsor drawings was not responsible for the whole scheme but only for the extension to be carried out after 1709. They show the Bishop's Palace and the nave of the church in yellow to indicate that these parts were completed or at least begun when the drawings were made.

The 'minuta di fede degli architetti' of 8 November 1716, when building activities were resumed, lists the parts that were then finished (Arch. Catt. fasc.XVI, no.4). The description of the Milan architects Giovanni Battista Pianezza and Francesco del Zoppo of the sections completed agrees only in part with the indications on the Windsor drawings, although basically the project shown in them was still valid. The written account confirms the drawings in that it describes the Bishop's Palace as 'resa abitabile', but the *cortile* 'Couerto, e Scouerto' had, as at present, an arcade on only one side. This leads to the conclusion that the plans must have been changed after the Windsor designs were finished, which meant sacrificing parts already built or begun in order to gain more space for the *cortile.* Part of the site on the right, which was to have been occupied by the left transept of the church and the rooms attached to it in depth, were incorporated in the courtyard.

The staircase still occupies the position indicated in the ground plan, but has been drastically restored in modern times. The bishop's apartments 'consistente in stanze num.o 6 di filo', connected by doors to the *Cancelleria* in the block on the street, also conform to the drawings. It is significant that the two architects refer to both the Bishop's Palace and the church as completed. The second staircase in the back wing was executed in accordance with the Windsor plans, and the rooms near it were completed in 1716. The refectory is considerably shorter than in no.713. The dormitory in the drawing was in the event divided into two dormitories.

What was envisaged in 1716 was therefore only a fragment of Martinelli's grandiose scheme, and even of this reduced project only a single wing on the right of the church was actually built. The sudden cessation of building activities was probably due to the death of Martinelli on 19 August 1715. His successor was more concerned with the restoration of the old cathedral, which was carried out between 1714 and 1716 (cf. Piccirilli, loc.cit.).

Research in the archives of the cathedral of Sulmona has, unfortunately, yielded no information about the architect of the Windsor project, nor about his predecessor, who was in charge of the first building phase. The financial donations of the Pope prove, however, that a direct link with Rome existed, and this is confirmed by the connection between the ground plan no.713, and the church of the Ospizio di S. Michele, Rome. Chronologically the Sulmona project is followed by Filippo Raguzzini's Ospedale di S. Gallicano in Trastevere (1725–26).

ADDITIONAL BIBLIOGRAPHY:
P. Piccirilli, *Monumenti architettonici Sulmonensi dal XIV al XVI Secolo*, Lanciano, 1886, pp.73ff.
Ignazio di Pietro, *Memorie storiche della Città di Sulmona*, Naples, 1804, pp.358f.

713 GROUND-FLOOR PLAN (*Figure* 544) [10322]
448×635 mm. Watermark no.9. Pen, yellow and pink wash, traces of chalk. With scale in Neapolitan *palmi* and annotations. Inscribed: *Prima / Pianta del Palazzo e Seminario Episcopale / di Sulmona.*

The left wing and the entrance to the church are indicated in yellow; the remainder is in pink. The rooms adjoining the left cross-arm of the church, which were incorporated in the staircase, are in pink.

714 FIRST-FLOOR PLAN (*Figure* 543) [10321]
439×654 mm. Watermark no.9. Pen, yellow and pink wash, traces of chalk. Inscribed: *Seconda / Pianta / seù del Apartam.o / civile.*

715 ELEVATION AND SECTION (*Figure* 542) [10323]
514×682 mm. Watermark no.9. Pen, grey, pink and yellow wash, traces of chalk. With annotations.

The Bishop's Palace as shown here corresponds essentially with its present appearance, though the window pediments have either been removed or were never executed. Three inscriptions are transcribed at the top of the drawing; they are indexed A, B and C, referring to three areas of the façade. The frame of the tablet above the middle window of the Bishop's Palace had been modified, but the inscription indicated on the drawing (index B) can still be seen (cf. above). The corresponding inscription for the façade of the Seminary (index C) is indicated on the right of the drawing. The section occupies the lower part of the sheet. Curiously enough the whole of the left cross-arm of the church up to the vault and the lower cornice of the drum is shown in yellow wash, which would lead one to assume that this left arm was already built, if the ground plan, no.713, did not show clearly at which point the new architect became involved. Because of the omission of the loggias on the three sides and of the left cross-arm of the church, the present courtyard is considerably larger than that shown in the drawing.

Terracina

716 Antonio Ludovisi
VIEW OF A SPRING IN THE CAMPAGNA IN THE VICINITY OF TERRACINA [10595]
476×362 mm. Two sheets joined horizontally. Watermark, no.9. Pen, coloured washes. With inscription and index.

The lower sheet contains a long description of the site, which is represented on the upper sheet. It is a copy of a text signed by 'Antonio Ludovisij di Cond.ne' (?), who was apparently asked to survey the spring at the request of the 'Contest-(abil)e Colonna'. The text is entitled: 'Pianta è dischritt:ne della fontana di San Marco, principio et uno de Capi del Fiume Maseno, posta è situata nel Teritorio della / Terra di S. Lorenzo, . . .'. The main features of the site, including the nearby church of S. Marco, are described at length and the other fountains on the course of the river are mentioned. This apparently ended at the port of Terracina, thirty miles distant.

Maps connected with fortification and warfare: Italy

717 MAP OF NORTHERN ITALY, ILLUSTRATING ROUTES FOR TRANSPORTING GRAIN TO SWITZERLAND [10626]
382×533 mm. Pen, coloured washes. With scale and annotations.

A panel in the bottom left-hand corner describes routes for the transport of grain; it is entitled: 'DELINEATIONE GEOGRAFICA. / Indicante il modo da pratticarsi per il trasporto / de Grani dal' nostro Stato Eccl'co nel Paese de Suizzeri quale puol essere per due Strade.'

718 SKETCH MAP OF PART OF LOMBARDY, SHOWING POSITIONS OF FRENCH AND GERMAN TROOPS [10309]
419×559 mm. Watermark no.8 (?). Pen, coloured washes. With annotations.

This clumsily-drawn map is of an area which includes the towns of Piacenza, Parma and Mantua.

719 MAP OF THE TERRITORY NORTH OF FERRARA [10625]
304×258 mm. Watermark no.5. Pen, coloured washes. With index.

The key to the index is in French; some of the letters refer to strategic points in a possible German advance across the Po.

720 Charles Smith of Carington
PLAN OF THE FORTRESS OF FERRARA [10314]
547×731 mm. Watermark, letters GLB in oval. Pen, coloured washes, gold leaf. With scale in Ferrarese feet and index. Inscribed at top *Disegno Primo* and signed, lower left: *Misurata, e disegnata da Carlo Smitheo di Carington Inglese*.

The key to the index is surmounted by the Albani arms (shown in part) and it is entitled: 'La uera Pianta della Fortezza di / FERRARA come si troua al presente'.

721 Charles Smith of Carington
PERSPECTIVE VIEW OF THE FORTRESS OF FERRARA (*Figure* 546) [10313]
480×705 mm. Watermark as preceding. Pen, coloured washes, gold leaf. With index. Inscribed at top *Disegno secondo*, and signed, bottom right, as in preceding drawing.

The Albani arms are again present on the key to the index, which is entitled: 'La Fortezza di FERRARA in / Prospettiua Caualiera con suo ue:/ro Profilo.'. The upper part of the sheet contains what appears to be a section taken across the moat of the citadel, showing the trajectory of a cannon ball fired from the parapet.

722 MAP OF THE FORTIFICATIONS OF FERRARA [10312]
385×523 mm. Watermark no.8. Pen and black ink, coloured washes. With index.

A cartouche containing the arms of Clement XI occurs in the upper left-hand corner. The key to the index, lower right, is entitled: 'Tauola delli nomi delle fortificazioni fatte/ in Ferrara, e di molte altre opere fatte / per rendere ben diffesa la d.[a] Citta e Citadella.'

723 COMACCHIO: PLANS AND VIEWS [10311]
653×523 mm. Pen, coloured washes. With index and annotations. Inscribed in capitals, bottom right: *Comacchio Sorpresa dalli Alemani Li XXIIII Maggio MDCCVIII*'.

Near the top of the sheet is a cartouche with an inscription referring to the Emperor Joseph and the taking of Comacchio. The Pope's youngest nephew Alessandro Albani was in command of a body of Papal troops at the taking of Comacchio (see L. Lewis, *Connoisseurs and Secret Agents in Rome*, 1961, p.38).

724 COMACCHIO: PLANS OF THREE FORTIFIED SITES [10310]
425×775 mm. Watermark, three graded crescents, with letters. Pen, coloured washes. With annotations.

The two plans at the bottom of the page are more careful renderings of the two fortified towers shown in the preceding drawing. The top of the page contains an inscription, dated 1708, which corresponds with that at the top of the preceding drawing, and the plan of a third fortified site, the church of *S. Agostino in Comachio.*

Maps connected with fortification and warfare outside Italy

725 MAP OF THE FRENCH COAST NEAR MARSEILLES, WITH KEY TO FORTIFICATIONS (1695) [10301]
435×750 mm. Watermark, small bunch of grapes. Two sheets joined vertically. Pen with black and brown ink, coloured washes. With scale in *toises* and full index.

The plan is inscribed, upper right: 'Plan de la Coste de Marseille / depuis le cap de la Croisette jusquau cap de / Niolon avec les differentes Batteries qui y ont eté Construite pour Sopposer aux / Ennemies En lannee 1695.'

726 OUTLINE MAP OF THE PORT OF ANTIBES [10303]
340×515 mm. Watermark, sun with face and ten rays. Pen and black ink, coloured washes. With scale in *toises* and full index of fortifications. Inscribed, upper left: '*PLAN / DE LA VILLE D'ANTIBES*'.

Innumerable small letters are inscribed on the site of the waters of the harbour; they are not explained in the index.

727 OUTLINE MAP OF THE TOWN OF TORTOSA (SPAIN) [10302]
278×436 mm. Watermark, large crown (?) of which only a small part is visible. Pen, coloured washes. With scale in Spanish feet and full index in Spanish, including references to the fortifications of the town.

728 Benedykt Renard
OUTLINE MAP OF THE TOWN OF KAMINIEC, POLAND (1713) (*Figure* 547) [10300]
452×575 mm. Partly laid down. Watermark, lily in oval with illegible letter. Pen, coloured washes. With scale in *toises* and full index in French. Signed, bottom left: *Benedictus Renard Polonus delineavit: Anno 1713.*

A scroll, bottom left, containing the key to the plan, is surmounted by the papal/Albani arms and inscribed at the top: 'Plan de la Ville et Chateau, / de Kaminiec le 25. 8bre 1713.' The index includes references to the fortifications of the town. Renard is presumably identifiable with the Polish architect and engineer, Benedykt Renard, who is recorded in Thieme Becker (vol.28, 1934, p.154), and as a participant in Accademia di S. Luca competitions in 1705, 1706 and 1708 (Marconi, etc.).

Unidentified drawings I: Drawings referring to ecclesiastical buildings

Designs for a convent

Two plans in Volume 185 record a project for the rebuilding of a small convent (Fig.548). The convent is possibly to be located in Urbino. The drawings are not greatly different from those produced in Fontana's workshop, but the inscriptions are in a different hand from his. The scale is in *palmi romani.*

729 GROUND-FLOOR PLAN [10315]
735×470 mm. Watermark no.7. Pen, grey wash, chalk. With annotations.

The existing buildings on the site appear to be those shown in outline in ink; the areas to be newly constructed are probably those shown in grey, with the exception of the church and the outer wall of the convent (see following drawing).

730 FIRST-FLOOR PLAN (*Figure* 548) [10316]
710×467 mm. Watermark no.7. Pen, grey wash, chalk. With scale in *p*:(almi) *Romani*, and annotations.

The church and the wall around the site are indicated in chalk and grey wash, the main convent block in brown ink and grey wash, with the existing (?) walls in chalk. This suggests that the main convent building was the only part where rebuilding is proposed in the present plan, up to and including an arch which passes across the street in front of the site and which here leads to a 'Vigna'.

Designs for a centralized church

Volume 185 contains two unsigned drawings, a ground plan (no.731) and a longitudinal section (no.732) of a church with the Albani coat-of-arms at several points (Figs 550, 551). The church was to be incorporated in an existing building, which is indicated in the ground plan.

The section (no.732) differs in several important respects from the plan. The apses leading out of the main octagon are omitted in the drawing; the chapels on the cross axis now seem to be shallow, rectangular spaces; the vestibule and choir are also rectangular, but slightly deeper, and in the latter case an apse is added to contain the high altar.

The decorative details suggest that the drawings are by an architect from Fontana's immediate circle. There are certain similarities, though the scale is about 20 *palmi* larger, with S. Maria del Suffragio in Ravenna, not only in the ground plan and the elevation, but also topographically (cf. Heinrich Strack, *Zentral-und Kuppelkirchen der Renaissance in Italien*, Berlin, 1882, pl.30, no.27). The assertions of Coudenhove-Erthal (p.131, note 240) and Ugo Donati (p.378) that Francesco Fontana was involved in the building of S. Maria del Suffragio, which was started in 1701 according to Gaetano Fabri, *Memorie Sacre di Ravenna*, 1852, pp.463ff., after a design by Carlo Fontana, have been confirmed in recent research by Werner Oechslin.

731 PLAN (*Figure* 550) [10344]
537×386 mm. Watermark no.9. Pen, grey and yellow wash, traces of chalk. With scale.

732 LONGITUDINAL SECTION (*Figure* 551) [10343]
388×540 mm. Watermark no.9. Pen, grey, yellow and pink wash, traces of chalk.

The differences between the plan and the section suggest that the section may belong to a different, possibly later, stage of the planning.

Drawing of a monastic building

733 SHEET OF SKETCHES [10646]
252×410 mm. Watermark no.7. Chalk, pen.

On the right of the sheet is a section of a building containing rooms which are labelled 'Capitolo', 'Refettorio' and 'Cantina'. On the left occurs what appears to be the elevation of the façade of a small church, with a section through an arcaded building beside it to the left.

Drawings referring to a library constructed by Sicilian Capuchins

Six drawings in Volume 188 appear to be connected with such a library, which is referred to in the inscription on drawing 734. Four of the drawings appear to be in a fairly clumsy hand, no.734 itself, and nos 737, 738 and 739, which are drawings of bookcases. The library was perhaps of the same kind as that founded by Clement XI in the Franciscan monastery at Urbino (see above), but the site has not been identified. It may conceivably have some connection with the Capuchin monastery at Sora (?) which is referred to in the inscriptions on plan no.712 (see above).

734 ELEVATION OF A DOORWAY (*Figure* 549) [10702]
432×375 mm. Watermark, lily in single oval, letters C (?) and B. Pen, traces of chalk. With scale labelled *Pede 6 –*. Inscribed on a square of paper laid beneath the sheet: *Disegni delle Scanzie / della Libraria fatti da / PP. Capuccini Siciliani.*

The doorway is surmounted by a cartouche bearing the Albani arms.

735 SKETCH OF THE SAME [10699]
210×138 mm. Watermark no.5. Pen, chalk.

This small sketch shows the left half of a door corresponding with the preceding.

736 STUDY OF A BOOKCASE [10700]
212×237 mm. Pen, traces of chalk. With scale (unfinished).

The drawing is of the same character as the preceding, and the bookcase is articulated with pilasters of the same kind as those flanking the doorway in the same drawing.

737 ELEVATION OF A BOOKCASE [10701]
351×498 mm. Pen, grey wash. With scale labelled *Parme* [sic] *Romane*.

In style the drawing resembles no.734 above. The bookcase resembles in its general shape that represented in drawing no.736. In design it would appear to be the work of a local craftsman.

738 ELEVATION OF ONE END OF THE SAME [10694]
276×203 mm. With illegible (?) watermark. Pen, grey wash, traces of chalk.

By the same hand as the preceding.

739 ELEVATION OF A BOOKCASE [10698]
263×385 mm. Pen, blue wash. With scale labelled *Palmi Romani.*

The drawing appears to be in a similar style as the two foregoing studies, and it may thus be connected with the same work.

Unidentified drawings II: Drawings referring to secular (?) buildings

740 STUDY OF A PANELLED CEILING [10333]
259×430 mm. Laid down. Ink. With annotations and scale in *palmi romani.*

The room is irregular in plan, with a single window, two doors and a 'Porticella della scala secreta'. The drawing may represent a room of the Palazzo Albani at Urbino.

741 PLAN AND SECTION OF AN ATTIC [10335]
268×193 mm. Watermark no.7. Pen, grey wash, traces of chalk. With scale.

The drawing may refer to the Palazzo Albani at Urbino.

742 ELEVATION OF A DOORWAY [10336]
312×224 mm. Watermark no.5. Pen, traces of chalk. With scale and measurements.

The relatively simple character of the case suggests that the drawing refers to an internal doorway. It may be connected with the Palazzo Albani at Urbino.

743 PLAN OF A SMALL CHAPEL AND OTHER ROOMS [10338]
*C.*200×267 mm. Pen, grey and yellow wash, some chalk. With scale and annotations.

The plan shows a group of rooms centered upon one labelled 'Capella'. It may illustrate a project for piercing two windows in the walls of this chapel; they are superimposed in ink on the grey wash and coloured grey at the sides.

744 SECTION IN PERSPECTIVE OF PART OF A RAMPART WITH A PARAPET [10341]
380×537 mm. Pen. With scale in *piedi.* Inscribed at top *Profilo in prospettiua dell terrapieno, e parapetto, e sue banchette, e camini di Ronda,* and on *verso, Disegni Stampe.*

The drawing may refer to the fortifications of Ferrara, which are illustrated in other drawings in Volume 185 (see above).

745 ELEVATION OF A WALL SURMOUNTED BY A VAULTED CEILING [10352]
274×416 mm. Laid down. Pen, grey washes, some chalk. With scale.

The drawing appears to be a project for the modification of a 15th-century room by the introduction of a modern doorway (surmounted by a star) and of matching windows to each side of it. The style of the frames of the door and windows appears to be too flamboyant for any architect in the immediate circle of Fontana. The project may be connected with the alteration of the Palazzo Albani at Urbino.

746 VIEW OF A TOWN (*Figure* 555) [10629]
243×378 mm. Watermark no.7. Pen, coloured washes.

An object near the centre of the drawing, lying near the river, appears to be a small watermill. It is inscribed: 'F.B / Paue:/sius'.

747 VIEW OF THE SAME (?), DETAIL [10627]
350×278 mm. Pen.

The present drawing appears to record the same watermill(?) as that represented in the foregoing view, and the area of the riverbank in its vicinity. There are, however, many discrepancies between the objects shown in the two drawings. This drawing resembles in the (very coarse) style of its draughtsmanship the site plan of Morciola no.675. It is possible that the present two views refer also to this town.

748 SITE PLAN OF A BUILDING ON A *STRADA DEL BALESTIERE* [10697]
194×330 mm. Pen, yellow wash. With scale labelled *Palmi Romani.*

The drawing shows the outline of a roughly rectangular site bounded on its longer sides by a 'Giardino' and a 'Strada del Balestiere', and marked on its shorter sides 'Muro diuisorio trà la Stalla, e la Scala' and 'Muro diuisorio trà le case doue habita il Sig: Stefano / Gini, e Monsù Giouanni'.

Project for an Albani villa

Two drawings in Volume 188 are of a small villa, of which the window frames are decorated with the *monti* and star of the Albani arms. It is not known for which site the villa was designed, or whether it was built. The style of the architecture suggests a good, probably North Italian architect of the early 18th century. The drawings themselves, as suggested by the watermark, may have been produced in Rome.

749 GROUND-FLOOR PLAN (*Figure* 554) [10725]
278×397 mm. Pen and grey ink, grey wash. With scale in *palmi romani*.

750 FRONT ELEVATION (*Figure* 553) [10709]
249×415 mm. Watermark no.7. Pen and grey ink, grey wash.

Unidentified drawings III: Drawings of church ornaments

Three projects for lamps

Drawings 751 to 753 (10318 to 10320 in Volume 185) are projects for lamps mounted in elaborate rococo settings – the first two sheets sketched in chalk and the third drawn more carefully in wash. The lower part of the setting incorporates a composition with figures, but this is too roughly drawn for any details to be made out. No arms or escutcheons are incorporated in the designs, but it can be assumed that they were commissioned by the Pope or by one of his family.

751 PROJECT FOR SMALL LAMP [10318]
718×275 mm. Two sheets joined horizontally. Watermark, *Agnus Dei* in circle. Black chalk.

752 PROJECT FOR LARGE LAMP WITH *PUTTI* (*Figure* 552) [10319]
755×281 mm. Two sheets joined horizontally. Watermark, lily on *monti* in circle. Black chalk.

753 PROJECT FOR DECORATED LAMP AND TWO *PUTTI* [10320]
549×*c*.411 mm. Watermark, no.9. Chalk, grey wash. Inscribed on the *verso: Disegni di lampa.*

The drawing is not laid down, but bound into Volume 185. The upper part of the sheet (not included in the measurement) had been trimmed and folded. Alternative designs are given for the upper part of the setting.

Drawings of a font (?) and a tabernacle

754 DESIGN FOR A FONT (?), PLAN AND ELEVATION [10353]
338×215 mm. Laid down. Pen, grey wash, traces of chalk. With scale.

The font (?) has handles at the sides, decorated with winged cherubs' heads. It is surmounted by what appears to be a lid in the shape of a domed circular temple with a statue above.

755 PLAN AND ELEVATION OF A TABERNACLE (*Figure* 557) [10581]
424×280 mm. Pen, coloured washes, traces of chalk. With scale labelled *Palmi Romani.*

Two designs for holy oil burners

756 PROJECT WITH PARTLY GILT ARM AND BURNER CASE [10584]
467×367 mm. Pen, coloured washes.

The burner is supported on a heavy arm of elaborately-wrought metal, partly gilt. Beneath the burner are the *monti* of the Albani arms, conceived as small rocks, and above the burner is a large star. This part of the drawing projects above the laid down sheet (it is not included in the measurement).

757 PROJECT WITH A WHOLLY GILT ARM AND BURNER CASE [10585]
546×*c*.415 mm. Watermark no.7. Pen, coloured wash.

The drawing forms a bound sheet in Volume 185. A square of paper pasted on the sheet is inscribed with notes on colours and materials to be used. The reference to only partial gilding in the inscription suggests that it refers to the foregoing drawing, not to no.757.

Studies of a statue of S. Andrew and its pedestal

There are two drawings of this subject in Volume 188. They appear to be in the hand of a painter or sculptor, rather than in that of an architect. Neither the artist nor the work itself has been identified.

758 ELEVATION OF THE STATUE ON ITS PEDESTAL [10588]
265×186 mm. Watermark no.2. Chalk. Inscribed on the pedestal: *Pmi 9.*

The measurement probably refers to the height or width of the pedestal, in which case the statue would be between 20 and 30 *palmi* in height.

759 ELEVATION OF THE PEDESTAL [10589]
194×225 mm. Chalk.

The drawing shows a representation on a larger scale of the pedestal of the preceding drawing. It is inscribed 'S ANDREA'.

Projects for an ornament on a pedestal

Two drawings in Volume 188 are studies for an ornament on a pedestal. The symbolism of the ornament alludes partly to the papacy and it is possible that it was intended for the decoration of S. Peter's or the Vatican.

760 PROJECT WITH A FLAMING HEART [10637]
364×165 mm. Watermark no.8. Pen and brown inks, traces of chalk.

The pedestal is eared and decorated with a cherub's head, a mitre and a papal tiara. The ornament it supports consists of two dolphins with a shell on which is displayed a flaming heart. A ribbon around the shell is inscribed 'TV FILIVS DEI VIVI'.

761 PROJECT WITH CROSS AND KEYS [10638]
361×153 mm. Pen and brown inks, traces of chalk.

The main variation between this and the preceding project lies in the substitution of a cross and keys for the heart within the shell at the top of the ornament.

Projects for a reliquary case (?)

762 STUDY OF THE CASE (?) [10655]
167×167 mm. Laid down. Chalk.

The drawing shows an elaborate pedestal over which is an oval frame surmounted by a cross. The oval probably represents a window through which a reliquary was to be made visible.

763 STUDY OF THE SAME (?) [10657]
111×91 mm. Chalk.

The drawing is laid down on the same page as two drawings which are connected above with the high altar of the Cathedral of Urbino, 635/636; it may be connected with the foregoing study.

Seven studies for candlesticks

Drawings 764 to 770 (10669 to 10675 in Volume 188) are studies for candlesticks, of which five are decorated with the Albani insignia. The drawings are bound immediately after the projects for the high altar of the Cathedral of Urbino (see above) and they are most probably connected with the candlesticks presented for the altar by Orazio Albani (see introduction to the high altar of Urbino Cathedral). The Treasury of the Cathedral now contains no candlesticks corresponding with any of the following projects.

764 FIRST PROJECT [10669]
312×185 mm. Laid down. Watermark no.7. Pen, blue wash.

765 SECOND PROJECT [10670]
320×209 mm. Pen, grey wash, traces of chalk.

By the same hand as the following drawing where the Albani insignia are present.

766 THIRD PROJECT [10671]
361×259 mm. Watermark no.7. Pen, grey wash.

767 FOURTH PROJECT [10672]
430×165 mm. Laid down. Watermark no.7. Pen, grey wash, traces of chalk.

By the same hand as the following drawing, where the Albani insignia are present.

768 FIFTH PROJECT [10673]
430×155 mm. Laid down. Watermark no.7. Pen, grey wash, chalk.

769 SIXTH PROJECT (*Figure* 556) [10674]
605×228 mm. Laid down; folded at the top. Watermark no.8(?) (cut on right). Pen, grey wash, traces of chalk.

770 SEVENTH PROJECT [10675]
580×247 mm. Laid down; folded at the top. Watermark no.7 (cut). Pen, grey wash, traces of chalk.

By the same hand as the preceding; both designs incorporate the Albani *monti* and star.

Study of a frame

771 STUDY OF A FRAME [10676]
237×360 mm. Watermark, coronet with six-pointed star. Pen. With two scales, the upper one labelled *Palmo con cui si e misurato*, the lower one *Scala di Palmi Romani*.

The frame is decorated with *putti* playing musical instruments and carrying flowers. The unusual watermark of the sheet and the presence of the upper scale suggests that the frame, which is probably that of a Holy Picture, was for (or existing in) a church outside Rome, possibly at Urbino.

Six drawings of reliquaries or pyxes and one of an ornament

Drawings 772 to 778 (10677 to 10683 in Volume 188) comprise six studies of reliquaries or pyxes (cf.Fig.558) and one study of an ornament decorated with a relief. The drawings may be connected with the furnishings of the Cathedral of Urbino.

772 FIRST PROJECT [10677]
260×152 mm. Laid down. Watermark no.12. Pen, grey wash.

The reliquary is in the shape of a *putto* holding aloft a glory.

773 SECOND PROJECT [10678]
235 × 188 mm. Laid down. Pen.

The pyx is encircled by a wreath supported on a base.

774 THIRD PROJECT [10679]
225 × 109 mm. Laid down. Watermark no.12. Pen, brown and yellow wash.

The pyx is encircled by a frame decorated with representations of the Albani *monti* and star.

775 VERSION OF THE SECOND PROJECT [10680]
239 × 199 mm. Watermark no.12. Pen, yellow wash.

776 FOURTH PROJECT (*Figure* 558) [10681]
421 × 279 mm. Laid down. Watermark no.8. Pen, brown wash, traces of chalk.

The reliquary is decorated with *putti* and *putti* heads.

777 STUDY OF AN ORNAMENT [10682]
549 × 415 mm. Watermark no.7. Chalk.

The base of the ornament is cut out and folded. The design is surmounted by angels supporting a large star; in the centre is an elaborate rococo frame enclosing a relief composition showing a pope(?) in procession.

778 FIFTH PROJECT [10683]
845 × *c*.415 mm. Three sheets joined horizontally. Watermark no.7. Pen, chalk. Inscribed on the *verso: Varij Disegni,* [(?)] *stemmij*, and with a sum.

The central part of the bottom of the sheet is folded (it is included in the measurement). The inscription appears to indicate that a group of drawings for *stemmij* was folded inside the present large sheet.

Unidentified drawings IV: Drawings of miscellaneous objects

779 STUDIES OF A SEXTANT (?) [10332]
314 × 466 mm. Pen.

The main studies on the sheet are diagrams of two scales, one semi-circular, and one a quarter circle with a movable arm attached to the drawing.

780 STUDY OF AN UNIDENTIFIED CONTAINER [10334]
455 × 310 mm. Chalk, Pen.

The object is represented within a frame in the centre of the page. It is roughly cylindrical and pierced with slits.

Two studies of Albani coats-of-arms

The following two drawings are widely separated within Volume 188 but they appear to be by the same draughtsman. The inscription on the *verso* of the first refers to a church of S. Isidoro, and it may be that the drawings are connected with the church of this name in Rome, of which the façade was redecorated during the papacy of Pope Clement XI to designs by Carlo Bizzacheri. Drawings for the church may, alternatively, have been wrapped in the first of these coats-of-arms drawings, and they may be missing or laid down in one of the Albani volumes and still to be identified. In style the present two drawings resemble the profile drawings for the doors of the church at Colbordolo, and they may be connected with that church, rather than with S. Isidoro.

781 STUDY OF THE COAT-OF-ARMS OF POPE CLEMENT XI [10579]
337 × 246 mm. Watermark no.7. Pen, traces of chalk. Inscribed on *verso: Varie piante di* [*S. Isidoro*].

The drawing acts as the frontispiece to Volume 188.

782 STUDY OF THE COAT-OF-ARMS OF THE ALBANI FAMILY WITH A DUCAL CORONET [10689]
387 × 258 mm. Pen, traces of chalk.

Study of a cubic block bearing a Latin inscription

783 PERSPECTIVE VIEW [10711]
274 × 284 mm. Chalk, brown wash, pen. Inscribed at bottom: *Il masso del Marmo della Sud.ª Inscrittione è alto palmi 3¾ largo p le altre parti palmi 3½.*

The inscription on the block reads as follows: 'M. Valerius. Messalla. Coruinus / P. Rutilius Lupus. L. Iunius Silanus / L. Pontus mela. D. Marius / Niger Heredes. C. Cesti & / L. Cestius quae ex parte ad: / Eum fratris Hereditas: / M. Agripae munere per: / Venit ex ea Pecunia Quam / Prosuis: partibus Receper / Ex uenditione Acta. Licor / Quae. Eis per edictum Aedit / In Sepulcrum. C. Cesti. ex / Testamento Eius inferre / non Licuit'.

Concordance of Numbers

Number of sheet in Windsor Inventory	Number in the present catalogue
Volume 168	
9271	318
9272	317
9273	324
9274	347
9275	348
9276	328
9277	323
9278	322
9279	321
9280	320
9281	319
9282	327
9283	329
9284	325
9285	326
9286	345
9287	346
9288	342
9289	341
9290	311
9291	312
9292	313
9293	314
9294	339
9295	343
9296	340
9297	349
9298	350
9299	351
9300	334
9301	335
9302	333
9303	338
9304	316
9305	336
9306	337
9307	315
9308	331
9309	344
9310	330
9311	332
Volume 169	
9312	517
9313	512
9314	513
9315	514
9316	510
9317	511
9318	518
9319	519
9320	520
9321	521
9322	522
9323	525
9324	523
9325	524
9326	529
9327	526
9328	527
9329	530
9330	531
9331	532
9332	528
9333	533
9334	515
9335	516
9336	534
Volume 170	
9337	366
9338	367
9339	369
9340	370
9341	371
9342	372
9343	368
9344	375
9345	373
9346	374
9347	376
9348	289
9349	290
9350	291
9351	292
9352	293
9353	137
9354	106
9355	107
9356	108
9357	101
9358	102
9359	104
9360	105
9361	103
9362	306
9363	310
9364	309
9365	308
9366	307
Volume 171	
9367	241
9368	242
9369	284
9370	280
9371	281
9372	283
9373	282
9374	243
9375	277
9376	278
9377	279
9378	245
9379	258
9380	261
9381	262
9382	263
9383	264
9384	265
9385	267
9386	269
9387	266
9388	268
9389	251
9390	254
9391	246
9392	248
9393	259
9394	260
9395	270
9396	271
9397	273
9398	274
9399	272
9400	275
9401	276
9402	244
9403	252
9404	253
9405	247
9406	249
9407	250
9408	257
9409	256
9410	255
Volume 172	
9411	81
9412	82
9413	176
9414	79
9415	80
9416	136
9417	134
9418	135
9419	449
9420	509
9421	452
9422	456
9423	455
9424	457
9425	472
9426	458
9427	461
9428	474
9429	475
9430	476

Number of sheet in Windsor Inventory	Number in the present catalogue	Number of sheet in Windsor Inventory	Number in the present catalogue	Number of sheet in Windsor Inventory	Number in the present catalogue	Number of sheet in Windsor Inventory	Number in the present catalogue
9431	477	9481	54	9529	93	9712	295
9432	478	9482	53	9530	94	9713	299
9433	464	9483	98	9531	83	9714 (9722)	38
9434	465	9484	97	9532	91	9715	34
9435	466	9485	50	9533	49	9716	35
9436	467	9486	51	9534	47	9717	40
9437	468	9487	590	9535	48	9718	41
9438	469			9536	84	9719	39
9439	470	*Volume 174*		9537	138	9720	43
9440	463	9488	482	9538	450	9721	36
9441	462	9489	480	9539	451	9722 (9714)	38
9442	473	9490	479	9540	575	9723	302
9443	460	9491	481	9541	385	9724	443
9444	471	9492	129	9542	386	9725	445
9445	454	9493	128	9543	383	9726	444
9446	459	9494	130	9544	388	9727	446
9447	453	9495	124	9545	384	9728	447
9448	508	9496	125	9546	379	9729	448
9449	507	9497	120	9547	387	9730	441
9450	303	9498	119	9548	378	9731	440
9451	544	9499	127	9549	382	9732	438
9452	239	9500	126	9550	380	9733	439
9453	235	9501	121	9551	381	9734	437
9454	238	9502	115	9552	359	9735	431
9455	237	9503	118	9553	360	9736	442
9456	240	9504	122	9554	361	9737	57
9457	234	9505	116	9555	358	9738	58
9458	236	9506	123	9556	357	9739	286
9459	233	9507	117	9557	356	9740	395
9460	232	9508	131	9558	352	9741	389
9461	582	9509	132	9559	354	9742	392
9462	576	9510	149	9560	364	9743	390
9463	583	9511	150	9561	365	9744	391
9464	578	9512	147	9562	362	9745	586
9465	579	9513	151	9563	363	9746	587
9466	577	9514	153	9564	353	9747	60
9467	580	9515	154	9565	355	9748	133
9468	581	9516	152			9749	42
9469	158	9517	148	*Volume 176*		9750	178
9470	164	9518	173	9701	504	9751	584
9471	162	9519	174	9702	505	9752	585
9472	167	9520	85	9703	502	9753	492
9473	169	9521	90	9704	503	9754	436
9474	168	9522	87	9705	506	9755	591
9475	166	9523	96	9706	300	9756	155
9476	163	9524	89	9707	301	9757	171
9477	160	9525	95	9708	298	9758	172
9478	161	9526	88	9709	297	9759	170
9479	165	9527	86	9710	296	9760	156
9480	159	9528	92	9711	294	9761	157

Number of sheet in Windsor Inventory	Number in the present catalogue
9762	377
9763	55
9764	56
9765	engraving
9765A	59
9766	61
9766A	113
9767	485
9768	488
9769	484
9770	486
9771	483
9772	487
9773	568
9774 (9780)	566
9775	569
9776	570
9777	567
9778	571
9779	572
9780 (9774)	566
9781	573
9782 9783	574
9784	52
9785	422
9786	427
9787	428
9788	423
9789	424
9790	421
9791	420
9792	429
9793	430
9794	433
9795	432
9796	425
9797	426
9798	589
9799	588
9800 (9806)	493
9801	496
9802	497
9803	494
9804	498
9805	495
9806 (9800)	493
Volume 177	
9807	180
9808	181
9809	182
9810	183
9811	184
9812	185
9813	186
9814	187
9815	188
9816	189
9817	190
9818	191
9819	192
9820	193
9821	194
9822	195
9823	196
9824	197
9825	198
9826	199
9827	200
9828	201
9829	202
9830	204
9831	205
9832	211
9833	207
9834	208
9835	206
9836	214
9837	213
9838	212
9839	203
9840	209
9841	218
9842 9843	216
9844	224
9845	217
9846	219
9847	210
9848	227
9849	226
9850	215
9851	225
9852	222
9853	223
9854	220
9855	221
9856	229
9857	230
9858	231
9859	228
Volume 178	
9860	558
9861	557
9862	556
9863	555
9864	536
9865	537
9866	538
9867	539
9868	540
9869	541
9870	542
9871	543
9872	545
9873	546
9874	547
9875	548
9876	549
9877	551
9878	552
9879	550
9880	560
9881	559
9882	554
9883	561
9884	562
9885	553
9886	564
9887	565
9888	563
Volume 179	
9889	74
9890	76
9891	75
9892	77
9893	63
9894	66
9895	65
9896	72
9897	67
9898	69
9899	73
9900	68
9901	64
9902	70
9903	62
9904	46
9905	71
9906	78
9907	535
9908	112
9909	111
9910	177
9911	288
9912	287
9913	110
9914	109
9915	285
9915A	44
9916	37
9917	99
9918	114
9919	175
Volume 180	
9920	1
9921	2
9922	3
9923	4
9924	5
9925	6
9926	7
9927	8
9928	9
9929	10
9930	11
9931A	12
9931	13
9932	14
9933	15
9934	16
9935	17
9936	18
9937	19
9938	20
9939	21
9940	22
9941	23
9942	24
9943	25
9944	26
9945	27
9946	28
9947	29

Number of sheet in Windsor Inventory	Number in the present catalogue	Number of sheet in Windsor Inventory	Number in the present catalogue	Number of sheet in Windsor Inventory	Number in the present catalogue	Number of sheet in Windsor Inventory	Number in the present catalogue
9948	30	10315	729	10588	758	10635	606
9949	31	10316	730	10589	759	10636	601
9950	32	10317	631	10590	611	10637	760
9951	33	10318	751	10591	612	10638	761
		10319	752	10592	500	10639	707
Volume 181		10320	753	10593	618	10640	710
9952	414	10321	714	10593a	629 (engraving)	10641	708
9953	415	10322	713			10642	709
9954	412	10323	715			10643	711
9955	413	10324	706	10594	630	10644	616
9956	416	10325	608	10595	716	10645	712
9957	398	10326	394	10596	501	10646	733
9958	406	10327	393	10597	139	10647	648
9959	409	10328	592	10598	435	10648	667
9960	408	10329	619	10599	305	10649	657
9961	407	10330	617	10600	146	10650	674
9962	399	10331	705	10601	144	10651	672
9963	397	10332	779	10602	141	10652	673
9964	396	10333	740	10603	140	10653	637
9965	404	10334	780	10604	142	10654	633
9966	410	10335	741	10605	143	10655	762
9967	405	10336	742	10606	145	10656	668
9968	411	10337	660	10607	696	10657	763
9969	400	10338	743	10608	597	10658	636
9970	402	10339	656	10609	596	10659	635
9971	418	10340	643	10610		10660	639
9972	403	10341	744	10611	593	10661	638
9973	401	10342	615	10612		10662	641
9974	419	10343	732	10613	594	10663	640
9975	417	10344	731	10614		10664	646
9975A & B	434	10345	609	10615		10665	644
		10346	610	10616	595	10666	642
Volume 185		10347	625	10617		10667	645
10298	627	10348	624	10618	626	10668	650
10299	628	10349	599	10619	489	10669	764
10300	728	10350	600	10620	490	10670	765
10301	725	10351	598	10621	491	10671	766
10302	727	10352	745	10622	614	10672	767
10303	726	10353	754	10623	613	10673	768
10304	703			10624	647	10674	769
10305	701	*Volume 188*		10625	719	10675	770
10306	702	10579	781	10626	717	10676	771
10307	704	10580	499	10627	747	10677	772
10308	700	10581	755	10628	304	10678	773
10309	718	10582	179	10629	746	10679	774
10310	724	10583	45	10630	602	10680	775
10311	723	10584	756	10631	603	10681	776
10312	722	10585	757	10632	607	10682	777
10313	721	10586	623	10633	604	10683	778
10314	720	10587	622	10634	605	10684	649

Number of sheet in Windsor Inventory	Number in the present catalogue	Number of sheet in Windsor Inventory	Number in the present catalogue	Number of sheet in Windsor Inventory	Number in the present catalogue	Number of sheet in Windsor Inventory	Number in the present catalogue
10685	653	10700	736	10715	699	10730	679
10686	651	10701	737	10716	695	10731	680
10687	652	10702	734	10717	694	10732	682
10688	634	10703	669	10718	686	10733	683
10689	782	10704	670	10719	687	10734	685
10690	654	10705	671	10720	688	10735	684
10691	655	10706	658	10721	689	10736	681
10692	665	10707	659	10722	690	10737	632
10693	663	10708	661	10723	692		
10694	738	10709	750	10724	691	*Volume 189*	
10695	662	10710	664	10725	749	10740	100
10696	666	10711	783	10726	675	10765	620
10697	748	10712	693	10727	676	10769	621
10698	739	10713	697	10728	677		
10699	735	10714	698	10729	678		

General Index

S. Peter's

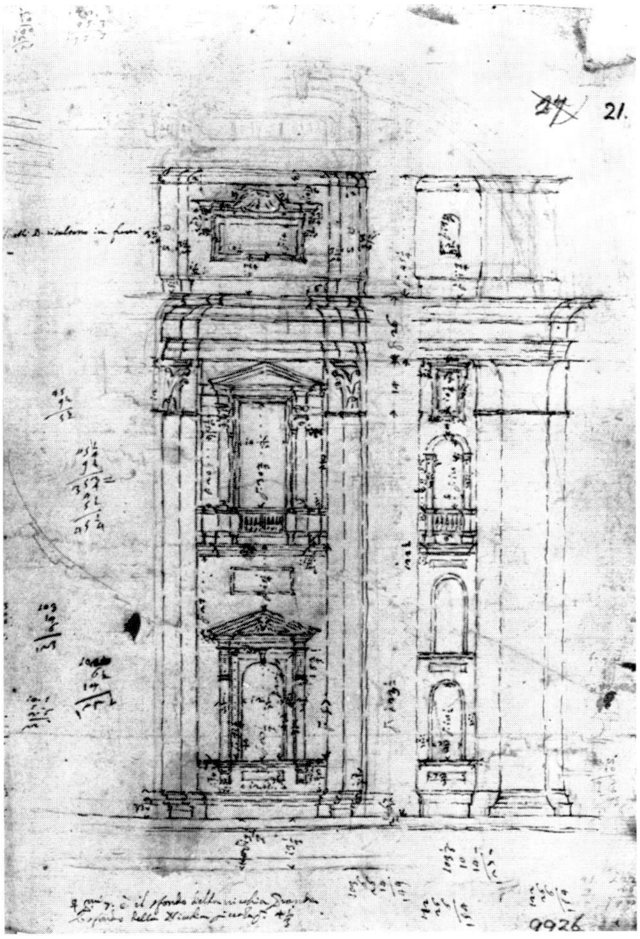

1 Elevation of two bays of a side façade of S. Peter's (no.7)

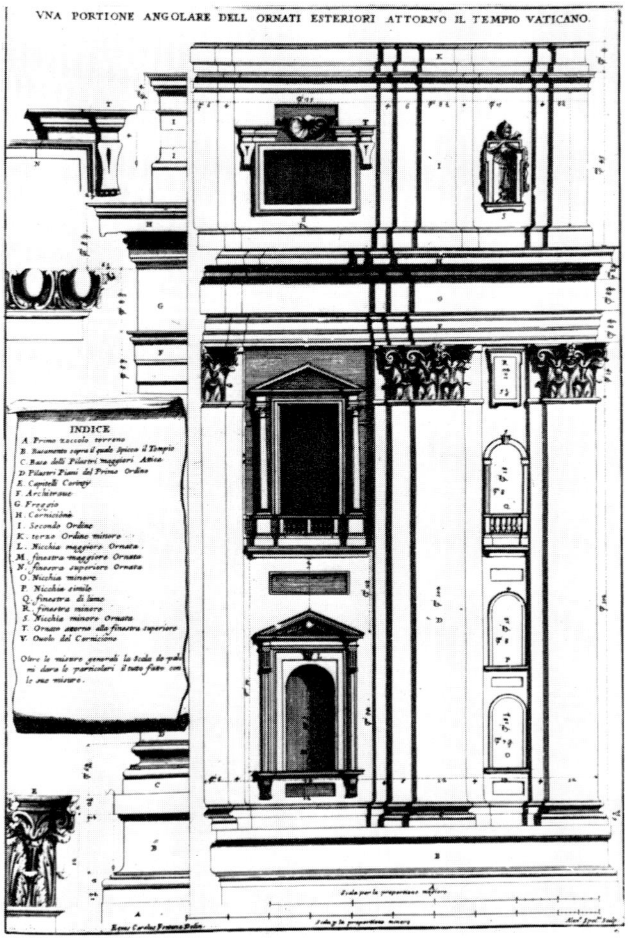

2 Sheet of studies from the *Tempio Vaticano* (engraving by Specchi after Fontana)

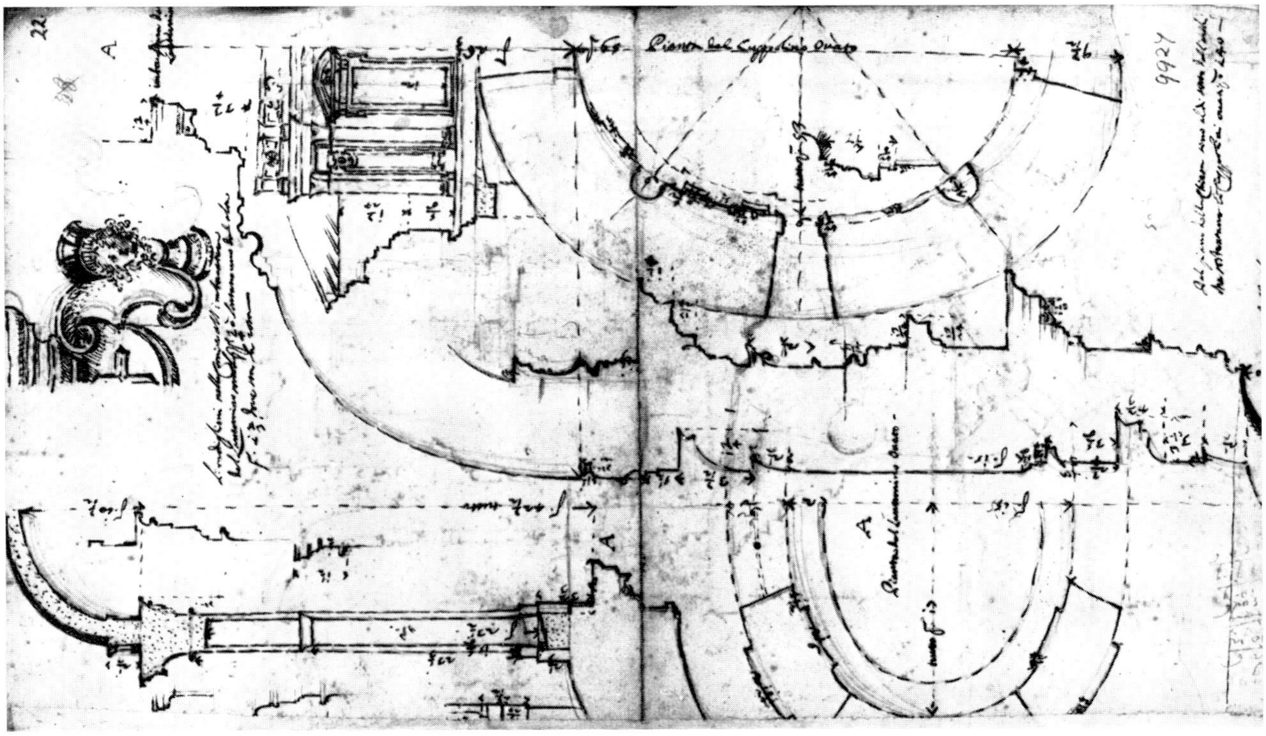

3 Studies of S. Peter's, mainly of the *cupolini* (no.8 *recto*)

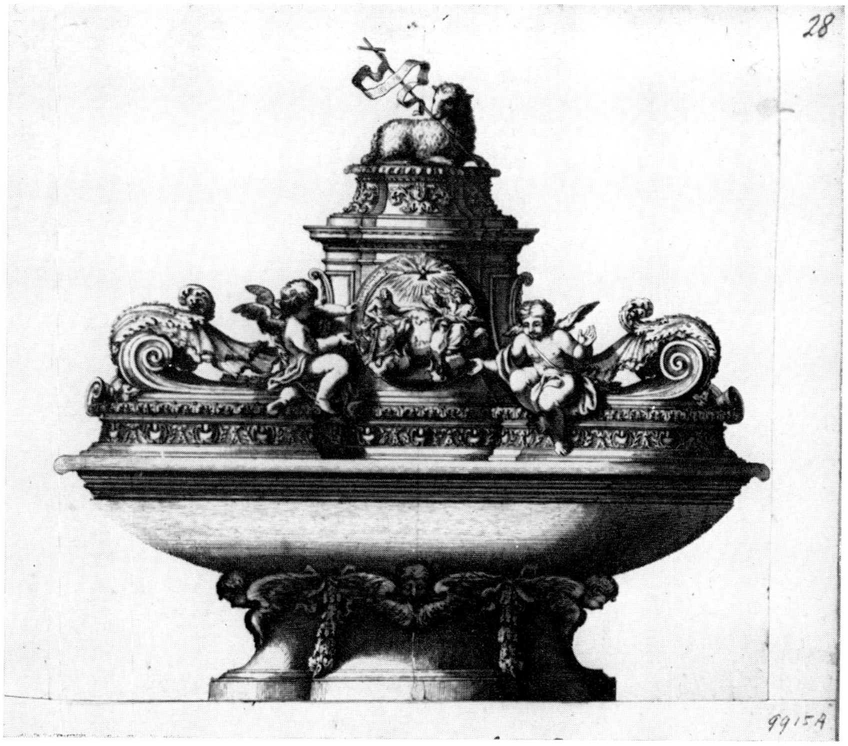

4 Elevation of the font (engraving, flap of no.44)

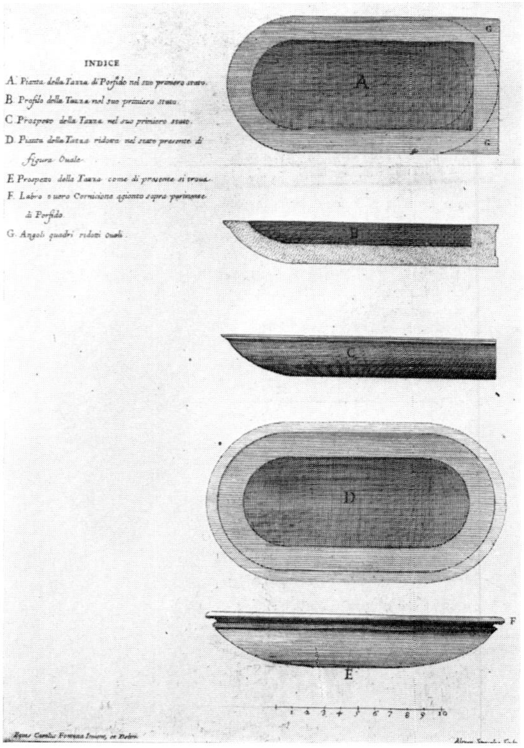

6 Diagrams of the basin (engraving by Specchi after Fontana)

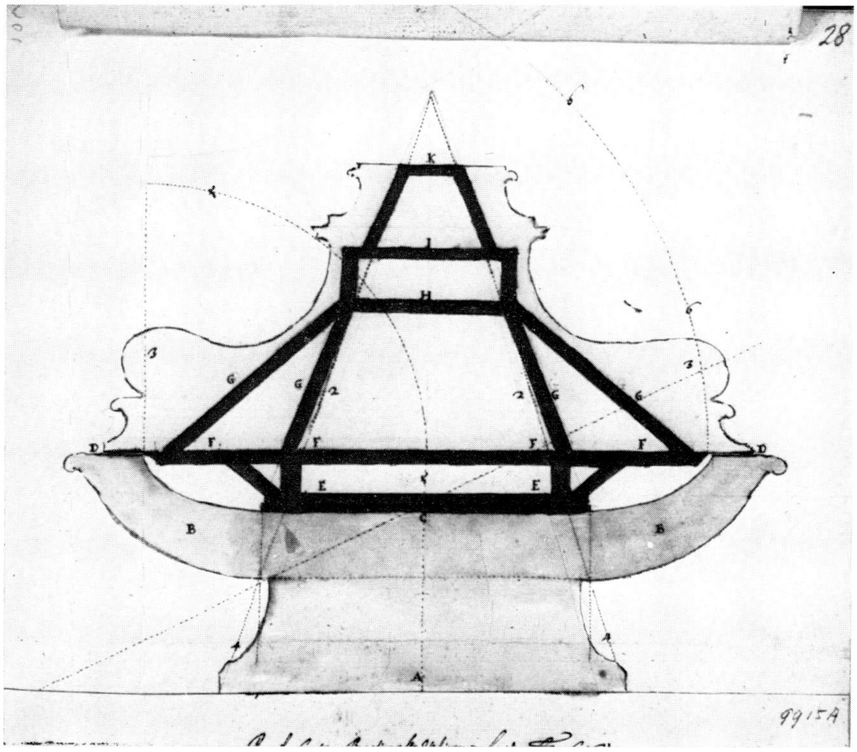

5 Section of the font (no.44)

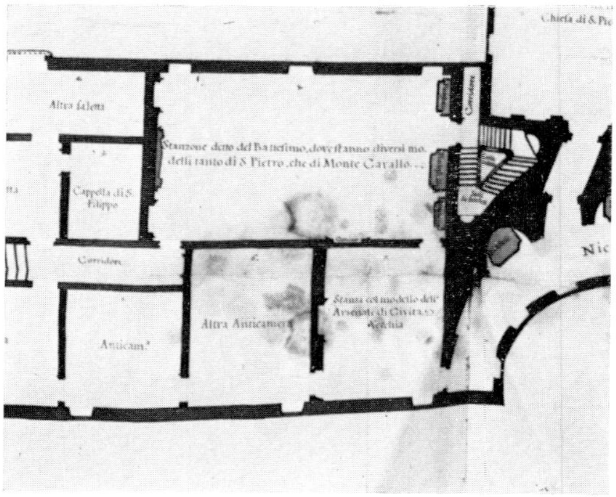

7 Plan of a room in the Vatican, showing model for Baptistry (anon. drawing; London, British Museum)

8 Section of the Baptistry (drawing by Fontana; Madrid, Biblioteca Nacional)

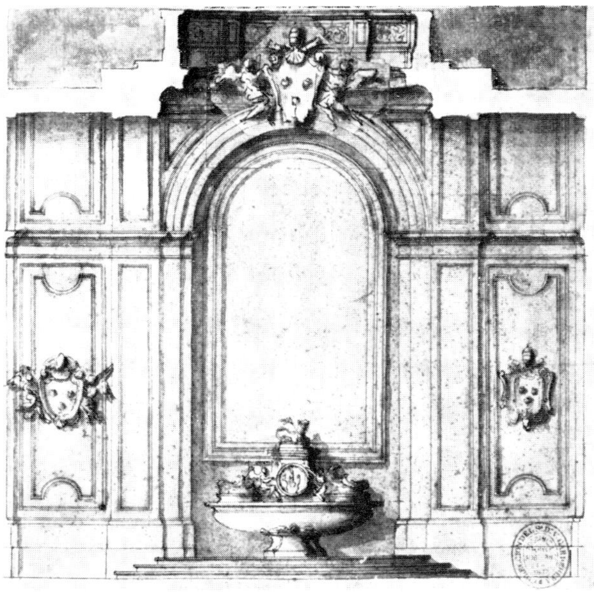

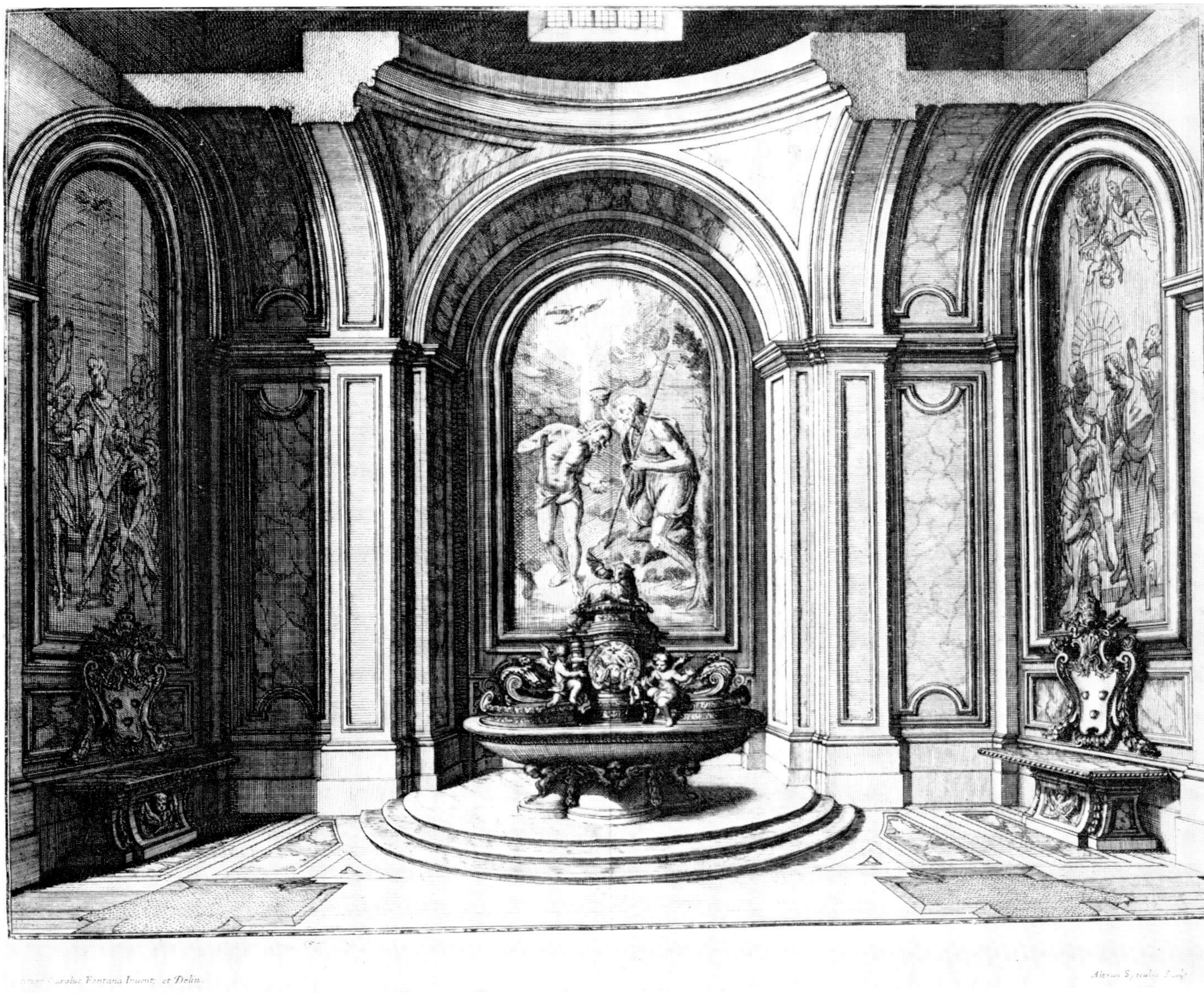

9 Perspective view of the Baptistry (engraving by Specchi after Fontana)

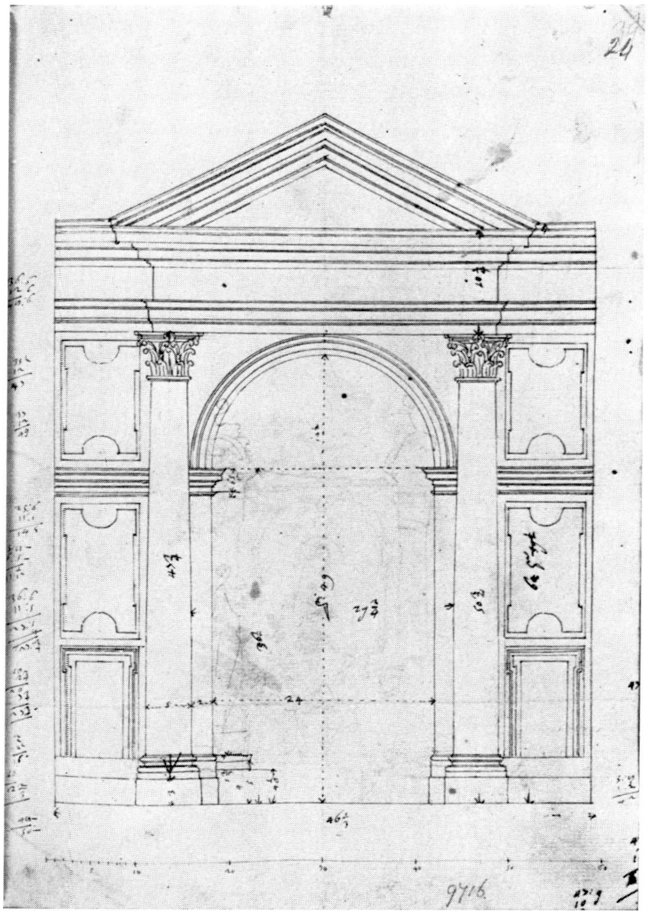

10 Elevation of the entrance (no.35)

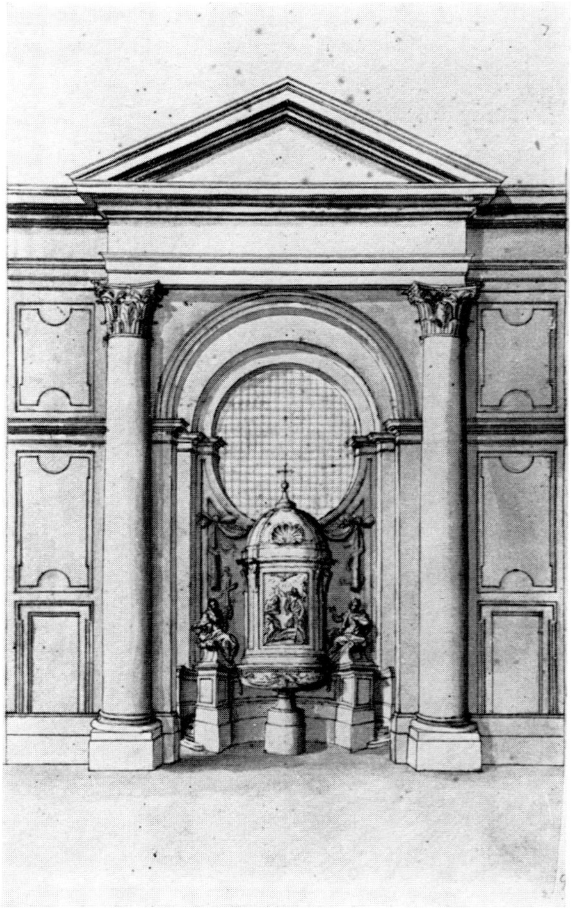

11 Elevation of the entrance (no.37)

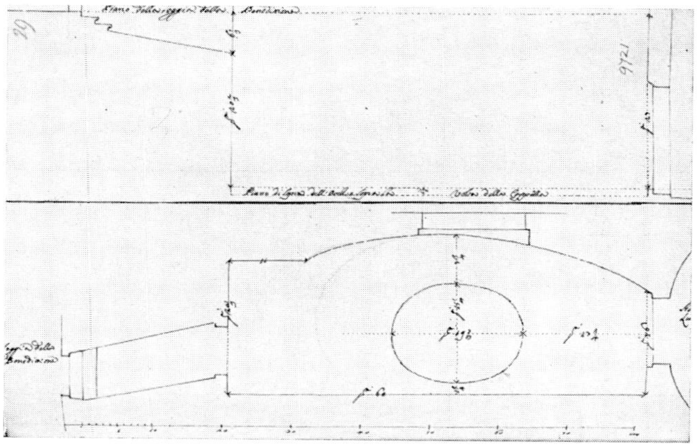

12 Sketch plan and section of the space above the chapel (no.36)

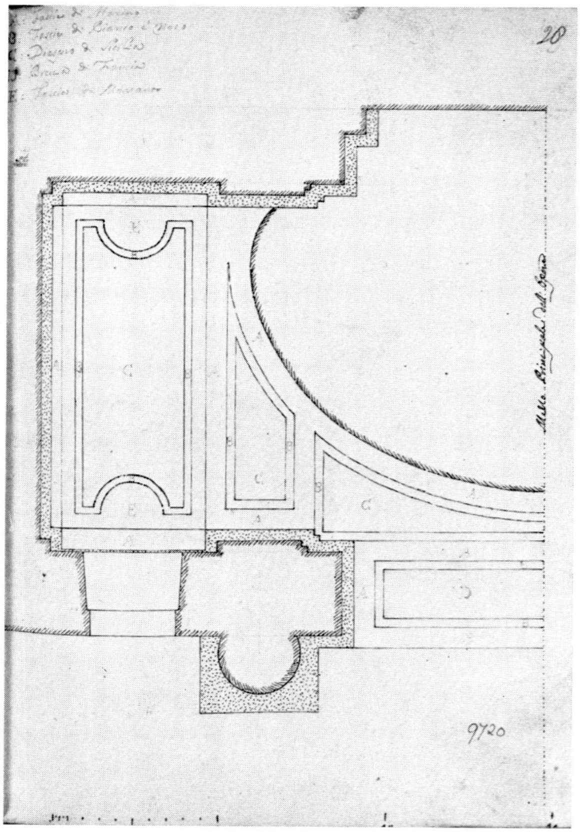

13 Half plan with project for floor decoration (no.43)

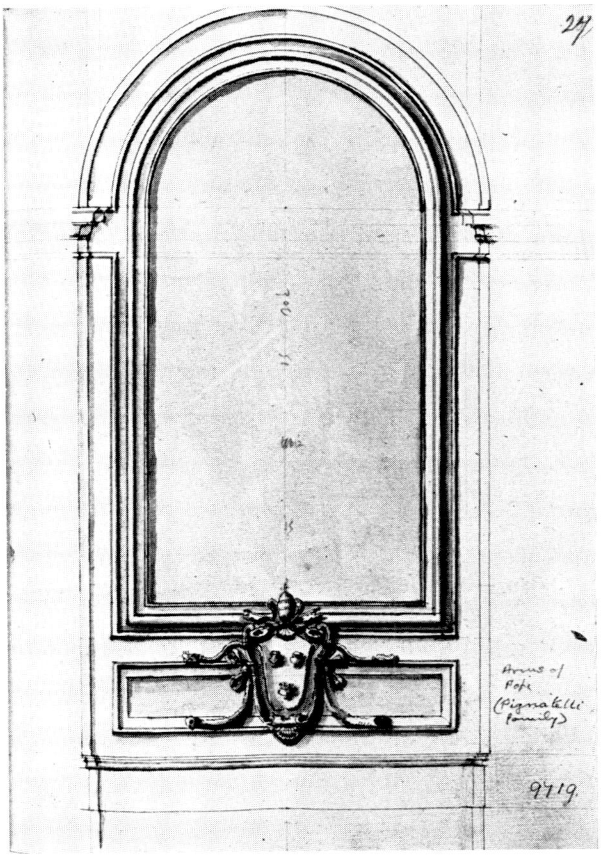

14 Project for the facing of a side wall (no.39)

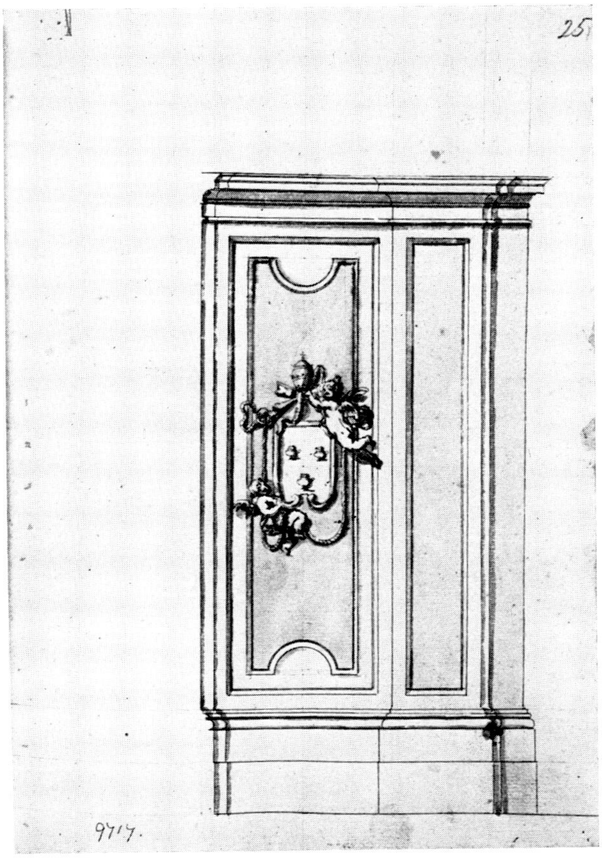

15 Project for a wall facing (no.40)

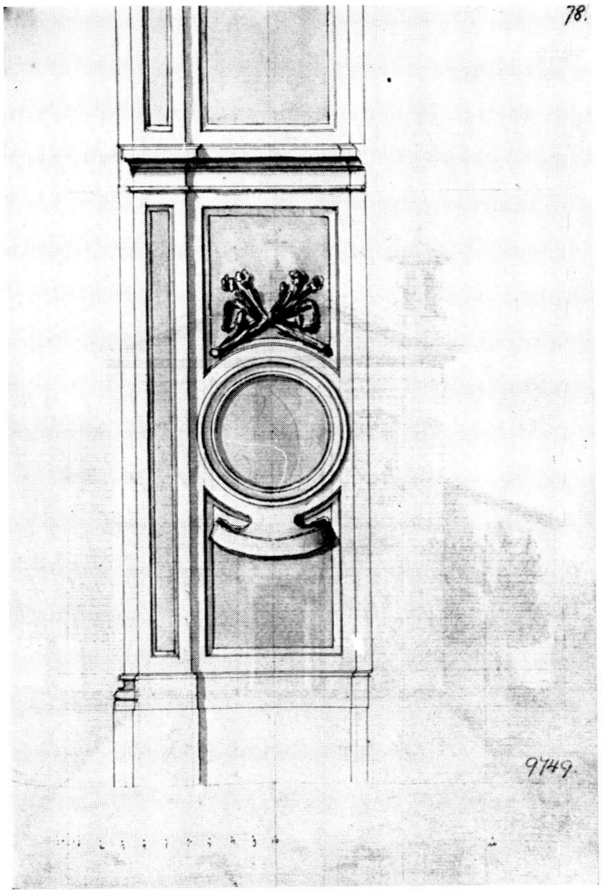

16 Project for a wall facing (no.42)

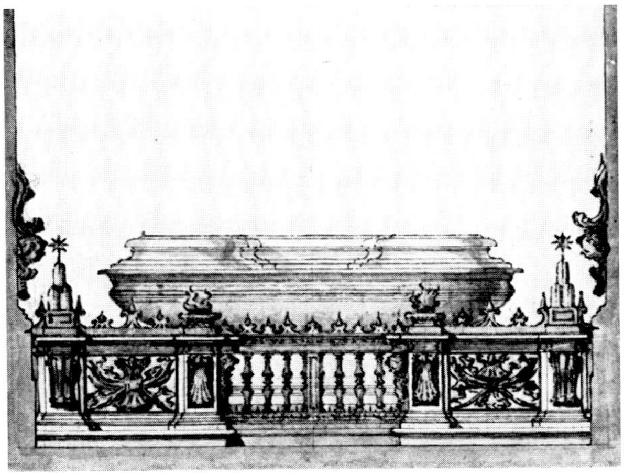

17 Project for the entrance screen (anon. drawing; no.45)

The tomb of Innocent XII (1692 and (?) after 1700)

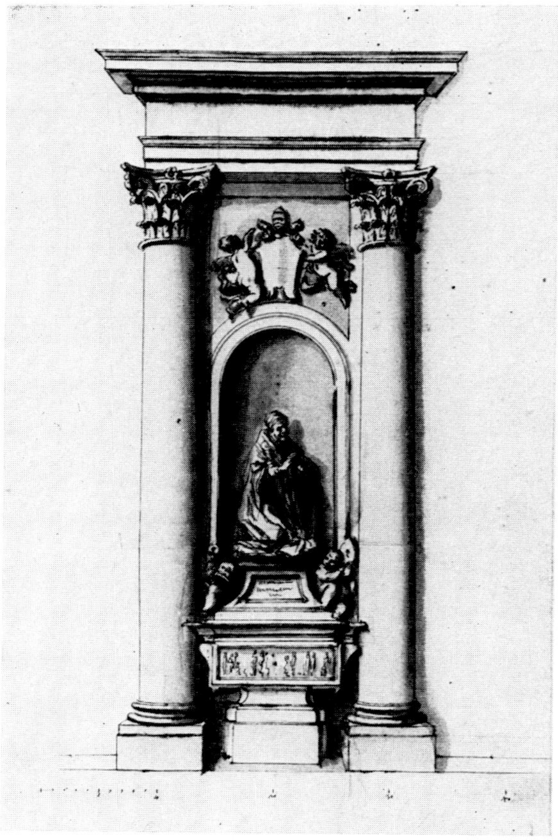

18 Project with a kneeling figure, perspective view (no.46)

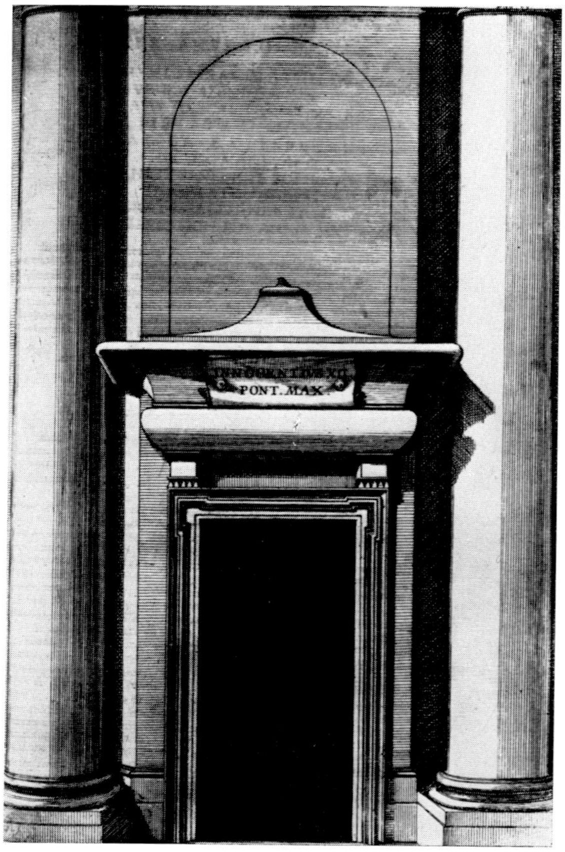

19 Perspective view of the tomb (engraving from Bonanni)

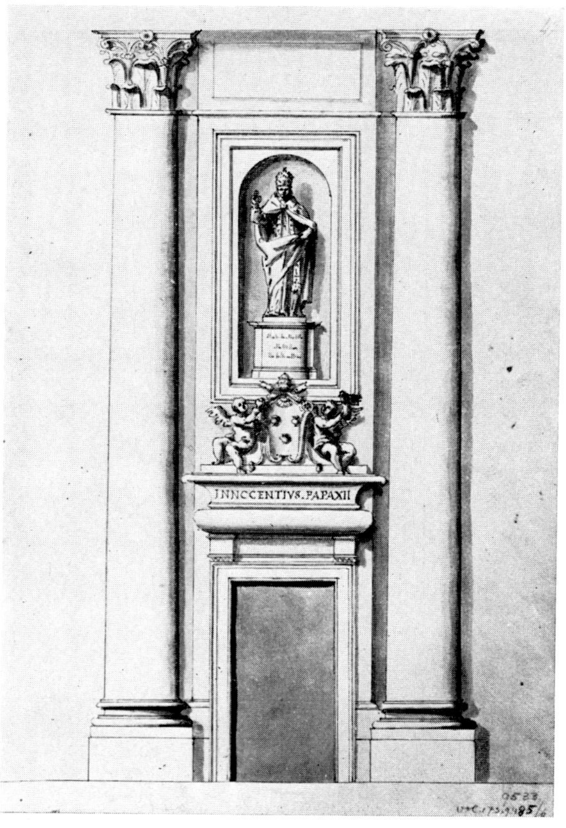

20 Project with a niche (1), elevation (no.49)

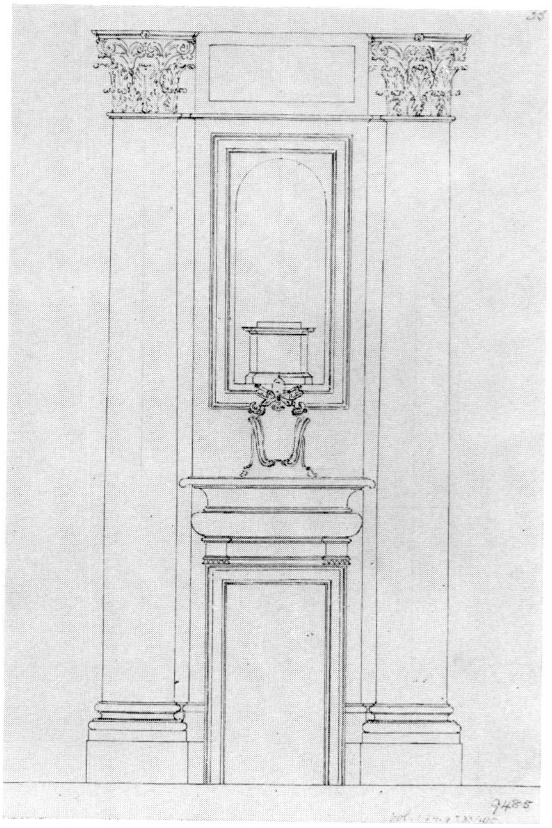

21 Project with a niche (2), elevation (no.50)

Projects for the Sacristy (1693 and 1706)

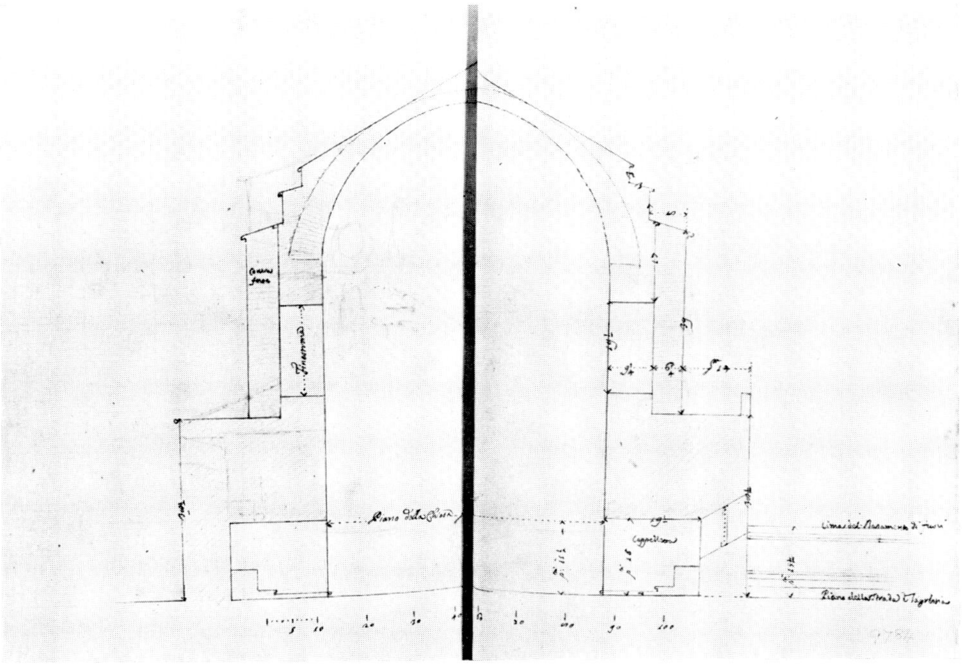

22 Section of the 'Madonna della Febbre' (no.52)

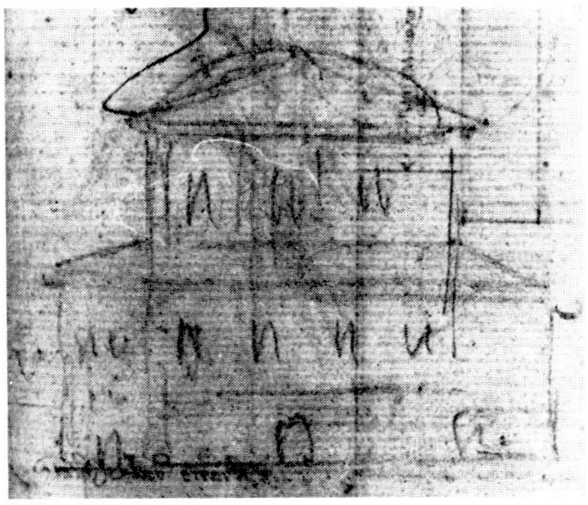

23 Sketch of Sacristy project (no.52 *verso*)

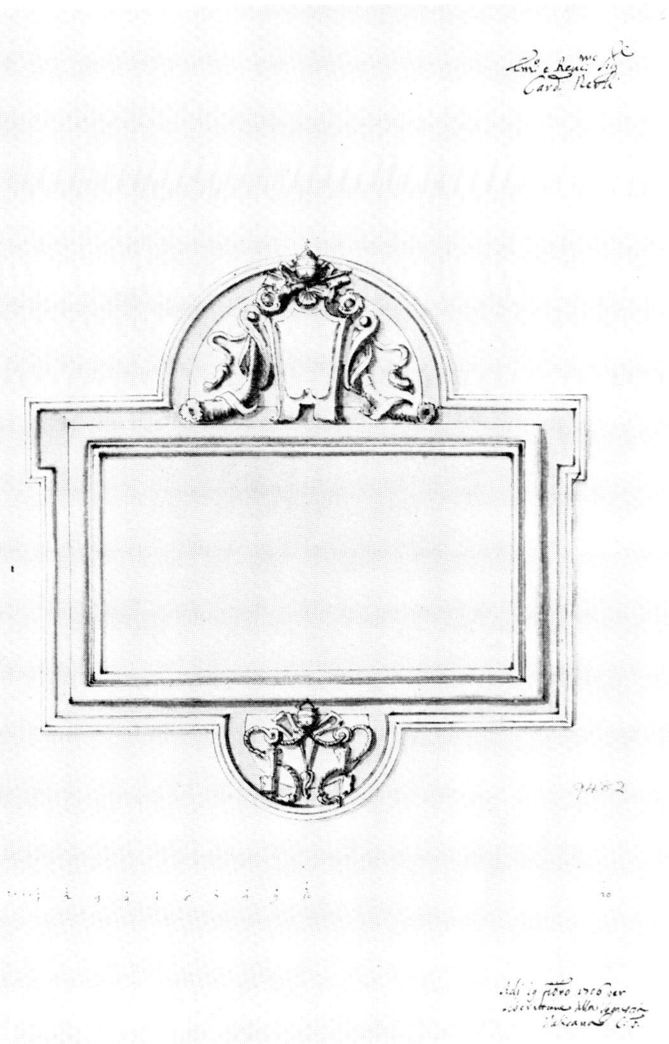

24 Project for an inscribed tablet (1706) (no.53)

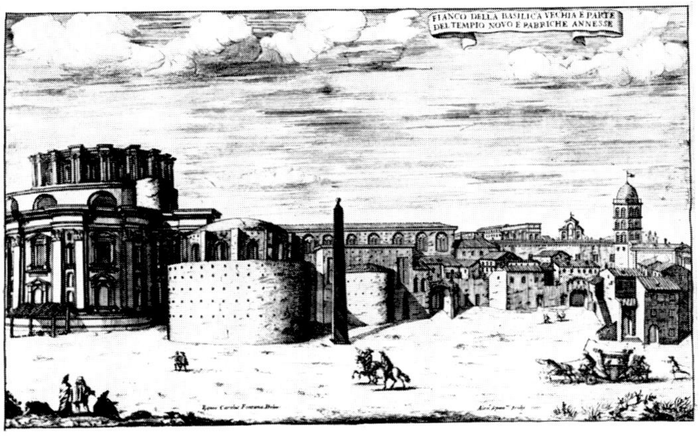

25 View of S. Peter's, showing the 'Madonna della Febbre' (engraving from Fontana's *Tempio Vaticano*)

Surveys of the lantern (1694 etc.) and cupola (1695)

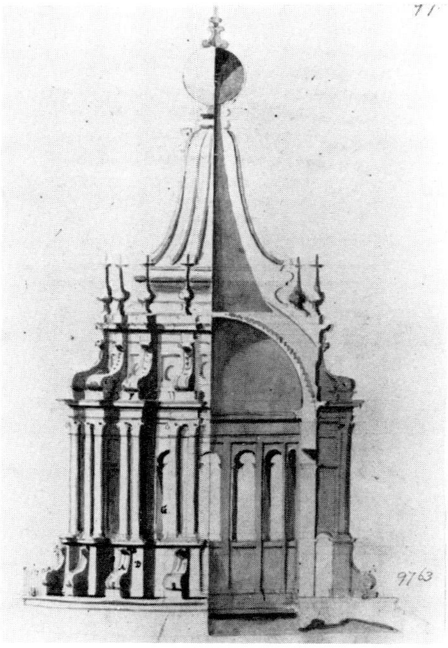

26 Elevation and section of the lantern (no.55)

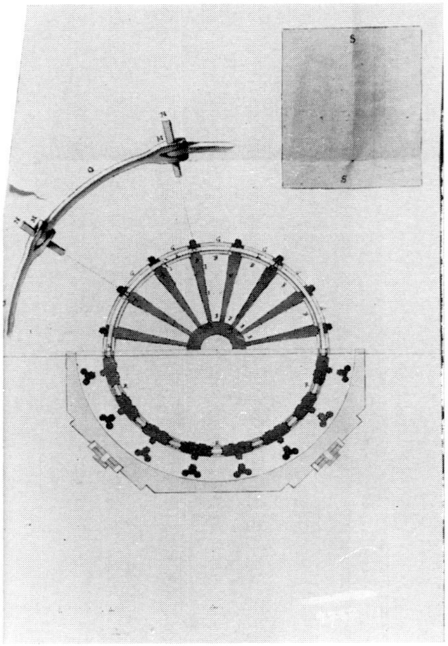

27 Plans of the cupola with diagrams of an iron brace (no.57)

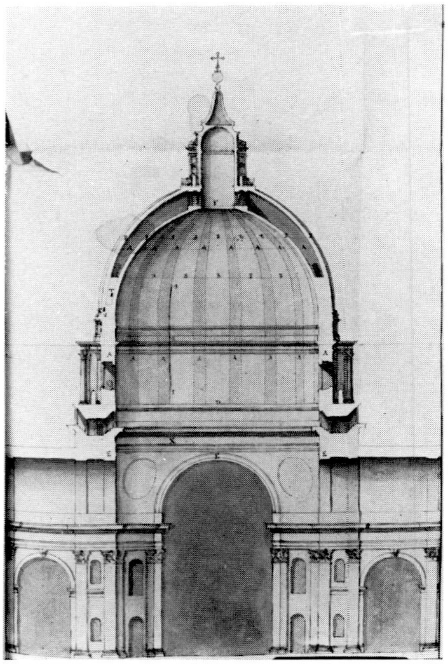

28 Section through the crossing and cupola (no.58)

Surveys of the tomb of Alexander VIII (1696 and 1699)

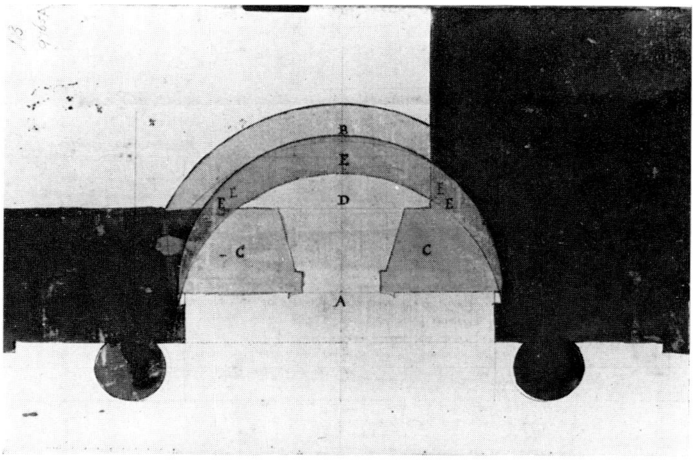

29 Plan of the tomb (1696) (no.59)

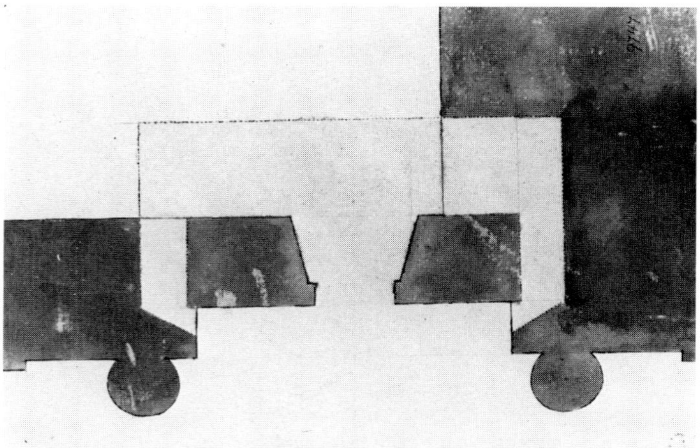

30 Plan of the site occupied by the tomb (no.60)

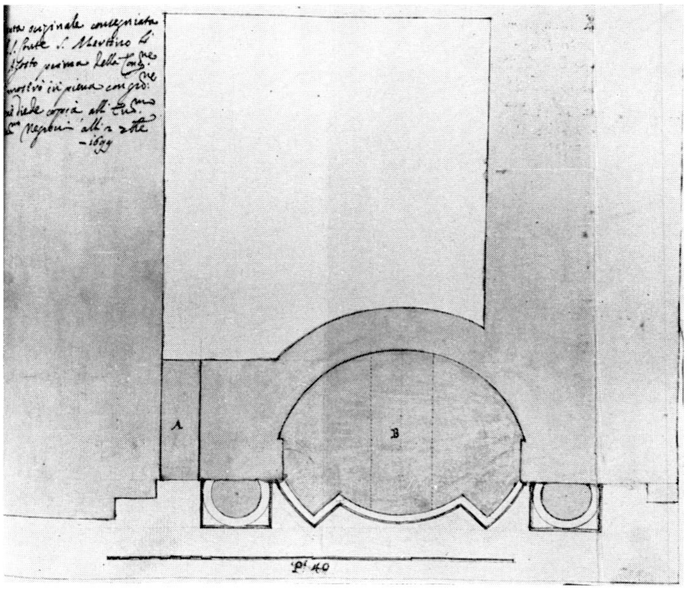

31 Plan of the tomb (1699) (anon. drawing; no.61)

The tomb of Queen Christina of Sweden (1696–1702)

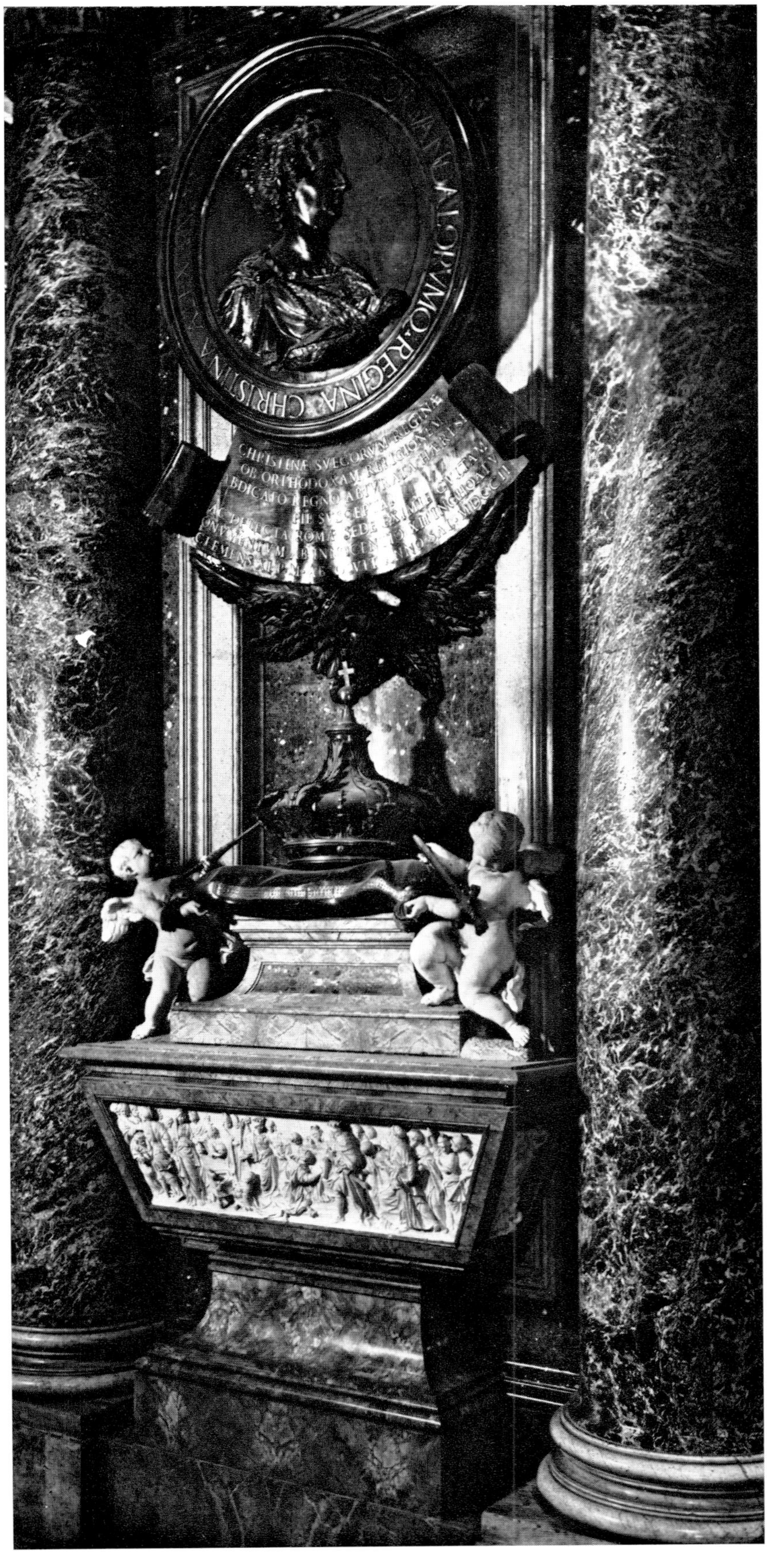

32 View of the tomb (photograph Alinari)

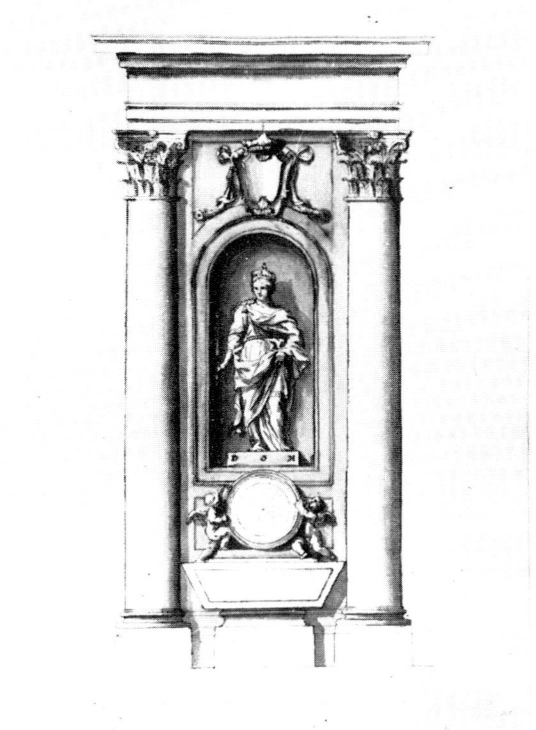

33 Project with a full-length statue (no.62)

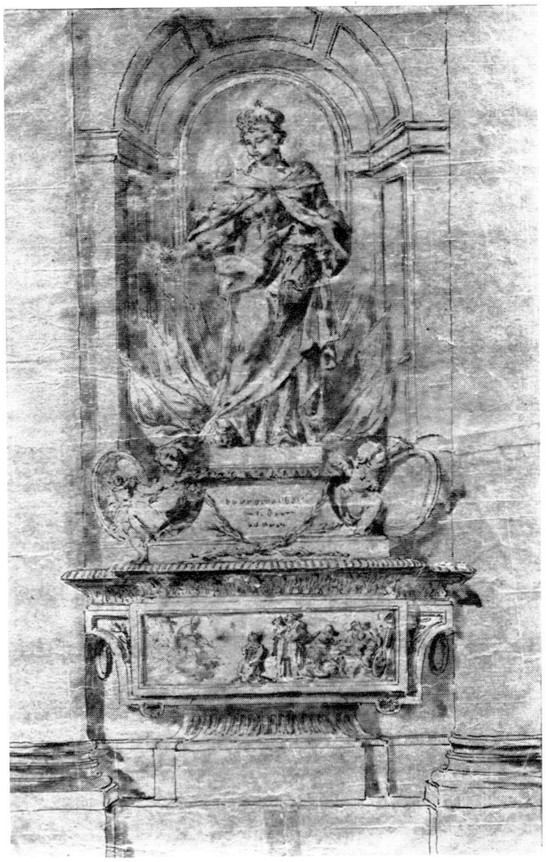

34 Tracing probably after a lost project by Fontana (Rome, Busiri Vici collection)

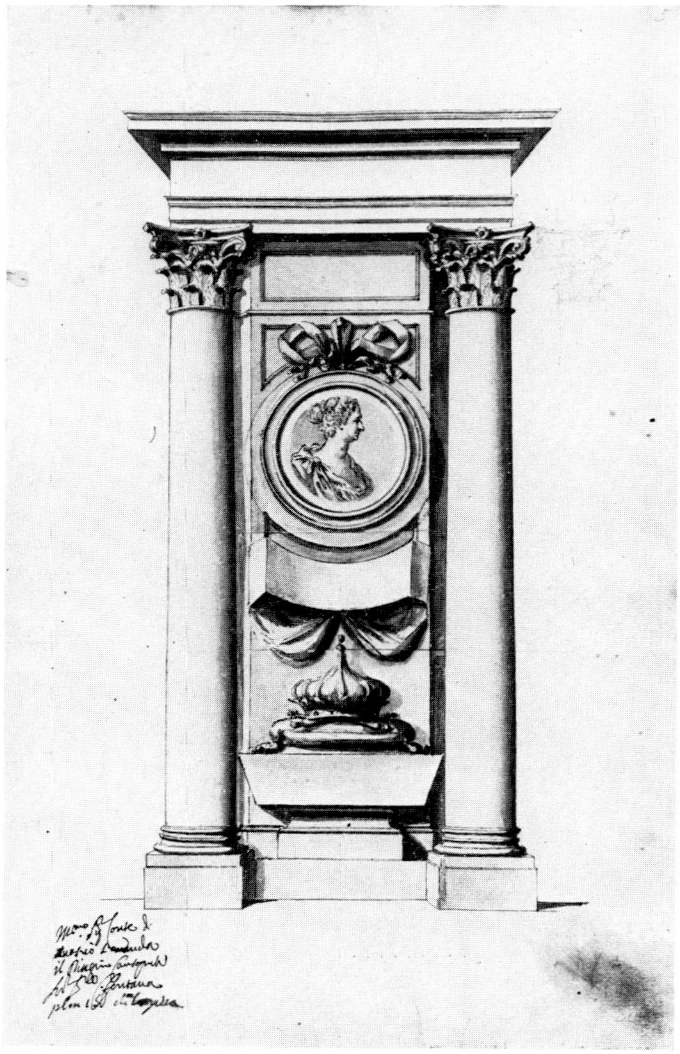

35 First project originally over a doorway (no.63)

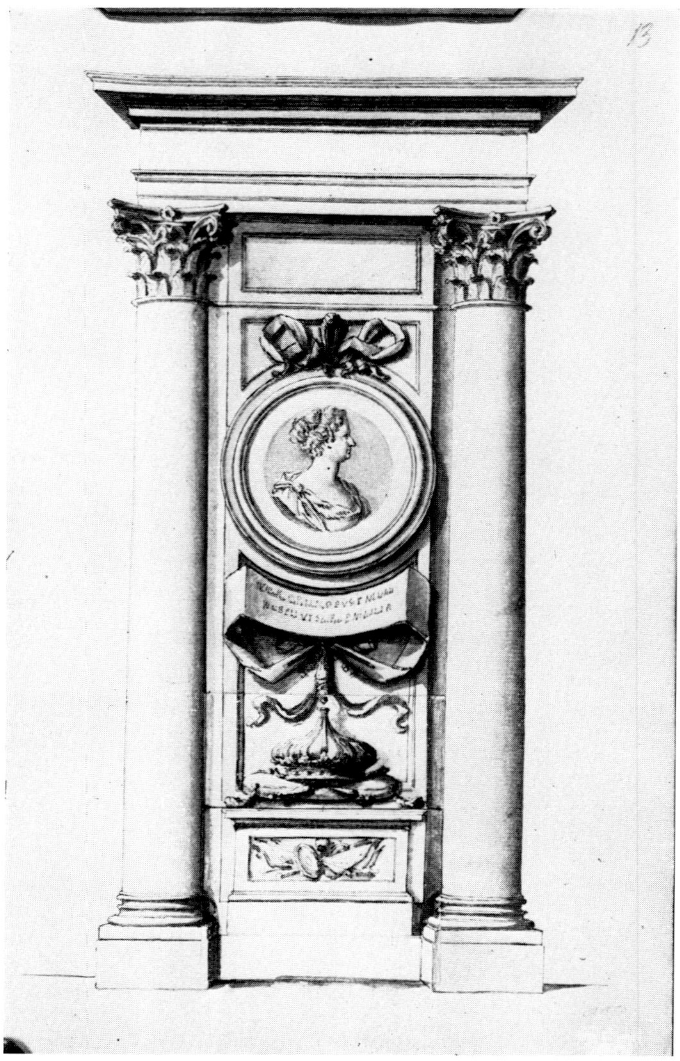

36 Second project originally over a doorway (no.64)

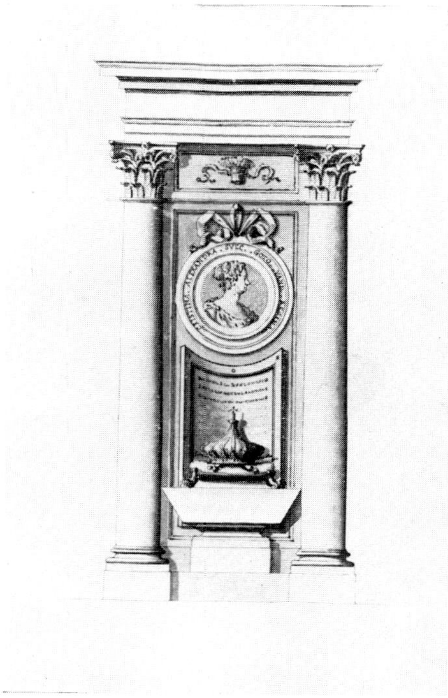

37 Project with a concave tablet (no.65)

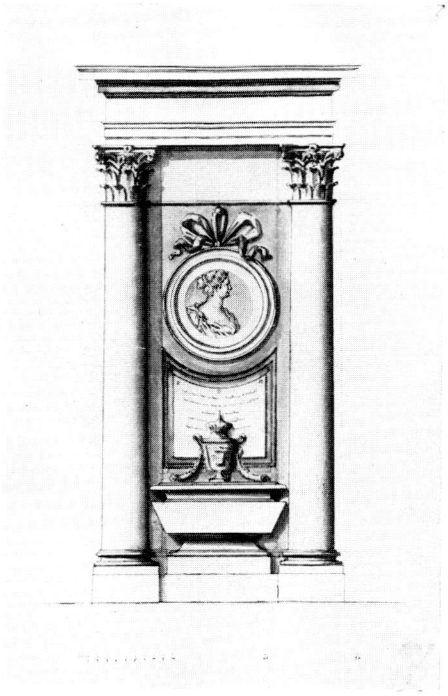

38 Project with an urn (no.66)

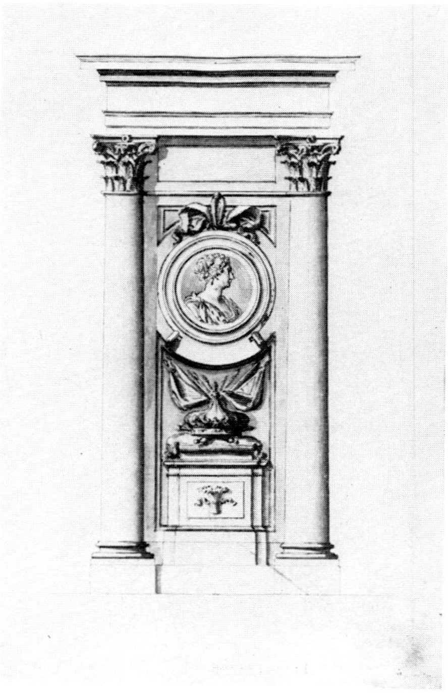

39 Project with a rectangular plinth (no.67)

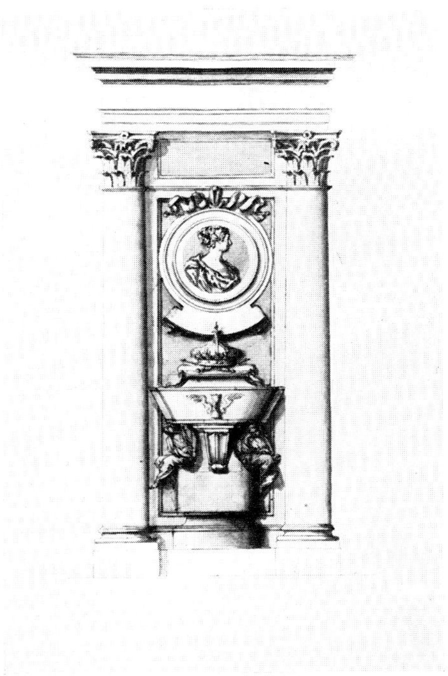

40 Project with two mourners (no.68)

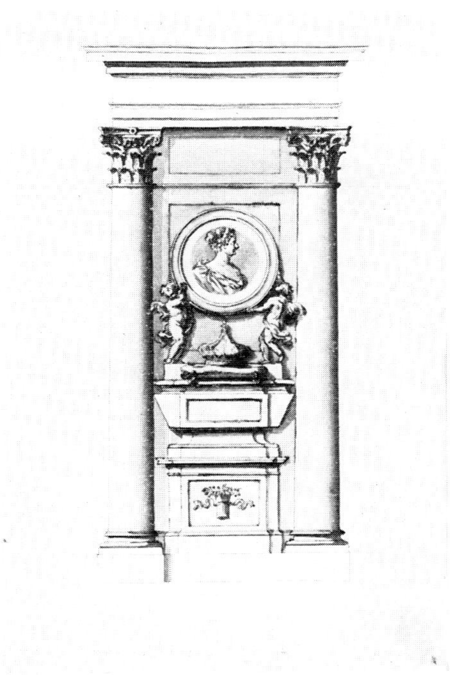

41 Project with *putti* supporting the medallion (no.69)

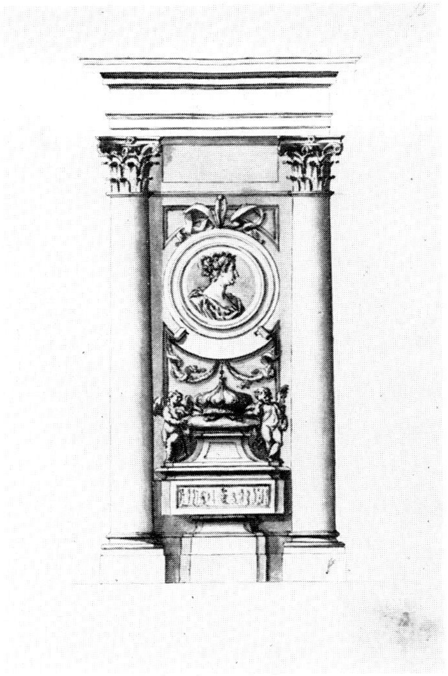

42 Project with a rectangular sarcophagus (no.70)

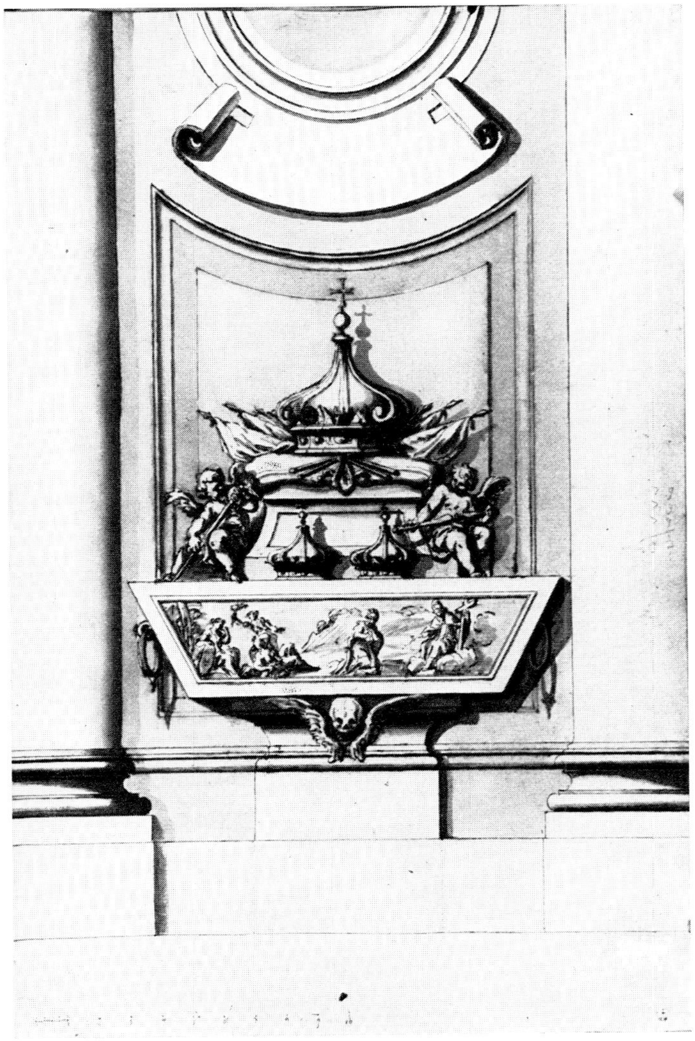

43 Project with three crowns, lower half (no.71)

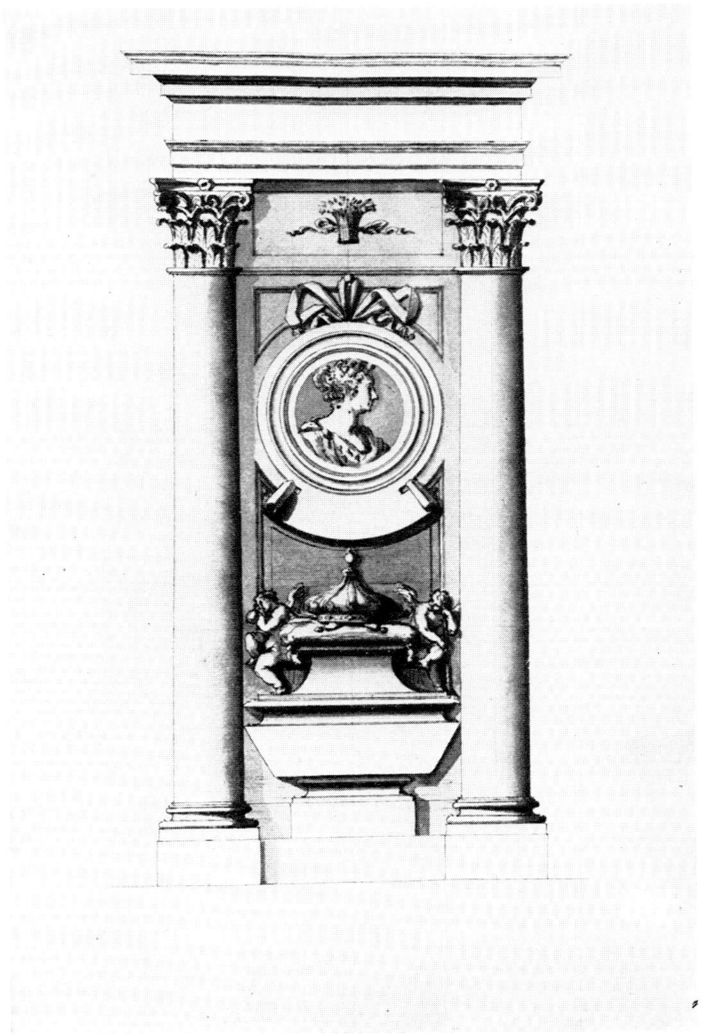

44 Project with reclining *putti* (no.72)

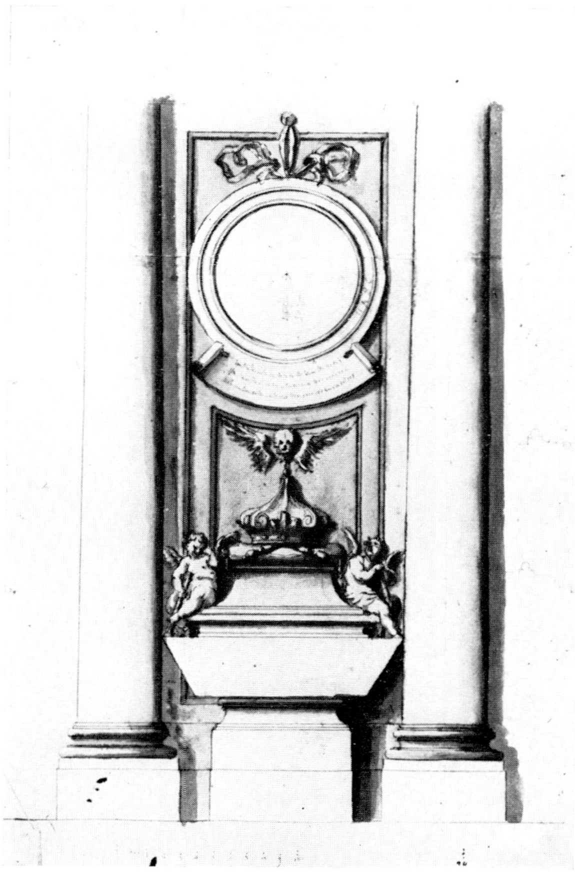

45 Project with a frontal death's-head (no.73)

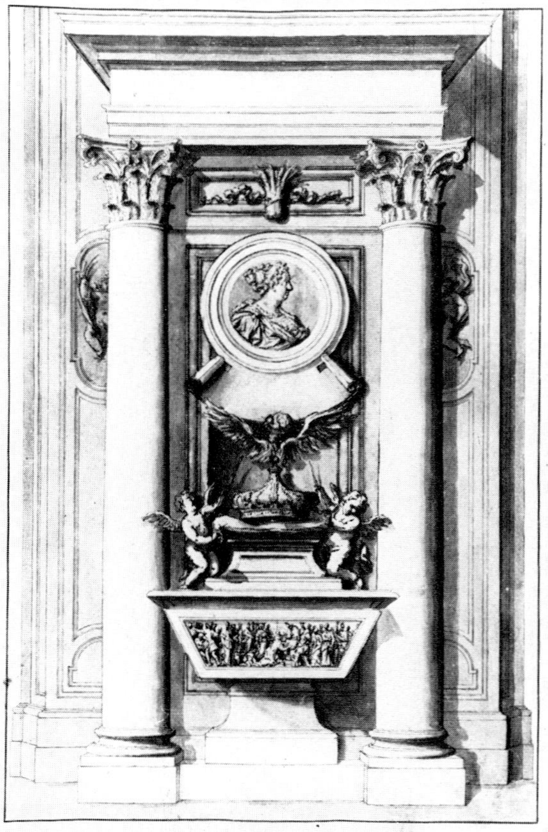

46 Perspective view of the final design (no.74)

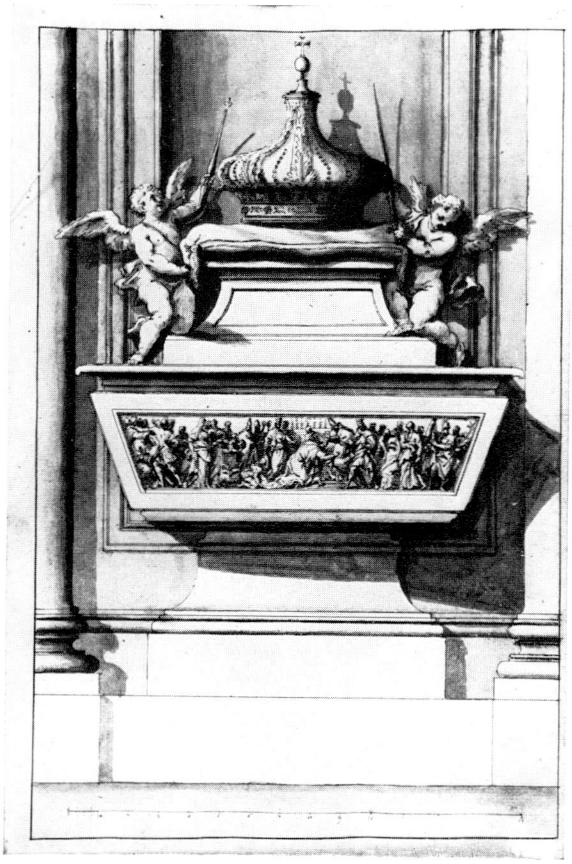

47 Elevation of the lower half of the final design (no.75)

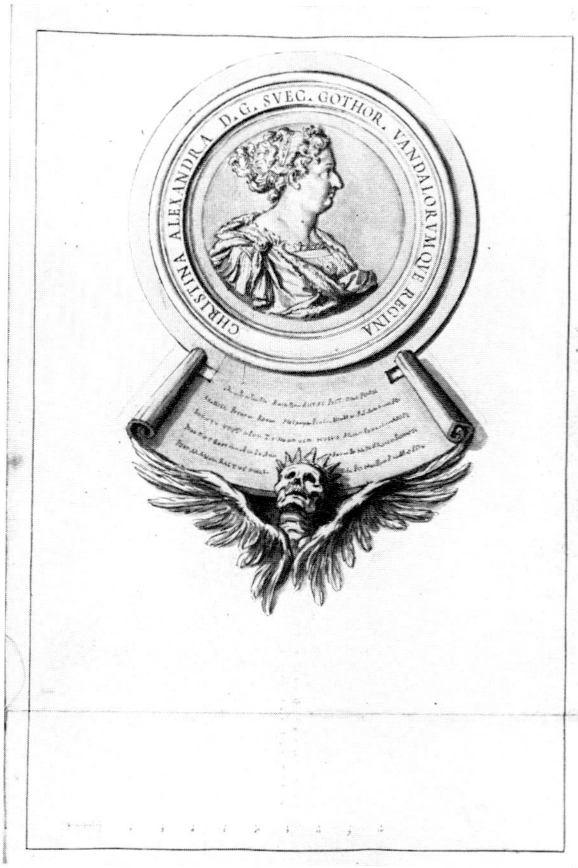

48 Study of the portrait medallion (no.77)

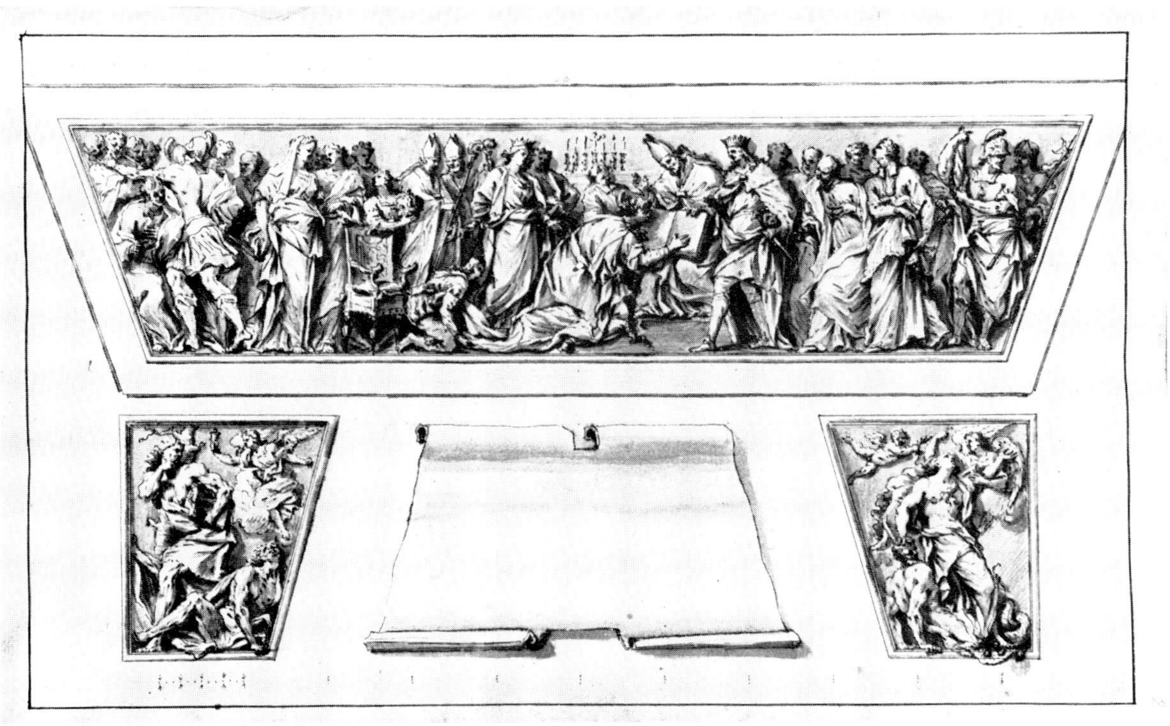

49 Studies of the sarcophagus reliefs (no.76)

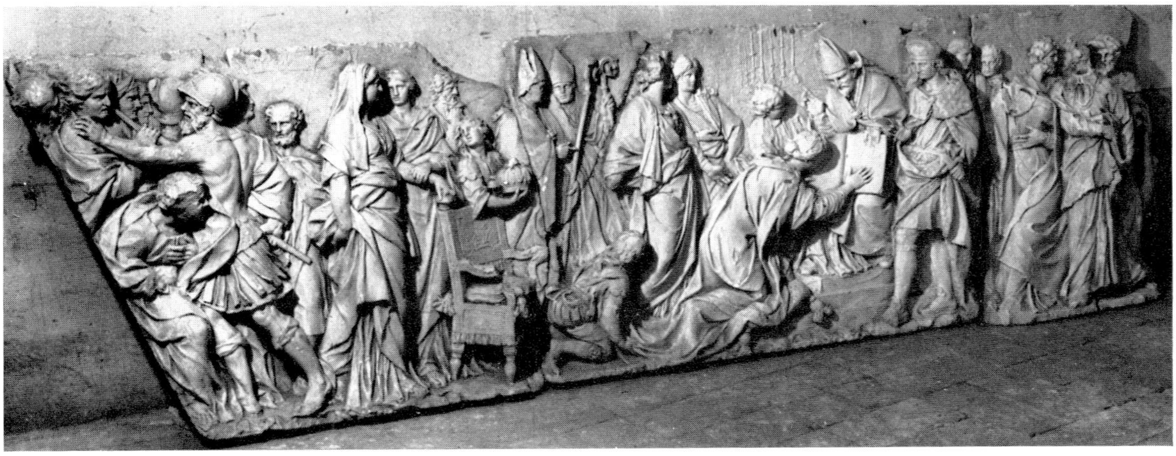

50 First model for the sarcophagus relief (by Jean Théodon)

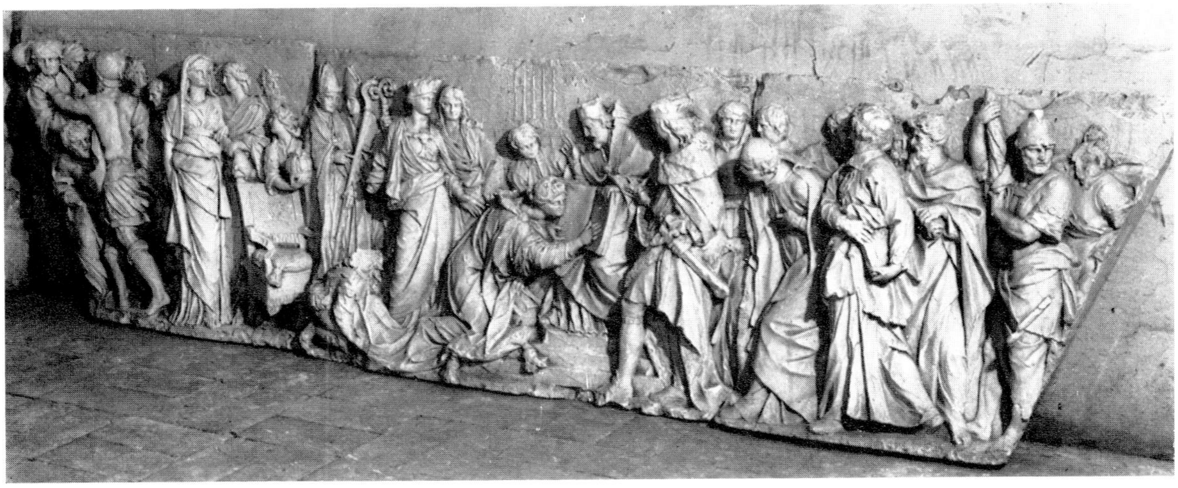

51 Second model for the sarcophagus relief (by Jean Théodon)

Drawings of the sarcophagus of Anicius Probus (1704) and of the 'Throne of S. Peter' (1705)

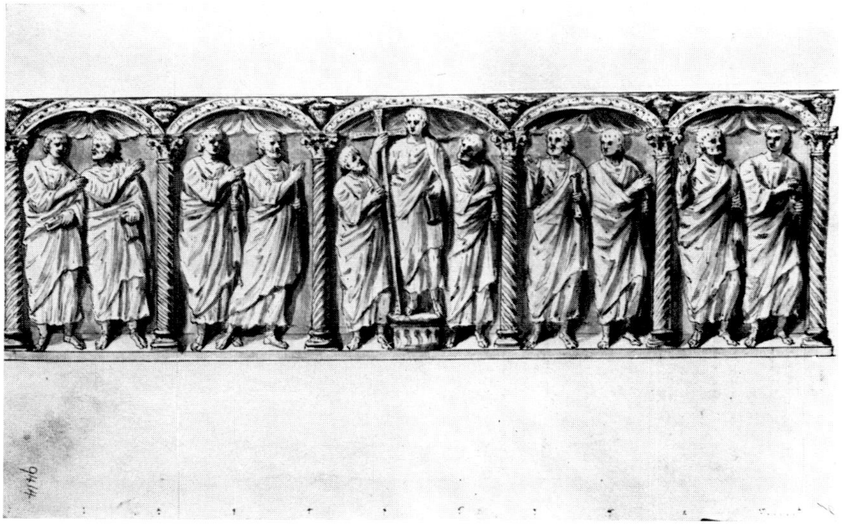

52 Elevation of the front of the sarcophagus (no.79)

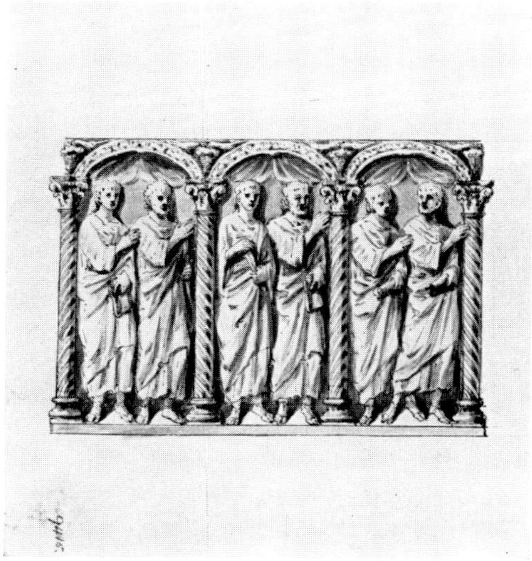

53 Elevation of the left side (detail of no.80)

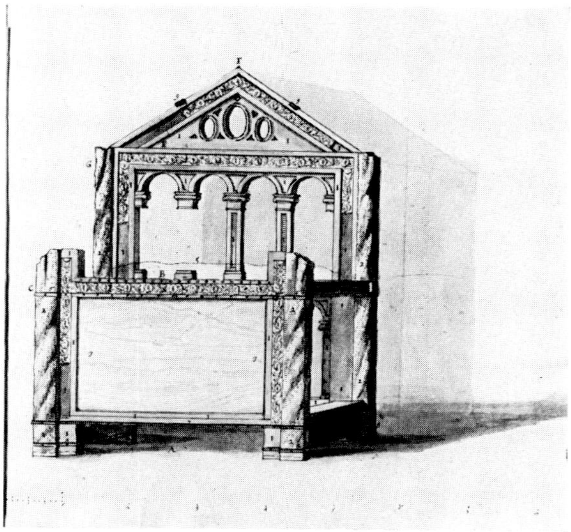

54 Perspective view of the throne (no.82)

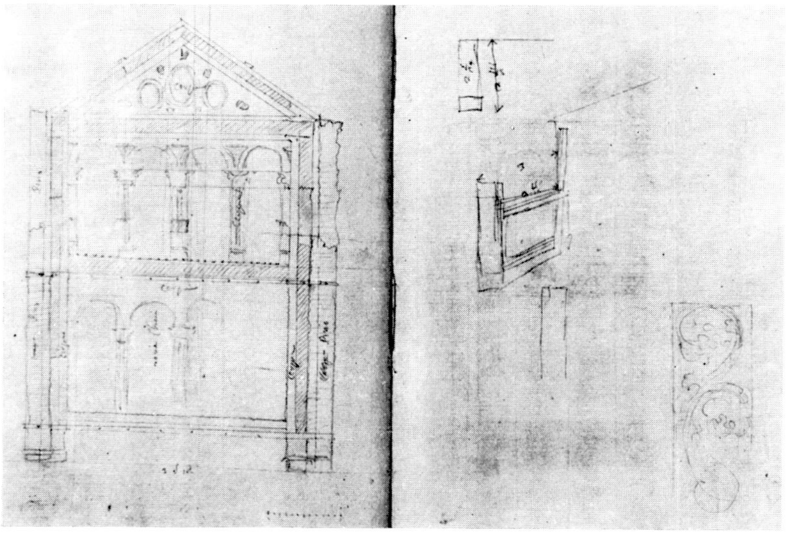

55 Front elevation of the throne, and four details (no.81)

Projects for the decoration of the piers

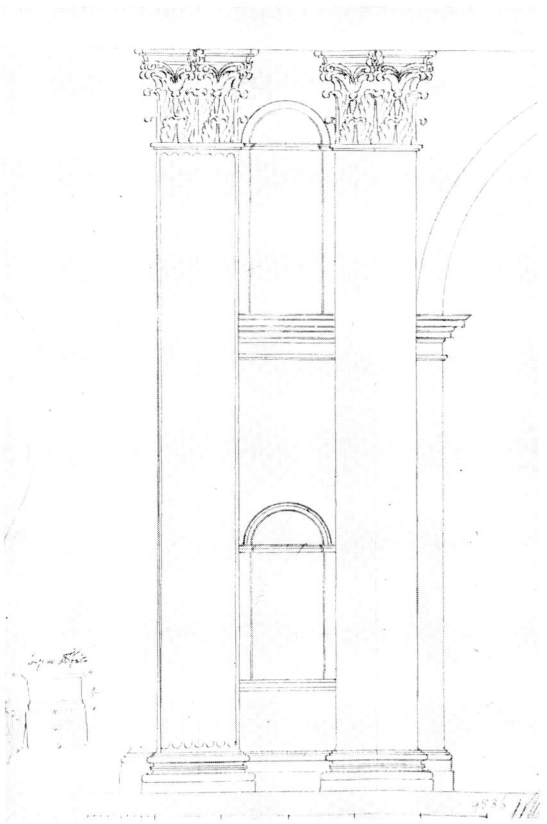

56 Elevation of a pier (2) (no.84)

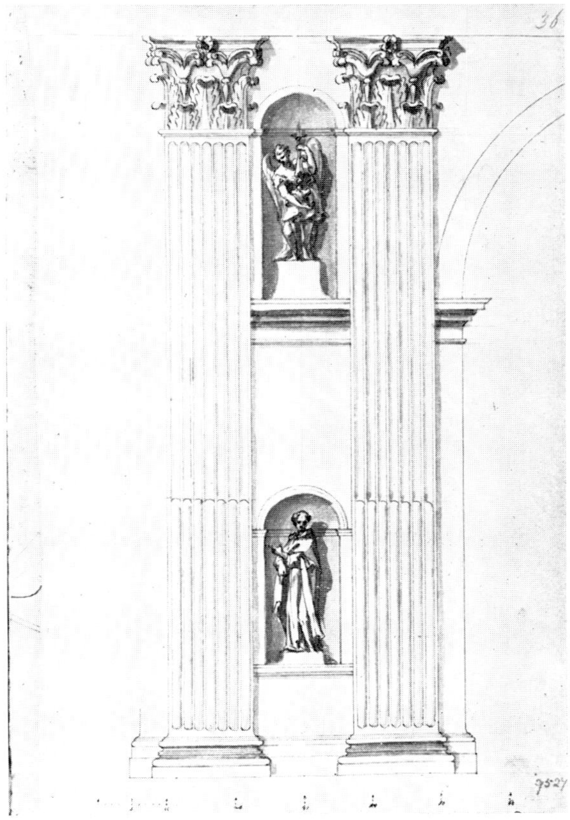

57 Project incorporating the extant niches, elevation (no.86)

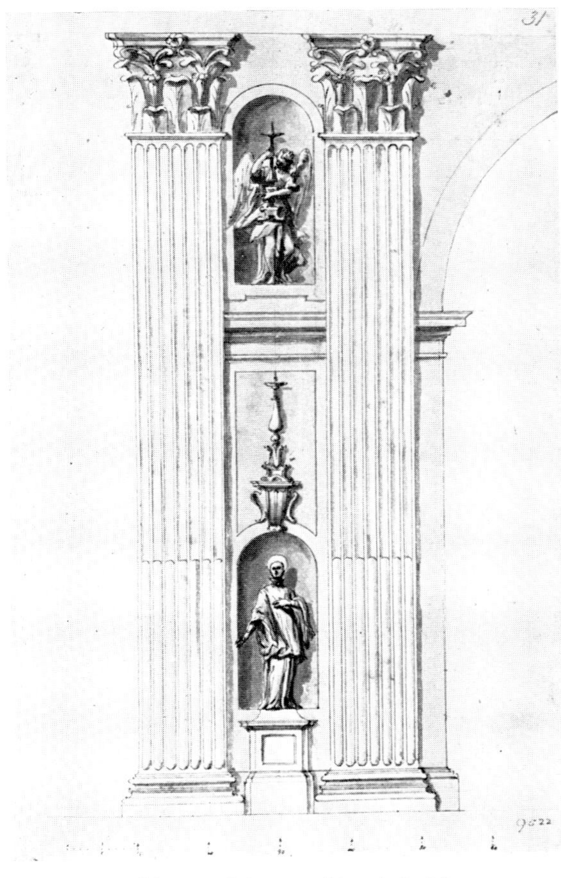

58 Project with two plain round-headed niches, 1 – elevation (no.87)

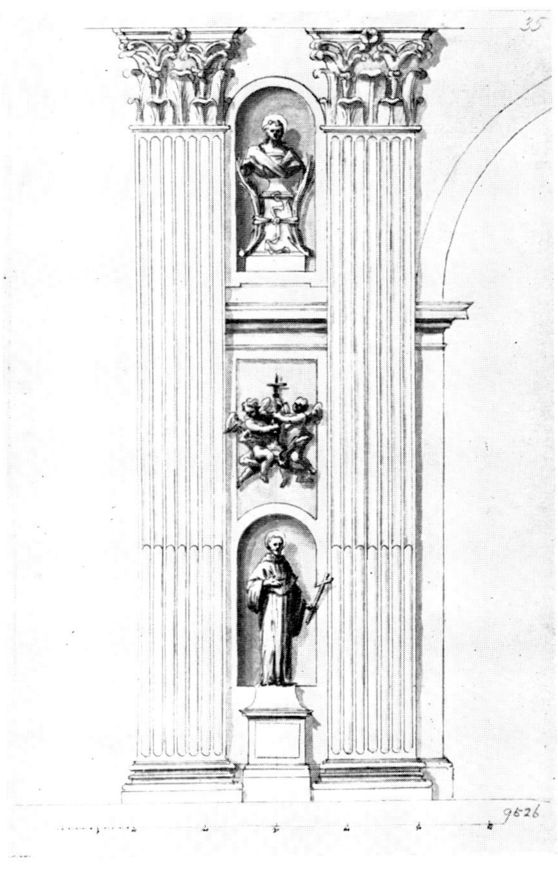

59 Project with two plain round-headed niches, 2 – elevation (no.88)

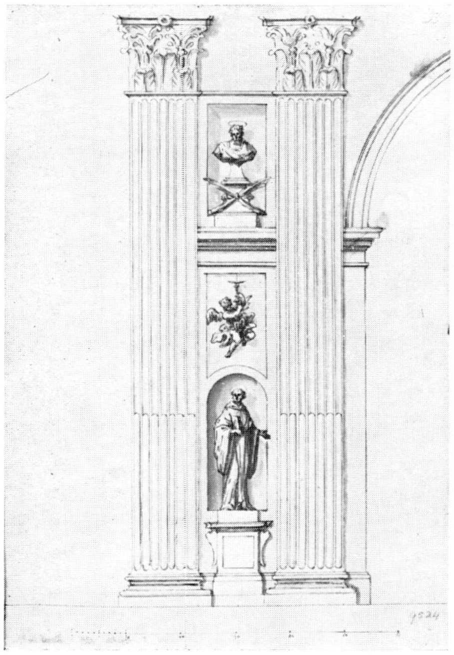

60 Project with a rectangular upper niche, 1 – elevation (no.89)

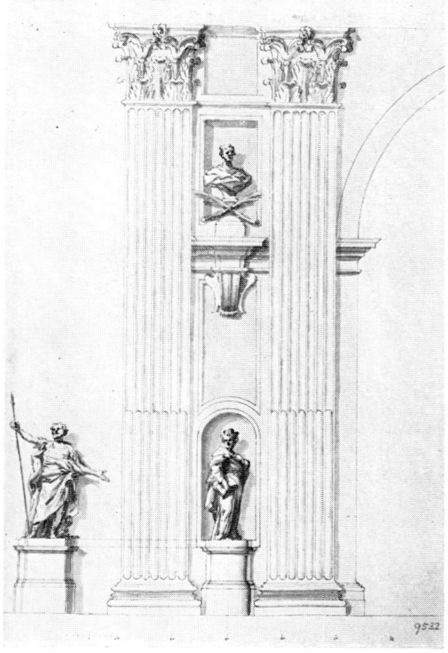

61 Project with a rectangular upper niche, 2 – elevation (no.91)

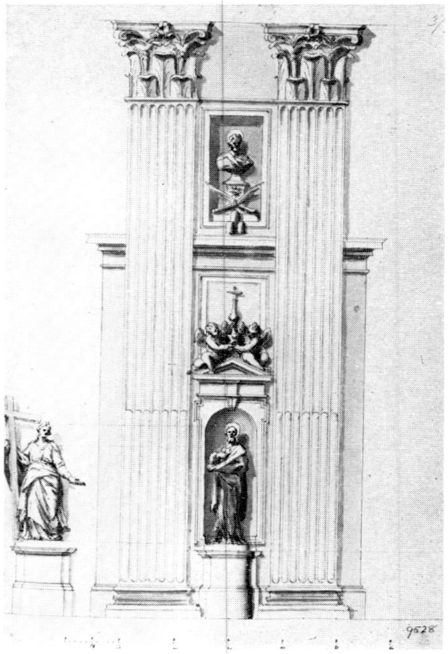

62 Project with a pedimented lower niche, 1 – elevation (no.92)

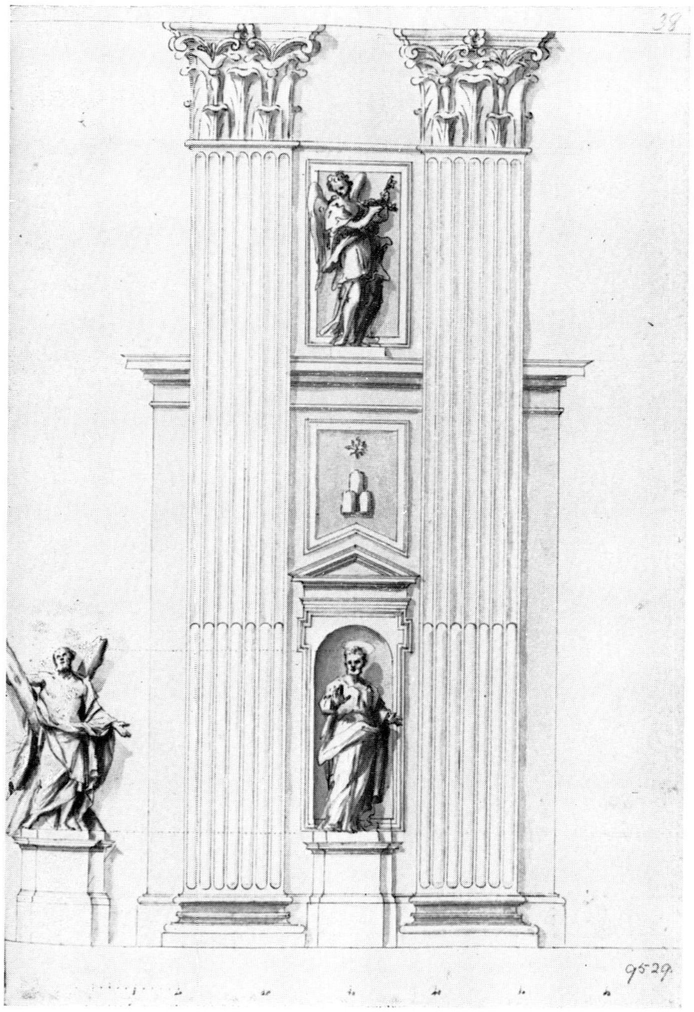

63 Project with a pedimented lower niche, 2 – elevation (no.93)

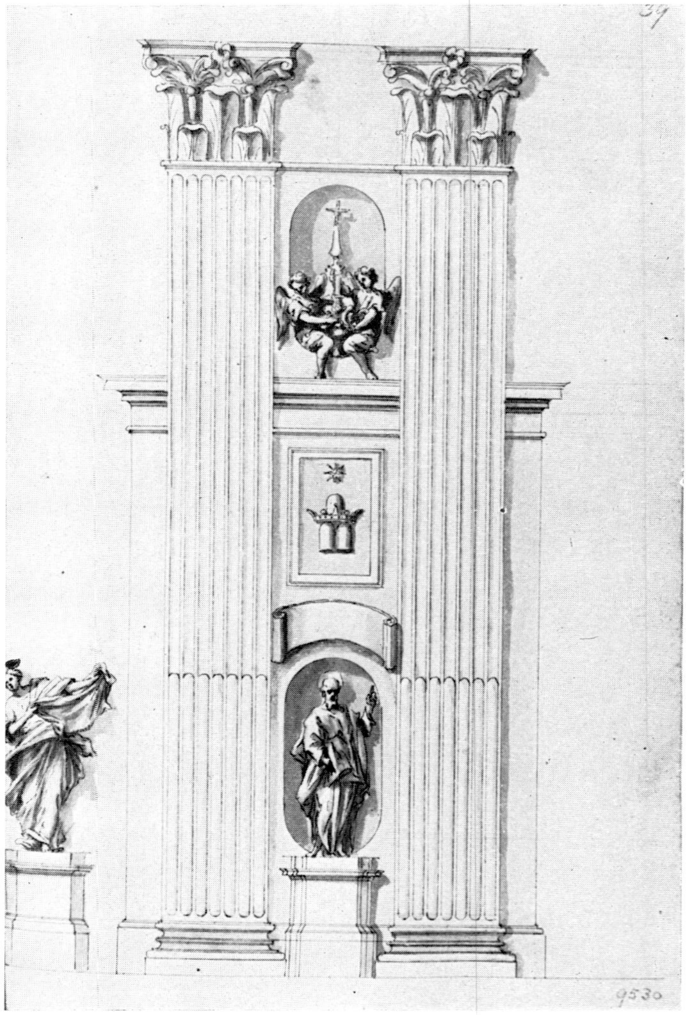

64 Project with two oval niches, elevation (no.94)

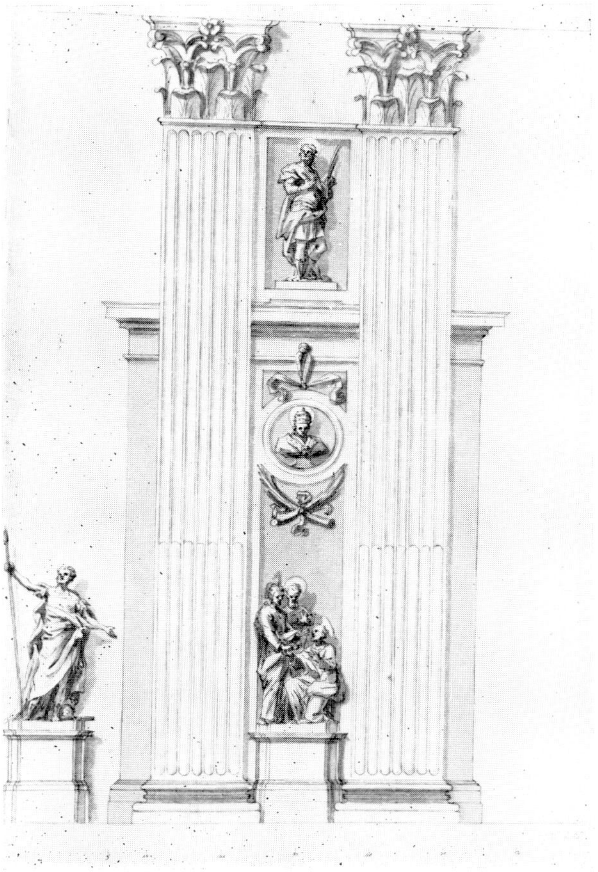

65 Project omitting the lower niche, elevation (no.95)

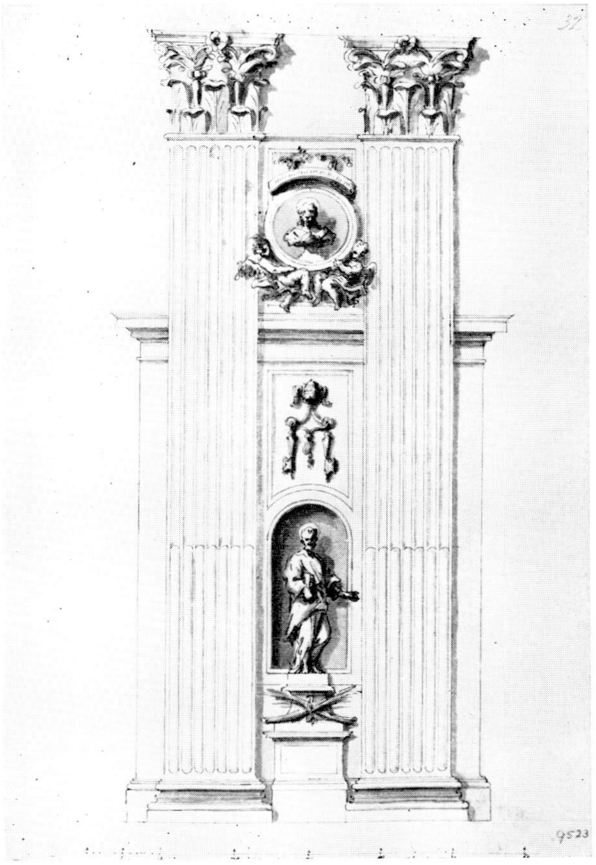

66 Project with a high pedestal, elevation (no.96)

Projects for decorating the vault roundels

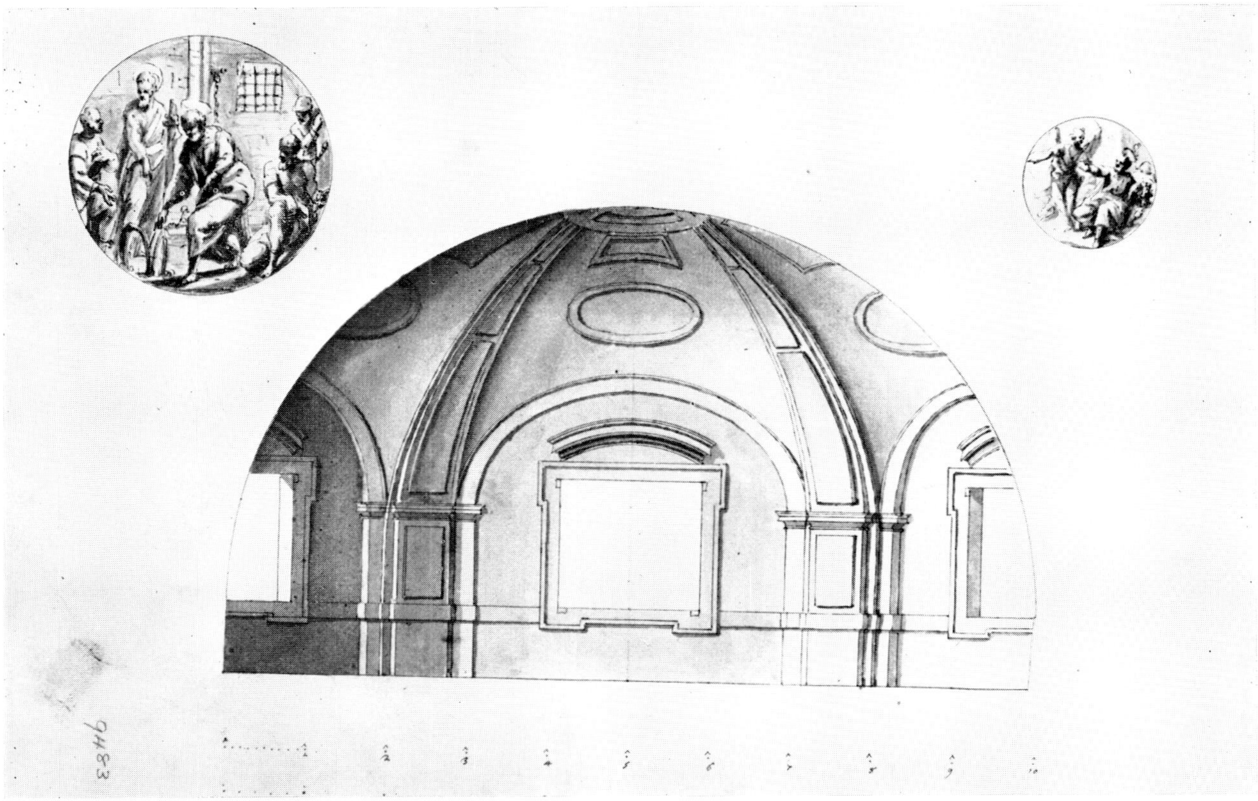

67 Elevation of the choir (?) vault, and two studies for a roundel (no.98)

Other Ecclesiastical Works

A project for S. Maria dei Miracoli, Rome (1673/4)

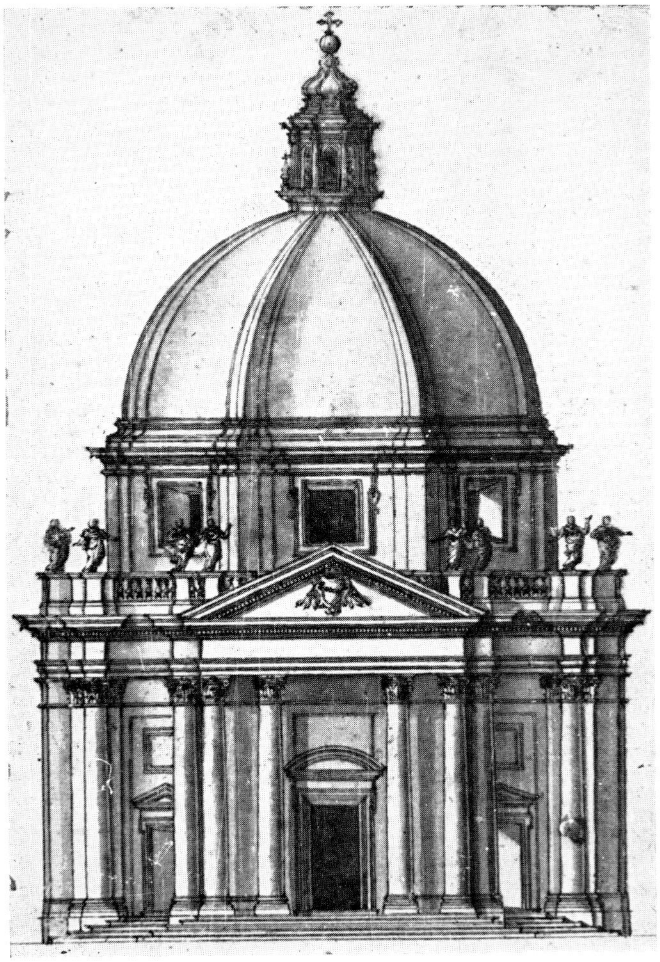

68 Elevation (after Fontana, no. 100)

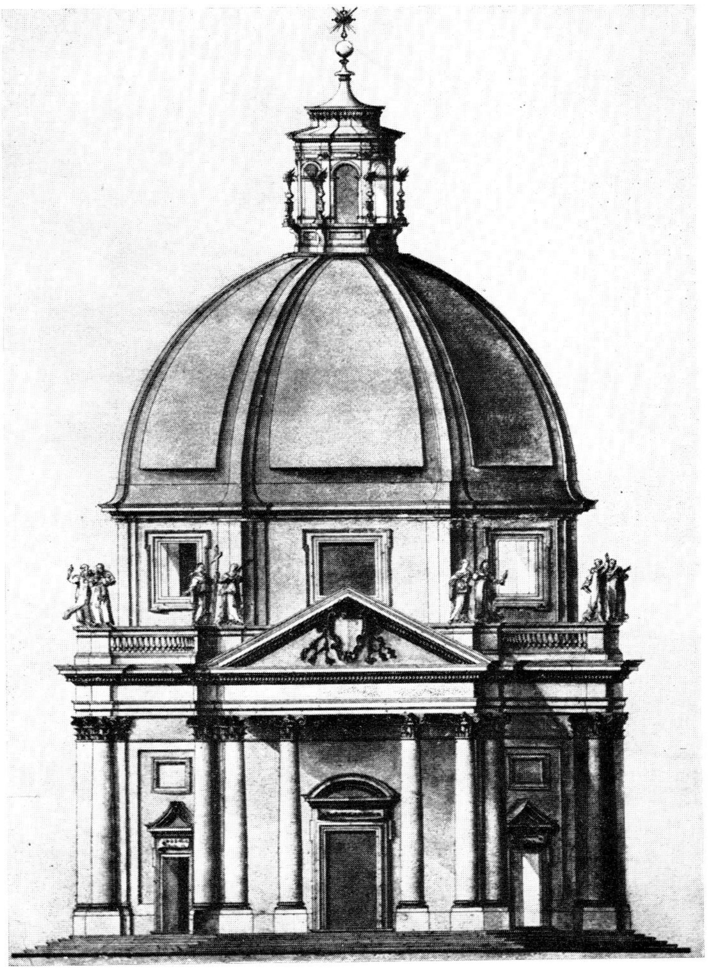

69 Elevation (drawing attributed to Gabriele Valvassori; Berlin, Kunstbibliothek)

Naples Cathedral, projects for the decoration of the apse (between 1691 and 1696)

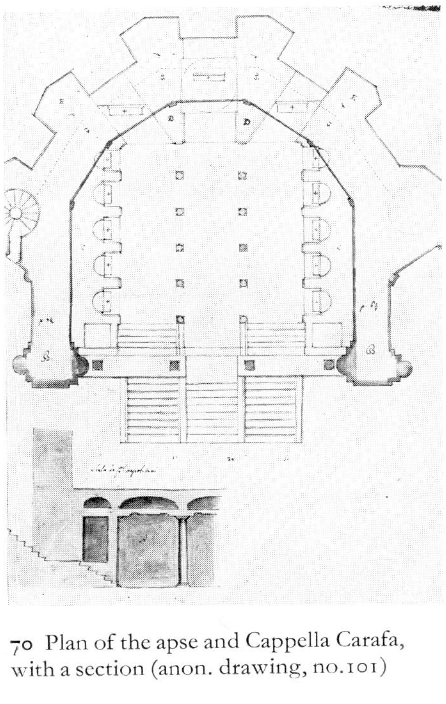

70 Plan of the apse and Cappella Carafa, with a section (anon. drawing, no. 101)

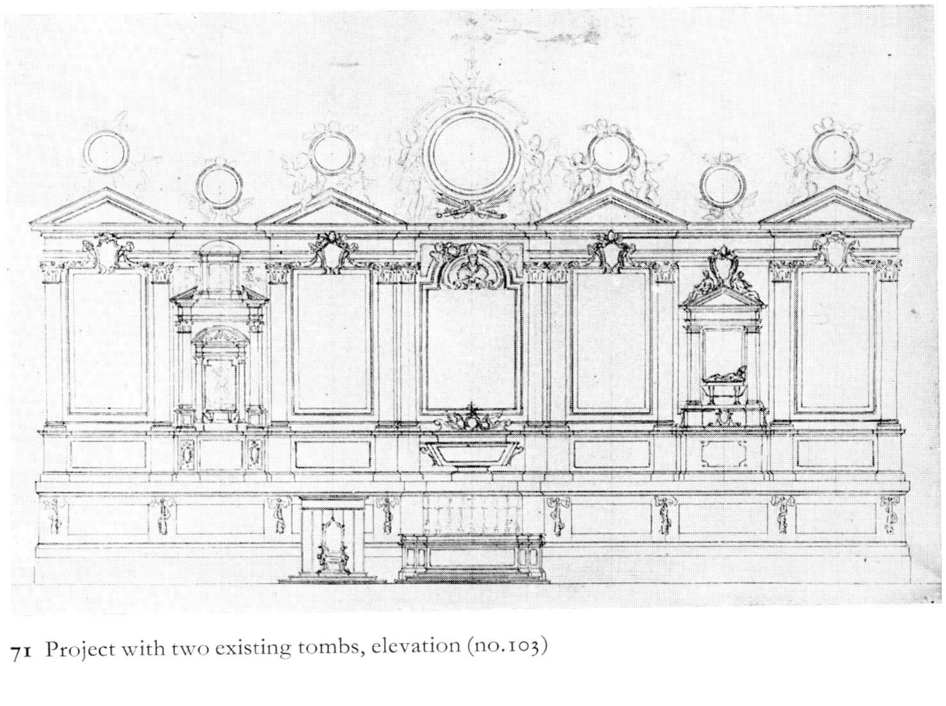

71 Project with two existing tombs, elevation (no. 103)

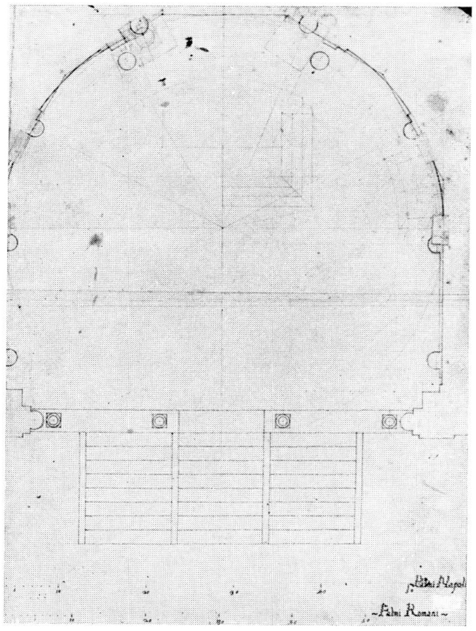

72 Plan project (no.102)

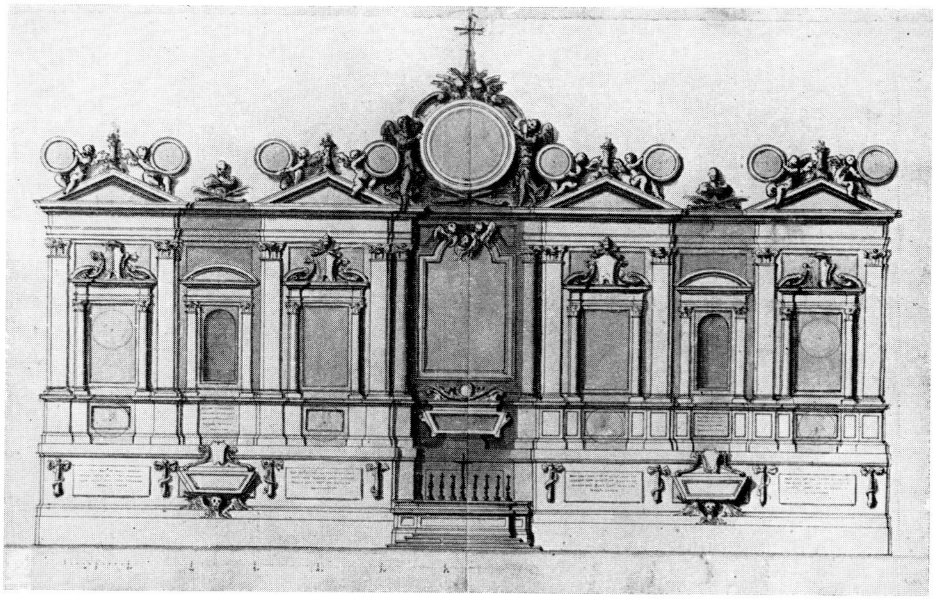

73 Project with two sarcophagi, elevation (no.104)

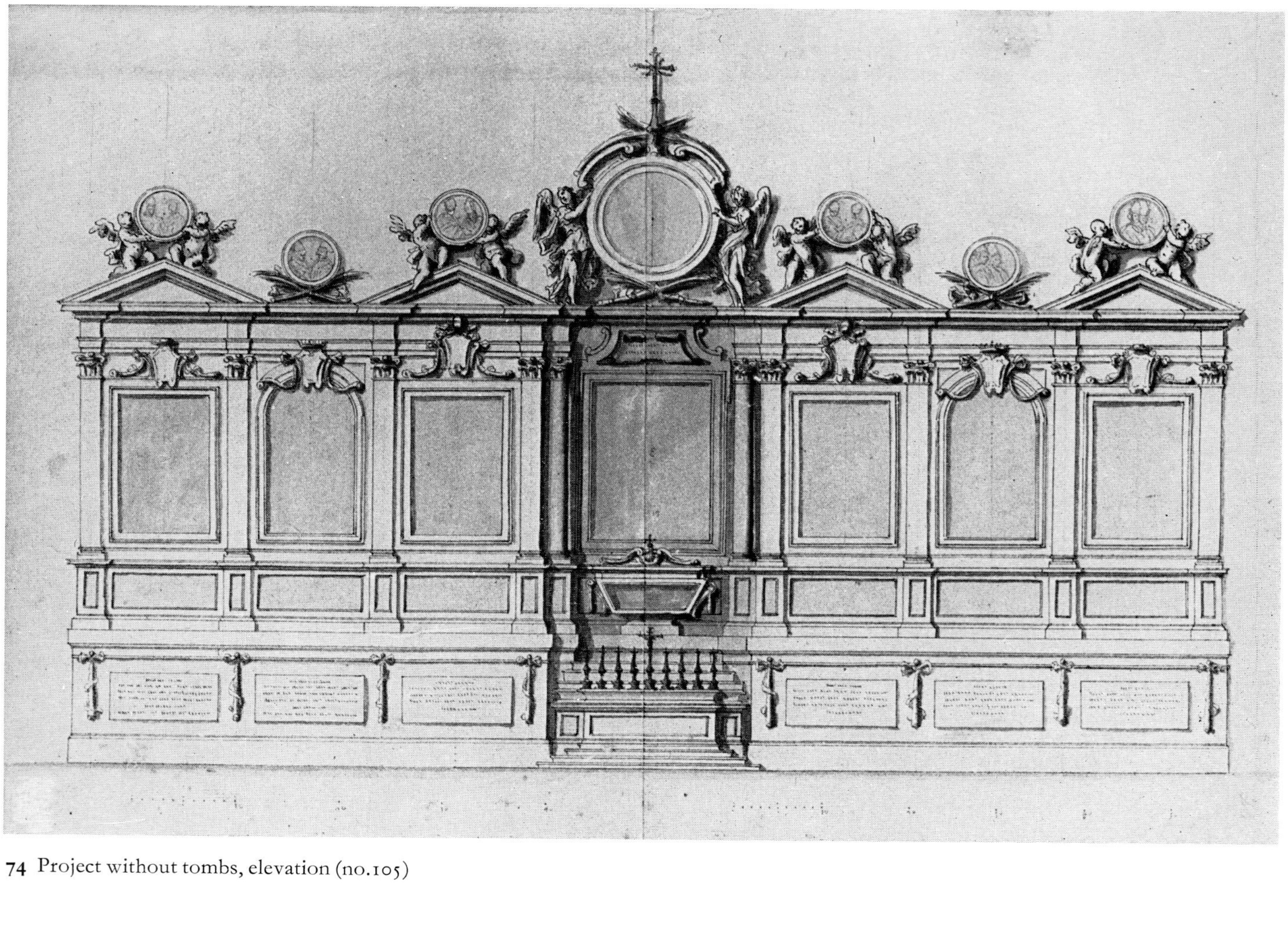

74 Project without tombs, elevation (no.105)

Project for the Jesuit church at Frascati (1694)

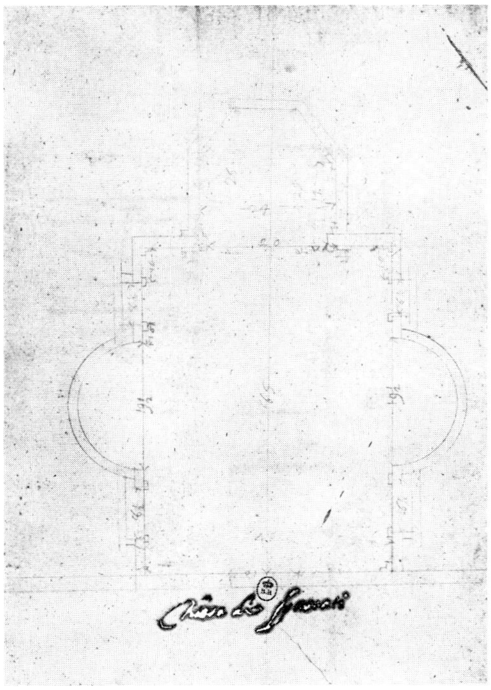

75 Plan of the church of 1608–1610 (anon. drawing, detail: Paris, Bibliothèque Nationale)

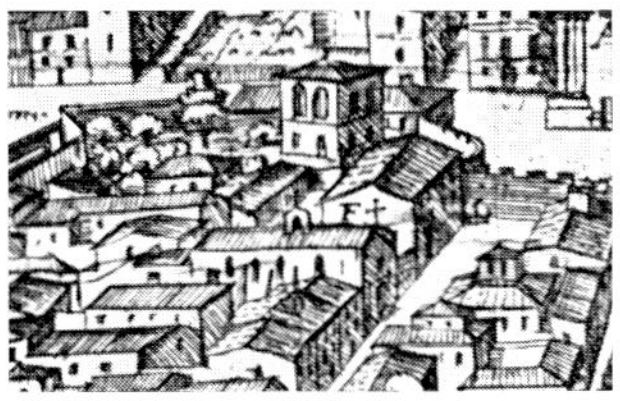

76 View of the church, 1620 (detail of the Greutter plan of Frascati)

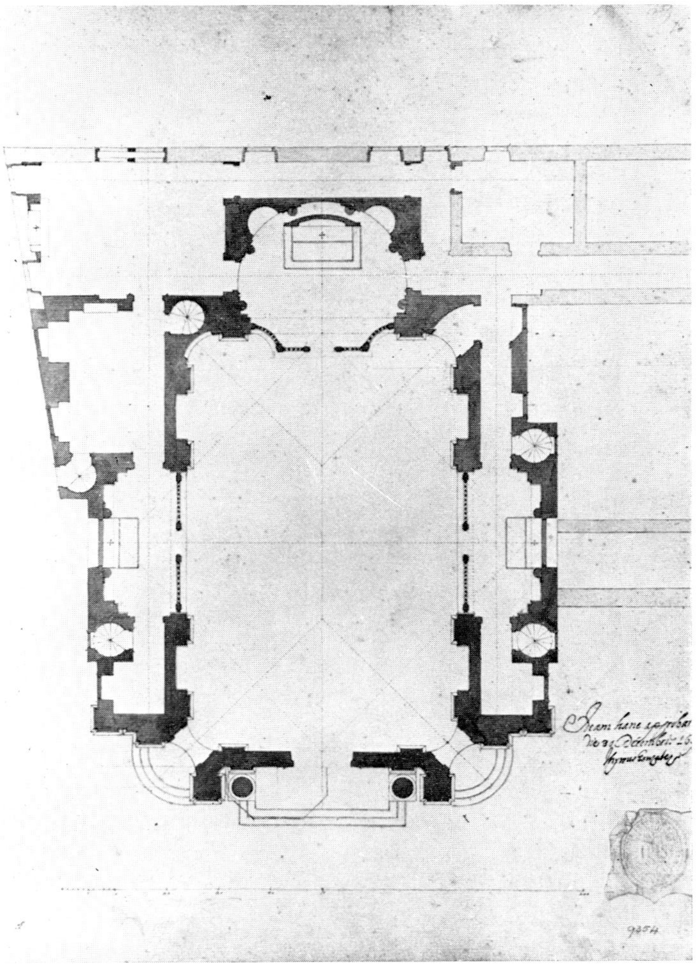

77 Plan (no.106)

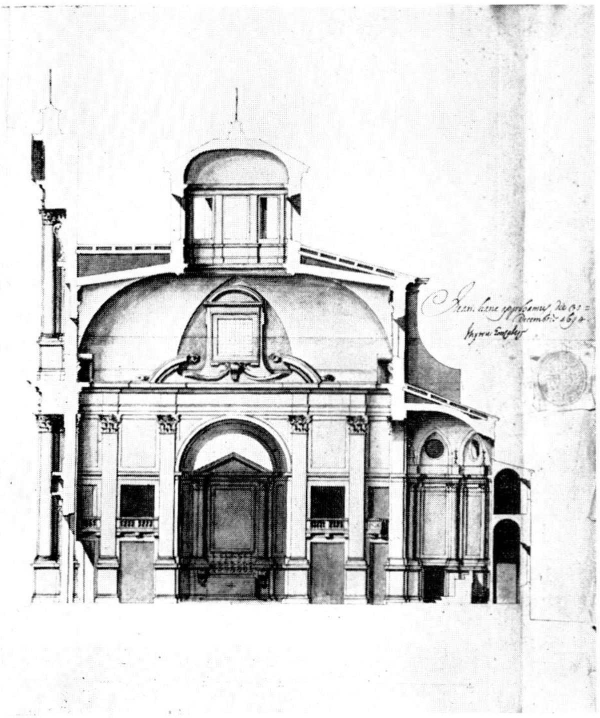

78 Longitudinal section (no.107)

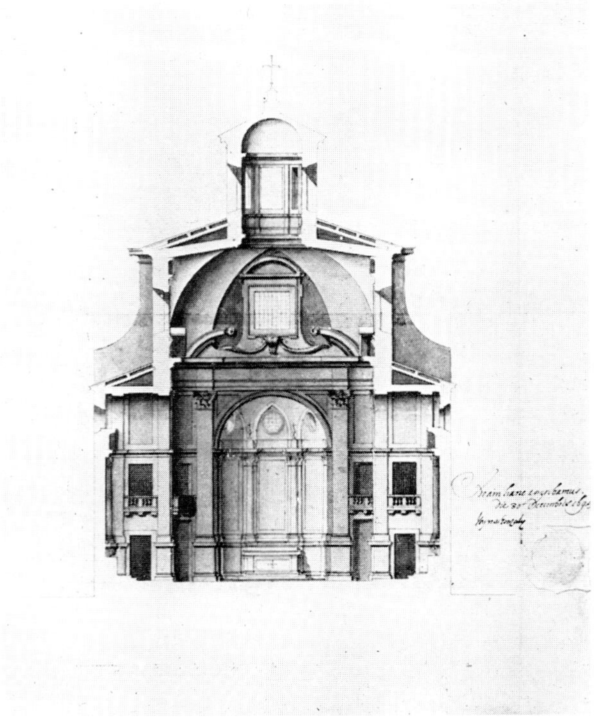

79 Transverse section (no.108)

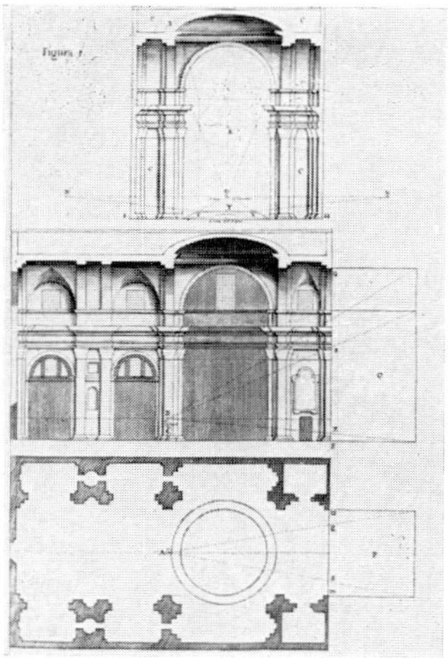

80 Project for a church (engraving from Pozzo, *Prospettiva*, 1700)

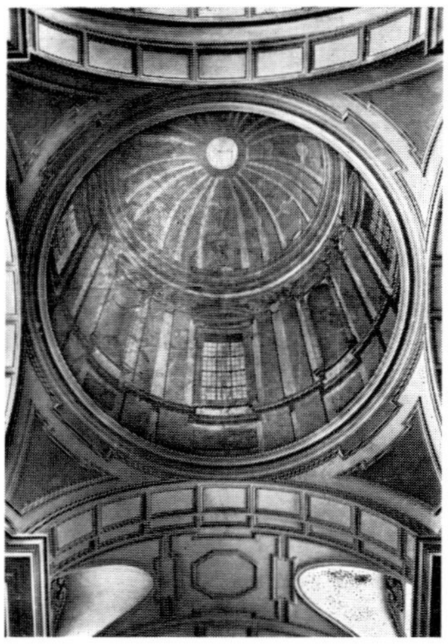

81 View of the painted dome

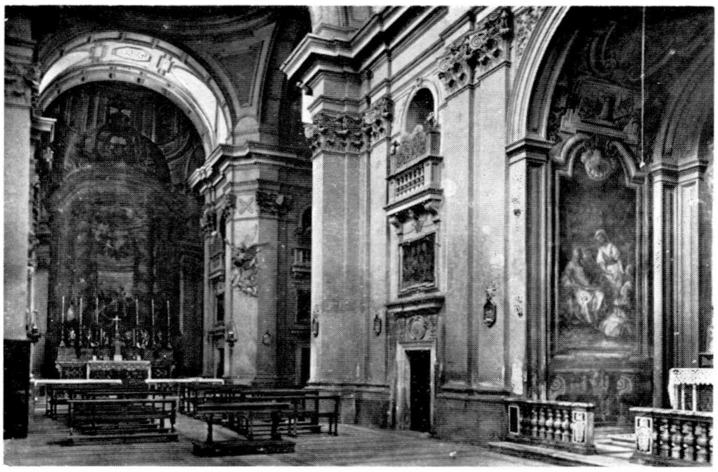

82 View of the interior

Parma, S. Maria della Steccata, project for the high altar (1696)

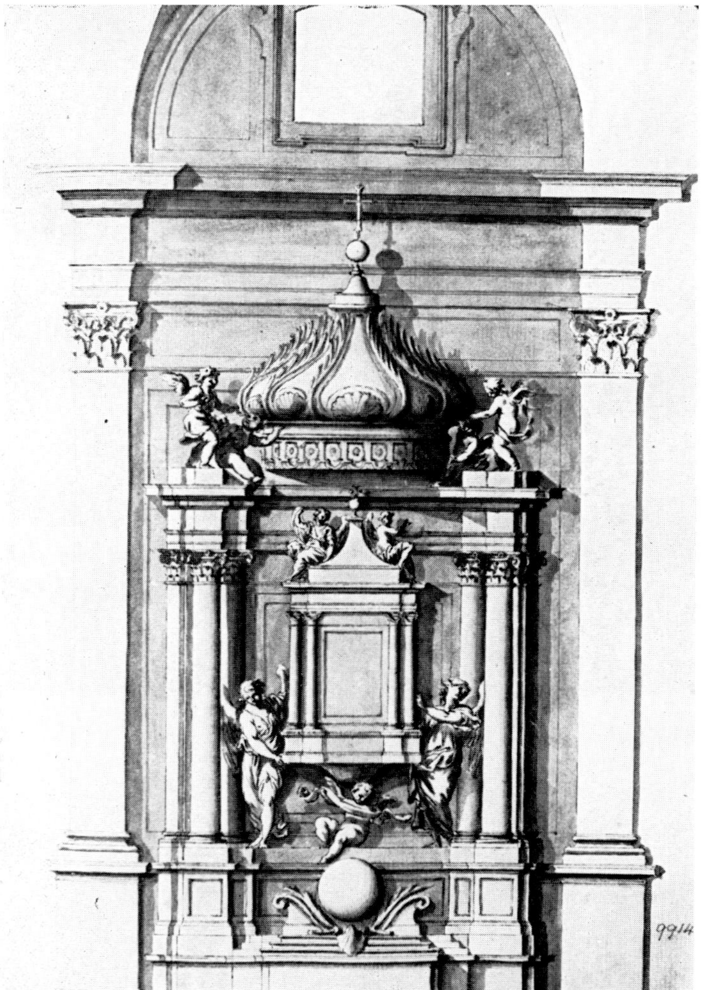

83 Elevation of the altar (no.109)

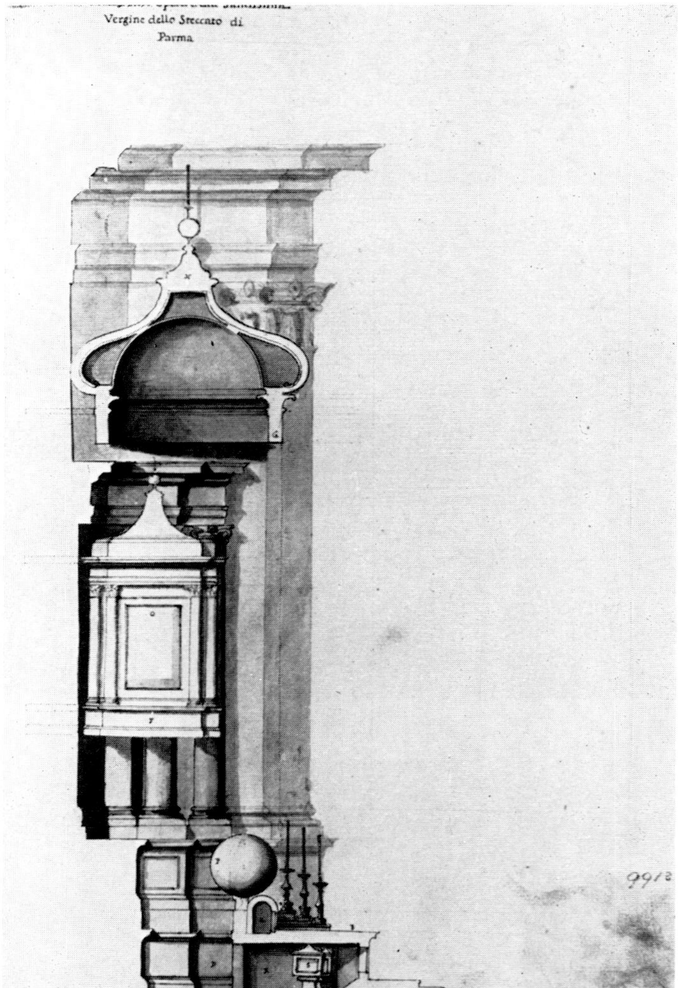

84 Section of the altar (no.110)

A church design for Cardinal Negroni (1697)

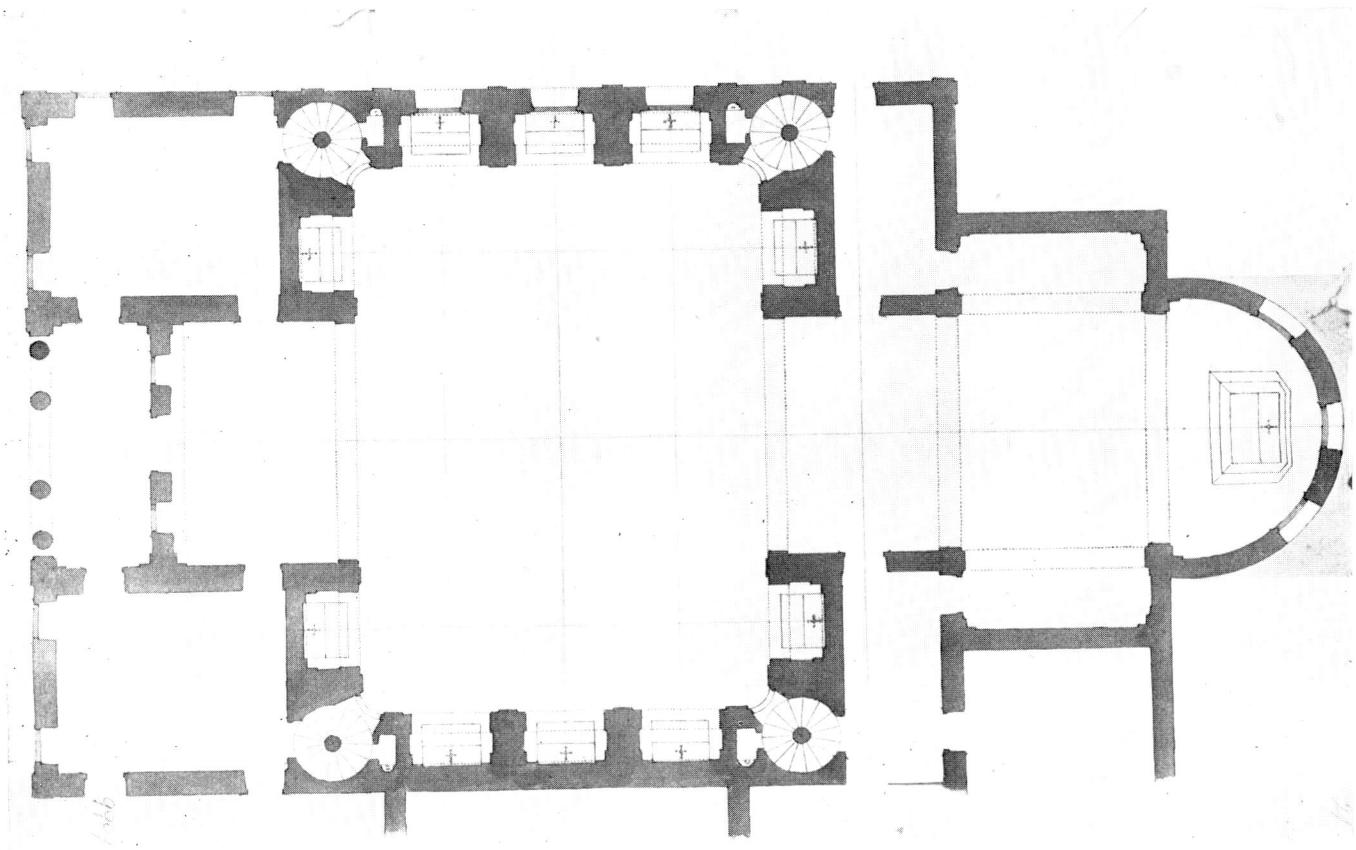

85 Plan of the church (no.111)

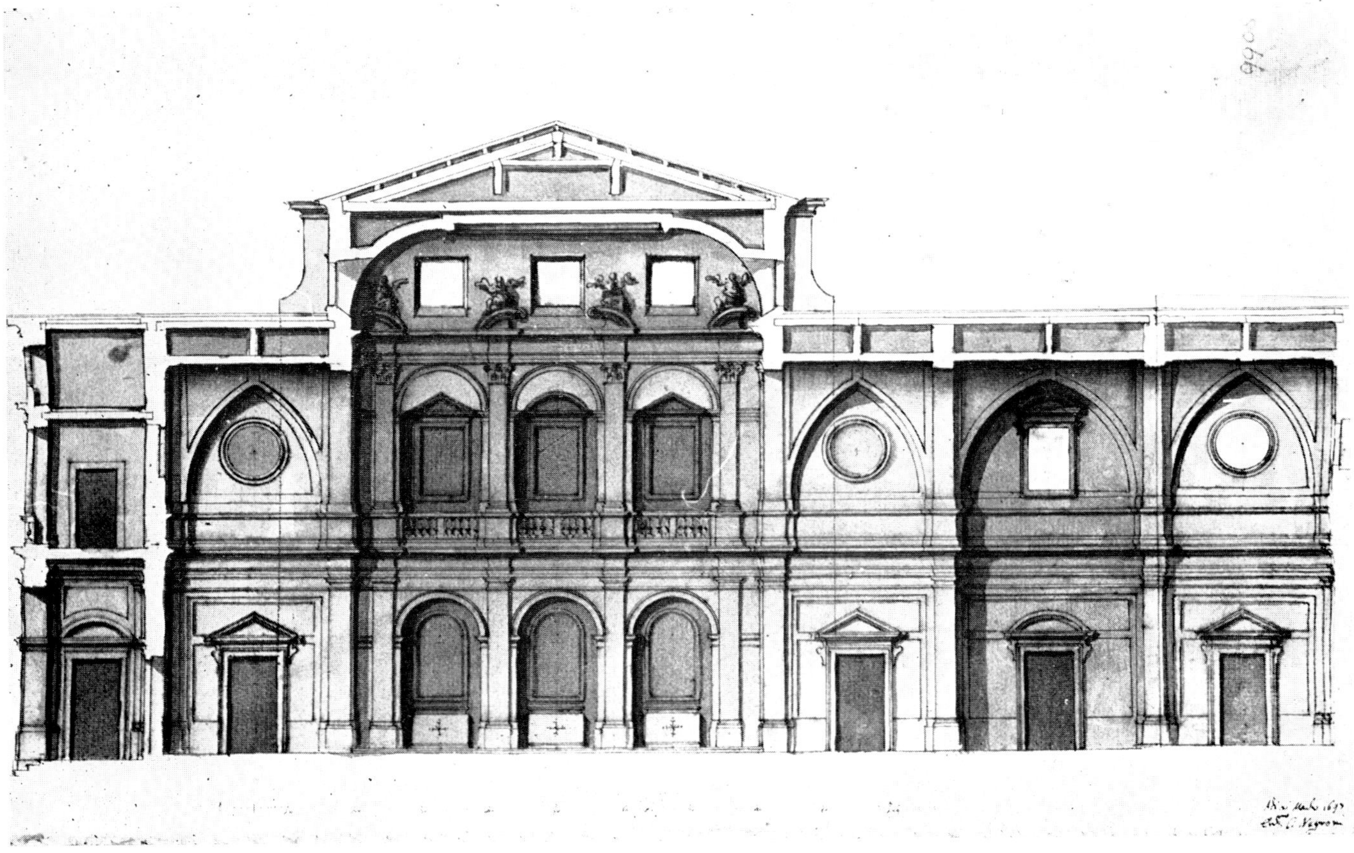

86 Longitudinal section of the church (no.112)

The restoration of S. Spirito dei Napolitani, Rome (*c.*1700/1702–1708)

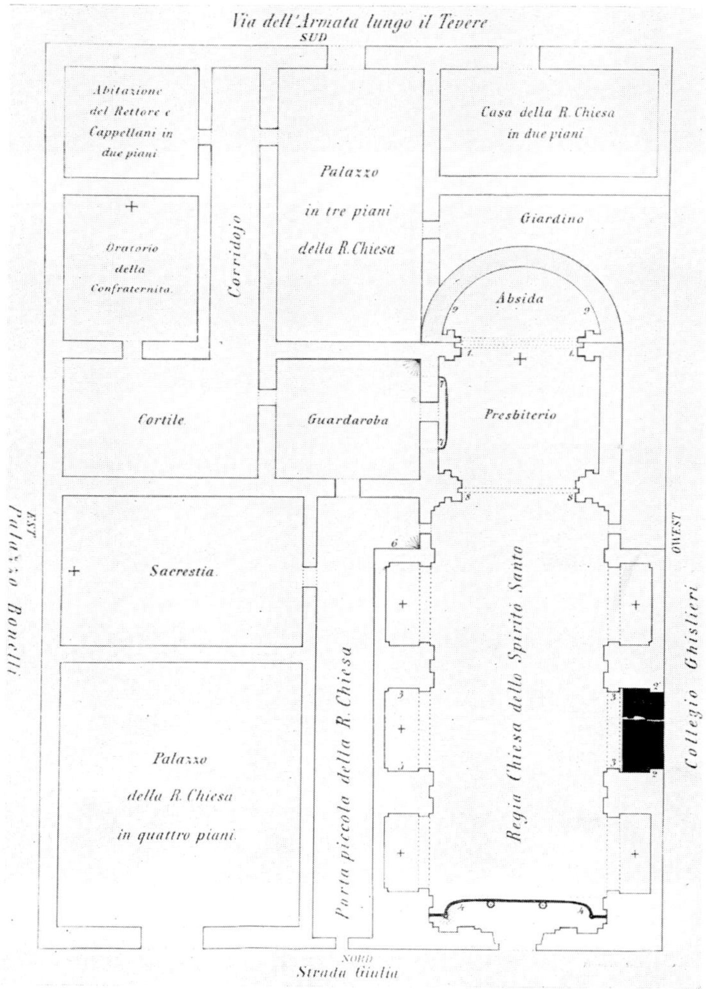

87 Plan of the church and neighbouring site, 1868 (engraving from Lancelotti)

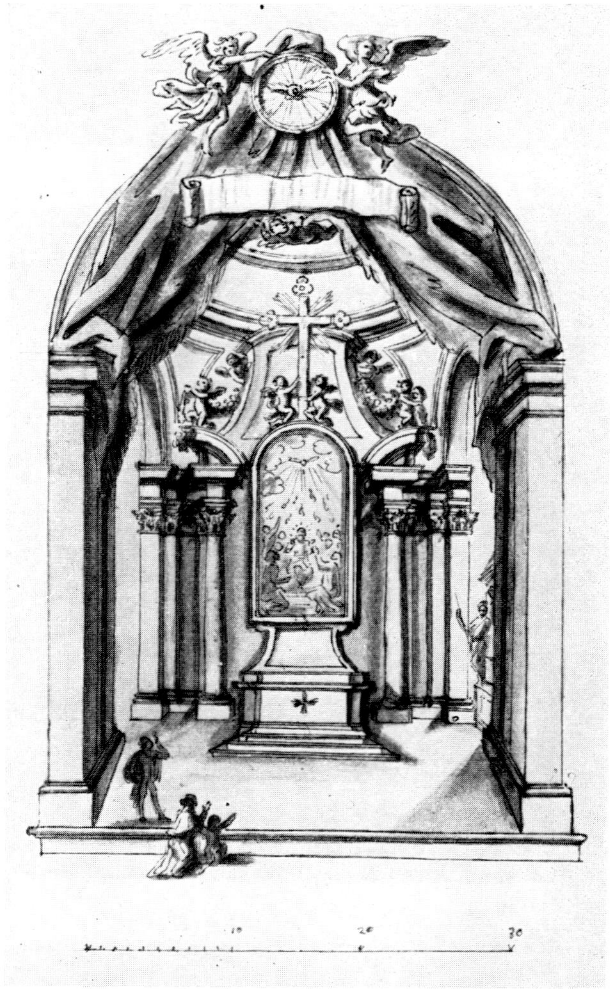

88 Perspective view of the choir (anon. drawing; Stockholm, Nationalmuseum)

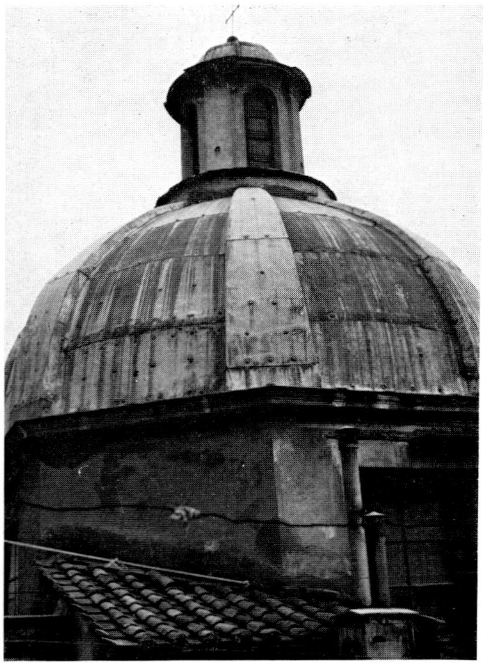

89 View of the cupola of the choir (photograph Nannini)

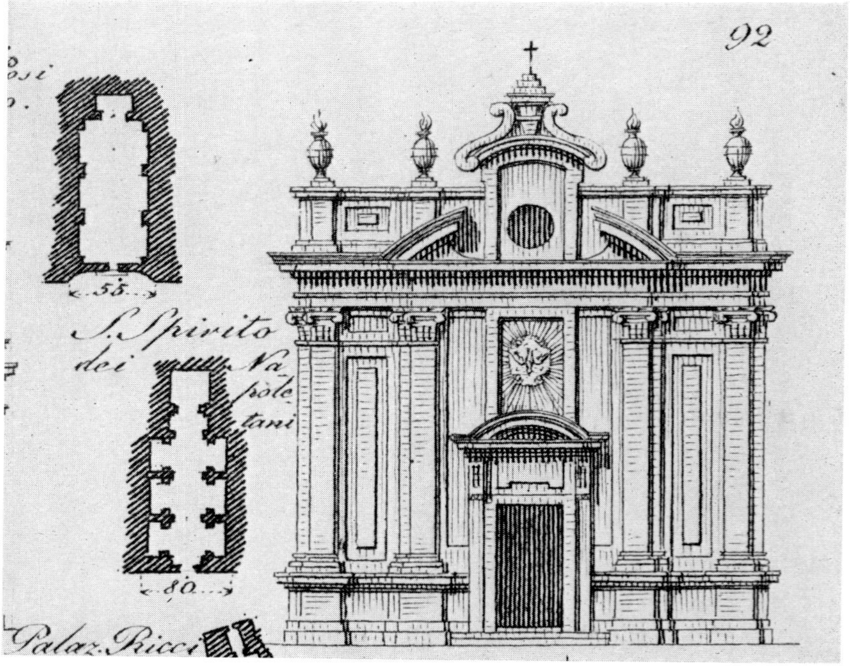

90 Elevation of the façade and two plans, 1835 (engraving from Cipriani)

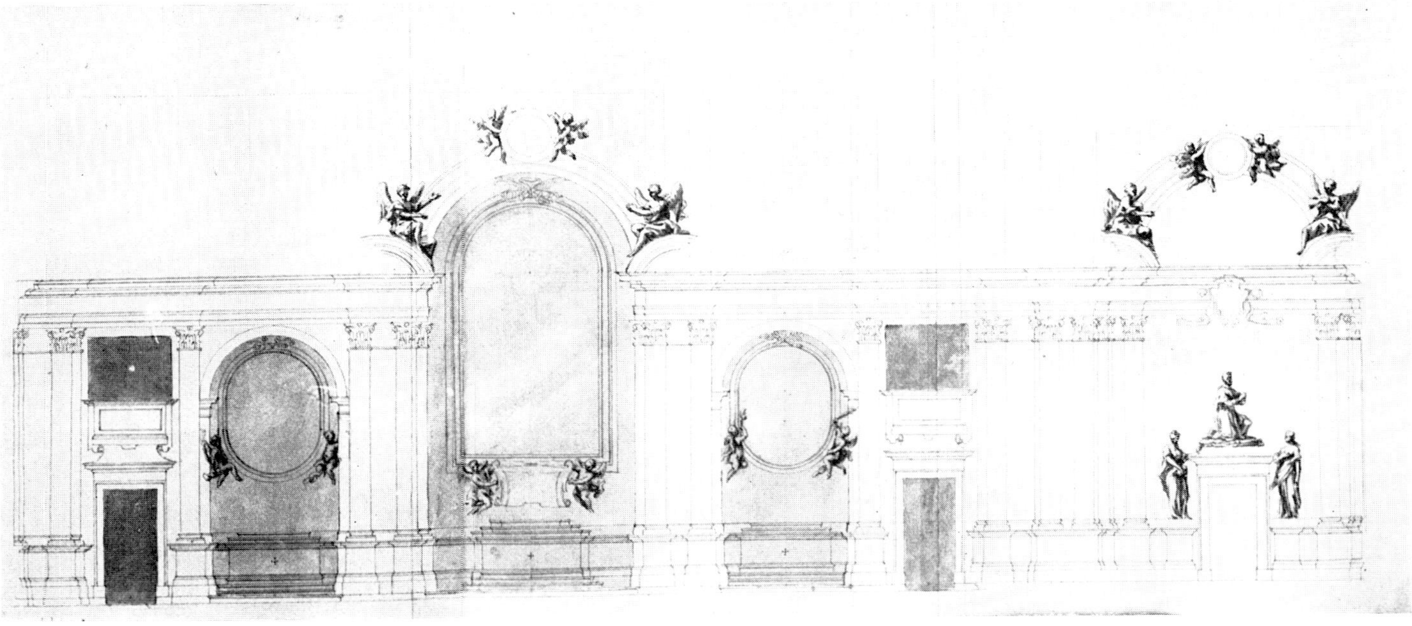

91 Longitudinal section of the nave and choir, stage 1 (no.114)

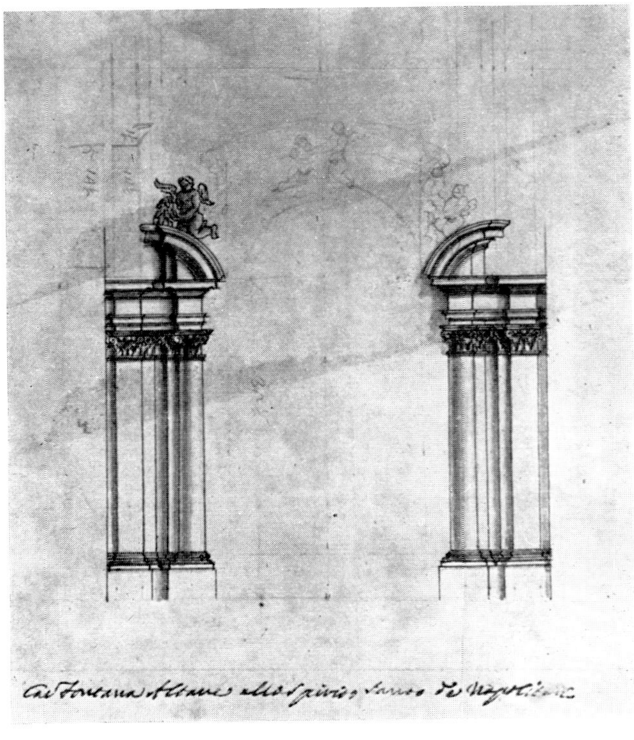

92 Elevation of the piers of the altar wall (anon. drawing; New York, Cooper Hewitt Museum)

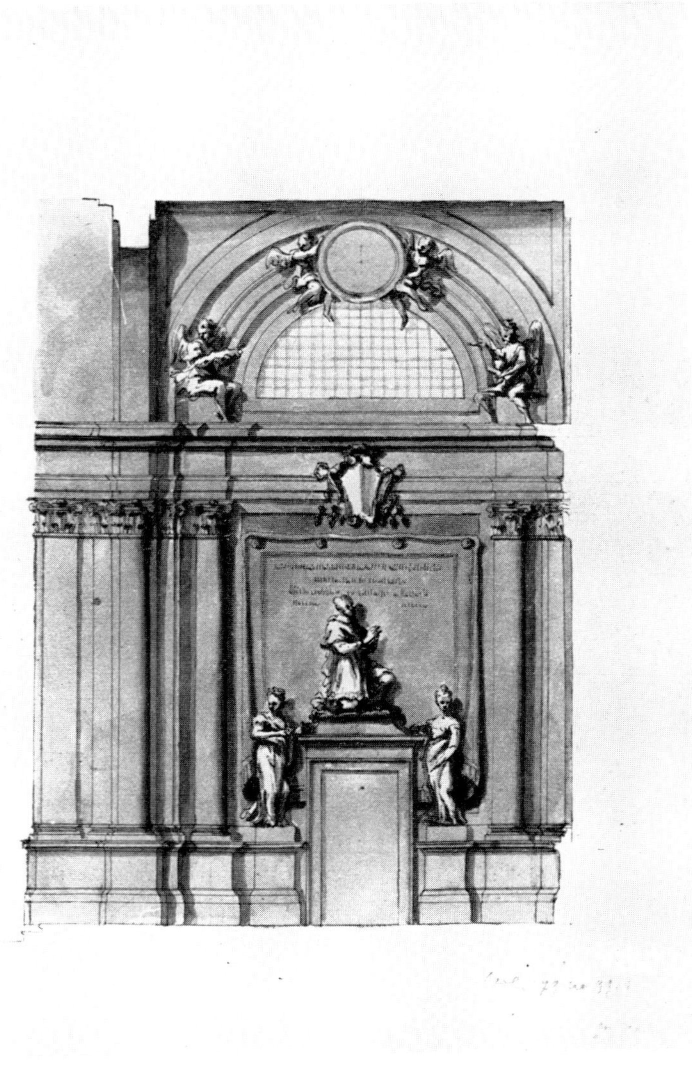

93 Section of the choir, stage 1 (no.115)

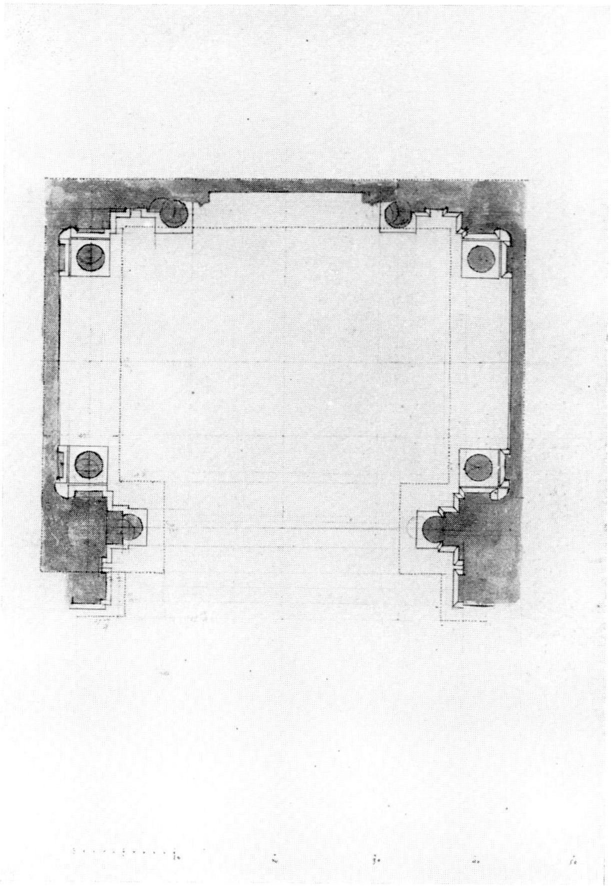

94 Plan of the choir, stage I (no.116)

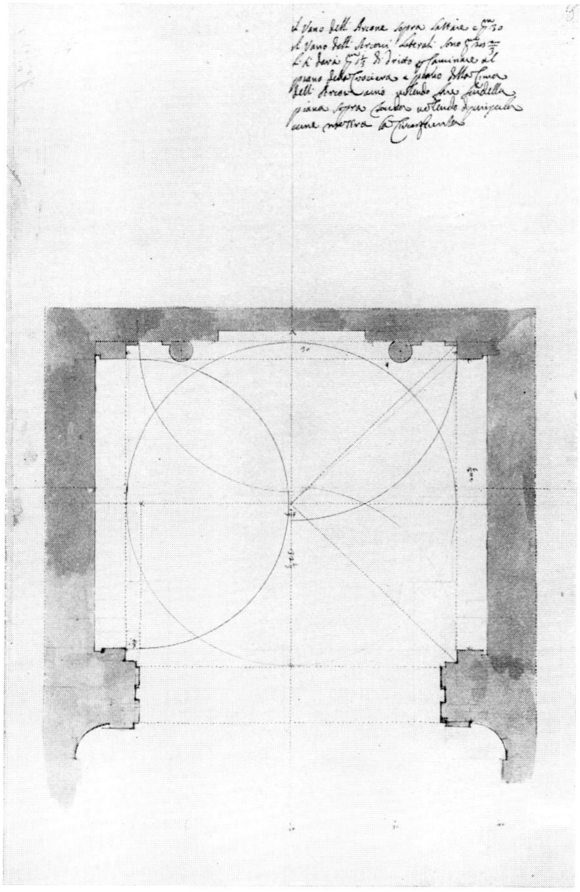

95 Plan of the choir, stage I (no.118)

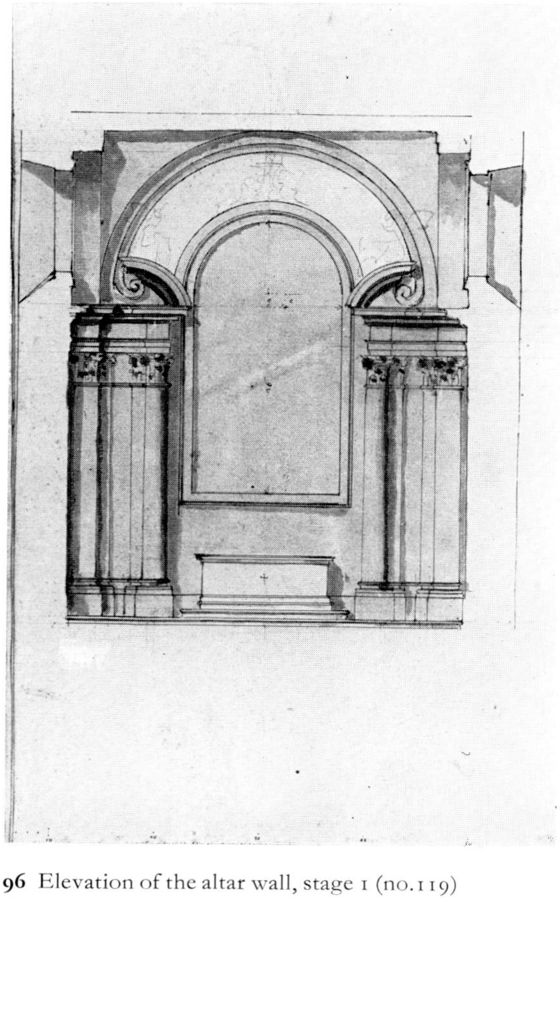

96 Elevation of the altar wall, stage I (no.119)

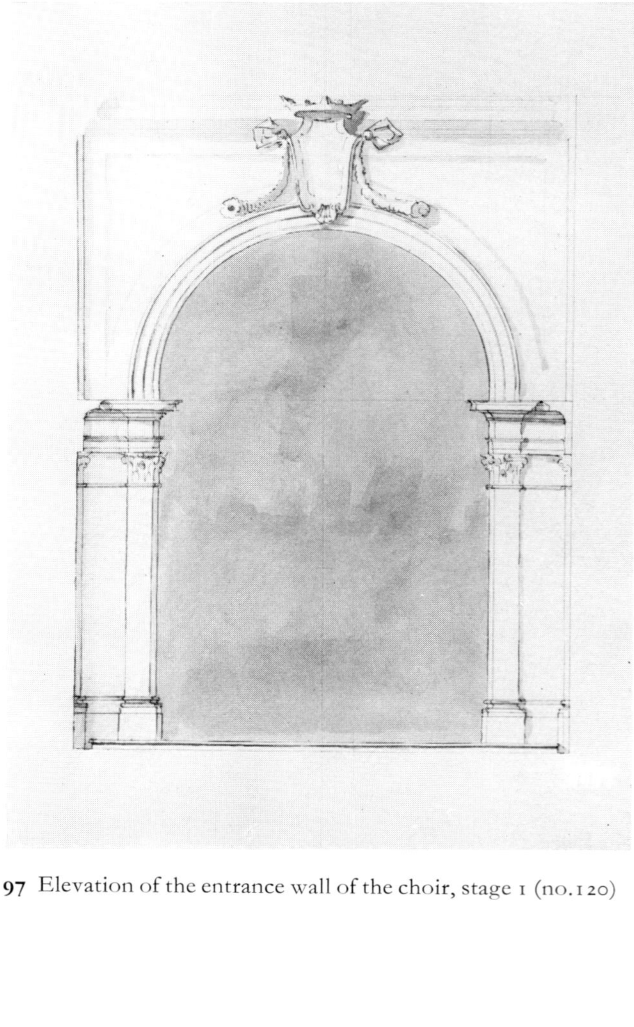

97 Elevation of the entrance wall of the choir, stage I (no.120)

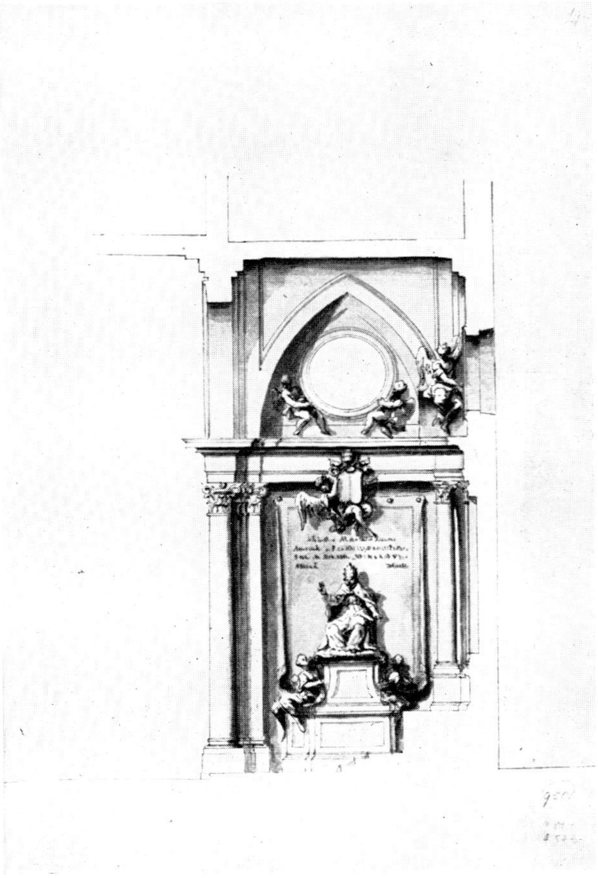

98 Section of the choir showing monument to Innocent XII, stage 1a (no.121)

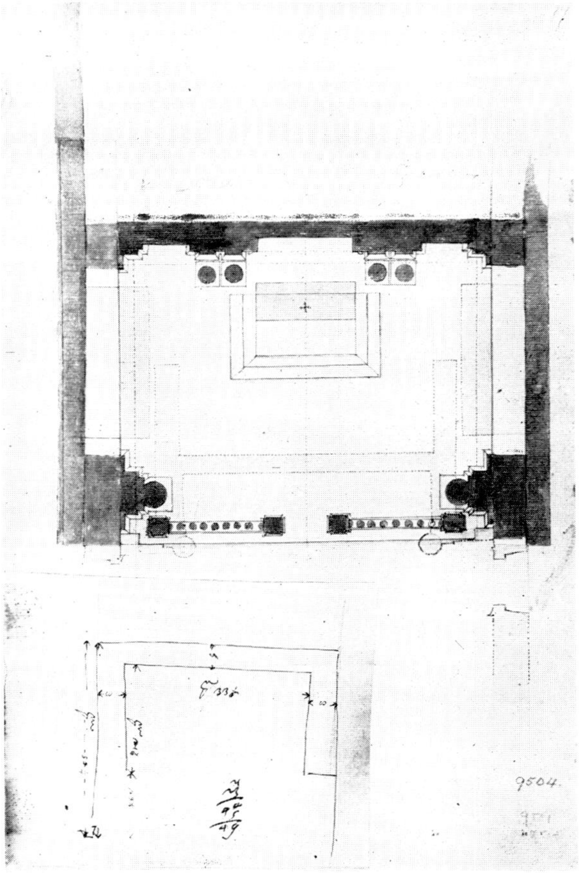

99 Plan of the choir, stage 1a (no.122)

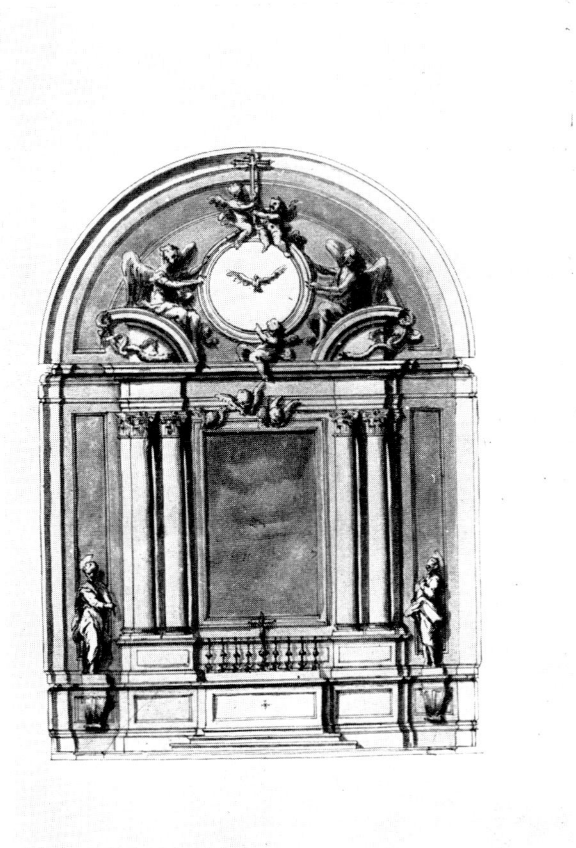

100 Elevation of the altar wall, stage 1a (no.124)

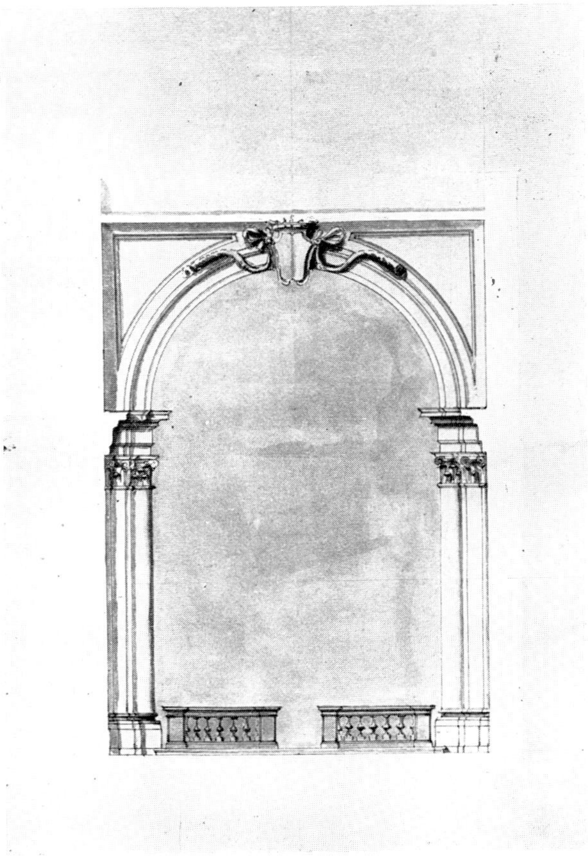

101 Elevation of the entrance wall of the choir, stage 1a (no.125)

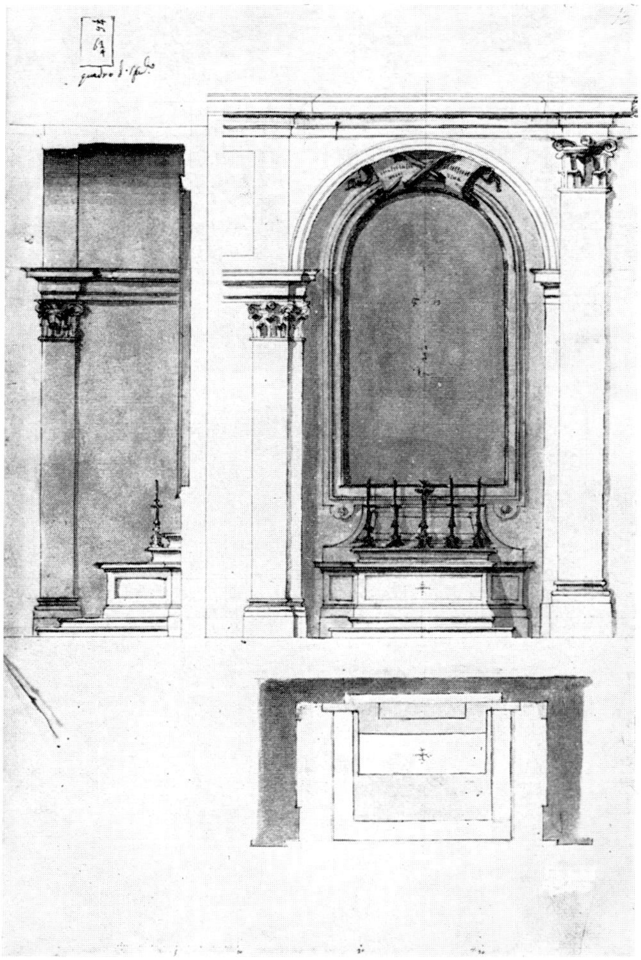

102 Plan, section and elevation of a side chapel, transitional stage (no.126)

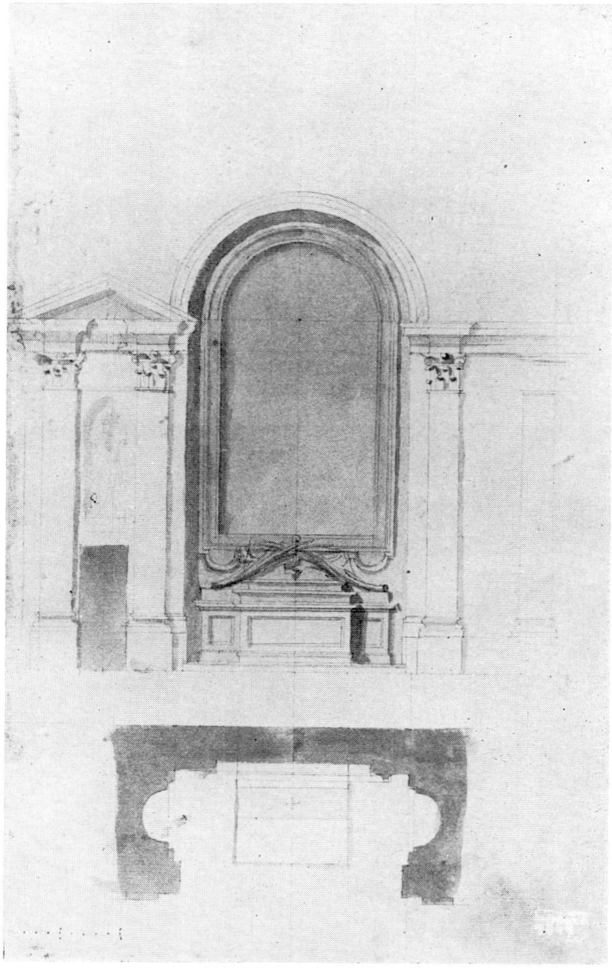

103 Part elevation of the nave, showing a side chapel in plan and elevation, transitional stage (no.127)

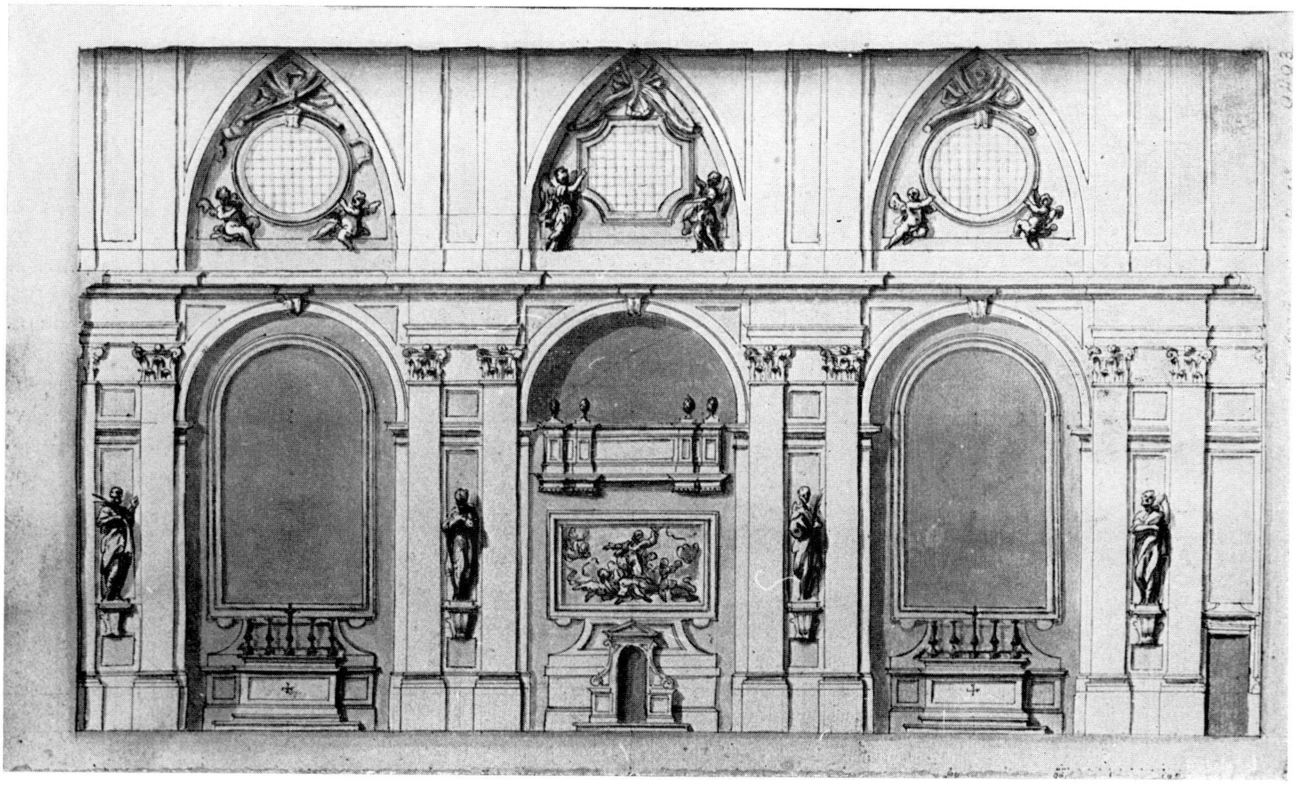

104 Section of the nave, stage 2 (no.128)

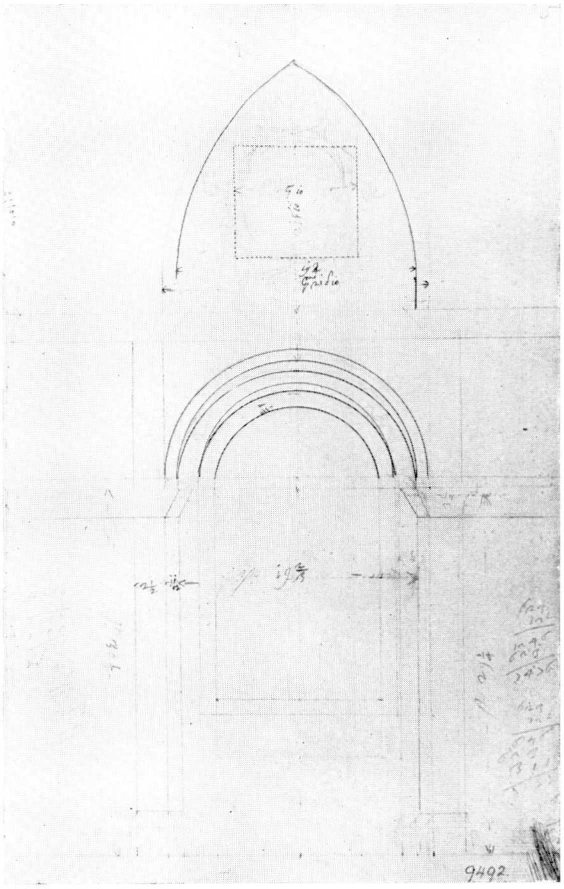

105 Sketch of one bay of the nave, elevation, stage 2 (no.129)

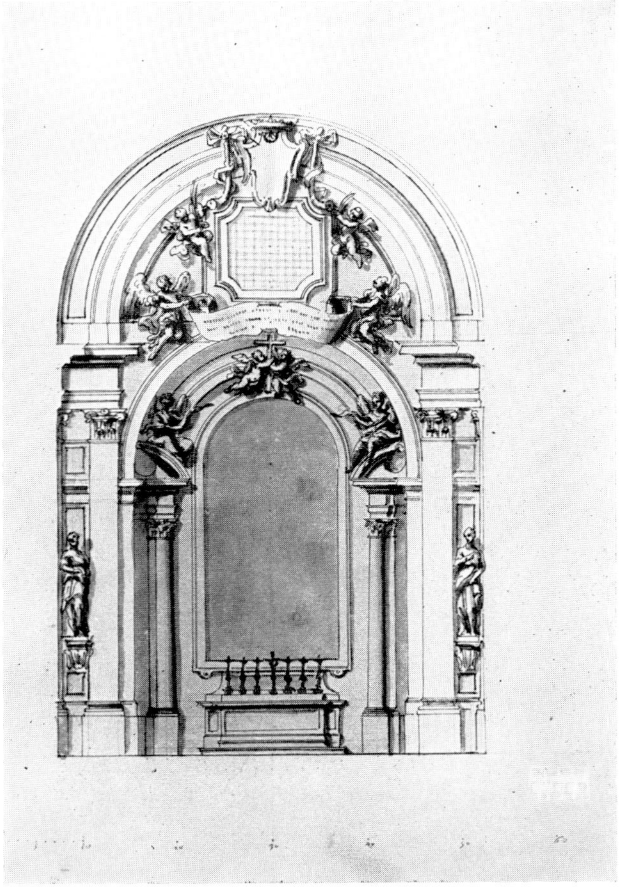

106 Elevation of the entrance wall of the choir, stage 2 (no.130)

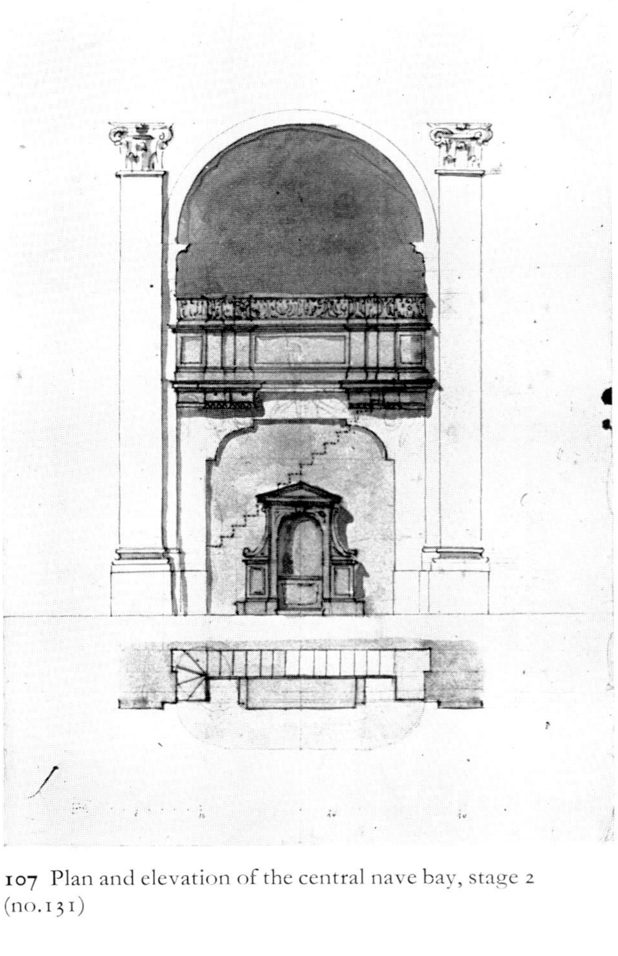

107 Plan and elevation of the central nave bay, stage 2 (no.131)

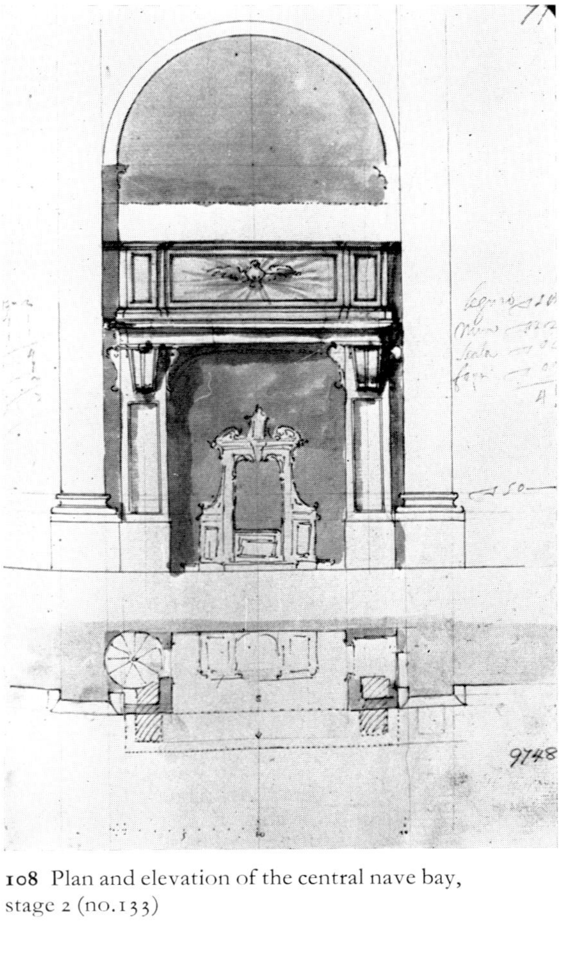

108 Plan and elevation of the central nave bay, stage 2 (no.133)

The portico of S. Maria in Trastevere, Rome (1701)

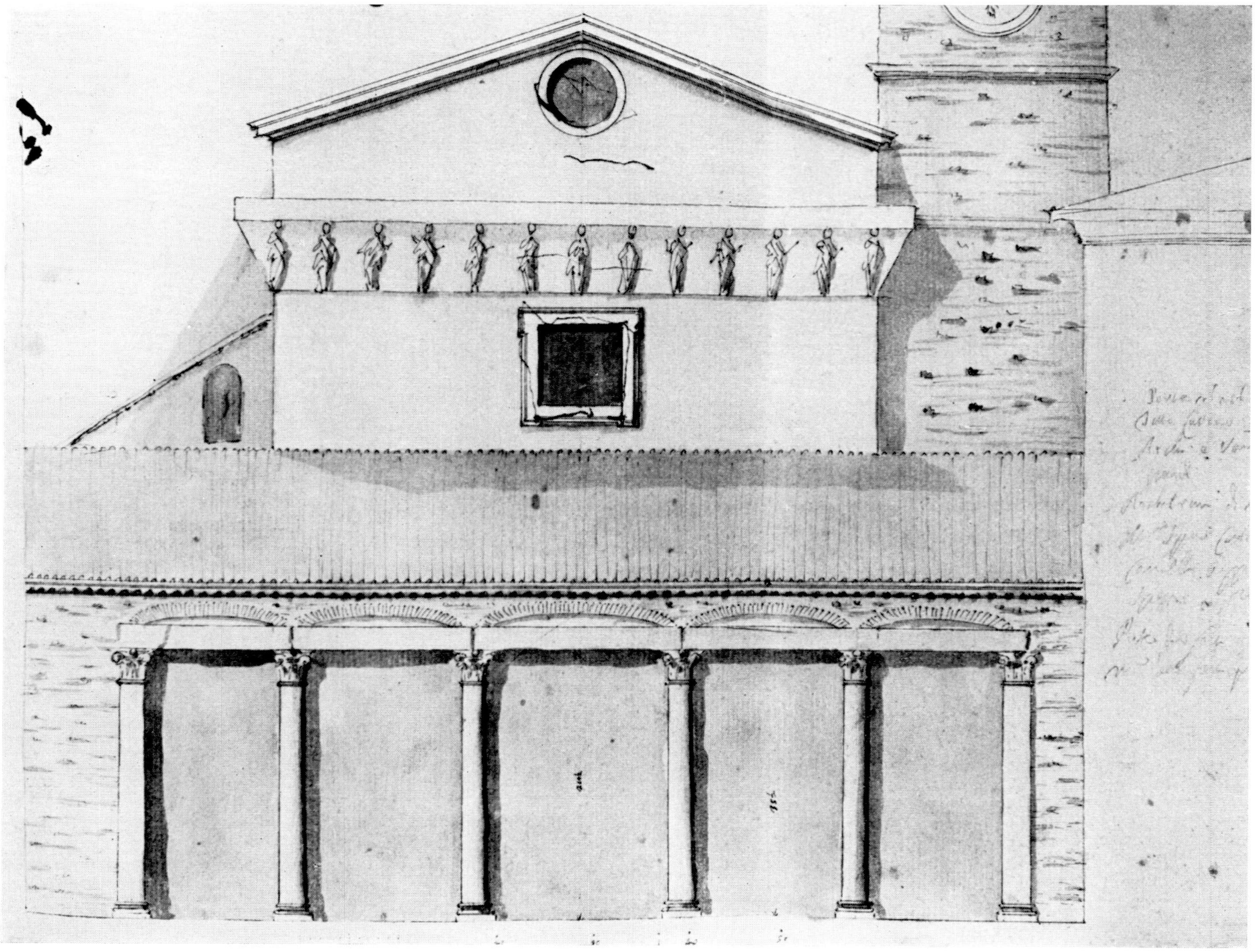

109 Elevation of the old façade (no.135)

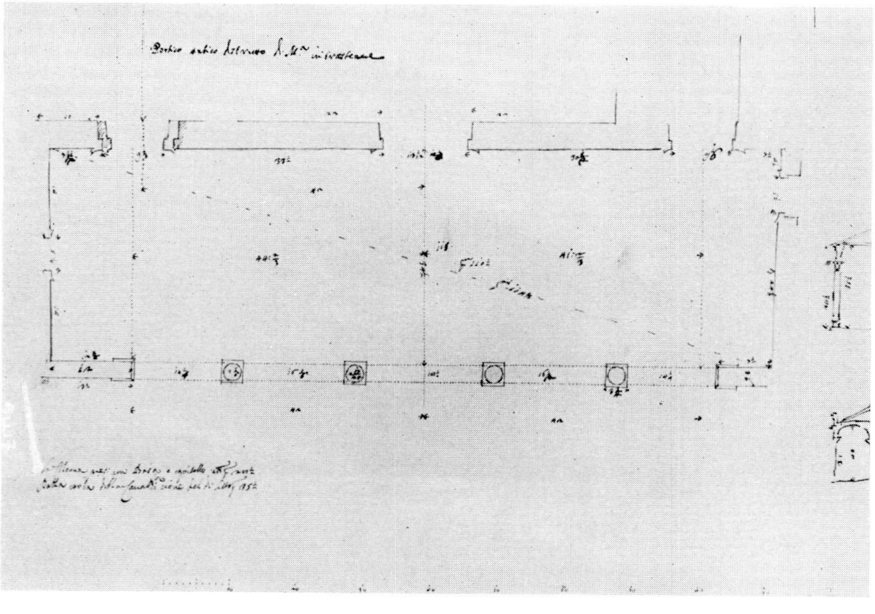

110 Plan of the old portico (no.134)

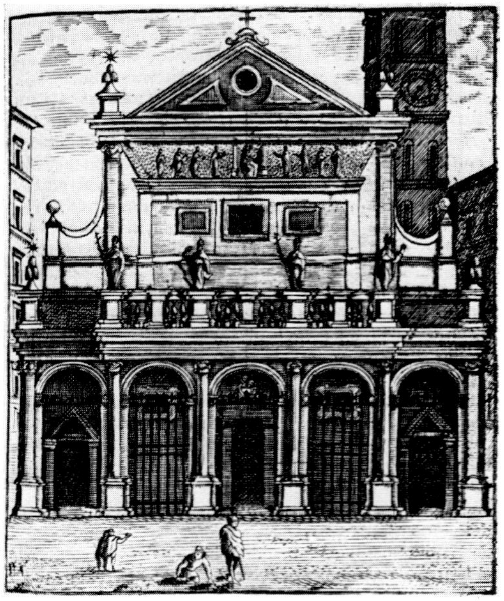

111 View of the new façade (engraving from *Roma moderna*, 1708)

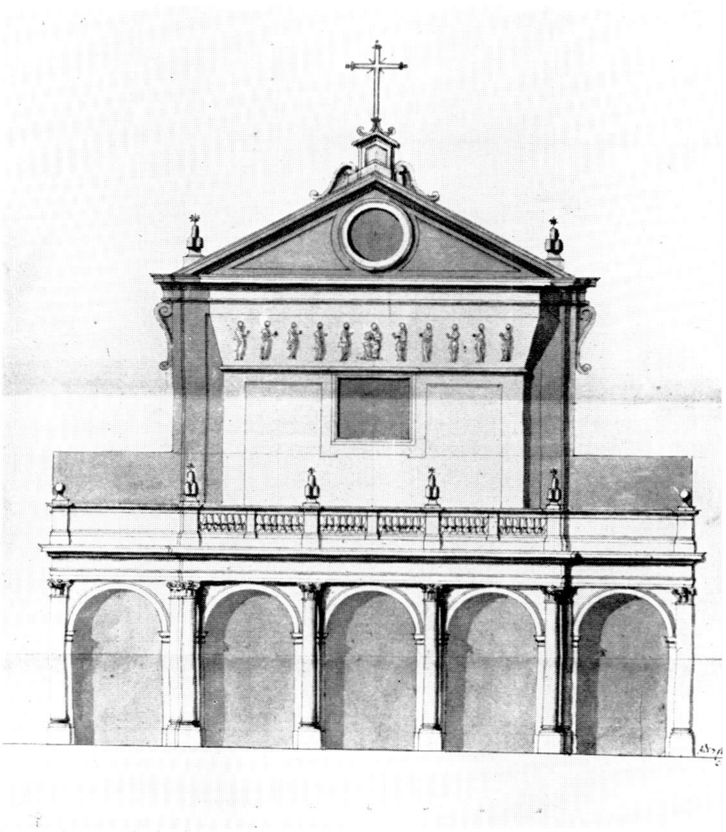

112 Project for the new portico, with Albani *monti*, elevation (no.136)

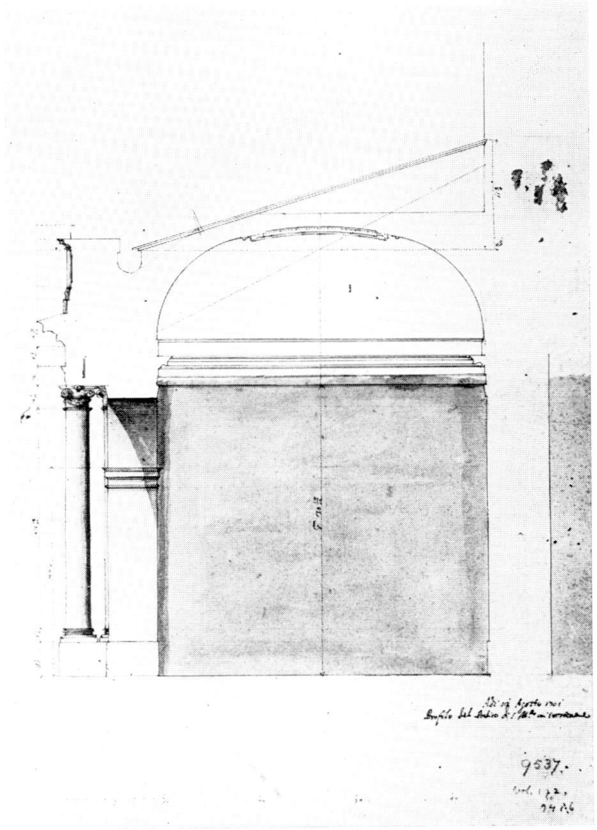

113 Section of the new portico (no.138)

The restoration of S. Teodoro al Palatino, Rome (1702–1704)

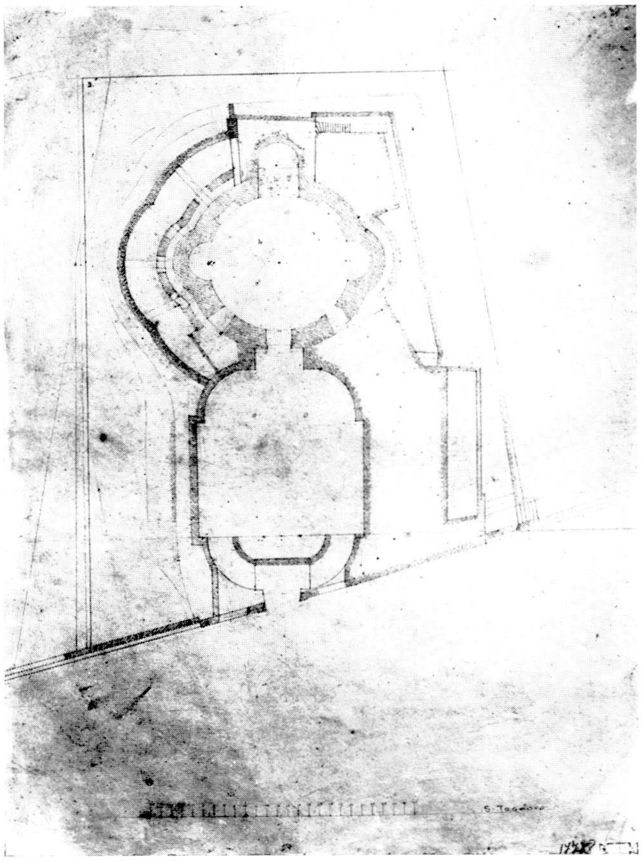

114 Plan of the church (anon. drawing; Rome, Biblioteca dell'Istituto Nazionale di Archeologia e Storia dell'Arte)

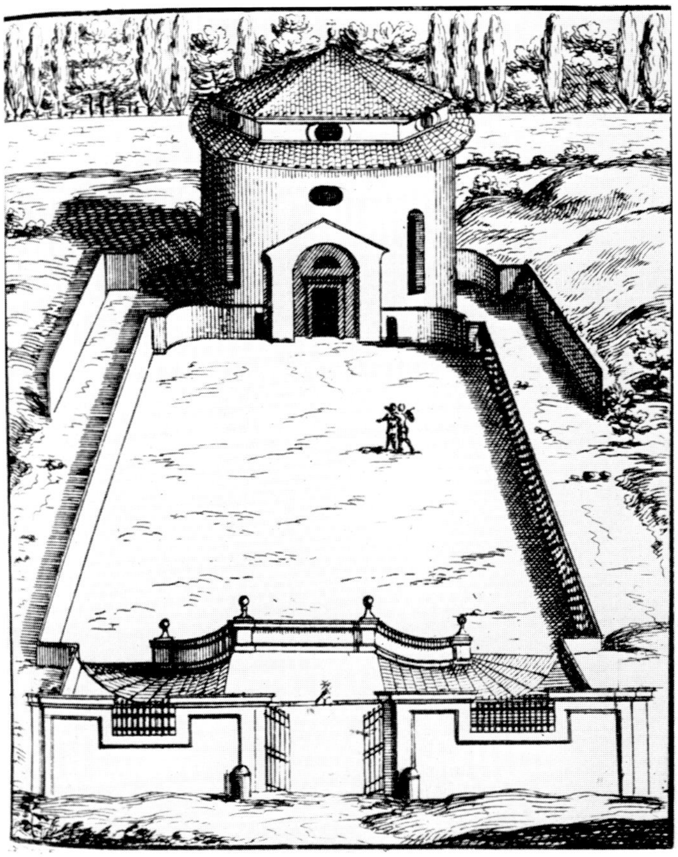

115 Perspective view (engraving from *Roma moderna*, 1708)

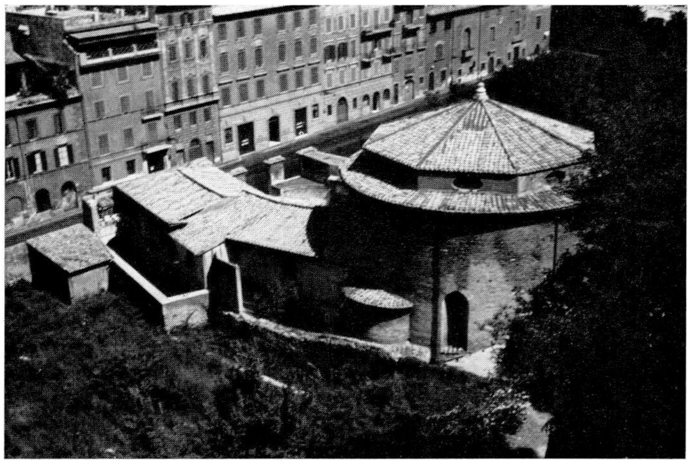

116 View of the church (photograph Nannini)

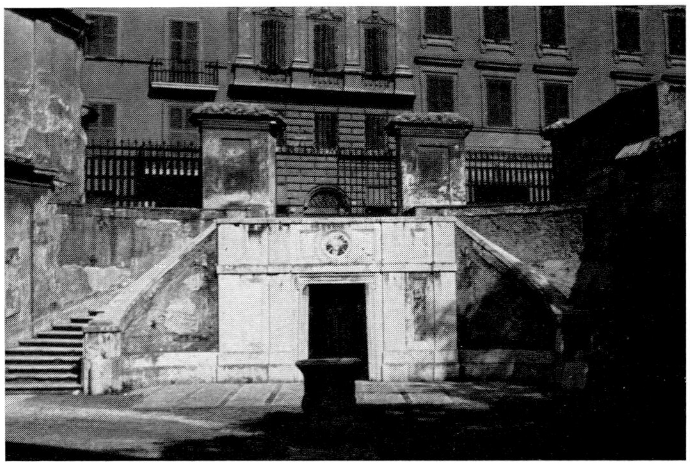

117 View of the entrance screen from the forecourt (photograph Nannini)

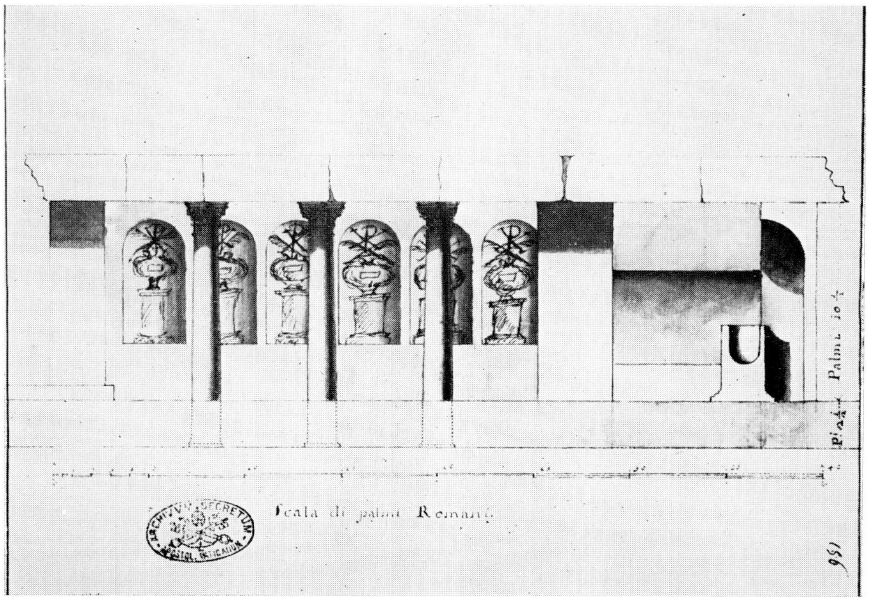

118 S. Maria in Cosmedin, section of the crypt (anon. drawing; Rome, Vatican, Fondo Albani)

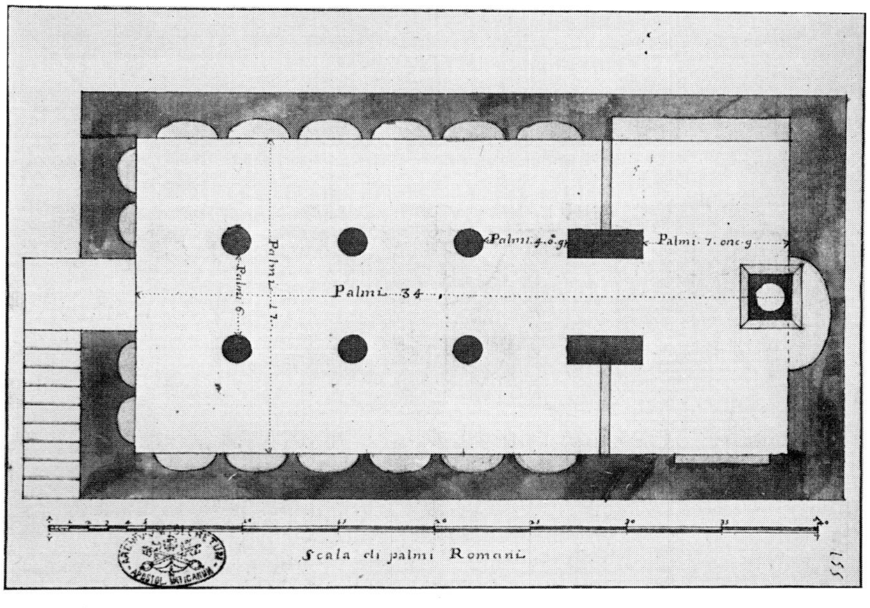

119 S. Maria in Cosmedin, plan of the crypt (anon. drawing; Rome, Vatican, Fondo Albani)

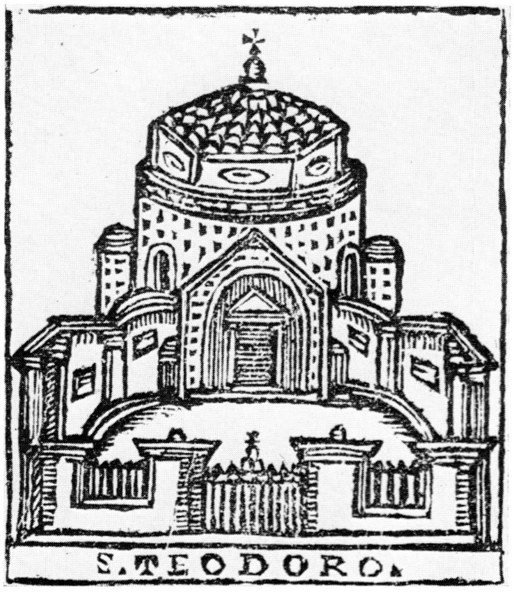

120 Perspective view (engraving from *Roma sacra e moderna*, 1725)

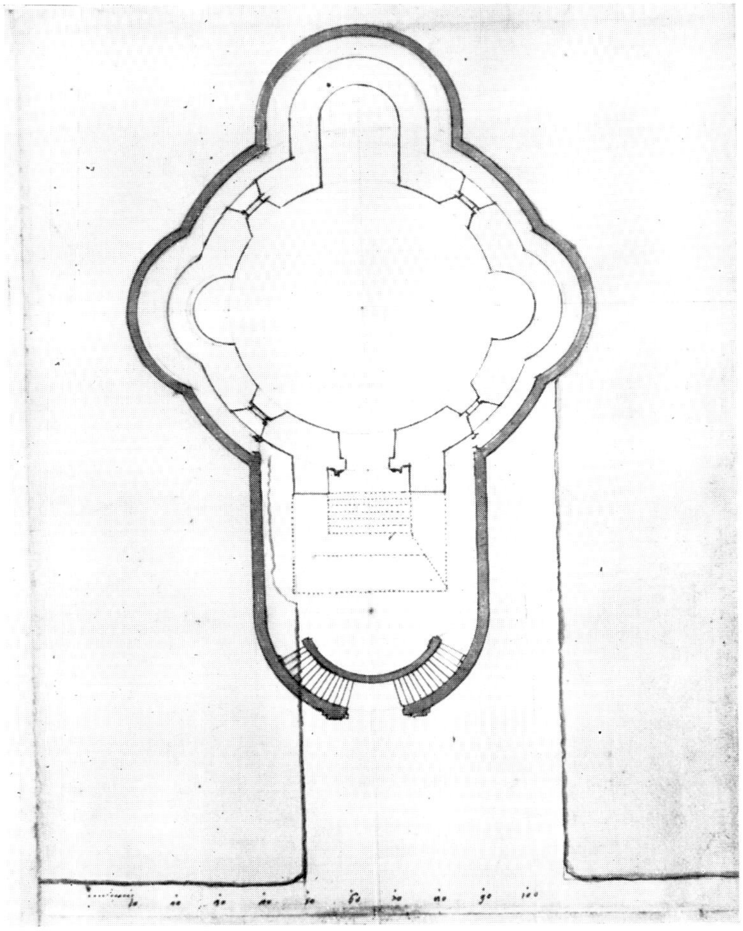

121 Project with short forecourt, plan, stage 1 (no.140)

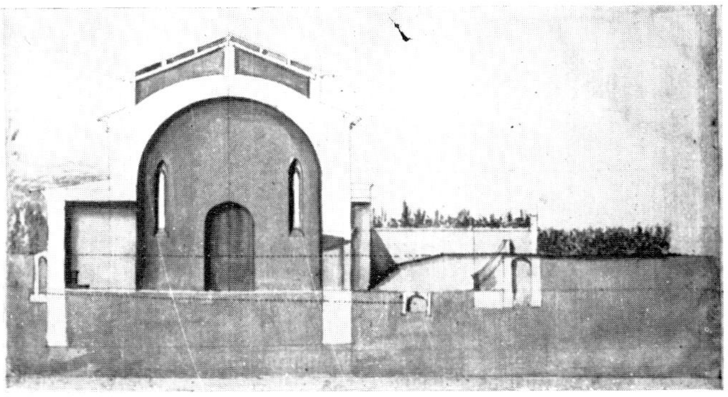

122 Project with short forecourt, section, stage 1 (no.141)

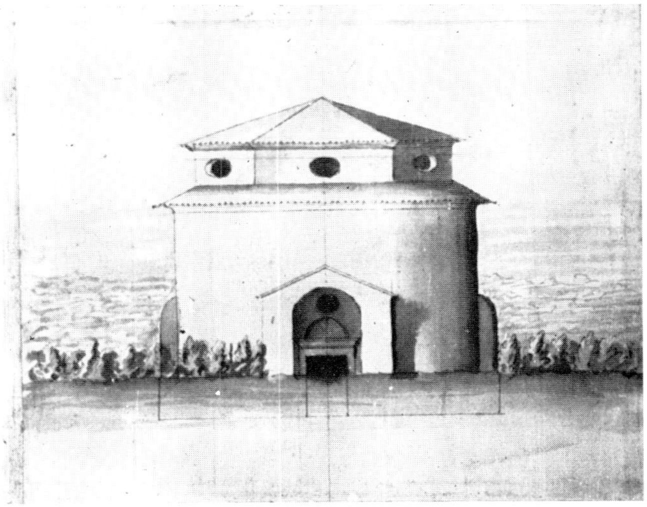

123 Front elevation, showing existing state (no.142)

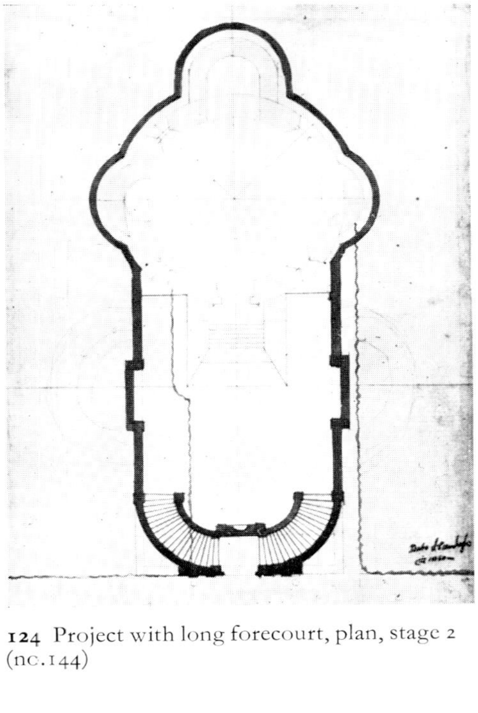

124 Project with long forecourt, plan, stage 2 (no.144)

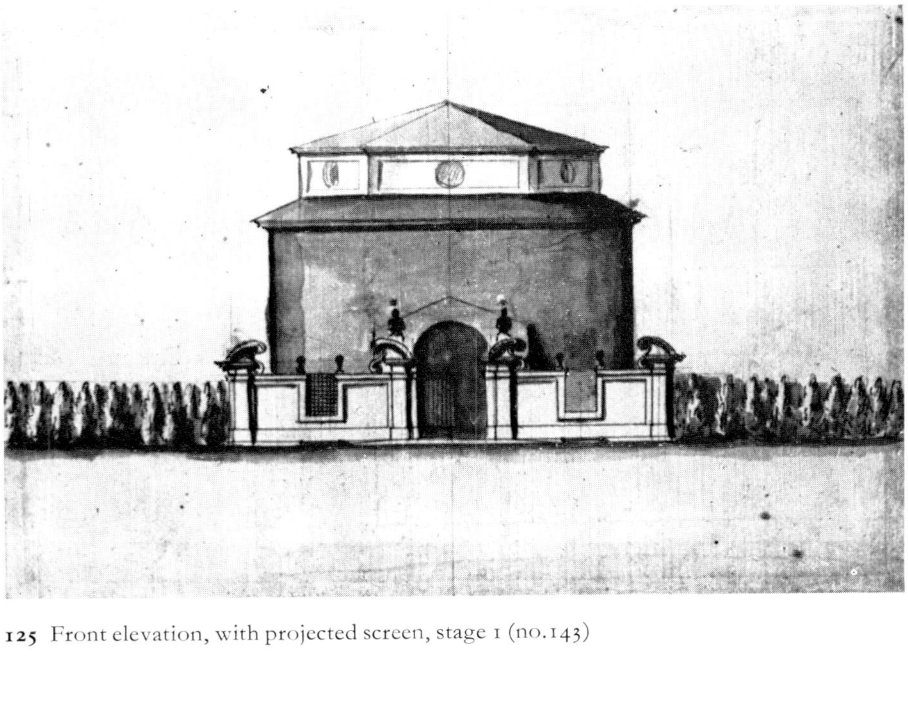

125 Front elevation, with projected screen, stage 1 (no.143)

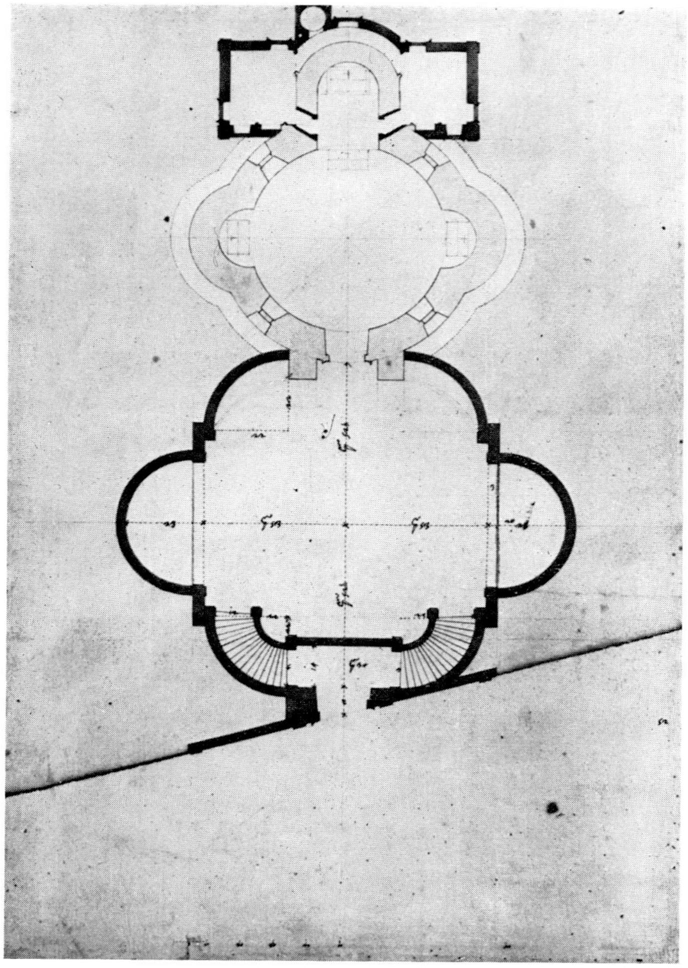

126 Project with *exedrae* for forecourt, stage 3 (no.145)

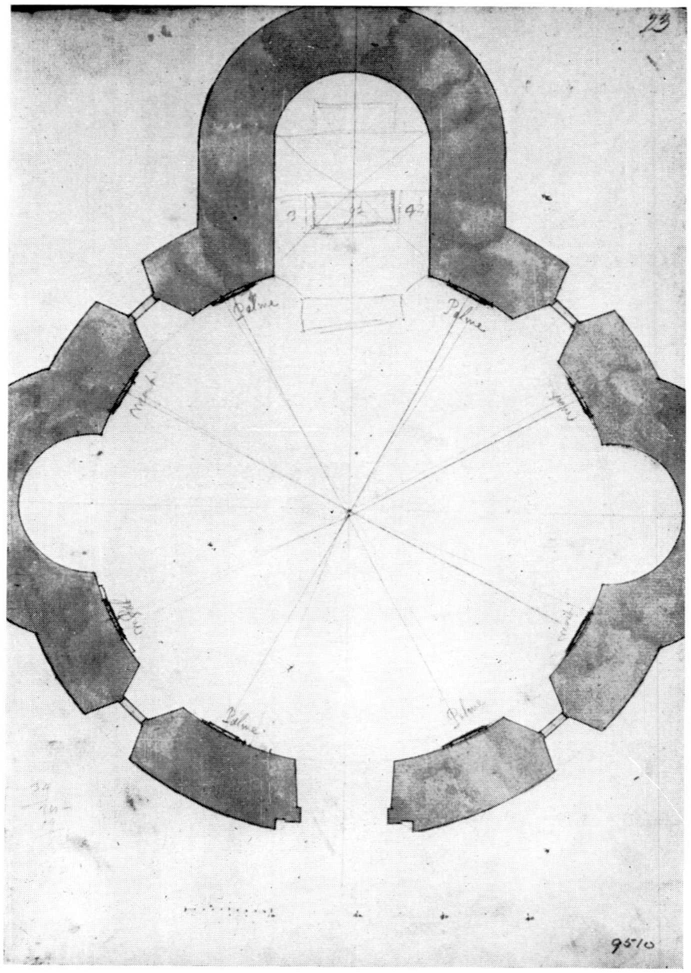

127 Plan of the church (no.149)

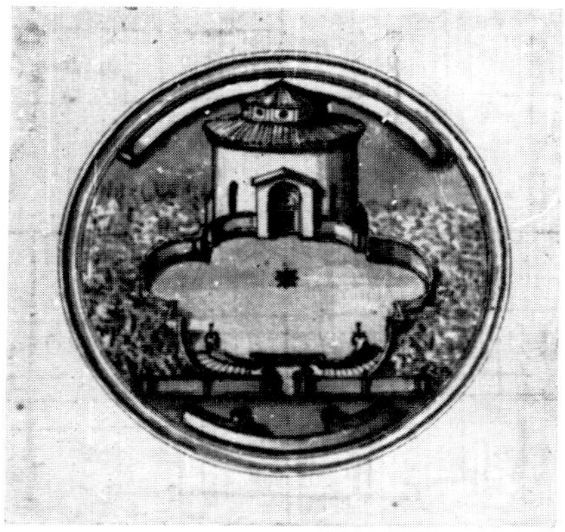

128 Project with *exedrae* for forecourt, stage 3, design for a medal (no.146)

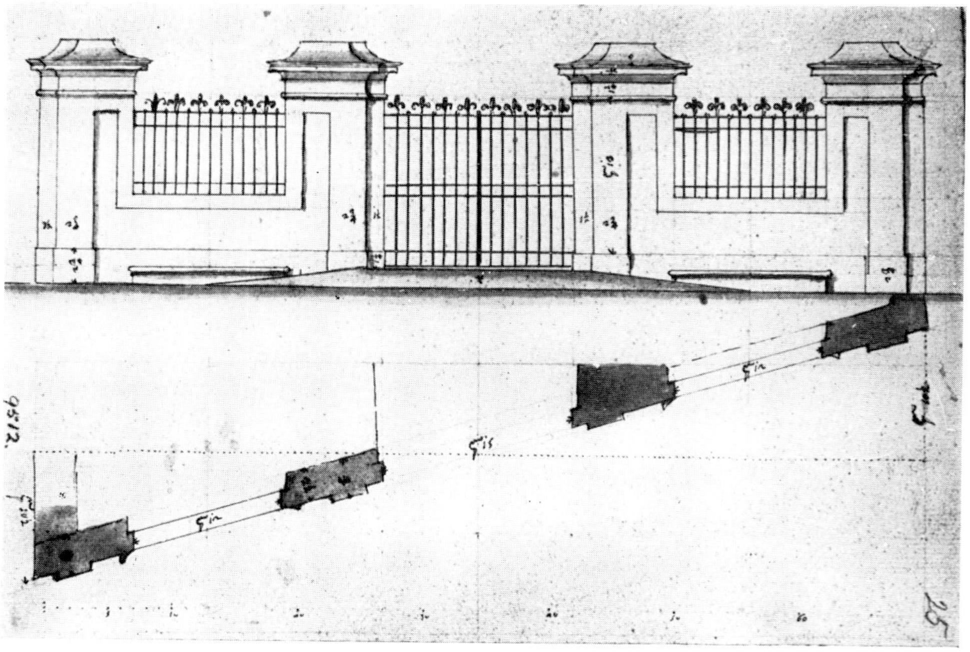

129 Plan and elevation of the screening wall, stage 4 (no.147)

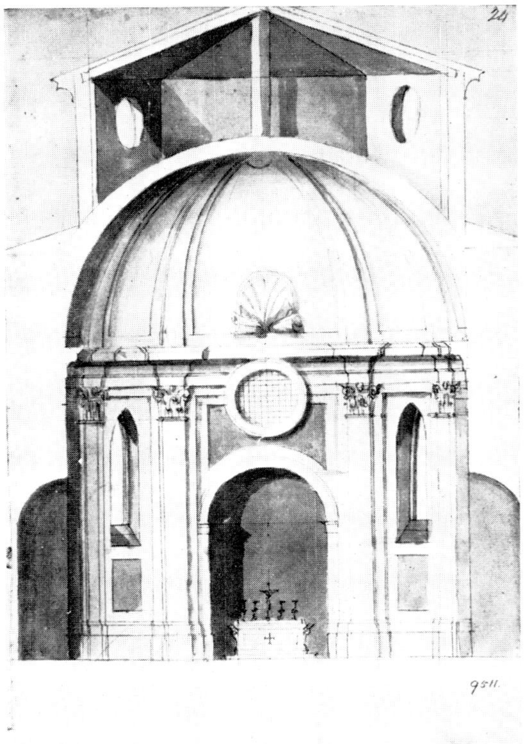

130 Transverse section (no.150)

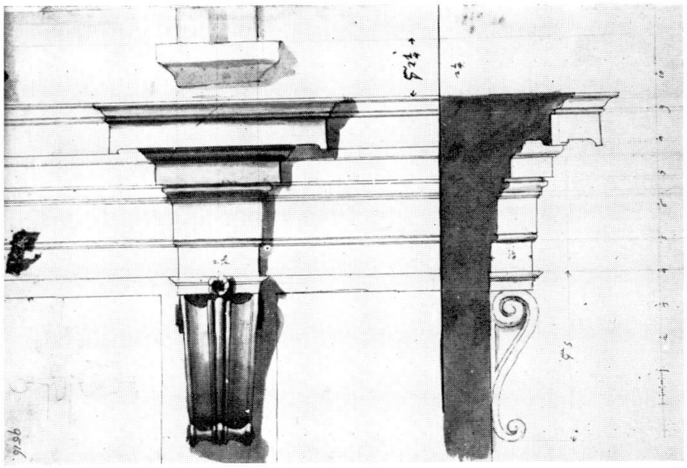

131 Elevation and section of part of the cornice, showing a console (no.152)

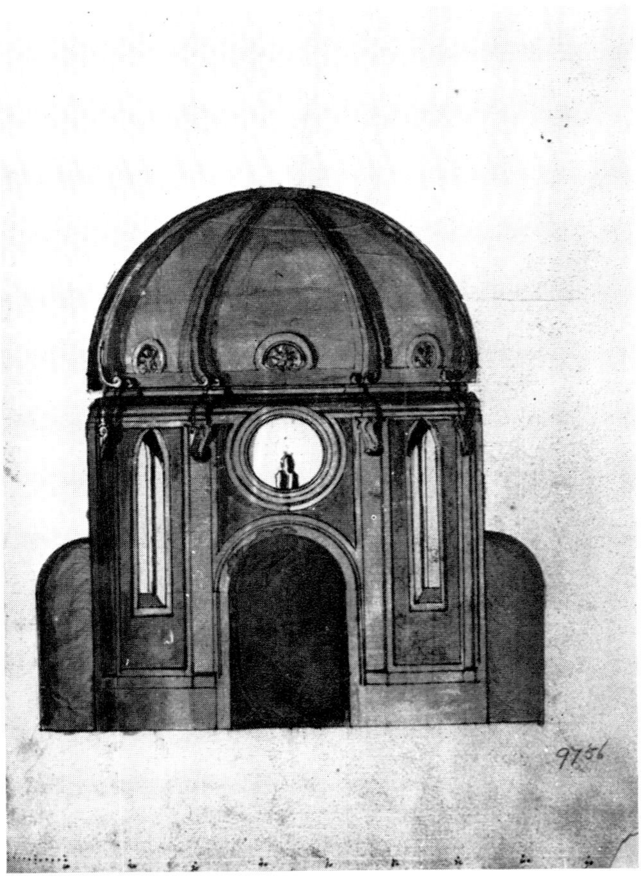

132 Transverse section (no.155)

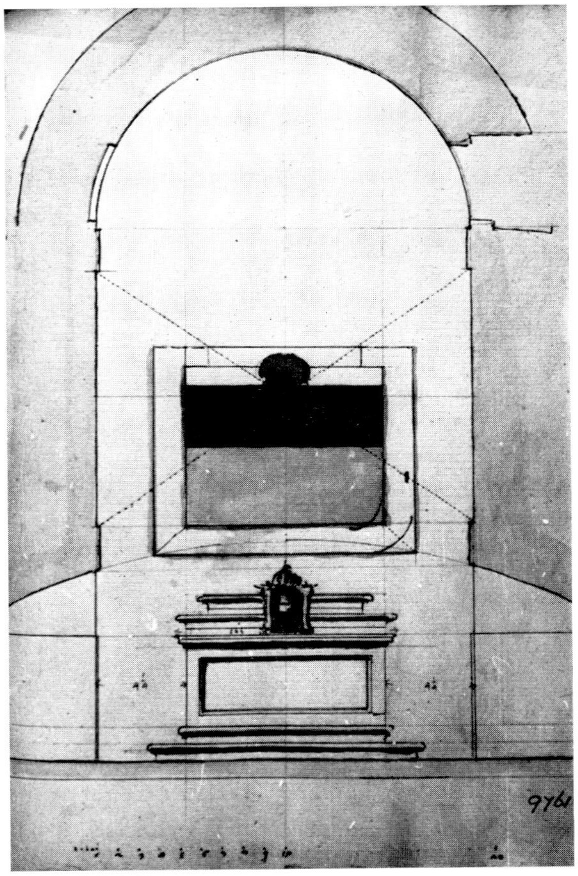

133 Plan of the choir, with project for the high altar (no.157)

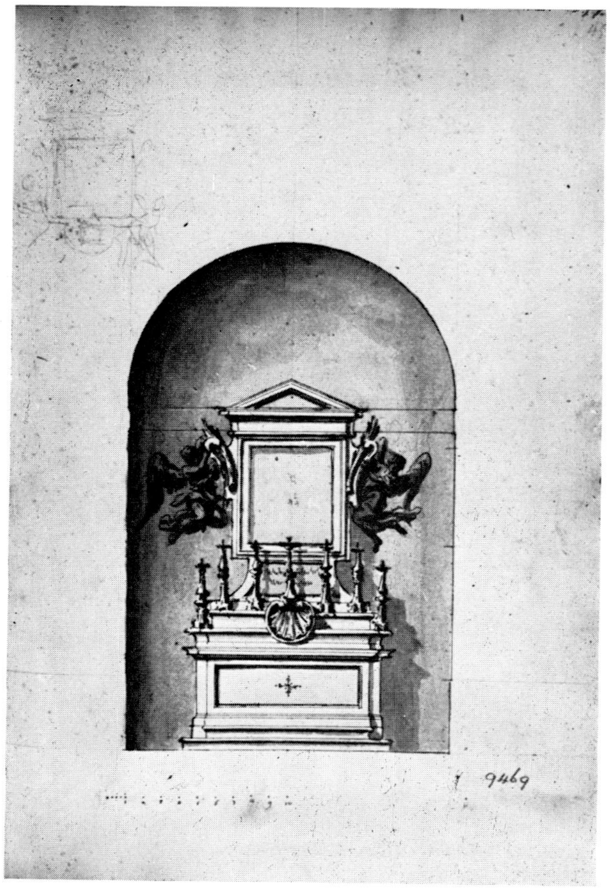

134 Project for the high altar, elevation (no.158)

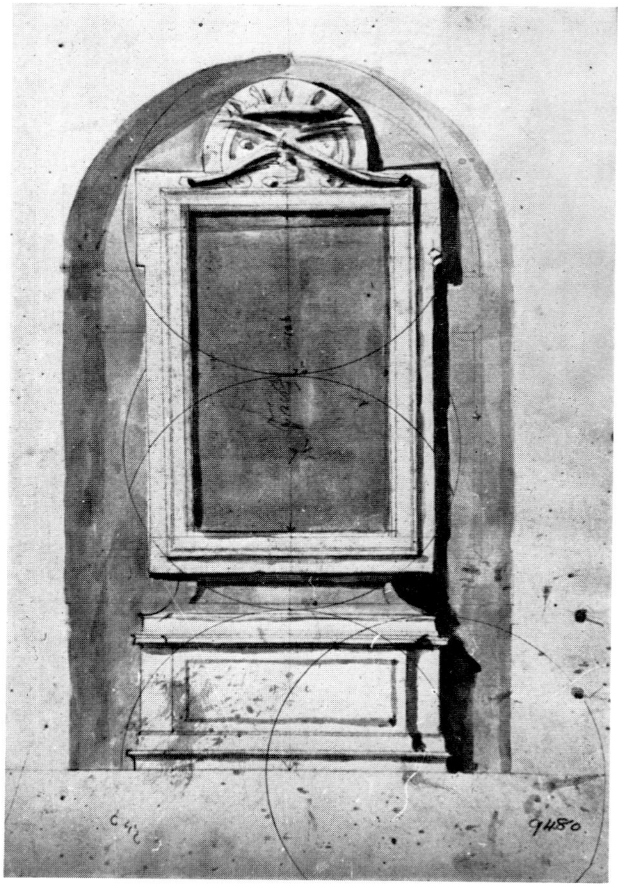

135 Project for a side altar, elevation (1) (no.159)

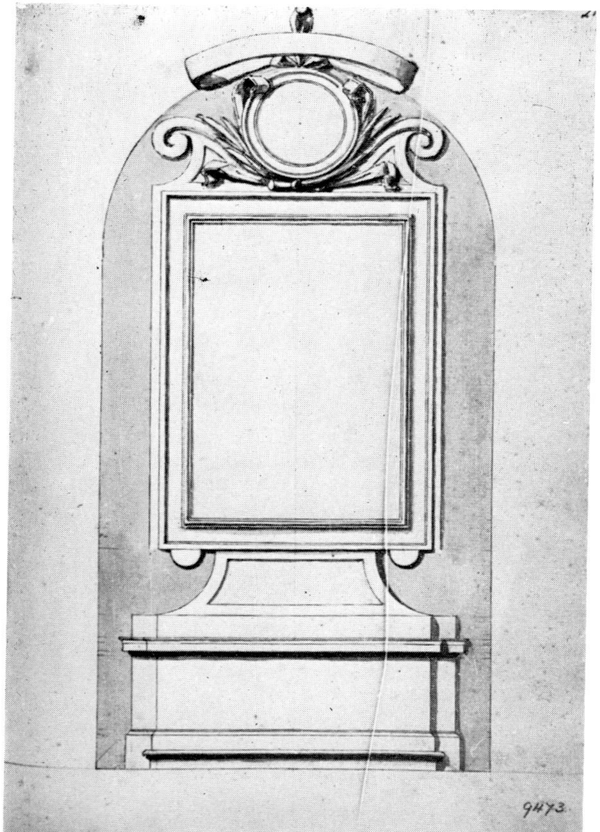

136 Project for a side altar, elevation (executed design) (no.169)

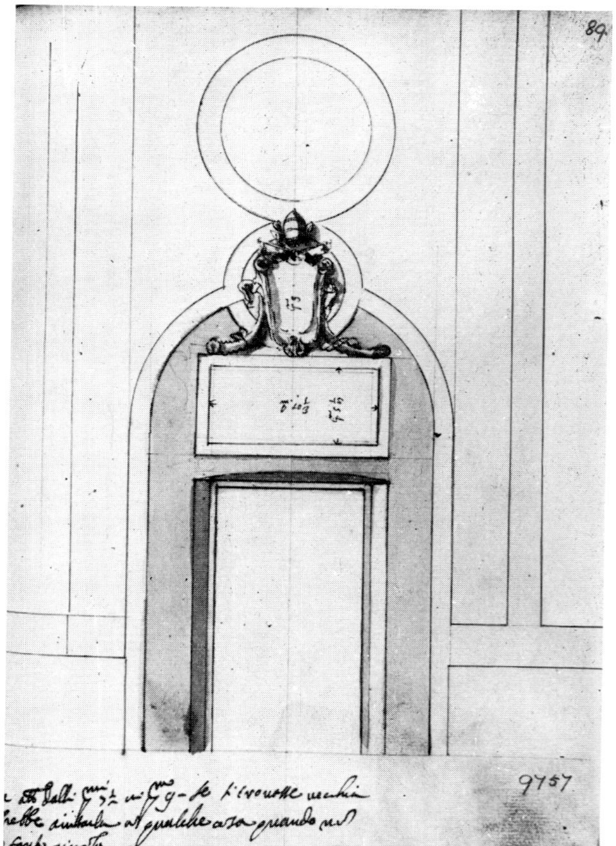

137 Project for the framing of the entrance door (no.171)

The façade of S. Maria dell'Umilità, Rome (1703)

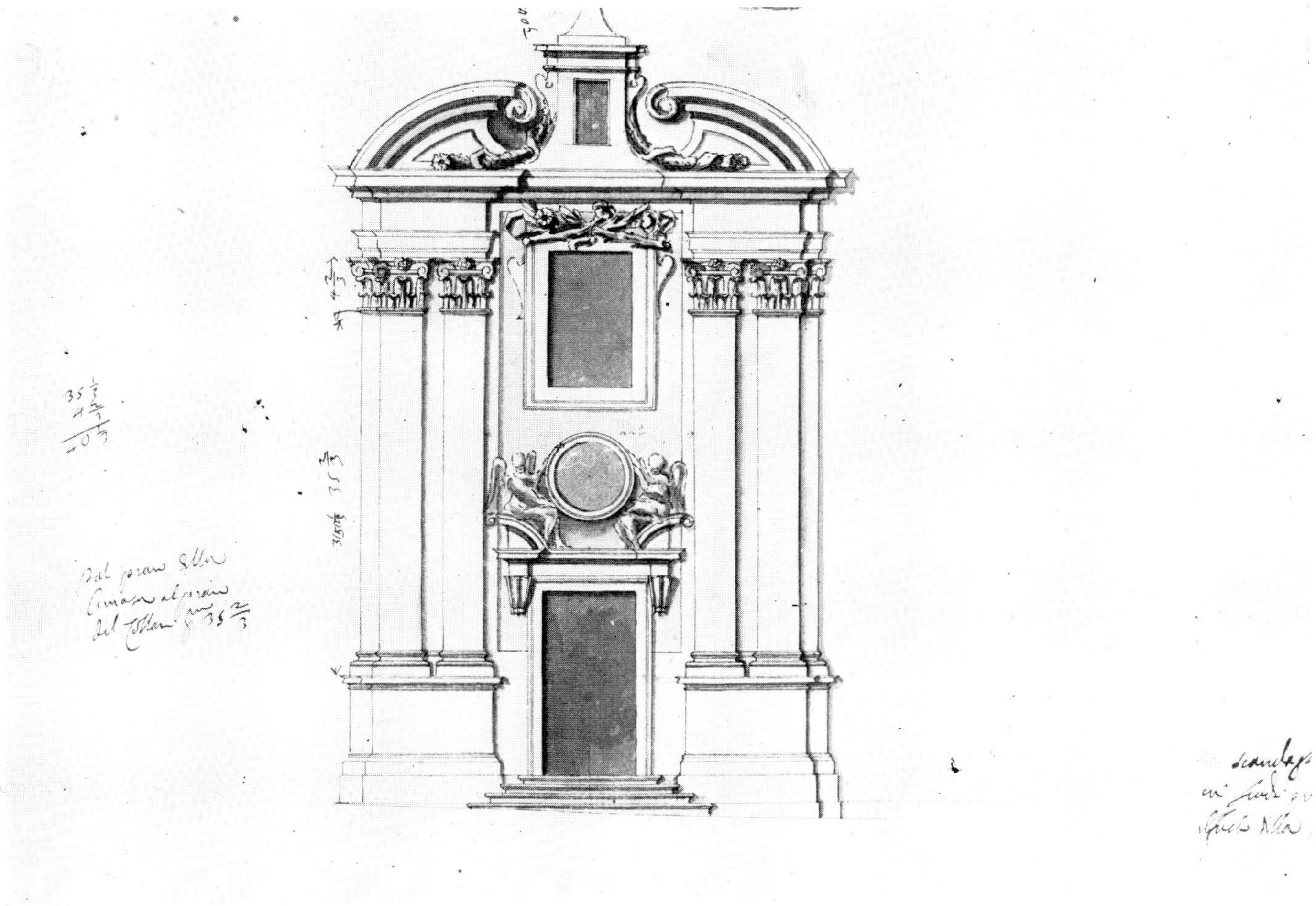

138 Elevation of the façade (no.173)

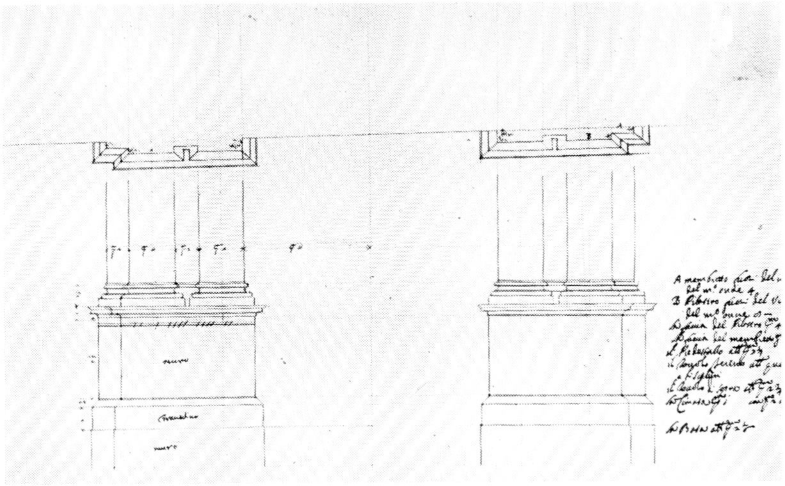

139 Diagram of the lower part of the façade, plan and elevation (no.174)

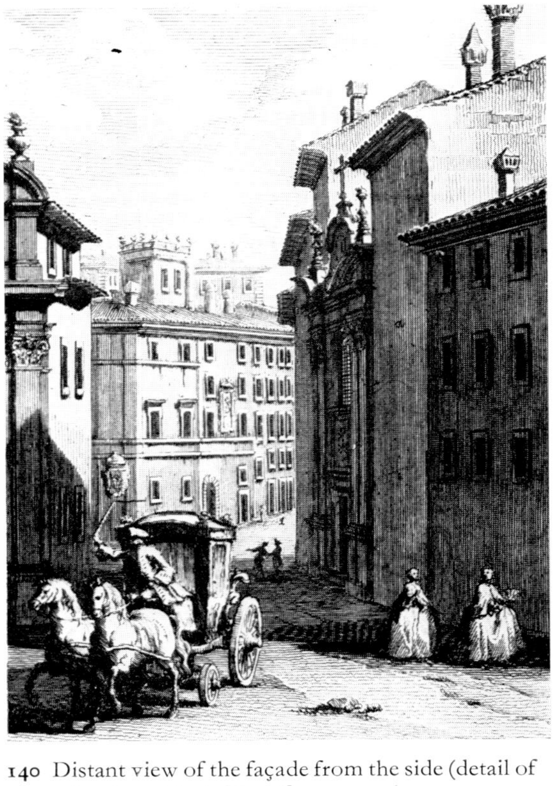

140 Distant view of the façade from the side (detail of engraving from Vasi, *Magnificenze*, 1753)

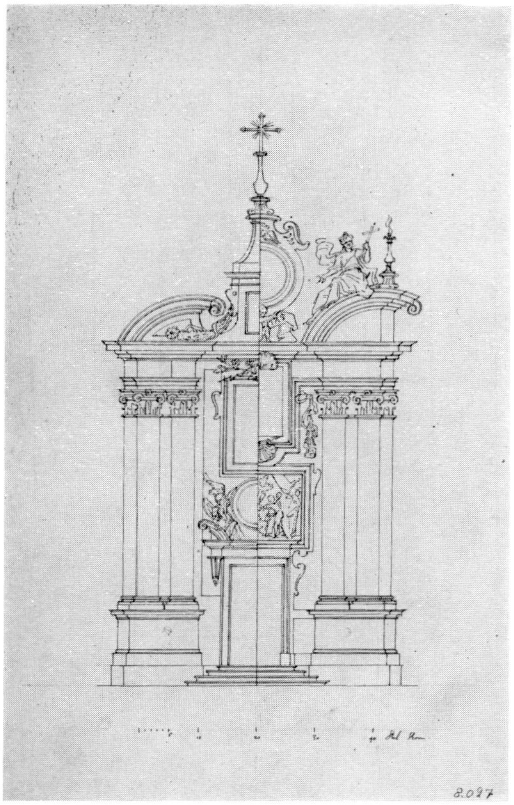

141 Projects for the façade (anon. drawing; Stockholm, Nationalmuseum)

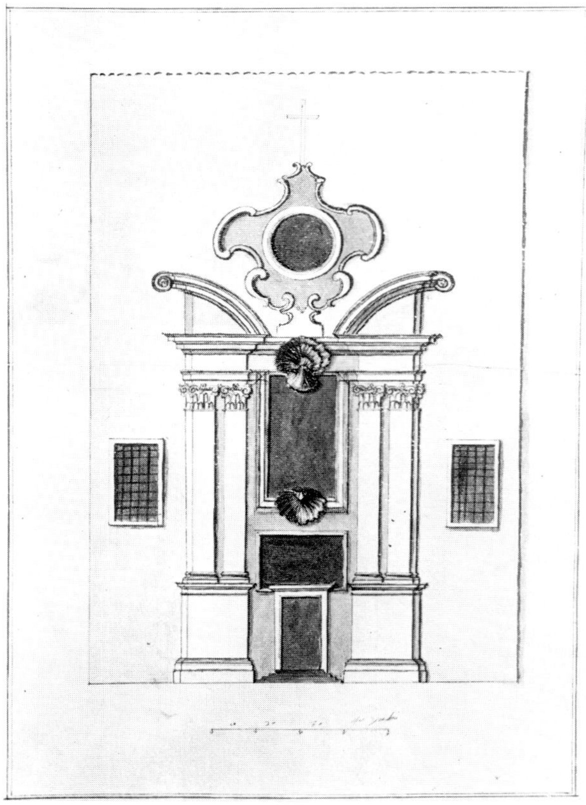

142 Elevation of the façade (anon. drawing; Vienna, Albertina)

Rome, S. Giovanni in Laterano, drawings of the nave niches (1703)

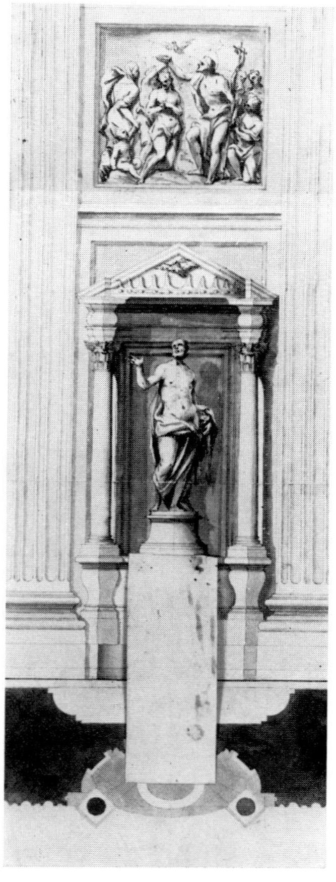

143 Plan and elevation of a tabernacle (no.175)

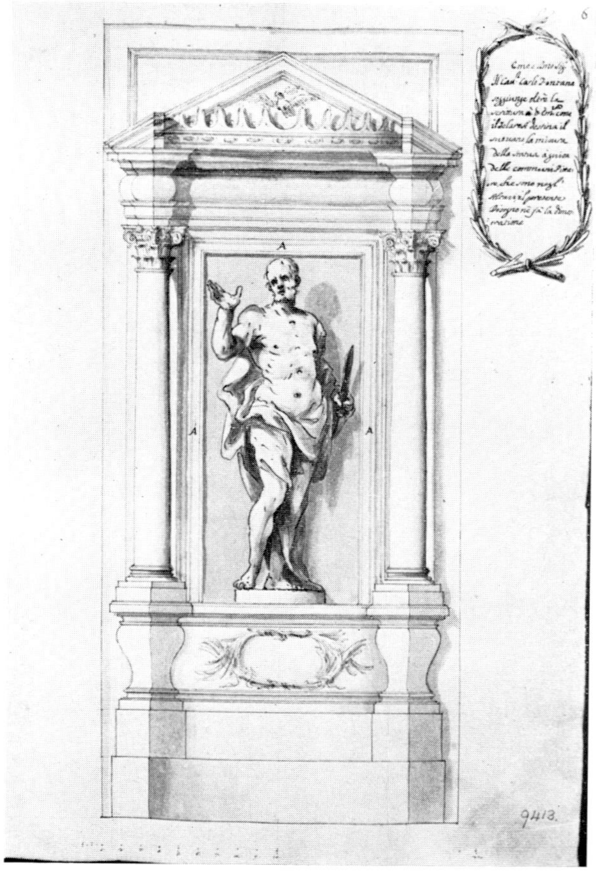

144 Elevation of a tabernacle (no.176)

Projects for SS. Marcellino e Pietro, Rome (1703?)

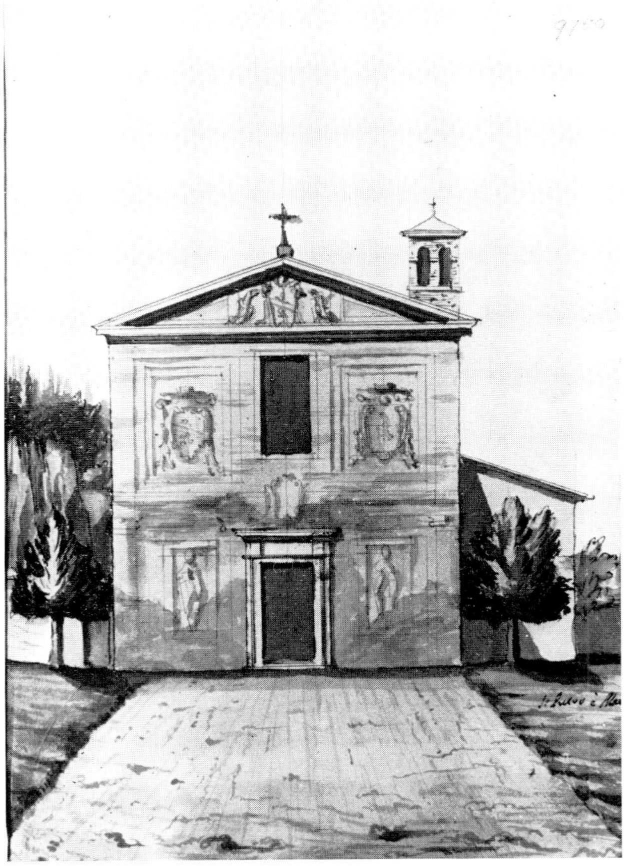

145 View of the façade and forecourt (no.178)

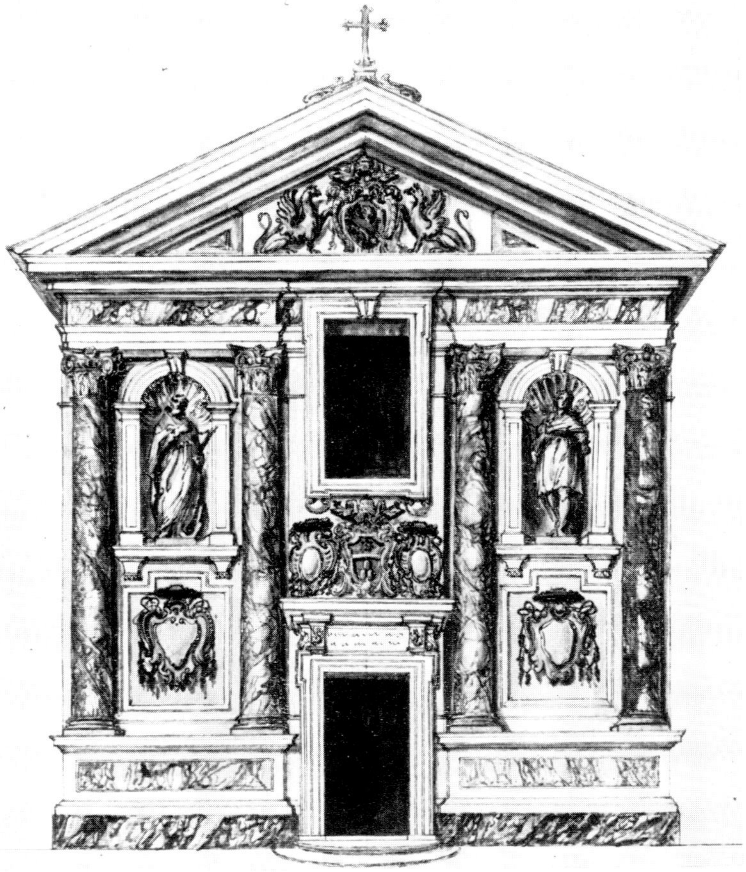

146 Project for the façade, perspective view (anon. drawing, no. 179)

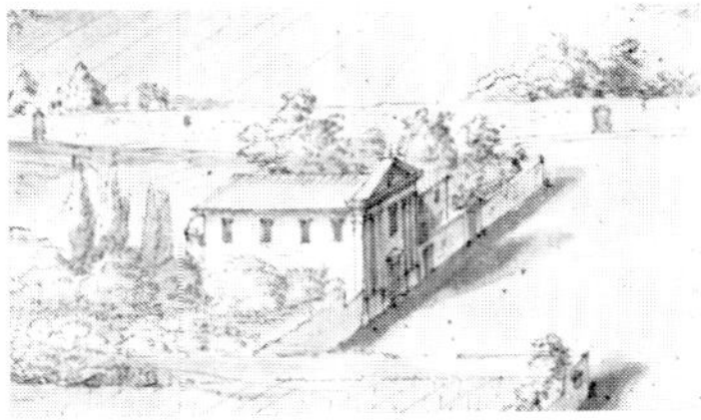

147 Distant view of the church (detail of a drawing by Juvarra; Rome, Vatican Library)

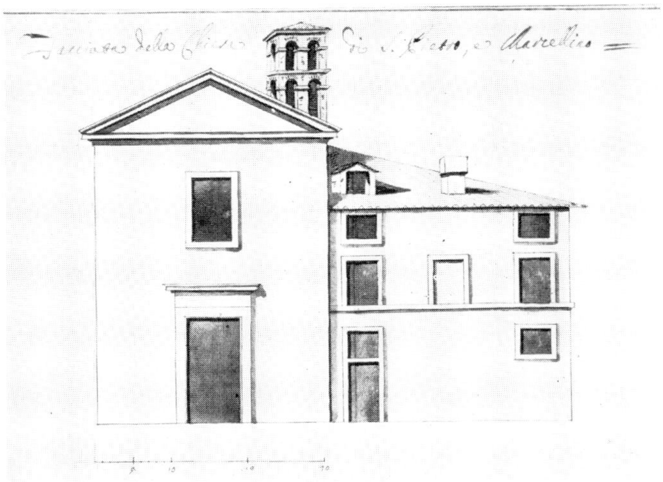

148 Elevation of the façade (anon. drawing; Vienna, Albertina)

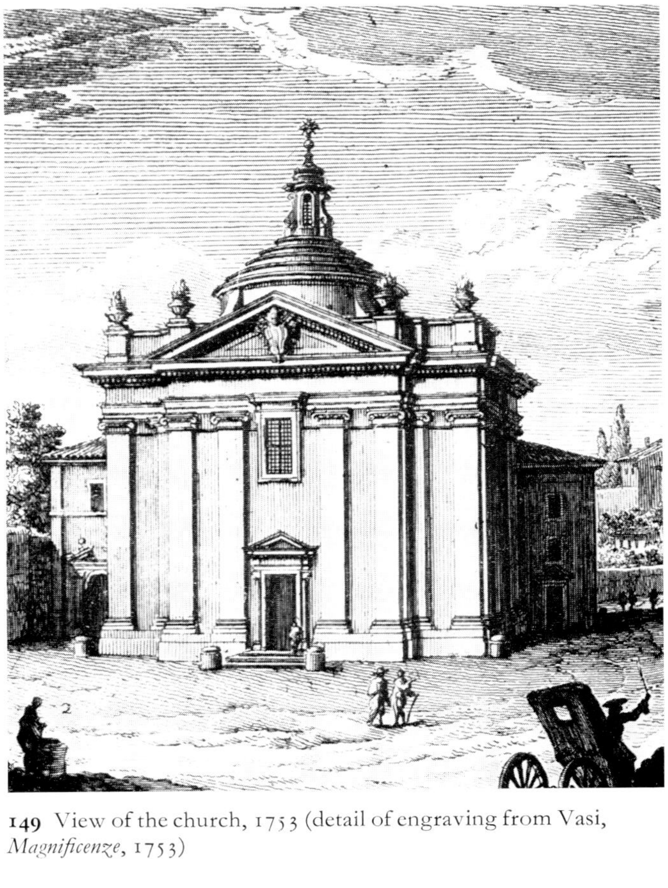

149 View of the church, 1753 (detail of engraving from Vasi, *Magnificenze*, 1753)

The decoration of S. Maria dell'Anima, Rome, for the memorial service to the Emperor Leopold I (1705)

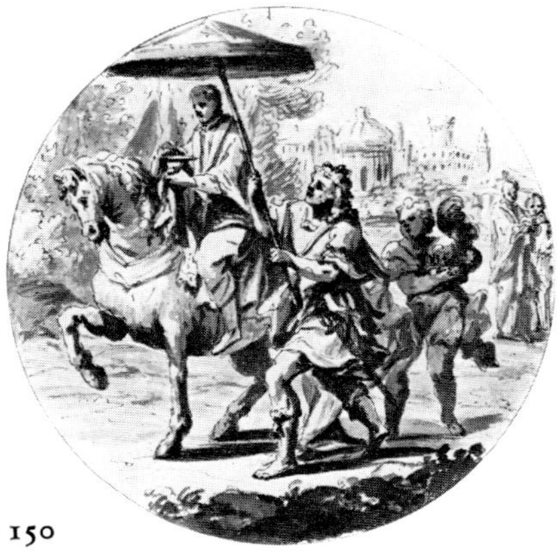

150

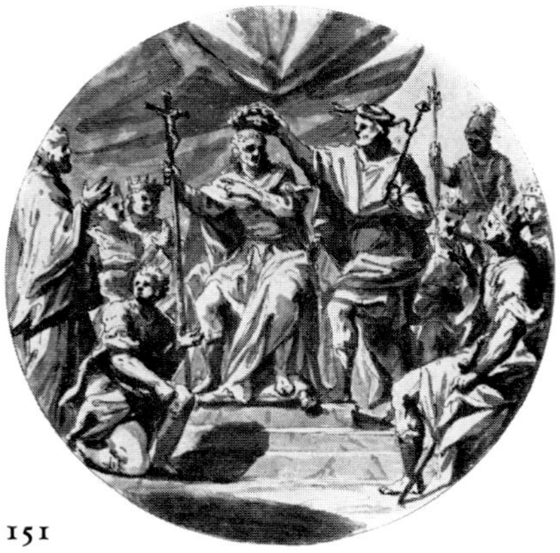

151

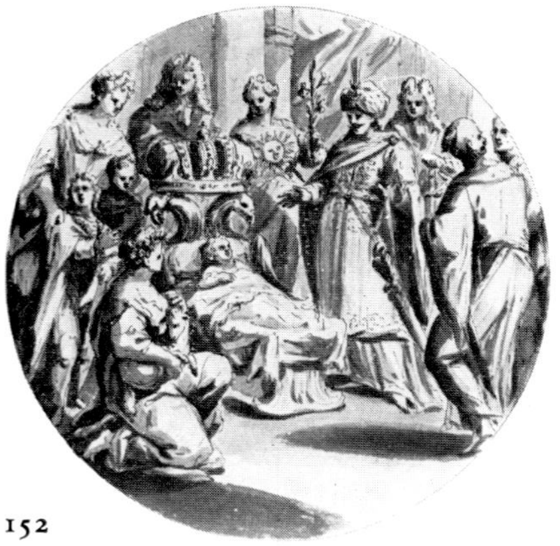

152

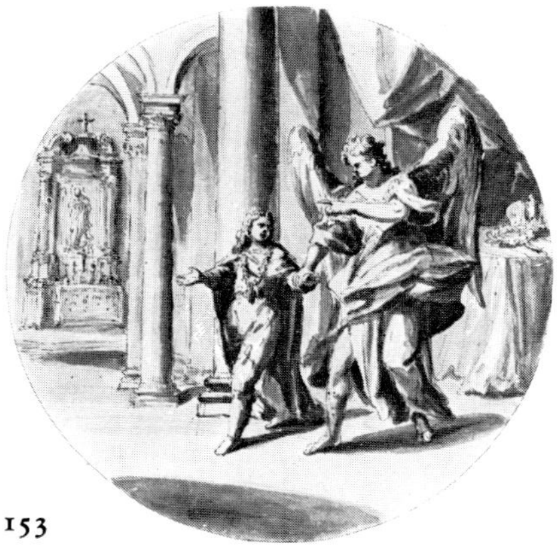

153

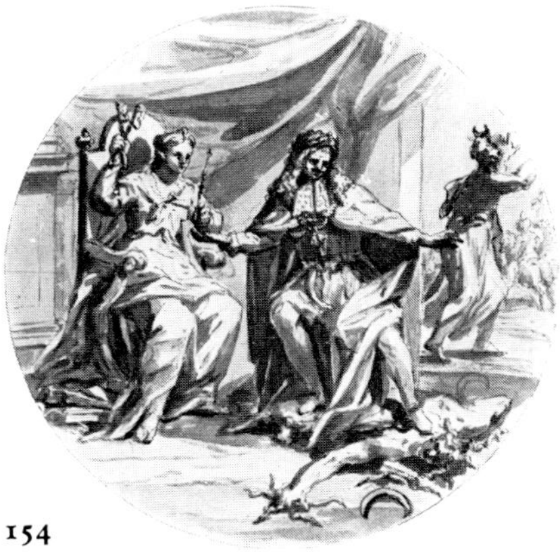

154

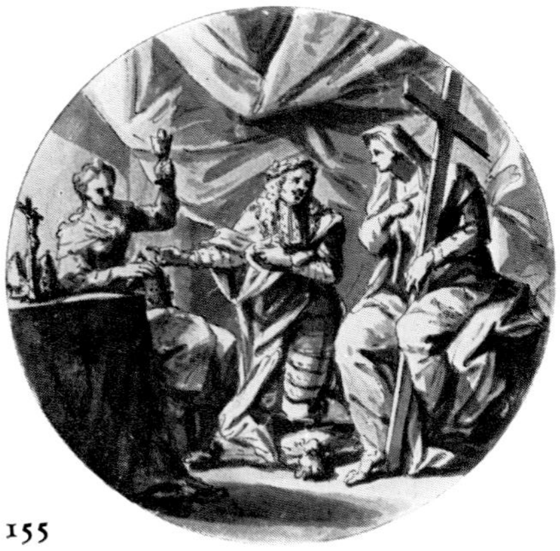

155

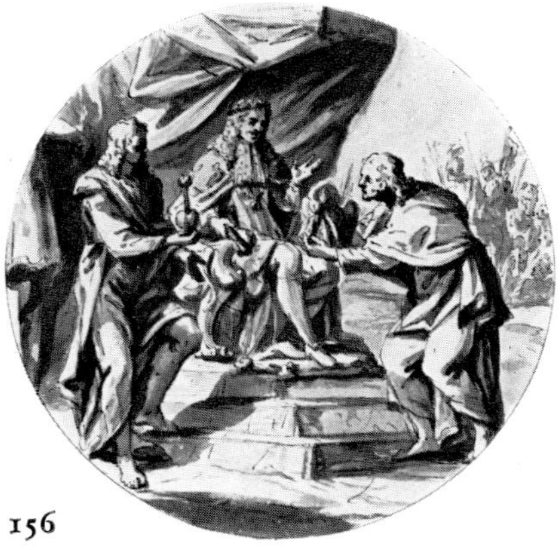

156

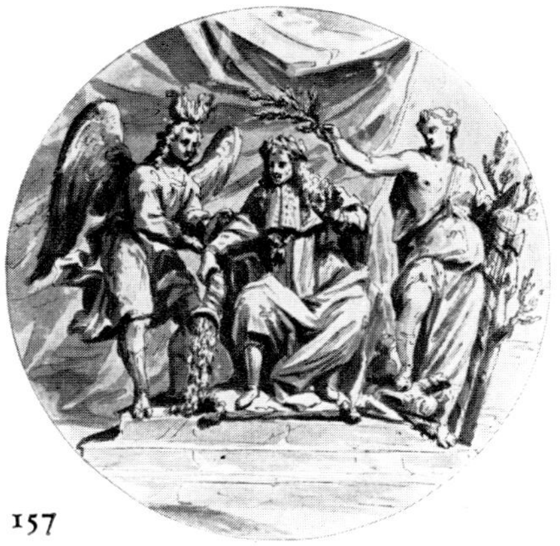

157

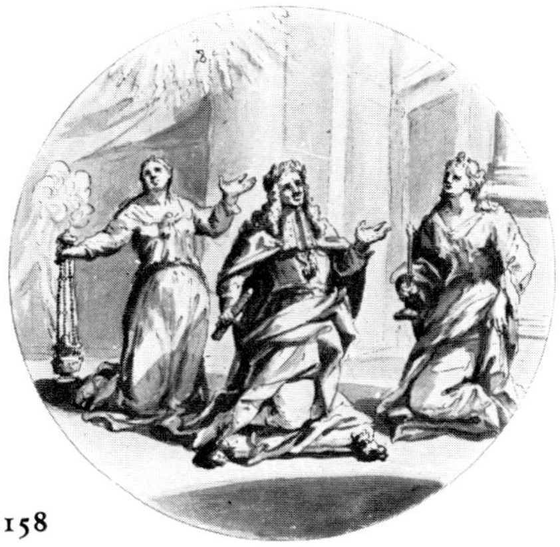

158

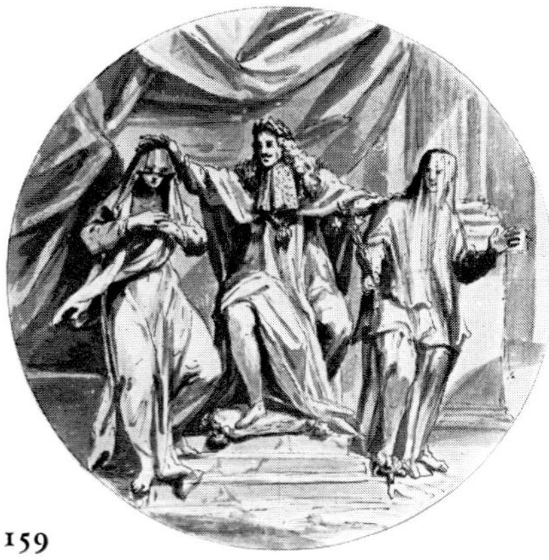

159

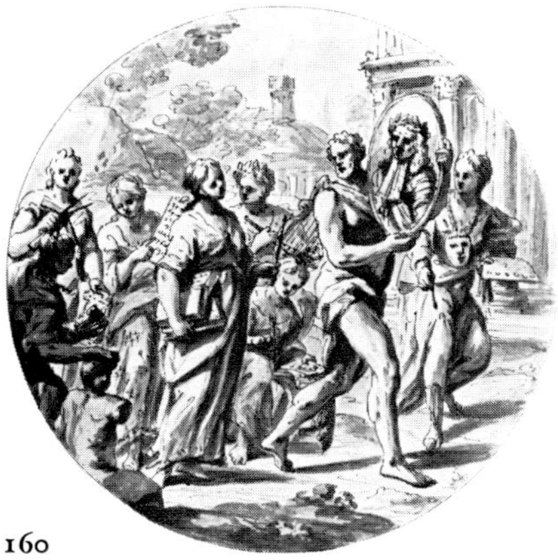

160

150 to 160 The roundels for the unexecuted scheme of decoration (nos 180–190)

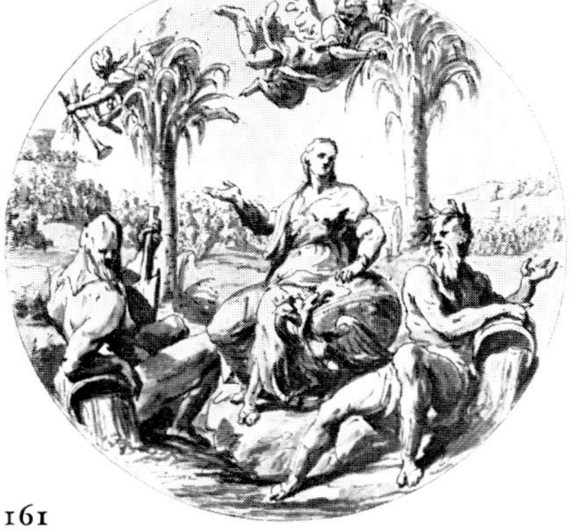

161

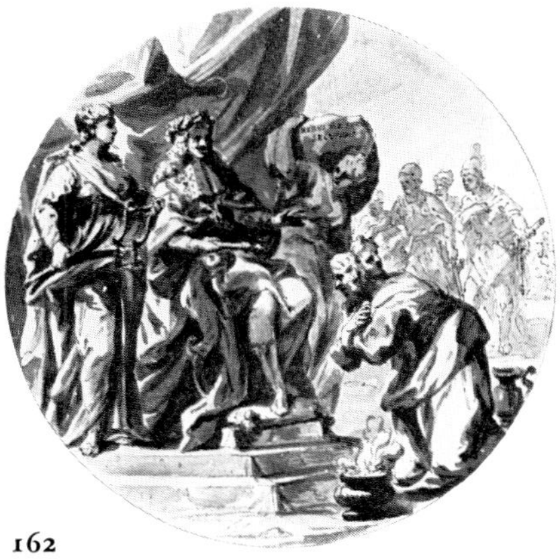

162

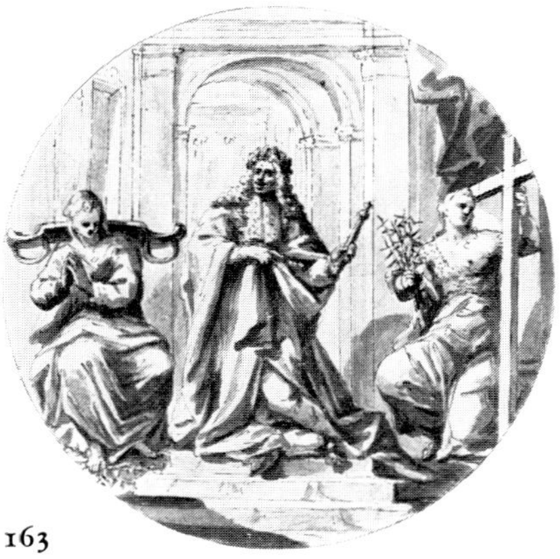

163

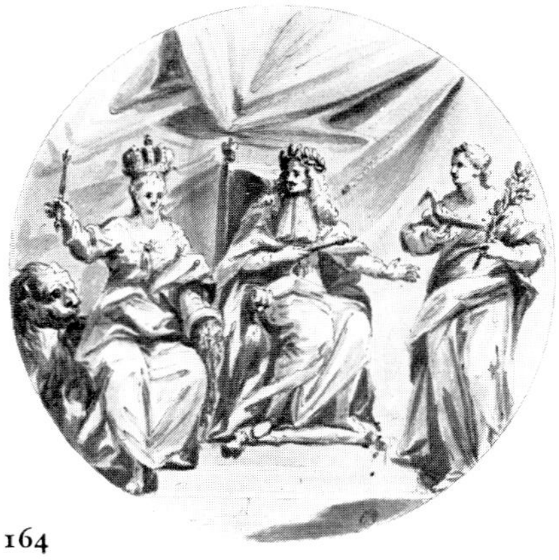

164

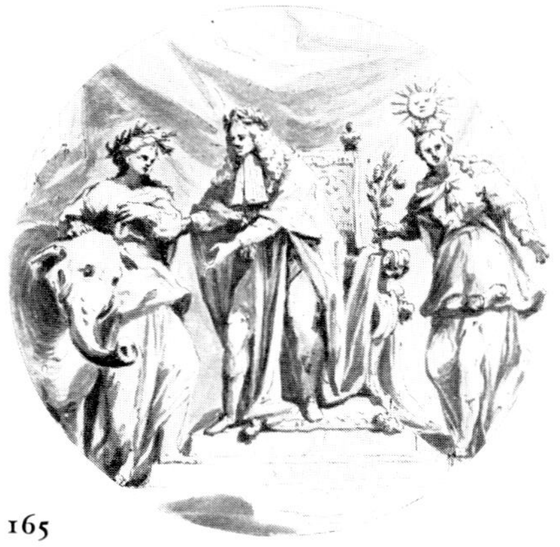

165

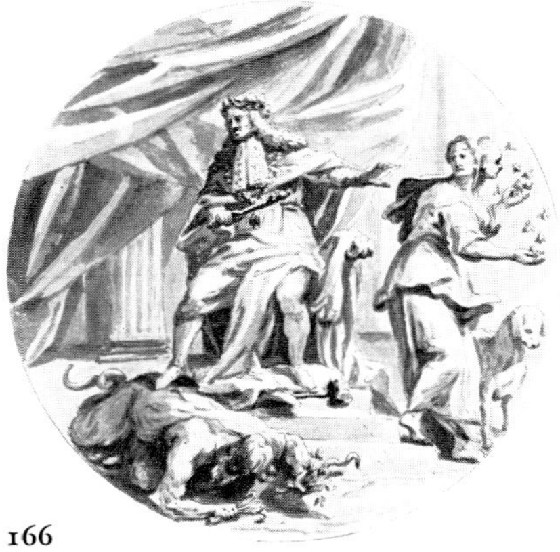

166

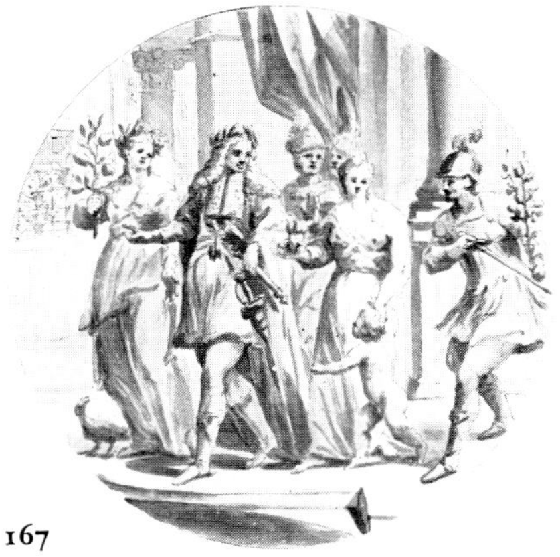

167

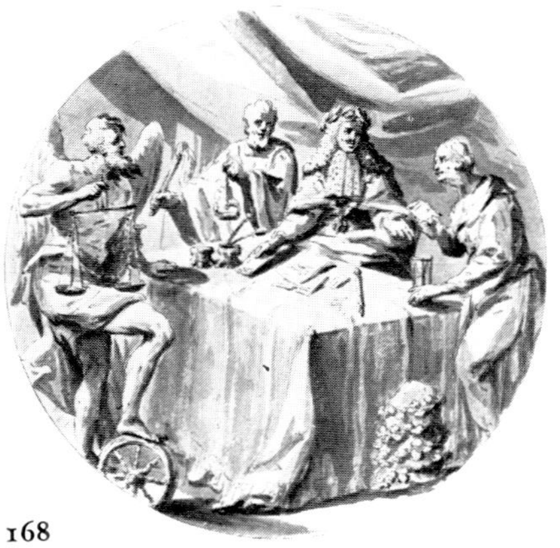

168

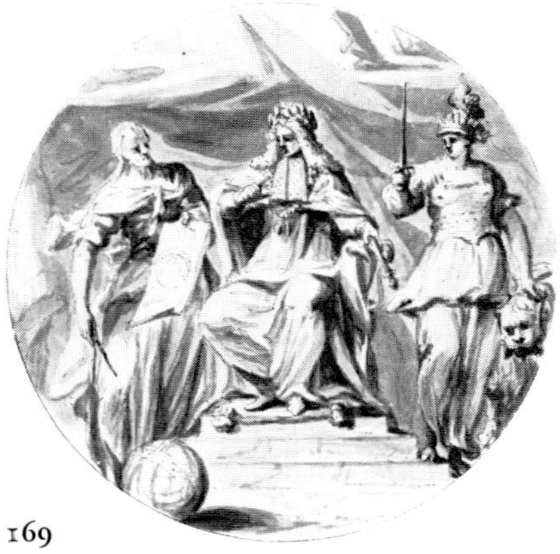

169

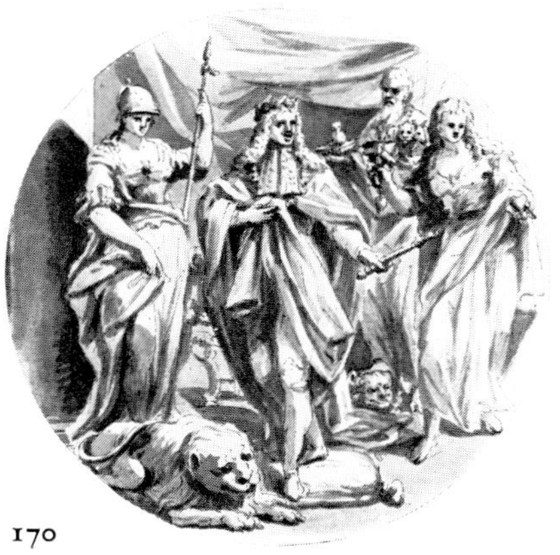

170

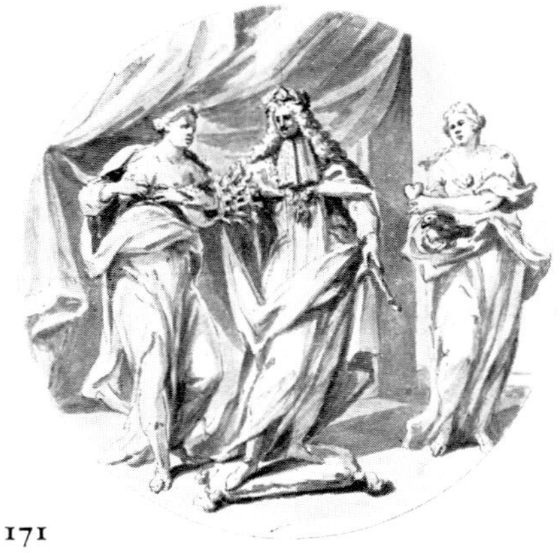

171

161 to 171 The roundels for the unexecuted scheme of decoration (nos 191–201)

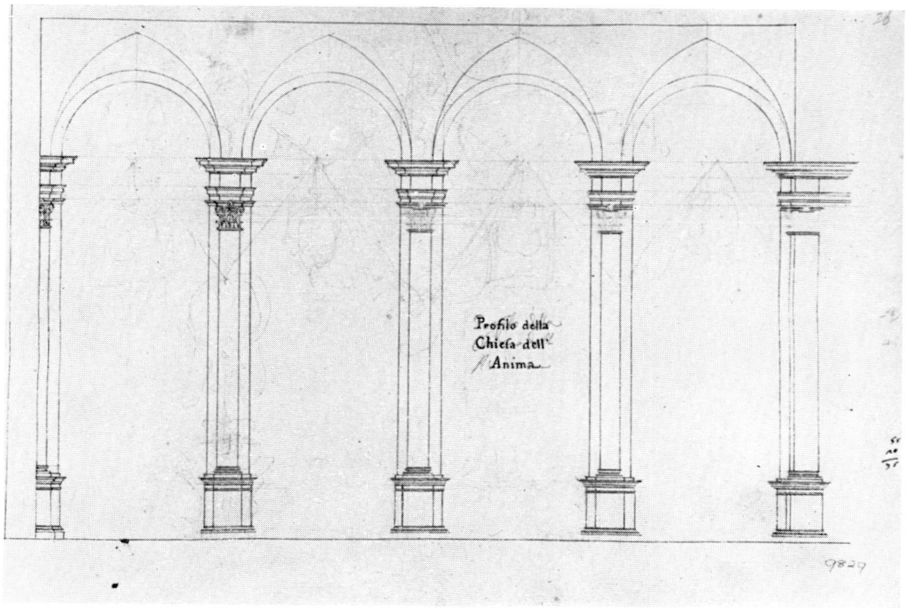

172 Elevation of the nave arcade (no.202)

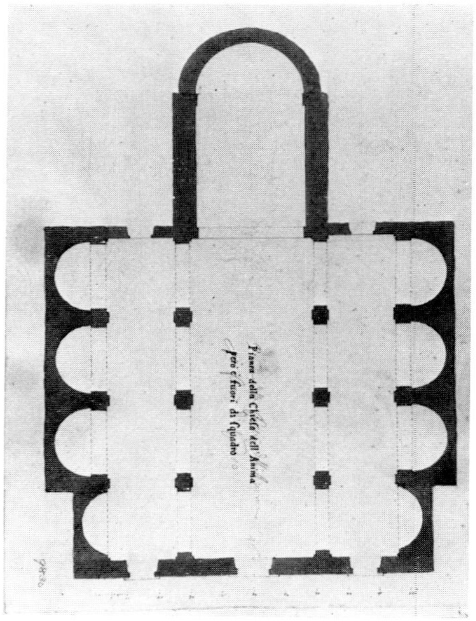

173 Plan of the church (no.204)

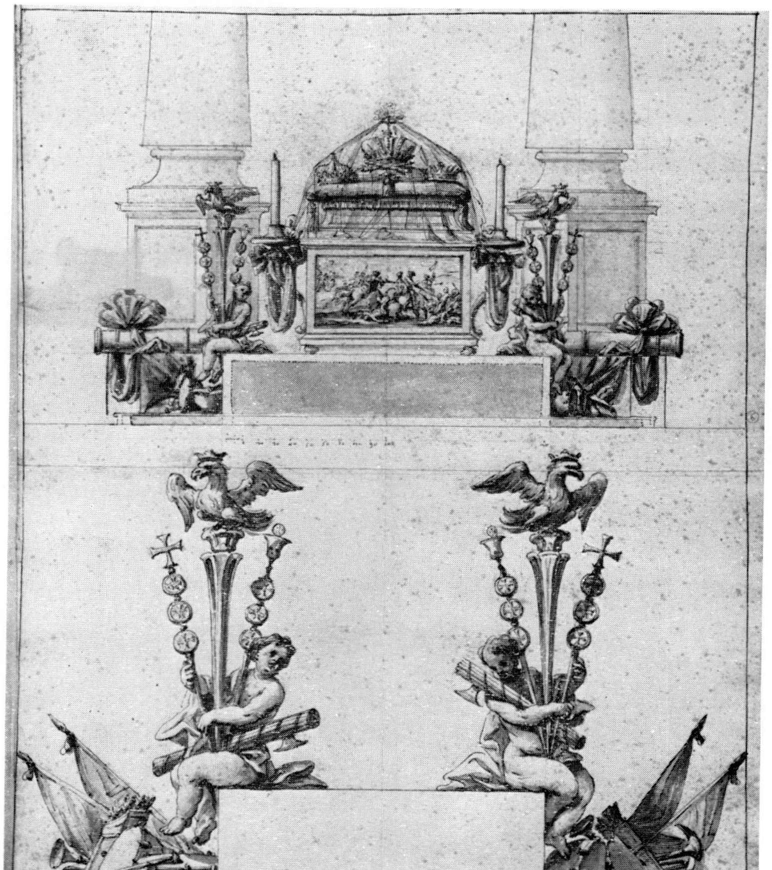

174 Elevation of the bier; studies of the *putti* (drawing after (?) Fontana; London, Victoria and Albert Museum)

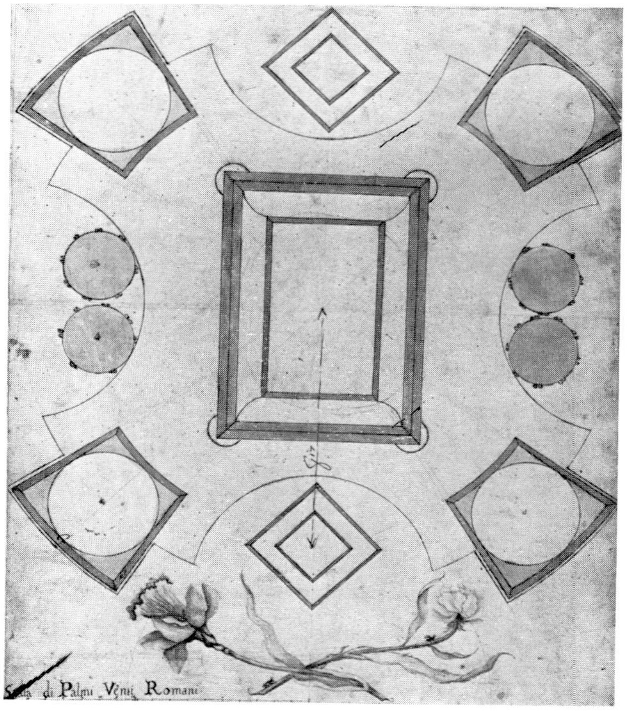

175 Plan of the bier (drawing after (?) Fontana; London, Victoria and Albert Museum)

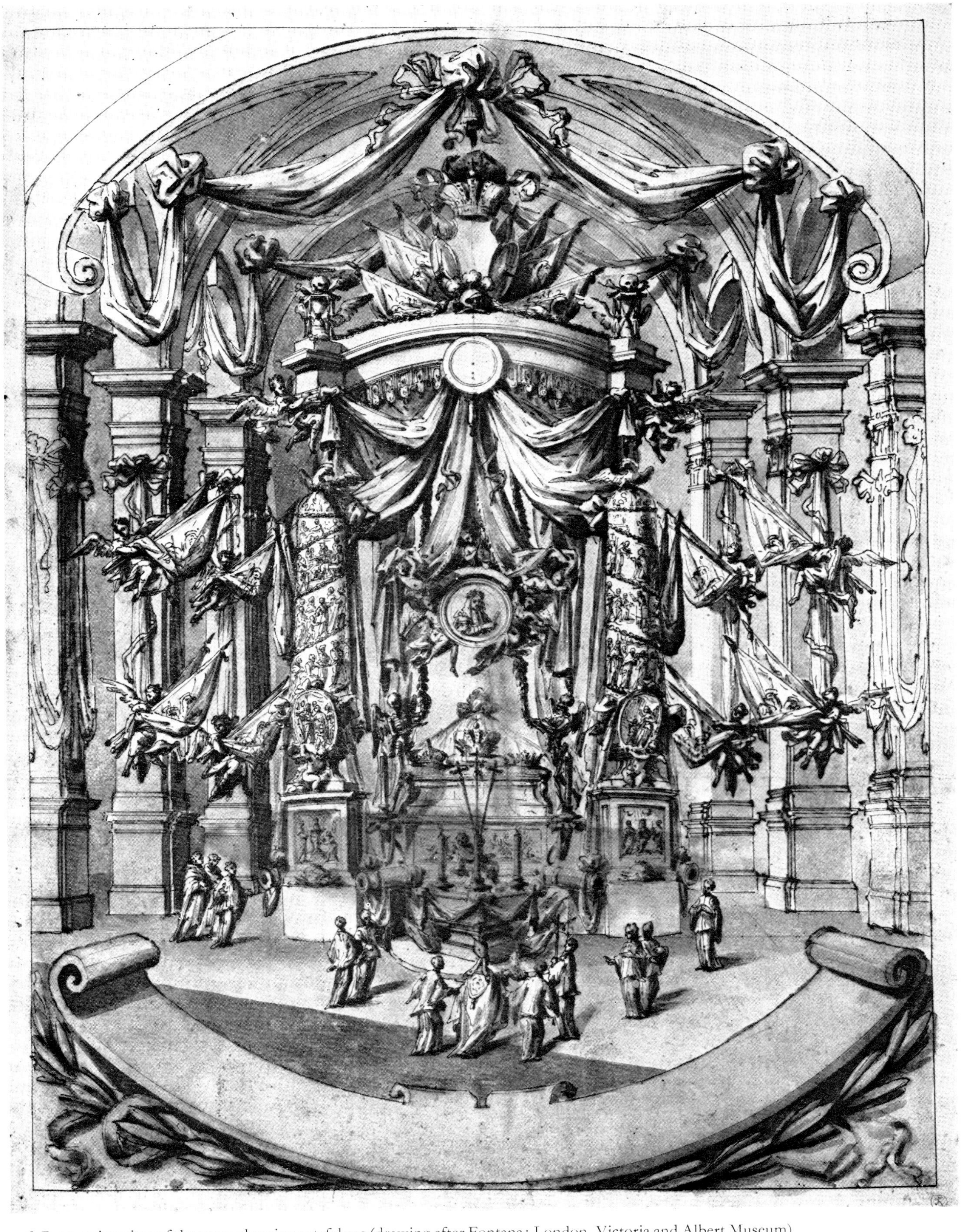

176 Perspective view of the nave, showing catafalque (drawing after Fontana; London, Victoria and Albert Museum)

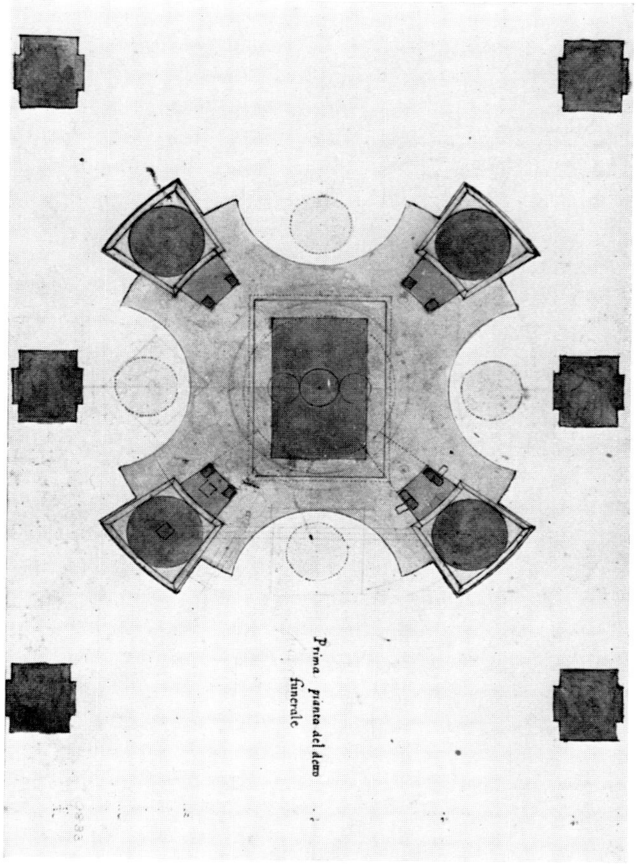

177 Plan of the central nave bays and of the catafalque (no.207)

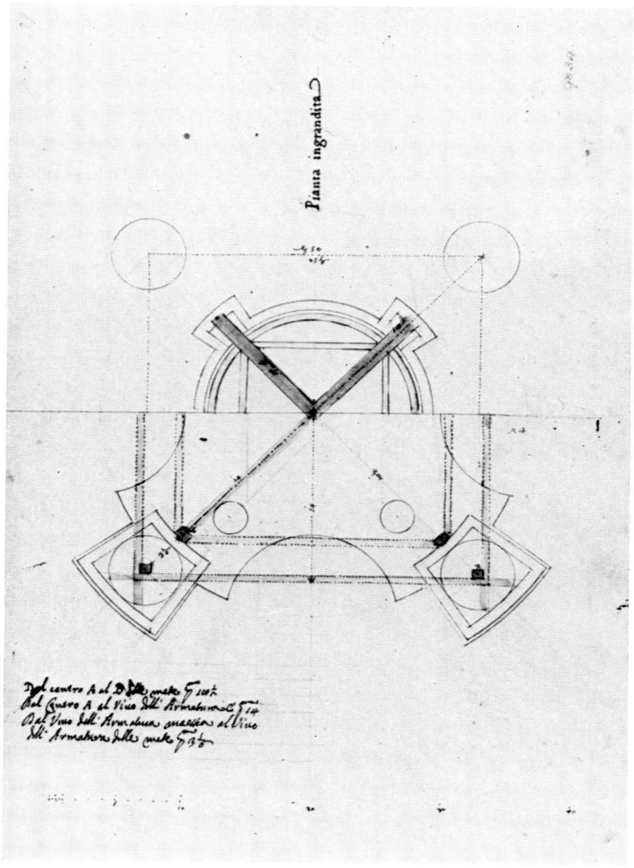

178 Plan of the catafalque at base and baldacchino level, showing structural support (no.208)

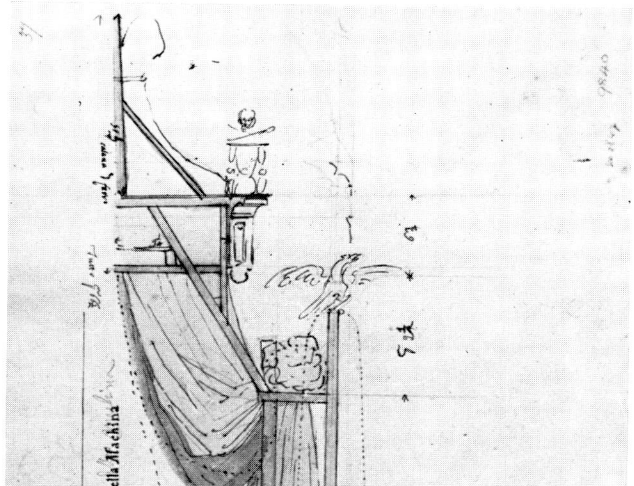

179 Diagonal half section of the catafalque, showing structural support (no.209)

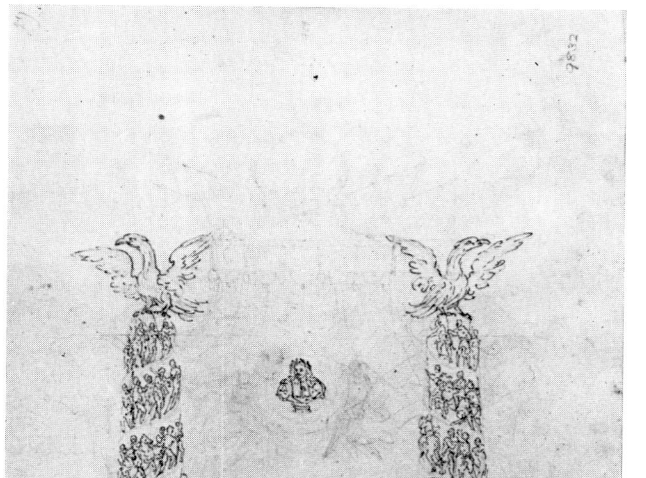

180 Elevation of the catafalque (no.211)

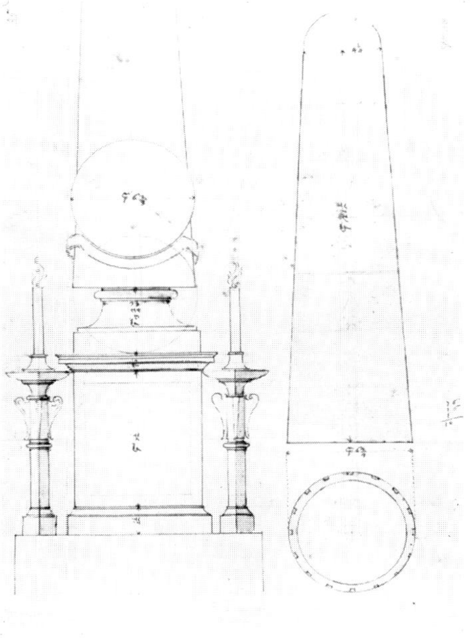

181 Elevation of a *meta*, with plan (no.212)

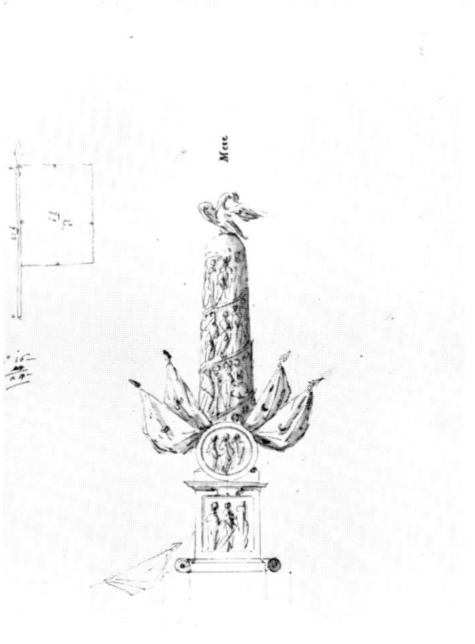

182 Elevation of a *meta* (no.214)

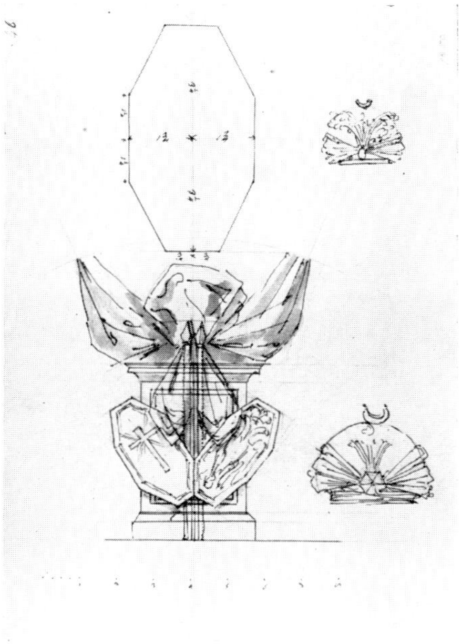

183 Studies for the decoration of a pedestal (no.215)

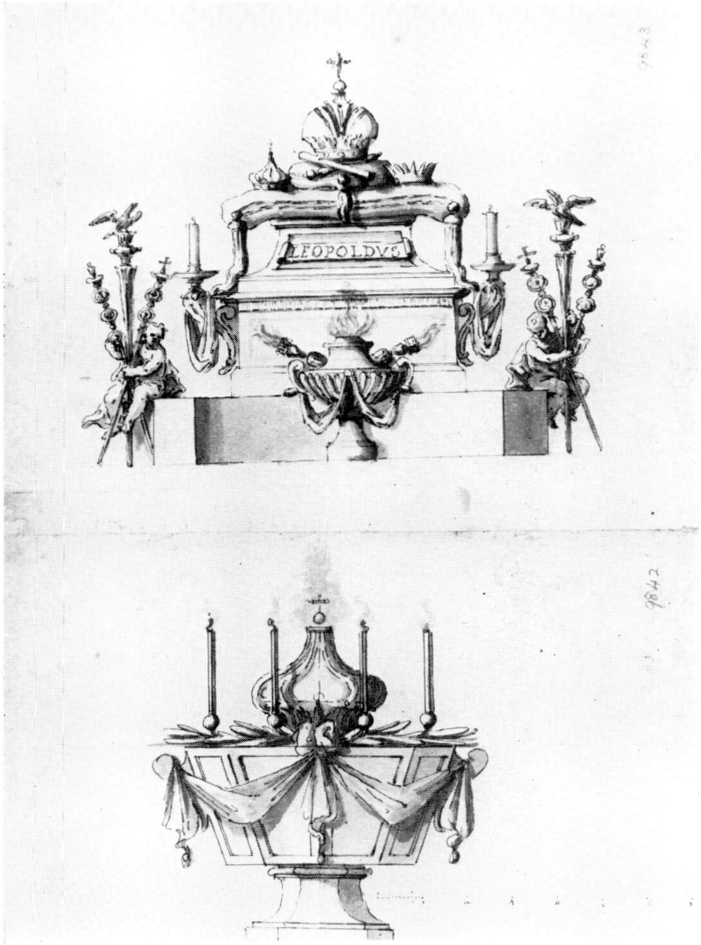

184 Elevation of the bier and an incense urn (no.216)

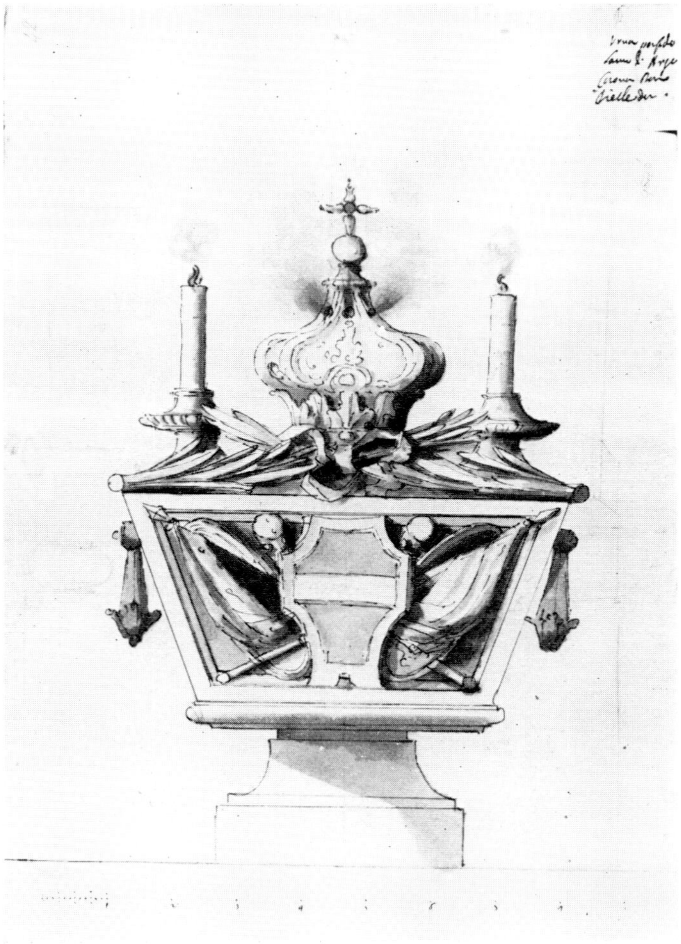

185 Elevation of a pedestal with incense crown (no.219)

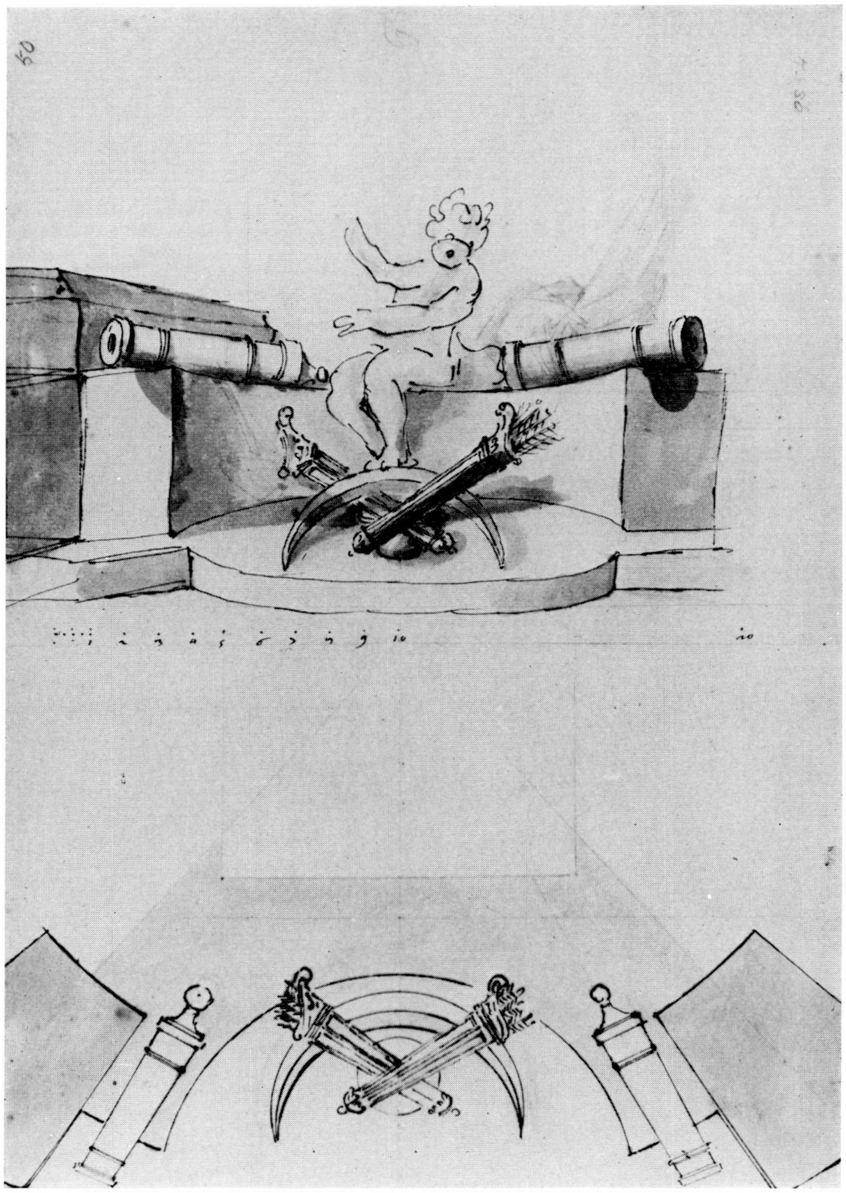

186 Plan and perspective view of a concave bay of the catafalque (no.220)

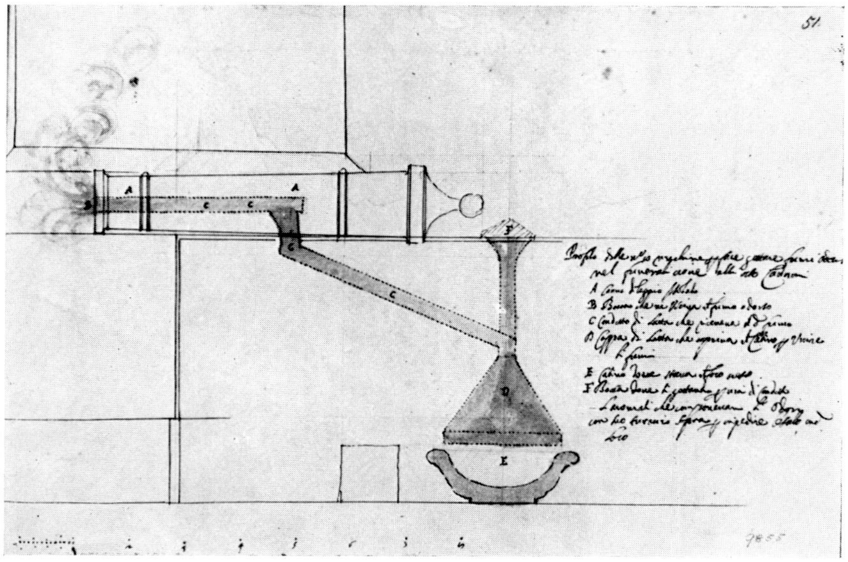

187 Section of an incense cannon (no.221)

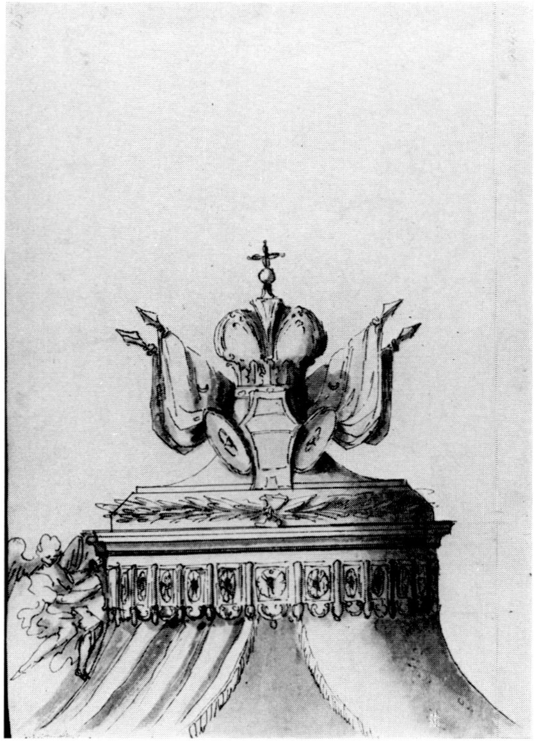

188 Elevation of the baldacchino, decorated with an Imperial crown (no.226)

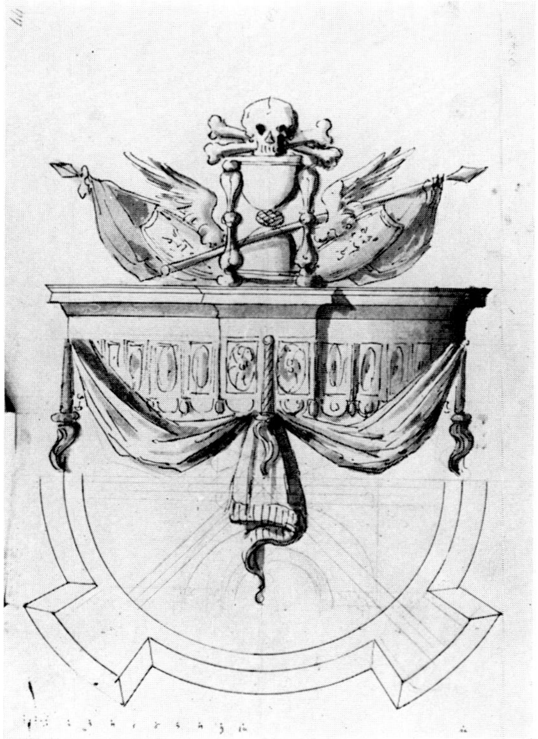

189 Elevation and half plan of the baldacchino, decorated with a death's head (no.227)

Rome, S. Egidio in Trastevere, the Origo Monument (1706)

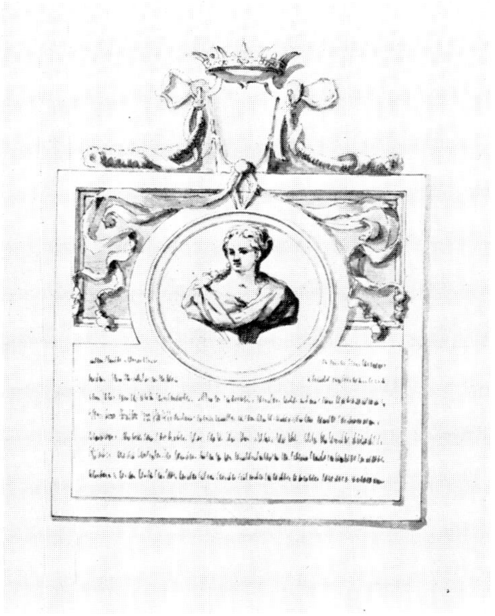

190 Project with a square frame (no.232)

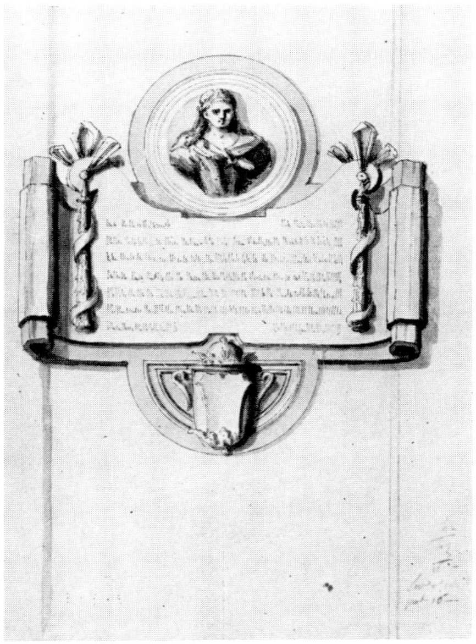

191 Project with an extended scroll (no.233)

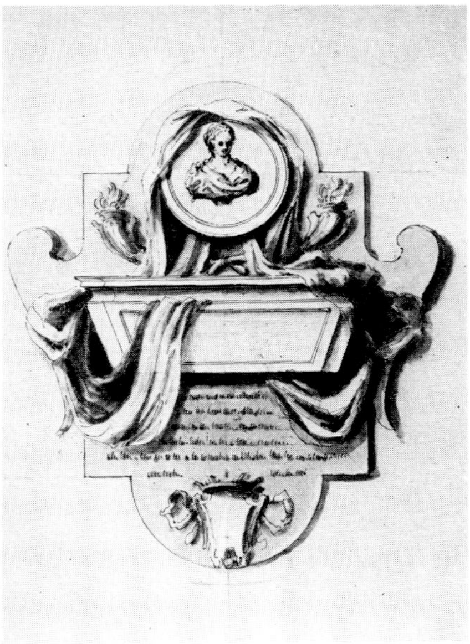

192 Project with a sarcophagus (no.234)

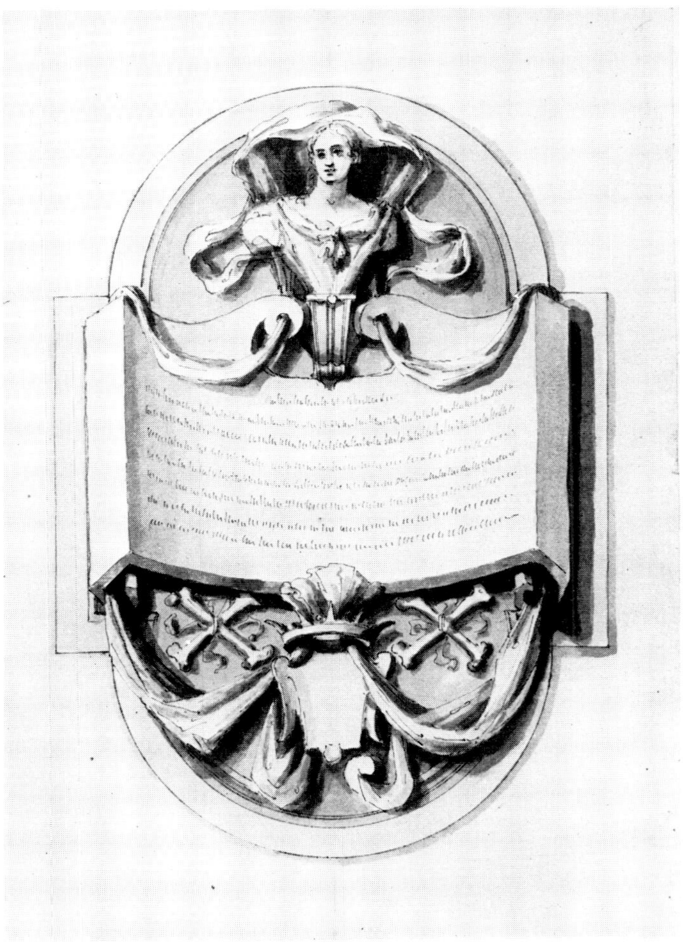

193 Project with a free-standing portrait bust (1) (no.235)

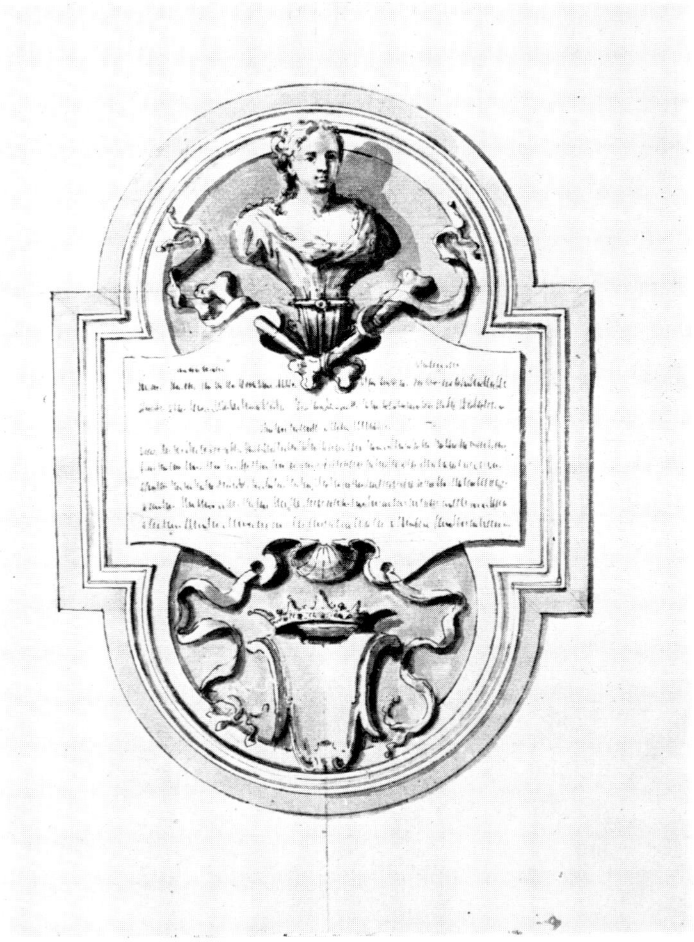

194 Project with a free-standing portrait bust (2) (no.236)

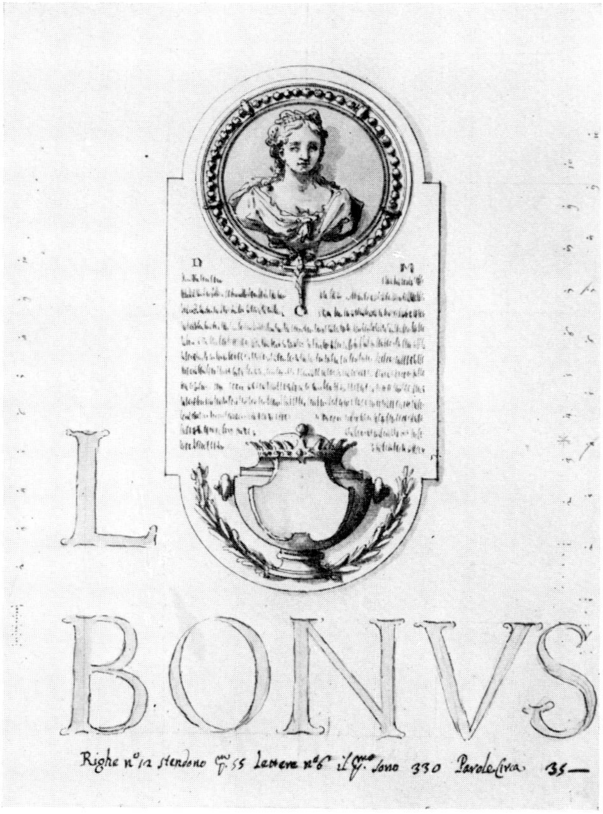

195 Project with an urn flanked by laurel branches (no.237)

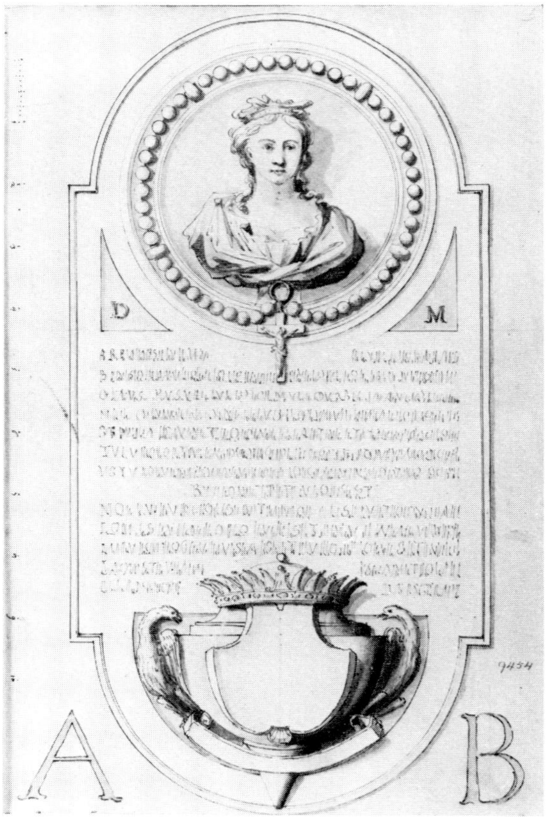

196 Project with an urn flanked by eagles (1) (no.238)

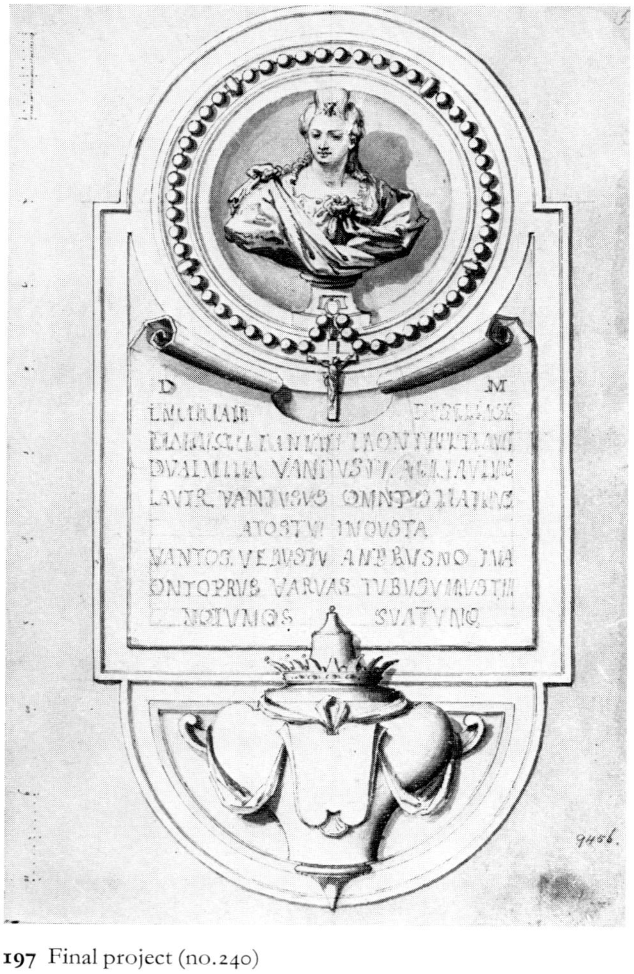

197 Final project (no.240)

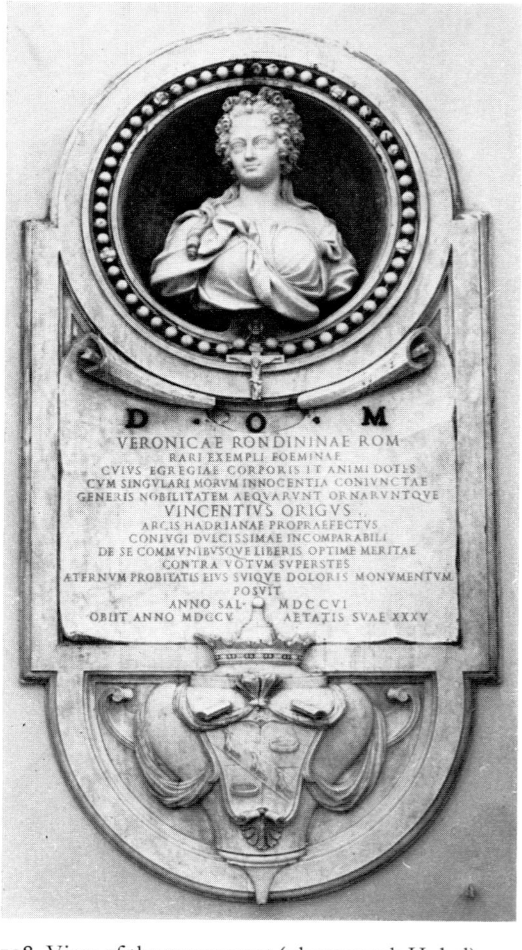

198 View of the monument (photograph Huhel)

The decoration of S. Antonio de'Portoghesi, Rome, for the memorial service to King Pedro II of Portugal (1707)

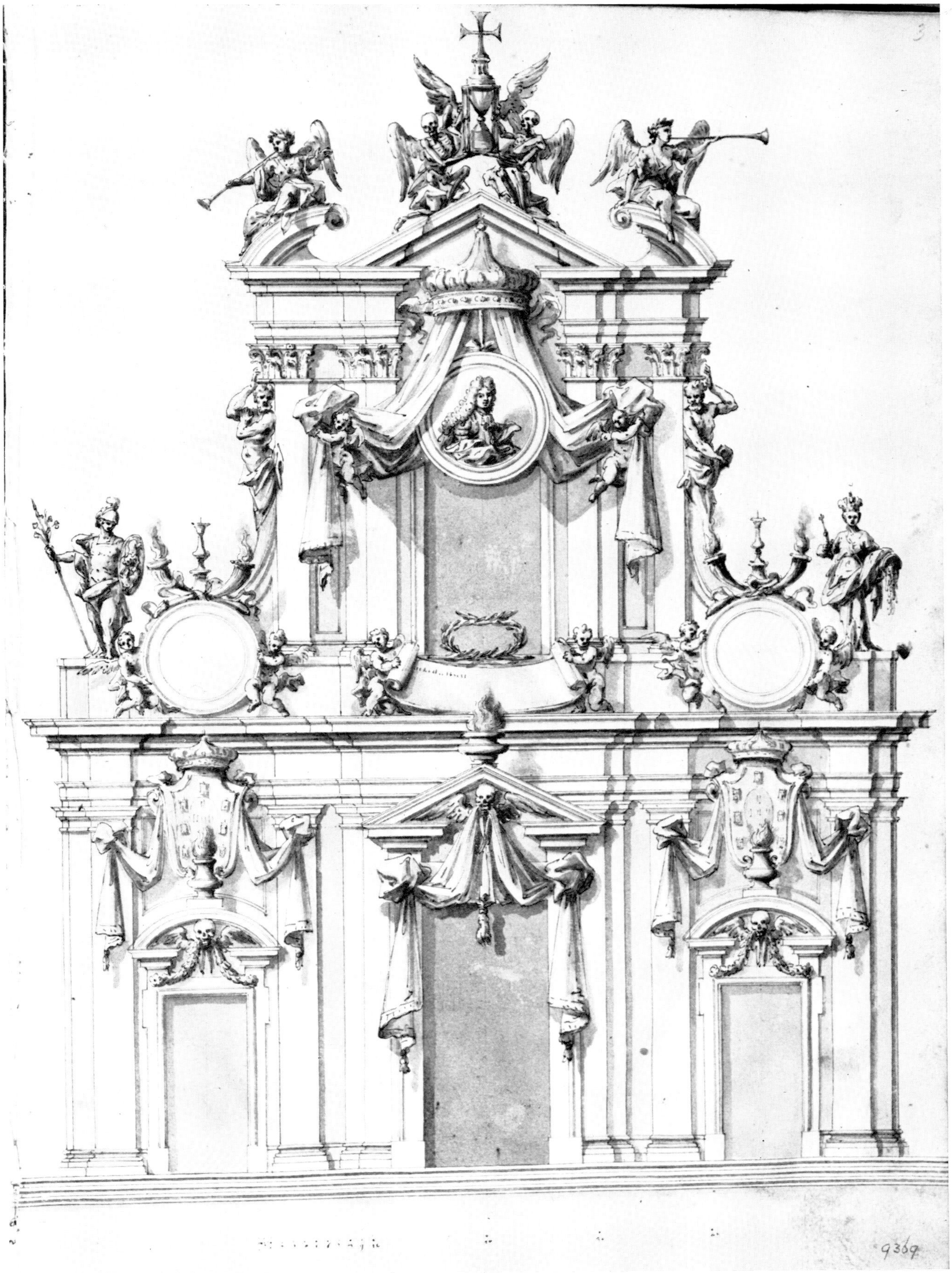

199 Elevation of the main façade (no.284)

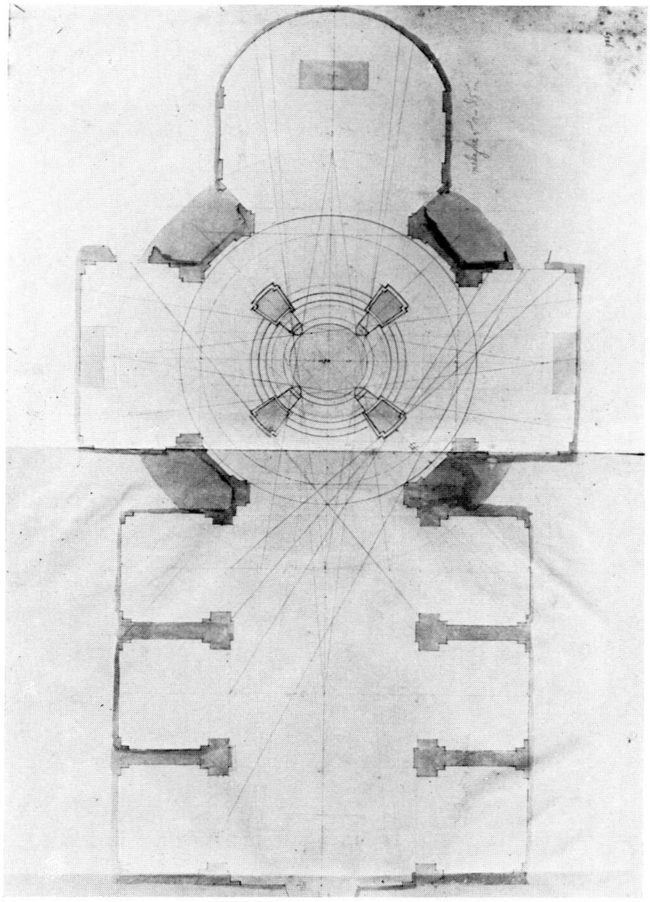

200 Plan of the interior of the church (no.241)

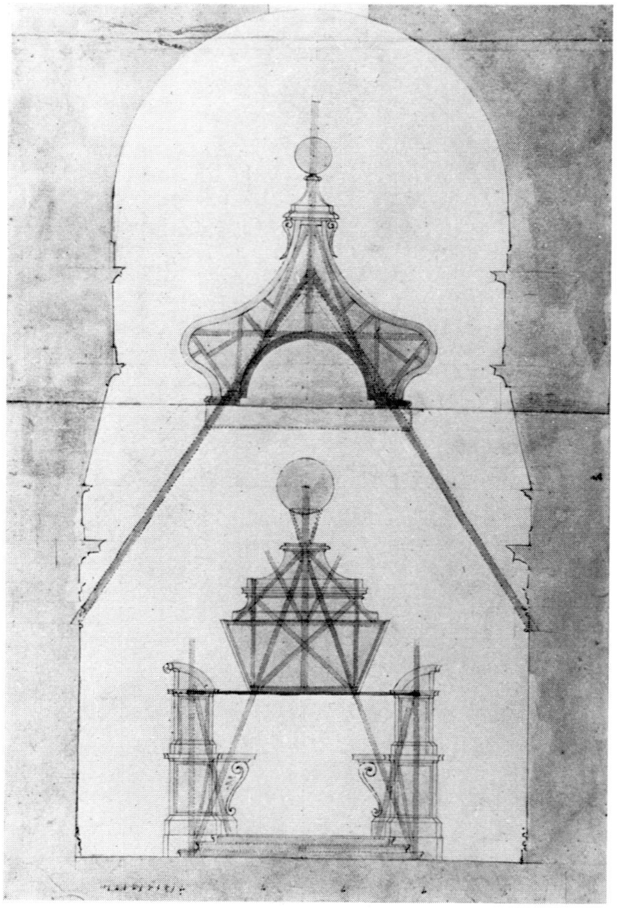

201 Section of the catafalque and baldacchino (no.246)

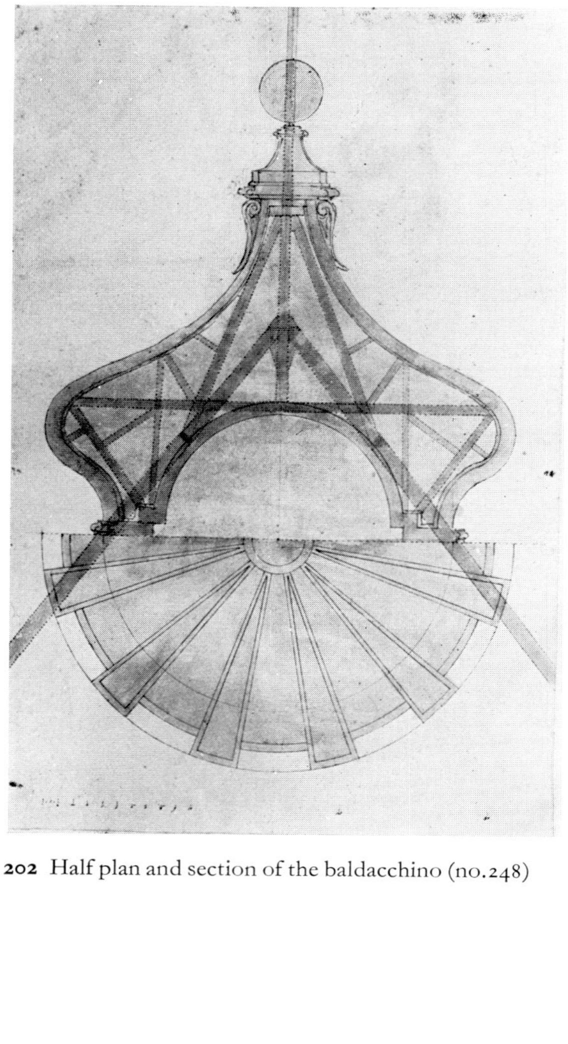

202 Half plan and section of the baldacchino (no.248)

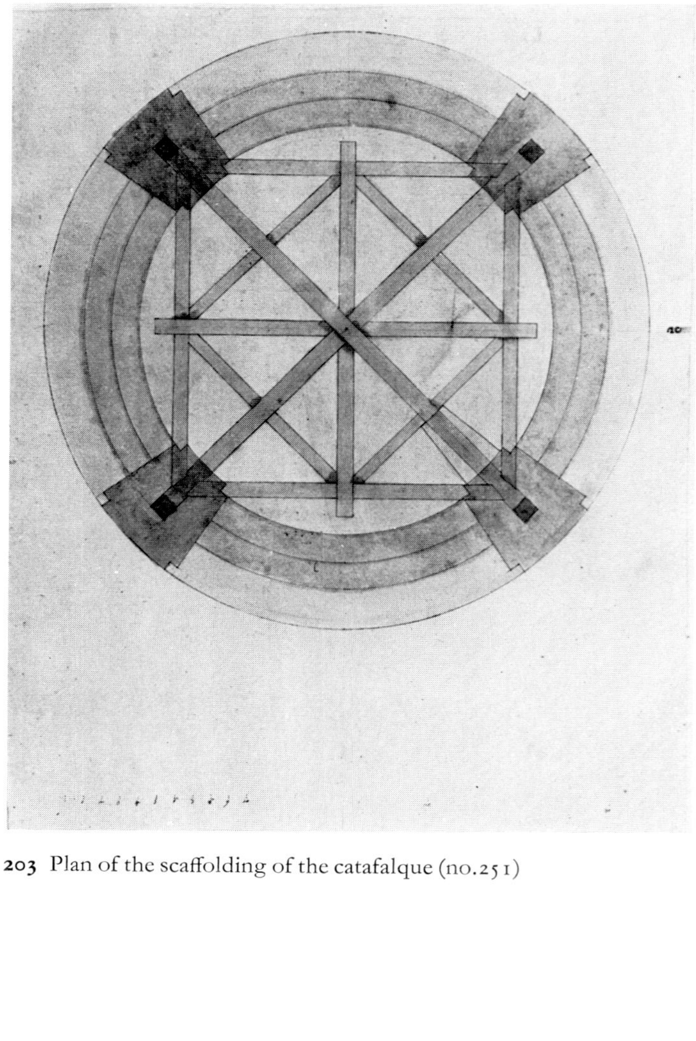

203 Plan of the scaffolding of the catafalque (no.251)

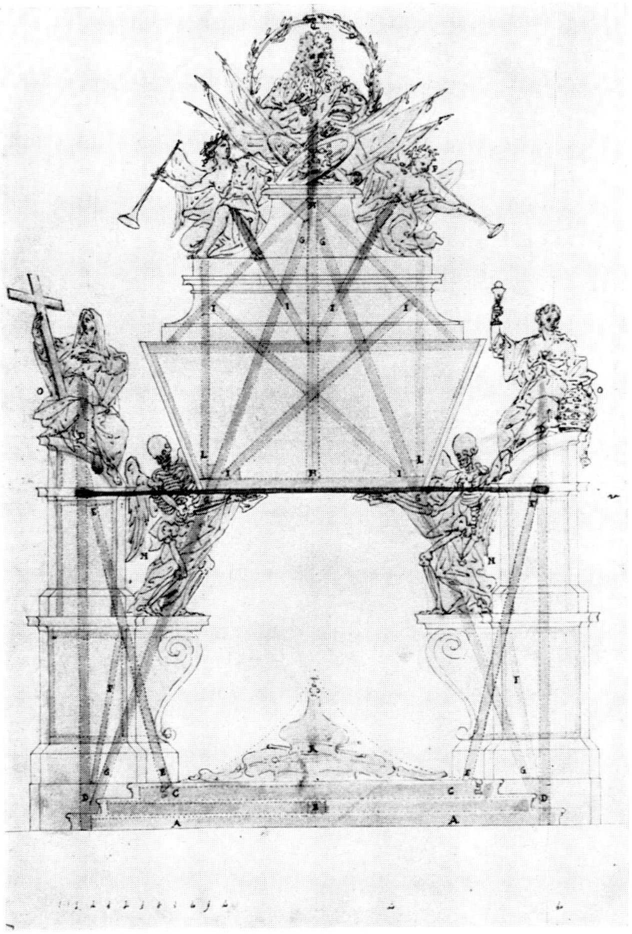

204 Section of the catafalque, showing sculptural decoration (no.254)

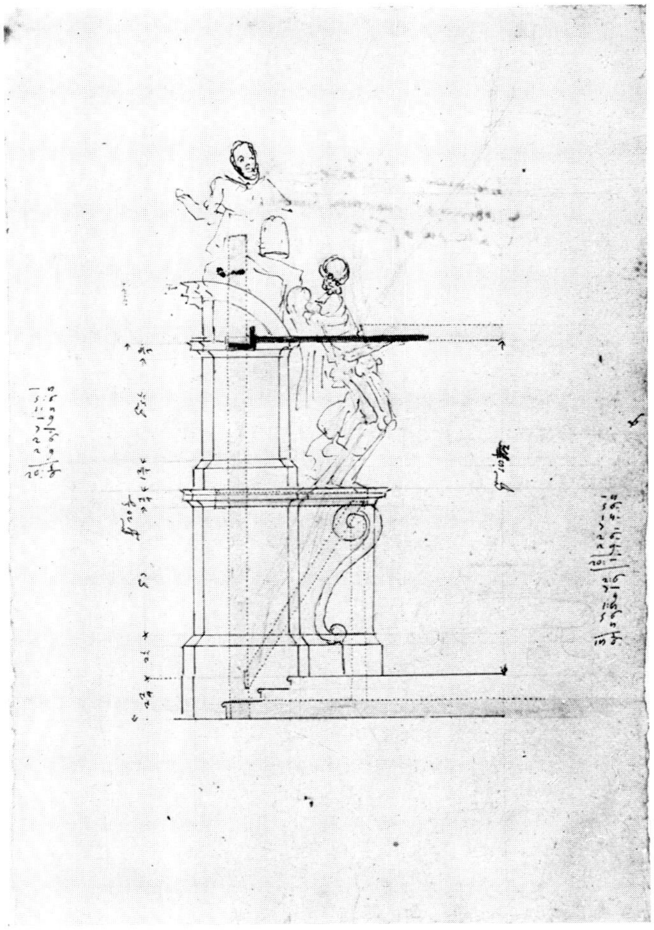

205 Elevation of a pedestal, showing scaffolding and some decoration (no.255)

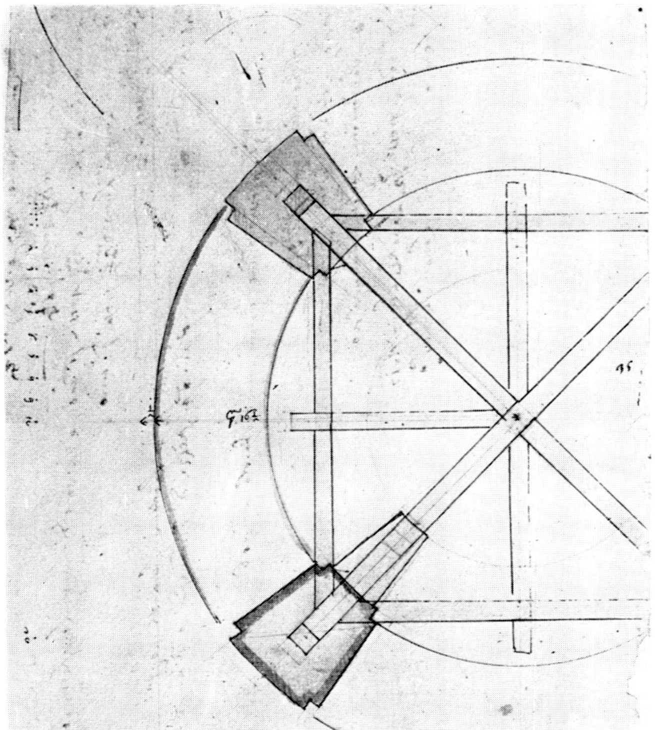

206 Plan of the scaffolding of the catafalque (no.256)

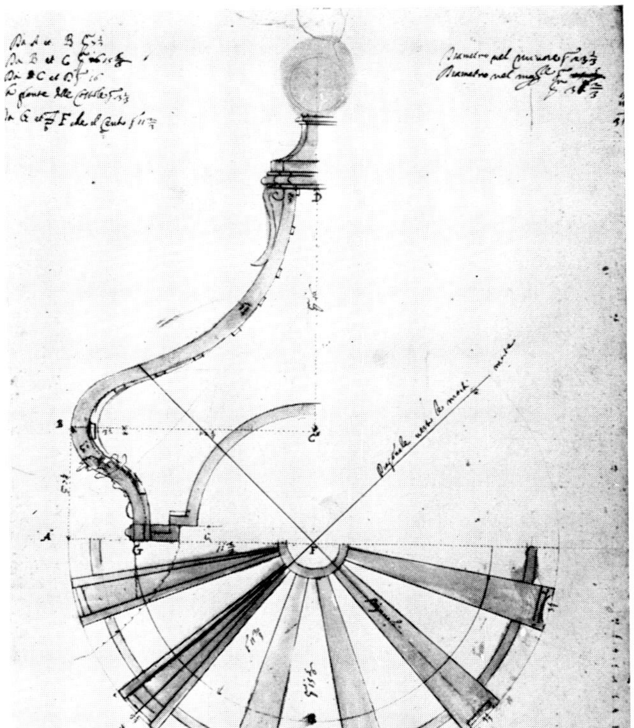

207 Half plan and half section of the baldacchino (no.257)

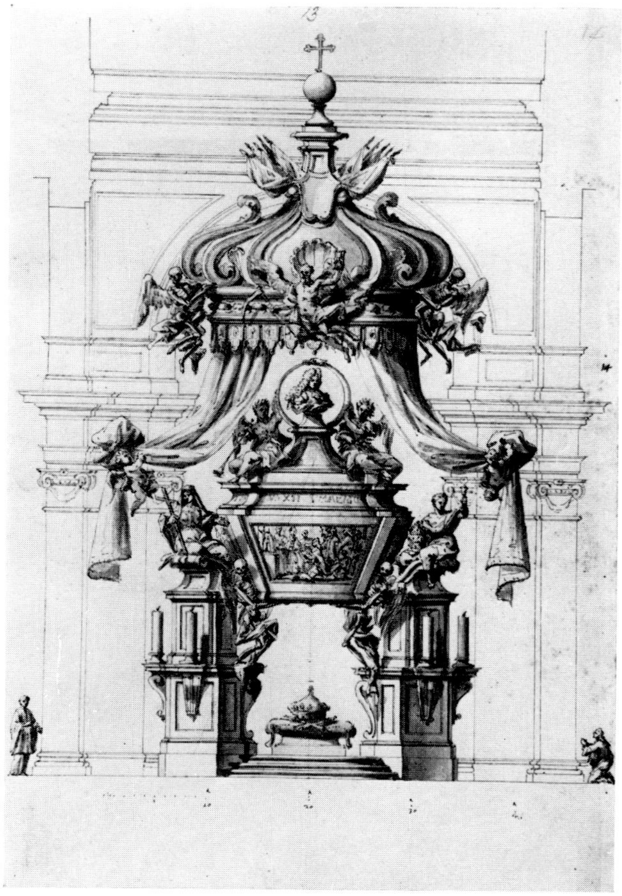

208 Elevation of the catafalque (no.258)

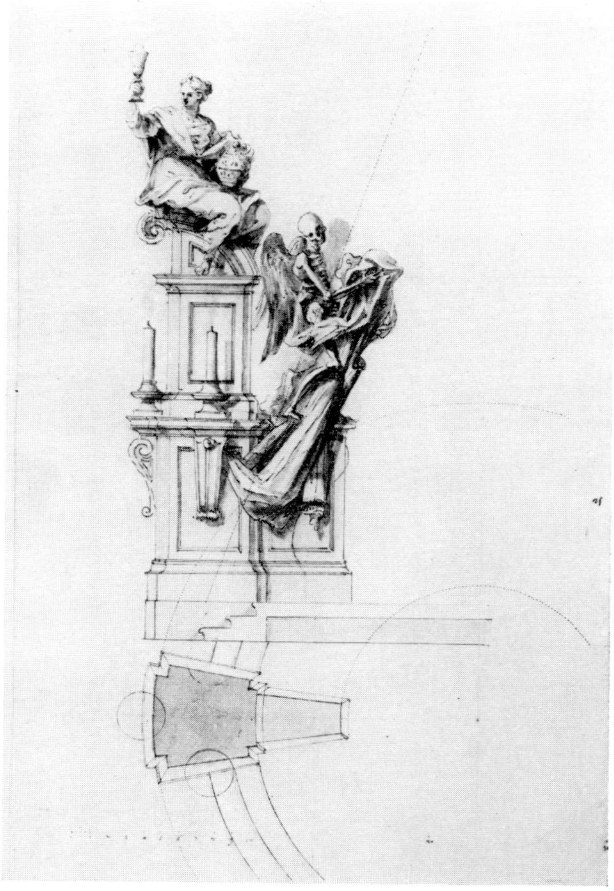

209 Plan and elevation of a pedestal (no.259)

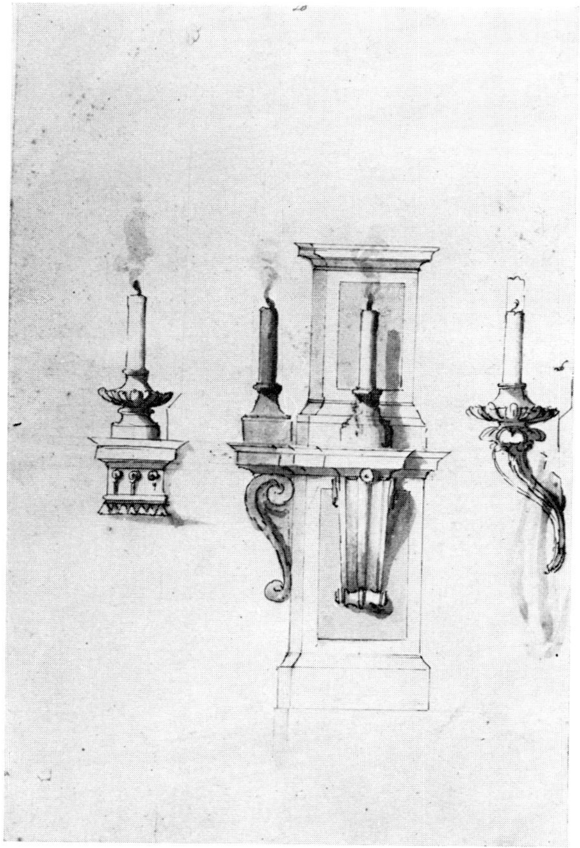

210 Studies of candle holders (no.260)

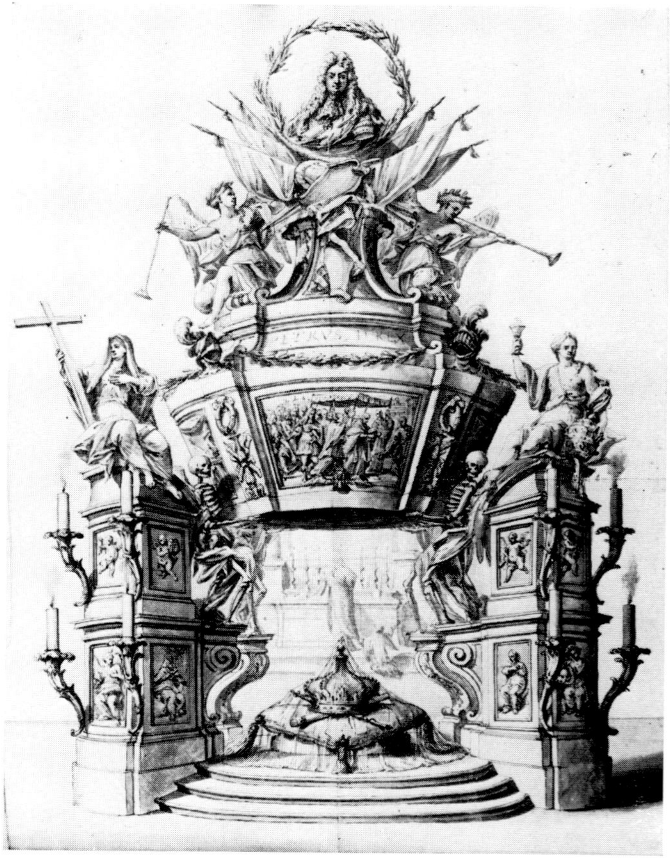

211 Perspective view of the catafalque (no.263)

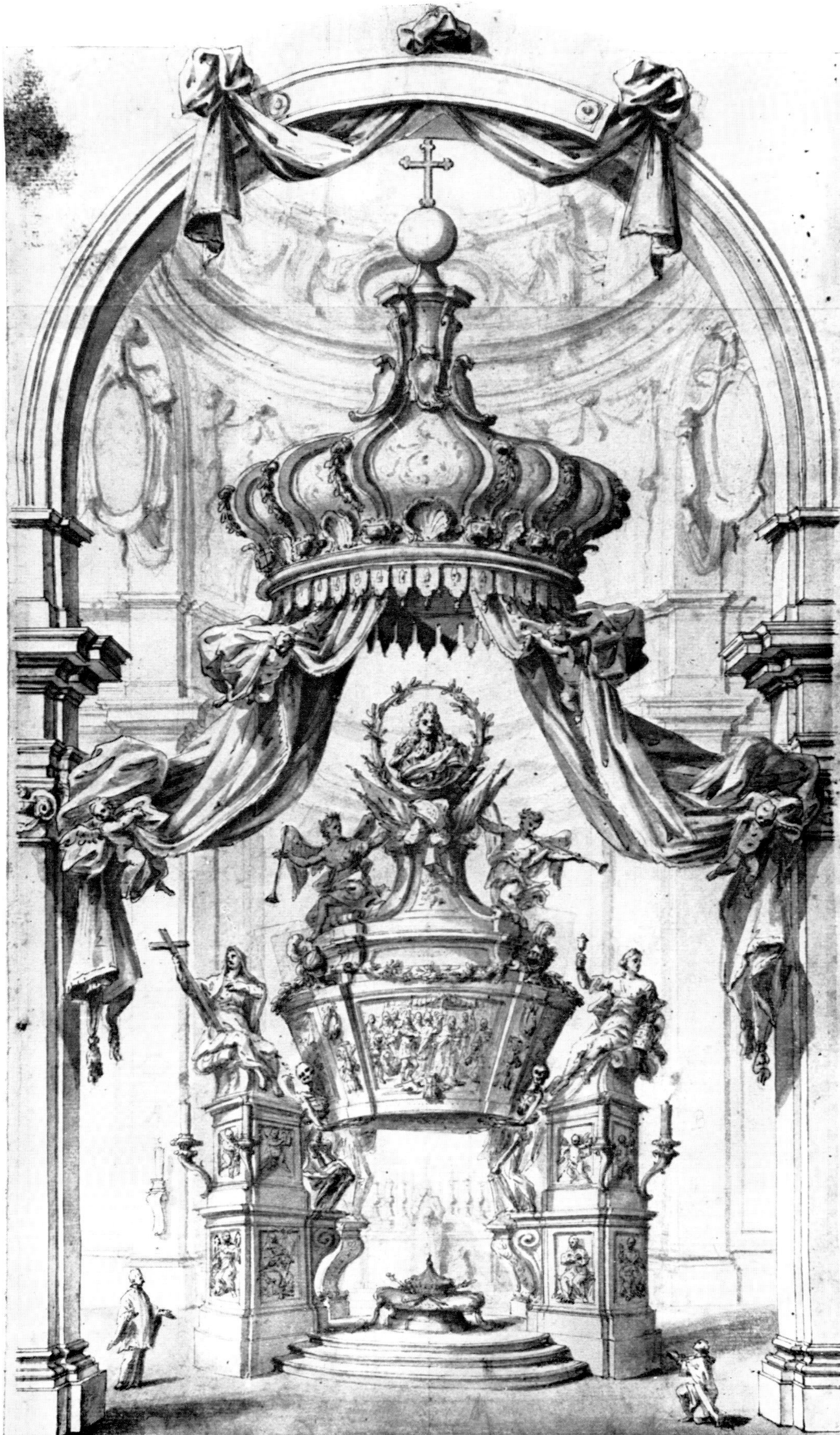

212 Perspective view of the catafalque and baldacchino in the crossing (no.261)

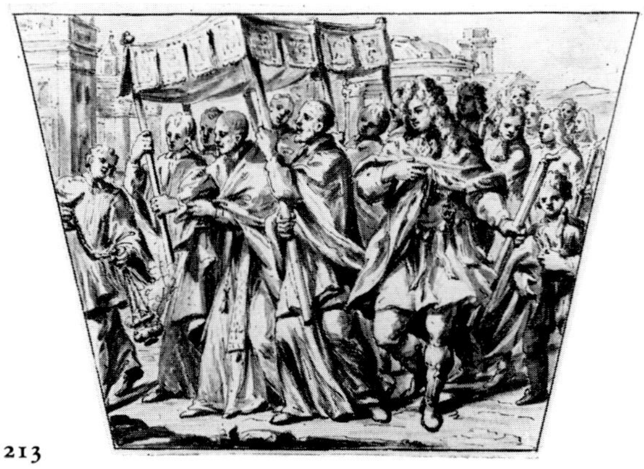

213

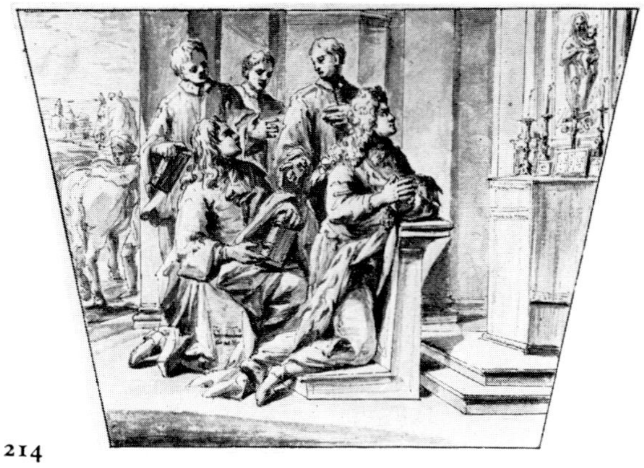

214

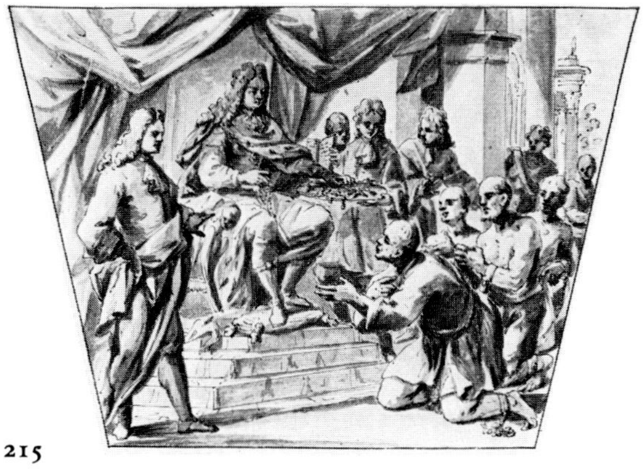

215

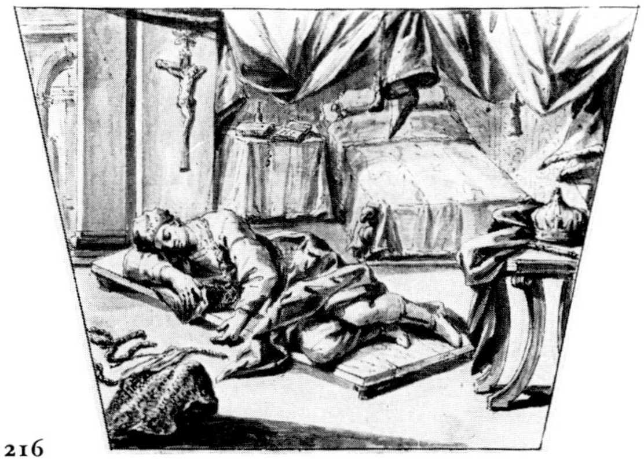

216

213 to 216 Drawings of the reliefs on the sarcophagus (nos 264, 265, 266 and 268)

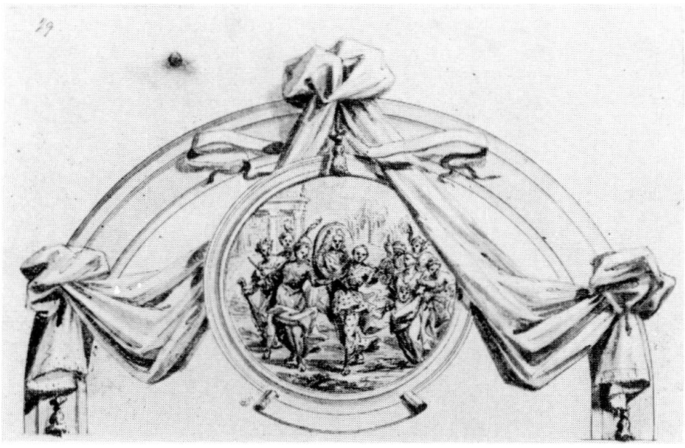

217

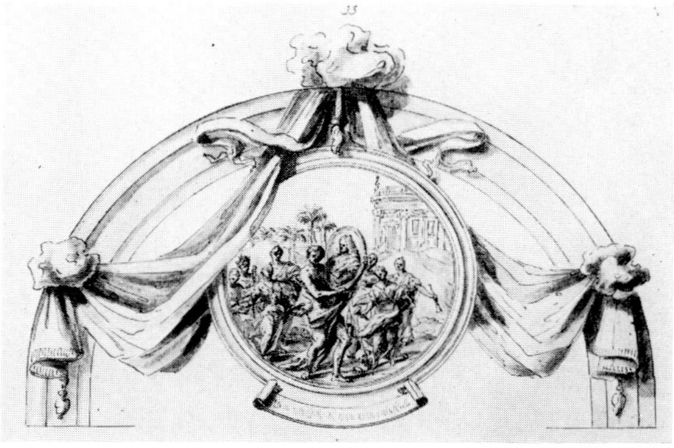

218

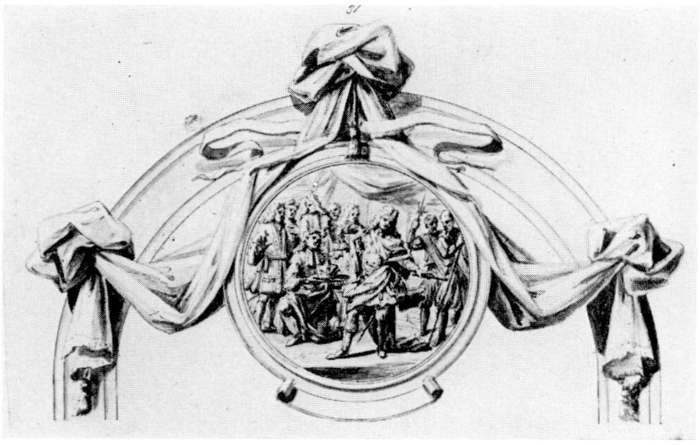

219

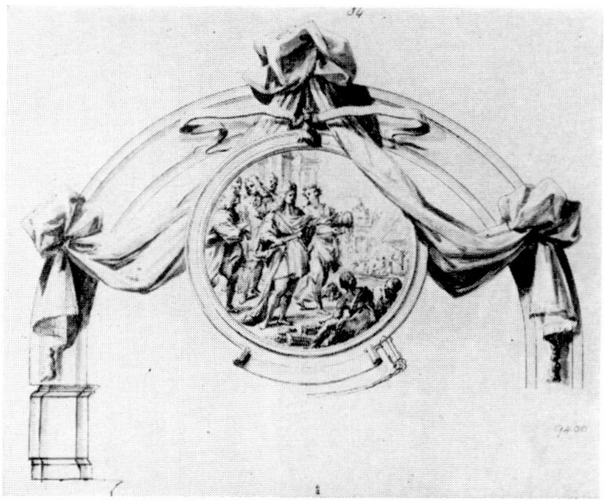

220

217 to 220 Drawings of the roundels suspended in the crossing (nos 270, 272, 273 and 275)

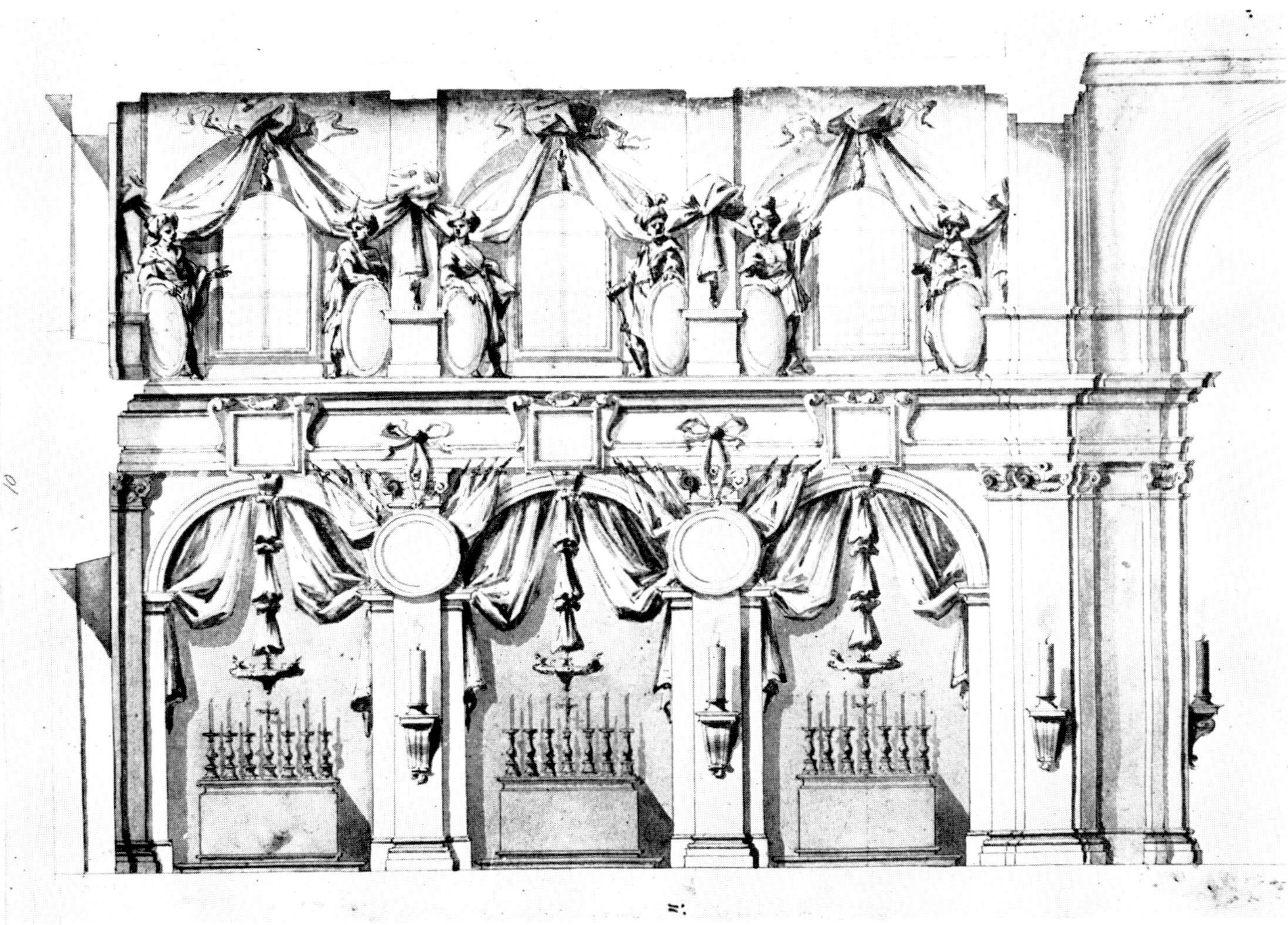

221 Elevation of the left wall of the nave (no.278)

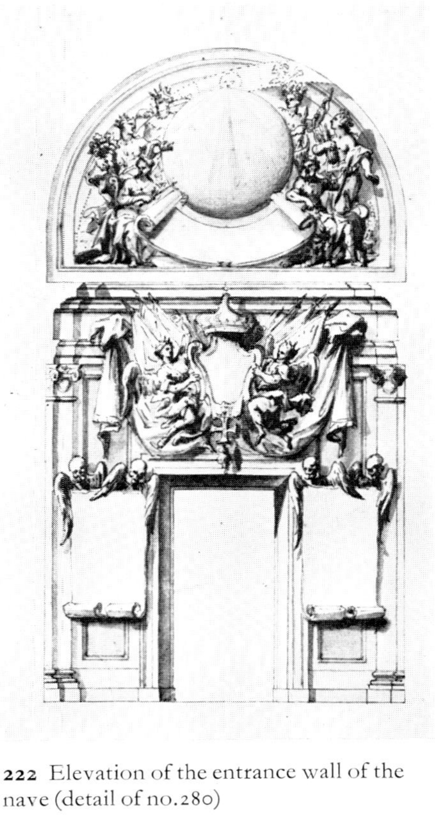

222 Elevation of the entrance wall of the nave (detail of no.280)

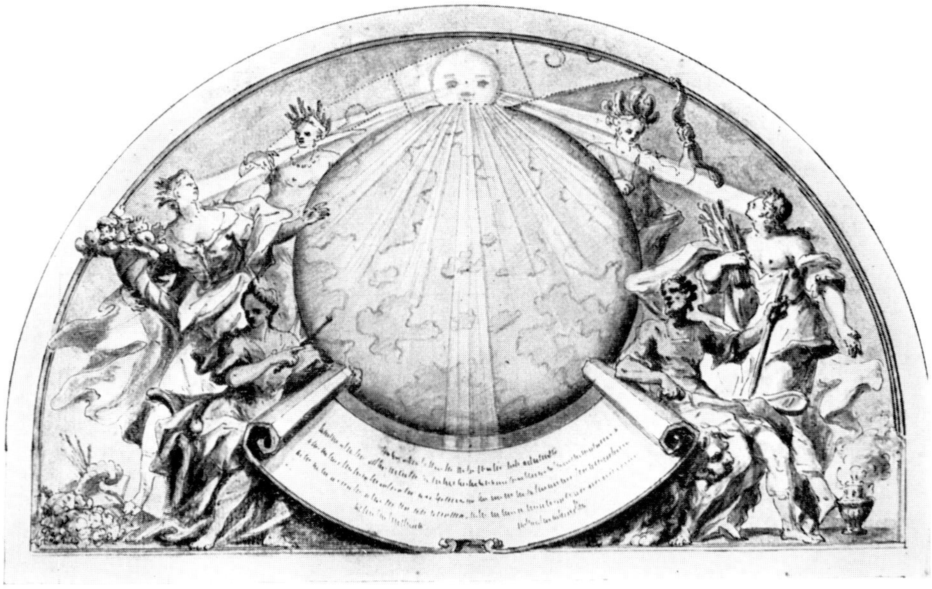

223 Study of the lunette over the doorway (no.282)

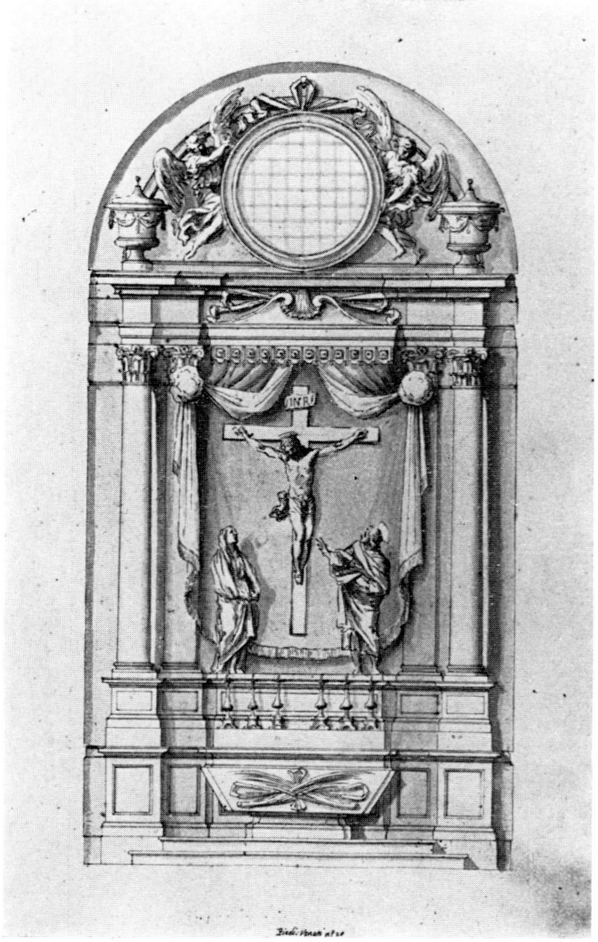

224 An altar for Venice (S. Maria dei Frari ?), elevation (no.285)

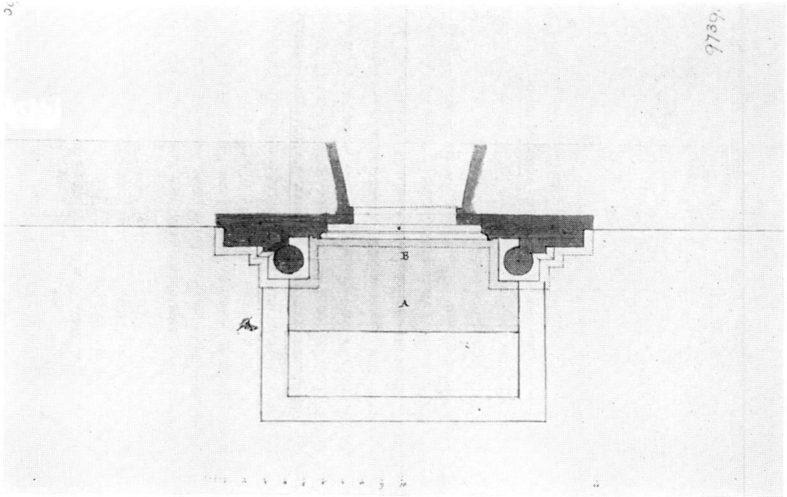

225 An altar for Cardinal Ferrari, for Manduria (?), plan (no.286)

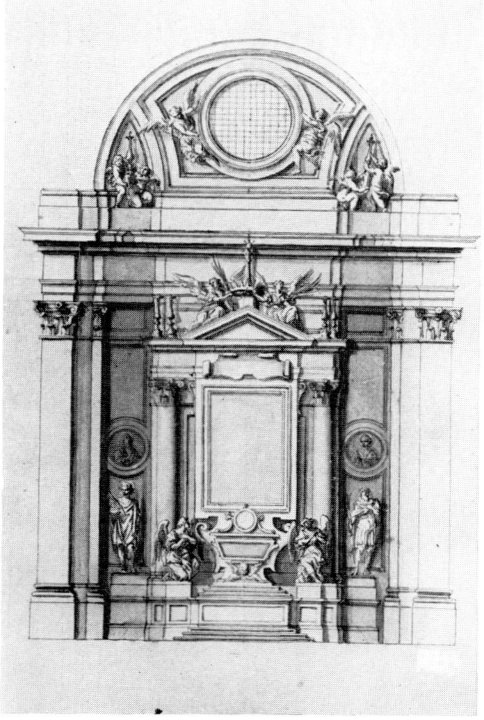

226 An altar with two martyrs, elevation (1) (no.287)

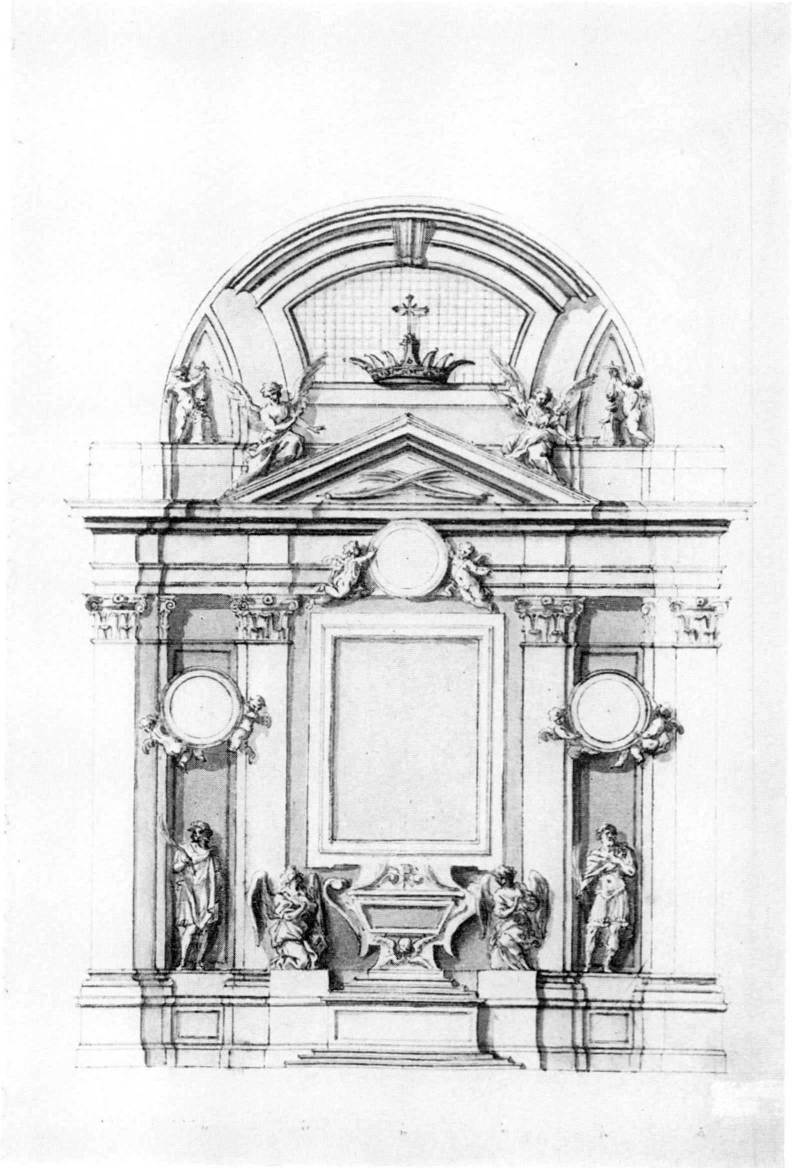

227 An altar with two martyrs, elevation (2) (no.288)

France, project for a cloistered building for Cardinal de Forbin Janson

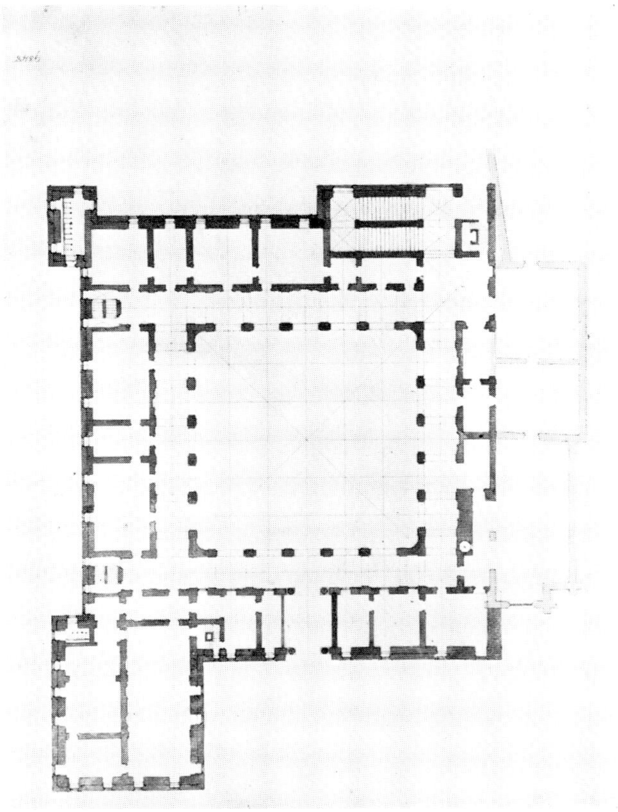

228 Ground-floor plan (no.289)

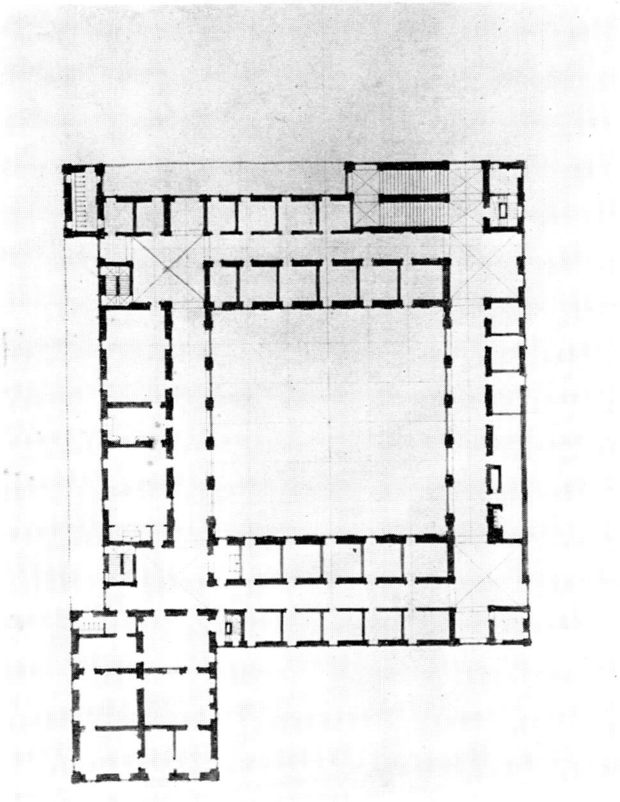

229 First-floor plan (no.290)

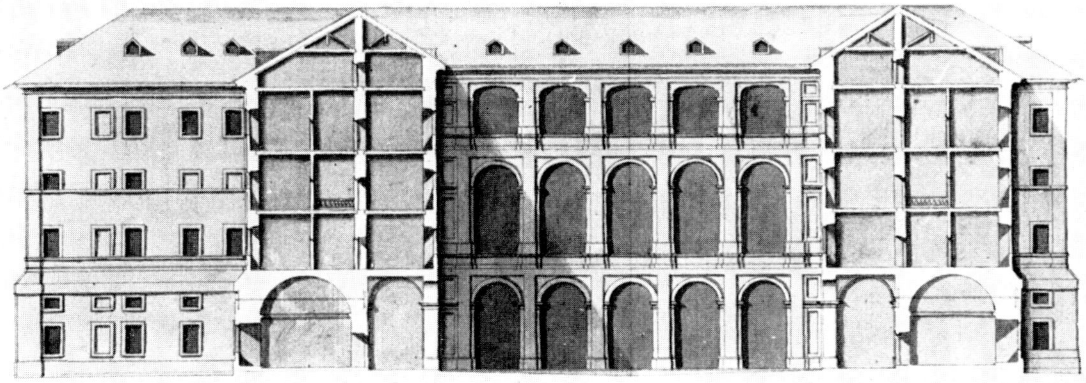

230 Longitudinal section (1) (no.292)

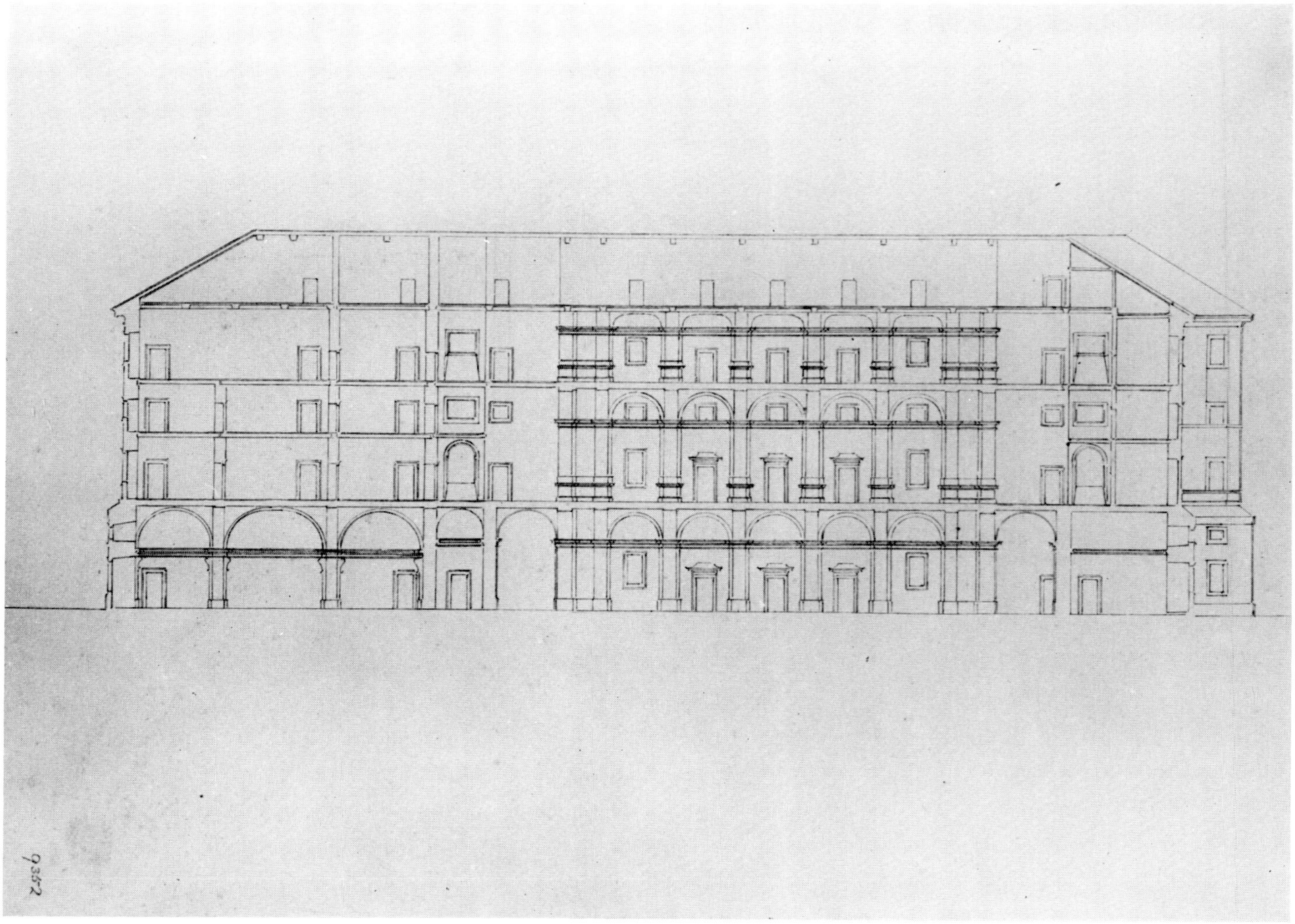

231 Longitudinal section (2) (no.293)

Secular Buildings

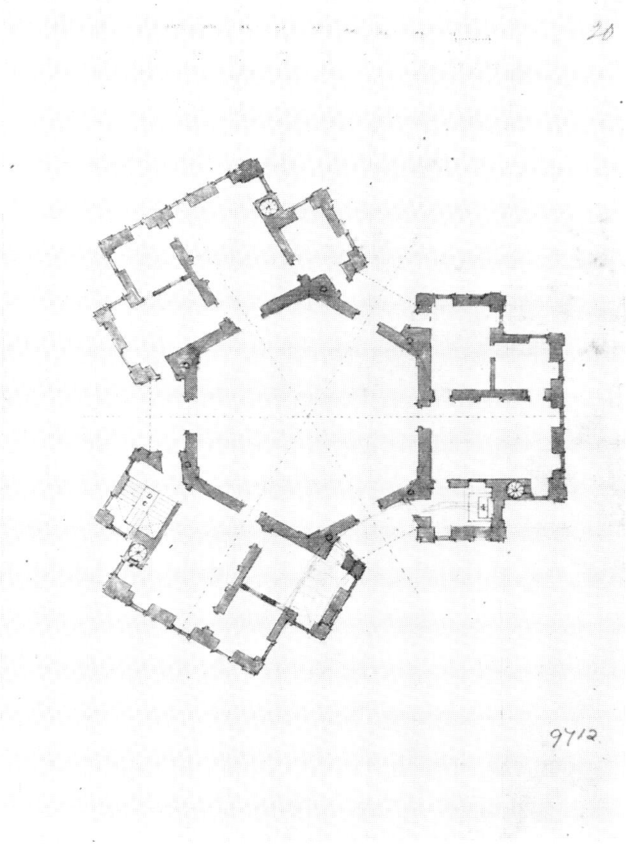

232 Ground-floor plan, first project (no.295)

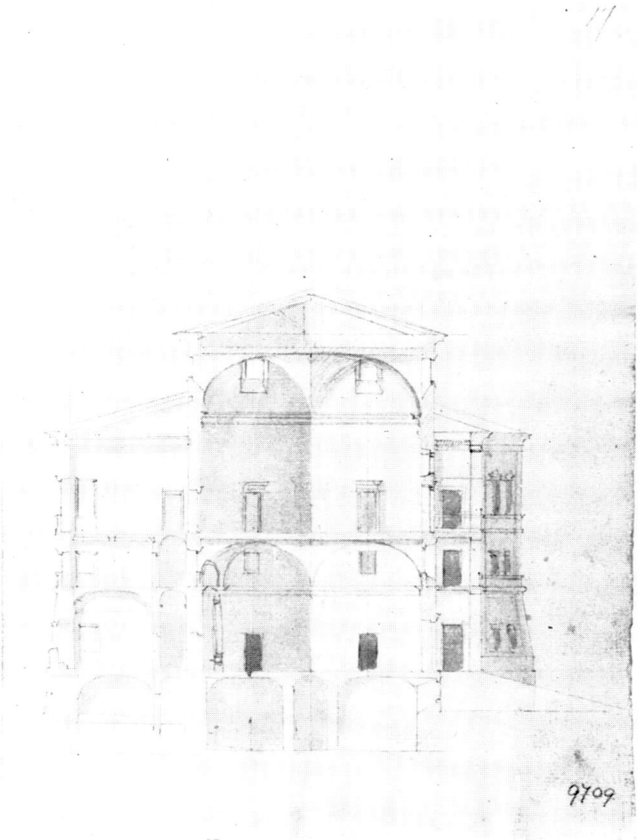

233 Section, first project (no.297)

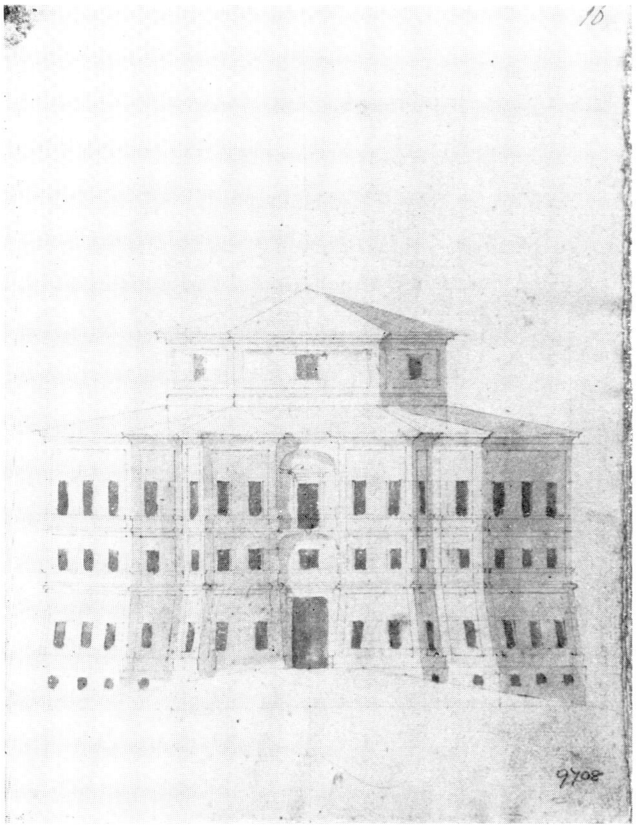

234 Elevation, first project (no.298)

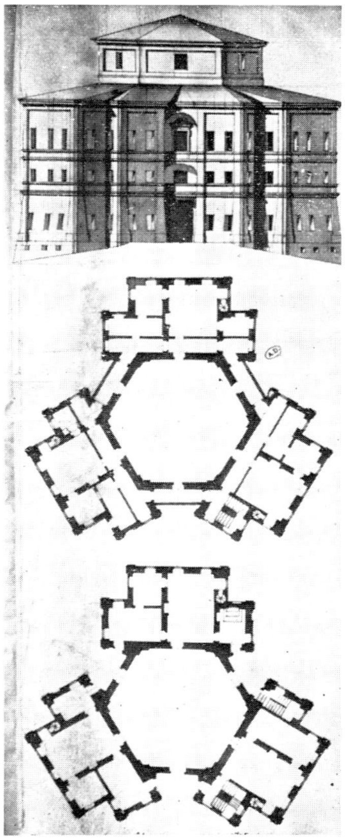

235 Plans of the ground and mezzanine floors, and elevation (drawing by Vittone after Fontana)

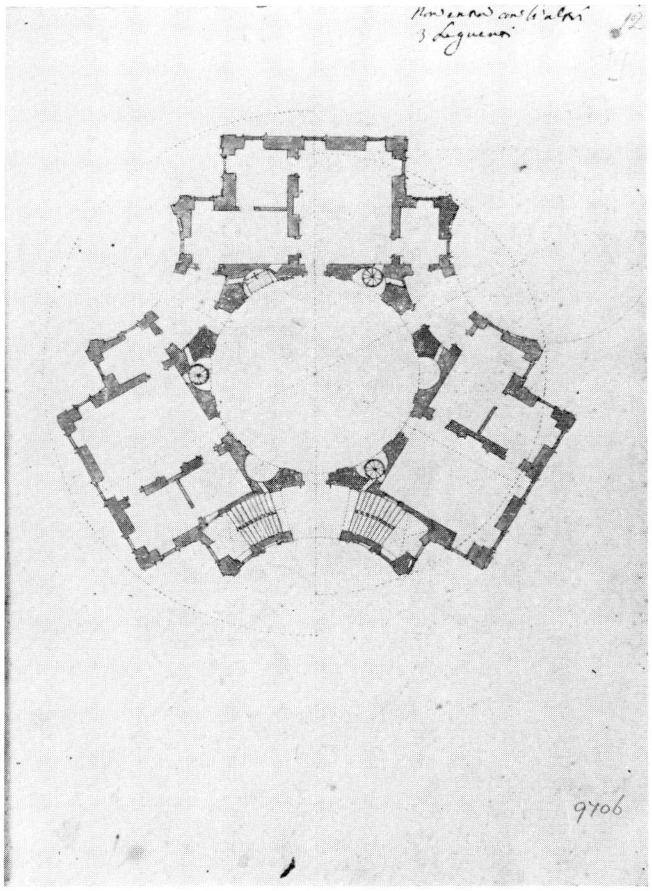

236 Ground-floor plan, later project (no.300)

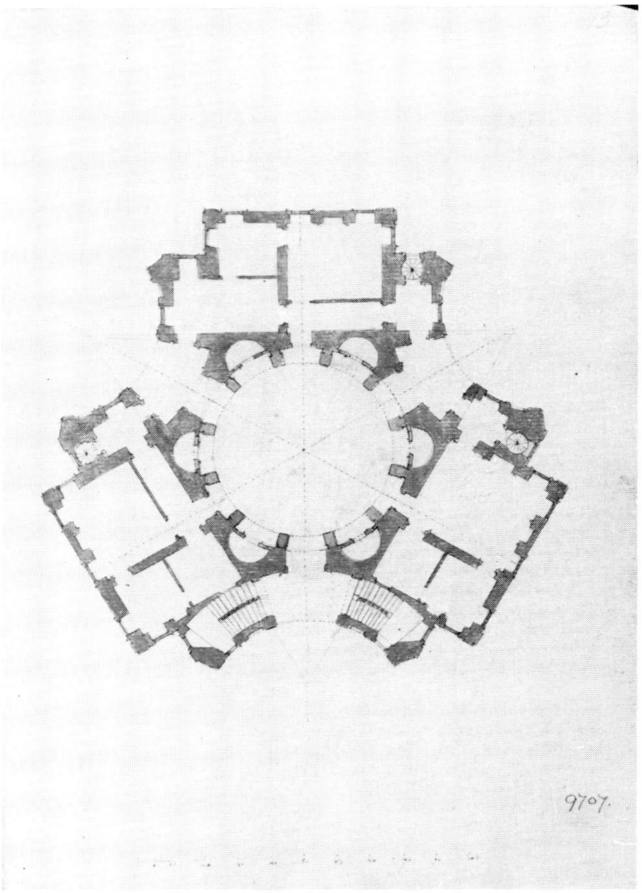

237 Ground-floor plan, later project (no.301)

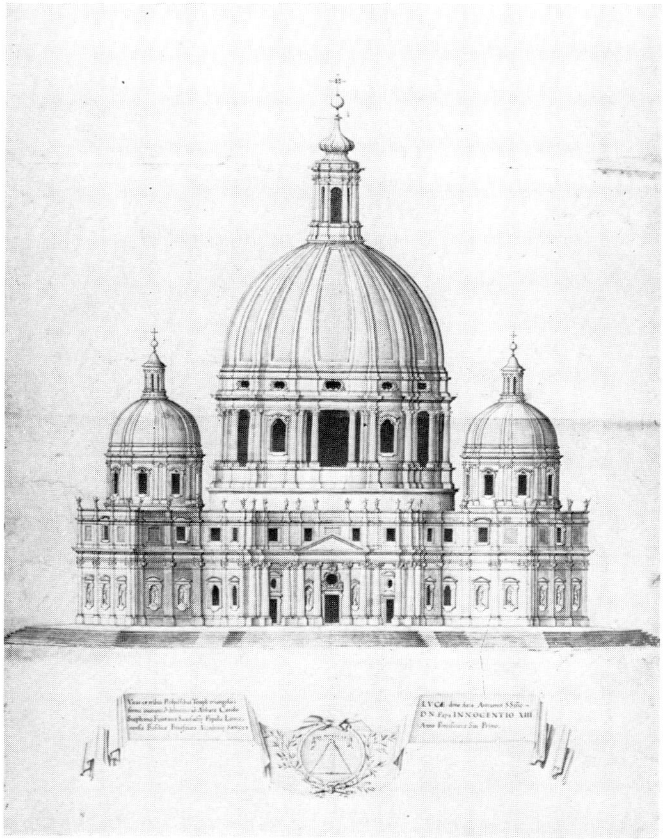

238 Project for a triangular church, elevation (drawing by Carlo Stefano Fontana; Rome, Accademia di S. Luca)

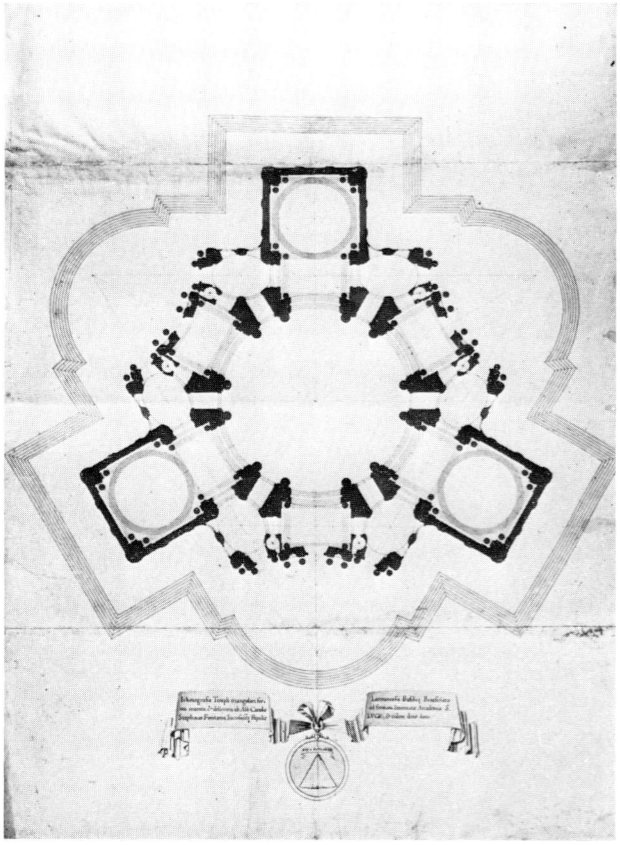

239 Project for a triangular church, plan (drawing by Carlo Stefano Fontana; Rome, Accademia di S. Luca)

Civitavecchia, the aqueduct (1692–1702)

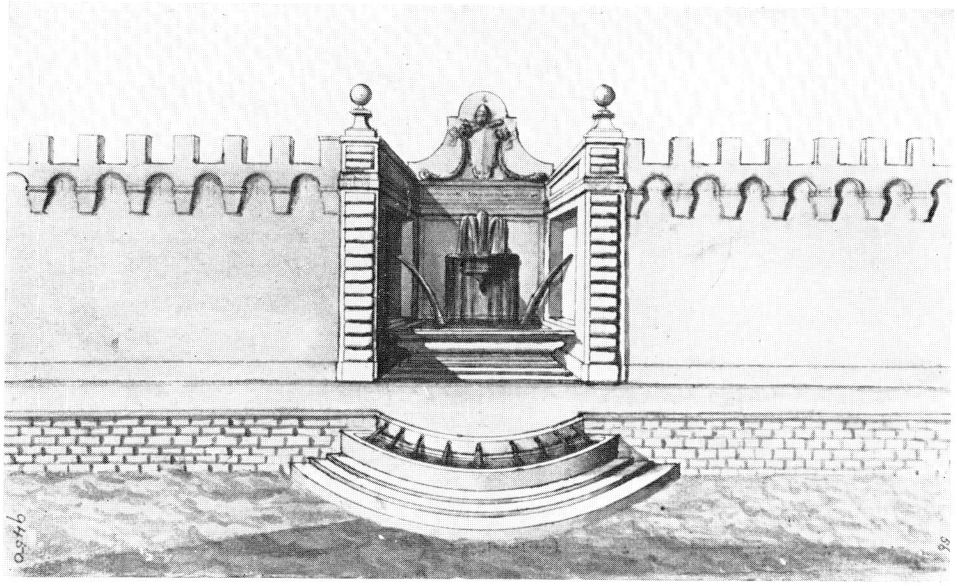

240 Project for a fountain, perspective view (no.303)

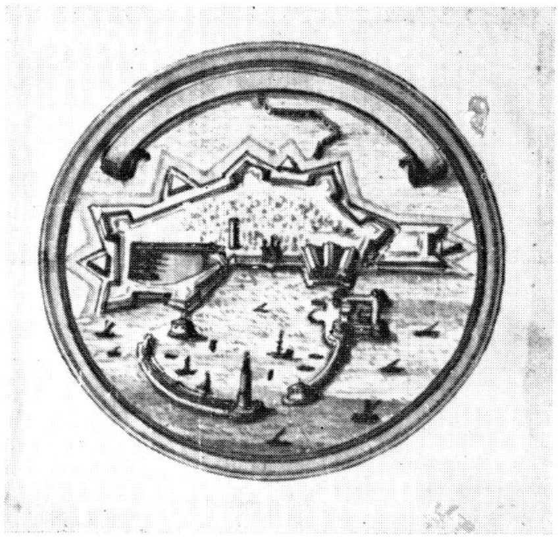

241 Civitavecchia: design for a medal (no.305)

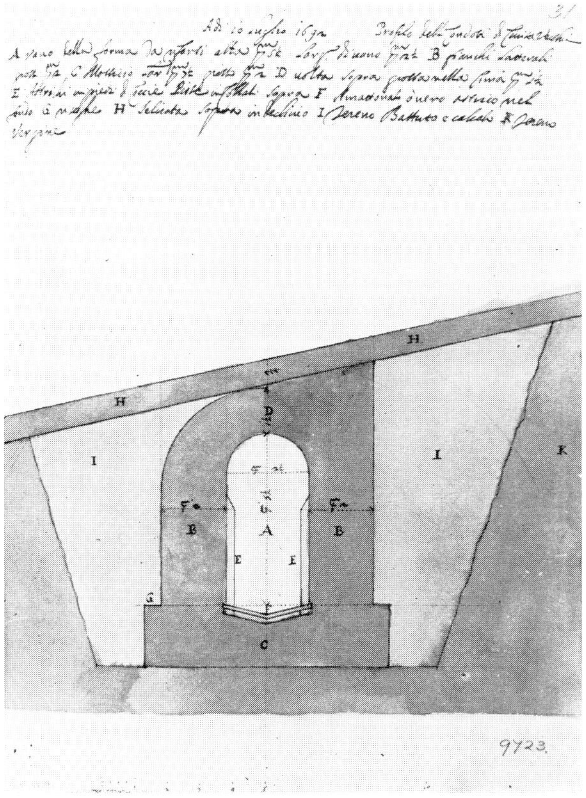

242 Section through the aqueduct (no.302)

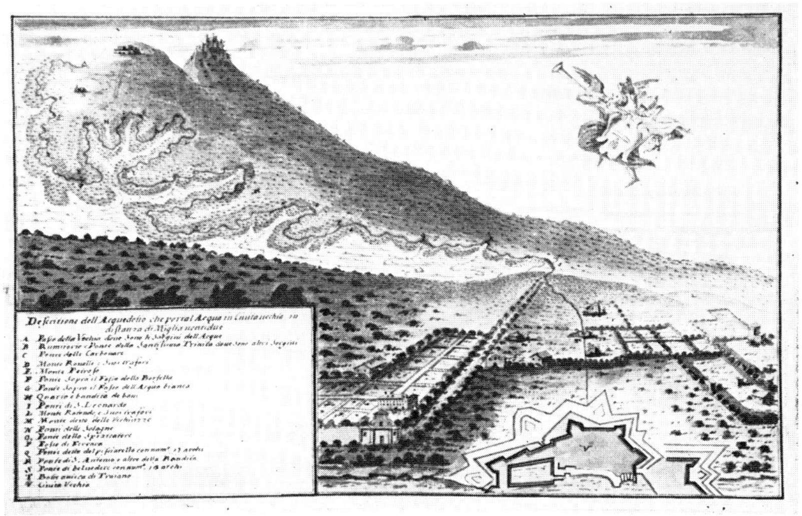

243 View of the aqueduct (anon. drawing; no.304)

Civitavecchia, project for the Arsenal and the Piazza

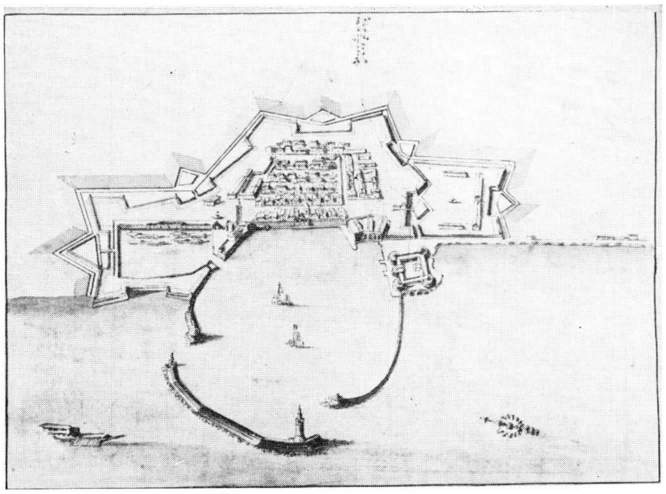

244 Perspective view of Civitavecchia (no.306)

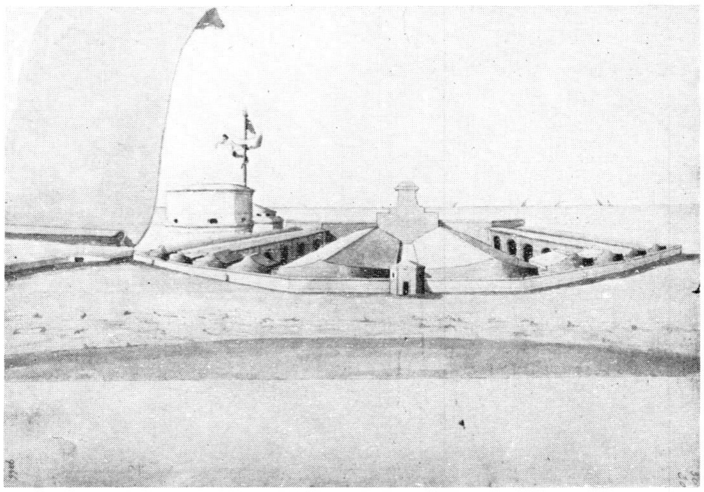

245 Perspective view of the arsenal (no.307)

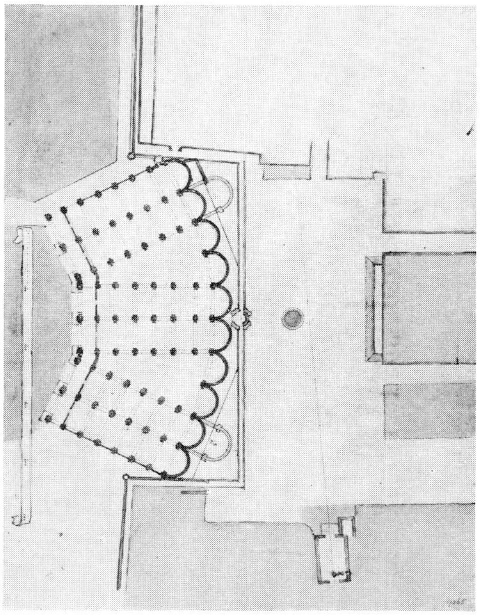

246 Plan of the arsenal and the Piazza (no.308)

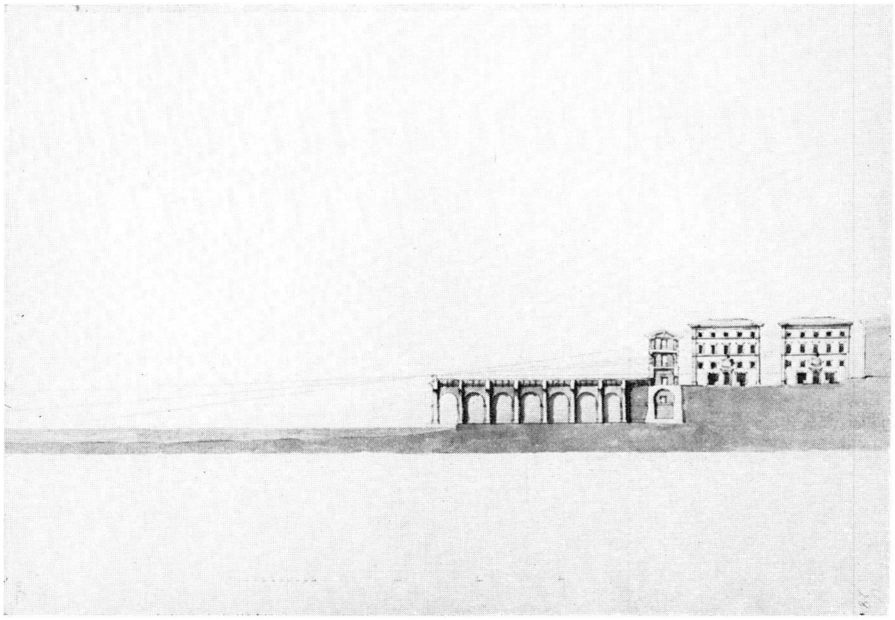

247 Section through the arsenal (no.309)

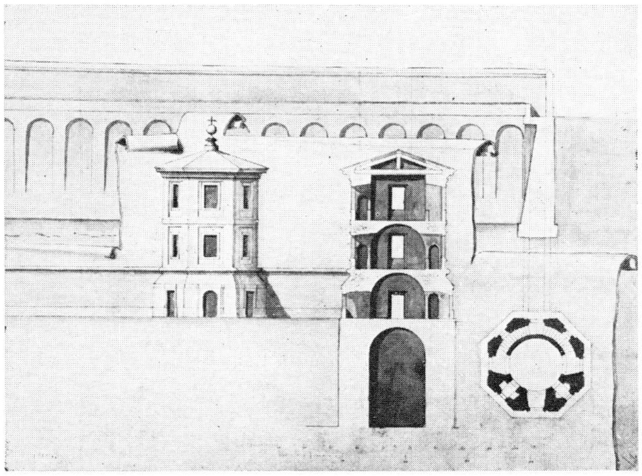

248 Studies of the tower and rampart (no.310)

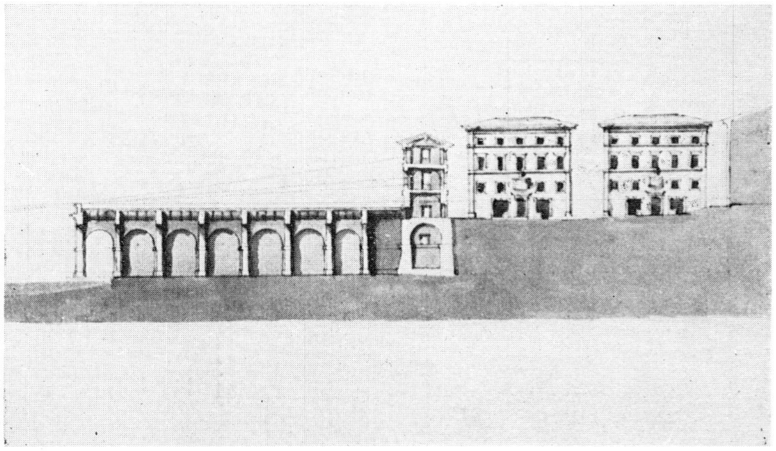

249 Detail of Fig.247

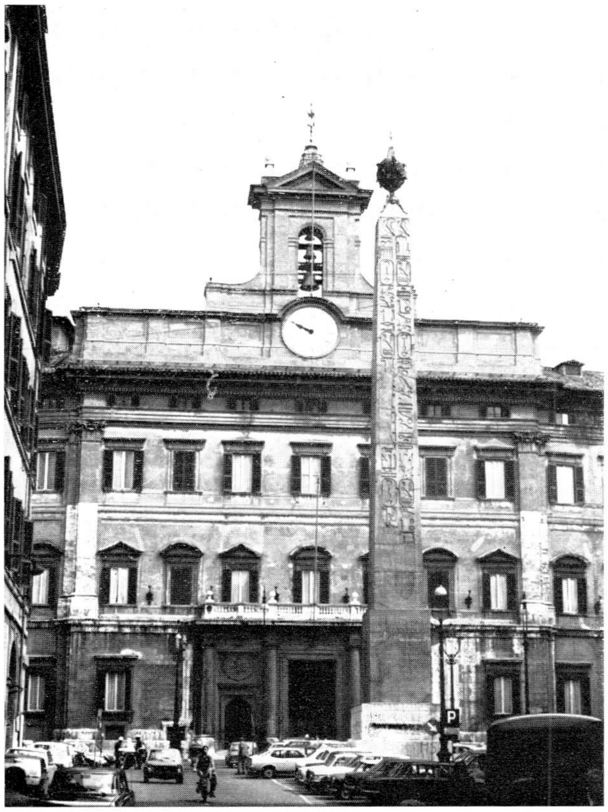

250 View of the central part of the façade

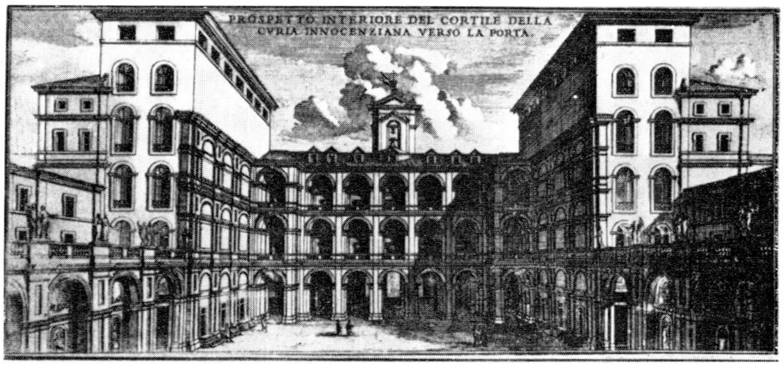

251 View of the court, facing south (engraving by Specchi)

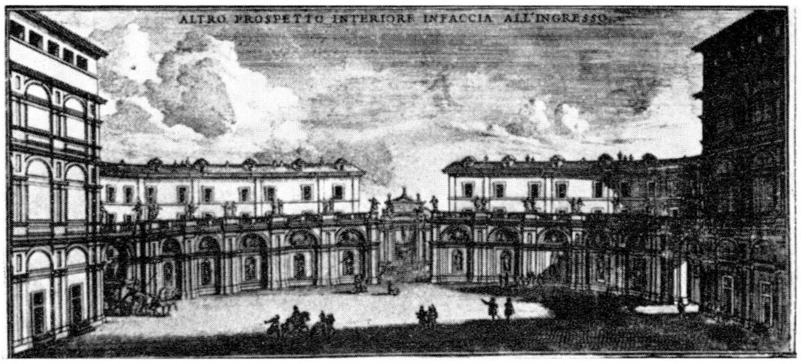

252 View of the court, facing north (engraving by Specchi)

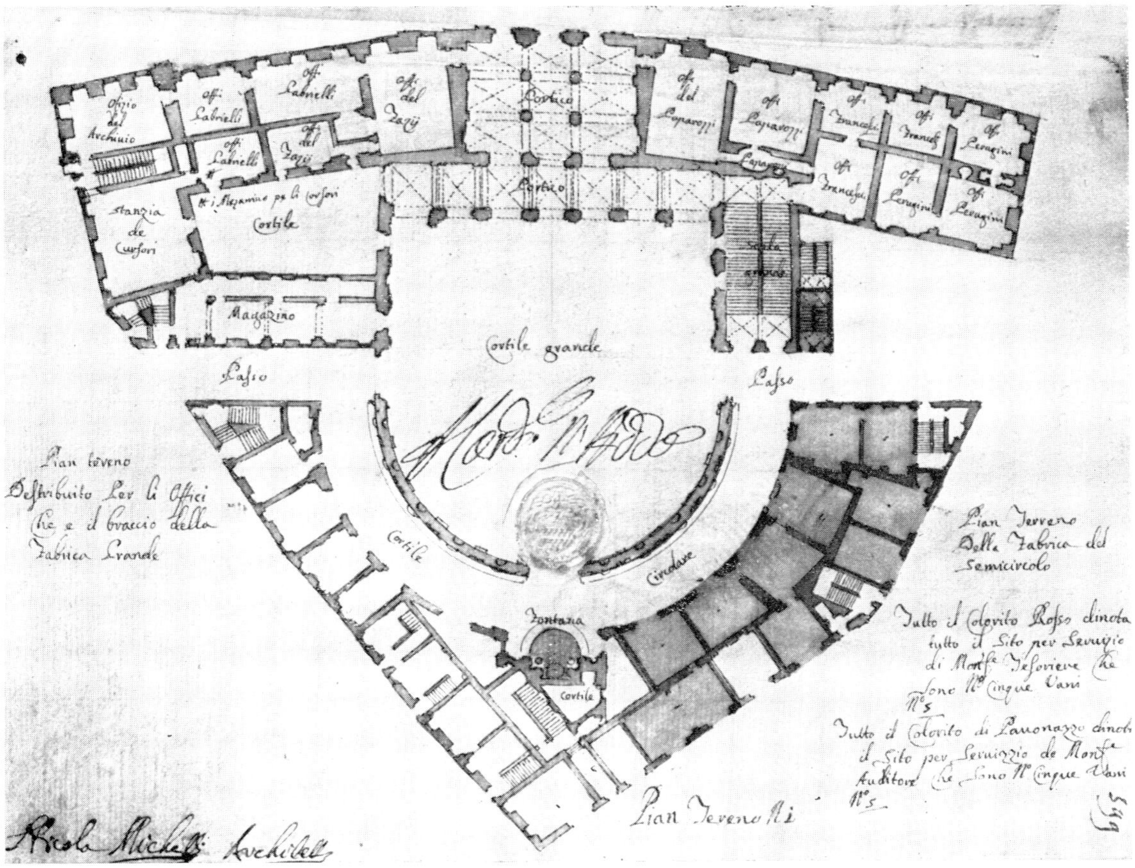

253 Plan of the ground floor, 1715 (drawing by Nicola Michetti; Rome, Archivio di Stato)

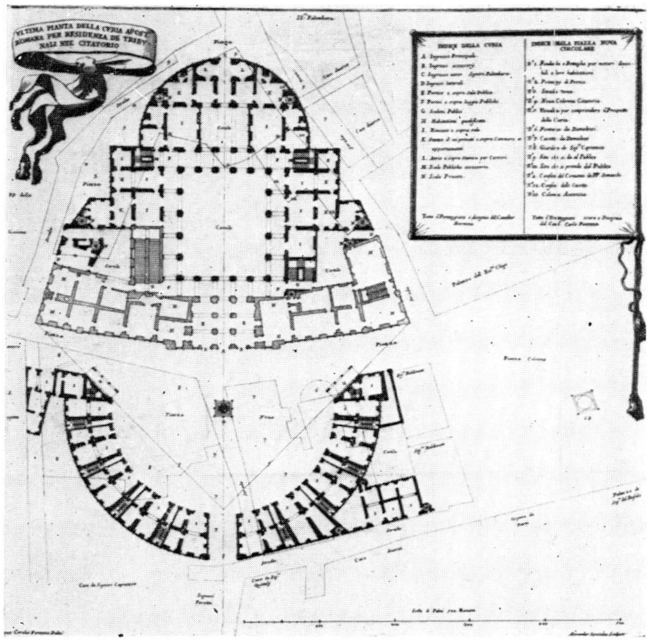

254 Project with semicircular forecourt (1694), plan (engraving by Specchi after Fontana)

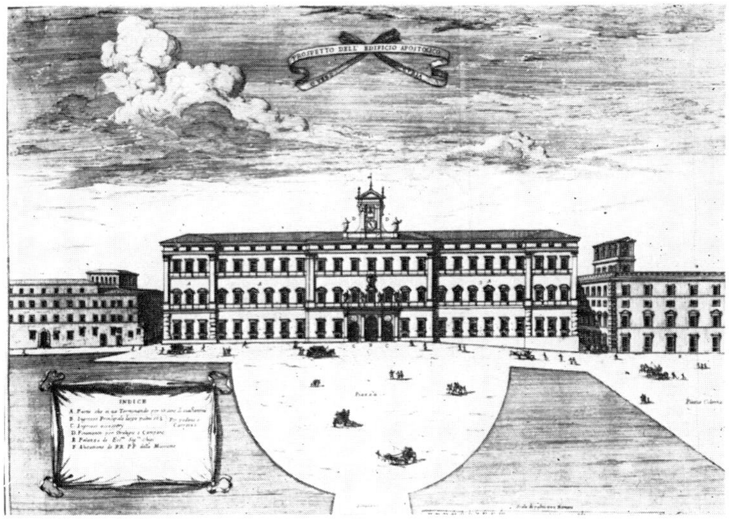

255 Project with semicircular forecourt (1694), elevation (engraving by Specchi after Fontana)

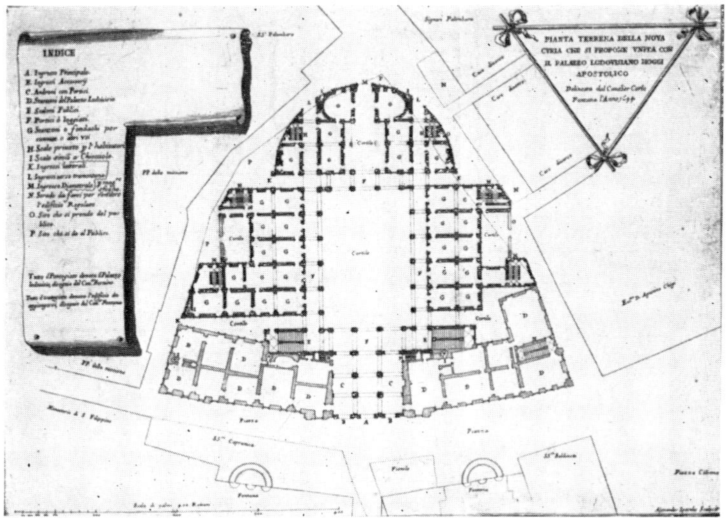

256 Project with rectangular court (1694), plan (engraving by Specchi after Fontana)

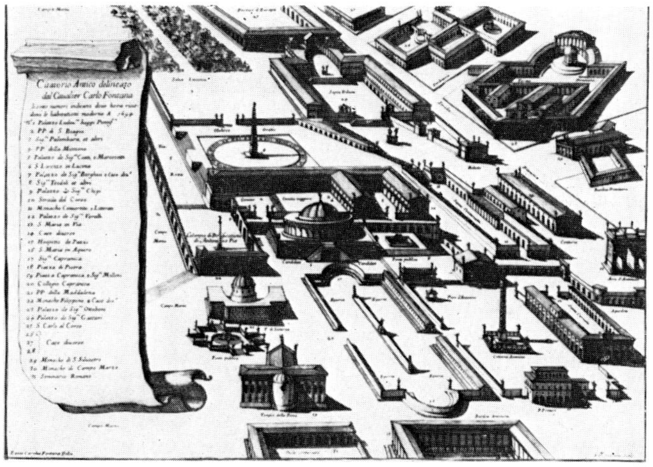

257 Reconstruction of the site in antiquity (engraving by Specchi after Fontana, 1694)

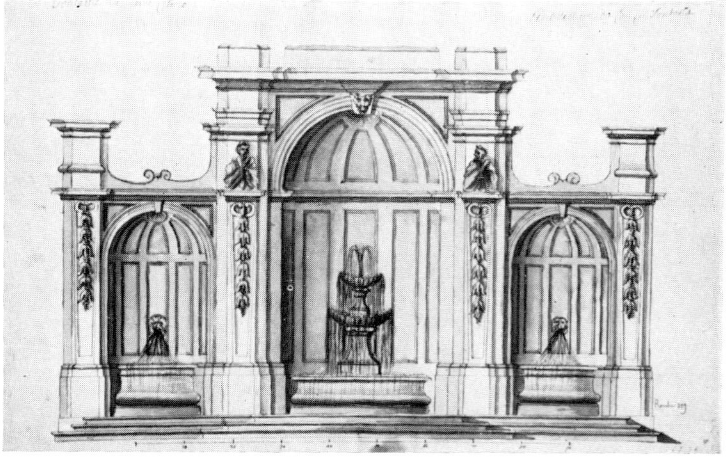

258 Project for a fountain, elevation (anon. drawing; Stockholm, Nationalmuseum)

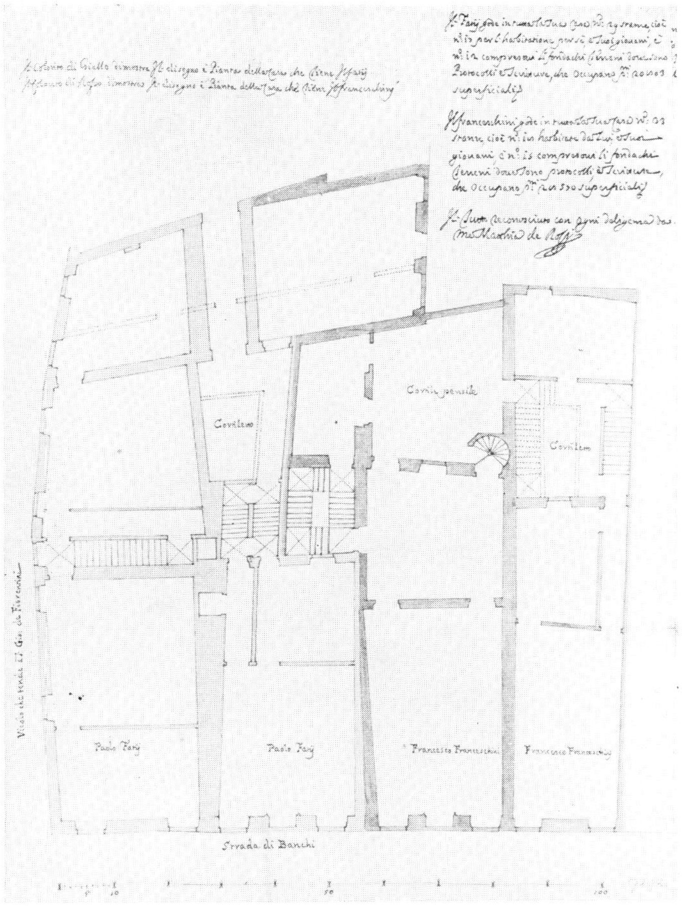

259 The offices of Fatii and Franceschini on the Strada di Banchi, plan (drawing by Mattia de' Rossi; no.313)

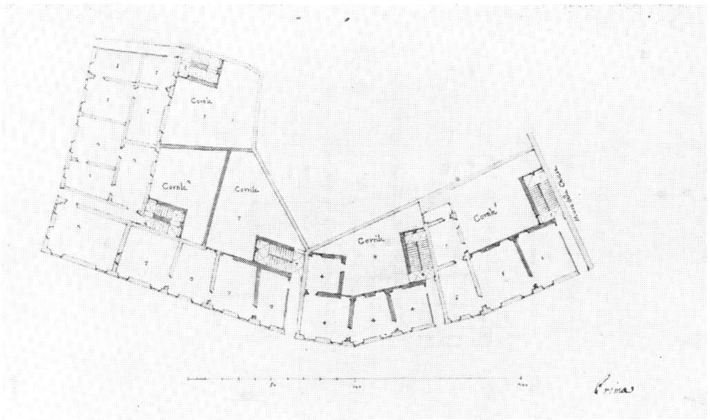

260 Ground-floor plan of the buildings at the northern border of the Curia site (drawing by Mattia de' Rossi; no.315)

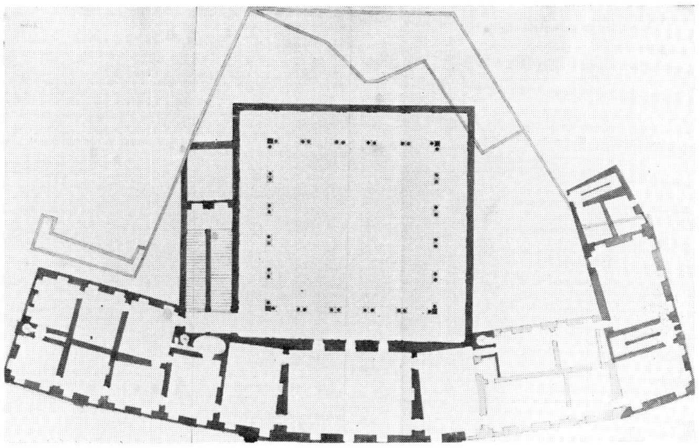

261 Ground-floor plan, with square court, after Bernini (?) (no.316)

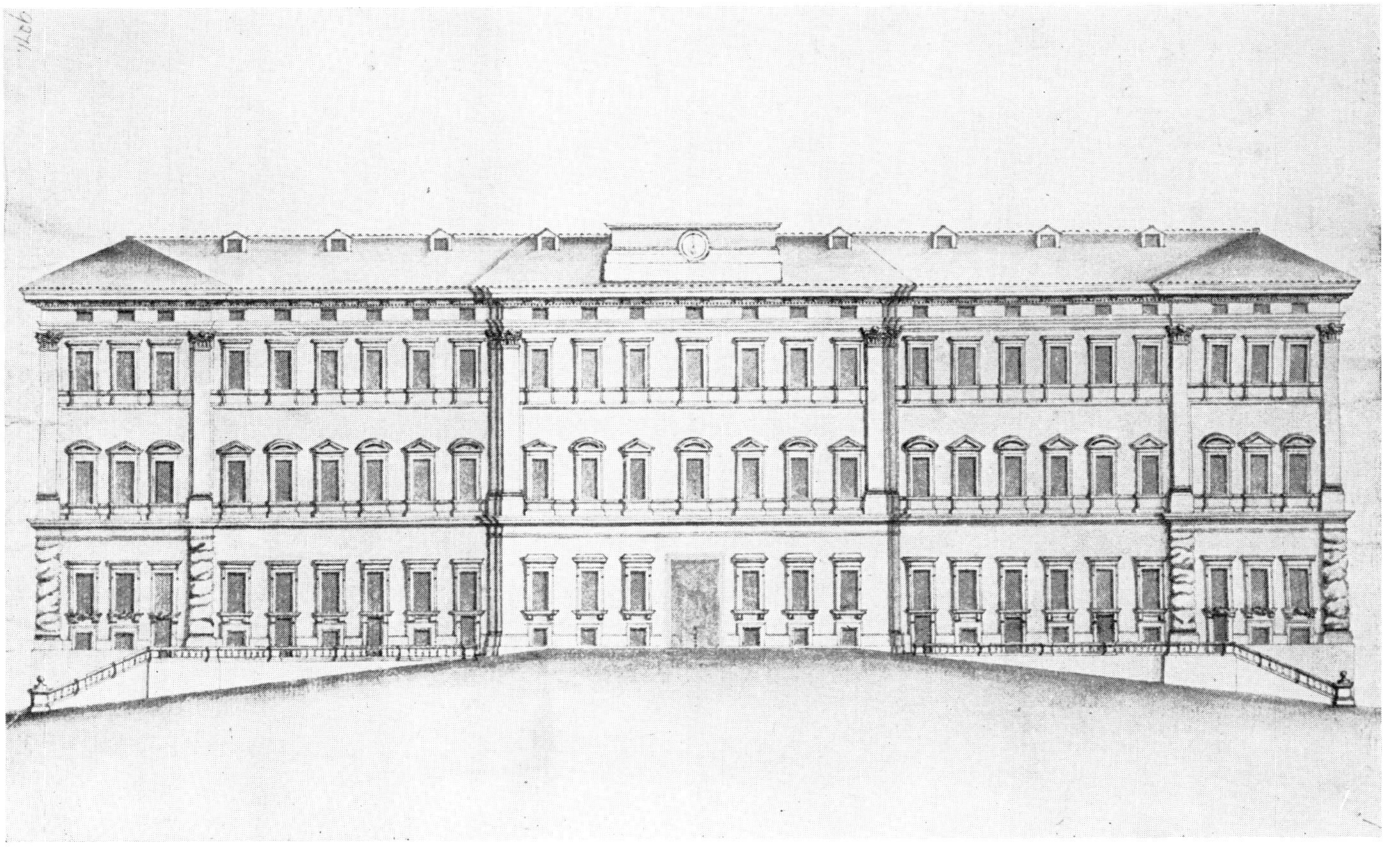

262 Elevation with single doorway (no.318)

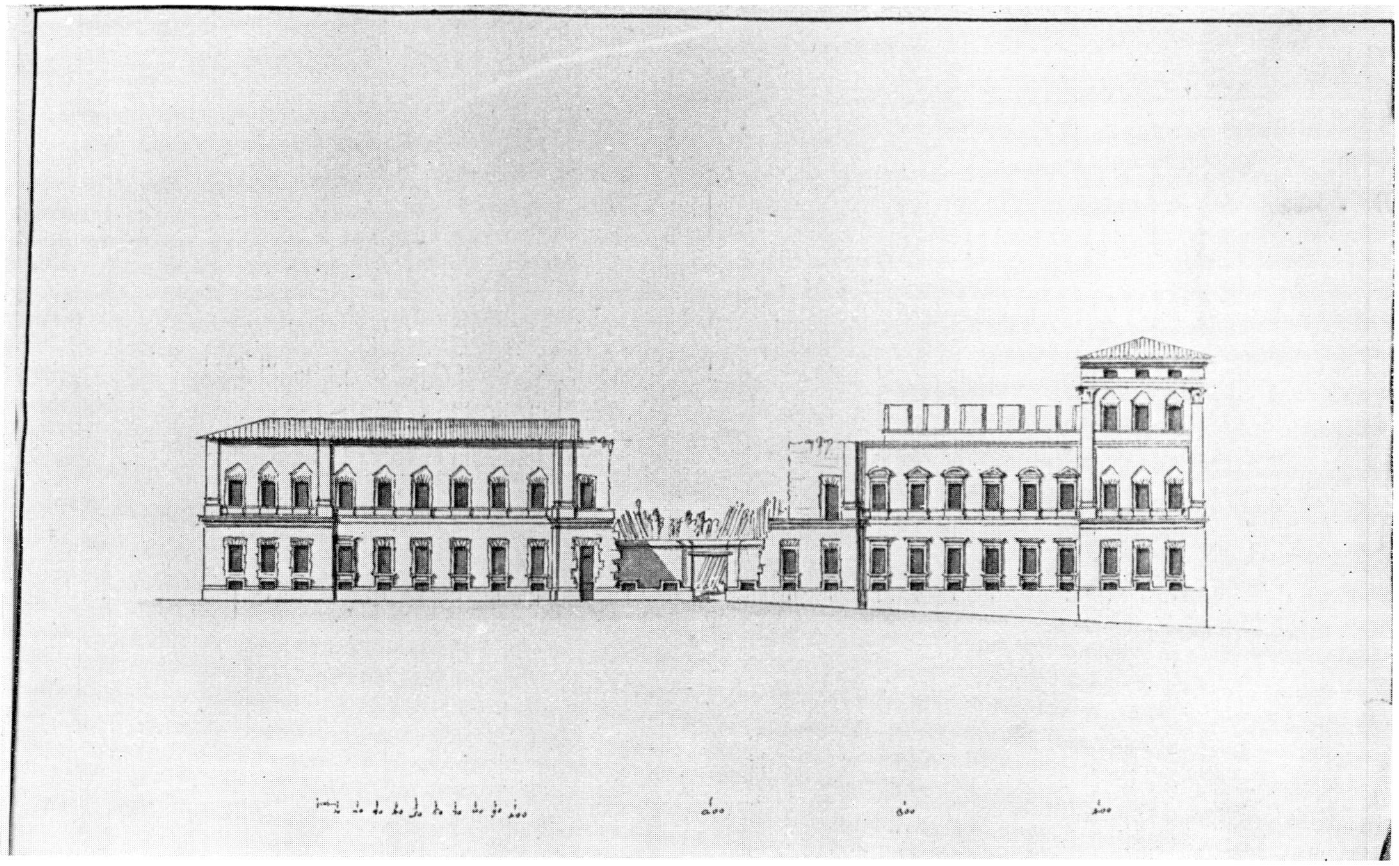

263 Elevation in unfinished state (no.317)

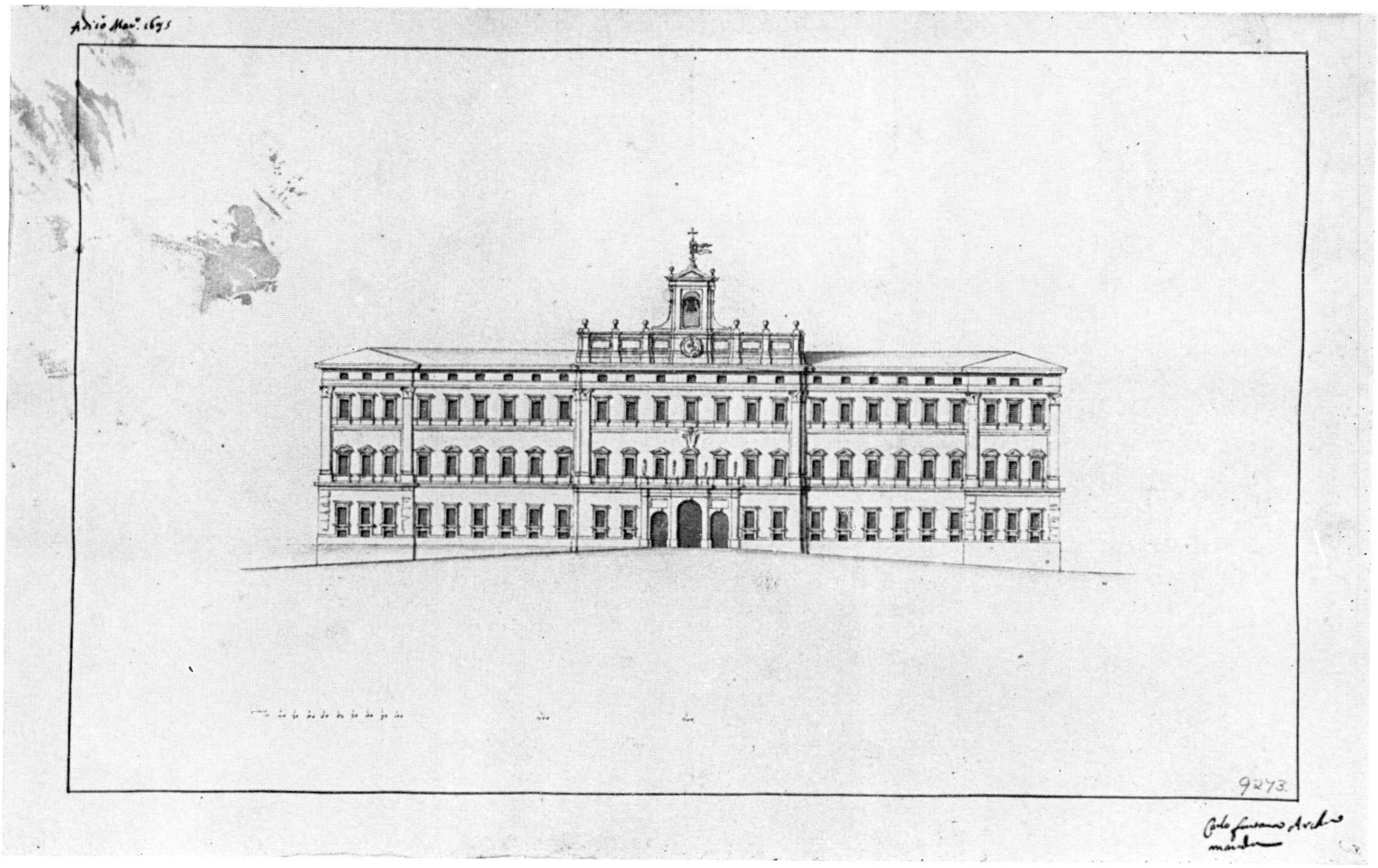

264 Elevation (March, 1695) (no.324)

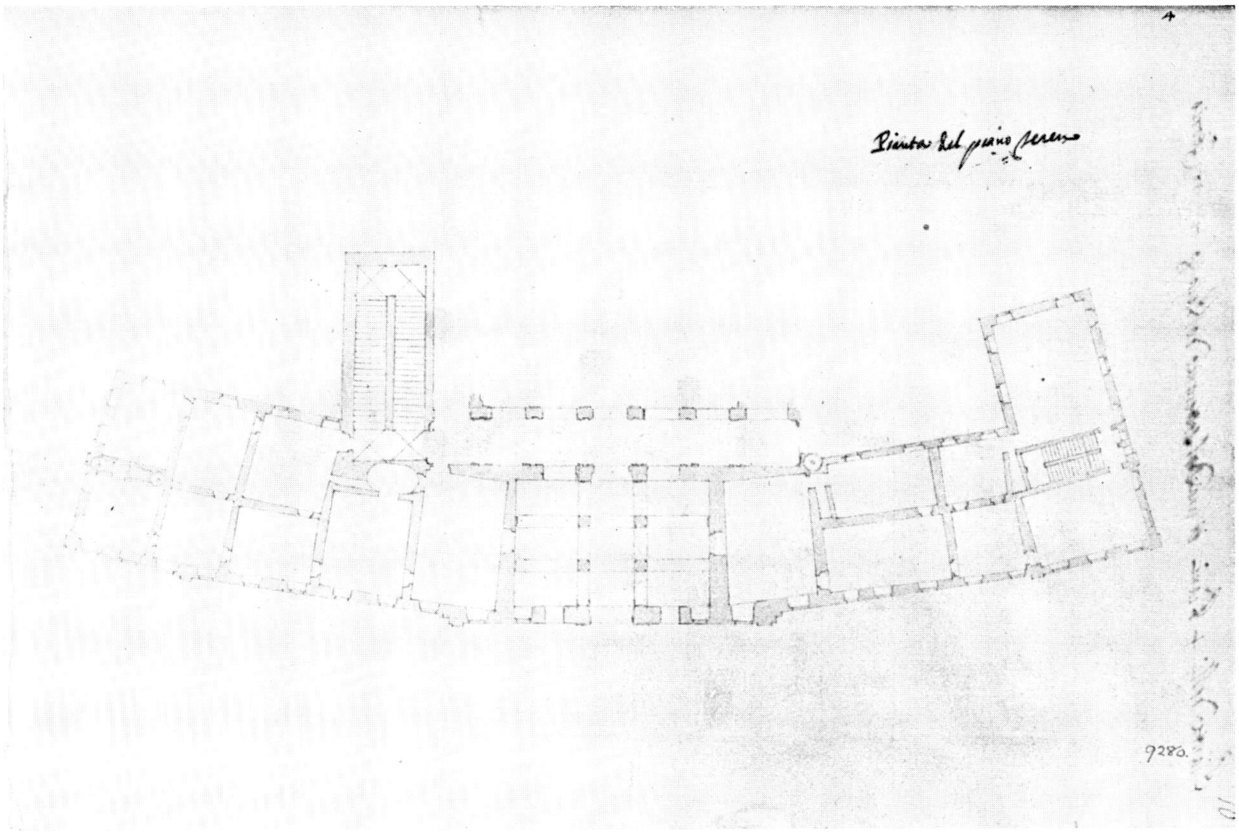

265 Ground-floor plan (no.320)

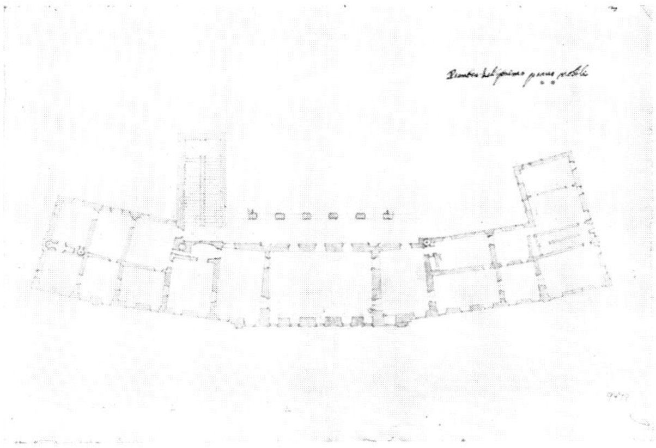

266 First-floor plan (no.321)

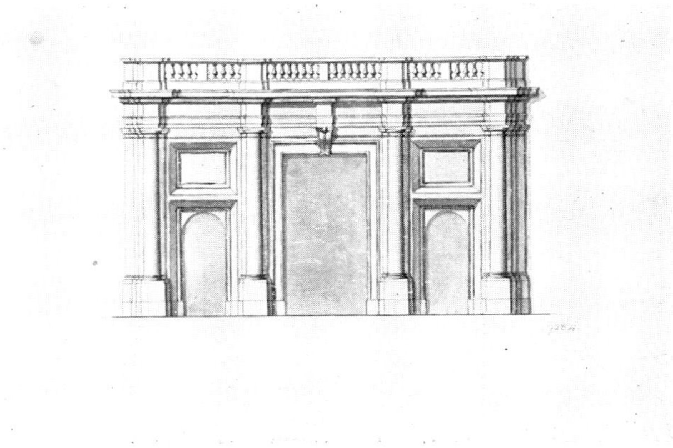

267 Project for the main doorway (1), elevation (no.325)

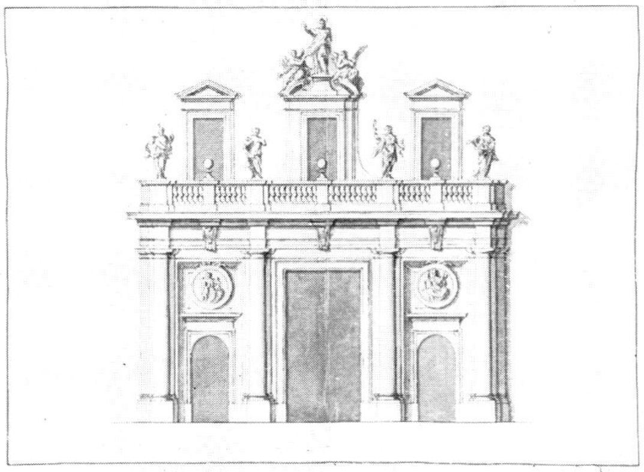

268 Project for the main doorway (2), elevation (no.326)

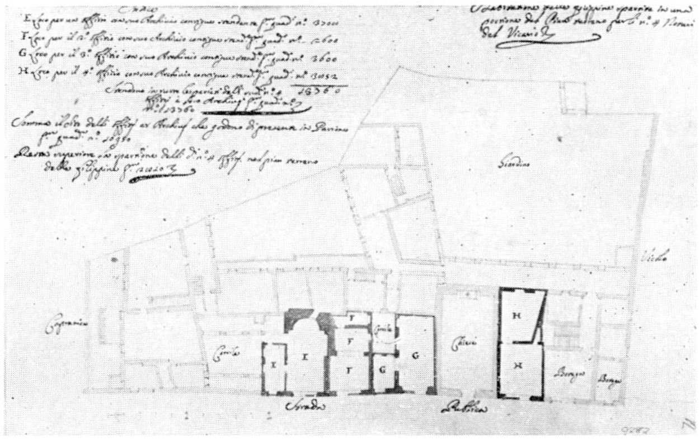

269 Ground-floor plan of the monastery of the Filippini (south at top) (no.327)

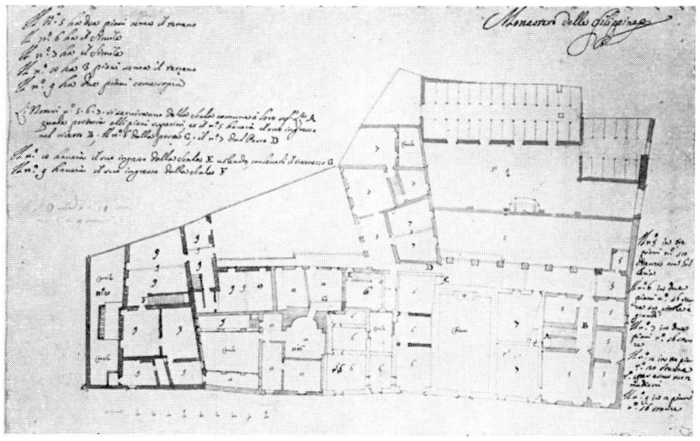

270 First-floor plan of the monastery of the Filippini (south at top) (no.329)

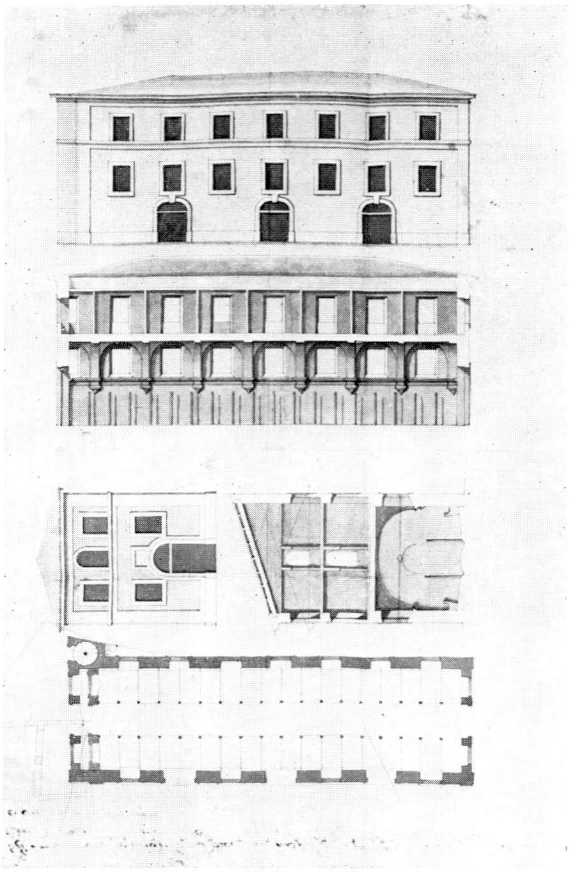

271 Plan, sections and elevations of stables at back of monastery (no.332)

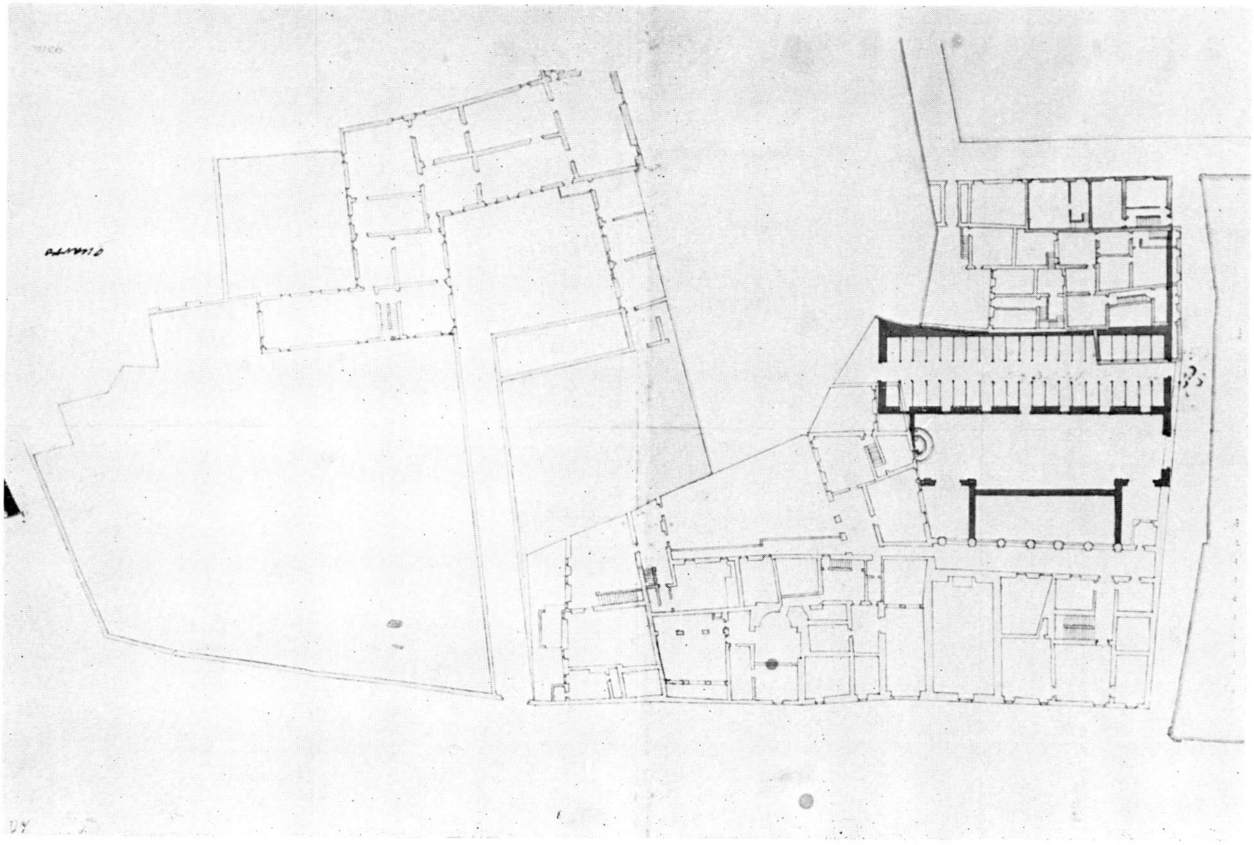

272 Site plan, showing new stables at the back of the monastery (south at top) (no.330)

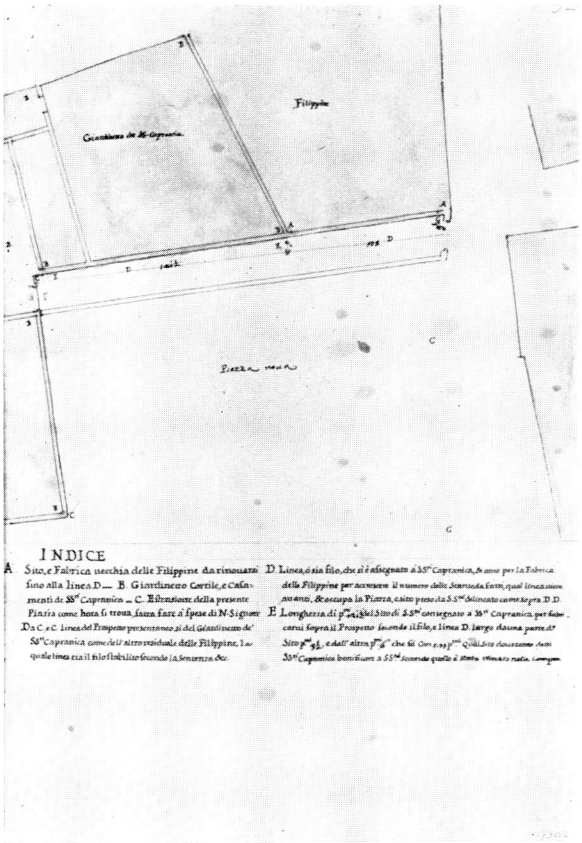

273 Half plan of the Piazza in front of the Curia (west at top) (no.333)

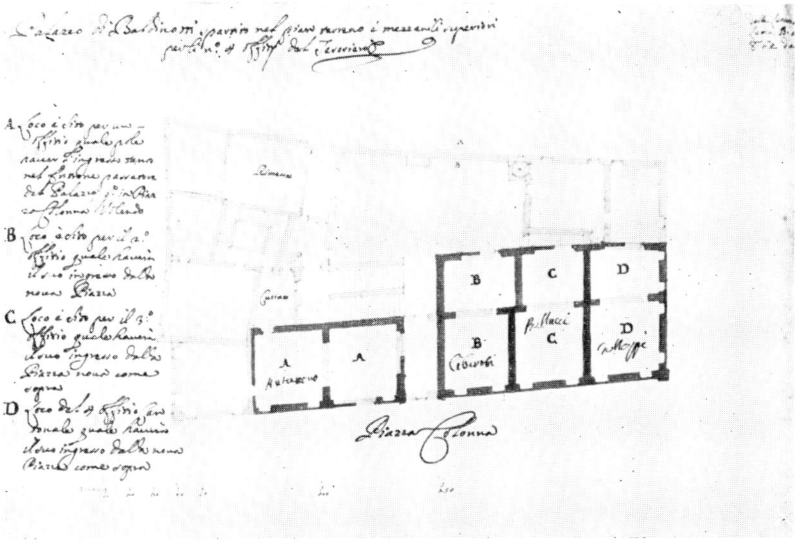

274 Plan of the Palazzo Baldinotti at (?) mezzanine level (west at top) (no.334)

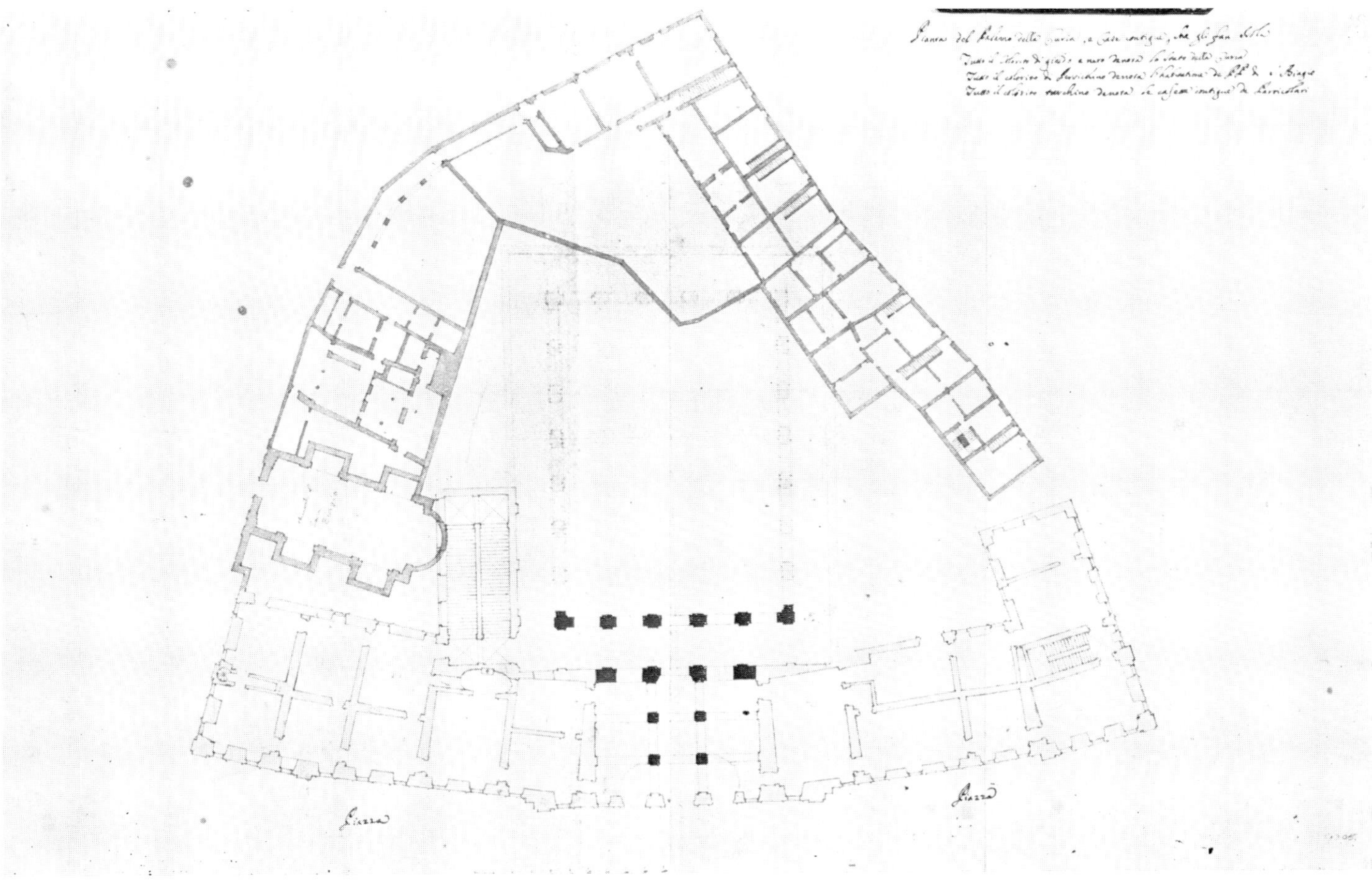

275 Court project 1, ground-floor plan (no.336)

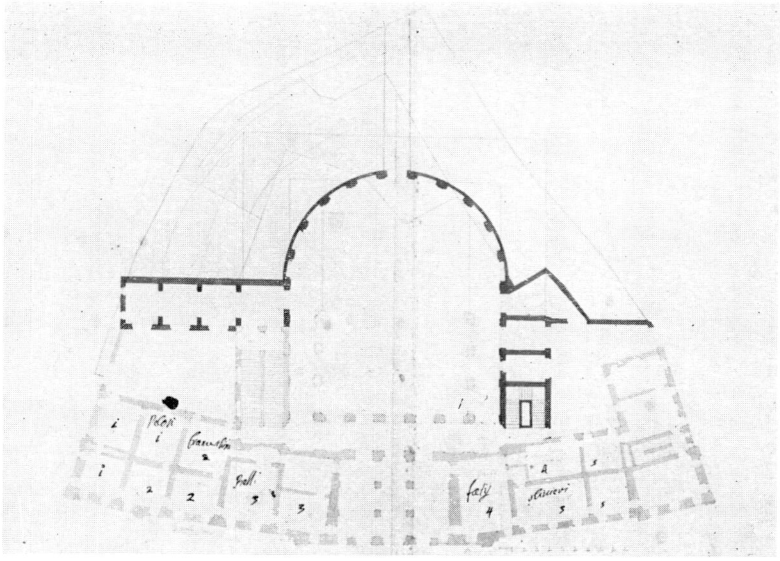

276 Court project 2, ground-floor plan (no.338)

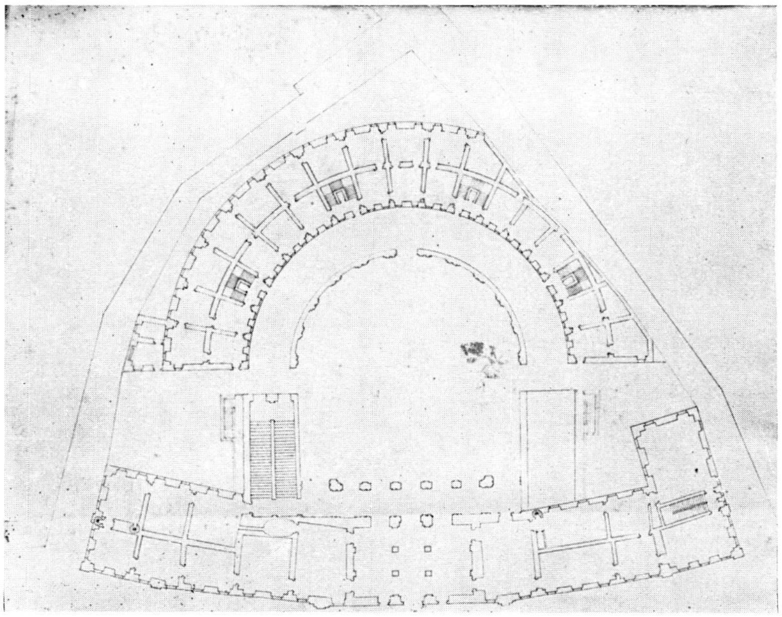

277 Court project 3, first version, ground-floor plan (no.340)

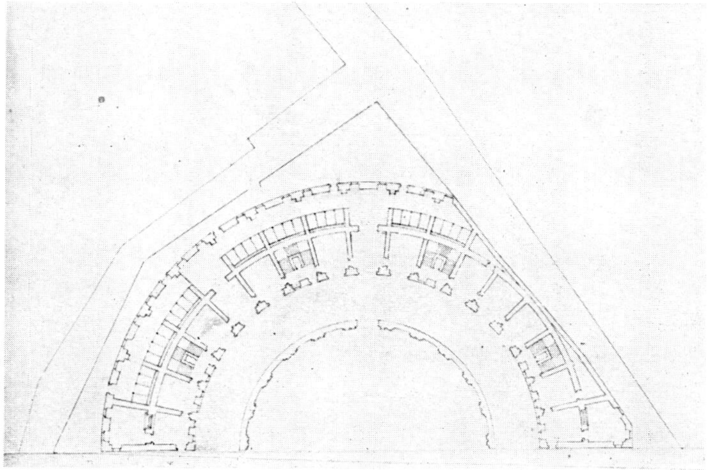

278 Court project 3, second version, ground-floor plan (detail of no.341)

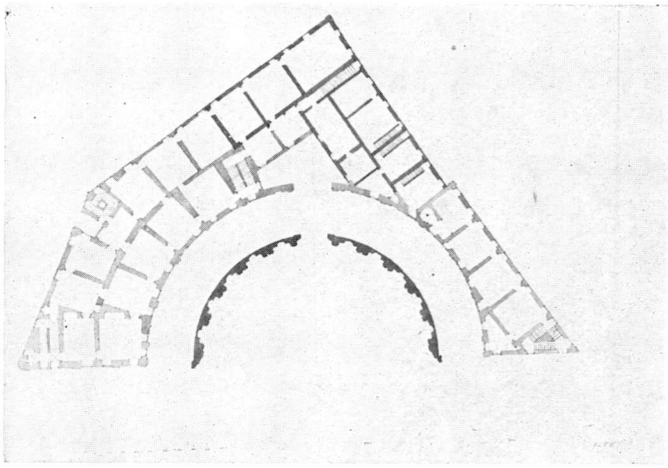

279 Court project 4, ground-floor plan (no.342)

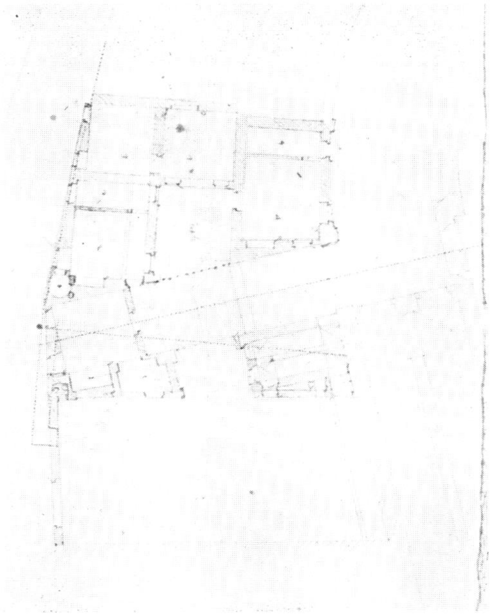

280 Plan of the area beside the main staircase (detail of no.343)

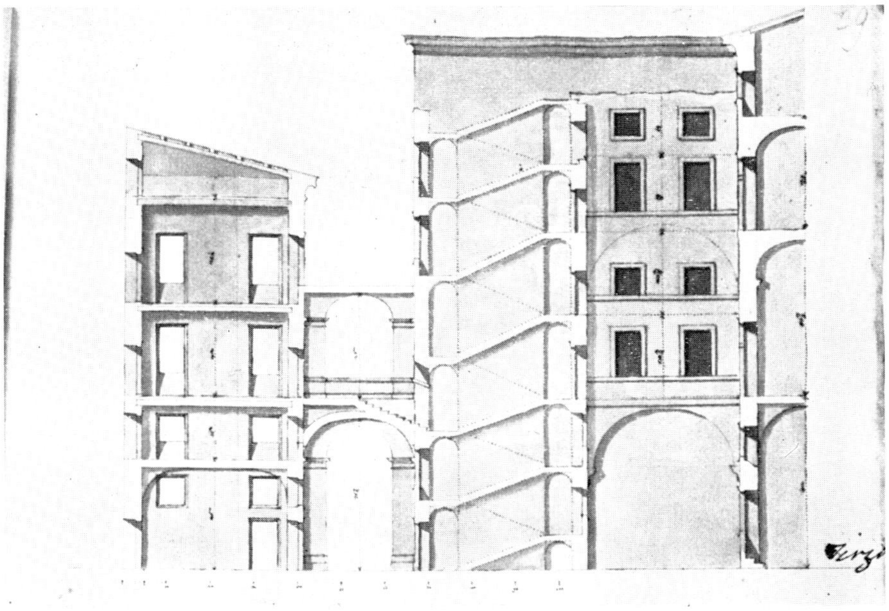

281 Section through an area beside the main staircase (no.344)

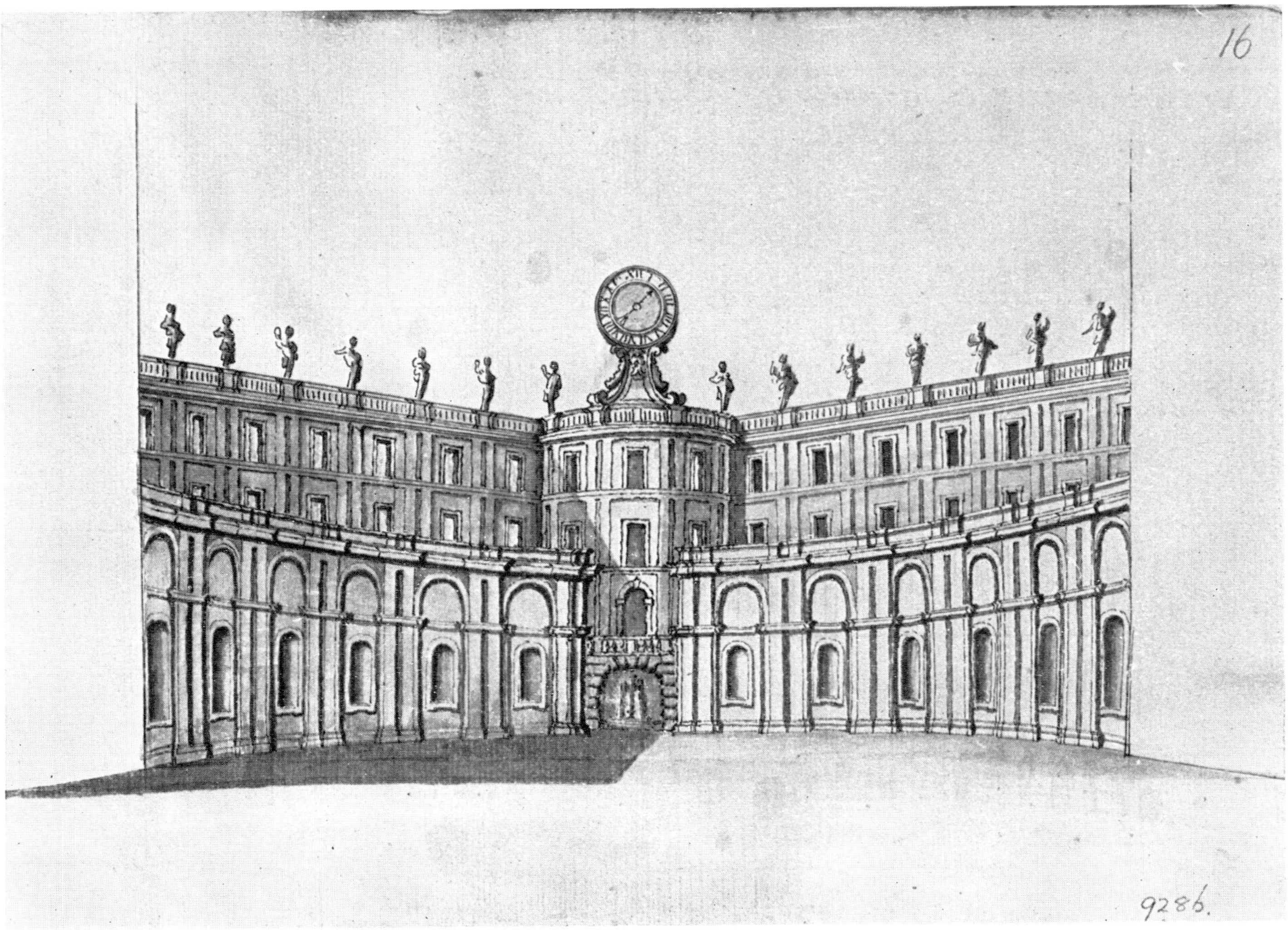

282 Perspective view of the rear part of the court (1) (no.345)

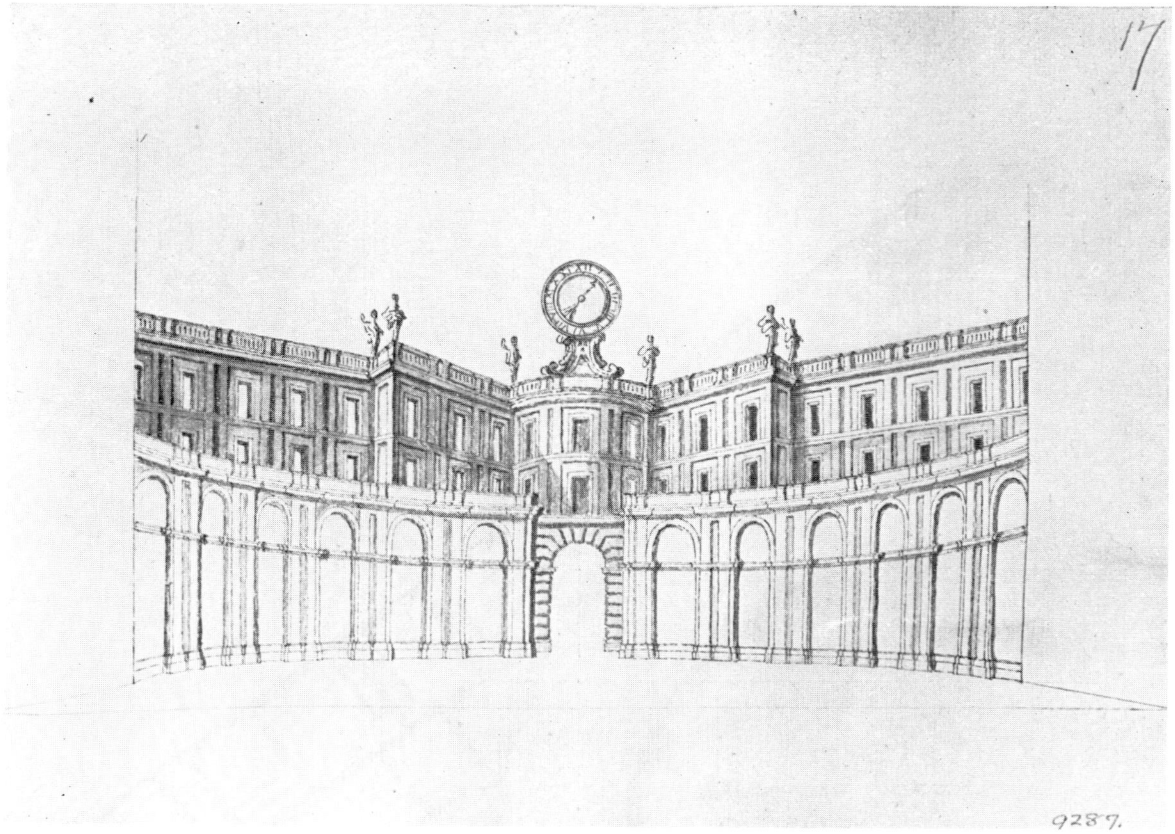

283 Perspective view of the rear part of the court (2) (no.346)

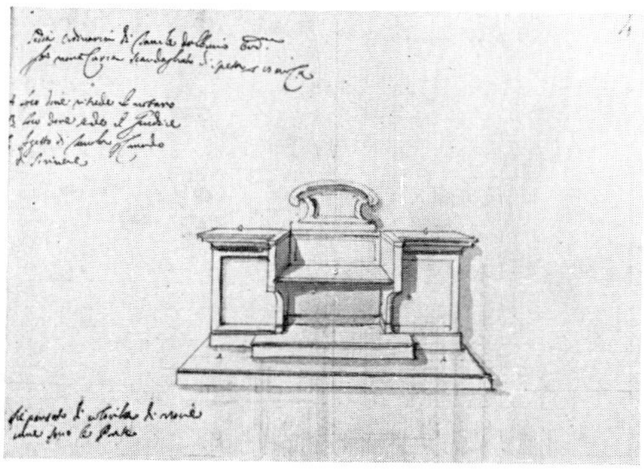

284

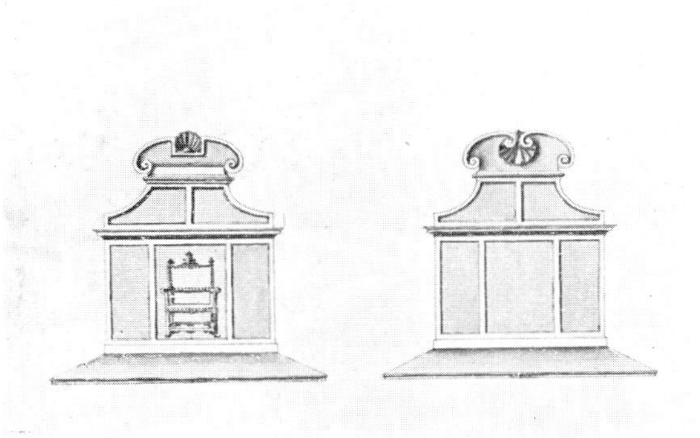

285

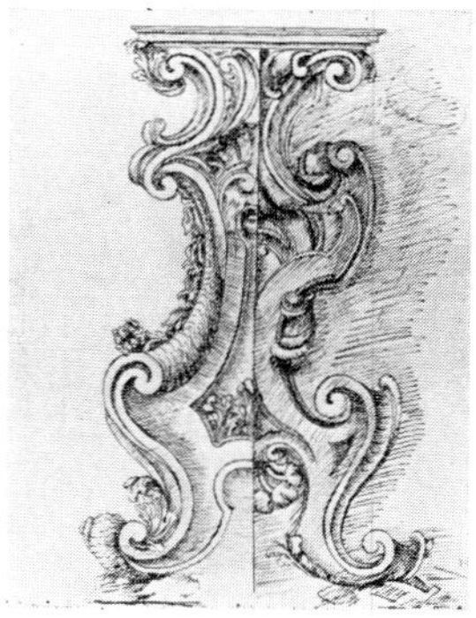

286

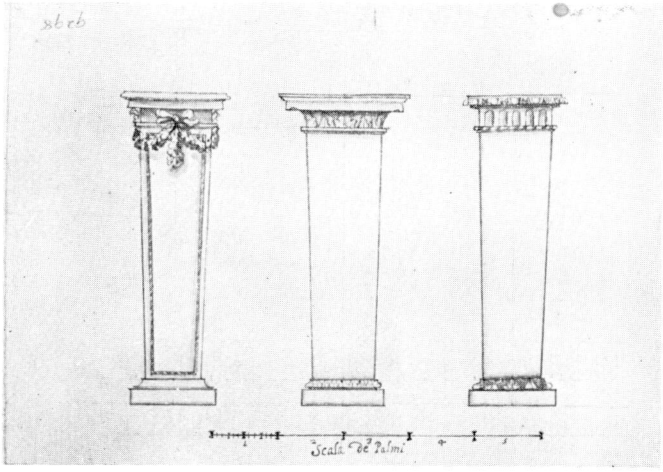

287

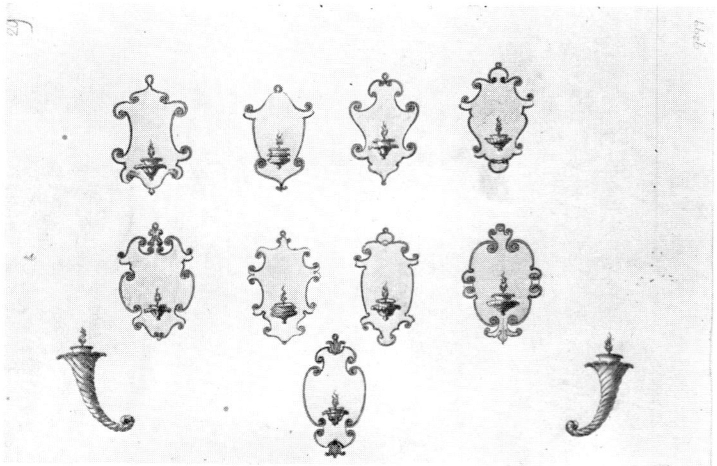

288

284 to 288 Drawings of the internal furnishings for the Curia (nos 347 to 351)

Projects for the Liechtenstein Palace, Landskron, Bohemia (1696)

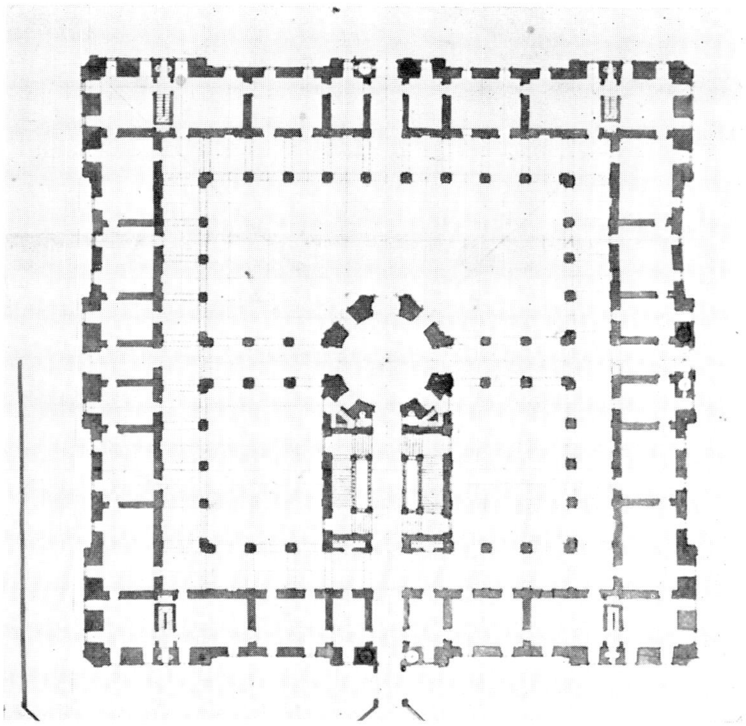

289 Ground-floor plan (no.352, basic version)

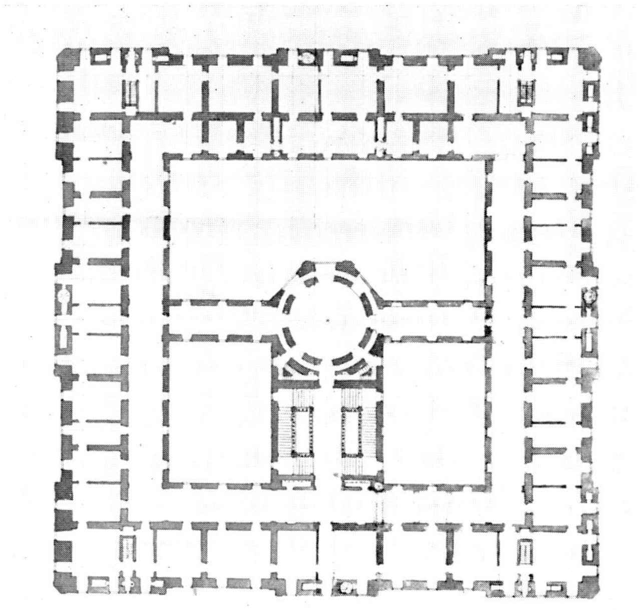

290 First-floor plan (no.354, basic version)

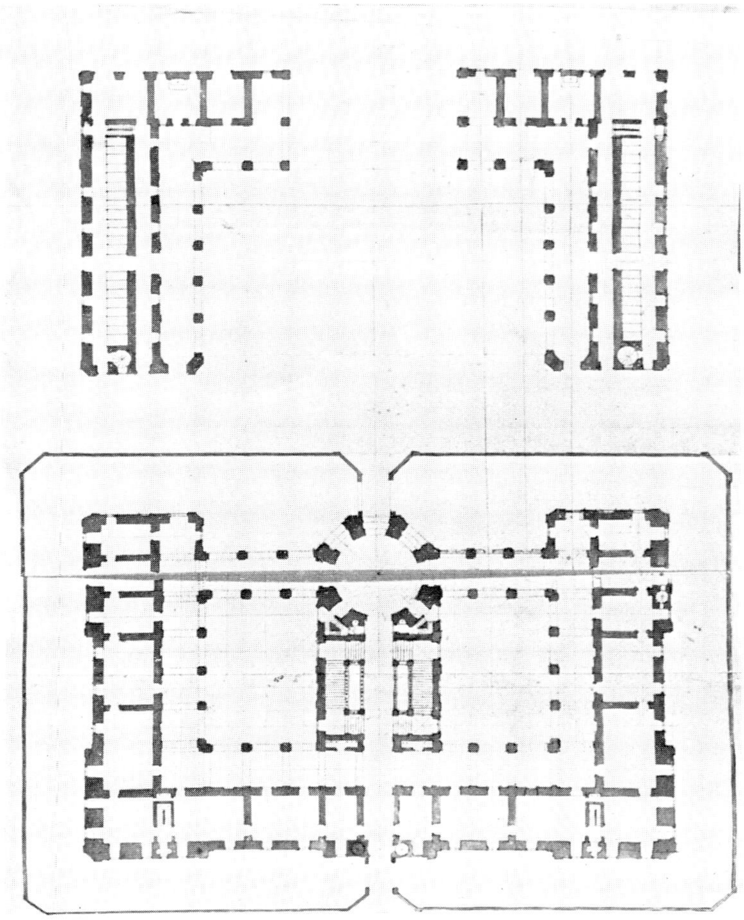

291 Ground-floor plan (no.352, project on flap)

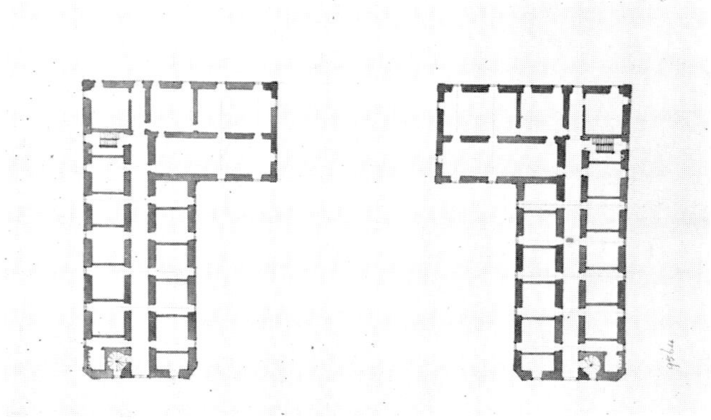

292 First-floor plan of the stables (no.353)

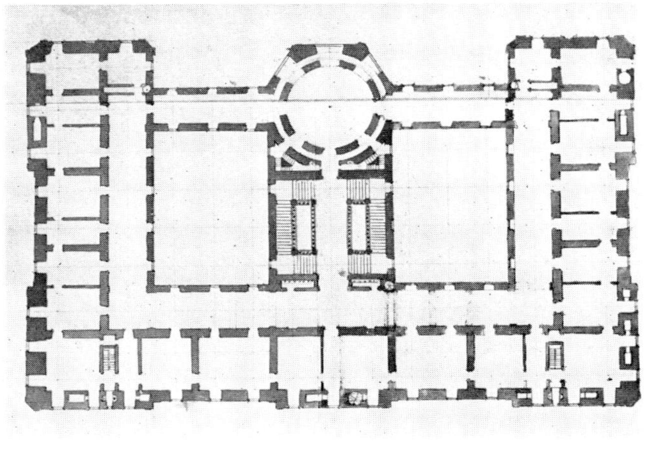

293 First-floor plan (no.354, project on flap)

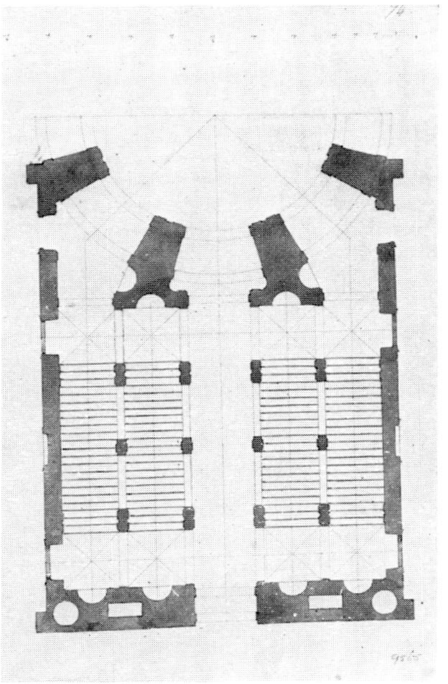

294 Plan of the staircase (no.355)

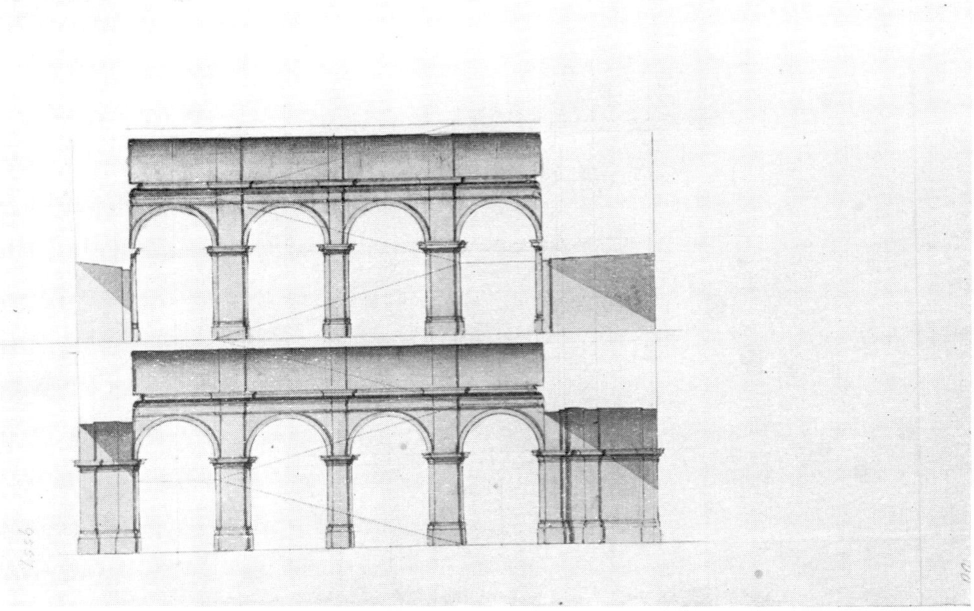

295 Section of the staircase (no.356)

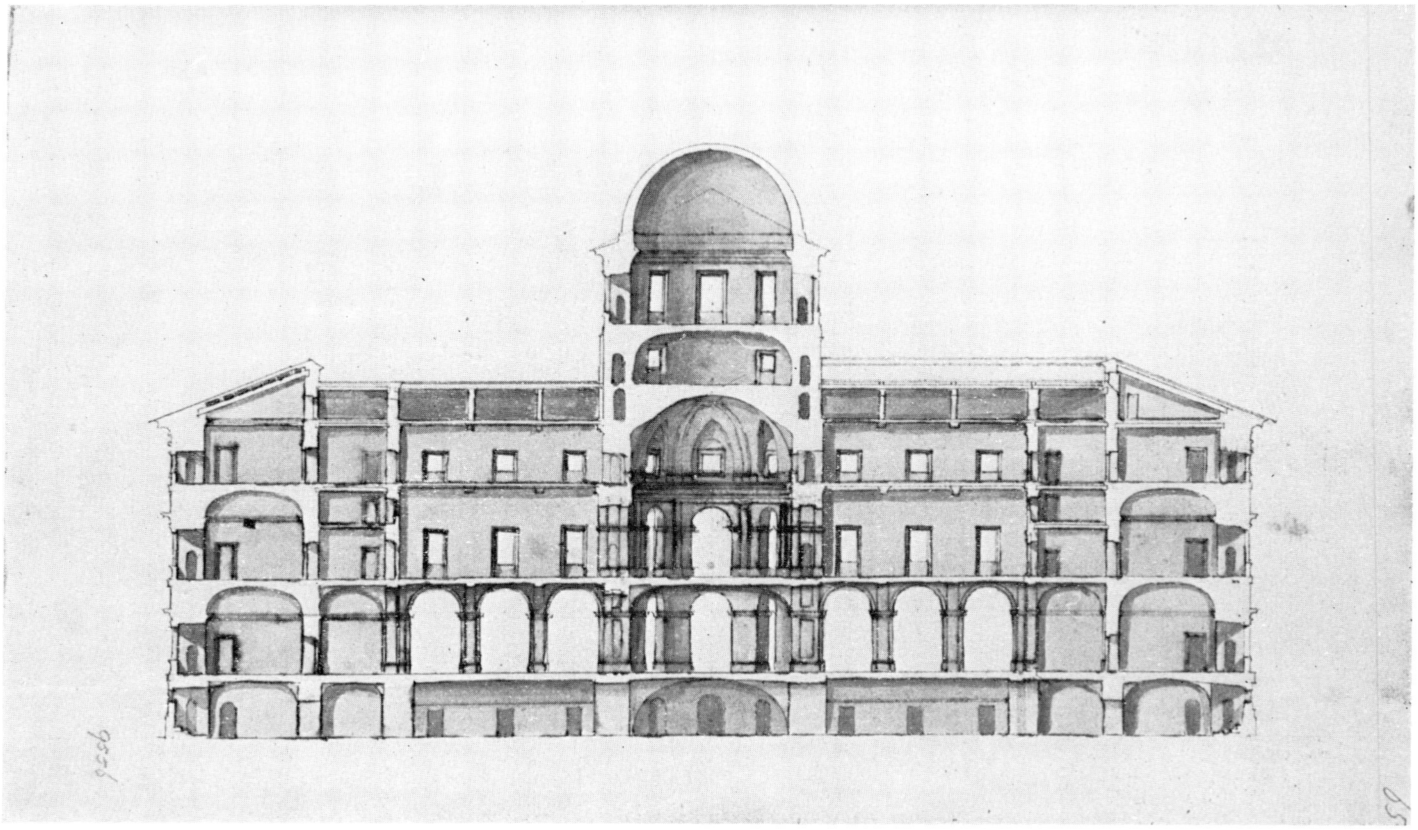

296 Transverse section (no.357)

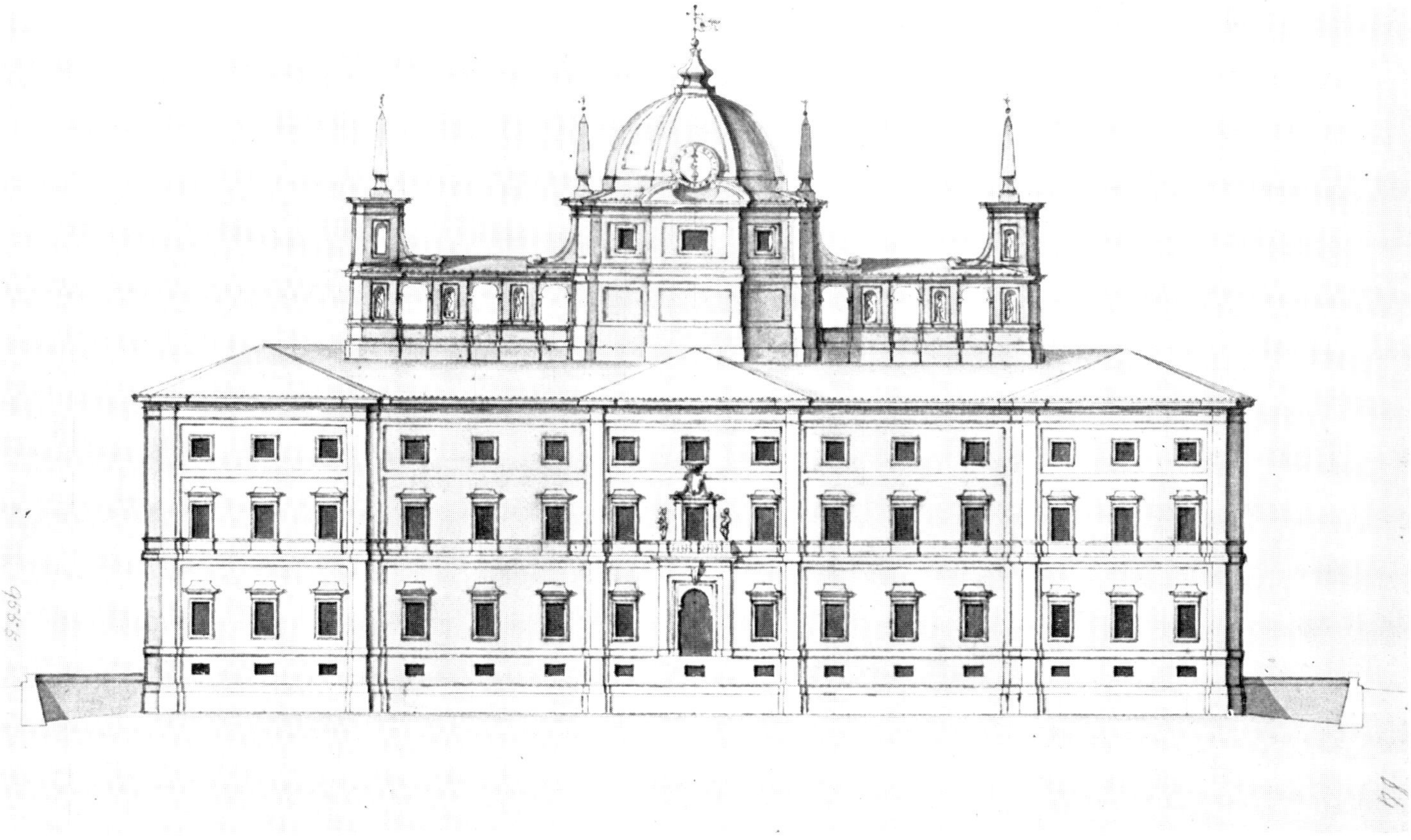

297 Front elevation (1) (no.358)

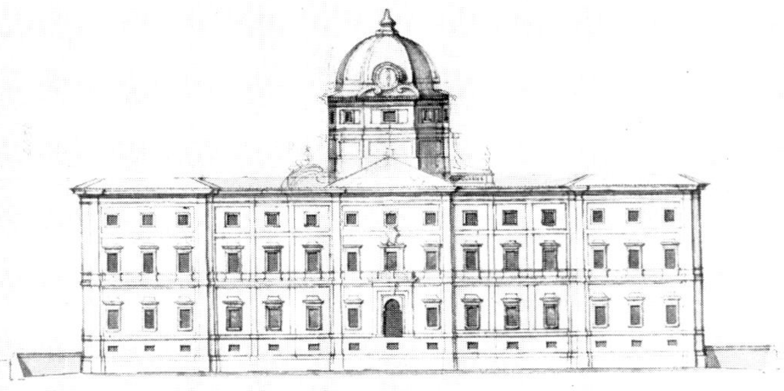

298 Front elevation (2) (no.359)

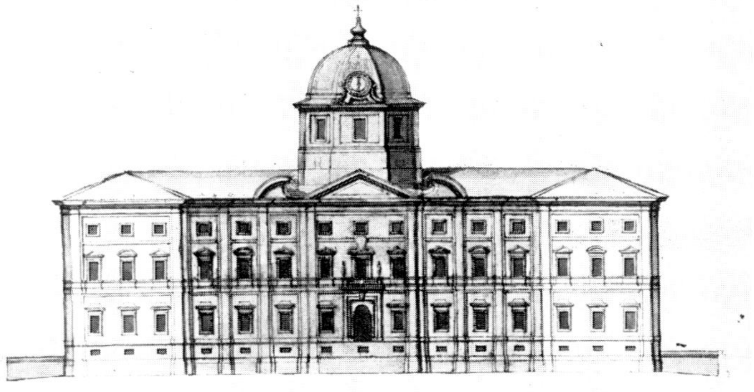

299 Front elevation (3, final design) (no.360)

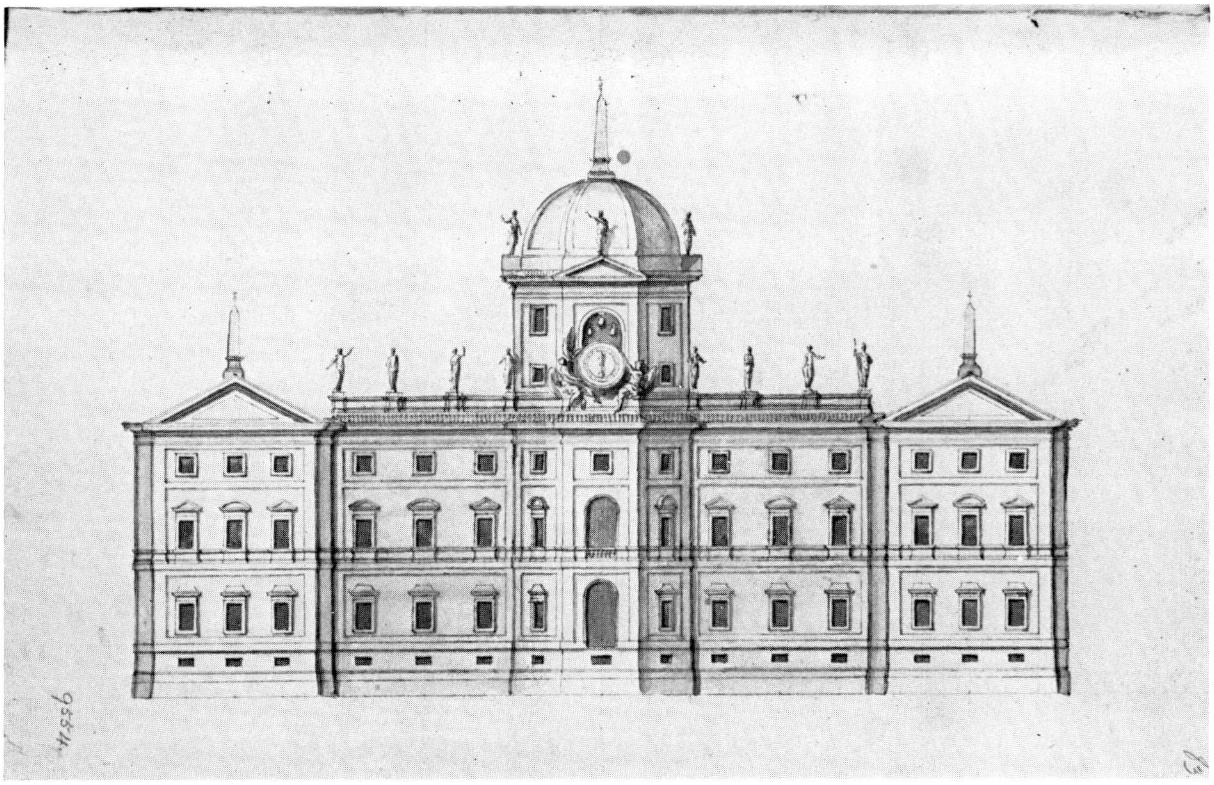

300 Rear elevation (no.361)

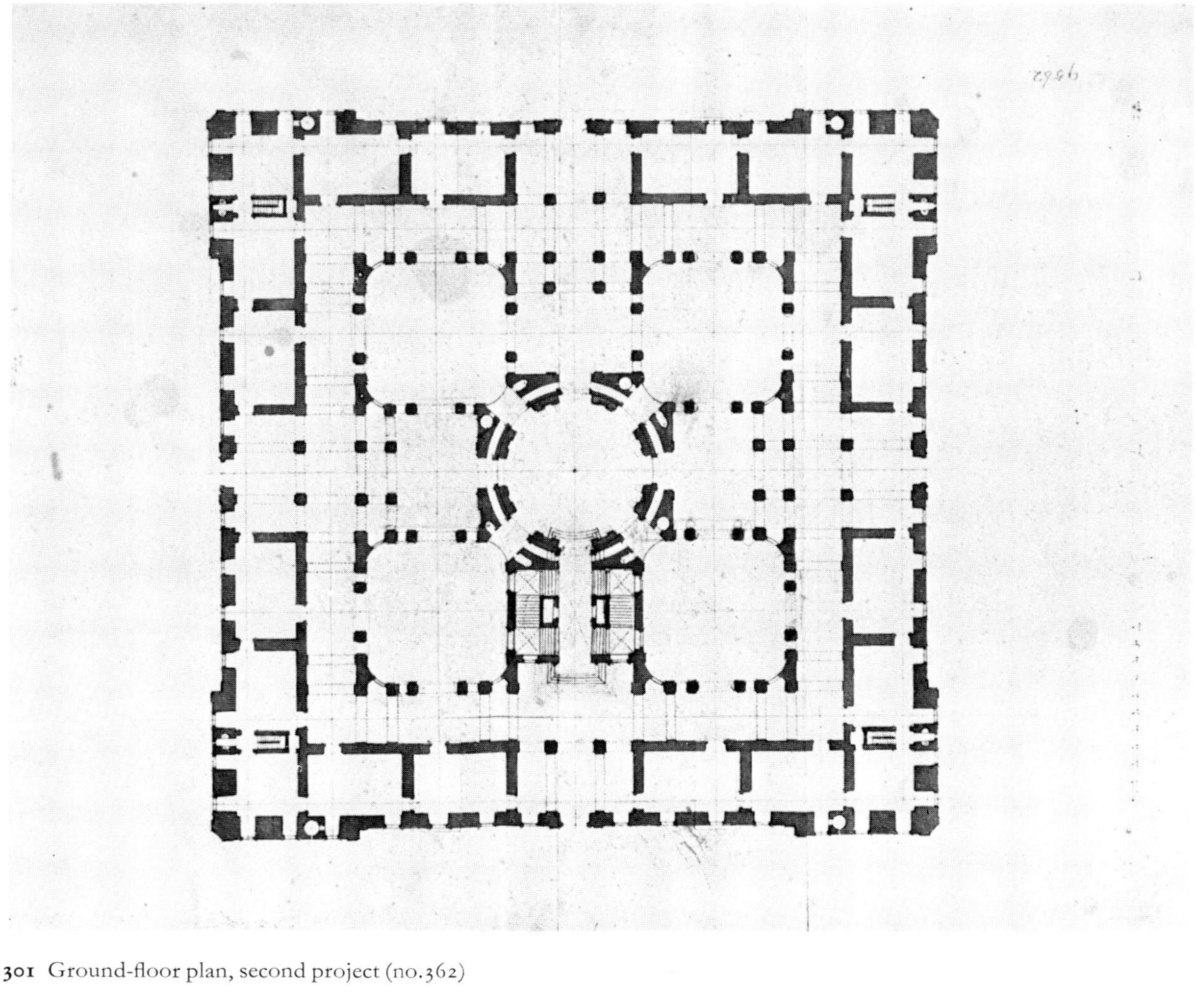

301 Ground-floor plan, second project (no.362)

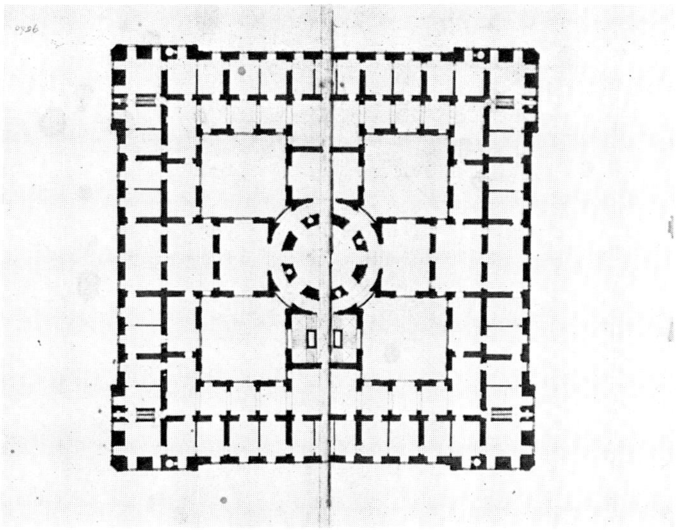

302 First-floor plan (1), second project (no.363)

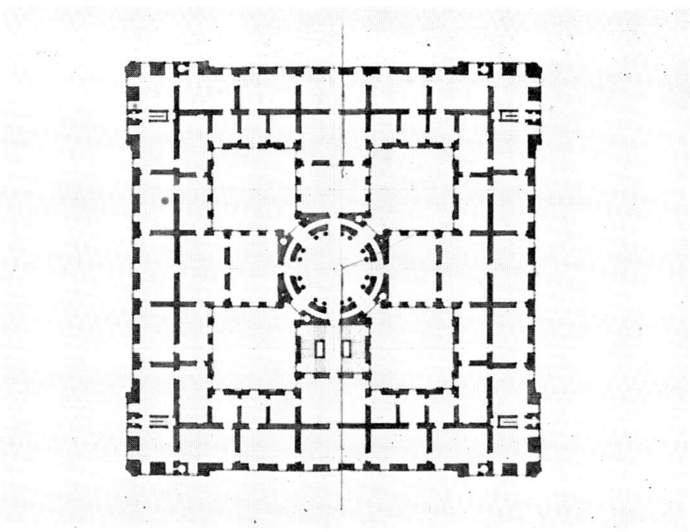

303 First-floor plan (2), second project (no.364)

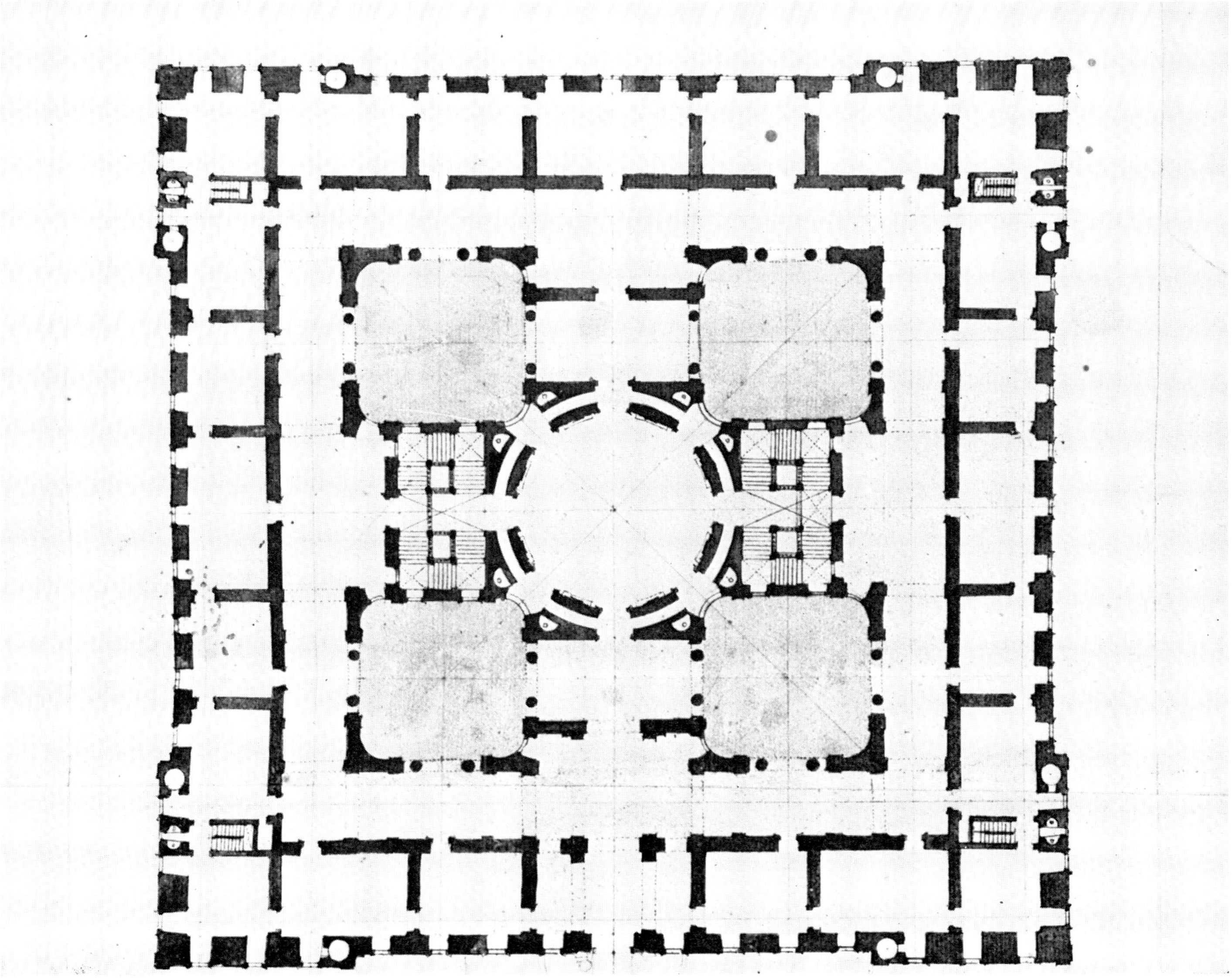

304 Ground-floor plan, revised version, second project (no.365)

Projects for a Sternberg palace, Prague (*c.*1696–1700)

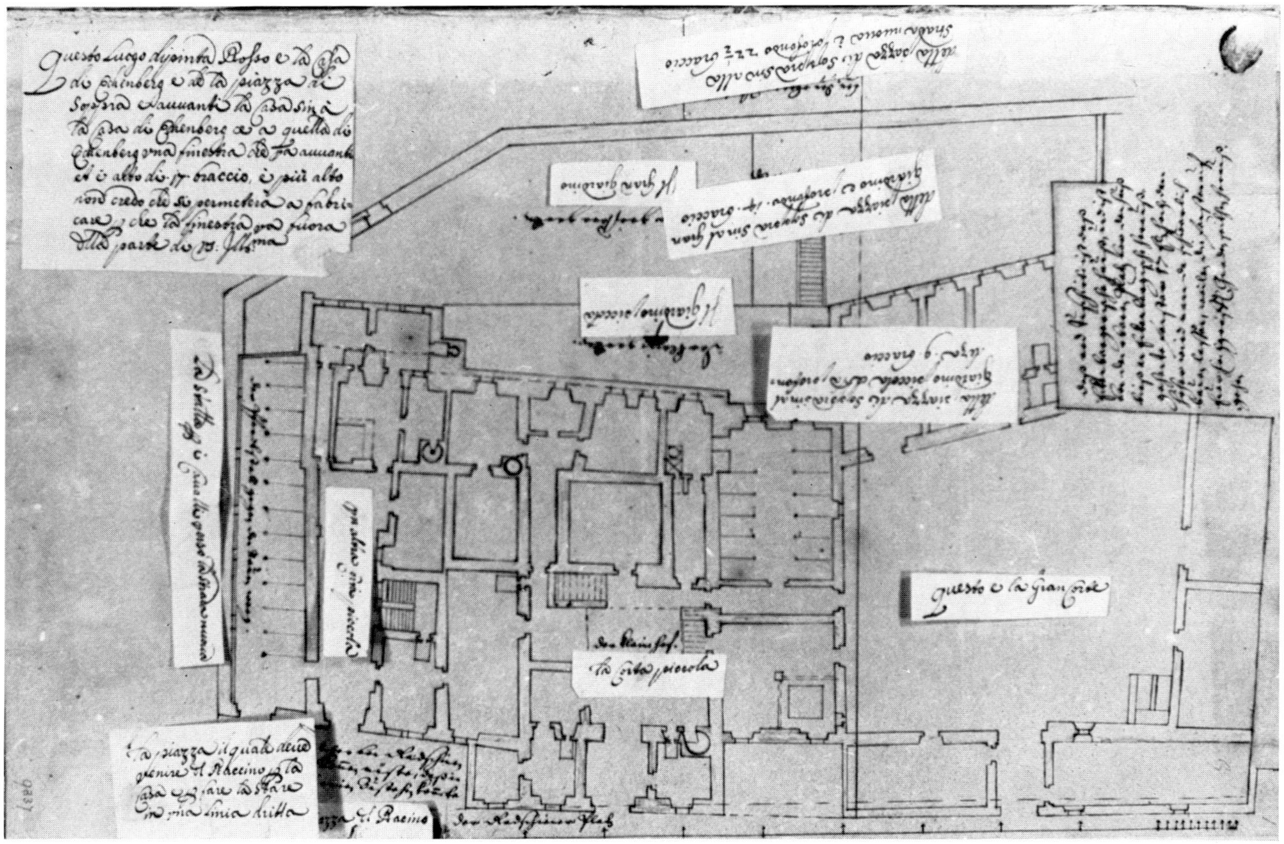

305 Site plan (anon. German drawing, no.366)

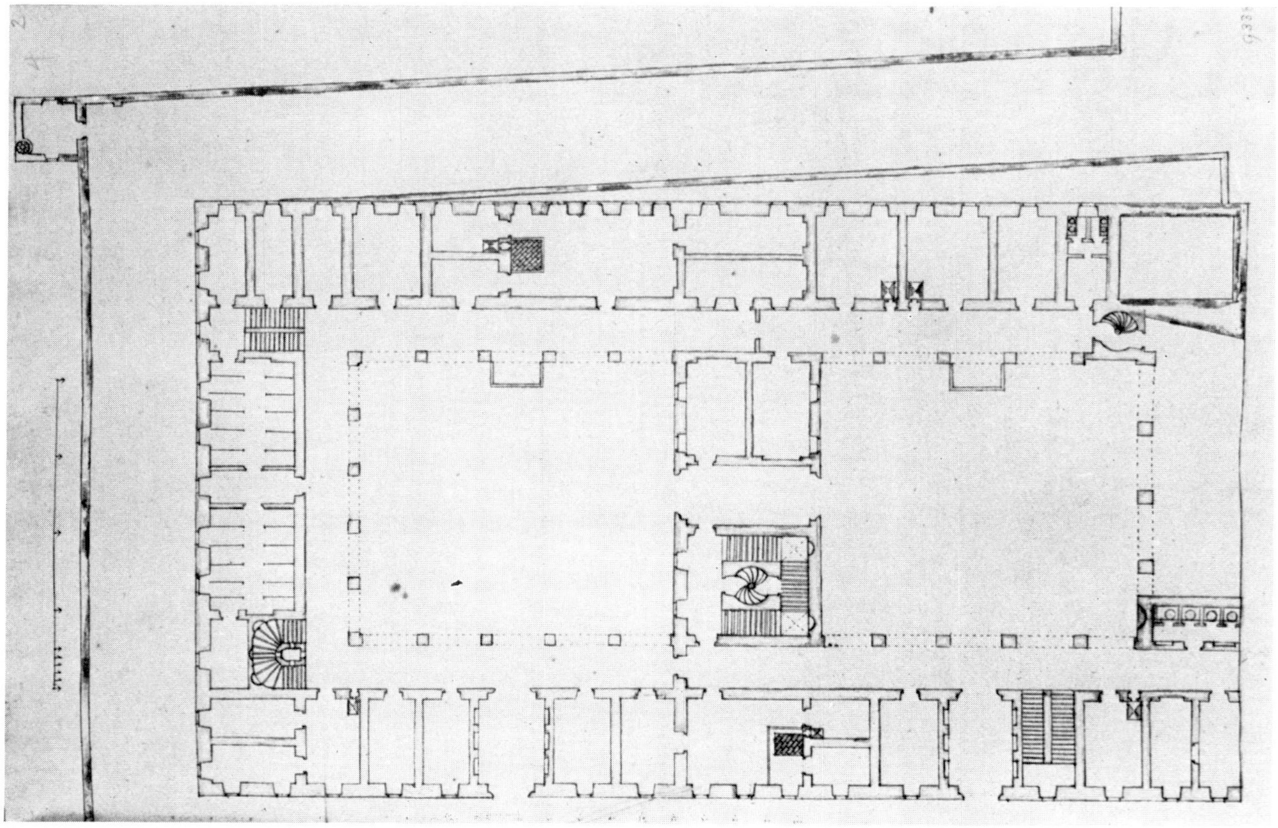

306 Plan project (anon. German drawing, no.367)

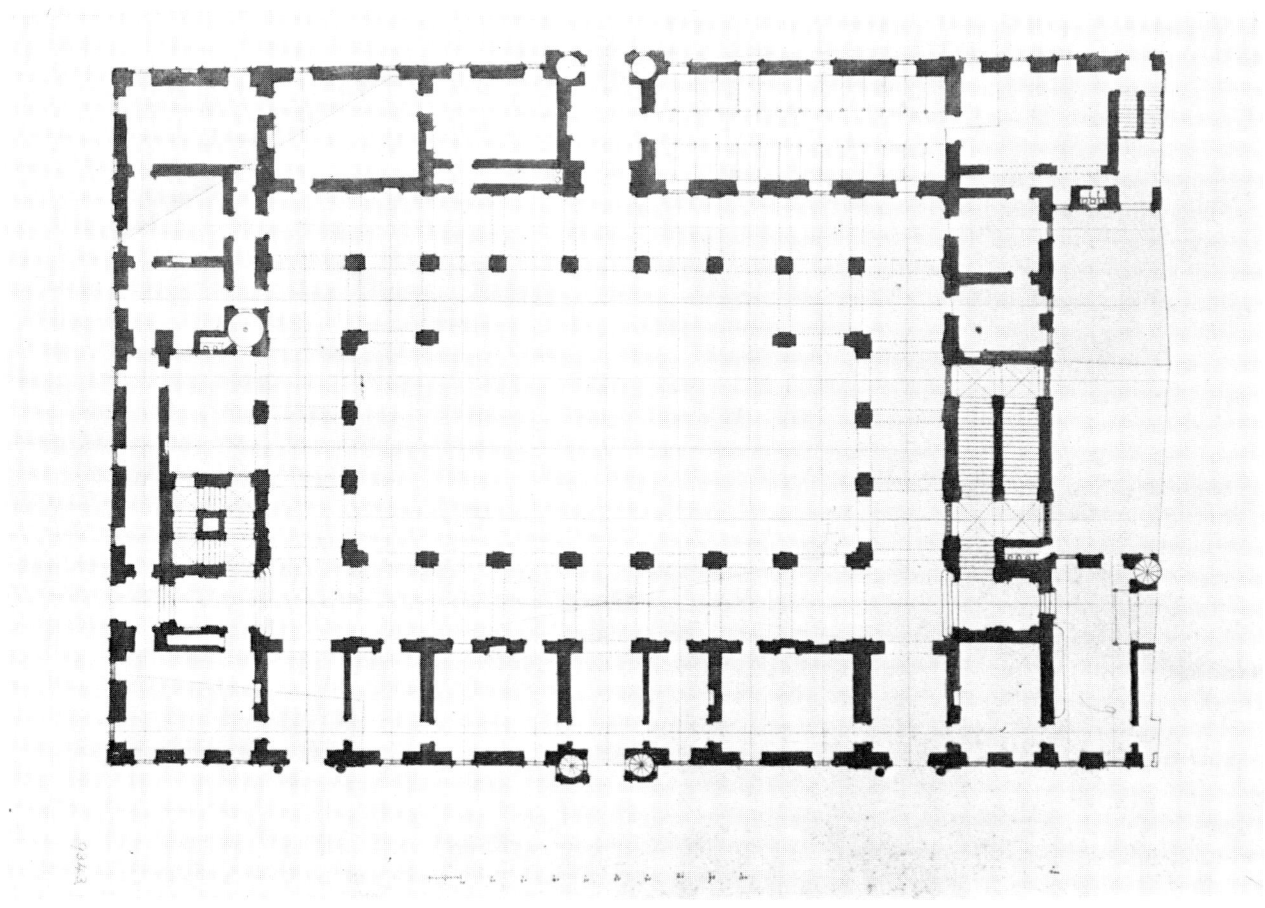

307 Ground-floor plan, first project (no.368)

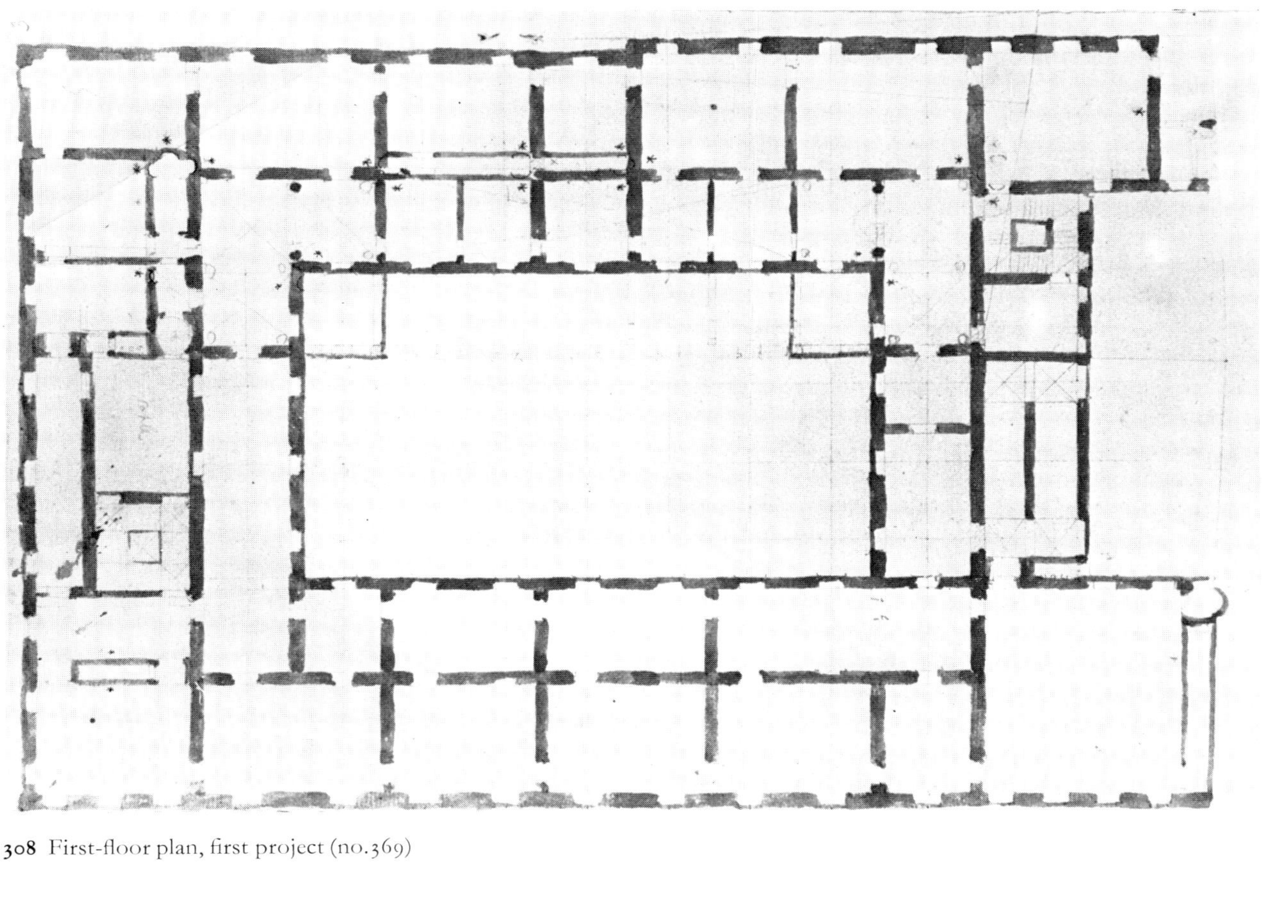

308 First-floor plan, first project (no.369)

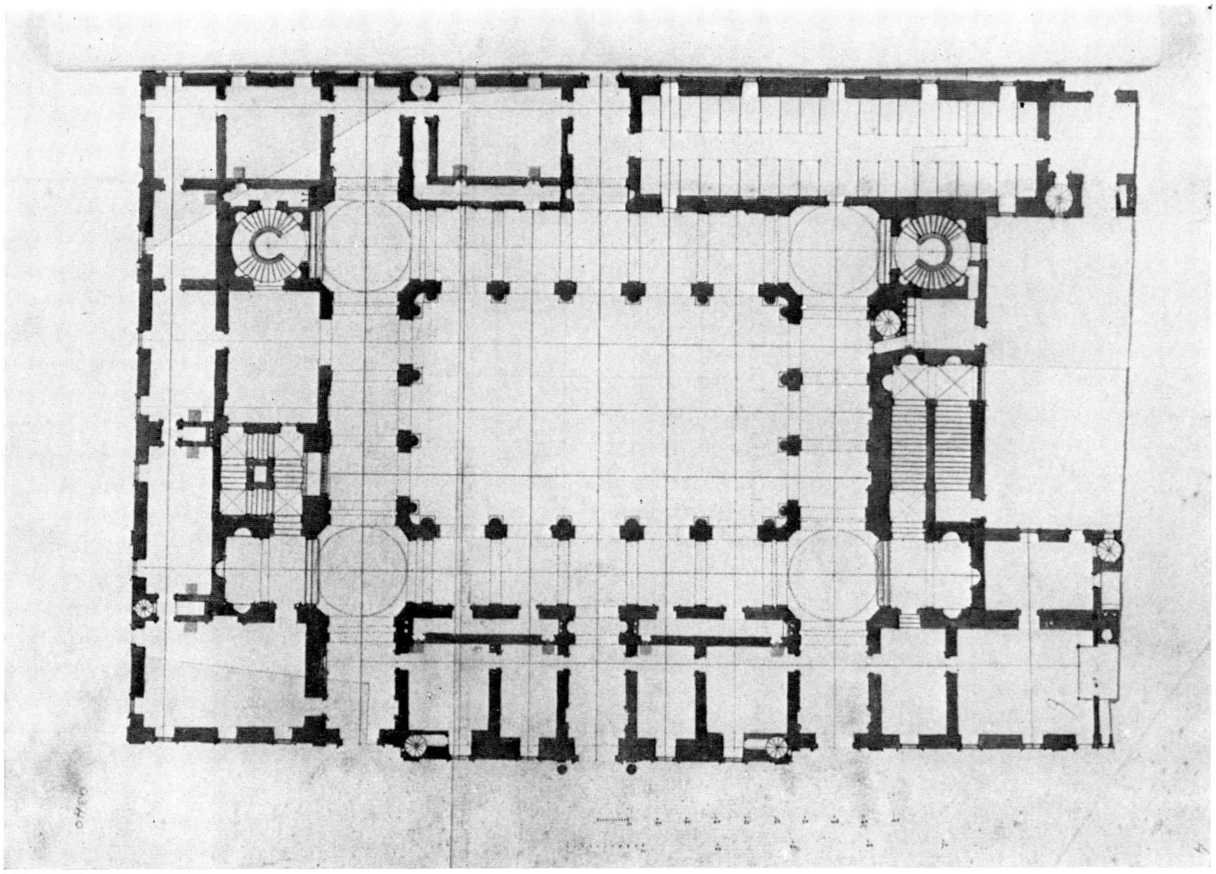

309 Ground-floor plan, second project (no.370)

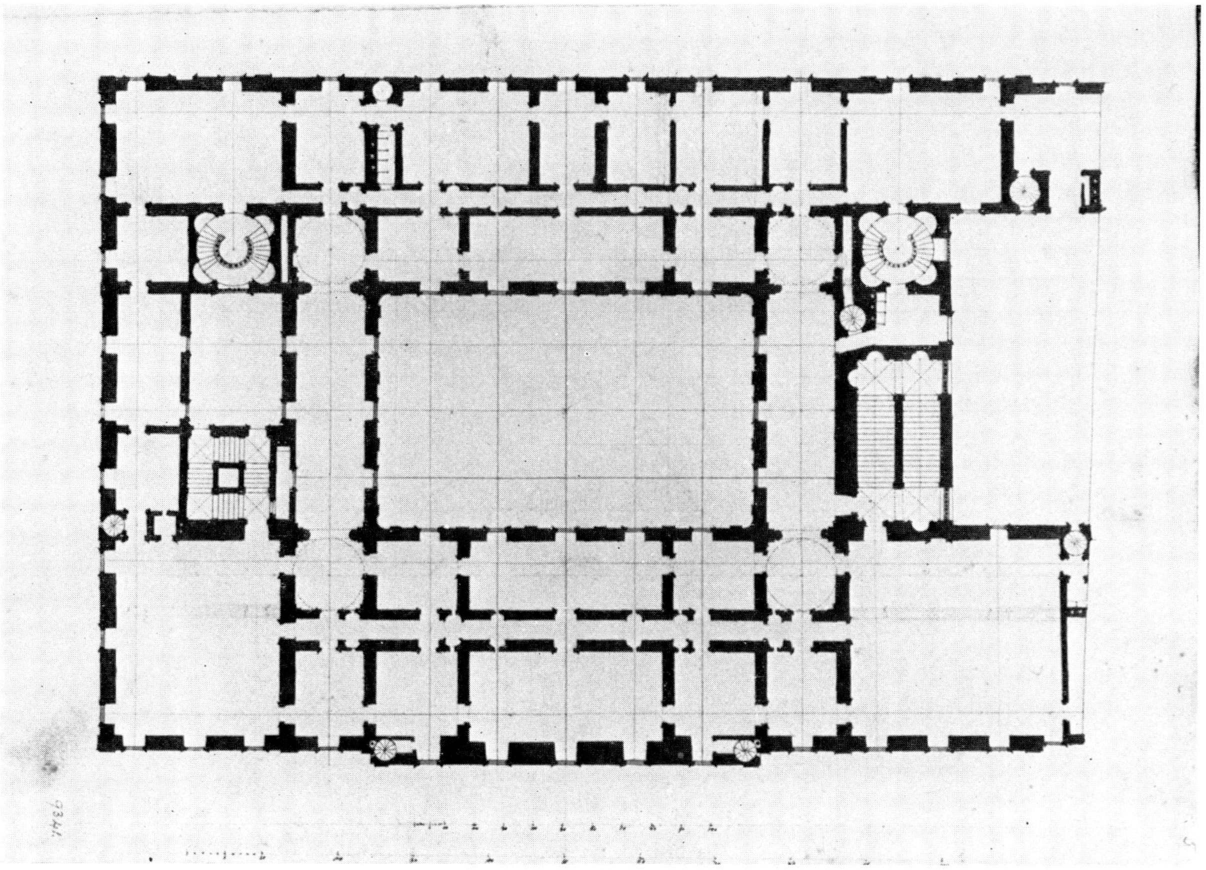

310 First-floor plan, second project (no.371)

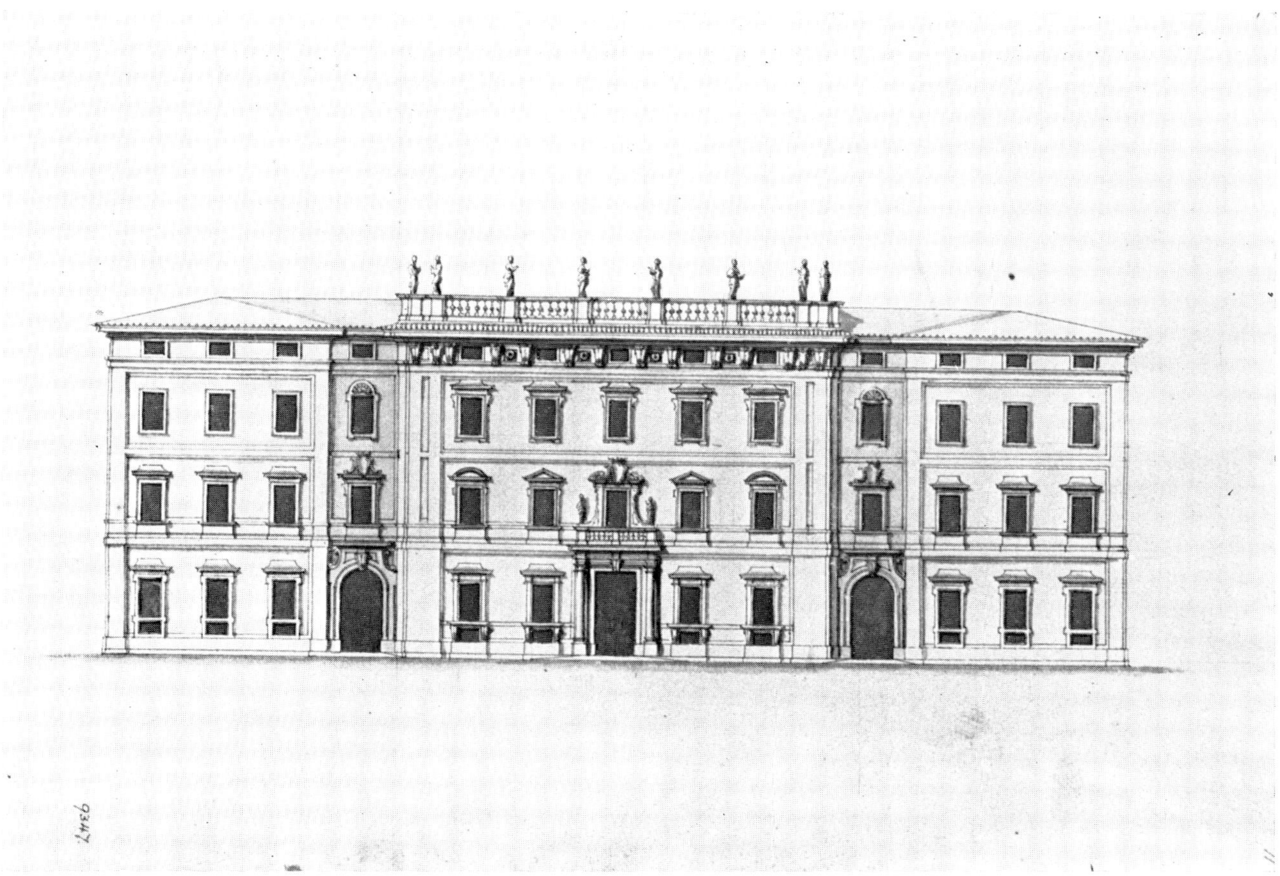

311 Elevation of the main façade, second project (no.376)

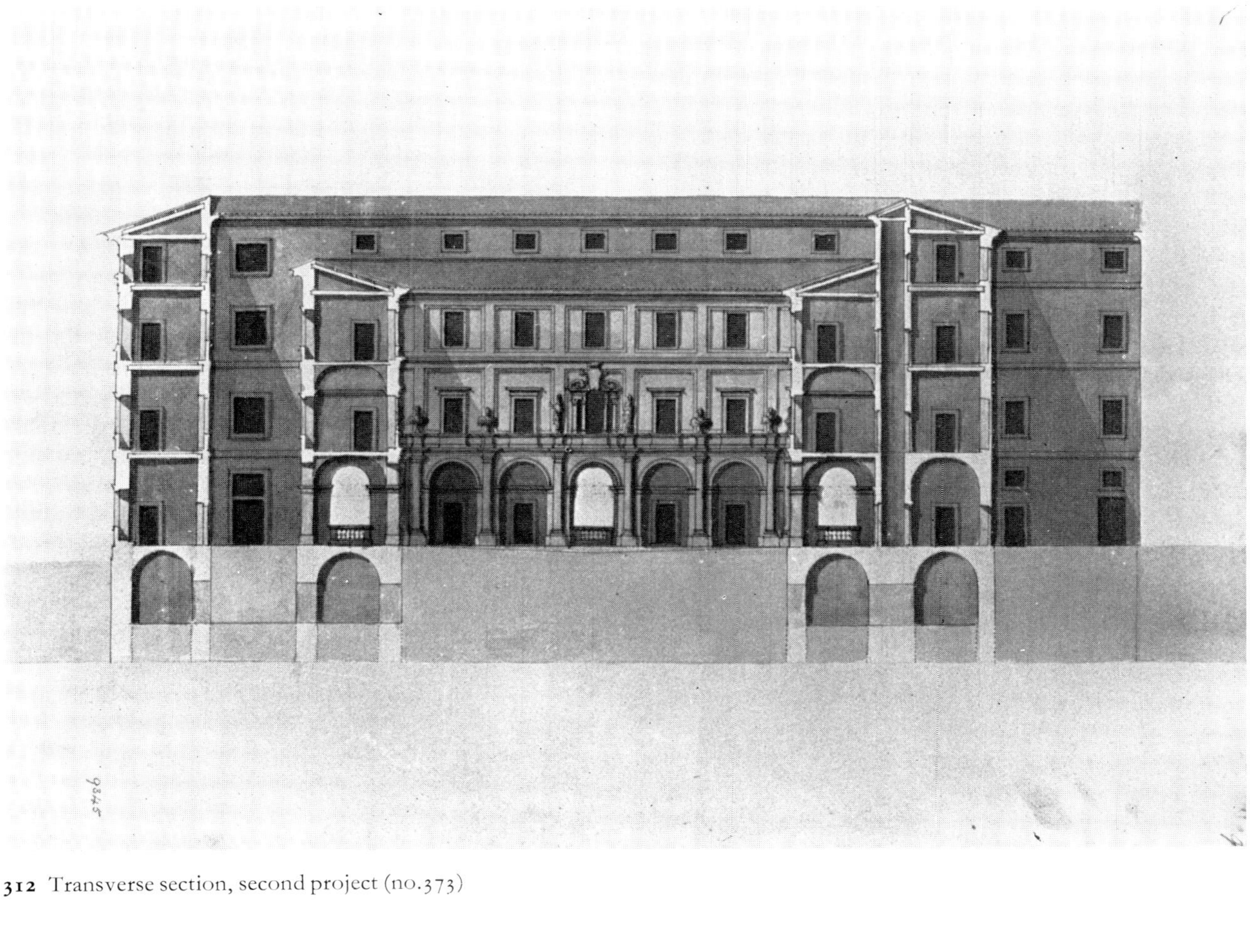

312 Transverse section, second project (no.373)

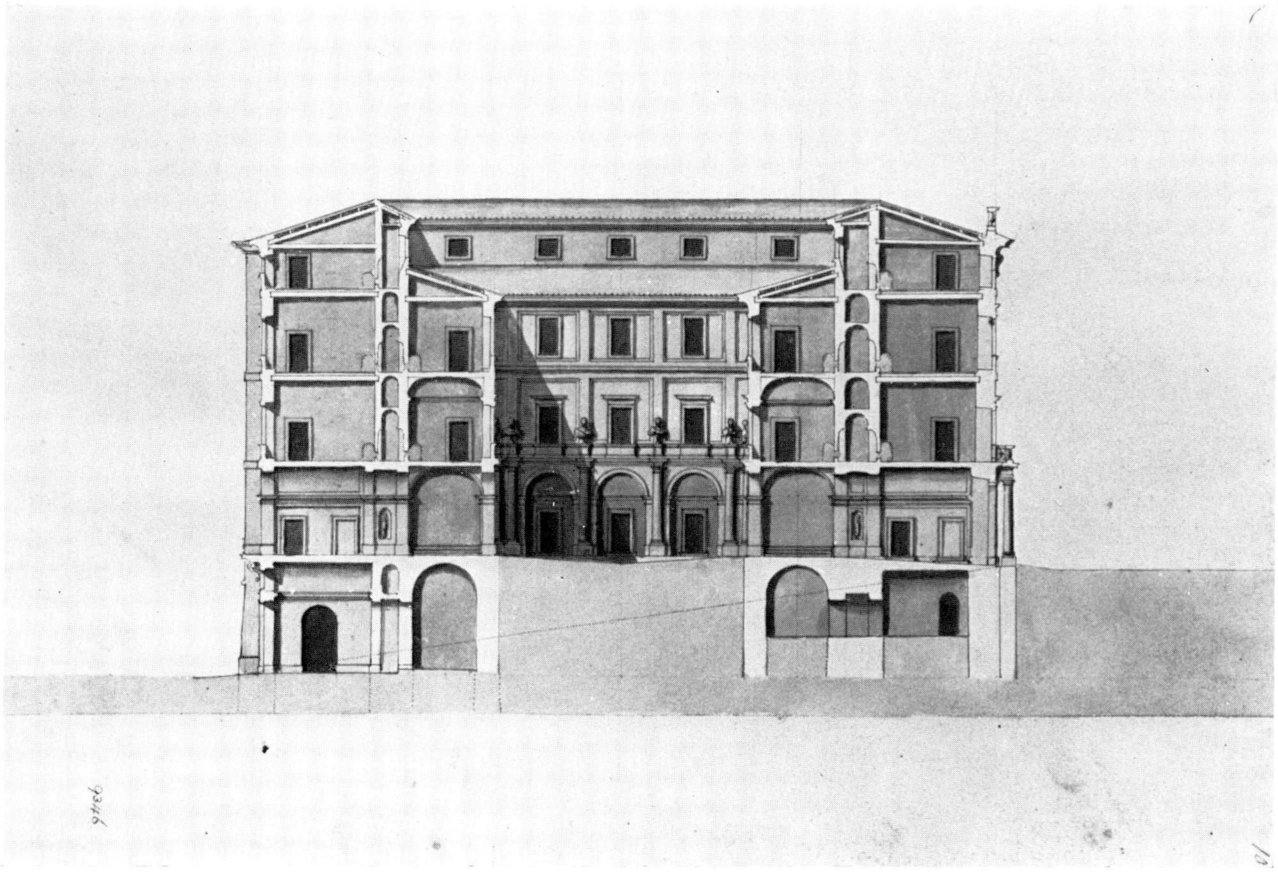

313 Longitudinal section, second project (no.374)

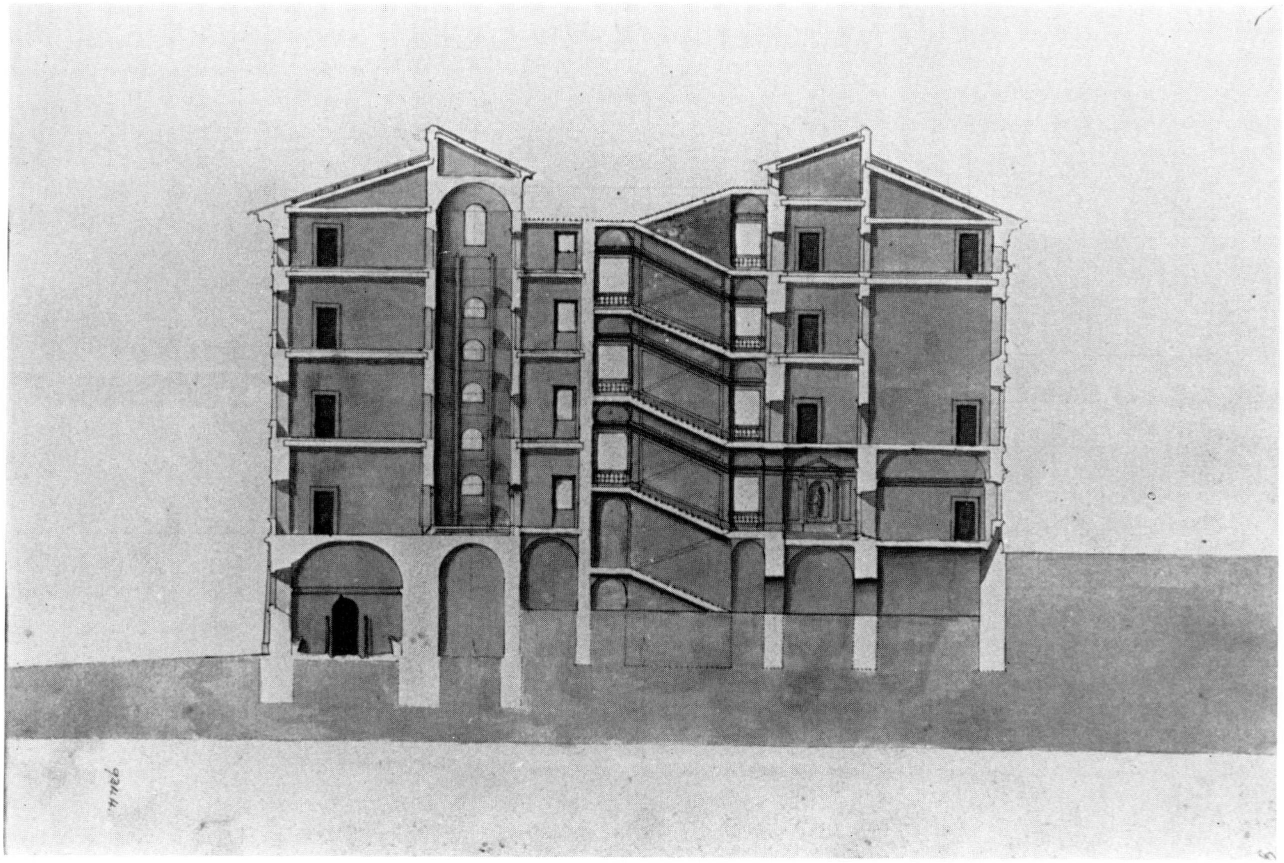

314 Longitudinal section, showing staircases, second project (no.375)

A study of primitive boats (*c.*1698?)

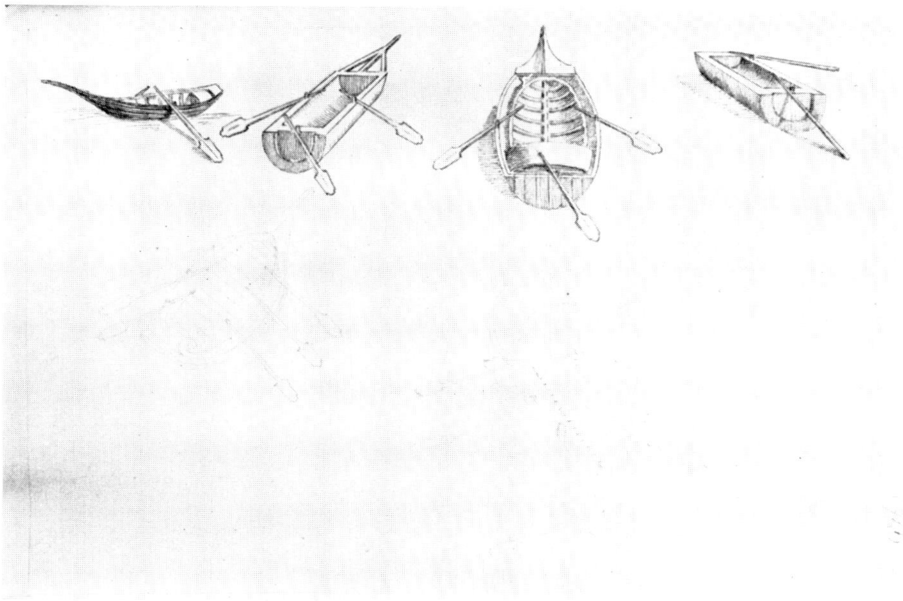

315 Studies of primitive boats (no.377)

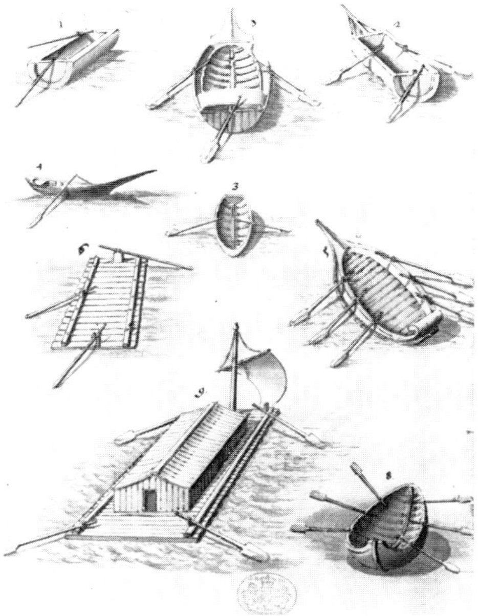

316 Studies of boats (drawing by Fontana; London, British Museum)

The Martinitz Palace, Prague (1700)

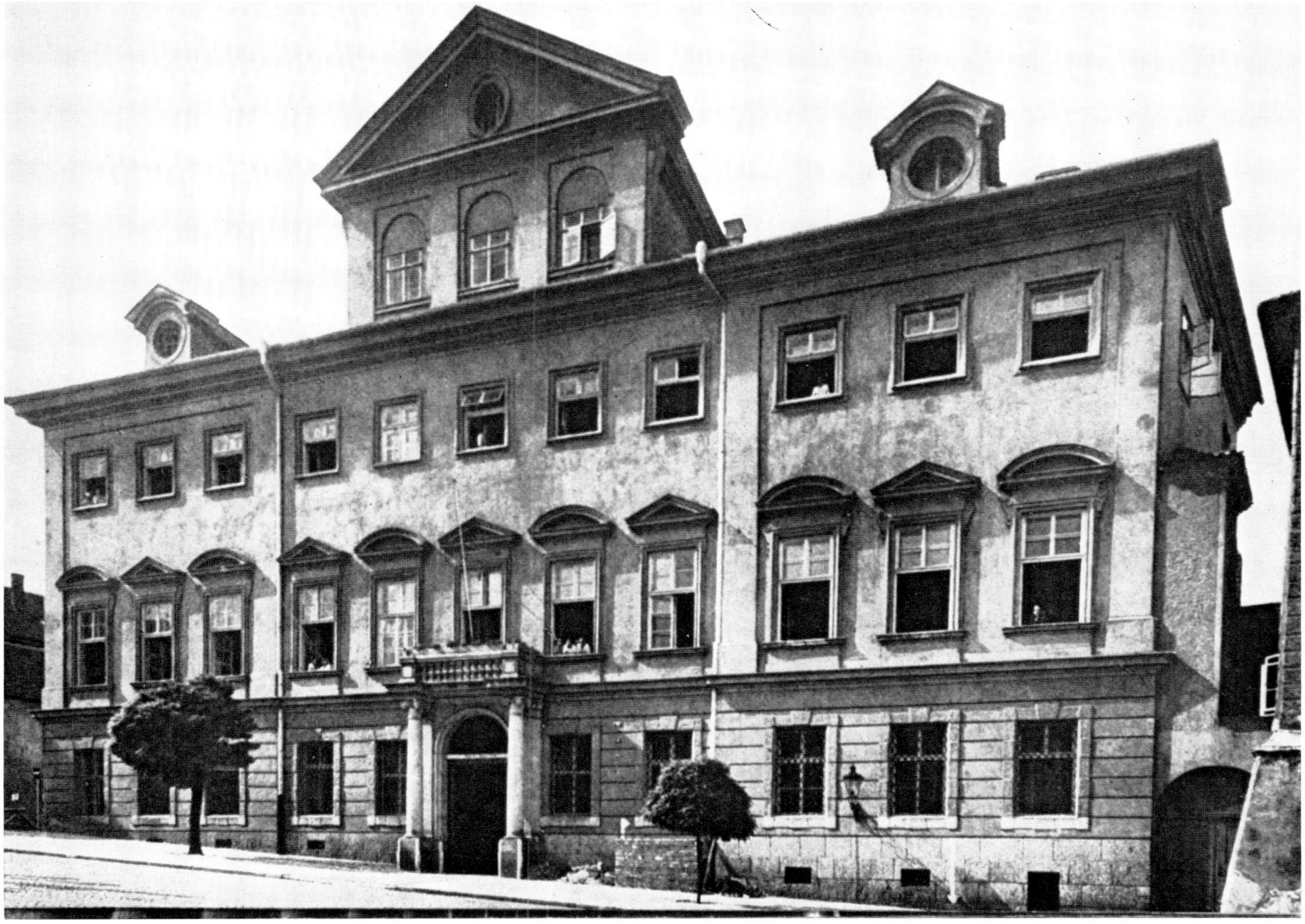

317 View of the palace

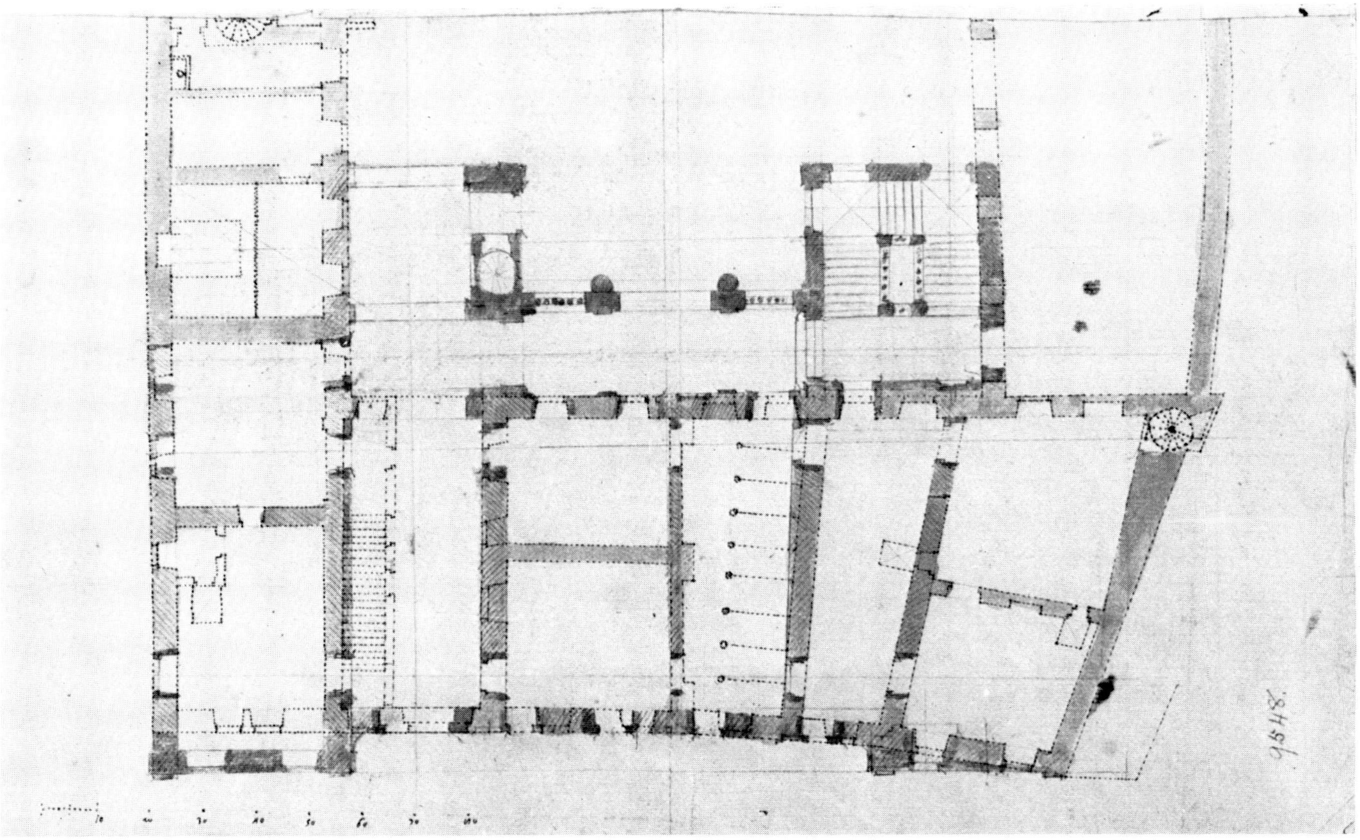

318 Ground-floor plan, first project (no.378)

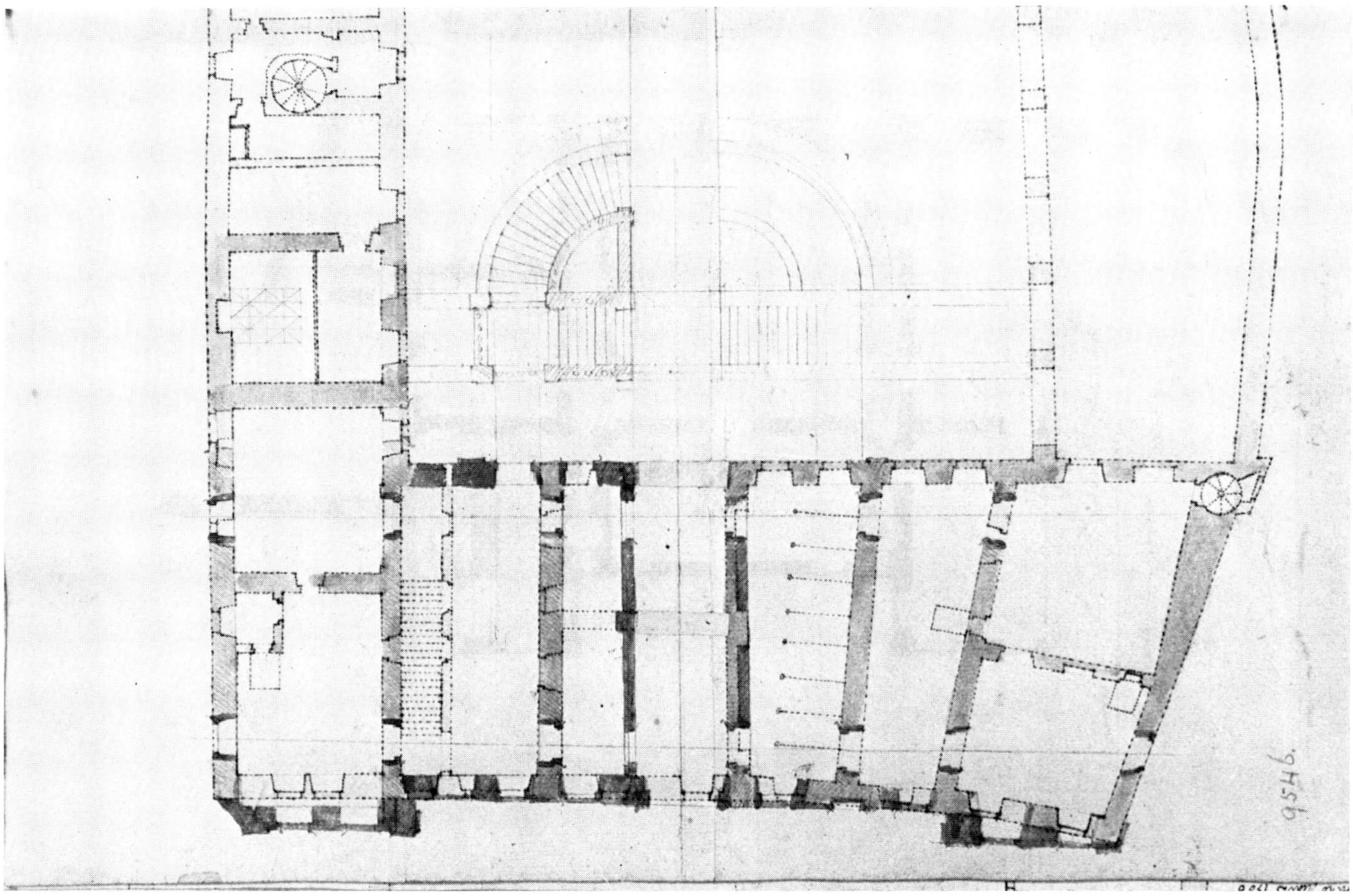

319 Ground-floor plan, second project (no.379)

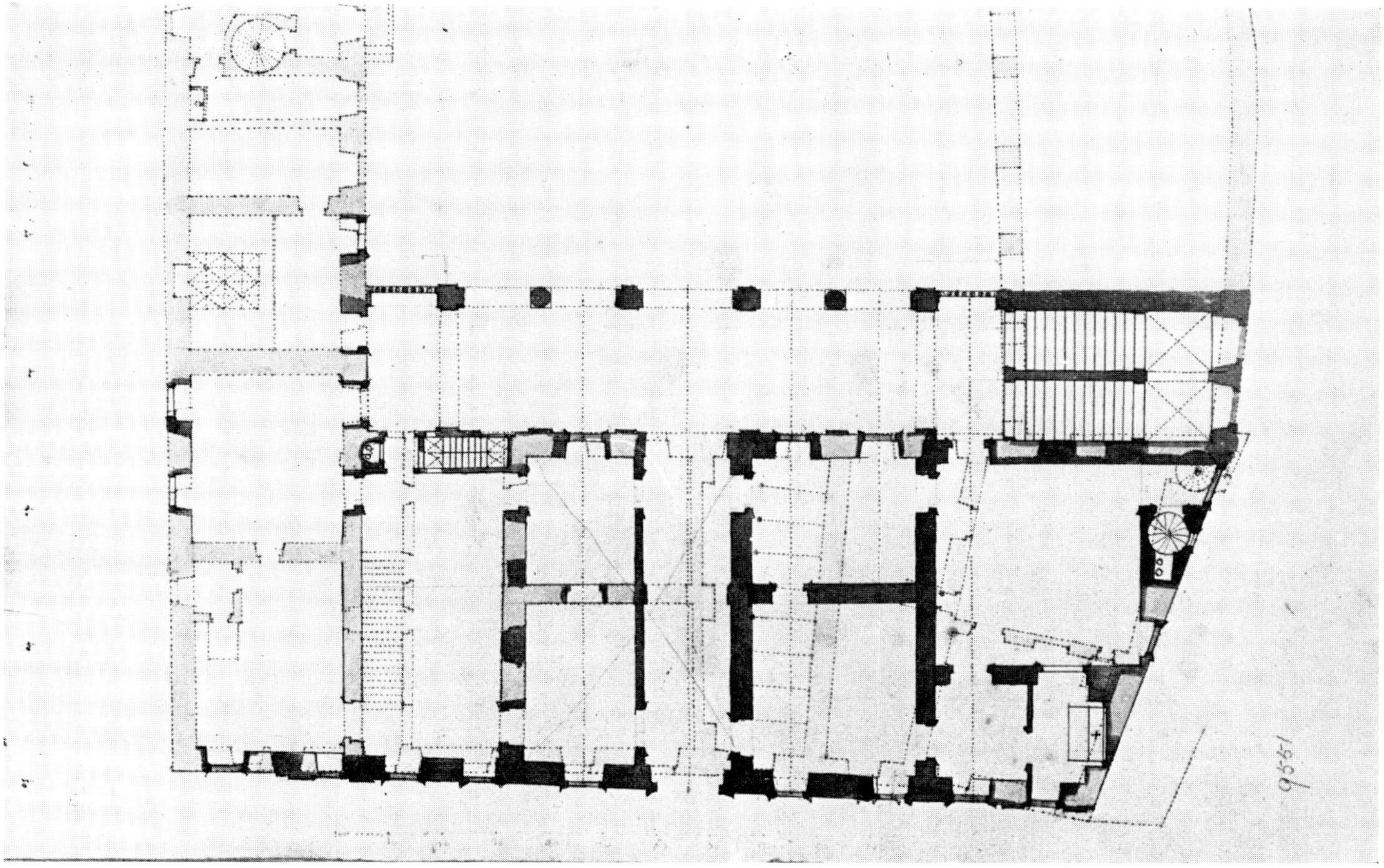

320 Ground-floor plan, third project (no.381)

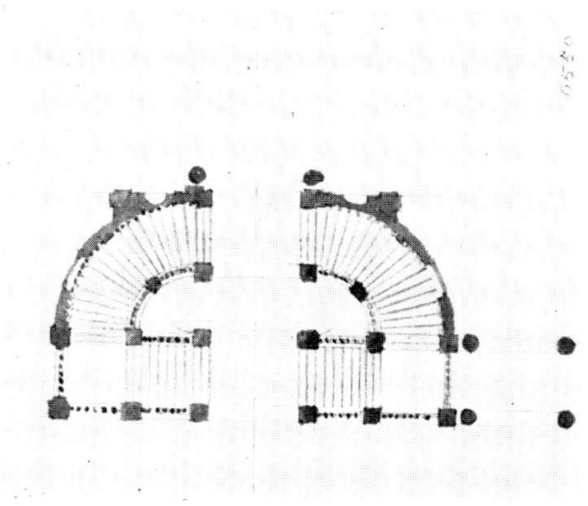

321 Plan of the staircase, second project (no.380)

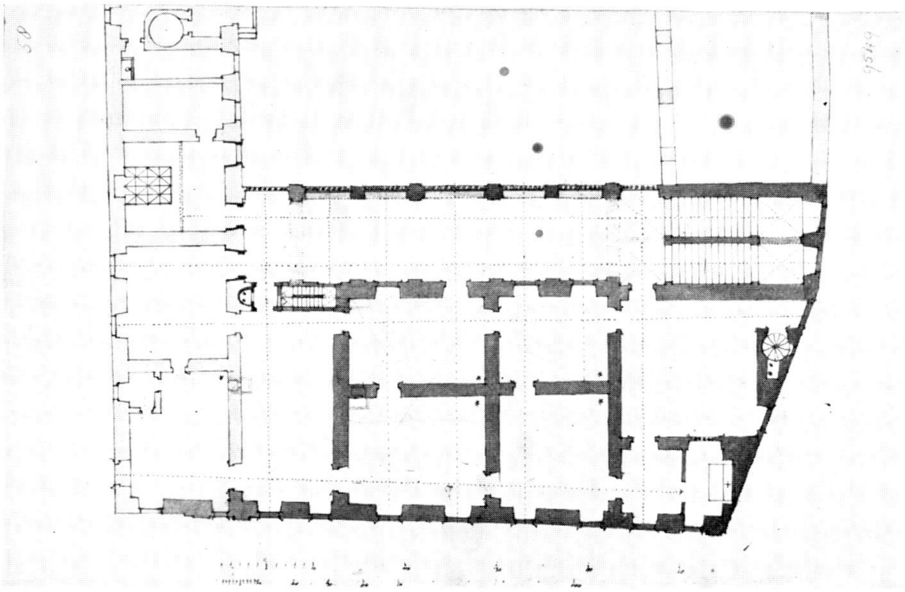

322 First-floor plan, third project (no.382)

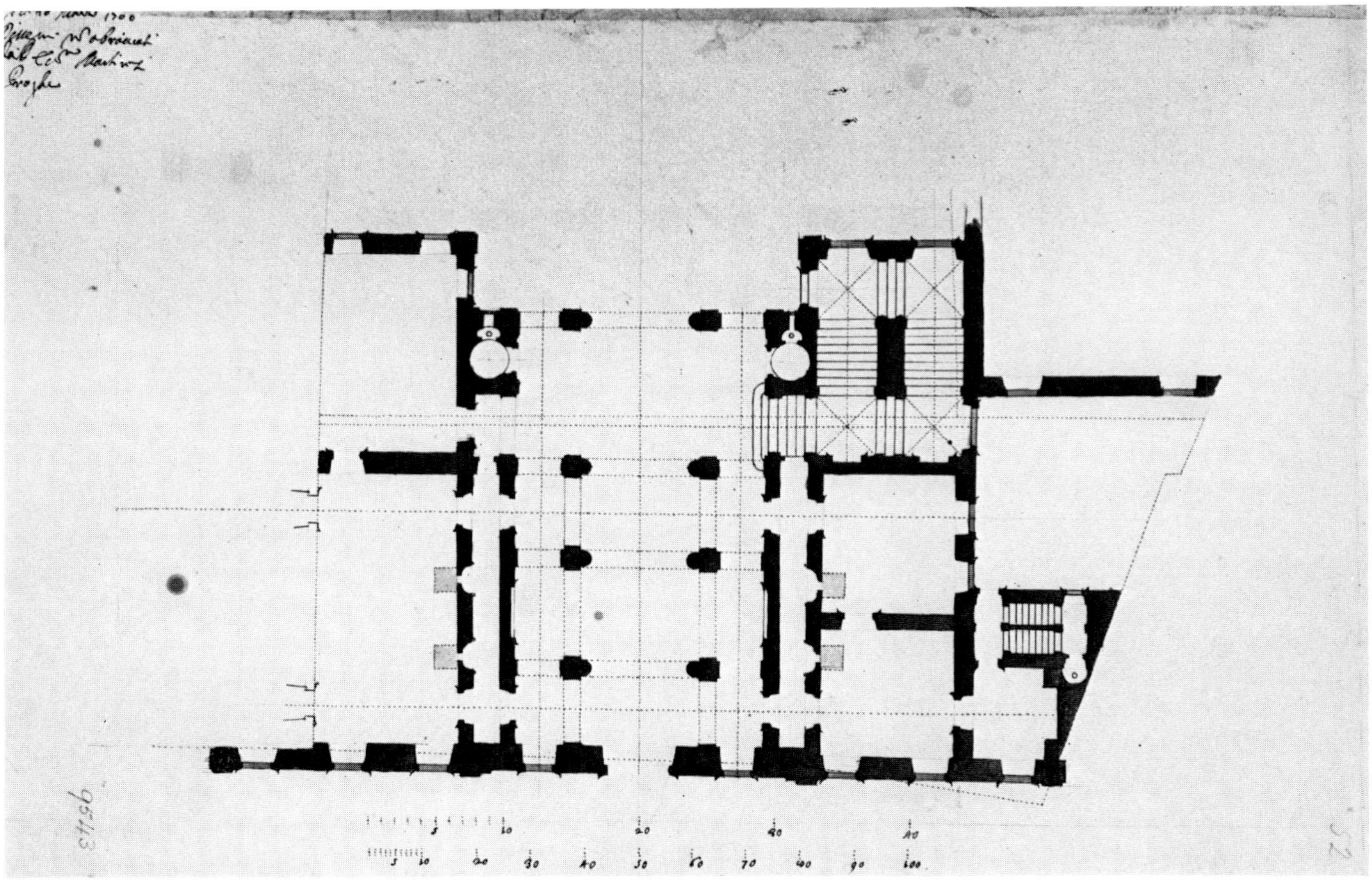

323 Ground-floor plan, fourth project (no.383)

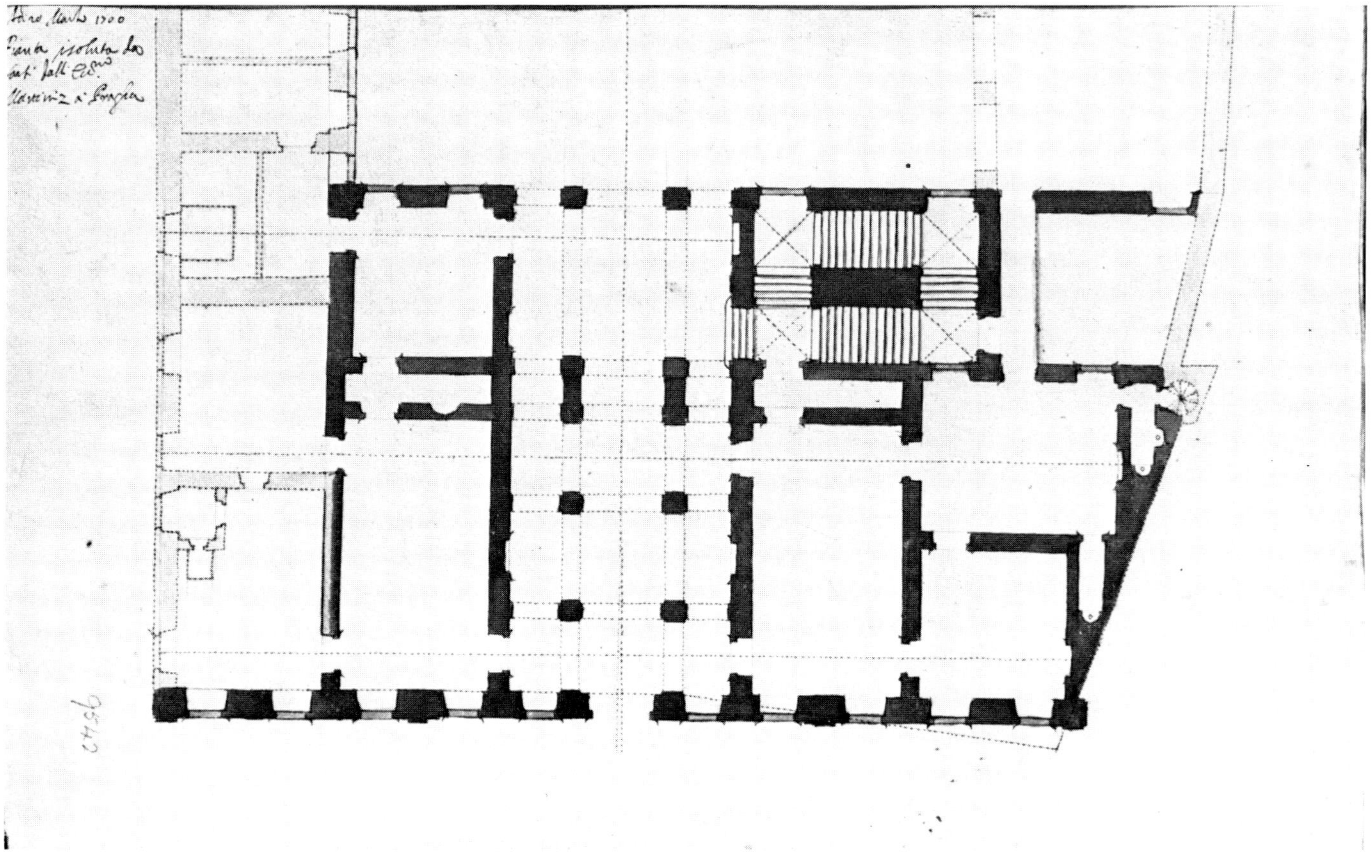

324 Ground-floor plan, final project (no.386)

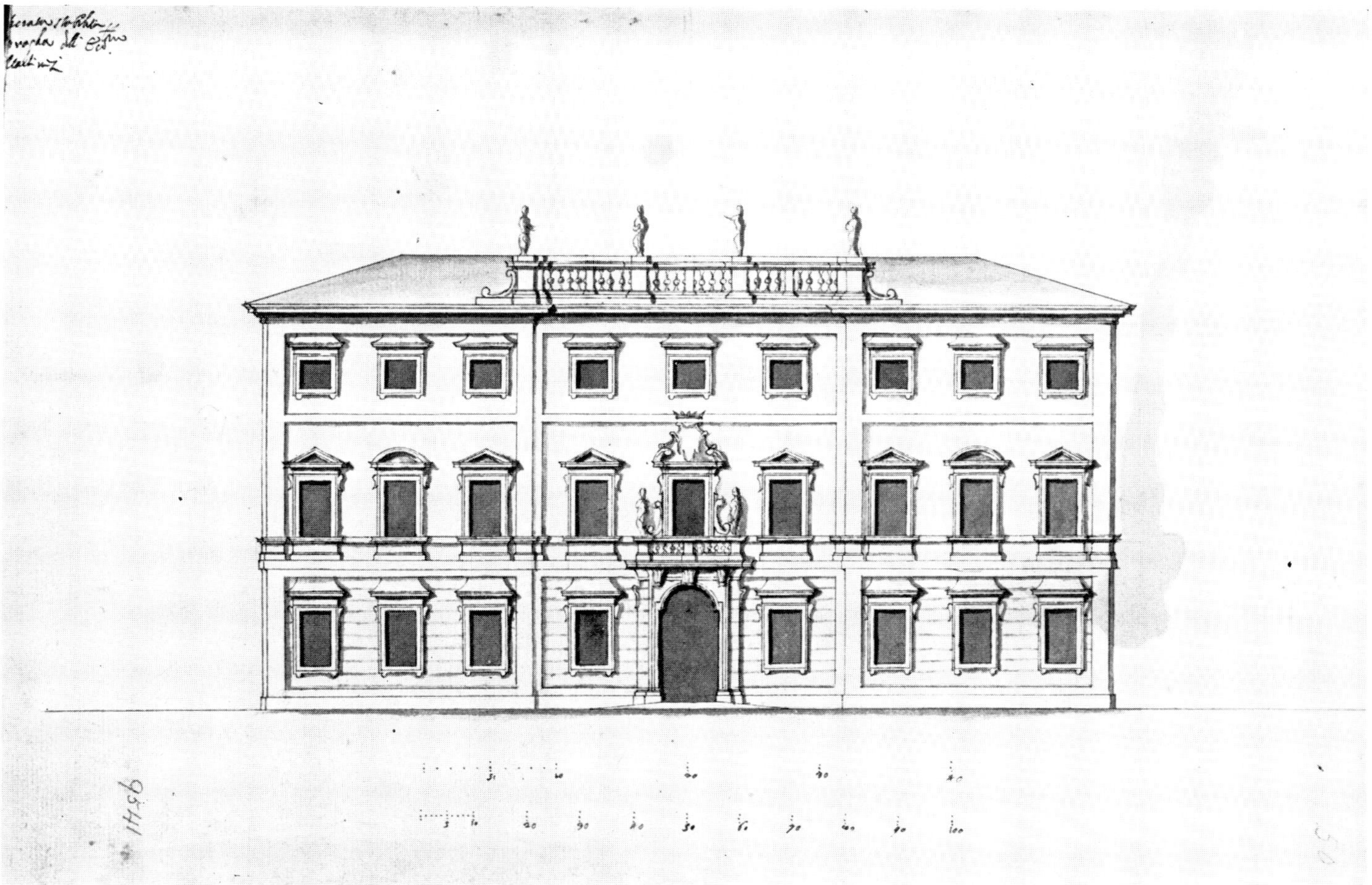

325 Front elevation, fourth project (no.385)

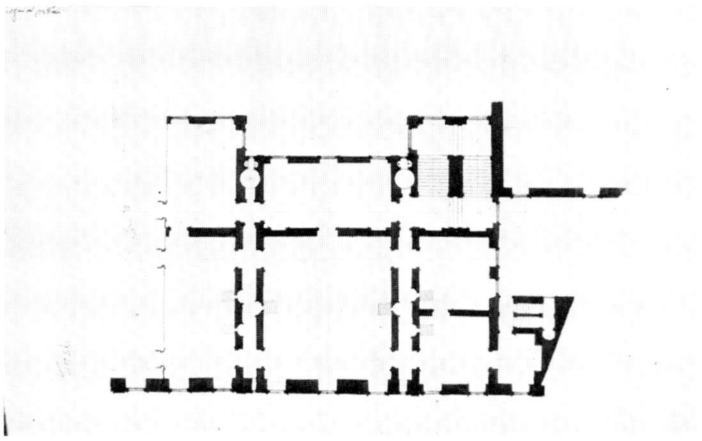

326 First-floor plan, fourth project (no.384)

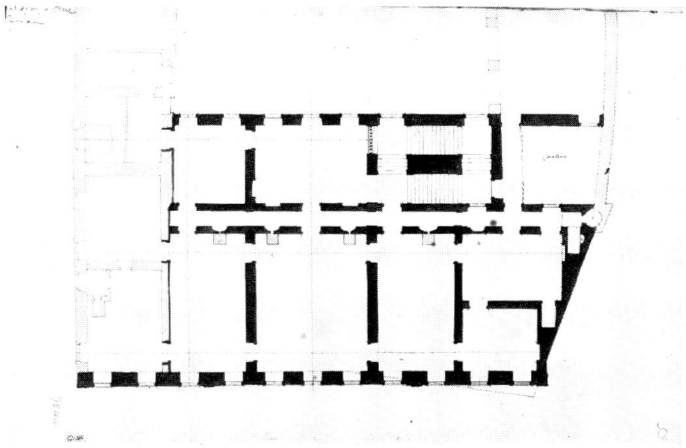

327 First-floor plan (2), final project (no.388)

Survey of the Torre Olevola, near Terracina (1700 and 1703)

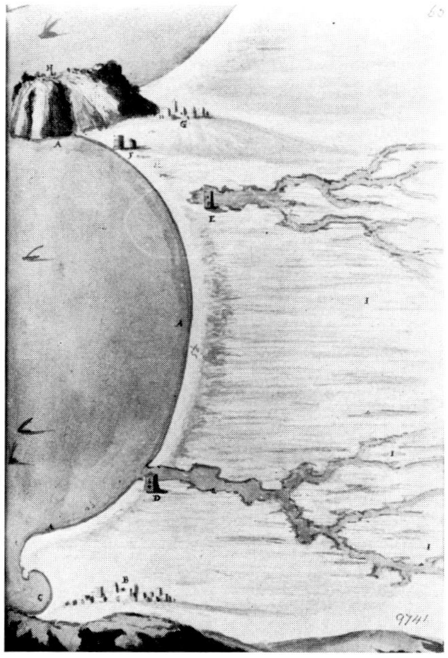

328 View from the east of the coast between Terracina and Monte Circeo (no.389)

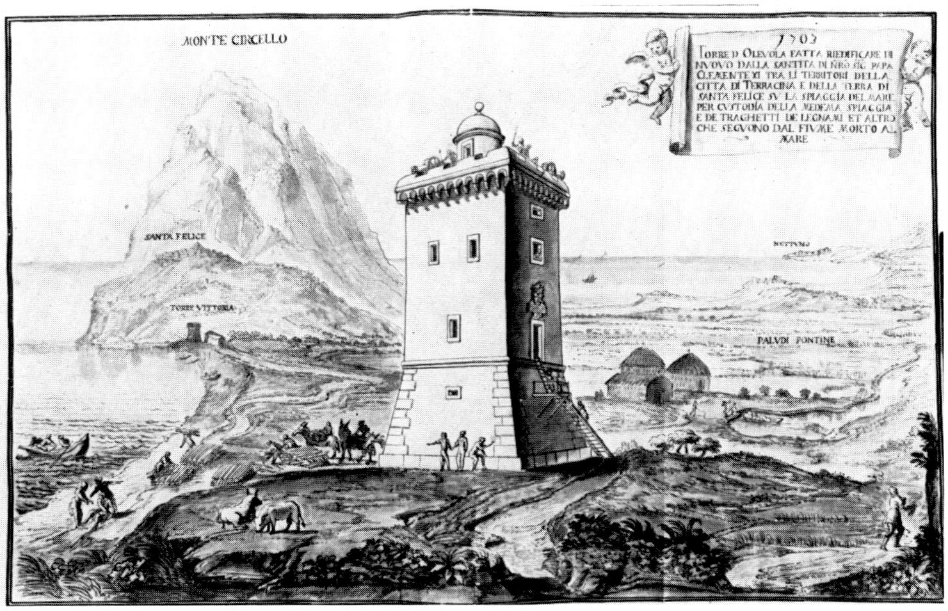

330 Perspective view of the tower and the neighbouring area, 1703 (anon. drawing; no.393)

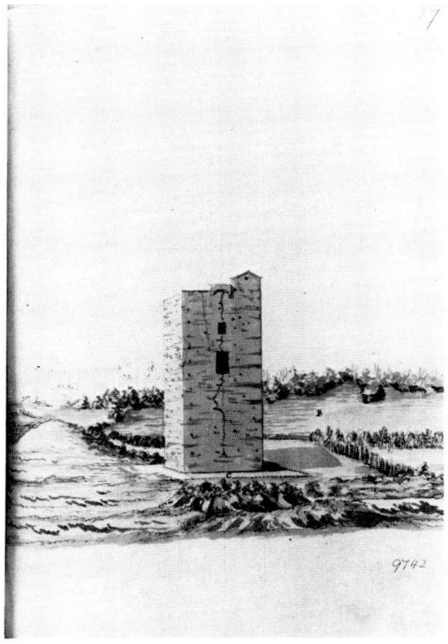

329 Perspective view of the tower (no.392)

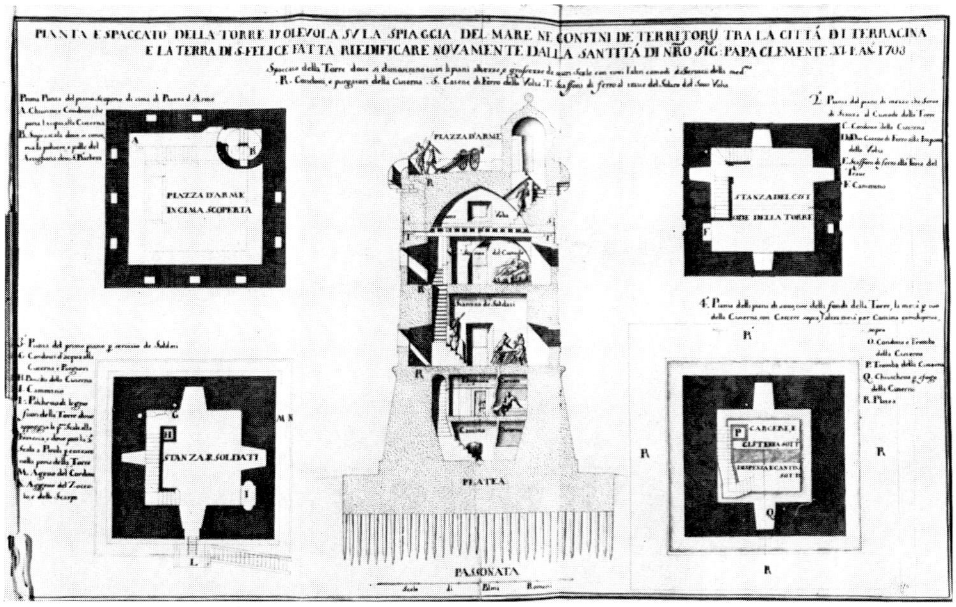

331 Section and four plans of the tower, 1703 (anon. drawing; no.394)

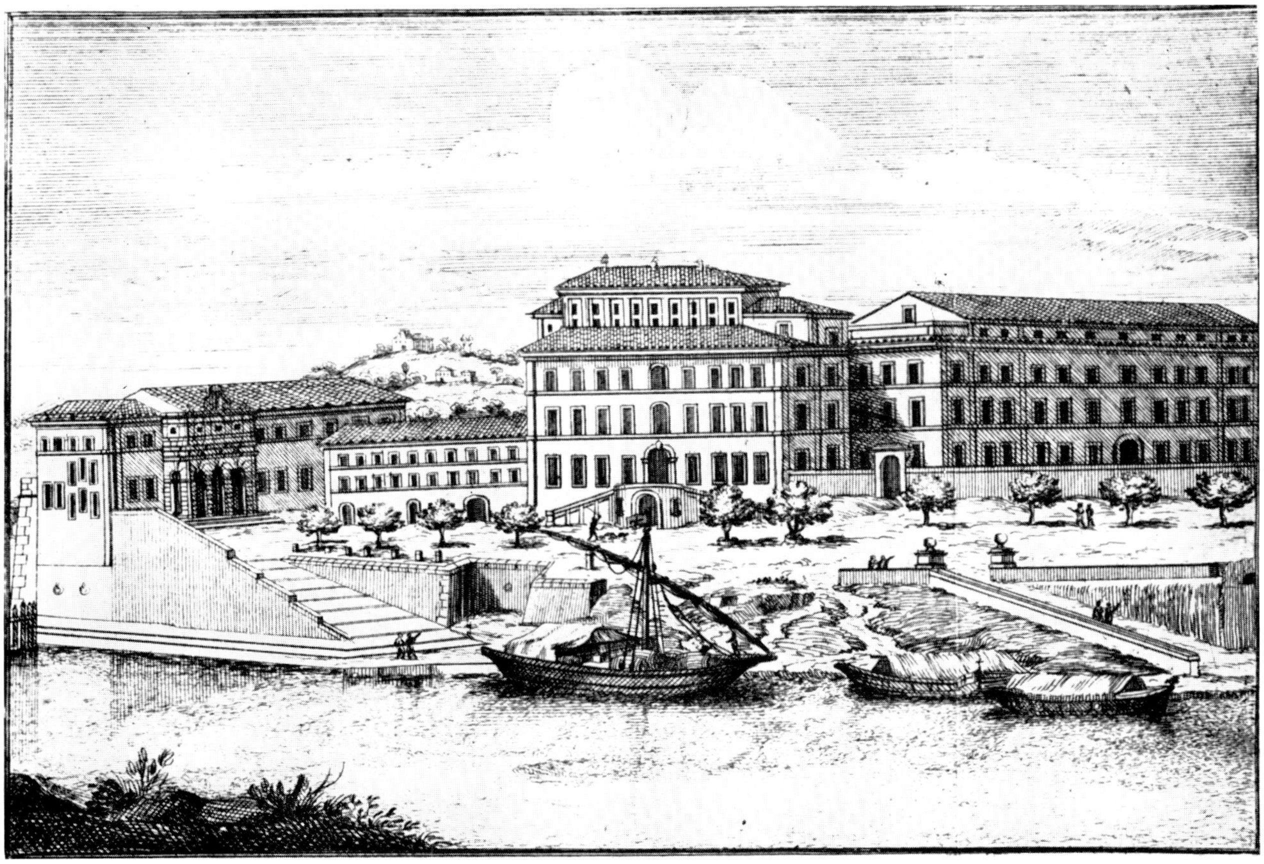

332 View of the Ospizio, 1708 (based on engraving by Specchi, 1699)

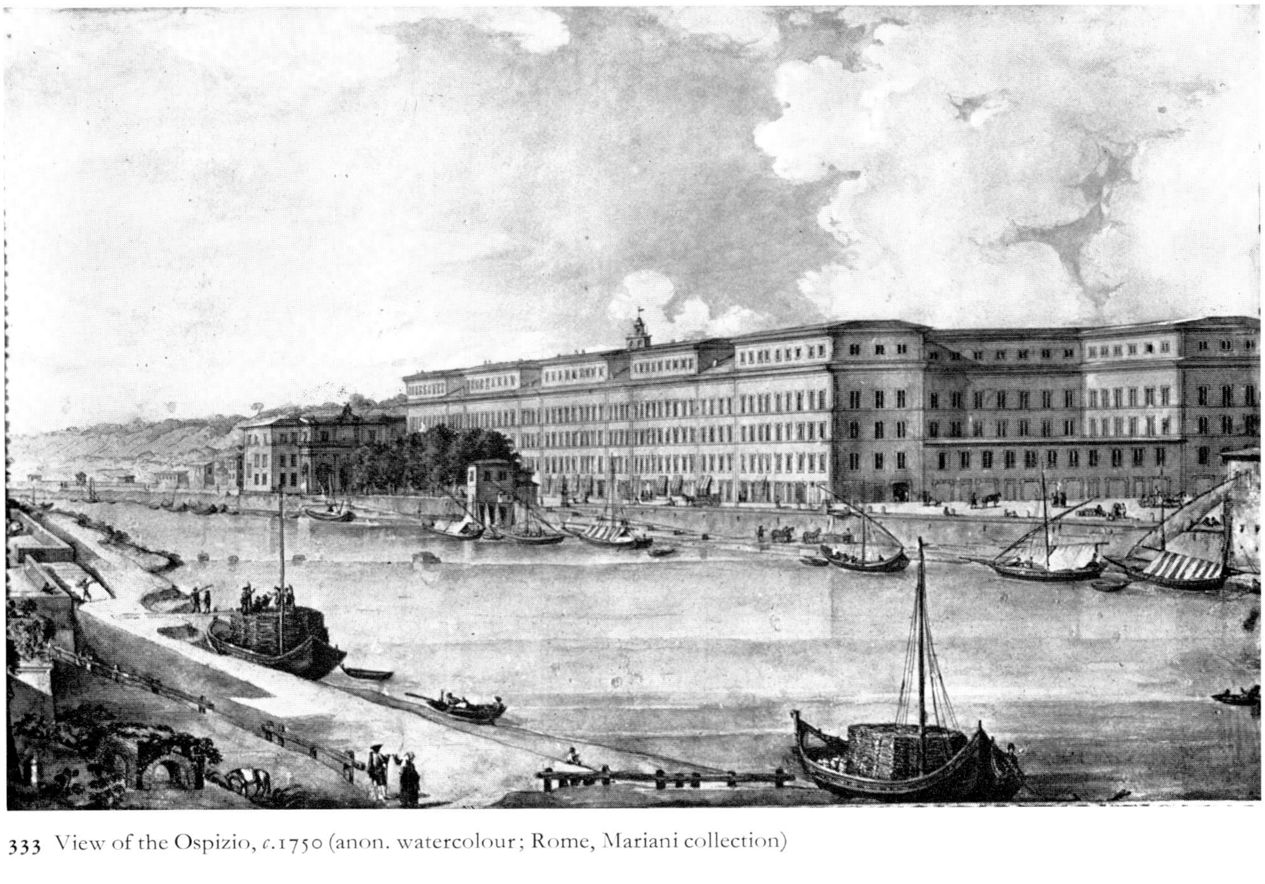

333 View of the Ospizio, *c.*1750 (anon. watercolour; Rome, Mariani collection)

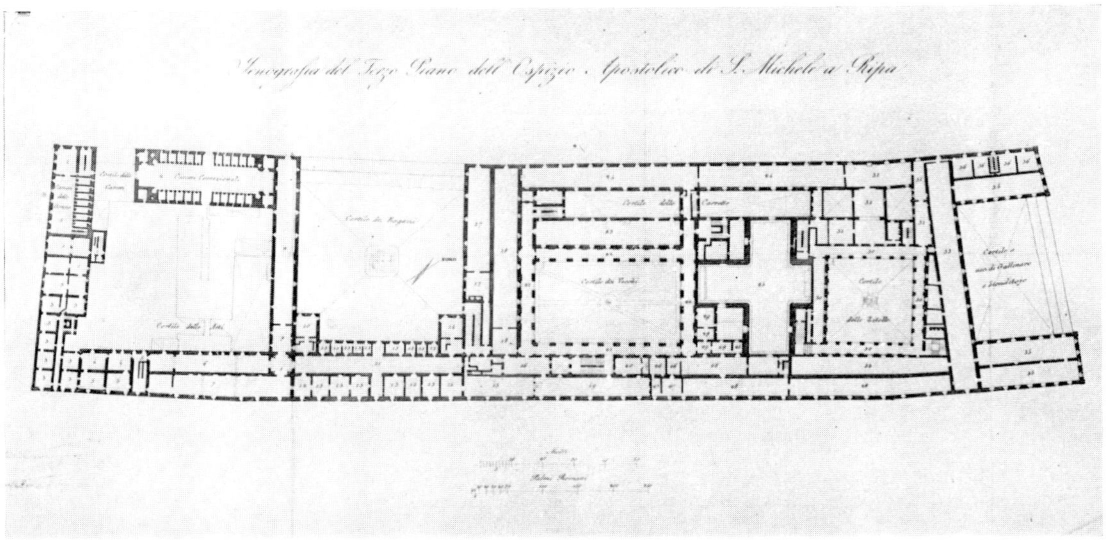

334 Plan of the Ospizio, showing prison (upper left), and south-west corner (lower left), 1832 (engraving from Tosti)

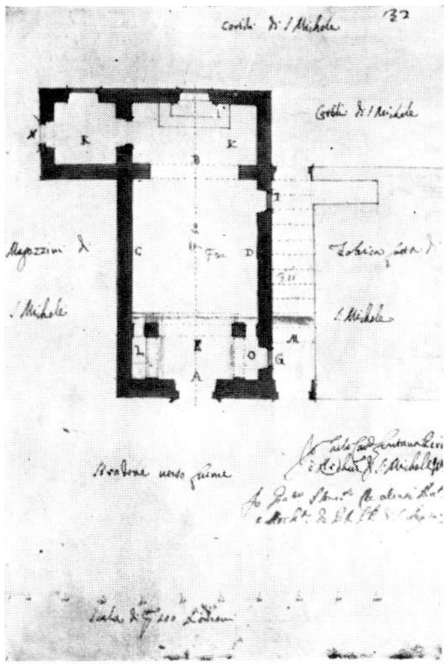

335 Madonna del Buon Viaggio (plan by Fontana)

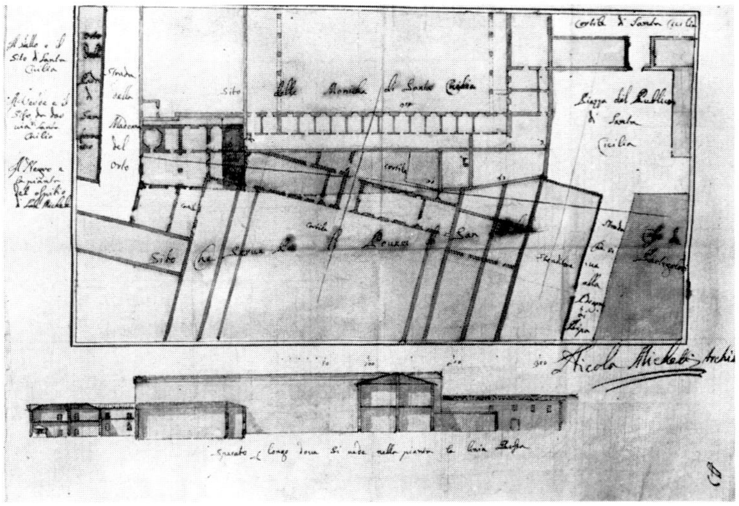

336 Project for the site to the north east of the Ospizio (drawing by Nicola Michetti; Rome, Archivio di Stato)

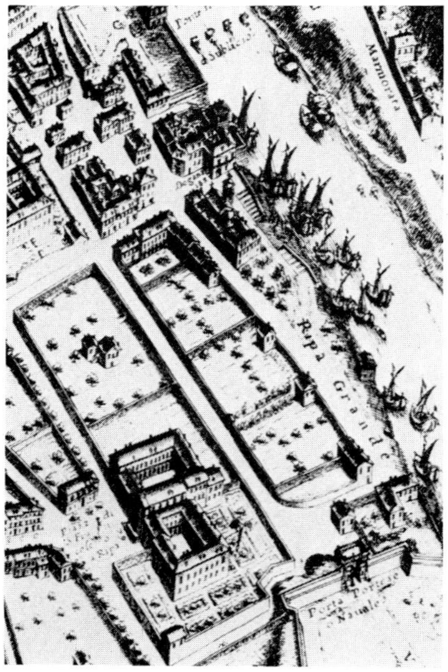

337 View of the site, 1676 (detail from the Falda plan of Rome)

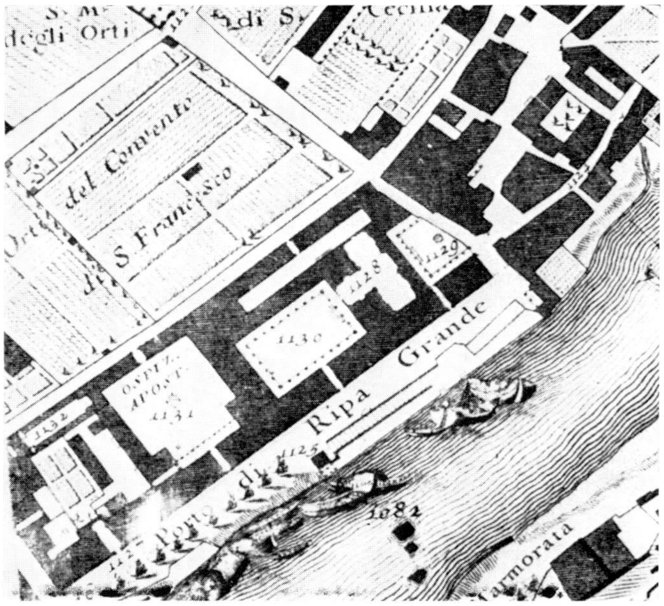

338 Plan of the Ospizio, 1748 (detail of the Nolli plan of Rome)

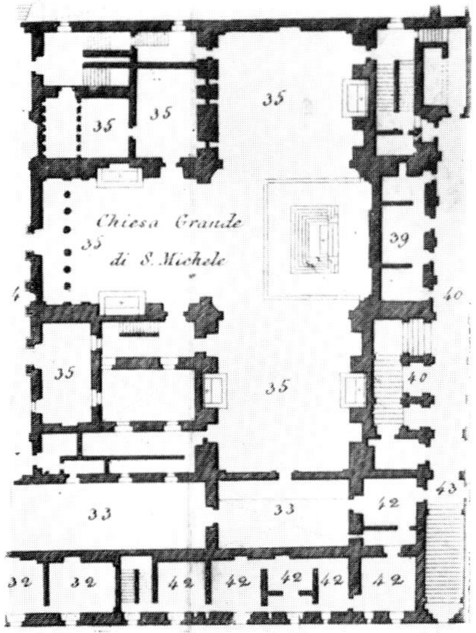

339 Plan of the church, 1832 (engraving from Tosti)

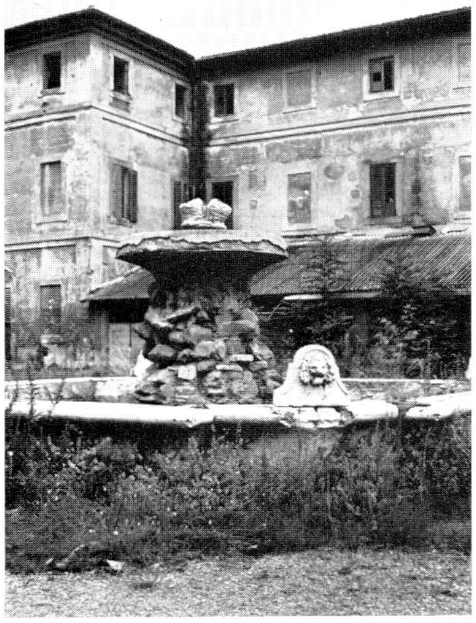

341 View of the fountain in the Cortile dei Ragazzi

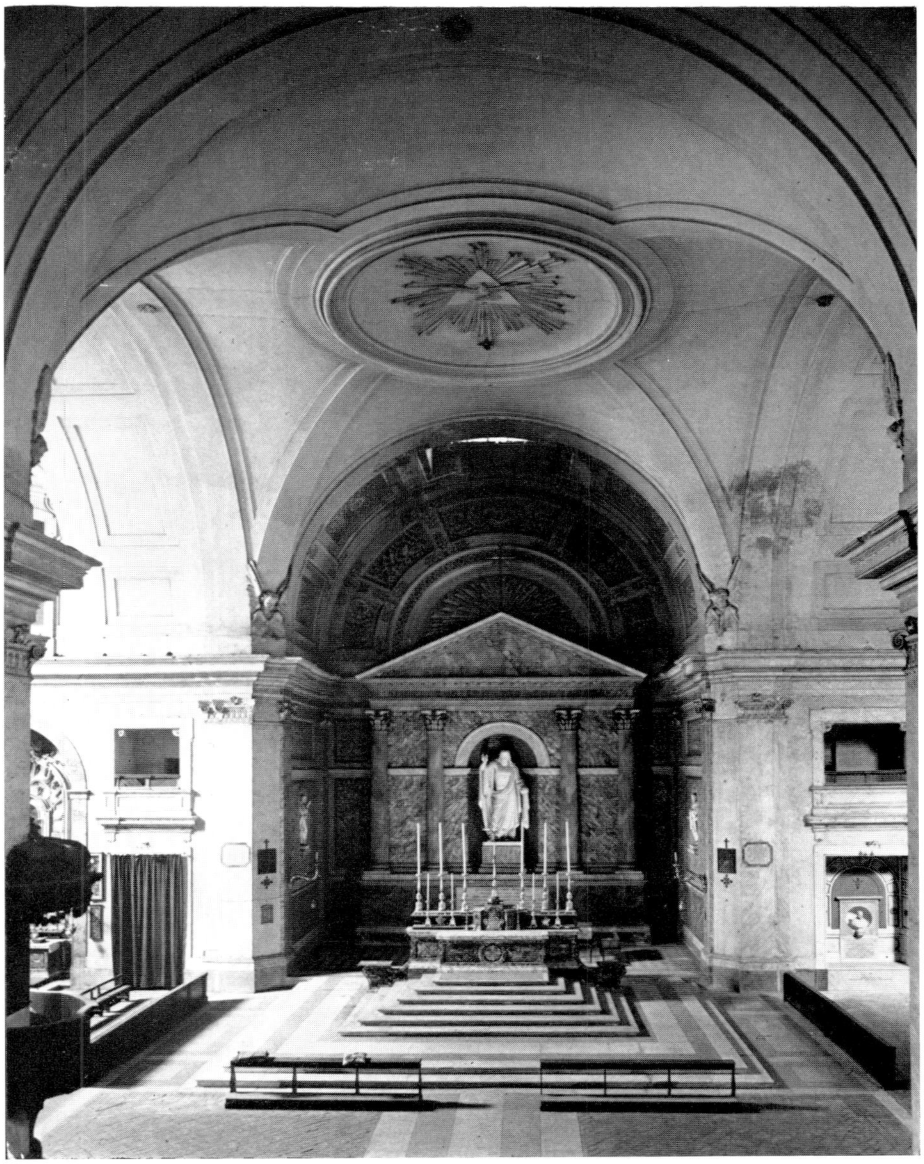

340 View of the interior of the church

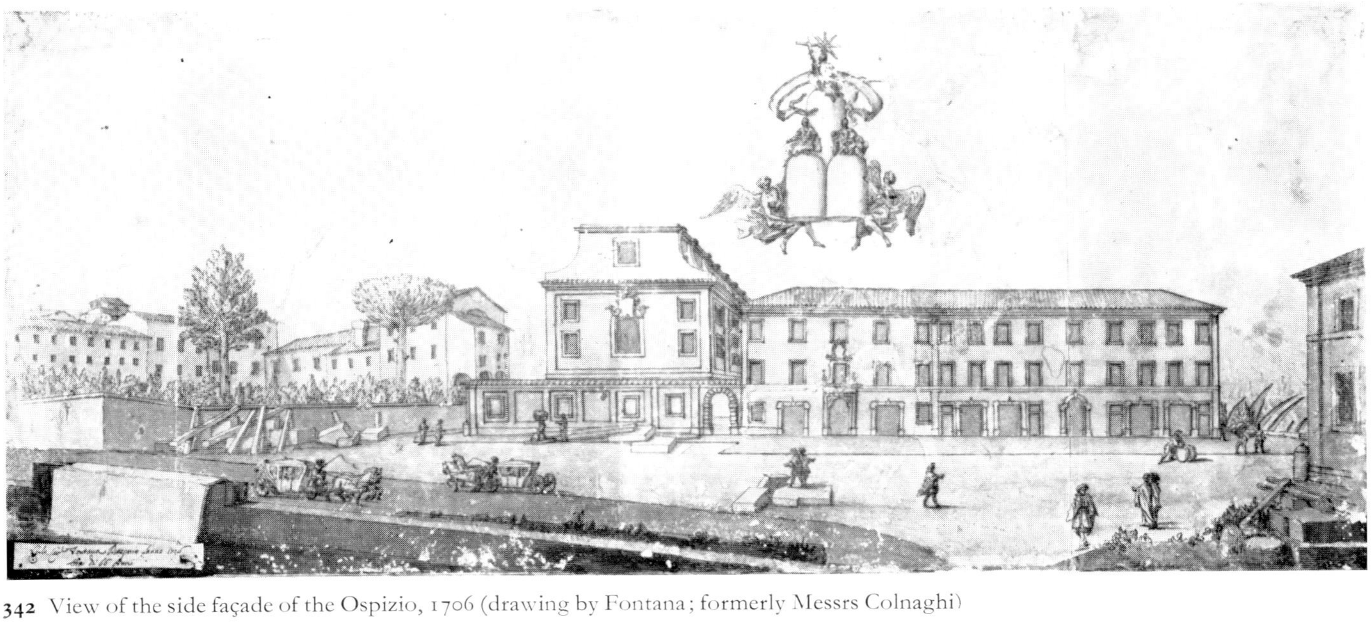

342 View of the side façade of the Ospizio, 1706 (drawing by Fontana; formerly Messrs Colnaghi)

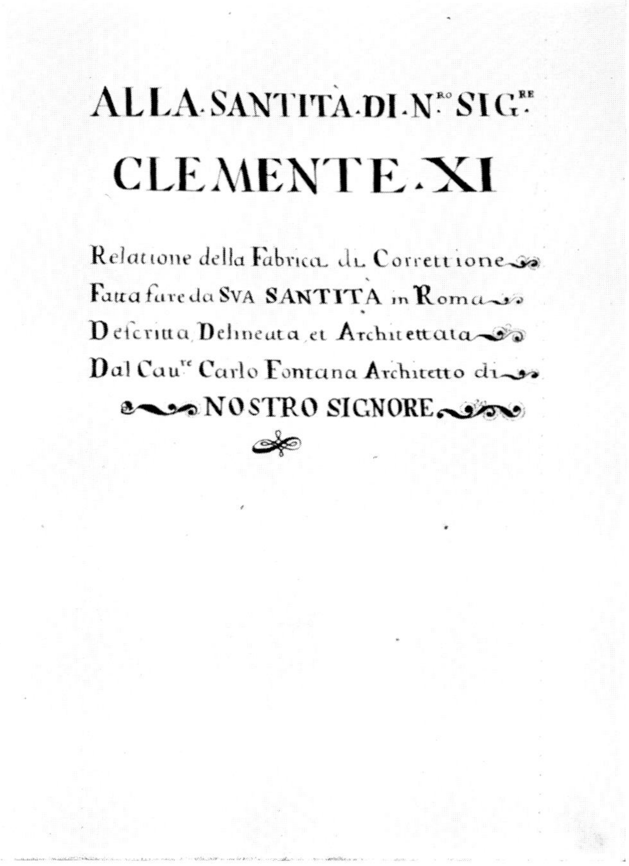

ALLA·SANTITÀ·DI·N.RO SIG.RE
CLEMENTE·XI
Relatione della Fabrica di Correttione
Fatta fare da SVA SANTITÀ in Roma
Descritta Delineata et Architettata
Dal Cav.re Carlo Fontana Architetto di
NOSTRO SIGNORE

343 Title page of Windsor Volume 181

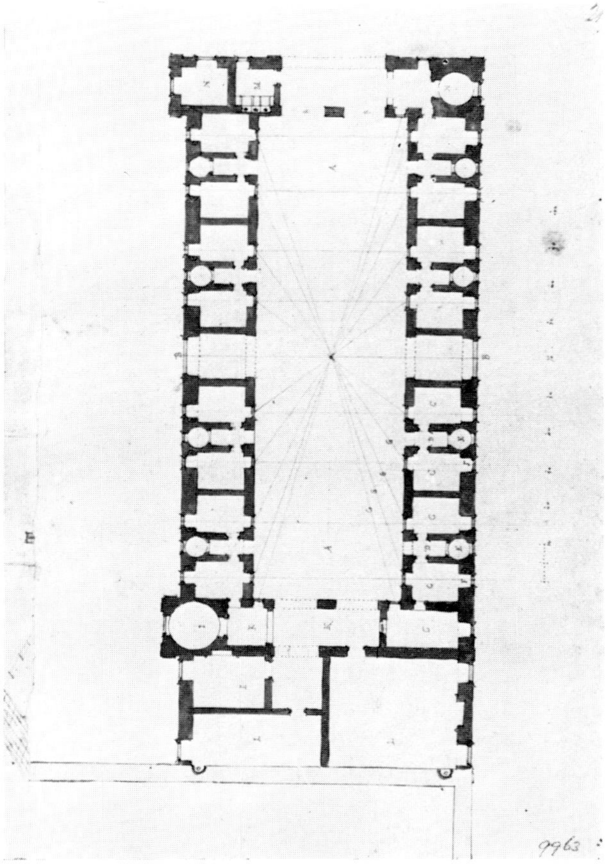

344 First (prison) floor plan, first project (no.397)

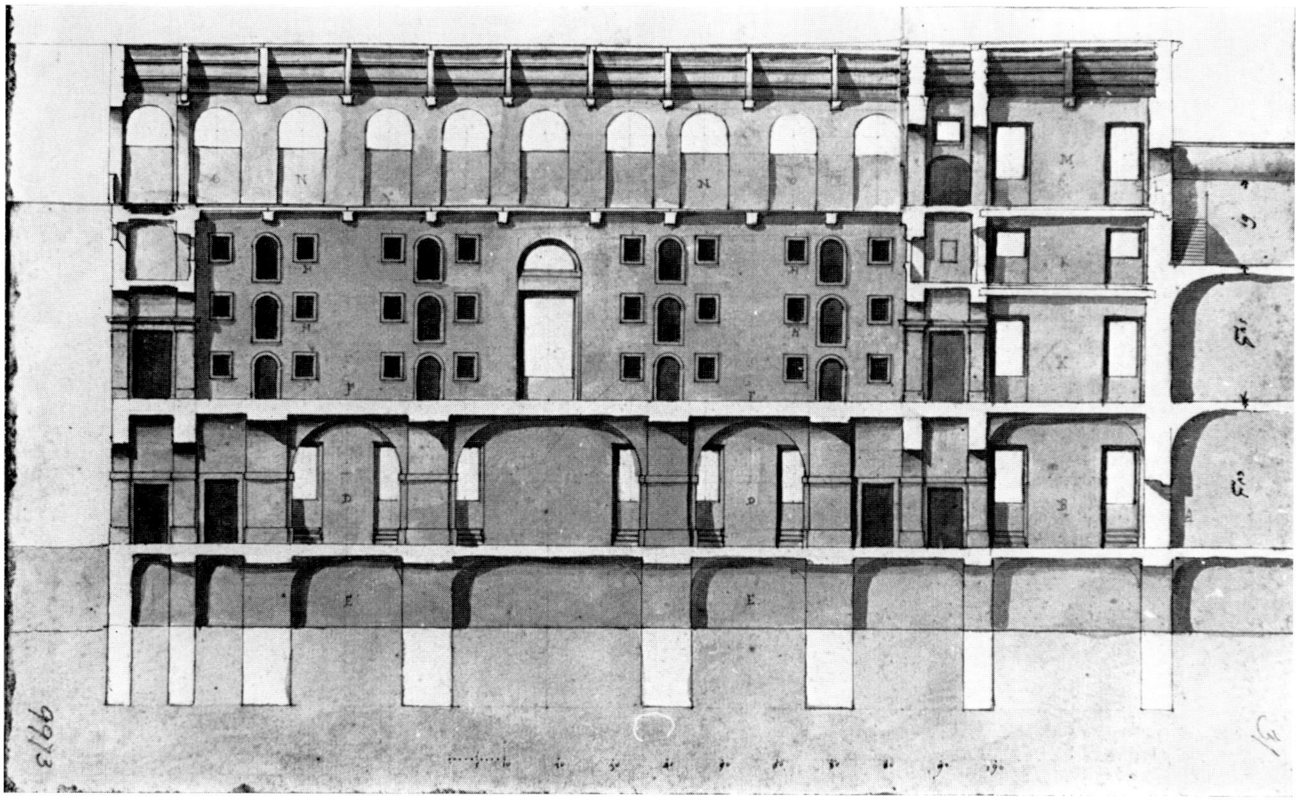

345 Longitudinal section, first project (no.401)

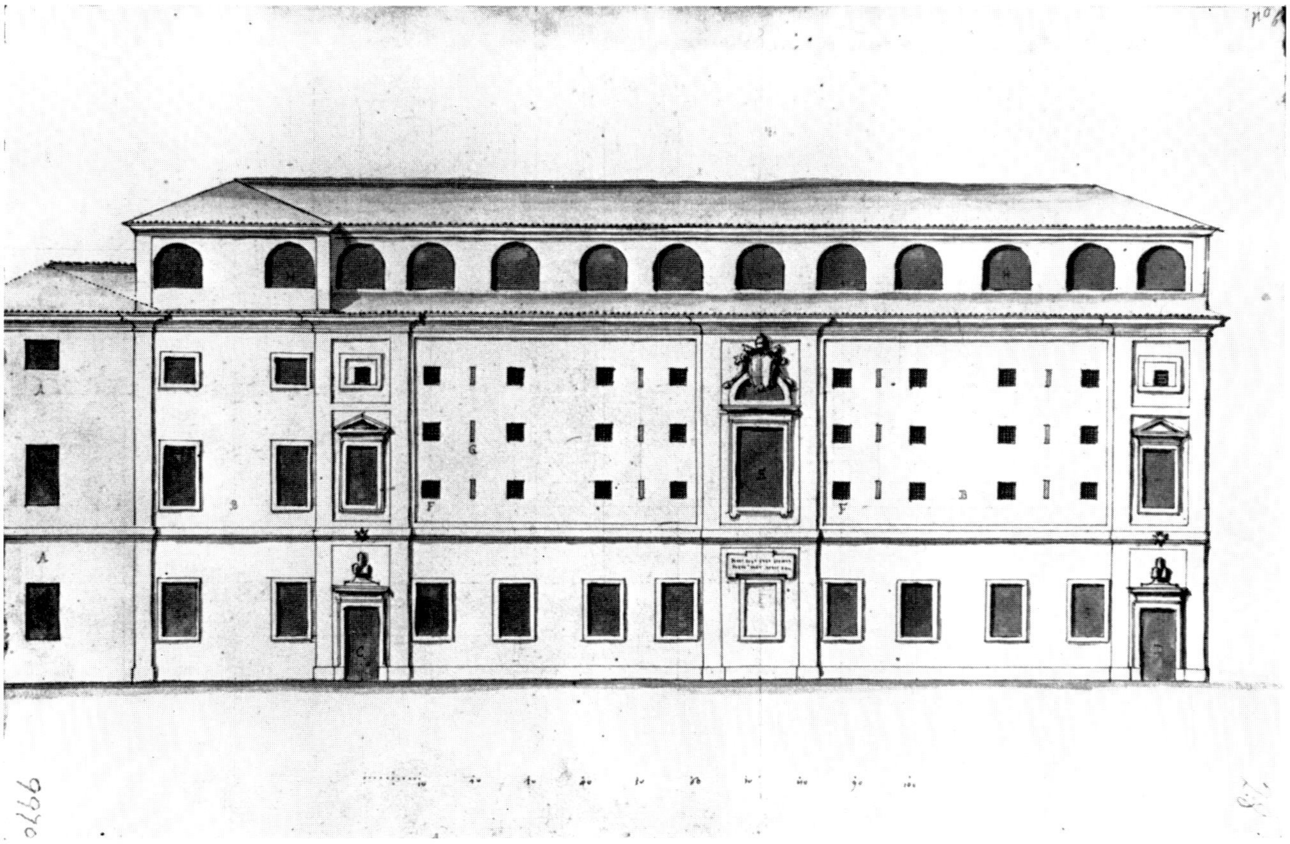

346 Street elevation, first project (no.402)

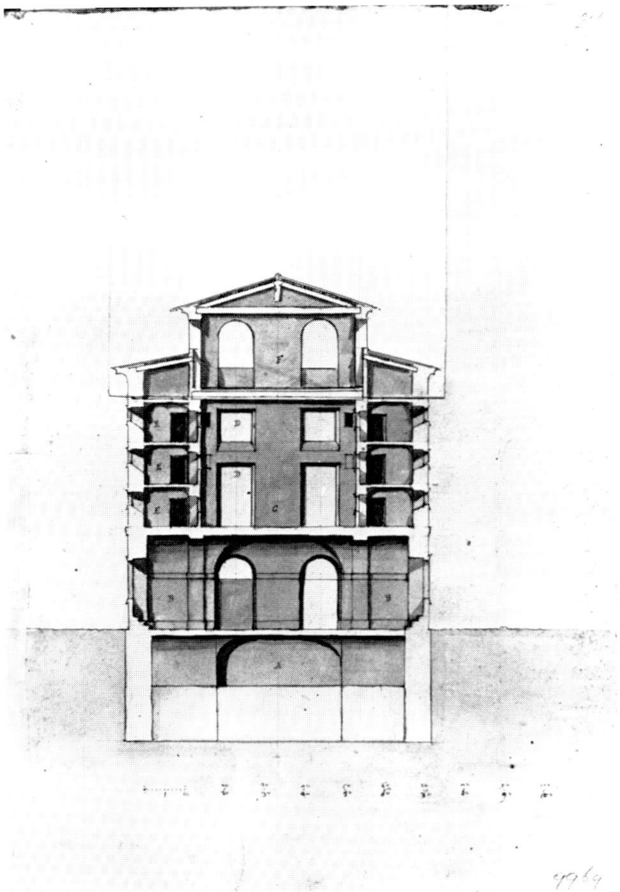

347 Transverse section, first project (no.400)

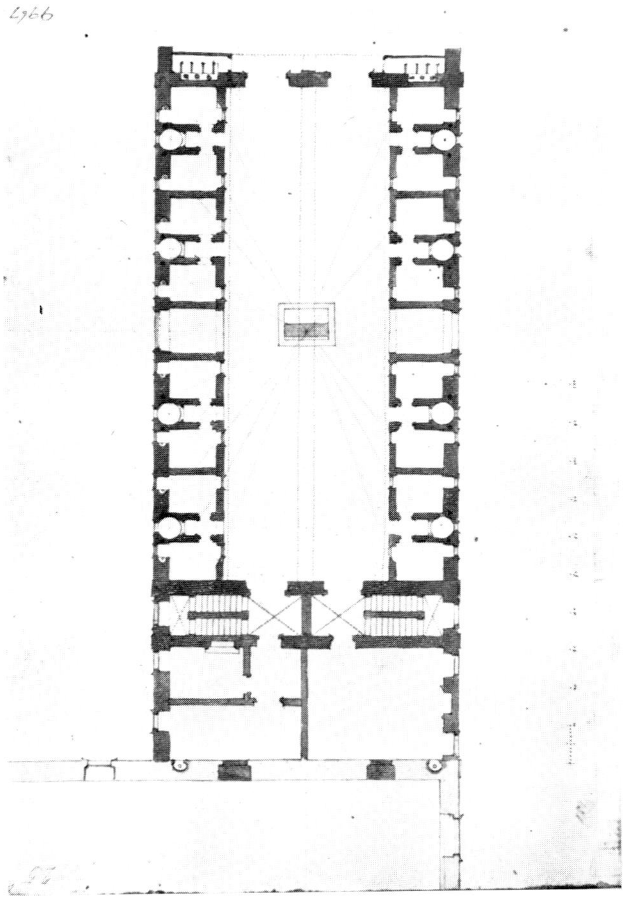

348 First (prison) floor plan, second project (no.405)

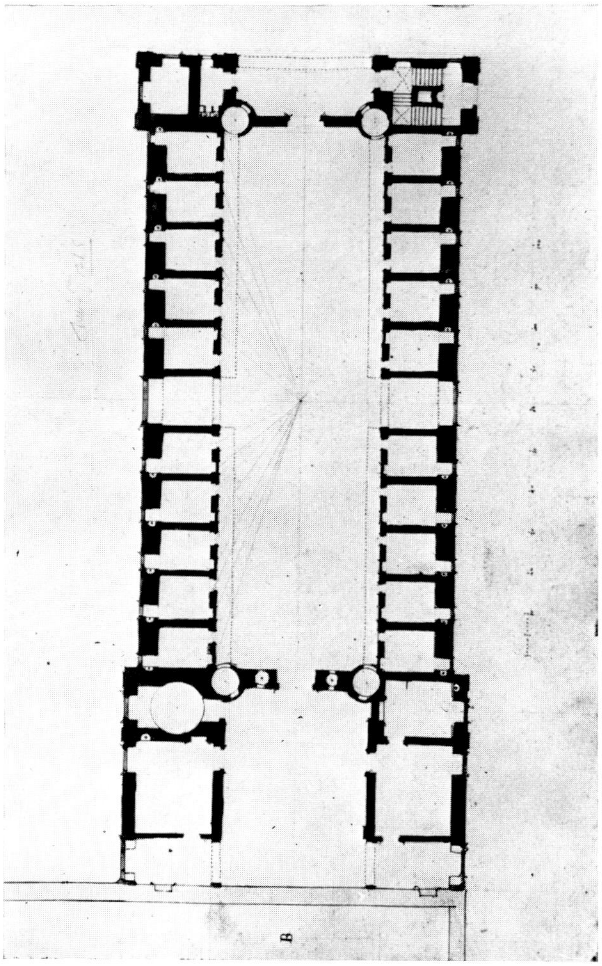

349 First (prison) floor plan, third project, B (no.409)

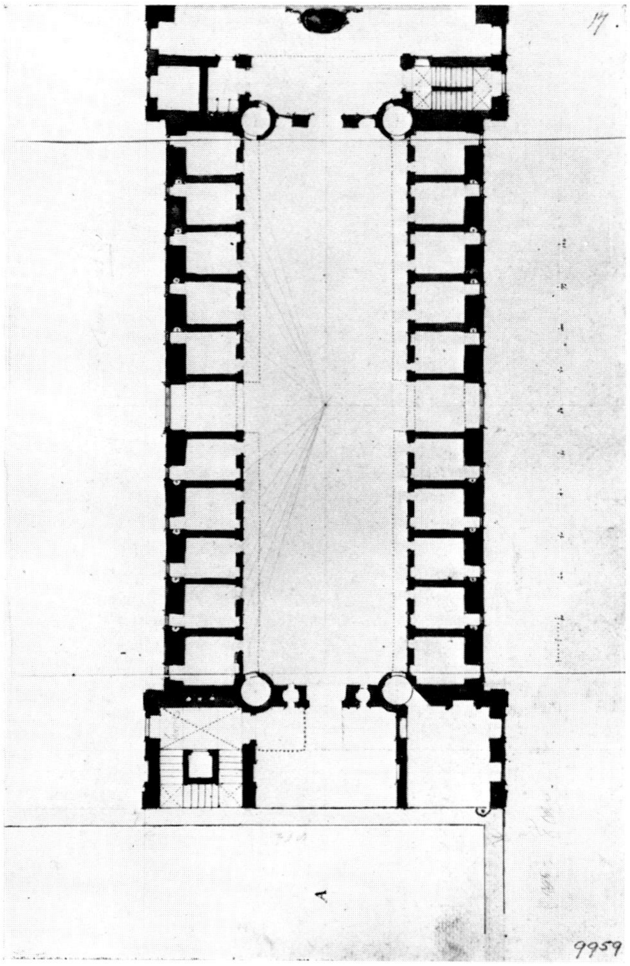

350 First (prison) floor plan, third project, A (no.409)

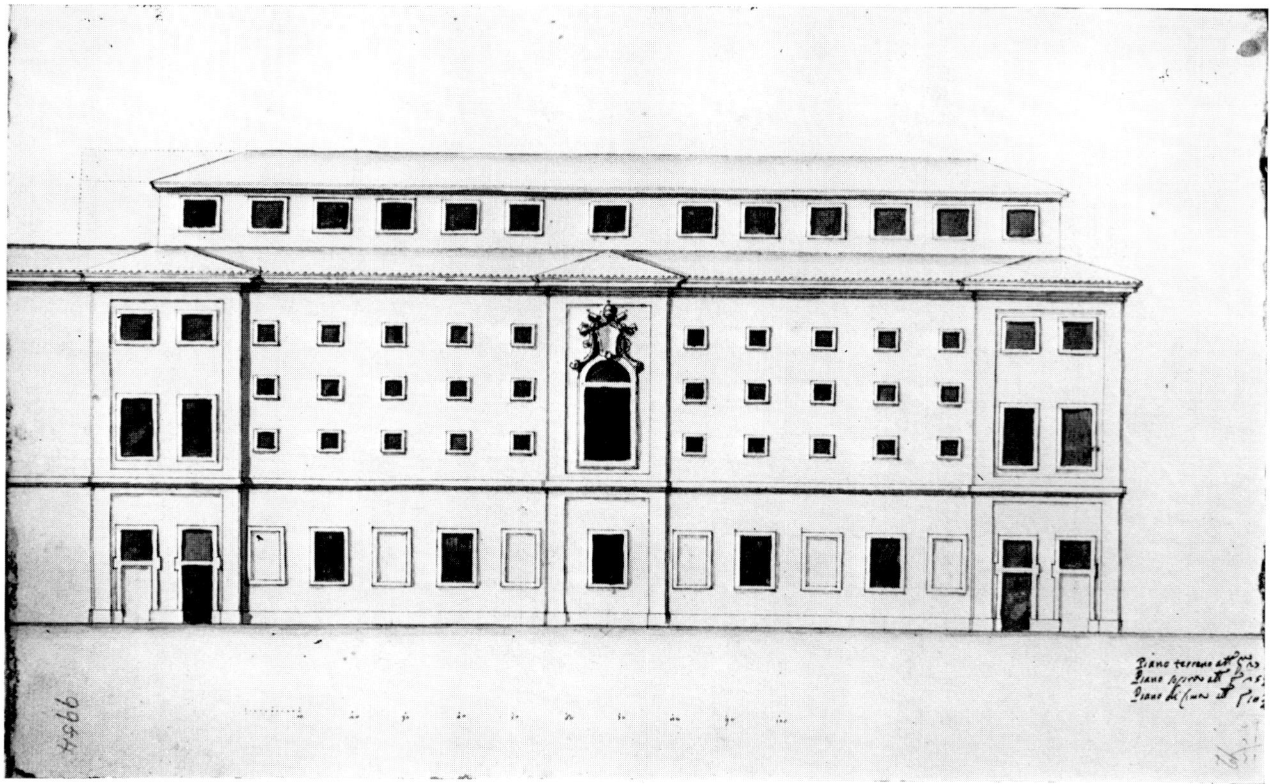

351 Street elevation, third project, A (no.412)

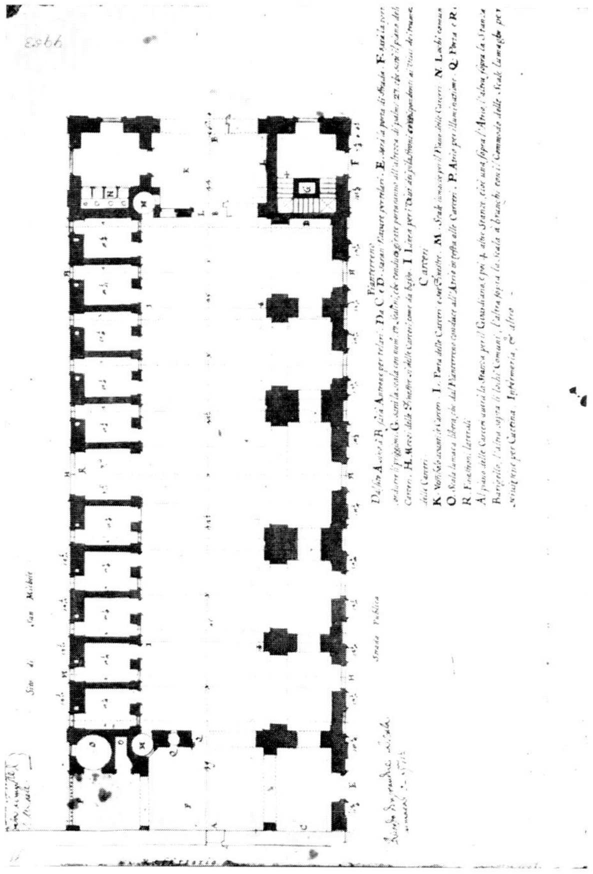

352 Ground and first (prison) floor plan, fourth project (no.415)

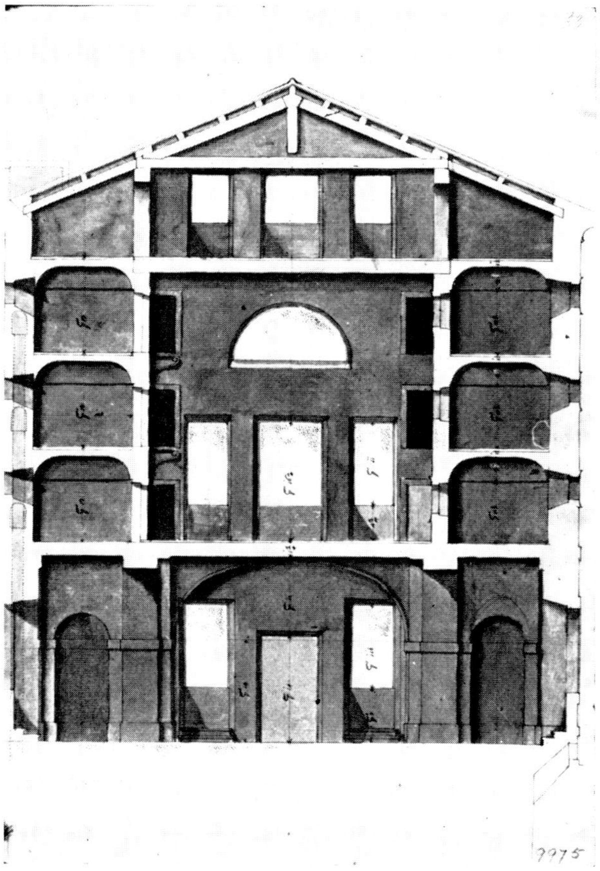

353 Transverse section, fourth project (no.417)

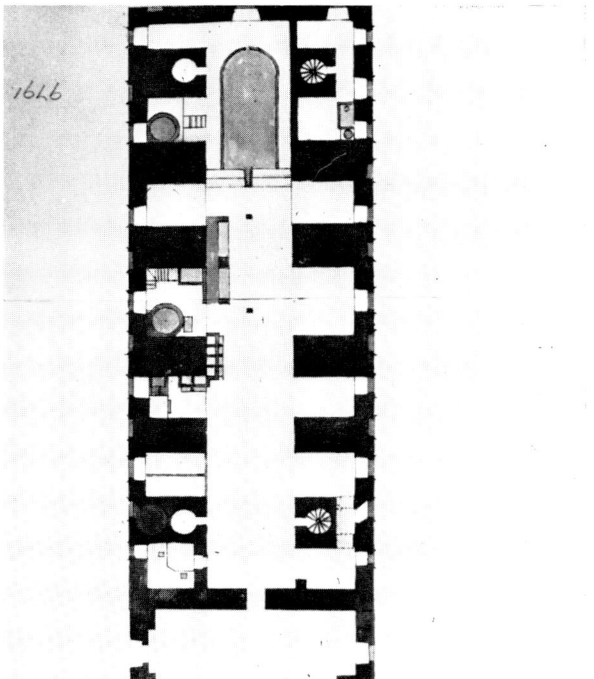

354 Basement plan, final project (no.420)

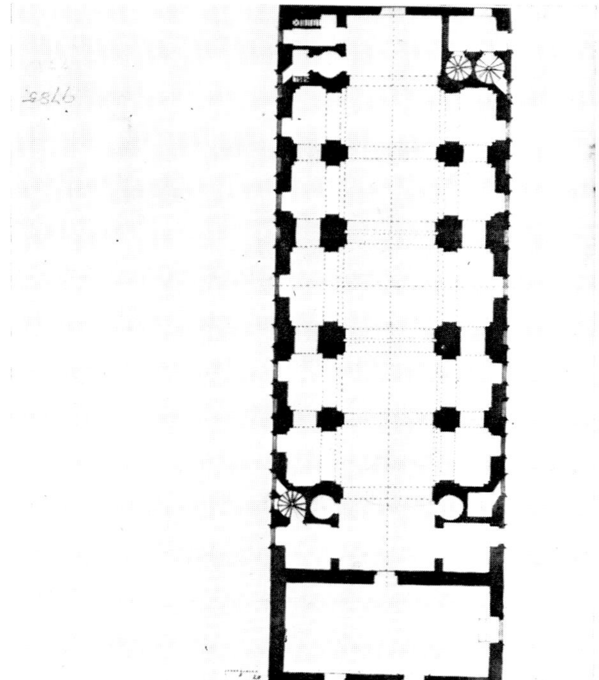

355 Ground-floor plan, final project (no.422)

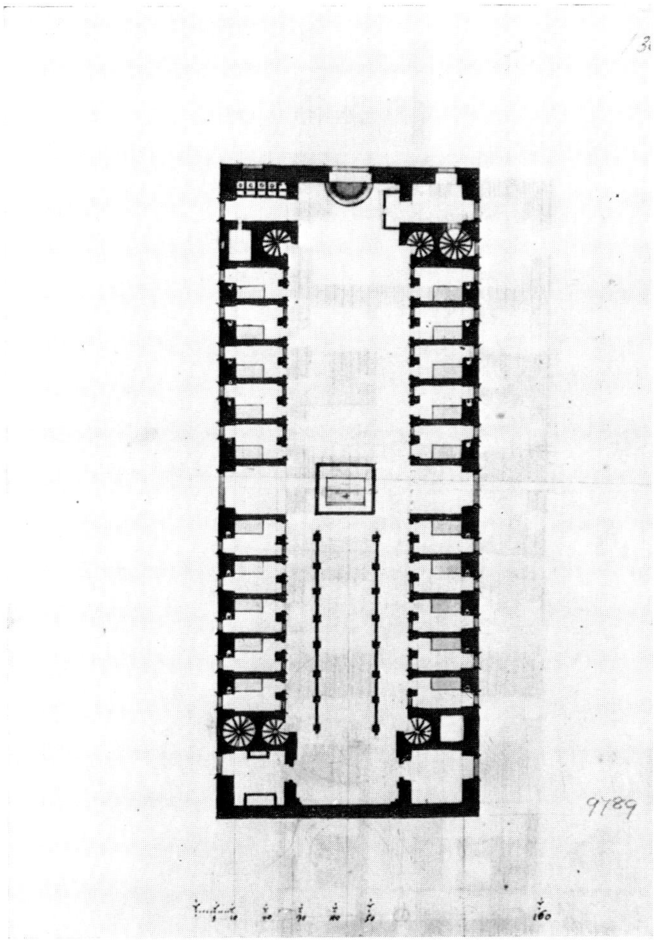

356 First (prison) floor plan, final project (no.424)

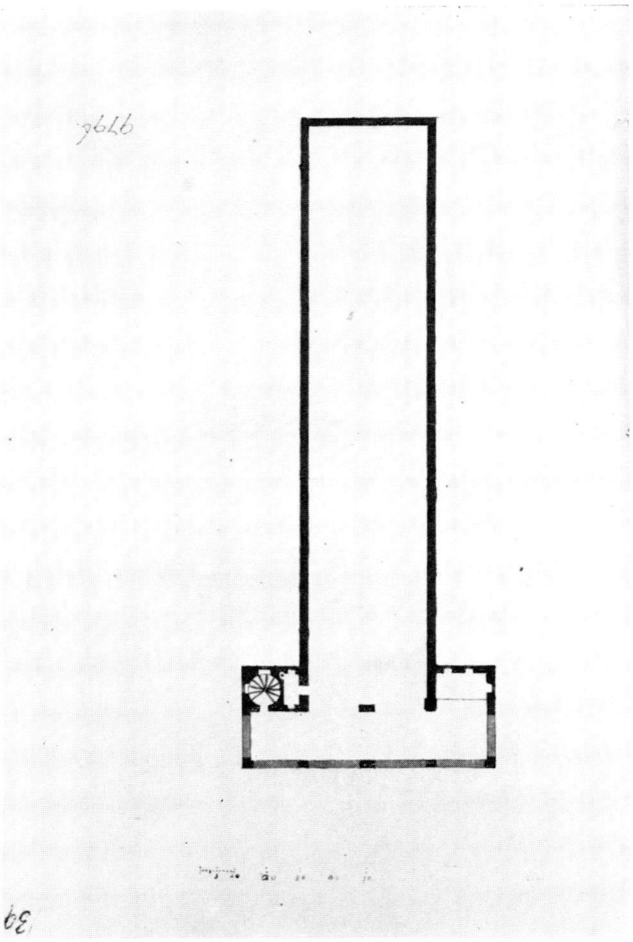

357 Plan of the loggia, final project (no.425)

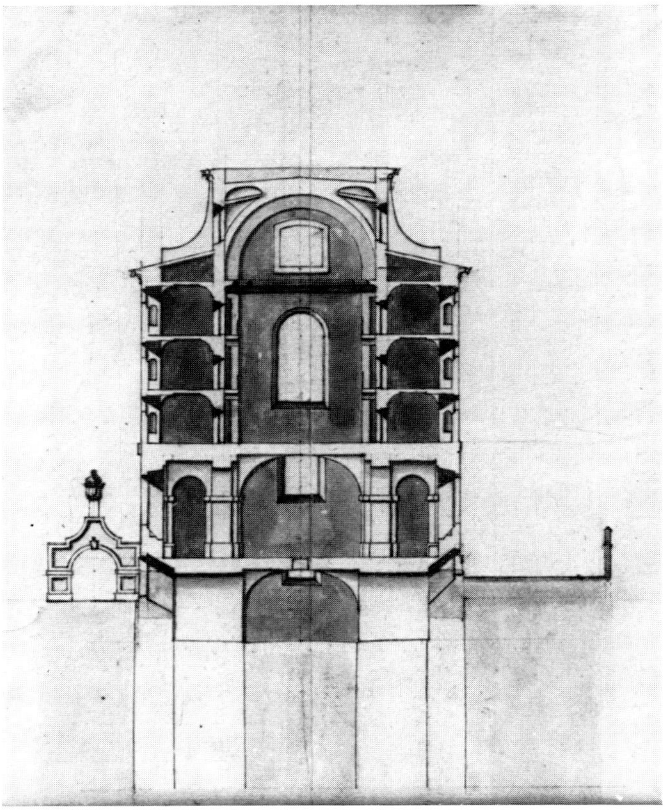

358 Transverse section, final project (detail of no.426)

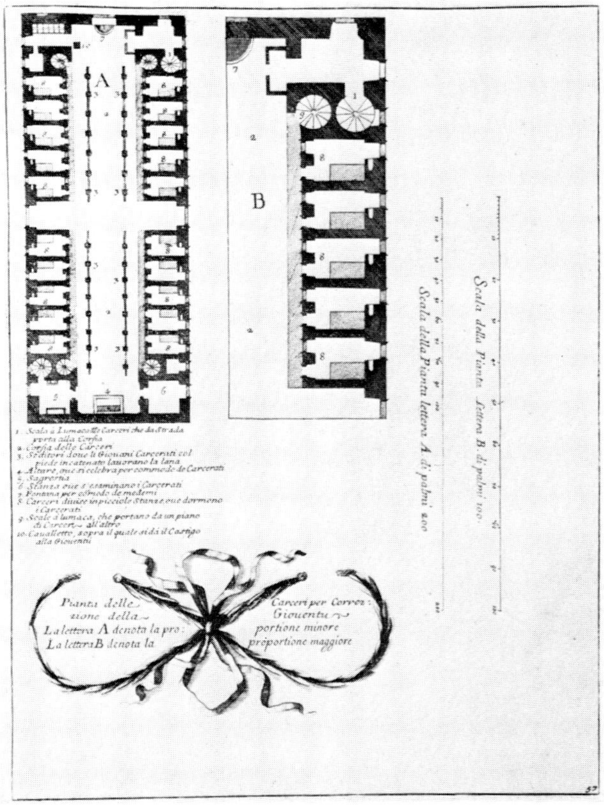

359 First-floor plan, with detail (engraving from de' Rossi, 1721)

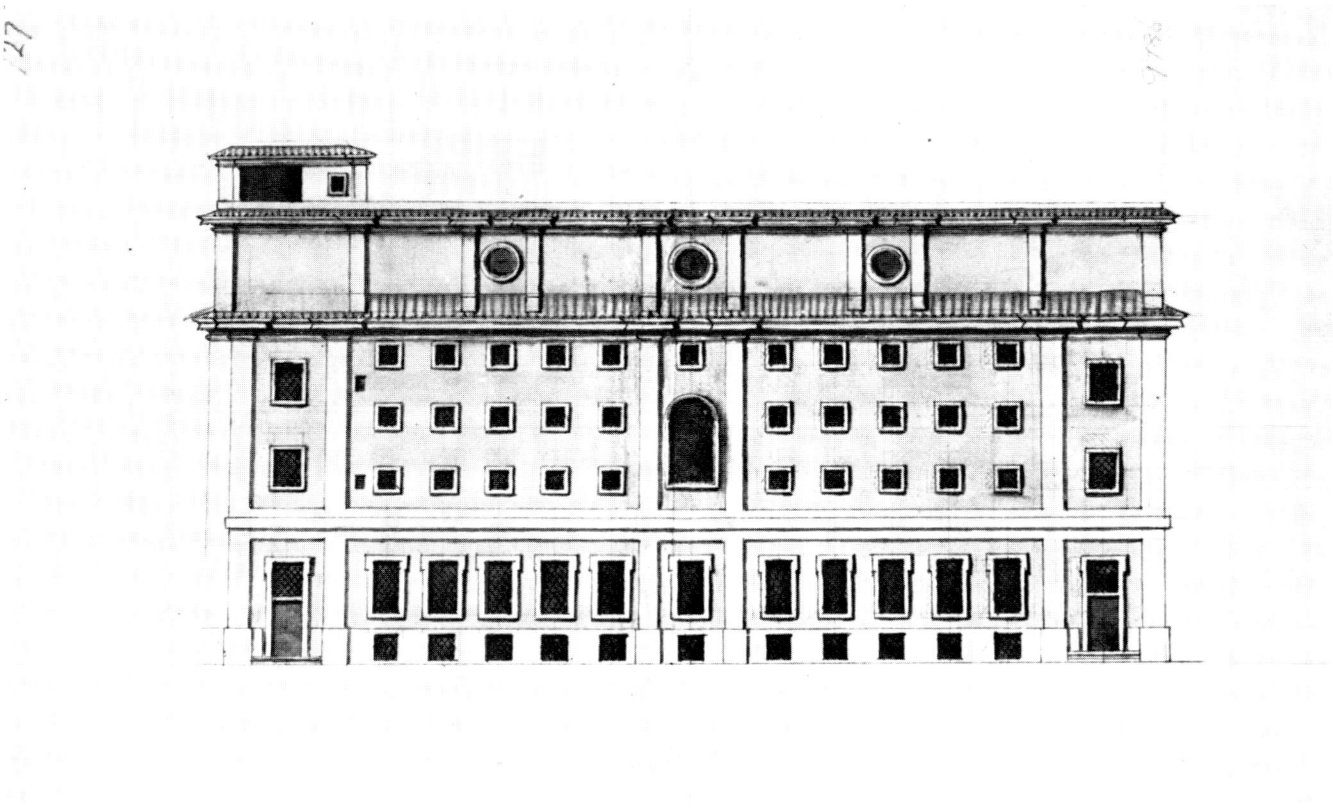

360 Street elevation, final project (no.427)

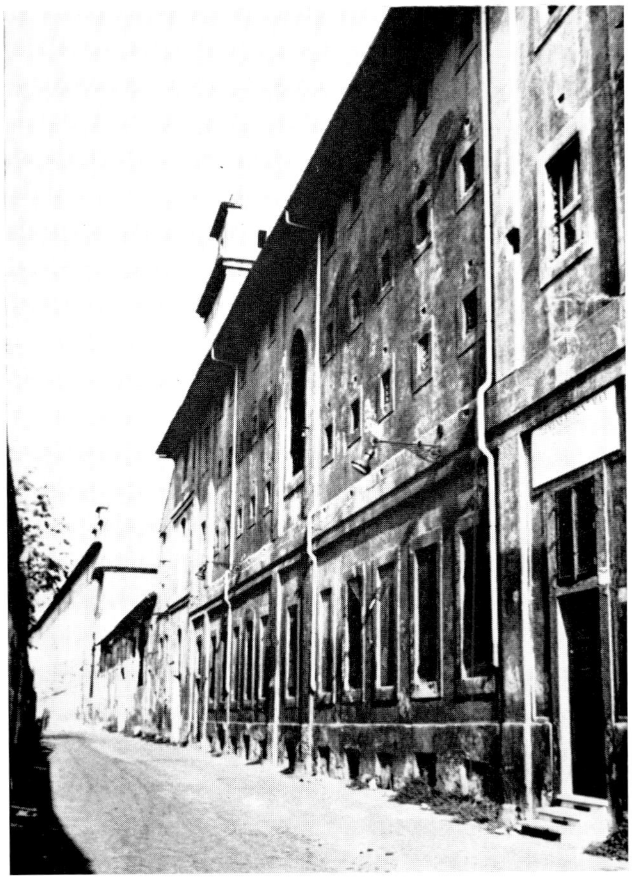

361 View of the street façade

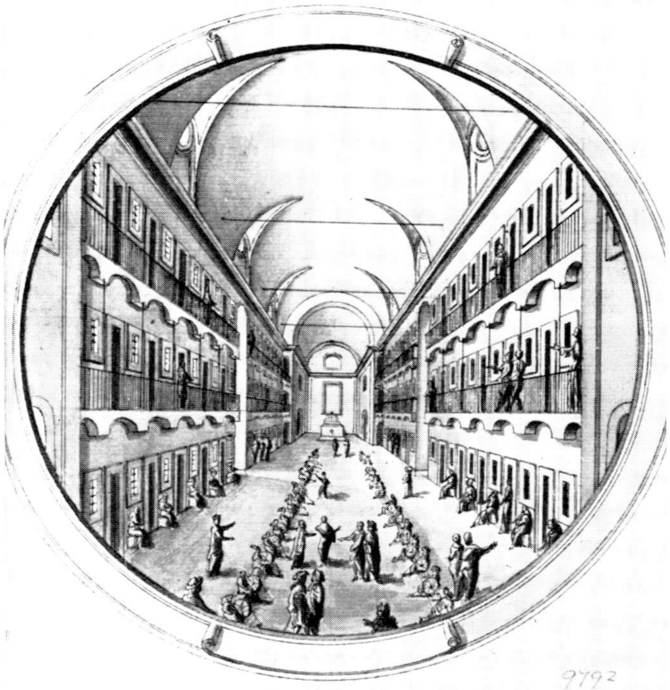

362 Perspective view inside the prison: design for a medal (no.429)

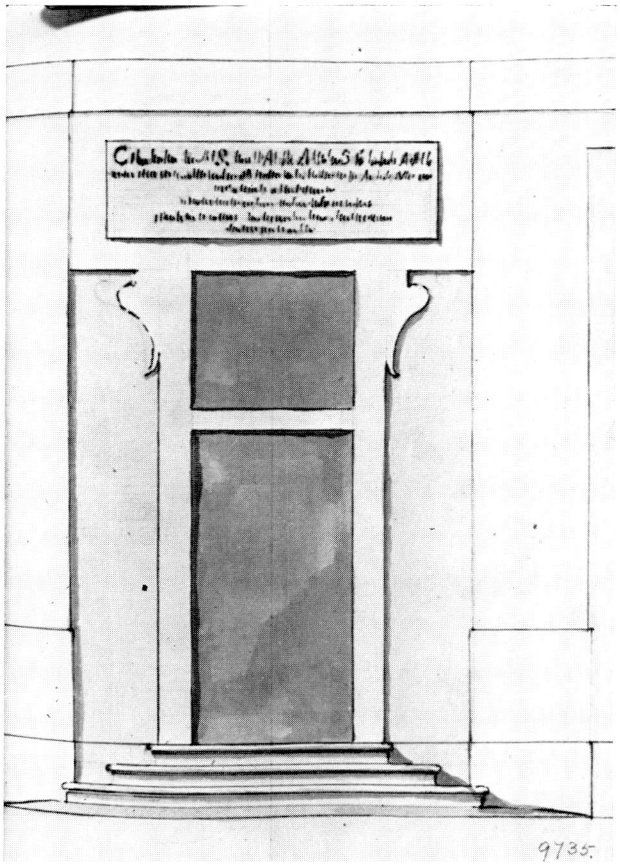

363 Elevation of the street doorway (no.431)

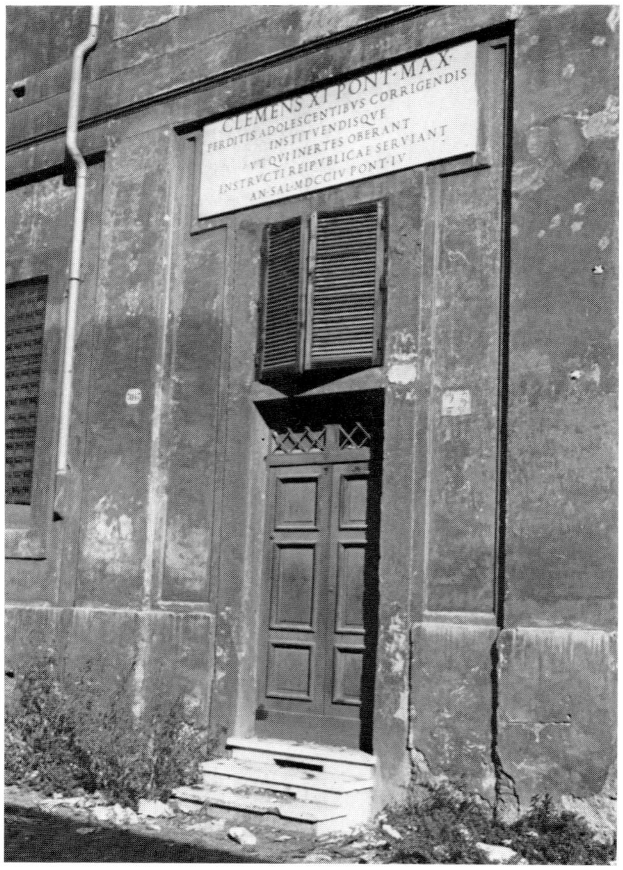

364 View of the street doorway

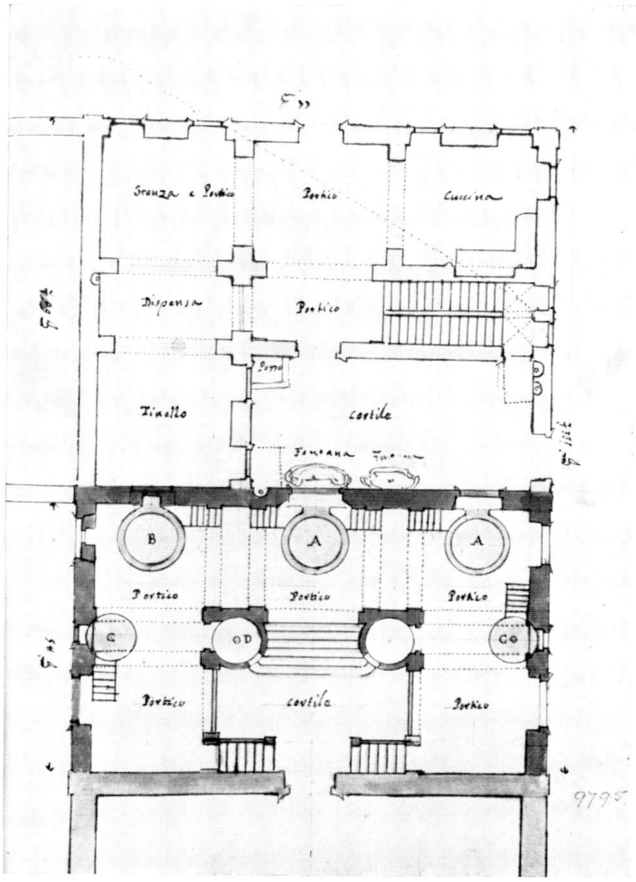

365 Annexe to the prison, ground-floor plan (no.432)

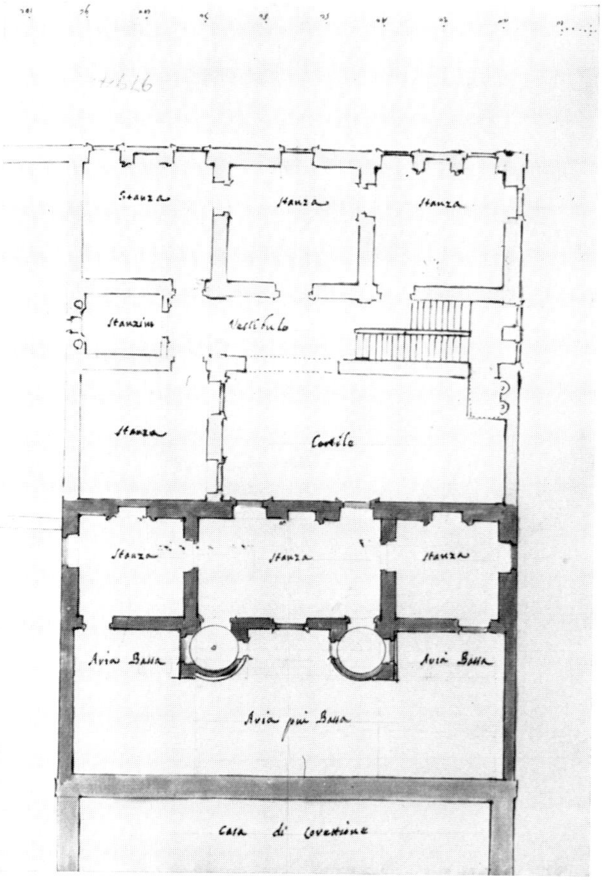

366 Annexe to the prison, first-floor plan (no.433)

The south-west corner of the Ospizio di S. Michele (1704)

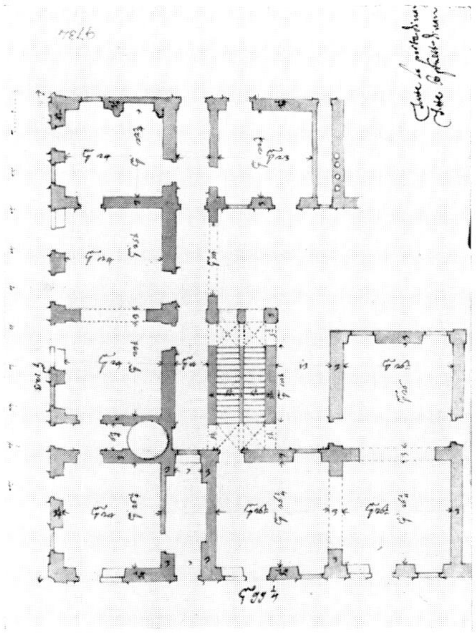

367 Ground-floor plan, first project (no.347)

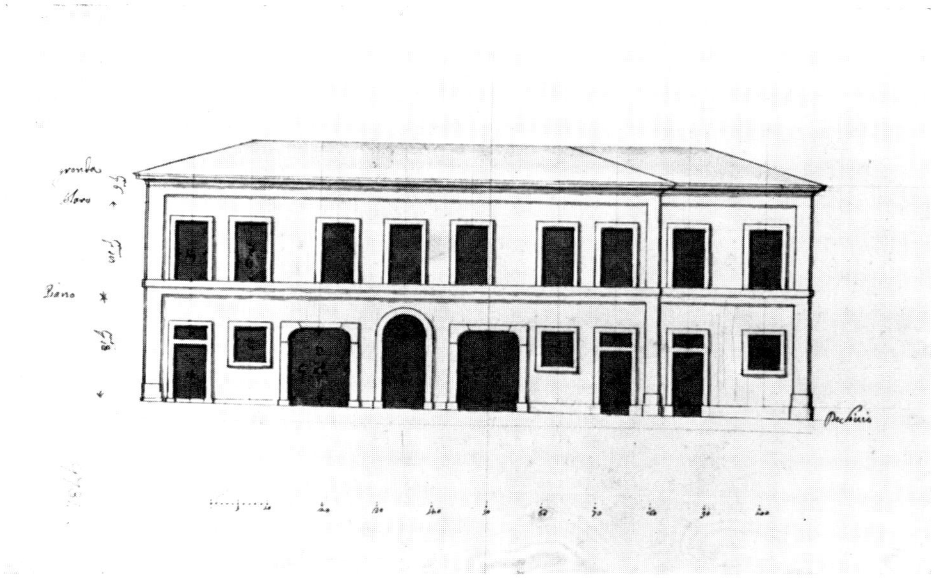

368 Elevation facing the Dogana, first project (no.440)

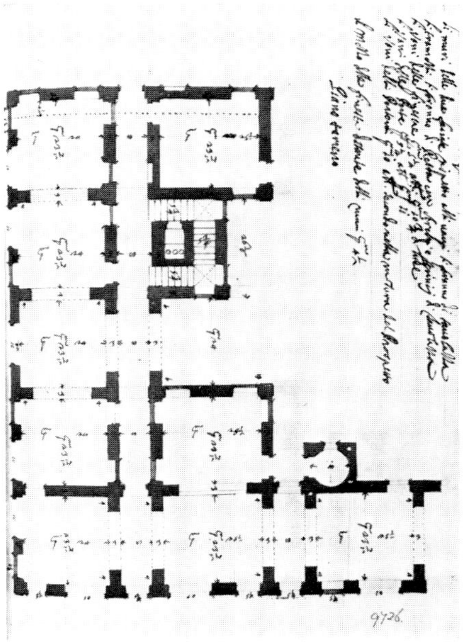

369 Ground-floor plan, second project (no.444)

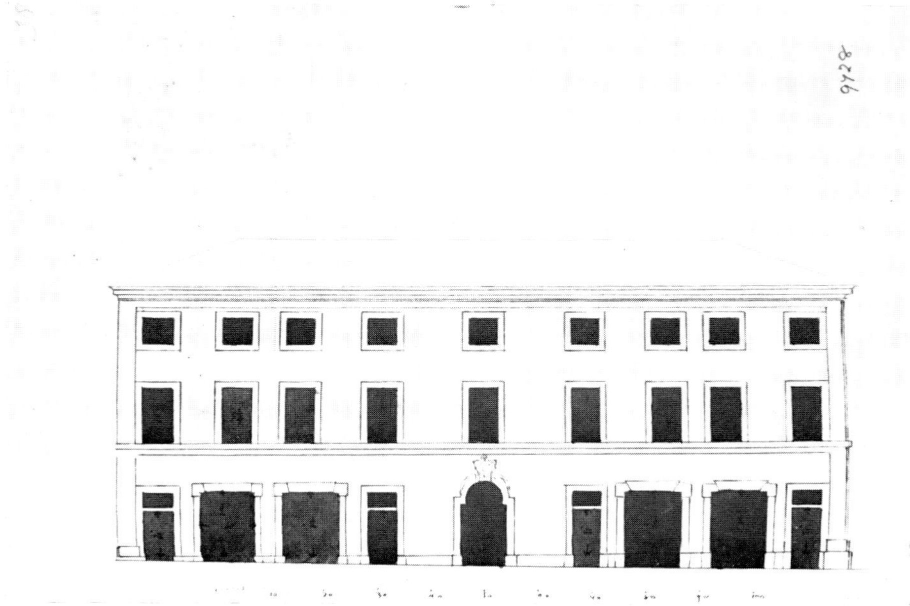

370 Elevation facing the Dogana, second project (no.447)

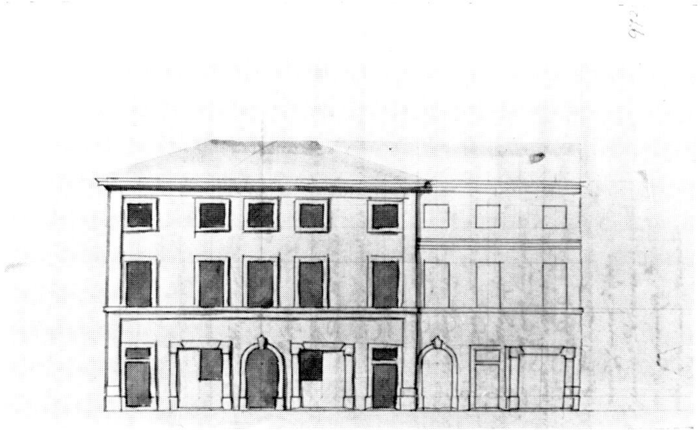

371 Elevation overlooking the river, second project (no.448)

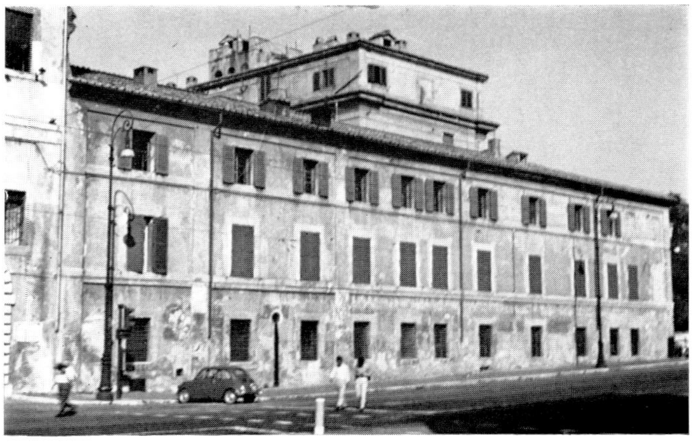

372 View of the south-west corner of the Ospizio

Fontana's coat-of-arms (1702?)

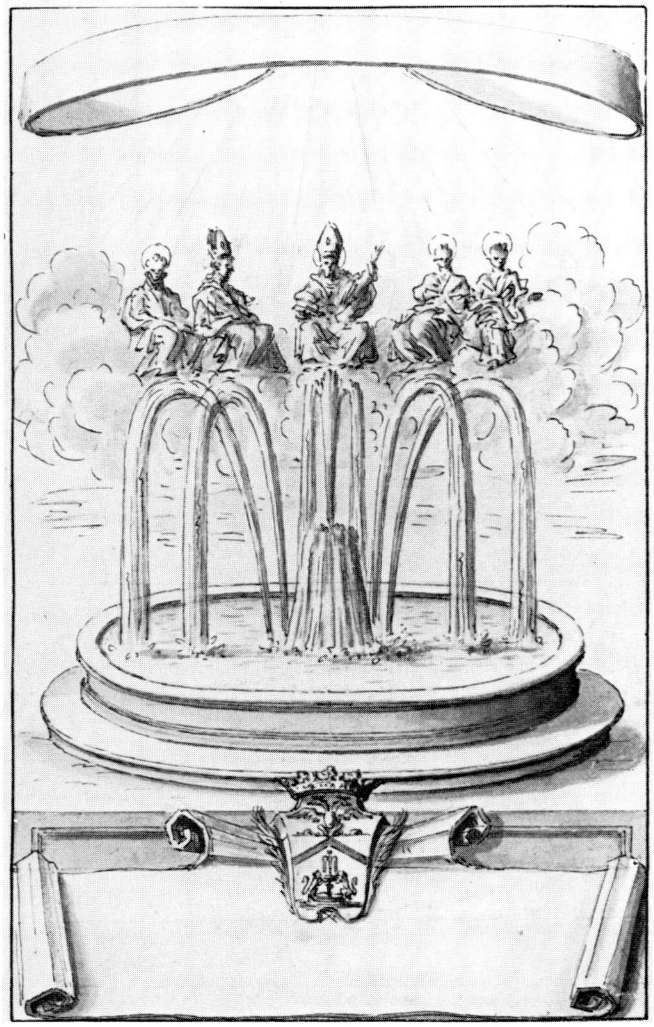

373 Design for the coat-of-arms (no.449)

A survey drawing of the Palazzo del Senatore (1703)

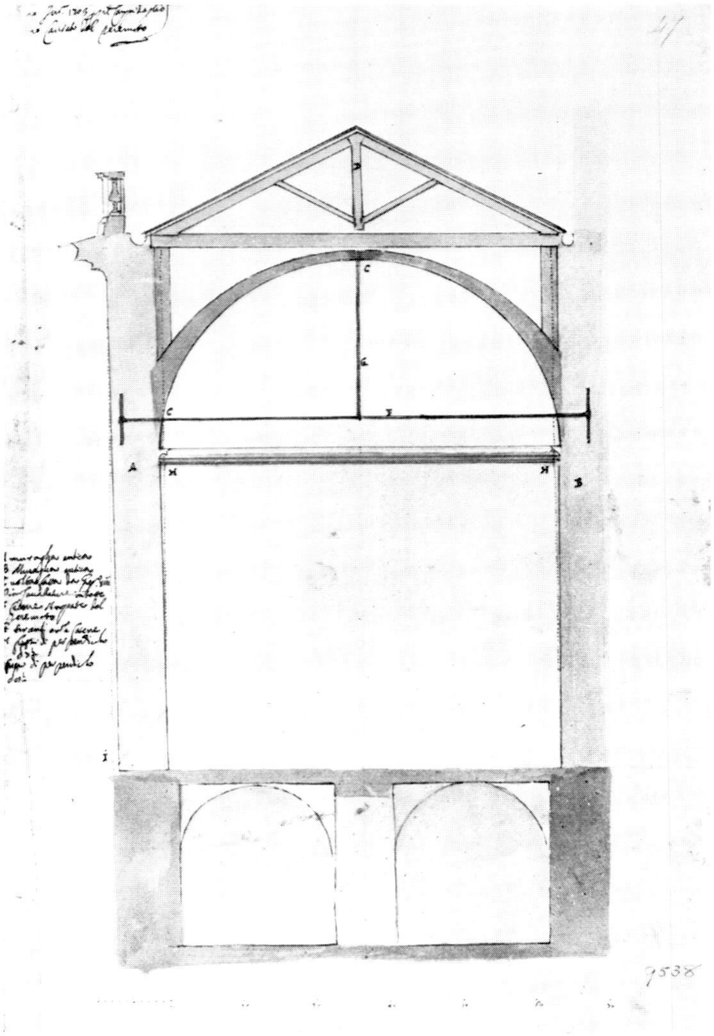

374 Section of the palace, recording damage by earthquake (no.450)

Project for the Porto di Ripetta (1703)

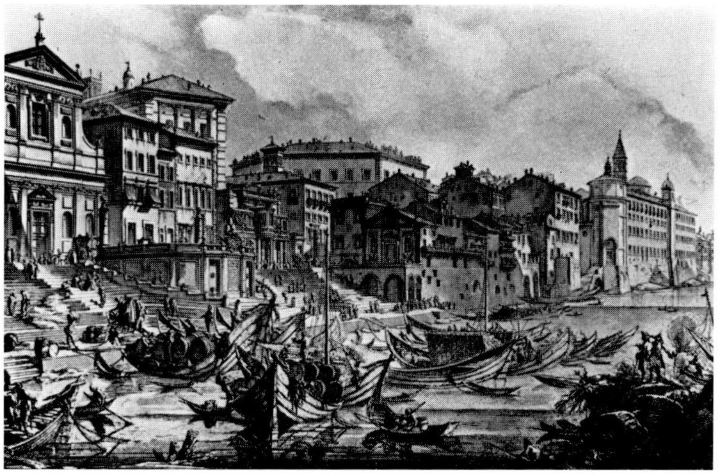

375 View of the port (engraving by Piranesi)

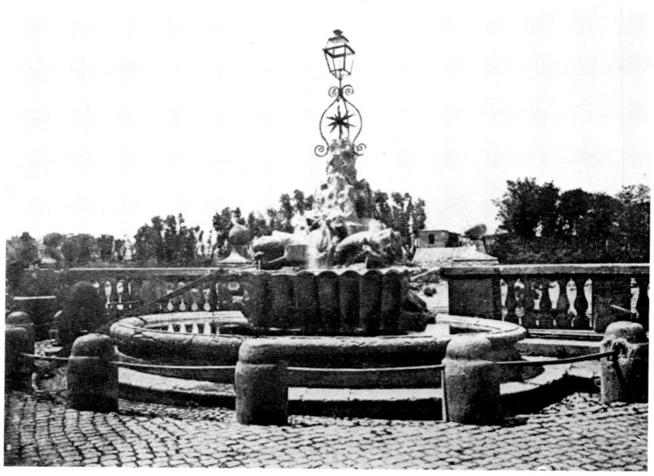

376 View of the fountain (photograph, *c.*1926, before demolition)

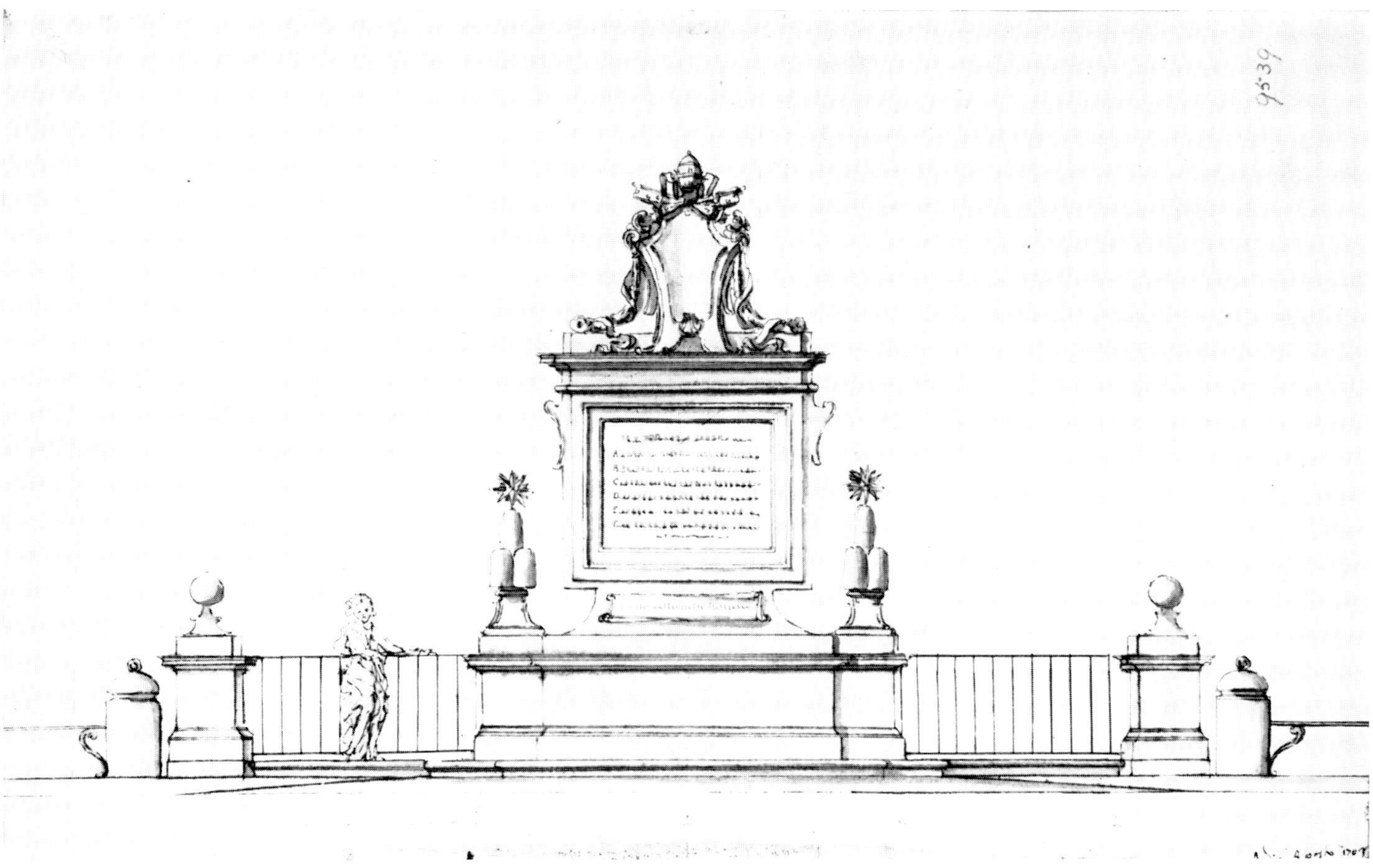

377 Elevation of the parapet (no.451)

The Granary, near the Baths of Diocletian (1703–1705)

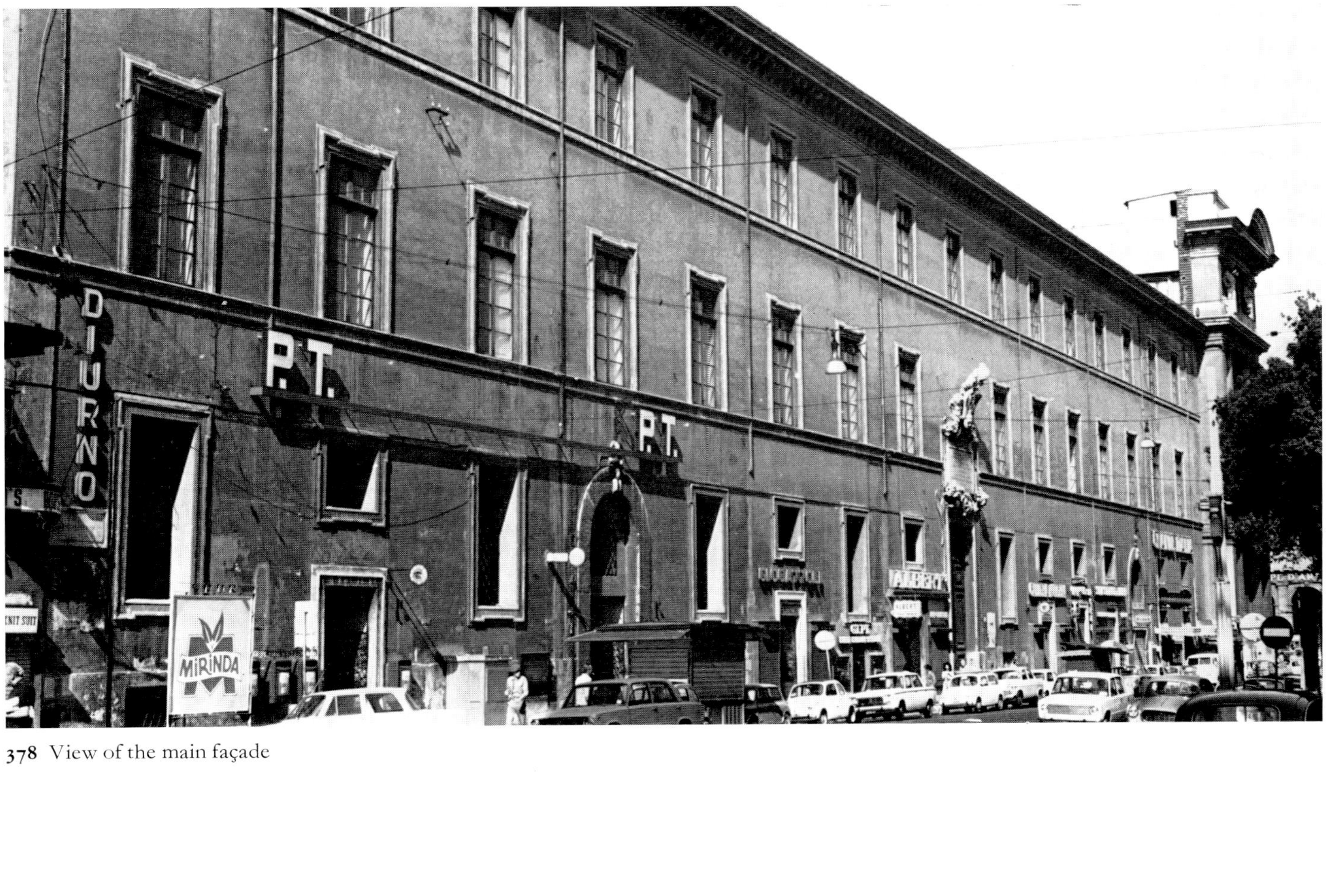

378 View of the main façade

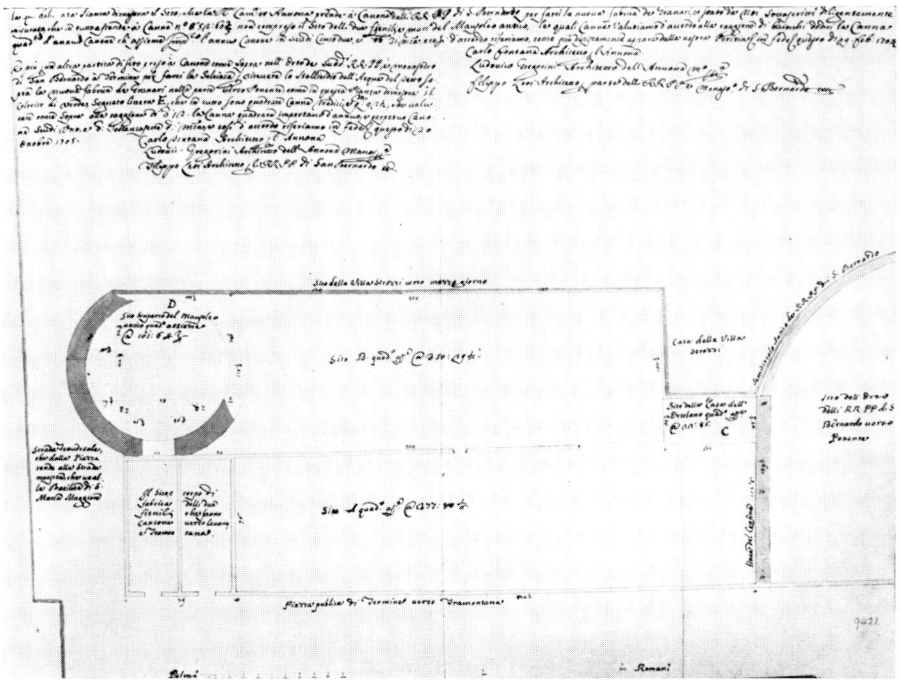

379 Plan of the site (no.452)

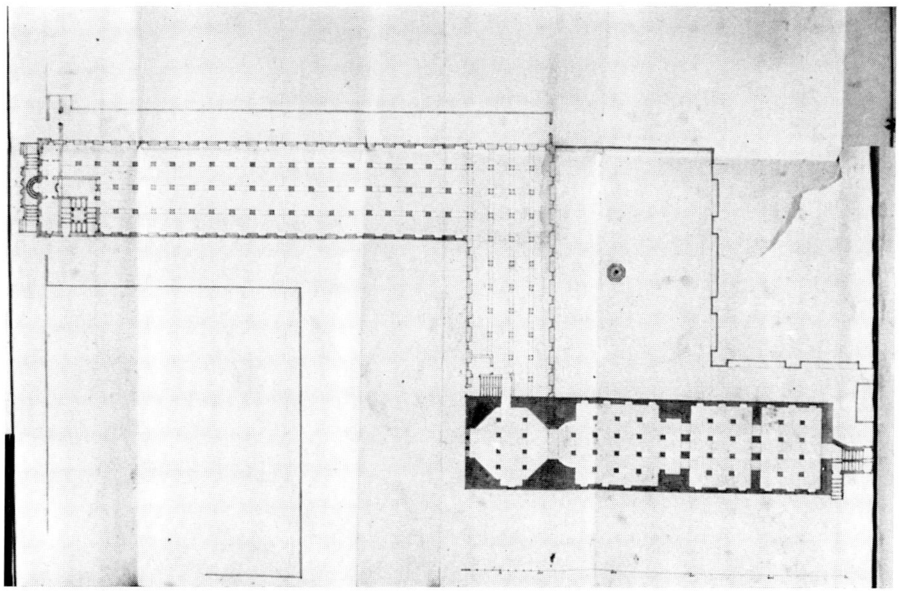

380 Plan of the old granaries (anon. drawing; no.453)

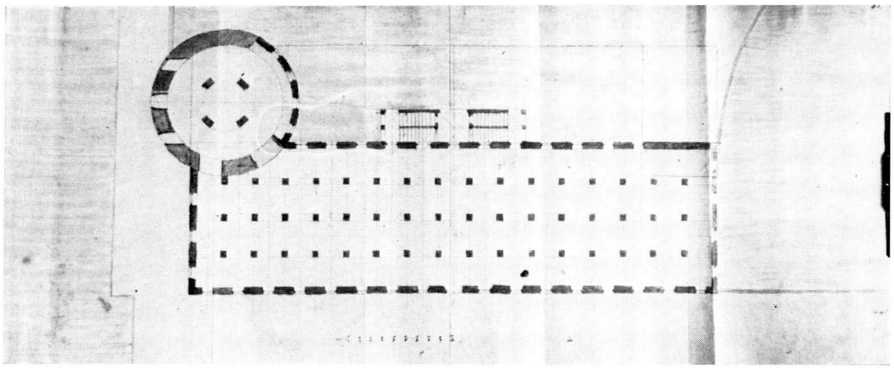

381 Plan, first project (no.454)

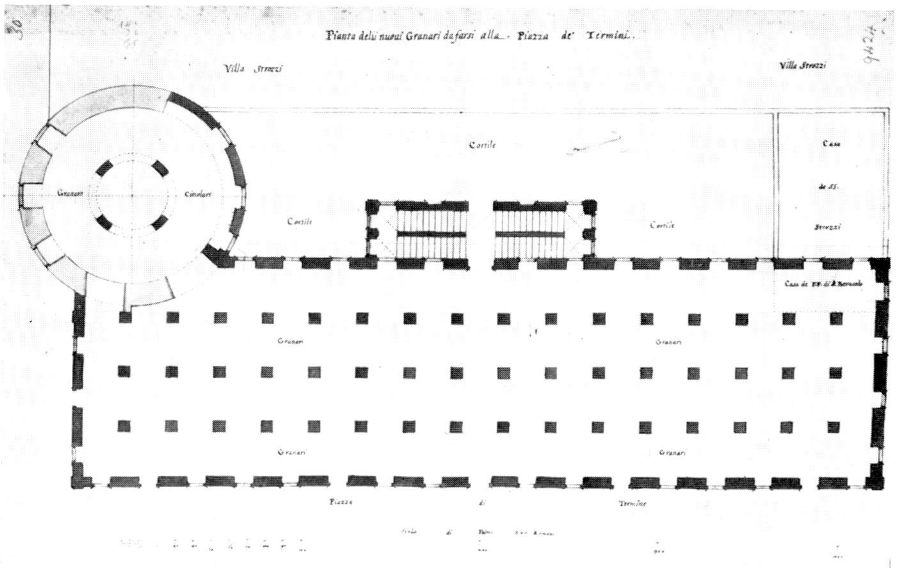

382 Plan, first project (no.457)

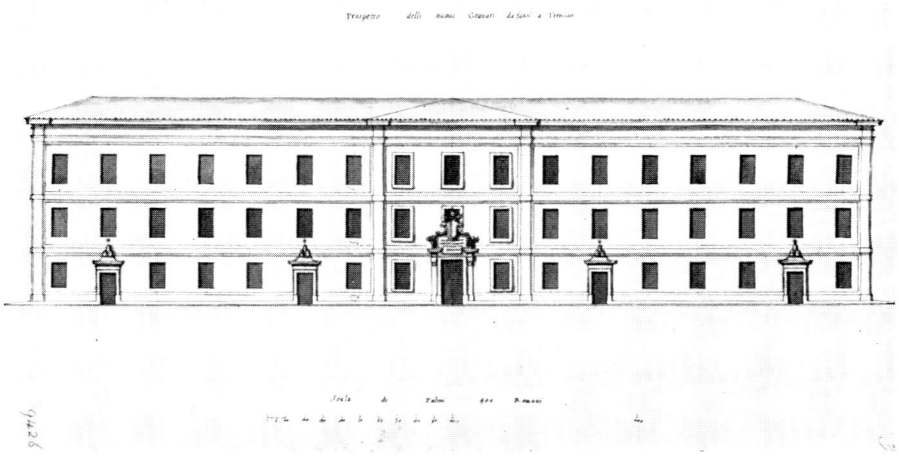

383 Elevation of the main façade, first project (no.458)

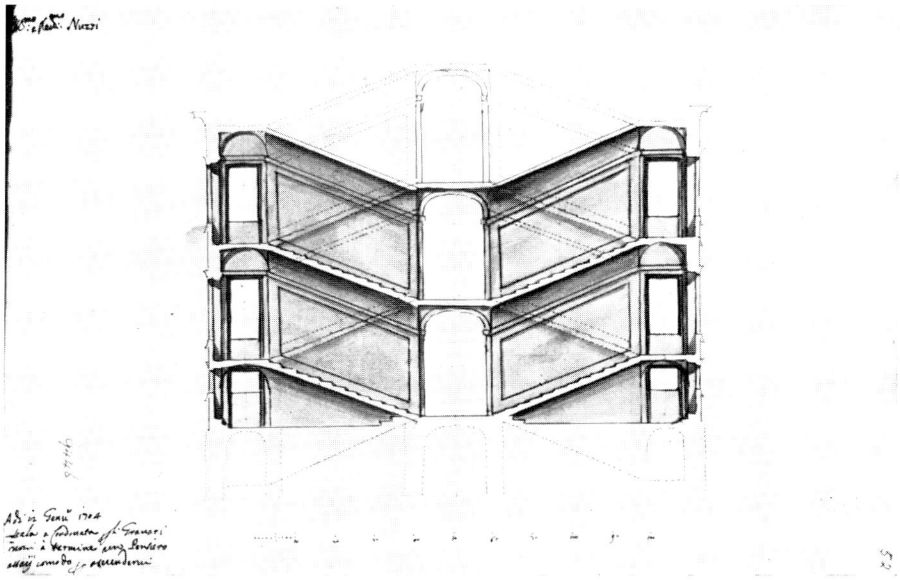

384 Section of the staircase, first project (no.459)

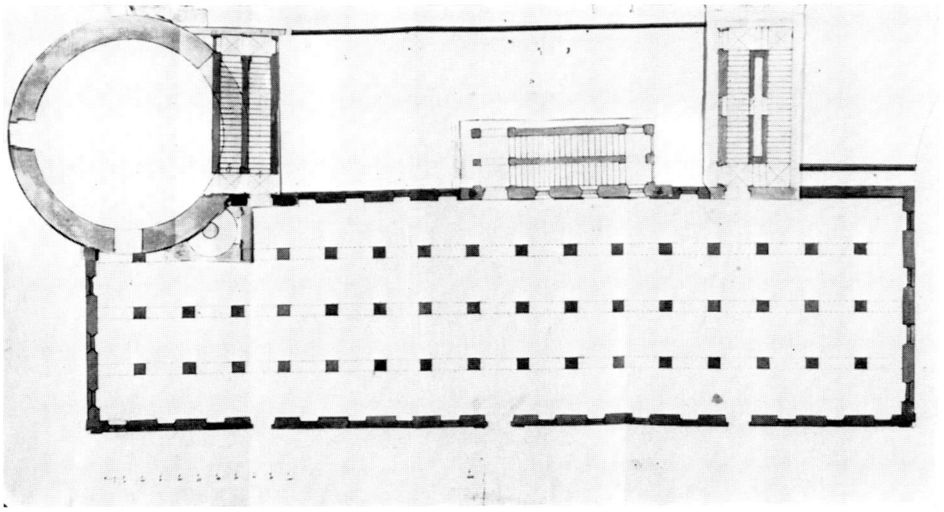

385 Plan with several trial staircases (no.460)

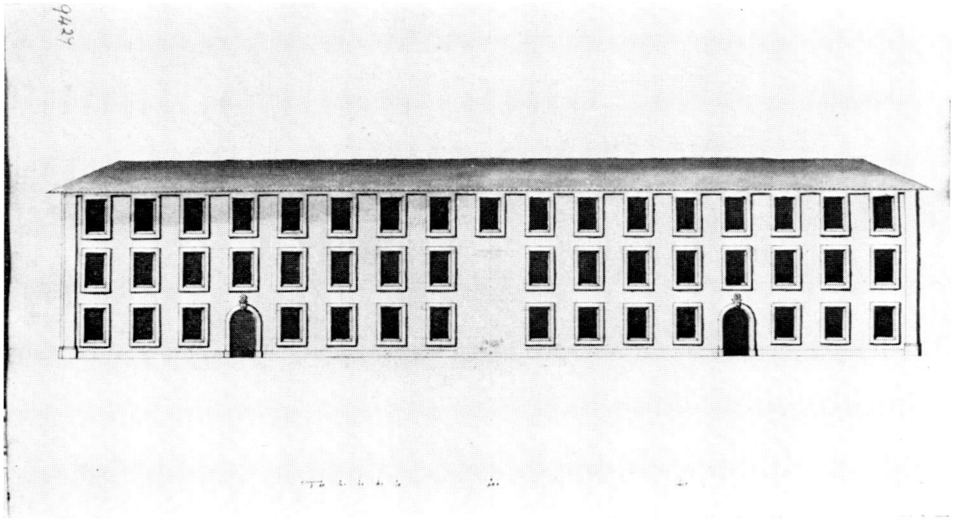

386 Elevation of the main façade (no.461)

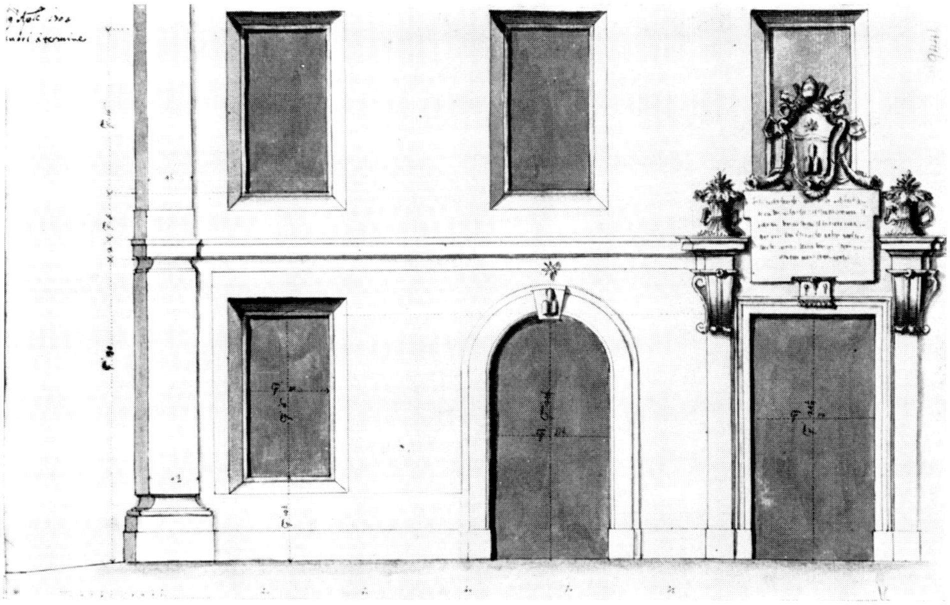

387 Study of the doors of the main façade, elevation (no.462)

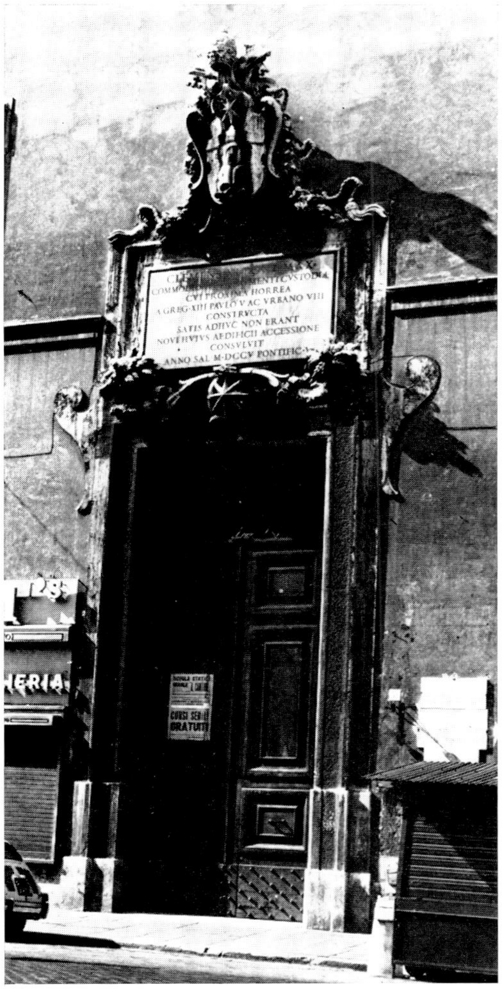

388 View of the central doorway

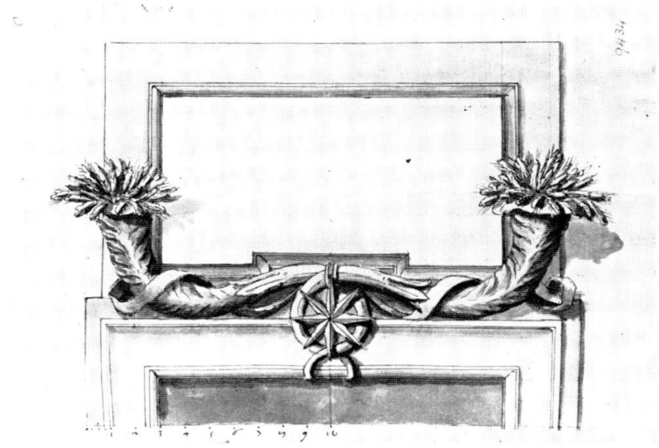

389 Study for the main doorway (no.465)

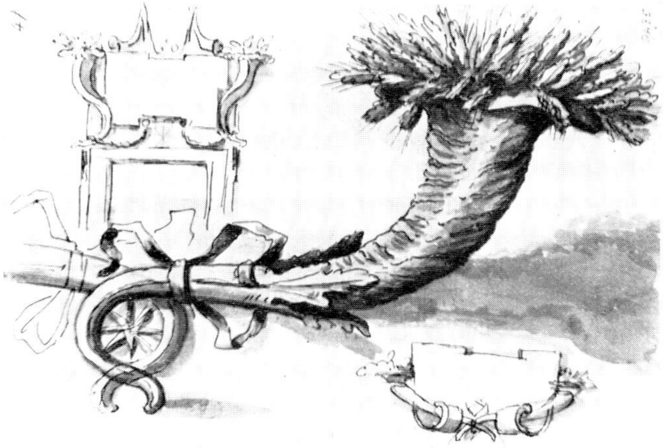

390 Studies of a double wheat cornucopia and two plaques (no.466)

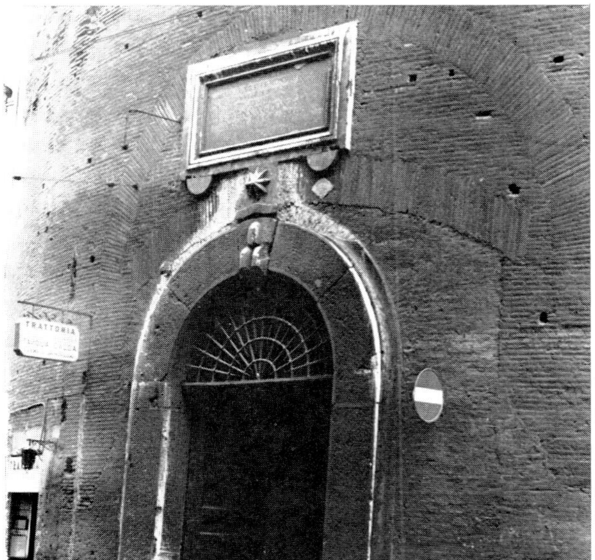

391 View of the door in the side of the 'Mausoleo'

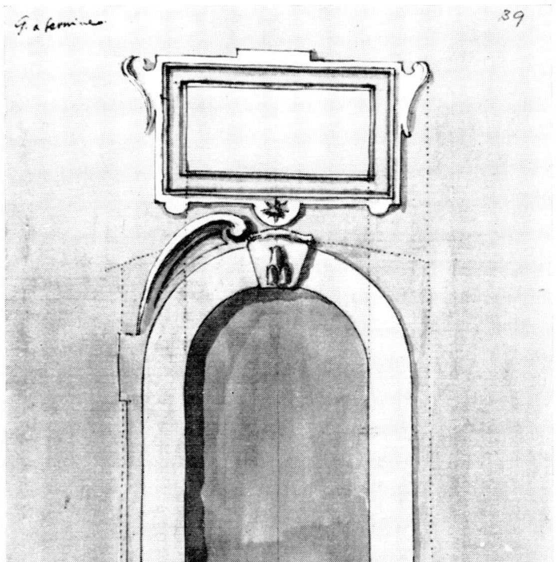

392 Study of the door in the side of the 'Mausoleo', elevation (no.464)

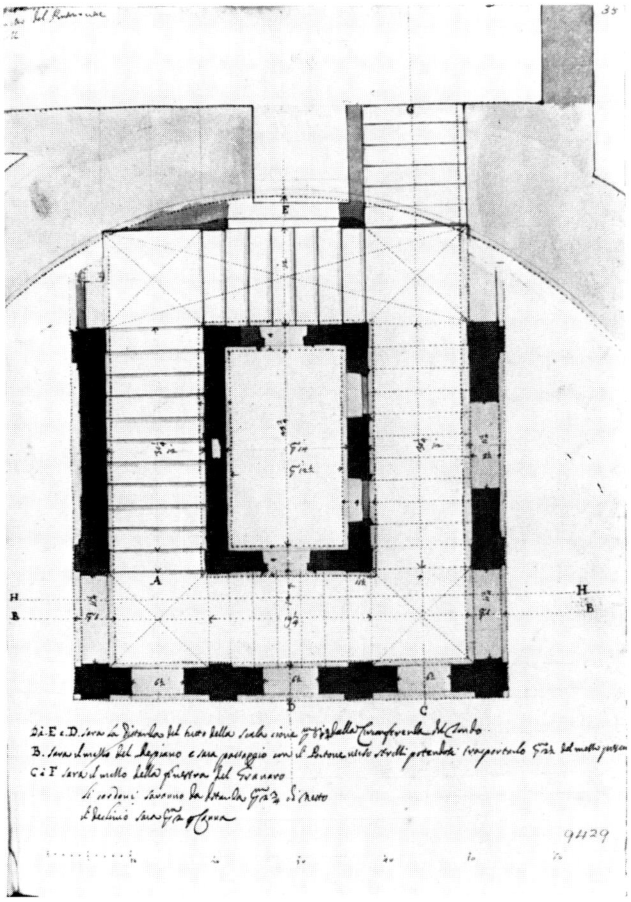

393 Plan of the first (and second) levels of the staircase (no.475)

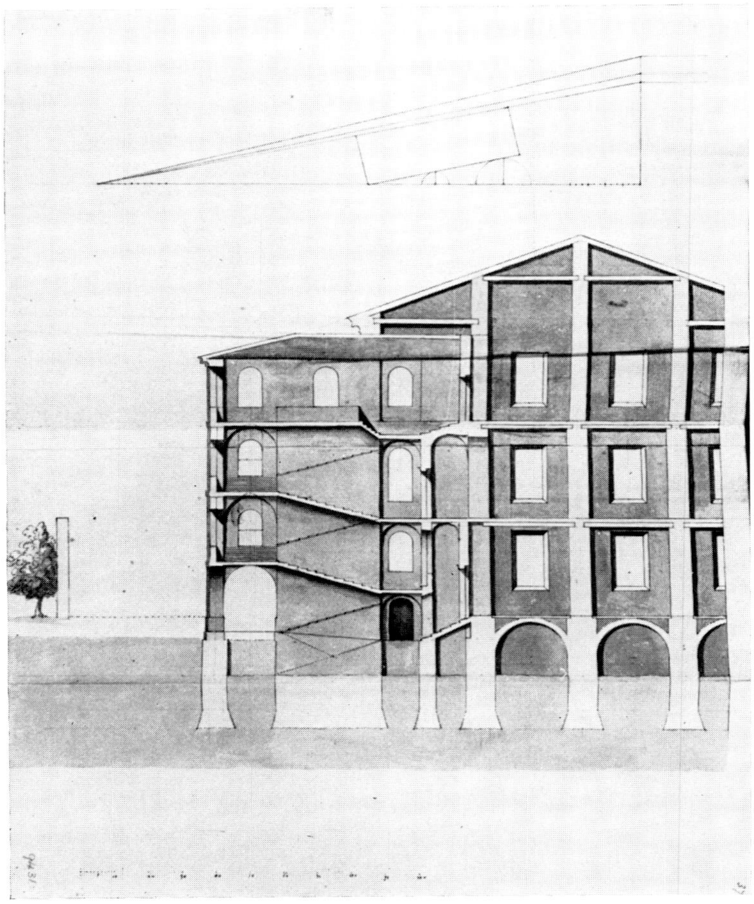

394 Section of the granary (detail) showing staircase (no.477)

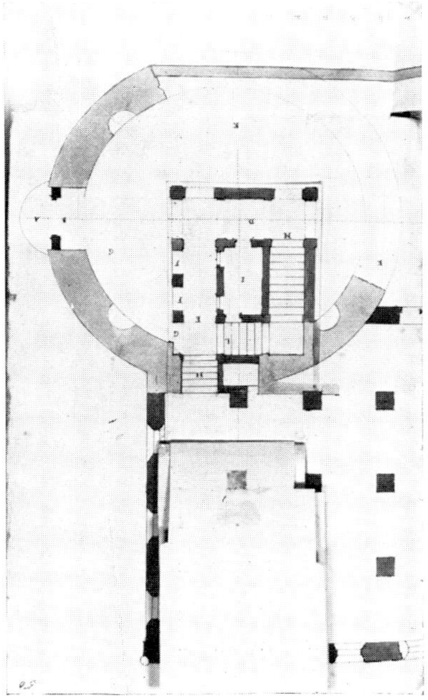

395 Plan of the eastern end of the granary (no.471)

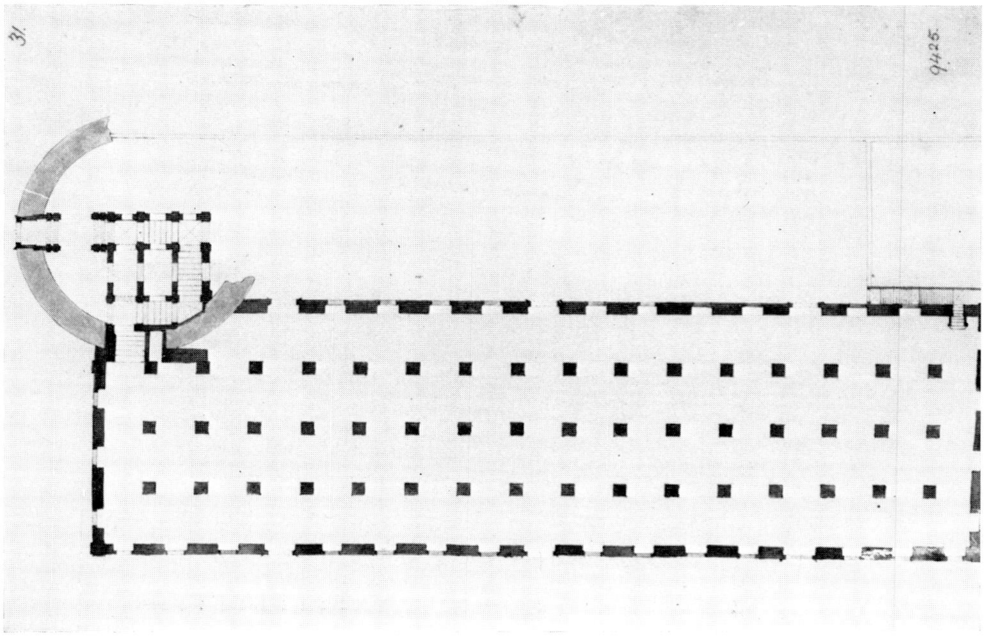

396 Plan of the granary (no.472)

Rome, the Palazzo del Quirinale, projects for the decoration of the gallery (*c.*1703)

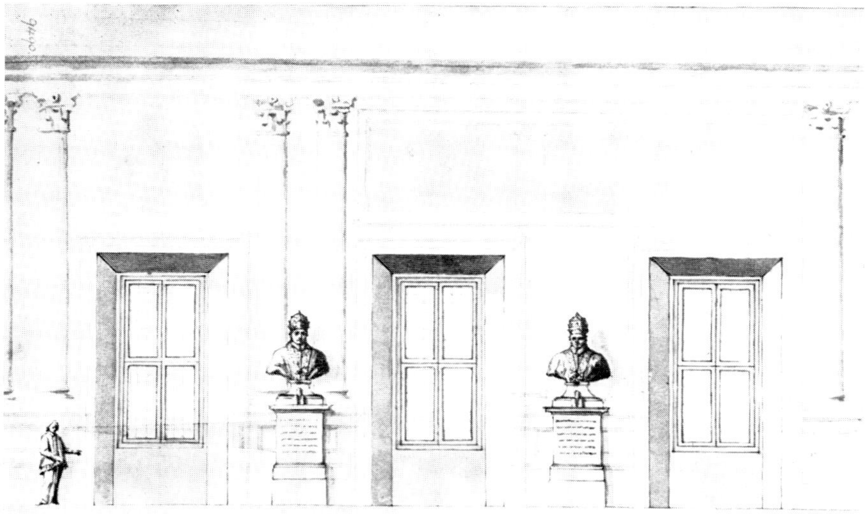

397 Elevation of part of the wall of the gallery (no.479)

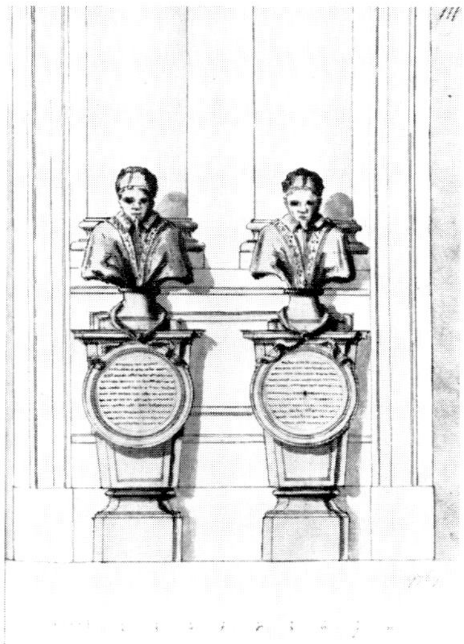

400 Project for pedestals with roundels, elevation (no.484)

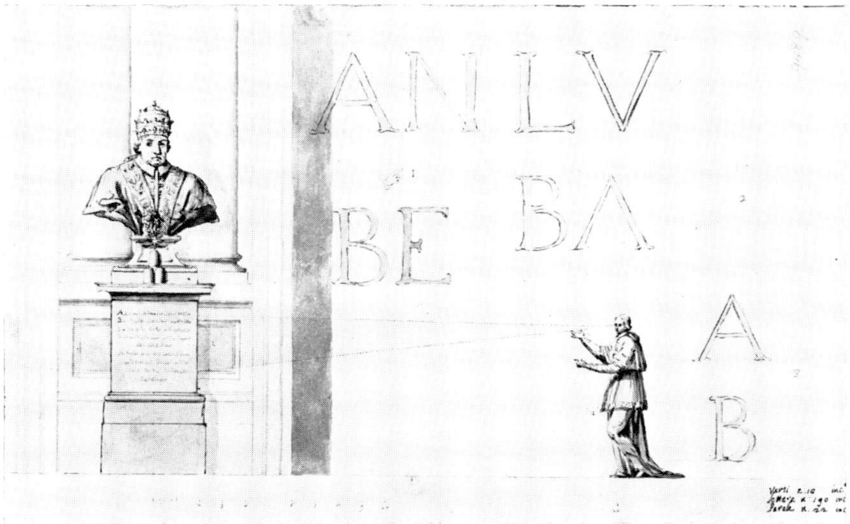

398 Elevation of a pedestal with a portrait bust (no.480)

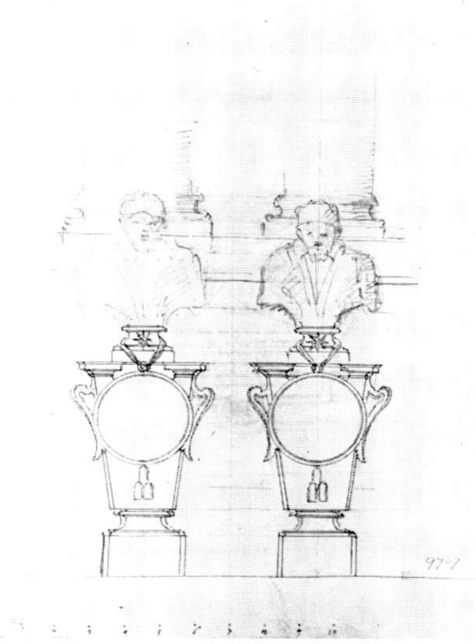

401 Project for pedestals with roundels and consoles (no.485)

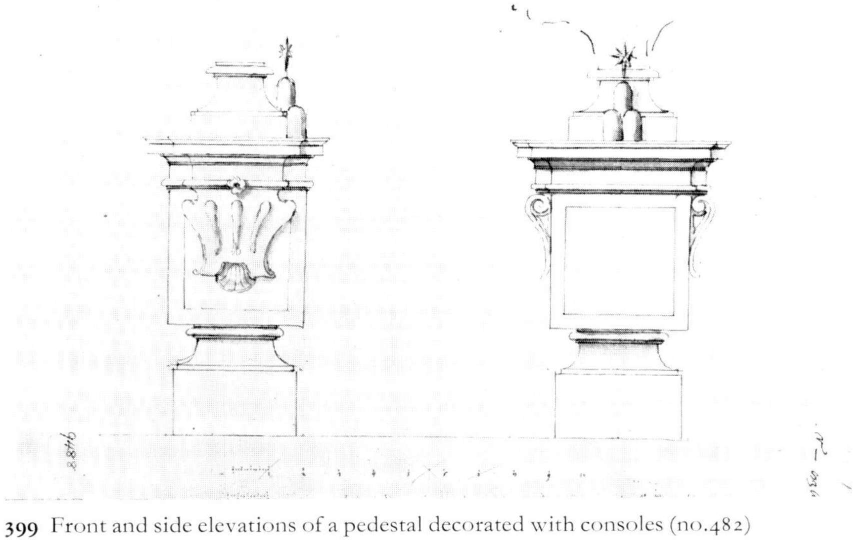

399 Front and side elevations of a pedestal decorated with consoles (no.482)

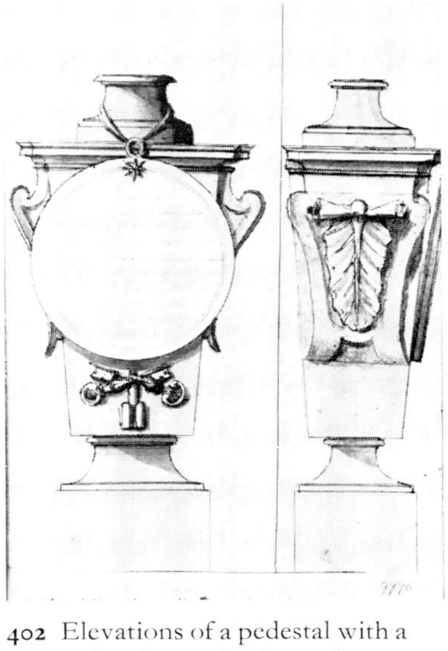

402 Elevations of a pedestal with a roundel and consoles (no.486)

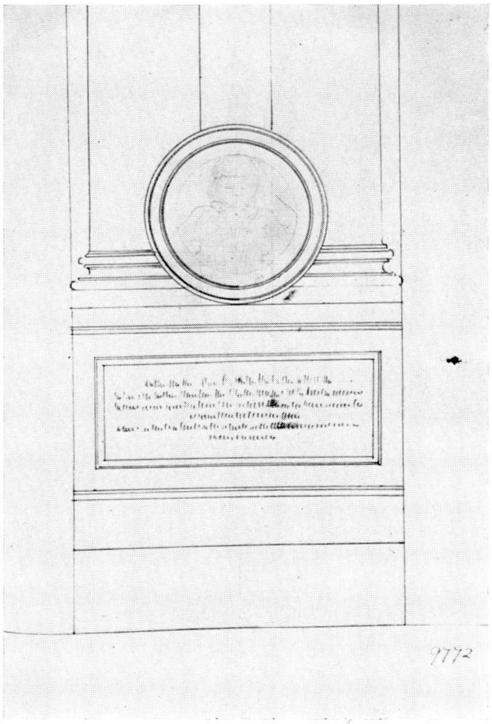

403 Project with a simple rectangular tablet, elevation (no.487)

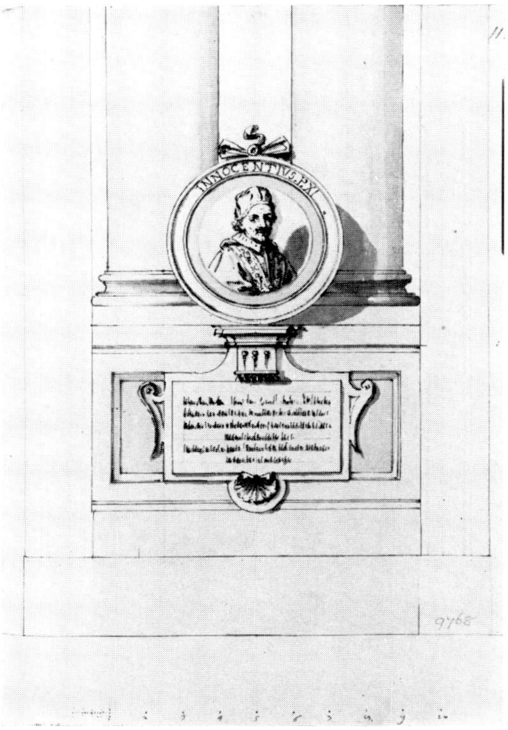

404 Project with a tablet decorated with consoles, elevation (no.488)

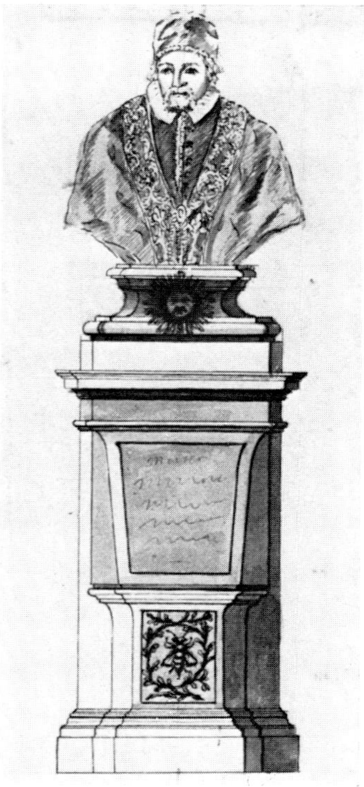

405 Elevation of apedestal with bust of Pope Urban VIII (anon. drawing; no.489)

Project for the Fontana dell'Organo in the Quirinal gardens

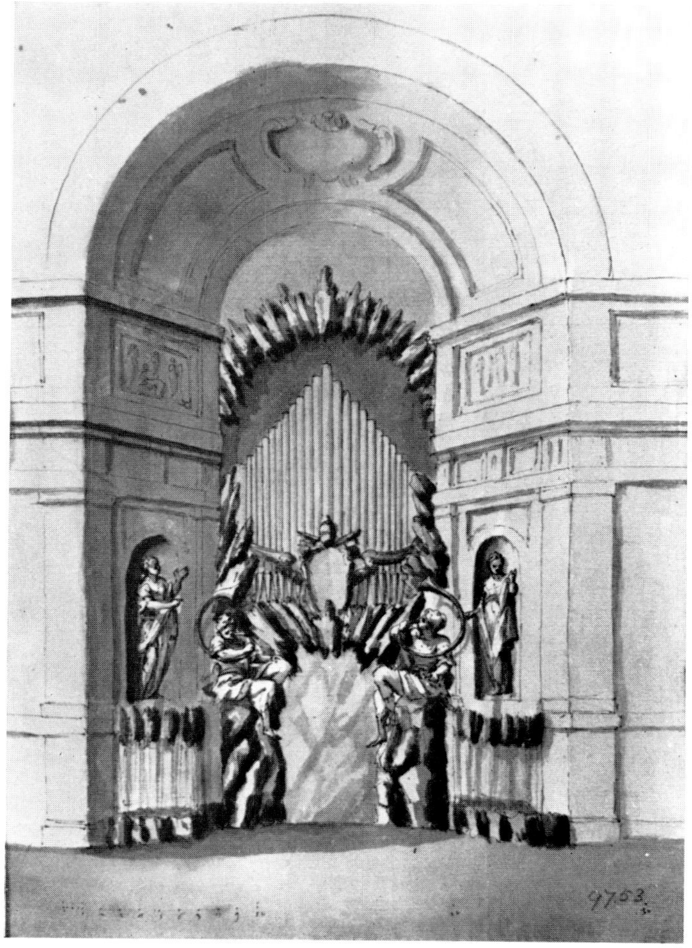

406 Elevation of the central bay of the fountain (no.492)

Drawings of the water drainage of the Quirinal gardens

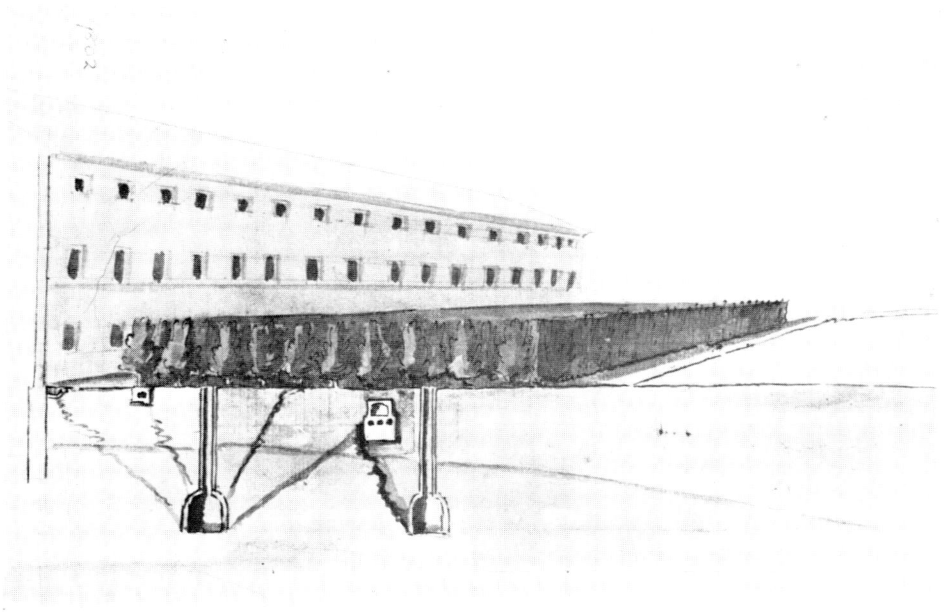

407 Section of part of the drainage system, with perspective view of one wing of the palace (no.497)

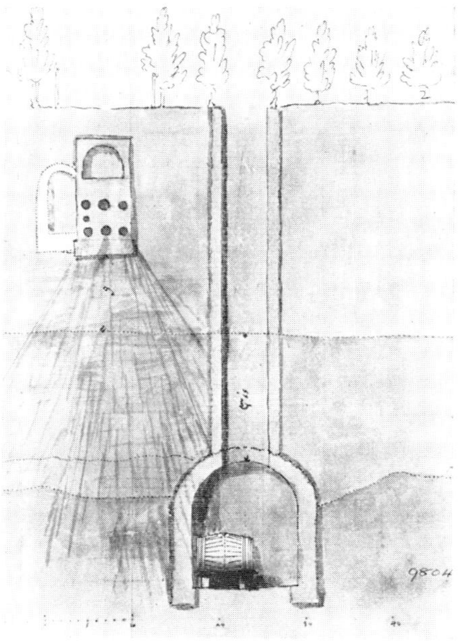

408 Section of part of the drainage system (no.498)

The coach houses of the Quirinal (1706) and a project for the stables

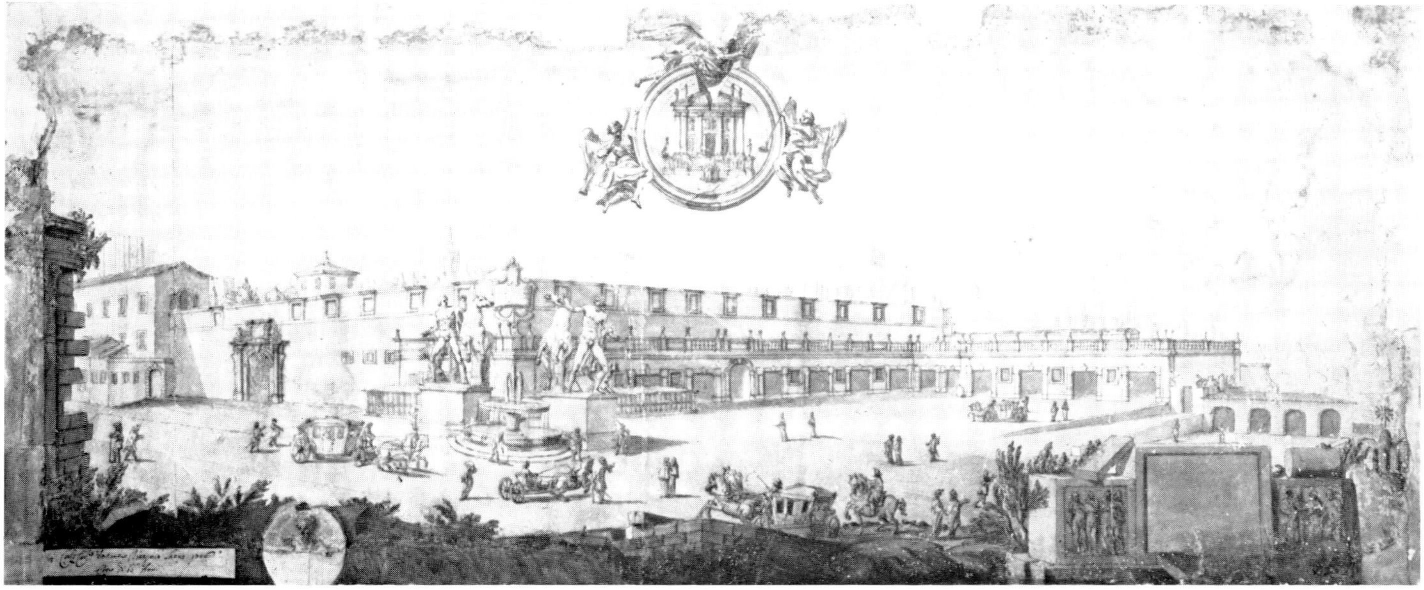

409 View of the Piazza di Montecavallo, 1706 (drawing by Fontana; formerly Messrs Colnaghi)

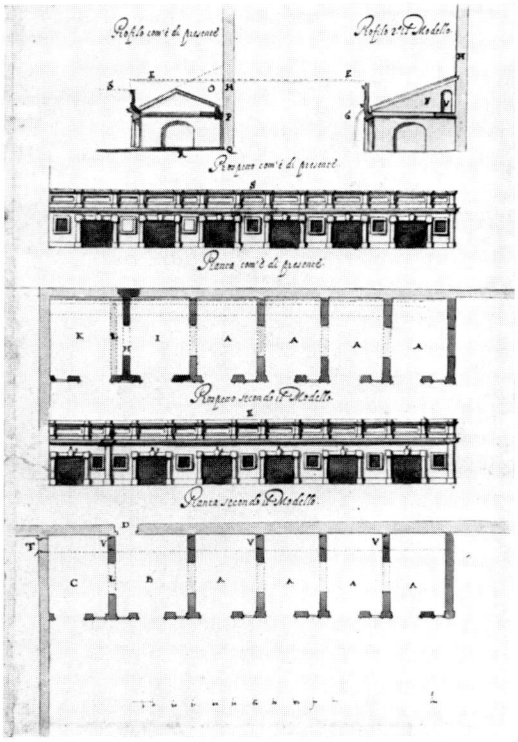

410 Studies of the coach houses (anon. drawing; no.499)

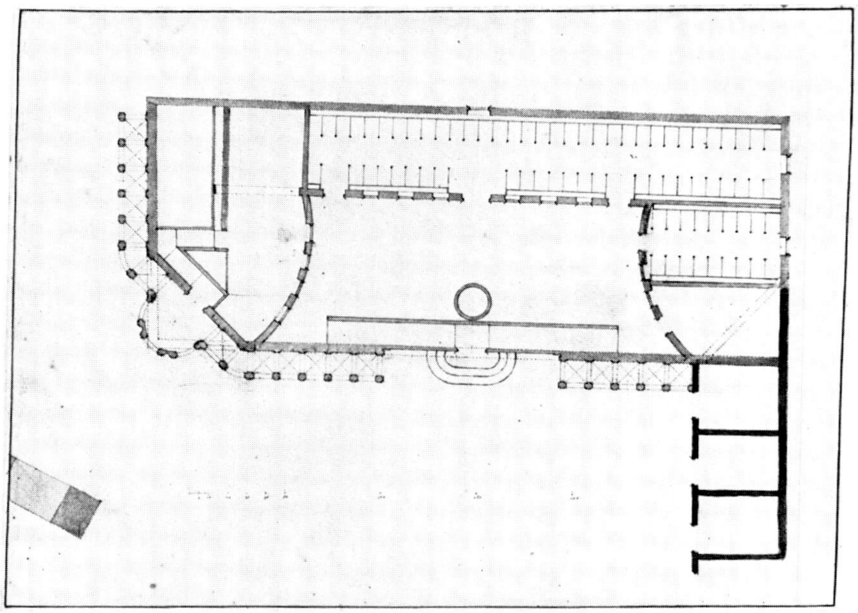

411 Project for the stables, plan (by Alessandro Specchi ?; no.500)

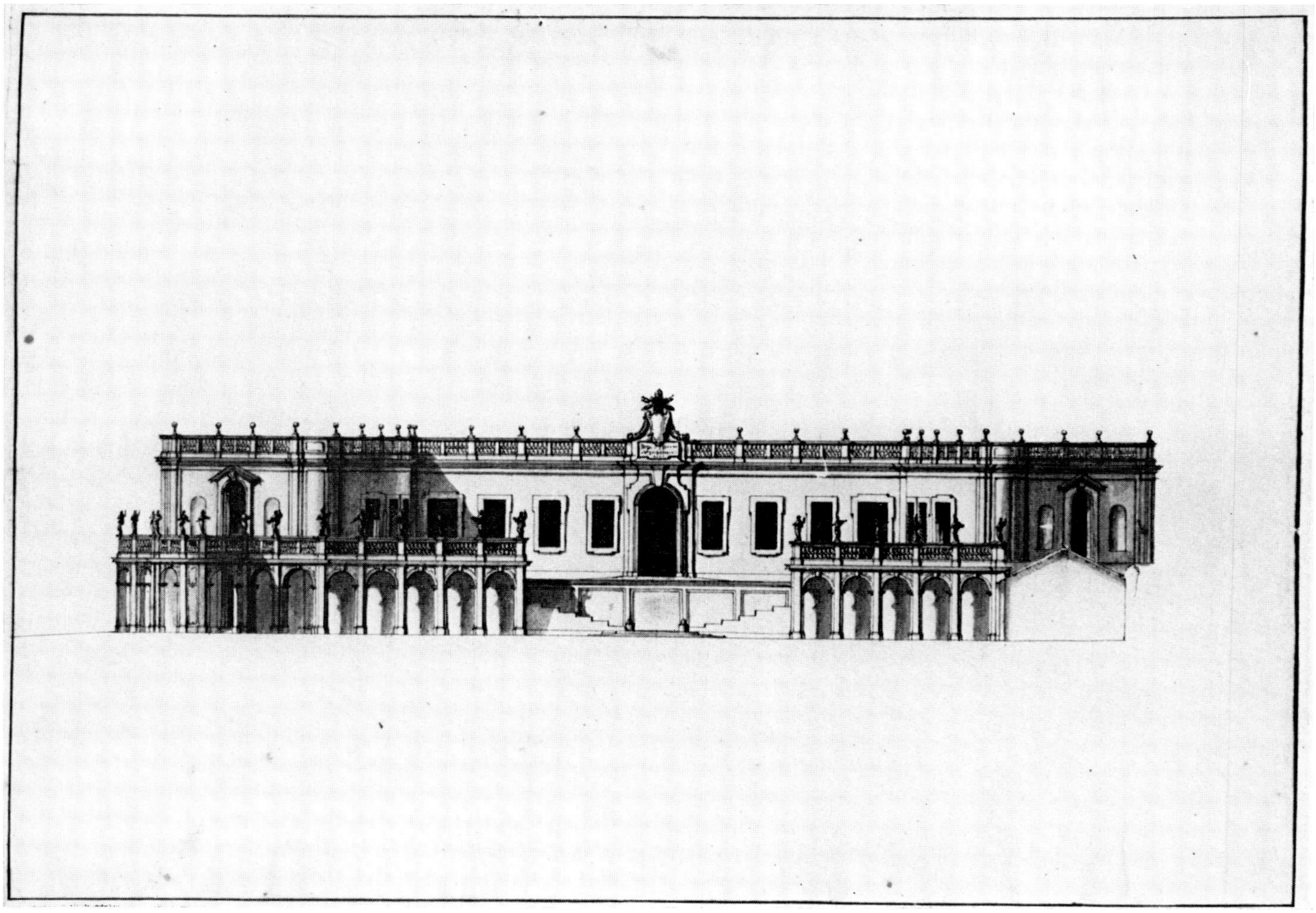

412 Project for the stables, elevation (by Alessandro Specchi ?; no.501)

Caprarola, survey of the stables (1704/5)

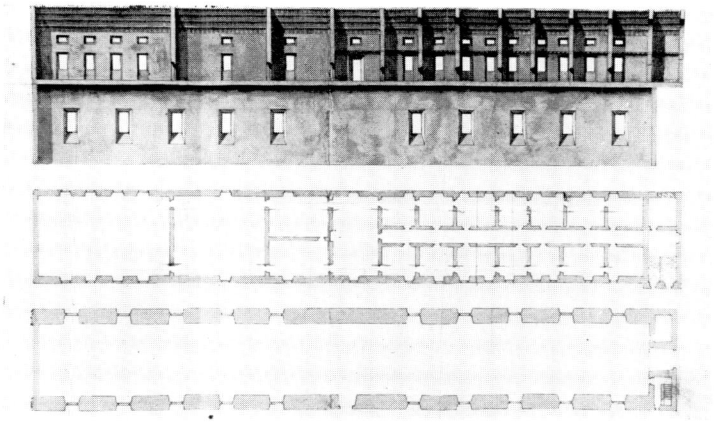

413 Plans of the ground and first floors, and longitudinal section (no.502)

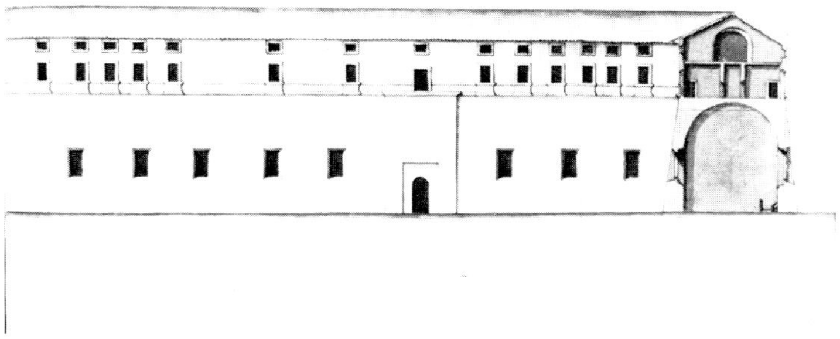

414 Elevation and transverse section (no.503)

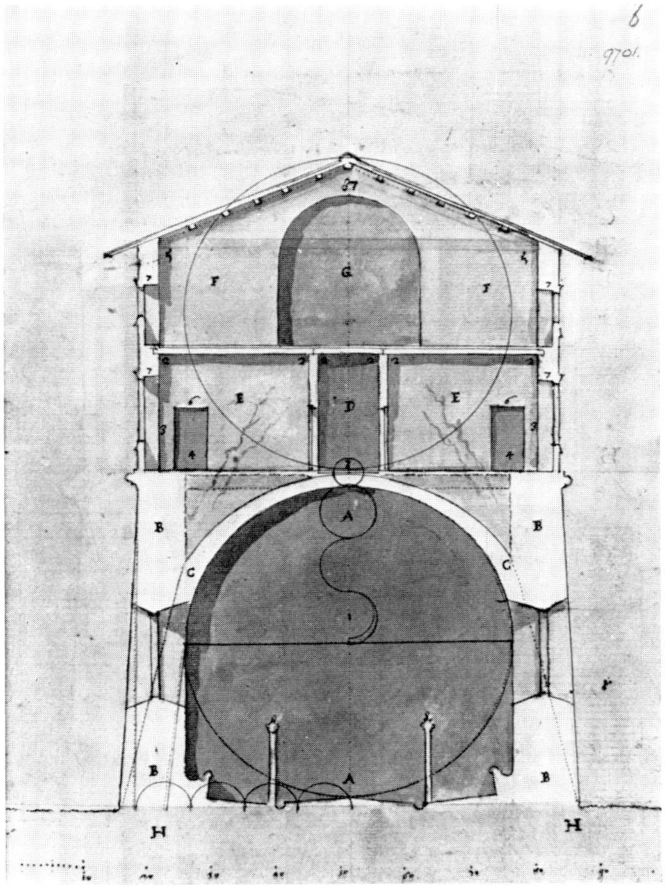

415 Transverse section (no.504)

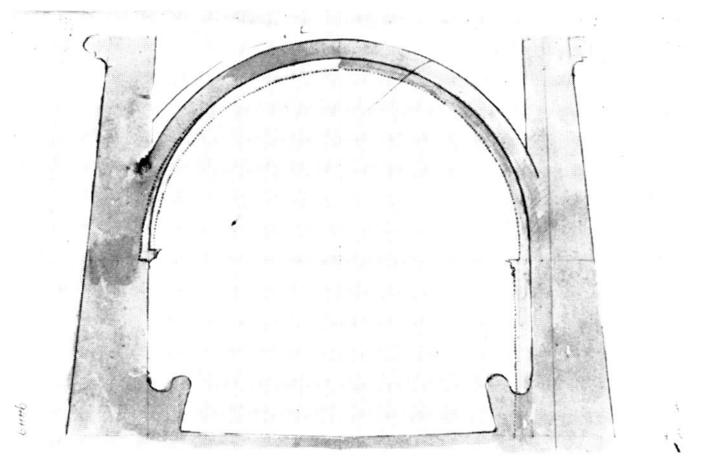

416 Transverse section of the ground floor (no.507)

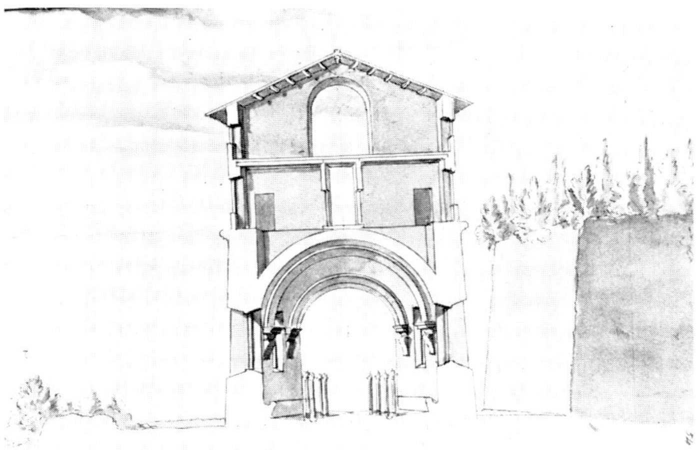

417 Transverse section in perspective (no.508)

A view of the Ponte dell'Abadia, near Castro (1705)

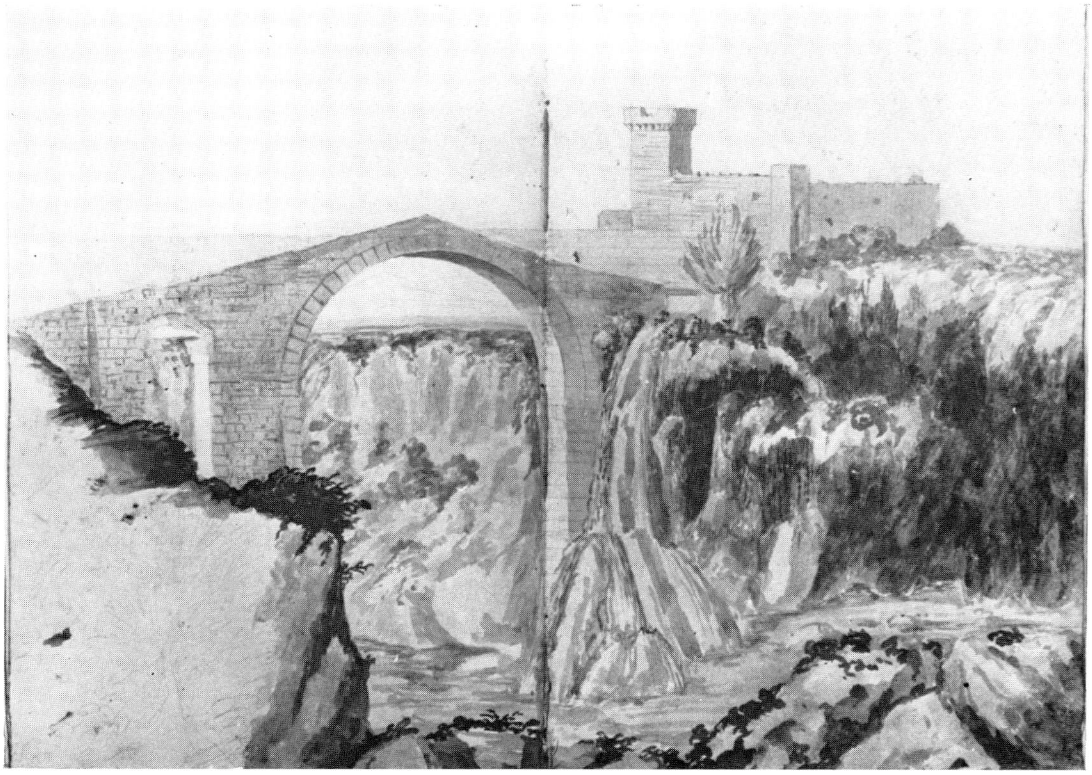

418 Perspective view of the bridge in a landscape (no.509)

Projects for the Fontana di Trevi (1706)

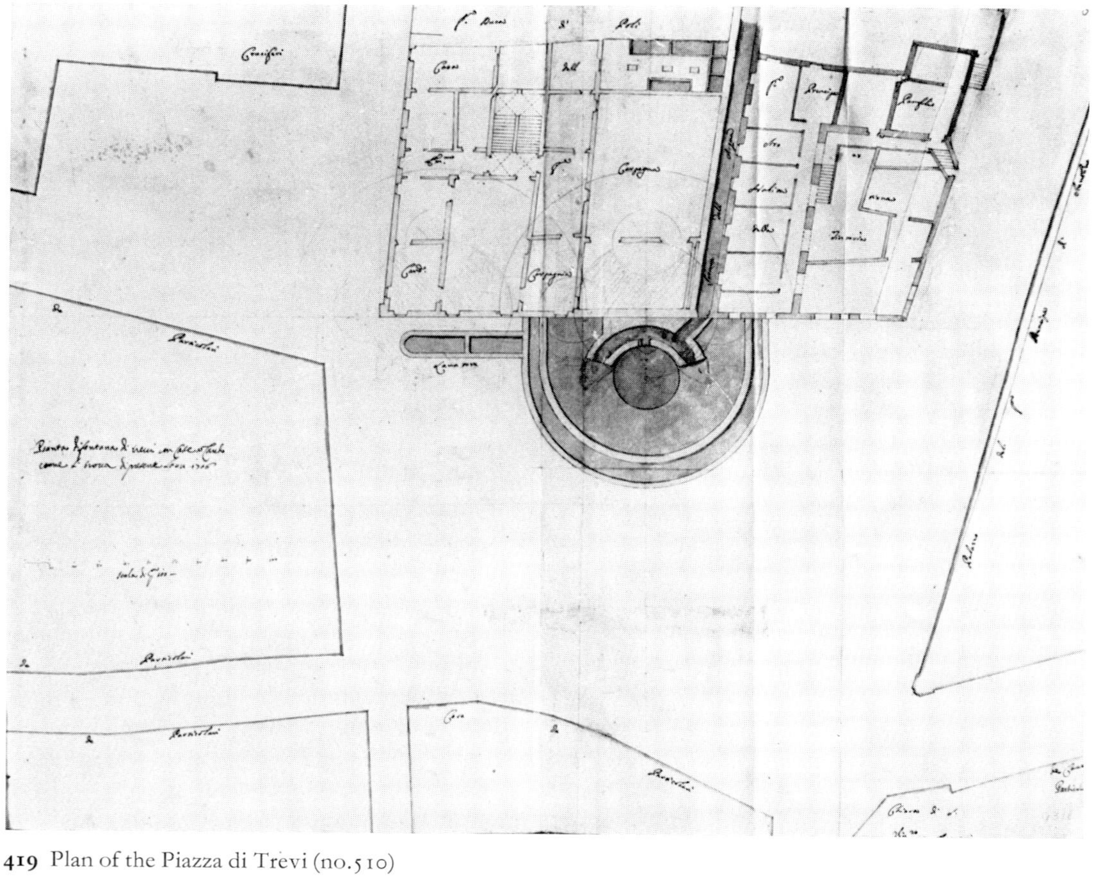

419 Plan of the Piazza di Trevi (no.510)

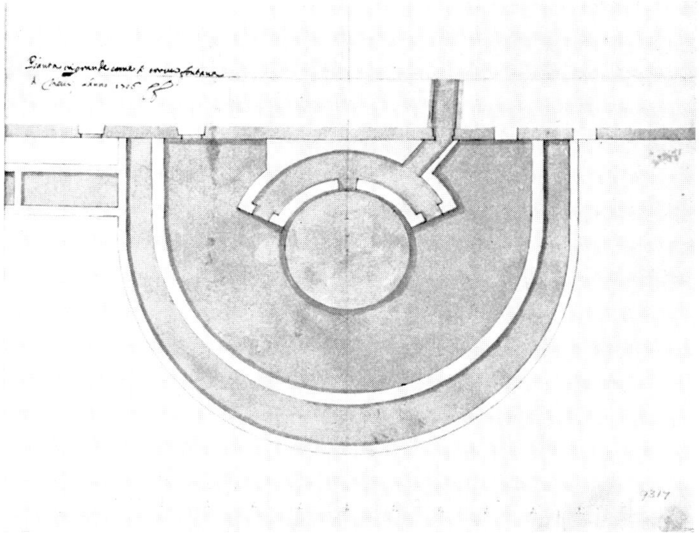

420 Plan of the fountain (no.511)

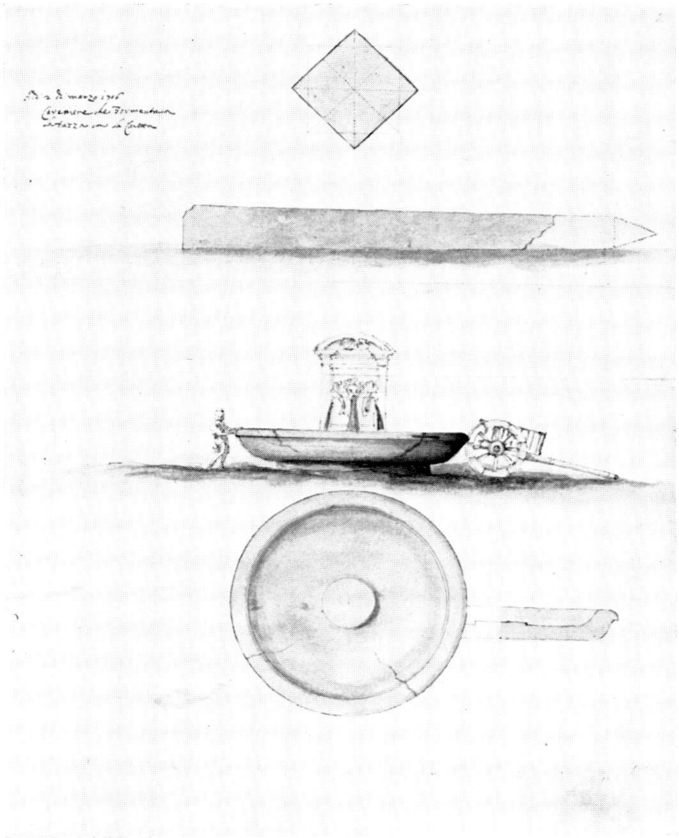

421 Four studies of the obelisk and the basin (no.512)

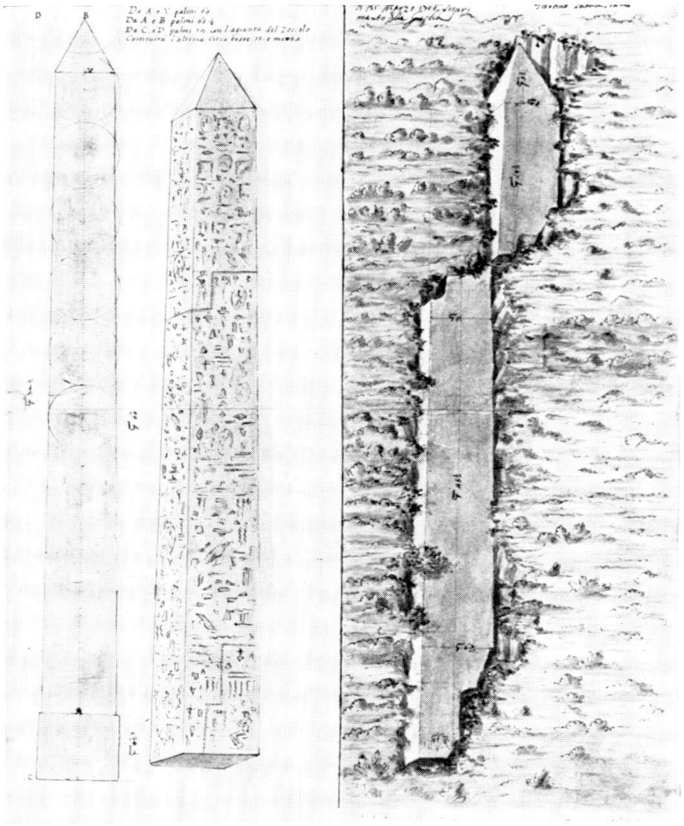

422 Three studies of the obelisk (no.513)

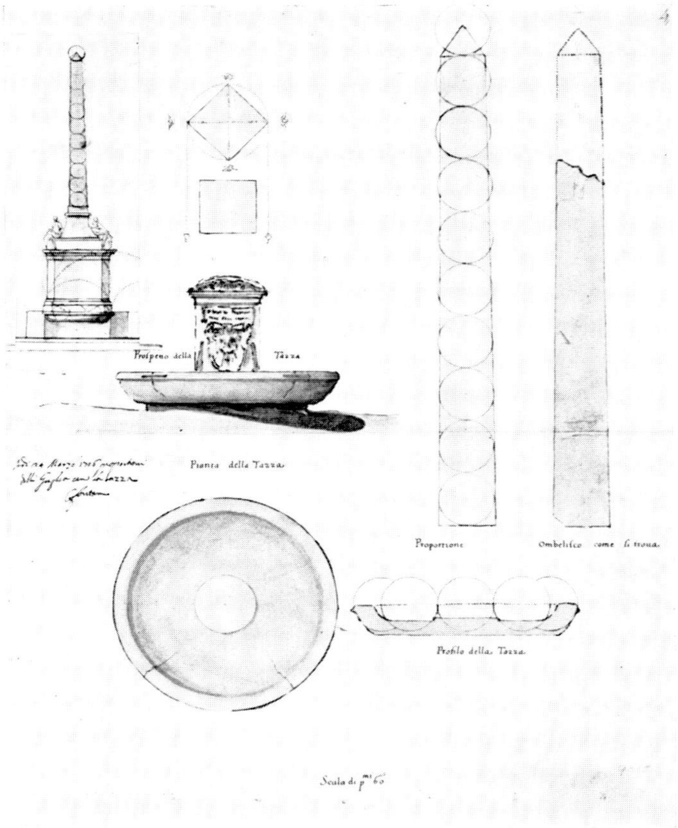

423 Seven studies of the obelisk and the basin (no.514)

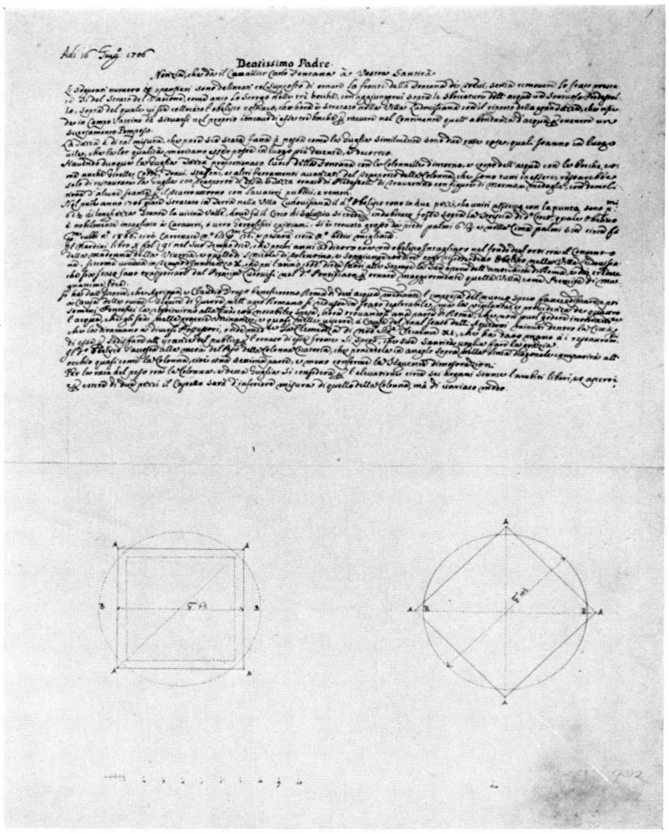

424 Introduction to Volume 169, with diagrammatic plans of the obelisk and a column (no.517)

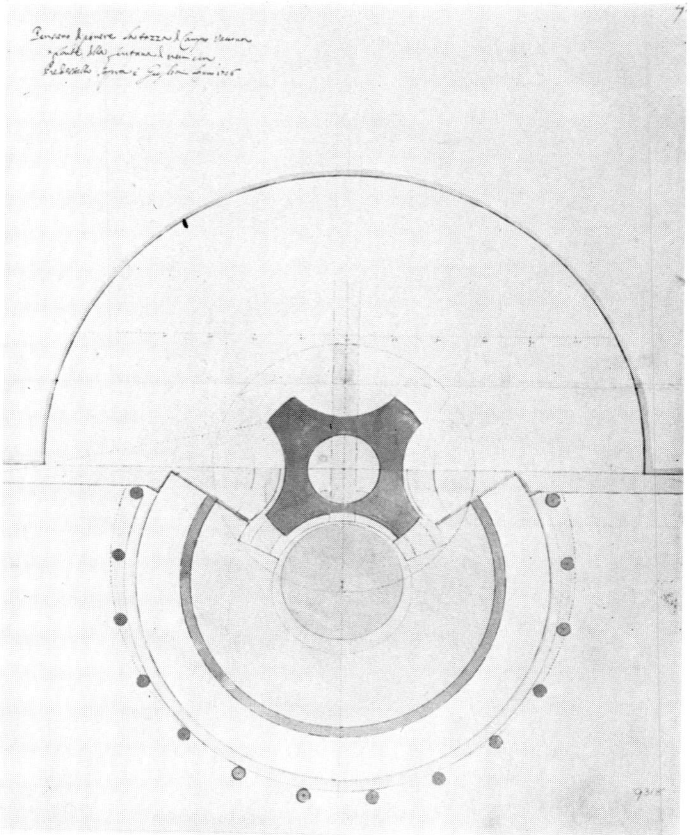

425 Project with a circular lower basin, plan (no.518)

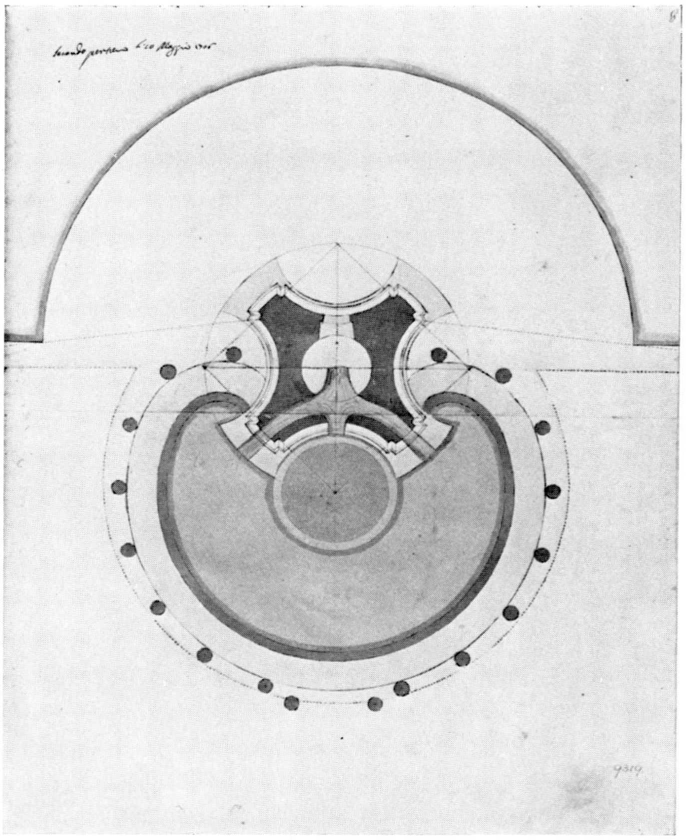

426 Project with a heart-shaped lower basin, plan (no.519)

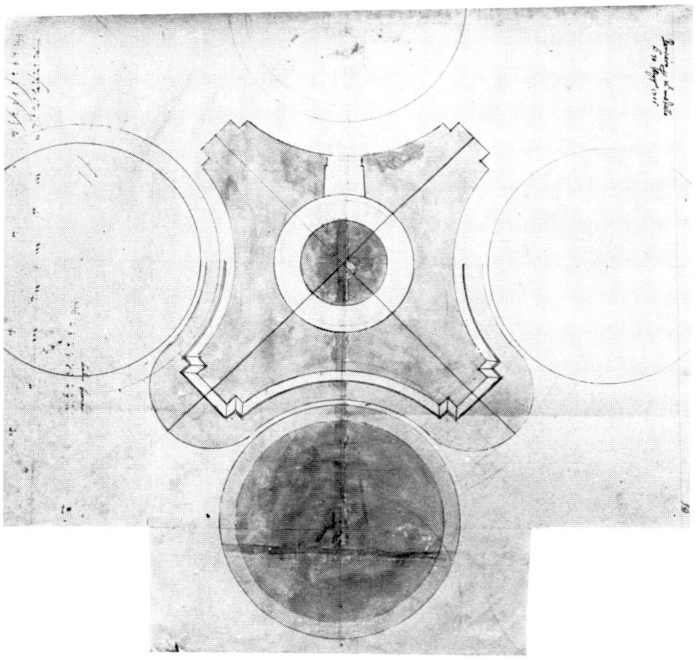

427 Project used for a model, plan (no.521)

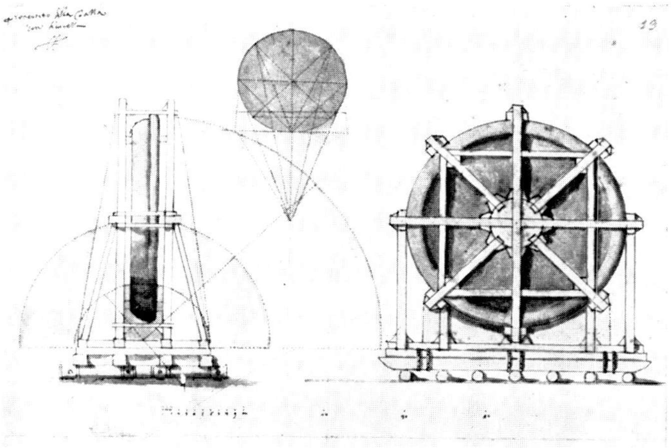

428 Demonstration of safe method of transporting the basin (no.515)

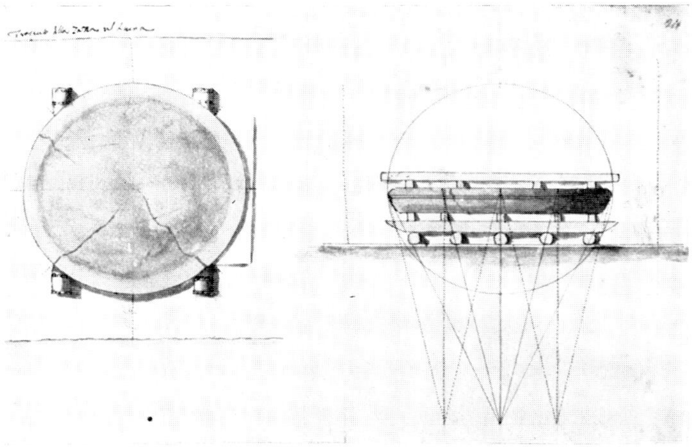

429 Demonstration of unsafe method of transporting the basin (no.516)

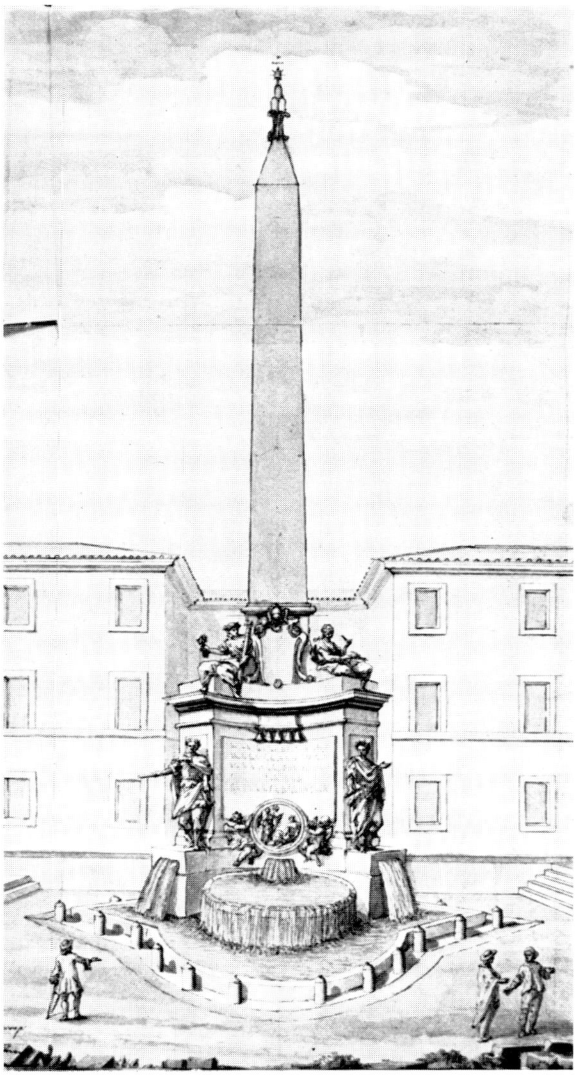

430 Project with statues of Roman Emperors (no.522)

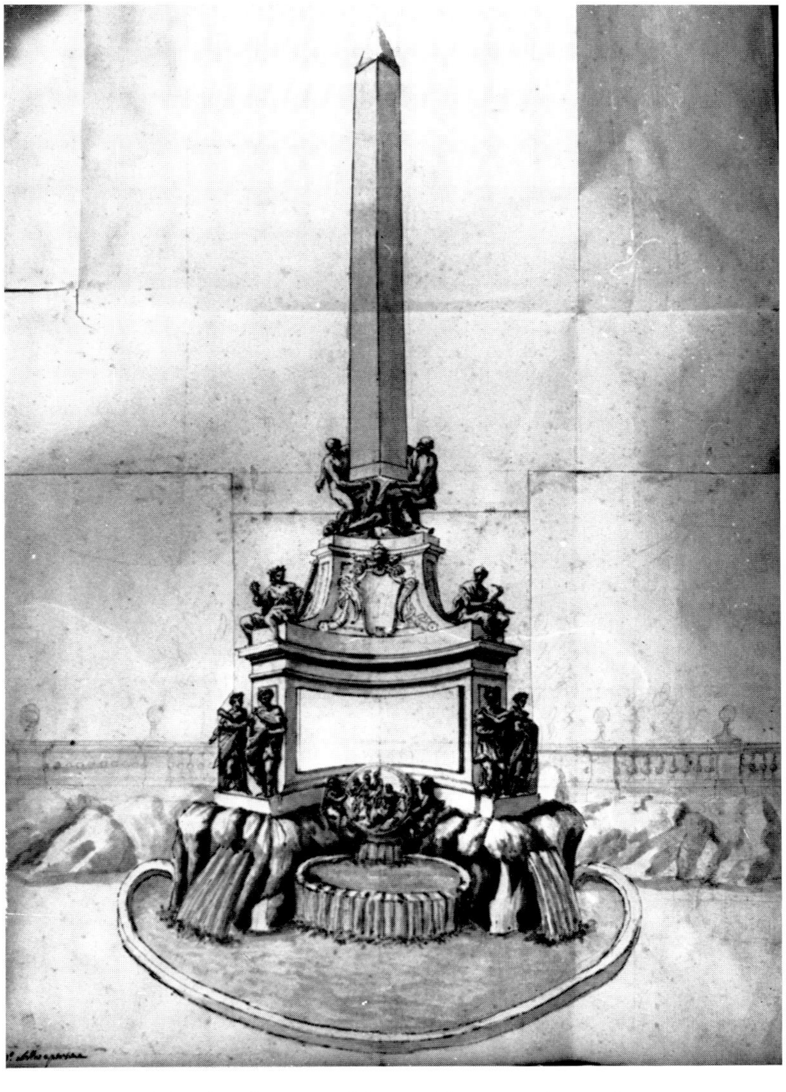

431 Project with pairs of statues of Roman Emperors (no.525)

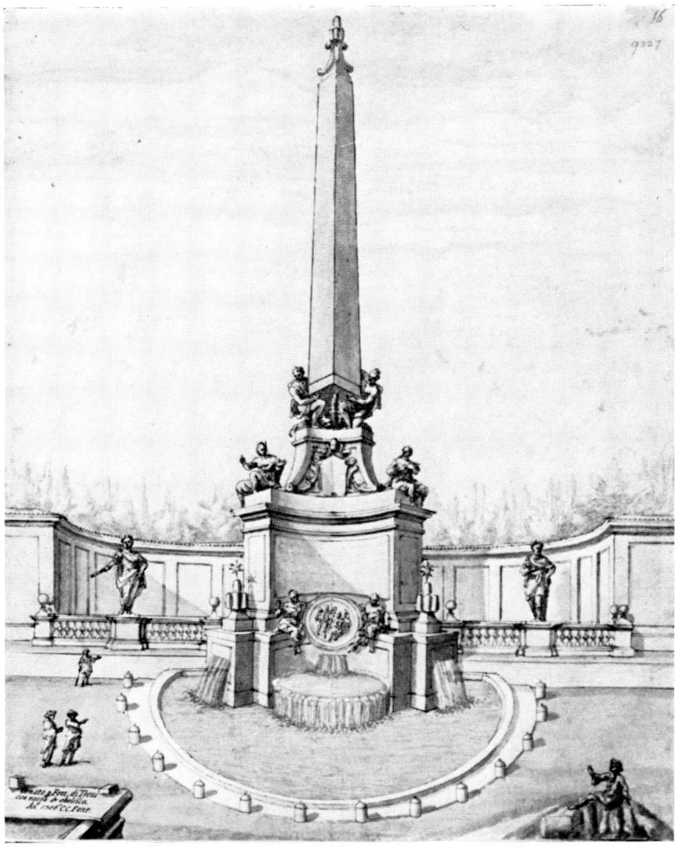

432 Project with statues of Roman Emperors in the background (no.526)

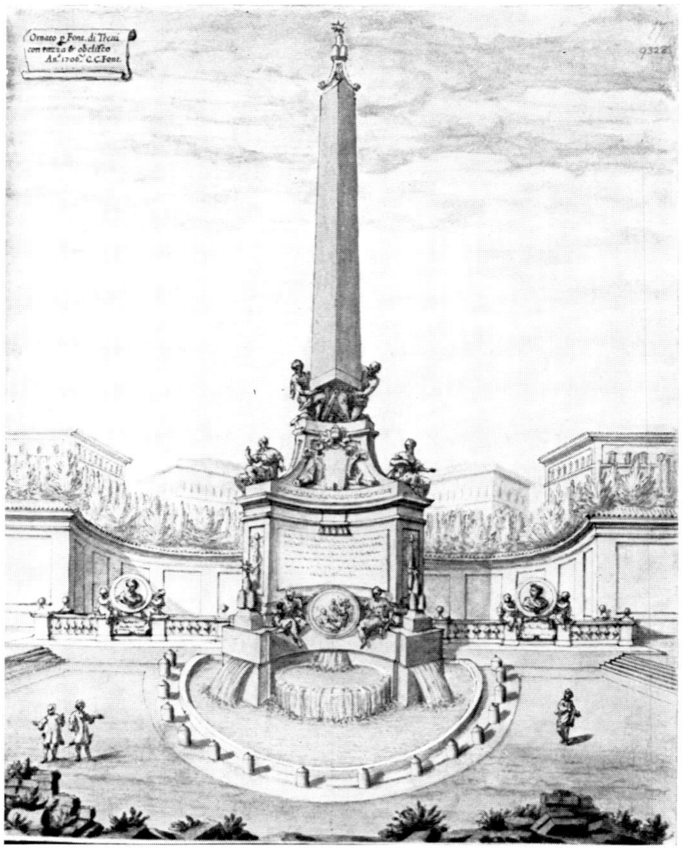

433 Project with roundels of Roman Emperors in the background (no.527)

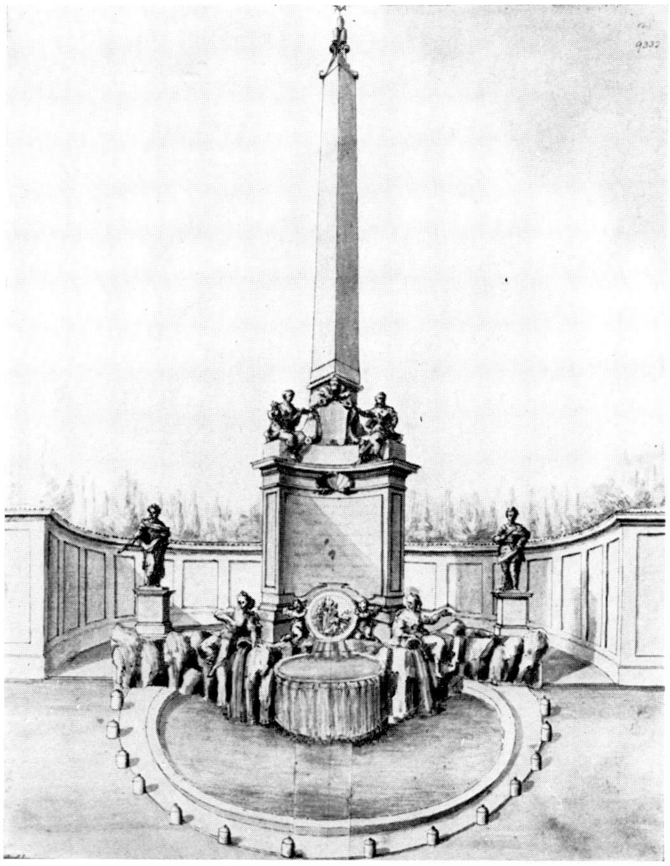

434 Project with statues of Roman Emperors on pedestals in the background (no.528)

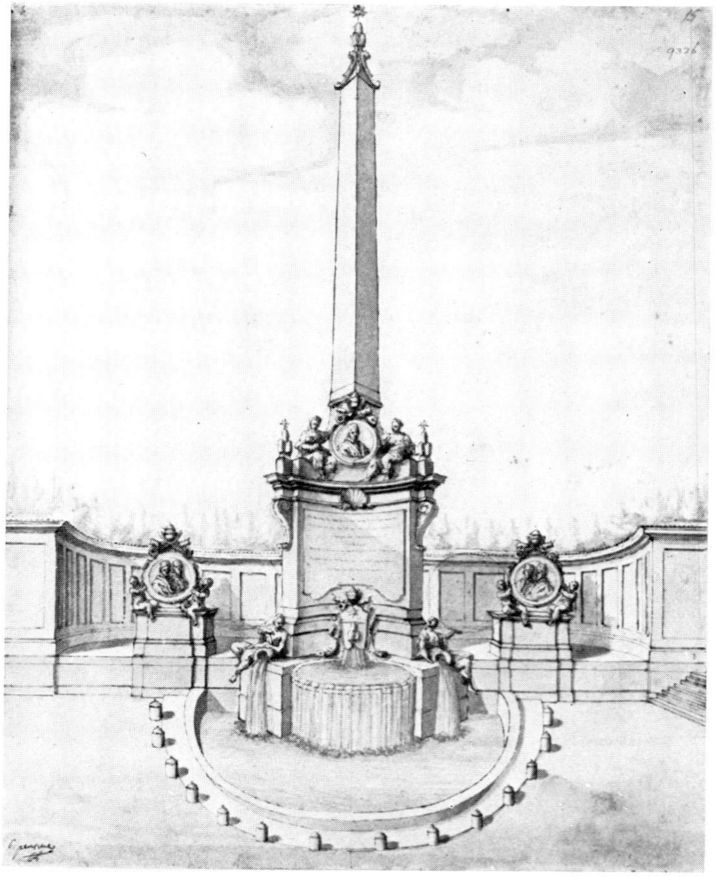

435 Project with roundels of Popes (no.529)

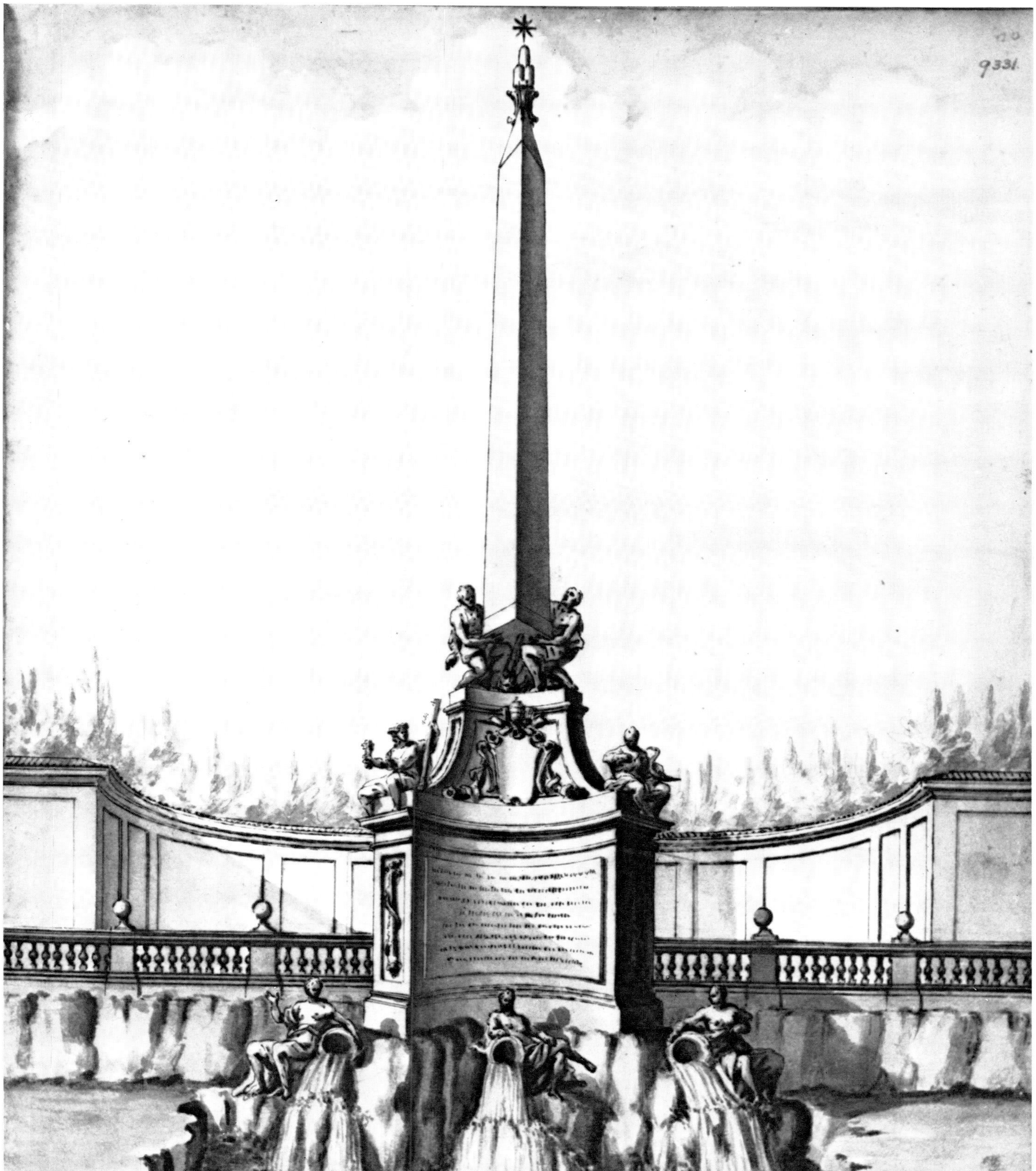

436 Project with a pool surrounded by rock (no.532)

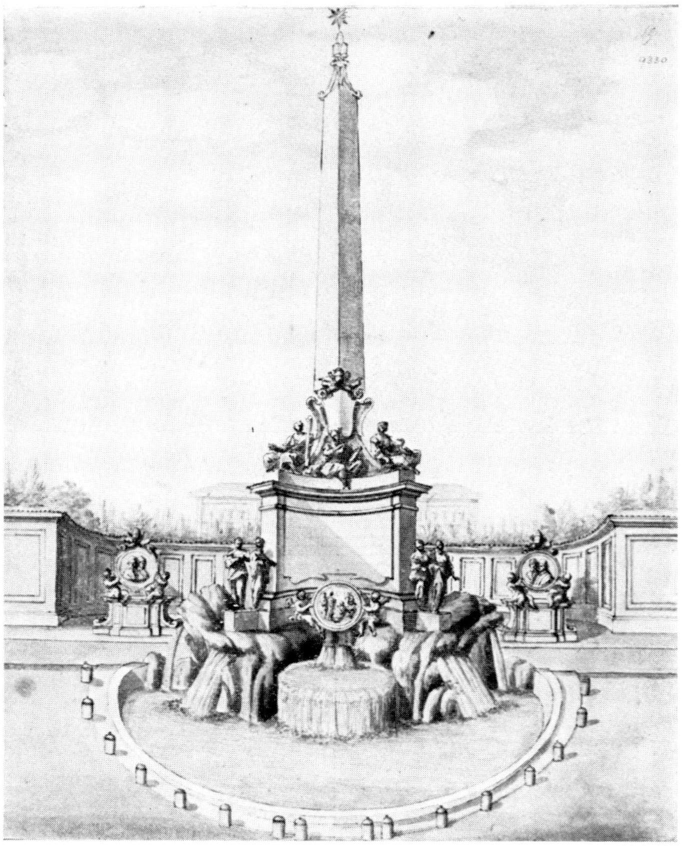

437 Project with five jets (no.531)

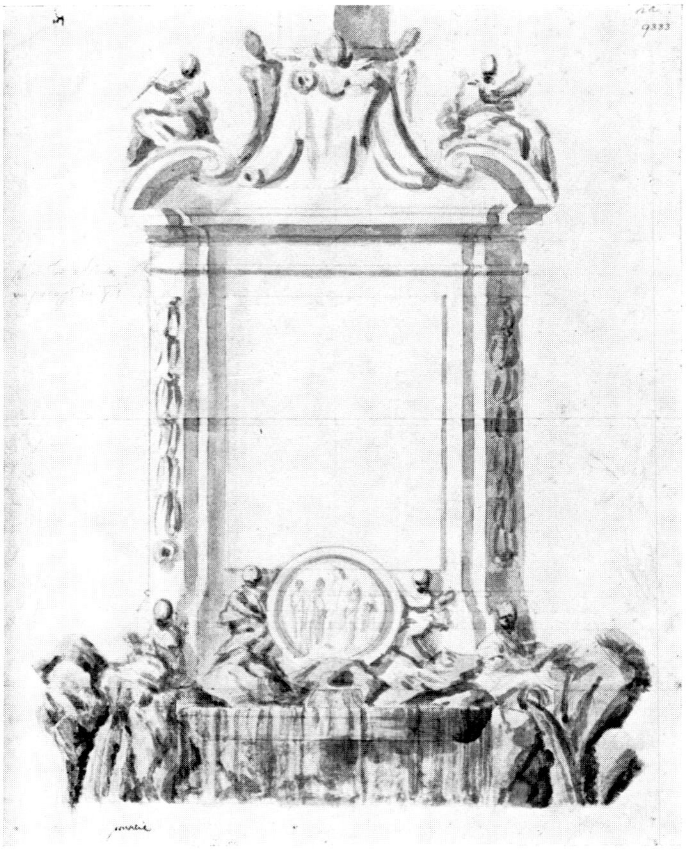

438 Project in elevation with a pedimented pedestal (detail) (no.533)

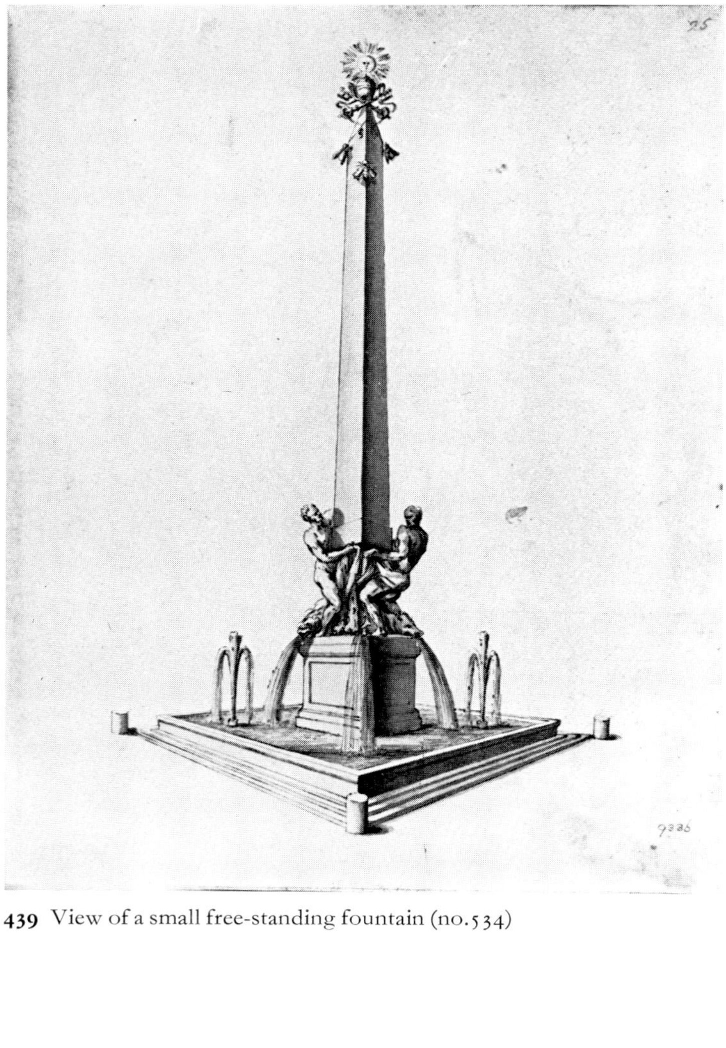

439 View of a small free-standing fountain (no.534)

Civitavecchia, survey of the 'Antimurale' (1708 and earlier)

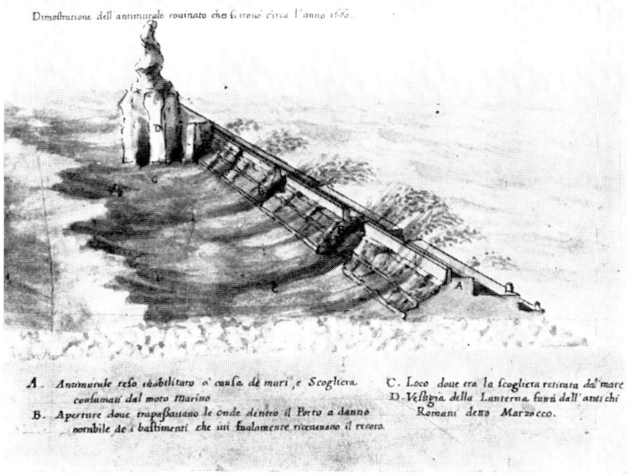

440 Section in perspective, facing north west (*c.*1660) (no.536)

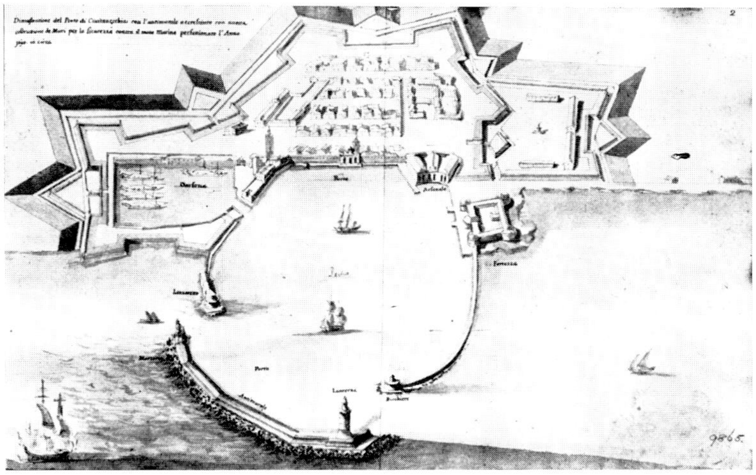

441 View of Civitavecchia (*c.*1690) (no.537)

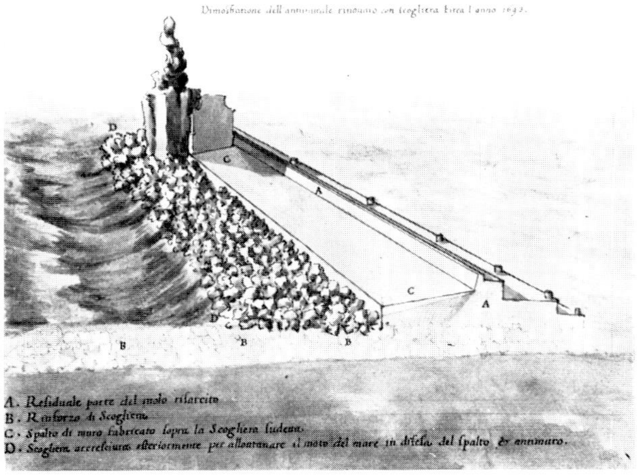

442 Section in perspective facing north west (*c.*1693) (no.539)

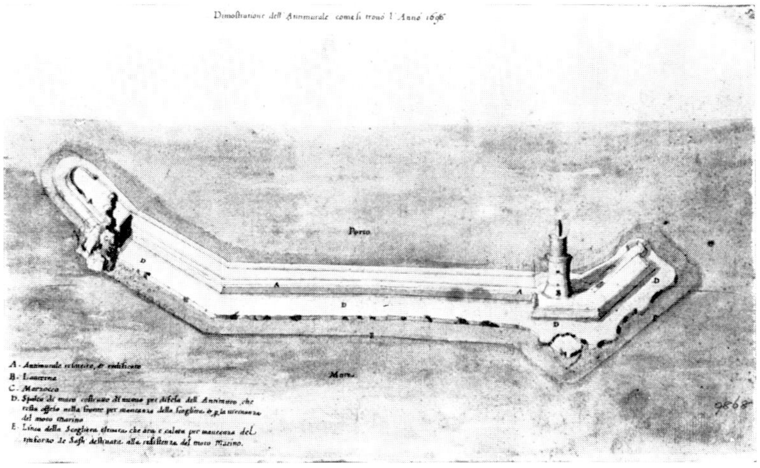

443 View from the south west (1698) (no.540)

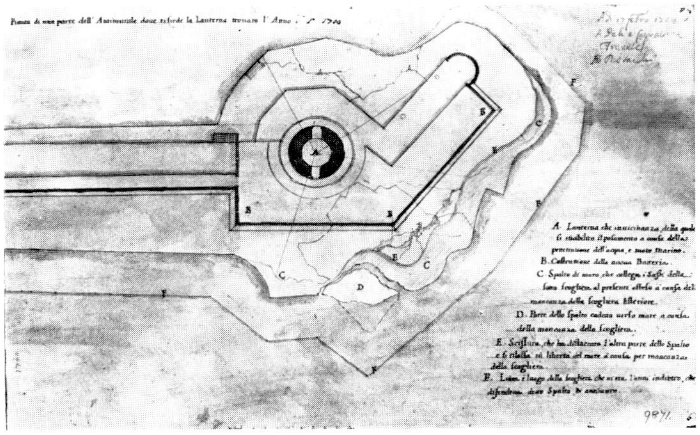

444 Plan of the lighthouse and south-east end of the 'antimurale' (no.543)

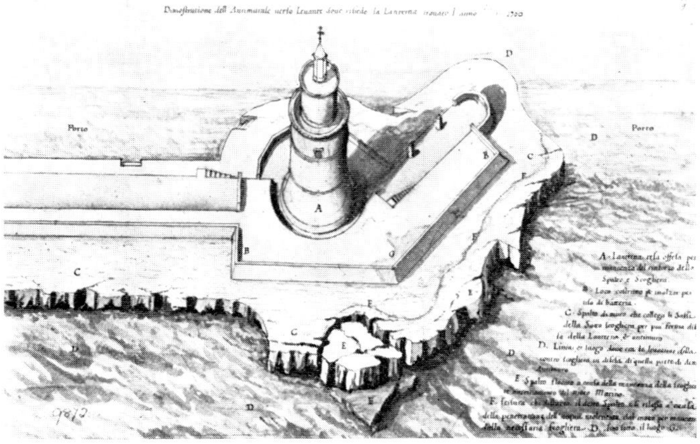

445 Perspective view of the lighthouse and south-east end of the 'antimurale' (no.545)

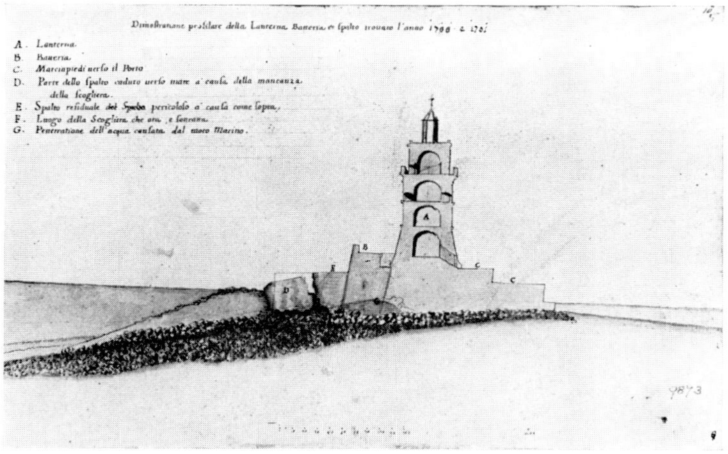

446 Section of the lighthouse and south-east end of the 'antimurale' (no.546)

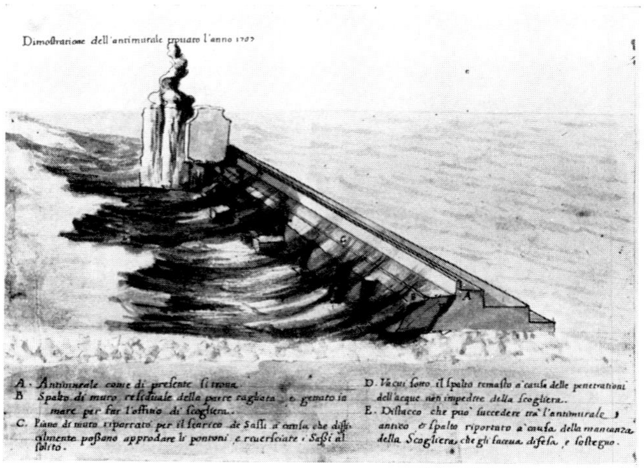

447 Section in perspective facing north west (1707) (no.548)

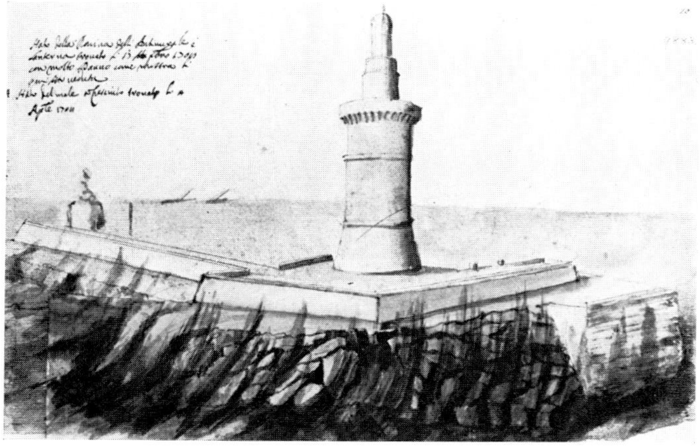

448 Perspective view of the lighthouse and south-east end of the 'antimurale' (no.561)

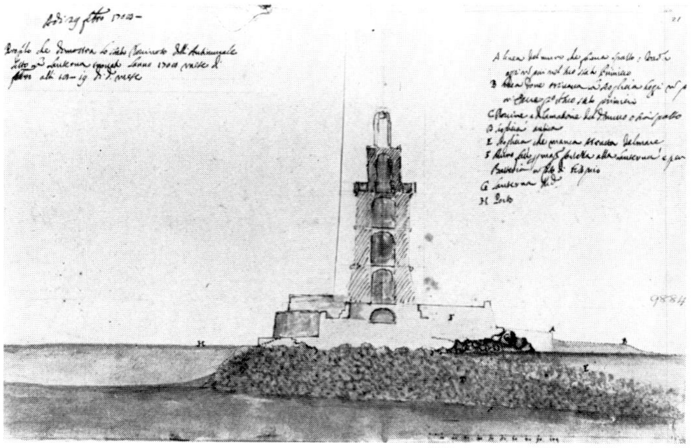

449 Section of the lighthouse and south-east end of the 'antimurale' (no.562)

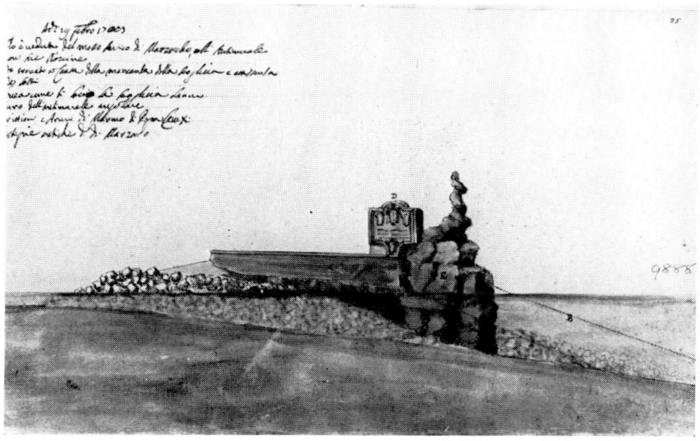

450 Section in perspective towards the 'Marzocco' (no.563)

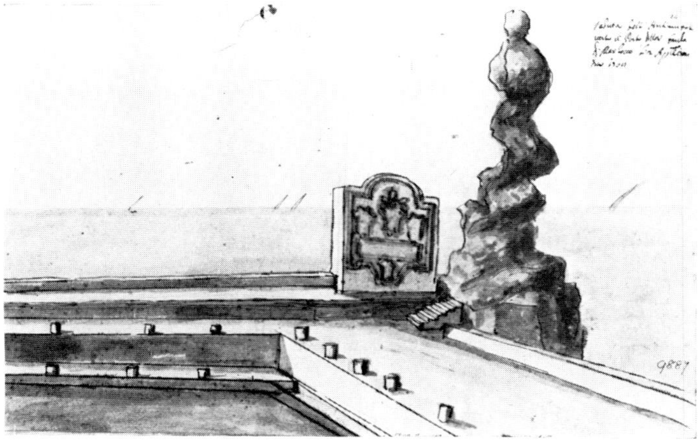

451 View of the north-west end of the 'antimurale' and the 'Marzocco' (no.565)

Civitavecchia, design for a papal galley (before 1704)

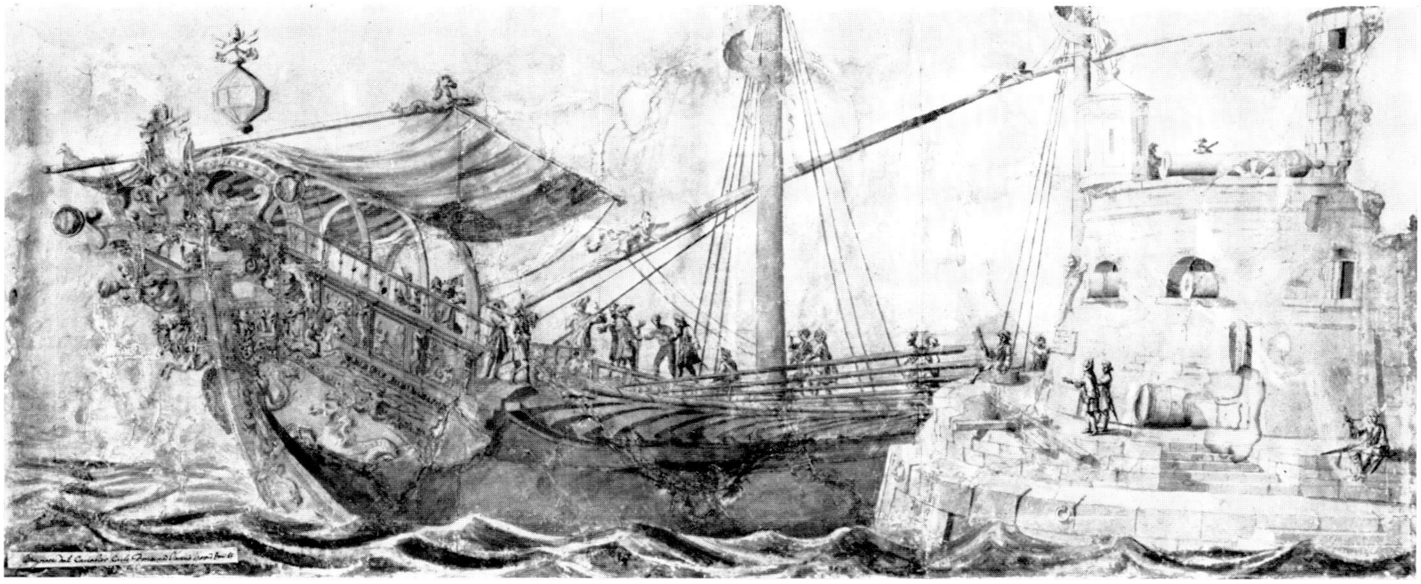

452 View of the galley, 1704 (drawing by Fontana; formerly Messrs Colnaghi)

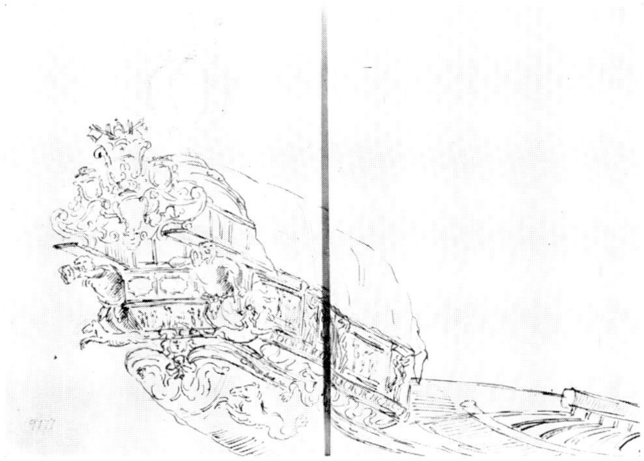

453 Study of the stern of the galley (no.567)

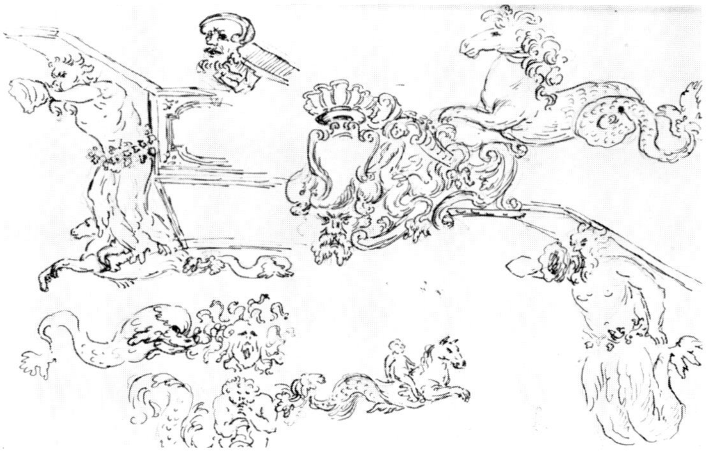

454 Studies for the decorations for the stern of the galley (no.570)

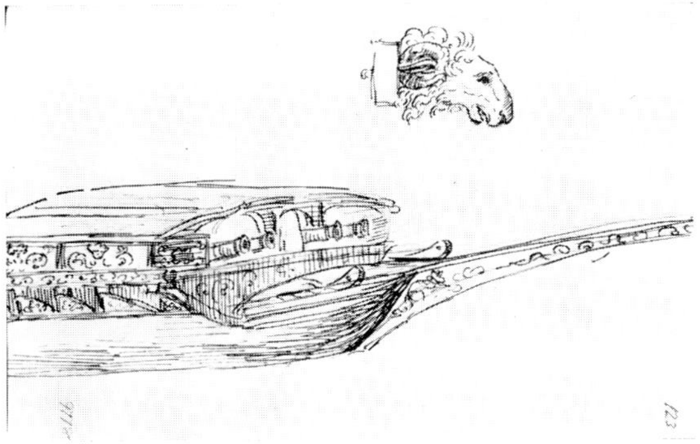

455 Study for the prow of the galley (no.571)

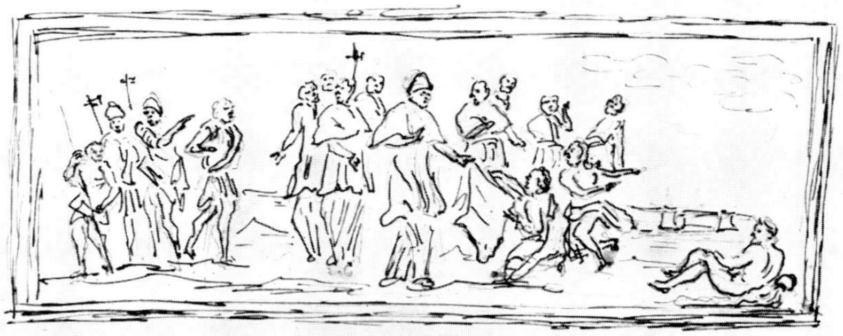

456 Study for a figure composition within a rectangular frame (no.574)

Project for a canopy for the Belvedere Torso

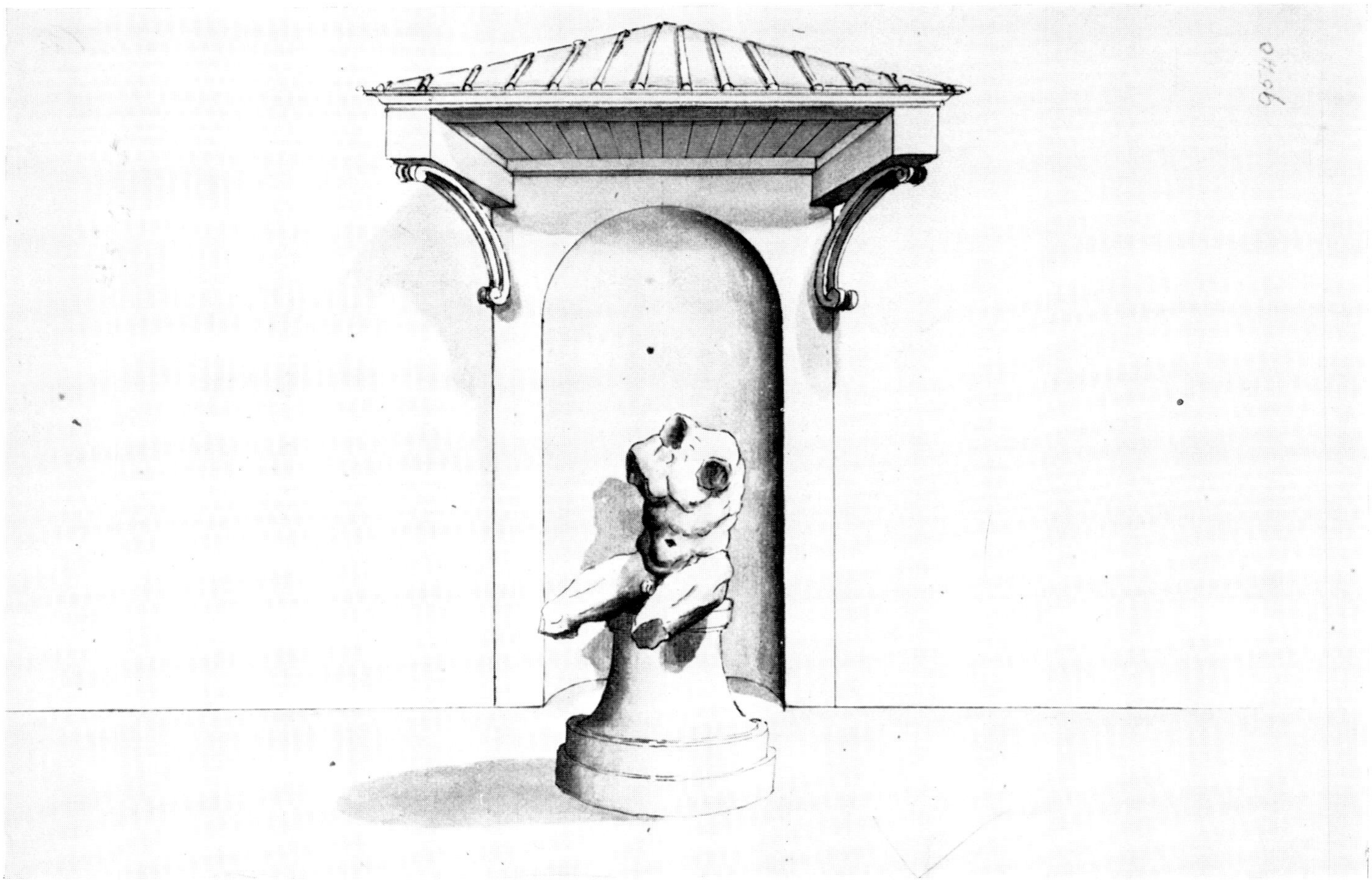

457 Perspective view of the torso and the canopy (no.575)

Projects for a doorway

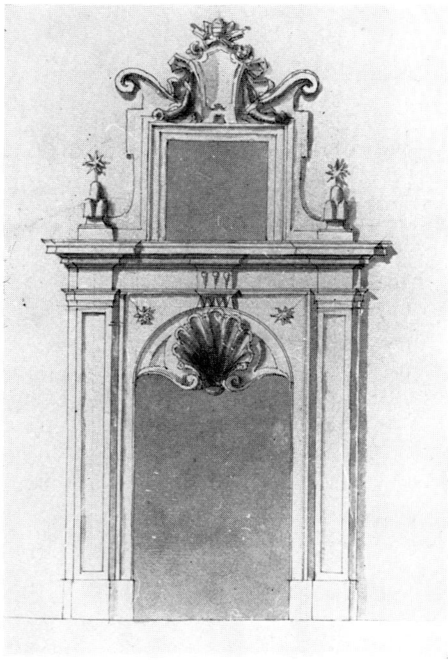

458 Project with the Albani arms (2) (no.577)

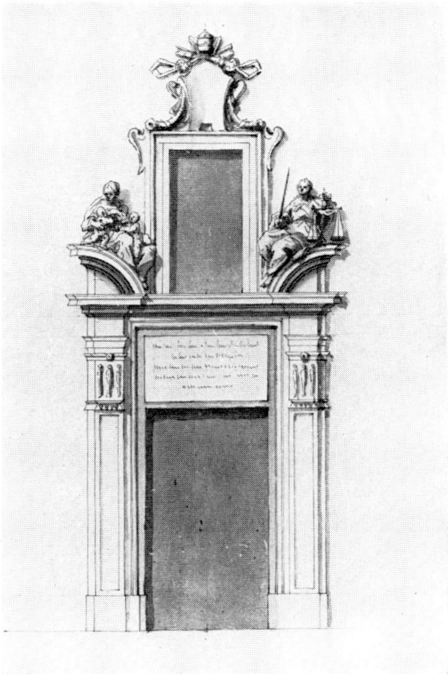

459 Project with seated figures of Charity and Justice (3) (no.580)

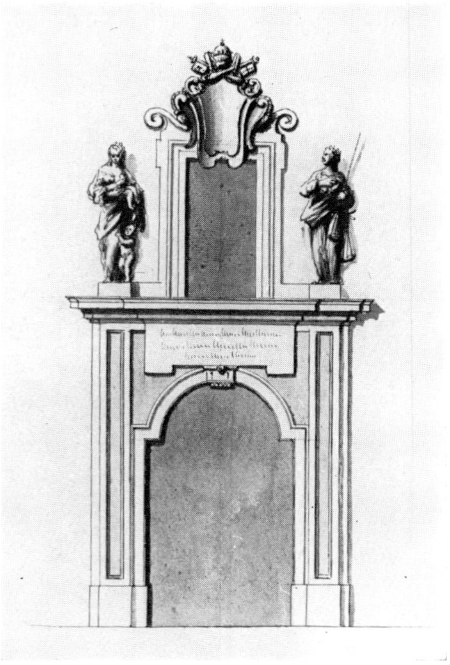

460 Project with standing figures of Charity and Justice (no.581)

Lago Maggiore, Isola Bella, projects for the Palazzo Borromeo

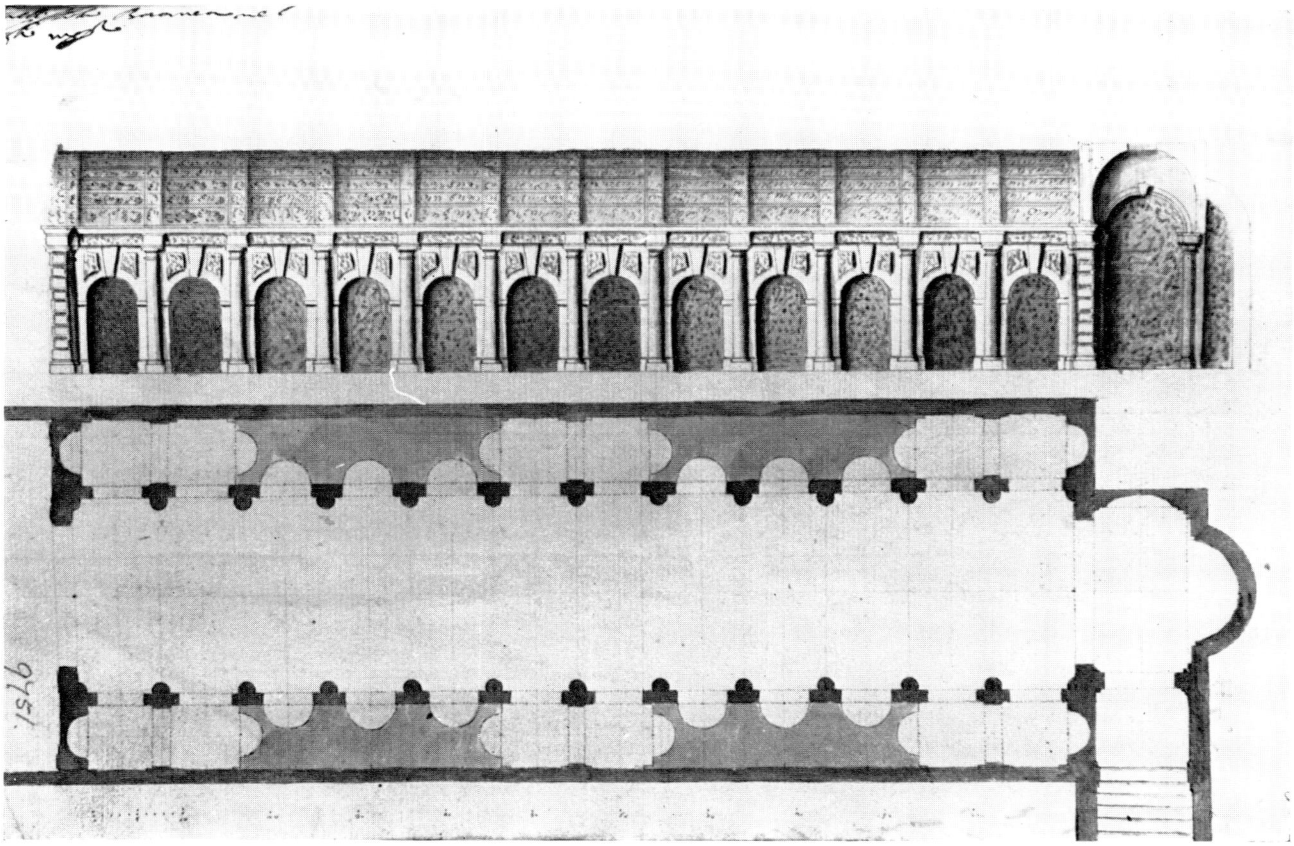

461 Plan and section of a garden gallery (no.584)

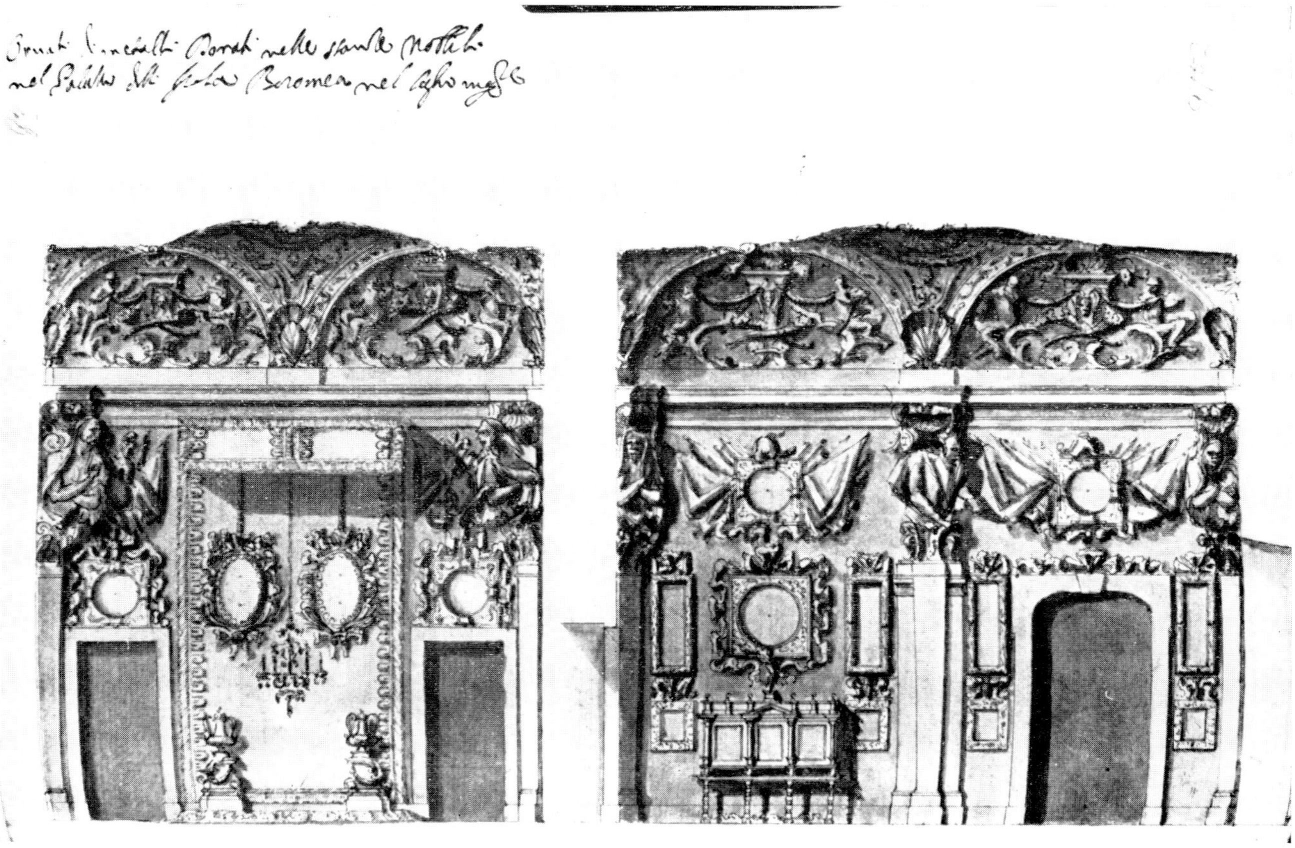

462 Sections of the 'Sala del Trono' (no.585)

The 'Albani' Volumes and additional illustrations

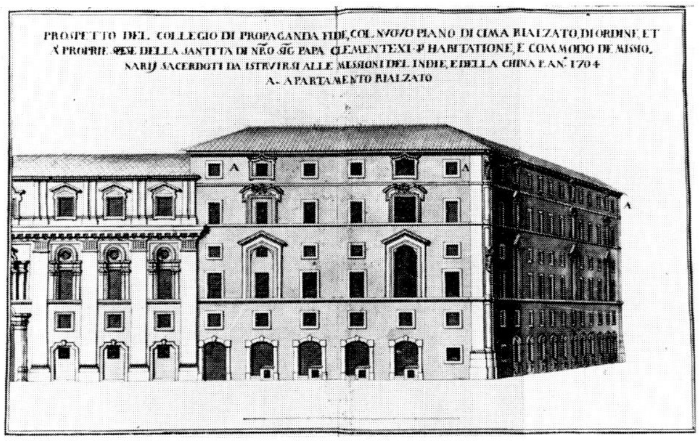

463 Perspective view of south half of Palazzo di Propaganda Fide, with new attic, 1704 (no.592)

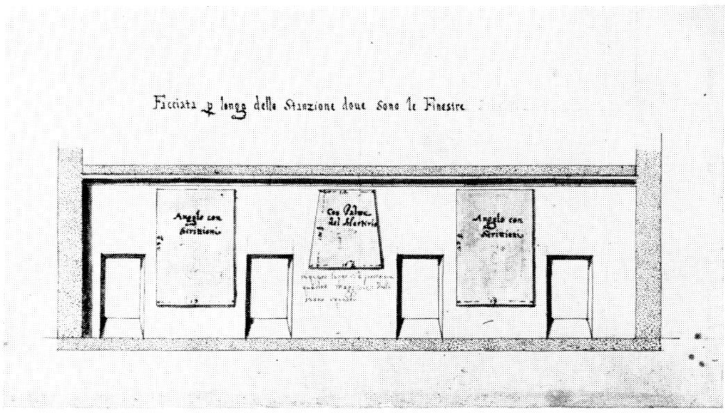

464 Elevation of a wall of the 'Stanzione contiguo alla stanza della Bologna' in the Vatican (no.597)

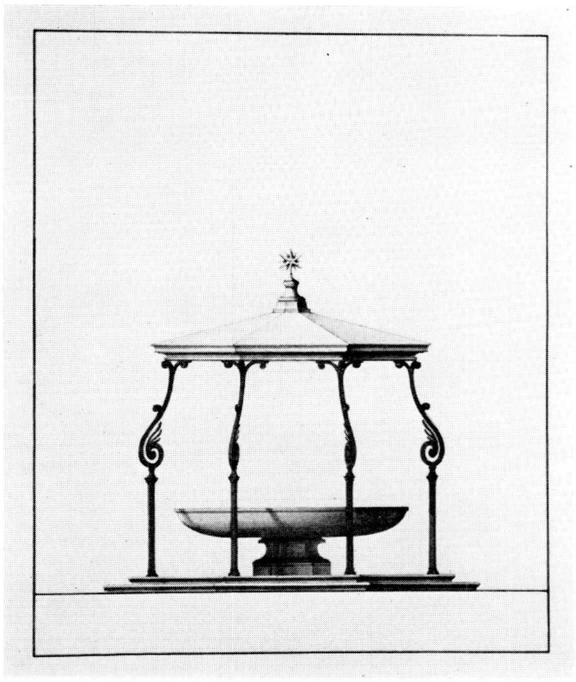

465 Project for pavilion for the 'Cortile Ottangolare' of the Vatican, elevation (no.600)

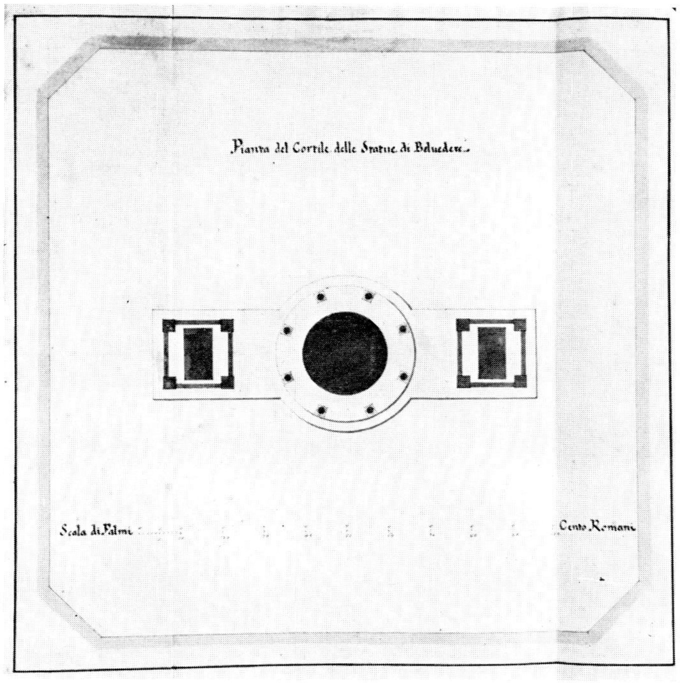

466 Project for a circular temple for the 'Cortile Ottangolare' of the Vatican, plan (no.598)

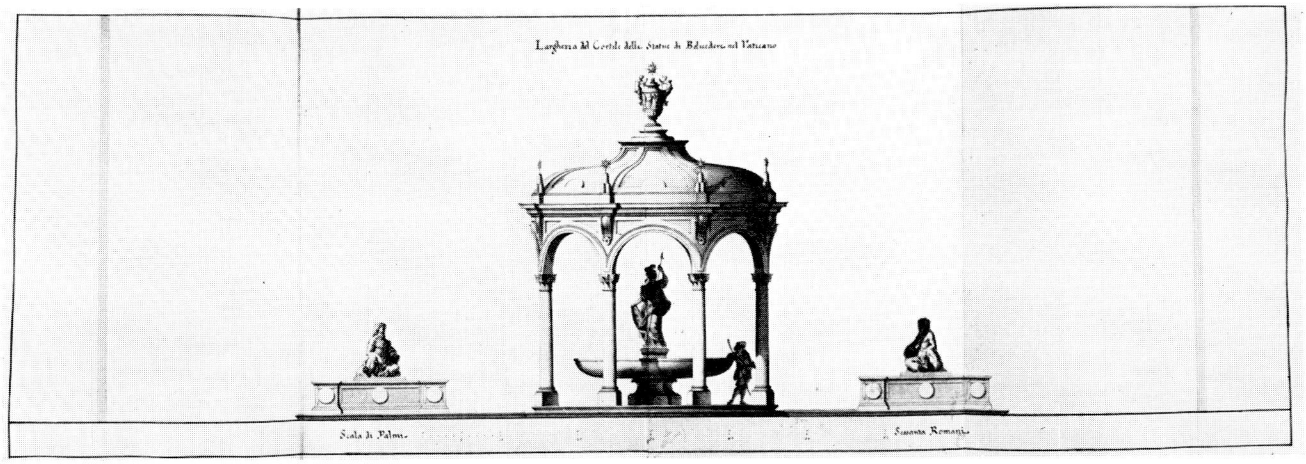

467 Project for a circular temple for the 'Cortile Ottangolare' of the Vatican, elevation (no.599)

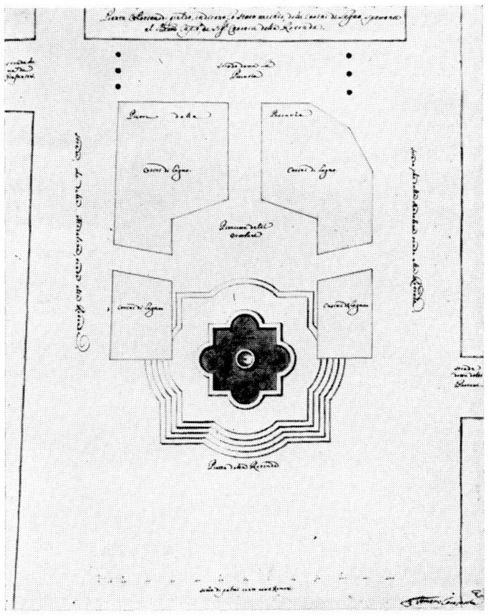

468 Plan of the existing site (by Romano Carapecchia; no.602)

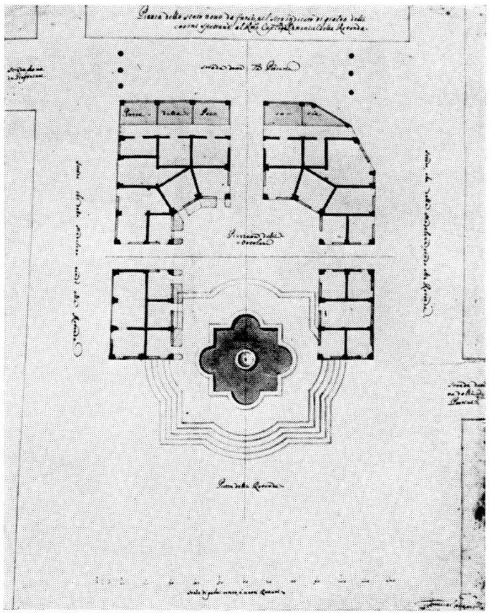

469 Project for new stalls, plan (by Romano Carapecchia; no.603)

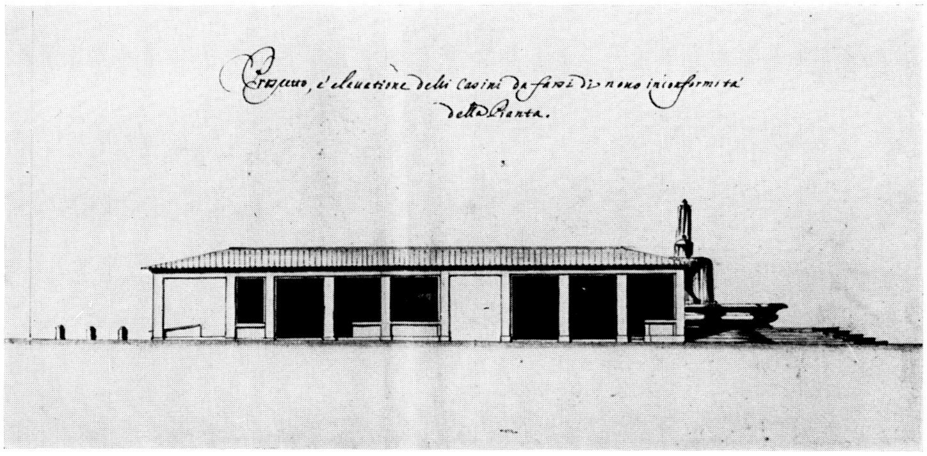

470 Project for new stalls, side elevation (by Romano Carapecchia; no.604)

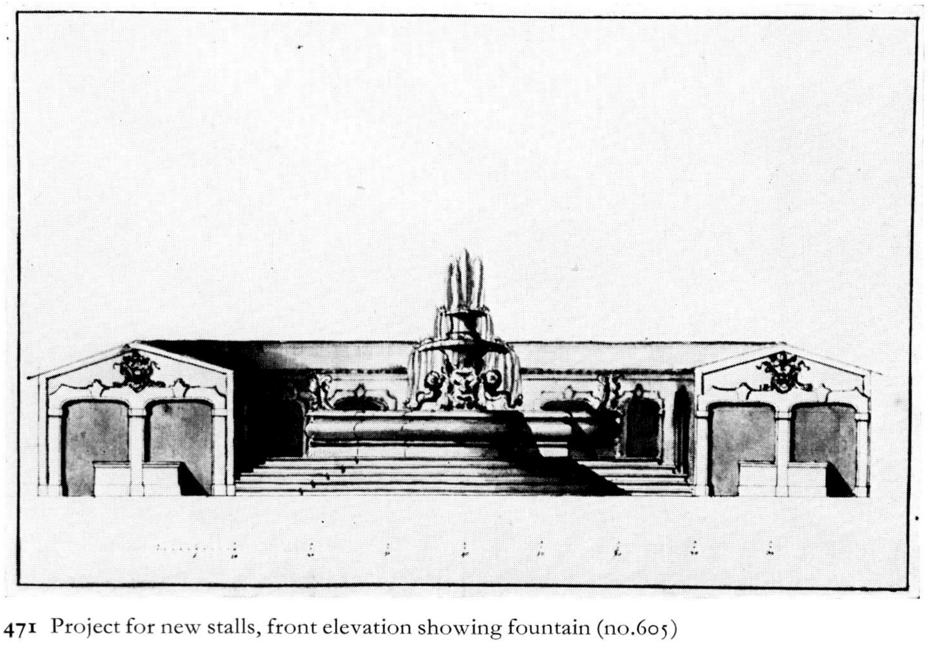

471 Project for new stalls, front elevation showing fountain (no.605)

SS. Apostoli, a survey drawing (1708)

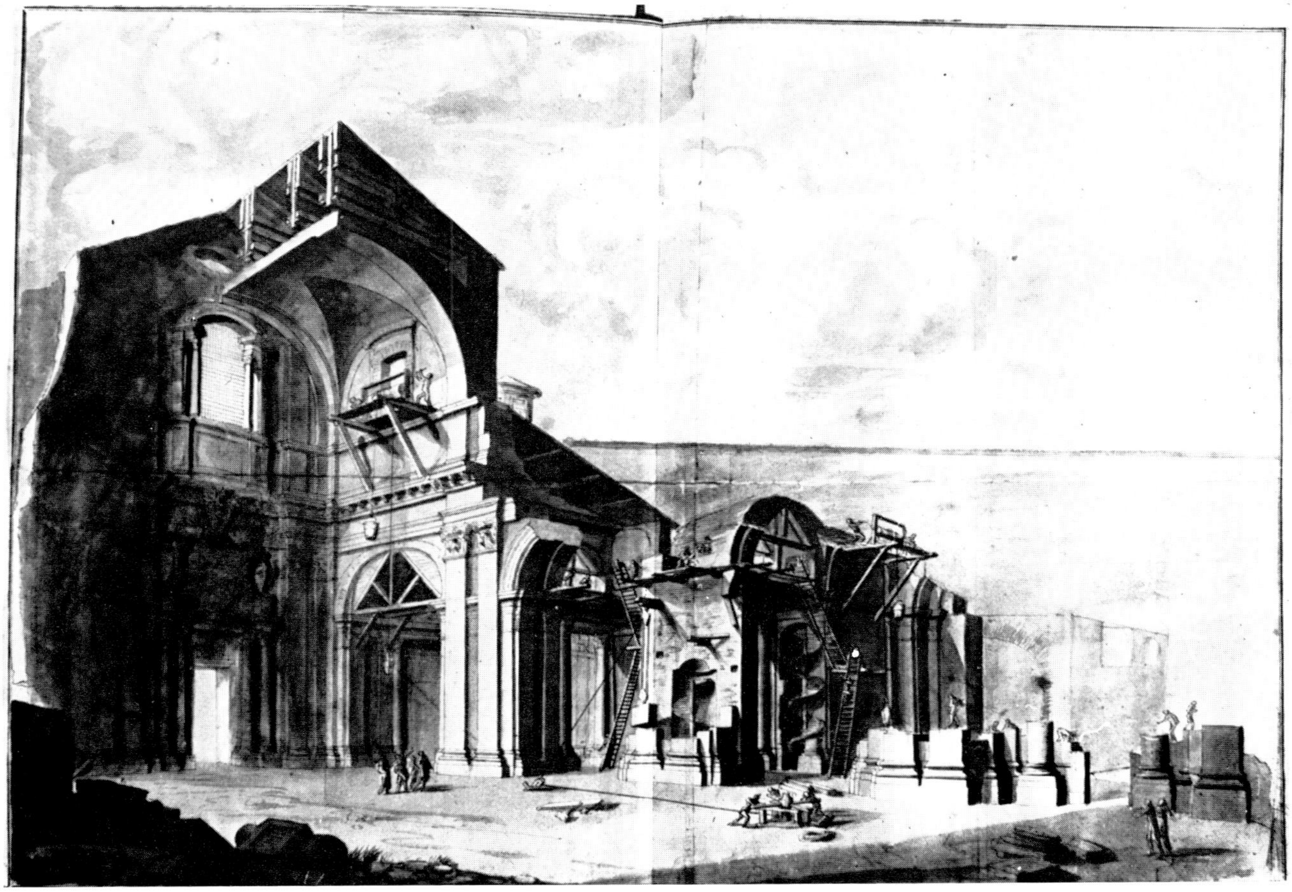

472 Perspective view of the church (by Nicola Michetti; no.608)

S. Maria della Concezione, project for the façade (1712?)

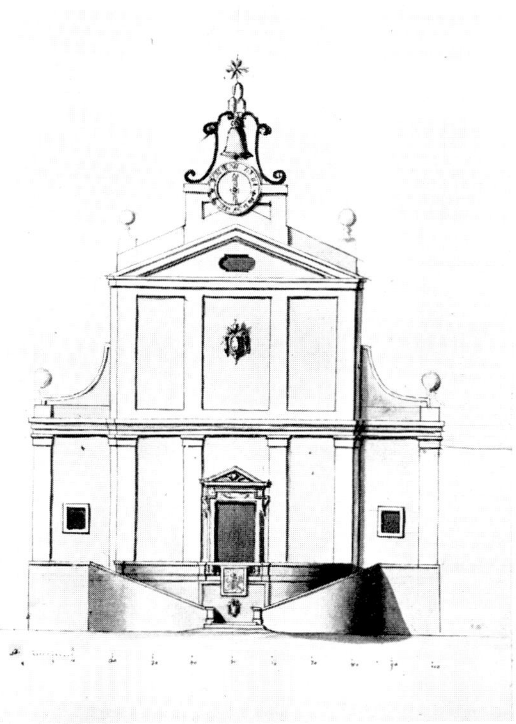

473 Elevation of the façade (no.612)

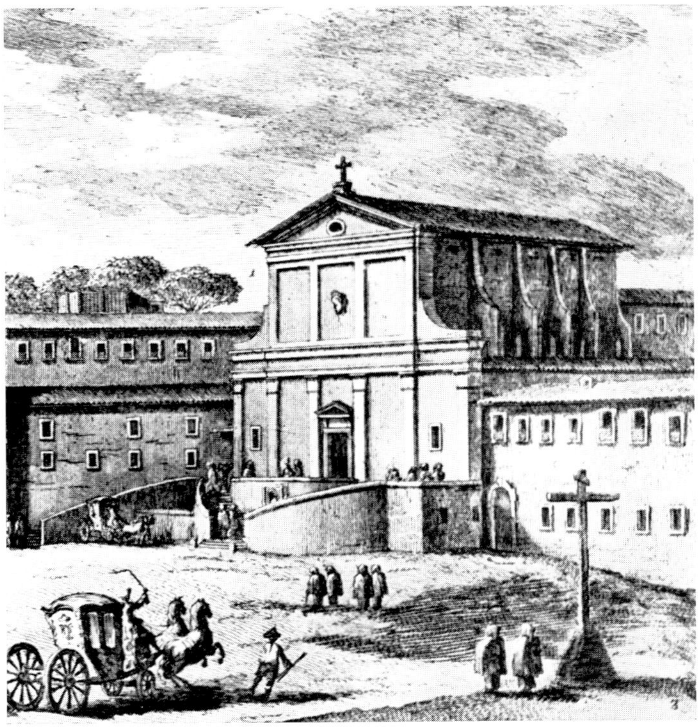

474 View of the façade (detail of engraving from Vasi, *Magnificenze*, 1757)

S. Maria Maggiore, project for the portico gates

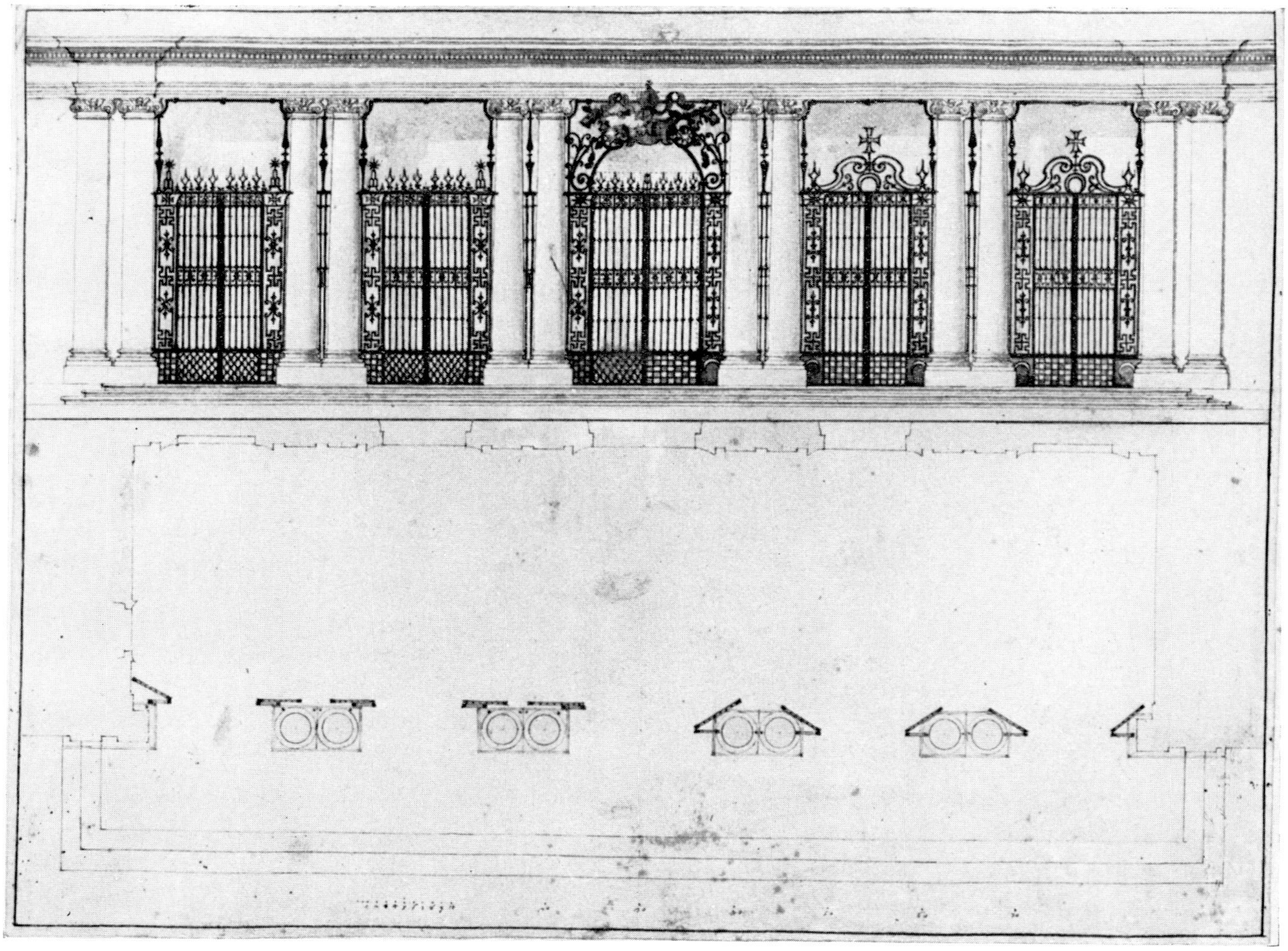

475 Plan and elevation of the portico (no.613)

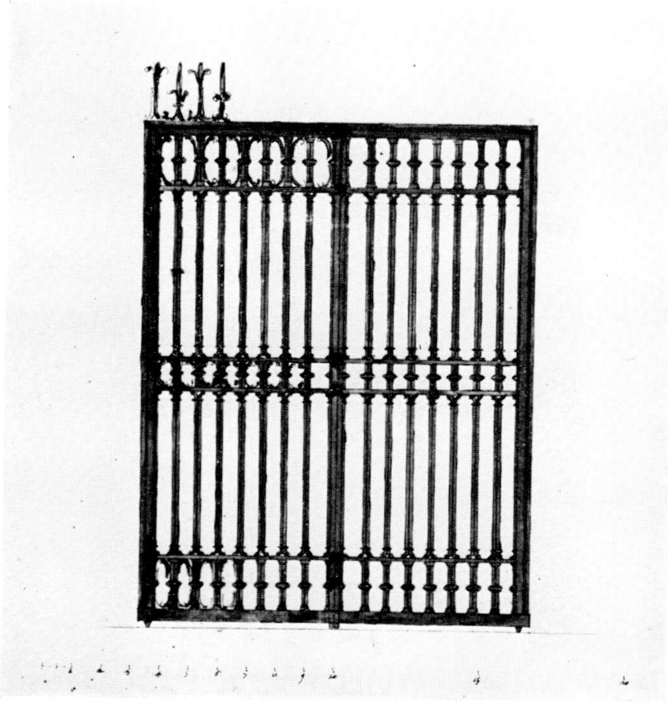

476 Project for a gate (no.614)

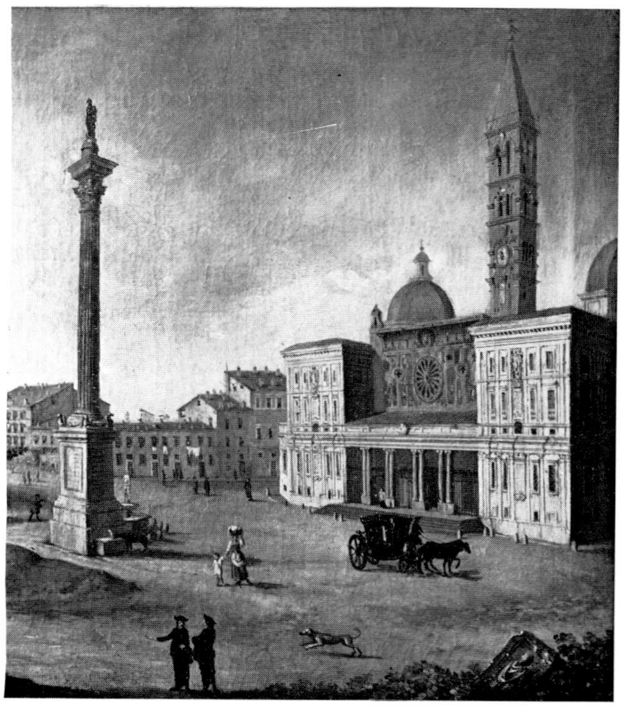

477 View of the façade before the 18th-century alterations (detail of anon. painting; Museo di Roma)

S. Maria in Monticelli, project for restoration (1714)

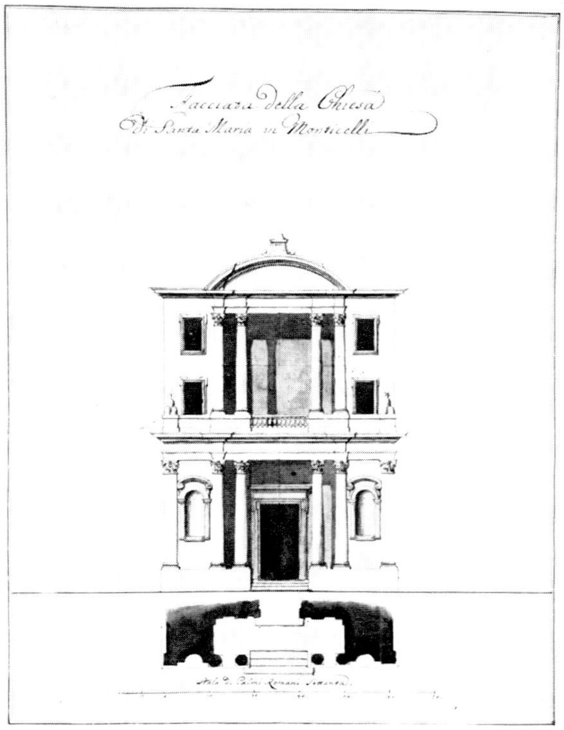

478 Project for the façade, elevation (anon. drawing; Vienna, Albertina)

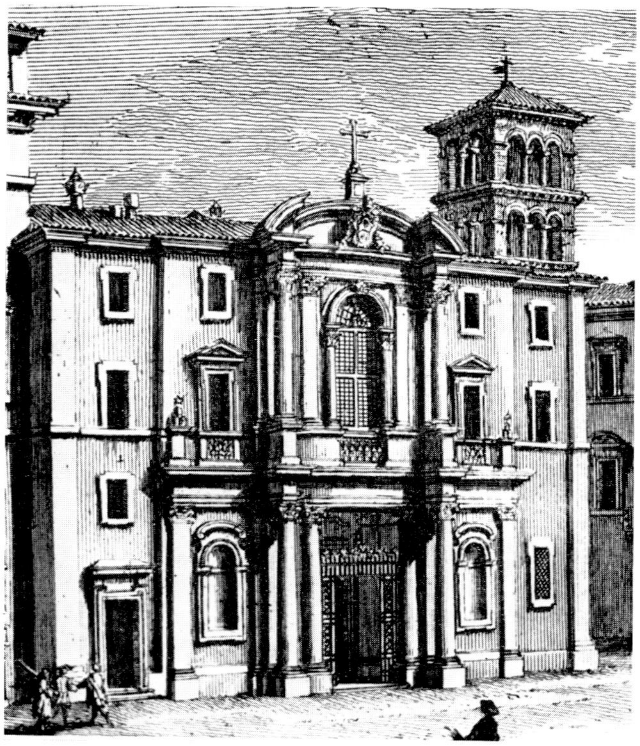

479 View of the façade (detail of engraving from Vasi, *Magnificenze*, 1756)

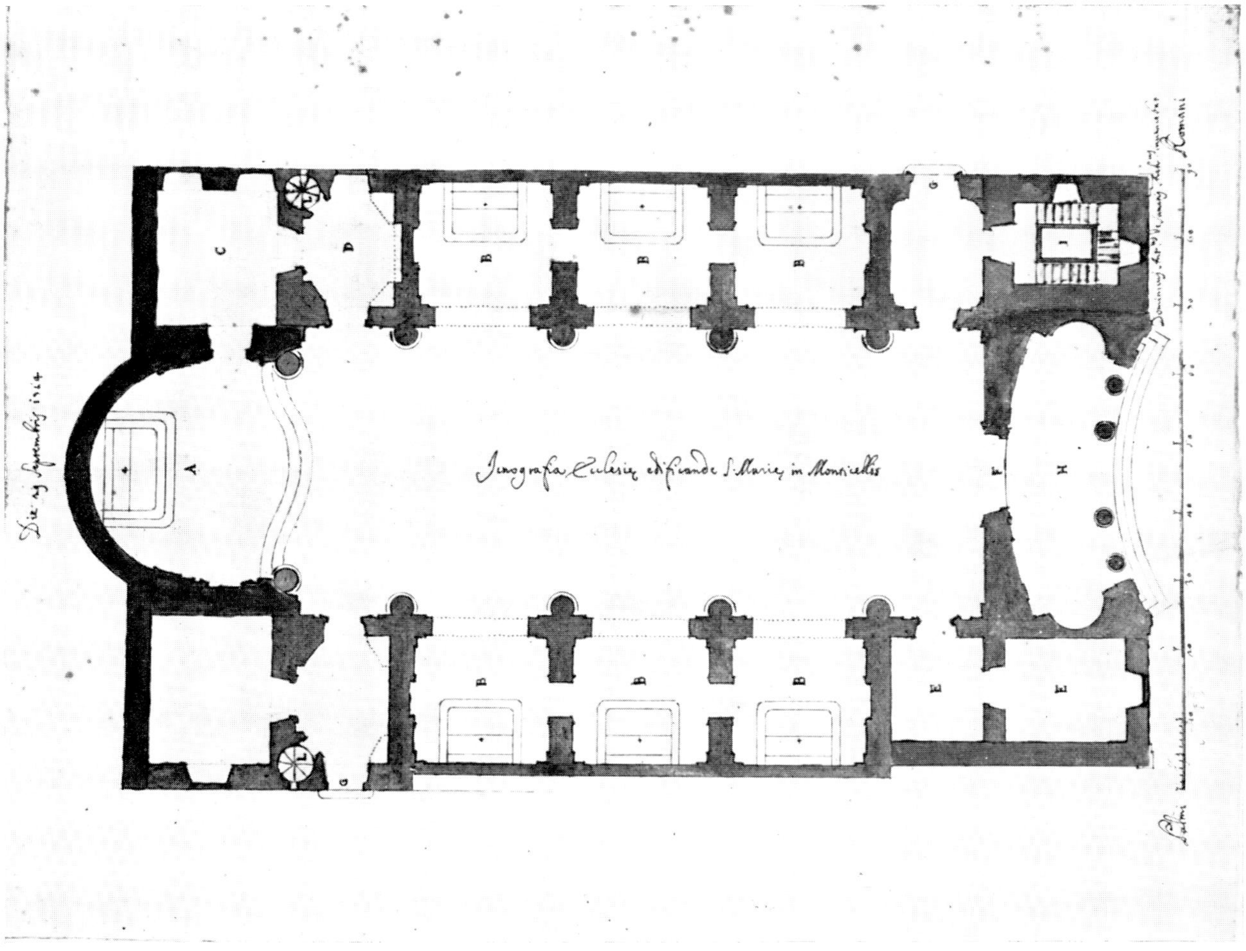

480 Plan project (by Domenico Antonio de Sanctis; no.615)

Rome, secular works: projects for using the Colonna Citatoria (1703–1705?)

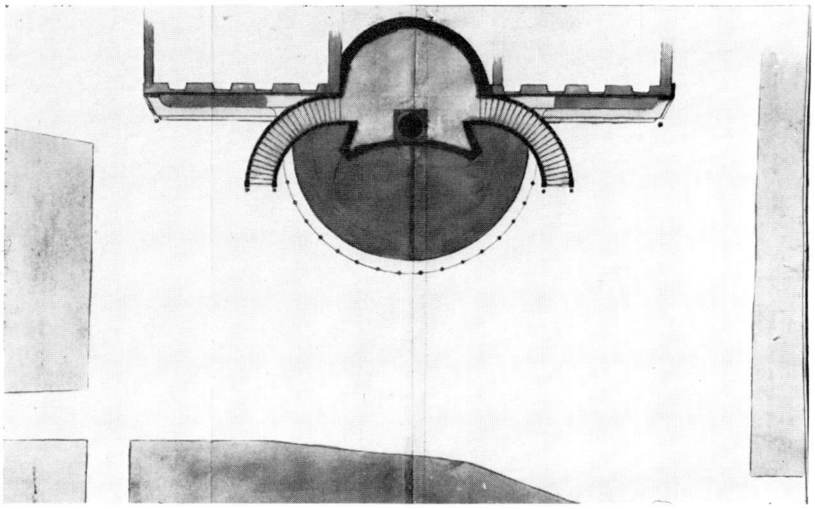

481 Project for the Fontana di Trevi, plan (by Nicola Michetti; no.619)

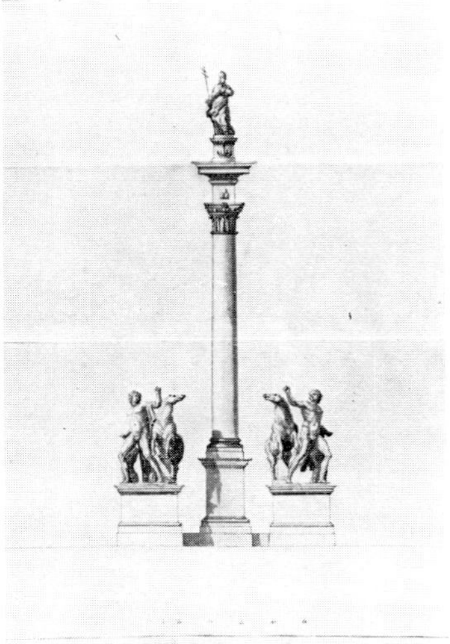

484 Project for the Piazza di Montecavallo, elevation (no.617)

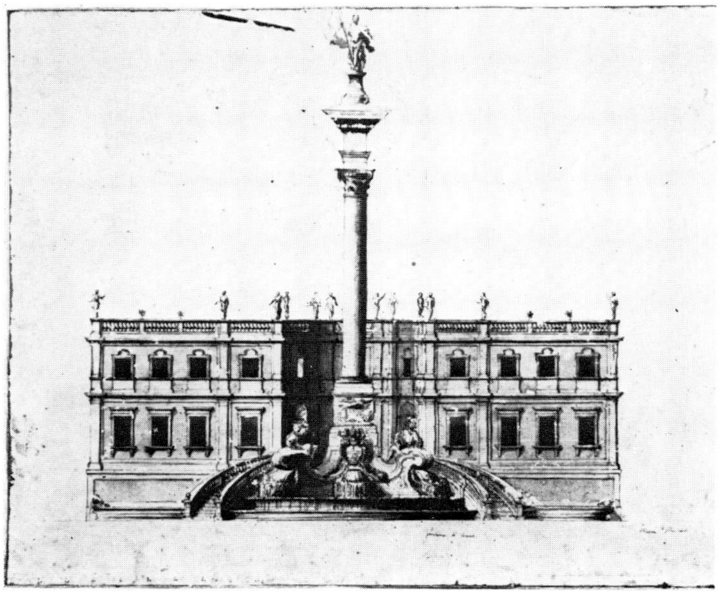

482 Project for the Fontana di Trevi, elevation (by Nicola Michetti; no.620)

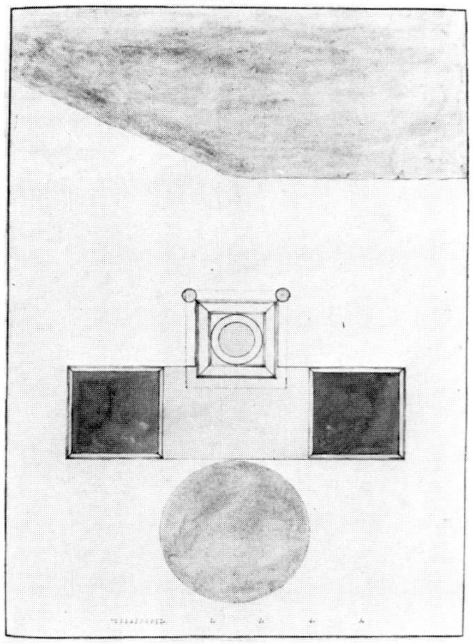

485 Project for the Piazza di Montecavallo, plan (no.618)

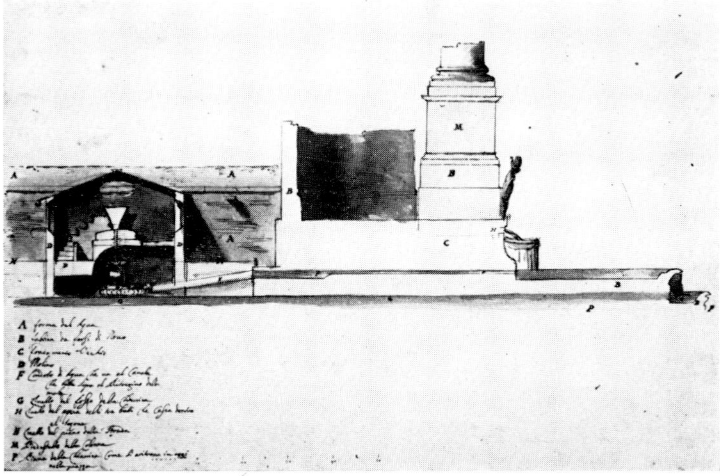

483 Project for the Fontana di Trevi, section (by Nicola Michetti; no.621)

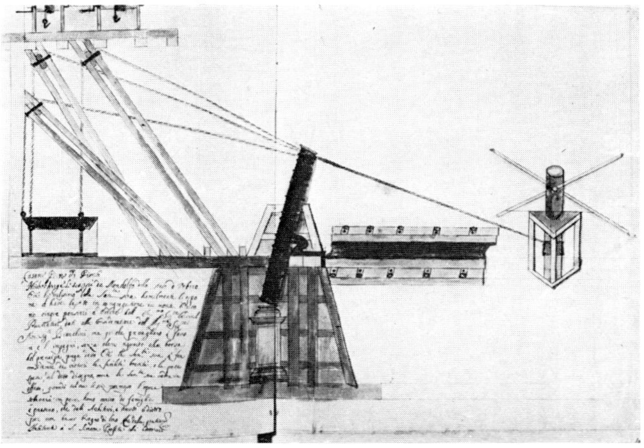

486 Project for raising the column (by 'Michel Angeli Scappi da Mondolfo'; no.616)

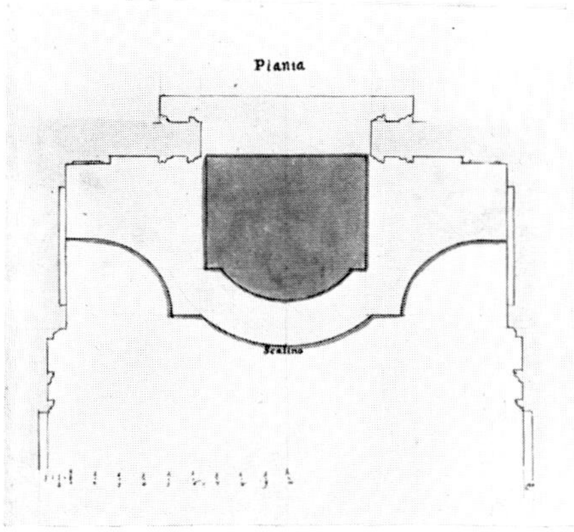

487 Site plan of statue of Paul IV in the Palazzo dei Conservatori (no.622)

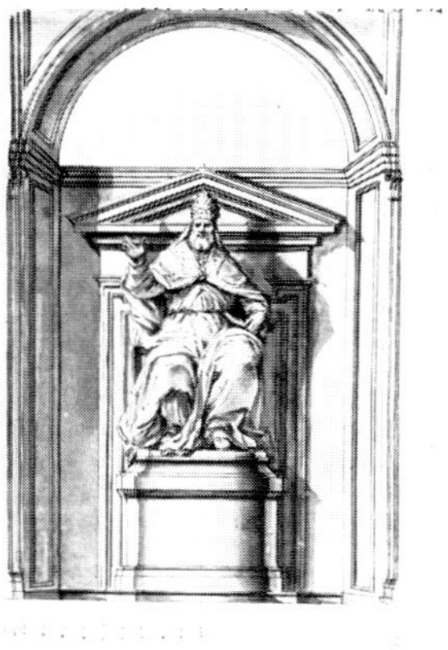

488 Perspective view of the statue on its dais (no.623)

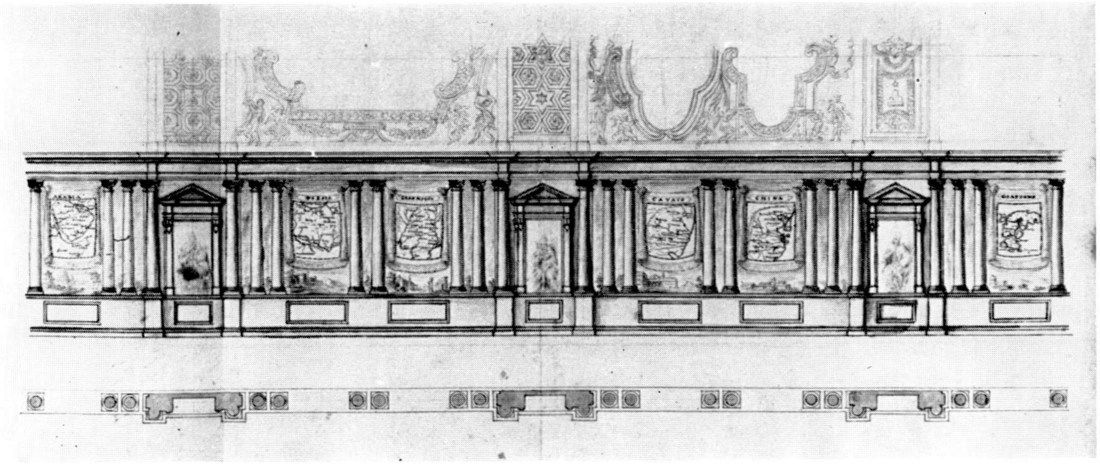

489 Plan and elevation of a wall of a Sala del Mappamondo in the Quirinal ? Palace (no.626)

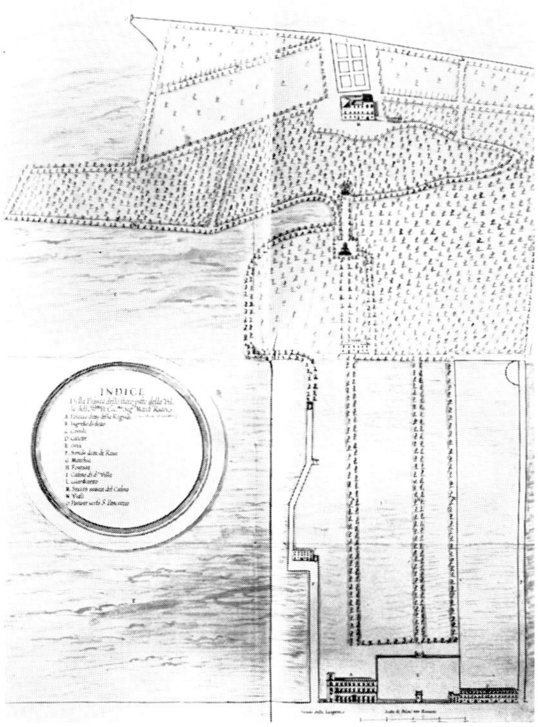

490 Plan of the grounds of the Palazzo Riario (no.627)

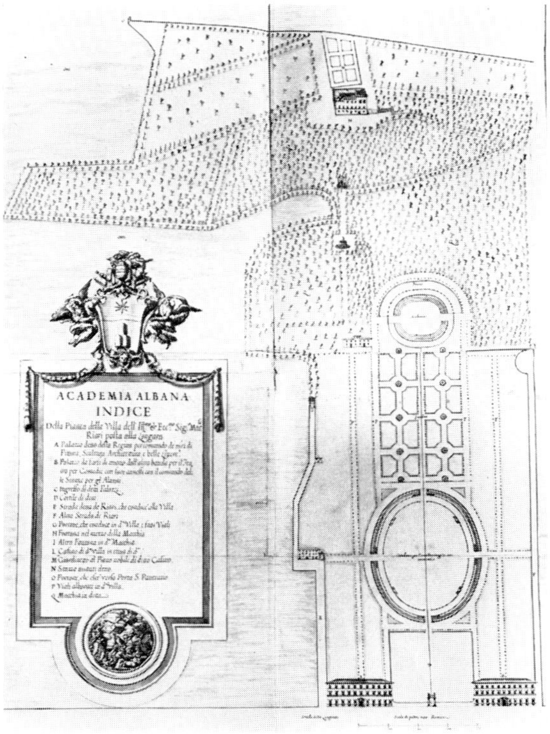

491 Plan of the grounds of the Palazzo Riario, showing projects for alterations (no.628)

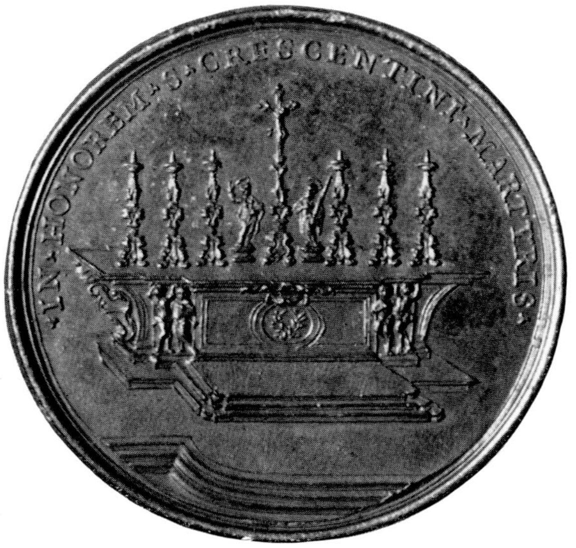

492 Medal of the altar, 1708 (Genoa, Gabinetto numismatico del Comune di Genoa)

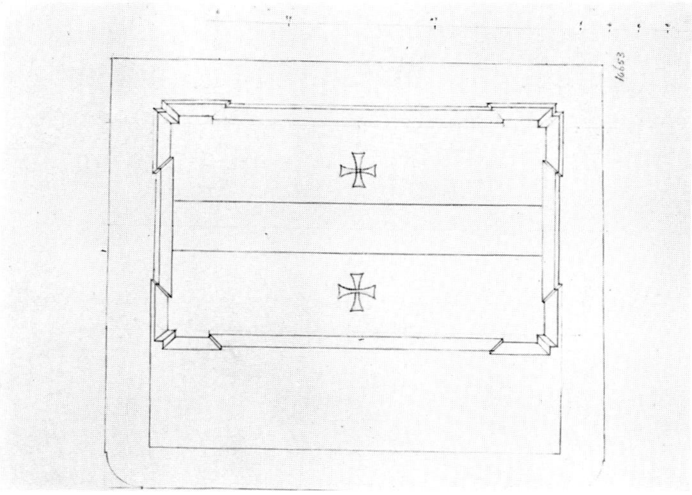

494 Project with a broad *mensa*, plan (no.637)

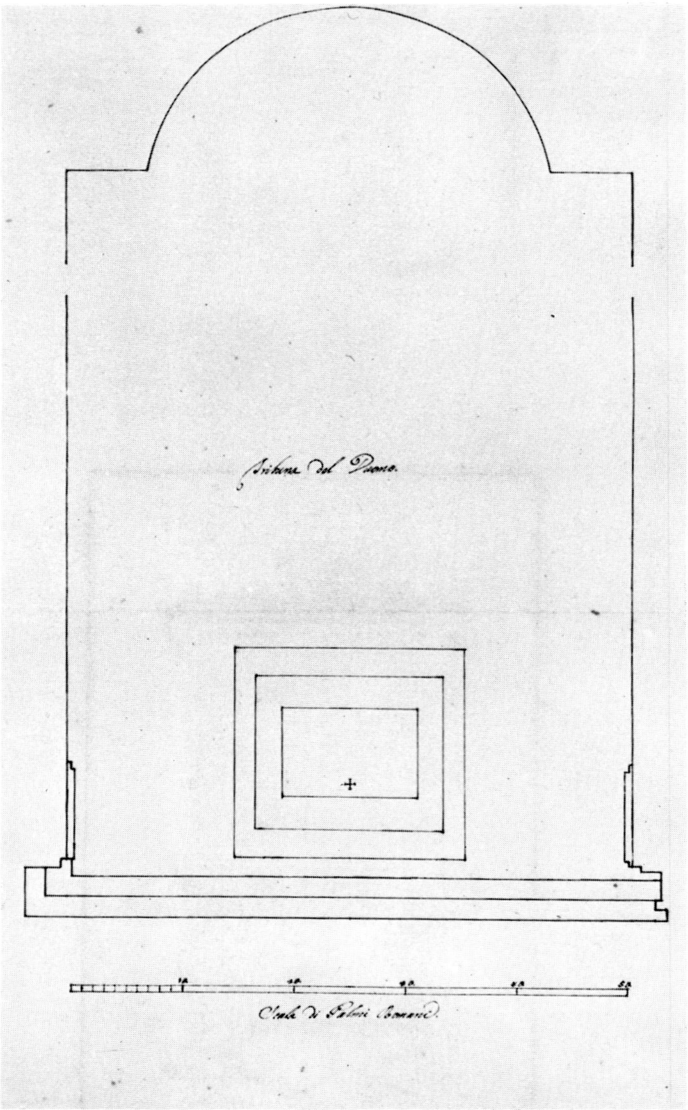

493 Plan of the choir (no.633)

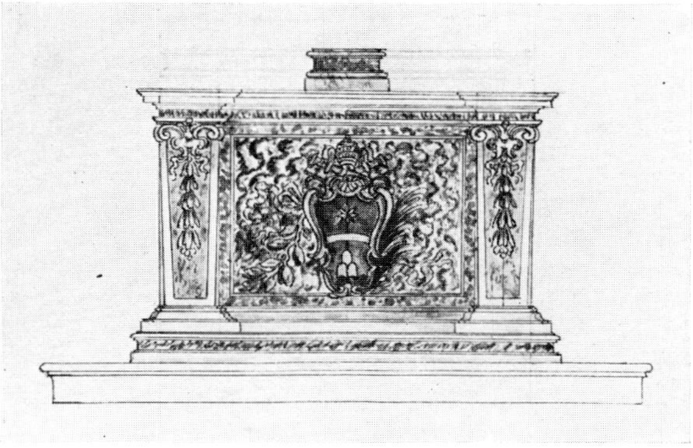

495 Project with a broad *mensa*, side elevation (no.636)

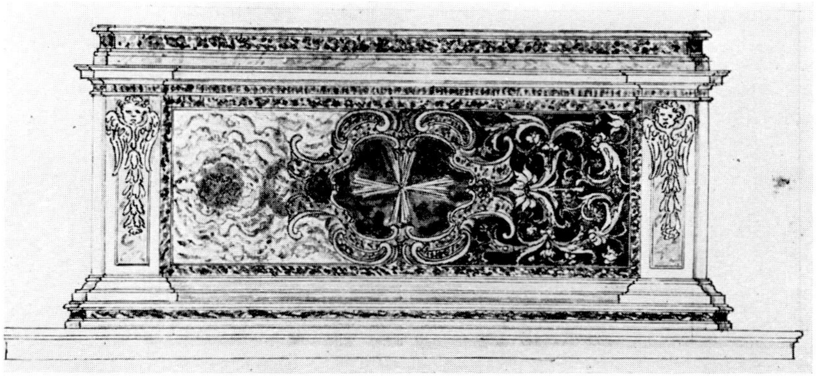

496 Project with a broad *mensa*, front elevation (no.635)

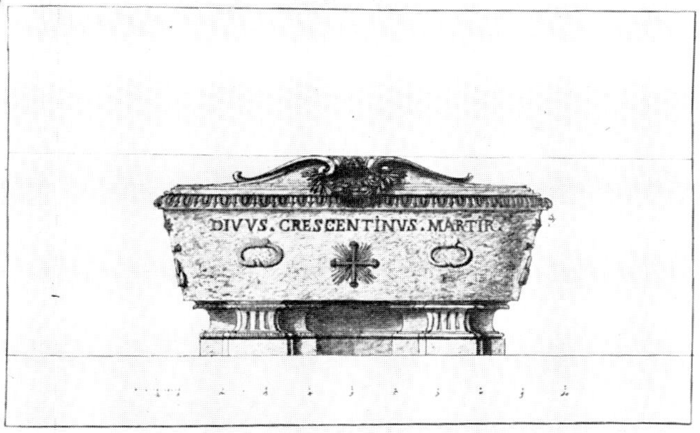

497 Project for a curved sarcophagus, elevation (no.640)

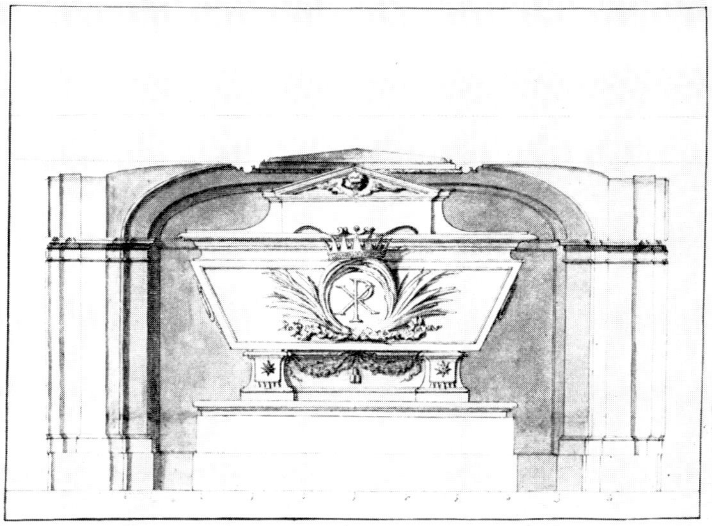

499 Section of the altar with project for urn sarcophagus (1), elevation (no.642)

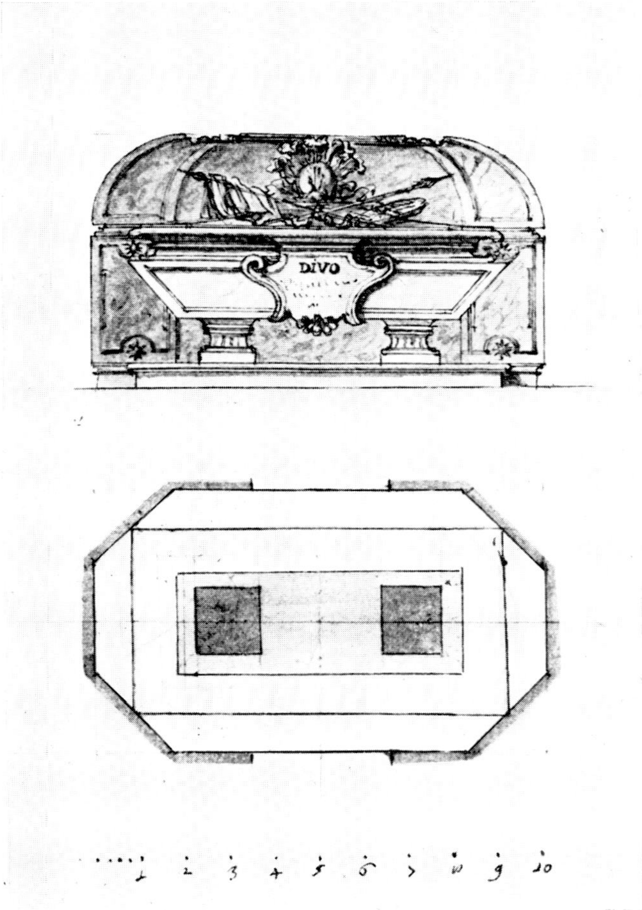

498 Section and plan of the altar with project for sarcophagus decorated with flags (no.641)

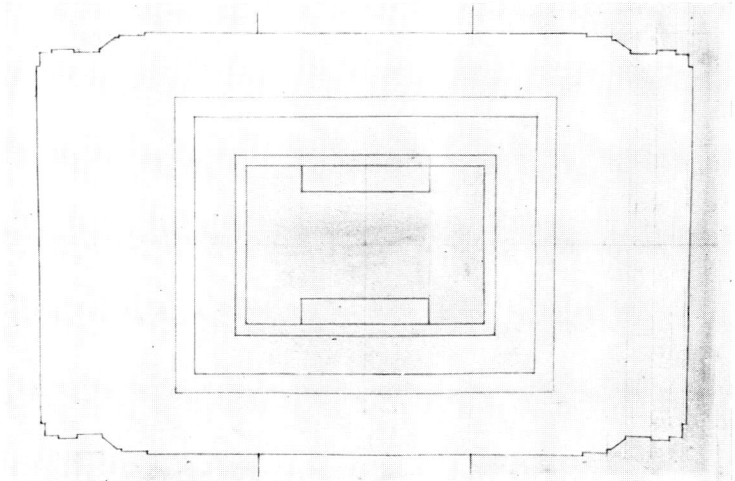

500 Plan of the altar with project for urn sarcophagus (1) (no.643)

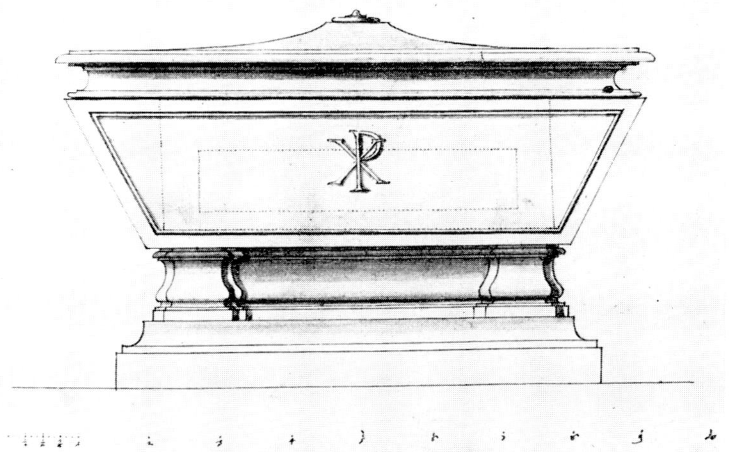

501 Project for urn sarcophagus (3), elevation (no.646)

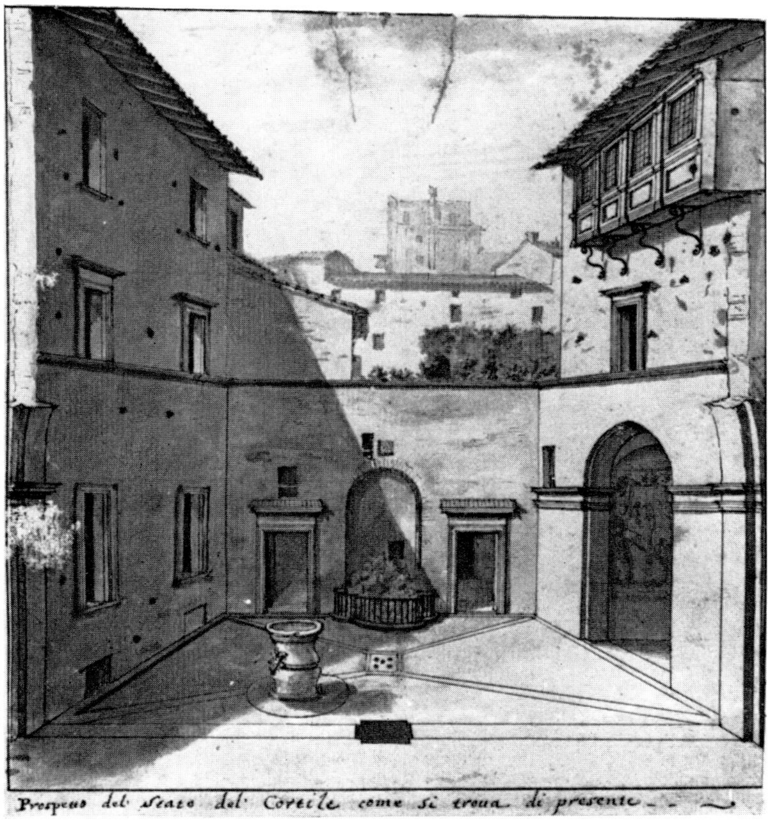

502 Perspective view of the courtyard (no.654)

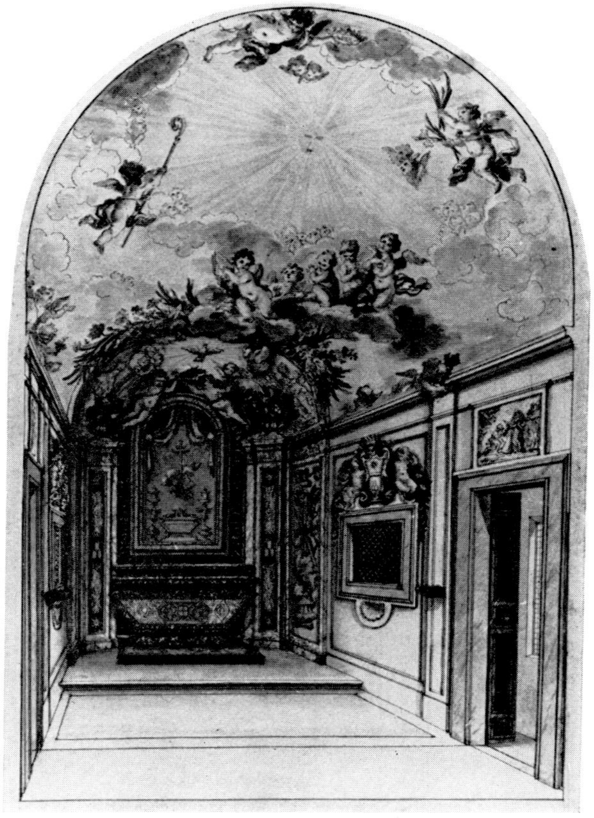

504 Perspective view of the chapel (no.658)

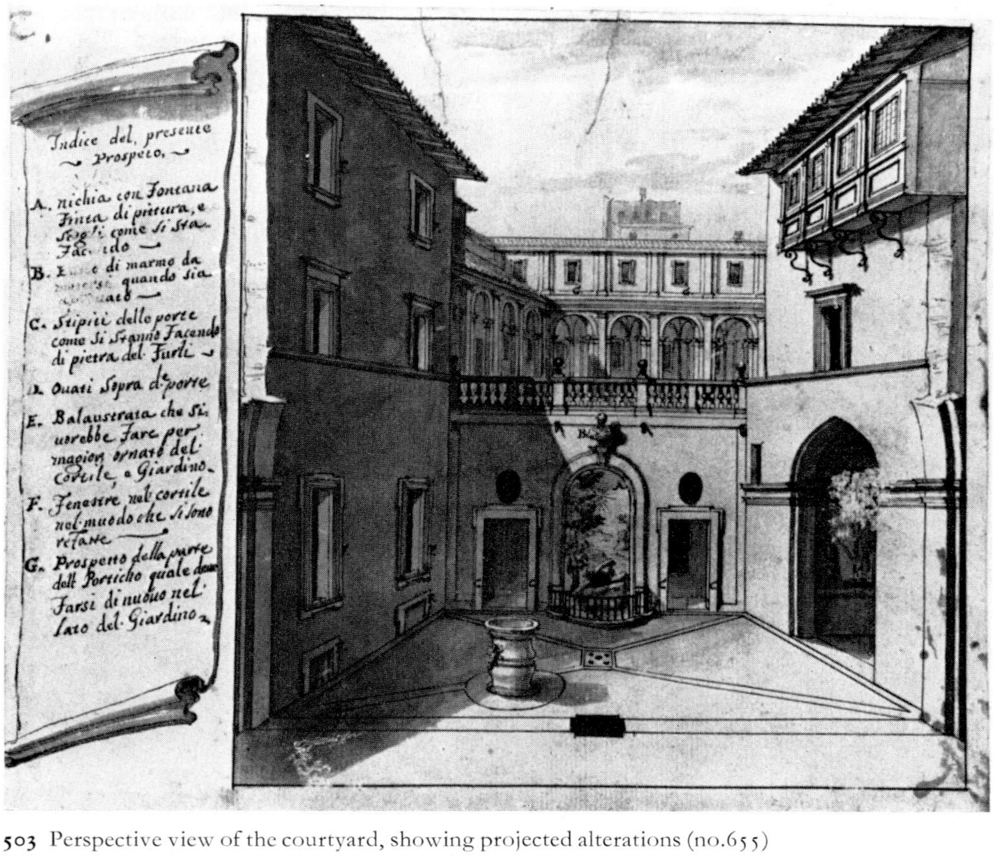

503 Perspective view of the courtyard, showing projected alterations (no.655)

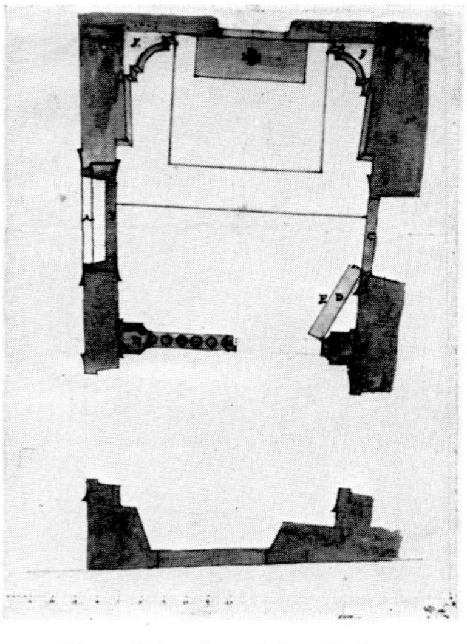

505 Plan of the chapel (no.656)

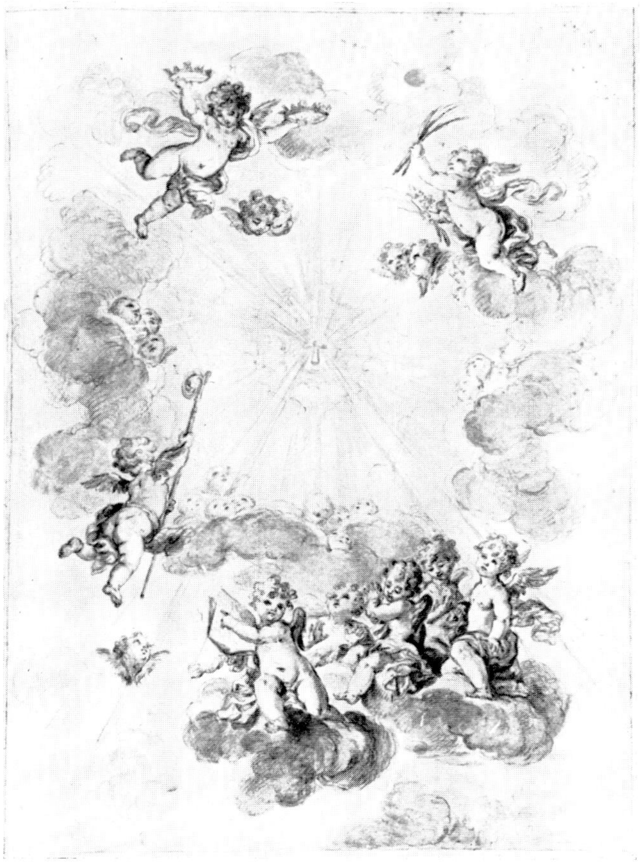

506 Study of the ceiling fresco of the chapel (no.659)

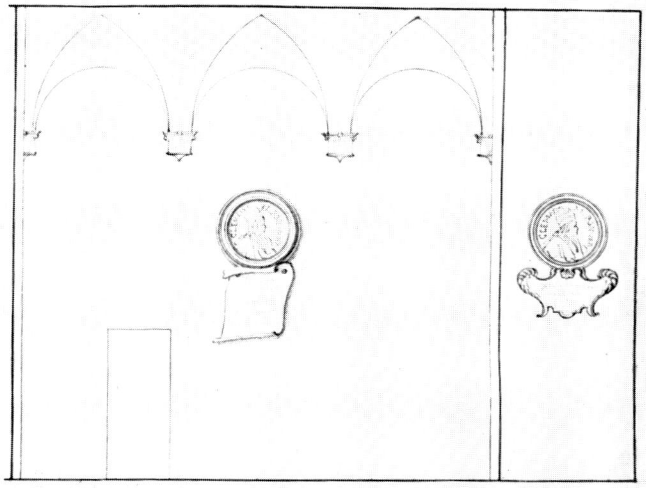

508 Elevation of a wall, with portrait medallions of Pope Clement XI (no.660)

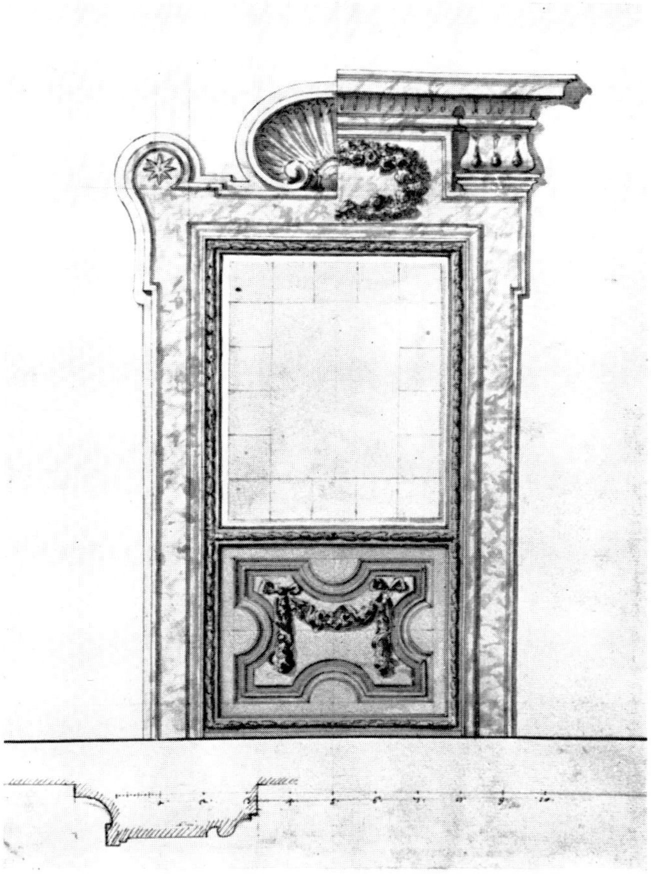

507 Project for a doorway, half plan and elevation (no.665)

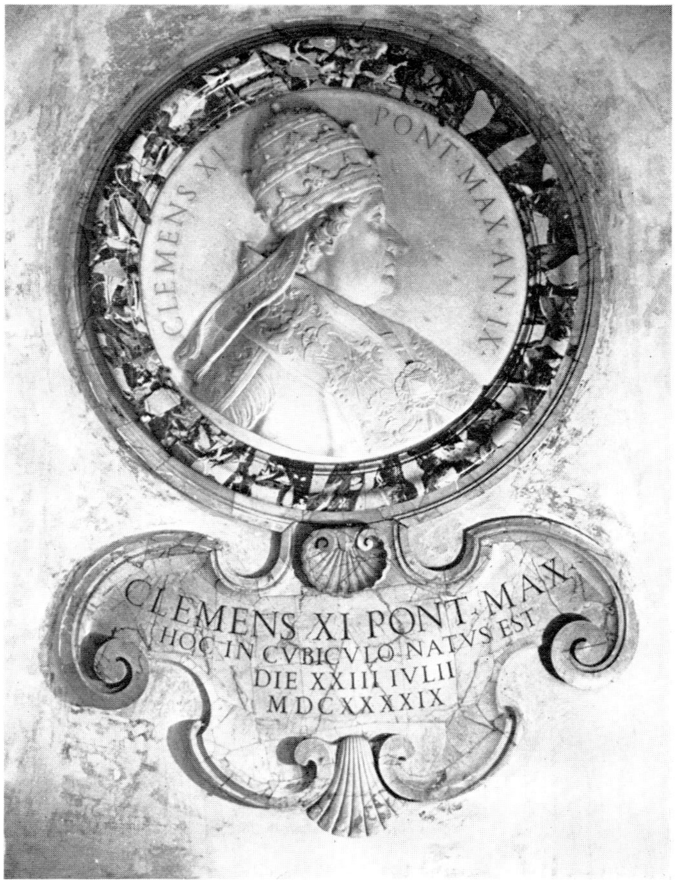

509 Medallion of Pope Clement XI

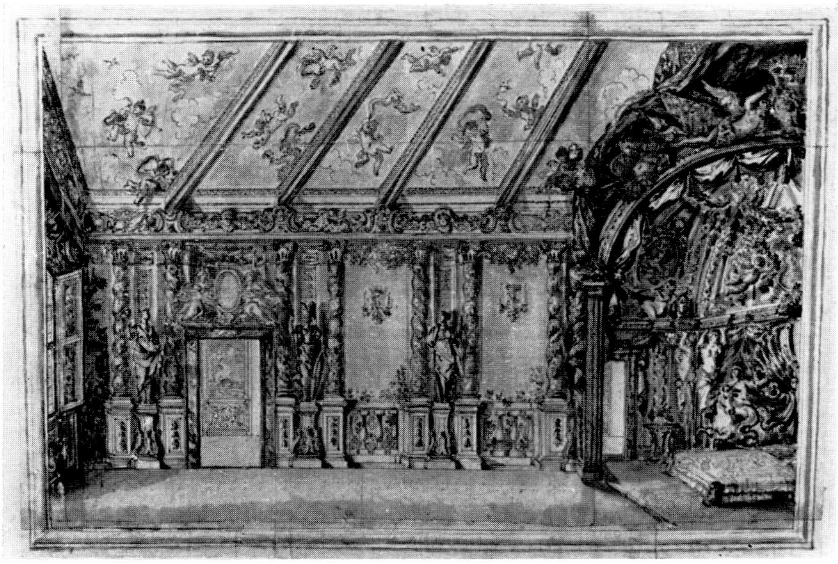

510 Study for the decoration of a bedroom (no.661)

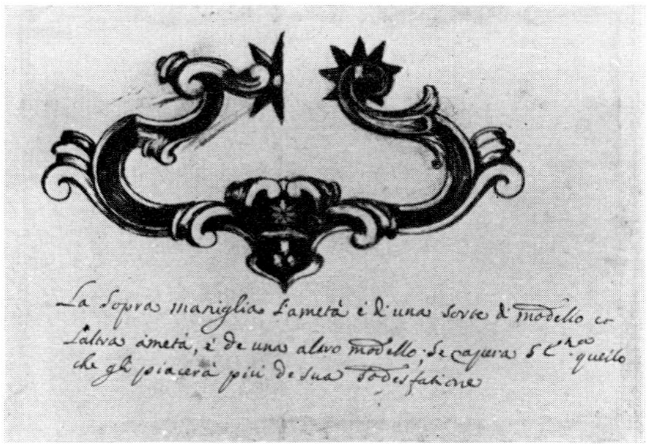

511 Design for a door-knocker (no.670)

The Porta Valbona, Urbino; The Metelli Altar, S. Francesco, Pesaro

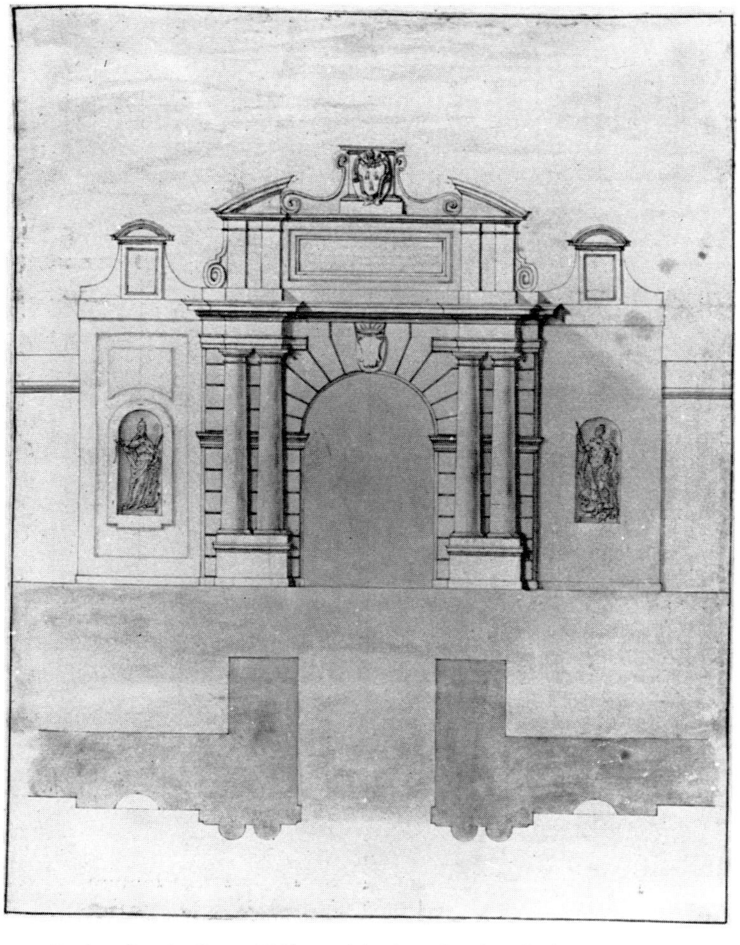

512 Project for the Porta Valbona (2), elevation (no.673)

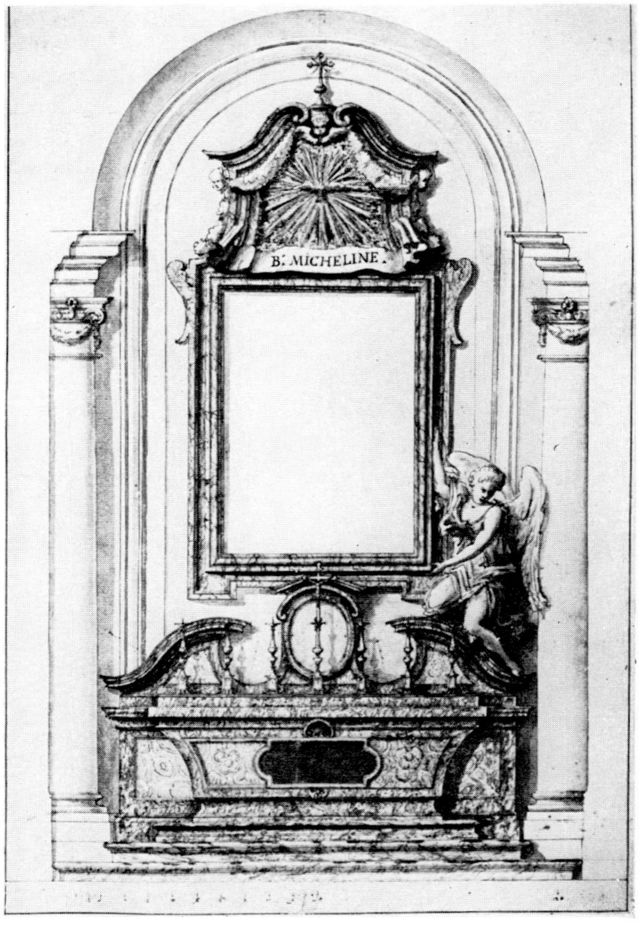

513 Project for the Metelli Altar, elevation (no.674)

The church and the Villa Albani near Colbordolo

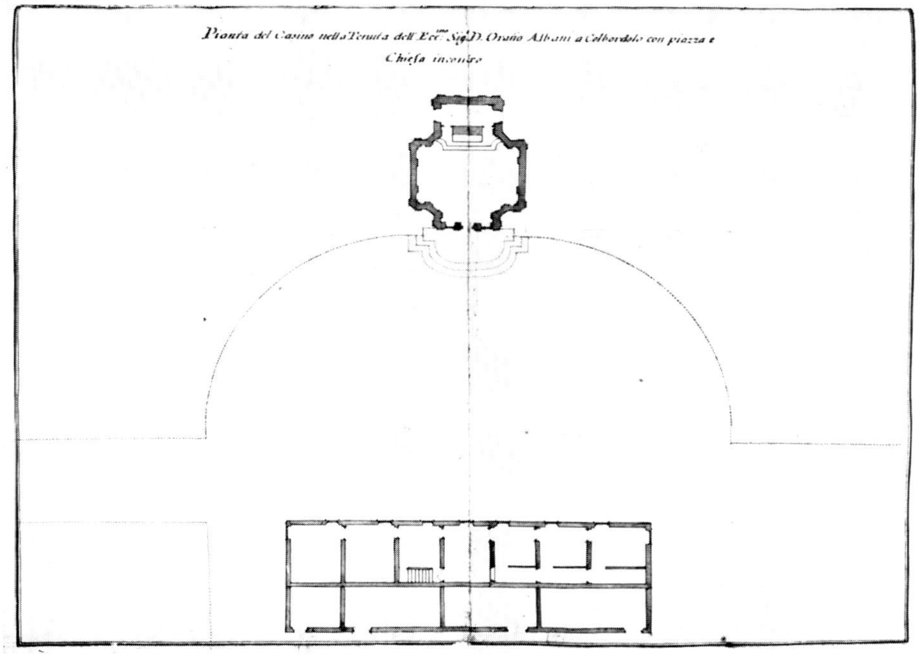

514 Plan of the Piazza with villa and church (no.676)

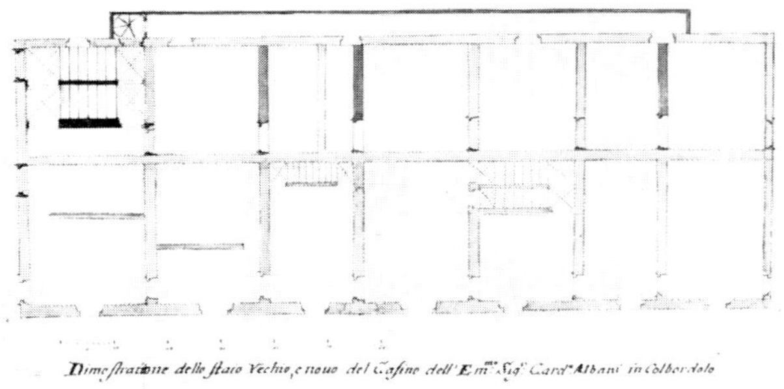

515 Ground plan of the villa (no.677)

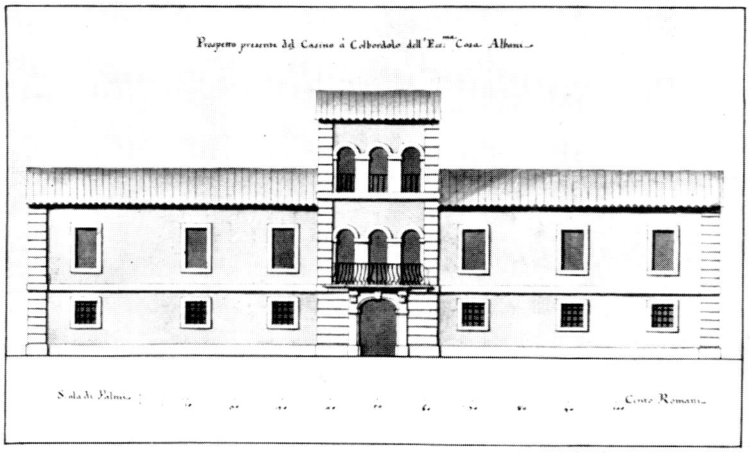

516 Elevation of the front of the villa (no.679)

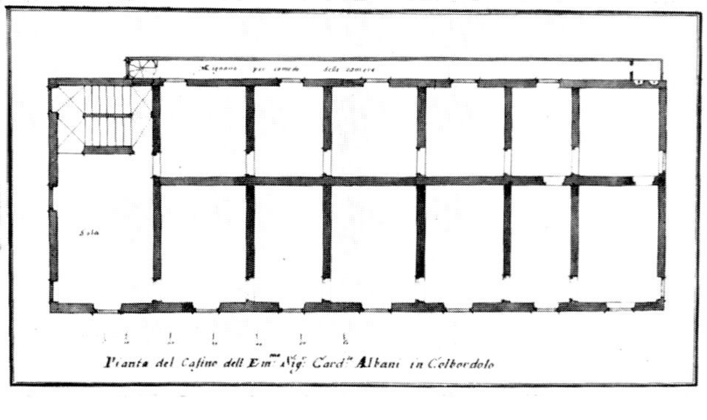

517 First-floor plan of the villa, incorporating alterations (no.678)

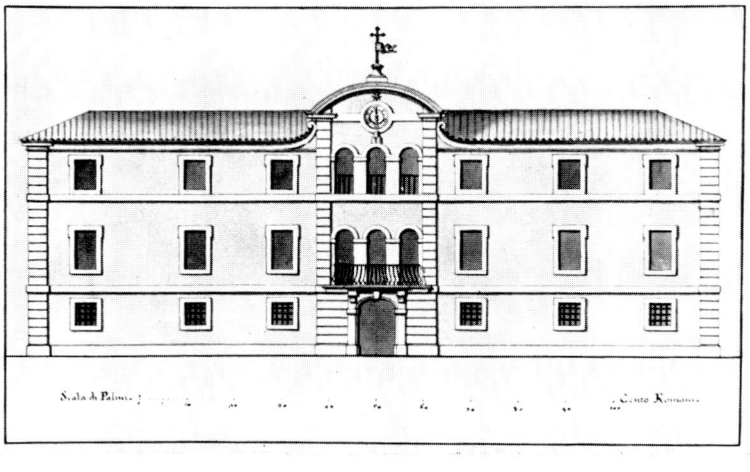

518 Elevation of the front of the villa, incorporating alterations (no.680)

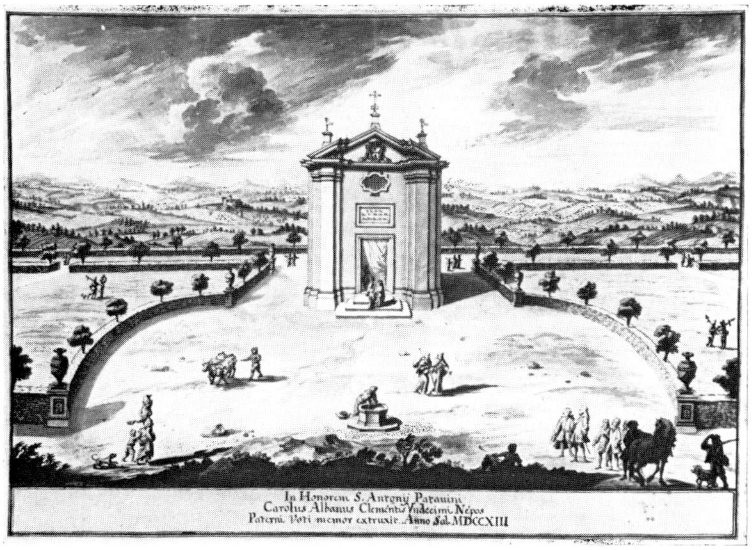

519 Perspective view of the church, executed project, 1713 (no.681)

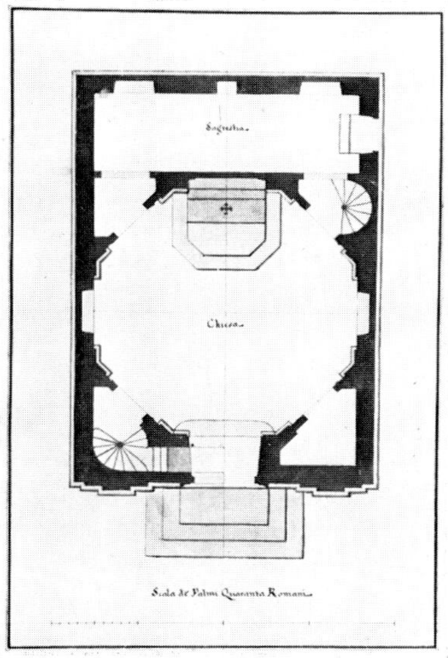

520 Ground plan of the church (no.682)

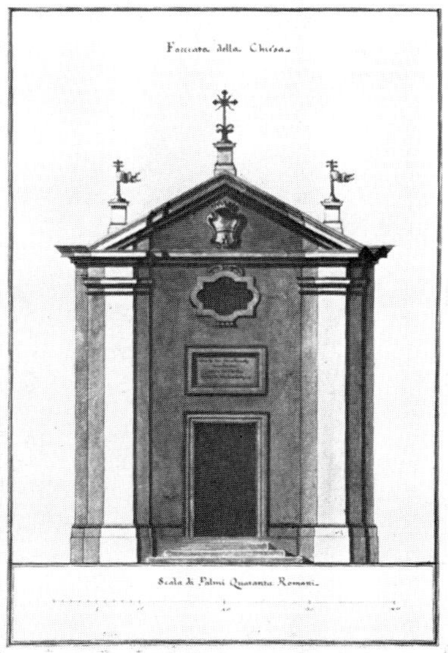

521 Front elevation of the church (no.683)

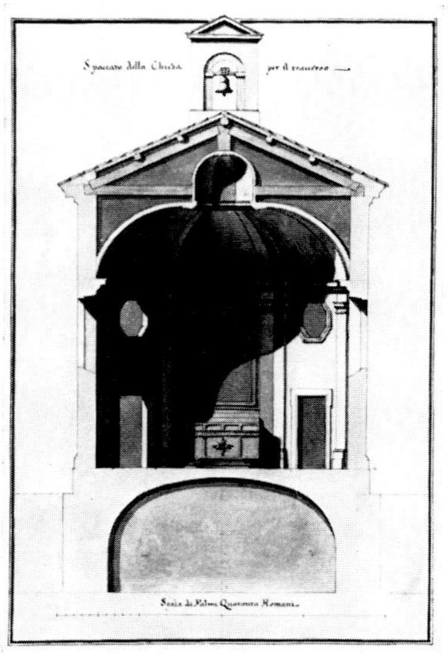

522 Transverse section of the church (no.685)

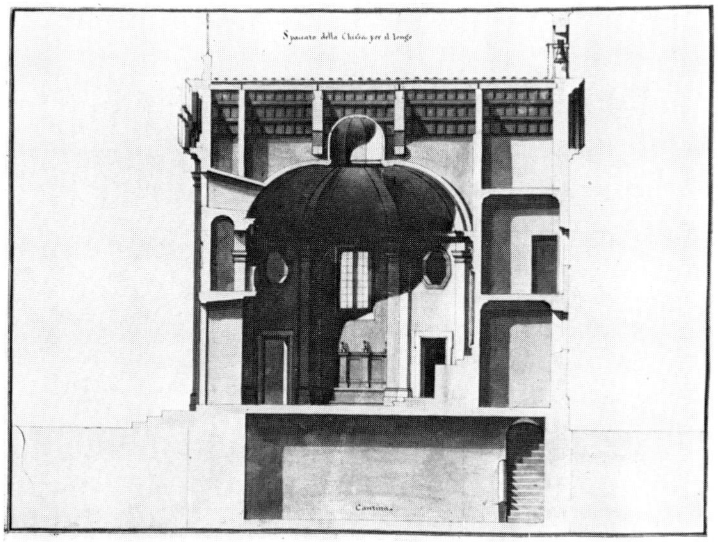

523 Longitudinal section of the church (no.684)

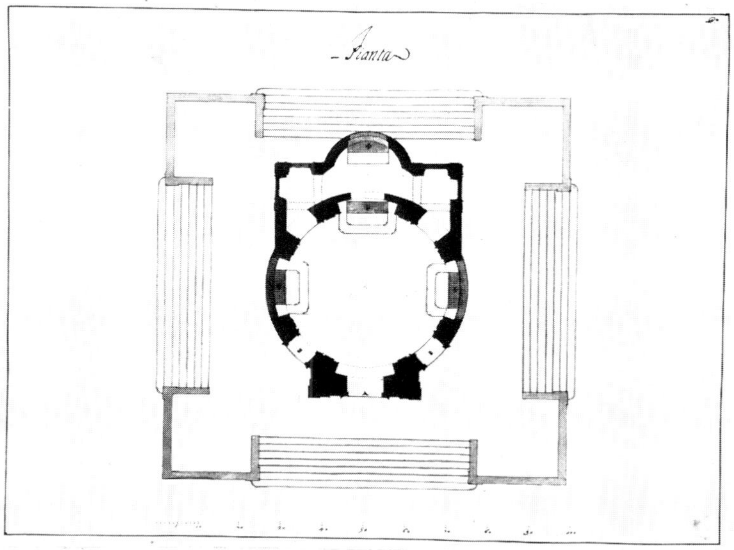

524 Ground plan of the church, unexecuted project (no.686)

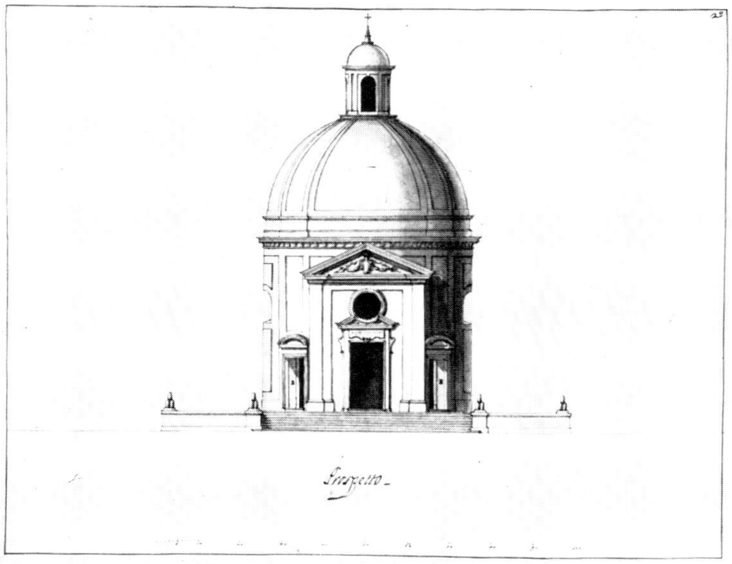

525 Front elevation (no.687)

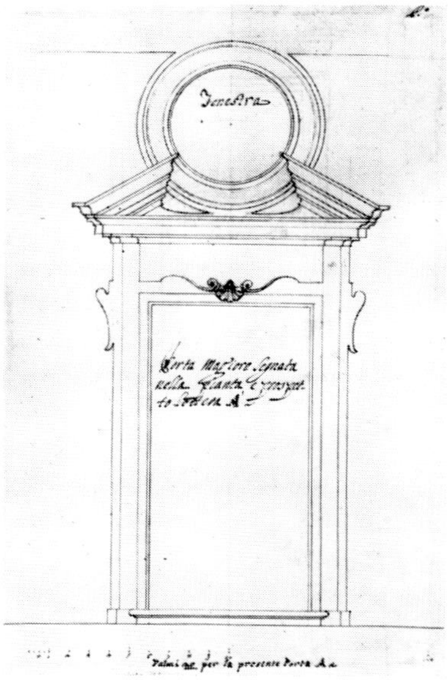

526 Elevation of the main door (no.693)

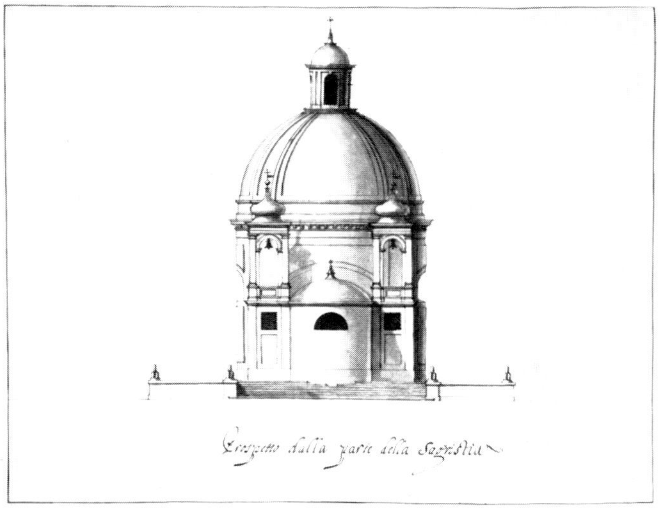

527 Rear elevation (no.688)

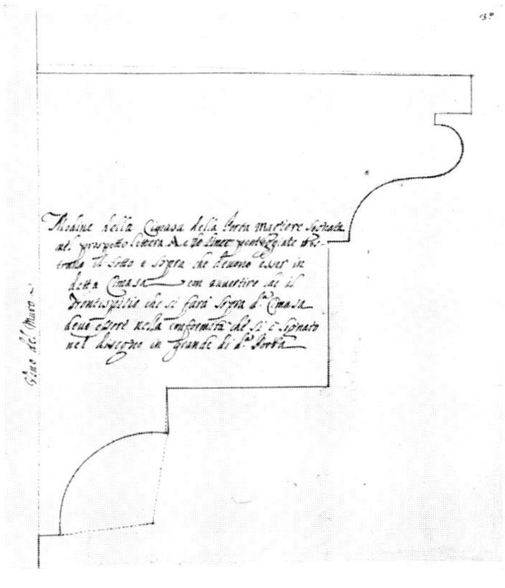

528 Profile of the cornice of the main door (no.695)

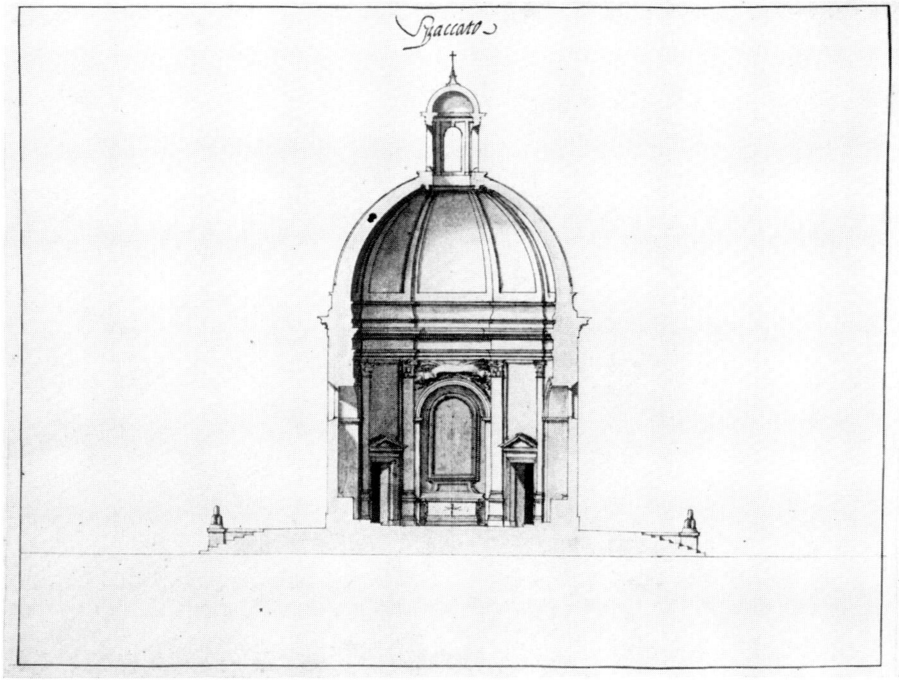

529 Transverse section (1) (no.689)

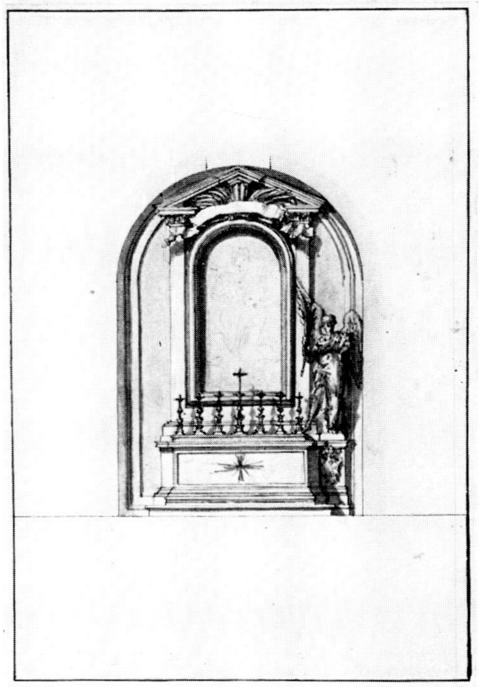

530 Section of the apse, showing high altar (2) (no.692)

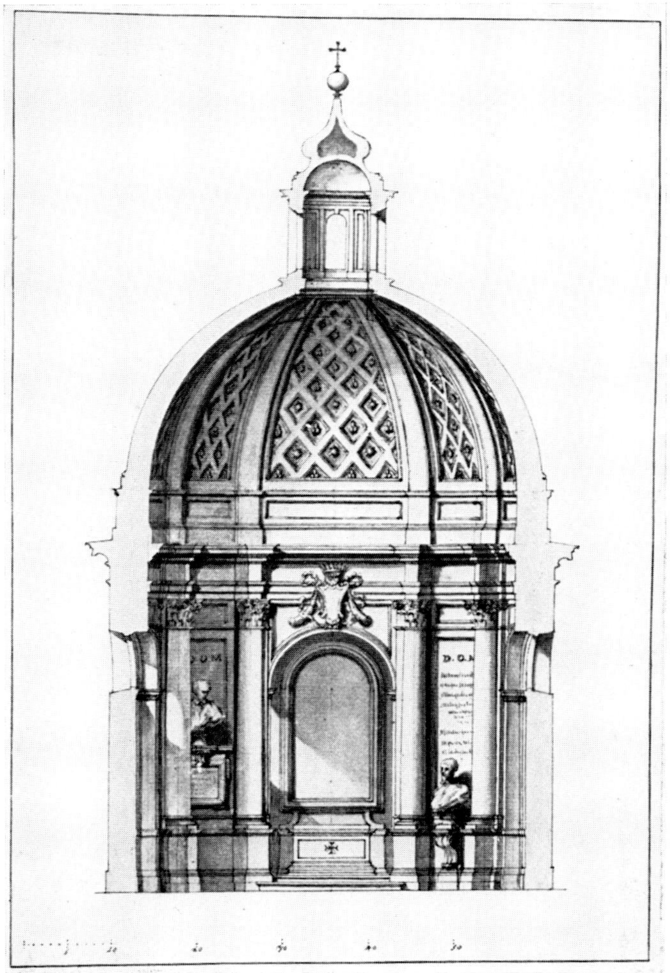

531 Transverse section (2) (no.690)

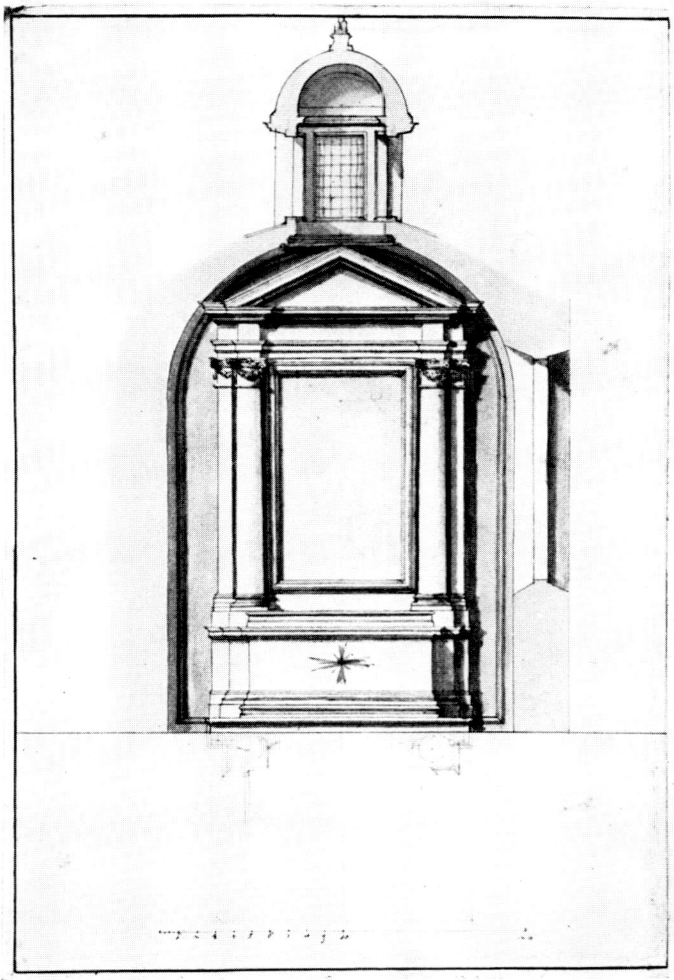

532 Section of the apse, showing high altar (1) (no.691)

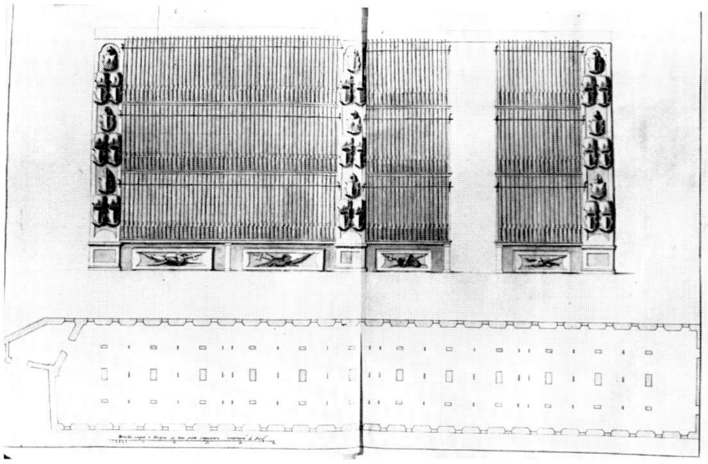

533 Plan, with elevation of musket racks (no.700)

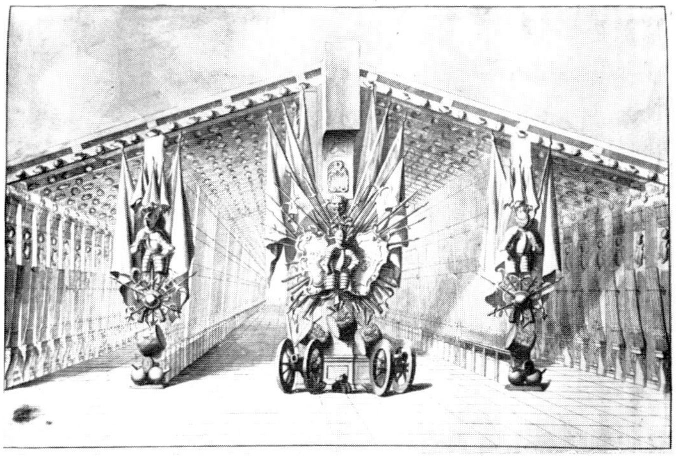

534 Cross section, with perspective view of interior (no.701)

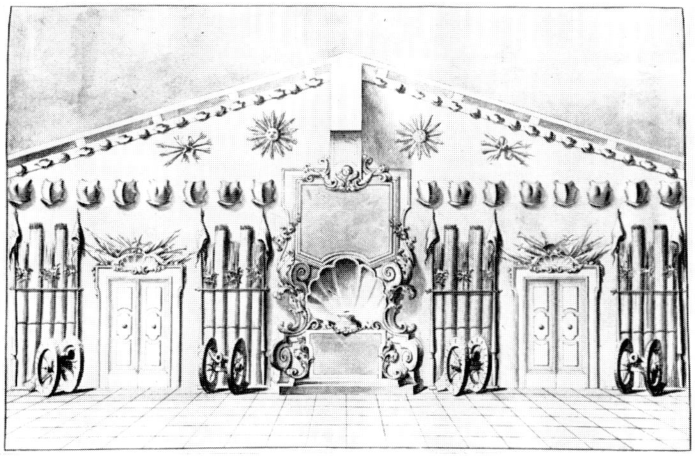

535 Elevation of the end wall (no.702)

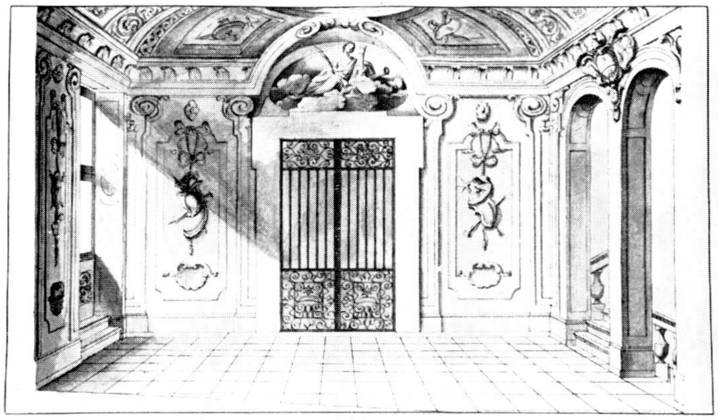

536 Perspective view of the entrance vestibule (no.704)

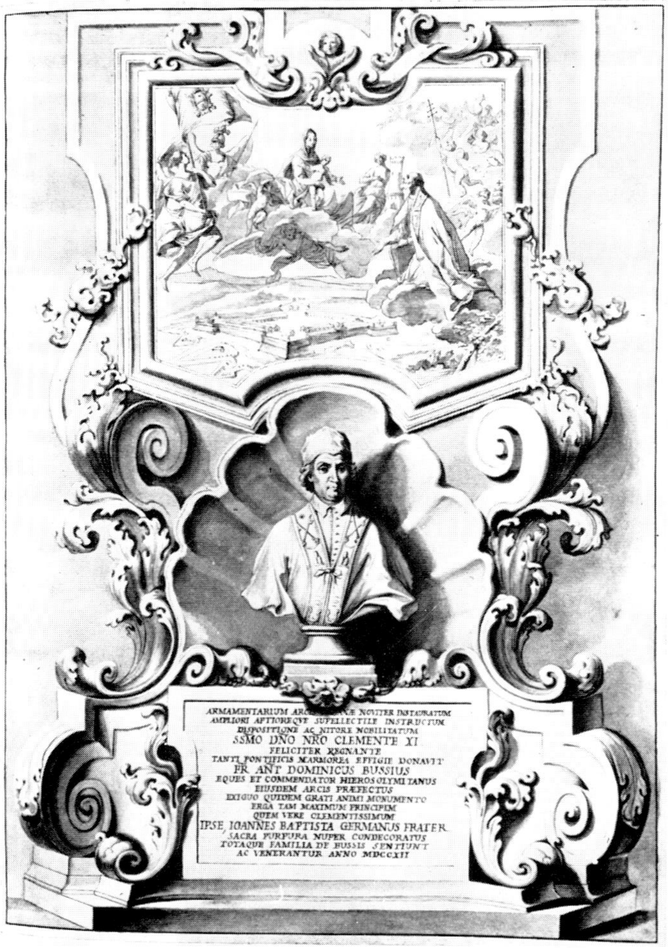

537 Elevation of the central feature of the end wall (no.703)

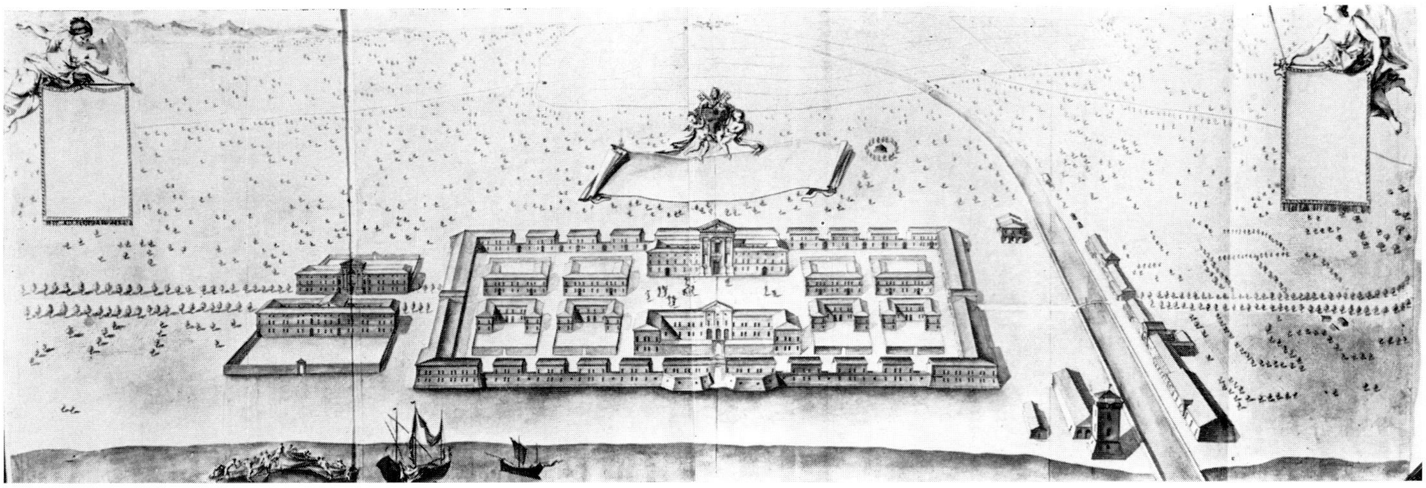

538 Perspective view of Cervia Nuova (no.705)

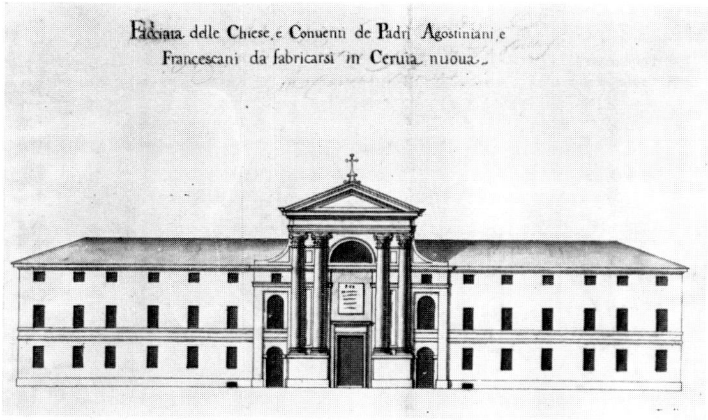

539 Project for the Franciscan and Augustinian foundations of Cervia Nuova, elevation (anon. drawing; Rome, Bibliotheca Corsini)

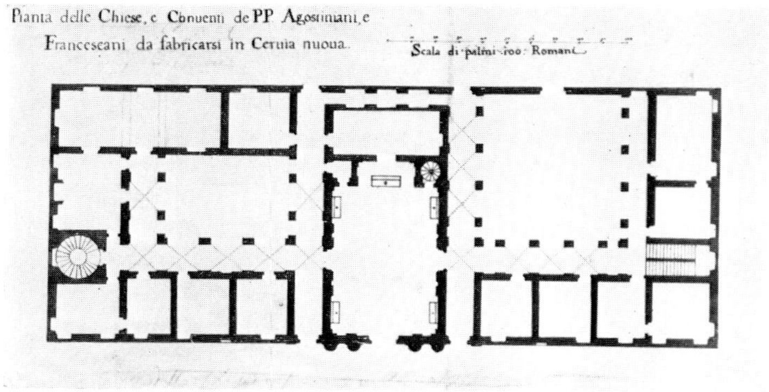

540 Project for the Franciscan and Augustinian foundations of Cervia Nuova, plan (anon. drawing; Rome, Bibliotheca Corsini)

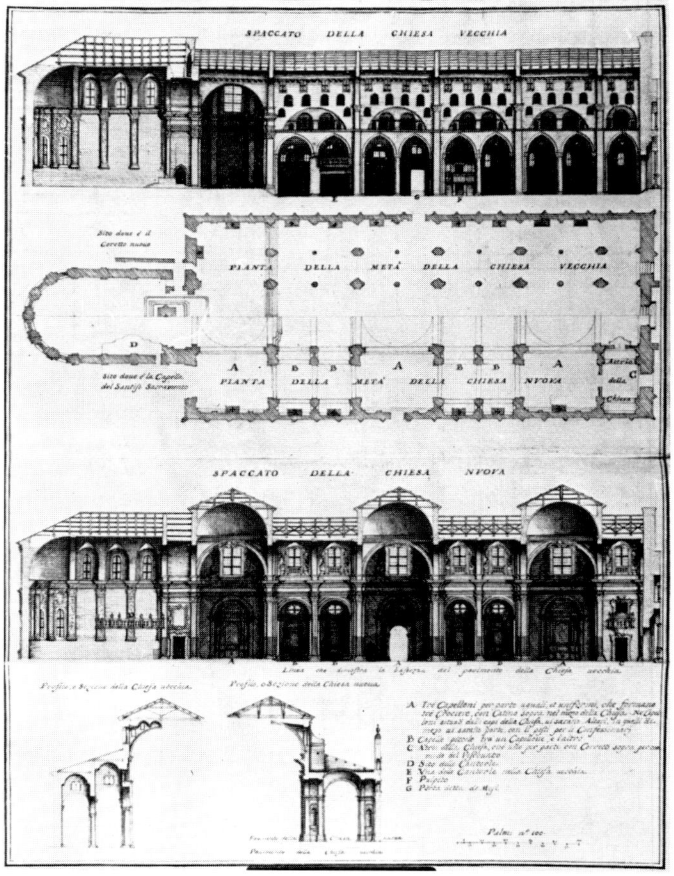

541 Plans and sections of Ferrara Cathedral showing the old and new states of the nave (no.706)

Sulmona, the Bishop's Palace

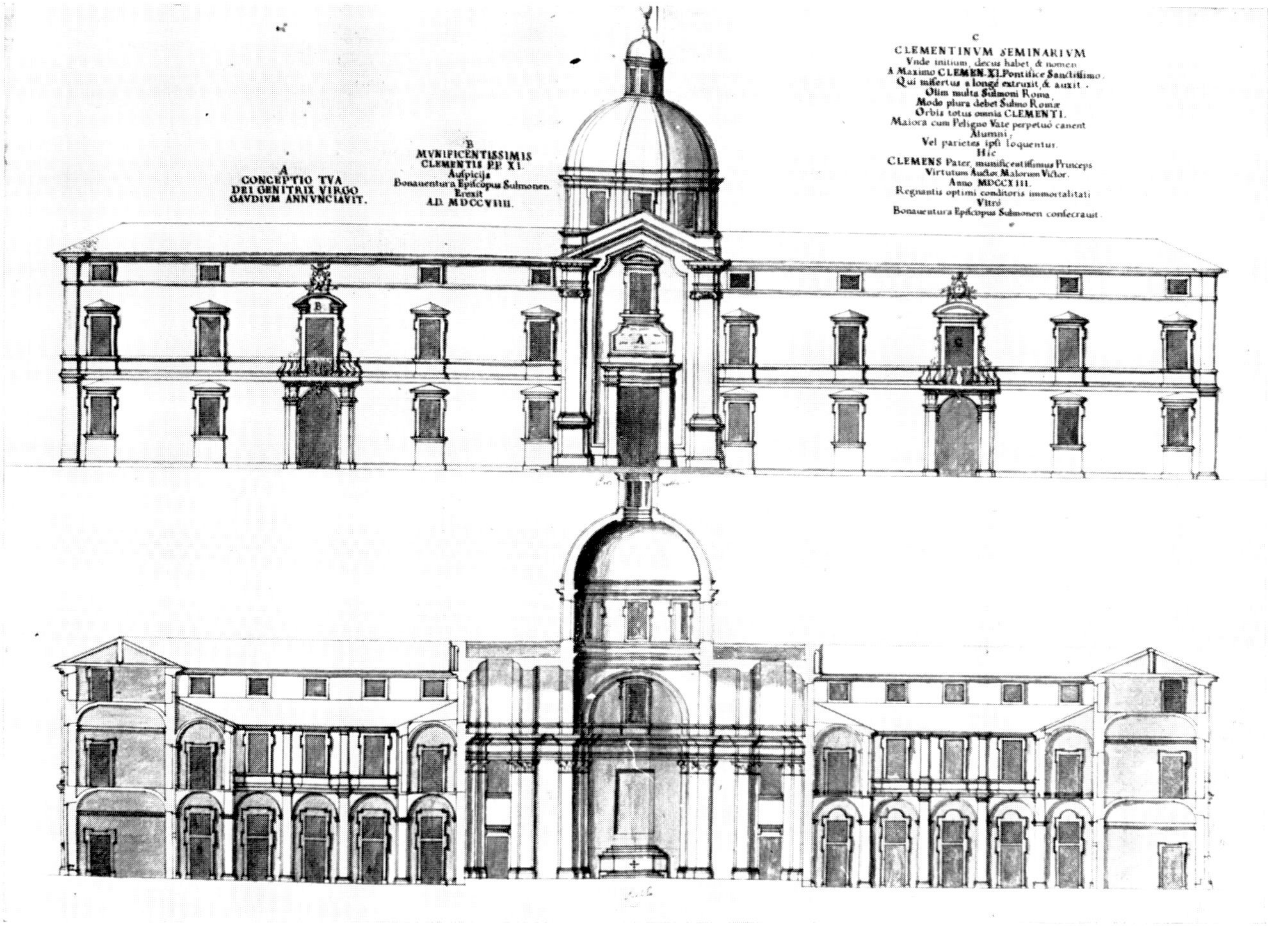

542 Elevation and section of the convent, palace and church (no.715)

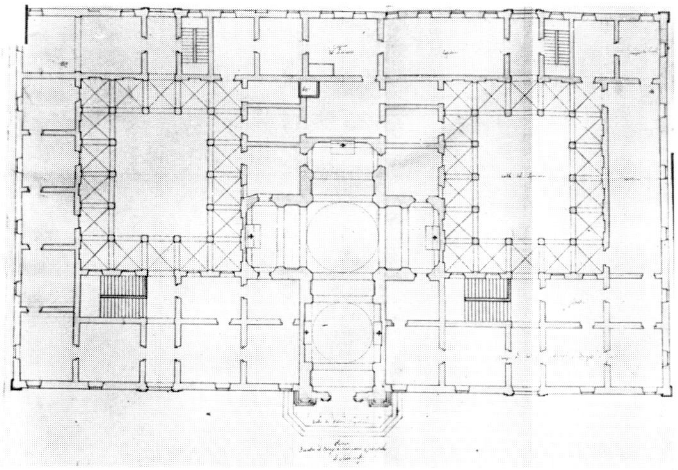

543 First-floor plan (no.714)

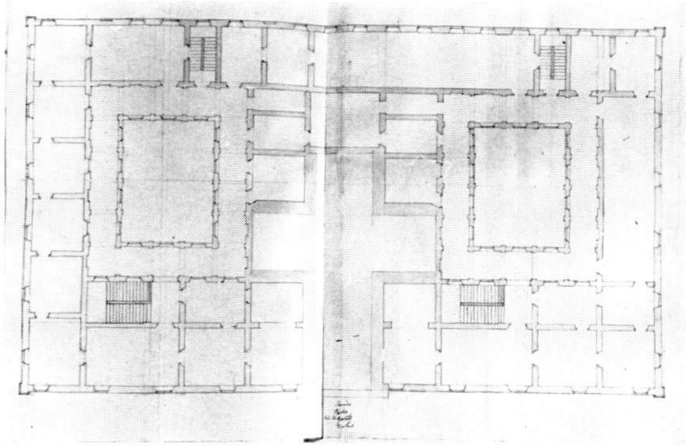

544 Ground-floor plan (no.713)

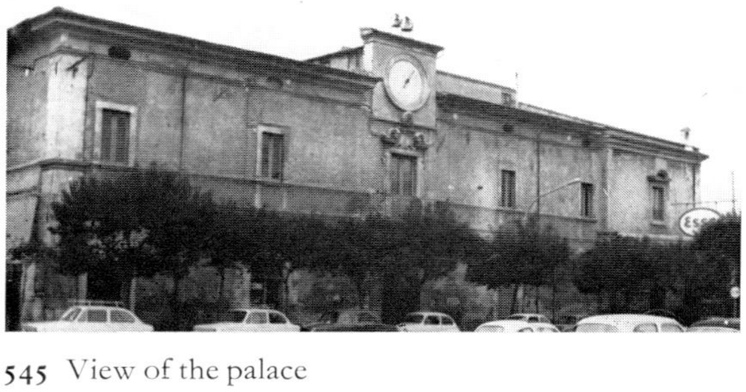

545 View of the palace

Maps connected with fortification and warfare

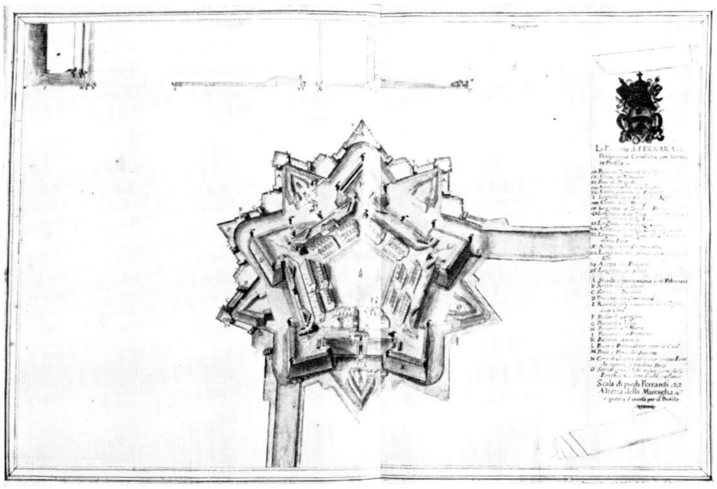

546 Perspective view of the fortress of Ferrara (by Charles Smith of Carington; no.721)

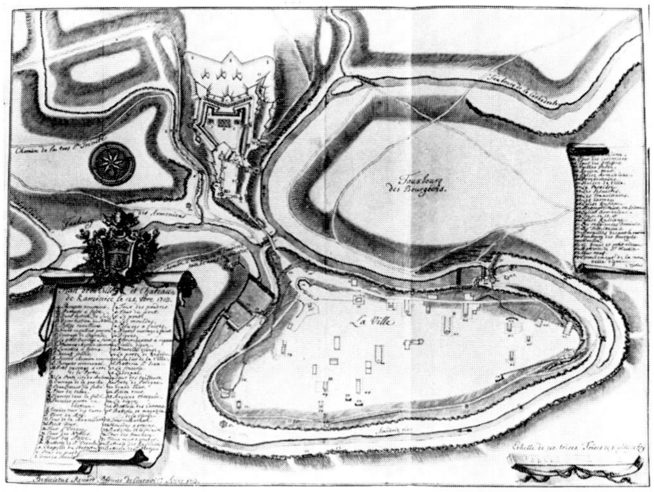

547 Outline map of the town of Kaminiec, Poland (1713) (by Benedykt Renard; no.728)

Unidentified drawings

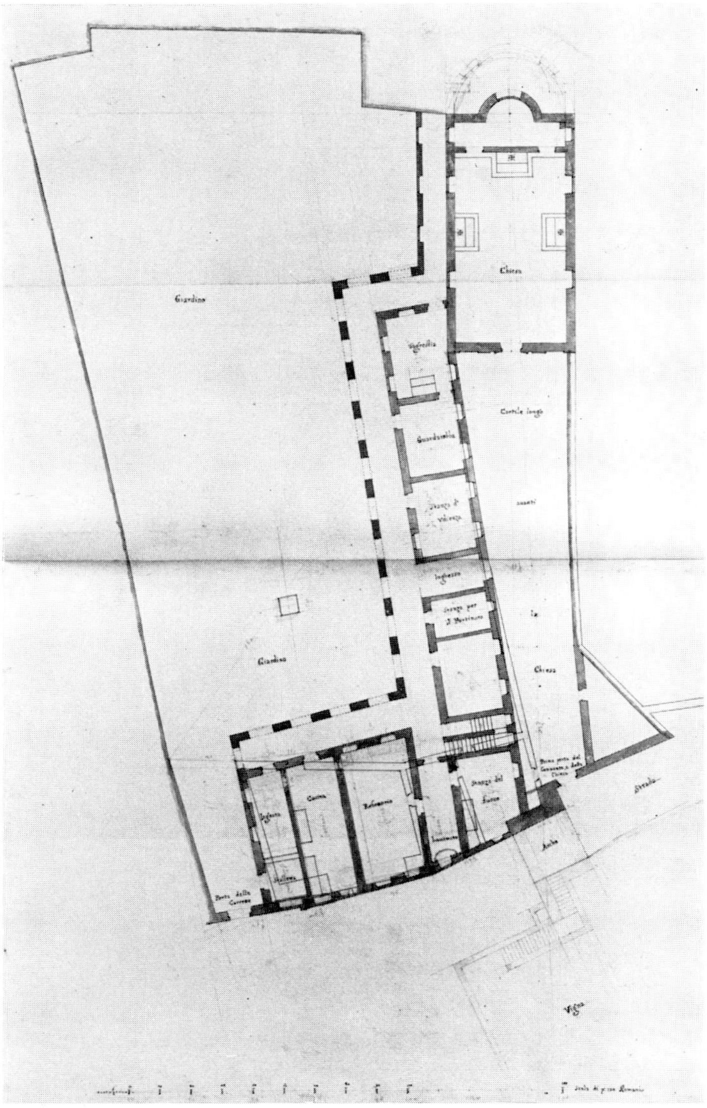

548 Project for the alterations of a convent, first-floor plan (no.730)

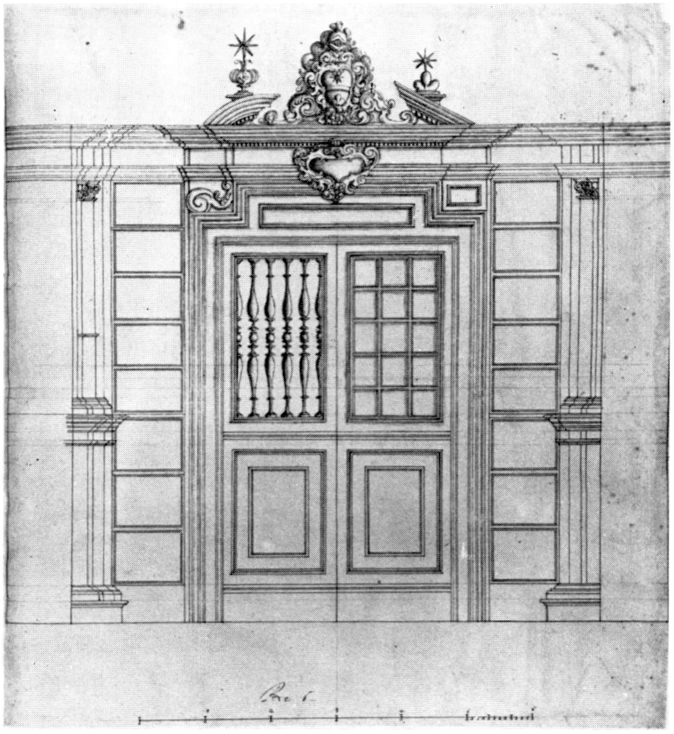

549 A library constructed by Sicilian Capuchins, elevation of a doorway (no.734)

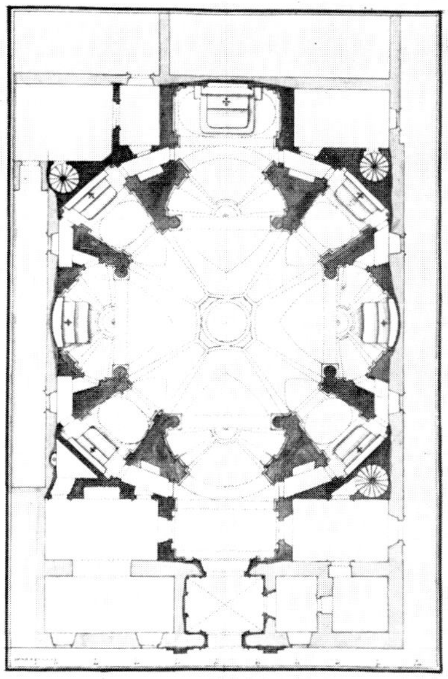

550 Designs for a centralized church, plan (no.731)

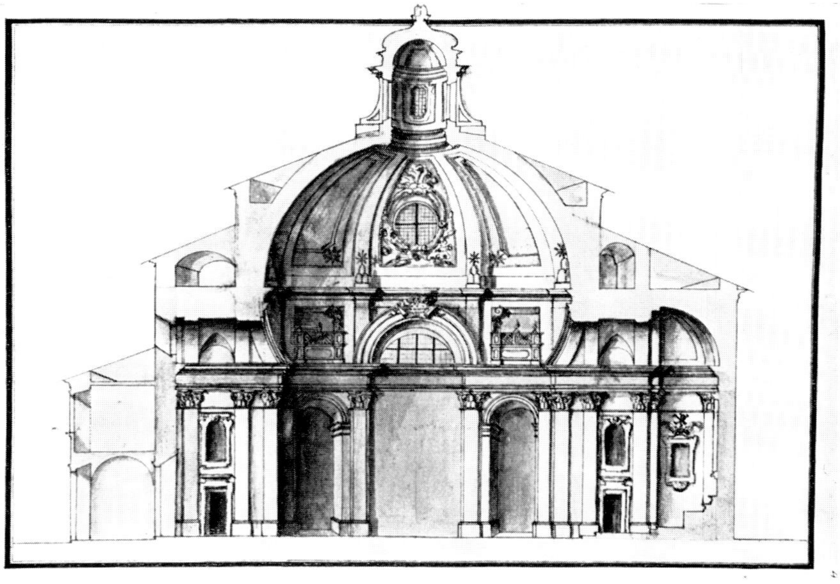

551 Designs for a centralized church, longitudinal section (no.732)

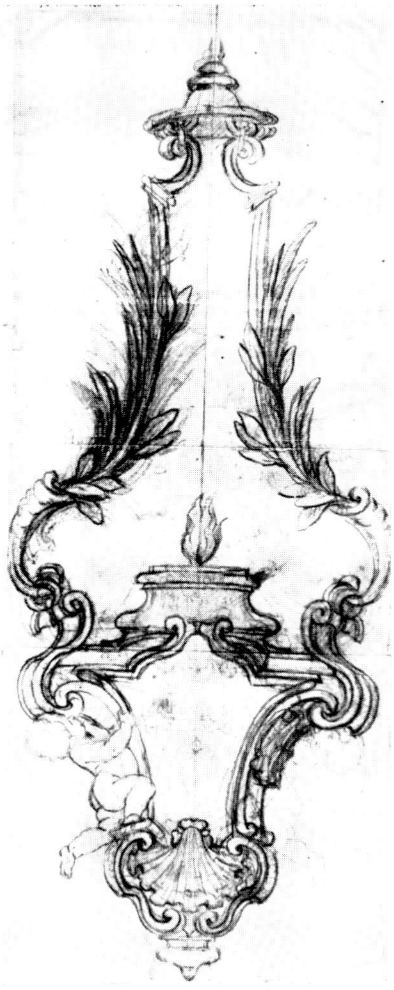

552 Project for large lamp with *putti* (no.752)

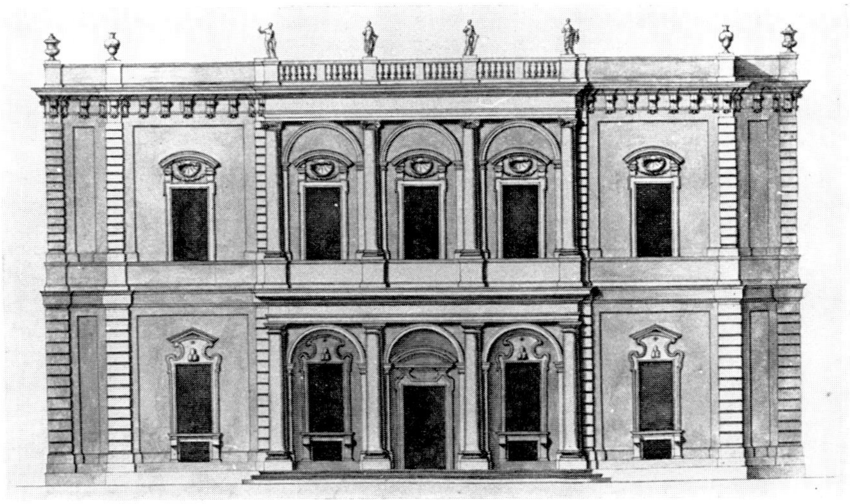

553 Project for an Albani villa, front elevation (no.750)

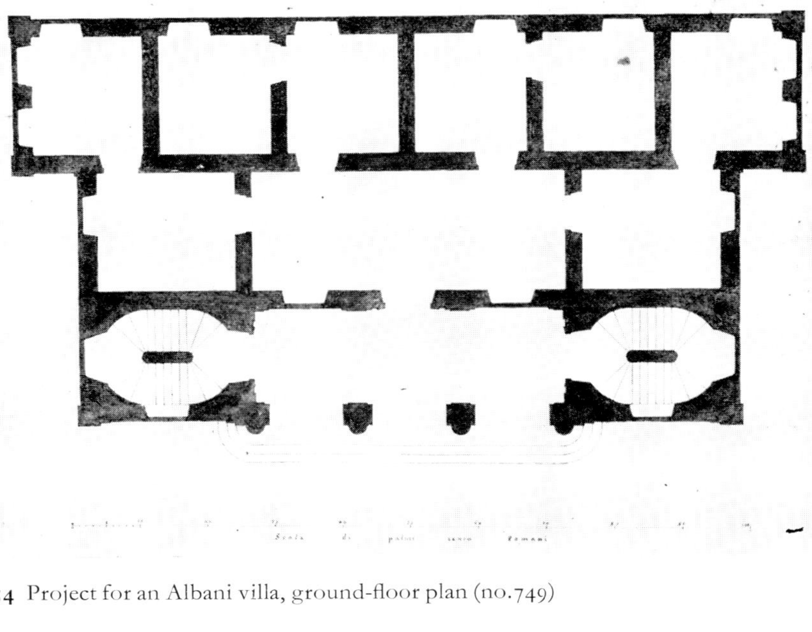

554 Project for an Albani villa, ground-floor plan (no.749)

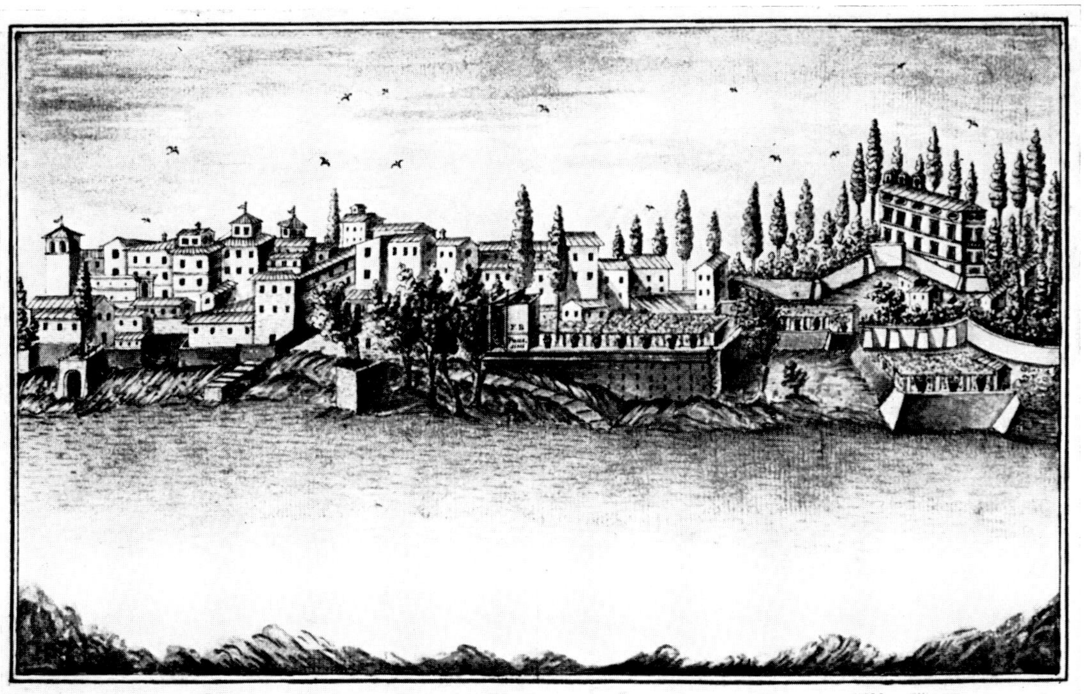

555 View of a town beside a river (no.746)

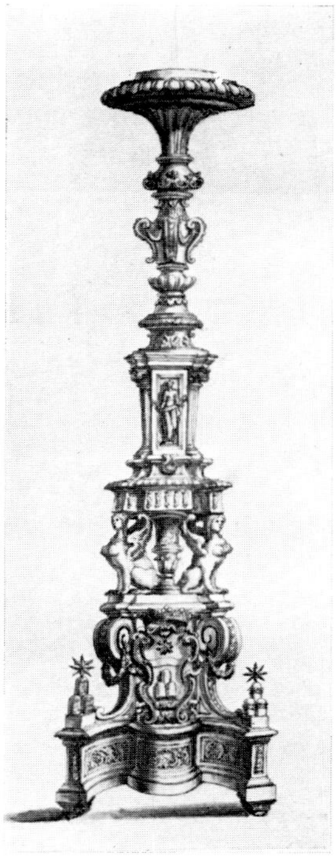

556 Studies for candlesticks, sixth project (no.769)

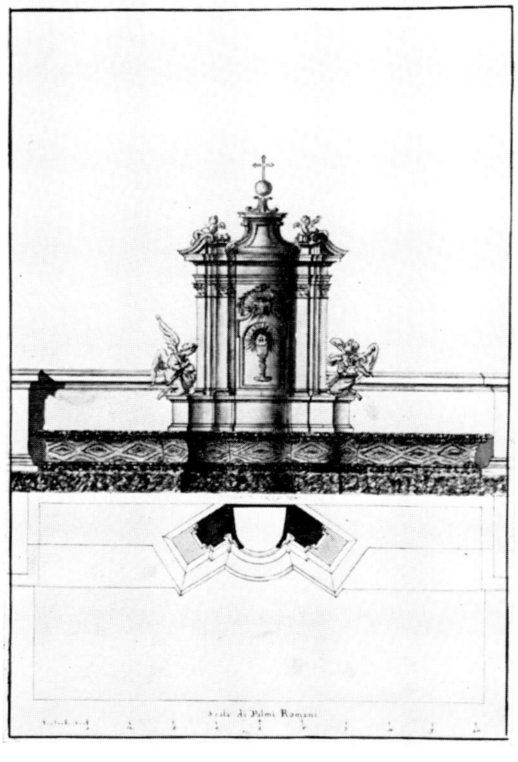

557 Plan and elevation of a tabernacle (no.755)

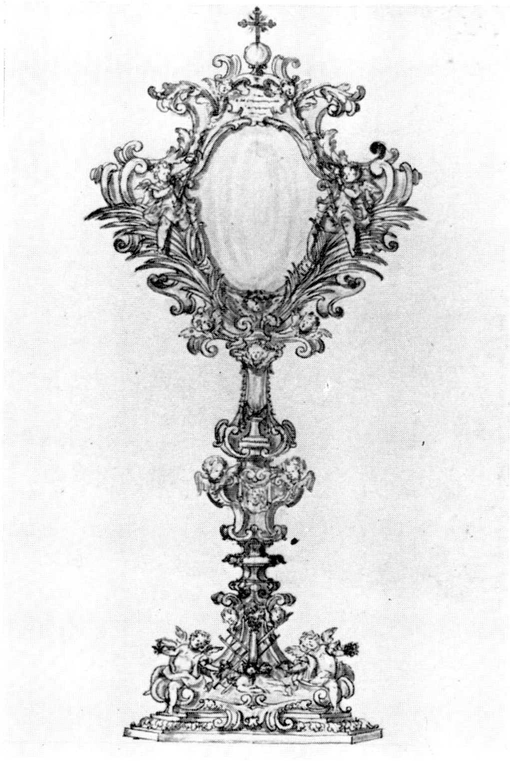

558 Drawings of reliquaries, fourth project (no.776)

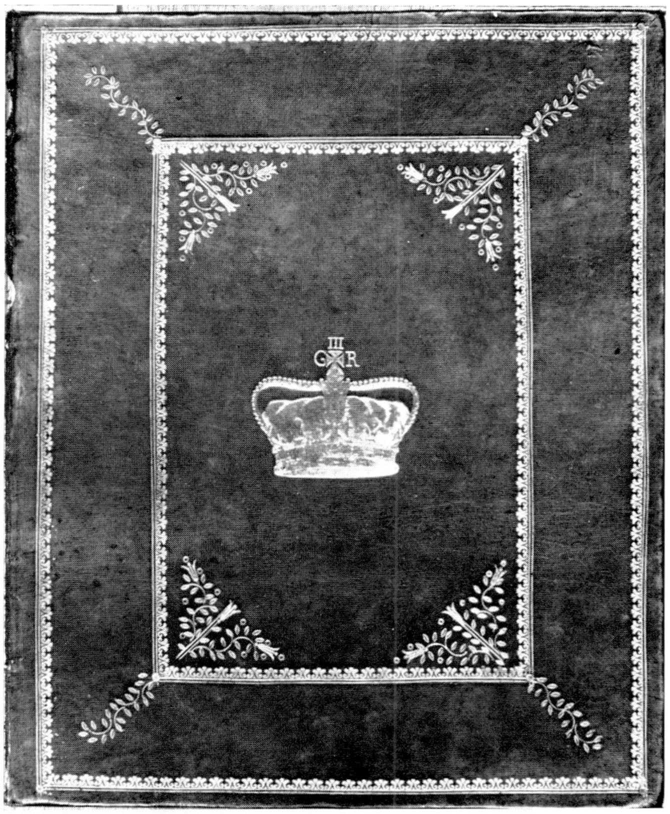

559 Windsor binding, type A (Volume 169)

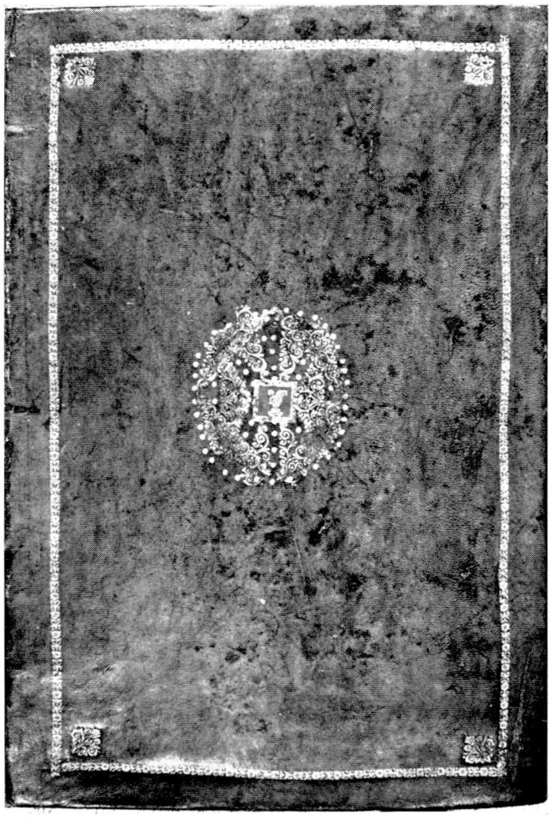

560 Windsor binding, type B 1 (Volume 172)

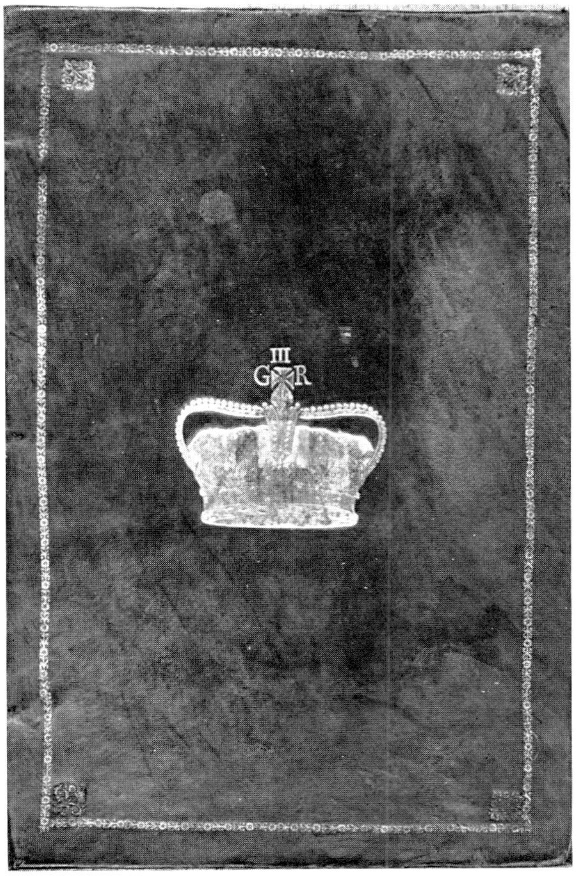

561 Windsor binding, type B 2 (Volume 174)

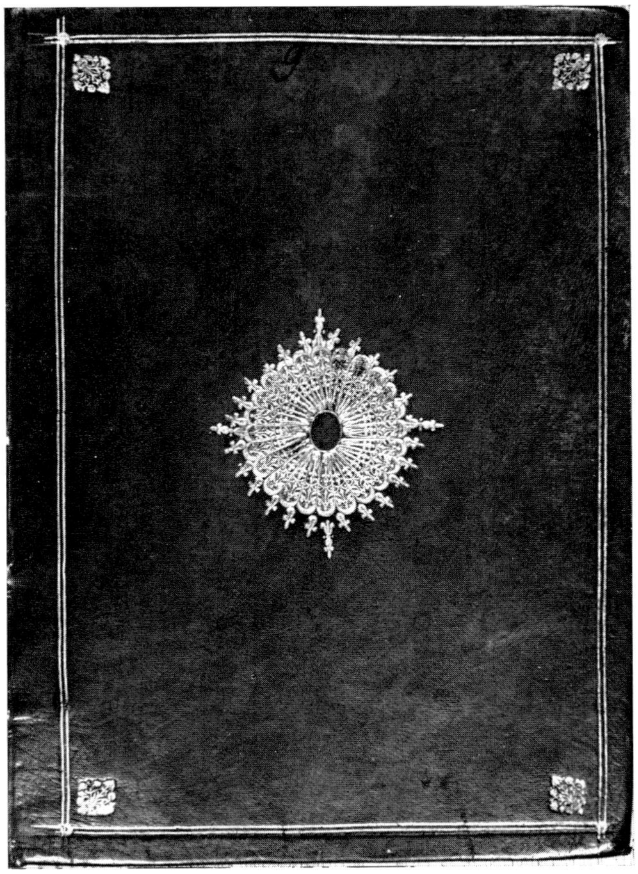

562 Windsor binding, type C (Volume 176)

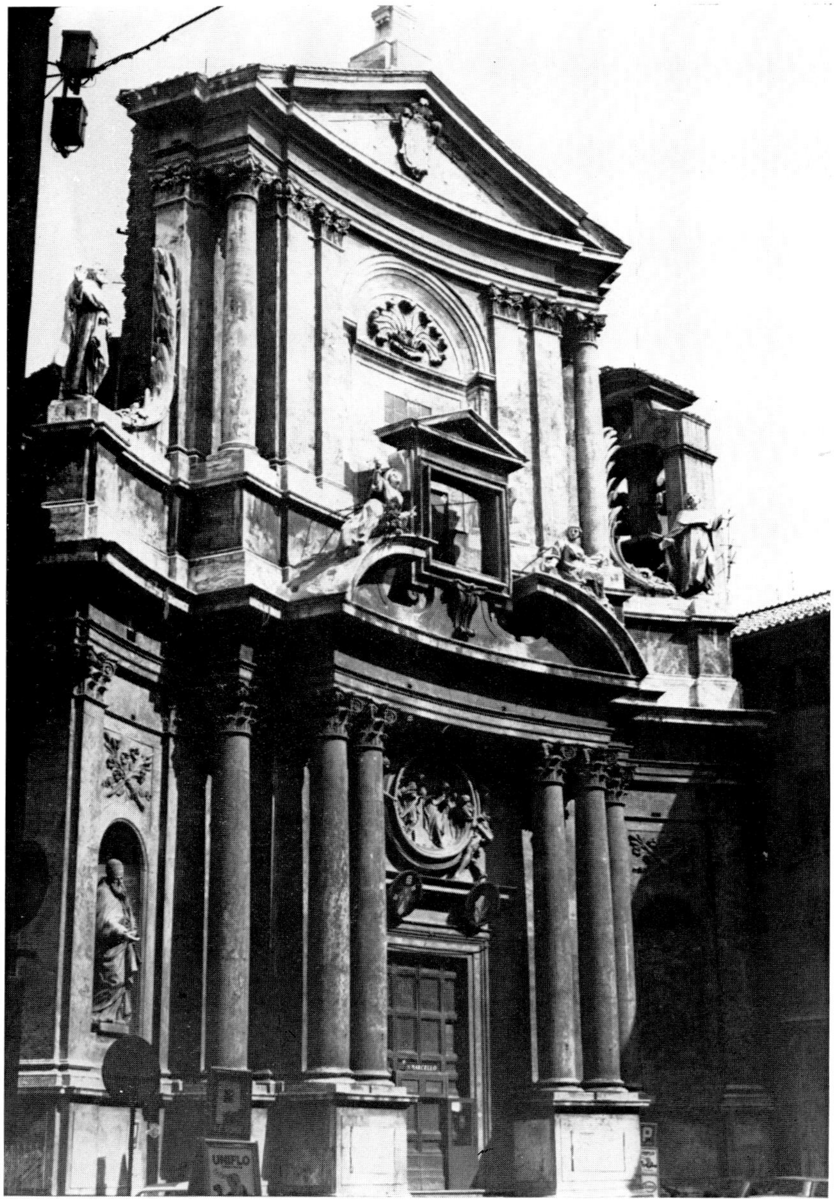

563 Rome, S. Marcello al Corso, view of the façade

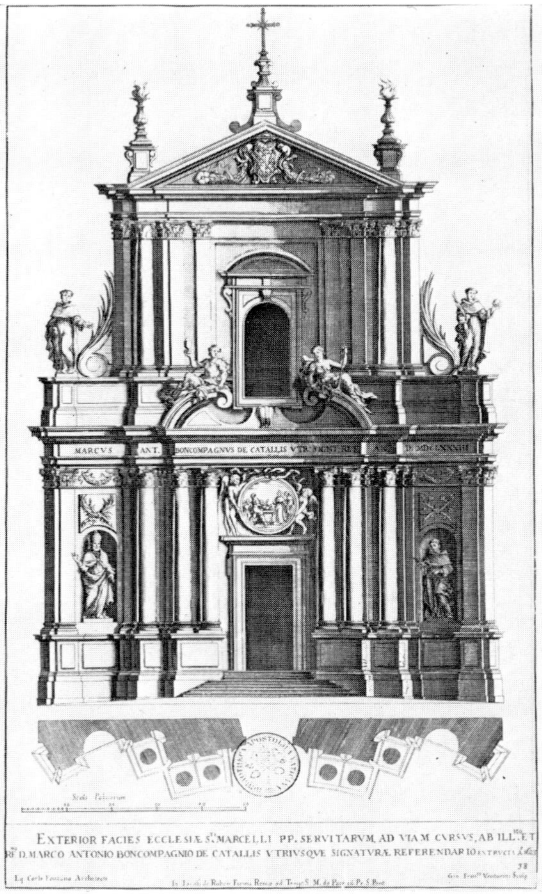

564 Rome, S. Marcello al Corso, project for the façade, 1684 (engraving by de' Rossi after Fontana)

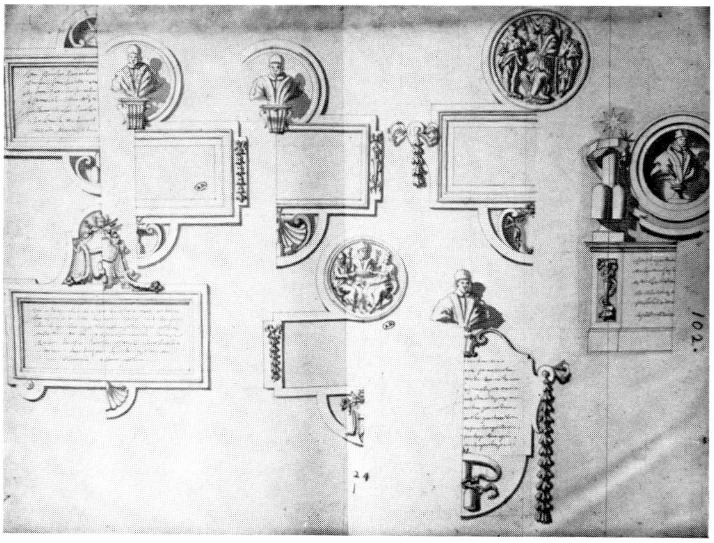

565 Projects for an inscribed tablet for Clement XI (drawing by Vittone after Fontana; Paris, Musée des Arts Décoratifs)

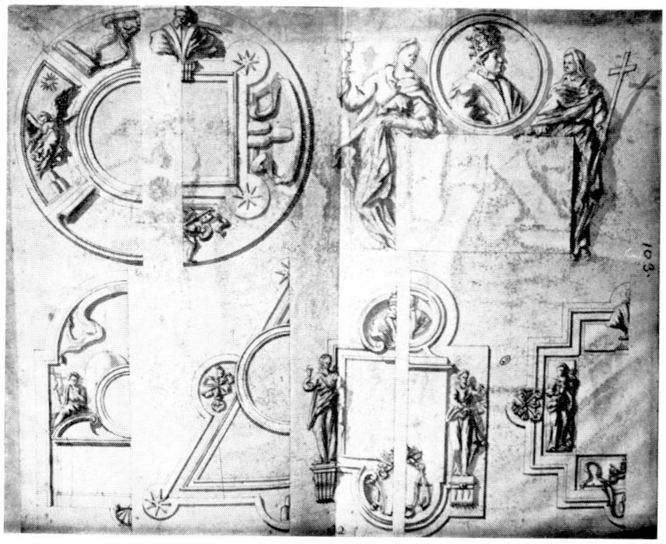

566 Projects for an inscribed tablet for Clement XI (drawing by Vittone after Fontana; Paris, Musée des Arts Décoratifs)

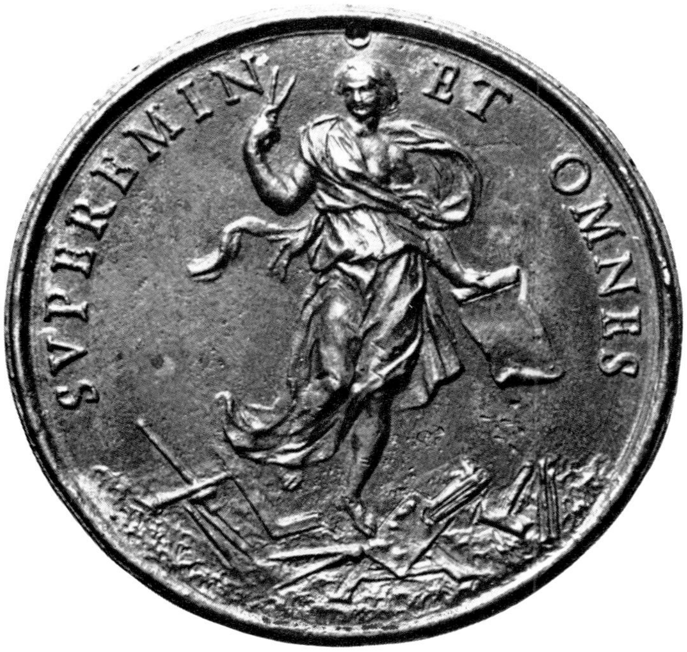

567 Medal of 1681, obverse (photograph Franco Cisterna)

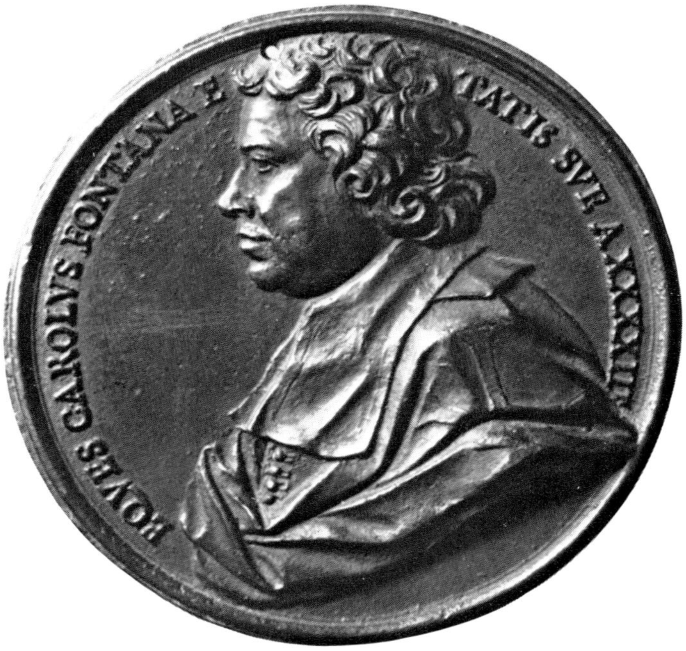

568 Medal of 1681 with portrait of Fontana (photograph Franco Cisterna)

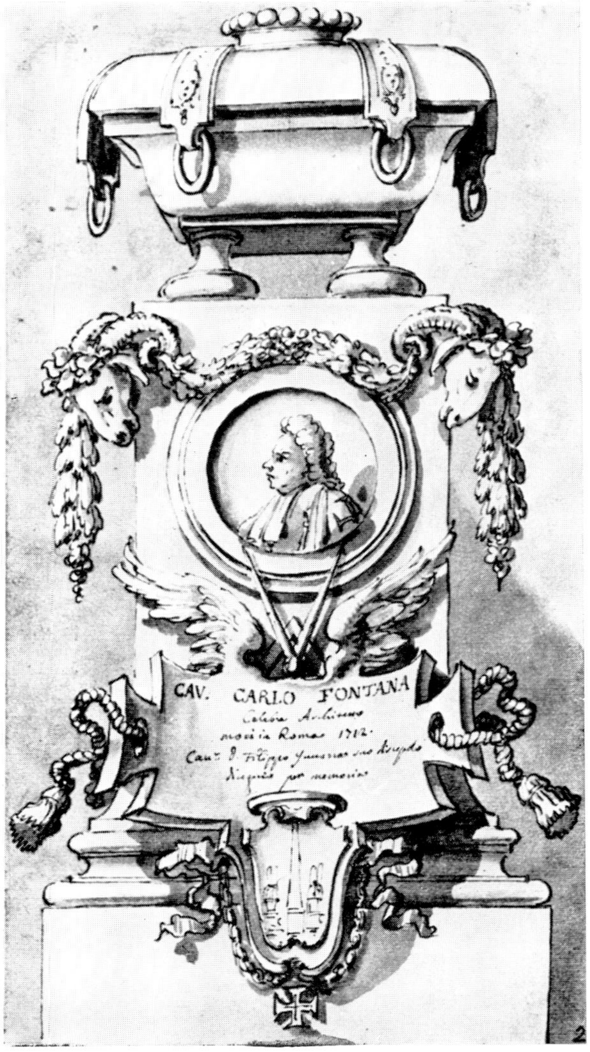

569 Project for a monument to Fontana (drawing by Juvarra; Turin, Biblioteca Nazionale)

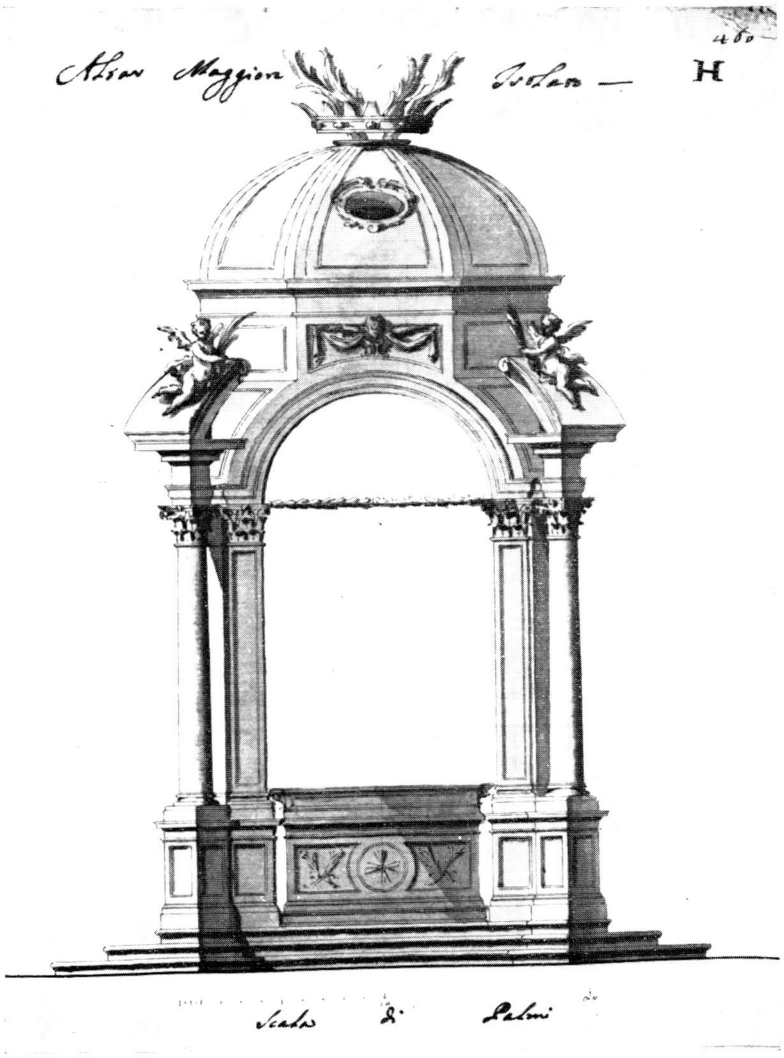

570 Elevation of the high altar of SS. Apostoli, 1702 (drawing by Francesco Fontana; Rome, Archivio di Stato)